Less managing. More teaching. Greater learning.

INSTRUCTORS...

Would you like your **students** to show up for class more **prepared**? *(Let's face it, class is much more fun if everyone is engaged and prepared...)*

Want ready-made application-level **interactive assignments,** student progress reporting, and auto-assignment grading? *(Less time grading means more time teaching...)*

Want an **instant view of student or class performance** relative to learning objectives? *(No more wondering if students understand...)*

Need to **collect data and generate reports** required for administration or accreditation? *(Say goodbye to manually tracking student learning outcomes...)*

Want to **record and post your lectures** for students to view online?

With **McGraw-Hill's *Connect*™ Management,**

INSTRUCTORS GET:

- Interactive Applications – **book-specific interactive assignments** that require students to APPLY concepts and tools of strategic analysis.

- Simple **assignment management,** allowing you to spend more time teaching.

- **Auto-graded** assignments, quizzes, and tests.

- **Detailed Visual Reporting** where student and section results can be viewed and analyzed.

- Sophisticated **online testing** capability.

- A **filtering and reporting** function that allows you to easily assign and report on materials that are correlated to accreditation standards, learning outcomes, and Bloom's taxonomy.

- An easy-to-use **lecture capture** tool.

STUDENTS...

Want to get more **value** from your textbook purchase?

Think learning strategic management should be a bit more **interesting**?

Check out the STUDENT RESOURCES section under the *Connect*™ Library tab.

Here you'll find a wealth of resources designed to help you achieve your goals in the course. You'll find things like **quizzes, PowerPoints, and Case Grid** to help you study. Every student has different needs, so explore the STUDENT RESOURCES to find the materials best suited to you.

INSTRUCTORS...

McGraw-Hill Higher Education and Blackboard have teamed up. What does this mean **for you**?

- **Your life, simplified.** Now you and your students can access McGraw-Hill's Connect™ and Create™ right from within your Blackboard course—all with one single sign-on.

- **Deep integration of content and tools.** Whether you're choosing a book for your course or building Connect™ assignments, all the tools you need are right where you want them—inside of Blackboard.

- **Seamless Gradebooks.** Multiple gradebooks? No thanks! When a student completes an integrated Connect™ assignment, the grade for that assignment automatically (and instantly) feeds your Blackboard grade center.

- **A solution for everyone.** Whether your institution is already using Blackboard or you just want to try Blackboard on your own, we have a solution for you. Be sure to ask your local McGraw-Hill representative for details.

The **Best** of **Both Worlds**

www.domorenow.com

Strategic Management

text and cases

sixth edition

Gregory G. Dess
University of Texas at Dallas

G. T. Lumpkin
Syracuse University

Alan B. Eisner
Pace University

Gerry McNamara
Michigan State University

Strategic Management

text and cases

sixth edition

McGraw-Hill Irwin

McGraw-Hill
Irwin

STRATEGIC MANAGEMENT: TEXT AND CASES
Published by McGraw-Hill/Irwin, a business unit of The McGraw-Hill Companies, Inc., 1221 Avenue of the Americas, New York, NY, 10020. Copyright © 2012, 2010, 2008, 2007, 2006, 2004 by The McGraw-Hill Companies, Inc. All rights reserved. Printed in the United States of America. No part of this publication may be reproduced or distributed in any form or by any means, or stored in a database or retrieval system, without the prior written consent of The McGraw-Hill Companies, Inc., including, but not limited to, in any network or other electronic storage or transmission, or broadcast for distance learning.

Some ancillaries, including electronic and print components, may not be available to customers outside the United States.

This book is printed on acid-free paper.

2 3 4 5 6 7 8 9 0 DOW/DOW 1 0 9 8 7 6 5 4 3 2

ISBN 978-0-07-802931-8
MHID 0-07-802931-7

Vice president and editor-in-chief: *Brent Gordon*
Editorial director: *Paul Ducham*
Executive editor: *Michael Ablassmeir*
Executive director of development: *Ann Torbert*
Development editor II: *Laura Griffin*
Editorial coordinator: *Andrea Heirendt*
Vice president and director of marketing: *Robin J. Zwettler*
Marketing director: *Amee Mosley*
Executive marketing manager: *Anke Braun Weekes*
Marketing specialist: *Elizabeth Steiner*
Vice president of editing, design, and production: *Sesha Bolisetty*
Lead project manager: *Harvey Yep*
Buyer II: *Debra R. Sylvester*
Interior designer: *Pam Verros*
Senior photo research coordinator: *Jeremy Cheshareck*
Lead media project manager: *Kerry Bowler*
Cover/interior design: *Pam Verros*
Cover image: © *Getty Images*
Typeface: *10/12 Times Roman*
Compositor: *Laserwords Private Limited*
Printer: *R. R. Donnelley*

Library of Congress Cataloging-in-Publication Data

Strategic management : text and cases / Gregory G. Dess ... [et al.]. — 6th ed.
    p. cm.
    Includes index.
    ISBN-13: 978-0-07-802931-8 (alk. paper)
    ISBN-10: 0-07-802931-7 (alk. paper)
    1. Strategic planning. I. Dess, Gregory G.
HD30.28.D4746 2012
658.4'012—dc23

2011027546

www.mhhe.com

Dedication

To my family, Margie and Taylor;
my parents, Bill and Mary Dess;
and Glenn F. Kirk
–Greg

To my lovely wife, Vicki,
and my students and colleagues
–Tom

To my family, Helaine, Rachel, and Jacob
–Alan

To my wonderful wife, Gaelen;
my children, Megan and AJ;
and my parents, Gene and Jane
–Gerry

About the Authors

Gregory G. Dess   is the Andrew R. Cecil Endowed Chair in Management at the University of Texas at Dallas. His primary research interests are in strategic management, organization–environment relationships, and knowledge management. He has published numerous articles on these subjects in both academic and practitioner-oriented journals. He also serves on the editorial boards of a wide range of practitioner-oriented and academic journals. In August 2000, he was inducted into the *Academy of Management Journal*'s Hall of Fame as one of its charter members. Professor Dess has conducted executive programs in the United States, Europe, Africa, Hong Kong, and Australia. During 1994 he was a Fulbright Scholar in Oporto, Portugal. In 2009, he received an honorary doctorate from the University of Bern (Switzerland). He received his PhD in Business Administration from the University of Washington (Seattle) and a BIE degree from Georgia Tech.

G. T. (Tom) Lumpkin   is the Chris J. Witting Chair and Professor of Entrepreneurship at Syracuse University in New York. Prior to joining the faculty at Syracuse, Tom was the Kent Hance Regents Endowed Chair and Professor of Entrepreneurship at Texas Tech University. His research interests include entrepreneurial orientation, opportunity recognition, strategy-making processes, social entrepreneurship, and innovative forms of organizing work. He has published numerous research articles in journals such as *Strategic Management Journal, Academy of Management Journal, Academy of Management Review, Journal of Business Venturing,* and *Entrepreneurship: Theory and Practice.* He is a member of the editorial review boards of *Strategic Entrepreneurship Journal, Entrepreneurship Theory & Practice,* and the *Journal of Business Venturing.* He received his PhD in management from the University of Texas at Arlington and MBA from the University of Southern California.

Alan B. Eisner is Professor of Management and Department Chair, Management and Management Science Department, at the Lubin School of Business, Pace University. He received his PhD in management from the Stern School of Business, New York University. His primary research interests are in strategic management, technology management, organizational learning, and managerial decision making. He has published research articles and cases in journals such as *Advances in Strategic Management, International Journal of Electronic Commerce, International Journal of Technology Management, American Business Review, Journal of Behavioral and Applied Management,* and *Journal of the International Academy for Case Studies.* He is the former Associate Editor of the Case Association's peer reviewed journal, *The CASE Journal.*

Gerry McNamara is a Professor of Management at Michigan State University. He received his PhD from the Carlson School of Management at the University of Minnesota. His research focuses on strategic decision making, organizational risk taking, and mergers and acquisitions. His research has been published in numerous journals, including the *Academy of Management Journal, Strategic Management Journal, Organization Science, Organizational Behavior and Human Decision Processes, Journal of Management,* and *Journal of International Business Studies.* His research on mergers and acquisitions has been abstracted in the *New York Times, Bloomberg Businessweek, The Economist,* and *Financial Week.* He is currently an Associate Editor for the *Academy of Management Journal*

Preface

Welcome to the Sixth Edition of *Strategic Management: Text and Cases*! We're very pleased with the positive market response to our previous editions. We are always striving to improve our work, and we appreciate the extensive and constructive feedback that many strategy professionals have graciously given us. We have worked hard to incorporate many of their ideas into the Sixth Edition—as we have in previous editions as well. We acknowledge these many contributions later in the Preface.

As you noticed on the cover, we have added Gerry McNamara of Michigan State University as a coauthor. We are very excited to welcome him—he has certainly added a lot of value to our collective work. Gerry has an outstanding record as a strategy scholar—and his writing style is consistent with that of the other authors on the book. As we worked on the Sixth Edition, it was great to have, in the vernacular, "fresh blood" to provide new perspectives. Gerry certainly did not let us down!

We'd like to revisit a fundamental question: Why did we write the book in the first place? All of us would agree that there have always been some solid strategy textbooks on the market. However, we felt that there was a strong need for a book that students and faculty would think satisfied the three *R*'s that we always kept in mind while we worked: relevant, rigorous, and readable. That is, our tagline (paraphrasing the well-known Secret deodorant commercial) is: "Strong enough for the professor; made for the student." We are quite pleased that we have received such feedback over the years from faculty who have used our book. Perhaps Professor Stephen Vitucci (Tarleton State University) said it best:

> I want it to be rigorous but something that they can read and understand. The Dess, Lumpkin, and Eisner text I am currently using is exactly what I like and, more importantly, what my students need and like.

We were also recently contacted by Liz Welch and Sabina Nawaz, former General Manager and Senior Director, respectively, at Microsoft. They are now external consultants who conduct course offerings for Microsoft, several divisions of ITT, and other well-known firms. The author team was very gratified by their strong support of our text, which we feel verifies the "external validity" and practical relevance of our work:

> As organizational and leadership development consultants, we are always looking for great tools, case studies, and examples to better deliver core strategy concepts to our clients. Not only does DLE's *Strategic Management* provide us with that, it is almost a "one-stop shop" in this regard. The book has a comprehensive conceptual model with timely, relevant, and well-researched examples and cases. We have found it to be of conceptual as well as practical use and highly recommend it to consultants and leaders alike.

We were quite pleased with such praise. But to continue to earn it, we strive to use an engaging writing style that minimizes unnecessary jargon and covers all of the traditional bases. We also integrate some central themes throughout the book—such as globalization, technology, ethics, environmental sustainability, and entrepreneurship—that are vital in understanding strategic management in today's global economy. We draw on short examples from business practice to bring concepts to life by providing 103 Strategy Spotlights (more detailed examples in sidebars).

Unlike other strategy texts, we provide three separate chapters that address timely topics about which business students should have a solid understanding. These are the role of intellectual assets in value creation (Chapter 4), entrepreneurial strategy and competitive dynamics (Chapter 8), and fostering entrepreneurship in established organizations (Chapter 12). We also provide an excellent set of cases to help students analyze, integrate, and apply strategic management concepts.

In developing *Strategic Management: Text and Cases,* we certainly didn't forget the instructors. As we all know, you have a most challenging (but rewarding) job. We did our best to help you. We provide a variety of supplementary materials that should help you in class preparation and delivery. For example, our chapter notes do not simply summarize the material in the text. Rather (and consistent with the concept of strategy!), we ask ourselves: "How can we add value?" Thus, for each chapter, we provide numerous questions to pose to help guide class discussion, at least 12 boxed examples to supplement chapter material, and three detailed "teaching tips" to further engage students. Also, the author team completed the chapter notes—along with the entire test bank—ourselves. That is, unlike many of our rivals, we didn't simply farm the work out to others. Instead, we felt that such efforts help to enhance quality and consistency—as well as demonstrate our personal commitment to provide a top-quality total package to strategy instructors.

Let's now address some of the key substantive changes in the Sixth Edition. Then we will cover some of the major features that we have had in previous editions.

What's New? Highlights of the Sixth Edition

We worked hard to add new material to the chapters that reflects both the feedback that we have received from reviewers as well as the challenges and opportunities that face today's managers. This involved an extensive amount of time carefully reviewing a wide variety of books, academic and practitioner journals, and the business press.

We also endeavored to avoid "chapter creep." That is, when we added new material, we deleted others (which included culling out redundant examples). We certainly benefited from the work of Rae Pinkham, a professional editor. She diligently pored over the chapter material and helped tighten our writing. The overall result was that we were able to update our material, add new material, as well as keep the chapters about the same length. We certainly appreciate her excellent contribution!

Here are some major changes in the Sixth Edition:

- **All of the 12 opening "Learning from Mistakes" vignettes that lead off each chapter are totally new.** Unique to this text, they are all examples of what can go wrong, and they serve as an excellent vehicle for clarifying and reinforcing strategy concepts. After all, what can be learned if one simply admires perfection!
- **Well over half of our "Strategy Spotlights" (sidebar examples) are brand new, and many others have been thoroughly updated.** We have a total of 103 Spotlights—by far the most sidebar examples in the strategy market. We are still able to conserve space because we focus on bringing the most important strategy concepts to life in a concise and highly readable manner. We work hard to eliminate unnecessary detail that detracts from the main point we are trying to make.
- **We have added 4 exhibits to the text and have carefully revised many other exhibits.** This, along with the four-color pictures in each chapter, aids learning and improves visual appeal. To further enhance readability, we focus on writing short paragraphs and provide many indented examples throughout the book.
- **We have increased the number of "Strategy Spotlights" that focus on three issues that are critical in today's leading-edge organizations—ethics, environmental sustainability, and crowdsourcing.** We have included an icon to identify each of these topics, We have 10 "Spotlights" on ethics that include

such issues as the role of nongovernmental organizations (NGOs) as an important stakeholder group (Chapter 1) and how some power companies engaged in "greenwashing"—making unsubstantiated claims about how environmental friendly their products or services really are (Chapter 11)! We include 10 "Spotlights" on environmental sustainability, such as Timberland's detoxification initiative as a means to create an efficient supply chain (Chapter 3) and why Shell's innovative gasoline product worked in Thailand—but failed miserably in Holland (Chapter 7). Finally, we have 8 "Spotlights" on crowdsourcing. These include topics such as how Goldcorp used crowdsourcing to strike gold (literally!) (Chapter 1) and how IBM's "Innovation Jam" helped it create new products and services (Chapter 12).

Key content changes for the chapters include:

- **Chapter 1 introduces the concept of "shared value," which was coined by Michael Porter and Mark Kramer in a 2011 *Harvard Business Review* article.** Shared value involves practices that enhance the competitiveness of a company while simultaneously advancing the economic and social conditions in which it operates. Such an approach goes beyond narrowly focusing on shareholder returns—it enhances the satisfaction of multiple shareholders.
- **Chapter 3 addresses a novel perspective—"The Prosumer"—that has important implications for today's organizations.** Here, the customer becomes engaged in the actual production process. Not only can this generate greater customer satisfaction, but also it has the potential to result in significant cost savings and generate innovative ideas for the firm.
- **Chapter 4 provides insights on how firms can successfully achieve integration when they engage in collaborative efforts.** We address four barriers (e.g., people aren't willing to provide help, people are unable to work with people they don't know well) that need to be overcome before effective collaboration can be achieved. Such barriers must be identified, and we discuss how managers can devise appropriate ways to overcome them.
- **Chapter 5 now includes a detailed discussion on the sustainability of competitive advantage that integrates key strategy concepts that are addressed in the first four chapters of the text.** We include the concepts of stakeholder analysis, industry five-forces analysis, the resource-base view of the firm, and social capital (both within and outside the firm's boundaries). We address how such strategic management concepts provide us with a means to address whether or not the strategy of a firm (Atlas Door) is sustainable over time.
- **Chapter 7 discusses "reverse innovation" a trend whereby many developing countries are becoming hotbeds for innovation.** Also referred to as "frugal innovation," such initiatives serve to expand potential markets in both developing and mature economies.
- **Chapter 9 addresses one of the most controversial topics in corporate governance—duality. That is, should a firm's Chief Executive Officer also serve as Chairman of the Board?** We address "pro" and "con" positions and explain why there is a trend toward less duality in large corporations as well as what the implications are for other governance mechanisms, such as the appointing of a lead director.
- **Chapter 11 introduces a rather new idea—the ambicultural leader.** Here, leaders can benefit by drawing on the best of different philosophies and business practices while avoiding the negatives of each. To illustrate, we provide the example of combining both Chinese and Western philosophies and practices.

- **Chapter 12 explains the idea of an "Innovator's D.N.A" and its importance in enhancing a firm's capacity for innovation and creativity.** We address the five key traits (e.g., questioning, observing, experimenting) and provide examples of how well-known entrepreneurs applied them to launch extremely successful enterprises.
- **Chapter 13 updates our Appendix: Sources of Company and Industry Information.** Here, we are most indebted to Ruthie Brock and Carol Byrne. These library professionals at the University of Texas at Arlington have graciously provided us with comprehensive and updated information that is organized in a range of issues. These include competitive intelligence, annual report collections, company rankings, business websites, and strategic and competitive analysis. Such information is invaluable in analyzing companies and industries.
- **Alan Eisner, our case editor, has worked hard to further enhance our excellent case package.**
  - Approximately half of the cases are author-written (much more than our competition). In addition, our case author, Alan Eisner, has carefully revised and edited most of the other cases. This promotes a tight linkage between chapter content and our cases and ensures that students effectively apply key strategic management concepts.
  - Updating our users' favorite cases (based on extensive market feedback) with new information and data to minimize instructor preparation time and "maximize freshness."
  - 9 new cases and significant updates on 27 cases, including Southwest, JetBlue, General Motors, Ford, Apple, eBay, and many others.
  - Providing an excellent mix of "tried and true classics" as well as shorter favorites from Harvard.
  - A major focus on fresh and current cases about familiar firms.
  - Cases of varying lengths to best fit instructor needs.
  - Many videos to match the cases.

WHAT REMAINS THE SAME: KEY FEATURES OF EARLIER EDITIONS

Let's now briefly address some of the exciting features that remain from the earlier editions.

- **Traditional organizing framework with three other chapters on timely topics.** Crisply written chapters cover all of the strategy bases and address contemporary topics. First, the chapters are divided logically into the traditional sequence: strategy analysis, strategy formulation, and strategy implementation. Second, we include three chapters on such timely topics as intellectual capital/knowledge management, entrepreneurial strategy and competitive dynamics, and fostering corporate entrepreneurship and new ventures.
- **"Learning from Mistakes" chapter-opening cases.** To enhance student interest, we begin each chapter with a case that depicts an organization that has suffered a dramatic performance drop, or outright failure, by failing to adhere to sound strategic management concepts and principles. We believe that this feature serves to underpin the value of the concepts in the course and that it is a preferred teaching approach to merely providing examples of outstanding companies that always seem to get it right! After all, isn't it better (and more challenging) to diagnose problems than admire perfection? As Dartmouth's Sydney Finkelstein, author of *Why Smart Executives Fail,* notes: "We live

in a world where success is revered, and failure is quickly pushed to the side. However, some of the greatest opportunities to learn—both for individuals and organizations— come from studying what goes wrong."* We'll see how, for example, Nokia, the Finnish phone manufacturer, saw its reputation as the industry's most powerful brand eroded when it failed to meet customers' needs in the emerging smartphone revolution. Clearly, its focus on mobile phones for voice communication was its most disastrous call in the past 10 years. We will also explore why AOL's $850 million acquisition of Bebo, a social networking firm, failed. AOL, a provider of Internet service, unloaded it two years later for only $10 million. Not a good return on their investment, to say the least! And we discuss why Carrefour, Europe's largest retailer, failed in both Thailand and Malaysia. Its key rival, Tesco, not only was much savvier in figuring out customer needs in these markets but also picked strong local partners.

- **Consistent chapter format and features to reinforce learning.** We have included several features in each chapter to add value and create an enhanced learning experience. First, each chapter begins with an overview and a set of bullets pointing to key learning objectives. Second, as previously noted, the opening case describes a situation in which a company's performance eroded because of a lack of proper application of strategy concepts. Third, at the end of each chapter there are four different types of questions/exercises that should help students assess their understanding and application of material:

  1. Summary review questions.
  2. Experiential exercises.
  3. Application questions and exercises.
  4. Ethics questions

Given the emergence of the Internet and e-commerce, each chapter contains at least one exercise that involves the use of the Internet.

- **"Reflecting on Career Implications" for each chapter.** This feature—at the end of each chapter—will help instructors drive home the immediate relevance/value of strategy concepts. It focuses on how an understanding of key concepts helps business students early in their careers.
- **Key Terms.** Approximately a dozen key terms for each chapter are identified in the margins of the pages. This addition was made in response to reviewer feedback and improves students' understanding of core strategy concepts.
- **Clear articulation and illustration of key concepts.** Key strategy concepts are introduced in a clear and concise manner and are followed by timely and interesting examples from business practice. Such concepts include value-chain analysis, the resource-based view of the firm, Porter's five-forces model, competitive advantage, boundaryless organizational designs, digital strategies, corporate governance, ethics, and entrepreneurship.
- **Extensive use of sidebars.** We include 103 sidebars (or about eight per chapter) called "Strategy Spotlights." The Strategy Spotlights not only illustrate key points but also increase the readability and excitement of new strategy concepts.
- **Integrative themes.** The text provides a solid grounding in ethics, globalization, environmental sustainability and technology. These topics are central themes throughout the book and form the basis for many of the Strategy Spotlights.
- **Implications of concepts for small businesses.** Many of the key concepts are applied to start-up firms and smaller businesses, which is particularly important since many students have professional plans to work in such firms.

*Personal communication, June 20, 2005.

- **Not just a textbook but an entire package.** *Strategic Management* features the best chapter teaching notes available today. Rather than merely summarizing the key points in each chapter, we focus on value-added material to enhance the teaching (and learning) experience. Each chapter includes dozens of questions to spur discussion, teaching tips, in-class group exercises, and about a dozen detailed examples from business practice to provide further illustrations of key concepts.
- **Excellent Case Studies.** We have selected an outstanding collection of current and classic cases for this edition, carefully including a wide variety of cases matched to key strategic concepts and organized to create maximum flexibility. We have a balance of short, concise and longer, comprehensive cases while maintaining currency and name recognition of our cases with many new and updated classroom-tested cases. We also have updated many of the favorites from the Fifth Edition, such as Southwest Airlines, JetBlue Airways, World Wrestling Entertainment, Ann Taylor, Apple, eBay in Asia, Nintendo, and many others, to further engage students.

Student Support Materials

Online Learning Center (OLC)

The following resources are available to students via the publisher's OLC at www.mhhe.com/dess6e:

- Chapter quizzes students can take to gauge their understanding of material covered in each chapter.
- A selection of PowerPoint slides for each chapter.
- Links to strategy simulations the Business Strategy Game & GLO-BUS. Both provide a powerful and constructive way of connecting students to the subject matter of the course with a competition among classmates on campus and around the world.

Instructor Support Materials

Instructor's Manual (IM)

Prepared by the textbook authors, the accompanying IM contains summary/objectives, lecture/discussion outlines, discussion questions, extra examples not included in the text, teaching tips, reflecting on career implications, experiential exercises, and more.

Test Bank

Prepared by the authors, the test bank contains more than 1,000 true/false, multiple-choice, and essay questions. It has now been tagged with learning objectives as well as Bloom's Taxonomy and AACSB criteria.

- **Assurance of Learning Ready.** Assurance of Learning is an important element of many accreditation standards. Dess 6e is designed specifically to support your Assurance of Learning initiatives. Each chapter in the book begins with a list of numbered learning objectives that appear throughout the chapter, as well as in the end-of-chapter questions and exercises. Every test bank question is also linked to one of these objectives, in addition to level of difficulty, topic area, Bloom's Taxonomy level, and AACSB skill area. *EZ Test,* McGraw-Hill's easy-to-use test bank software, can search the test bank by these and other categories, providing an engine for targeted Assurance of Learning analysis and assessment.

- **AACSB Statement.** The McGraw-Hill Companies is a proud corporate member of AACSB International. Understanding the importance and value of AACSB accreditation, Dess 6e has sought to recognize the curricula guidelines detailed in the AACSB standards for business accreditation by connecting selected questions in Dess 6e and the test bank to the general knowledge and skill guidelines found in the AACSB standards. The statements contained in Dess 6e are provided only as a guide for the users of this text. The AACSB leaves content coverage and assessment within the purview of individual schools, the mission of the school, and the faculty. While Dess 6e and the teaching package make no claim of any specific AACSB qualification or evaluation, we have labeled selected questions within Dess 6e according to the six general knowledge and skills areas.

- **Computerized Test Bank Online.** A comprehensive bank of test questions is provided within a computerized test bank powered by McGraw-Hill's flexible electronic testing program, *EZ Test Online* (www.eztestonline.com). *EZ Test Online* allows you to create paper and online tests or quizzes in this easy-to-use program! Imagine being able to create and access your test or quiz anywhere, at any time without installing the testing software. Now, with *EZ Test Online,* instructors can select questions from multiple McGraw-Hill test banks or author their own, and then either print the test for paper distribution or give it online.

- **Test Creation.**
  - Author/edit questions online using the 14 different question type templates.
  - Create printed tests or deliver online to get instant scoring and feedback.
  - Create questions pools to offer multiple versions online – great for practice.
  - Export your tests for use in *WebCT, Blackboard, PageOut,* and Apple's *iQuiz.*
  - Compatible with *EZ Test Desktop* tests you've already created.
  - Sharing tests with colleagues, adjuncts, TAs is easy.

- **Online Test Management.**
  - Set availability dates and time limits for your quiz or test.
  - Control how your test will be presented.
  - Assign points by question or question type with drop-down menu.
  - Provide immediate feedback to students or delay until all finish the test.
  - Create practice tests online to enable student mastery.
  - Your roster can be uploaded to enable student self-registration.

- **Online Scoring and Reporting.**
  - Automated scoring for most of *EZ Test*'s numerous question types.
  - Allows manual scoring for essay and other open response questions.
  - Manual rescoring and feedback is also available.
  - *EZ Test*'s grade book is designed to easily export to your grade book.
  - View basic statistical reports.

- **Support and Help.**
  - User's guide and built-in page-specific help.
  - Flash tutorials for getting started on the support site.
  - Support website: *www.mhhe.com/eztest.*
  - Product specialist available at 1-800-331-5094.
  - Online Training: *http://auth.mhhe.com/mpss/workshops/.*

PowerPoint Presentation

Prepared by Brad Cox of Midlands Tech, it consists of more than 400 slides incorporating an outline for the chapters tied to learning objectives. Also included are multiple-choice questions that can be used as Classroom Performance System (CPS) questions as well as additional examples outside of the text to promote class discussion. Case Study PowerPoint slides are available to facilitate case study coverage.

Instructor's Resource CD-ROM

All instructor supplements are available in this one-stop multimedia resource, which includes the Instructor's Manual, Test Bank, PowerPoint Presentations, and Case Study Teaching Notes.

McGraw-Hill Connect™ Management

Less Managing. More Teaching. Greater Learning. McGraw-Hill *Connect Management* is an online assignment and assessment solution that connects students with the tools and resources they'll need to achieve success.

- **McGraw-Hill *Connect Management* Features.** *Connect Management* offers a number of powerful tools and features to make managing assignments easier, so faculty can spend more time teaching. With *Connect Management,* students can engage with their coursework anytime and anywhere, making the learning process more accessible and efficient. *Connect Management* offers you the features described below.

  - There are chapter quizzes for the 12 chapters, consisting of 15–25 multiple-choice questions, testing students' overall comprehension of concepts presented in the chapter.
  - There are 2 specially crafted interactives for each of the 12 chapters that drill students in the use and application of the concepts and tools of strategic analysis.
  - *Connect* also includes special case exercises for approximately one-third of the 36 cases in this edition that require students to develop answers to a select number of the assignment questions.
  - Additionally, there will be financial remediation exercises related to the case exercises.
  - The majority of the *Connect* exercises are automatically graded, thereby simplifying the task of evaluating each class member's performance and monitoring the learning outcomes.

- **Student Progress Tracking.** *Connect Management* keeps instructors informed about how each student, section, and class is performing, allowing for more productive use of lecture and office hours. The progress-tracking function enables you to

  - View scored work immediately and track individual or group performance with assignment and grade reports.
  - Access an instant view of student or class performance relative to learning objectives.
  - Collect data and generate reports required by many accreditation organizations, such as AACSB.

- **Smart Grading.** When it comes to studying, time is precious. *Connect Management* helps students learn more efficiently by providing feedback and practice material when they need it, where they need it. When it comes to teaching, your time also is precious. The grading function enables you to

- Have assignments scored automatically, giving students immediate feedback on their work and side-by-side comparisons with correct answers.
- Access and review each response, manually change grades, or leave comments for students to review.
- Reinforce classroom concepts with practice tests and instant quizzes.

- **Simple Assignment Management.** With *Connect Management,* creating assignments is easier than ever, so you can spend more time teaching and less time managing. The assignment management function enables you to

  - Create and deliver assignments easily with selectable test bank items.
  - Streamline lesson planning, student progress reporting, and assignment grading to make classroom management more efficient than ever.
  - Go paperless with online submission and grading of student assignments.

- **Instructor Library.** The *Connect Management* Instructor Library is your repository for additional resources to improve student engagement in and out of class. You can select and use any asset that enhances your lecture. The *Connect Management* Instructor Library includes

  - Instructor Manual
  - Case Teaching Notes
  - PowerPoint® files
  - Test Bank

Case Videos

A set of videos related to selected cases accompanies the text to support your classroom, student lab, or for home viewing. These thought-provoking video clips are available upon adoption of this text.

Online Learning Center (OLC)

The instructor section of *www.mhhe.com/dess6e* also includes the Instructor's Manual, PowerPoint Presentations, Case Grid, and Case Study Teaching Notes as well as additional resources.

The Business Strategy Game and GLO-BUS Online Simulations

Both allow teams of students to manage companies in a head-to-head contest for global market leadership. These simulations give students the immediate opportunity to experiment with various strategy options and to gain proficiency in applying the concepts and tools they have been reading about in the chapters. To find out more or to register, please visit *www.mmhe.com/thompsonsims*.

Additional Resources

Create

Craft your teaching resources to match the way you teach! With McGraw-Hill *Create, www.mcgrawhillcreate.com* you can easily rearrange chapters, combine material from other content sources, and quickly upload content you have written, like your course syllabus or teaching notes. Find the content you need in *Create* by searching through thousands of leading McGraw-Hill textbooks. Arrange your book to fit your teaching style. *Create* even allows you to personalize your book's appearance by selecting the cover and adding your name, school, and course information. Order a *Create* book and you'll receive a complimentary print review copy in 3–5 business days or a complimentary electronic review copy (eComp) via e-mail in about one hour. Go to *www.mcgrawhillcreate.com* today and register. Experience how McGraw-Hill *Create* empowers you to teach *your* students *your* way.

McGraw-Hill Higher Education and Blackboard

McGraw-Hill Higher Education and Blackboard have teamed up. What does this mean for you?

1. **Your life, simplified.** Now you and your students can access McGraw-Hill's *Connect* and *Create* right from within your Blackboard course—all with one single sign-on. Say goodbye to the days of logging in to multiple applications.
2. **Deep integration of content and tools.** Not only do you get single sign-on with *Connect* and *Create,* you also get deep integration of McGraw-Hill content and content engines right in Blackboard. Whether you're choosing a book for your course or building Connect assignments, all the tools you need are right where you want them—inside of Blackboard.
3. **Seamless gradebooks.** Are you tired of keeping multiple gradebooks and manually synchronizing grades into Blackboard? We thought so. When a student completes an integrated Connect assignment, the grade for that assignment automatically (and instantly) feeds your Blackboard grade center.
4. **A solution for everyone.** Whether your institution is already using Blackboard or you just want to try Blackboard on your own, we have a solution for you. McGraw-Hill and Blackboard can now offer you easy access to industry-leading technology and content, whether your campus hosts it or we do. Be sure to ask your local McGraw-Hill representative for details.

The **Best** of **Both Worlds**

Mc Graw Hill

Bb
Blackboard

Do More

McGraw-Hill Customer Care Contact Information

At McGraw-Hill, we understand that getting the most from new technology can be challenging. That's why our services don't stop after you purchase our products. You can e-mail our product specialists 24 hours a day to get product training online. Or you can search our knowledge bank of Frequently Asked Questions on our support website. For customer support, call 800-331-5094, e-mail *hmsupport@mcgraw-hill.com*, or visit *www.mhhe.com/support*. One of our technical support analysts will be able to assist you in a timely fashion.

Acknowledgments

Strategic Management represents far more than just the joint efforts of the four co-authors. Rather, it is the product of the collaborative input of many people. Some of these individuals are academic colleagues, others are the outstanding team of professionals at McGraw-Hill/Irwin, and still others are those who are closest to us—our families. It is time to express our sincere gratitude.

First, we'd like to acknowledge the dedicated instructors who have graciously provided their insights since the inception of the text. Their input has been very helpful in both pointing out errors in the manuscript and suggesting areas that needed further development as additional topics. We sincerely believe that the incorporation of their ideas has been critical to improving the final product. These professionals and their affiliations are:

The Reviewer Hall of Fame

Moses Acquaah, *University of North Carolina–Greensboro*

Todd Alessandri, *Northeastern University*

Larry Alexander, *Virginia Polytechnic Institute*

Brent B. Allred, *College of William & Mary*

Allen C. Amason, *University of Georgia*

Kathy Anders, *Arizona State University*

Peter H. Antoniou, *California State University, San Marcos*

Dave Arnott, *Dallas Baptist University*

Marne L. Arthaud-Day, *Kansas State University*

Jay Azriel, *York University of Pennsylvania*

Jeffrey J. Bailey, *University of Idaho*

Dennis R. Balch, *University of North Alabama*

Bruce Barringer, *University of Central Florida*

Barbara R. Bartkus, *Old Dominion University*

Barry Bayon, *Bryant University*

Brent D. Beal, *Louisiana State University*

Joyce Beggs, *University of North Carolina–Charlotte*

Michael Behnam, *Suffolk University*

Kristen Bell DeTienne, *Brigham Young University*

Eldon Bernstein, *Lynn University*

Daniela Blettner, *Tilburg University*

Dusty Bodie, *Boise State University*

William Bogner, *Georgia State University*

Jon Bryan, *Bridgewater State College*

Charles M. Byles, *Virginia Commonwealth University*

Mikelle A. Calhoun, *Valparaiso University*

Thomas J. Callahan, *University of Michigan, Dearborn*

Samuel D. Cappel, *Southeastern Louisiana State University*

Gary Carini, *Baylor University*

Shawn M. Carraher, *Texas A&M University, Commerce*

Tim Carroll, *University of South Carolina*

Don Caruth, *Amberton University*

Maureen Casile, *Bowling Green State University*

Gary J. Castrogiovanni, *Florida Atlantic University*

Radha Chaganti, *Rider University*

Erick PC Chang, *Arkansas State University*

Theresa Cho, *Rutgers University*

Bruce Clemens, *Western New England College*

Betty S. Coffey, *Appalachian State University*

Wade Coggins, *Webster University, Fort Smith Metro Campus*

Susan Cohen, *University of Pittsburgh*

George S. Cole, *Shippensburg University*

Joseph Coombs, *Texas A & M University*

Christine Cope Pence, *University of California, Riverside*

James J. Cordeiro, *SUNY Brockport*

Jeffrey Covin, *Indiana University*

Keith Credo, *Auburn University*

Deepak Datta, *University of Texas at Arlington*

James Davis, *University of Notre Dame*

David Dawley, *West Virginia University*

Helen Deresky, *State University of New York, Plattsburgh*

Rocki-Lee DeWitt, *University of Vermont*

Jay Dial, *Ohio State University*

Michael E. Dobbs, *Arkansas State University*

Jonathan Doh, *Villanova University*

Tom Douglas, *Clemson University*

Jon Down, *Oregon State University*

Alan E. Ellstrand, *University of Arkansas*

Dean S. Elmuti, *Eastern Illinois University*

Clare Engle, *Concordia University*

Tracy Ethridge, *Tri-County Technical College*

William A. Evans, *Troy State University, Dothan*

Frances H. Fabian, *University of Memphis*

Angelo Fanelli, *Warrington College of Business*

Michael Fathi, *Georgia Southwestern University*

Carolyn J. Fausnaugh, *Florida Institute of Technology*

Tamela D. Ferguson, *University of Louisiana at Lafayette*

David Flanagan, *Western Michigan University*

Dave Foster, *Montana State University*

Isaac Fox, *University of Minnesota*

Deborah Francis, *Brevard College*

Steven A. Frankforter, *Winthrop University*

Vance Fried, *Oklahoma State University*

Naomi A. Gardberg, *CNNY Baruch College*

Mehmet Erdem Genc, *Baruch College, CUNY*

J. Michael Geringer, *California Polytechnic State University*

Diana L. Gilbertson, *California State University, Fresno*

Matt Gilley, *St. Mary's University*

Debbie Gilliard, *Metropolitan State College–Denver*

Yezdi H. Godiwalla, *University of Wisconsin–Whitewater*

Sanjay Goel, *University of Minnesota, Duluth*

Sandy Gough, *Boise State University*

Allen Harmon, *University of Minnesota, Duluth*

Niran Harrison, *University of Oregon*

Paula Harveston, *Berry College*

Ahmad Hassan, *Morehead State University*

Donald Hatfield, *Virginia Polytechnic Institute*

Kim Hester, *Arkansas State University*

John Hironaka, *California State University, Sacramento*

Alan Hoffman, *Bentley College*

Gordon Holbein, *University of Kentucky*

Stephen V. Horner, *Arkansas State University*

Jill Hough, *University of Tulsa*

John Humphreys, *Eastern New Mexico University*

James G. Ibe, *Morris College*

Jay J. Janney, *University of Dayton*

Lawrence Jauch, *University of Louisiana–Monroe*

Dana M. Johnson, *Michigan Technical University*

Homer Johnson, *Loyola University, Chicago*

James Katzenstein, *California State University, Dominguez Hills*

Joseph Kavanaugh, *Sam Houston State University*

Franz Kellermanns, *University of Tennessee*

Craig Kelley, *California State University, Sacramento*

Donna Kelley, *Babson College*

Dave Ketchen, *Auburn University*

John A. Kilpatrick, *Idaho State University*

Helaine J. Korn, *Baruch College,CUNY*

Stan Kowalczyk, *San Francisco State University*

Daniel Kraska, *North Central State College*

Donald E. Kreps, *Kutztown University*

Jim Kroeger, *Cleveland State University*

Subdoh P. Kulkarni, *Howard University*

Ron Lambert, *Faulkner University*

Theresa Lant, *New York University*

Ted Legatski, *Texas Christian University*

David J. Lemak, *Washington State University–Tri-Cities*

Cynthia Lengnick-Hall, *University of Texas at San Antonio*

Donald L. Lester, *Arkansas State University*

Wanda Lester, *North Carolina A&T State University*

Benyamin Lichtenstein, *University of Massachusetts at Boston*

Jun Lin, *SUNY at New Paltz*

Zhiang (John) Lin, *University of Texas at Dallas*

Dan Lockhart, *University of Kentucky*

John Logan, *University of South Carolina*

Kevin Lowe, *University of North Carolina, Greensboro*

Doug Lyon, *Fort Lewis College*

Hao Ma, *Bryant College*

Rickey Madden, *Ph.D., Presbyterian College*

James Maddox, *Friends University*

Ravi Madhavan, *University of Pittsburgh*

Paul Mallette, *Colorado State University*

Santo D. Marabella, *Moravian College*

Catherine Maritan, *Syracuse University*

Daniel Marrone, *Farmingdale State College, SUNY*

Sarah Marsh, *Northern Illinois University*

John R. Massaua, *University of Southern Maine*

Larry McDaniel, *Alabama A&M University*

Abagail McWilliams, *University of Illinois, Chicago*

John E. Merchant, *California State University, Sacramento*

John M. Mezias, *University of Miami*

Michael Michalisin, *Southern Illinois University at Carbondale*

Doug Moesel, *University of Missouri–Columbia*

Fatma Mohamed, *Morehead State University*

Mike Montalbano, *Bentley University*

Debra Moody, *University of North Carolina, Charlotte*

Gregory A. Moore, *Middle Tennessee State University*

James R. Morgan, *Dominican University and UC Berkeley Extension*

Sara A. Morris, *Old Dominion University*

Carolyn Mu, *Baylor University*

Stephen Mueller, *Northern Kentucky University*

John Mullane, *Middle Tennessee State University*

Gerry Nkombo Muuka, *Murray State University*

Chandran Mylvaganam, *Northwood University*

Anil Nair, *Old Dominion University*

V.K. Narayanan, *Drexel University*

Maria L. Nathan, *Lynchburg College*

Louise Nemanich, *Arizona State University*

Charles Newman, *University of Maryland, University College*

Stephanie Newport, *Austin Peay State University*

Bill Norton, *University of Louisville*

Yusuf A. Nur, *SUNY Brockport*

Jeffrey R. Nystrom, *University of Colorado*

d.t. ogilvie, *Rutgers University*

William Ross O'Brien, *Dallas Baptist University*

Floyd Ormsbee, *Clarkson University*

Karen L. Page, *University of Wyoming*

Jacquelyn W. Palmer, *University of Cincinnati*

Julie Palmer, *University of Missouri, Columbia*

Daewoo Park, *Xavier University*

Gerald Parker, *Saint Louis University*

Ralph Parrish, *University of Central Oklahoma*

Douglas K. Peterson, *Indiana State University*

Edward Petkus, *Mary Baldwin College*

Michael C. Pickett, *National University*

Peter Ping Li, *California State University, Stanislaus*

Michael W. Pitts, *Virginia Commonwealth University*

Laura Poppo, *Virginia Tech*

Steve Porth, *Saint Joseph's University*

Jodi A. Potter, *Robert Morris University*

Scott A. Quatro, *Grand Canyon University*

Nandini Rajagopalan, *University of Southern California*

Annette L. Ranft, *Florida State University*

Abdul Rasheed, *University of Texas at Arlington*

Devaki Rau, *Northern Illinois University*

George Redmond, *Franklin University*

Kira Reed, *Syracuse University*

Clint Relyea, *Arkansas State University*

Barbara Ribbens, *Western Illinois University*

Maurice Rice, *University of Washington*

Violina P. Rindova, *University of Maryland, College Park*

Ron Rivas, *Canisius College*

David Robinson, *Indiana State University–Terre Haute*

Kenneth Robinson, *Kennesaw State University*

Simon Rodan, *San Jose State University*

Patrick R. Rogers, *North Carolina A&T State University*

John K. Ross III, *Texas State University, San Marcos*

Robert Rottman, *Kentucky State University*

Matthew R. Rutherford, *Gonzaga University*

Carol M. Sanchez, *Grand Valley State University*

William W. Sannwald, *San Diego State University*

Yolanda Sarason, *Colorado State University*

Marguerite Schneider, *New Jersey Institute of Technology*

Roger R. Schnorbus, *University of Richmond*

Terry Sebora, *University of Nebraska–Lincoln*

John Seeger, *Bentley College*

Jamal Shamsie, *Michigan State University*

Mark Shanley, *University of Illinois at Chicago*

Lois Shelton, *California State University, Northridge*

Herbert Sherman, *Long Island University*
Weilei Shi, *Baruch College–CUNY*
Chris Shook, *Auburn University*
Jeremy Short, *Texas Tech University*
Mark Simon, *Oakland University, Michigan*
Rob Singh, *Morgan State University*
Bruce Skaggs, *University of Kentucky*
Wayne Smeltz, *Rider University*
Anne Smith, *University of Tennessee*
Andrew Spicer, *University of South Carolina*
James D. Spina, *University of Maryland*
John Stanbury, *George Mason University & Inter-University Institute of Macau, SAR China*
Timothy Stearns, *California State University, Fresno*
Elton Stephen, *Austin State University*
Alice Stewart, *Ohio State University*
Ram Subramanian, *Grand Valley State University*
Roy Suddaby, *University of Iowa*
Michael Sullivan, *UC Berkeley Extension*
Marta Szabo White, *Georgia State University*
Justin Tan, *York University, Canada*
Qingju Tao, *Lehigh University*
Linda Teagarden, *Virginia Tech*
Bing-Sheng Teng, *George Washington University*
Alan Theriault, *University of California–Riverside*
Tracy Thompson, *University of Washington, Tacoma*
Karen Torres, *Angelo State University*
Robert Trumble, *Virginia Commonwealth University*

K.J. Tullis, *University of Central Oklahoma*
Craig A. Turner, *Ph.D., East Tennessee State University*
Beverly Tyler, *North Carolina State University*
Rajaram Veliyath, *Kennesaw State University*
S. Stephen Vitucci, *Tarleton State University–Central Texas*
Jay A. Vora, *St. Cloud State University*
Jorge Walter, *Portland State University*
Bruce Walters, *Louisiana Tech University*
Edward Ward, *St. Cloud State University*
N. Wasilewski, *Pepperdine University*
Andrew Watson, *Northeastern University*
Larry Watts, *Stephen F. Austin University*
Paula S. Weber, *St. Cloud State University*
Kenneth E. A. Wendeln, *Indiana University*
Robert R. Wharton, *Western Kentucky University*
Laura Whitcomb, *California State University–Los Angeles*
Scott Williams, *Wright State University*
Diana Wong, *Bowling Green State University*
Beth Woodard, *Belmont University*
John E. Wroblewski, *State University of New York–Fredonia*
Anne York, *University of Nebraska, Omaha*
Michael Zhang, *Sacred Heart University*
Monica Zimmerman, *Temple University*

Second, the authors would like to thank several faculty colleagues who were particularly helpful in the review, critique, and development of the book and supplementary materials. Greg's colleagues at the University of Texas at Dallas also have been helpful and supportive. These individuals include Mike Peng, Joe Picken, Kumar Nair, John Lin, Roberto Ragozzino, Seung-Hyun Lee, Tev Dalgic, and Jane Salk. His administrative assistant, Mary Vice, has been extremely helpful. Two doctoral students, Brian Pinkham and Ciprian Stan, have provided many useful inputs and ideas, along with a research associate, Yolanda Tsang. He also appreciates the support of his dean and associate dean, Hasan Pirkul and Varghese Jacob, respectively. Tom would like to thank Gerry Hills, Abagail McWilliams, Rod Shrader, Mike Miller, James Gillespie, Ron Mitchell, Kim Boal, Keith Brigham, Jeremy Short, Tyge Payne, Bill Wan, Andy Yu, Abby Wang, Johan Wiklund, Mike Haynie, Alex McKelvie, Cathy Maritan, Ravi Dharwadkar, and Pam Brandes. Special thanks also to Jeff Stambaugh for his vital contribution to new materials. Tom also extends a special thanks to Benyamin Lichtenstein for his support and encouragement. Both Greg and Tom wish to thank a special colleague, Abdul Rasheed at the University of Texas at Arlington, who certainly has been a valued source of friendship and ideas for us for many years. He provided many valuable contributions to all editions. Alan thanks his colleagues at Pace University and the Case Association for their support in developing these fine case selections. Special thanks go to Jamal Shamsie at Michigan State University for his support in developing the case selections for this edition. He is also very grateful to Pauline Assenza at Berkeley College for her superb work as case teaching notes and powerpoints editor. And we appreciate Doug Sanford, at University of Towson for his expertise with one of our key pedagogical features—the key terms in each chapter. Gerry thanks all of his colleagues at Michigan State University for their help and support over the years. He also thanks his co-authors, including Phil Bromiley, Paul Vaaler, Cindy Devers, Federico Aime, Mike Mannor, John Haleblian, Kalin Kolev, Seungho Choi, Don Conlon, Bob Wiseman, Rebecca Luce, Kathie Sutcliffe, Jody Tompson, David Deephouse, Bernadine Dykes, Mathias Arrfelt, Mason Carpenter, Rob Davison, and Dustin Sleesman, for their role in helping him grow as a scholar.

Third, we would like to thank the team at McGraw-Hill/Irwin for their outstanding support throughout the process. This begins with John Biernat, formerly Publisher, who signed us to our original contract. John was always available to provide support and valued input during the entire process. In editorial, Paul Ducham, editorial director, executive editor Mike Ablassmeir, development editor Laura Griffin, and editorial coordinator Andrea Heirendt, kept things on track, responded quickly to our never-ending needs and requests, and offered insights and encouragement. Once the manuscript was completed and revised, lead project manager Harvey Yep expertly guided us through the production process. Rachel Townsend, media project manager, did an outstanding job in helping us with the digital materials. Jeremy Cheshareck, senior photo research coordinator, and freelance designer Pam Verros provided excellent design, photo, and art work. We also appreciate executive marketing manager Anke Weekes and marketing specialist Liz Steiner for their energetic, competent, and thorough marketing efforts. Last, but certainly not least, we thank MHI's 70 plus outstanding book reps—who serve on the "front lines"—as well as many in-house sales professionals based in Dubuque, Iowa. Clearly, they deserve a lot of credit for our success.

Finally, we would like to thank our families. For Greg this includes his parents, William and Mary Dess, who have always been there for him. His wife, Margie, and daughter, Taylor, have been a constant source of love and companionship. Greg would also like to recognize Glenn F. Kirk. He was one of Greg's first managers in industry (Western Electric Company), and he certainly led by example. Glenn was also very patient (and forgiving) with Greg's limited engineering and "collaboration" skills(!). Tom thanks his wife Vicki for her constant love and companionship. Tom also thanks Lee Hetherington and Thelma Lumpkin for their inspiration, as well as his mom Katy, and his sister Kitty, for a lifetime of support. Alan thanks his family—his wife Helaine and his children Rachel and Jacob—for their love and support. He also thanks his parents, Gail Eisner and the late Marvin Eisner, for their support and encouragement. Gerry thanks his wife, Gaelen, for her love, support, and friendship and his children, Megan and AJ, for their love and the joy they bring to his life. He also thanks his parents, Gene and Jane, for their encouragement and support in all phases of his life. Finally, he thanks Phil Bromiley, his academic mentor, for helping him grow as a scholar.

guided tour

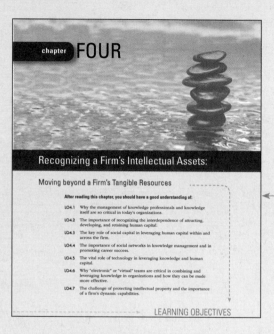

Learning Objectives

Learning Objectives numbered LO4.1, LO4.2, LO4.3, etc. with corresponding icons in the margins to indicate where learning objectives are covered in the text.

Learning from Mistakes

Learning from Mistakes are examples of where things went wrong. Failures are not only interesting but also sometimes easier to learn from. And students realize strategy is not just about "right or wrong" answers, but requires critical thinking.

Learning from Mistakes

Toyota Motor Company had developed an industry-leading strategy that focused on value innovation and cost reduction.[1] For many years it was a solid strategy for both the company and its customers. Over the years, Toyota built a reputation for engineering excellence and cost cutting. Its engineers collaborated with suppliers to extract cost-savings without compromising quality. Yet, by the middle of the last decade, Toyota's virtue had become a vice and eventually led to recalled vehicles, lawsuits, and a damaged reputation. What went wrong?

Toyota's problems stemmed from an overwhelming desire to cut costs. This, in turn, led to a product that did not meet the same high quality that its customers had come to expect. When a North American parts supplier interested in working with the automaker did a teardown of a 2007 Camry, its engineers were surprised by how much the traditional Toyota craftsmanship had been watered down by years of nips and tucks. One example of this came to light in 2006, when a redesigned Camry revealed an embarrassing flaw in its headliner (the lining that covers the inside of the roof). Under pressure to cut costs, a Toyota affiliate chose a carbon fiber material that had not yet been approved by Toyota engineers. Unfortunately, the new carbon fiber material required so much heat to mold during production that it would catch fire. Thus, as many as 30 percent of the parts were scrapped—compared to a normal scrap rate for headliners of about 5 percent.

6.6 strategy spotlight

Crowdsourcing: How a Strategic Alliance Will Benefit Both Parties

MRM Worldwide, a New York–based advertising firm, has entered into a strategic alliance with Aniboom, a "virtual" animation company. The alliance is designed to bring MRM's clients quicker and more cost-efficient animation services.

Sources: Van Hoven, M. 2009. Strategic Alliance: MRM and Aniboom Team Up, *Crowdsource*, www.mediabistro.com. August 31. np; and McClellan, S. 2009. MRM, Aniboom Team Up. www.adweek.com. August 31. np.

in the future as clients seek more efficient ways of doing business.

MRM's plans are to have animators compete for work: "MRMs clients can launch a content creation competition in the Aniboom community for advertising solutions and have the community at large or a panel of judges select the top finalists and ultimate winner of the assign-

Strategy Spotlight

These boxes weave themes of ethics, globalization, and technology into every chapter of the text, providing students with a thorough grounding necessary for understanding strategic management. Select boxes incorporating crowdsourcing, environmental sustainability, and ethical themes include the following icons:

8.2 strategy spotlight

Entrepreneurial Vision to Revitalize Detroit

Detroit is the poorest major city in America. With an unemployment rate of 26 percent and a declining population, it

Sources: Sohail, F. 2010. Alternative Energy: Creating Non-exportable Jobs. *Forbes.com*, June 30. np; Easton, N. 2010. If You Can Remake Yourself Here. *Fortune*, November 1: 59–63; Gray, S. 2010. When Entrepreneurs Need Nerves of Steel. *Fortune*, October 18: 63–66; Saulny, S. 2010. Detroit Entrepreneurs Opt to Look Up. *The New York Times*, January 10: A18; Anonymous. 2010. Champions of the New Economy. *eBusiness*, May/June: np; Whitford, D. 2010. Can Farming Save Detroit? *Fortune*, January 18: 78–84.

that is surrounded by the Great Lakes and having served as a member of the Detroit Water and Sewerage Board of Commissioners, Oliver appreciated the value of water as a critical resource needed for economic development. Fresh water is a commodity increasingly demanded around the world.

Although these businesses span a wide range of industries, they demonstrate that entrepreneurial vision often arises out an individual's experiences and can encompass both a business idea as well as a vehicle with which to improve conditions in a larger community.

Key Terms

Key Terms defined in the margins have been added to improve students' understanding of core strategy concepts.

> **human capital** the individual capabilities, knowledge, skills, and experience of a company's employees and managers.

Reflecting on Career Implications

This new section before the summary of every chapter consists of examples on how understanding of key concepts helps business students early in their careers.

Reflecting on Career Implications . . .

- **Creating the Environmentally Aware Organization:** In your career, what are some ways in which you can engage in scanning, monitoring, and intelligence gathering for future job opportunities? Consider, for example, subscribing to your field's professional publications and becoming actively involved in relevant professional organizations.
- **SWOT Analysis:** From a career standpoint, periodically evaluate your strengths and weaknesses as well as potential opportunities and threats to your career. In addition, strive to seek input from trusted peers and superiors.
- **General Environment:** Carefully evaluate the elements of the general environment facing your firm. Identify factors (e.g., rapid technological change) that can provide promising career opportunities as well as possibilities for you to add value for your organization. In doing this, don't focus solely on "internal factors" of your organization.
- **Five-Forces Analysis:** Consider the five forces affecting the industry within which your organization competes. If the "forces" are unfavorable, the long-term profit potential of the industry may be unattractive. And, there will likely be fewer resources available and—all other things being equal—fewer career opportunities.

Exhibit 7.4 Opposing Pressures and Four Strategies

Exhibits

Both new and improved exhibits in every chapter provide visual presentations of the most complex concepts covered to support student comprehension.

Cases

Updated case lineup provides 9 new cases. The remaining have been revised to "maximize freshness" and minimize instructor preparation time. New cases for this edition include well-known companies such as Yahoo!, the movie exhibition industry, Geely Automotive, and microfinance banks.

support materials

Online Learning Center (OLC)

The website *www.mhhe.com/dess6e* follows the text chapter-by-chapter. OLC content is ancillary and supplementary germane to the textbook. As students read the book, they can go online to take self-grading quizzes, review material, or work through interactive exercises. It includes chapter quizzes, student PowerPoint slides, and links to strategy simulations The *Business Strategy Game* and GLO-BUS.

The instructor section also includes the Instructor's Manual, PowerPoint Presentations, Case Study Teaching Notes, Case Grid, and Video Guide as well as all student resources.

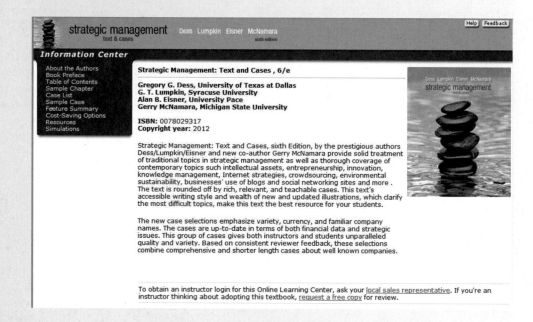

Brief Contents

Contents

part 2 Strategic Formulation

Chapter 7
International Strategy: Creating Value in Global Markets 238

Chapter 8
Entrepreneurial Strategy and Competitive Dynamics 278

part 3 Strategic
Implementation

Chapter 9
Strategic Control and Corporate
Governance 316

Chapter 10
Creating Effective Organizational
Designs 354

part 4 Case Analysis

Cases

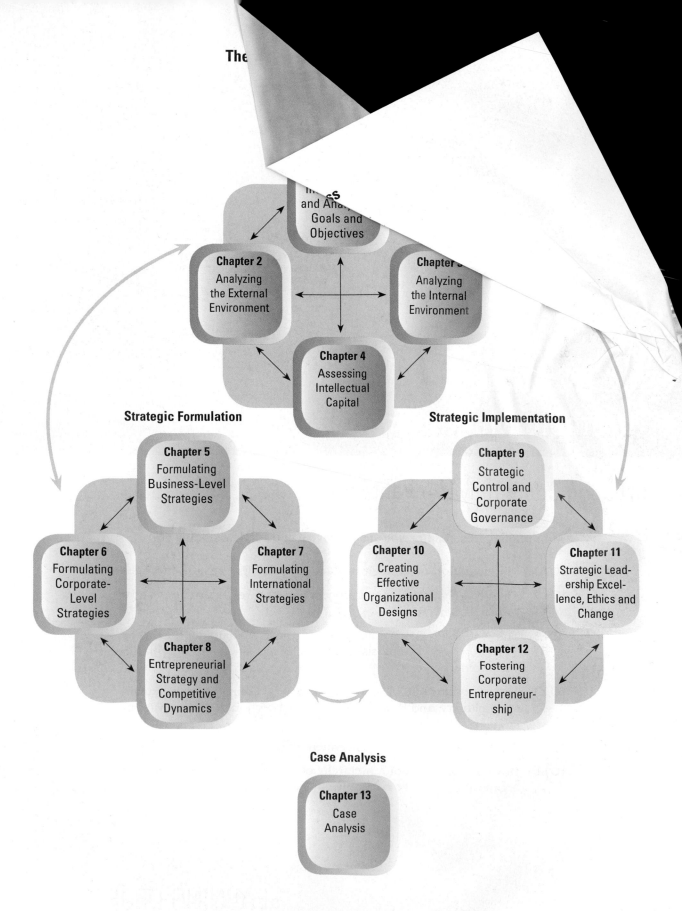

The

Chapter 1
...cess
and Ana...
Goals and
Objectives

Chapter 2
Analyzing
the External
Environment

Chapter 3
Analyzing
the Internal
Environment

Chapter 4
Assessing
Intellectual
Capital

Strategic Formulation

Chapter 5
Formulating
Business-Level
Strategies

Chapter 6
Formulating
Corporate-
Level
Strategies

Chapter 7
Formulating
International
Strategies

Chapter 8
Entrepreneurial
Strategy and
Competitive
Dynamics

Strategic Implementation

Chapter 9
Strategic
Control and
Corporate
Governance

Chapter 10
Creating
Effective
Organizational
Designs

Chapter 11
Strategic Lead-
ership Excel-
lence, Ethics and
Change

Chapter 12
Fostering
Corporate
Entrepreneur-
ship

Case Analysis

Chapter 13
Case
Analysis

chapter

Strategic Management:

Creating Competitive Advantages

After reading this chapter, you should have a good understanding of:

LO1.1 The definition of strategic management and its four key attributes.

LO1.2 The strategic management process and its three interrelated and principal activities.

LO1.3 The vital role of corporate governance and stakeholder management as well as how "symbiosis" can be achieved among an organization's stakeholders.

LO1.4 The importance of social responsibility, including environmental sustainability, and how it can enhance a corporation's innovation strategy.

LO1.5 The need for greater empowerment throughout the organization.

LO1.6 How an awareness of a hierarchy of strategic goals can help an organization achieve coherence in its strategic direction.

LEARNING OBJECTIVES

The Strategic Management Process

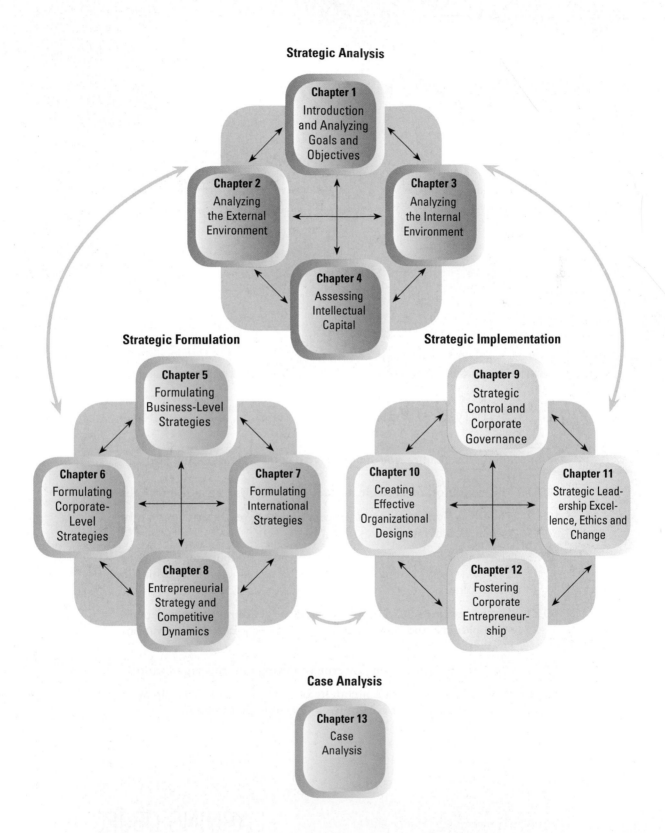

Strategic Analysis

Chapter 1
Introduction and Analyzing Goals and Objectives

Chapter 2
Analyzing the External Environment

Chapter 3
Analyzing the Internal Environment

Chapter 4
Assessing Intellectual Capital

Strategic Formulation

Chapter 5
Formulating Business-Level Strategies

Chapter 6
Formulating Corporate-Level Strategies

Chapter 7
Formulating International Strategies

Chapter 8
Entrepreneurial Strategy and Competitive Dynamics

Strategic Implementation

Chapter 9
Strategic Control and Corporate Governance

Chapter 10
Creating Effective Organizational Designs

Chapter 11
Strategic Leadership Excellence, Ethics and Change

Chapter 12
Fostering Corporate Entrepreneurship

Case Analysis

Chapter 13
Case Analysis

chapter ONE

Strategic Management:

Creating Competitive Advantages

After reading this chapter, you should have a good understanding of:

LO1.1   The definition of strategic management and its four key attributes.

LO1.2   The strategic management process and its three interrelated and principal activities.

LO1.3   The vital role of corporate governance and stakeholder management as well as how "symbiosis" can be achieved among an organization's stakeholders.

LO1.4   The importance of social responsibility, including environmental sustainability, and how it can enhance a corporation's innovation strategy.

LO1.5   The need for greater empowerment throughout the organization.

LO1.6   How an awareness of a hierarchy of strategic goals can help an organization achieve coherence in its strategic direction.

LEARNING OBJECTIVES

We define strategic management as *consisting of the analyses, decisions, and actions an organization undertakes in order to create and sustain competitive advantages.* At the heart of strategic management is the question: How and why do some firms outperform others? Thus, the challenge to managers is to decide on strategies that provide advantages that can be sustained over time. There are four key attributes of strategic management. It is directed at overall organizational goals, includes multiple stakeholders, incorporates short-term as well as long-term perspectives, and recognizes trade-offs between effectiveness and efficiency. We discuss the above definition and the four key attributes in the first section.

The second section addresses the strategic management process. The three major processes are strategy analysis, strategy formulation, and strategy implementation. These three components parallel the analyses, decisions, and actions in the above definition. We discuss how each of the 12 chapters addresses these three processes and provide examples from each chapter.

The third section discusses two important and interrelated concepts: corporate governance and stakeholder management. Corporate governance addresses the issue of who "governs" the corporation and determines its direction. It consists of three primary participants: stockholders (owners), management (led by the chief executive officer), and the board of directors (elected to monitor management). Stakeholder management recognizes that the interests of various stakeholders, such as owners, customers, and employees, can often conflict and create challenging decision-making dilemmas for managers. However, we discuss how some firms have been able to achieve "symbiosis" among stakeholders wherein their interests are considered interdependent and can be achieved simultaneously. We also discuss the important role of social responsibility and explain the concept of "shared value." Further, we emphasize the need for corporations to incorporate environmental sustainability in their strategic actions.

The fourth section addresses factors in the business environment that have increased the level of unpredictable change for today's leaders. Such factors have also created the need for a greater strategic management perspective and reinforced the role of empowerment throughout the organization.

The final section focuses on the need for organizations to ensure consistency in their vision, mission, and strategic objectives which, collectively, form a hierarchy of goals. While visions may lack specificity, they must evoke powerful and compelling mental images. Strategic objectives are much more specific and are essential for driving toward overall goals.

How CEO George Buckley Turned Around 3M

Why is innovation important to 3M? As their older products become outmoded or become commodities, they must be replaced. According to Larry Wendling, head of 3M's corporate research, "Our business model is literally new-product innovation." However, when James McNerney left the company to become Boeing's CEO, the percentage had slid to 21 percent. And, what's worse, much of the new product revenue came from a single category: optical films.

The board went outside the firm for its new CEO and appointed George Buckley, who had previously served as CEO of Brunswick, an Illinois company known for bowling gear and boats. What is perhaps most important to know about Buckley, however, is that he has a Ph.D. in electrical engineering and is a scientist at heart, with several patents to his name. He states: "This is to me an engineer's and scientist's Toys'R'Us," and "There is no company like it in America. There is no company like it in the world."

When Buckley took over 3M, he quickly set some clear business goals for the company. He wanted his managers to protect and strengthen 3M's core businesses, which included abrasives, optical film, and industrial tapes. He also wanted 3M to develop lower-cost

products to compete in emerging markets, as well as for the firm to play a key role in future growth markets such as renewable energy, water infrastructure, and mobile digital media.

Perhaps most important, Buckley has been an outspoken champion for 3M's labs. In 2009, despite the deep recession, he kept R&D spending at more than $1 billion and asserted that "even in the worst economic times in memory, we released over 1,000 new products." He also removed the stringent focus on efficiency, particularly in basic research. This had a huge psychic payoff for staff at the science-centric company. Ram Charan, a world-famous consultant who advises the firm claims "George has accelerated the innovation machine by devoting his personal time, his energy, his focus, to empowering the researchers, opening up their minds and urging them to restore the luster of 3M." Buckley's results are impressive: The percentage of 3M's revenue from products introduced in the past five years is back to 30 percent and is expected to reach the mid-30s by 2012.

In closing, Marc Gunther, a contributing editor at *Fortune* magazine, provides some interesting personal insights: "Buckley is a charming and, above all, enthusiastic guy . . . who, in his spare time, likes taking apart and putting together old motorcycles or restoring Victorian furniture . . . While he surely needs traditional management skills to oversee a global company of 75,000 people, my sense is that his scientific curiosity about how the world works and boyish delight in how things get invented make him a perfect fit for 3M."

Sources: Gunther, M. 2010. 3M's innovation revival. *Fortune.* September 27: 73–76; Hindo, B. 2007. 3M chief plants a money tree. *www.businessweek.com.* June 11: np; and, Gunther, M. Why 3M is unique. *theenergycollective.com.* December 10: np.

On the other hand, when things don't go well, much of the failure of an organization can also, rightfully, be attributed to the leader.[8] Nokia's leadership failed to see the changes taking place in the mobile phone industry. In contrast, Apple fully capitalized on the emerging trend toward sophisticated smartphones.

The contrasting fortunes of Hewlett-Packard under two different CEOs also demonstrate the influence leadership has on firm performance.[9] When Carly Fiorina was fired as CEO of the firm, HP enjoyed an immediate increase in its stock price of 7 percent—hardly a strong endorsement of her leadership! Her successor, Mark Hurd, led the firm to five years of outstanding financial results. Interestingly, when he abruptly resigned on August 6, 2010, the firm's stock dropped 12 percent almost instantly! (To provide some perspective, this represents a decrease in HP's market value of about $12 billion.)

However, this reflects only part of the picture. Consider another perspective called the **external control view of leadership.** Here, rather than making the implicit assumption that the leader is the most important factor in determining organizational outcomes, the focus is on external factors that may positively (or negatively) affect a firm's success. We don't have to look far to support this perspective. Developments in the general environment,

external control view of leadership situations in which external forces—where the leader has limited influence—determine the organization's success.

such as economic downturns, governmental legislation, or an outbreak of major internal conflict or war, can greatly restrict the choices that are available to a firm's executives. In addition, major unanticipated developments can often have very negative consequences for businesses regardless of how well formulated their strategies are.

Let's look at a few recent examples:[10]

- Hurricane Katrina in 2007 had a disastrous effect on businesses located along the Gulf Coast.
- The financial meltdown of 2008 and the resultant deep recession during the following two years forced once proud corporations like General Motors and Citigroup to ask for government bailouts. Others, such as Merrill Lynch and Washington Mutual, had to be acquired by other firms.
- In the aftermath of BP's disastrous oil well explosion on April 20, 2010, the fishing and tourism industries in the region suffered significant downturns. BP itself was forced to pay a $20 billion fine to the U.S. government.
- In April 2010, a volcanic eruption in Iceland disrupted air traffic all over Europe for well over a week. It is estimated that major airlines lost approximately $1.7 billion.
- On March 11, 2011, a 9.0 earthquake and tsunami devastated Japan and resulted in the loss of more than 20,000 lives. During the next two trading days, the country's stock exchange (Nikkei) suffered its biggest loss in 40 years. The disaster hit nearly every industry hard—especially energy companies. For example, Tokyo Electric Power Co., which operates a nuclear power plant that was severly damaged, fell 24.7 percent, and Toshiba Corp., a maker of nuclear power plants, slid 19.5 percent. Firms as diverse as Toyota, Honda, and Sony were forced to halt production because extensive damage to roads and distribution systems made it nearly impossible to move products.

Before moving on, it is important to point out that successful executives are often able to navigate around the difficult circumstances that they face. At times it can be refreshing to see the optimistic position they take when they encounter seemingly insurmountable odds. Of course, that's not to say that one should be naïve or Pollyannaish. Consider, for example, how one CEO is handling trying times:[11]

Name a general economic woe, and the chances are that Charles Needham is dealing with it.

- Market turmoil has knocked 80 percent off the shares of South Africa's Metorex, the mining company that he heads.
- The plunge in global commodities is slamming prices for the copper, cobalt, and other minerals Metorex unearths across Africa. The credit crisis makes it harder to raise money.
- And fighting has again broken out in the Democratic Republic of Congo, where Metorex has a mine and several projects in development.

Such problems might send many executives to the window ledge. Yet Needham appears unruffled as he sits down at a conference table in the company's modest offices in a Johannesburg suburb. The combat in northeast Congo, he notes, is far from Metorex's mine. Commodity prices are still high, in historical terms. And Needham is confident he can raise enough capital, drawing on relationships with South African banks. "These are the kinds of things you deal with, doing business in Africa," he says.

What Is Strategic Management?

Given the many challenges and opportunities in the global marketplace, today's managers must do more than set long-term strategies and hope for the best.[12] They must go beyond what some have called "incremental management," whereby they view their job as making markets can exert significant pressures on executives to meet short-term performance targets. Studies have shown that corporate leaders often take a short-term approach to the detriment of creating long-term shareholder value. Consider the following:

> According to recent studies, only 59 percent of financial executives say they would pursue a positive net present value project if it meant missing the quarter's consensus earnings per-share estimate. Worse, 78 percent say they would sacrifice value—often a great deal of value—to smooth earnings. Similarly, managers are more likely to cut R&D to reverse an earning slide if a significant amount of the company's equity is owned by institutions with high portfolio turnover. Many companies have the same philosophy about long-term investments such as infrastructure and employee training.[21]

Fourth, strategic management *involves the recognition of trade-offs between effectiveness and efficiency.* Some authors have referred to this as the difference between "doing the right thing" **(effectiveness)** and "doing things right" **(efficiency).**[22] While managers must allocate and use resources wisely, they must still direct their efforts toward the attainment of overall organizational objectives. Managers who only focus on meeting short-term budgets and targets may fail to attain the broader goals. Consider the following amusing story told by Norman Augustine, former CEO of defense giant Martin Marietta (now Lockheed Martin):

> I am reminded of an article I once read in a British newspaper which described a problem with the local bus service between the towns of Bagnall and Greenfields. It seemed that, to the great annoyance of customers, drivers had been passing long queues of would-be passengers with a smile and a wave of the hand. This practice was, however, clarified by a bus company official who explained, "It is impossible for the drivers to keep their timetables if they must stop for passengers."[23]

Clearly, the drivers who were trying to stay on schedule had ignored the overall mission. As Augustine noted, "Impeccable logic but something seems to be missing!"

Successful managers must make many trade-offs. It is central to the practice of strategic management. At times, managers must focus on the short term and efficiency; at other times the emphasis is on the long term and expanding a firm's product-market scope in order to anticipate opportunities in the competitive environment. For example, consider Kevin Sharer's perspective. He is CEO of Amgen, the giant $15 billion biotechnology firm:

> A CEO must always be switching between what I call different altitudes—tasks of different levels of abstraction and specificity. At the highest altitude you're asking the big questions: What are the company's mission and strategy? Do people understand and believe in these aims? Are decisions consistent with them? At the lowest altitude, you're looking at on-the-ground operations: Did we make that sale? What was the yield on that last lot in the factory? How many days of inventory do we have for a particular drug? And then there's everything in between: How many chemists do we need to hire this quarter? What should we pay for a small biotech company that has a promising new drug? Is our production capacity adequate to roll out a product in a new market?[24]

Some authors have developed the concept of **"ambidexterity"** which refers to a manager's challenge to both align resources to take advantage of existing product markets as well as proactively explore new opportunities.[25] Strategy Spotlight 1.2 discusses ambidextrous behaviors that are required for success in today's challenging marketplace.

The Strategic Management Process

We've identified three ongoing processes—analyses, decisions, and actions—that are central to strategic management. In practice, these three processes—often referred to as strategy analysis, strategy formulation, and strategy implementation—are highly interdependent and do not take place one after the other in a sequential fashion in most companies.

---

effectiveness tailoring actions to the needs of an organization rather than wasting effort, or "doing the right thing."

efficiency performing actions at a low cost relative to a benchmark, or "doing things right."

ambidexterity the challenge managers face of both aligning resources to take advantage of existing product markets as well as proactively exploring new opportunities.

strategic management process strategy analysis, strategy formulation, and strategy implementation

>LO1.2
The strategic management process and its three interrelated and principal activities.

- Olam International, a leading cash[...]
Africa to Asia for processing. By c[...]
ers in Tanzania, Mozambique, Nig[...]
and shipping costs by as much as 2[...]
Further, Olam built preferred relati[...]
employment to 17,000 people—95[...]
employment to an equal number o[...]
not available.

**The Triple Bottom Line: Incorpo[...]
and Social Costs** Many companie[...]
bottom line."** This involves assessing[...]
Shell, NEC, Procter & Gamble, and [...]
the environmental and social costs of[...]
community.[68]

The environmental revolution has[...]
1960s and 1970s, companies were in a[...]
natural environment. However, a serie[...]
swell for strict governmental regulatio[...]
people died of mercury poisoning. Cl[...]
throughout the world. Some other exan[...]

- Ice roads are melting, so Canadian[...]
diamond miners must airlift equip[...]
at great cost instead of trucking it[...]
- More severe storms and rising sea[...]
mean oil companies must build str[...]
ger rigs, and cities must build high[...]
seawalls.
- The loss of permafrost and protect[...]
sea ice may force villages like Ala[...]
Shismaref to relocate.
- Yukon River salmon and fisheries[...]
are threatened by a surge of para-[...]
sites associated with a jump in wa[...]
temperature.
- Later winters have let beetles spre[...]
in British Columbia, killing 22 mi[...]
acres of pine forests, an area the s[...]
of Maine.
- In Mali, Africa, crops are threaten[...]
the dry season is too hot for potat[...]

Stuart Hart, writing in the *Harvar*[...]
lems and challenges associated with th[...]

The challenge is to develop a *sustain*[...]
capable of supporting indefinitely. Alt[...]
the developed world, the planet as a wl[...]
the scourges of the late twentieth centu[...]
urban pollution; poverty; infectious d[...]
borders. The simple fact is this: in mee[...]
generations to meet theirs . . . corpo[...]
the technology, the global reach, and, [...]

Intended versus Realized Strategies

Henry Mintzberg, a management scholar at McGill University, argues that viewing the strategic management process as one in which analysis is followed by optimal decisions and their subsequent meticulous implementation neither describes the strategic management process accurately nor prescribes ideal practice.[26] He sees the business environment as far from predictable, thus limiting our ability for analysis. Further, decisions are seldom based on optimal rationality alone, given the political processes that occur in all organizations.[27]

Taking into consideration the limitations discussed above, Mintzberg proposed an alternative model. As depicted in Exhibit 1.2, decisions following from analysis, in this model, constitute the *intended* **strategy** of the firm. For a variety of reasons, the intended strategy rarely survives in its original form. Unforeseen environmental developments,

intended strategy
strategy in which organizational decisions are determined only by analysis.

Shared value
petitiveness of a c
tions in which it c
connections betw

Shared value
by firms—a redis
nomic and social

Fair trade aim:
them higher p
is mostly abou

A shared valu
strengthening
increase farme
ger pie of reve
them. Early st
fair trade can i
raise their inco
to implement r
be greater ecor

A firm's valu
Opportunities to c
costs in the firm's
in the absence of
greenhouse gases

The shared v
progress and valu
increases when fi
new ways of oper
the full productivi

Let's look at v
societal challenge

- Hindustan Ui
  ated by under
  people. The f
  preneurs cove
  the name of tl
  giving womer
  the spread of
  Thus, the uni
  efit society by
  Project Shakt
  also extended
  regions, creat
- Leading comp
  employee pro
  For example,
  reduction in t
  grams. Such i
  return of $2.7
  son & Johnso

Experiential Exercise

Using the Internet or library sources, select four organizations—two in the private sector and two in the public sector. Find their mission statements. Complete the following exhibit by identifying the stakeholders that are mentioned. Evaluate the differences between firms in the private sector and those in the public sector.

Name			
Mission Statement			
Stakeholders (✓ = mentioned)			
1. Customers			
2. Suppliers			
3. Managers/employees			
4. Community-at-large			
5. Owners			
6. Others?			
7. Others?			

Application Questions & Exercises

1. Go to the Internet and look up one of these company sites: *www.walmart.com*, *www.ge.com*, or *www.fordmotor.com*. What are some of the key events that would represent the "romantic" perspective of leadership? What are some of the key events that depict the "external control" perspective of leadership?

2. Select a company that competes in an industry in which you are interested. What are some of the recent demands that stakeholders have placed on this company? Can you find examples of how the company is trying to develop "symbiosis" (interdependence and mutual benefit) among its stakeholders? (Use the Internet and library resources.)

3. Provide examples of companies that are actively trying to increase the amount of empowerment in the strategic management process throughout the organization. Do these companies seem to be having positive outcomes? Why? Why not?

4. Look up the vision statements and/or mission statements for a few companies. Do you feel that they are constructive and useful as a means of motivating employees and providing a strong strategic direction? Why? Why not? (*Note:* Annual reports, along with the Internet, may be good sources of information.)

Ethics Questions

1. A company focuses solely on short-term profits to provide the greatest return to the owners of the business (i.e., the shareholders in a publicly held firm). What ethical issues could this raise?

2. A firm has spent some time—with input from managers at all levels—in developing a vision statement and a mission statement. Over time, however, the behavior of some executives is contrary to these statements. Could this raise some ethical issues?

References

1. Gunther, M. 2010. Fallen angels. *Fortune,* November 1: 75–78.

2. Sidhu, I. 2010. *Doing both.* East Saddle River, NJ & London: FT Press; ben-Aaron, D. 2010. After Nokia, can angry birds propel Finland? *Bloomberg BusinessWeek.* December 6–December 12: 48–50; ben-Aaron, D. 2010. Nokia board faces call for change on $77 billion lost value. *http://www.bloomberg.com/news.* July 15: np; Anonymous. 2010. The curse of the alien boss. *The Economist.* August 7: 65; and, Lynn, M. 2010. The fallen king of Finland. *Bloomberg BusinessWeek.* September 26: 6–7. We thank Pratik Kapadia for his valued contribution.

3. For a discussion of the "romantic" versus "external control" perspective, refer to Meindl, J. R. 1987. The romance of leadership and the evaluation of organizational performance. *Academy of Management Journal* 30: 92–109; and Pfeffer, J. & Salancik, G. R. 1978. *The external control of organizations: A resource dependence perspective.* New York: Harper & Row.

4. A recent perspective on the "romantic view" of leadership is provided by Mintzberg, H. 2004. Leadership and management development: An afterword. *Academy of Management Executive,* 18(3): 140–142.

5. For a discussion of the best and worst managers for 2008, read: Anonymous. 2009. The best managers. *BusinessWeek,* January 19: 40–41; and, The worst managers. On page 42 in the same issue.

6. Burrows, P. 2009. Apple without its core? *BusinessWeek.* January 26/February 2: 31.

7. For an insightful discussion of Steve Jobs's impact on Apple, read: Satariano, A. 2011. The essence of Apple. *Bloomberg BusinessWeek.* January 24–January 30: 6–8.

8. For a study on the effects of CEOs on firm performance, refer to: Kor, Y. Y. & Misangyi, V. F. 2008. *Strategic Management Journal,* 29(11):1357–1368.

9. Charan, R. & Colvin, G. 2010. Directors: A harsh new reality. *money.cnn.com.* October 6: np.

10. Dobson, C. 2010. Global airlines lost $1.7 billion due to Iceland ash cloud. *www.theepochtimes.com.* May 23: np, and Pylas, P. 2011. Nikkei slides 11 percent on radiation fears. *www.finance.yahoo.com.* March 14: np.

11. Ewing, J. 2008. South Africa emerges from the shadows. *BusinessWeek.* December 15: 52–56.

12. For an interesting perspective on the need for strategists to maintain a global mind-set, refer to Begley, T. M. & Boyd, D. P. 2003. The need for a global mind-set. *MIT Sloan Management Review* 44(2): 25–32.

13. Porter, M. E. 1996. What is strategy? *Harvard Business Review* 74(6): 61–78.

14. See, for example, Barney, J. B. & Arikan, A. M. 2001. The resource-based view: Origins and implications. In Hitt, M. A., Freeman, R. E., & Harrison, J. S. (Eds.), *Handbook of strategic management:* 124–189. Malden, MA: Blackwell.

15. Porter, M. E. 1996. What is strategy? *Harvard Business Review,* 74(6): 61–78; and Hammonds, K. H. 2001. Michael Porter's big ideas. *Fast Company,* March: 55–56.

16. This section draws upon Dess, G. G. & Miller, A. 1993. *Strategic management.* New York: McGraw-Hill.

17. See, for example, Hrebiniak, L. G. & Joyce, W. F. 1986. The strategic importance of managing myopia. *Sloan Management Review,* 28(1): 5–14.

18. For an insightful discussion on how to manage diverse stakeholder groups, refer to Rondinelli, D. A. & London, T. 2003. How corporations and environmental groups cooperate: Assessing cross-sector alliances and collaborations. *Academy of Management Executive,* 17(1): 61–76.

19. Some dangers of a short-term perspective are addressed in: Van Buren, M. E. & Safferstone, T. 2009. The quick wins paradox. *Harvard Business Review,* 67(1): 54–61.

20. Senge, P. 1996. Leading learning organizations: The bold, the powerful, and the invisible. In Hesselbein, F., Goldsmith, M., & Beckhard, R. (Eds.), *The leader of the future:* 41–58. San Francisco: Jossey-Bass.

21. Samuelson, J. 2006. A critical mass for the long term. *Harvard Business Review,* 84(2): 62, 64; and, Anonymous. 2007. Power play. *The Economist,* January 20: 10–12.

22. Loeb, M. 1994. Where leaders come from. *Fortune,* September 19: 241 (quoting Warren Bennis).

23. Address by Norman R. Augustine at the Crummer Business School, Rollins College, Winter Park, FL, October 20, 1989.

24. Hemp, P. 2004. An Interview with CEO Kevin Sharer. *Harvard Business Review,* 82(7/8): 66–74.

25. New perspectives on "management models" are addressed in: Birkinshaw, J. & Goddard, J. 2009. What is your management model? *MIT Sloan Management Review,* 50(2): 81–90.

26. Mintzberg, H. 1985. Of strategies: Deliberate and emergent. *Strategic Management Journal,* 6: 257–272.

27. Some interesting insights on decision-making processes are found in: Nutt, P. C. 2008. Investigating the success of decision making processes. *Journal of Management Studies,* 45(2): 425–455.

28. Aston, A. 2009. How to bet on cleantech. *BusinessWeek,* January 5: 70–71.

29. A study investigating the sustainability of competitive advantage is: Newbert, S. L. 2008. Value, rareness, competitive advantages, and performance: A conceptual-level empirical investigation of the resource-based view of the firm. *Strategic Management Journal,* 29(7): 745–768.

30. Good insights on mentoring are addressed in: DeLong, T. J., Gabarro, J. J., & Lees, R. J. 2008. Why mentoring matters in a hypercompetitive world. *Harvard Business Review,* 66(1): 115–121.

31. A unique perspective on differentiation strategies is: Austin, R. D. 2008. High margins and the quest for aesthetic coherence. *Harvard Business Review,* 86(1): 18–19.

Tuition Increases: Sometimes Students Have Low Bargaining Power

Students at the University of California at Berkeley got hit with a 32 percent tuition fee increase in 2010. They protested by taking over a classroom building. As noted by *Forbes* writer Asher Hawkins: "It was a futile effort. Students who are already embarked on a four-year program are something of a captive audience, and California's state coffers are empty."

After the increase, the tuition and fees for in-state undergraduate students will come to about $10,000 for the academic year. (This represents a compound annual increase of nearly 10 percent over the past decade.) Although this may still seem like a reasonable price for a high-quality education, there could be more price increases ahead.

At some state schools, the risk of sharp tuition increases is quite high. *Forbes* conducted a study that

analyzed university financial data, state budgets, and tuition levels to come up with a "danger list." These are state schools that are most likely to raise tuition or cut the quality of the educational experience over the next four-year period. It should be something for students to consider when deciding where to go for undergraduate school.

Five of the 10 schools on the high-risk short list were part of the University of California system. A big contributing factor is the state's enormous budget deficit. And since Berkeley and UCLA have 10 to 12 applicants for every available spot, they are easy targets for legislators looking for ways to balance the budget. A spokesman for the UC system, Peter King, agrees: "The factors employed by *Forbes* to generate this ranking list capture well the perfect storm that has enveloped the University of California system."

On January 8, 2011, California Governor Jerry Brown proposed cutting a combined $1 billion from the University of California and California State systems, which had a combined $5.6 billion general fund budget in 2010. Mark Yudof, president of the UC system stated, "The collective tuition payments made by UC students for the first time in history would exceed what the state contributes to the system's general fund."

Sources: Staley, O. 2011. California universities feel the squeeze. *Bloomberg Businessweek*. January 24–January 30: 29–30; Hawkins, A. 2010. Tuition risk. *Forbes*. May 10: 36; and, Woo, S. 2011. California governor unveils spending plan. *www.wsj.com*. January 11: np.

packaging materials, metal stampings, and services. By aggregating buyers, FreeMarkets increases the buyers' bargaining power. The results are impressive. In its first 48 auctions, most participating companies saved over 15 percent; some saved as much as 50 percent.

Although a firm may be tempted to take advantage of its suppliers because of high buyer power, it must be aware of the potential long-term backlash from such actions. A recent example (Strategy Spotlight 2.7) is the growing resentment that students have toward state universities in California because of steep increases in tuition. Unfortunately, students are essentially a captive market and have relatively little bargaining power.

bargaining power of suppliers the threat that suppliers may raise prices or reduce the quality of purchased goods and services.

The Bargaining Power of Suppliers   Suppliers can exert bargaining power by threatening to raise prices or reduce the quality of purchased goods and services. Powerful suppliers can squeeze the profitability of firms so far that they can't recover the costs of raw material inputs.[57] The factors that make suppliers powerful tend to mirror those that make buyers powerful. A supplier group will be powerful when:

- *The supplier group is dominated by a few companies and is more concentrated (few firms dominate the industry) than the industry it sells to.* Suppliers selling to fragmented industries influence prices, quality, and terms.
- *The supplier group is not obliged to contend with substitute products for sale to the industry.* The power of even large, powerful suppliers can be checked if they compete with substitutes.
- *The industry is not an important customer of the supplier group.* When suppliers sell to several industries and a particular industry does not represent a significant fraction of its sales, suppliers are more prone to exert power.

- *The supplier's product is an important input to the buyer's business.* When such inputs are important to the success of the buyer's manufacturing process or product quality, the bargaining power of suppliers is high.
- *The supplier group's products are differentiated or it has built up switching costs for the buyer.* Differentiation or switching costs facing the buyers cut off their options to play one supplier against another.
- *The supplier group poses a credible threat of forward integration.* This provides a check against the industry's ability to improve the terms by which it purchases.

The Threat of Substitute Products and Services   All firms within an industry compete with industries producing substitute products and services.[58] Substitutes limit the potential returns of an industry by placing a ceiling on the prices that firms in that industry can profitably charge. The more attractive the price/performance ratio of substitute products, the tighter the lid on an industry's profits.

Identifying substitute products involves searching for other products or services that can perform the same function as the industry's offerings. This may lead a manager into businesses seemingly far removed from the industry. For example, the airline industry might not consider video cameras much of a threat. But as digital technology has improved and wireless and other forms of telecommunication have become more efficient, teleconferencing has become a viable substitute for business travel. That is, the rate of improvement in the price–performance relationship of the substitute product (or service) is high.

Teleconferencing can save both time and money, as IBM found out with its "Manager Jam" idea.[59] With 319,000 employees scattered around six continents, it is one of the world's largest businesses (including 32,000 managers) and can be a pretty confusing place. The shift to an increasingly mobile workplace means many managers supervise employees they rarely see face-to-face. To enhance coordination, Samuel Palmisano, IBM's new CEO, launched one of his first big initiatives: a two-year program exploring the role of the manager in the 21st century. "Manager Jam," as the project was nicknamed, was a 48-hour real-time Web event in which managers from 50 different countries swapped ideas and strategies for dealing with problems shared by all of them, regardless of geography. Some 8,100 managers logged on to the company's intranet to participate in the discussion forums.

Renewable energy resources are also a promising substitute product and are rapidly becoming more economically competitive with fossil fuels. Strategy Spotlight 2.8 addresses this critical issue.

The Intensity of Rivalry among Competitors in an Industry   Firms use tactics like price competition, advertising battles, product introductions, and increased customer service or warranties. Rivalry occurs when competitors sense the pressure or act on an opportunity to improve their position.[60]

Some forms of competition, such as price competition, are typically highly destabilizing and are likely to erode the average level of profitability in an industry.[61] Rivals easily match price cuts, an action that lowers profits for all firms. On the other hand, advertising battles expand overall demand or enhance the level of product differentiation for the benefit of all firms in the industry. Rivalry, of course, differs across industries. In some instances it is characterized as warlike, bitter, or cutthroat, whereas in other industries it is referred to as polite and gentlemanly. Intense rivalry is the result of several interacting factors, including the following:

- *Numerous or equally balanced competitors.* When there are many firms in an industry, the likelihood of mavericks is great. Some firms believe they can make moves without being noticed. Even when there are relatively few firms, and they are nearly equal in size and resources, instability results from fighting among companies having the resources for sustained and vigorous retaliation.

threat of substitute products and services the threat of limiting the potential returns of an industry by placing a ceiling on the prices that firms in that industry can profitably charge without losing too many customers to substitute products.

substitute products and services products and services outside the industry that serve the same customer needs as the industry's products and services.

intensity of rivalry among competitors in an industry the threat that customers will switch their business to competitors within the industry.

The Growing Viability of Renewable Resources as Substitutes for Fossil Fuels

Renewable resources currently provide just over 6 percent of total U.S. energy. However, that figure could increase rapidly in the years ahead, according to a joint report issued in September 2006 by the Worldwatch Institute and the Center for Progress, entitled "American Energy: The Renewable Path to Energy Security."

The report indicates that many of the new technologies that harness renewables are, or soon will be, economically competitive with fossil fuels. Dynamic growth rates are driving down costs and spurring rapid advances in technologies. And, since 2000, global wind energy generation has more than tripled, solar cell production has risen six-fold, production of fuel ethanol from crops has more than doubled, and biodiesel production has expanded nearly four-fold. Annual global investment in "new" renewable energy has risen almost six-fold since 1995, with cumulative investment over the period nearly $180 billion.

A November 2006 study by the RAND Corporation is consistent with the aforementioned report. It asserts that

the economy of the United States would likely benefit, rather than be slowed, if the nation attained the goal of supplying 25 percent of its energy needs from renewable sources by 2025. Such developments would also reduce U.S. dependence on oil, which would mean a substantial start on capping greenhouse gas emissions, which most scientists link to global warming.

Deep Patel, founder of Los Angeles–based online clean-energy technologies retailer *GoGreenSolar.com*, provides some practical insights:

- *Clean energy is regional:* Think solar in sunny climates like California, geothermal in Nevada, and wind in blustery states such as Oklahoma.

- *Big corporations tend to hire established, renewable energy companies.* "But no one's paying as much attention to smaller businesses and homeowners that want to go solar. For entrepreneurs, that represents the biggest untapped market."

- *Consumers need help "taking a staged approach to going solar."* At GoGreenSolar, a "Plug N Play Solar Power Kit" starts consumers off with two solar panels that they can add to later. Patel's prediction: more such modular solutions will become available.

Sources: Anonymous. 2008. Clean Energy. *Entrepreneur,* December: 59; Clayton, M. 2006. Greener, cleaner . . . and competitive. *www.csmonitor.com.* December 4; and, Anonymous. 2006. Renewables becoming cost-competitive with fossil fuels in the U.S. *www.worldwatch.org.* September 18.

 environmental sustainability

- ***Slow industry growth.*** Slow industry growth turns competition into a fight for market share, since firms seek to expand their sales.

- ***High fixed or storage costs.*** High fixed costs create strong pressures for all firms to increase capacity. Excess capacity often leads to escalating price cutting.

- ***Lack of differentiation or switching costs.*** Where the product or service is perceived as a commodity or near commodity, the buyer's choice is typically based on price and service, resulting in pressures for intense price and service competition. Lack of switching costs, described earlier, has the same effect.

- ***Capacity augmented in large increments.*** Where economies of scale require that capacity must be added in large increments, capacity additions can be very disruptive to the industry supply/demand balance.

- ***High exit barriers.*** Exit barriers are economic, strategic, and emotional factors that keep firms competing even though they may be earning low or negative returns on their investments. Some exit barriers are specialized assets, fixed costs of exit, strategic interrelationships (e.g., relationships between the business units and others within a company in terms of image, marketing, shared facilities, and so on), emotional barriers, and government and social pressures (e.g., governmental discouragement of exit out of concern for job loss).

Rivalry between firms is often based solely on price, but it can involve other factors. Take Pfizer's market position in the impotence treatment market. Pfizer was the first pharmaceutical firm to develop Viagra, a highly successful drug that treats impotence.

In several countries, the United Kingdom among them, Pfizer faced a lawsuit by Eli Lilly & Co. and Icos Corp. challenging its patent protection. These two pharmaceutical firms recently entered into a joint venture to market Cialis, a drug to compete with Viagra. The U.K. courts agreed and lifted the patent.

This opened the door for Eli Lilly and Icos to proceed with challenging Pfizer's market position. Because Cialis has fewer side effects than Viagra, the drug has the potential to rapidly decrease Pfizer's market share in the United Kingdom if physicians switch prescriptions from Viagra to Cialis. If future patent challenges are successful, Pfizer may see its sales of Viagra erode rapidly.[62] But Pfizer is hardly standing still. It recently doubled its advertising expenditures on Viagra.

Exhibit 2.8 summarizes our discussion of industry five-forces analysis. It points out how various factors such as economies of scale and capital requirements affect each "force."

> **Internet** a global network of linked computers that use a common transmission format, exchange information and store data.

How the Internet and Digital Technologies Are Affecting the Five Competitive Forces

> **>LO2.6**
> How the Internet and digitally based capabilities are affecting the five competitive forces and industry profitability.

The Internet and other digital technologies are having a significant impact on nearly every industry. These technologies have fundamentally changed the ways businesses interact with each other and with consumers. In most cases, these changes have affected industry forces in ways that have created many new strategic challenges. In this section, we will evaluate Michael Porter's five-forces model in terms of the actual use of the Internet and the new technological capabilities that it makes possible.

The Threat of New Entrants In most industries, the threat of new entrants has increased because digital and Internet-based technologies lower barriers to entry. For example, businesses that reach customers primarily through the Internet may enjoy savings on other traditional expenses such as office rent, sales-force salaries, printing, and postage. This may encourage more entrants who, because of the lower start-up expenses, see an opportunity to capture market share by offering a product or performing a service more efficiently than existing competitors. Thus, a new cyber entrant can use the savings provided by the Internet to charge lower prices and compete on price despite the incumbent's scale advantages.

Alternatively, because digital technologies often make it possible for young firms to provide services that are equivalent or superior to an incumbent, a new entrant may be able to serve a market more effectively, with more personalized services and greater attention to product details. A new firm may be able to build a reputation in its niche and charge premium prices. By so doing, it can capture part of an incumbent's business and erode profitability. Consider Voice Over Internet Protocol (VOIP), a fast growing alternative to traditional phone service, which is expected to reach 25 million U.S. households by 2012.[63] Savings of 20 to 30 percent are common for VOIP consumers. This is driving prices down and lowering telecom industry profits. More importantly it threatens the value of the phone line infrastructure that the major carriers have invested in so heavily.

Another potential benefit of Web-based business is access to distribution channels. Manufacturers or distributors that can reach potential outlets for their products more efficiently by means of the Internet may enter markets that were previously closed to them. Access is not guaranteed, however, because strong barriers to entry exist in certain industries.[64]

The Bargaining Power of Buyers The Internet and wireless technologies may increase buyer power by providing consumers with more information to make buying decisions and by lowering switching costs. But these technologies may also suppress the power

Threat of New Entrants Is High When:	High	Low
Economies of scale are		X
Product differentiation is		X
Capital requirements are		X
Switching costs are		X
Incumbent's control of distribution channels is		X
Incumbent's proprietary knowledge is		X
Incumbent's access to raw materials is		X
Incumbent's access to government subsidies is		X

Power of Buyers Is High When:	High	Low
Concentration of buyers relative to suppliers is	X	
Switching costs are		X
Product differentiation of suppliers is		X
Threat of backward integration by buyers is	X	
Extent of buyer's profits is		X
Importance of the supplier's input to quality of buyer's final product is		X

Power of Suppliers Is High When:	High	Low
Concentration relative to buyer industry is	X	
Availability of substitute products is		X
Importance of customer to the supplier is		X
Differentiation of the supplier's products and services is	X	
Switching costs of the buyer are	X	
Threat of forward integration by the supplier is	X	

Threat of Substitute Products Is High When:	High	Low
The differentiation of the substitute product is	X	
Rate of improvement in price–performance relationship of substitute product is	X	

Intensity of Competitive Rivalry Is High When:	High	Low
Number of competitors is	X	
Industry growth rate is		X
Fixed costs are	X	
Storage costs are	X	
Product differentiation is		X
Switching costs are		X
Exit barriers are	X	
Strategic stakes are	X	

Exhibit 2.8   Competitive Analysis Checklist

of traditional buyer channels that have concentrated buying power in the hands of a few, giving buyers new ways to access sellers. To sort out these differences, let's first distinguish between two types of buyers: end users and buyer channel intermediaries.

End users are the final customers in a distribution channel. Internet sales activity that is labeled "B2C"—that is, business-to-consumer—is concerned with end users. The Internet is likely to increase the power of these buyers for several reasons. First, the Internet provides large amounts of consumer information. This gives end users the information they need to shop for quality merchandise and bargain for price concessions. The automobile industry provides an excellent example. For a small fee, agencies such as Consumers Union (publishers of *Consumer Reports*) will provide customers with detailed information about actual automobile manufacturer costs.[65] This information, available online, can be used to bid down dealers' profits. Second, an end user's switching costs are also potentially much lower because of the Internet. Switching may involve only a few clicks of the mouse to find and view a competing product or service online.

In contrast, the bargaining power of distribution channel buyers may decrease because of the Internet. *Buyer channel intermediaries* are the wholesalers, distributors, and retailers who serve as intermediaries between manufacturers and end users. In some industries, they are dominated by powerful players that control who gains access to the latest goods or the best merchandise. The Internet and wireless communications, however, make it much easier and less expensive for businesses to reach customers directly. Thus, the Internet may increase the power of incumbent firms relative to that of traditional buyer channels. Strategy Spotlight 2.9 illustrates some of the changes brought on by the Internet that have affected the industry's two types of buyers.

The Bargaining Power of Suppliers   Use of the Internet and digital technologies to speed up and streamline the process of acquiring supplies is already benefiting many sectors of the economy. But the net effect of the Internet on supplier power will depend on the nature of competition in a given industry. As with buyer power, the extent to which the Internet is a benefit or a detriment also hinges on the supplier's position along the supply chain.

The role of suppliers involves providing products or services to other businesses. The term "B2B"—that is, business-to-business—often refers to businesses that supply or sell to other businesses. The effect of the Internet on the bargaining power of suppliers is a double-edged sword. On the one hand, suppliers may find it difficult to hold onto customers because buyers can do comparative shopping and price negotiations so much faster on the Internet. This is especially damaging to supply-chain intermediaries, such as product distributors, who cannot stop suppliers from directly accessing other potential business customers. In addition, the Internet inhibits the ability of suppliers to offer highly differentiated products or unique services. Most procurement technologies can be imitated by competing suppliers, and the technologies that make it possible to design and customize new products rapidly are being used by all competitors.

On the other hand, several factors may also contribute to stronger supplier power. First, the growth of new Web-based business may create more downstream outlets for suppliers to sell to. Second, suppliers may be able to create Web-based purchasing arrangements that make purchasing easier and discourage their customers from switching. Online procurement systems directly link suppliers and customers, reducing transaction costs and paperwork.[66] Third, the use of proprietary software that links buyers to a supplier's website may create a rapid, low-cost ordering capability that discourages the buyer from seeking other sources of supply. *Amazon.com*, for example, created and patented One-Click purchasing technology that speeds up the ordering process for customers who enroll in the service.[67]

Finally, suppliers will have greater power to the extent that they can reach end users directly without intermediaries. Previously, suppliers often had to work through intermediaries who brought their products or services to market for a fee. But a process known as

strategy spotlight

Buyer Power in the Book Industry: The Role of the Internet

The $25 billion book publishing industry illustrates some of the changes brought on by the Internet that have affected buying power among two types of buyers—end users and buyer channel intermediaries. Prior to the Internet, book publishers worked primarily through large distributors. These intermediaries such as Tennessee-based Ingram, one of the largest and most powerful distributors, exercised strong control over the movement of books from publishers to bookstores. This power was especially strong relative to small, independent publishers who often found it difficult to get their books into bookstores and in front of potential customers.

Sources: Healy, M. 2009. Book Industry Trends 2009 shows publishers' net revenues rose 1.0 percent in 2007 to reach $40.3 billion. *www.bisg.org.* May 29: np; Books "most popular online buy." 2008. *newsvote.bbc.co.uk.* January 29: np. Hoynes, M. 2002. Is it the same for book sales? *BookWeb.org, www.bookweb.org,* March 20; *www.parapublishing.com;* Teague, D. 2005. U.S. book production reaches new high of 195,000 titles in 2004; Fiction soars.*Bowker.com, www.bowker.com,* May 24; and Teicher, C. M. 2007. March of the small presses. *Publishers Weekly, www.publishersweekly.com,* March 26; and The Nielsen Company, 2010. Global trends in online: A Nielsen global consumer report.

The Internet has significantly changed these relationships. Publishers can now negotiate distribution agreements directly with online retailers such as Amazon and Books-A-Million. Such online bookstores now account for about $4 billion in annual sales. And small publishers can use the Internet to sell directly to end users and publicize new titles, without depending on buyer channel intermediaries to handle their books. By using the Internet to appeal to niche markets, 63,000 small publishers with revenues of less than $50 million each generated $14.2 billion in sales in 2005—over half of the industry's total sales.

Future trends for the industry do not look favorable. The Book Industry Study Group (BISG) released figures in May 2009 which estimated that publishers' revenues in 2008 reached $40.3 billion, up 1 percent from 2007's total. BISG expects revenues to increase to $43.5 billion by the end of 2012. There is also good news for online book sellers: According to results from a 2010 worldwide survey by Nielsen Online, 44 percent of users had bought books online—up from 34 percent just three years earlier.

---

disintermediation is removing the organizations or business process layers responsible for intermediary steps in the value chain of many industries.[68] Just as the Internet is eliminating some business functions, it is creating an opening for new functions. These new activities are entering the value chain by a process known as *reintermediation*—the introduction of new types of intermediaries. Many of these new functions are affecting traditional supply chains. For example, delivery services are enjoying a boom because of the Internet. Many more consumers are choosing to have products delivered to their door rather than going out to pick them up.

The Threat of Substitutes   Along with traditional marketplaces, the Internet has created a new marketplace and a new channel. In general, therefore, the threat of substitutes is heightened because the Internet introduces new ways to accomplish the same tasks.

Consumers will generally choose to use a product or service until a substitute that meets the same need becomes available at a lower cost. The economies created by Internet technologies have led to the development of numerous substitutes for traditional ways of doing business. For example, a company called Conferenza is offering an alternative way to participate in conferences for people who don't want to spend the time and money to attend. Conferenza's website provides summaries of many conference events, quality ratings using an "event intelligence" score, and schedules of upcoming events.[69]

Another example of substitution is in the realm of electronic storage. With expanded desktop computing, the need to store information electronically has increased dramatically. Until recently, the trend has been to create increasingly larger desktop storage capabilities and techniques for compressing information that create storage efficiencies. But a viable substitute has recently emerged: storing information digitally on the Internet. Companies such as My Docs Online Inc. are providing Web-based storage that firms can access simply by leasing space online. Since these storage places are virtual, they can be accessed anywhere the Web can be accessed. Travelers can access important documents and files without transporting them physically from place to place. Cyberstorage is not free, but it is cheaper and more convenient than purchasing and carrying disk storage.[70]

The Intensity of Competitive Rivalry   Because the Internet creates more tools and means for competing, rivalry among competitors is likely to be more intense. Only those competitors that can use digital technologies and the Web to give themselves a distinct image, create unique product offerings, or provide "faster, smarter, cheaper" services are likely to capture greater profitability with the new technology. Such gains are hard to sustain, however, because in most cases the new technology can be imitated quickly. Thus, the Internet tends to increase rivalry by making it difficult for firms to differentiate themselves and by shifting customer attention to issues of price.

Rivalry is more intense when switching costs are low and product or service differentiation is minimized. Because the Internet makes it possible to shop around, it has "commoditized" products that might previously have been regarded as rare or unique. Since the Internet reduces the importance of location, products that previously had to be sought out in geographically distant outlets are now readily available online. This makes competitors in cyberspace seem more equally balanced, thus intensifying rivalry.

The problem is made worse for marketers by the presence of shopping robots ("bots") and infomediaries that search the Web for the best possible prices. Consumer websites like mySimon and PriceSCAN seek out all the Web locations that sell similar products and provide price comparisons.[71] Obviously, this focuses the consumer exclusively on price. Some shopping infomediaries, such as BizRate and CNET, not only search for the lowest prices on many different products but also rank the customer service quality of different sites that sell similarly priced items.[72] Such infomediary services are good for consumers because they give them the chance to compare services as well as price. For businesses, however, they increase rivalry by consolidating the marketing message that consumers use to make a purchase decision into a few key pieces of information over which the selling company has little control.

Exhibit 2.9 summarizes many of the ways the Internet is affecting industry structure. These influences will also change how companies develop and deploy strategies to generate above-average profits and sustainable competitive advantage.

Using Industry Analysis: A Few Caveats

For industry analysis to be valuable, a company must collect and evaluate a wide variety of information. As the trend toward globalization accelerates, information on foreign markets as well as on a wider variety of competitors, suppliers, customers, substitutes, and potential new entrants becomes more critical. Industry analysis helps a firm not only to evaluate the profit potential of an industry but also consider various ways to strengthen its position vis-à-vis the five forces. However, we'd like to address a few caveats.

First, *managers must not always avoid low profit industries (or low profit segments in profitable industries).*[73] Such industries can still yield high returns for some players who pursue sound strategies. As examples, consider Paychex, a payroll-processing company, and WellPoint Health Network, a huge health care insurer:[74]

> Paychex, with $2 billion in revenues, became successful by serving small businesses. Existing firms had ignored them because they assumed that such businesses could not afford the service. When Paychex's founder, Tom Golisano, failed to convince his bosses at Electronic Accounting Systems that they were missing a great opportunity, he launched the firm. It now serves nearly 600,000 clients in the United States and Germany. Paychex's after-tax-return on sales is a stunning 24 percent.

Exhibit 2.9　How the Internet and Digital Technologies Influence Industry

	Benefits to Industry (+)	Disadvantages to Industry (−)
Threat of New Entrants		• Lower barriers to entry increase number of new entrants. • Many Internet-based capabilities can be easily imitated.
Bargaining Power of Buyers	• Reduces the power of buyer intermediaries in many distribution channels.	• Switching costs decrease. • Information availability online empowers end users.
Bargaining Power of Suppliers	• Online procurement methods can increase bargaining power over suppliers.	• The Internet gives suppliers access to more customers and makes it easier to reach end users. • Online procurement practices deter competition and reduce differentiating features.
Threat of Substitutes	• Internet-based increases in overall efficiency can expand industry sales.	• Internet-based capabilities create more opportunities for substitution.
Intensity of Rivalry		• Since location is less important, the number of competitors increases. • Differences among competitors are harder to perceive online. • Rivalry tends to focus on price and differentiating features are minimized.

Sources: Bodily, S. & Venkataraman, S. 2004. Not walls, windows: Capturing value in the digital age. *Journal of Business Strategy,* 25(3): 15–25; Lumpkin, G. T., Droege, S. B., & Dess, G. G. 2002. E-commerce strategies: Achieving sustainable competitive advantage and avoiding pitfalls. *Organizational Dynamics,* 30 (Spring): 1–17.

In 1986, WellPoint Health Network (when it was known as Blue Cross of California) suffered a loss of $160 million. That year, Leonard Schaeffer became CEO and challenged the conventional wisdom that individuals and small firms were money losers. (This was certainly "heresy" at the time—the firm was losing $5 million a year insuring 65,000 individuals!) However, by the early 1990s, the health insurer was leading the industry in profitability. The firm has continued to grow and outperform its rivals even during economic downturns. By 2010, its revenues and profits were $65 billion and $4.8 billion, respectively—each figure representing an *annual* increase of over 18 percent for the most recent four-year period.

zero-sum game a situation in which multiple players interact, and winners win only by taking from other players.

Second, five-forces analysis implicitly *assumes a zero-sum game, determining how a firm can enhance its position relative to the forces.* Yet such an approach can often be short-sighted; that is, it can overlook the many potential benefits of developing constructive win–win relationships with suppliers and customers. Establishing long-term mutually beneficial relationships with suppliers improves a firm's ability to implement just-in-time (JIT) inventory systems, which let it manage inventories better and respond quickly to market demands. A recent study found that if a company exploits its powerful position against a supplier, that action may come back to haunt the company.[75] Consider, for example, General Motors' heavy-handed dealings with its suppliers:[76]

> GM has a reputation for particularly aggressive tactics. Although it is striving to crack down on the most egregious of these, it continues to rank dead last in the annual supplier satisfaction survey. "It's a brutal process," says David E. Cole, who is head of the Center for Automotive Research in Ann Arbor. "There are bodies lying by the side of the road."
>
> Suppliers point to one particularly nasty tactic: shopping their technology out the back door to see if rivals can make it cheaper. In one case, a GM purchasing manager showed a supplier's new brake design to Delphi Corporation. He was fired. However, in a recent survey, parts executives said they tend to bring hot new technology to other carmakers first. This is yet another reason GM finds it hard to compete in an intensely competitive industry.

Third, the five-forces analysis also has been criticized for *being essentially a static analysis.* External forces as well as strategies of individual firms are continually changing the structure of all industries. The search for a dynamic theory of strategy has led to greater use of game theory in industrial organization economics research and strategy research.

Based on game-theoretic considerations, Brandenburger and Nalebuff recently introduced the concept of the value net,[77] which in many ways is an extension of the five-forces analysis. It is illustrated in Exhibit 2.10. The value net represents all the players in the game and analyzes how their interactions affect a firm's ability to generate and appropriate value. The vertical dimension of the net includes suppliers and customers. The firm has direct transactions with them. On the horizontal dimension are substitutes and complements, players with whom a firm interacts but may not necessarily transact. The concept of complementors is perhaps the single most important contribution of value net analysis and is explained in more detail below.

Complements typically are products or services that have a potential impact on the value of a firm's own products or services. Those who produce complements are usually referred to as complementors.[78] Powerful hardware is of no value to a user unless there is software that runs on it. Similarly, new and better software is possible only if the hardware on which it can be run is available. This is equally true in the video game industry, where the sales of game

complements
products or services that have an impact on the value of a firm's products or services.

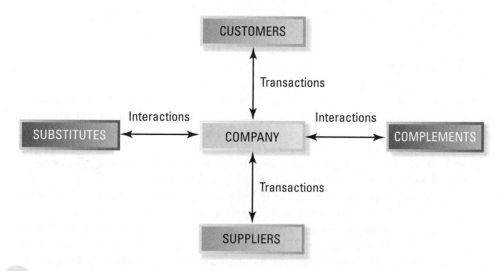

Exhibit 2.10   The Value Net

Source: Reprinted by permission of *Harvard Business Review.* Exhibit from "The Right Game: Use Game Theory to Shape Strategy," by A. Brandenburger and B. J. Nalebuff, July–August 1995. Copyright © 1995 by the Harvard Business School Publishing Corporation. All rights reserved.

consoles and video games complement each other. Nintendo's success in the early 1990s was a result of their ability to manage their relationship with their complementors. They built a security chip into the hardware and then licensed the right to develop games to outside firms. These firms paid a royalty to Nintendo for each copy of the game sold. The royalty revenue enabled Nintendo to sell game consoles at close to their cost, thereby increasing their market share, which, in turn, caused more games to be sold and more royalties to be generated.[79]

Despite efforts to create win–win scenarios, conflict among complementors is inevitable.[80] After all, it is naive to expect that even the closest of partners will do you the favor of abandoning their own interests. And even the most successful partnerships are seldom trouble free. Power is a factor that comes into play as we see in Strategy Spotlight 2.10 with the example of Apple's iPod—an enormously successful product.

We would like to close this section with some recent insights from Michael Porter, the originator of the five-forces analysis.[81] He addresses two critical issues in conducting a good industry analysis, which will yield an improved understanding of the root causes of profitability: (1) choosing the appropriate time frame and (2) a rigorous quantification of the five forces.

- *Good industry analysis looks rigorously at the structural underpinnings of profitability. A first step is to understand the time horizon.* One of the essential tasks in industry analysis is to distinguish short-term fluctuations from structural changes. A good guideline for the appropriate time horizon is the full business cycle for the particular industry. For most industries, a three- to five-year horizon is appropriate. However, for some industries with long lead times, such as mining, the appropriate horizon may be a decade or more. It is average profitability over this period, not profitability in any particular year, which should be the focus of analysis.
- *The point of industry analysis is not to declare the industry attractive or unattractive but to understand the underpinnings of competition and the root causes of profitability.* As much as possible, analysts should look at industry structure quantitatively, rather than be satisfied with lists of qualitative factors. Many elements of five forces can be quantified: the percentage of the buyer's total cost accounted for by the industry's product (to understand buyer price sensitivity); the percentage of industry sales required to fill a plant or operate a logistical network to efficient scale (to help assess barriers to entry); and the buyer's switching cost (determining the inducement an entrant or rival must offer customers).

Strategic Groups within Industries

In an industry analysis, two assumptions are unassailable: (1) No two firms are totally different, and (2) no two firms are exactly the same. The issue becomes one of identifying groups of firms that are more similar to each other than firms that are not, otherwise known as **strategic groups.**[82] This is important because rivalry tends to be greater among firms that are alike. Strategic groups are clusters of firms that share similar strategies. After all, is Kmart more concerned about Nordstrom or Walmart? Is Mercedes more concerned about Hyundai or BMW? The answers are straightforward.[83]

These examples are not meant to trivialize the strategic groups concept.[84] Classifying an industry into strategic groups involves judgment. If it is useful as an analytical tool, we must exercise caution in deciding what dimensions to use to map these firms. Dimensions include breadth of product and geographic scope, price/quality, degree of vertical integration, type of distribution (e.g., dealers, mass merchandisers, private label), and so on. Dimensions should also be selected to reflect the variety of strategic combinations in an industry. For example, if all firms in an industry have roughly the same level of product differentiation (or R&D intensity), this would not be a good dimension to select.

What value is the strategic groups concept as an analytical tool? *First, strategic groupings help a firm identify barriers to mobility that protect a group from attacks by other*

strategic groups
clusters of firms that share similar strategies.

>LO2.7
The concept of strategic groups and their strategy and performance implications.

2.10

Apple's iPod: Relationships with Its Complementors

In 2002, Steve Jobs began his campaign to cajole the major music companies into selling tracks to iPod users through the iTunes Music Store, an online retail site. Most industry executives, after being burned by illegal file-sharing services like Napster and Kazaa, just wanted digital music to disappear. However, Jobs's passionate vision persuaded them to climb on board. He promised to reduce the risks that they faced by offering safeguards against piracy, as well as a hip product (iPod and iPad Touch) that would drive sales.

However, Apple had a much stronger bargaining position when its contracts with the music companies came up for renewal in April 2005. By then, iTunes had captured 80 percent of the market for legal downloads. The music companies, which were receiving between 60 and 70 cents per download, wanted more. Their reasoning: If the iTunes Music Store would only charge $1.50 or $2.00 per track, they could double or triple their revenues and profits. Since Jobs knew that he could sell more iPods if the music was cheap, he was determined to keep the price of a download at 99 cents and to maintain Apple's

Source: Hesseldahl, A. 2008. Now that we all have iPods. *BusinessWeek*, December 15: 36; Apple Computer Inc. 10-K, 2010; and, Yoffie, D. B. & Kwak, M. 2006. With friends like these: The art of managing complementors. *Harvard Business Review*, 84(9): 88–98.

margins. Given iTunes' dominant position, the music companies had little choice but to relent.

Apple's foray into music has been tremendously successful. Between 2006 and 2009, iPod sales increased from $7.7 billion to $9.4 billion—a 22 percent increase. And, other music related products and services soared from $4 billion to $5 billion over the same period. Despite tough competition, Apple still dominates the music player business.

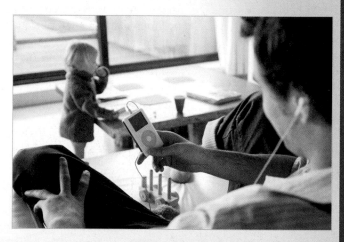

● The iPod is largely responsible for Apple's recent stellar financial performance.

---

groups.[85] Mobility barriers are factors that deter the movement of firms from one strategic position to another. For example, in the chainsaw industry, the major barriers protecting the high-quality/dealer-oriented group are technology, brand image, and an established network of servicing dealers.

The second value of strategic grouping is that it *helps a firm identify groups whose competitive position may be marginal or tenuous*. We may anticipate that these competitors may exit the industry or try to move into another group. In recent years in the retail department store industry, firms such as JCPenney and Sears have experienced extremely difficult times because they were stuck in the middle, neither an aggressive discount player like Walmart nor a prestigious upscale player like Neiman Marcus.

Third, strategic groupings *help chart the future directions of firms' strategies*. Arrows emanating from each strategic group can represent the direction in which the group (or a firm within the group) seems to be moving. If all strategic groups are moving in a similar direction, this could indicate a high degree of future volatility and intensity of competition. In the automobile industry, for example, the competition in the minivan and sport utility segments has intensified in recent years as many firms have entered those product segments.

Fourth, strategic groups are *helpful in thinking through the implications of each industry trend for the strategic group as a whole*. Is the trend decreasing the viability of a group? If so, in what direction should the strategic group move? Is the trend increasing or decreasing entry barriers? Will the trend decrease the ability of one group to separate itself from other groups? Such analysis can help in making predictions about industry evolution. A sharp increase in interest rates, for example, tends to have less impact on providers of higher-priced goods (e.g., Porsches) than on providers of lower-priced goods (e.g., Chevrolet Cobalt) whose customer base is much more price sensitive.

Exhibit 2.11 provides a strategic grouping of the worldwide automobile industry.[86] The firms in each group are representative; not all firms are included in the mapping. We have identified four strategic groups. In the top left-hand corner are high-end luxury automakers who focus on a very narrow product market. Most of the cars produced by the members of this group cost well over $100,000. Some cost many times that amount. The 2010 45B Ferrari Italia starts at $225,000, and the 2010 Lamborghini Gallardo will set you back about $221,000 (in case you were wondering how to spend your employment signing bonus). Players in this market have a very exclusive clientele and face little rivalry from other strategic groups. At the other extreme, in the lower left-hand corner is a strategic group that has low-price/quality attributes and targets a narrow market. These players, Hyundai and Kia, limit competition from other strategic groups by pricing their products very low. The third group (near the middle) consists of firms high in product pricing/quality and average in their product-line breadth. The final group (at the far right) consists of firms with a broad range of products and multiple price points. These firms have entries that compete at both the lower end of the market (e.g., the Ford Focus) and the higher end (e.g., Chevrolet Corvette).

The auto market has been very dynamic and competition has intensified in recent years.[87] Many firms in different strategic groups compete in the same product markets, such as minivans and sport utility vehicles. In the late 1990s Mercedes entered the fray with its M series, and Porsche has a recent entry as well with its Cayenne, a 2004 model.

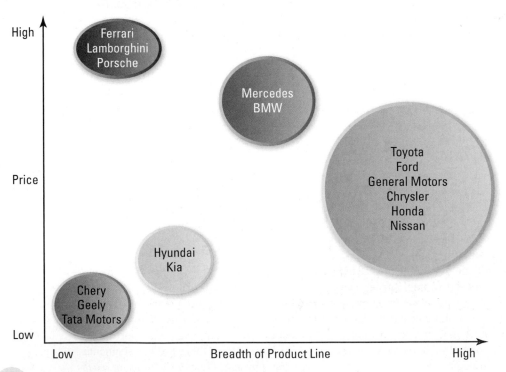

Exhibit 2.11   **The World Automobile Industry: Strategic Groups**

Note: Members of each strategic group are not inclusive, only illustrative.

Some players are also going more upscale with their product offerings. Recently, Hyundai introduced its Genesis, starting at $33,000. This brings Hyundai into direct competition with entries from other strategic groups such as Toyota's Camry and Honda's Accord. Hyundai is offering an extensive warranty (10 years, 100,000 miles) in an effort to offset customer perceptions of their lower quality. To further intensify competition, some key automakers are providing offerings in lower-priced segments. BMW, with their 1-series, is a well-known example. Such cars, priced in the low $30,000s, compete more directly with products from broad-line manufacturers like Ford, General Motors, and Toyota.

Such models are competing in an industry that has experienced relatively flat unit sales in the first half of the last decade. However, in recent years things have turned increasingly sour. U.S. automobile sales dropped from 13.2 million units in 2008 to only 10.4 million units in 2009 (the fewest units since 1982) and 11.3 million units in 2010. This compares to an average of 16.4 million units between 2000 and 2007. And J. D. Power predicts sales of only 13.2 million units for 2011, as the economy emerges from the recession.[88] One can certainly expect incentive-laden offerings to appear on dealer lots for some time to come.

Our discussion would not be complete, of course, without paying some attention to recent entries in the automobile industry that will likely lead to the formation of a new strategic group—placed at the bottom left corner of the grid in Exhibit 2.11. Three firms—China's Zhejiang Geely Holding Company, China's Chery Automobile Company, and India's Tata Motors—have introduced models that bring new meaning to the term "subcompact."[89] Let's take a look at these econoboxes.

Chery's QQ model sells for between $4,000 and $7,000 in the Chinese market and sports horsepower in the range of 51 to 74. Geely's best-selling four-door sedan, the Free Cruiser, retails from $6,300 and $6,900. The firm is planning to go more upscale with the Geely KingKong ($7,500−$10,000), a four-door 1.5- to 1.8-liter sedan, and the Vision ($9,700−$15,300), a 1.8-liter four-door sedan. But, for price-points, India's Tata Motors has everyone beat. In January 2008, it unveiled the Nano with an astonishing retail price of only $2,500. It is a four-door, five-seat hatchback that gets 54 miles per gallon. But before you order one—keep in mind that it only comes with a 30 horsepower engine.

Reflecting on Career Implications . . .

- *Creating the Environmentally Aware Organization:* In your career, what are some ways in which you can engage in scanning, monitoring, and intelligence gathering for future job opportunities? Consider, for example, subscribing to your field's professional publications and becoming actively involved in relevant professional organizations.
- *SWOT Analysis:* From a career standpoint, periodically evaluate your strengths and weaknesses as well as potential opportunities and threats to your career. In addition, strive to seek input from trusted peers and superiors.
- *General Environment:* Carefully evaluate the elements of the general environment facing your firm. Identify factors (e.g., rapid technological change) that can provide promising career opportunities as well as possibilities for you to add value for your organization. In doing this, don't focus solely on "internal factors" of your organization.
- *Five-Forces Analysis:* Consider the five forces affecting the industry within which your organization competes. If the "forces" are unfavorable, the long-term profit potential of the industry may be unattractive. And, there will likely be fewer resources available and—all other things being equal—fewer career opportunities.

Summary

Managers must analyze the external environment to minimize or eliminate threats and exploit opportunities. This involves a continuous process of environmental scanning and monitoring as well as obtaining competitive intelligence on present and potential rivals. These activities provide valuable inputs for developing forecasts. In addition, many firms use scenario planning to anticipate and respond to volatile and disruptive environmental changes.

We identified two types of environments: the general environment and the competitive environment. The six segments of the general environment are demographic, sociocultural, political/legal, technological, economic, and global. Trends and events occurring in these segments, such as the aging of the population, higher percentages of women in the workplace, governmental legislation, and increasing (or decreasing) interest rates, can have a dramatic effect on a firm. A given trend or event may have a positive impact on some industries and a negative, neutral, or no impact at all on others.

The competitive environment consists of industry-related factors and has a more direct impact than the general environment. Porter's five-forces model of industry analysis includes the threat of new entrants, buyer power, supplier power, threat of substitutes, and rivalry among competitors. The intensity of these factors determines, in large part, the average expected level of profitability in an industry. A sound awareness of such factors, both individually and in combination, is beneficial not only for deciding what industries to enter but also for assessing how a firm can improve its competitive position. We discuss how many of the changes brought about by the digital economy can be understood in the context of five-forces analysis. The limitations of five-forces analysis include its static nature and its inability to acknowledge the role of complementors. Although we addressed the general environment and competitive environment in separate sections, they are quite interdependent. A given environmental trend or event, such as changes in the ethnic composition of a population or a technological innovation, typically has a much greater impact on some industries than on others.

The concept of strategic groups is also important to the external environment of a firm. No two organizations are completely different nor are they exactly the same. The question is how to group firms in an industry on the basis of similarities in their resources and strategies. The strategic groups concept is valuable for determining mobility barriers across groups, identifying groups with marginal competitive positions, charting the future directions of firm strategies, and assessing the implications of industry trends for the strategic group as a whole.

Summary Review Questions

1. Why must managers be aware of a firm's external environment?
2. What is gathering and analyzing competitive intelligence and why is it important for firms to engage in it?
3. Discuss and describe the six elements of the external environment.
4. Select one of these elements and describe some changes relating to it in an industry that interests you.
5. Describe how the five forces can be used to determine the average expected profitability in an industry.
6. What are some of the limitations (or caveats) in using five-forces analysis?
7. Explain how the general environment and industry environment are highly related. How can such interrelationships affect the profitability of a firm or industry?
8. Explain the concept of strategic groups. What are the performance implications?

Key Terms

threat of substitute products and services, 59
substitute products and services, 59
intensity of rivalry among

competitors in an industry, 59
Internet, 61
zero-sum game, 66
complements, 67
strategic groups, 68

Experiential Exercise

Select one of the following industries: personal computers, airlines, or automobiles. For this industry, evaluate the strength of each of Porter's five forces as well as complementors.

Industry Force	High? Medium? Low?	Why?
1. Threat of new entrants		
2. Power of buyers		
3. Power of suppliers		
4. Power of substitutes		
5. Rivalry among competitors		
6. Complementors		

Application Questions & Exercises

1. Imagine yourself as the CEO of a large firm in an industry in which you are interested. Please (1) identify major trends in the general environment, (2) analyze their impact on the firm, and (3) identify major sources of information to monitor these trends. (Use Internet and library resources.)

2. Analyze movements across the strategic groups in the U.S. retail industry. How do these movements within this industry change the nature of competition?

3. What are the major trends in the general environment that have impacted the U.S. pharmaceutical industry?

4. Go to the Internet and look up *www.kroger.com*. What are some of the five forces driving industry competition that are affecting the profitability of this firm?

Ethics Questions

1. What are some of the legal and ethical issues involved in collecting competitor intelligence in the following situations?

   a. Hotel A sends an employee posing as a potential client to Hotel B to find out who Hotel B's major corporate customers are.

   b. A firm hires an MBA student to collect information directly from a competitor while claiming the information is for a course project.

   c. A firm advertises a nonexistent position and interviews a rival's employees with the intention of obtaining competitor information.

2. What are some of the ethical implications that arise when a firm tries to exploit its power over a supplier?

References

1. Heimbuch, J. 2010. Hooray! Hawaii outlaws shark fin soup. *www.treehugger.com,* October 27: np.; Anonymous. 2006. The value of China's emerging middle class. *www.mkqpreview.com.* June: np; and, Wassener, B. 2010. A shark fin promotion backfires. *www.green.blogs.nytimes.com.* July 22: np; and, *www.citigroup.com.* We thank Kimberly Kentfield for her valued contributions.

2. Hamel, G. & Prahalad, C. K. 1994. *Competing for the future.* Boston: Harvard Business School Press.

3. Drucker, P. F. 1994. Theory of the business. *Harvard Business Review,* 72: 95–104.

4. For an insightful discussion on managers' assessment of the external environment, refer to Sutcliffe, K. M. & Weber, K. 2003. The high cost of accurate knowledge. *Harvard Business Review,* 81(5): 74–86.

5. For insights on recognizing and acting on environmental opportunities, refer to: Alvarez, S. A. & Barney, J. B. 2008. Opportunities, organizations, and entrepreneurship: Theory and debate. *Strategic Entrepreneurship Journal,* 2(3): entire issue.

6. Charitou, C. D. & Markides, C. C. 2003. Responses to disruptive strategic innovation. *MIT Sloan Management Review,* 44(2): 55–64.

7. Our discussion of scanning, monitoring, competitive intelligence, and forecasting concepts draws on several sources. These include Fahey, L. & Narayanan, V. K. 1983. *Macroenvironmental analysis for strategic management.* St. Paul, MN: West; Lorange, P., Scott, F. S., & Ghoshal,

S. 1986. *Strategic control.* St. Paul, MN: West; Ansoff, H. I. 1984. *Implementing strategic management.* Englewood Cliffs, NJ: Prentice Hall; and Schreyogg, G. & Stienmann, H. 1987. Strategic control: A new perspective. *Academy of Management Review,* 12: 91–103.

8. An insightful discussion on how leaders can develop "peripheral vision" in environmental scanning is found in: Day, G. S. & Schoemaker, P. J. H. 2008. Are you a "vigilant leader"? *MIT Sloan Management Review,* 49 (3): 43–51.

9. Elenkov, D. S. 1997. Strategic uncertainty and environmental scanning: The case for institutional influences on scanning behavior. *Strategic Management Journal,* 18: 287–302.

10. For an interesting perspective on environmental scanning in emerging economies see May, R. C., Stewart, W. H., & Sweo, R. 2000. Environmental scanning behavior in a transitional economy: Evidence from Russia. *Academy of Management Journal,* 43(3): 403–27.

11. Bryon, E. 2010. For insight into P&G, check Olay numbers. *Wall Street Journal.* October 27: C1.

12. Tang, J. 2010. How entrepreneurs discover opportunities in China: An institutional view. *Asia Pacific Journal of Management.* 27(3): 461–480.

13. Walters, B. A. & Priem, R. L. 1999. Business strategy and CEO intelligence acquisition. *Competitive Intelligence Review,* 10(2): 15–22.

14. Prior, V. 1999. The language of competitive intelligence, Part 4. *Competitive Intelligence Review,* 10(1): 84–87.

15. Zahra, S. A. & Charples, S. S. 1993. Blind spots in competitive analysis. *Academy of Management Executive* 7(2): 7–27.

16. Wolfenson, J. 1999. The world in 1999: A battle for corporate honesty. *The Economist* 38: 13–30.

17. Drucker, P. F. 1997. The future that has already happened. *Harvard Business Review,* 75(6): 22.

18. Evans, P. B. & Wurster, T. S. 1997. Strategy and the new economics of information. *Harvard Business Review,* 75(5): 71–82.

19. Fahey & Narayanan, op. cit., p. 41.

20. Insights on how to improve predictions can be found in: Cross, R., Thomas, R. J., & Light, D. A. 2009. The prediction lover's handbook. *MIT Sloan Management Review,* 50 (2): 32–34.

21. Courtney, H., Kirkland, J., & Viguerie, P. 1997. Strategy under uncertainty. *Harvard Business Review,* 75(6): 66–79.

22. Odlyzko, A. 2003. False hopes. *Red Herring,* March: 31.

23. Coy, P. 2009. Worst predictions about 2008. *BusinessWeek,* January 12: 15–16.

24. For an interesting perspective on how Accenture practices and has developed its approach to scenario planning, refer to Ferguson, G., Mathur, S., & Shah, B. 2005. Evolving from information to insight. *MIT Sloan Management Review,* 46(2): 51–58.

25. Dean, T. J., Brown, R. L., & Bamford, C. E. 1998. Differences in large and small firm responses to environmental context: Strategic implications from a comparative analysis of business formations. *Strategic Management Journal,* 19: 709–728.

26. Some insights on management during economic downturns are in: Colvin, G. 2009. How to manage your business in a recession. *Fortune,* January 19: 88–93.

27. Colvin, G. 1997. How to beat the boomer rush. *Fortune,* August 18: 59–63.

28. Porter, M. E. 2010. Discovering—and lowering—the real costs of health care. *Harvard Business Review,* 89 (1/2): 49–50.

29. U.S. Bureau of Labor Statistics. 2009. *Occupational handbook, 2010–2011 edition.* December 19. www.bls.gov/oco/oco203.htm.

30. Challenger, J. 2000. Women's corporate rise has reduced relocations. *Lexington (KY) Herald-Leader,* October 29: D1.

31. Tsao, A. 2005. Retooling home improvement, *Businessssweek.com,* February, 14; and, Grow, B. 2004. Who wears the wallet in the family? *BusinessWeek,* August 16:10.

32. Watkins, M. D. 2003. Government games. *MIT Sloan Management Review* 44(2): 91–95.

33. A discussion of the political issues surrounding caloric content on meals is in: Orey, M. 2008. A food fight over calorie counts. *BusinessWeek,* February 11: 36.

34. For a discussion of the linkage between copyright law and innovation, read: Guterman, J. 2009. Does copyright law hinder innovation? *MIT Sloan Management Review,* 50(2): 14–15.

35. Davies, A. 2000. The welcome mat is out for nerds. *BusinessWeek,* May 21: 17; Broache, A. 2007. Annual H-1B visa cap met—already. *news.cnet.com,* April 3: np; and, Anonymous. Undated. Cap count for H-1B and H-2B workers for fiscal year 2009. *www.uscis.gov:* np.

36. Hout, T. M., Ghemawat, P. 2010. China vs. the world: Whose technology is it? *Harvard Business Review,* 88(12): 94–103.

37. Anonymous. Business ready for Internet revolution. 1999. *Financial Times,* May 21: 17.

38. A discussion of an alternate energy—marine energy—is the topic of: Boyle, M. 2008. Scottish power. *Fortune.* March 17: 28.

39. Baker, S. & Aston, A. 2005. The business of nanotech. *BusinessWeek,* February 14: 64–71.

40. Morse, G. 2009. The power of unwitting workers. *Harvard Business Review,* 87(10): 26.

41. For an insightful discussion of the causes of the global financial crisis, read: Johnson, S. 2009. The global financial crisis—What really precipitated it? *MIT Sloan Management Review.* 50(2): 16–18.

42. Tyson, L. D. 2011. A better stimulus for the U.S. economy. *Harvard Business Review,* 89(1/2): 53.

43. A interesting and balanced discussion on the merits of multinationals to the U.S. economy is found in: Mandel, M. 2008. Multinationals: Are they good for America? *BusinessWeek,* March 10: 41–64.

44. Insights on risk perception across countries are addressed in: Purda, L. D. 2008. Risk perception and the financial system. *Journal of International Business Studies,* 39(7): 1178–1196.

45. Gogoi, P. 2010. Many U.S. companies are hiring . . . overseas. *www.msn.com.* December 28: np.

46. Byrnes, N. 2006. The high cost of fear. *BusinessWeek,* November 6: 16.

47. Goll, I. & Rasheed, M. A. 1997. Rational decision-making and firm performance: The moderating role of environment. *Strategic Management Journal,* 18: 583–591.

48. This discussion draws heavily on Porter, M. E. 1980. *Competitive strategy:* Chapter 1. New York: Free Press.

49. Ibid.

50. Rivalry in the airline industry is discussed in: Foust, D. 2009. Which airlines will disappear in 2009? *BusinessWeek,* January 19: 46–47.

51. Fryer, B. 2001. Leading through rough times: An interview with Novell's Eric Schmidt. *Harvard Business Review,* 78(5): 117–123.

52. For a discussion on the importance of barriers to entry within industries, read Greenwald, B. & Kahn, J. 2005. *Competition demystified: A radically simplified approach to business strategy.* East Rutherford, NJ: Portfolio.

53. A discussion of how the medical industry has erected entry barriers that have resulted in lawsuits is found in: Whelan, D. 2008. Bad medicine. *BusinessWeek,* March 10: 86–98.

54. The ProCD example draws heavily upon Shapiro, C. & Varian, H. R. 2000. Versioning: The smart way to sell information. *Harvard Business Review,* 78(1): 106–114.

55. Wise, R. & Baumgarter, P. 1999. Go downstream: The new profit imperative in manufacturing. *Harvard Business Review,* 77(5): 133–141.

56. Salman, W. A. 2000. The new economy is stronger than you think. *Harvard Business Review,* 77(6): 99–106.

57. Mudambi, R. & Helper, S. 1998. The "close but adversarial" model of supplier relations in the U.S. auto industry. *Strategic Management Journal,* 19: 775–792.

58. Trends in the solar industry are discussed in: Carey, J. 2009. Solar: The sun will come out tomorrow. *BusinessWeek,* January 12: 51.

59. Tischler, L. 2002. IBM: Manager jam. *Fast Company,* October: 48.

60. An interesting analysis of self-regulation in an industry (chemical) is in: Barnett, M. L. & King, A. A. 2008. Good fences make good neighbors: A longitudinal analysis of an industry self-regulatory institution. *Academy of Management Journal,* 51(6): 1053–1078.

61. For an interesting perspective on the intensity of competition in the supermarket industry, refer to Anonymous. 2005. Warfare in the aisles. *The Economist,* April 2: 6–8.

62. Marcial, G. 2000. Giving Viagra a run for its money. *BusinessWeek,* October 23: 173.

63. McGann, R. 2005. VOIP poised to take flight? *ClickZ.com,* February 23, *www.clickz.com.*

64. For an interesting perspective on changing features of firm boundaries, refer to Afuah, A. 2003. Redefining firm boundaries in the face of Internet: Are firms really shrinking? *Academy of Management Review,* 28(1): 34–53.

65. *www.consumerreports.org.*

66. Time to rebuild. 2001. *Economist,* May 19: 55–56.

67. *www.amazon.com.*

68. For more on the role of the Internet as an electronic intermediary, refer to Carr, N. G. 2000. Hypermediation: Commerce as clickstream. *Harvard Business Review,* 78(1): 46–48.

69. Olofson, C. 2001. The next best thing to being there. *Fast Company,* April: 175; and *www.conferenza.com.*

70. Lelii, S. R. 2001. Free online storage a thing of the past *? eWEEK,* April 22.

71. *www.mysimon.com;* and *www.pricescan.com.*

72. *www.cnet.com;* and *www.bizrate.com.*

73. For insights into strategies in a low-profit industry, refer to: Hopkins, M. S. 2008. The management lessons of a beleaguered industry. *MIT Sloan Management Review,* 50(1): 25–31.

74. Foust, D. 2007. The best performers. *BusinessWeek,* March 26: 58–95; Rosenblum, D., Tomlinson, D., & Scott, L. 2003. Bottom-feeding for blockbuster businesses. *Harvard Business Review,* 81(3): 52–59; Paychex 2006 Annual Report; and, WellPoint Health Network 2005 Annual Report.

75. Kumar, N. 1996. The power of trust in manufacturer-retailer relationship. *Harvard Business Review,* 74(6): 92–110.

76. Welch, D. 2006. Renault-Nissan: Say hello to Bo. *BusinessWeek,* July 31: 56–57.

77. Brandenburger, A. & Nalebuff, B. J. 1995. The right game: Use game theory to shape strategy. *Harvard Business Review,* 73(4): 57–71.

78. For a scholarly discussion of complementary assets and their relationship to competitive advantage, refer to Stieglitz, N. & Heine, K. 2007. Innovations and the role of complementarities in a strategic theory of the firm. *Strategic Management Journal,* 28(1): 1–15.

79. A useful framework for the analysis of industry evolution has been proposed by Professor Anita McGahan of Boston University. Her analysis is based on the identification of the core activities and the core assets of an industry and the threats they face. She suggests that an industry may follow one of four possible evolutionary trajectories—radical change, creative change, intermediating change, or progressive change—based on these two types of threats of obsolescence. Refer to: McGahan, A. M. 2004. How industries change. *Harvard Business Review,* 82(10): 87–94.

80. Yoffie, D. B. & Kwak, M. 2006. With friends like these: The art of managing complementors. *Harvard Business Review,* 84(9): 88–98.

81. Porter, M. I. 2008. The five competitive forces that shape strategy. *Harvard Business Review,* 86 (1): 79–93.

82. Peteraf, M. & Shanley, M. 1997. Getting to know you: A theory of strategic group identity. *Strategic Management Journal,* 18 (Special Issue): 165–186.

83. An interesting scholarly perspective on strategic groups may be found in

Dranove, D., Perteraf, M., & Shanley, M. 1998. Do strategic groups exist? An economic framework for analysis. *Strategic Management Journal,* 19(11): 1029–1044.

84. For an empirical study on strategic groups and predictors of performance, refer to Short, J. C., Ketchen, D. J., Jr., Palmer, T. B., & Hult, T. M. 2007. Firm, strategic group, and industry influences on performance. *Strategic Management Journal,* 28(2): 147–167.

85. This section draws on several sources, including Kerwin, K. R. & Haughton, K. 1997. Can Detroit make cars that baby boomers like? *BusinessWeek,* December 1: 134–148; and Taylor, A., III. 1994. The new golden age of autos. *Fortune,* April 4: 50–66.

86. Csere, C. 2001. Supercar supermarket. *Car and Driver,* January: 118–127.

87. For a discussion of the extent of over-capacity in the worldwide automobile industry, read: Roberts, D., Matlack, C., Busyh, J., & Rowley, I. 2009. A hundred factories too many. *BusinessWeek,* January 19: 42–43.

88. Naughton, K. 2010. HIS auto trims 2010 U.S. vehicle sales forecast to 11.3 million units. *www.bloomberg.com/news.* September 27: np; and, Woodall, B. 2011. J. D. Power lowers U.S. auto sales forecast. *www.reuters.com.* August 10: np.

89. This discussion draws on: Wojdyla, B. 2008. The $2500 Tata Nano, unveiled in India. *jalopnik.com,* January 10: np; Roberts, D. 2008. China's Geely has global auto ambitions. *businessweek.com,* July 27: np; and, Fairclough, G. 2007. In China, Chery automobile drives an industry shift. *The Wall Street Journal,* December 4: A1, A17.

chapter THREE

Assessing the Internal Environment of the Firm

After reading this chapter, you should have a good understanding of:

LO3.1 The benefits and limitations of SWOT analysis in conducting an internal analysis of the firm.

LO3.2 The primary and support activities of a firm's value chain.

LO3.3 How value-chain analysis can help managers create value by investigating relationships among activities within the firm and between the firm and its customers and suppliers.

LO3.4 The resource-based view of the firm and the different types of tangible and intangible resources, as well as organizational capabilities.

LO3.5 The four criteria that a firm's resources must possess to maintain a sustainable advantage and how value created can be appropriated by employees and managers.

LO3.6 The usefulness of financial ratio analysis, its inherent limitations, and how to make meaningful comparisons of performance across firms.

LO3.7 The value of the "balanced scorecard" in recognizing how the interests of a variety of stakeholders can be interrelated.

LO3.8 How firms are using Internet technologies to add value and achieve unique advantages. (Appendix)

LEARNING OBJECTIVES

Two firms compete in the same industry and both have many strengths in a variety of functional areas: marketing, operations, logistics, and so on. However, one of these firms outperforms the other by a wide margin over a long period of time. How can this be so? This chapter endeavors to answer that question.

We begin with two sections that include frameworks for gaining key insights into a firm's internal environment: value-chain analysis and the resource-based view of the firm. In value-chain analysis, we divide a firm's activities into a series of value-creating steps. We then explore how individual activities within the firm add value, and also how *interrelationships* among activities within the firm, and between the firm and its suppliers and customers, create value.

In the resource-based view of the firm, we analyze the firm as a collection of tangible and intangible resources as well as organizational capabilities. Advantages that tend to be sustainable over time typically arise from creating *bundles* of resources and capabilities that satisfy four criteria: they are valuable, rare, difficult to imitate, and difficult to substitute. Not all of the value created by a firm will necessarily be kept (or appropriated) by the owners. We discuss the four key factors that determine how profits will be distributed between owners as well as employees and managers.

In the closing sections, we discuss how to evaluate a firm's performance and make comparisons across firms. We emphasize both the inclusion of financial resources and the interests of multiple stakeholders. Central to our discussion is the concept of the balanced scorecard, which recognizes that the interests of different stakeholders can be interrelated. We also consider how a firm's performance evolves over time and how it compares with industry norms and key competitors.

In an appendix to this chapter, we explore how Internet-based businesses and incumbent firms are using digital technologies to add value. We consider four activities—search, evaluation, problem solving, and transaction—as well as three types of content—customer feedback, expertise, and entertainment programming. Such technology-enhanced capabilities are providing new means with which firms can achieve competitive advantages.

Learning from Mistakes

Toyota Motor Company had developed an industry-leading strategy that focused on value innovation and cost reduction.[1] For many years it was a solid strategy for both the company and its customers. Over the years, Toyota built a reputation for engineering excellence and cost cutting. Its engineers collaborated with suppliers to extract cost-savings without compromising quality. Yet, by the middle of the last decade, Toyota's virtue had become a vice and eventually led to recalled vehicles, lawsuits, and a damaged reputation. What went wrong?

Toyota's problems stemmed from an overwhelming desire to cut costs. This, in turn, led to a product that did not meet the same high quality that its customers had come to expect. When a North American parts supplier interested in working with the automaker did a teardown of a 2007 Camry, its engineers were surprised by how much the traditional Toyota craftsmanship had been watered down by years of nips and tucks. One example of this came to light in 2006, when a redesigned Camry revealed an embarrassing flaw in its headliner (the lining that covers the inside of the roof). Under pressure to cut costs, a Toyota affiliate chose a carbon fiber material that had not yet been approved by Toyota engineers. Unfortunately, the new carbon fiber material required so much heat to mold during production that it would catch fire. Thus, as many as 30 percent of the parts were scrapped—compared to a normal scrap rate for headliners of about 5 percent.

The worst of Toyota's problems came in early 2010 when the company recalled around 3.8 million vehicles. The problem with these vehicles occurred when customers complained that their car would suddenly accelerate to speeds of over 100 mph without warning. This recall included America's most popular passenger vehicle, the Camry, and the best-selling gas-electric hybrid, the Prius. Recalls came after the National Highway Traffic Safety Administration received reports of 102 incidents in which the accelerator became stuck. However, safety analysts estimated that there were approximately 2,000 cases in which owners of Toyota vehicles, including Camry, Prius, and Lexus, experienced "runaway cars."

A well-publicized incident that further tarnished Toyota's reputation was the tragic death of the Saylor family. On August 28, 2009, Mark Saylor died alongside his wife Cleofe, and their daughter Mahala, 13, and Mrs. Saylor's brother, Chris Lastrella when the Lexus they had rented accelerated out of control on a highway in San Diego. In the emergency call, Mr. Lastrella was heard saying: "We're in a Lexus . . . and we're going north on 125 and our accelerator is stuck . . . there's no brakes . . . we're approaching the intersection . . . Hold on . . . hold on and pray . . . pray."

Clearly, Toyota got carried away chasing high-speed growth, market share, and productivity gains year in and year out. This focus slowly dulled the commitment to quality embedded in Toyota's corporate culture. In February 2010, Kiichiro Toyoda, the grandson of the company's founder, told a congressional committee: "I fear the pace at which we have grown may have been too quick . . . Priorities became confused, and we were not able to stop, think and make improvements as much as we were able to do before."

Toyota aggressively tried to cut costs at a rate their product could not keep up with. By ignoring key aspects of the value chain, such as operations and R&D, quality was sacrificed within Toyota. This led to products that were faulty as well as a recall that has cost them billions of dollars in repairs and lost revenue—plus a damaged reputation.

In this chapter we will place heavy emphasis on the value-chain concept. That is, we focus on the key value-creating activities (e.g., operations, marketing and sales, and procurement) that a firm must effectively manage and integrate in order to attain competitive advantages in the marketplace. However, firms must not only pay close attention to their own value-creating activities but must also maintain close and effective relationships with key organizations outside the firm boundaries such as suppliers, customers, and alliance partners. Clearly, Toyota's overemphasis on cost cutting—both within the firm and with their suppliers—eroded the quality of their cars as well as their reputation with customers.

Before moving to value-chain analysis, let's briefly revisit the benefits and limitations of SWOT analysis. As discussed in Chapter 2, a SWOT analysis consists of a careful listing of a firm's strengths, weaknesses, opportunities, and threats. While we believe SWOT analysis is very helpful as a starting point, it should not form the primary basis for evaluating a firm's internal strengths and weaknesses or the opportunities and threats in the environment. Strategy Spotlight 3.1 elaborates on the limitations of the traditional SWOT approach.

We will now turn to value-chain analysis. As you will see, it provides greater insights into analyzing a firm's competitive position than SWOT analysis does by itself.

>LO3.1
The benefits and limitations of SWOT analysis in conducting an internal analysis of the firm.

Value-Chain Analysis

Value-chain analysis views the organization as a sequential process of value-creating activities. The approach is useful for understanding the building blocks of competitive advantage and was described in Michael Porter's seminal book *Competitive Advantage*.[2] Value is the amount that buyers are willing to pay for what a firm provides them and is measured by total revenue, a reflection of the price a firm's product commands and the quantity it can sell. A firm is profitable when the value it receives exceeds the total costs involved in creating its product or service. Creating value for buyers that exceeds the costs of production (i.e., margin) is a key concept used in analyzing a firm's competitive position.

Porter described two different categories of activities. First, five **primary activities**—inbound logistics, operations, outbound logistics, marketing and sales, and service—contribute to the physical creation of the product or service, its sale and transfer to the buyer, and its service after the sale. Second, **support activities**—procurement, technology development, human resource management, and general administration—either add value by themselves or add value through important relationships with both primary activities and other support activities. Exhibit 3.1 illustrates Porter's value chain.

value-chain analysis a strategic analysis of an organization that uses value-creating activities.

primary activities sequential activities of the value chain that refer to the physical creation of the product or service, its sale and transfer to the buyer, and its service after sale, including inbound logistics, operations, outbound logistics, marketing and sales, and service.

support activities activities of the value chain that either add value by themselves or add value through important relationships with both primary activities and other support activities; including procurement, technology development, human resource management, and general administration.

The Value Chain

Exhibit 3.1 The Value Chain: Primary and Support Activities

Source: Reprinted with the permission of Free Press, a division of Simon & Schuster Inc., from *Competitive Advantage: Creating and Sustaining Superior Performance* by Michael E. Porter. Copyright © 1985, 1998 The Free Press. All rights reserved.

The Limitations of SWOT Analysis

SWOT analysis is a tried-and-true tool of strategic analysis. SWOT (strengths, weaknesses, opportunities, threats) analysis is used regularly in business to initially evaluate the opportunities and threats in the business environment as well as the strengths and weaknesses of a firm's internal environment. Top managers rely on SWOT to stimulate self-reflection and group discussions about how to improve their firm and position it for success.

But SWOT has its limitations. It is just a starting point for discussion. By listing the firm's attributes, managers have the raw material needed to perform more in-depth strategic analysis. However, SWOT cannot show them how to achieve a competitive advantage. They must not make SWOT analysis an end in itself, temporarily raising awareness about important issues but failing to lead to the kind of action steps necessary to enact strategic change.

Consider the ProCD example from Chapter 2, page 57. A brief SWOT analysis might include the following:

Strengths	Opportunities
First-mover advantage	Demand for electronic phone books
Low labor cost	Sudden growth in use of digital technology

Weaknesses	Threats
Inexperienced new company	Easily duplicated product
No proprietary information	Market power of incumbent firms

The combination of low production costs and an early-mover advantage in an environment where demand for CD-based phone books was growing rapidly seems to indicate that ProCD founder James Bryant had a golden opportunity. But the SWOT analysis did not reveal how to turn those strengths into a competitive advantage, nor did it highlight how rapidly the environment would change, allowing imitators to come into the market and erode his first-mover advantage. Let's look at some of the limitations of SWOT analysis.

Strengths May Not Lead to an Advantage

A firm's strengths and capabilities, no matter how unique or impressive, may not enable it to achieve a competitive advantage in the marketplace. It is akin to recruiting a concert pianist to join a gang of thugs—even though such

an ability is rare and valuable, it hardly helps the organization attain its goals and objectives! Similarly, the skills of a highly creative product designer would offer little competitive advantage to a firm that produces low-cost commodity products. Indeed, the additional expense of hiring such an individual could erode the firm's cost advantages. If a firm builds its strategy on a capability that cannot, by itself, create or sustain competitive advantage, it is essentially a wasted use of resources. ProCD had several key strengths, but it did not translate them into lasting advantages in the marketplace.

SWOT's Focus on the External Environment Is Too Narrow

Strategists who rely on traditional definitions of their industry and competitive environment often focus their sights too narrowly on current customers, technologies, and competitors. Hence they fail to notice important changes on the periphery of their environment that may trigger the need to redefine industry boundaries and identify a whole new set of competitive relationships. Reconsider the example from Chapter 2 of *Encyclopaedia Britannica,* whose competitive position was severely eroded by a "nontraditional" competitor—CD-based encyclopedias (e.g., Microsoft *Encarta*) that could be used on home computers.

SWOT Gives a One-Shot View of a Moving Target

A key weakness of SWOT is that it is primarily a static assessment. It focuses too much of a firm's attention on one moment in time. Essentially, this is like studying a single frame of a motion picture. You may be able to identify the principal actors and learn something about the setting, but it doesn't tell you much about the plot. Competition among organizations is played out over time. As circumstances, capabilities, and strategies change, static analysis techniques do not reveal the dynamics of the competitive environment. Clearly, ProCD was unaware that its competitiveness was being eroded so quickly.

SWOT Overemphasizes a Single Dimension of Strategy

Sometimes firms become preoccupied with a single strength or a key feature of the product or service they are offering and ignore other factors needed for competitive success. For example, Toyota, the giant automaker, paid a heavy price for its excessive emphasis on cost control. The resulting problems with quality and the negative publicity led to severe financial losses and an erosion of its reputation in many markets.

SWOT analysis has much to offer, but only as a starting point. By itself, it rarely helps a firm develop competitive advantages that it can sustain over time.

Sources: Shapiro, C. & Varian, H. R. 2000. Versioning: The Smart Way to Sell Information. *Harvard Business Review,* 78(1): 99–106; and Picken, J. C. & Dess, G. G. 1997. *Mission Critical.* Burr Ridge, IL: Irwin Professional Publishing.

To get the most out of value-chain analysis, view the concept in its broadest context, without regard to the boundaries of your own organization. That is, place your organization within a more encompassing value chain that includes your firm's suppliers, customers, and alliance partners. Thus, in addition to thoroughly understanding how value is created within the organization, be aware of how value is created for other organizations in the overall supply chain or distribution channel.[3]

>LO3.2
The primary and support activities of a firm's value chain.

Next, we'll describe and provide examples of each of the primary and support activities. Then, we'll provide examples of how companies add value by means of relationships among activities within the organization as well as activities outside the organization, such as those activities associated with customers and suppliers.[4]

Primary Activities

Five generic categories of primary activities are involved in competing in any industry, as shown in Exhibit 3.2. Each category is divisible into a number of distinct activities that depend on the particular industry and the firm's strategy.[5]

Inbound Logistics Inbound logistics is primarily associated with receiving, storing, and distributing inputs to the product. It includes material handling, warehousing, inventory control, vehicle scheduling, and returns to suppliers.

inbound logistics receiving, storing, and distributing inputs of a product.

Just-in-time (JIT) inventory systems, for example, were designed to achieve efficient inbound logistics. In essence, Toyota epitomizes JIT inventory systems, in which parts deliveries arrive at the assembly plants only hours before they are needed. JIT systems will play a vital role in fulfilling Toyota's commitment to fill a buyer's new car order in just five days.[6] This standard is in sharp contrast to most competitors that require approximately 30 days' notice to build vehicles. Toyota's standard is three times faster than even Honda Motors, considered to be the industry's most efficient in order follow-through. The five

---

Inbound Logistics

- Location of distribution facilities to minimize shipping times.
- Warehouse layout and designs to increase efficiency of operations for incoming materials.

Operations

- Efficient plant operations to minimize costs.
- Efficient plant layout and workflow design.
- Incorporation of appropriate process technology.

Outbound Logistics

- Effective shipping processes to provide quick delivery and minimize damages.
- Shipping of goods in large lot sizes to minimize transportation costs.

Marketing and Sales

- Innovative approaches to promotion and advertising.
- Proper identification of customer segments and needs.

Service

- Quick response to customer needs and emergencies.
- Quality of service personnel and ongoing training.

Source: Adapted from Porter, M.E. 1985. *Competitive Advantage: Creating and Sustaining Superior Performance.* New York: Free Press.

Exhibit 3.2
The Value Chain: Some Factors to Consider in Assessing a Firm's Primary Activities

days represent the time from the company's receipt of an order to the time the car leaves the assembly plant. Actual delivery may take longer, depending on where a customer lives. How can Toyota achieve such fast turnaround?

- Its 360 key suppliers are now linked to the company by way of computer on a virtual assembly line.
- Suppliers load parts onto trucks in the order in which they will be installed.
- Parts are stacked on trucks in the same place each time to help workers unload them quickly.
- Deliveries are required to meet a rigid schedule with as many as 12 trucks a day and no more than four hours between trucks.

operations all activities associated with transforming inputs into the final product form.

Operations   Operations include all activities associated with transforming inputs into the final product form, such as machining, packaging, assembly, testing, printing, and facility operations.

Creating environmentally friendly manufacturing is one way to use operations to achieve competitive advantage. Shaw Industries (now part of Berkshire Hathaway), a world-class competitor in the floor-covering industry, is well known for its concern for the environment.[7] It has been successful in reducing the expenses associated with the disposal of dangerous chemicals and other waste products from its manufacturing operations. Its environmental endeavors have multiple payoffs. Shaw has received many awards for its recycling efforts—awards that enhance its reputation.

outbound logistics collecting, storing, and distributing the product or service to buyers.

Outbound Logistics   Outbound logistics is associated with collecting, storing, and distributing the product or service to buyers. These activities include finished goods, warehousing, material handling, delivery vehicle operation, order processing, and scheduling.

● Despite superb logistics and excellent manufacturing operations, Dell's competitive position in personal computers—including desktops and laptops—has eroded in recent years.

Campbell Soup uses an electronic network to facilitate its continuous-replenishment program with its most progressive retailers.[8] Each morning, retailers electronically inform Campbell of their product needs and of the level of inventories in their distribution centers. Campbell uses that information to forecast future demand and to determine which products require replenishment (based on the inventory limits previously established with each retailer). Trucks leave Campbell's shipping plant that afternoon and arrive at the retailers' distribution centers the same day. The program cuts the inventories of participating retailers from about a four- to a two-weeks' supply. Campbell Soup achieved this improvement because it slashed delivery time and because it knows the inventories of key retailers and can deploy supplies when they are most needed.

The Campbell Soup example also illustrates the win–win benefits of exemplary value-chain activities. Both the supplier (Campbell) and its buyers (retailers) come out ahead. Since the retailer makes more money on Campbell products delivered through continuous replenishment, it has an incentive to carry a broader line and give the company greater shelf space. After Campbell introduced the program, sales of its products grew twice as fast through participating retailers as through all other retailers. Not surprisingly, supermarket chains love such programs.

Security Risks in Mexico Have Led to Higher Shipping Costs

A report in January 2009 by the U.S. Joint Forces Command caught some by surprise with its warning about Mexico's political instability. It stated: "In terms of worst-case scenarios for the Joint Force and indeed the world, two large and important states bear consideration for a rapid and sudden collapse: Pakistan and Mexico." While the report stated that a collapse in Mexico was considered less likely, it went on to say, "The government, its politicians and judicial infrastructure are all under sustained assault and pressure by criminal gangs and drug cartels. How that internal conflict turns out over the next several years will have a major impact on the stability of the Mexican state."

A December 17, 2010, *Wall Street Journal* article also claimed that fights between drug cartels claimed more than 31,000 lives over the most recent four-year period—including 11,000 lives in 2010. Further, crimes such as robbery, extortion, and kidnapping increased. For some companies—especially those that don't yet have operations in Mexico—the violence has become daunting.

Sources: Casey, N., & Hagerty, J. R. 2010. Companies Shun Violent Mexico. *www.wsj.com*. December 17: np; Anonymous. 2009. Just How Risky Has Mexico Become as a Sourcing Location? *www.scdigest.com*. February 9: np; and Villagran, L. 2010. Companies Grapple with Mexico Security Risks. *Dallas Morning News*. August 20: 1D, 3D.

Not surprisingly, such instability has implications for quality of life and economic development—as well as the cost of doing business. Let's take a look at how logistics costs are affected.

Ryder Systems, for example, doesn't take any chances when it comes to securing its shipping operations in Mexico. It uses GPS to track every one of its trucks moving manufactured goods in Mexico to the border. Private security agents escort every container before it heads to Texas or elsewhere. It handles about 3,000 border crossings weekly. And if a load arrives late, alarms are raised and the dogs do their inspections—not once, but three times.

Faced with the threat of smuggling attempts by criminal organizations in Mexico, foreign companies are simply forced to do more and spend more. In the process, they are charging consumers more to shore up security in a country where killings, extortions, and kidnappings have become part of daily life. While it is difficult to define the full scope of the problem, those who provide risk analysis can offer some insights.

The share of corporate operating costs dedicated to security has risen by roughly a third in the past two years, according to Julio Millan, a Mexico City–based business consultant. He estimates that security spending in 2010 accounted for 3 percent of corporate operating costs in the northern part of the country, versus only 2 percent in 2009. "That's a huge jump," claims Millan. "The public is paying the cost of security through the price of products."

Many U.S. companies with manufacturing plants in Mexico took advantage of low labor costs. However, they have experienced a sharp increase in their shipping costs. This is because they have been forced to spend more on security as a result of increasing drug-related violence (see Strategy Spotlight 3.2).

Marketing and Sales   These activities are associated with purchases of products and services by end users and the inducements used to get them to make purchases.[9] They include advertising, promotion, sales force, quoting, channel selection, channel relations, and pricing.[10,11]

It is not always enough to have a great product.[12] The key is to convince your channel partners that it is in their best interests not only to carry your product but also to market it in a way that is consistent with your strategy.[13] Consider Monsanto's efforts at educating distributors to improve the value proposition of its line of Saflex® windows.[14] The products had a superior attribute: The window design permitted laminators to form an exceptional type of glass by sandwiching a plastic sheet interlayer between two pieces of glass. This product is not only stronger and offers better ultraviolet protection than regular glass, but also when cracked, it adheres to the plastic sheet—an excellent safety feature for both cars and homes.

> **marketing and sales** activities associated with purchases of products and services by end users and the inducements used to get them to make purchases.

Despite these benefits, Monsanto had a hard time convincing laminators and window manufacturers to carry these products. According to Melissa Toledo, brand manager at Monsanto, "Saflex was priced at a 30 percent premium above traditional glass, and the various stages in the value chain (distributors and retailers) didn't think there would be a demand for such an expensive glass product." What did Monsanto do? It reintroduced Saflex as KeepSafe® and worked to coordinate the product's value propositions. By analyzing the experiences of all of the players in the supply chain, it was able to create marketing programs that helped each build a business aimed at selling its products. Said Toledo, "We want to know how they go about selling those types of products, what challenges they face, and what they think they need to sell our products. This helps us a lot when we try to provide them with these needs."[15]

At times, a firm's marketing initiatives may become overly aggressive and lead to actions that are both unethical and illegal.[16] For example:

- **Burdines.** This department store chain is under investigation for allegedly adding club memberships to its customers' credit cards without prior approval.
- **Fleet Mortgage.** This company has been accused of adding insurance fees for dental coverage and home insurance to its customers' mortgage loans without the customers' knowledge.
- **HCI Direct.** Eleven states have accused this direct-mail firm with charging for panty hose samples that customers did not order.
- **Juno Online Services.** The Federal Trade Commission brought charges against this Internet service provider for failing to provide customers with a telephone number to cancel service.

Strategy Spotlight. 3.3 discusses RYZ, a company which has almost no marketing costs. Why? It relies exclusively on social media such as Myspace and Facebook to create demand for its products.

service actions associated with providing service to enhance or maintain the value of the product.

Service   This primary activity includes all actions associated with providing service to enhance or maintain the value of the product, such as installation, repair, training, parts supply, and product adjustment.

Let's see how two retailers are providing exemplary customer service. At Sephora. com, a customer service representative taking a phone call from a repeat customer has instant access to what shade of lipstick she likes best. This will help the rep cross-sell by suggesting a matching shade of lip gloss. CEO Jim Wiggett expects such personalization to build loyalty and boost sales per customer. Nordstrom, the Seattle-based department store chain, goes even a step further. It offers a cyber-assist: A service rep can take control of a customer's Web browser and literally lead her to just the silk scarf that she is looking for. CEO Dan Nordstrom believes that such a capability will close enough additional purchases to pay for the $1 million investment in software.

Support Activities

Support activities in the value chain can be divided into four generic categories, as shown in Exhibit 3.3. Each category of the support activity is divisible into a number of distinct value activities that are specific to a particular industry. For example, technology development's discrete activities may include component design, feature design, field testing, process engineering, and technology selection. Similarly, procurement may include activities such as qualifying new suppliers, purchasing different groups of inputs, and monitoring supplier performance.

procurement the function of purchasing inputs used in the firm's value chain, including raw materials, supplies, and other consumable items as well as assets such as machinery, laboratory equipment, office equipment, and buildings.

Procurement   Procurement refers to the function of purchasing inputs used in the firm's value chain, not to the purchased inputs themselves.[17] Purchased inputs include raw materials, supplies, and other consumable items as well as assets such as machinery, laboratory equipment, office equipment, and buildings.[18,19]

Crowdsourcing: RYZ's Potential Customers Become Its Marketing and Design Staff

What happens when a company lets consumers design and vote on their own products? Quite often, the firm's overhead goes down and profits go up. This business model is an example of using crowdsourcing as a means of community-based design.

One of these companies is RYZ, founded in 2008, with over $1 million in revenues. It doesn't need a large marketing or design staff. Rather, it relies on potential customers for that. Would-be designers use a template from the company's website to create a pair of high-rise sneakers. The designs are posted online, and viewers vote on which ones they like. Winning designs are produced, and designers get $1,000 plus 1 percent of royalties for their efforts.

Sources: Britten, F. 2010. The Youdesign Movement. *www.nyt.com*. February 25: np; Kaufman, W. 2009. Crowdsourcing Turns Business on Its Head. *www.npr.org*. August 20: np; and *RYZwear.com*.

RYZ runs a weekly contest to cherry pick the best submitted sneaker design, which is then manufactured in a limited edition and sold for $54.99 to $99. And encouraging winners to promote their work makes sense: After all, you are more likely to try to make your design a success when you've invested time and effort. As an additional inducement, the winners get their picture on the company's website—along with a statement touting their work.

Not surprisingly, marketing costs are virtually nil, and relying on customers for design and market research enables the firm to move much more quickly, claims Rob Langstaff, the firm's founder and CEO. Previously head of Adidas North America, he says that it would take about 12 months and a substantial investment to get a design to market in the traditional, large shoe companies. In contrast, he asserts that RYZ can go from design to final product in only about six weeks.

crowdsourcing

Exhibit 3.3   The Value Chain: Some Factors to Consider in Assessing a Firm's Support Activities

General Administration

- Effective planning systems to attain overall goals and objectives.
- Excellent relationships with diverse stakeholder groups.
- Effective information technology to integrate value-creating activities.

Human Resource Management

- Effective recruiting, development, and retention mechanisms for employees.
- Quality relations with trade unions.
- Reward and incentive programs to motivate all employees.

Technology Development

- Effective R&D activities for process and product initiatives.
- Positive collaborative relationships between R&D and other departments.
- Excellent professional qualifications of personnel.

Procurement

- Procurement of raw material inputs to optimize quality and speed and to minimize the associated costs.
- Development of collaborative win-win relationships with suppliers.
- Analysis and selection of alternative sources of inputs to minimize dependence on one supplier.

Source: Adapted from Porter, M.E. 1985. *Competitive Advantage: Creating and Sustaining Superior Performance.* New York: Free Press.

Microsoft has improved its procurement process (and the quality of its suppliers) by providing formal reviews of its suppliers. One of Microsoft's divisions has extended the review process used for employees to its outside suppliers.[20] The employee services group, which is responsible for everything from travel to 401(k) programs to the on-site library, outsources more than 60 percent of the services it provides. Unfortunately, the employee services group was not providing them with enough feedback. This was feedback that the suppliers wanted to get and that Microsoft wanted to give.

The evaluation system that Microsoft developed helped clarify its expectations to suppliers. An executive noted: "We had one supplier—this was before the new system—that would have scored a 1.2 out of 5. After we started giving this feedback, and the supplier understood our expectations, its performance improved dramatically. Within six months, it scored a 4. If you'd asked me before we began the feedback system, I would have said that was impossible."

technology development activities associated with the development of new knowledge that is applied to the firm's operations.

Technology Development   Every value activity embodies technology.[21] The array of technologies employed in most firms is very broad, ranging from technologies used to prepare documents and transport goods to those embodied in processes and equipment or the product itself.[22] Technology development related to the product and its features supports the entire value chain, while other technology development is associated with particular primary or support activities.

The Allied Signal and Honeywell merger brought together roughly 13,000 scientists and an $870 million R&D budget that should lead to some innovative products and services in two major areas: performance materials and control systems. Some of the possible innovations include:

- *Performance materials.* The development of uniquely shaped fibers with very high absorption capability. When employed in the company's Fram oil filters, they capture 50 percent more particles than ordinary filters. This means that cars can travel further with fewer oil changes.
- *Control systems.* Working with six leading oil companies, Honeywell developed software using "self-learning" algorithms that predict when something might go wrong in an oil refinery before it actually does. Examples include a faulty gas valve or hazardous spillage.[23]

human resource management activities involved in the recruiting, hiring, training, development and compensation of all types of personnel.

Human Resource Management   Human resource management consists of activities involved in the recruiting, hiring, training, development, and compensation of all types of personnel.[24] It supports both individual primary and support activities (e.g., hiring of engineers and scientists) and the entire value chain (e.g., negotiations with labor unions).[25]

Like all great service companies, JetBlue Airways Corporation is obsessed with hiring superior employees.[26] But they found it difficult to attract college graduates to commit to careers as flight attendants. JetBlue developed a highly innovative recruitment program for flight attendants—a one-year contract that gives them a chance to travel, meet lots of people, and then decide what else they might like to do. They also introduced the idea of training a friend and employee together so that they could share a job. With such employee-friendly initiatives, JetBlue has been very successful in attracting talent.

Jeffrey Immelt, GE's chairman, addresses the importance of effective human resource management:[27]

> Human resources has to be more than a department. GE recognized early on—50 or 60 years ago—that in a multibusiness company, the common denominators are people and culture. From an employee's first day at GE, she discovers that she's in the people-development business as much as anything else. You'll find that most good companies have the same basic HR processes that we have, but they're discrete. HR at GE is not an agenda item; it is the agenda.

Removing Individual Metrics in Performance Evaluations

ITT China President William Taylor wanted to know why employee turnover was so high in the Shanghai sales office. The local manager knew the answer: If the sales manager gave workers an average "3" on the 1-5 performance scale, they'd stop talking to him and, in some cases, quit shortly thereafter. The manager lamented: "They're losing face in the organization. It would be great if we could do something about the scores."

Comments like that popped up around the world. For example, in southern Europe, the focus on individual performance didn't sit well with the region's more "collective ethos," claims James Duncan, director of ITT's talent development. And in Scandinavia, where there's more of "a sense of equality between bosses and workers," says Duncan, some workers asked, "What gives you the right to rate me a 3?" That led ITT to make the radical decision to ditch performance ratings altogether.

Most employees, who still require a detailed evaluation, cheered the changes. In one of the ITT plants in Shenyang, China, the new system has helped to cut the plant's attrition rate in half. The change isn't as popular in the U.S., where some metrics-loving engineers in the defense business remain attached to the old rankings. Still, most people have come around. Says Duncan, "It's not just Asia and Europe." No matter what culture you are from, everyone "likes the fact that they're treated like an adult in this discussion."

Source: McGregor, J. 2008. Case study: To Adapt, ITT Lets Go of Unpopular Ratings. *BusinessWeek*, January 28: 46.

Strategy Spotlight 3.4 discusses a rather unique approach to individual performance evaluations: eliminate the metrics!

General Administration   General administration consists of a number of activities, including general management, planning, finance, accounting, legal and government affairs, quality management, and information systems. Administration (unlike the other support activities) typically supports the entire value chain and not individual activities.[28]

Although general administration is sometimes viewed only as overhead, it can be a powerful source of competitive advantage. In a telephone operating company, for example, negotiating and maintaining ongoing relations with regulatory bodies can be among the most important activities for competitive advantage. Also, in some industries top management plays a vital role in dealing with important buyers.[29]

The strong and effective leadership of top executives can also make a significant contribution to an organization's success. As we discussed in Chapter 1, chief executive officers (CEOs) such as Herb Kelleher, Andrew Grove, and Jack Welch have been credited with playing critical roles in the success of Southwest Airlines, Intel, and General Electric.

Information systems can also play a key role in increasing operating efficiencies and enhancing a firm's performance.[30] Consider Walgreen Co.'s introduction of Intercom Plus, a computer-based prescription management system. Linked by computer to both doctors' offices and third-party payment plans, the system automates telephone refills, store-to-store prescription transfers, and drug reordering. It also provides information on drug interactions and, coupled with revised workflows, frees up pharmacists from administrative tasks to devote more time to patient counseling.[31]

Interrelationships among Value-Chain Activities within and across Organizations

We have defined each of the value-chain activities separately for clarity of presentation. Managers must not ignore, however, the importance of relationships among value-chain

> **>LO3.3**
> How value-chain analysis can help managers create value by investigating relationships among activities within the firm and between the firm and its customers and suppliers.

> **general administration** general management, planning, finance, accounting, legal and government affairs, quality management, and information systems; activities that support the entire value chain and not individual activities.

activities.[32] There are two levels: (1) **interrelationships** among activities within the firm and (2) relationships among activities within the firm and with other stakeholders (e.g., customers and suppliers) that are part of the firm's expanded value chain.[33]

With regard to the first level, consider AT&T's innovative Resource Link program. Here, employees who have reached their plateau may apply for temporary positions in other parts of the organization. Clearly, this program has the potential to benefit all activities within the firm's value chain because it creates opportunities for top employees to lend their expertise to all of the organization's value-creating activities.

With regard to the second level, Campbell Soup's use of electronic networks enabled it to improve the efficiency of outbound logistics.[34] However, it also helped Campbell manage the ordering of raw materials more effectively, improve its production scheduling, and help its customers better manage their inbound logistics operations.

Strategy Spotlight 3.5 discusses an innovative initiative by Timberland, a leading shoe manufacturer, to eliminate toxic adhesives from its shoes. This effort has the potential for long-term cost savings for their suppliers as well as increased market share for their product line.

The "Prosumer" Concept: Integrating Customers into the Value Chain

When addressing the value-chain concept, it is important to focus on the interrelationship between the organization and its most important stakeholder—its customers.[35] A key to success for some leading-edge firms is to team up with their customers to satisfy their particular need(s). As stated in a recent IBM Global CEO Study:

> In the future, we will be talking more and more about the "prosumer"—a customer/producer who is even more extensively integrated into the value chain. As a consequence, production processes will be customized more precisely and individually.[36]

Including customers in the actual production process can create greater satisfaction among them. It also has the potential to result in significant cost savings and to generate innovative ideas for the firm, which can be transferred to the customer in terms of lower prices and higher quality products and services.

In terms of how a firm views its customers, the move to create the prosumer stands in rather stark contrast to the conventional marketing approach in which the customer merely consumes the products produced by the company. Another area where this approach differs from conventional thinking concerns the notion of tying the customer into the company through, for example, loyalty programs and individualized relationship marketing.

How Procter & Gamble Embraced the Prosumer Concept   In the early 2000s P&G's people were not clearly oriented toward any common purpose. The corporate mission "To meaningfully improve the everyday lives of the customers" had not been explicitly or inspirationally rolled out to the employees. To more clearly focus everyone's efforts, P&G expanded the mission to include the idea that "the consumer is the boss." This philosophy became one in which people who buy and use P&G products are valued not just for their money but also as *a rich source of information and direction*. "The consumer is the boss" became far more than a slogan in P&G. It became a clear, simple, and inclusive cultural priority for both employees and the external stakeholders such as suppliers.

The P&G efforts in the fragrance areas are one example. P&G transformed this small underperforming business area into a global leader and the world's largest fine fragrance company. They accomplished this by clearly and precisely defining the target consumer for each fragrance brand and by identifying subgroups of consumers for some brands. P&G still kept the partnerships with established fashion houses such as Dolce & Gabbana, Gucci, and Lacoste. However, the main point was to make the consumer the boss, focusing on innovations that were meaningful to consumers, including, for instance, fresh new

Timberland's Detoxification Initiative

Making shoes is a surprisingly toxic business. Both the materials and the adhesives that connect them are made of chemicals that are known dangers to the cardiac, respiratory, and nervous systems. One pair of running shoes will hardly harm you. However, workers in the industry face real risks.

Timberland, the second largest company in the outdoor industry, with $1.3 billion in revenues, realized that it needed to rethink the industry's traditional reliance on toxic chemicals. It became the first footwear company to test new water-based adhesives on nonathletic shoes. (Nike and others had already taken the initiatives in the "white shoe," or athletic, part of the industry.) Making such a change required the firm to work closely with Asian suppliers. According to Timberland's website, the company released its long-term strategy in 2008, which included its goal to create products at lower cost and with less harm to the environment. The strategy included eliminating polyvinylchloride (PVC) from its product line and increasing the use of water-based adhesives in its footwear in order to reduce the use of solvents.

Common sense would suggest that Timberland's detoxification efforts would be very costly for its suppliers. And during the test phase it was quite expensive. The new adhesives cost more because economies of scale hadn't yet been achieved. However, over time, Timberland fully expects the process to be at least cost neutral for its business and a money maker for the full value chain.

Sources: Esty, D. C. & Winston, A. S. *Green to Gold.* Hoboken, NJ: Wiley, p: 112–113; *www.community.timberland.com*; and *finance.yahoo.com*.

Why? Water-based adhesives eliminate almost entirely the supplier's expense for handling hazardous materials, including waste disposal, insurance, and training. Manufacturing expenses had already declined during the testing phase, because water-based adhesives go on with one coat instead of two, and the application equipment requires less cleaning. Thus, suppliers can run

● Timberland is well known for their environmental sustainability initiatives.

longer without interruption. The change also improves worker safety as well as reduces both labor costs and time.

Sounds good. But will Timberland be able to capture these supplier savings down the road? Probably not, but over time this strategy should help the firm win market share and drive revenues.

environmental sustainability

---

scents, distinctive packaging, and proactive marketing. In addition, P&G streamlined the supply chain to reduce complexity and lower its cost structure.

"The consumer is the boss" idea goes even further. It also means that P&G tries to build social connections through digital media and other forms of interactions (thus incorporating the crowdsourcing concept that we introduced in Chapter 1). Baby diapers are one example. P&G used to use handmade diapers for its product tests. Today, however, this product is shown digitally and created in alternatives in an on-screen virtual world. Changes can be made immediately as new ideas emerge, and it can be redesigned on screen. Thus, P&G is creating a social system with the consumers (and potential consumers) that enable the firm to co-design and co-engineer new innovations with buyers. At P&G the philosophy of "the consumer is the boss" set a new standard.

Applying the Value Chain to Service Organizations

The concepts of inbound logistics, operations, and outbound logistics suggest managing the raw materials that might be manufactured into finished products and delivered to customers. However, these three steps do not apply only to manufacturing. They correspond to any transformation process in which inputs are converted through a work process into outputs that add value. For example, accounting is a sort of transformation process that converts daily records of individual transactions into monthly financial reports. In this example, the transaction records are the inputs, accounting is the operation that adds value, and financial statements are the outputs.

What are the "operations," or transformation processes, of service organizations? At times, the difference between manufacturing and service is in providing a customized solution rather than mass production as is common in manufacturing. For example, a travel agent adds value by creating an itinerary that includes transportation, accommodations, and activities that are customized to your budget and travel dates. A law firm renders services that are specific to a client's needs and circumstances. In both cases, the work process (operation) involves the application of specialized knowledge based on the specifics of a situation (inputs) and the outcome that the client desires (outputs).

The application of the value chain to service organizations suggests that the value-adding process may be configured differently depending on the type of business a firm is engaged in. As the preceding discussion on support activities suggests, activities such as procurement and legal services are critical for adding value. Indeed, the activities that may only provide support to one company may be critical to the primary value-adding activity of another firm.

Exhibit 3.4 provides two models of how the value chain might look in service industries. In the retail industry, there are no manufacturing operations. A firm, such as Best Buy, adds value by developing expertise in the procurement of finished goods and by displaying them in their stores in a way that enhances sales. Thus, the value chain makes procurement activities (i.e., partnering with vendors and purchasing goods) a primary rather than a support activity. Operations refer to the task of operating Best Buy's stores.

Retail: Primary Value-Chain Activities

Partnering with vendors → Purchasing goods → Managing and distributing inventory → Operating stores → Marketing and selling

Engineering Services: Primary Value-Chain Activities

Research and development → Engineering → Designs and solutions → Marketing and sales → Service

Exhibit 3.4 Some Examples of Value Chains in Service Industries

For an engineering services firm, research and development provides inputs, the transformation process is the engineering itself, and innovative designs and practical solutions are the outputs. Arthur D. Little, for example, is a large consulting firm with offices in 20 countries. In its technology and innovation management practice, A. D. Little strives to make the best use of the science, technology and knowledge resources available to create value for a wide range of industries and client sectors. This involves activities associated with research and development, engineering, and creating solutions as well as downstream activities such as marketing, sales, and service. How the primary and support activities of a given firm are configured and deployed will often depend on industry conditions and whether the company is service and/or manufacturing oriented.

Resource-Based View of the Firm

The **resource-based view (RBV) of the firm** combines two perspectives: (1) the internal analysis of phenomena within a company and (2) an external analysis of the industry and its competitive environment.[37] It goes beyond the traditional SWOT (strengths, weaknesses, opportunities, threats) analysis by integrating internal and external perspectives. The ability of a firm's resources to confer competitive advantage(s) cannot be determined without taking into consideration the broader competitive context. A firm's resources must be evaluated in terms of how valuable, rare, and hard they are for competitors to duplicate. Otherwise, the firm attains only competitive parity.

As noted earlier (in Strategy Spotlight 3.1), a firm's strengths and capabilities—no matter how unique or impressive—do not necessarily lead to competitive advantages in the marketplace. The criteria for whether advantages are created and whether or not they can be sustained over time will be addressed later in this section. Thus, the RBV is a very useful framework for gaining insights as to why some competitors are more profitable than others. As we will see later in the book, the RBV is also helpful in developing strategies for individual businesses and diversified firms by revealing how core competencies embedded in a firm can help it exploit new product and market opportunities.

In the two sections that follow, we will discuss the three key types of resources that firms possess (summarized in Exhibit 3.5): tangible resources, intangible resources, and organizational capabilities. Then we will address the conditions under which such assets and capabilities can enable a firm to attain a sustainable competitive advantage.[38]

It is important to note that resources by themselves typically do not yield a competitive advantage. Even if a basketball team recruited an all-star center, there would be little chance of victory if the other members of the team were continually outplayed by their opponents or if the coach's attitude was so negative that everyone, including the center, became unwilling to put forth their best efforts.

In a business context, a firm's excellent value-creating activities (e.g., logistics) would not be a source of competitive advantage if those activities were not integrated with other important value-creating activities such as marketing and sales. Thus, a central theme of the resource-based view of the firm is that competitive advantages are created (and sustained) through the bundling of several resources in unique combinations.[39]

Types of Firm Resources

Firm resources are all assets, capabilities, organizational processes, information, knowledge, and so forth, controlled by a firm that enable it to develop and implement value-creating strategies.

Tangible Resources These are assets that are relatively easy to identify. They include the physical and financial assets that an organization uses to create value for its

resource-based view of the firm perspective that firms' competitive advantages are due to their endowment of strategic resources that are valuable, rare, costly to imitate, and costly to substitute.

>LO3.4
The resource-based view of the firm and the different types of tangible and intangible resources, as well as organizational capabilities.

tangible resources organizational assets that are relatively easy to identify, including physical assets, financial resources, organizational resources, and technological resources.

Tangible Resources

Financial	• Firm's cash account and cash equivalents.
	• Firm's capacity to raise equity.
	• Firm's borrowing capacity.
Physical	• Modern plant and facilities.
	• Favorable manufacturing locations.
	• State-of-the-art machinery and equipment.
Technological	• Trade secrets.
	• Innovative production processes.
	• Patents, copyrights, trademarks.
Organizational	• Effective strategic planning processes.
	• Excellent evaluation and control systems.

Intangible Resources

Human	• Experience and capabilities of employees.
	• Trust.
	• Managerial skills.
	• Firm-specific practices and procedures.
Innovation and creativity	• Technical and scientific skills.
	• Innovation capacities.
Reputation	• Brand name.
	• Reputation with customers for quality and reliability.
	• Reputation with suppliers for fairness, non–zero-sum relationships.

Organizational Capabilities

- Firm competencies or skills the firm employs to transfer inputs to outputs.
- Capacity to combine tangible and intangible resources, using organizational processes to attain desired end.

EXAMPLES:

- Outstanding customer service.
- Excellent product development capabilities.
- Innovativeness of products and services.
- Ability to hire, motivate, and retain human capital.

Source: Adapted from Barney, J. B. 1991. Firm Resources and Sustained Competitive Advantage. *Journal of Management:* 17: 101; Grant, R. M. 1991. *Contemporary Strategy Analysis:* 100–102. Cambridge England: Blackwell Business and Hitt, M. A., Ireland, R. D., & Hoskisson, R. E. 2001. *Strategic Management: Competitiveness and Globalization* (4th ed.). Cincinnati: South-Western College Publishing.

customers. Among them are financial resources (e.g., a firm's cash, accounts receivables, and its ability to borrow funds); physical resources (e.g., the company's plant, equipment, and machinery as well as its proximity to customers and suppliers); organizational resources (e.g., the company's strategic planning process and its employee development, evaluation, and reward systems); and technological resources (e.g., trade secrets, patents, and copyrights).

Many firms are finding that high-tech, computerized training has dual benefits: It develops more effective employees and reduces costs at the same time. Employees at FedEx take computer-based job competency tests every 6 to 12 months.[40] The 90-minute computer-based tests identify areas of individual weakness and provide input to a computer database of employee skills—information the firm uses in promotion decisions.

Intangible Resources   Much more difficult for competitors (and, for that matter, a firm's own managers) to account for or imitate are **intangible resources**, which are typically embedded in unique routines and practices that have evolved and accumulated over time. These include human resources (e.g., experience and capability of employees, trust, effectiveness of work teams, managerial skills), innovation resources (e.g., technical and scientific expertise, ideas), and reputation resources (e.g., brand name, reputation with suppliers for fairness and with customers for reliability and product quality).[41] A firm's culture may also be a resource that provides competitive advantage.[42]

For example, you might not think that motorcycles, clothes, toys, and restaurants have much in common. Yet Harley-Davidson has entered all of these product and service markets by capitalizing on its strong brand image—a valuable intangible resource.[43] It has used that image to sell accessories, clothing, and toys, and it has licensed the Harley-Davidson Café in New York City to provide further exposure for its brand name and products.

Strategy Spotlight 3.6 discusses how various social networking sites have the potential to play havoc with a firm's reputation.

Organizational Capabilities   **Organizational capabilities** are not specific tangible or intangible assets, but rather the competencies or skills that a firm employs to transform inputs into outputs.[44] In short, they refer to an organization's capacity to deploy tangible and intangible resources over time and generally in combination, and to leverage those capabilities to bring about a desired end.[45] Examples of organizational capabilities are outstanding customer service, excellent product development capabilities, superb innovation processes, and flexibility in manufacturing processes.[46]

In the case of Apple, the majority of components used in their products can be characterized as proven technology, such as touch screen and MP3 player functionality.[47] However, Apple combines and packages these in new and innovative ways while also seeking to integrate the value chain. This is the case with iTunes, for example, where suppliers of downloadable music are a vital component of the success Apple has enjoyed with their iPod series of MP3 players. Thus, Apple draws on proven technologies and their ability to offer innovative combinations of these.

Firm Resources and Sustainable Competitive Advantages

As we have mentioned, resources alone are not a basis for competitive advantages, nor are advantages sustainable over time.[48] In some cases, a resource or capability helps a firm to increase its revenues or to lower costs but the firm derives only a temporary advantage because competitors quickly imitate or substitute for it.[49] Many e-commerce businesses in the early 2000s saw their profits seriously eroded because new (or existing) competitors easily duplicated their business model. For example, Priceline.com, expanded its offerings from enabling customers to place bids online for airline tickets to a wide variety of other products. However, it was easy for competitors (e.g., a consortium of major airlines) to duplicate Priceline's products and services. Ultimately, its market capitalization had plummeted roughly 98 percent from its all-time high.

For a resource to provide a firm with the potential for a sustainable competitive advantage, it must have four attributes.[50] First, the resource must be valuable in the sense that it exploits opportunities and/or neutralizes threats in the firm's environment. Second, it must be rare among the firm's current and potential competitors. Third, the resource must be difficult for competitors to imitate. Fourth, the resource must have no strategically equivalent

intangible resources organizational assets that are difficult to identify and account for and are typically embedded in unique routines and practices, including human resources, innovation resources, and reputation resources.

organizational capabilities the competencies and skills that a firm employs to transform inputs into outputs.

strategic resources (also firm resources or organizational resources) firms' capabilities that are valuable, rare, costly to imitate, and costly to substitute.

> **LO3.5**
The four criteria that a firm's resources must possess to maintain a sustainable advantage and how value created can be appropriated by employees and managers.

Blogs, Social Networking Sites, and Corporate Reputations: A Lethal Combination?

Customers are now connecting with and drawing power from one another. The mechanism: online social technologies such as blogs, social networking sites like MySpace, user-generated content sites like YouTube, and countless communities across the web. They are defining their own perspective on companies and brands—a perspective that is often at odds with the image a company wants to project. This groundswell of people using technologies to get the things they need from one another, rather than from the companies, has tilted the balance of power from company to customer.

Let's look at an example: Brian Finkelstein, a law student, had trouble with the cable modem in his home. A Comcast Cable repairman arrived to fix the problem. However, when the technician had to call the home office for a key piece of information, he was put on hold for so long that he fell asleep on Finkelstein's couch. Outraged, Finkelstein made a video of the sleeping technician and posted it on YouTube. The clip became a hit—with more than a million viewings. And, to this day, it continues to undermine Comcast's efforts to improve its reputation for customer service.

Source: Bernoff, J. & Li, C. 2008. Harnessing the Power of the Oh-So-Social Web. *MIT Sloan Management Review,* 49(3): 36–42; and, Stelter, B. 2008. Griping Online? Comcast Hears and Talks Back. nytimes.com, July 25: np.

But Comcast is working hard to improve its reputation. It has a lot of work to do—after all, the company was ranked at the bottom of a recent American Customer Satisfaction Index, which tracks consumer opinions of more than 200 companies. And hundreds of customers have filed grievances on a site called comcastmustdie.com.

One of Comcast's initiatives to try to turn things around is headed by Frank Eliason, its digital care manager. He uses readily available online tools to monitor public comments on blogs, message boards, and social networks for any mention of Comcast. When Eliason sees a complaint, he contacts the source and tries to defuse the problem. "When you're having a two-way conversation, you really get to clear the air," says Eliason.

Comcast says the online outreach is part of a larger effort to revamp its customer service. In just five months, Eliason, whose job redefines customer service, has reached out to well over 1,000 customers online.

Comcast is not the only company trying to reach out to customers online. Using the social messaging service Twitter, Southwest Airlines answers customer questions about ticket prices and flight delays, Whole Foods Market posts details about discounts, and the chief executive of the online shoe store Zappos shares details of his life with 7,200 "followers." Many other companies also monitor online discussion groups. But given its track record, Comcast felt they needed to take the extra step: contacting customers who are discussing the company online.

---

substitutes. These criteria are summarized in Exhibit 3.6. We will now discuss each of these criteria. Then, we will examine how Dell's competitive advantage, which seemed secure as late as 2006, has eroded.

Is the Resource Valuable?   Organizational resources can be a source of competitive advantage only when they are valuable. Resources are valuable when they enable a firm to formulate and implement strategies that improve its efficiency or effectiveness. The SWOT framework suggests that firms improve their performance only when they exploit opportunities or neutralize (or minimize) threats.

The fact that firm attributes must be valuable in order to be considered resources (as well as potential sources of competitive advantage) reveals an important complementary relationship among environmental models (e.g., SWOT and five-forces analyses) and the resource-based model. Environmental models isolate those firm attributes that exploit opportunities and/or neutralize threats. Thus, they specify what firm attributes may be considered as resources. The resource-based model then suggests what additional characteristics these resources must possess if they are to develop a sustained competitive advantage.

Exhibit 3.6
Four Criteria for
Assessing
Sustainability of
Resources and
Capabilities

Is the resource or capability . . .	Implications
Valuable?	• Neutralize threats and exploit opportunities
Rare?	• Not many firms possess
Difficult to imitate?	• Physically unique
	• Path dependency (how accumulated over time)
	• Causal ambiguity (difficult to disentangle what it is or how it could be re-created)
	• Social complexity (trust, interpersonal relationships, culture, reputation)
Difficult to substitute?	• No equivalent strategic resources or capabilities

Is the Resource Rare?   If competitors or potential competitors also possess the same valuable resource, it is not a source of a competitive advantage because all of these firms have the capability to exploit that resource in the same way. Common strategies based on such a resource would give no one firm an advantage. For a resource to provide competitive advantages, it must be uncommon, that is, rare relative to other competitors.

This argument can apply to bundles of valuable firm resources that are used to formulate and develop strategies. Some strategies require a mix of multiple types of resources—tangible assets, intangible assets, and organizational capabilities. If a particular bundle of firm resources is not rare, then relatively large numbers of firms will be able to conceive of and implement the strategies in question. Thus, such strategies will not be a source of competitive advantage, even if the resource in question is valuable.

Can the Resource Be Imitated Easily?   Inimitability (difficulty in imitating) is a key to value creation because it constrains competition.[51] If a resource is inimitable, then any profits generated are more likely to be sustainable.[52] Having a resource that competitors can easily copy generates only temporary value.[53] This has important implications. Since managers often fail to apply this test, they tend to base long-term strategies on resources that are imitable. IBP (Iowa Beef Processors) became the first meatpacking company in the United States to modernize by building a set of assets (automated plants located in cattle-producing states) and capabilities (low-cost "disassembly" of carcasses) that earned returns on assets of 1.3 percent in the 1970s. By the late 1980s, however, ConAgra and Cargill had imitated these resources, and IBP's profitability fell by nearly 70 percent, to 0.4 percent.

Monster.com entered the executive recruiting market by providing, in essence, a substitute for traditional bricks-and-mortar headhunting firms. Although Monster.com's resources are rare and valuable, they are subject to imitation by new rivals—other dot-com firms. Why? There are very low entry barriers for firms wanting to try their hand at recruitment. For example, many job search dot-coms have emerged in recent years, including jobsearch.com, headhunter.com, nationjob.com, and hotjobs.com. In all, there are more than 40,000 online job boards available to job seekers. It would be most difficult for a firm to attain a sustainable advantage in this industry.

Clearly, an advantage based on inimitability won't last forever. Competitors will eventually discover a way to copy most valuable resources. However, managers can forestall them and sustain profits for a while by developing strategies around resources that have at least one of the following four characteristics.[54]

Physical Uniqueness The first source of inimitability is physical uniqueness, which by definition is inherently difficult to copy. A beautiful resort location, mineral rights, or Pfizer's pharmaceutical patents simply cannot be imitated. Many managers believe that several of their resources may fall into this category, but on close inspection, few do.

Path Dependency A greater number of resources cannot be imitated because of what economists refer to as **path dependency.** This simply means that resources are unique and therefore scarce because of all that has happened along the path followed in their development and/or accumulation. Competitors cannot go out and buy these resources quickly and easily; they must be built up over time in ways that are difficult to accelerate.

The Gerber Products Co. brand name for baby food is an example of a resource that is potentially inimitable. Re-creating Gerber's brand loyalty would be a time-consuming process that competitors could not expedite, even with expensive marketing campaigns. Similarly, the loyalty and trust that Southwest Airlines employees feel toward their firm and its cofounder, Herb Kelleher, are resources that have been built up over a long period of time. Also, a crash R&D program generally cannot replicate a successful technology when research findings cumulate. Clearly, these path-dependent conditions build protection for the original resource. The benefits from experience and learning through trial and error cannot be duplicated overnight.

Causal Ambiguity The third source of inimitability is termed **causal ambiguity**. This means that would-be competitors may be thwarted because it is impossible to disentangle the causes (or possible explanations) of either what the valuable resource is or how it can be re-created. What is the root of 3M's innovation process? You can study it and draw up a list of possible factors. But it is a complex, unfolding (or folding) process that is hard to understand and would be hard to imitate.

Often, causally ambiguous resources are organizational capabilities, involving a complex web of social interactions that may even depend on particular individuals. When Continental and United tried to mimic the successful low-cost strategy of Southwest Airlines, the planes, routes, and fast gate turnarounds were not the most difficult aspects for them to copy. Those were all rather easy to observe and, at least in principle, easy to duplicate. However, they could not replicate Southwest's culture of fun, family, frugality, and focus since no one can clearly specify exactly what that culture is or how it came to be.

Strategy Spotlight 3.7 describes Amazon's continued success as the world's largest online marketplace. Competitors recently tried to imitate Amazon's free shipping strategy, but with limited success. The reason is that Amazon has developed an array of interrelated elements of strategy which their rivals find too difficult to imitate.

Social Complexity A firm's resources may be imperfectly inimitable because they reflect a high level of **social complexity**. Such phenomena are typically beyond the ability of firms to systematically manage or influence. When competitive advantages are based on social complexity, it is difficult for other firms to imitate them.

A wide variety of firm resources may be considered socially complex. Examples include interpersonal relations among the managers in a firm, its culture, and its reputation with its suppliers and customers. In many of these cases, it is easy to specify how these socially complex resources add value to a firm. Hence, there is little or no causal ambiguity surrounding the link between them and competitive advantage. But an understanding that certain firm attributes, such as quality relations among managers, can improve a firm's efficiency does not necessarily lead to systematic efforts to imitate them. Such social engineering efforts are beyond the capabilities of most firms.

Although complex physical technology is not included in this category of sources of imperfect inimitability, the exploitation of physical technology in a firm typically involves the use of socially complex resources. That is, several firms may possess the same physical technology, but only one of them may have the social relations, culture, group norms, and so on to fully exploit the technology in implementing its strategies. If such complex social resources are not subject to imitation (and assuming they are valuable and rare and no substitutes exist), this firm may obtain a sustained competitive advantage from exploiting its physical technology more effectively than other firms.

strategy spotlight

Amazon Prime: Very Difficult for Rivals to Copy

Amazon Prime is a free shipping service which guarantees delivery of products within two days for an annual fee of $79. According to *Bloomberg Businessweek,* it may be the most ingenious and effective customer loyalty program in all of e-commerce, if not retail in general. It converts casual shoppers, who gorge on the gratification of having purchases reliably appear two days after they order, into Amazon addicts. Analysts describe Prime as one of the main factors driving Amazon's stock price—up nearly 300 percent from 2008 to 2010. Also, it is one of the main reasons why Amazon's sales grew 30 percent during the recession while other retailers suffered.

Analysts estimate that Amazon Prime has more than 4 million members in the United States, a small slice of Amazon's 121 million active buyers worldwide. However, analysts claim that Prime members increase their purchases on the site by about 150 percent after they join and may be responsible for as much as 20 percent of Amazon's overall sales in the United States. Such shoppers are considered the "whales" of the $140 billion U.S. e-commerce market, one of the fastest-growing parts of U.S. retail. And, according to Hudson Square Research, Amazon, with a hefty 8 percent of the U.S. e-commerce market, is the single biggest online retailer in the United States.

Source: Stone, B. 2010. What's in the box? Instant gratification. *Bloomberg Businessweek.* November 29–December 5: 39–40; Klein, E. 2010. The genius of Amazon Prime. *www.voices.washingtonpost.com.* November 29: np; and Fowler, G. A. 2010. Retailers team up against Amazon. *www.wsj.com.* October 6: np.

Prime was introduced in 2004. It was the result of a years-long search for the right loyalty program. An Amazon software engineer named Charlie Ward first suggested the idea of a free shipping service via a suggestion box feature on Amazon's internal website. Bing Gordon, an Amazon board member and venture capitalist, came up with the "Prime" name. Other executives, including Chief Executive Jeffrey Bezos, devised the two-day shipping offer—which exploited Amazon's ability to accelerate the handling of individual items in its distribution centers.

Amazon Prime has proven to be extremely hard for rivals to copy. Why? It enables Amazon to exploit its wide selection, low prices, network of third-party merchants, and finely tuned distribution system. All that while also keying off that faintly irrational human need to maximize the benefits of a club that you have already paid to join.

Now, several years after the program's creation, rivals—both online and off—have realized the increasing threat posed by Prime and are rushing to try to respond. For example, in October 2010, a consortium of more than 20 retailers, including Barnes & Noble, Sports Authority, and Toys 'R' Us, banded together to offer their own copycat $79, two-day shipping program, ShopRunner, which applies to products across their websites. However, as noted by Fiona Dias, the executive who administers the program, "As Amazon added more merchandising categories to Prime, retailers started feeling the pain. They have finally come to understand that Amazon is an existential threat and that Prime is the fuel of the engine."

Strategy Spotlight 3.8 describes how a Chinese beverage firm captured a significant market share in rural China by establishing close relationships with its distributors.

Are Substitutes Readily Available?   The fourth requirement for a firm resource to be a source of sustainable competitive advantage is that there must be no strategically equivalent valuable resources that are themselves not rare or inimitable. Two valuable firm resources (or two bundles of resources) are strategically equivalent when each one can be exploited separately to implement the same strategies.

Substitutability may take at least two forms. First, though it may be impossible for a firm to imitate exactly another firm's resource, it may be able to substitute a similar resource that enables it to develop and implement the same strategy. Clearly, a firm seeking to imitate another firm's high-quality top management team would be unable to copy the team exactly. However, it might be able to develop its own unique management team. Though these two teams would have different ages, functional backgrounds, experience, and so on, they could be strategically equivalent and thus substitutes for one another.

How a Chinese Beverage Company Succeeded by Creating Close Partnerships with Its Distributors

In 1998, when Hangzhou Wahaha Co. Ltd (Wahaha), the largest Chinese beverage producer, decided to take on Coca-Cola and PepsiCo, they began their attack in the rural areas of China. Why? They believed that they possessed a competitive advantage over the international giants because of the partnerships that they had built with the distributors across the more remote locations in China. ("Wa ha ha," which sounds like a child laughing, comes from a children's folk song.)

Four years prior to the launch of the "Wahaha Future Cola," the firm developed a policy for how to tie in "channel members" over the long term as a response to the increasing problem of accounts receivable and bad debt. This policy provided incentives for the channel members to pay an annual deposit in advance to cover any potential future bad debt and to operate according to Wahaha's payment policy.

Sounds OK, but what did the distributors get in return? They received an interest rate from Wahaha that was superior to the bank rate. In addition, further discounts were offered for early payment, and annual bonuses were awarded to distributors that met the criterion for prompt payment.

Wahaha implemented this model over a two-year period. It effectively struck financial partnerships with existing distributors that led to higher commitment from distributors. This creative strategy became instrumental to Wahaha's success and their ability to deliver products to the rural areas of China. Here, logistics often create unique challenges.

Wahaha's distribution network now consists of about 4,000 first-tier domestic wholesalers and a large number of second- and third-tier wholesalers and outlets to ensure that Wahaha's products reach millions of retailers nationwide within one week of leaving the factory—no small feat with China's vast rural areas and provinces as far out as Xinjiang and Tibet. As CEO Zong Qinghou colorfully points out: "Our rapid and sound network serves as human blood vessels which circulate the bloodstream to every part of the body once the products are ready."

In contrast, domestic and multinational companies established their own distribution networks—not partnerships with local distributors as Wahaha had done. Not surprisingly, Wahaha has managed to capture impressive market share increases in markets traditionally dominated by Coca-Cola and PepsiCo. And its financial results have been stunning. From 2003 to 2009, its revenues have increased from $1.24 billion to $5.2 billion, and its profits have increased from $165 million to $1.5 billion. These figures represent annual compound rate increases of 27 and 45 percent, respectively!

Source: Anonymous. 2010. Wahaha . . . China's leading beverage producer. *www.chinabevnews.com*. April 11: np; Andersen, M. M., Froholdt, M. & Poulfelt, F. 2010. *Return on Strategy*. New York: Routledge; and Miller, P. M. 2004. The Chinese beverage company's expansion is no laughing matter. *www.chinabuisnessreview*. September–October: np.

Second, very different firm resources can become strategic substitutes. For example, Internet booksellers such as Amazon.com compete as substitutes for bricks-and-mortar booksellers such as B. Dalton. The result is that resources such as premier retail locations become less valuable. In a similar vein, several pharmaceutical firms have seen the value of patent protection erode in the face of new drugs that are based on different production processes and act in different ways, but can be used in similar treatment regimes. The coming years will likely see even more radical change in the pharmaceutical industry as the substitution of genetic therapies eliminates certain uses of chemotherapy.[55]

To recap this section, recall that resources and capabilities must be rare and valuable as well as difficult to imitate or substitute in order for a firm to attain competitive advantages that are sustainable over time.[56] Exhibit 3.7 illustrates the relationship among the four criteria of sustainability and shows the competitive implications.

In firms represented by the first row of Exhibit 3.7, managers are in a difficult situation. When their resources and capabilities do not meet any of the four criteria, it would be difficult to develop any type of competitive advantage, in the short or long term. The

Is a resource or capability . . .				
Valuable?	Rare?	Difficult to Imitate?	Without Substitutes?	Implications for Competitiveness?
No	No	No	No	Competitive disadvantage
Yes	No	No	No	Competitive parity
Yes	Yes	No	No	Temporary competitive advantage
Yes	Yes	Yes	Yes	Sustainable competitive advantage

Source: Adapted from Barney, J. B. 1991. Firm Resources and Sustained Competitive Advantage. *Journal of Management,* 17: 99–120.

resources and capabilities they possess enable the firm neither to exploit environmental opportunities nor neutralize environmental threats. In the second and third rows, firms have resources and capabilities that are valuable as well as rare, respectively. However, in both cases the resources and capabilities are not difficult for competitors to imitate or substitute. Here, the firms could attain some level of competitive parity. They could perform on par with equally endowed rivals or attain a temporary competitive advantage. But their advantages would be easy for competitors to match. It is only in the fourth row, where all four criteria are satisfied, that competitive advantages can be sustained over time. Next, let's look at Dell and see how its competitive advantage, which seemed to be sustainable for a rather long period of time, has eroded.

Dell's Eroding (Sustainable?) Competitive Advantage   In 1984, Michael Dell started Dell Inc. in a University of Texas dorm room with an investment of $1,000.[57] By 2006, Dell had attained annual revenues of $56 billion and a net income of $3.6 billion—making Michael Dell one of the richest people in the world. Dell achieved this meteoric growth by differentiating itself through the direct sales approach that it pioneered. Its user-configurable products met the diverse needs of its corporate and institutional customer base. Exhibit 3.8 summarizes how Dell achieved its remarkable success by integrating its tangible resources, intangible resources, and organizational capabilities.

Dell continued to maintain this competitive advantage by strengthening its value-chain activities and interrelationships that are critical to satisfying the largest market opportunities. It achieved this by (1) implementing e-commerce direct sales and support processes that accounted for the sophisticated buying habits of the largest markets and (2) matching its inventory management to its extensive supplier network. Dell also sustained these advantages by investing in intangible resources, such as proprietary assembly methods and packaging configurations, that helped to protect against the threat of imitation.

Dell recognized that the PC is a complex product with components sourced from several different technologies and manufacturers. Thus, in working backward from the customer's purchasing habits, Dell saw that the company could build valuable solutions by organizing its resources and capabilities around build-to-specification tastes, making both the sales and integration processes flexible, and passing on overhead expenses to its suppliers. Even as the PC industry became further commoditized, Dell was one of the few competitors that was able to retain solid margins. It accomplished this by adapting its manufacturing and assembly capabilities to match the PC market's trend toward user compatibility.

For many years, it looked as if Dell's competitive advantage over its rivals would be sustainable for a very long period of time. However, by early 2007, Dell began falling

Resource		Competitive Advantage

Tangible Resources

Direct Sales/Support Systems → Simplification of the purchasing process and conveying strong support compresses the sales cycle and enables higher volume orders.

Just-In-Time Operations → Facility management is reduced only to the operations that are supported in-house, thus protecting margins against the continuous commoditization of PCs.

Intangible Resources

Proprietary Assembly Technology → Dell now has hundreds of patents that focus specifically on flexible assembly technologies, thus limiting the threat of imitation.

Organizational Capabilities

Adaptability to Customer Buying Habits → As e-commerce pioneers, Dell's flexible sales support and operations infrastructure allow them to flexibly support their customers' growing needs without strain since SG&A costs are already so low.

Supplier Management Processes → By having suppliers carry or share inventory costs, Dell reduces their working capital requirements.

Exhibit 3.8 Dell's Tangible Resources, Intangible Resources, and Organizational Capabilities

behind its rivals in market share. This led to a significant decline in its stock price—followed by a complete shake-up of the top management team. But what led to Dell's competitive decline in the first place?[58]

- Dell had become so focused on cost that it failed to pay attention to the design of the brand. Customers increasingly began to see the product as a commodity.
- Much of the growth in the PC industry today is in laptops. Customers demand a sleeker, better-designed machine instead of just the cheapest laptop. Also, they often want to see the laptop before they buy it.
- When Dell outsourced its customer service function to foreign locations, it led to a decline in customer support. This eroded Dell's brand value.
- Dell's efforts to replicate its made-to-order, no middleman strategy to other products such as printers and storage devices proved to be a failure. This is because customers saw little need for customization of these products.
- Rivals such as HP have been improving their product design and reducing their costs.[59] Thus, they now have cost parity with Dell, while enjoying a better brand image and the support of an extensive dealer network.

Not surprisingly, Dell's performance has suffered. Between 2006 and 2010, its revenues and net income have slumped from $56 billion to $53 billion and $3.6 billion and $1.4 billion, respectively. Inder Sidhu, the author of *Doing Both* (2010), provides a succinct summary of the central lesson in the Dell story:[60]

> Dell illustrates what can happen when a company emphasizes optimization to the exclusion of reinvention. Dell's obsession with operational excellence prevented it from delivering innovations that the market wanted, costing it a great deal of goodwill and prestige. When *Fortune* announced its annual list of "Most Admired Companies" in 2009, Dell, the leader from just four years prior, wasn't even mentioned in the top 50.

The Generation and Distribution of a Firm's Profits: Extending the Resource-Based View of the Firm

The resource-based view of the firm has been useful in determining when firms will create competitive advantages and enjoy high levels of profitability. However, it has not been developed to address how a firm's profits (often referred to as "rents" by economists) will be distributed to a firm's management and employees or other stakeholders such as customers, suppliers, or governments.[61] This becomes an important issue because firms may be successful in creating competitive advantages that can be sustainable for a period of time. However, much of the profits can be retained (or "appropriated") by its employees and managers or other stakeholders instead of flowing to the owners of the firm (i.e., the stockholders).*

Consider Viewpoint DataLabs International, a Salt Lake City–based company that makes sophisticated three-dimensional models and textures for film production houses, video games, and car manufacturers. This example will help to show how employees are often able to obtain (or "appropriate") a high proportion of a firm's profits:

> Walter Noot, head of production, was having trouble keeping his highly skilled Generation X employees happy with their compensation. Each time one of them was lured away for more money, everyone would want a raise. "We were having to give out raises every six months—30 to 40 percent—then six months later they'd expect the same. It was a big struggle to keep people happy."[62]

At Viewpoint DataLabs, much of the profits are being generated by the highly skilled professionals working together. They are able to exercise their power by successfully demanding more financial compensation. In part, management has responded favorably because they are united in their demands, and their work involves a certain amount of social complexity and causal ambiguity—given the complex, coordinated efforts that their work entails.

Four factors help explain the extent to which employees and managers will be able to obtain a proportionately high level of the profits that they generate:[63]

- **Employee Bargaining Power.** If employees are vital to forming a firm's unique capability, they will earn disproportionately high wages. For example, marketing professionals may have access to valuable information that helps them to understand the intricacies of customer demands and expectations, or engineers may understand unique technical aspects of the products or services. Additionally, in some industries such as consulting, advertising, and tax preparation, clients tend to be very loyal to individual professionals employed by the firm, instead of to the firm itself. This enables them to "take the clients with them" if they leave. This enhances their bargaining power.
- **Employee Replacement Cost.** If employees' skills are idiosyncratic and rare (a source of resource-based advantages), they should have high bargaining power based on the high cost required by the firm to replace them. For example, Raymond Ozzie, the software designer who was critical in the development of Lotus Notes, was able to dictate the terms under which IBM acquired Lotus.
- **Employee Exit Costs.** This factor may tend to reduce an employee's bargaining power. An individual may face high personal costs when leaving the organization. Thus, that individual's threat of leaving may not be credible. In addition, an employee's expertise may be firm-specific and of limited value to other firms. Causal ambiguity may make it difficult for the employee to explain his or her specific contribution to a given project. Thus, a rival firm might be less likely to pay a high wage premium since it would be unsure of the employee's unique contribution.

---

*Economists define rents as profits (or prices) in excess of what is required to provide a normal return.

- ***Manager Bargaining Power.*** Managers' power is based on how well they create resource-based advantages. They are generally charged with creating value through the process of organizing, coordinating, and leveraging employees as well as other forms of capital such as plant, equipment, and financial capital (addressed further in Chapter 4). Such activities provide managers with sources of information that may not be readily available to others. Thus, although managers may not know as much about the specific nature of customers and technologies, they are in a position to have a more thorough, integrated understanding of the total operation.

Chapter 9 addresses the conditions under which top-level managers (such as CEOs) of large corporations have been, at times, able to obtain levels of total compensation that would appear to be significantly disproportionate to their contributions to wealth generation as well as to top executives in peer organizations. Here, corporate governance becomes a critical control mechanism. For example, William Esrey and Ronald T. LeMay (the former two top executives at Sprint Corporation) earned more than $130 million in stock options because of "cozy" relationships with members of their board of directors, who tended to approve with little debate huge compensation packages.[64]

Such diversion of profits from the owners of the business to top management is far less likely when the board members are truly independent outsiders (i.e., they do not have close ties to management). In general, given the external market for top talent, the level of compensation that executives receive is based on factors similar to the ones just discussed that determine the level of their bargaining power.[65]

In addition to employees and managers, other stakeholder groups can also appropriate a portion of the rents generated by a firm. If, for example, a critical input is controlled by a monopoly supplier or if a single buyer accounts for most of a firm's sales, their bargaining power can greatly erode the potential profits of a firm. Similarly, excessive taxation by governments can also reduce what is available to a firm's stockholders.

Evaluating Firm Performance: Two Approaches

This section addresses two approaches to use when evaluating a firm's performance. The first is financial ratio analysis, which, generally speaking, identifies how a firm is performing according to its balance sheet, income statement, and market valuation. As we will discuss, when performing a financial ratio analysis, you must take into account the firm's performance from a historical perspective (not just at one point in time) as well as how it compares with both industry norms and key competitors.[66]

The second perspective takes a broader stakeholder view. Firms must satisfy a broad range of stakeholders, including employees, customers, and owners, to ensure their long-term viability. Central to our discussion will be a well-known approach—the balanced scorecard—that has been popularized by Robert Kaplan and David Norton.[67]

financial ratio analysis a technique for measuring the performance of a firm according to its balance sheet, income statement, and market valuation.

Financial Ratio Analysis

The beginning point in analyzing the financial position of a firm is to compute and analyze five different types of financial ratios:

- Short-term solvency or liquidity
- Long-term solvency measures
- Asset management (or turnover)
- Profitability
- Market value

Exhibit 3.9 summarizes each of these five ratios.

I. Short-term solvency, or liquidity, ratios

$$\text{Current ratio} = \frac{\text{Current assets}}{\text{Current liabilities}}$$

$$\text{Quick ratio} = \frac{\text{Current assets} - \text{Inventory}}{\text{Current liabilities}}$$

$$\text{Cash ratio} = \frac{\text{Cash}}{\text{Current liabilities}}$$

II. Long-term solvency, or financial leverage, ratios

$$\text{Total debt ratio} = \frac{\text{Total assets} - \text{Total equity}}{\text{Total assets}}$$

$$\text{Debt-equity ratio} = \text{Total debt/Total equity}$$

$$\text{Equity multiplier} = \text{Total assets/Total equity}$$

$$\text{Times interest earned ratio} = \frac{\text{EBIT}}{\text{Interest}}$$

$$\text{Cash coverage ratio} = \frac{\text{EBIT} + \text{Depreciation}}{\text{Interest}}$$

III. Asset utilization, or turnover, ratios

$$\text{Inventory turnover} = \frac{\text{Cost of goods sold}}{\text{Inventory}}$$

$$\text{Days' sales in inventory} = \frac{365 \text{ days}}{\text{Inventory turnover}}$$

$$\text{Receivables turnover} = \frac{\text{Sales}}{\text{Accounts receivable}}$$

$$\text{Days' sales in receivables} = \frac{365 \text{ days}}{\text{Receivables turnover}}$$

$$\text{Total asset turnover} = \frac{\text{Sales}}{\text{Total assets}}$$

$$\text{Capital intensity} = \frac{\text{Total assets}}{\text{Sales}}$$

IV. Profitability ratios

$$\text{Profit margin} = \frac{\text{Net income}}{\text{Sales}}$$

$$\text{Return on assets (ROA)} = \frac{\text{Net income}}{\text{Total assets}}$$

$$\text{Return on equity (ROE)} = \frac{\text{Net income}}{\text{Total equity}}$$

$$\text{ROE} = \frac{\text{Net income}}{\text{Sales}} \times \frac{\text{Sales}}{\text{Assets}} \times \frac{\text{Assets}}{\text{Equity}}$$

V. Market value ratios

$$\text{Price-earnings ratio} = \frac{\text{Price per share}}{\text{Earnings per share}}$$

$$\text{Market-to-book ratio} = \frac{\text{Market value per share}}{\text{Book value per share}}$$

Exhibit 3.9 A Summary of Five Types of Financial Ratios

Appendix 1 to Chapter 13 (the Case Analysis chapter) provides detailed definitions for and discussions of each of these types of ratios as well as examples of how each is calculated. Refer to pages 491 to 500.

A meaningful ratio analysis must go beyond the calculation and interpretation of financial ratios.[68] It must include how ratios change over time as well as how they are interrelated. For example, a firm that takes on too much long-term debt to finance operations will see an immediate impact on its indicators of long-term financial leverage. The additional debt will negatively affect the firm's short-term liquidity ratio (i.e., current and quick ratios) since the firm must pay interest and principal on the additional debt each year until it is retired. Additionally, the interest expenses deducted from revenues reduce the firm's profitability.

A firm's financial position should not be analyzed in isolation. Important reference points are needed. We will address some issues that must be taken into account to make financial analysis more meaningful: historical comparisons, comparisons with industry norms, and comparisons with key competitors.

Historical Comparisons   When you evaluate a firm's financial performance, it is very useful to compare its financial position over time. This provides a means of evaluating trends. For example, Apple Inc. reported revenues of $65 billion and net income of $14 billion in 2010. Virtually all firms would be very happy with such financial success. These

>LO3.6
The usefulness of financial ratio analysis, its inherent limitations, and how to make meaningful comparisons of performance across firms.

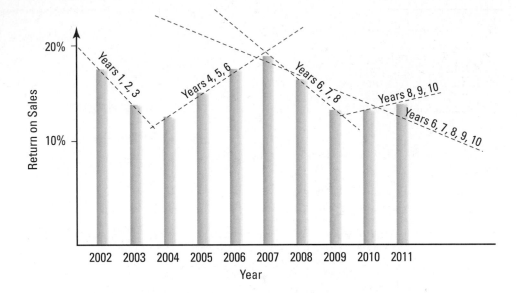

Exhibit 3.10
Historical Trends: Return on Sales (ROS) for a Hypothetical Company

figures represent a stunning annual growth in revenue and net income of 100 percent and 190 percent, respectively, for the 2008 to 2010 time period. Had Apple's revenues and net income in 2010 been $40 billion and $6 billion, respectively, it would still be a very large and highly profitable enterprise. However, such performance would have significantly damaged Apple's market valuation and reputation as well as the careers of many of its executives.

Exhibit 3.10 illustrates a 10-year period of return on sales (ROS) for a hypothetical company. As indicated by the dotted trend lines, the rate of growth (or decline) differs substantially over time periods.

Comparison with Industry Norms　When you are evaluating a firm's financial performance, remember also to compare it with industry norms. A firm's current ratio or profitability may appear impressive at first glance. However, it may pale when compared with industry standards or norms.

Comparing your firm with all other firms in your industry assesses relative performance. Banks often use such comparisons when evaluating a firm's creditworthiness. Exhibit 3.11 includes a variety of financial ratios for three industries: semiconductors, grocery stores, and skilled-nursing facilities. Why is there such variation among the financial ratios for these three industries? There are several reasons. With regard to the collection period, grocery stores operate mostly on a cash basis, hence a very short collection period. Semiconductor manufacturers sell their output to other manufacturers (e.g., computer makers) on terms such as 2/15 net 45, which means they give a 2 percent discount on bills paid within 15 days and start charging interest after 45 days. Skilled-nursing facilities also have a longer collection period than grocery stores because they typically rely on payments from insurance companies.

The industry norms for return on sales also highlight differences among these industries. Grocers, with very slim margins, have a lower return on sales than either skilled-nursing facilities or semiconductor manufacturers. But how might we explain the differences between skilled-nursing facilities and semiconductor manufacturers? Health care facilities, in general, are limited in their pricing structures by Medicare/Medicaid regulations and by insurance reimbursement limits, but semiconductor producers have pricing structures determined by the market. If their products have superior performance, semiconductor manufacturers can charge premium prices.

Exhibit 3.11
How Financial Ratios
Differ across Industries

Financial Ratio	Semiconductors	Grocery Stores	Skilled-Nursing Facilities
Quick ratio (times)	1.9	0.6	1.2
Current ratio (times)	3.9	1.9	1.6
Total liabilities to net worth (%)	30.2	71.4	156.9
Collection period (days)	49.0	2.6	30.3
Assets to sales (%)	147.3	19.5	113.9
Return on sales (%)	24	1.1	2.4

Source: Dun & Bradstreet. *Industry Norms and Key Business Ratios, 2007–2008*. One Year Edition, SIC #3600–3699 (Semiconductors); SIC #5400–5499 (Grocery Stores); SIC #8000–8099 (Skilled-Nursing Facilities). New York: Dun & Bradstreet Credit Services.

Comparison with Key Competitors   Recall from Chapter 2 that firms with similar strategies are members of a strategic group in an industry. Furthermore, competition is more intense among competitors within groups than across groups. Thus, you can gain valuable insights into a firm's financial and competitive position if you make comparisons between a firm and its most direct rivals. Consider a firm trying to diversify into the highly profitable pharmaceutical industry. Even if it was willing to invest several hundred million dollars, it would be virtually impossible to compete effectively against industry giants such as Pfizer and Merck. These two firms have 2010 revenues of $68 billion and $46 billion, respectively, and R&D budgets of $9 billion and $11 billion, respectively.[69]

Integrating Financial Analysis and Stakeholder Perspectives: The Balanced Scorecard

>LO3.7
The value of the "balanced scorecard" in recognizing how the interests of a variety of stakeholders can be interrelated.

It is useful to see how a firm is performing over time in terms of several ratios. However, such traditional approaches to performance assessments can be a double-edged sword.[70] Many important transactions that managers make—investments in research and development, employee training and development, and, advertising and promotion of key brands—may greatly expand a firm's market potential and create significant long-term shareholder value. But such critical investments are not reflected positively in short-term financial reports. Financial reports typically measure expenses, not the value created. Thus, managers may be penalized for spending money in the short term to improve their firm's long-term competitive viability!

Now consider the other side of the coin. A manager may destroy the firm's future value by dissatisfying customers, depleting the firm's stock of good products coming out of R&D, or damaging the morale of valued employees. Such budget cuts, however, may lead to very good short-term financials. The manager may look good in the short run and even receive credit for improving the firm's performance. In essence, such a manager has mastered "denominator management," whereby decreasing investments makes the return on investment (ROI) ratio larger, even though the actual return remains constant or shrinks.

balanced scorecard
a method of evaluating a firm's performance using performance measures from the customers', internal, innovation and learning, and financial perspectives.

The Balanced Scorecard: Description and Benefits   To provide a meaningful integration of the many issues that come into evaluating a firm's performance, Kaplan and Norton developed a **"balanced scorecard."**[71] This provides top managers with a fast but comprehensive view of the business. In a nutshell, it includes financial measures that reflect the results of actions already taken, but it complements these indicators with measures of customer satisfaction, internal processes, and the organization's innovation and improvement activities—operational measures that drive future financial performance.

Exhibit 3.12
The Balanced Scorecard's Four Perspectives

- How do customers see us? (customer perspective)
- What must we excel at? (internal business perspective)
- Can we continue to improve and create value? (innovation and learning perspective)
- How do we look to shareholders? (financial perspective)

customer perspective
measures of firm performance that indicate how well firms are satisfying customers' expectations.

internal business perspective
measures of firm performance that indicate how well firms' internal processes, decisions and actions are contributing to customer satisfaction.

innovation and learning perspective
measures of firm performance that indicate how well firms are changing their product and service offerings to adapt to changes in the internal and external environments.

financial perspective
measures of firms' financial performance that indicate how well strategy, implementation and execution are contributing bottom-line improvement.

The balanced scorecard enables managers to consider their business from four key perspectives: customer, internal, innovation and learning, and financial. These are briefly described in Exhibit 3.12.

Customer Perspective Clearly, how a company is performing from its customers' perspective is a top priority for management. The balanced scorecard requires that managers translate their general mission statements on customer service into specific measures that reflect the factors that really matter to customers. For the balanced scorecard to work, managers must articulate goals for four key categories of customer concerns: time, quality, performance and service, and cost. For example, lead time may be measured as the time from the company's receipt of an order to the time it actually delivers the product or service to the customer.

Internal Business Perspective Customer-based measures are important. However, they must be translated into indicators of what the firm must do internally to meet customers' expectations. Excellent customer performance results from processes, decisions, and actions that occur throughout organizations in a coordinated fashion, and managers must focus on those critical internal operations that enable them to satisfy customer needs. The internal measures should reflect business processes that have the greatest impact on customer satisfaction. These include factors that affect cycle time, quality, employee skills, and productivity. Firms also must identify and measure the key resources and capabilities they need for continued success.

Innovation and Learning Perspective Given the rapid rate of markets, technologies, and global competition, the criteria for success are constantly changing. To survive and prosper, managers must make frequent changes to existing products and services as well as introduce entirely new products with expanded capabilities. A firm's ability to improve, innovate, and learn is tied directly to its value. Simply put, only by developing new products and services, creating greater value for customers, and increasing operating efficiencies can a company penetrate new markets, increase revenues and margins, and enhance shareholder value. A firm's ability to do well from an innovation and learning perspective is more dependent on its intangible than tangible assets. Three categories of intangible assets are critically important: human capital (skills, talent, and knowledge), information capital (information systems, networks), and organization capital (culture, leadership).

Financial Perspective Measures of financial performance indicate whether the company's strategy, implementation, and execution are indeed contributing to bottom-line improvement. Typical financial goals include profitability, growth, and shareholder value. Periodic financial statements remind managers that improved quality, response time, productivity, and innovative products benefit the firm only when they result in improved sales, increased market share, reduced operating expenses, or higher asset turnover.[72]

Consider how Sears, the huge retailer, found a strong causal relationship between employee attitudes, customer attitudes, and financial outcomes.[73] Through an ongoing study, Sears developed (and continues to refine) what it calls its total performance indicators, or

TPI—a set of indicators for assessing their performance with customers, employees, and investors. Sears's quantitative model has shown that a 5.0 percent improvement in employee attitudes leads to a 1.3 percent improvement in customer satisfaction, which in turn drives a 0.5 percent improvement in revenue. Thus, if a single store improved its employee attitude by 5.0 percent, Sears could predict with confidence that if the revenue growth in the district as a whole were 5.0 percent, the revenue growth in this particular store would be 5.5 percent. Interestingly, Sears's managers consider such numbers as rigorous as any others that they work with every year. The company's accounting firm audits management as closely as it audits the financial statements.

A key implication is that managers do not need to look at their job as balancing stakeholder demands. They must avoid the following mind-set: "How many units in employee satisfaction do I have to give up to get some additional units of customer satisfaction or profits?" Instead, the balanced scorecard provides a win–win approach—increasing satisfaction among a wide variety of organizational stakeholders, including employees (at all levels), customers, and stockholders.

Limitations and Potential Downsides of the Balanced Scorecard   There is general agreement that there is nothing inherently wrong with the concept of the balanced scorecard.[74] The key limitation is that some executives may view it as a "quick fix" that can be easily installed. However, implementing a balanced metrics system is an evolutionary process. It is not a one-time task that can be quickly checked off as "completed." If managers do not recognize this from the beginning and fail to commit to it long term, the organization will be disappointed. Poor execution becomes the cause of such performance outcomes. And organizational scorecards must be aligned with individuals' scorecards to turn the balanced scorecards into a powerful tool for sustained performance.[*]

In a recent study of 50 Canadian medium-size and large organizations, the number of users expressing skepticism about scorecard performance was much greater than the number claiming positive results. However, the overwhelming perspective was that balanced scorecards can be worthwhile in clarifying an organization's strategy, and if this can be accomplished, better results will follow. A few companies stated categorically that scorecards have improved their firm's financial results. For example, one respondent claimed that "We did not meet our financial goals previously, but since implementing our balanced scorecard, we have now met our goals three years running."

On the other hand, a greater number of respondents agreed with the statement "Balanced scorecards don't really work." Some representative comments included: "It became just a number-crunching exercise by accountants after the first year," "It is just the latest management fad and is already dropping lower on management's list of priorities as all fads eventually do," and "If scorecards are supposed to be a measurement tool, why is it so hard to measure their results?" There is much work to do before scorecards can become a viable framework to measure sustained strategic performance.

Problems often occur in the balanced scorecard implementation efforts when there is an insufficient commitment to learning and the inclusion of employees' personal ambitions. Without a set of rules for employees that address continuous process improvement and the personal improvement of individual employees, there will be limited employee buy-in and insufficient cultural change. Thus, many improvements may be temporary and superficial. Often, scorecards that failed to attain alignment and improvements dissipated

---

[*] Building on the concepts that are the foundation of the balanced scorecard approach, Kaplan and Norton have recently developed a useful tool called the strategy map. Strategy maps show the cause and effect links by which specific improvements in different areas lead to a desired outcome. Strategy maps also help employees see how their jobs are related to the overall objectives of the organization. They also help us understand how an organization can convert its assets—both tangible and intangible—into tangible outcomes. Refer to Kaplan, R. S. & Norton, D. P. 2000. Having Trouble with Your Strategy? Then Map It. *Harvard Business Review,* 78(10): 167–176.

Key Terms

Experiential Exercise

Dell Computer is a leading firm in the personal computer industry, with annual revenues of $53 billion during its 2010 fiscal year. Dell had created a very strong competitive position via its "direct model," whereby it manufactures its personal computers to detailed customer specifications. However, its advantage has been eroded recently by strong rivals such as HP.

Below we address several questions that focus on Dell's value-chain activities and interrelationships among them as well as whether they are able to attain sustainable competitive advantage(s). (We discuss Dell in this chapter on pages 101–102.)

1. Where in Dell's value chain are they creating value for their customer?

Value-Chain Activity	Yes/No	How Does Dell Create Value for the Customer?
Primary:		
Inbound logistics		
Operations		
Outbound logistics		
Marketing and sales		
Service		
Support:		
Procurement		
Technology development		
Human resource management		
General administration		

2. What are the important relationships among Dell's value-chain activities? What are the important interdependencies? For each activity, identify the relationships and interdependencies.

	Inbound logistics	Operations	Outbound logistics	Marketing and sales	Service	Procurement	Technology development	Human resource management	General administration
Inbound logistics									
Operations									
Outbound logistics									
Marketing and sales									
Service									
Procurement									
Technology development									
Human resource management									
General administration									

3. What resources, activities, and relationships enable Dell to achieve a sustainable competitive advantage?

Resource/Activity	Is It Valuable?	Is It Rare?	Are There Few Substitutes?	Is It Difficult to Make?
Inbound logistics				
Operations				
Outbound logistics				
Marketing and sales				
Service				
Procurement				
Technology development				
Human resource management				
General administration				

Application Questions & Exercises

1. Using published reports, select two CEOs who have recently made public statements regarding a major change in their firm's strategy. Discuss how the successful implementation of such strategies requires changes in the firm's primary and support activities.

2. Select a firm that competes in an industry in which you are interested. Drawing upon published financial reports, complete a financial ratio analysis. Based on changes over time and a comparison with industry norms, evaluate the firm's strengths and weaknesses in terms of its financial position.

3. How might exemplary human resource practices enhance and strengthen a firm's value-chain activities?

4. Using the Internet, look up your university or college. What are some of its key value-creating activities that provide competitive advantages? Why?

Ethics Questions

1. What are some of the ethical issues that arise when a firm becomes overly zealous in advertising its products?

2. What are some of the ethical issues that may arise from a firm's procurement activities? Are you aware of any of these issues from your personal experience or businesses you are familiar with?

References

1. Anonymous. 2010. 'There's no brakes . . . hold on and pray': Last words of man before he and his family died in Toyota Lexus crash. *www.dailymail. co.uk.* February 3: np. Ohnsman, A. 2010. The Humbling of Toyota. *BusinessWeek,* March 22: 32–36; Anonymous. 2009. Toyota recalls 3.8 million vehicles, *www.msnbc.com.* September 29: np; Ross, B. 2009. Owners of Toyota cars in rebellion over series of accidents caused by sudden acceleration, Part one. *www.abcnews.go.com.* November 3: np; and, Ohnsman, A. 2009. Toyota recall crisis said to lie in cost cuts, growth ambitions, *www. bloomberg.com.* February 26: np. We thank Jason Hirsch for his valued contributions.

2. Our discussion of the value chain will draw on Porter, M. E. 1985. *Competitive advantage:* chap. 2. New York: Free Press.

3. Dyer, J. H. 1996. Specialized supplier networks as a source of competitive advantage: Evidence from the auto industry. *Strategic Management Journal,* 17: 271–291.

4. For an insightful perspective on value-chain analysis, refer to Stabell, C. B. & Fjeldstad, O. D. 1998. Configuring value for competitive advantage: On chains, shops, and networks. *Strategic Management Journal,* 19: 413–437. The authors develop concepts of value chains, value shops, and value networks to extend the value-creation logic across a broad range of industries. Their work builds on the seminal contributions of Porter, 1985, op. cit., and others who have addressed how firms create value through key interrelationships among value-creating activities.

5. Ibid.

6. Maynard, M. 1999. Toyota promises custom order in 5 days. *USA Today,* August 6: B1.

7. Shaw Industries. 1999. Annual report: 14–15.

8. Fisher, M. L. 1997. What is the right supply chain for your product? *Harvard Business Review,* 75(2): 105–116.

9. Jackson. M. 2001. Bringing a dying brand back to life. *Harvard Business Review,* 79(5): 53–61.

10. Anderson, J. C. & Nmarus, J. A. 2003. Selectively pursuing more of your customer's business. *MIT Sloan Management Review,* 44(3): 42–50.

11. Insights on advertising are addressed in: Rayport, J. F. 2008. Where is advertising? Into 'stitials. *Harvard Business Review,* 66(5): 18–20.

12. An insightful discussion of the role of identity marketing—that is, the myriad labels that people use to express who they are—in successful marketing activities is found in Reed, A., II & Bolton, L. E. 2005. The complexity of identity. *MIT Sloan Management Review,* 46(3): 18–22.

13. Insights on the usefulness of off-line ads are the focus of: Abraham, M. 2008. The off-line impact of online ads. *Harvard Business Review,* 66(4): 28.

14. Berggren, E. & Nacher, T. 2000. Why good ideas go bust. *Management Review,* February: 32–36.

15. For an insightful perspective on creating effective brand portfolios, refer to Hill, S., Ettenson, R., & Tyson, D. 2005. Achieving the ideal brand portfolio. *MIT Sloan Management Review,* 46(2): 85–90.

16. Haddad, C. & Grow, B. 2001. Wait a second—I didn't order that! *BusinessWeek,* July 16: 45.

17. For a scholarly discussion on the procurement of technology components, read Hoetker, G. 2005. How much you know versus how well I know you: Selecting a supplier for a technically innovative component. *Strategic Management Journal,* 26(1): 75–96.

18. For a discussion on criteria to use when screening suppliers for back-office functions, read Feeny, D., Lacity, M., & Willcocks, L. P. 2005. Taking the measure of outsourcing providers. *MIT Sloan Management Review,* 46(3): 41–48.

19. For a study investigating sourcing practices, refer to: Safizadeh, M. H., Field, J. M., & Ritzman, L. P. 2008. Sourcing practices and boundaries of the firm in the financial services industry. *Strategic Management Journal,* 29(1): 79–92.

20. Imperato, G. 1998. How to give good feedback. *Fast Company,* September: 144–156.

21. Bensaou, B. M. & Earl, M. 1998. The right mindset for managing information technology. *Harvard Business Review,* 96(5): 118–128.

22. A discussion of R&D in the pharmaceutical industry is in: Garnier, J-P. 2008. Rebuilding the R&D engine in big pharma. *Harvard Business Review,* 66(5): 68–76.

23. Donlon, J. P. 2000. Bonsignore's bid for the big time. *Chief Executive,* March: 28–37.

24. Ulrich, D. 1998. A new mandate for human resources. *Harvard Business Review,* 96(1): 124–134.

25. A study of human resource management in China is: Li, J., Lam, K., Sun, J. J. M., & Liu, S. X. Y. 2008. Strategic resource management, institutionalization, and employment modes: An empirical study in China. *Strategic Management Journal,* 29(3): 337–342.

26. Wood, J. 2003. Sharing jobs and working from home: The new face of the airline industry. AviationCareer. net, February 21.

27. Green, S., Hasan, F., Immelt, J. Marks, M., & Meiland, D. 2003. In search of global leaders. *Harvard Business Review,* 81(8): 38–45.

28. For insights on the role of information systems integration in fostering innovation refer to: Cash, J. I. Jr., Earl, M. J., & Morison, R. 2008. Teaming up to crack innovation and enterprise integration. *Harvard Business Review,* 66(11): 90–100.

29. For a cautionary note on the use of IT, refer to McAfee, A. 2003. When too much IT knowledge is a dangerous thing. *MIT Sloan Management Review,* 44(2): 83–90.

30. Walgreen Co. 1996. *Information technology and Walgreens: Opportunities for employment,* January; and Dess, G. G. & Picken, J. C. 1997. *Beyond productivity.* New York: AMACOM.

31. The important role in IT for a Japanese bank is addressed in: Upton, D. M. & Staats, B. R. 2008. Radically simple IT. *Harvard Business Review,* 66(3): 118–124.

32. For an interesting perspective on some of the potential downsides of close customer and supplier relationships, refer to Anderson, E. & Jap, S. D. 2005. The dark side of close relationships. *MIT Sloan Management Review,* 46(3): 75–82.

33. Day, G. S. 2003. Creating a superior customer-relating capability. *MIT Sloan Management Review,* 44(3): 77–82.

34. To gain insights on the role of electronic technologies in enhancing a firm's connections to outside suppliers and customers, refer to Lawrence, T. B., Morse, E. A., & Fowler, S. W. 2005. Managing your portfolio of connections. *MIT Sloan Management Review,* 46(2): 59–66.

35. This section draws on Andersen, M. M., Froholdt, M. & Poulfelt, F. 2010. *Return on strategy.* New York: Routledge: 96–100.

36. Quote from Hartmut Jenner, CEO, Alfred Karcher GmbH, IBM Global CEO Study, P. 27.

37. Collis, D. J. & Montgomery, C. A. 1995. Competing on resources: Strategy in the 1990's. *Harvard Business Review,* 73(4): 119–128; and Barney, J. 1991. Firm resources and sustained competitive advantage. *Journal of Management,* 17(1): 99–120.

38. For recent critiques of the resource-based view of the firm, refer to: Sirmon, D. G., Hitt, M. A., & Ireland, R. D. 2007. Managing firm resources in dynamic environments to create value: Looking inside the black box. *Academy of Management Review,* 32(1): 273–292; and Newbert, S. L. Empirical research on the resource-based view of the firm: An assessment and suggestions for future research. *Strategic Management Journal,* 28(2): 121–146.

39. For insights into research findings on the linkage between resources and performance, refer to: Crook, T. R., Ketchen, D. J., Jr., Combs, J. G., & Todd, S. Y. 2008. Strategic resources and performance: A meta-analysis. *Strategic Management Journal,* 29(11): 1141–1154.

40. Henkoff, R. 1993. Companies that train the best. *Fortune,* March 22: 83; and Dess & Picken, *Beyond productivity,* p. 98.

41. Gaines-Ross, L. 2010. Reputation warfare. *Harvard Business Review,* 88(12): 70–76.

42. Barney, J. B. 1986. Types of competition and the theory of strategy: Towards an integrative framework. *Academy of Management Review,* 11(4): 791–800.

43. Harley-Davidson. 1993. Annual report.

44. For a rigorous, academic treatment of the origin of capabilities, refer to Ethiraj, S. K., Kale, P., Krishnan, M. S., & Singh, J. V. 2005. Where do capabilities come from and how do they matter? A study of the software services industry. *Strategic Management Journal,* 26(1): 25–46.

45. For an academic discussion on methods associated with organizational capabilities, refer to Dutta, S., Narasimhan, O., & Rajiv, S. 2005. Conceptualizing and measuring capabilities: Methodology and empirical application. *Strategic Management Journal,* 26(3): 277–286.

46. Lorenzoni, G. & Lipparini, A. 1999. The leveraging of interfirm relationships as a distinctive organizational capability: A longitudinal study. *Strategic Management Journal,* 20: 317–338.

47. Andersen, M. M. op. cit. 209.

48. A study investigating the sustainability of competitive advantage is: Newbert, S. L. 2008. Value, rareness, competitive advantages, and performance: A conceptual-level empirical investigation of the resource-based view of the firm. *Strategic Management Journal,* 29(7): 745–768.

49. Arikan, A. M. & McGahan, A. M. 2010. The development of capabilities in new firms. *Strategic Management Journal,* 31(1): 1–18.

50. Barney, J. 1991. Firm resources and sustained competitive advantage. *Journal of Management,* 17(1): 99–120.

51. Barney, 1986, op. cit. Our discussion of inimitability and substitution draws upon this source.

52. A study that investigates the performance implications of imitation is: Ethiraj, S. K. & Zhu, D. H. 2008. Performance effects of imitative

entry. *Strategic Management Journal,* 29(8): 797–818.

53. Sirmon, D. G., Hitt, M. A., Arregale, J.-L. & Campbell, J. T. 2010. The dynamic interplay of capability strengths and weaknesses: Investigating the bases of temporary competitive advantage. *Strategic Management Journal,* 31(13): 1386–1409.

54. Deephouse, D. L. 1999. To be different, or to be the same? It's a question (and theory) of strategic balance. *Strategic Management Journal,* 20: 147–166.

55. Yeoh, P. L. & Roth, K. 1999. An empirical analysis of sustained advantage in the U.S. pharmaceutical industry: Impact of firm resources and capabilities. *Strategic Management Journal,* 20: 637–653.

56. Robins, J. A. & Wiersema, M. F. 2000. Strategies for unstructured competitive environments: Using scarce resources to create new markets. In Bresser, R. F., et al., (Eds.), *Winning strategies in a deconstructing world:* 201–220. New York: John Wiley.

57. For an insightful case on how Dell was able to build its seemingly sustainable competitive advantage in the marketplace, refer to "Matching Dell" by Jan W. Rivkin and Michael E. Porter, Harvard Business School Case 9-799-158 (June 6, 1999).

58. Byrnes, N. & Burrows, P. 2007. Where Dell went wrong. *BusinessWeek,* February 18: 62–63; and Smith, A. D. 2007. Dell's moves create buzz. *Dallas Morning News.* February 21: D1.

59. For an insightful perspective on how HP has increased its market share and profitability in the personal computer market, refer to: Edwards, C. 2008. How HP got the wow! back. *BusinessWeek,* December 22: 60–61. HP surpassed Dell in fall 2006 to become the world's largest PC manufacturer, and it increased its market share from 14.5 percent to 18.8 percent between June 2005 and September 2008.

60. Sidhu, I. op. cit., 61.

61. Amit, R. & Schoemaker, J. H. 1993. Strategic assets and organizational rent. *Strategic Management Journal,* 14(1): 33–46; Collis, D. J. & Montgomery, C. A. 1995. Competing on resources: Strategy in the 1990's. *Harvard Business Review,* 73(4): 118–128; Coff, R. W. 1999. When competitive advantage doesn't lead to performance: The resource-based view and stakeholder bargaining power. *Organization Science,* 10(2): 119–133; and Blyler, M. & Coff, R. W. 2003. Dynamic capabilities, social capital, and rent appropriation: Ties that split pies. *Strategic Management Journal,* 24: 677–686.

62. Munk, N. 1998. The new organization man. *Fortune,* March 16: 62–74.

63. Coff, op. cit.

64. Lavelle, L. 2003. Sprint's board needs a good sweeping, too. *BusinessWeek,* February 24: 40; Anonymous. 2003. Another nail in the coffin. *The Economist,* February 15: 69–70; and Byrnes, N., Dwyer, P., & McNamee, M. 2003. Hacking away at tax shelters, *BusinessWeek,* February 24: 41.

65. We have focused our discussion on how internal stakeholders (e.g., employees, managers, and top executives) may appropriate a firm's profits (or rents).

For an interesting discussion of how a firm's innovations may be appropriated by external stakeholders (e.g., customers, suppliers) as well as competitors, refer to Grant, R. M. 2002. *Contemporary strategy analysis* (4th ed.): 335–340. Malden, MA: Blackwell.

66. Luehrman, T. A. 1997. What's it worth? A general manager's guide to valuation. *Harvard Business Review,* 45(3): 132–142.

67. See, for example, Kaplan, R. S. & Norton, D. P. 1992. The balanced scorecard: Measures that drive performance. *Harvard Business Review,* 69(1): 71–79.

68. Hitt, M. A., Ireland, R. D., & Stadter, G. 1982. Functional importance of company performance: Moderating effects of grand strategy and industry type. *Strategic Management Journal,* 3: 315–330.

69. *finance.yahoo.com.*

70. Kaplan & Norton, op. cit.

71. Ibid.

72. For a discussion of the relative value of growth versus increasing margins, read Mass, N. J. 2005. The relative value of growth. *Harvard Business Review,* 83(4): 102–112.

73. Rucci, A. J., Kirn, S. P., & Quinn, R. T. 1998. The employee-customer-profit chain at Sears. *Harvard Business Review,* 76(1): 82–97.

74. Our discussion draws upon: Angel, R. & Rampersad, H. 2005. Do scorecards add up? *camagazine.com.* May: np.; and Niven, P. 2002. *Balanced scorecard step by step: Maximizing performance and maintaining results.* New York: John Wiley & Sons.

APPENDIX TO CHAPTER 3

>LO3.8

How firms are using Internet technologies to add value and achieve unique advantages. (Appendix)

How the Internet and Digital Technologies Add Value

The Internet has changed the way business is conducted. By providing new ways to interact with customers and using digital technologies to streamline operations, the Internet is helping companies create new value propositions. Let's take a look at several ways these changes have added new value. Exhibit 3A.1 illustrates four related activities that are being revolutionized by the Internet—search, evaluation, problem solving, and transactions.[1]

---

[1] The ideas in this section draw on several sources, including Zeng, M. & Reinartz, W. 2003. Beyond Online Search: The Road to Profitability. *California Management Review,* Winter: 107–130; and Stabell, C. B. & Fjeldstad, O. D. 1998. Configuring Value for Competitive Advantage: On Chains, Shops, and Networks. *Strategic Management Journal,* 19: 413–437.

Exhibit 3A.1 Internet Activities that Add Value

Sources: Adapted from Zeng, M., & Reinartz, W. 2003. Beyond online search: The road to profitability. *California Management Review.* Winter: 107–130; and Stabell, C. B., & Fjeldstad, O. D. 1998. Configuring value for competitive advantage: On chains, shops, and networks. *Strategic Management Journal,* 19: 413–437.

Search Activities

Search refers to the process of gathering information and identifying purchase options. The Internet has enhanced both the speed of information gathering and the breadth of information that can be accessed. This enhanced search capability is one of the key reasons the Internet has lowered switching costs—by decreasing the cost of search. These efficiency gains have greatly benefited buyers. Suppliers also have benefited. Small suppliers that had difficulty getting noticed can be found more easily, and large suppliers can publish thousands of pages of information for a fraction of the cost that hard-copy catalogs once required. Additionally, online search engines such as Google, Yahoo and Bing have accelerated the search process to incredible speeds.

> **search activities** a way that digital technologies and the Internet have added value to firms' operations by enhancing the gathering of information and identifying purchase options.

Evaluation Activities

Evaluation refers to the process of considering alternatives and comparing the costs and benefits of various options. Online services that facilitate comparative shopping, provide product reviews, and catalog customer evaluations of performance have made the Internet a valuable resource.[2] For example, BizRate.com offers extensive product ratings that can help evaluate products. Sites such as CNET that provide comparative pricing have helped lower prices even for quality products that have traditionally maintained premium prices. Opinion-based sites such as ePinions.com and PlanetFeedback.com provide reports of consumer experiences with various vendors.

Many Internet businesses, according to digital business experts Ming Zeng and Werner Reinartz, could improve their performance by making a stronger effort to help buyers evaluate purchases.[3] Even so, only certain types of products can be evaluated online. Products such as CDs that appeal primarily to the sense of sound sell well on the Internet. But products that appeal to multiple senses are harder to evaluate online. This explains why products such as furniture and fashion have never been strong online sellers. It's one thing to look at a leather sofa, but to be able to sit on it, touch, and smell the leather online are impossible.

> **evaluation activities** a way that digital technologies and the Internet have added value to firms' operations by facilitating the comparison of the costs and benefits of various options.

Problem-Solving Activities

Problem solving refers to the process of identifying problems or needs and generating ideas and action plans to address those needs. Whereas evaluation is primarily product-related, problem solving is typically used in the context of services. Customers usually have unique problems that are handled one at a time. For example, online travel services such as Travelocity help customers select from many options to form a unique travel package. Furthermore, problem solving often involves providing answers immediately (compared to the creation of a new product). Firms in industries such as medicine, law, and engineering are using the Internet and digital technologies to deliver many new solutions.

> **problem-solving activities** a way that digital technologies and the Internet have added value to firms' operations by identifying problems or needs and generating ideas and action plans to address those needs.

[2] For an interesting discussion of how successful Internet-based companies are using evaluation to add value see Weiss, L. M., Capozzi, M. M., & Prusak, L. 2004. Learning from the Internet Giants. *Sloan Management Review,* 45(4): 79–84.
[3] Zeng & Reinartz, op.cit.

Many products involve both a service and a product component; therefore, both problem solving and evaluation may be needed. Dell Computer's website is an example of a site that has combined the benefits of both. By creating a website that allows for customization of individual computers, they address the unique concerns of customers "one computer at a time." But the site also features a strong evaluative component because it allows users to compare the costs and features of various options. Shoppers can even compare their customized selection to refurbished Dell computers that are available at a substantially lower cost.

Transaction Activities

transaction activities a way that digital technologies and the Internet have added value to firms' operations by completing sales efficiently, including negotiating and agreeing contractually, making payments, and taking delivery.

Transaction refers to the process of completing the sale, including negotiating and agreeing contractually, making payments, and taking delivery. Numerous types of Internet-enabled activities have contributed to lowering this aspect of overall transaction costs. Auctions of various sorts, from raw materials used in manufacturing to collectibles sold on eBay, facilitate the process of arriving at mutually agreed-on prices. Services such as PayPal provide a third-party intermediary that facilitates transactions between parties who never have (and probably never will) meet. Amazon.com's One-Click technology allows for very rapid purchases, and Amazon's overall superiority in managing order fulfillment has made its transactions process rapid and reliable. Amazon's success today can be attributed to a large extent to its having sold this transaction capability to other companies such as Target, Toys "R" Us and even Borders (another bookseller!).[4]

Other Sources of Competitive Advantage

There are other factors that can be important sources of competitive advantage. One of the most important of these is content. The Internet makes it possible to capture vast amounts of content at a very low cost. Three types of content can improve the value proposition of a website—customer feedback, expertise, and entertainment programming.

- *Customer Feedback.* Buyers often trust what other buyers say more than a company's promises. One type of content that can enhance a website is customer testimonials. Remember the leather sofa online? The testimonials of other buyers can build confidence and add to the chances that the purchaser will buy online sight unseen. This is one way that content can be a source of competitive advantage. Being able to interact with like-minded customers by reading their experiences or hearing how they have responded to a new product offering builds a sense of belonging that is otherwise hard to create.
- *Expertise.* The Internet has emerged as a tremendously important learning tool. Fifty-one percent of users compare the Internet to a library.[5] The prime reason many users go to the Web is to gain expertise. Websites that provide new knowledge or unbiased information are highly valuable. Additionally the problem-solving function often involves educating consumers regarding options and implications of various choices. For example, LendingTree.com, the online loan company, provides a help center that includes extensive information and resources about obtaining loans, maintaining good credit, and so forth. Further, the expertise function is not limited to consumer sites. In the case of B2B businesses, websites that facilitate sharing expert knowledge help build a sense of community in industry or professional groups.
- *Entertainment Programming.* The Internet is being used by more and more people as an entertainment medium. With technologies such as streaming media, which allows the Internet to send televisionlike images and sound, computers can provide everything from breaking news to video games to online movies. A study by the Pew Internet and American Life Project indicates that among people using high-speed broadband service, TV viewing is down and online activity has increased. One reason is that the technology is interactive, which means that viewers don't just passively watch, but they use the Web to create art or play online games. Businesses have noticed this trend, of course, and are creating Web content that is not just informative but entertaining.

These three types of content—customer feedback, expertise, and entertainment programming—are potential sources of competitive advantage. That is, they create advantages by making the value creation process even stronger. Or, if they are handled poorly, they diminish performance.

[4] Bayers, C. 2002. The Last Laugh. *Business 2.0,* September: 86–93.
[5] Greenspan, R. 2003. Internet Not for Everyone. *CyberAtlas,* April 16, *www.cyberatlas.com.*

Business Models

The Internet provides a unique platform or staging area for business activity, which has become, in some ways, like a new marketplace. How do firms conduct business in this new arena? One way of addressing this question is by describing various Internet business models. A business model is a method and a set of assumptions that explain how a business creates value and earns profits in a competitive environment. Some of these models are quite simple and traditional even when applied in an Internet context. Others have features that are unique to the digitally networked, online environment. In this section, we discuss seven Internet business models that account for the vast majority of business conducted online.[6]

- **Commission-Based** Models are used by businesses that provide services for a fee. The business is usually a third-party intermediary, and the commission charged is often based on the size of the transaction. The most common type is a brokerage service, such as a stockbroker (e.g., Schwab.com), real estate broker (e.g., Remax.com), or transaction broker (e.g., PayPal.com). This category also includes auction companies such as eBay. In exchange for putting buyers and sellers together, eBay earns a commission.

- **Advertising-Based** Models are used by companies that provide content and/or services to visitors and sell advertising to businesses that want to reach those visitors. It is similar to the broadcast television model, in which viewers watch shows produced with advertising dollars. A key difference is that online visitors can interact with both the ads and the content. Large portals such as Yahoo.com are in this category as well as specialty portals such as iNest.com, which provides services for buyers of newly constructed homes. Epinions.com, a recommender system, is just one example of the many types of content that are often available.

- **Markup-Based** Models are used by businesses that add value in marketing and sales (rather than production) by acquiring products, marking up the price, and reselling them at a profit. Also known as the merchant model, it applies to both wholesalers and retailers. Amazon.com is the best-known example in this category. It also includes bricks-and-mortar companies such as Walmart, which has a very successful online operation, and vendors whose products are purely digital such as Fonts.com, which sells downloadable fonts and photographs.

- **Production-Based** Models are used by companies that add value in the production process by converting raw materials into value-added products. Thus, it is also referred to as the manufacturing model. The Internet adds value to this model in two key ways. First, it lowers marketing costs by enabling direct contact with end users. Second, such direct contact facilitates customization and problem solving. Dell's online ordering system is supported by a state-of-the-art customized manufacturing process. Travelocity uses its rich database of travel options and customer profiles to identify, produce, and deliver unique solutions.

- **Referral-Based** Models are used by firms that steer customers to another company for a fee. One type is the affiliate model, in which a vendor pays an affiliate a fee each time a visitor clicks through the affiliate's website and makes a purchase from the vendor. Many name-brand companies use affiliate programs. For example, WeddingChannel.com, which provides a bridal registry where wedding guests can buy gifts from companies such as Tiffany's, Macy's, or Crate & Barrel, receives a fee each time a sale is made through its website. Another referral-based example is Yesmail.com, which generates leads using e-mail marketing.

- **Subscription-Based** Models are used by businesses that charge a flat fee for providing either a service or proprietary content. Internet service providers are one example of this model. Companies such as America Online and Earthlink supply Internet connections for fees that are charged whether buyers use the service or not. Subscription-based models are also used by content creators such as the *Economist* or the *New York Times*. Although these recognizable brands often provide free content, only a small portion is available free. The *Economist,* for example, advertises that 70 percent of its content is available only to subscribers.

- **Fee-for-Service–Based** Models are used by companies that provide ongoing services similar to a utility company. Unlike the commission-based model, the fee-for-service model involves a pay-as-you-go system. That is, activities are metered and companies pay only for the amount of service used. Application service providers fall in this category. For example, eProject.com

---

[6] Afuah, A. & Tucci, C.L. 2003. *Internet Business Models and Strategies* (2nd ed). New York: McGraw-Hill; and, Timmers, P. 1999. *Electronic Commerce.* New York: Wiley.

provides virtual work space where people in different physical locations can collaborate online. Users essentially rent Internet space, and a host of tools that make it easy to interact, for a fee based on their usage.

Exhibit 3A.2 summarizes the key feature of each Internet business model, suggests what role content may play in the model, and addresses how the four value-adding activities—search, evaluation, problem solving, and transaction—can be sources of competitive advantage.

Exhibit 3A.2
Internet Business Models

Type	Features and Content	Sources of Competitive Advantage
Commission-Based	Charges commissions for brokerage or intermediary services. Adds value by providing expertise and/or access to a wide network of alternatives.	Search Evaluation Problem solving Transaction
Advertising-Based	Web content paid for by advertisers. Adds value by providing free or low-cost content—including customer feedback, expertise, and entertainment programming—to audiences that range from very broad (general content) to highly targeted (specialized content).	Search Evaluation
Markup-Based	Resells marked-up merchandise. Adds value through selection, through distribution efficiencies, and by leveraging brand image and reputation. May use entertainment programming to enhance sales.	Search Transaction
Production-Based	Sells manufactured goods and custom services. Adds value by increasing production efficiencies, capturing customer preferences, and improving customer service.	Search Problem solving
Referral-Based	Charges fees for referring customers. Adds value by enhancing a company's product or service offering, tracking referrals electronically, and generating demographic data. Expertise and customer feedback often included with referral information.	Search Problem solving Transaction
Subscription-Based	Charges fees for unlimited use of service or content. Adds value by leveraging strong brand name, providing high-quality information to specialized markets, or providing access to essential services. May consist entirely of entertainment programming.	Evaluation Problem solving
Fee-for-Service–Based	Charges fees for metered services. Adds value by providing service efficiencies, expertise, and practical outsourcing solutions.	Problem solving Transaction

Sources: Afuah, A. & Tucci, C. L. 2003. *Internet Business Models and Strategies* (2nd ed). New York: McGraw-Hill; Rappa, M. 2005. *Business Models on the Web,* digitalenterprise.org/models/models.html; and Timmers, P. 1999. *Electronic Commerce.* New York: Wiley.

Learning from Mistakes

Hitachi Ltd., a Japanese multinational corporation, is the world's third largest tech firm.[1] Its first president, Namihei Odaira, believed that "inventions are an engineer's lifeblood," and, not surprisingly, he focused on the company's inventions from the very beginning. He demanded that his tech people apply their engineering skills toward generating inventions and patents. This, he felt, could be the key to value creation and competitive advantage. Sounds good . . . but what problems arose?

In 1970 alone, Hitachi filed 20,000 patent applications. Unfortunately, the emphasis was on the sheer number rather than the quality of each patent. At that time, the company earned a mere $5 million in licensing income but paid out $95 million in licensing fees.

In 1979, Hitachi faced major patent litigation. Westinghouse charged Hitachi, a Hitachi-GE joint venture, and a few other companies with patent infringement and petitioned the U.S. International Trade Commission to block the import of circuit breakers from Japan. By then, Hitachi already had several dozen U.S. patents for electrical power transmission equipment. However, it found that they were all patents for features distinctive to Hitachi products and were not the type that other companies could use. Thus, there were no grounds for countersuing Westinghouse for patent infringement.

Hitachi's second big patent problem occurred in 1986. Texas Instruments sued a total of nine Japanese and Korean semiconductor manufacturers in the U.S. International Trade Commission and Texas courts, arguing that its licensing fee was too low and that it could not renew Hitachi's contract at the terms proposed. It demanded to set the licensing fee for DRAM manufacturing technology at 10 percent of sales.

These were bitter lessons for Hitachi. It initiated four campaigns to double its number of "strategic patents" in 1981, 1985, 1990, and 1995, respectively. The goal was to focus their resources on patents that would create the most value for the firm as well as to gain global patent coverage for the company's world-class products and technologies.

Patents can be very valuable. However, a company must effectively use them to create value. Hitachi realized that there was no point in obtaining a mountain of patents if they were not going to help the company compete in the competitive marketplace.

Managers are always looking for stellar professionals who can take their organizations to the next level. However, attracting talent is a necessary but *not* sufficient condition for success. In today's knowledge economy, it does not matter how big your stock of resources is—whether it be top talent, physical resources, or financial capital. Rather, the question becomes: How good is the organization at attracting top talent and leveraging that talent to produce a stream of products and services valued by the marketplace?

We also address issues associated with intellectual property (IP) and its potential to create value for the firm. The Hitachi example shows how heavy investment in IP alone is insufficient for value creation in the competitive marketplace.

>LO4.1
Why the management of knowledge professionals and knowledge itself are so critical in today's organizations.

The Central Role of Knowledge in Today's Economy

Central to our discussion is an enormous change that has accelerated over the past few decades and its implications for the strategic management of organizations.[2] For most of the 20th century, managers focused on tangible resources such as land, equipment, and money as well as intangibles such as brands, image, and customer loyalty. Efforts were directed more toward the efficient allocation of labor and capital—the two traditional factors of production.

How times have changed. Today, more than 50 percent of the gross domestic product (GDP) in developed economies is knowledge-based; it is based on intellectual assets and intangible people skills.[3] In the U.S., intellectual and information processes create most of the value for firms in large service industries (e.g., software, medical care, communications, and education), which make up 77 percent of the U.S. GDP. In the manufacturing sector, intellectual activities like R&D, process design, product design, logistics, marketing, and technological innovation produce the preponderance of value added.[4] To drive home the point, Gary Hamel and the late C. K. Prahalad, two leading writers in strategic management state:

> The machine age was a physical world. It consisted of things. Companies made and distributed things (physical products). Management allocated things (capital budgets); management invested in things (plant and equipment).
>
> In the machine age, people were ancillary, and things were central. In the information age, things are ancillary, knowledge is central. A company's value derives not from things, but from knowledge, know-how, intellectual assets, competencies—all embedded in people.[5]

In the **knowledge economy,** wealth is increasingly created by effective management of knowledge workers instead of by the efficient control of physical and financial assets. The growing importance of knowledge, coupled with the move by labor markets to reward knowledge work, tells us that investing in a company is, in essence, buying a set of talents, capabilities, skills, and ideas—intellectual capital—not physical and financial resources.[6]

Let's provide a few examples. People don't buy Microsoft's stock because of its software factories; it doesn't own any. Rather, the value of Microsoft is bid up because it sets standards for personal-computing software, exploits the value of its name, and forges alliances with other companies. Similarly, Merck didn't become the "Most Admired" company, for seven consecutive years in *Fortune*'s annual survey, because it can manufacture pills, but because its scientists can discover medicines. P. Roy Vagelos, who was CEO of Merck, the $44 billion pharmaceutical giant, during its long run atop the "Most Admired" survey, said, "A low-value product can be made by anyone anywhere. When you have knowledge no one else has access to—that's dynamite. We guard our research even more carefully than our financial assets."[7]

To apply some numbers to our arguments, let's ask, What's a company worth?[8] Start with the "big three" financial statements: income statement, balance sheet, and statement of cash flow. If these statements tell a story that investors find useful, then a company's market value* should roughly (but not precisely, because the market looks forward and the books look backward) be the same as the value that accountants ascribe to it—the book value of the firm. However, this is not the case. A study compared the market value with the book value of 3,500 U.S. companies over a period of two decades. In 1978 the two were similar: Book value was 95 percent of market value. However, market values and book values have diverged significantly. Within 20 years, the S&P industrials were—on average—trading at 2.2 times book value.[9] Robert A. Howell, an expert on the changing role of finance and accounting, muses that "The big three financial statements . . . are about as useful as an 80-year-old Los Angeles road map."

The gap between a firm's market value and book value is far greater for knowledge-intensive corporations than for firms with strategies based primarily on tangible assets.[10] Exhibit 4.1 shows the ratio of market-to-book value for some well-known companies. In

knowledge economy an economy where wealth is created through the effective management of knowledge workers instead of by the efficient control of physical and financial assets.

* The market value of a firm is equal to the value of a share of its common stock times the number of shares outstanding. The book value of a firm is primarily a measure of the value of its tangible assets. It can be calculated by the formula: total assets − total liabilities.

firms where knowledge and the management of knowledge workers are relatively important contributors to developing products and services—and physical resources are less critical—the ratio of market-to-book value tends to be much higher.

As shown in Exhibit 4.1, firms such as Apple, Google, Microsoft, and Oracle have very high market value to book value ratios because of their high investment in knowledge resources and technological expertise. In contrast, firms in more traditional industry sectors such as International Paper, Nucor, and Southwest Airlines have relatively low market to book ratios. This reflects their greater investments in physical resources and lower investment in knowledge resources. A firm like Intel has a market to book value ratio that falls between the above two groups of firms. This is because their high level of investment in knowledge resources is matched by a correspondingly huge investment in plant and equipment. For example, in 2007, Intel invested $3 billion to build a fabrication facility in Chandler, Arizona.[11]

Many writers have defined **intellectual capital** as the difference between a firm's market value and book value—that is, a measure of the value of a firm's intangible assets.[12] This broad definition includes assets such as reputation, employee loyalty and commitment, customer relationships, company values, brand names, and the experience and skills of employees.[13] Thus, simplifying, we have:

$$\text{Intellectual capital} = \text{Market value of firm} - \text{Book value of the firm}$$

How do companies create value in the knowledge-intensive economy? The general answer is to attract and leverage human capital effectively through mechanisms that create products and services of value over time.

First, **human capital** is the "*individual* capabilities, knowledge, skills, and experience of the company's employees and managers."[14] This knowledge is relevant to the task at hand, as well as the capacity to add to this reservoir of knowledge, skills, and experience through learning.[15]

Second, **social capital** is "the network of relationships that individuals have throughout the organization." Relationships are critical in sharing and leveraging knowledge and in acquiring resources.[16] Social capital can extend beyond the organizational boundaries to include relationships between the firm and its suppliers, customers, and alliance partners.[17]

Exhibit 4.1 Ratio of Market Value to Book Value for Selected Companies

Company	Annual Sales ($ billions)	Market Value ($ billions)	Book Value ($ billions)	Ratio of Market to Book Value
Apple	65.2	314.6	47.8	6.6
Google	20.9	196.4	36.0	5.4
Microsoft	65.8	241.3	46.2	5.2
Oracle	32.0	157.0	30.8	5.1
Intel	42.7	116.1	41.7	2.8
International Paper	24.6	12.3	6.0	2.1
Nucor	14.9	13.8	7.4	1.9
Southwest Airlines	11.7	9.9	5.5	1.8

Note: The data on market valuations are as of January 11, 2011. All other financial data are based on the most recently available balance sheets and income statements.

Source: *www.finance.yahoo.com.*

Third is the concept of "knowledge," which comes in two different forms. First, there is **explicit knowledge** that is codified, documented, easily reproduced, and widely distributed, such as engineering drawings, software code, and patents.[18] The other type of knowledge is **tacit knowledge.** That is in the minds of employees and is based on their experiences and backgrounds.[19] Tacit knowledge is shared only with the consent and participation of the indivivdual.

explicit knowledge knowledge that is codified, documented, easily reproduced, and widely distributed.

New knowledge is constantly created through the continual interaction of explicit and tacit knowledge. Consider, two software engineers working together on a computer code. The computer code is the explicit knowledge. By sharing ideas based on each individual's experience—that is, their tacit knowledge—they create new knowledge when they modify the code. Another important issue is the role of "socially complex processes," which include leadership, culture, and trust.[20] These processes play a central role in the creation of knowledge.[21] They represent the "glue" that holds the organization together and helps to create a working environment where individuals are more willing to share their ideas, work in teams, and, in the end, create products and services of value.[22]

tacit knowledge knowledge that is in the minds of employees and is based on their experiences and backgrounds.

Numerous books have been written on the subject of knowledge management and the central role that it has played in creating wealth in organizations and countries throughout the developed world.[23] Here, we focus on some of the key issues that organizations must address to compete through knowledge.

We will now turn our discussion to the central resource itself—human capital—and some guidelines on how it can be attracted/selected, developed, and retained.[24] Tom Stewart, editor of the *Harvard Business Review,* noted that organizations must also undergo significant efforts to protect their human capital. A firm may "diversify the ownership of vital knowledge by emphasizing teamwork, guard against obsolescence by developing learning programs, and shackle key people with golden handcuffs."[25] In addition, people are less likely to leave an organization if there are effective structures to promote teamwork and information sharing, strong leadership that encourages innovation, and cultures that demand excellence and ethical behavior. Such issues are central to this chapter. Although we touch on these issues throughout this chapter, we provide more detail in later chapters. We discuss organizational controls (culture, rewards, and boundaries) in Chapter 9, organization structure and design in Chapter 10, and a variety of leadership and entrepreneurship topics in Chapters 11 and 12.

Human Capital: The Foundation of Intellectual Capital

Organizations must recruit talented people—employees at all levels with the proper sets of skills and capabilities coupled with the right values and attitudes. Such skills and attitudes must be continually developed, strengthened, and reinforced, and each employee must be motivated and her efforts focused on the organization's goals and objectives.[26]

The rise to prominence of knowledge workers as a vital source of competitive advantage is changing the balance of power in today's organization.[27] Knowledge workers place professional development and personal enrichment (financial and otherwise) above company loyalty. Attracting, recruiting, and hiring the "best and the brightest," is a critical first step in the process of building intellectual capital. At a symposium for CEOs, Bill Gates said, "The thing that is holding Microsoft back . . . is simply how [hard] we find it to go out and recruit the kind of people we want to grow our research team."[28]

Hiring is only the first of three processes in which all successful organizations must engage to build and leverage their human capital. Firms must also *develop* employees to fulfill their full potential to maximize their joint contributions.[29] Finally, the first two processes are for naught if firms can't provide the working environment and intrinsic and extrinsic rewards to *retain* their best and brightest.[30]

>LO4.2 The importance of recognizing the interdependence of attracting, developing, and retaining human capital.

These activities are highly interrelated. We would like to suggest the imagery of a three-legged stool (see Exhibit 4.2).[31]If one leg is weak or broken, the stool collapses.

To illustrate such interdependence, poor hiring impedes the effectiveness of development and retention processes. In a similar vein, ineffective retention efforts place additional burdens on hiring and development. Consider the following anecdote, provided by Jeffrey Pfeffer of the Stanford University Business School:

> Not long ago, I went to a large, fancy San Francisco law firm—where they treat their associates like dog doo and where the turnover is very high. I asked the managing partner about the turnover rate. He said, "A few years ago, it was 25 percent, and now we're up to 30 percent." I asked him how the firm had responded to that trend. He said, "We increased our recruiting." So I asked him, "What kind of doctor would you be if your patient was bleeding faster and faster, and your only response was to increase the speed of the transfusion?"[32]

Clearly, stepped-up recruiting is a poor substitute for weak retention.[33] Although there are no simple, easy-to-apply answers, we can learn from what leading-edge firms are doing to attract, develop, and retain human capital in today's highly competitive marketplace.[34] Before moving on, Strategy Spotlight 4.1 addresses the importance of a firm's "green" or environmental sustainability strategy in attracting young talent.

Attracting Human Capital

> All we can do is bet on the people we pick. So my whole job is picking the right people.
>
> **Jack Welch,** former chairman, General Electric Company[35]

The first step in the process of building superior human capital is input control: attracting and selecting the right person.[36] Human resource professionals often approach employee selection from a "lock and key" mentality—that is, fit a key (a job candidate) into a lock (the job). Such an approach involves a thorough analysis of the person and the job. Only then can the right decision be made as to how well the two will fit together. How can you fail, the theory goes, if you get a precise match of knowledge, ability, and skill profiles? Frequently, however, the precise matching approach places its emphasis on task-specific skills (e.g., motor skills, specific information processing capabilities, and communication skills) and puts less emphasis on the broad general knowledge and experience, social skills, values, beliefs, and attitudes of employees.[37]

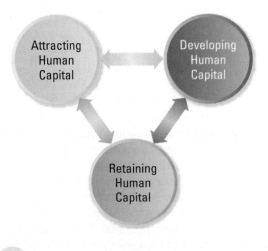

Exhibit 4.2 Human Capital: Three Interdependent Activities

strategy spotlight

Going "Green" Helps Attract Talent

When companies go "green," they often find that the benefits extend beyond the environment. Eco-friendly strategies can also help attract young talent and reduce costs. According to Lindsey Pollack, author of *Getting from College to Career:*

> Students are looking to work for companies that care about the environment. They are almost expecting greenness like they expect work-life balance, ethnic diversity, and globalization.

A recent poll on green employment by MonsterTRAK.com, a job website geared toward students and entry-level hires, found that 80 percent of young professionals are interested in securing a job that has a positive impact on the environment, and 92 percent would be more inclined to work for a company that is environmentally friendly. And, in another survey, 68 percent of Millennials said they would refuse to work for an employer that is not socially responsible.

In response, paper maker NewPage Corp. distributes a brochure that highlights the firm's commitment to environmental responsibility when it recruits on campuses. It showcases the company's new corporate headquarters, in Miamisburg, Ohio, that uses 28 percent to 39 percent less energy than a standard office building and is furnished with environmentally friendly materials. Says NewPage CEO Mark Sunwyn, "At the end of the day, we are competing with everyone else for the best talent, and this is a generation that is very concerned with the environment."

To meet the growing demand for students interested in working for green companies, MonsterTRAK, a unit of the giant employment firm Monster.com, launched GreenCareers. It was the first online recruitment service that focuses on green employment. EcoAmerica and the Environmental Defense Fund, two environmental nonprofits, are adding their expertise in partnership with Monster-TRAK. "EcoAmerica approached MonsterTRAK to create GreenCareers because there is an urgent need to reach and educate environmentally 'agnostic' audiences, in this case college students, about the ways they can address climate change and other serious environmental problems," claims Mark Charnock, vice president and general manager at MonsterTRAK.

Sources: Luhby, T. 2008. How to Lure Gen Y Workers? *CNNMoney.com,* August 17: np; Mattioli. 2007. How Going Green Draws Talent, Cut Costs. *Wall Street Journal,* November 13: B10; and, Odell, A. M. 2007. Working for the Earth: Green Companies and Green Jobs Attract Employees. *www. socialfunds.com,* October 9: np.

environmental sustainability

Many have questioned the precise matching approach. They argue that firms can identify top performers by focusing on key employee mind-sets, attitudes, social skills, and general orientations. If they get these elements right, the task-specific skills can be learned quickly. (This does not imply, however, that task-specific skills are unimportant; rather, it suggests that the requisite skill sets must be viewed as a necessary but not sufficient condition.) This leads us to a popular phrase today that serves as the title of the next section.

"Hire for Attitude, Train for Skill" Organizations are increasingly emphasizing general knowledge and experience, social skills, values, beliefs, and attitudes of employees.[38] Consider Southwest Airlines' hiring practices, which focus on employee values and attitudes. Given its strong team orientation, Southwest uses an "indirect" approach. For example, the interviewing team asks a group of employees to prepare a five-minute presentation about themselves. During the presentations, interviewers observe which candidates enthusiastically support their peers and which candidates focus on polishing their own presentations while the others are presenting.[39] The former are, of course, favored.

Alan Cooper, president of Cooper Software, Inc., in Palo Alto, California, goes further. He cleverly *uses technology* to hone in on the problem-solving ability of his applicants and their attitudes before an interview even takes place. He has devised a "Bozo

Filter," an online test that can be applied to any industry. Before you spend time on whether job candidates will work out satisfactorily, find out how their minds work. Cooper advised, "Hiring was a black hole. I don't talk to bozos anymore, because 90 percent of them turn away when they see our test. It's a self-administering bozo filter."[40] How does it work?

> The online test asks questions designed to see how prospective employees approach problem-solving tasks. For example, one key question asks software engineer applicants to design a table-creation software program for Microsoft Word. Candidates provide pencil sketches and a description of the new user interface. Another question used for design communicators asks them to develop a marketing strategy for a new touch-tone phone—directed at consumers in the year 1850. Candidates e-mail their answers back to the company, and the answers are circulated around the firm to solicit feedback. Only candidates with the highest marks get interviews.

Sound Recruiting Approaches and Networking   Companies that take hiring seriously must also take recruiting seriously. The number of jobs that successful knowledge-intensive companies must fill is astonishing. Ironically, many companies still have no shortage of applicants. For example, Google, ranked fourth on *Fortune*'s 2011 "100 Best Companies to Work For," is planning to hire thousands of employees—even though its hiring rate has slowed.[41] The challenge becomes having the right job candidates, not the greatest number of them.

GE Medical Systems, which builds CT scanners and magnetic resonance imaging (MRI) systems, relies extensively on networking. They have found that current employees are the best source for new ones. Recently, Steven Patscot, head of staffing and leadership development, made a few simple changes to double the number of referrals. First, he simplified the process—no complex forms, no bureaucracy, and so on. Second, he increased incentives. Everyone referring a qualified candidate received a gift certificate from Sears. For referrals who were hired, the "bounty" increases to $2,000. Although this may sound like a lot of money, it is "peanuts" compared to the $15,000 to $20,000 fees that GE typically pays to headhunters for each person hired.[42] Also, when someone refers a former colleague or friend for a job, his or her credibility is on the line. Thus, employees will be careful in recommending people for employment unless they are reasonably confident that these people are good candidates. This provides a good "screen" for the firm in deciding whom to hire. Hiring the right people makes things a lot easier: fewer rules and regulations, less need for monitoring and hierarchy, and greater internalization of organizational norms and objectives.

Consider some of the approaches that companies are currently using to recruit and retain young talent. As baby boomers retire, people in this demographic group are becoming more and more important in today's workforce. We also provide some "tips" on how to get hired. We address these issues in Exhibit 4.3.

Developing Human Capital

It is not enough to hire top-level talent and expect that the skills and capabilities of those employees remain current throughout the duration of their employment. Rather, training and development must take place at all levels of the organization.[43] For example, Solectron assembles printed circuit boards and other components for its Silicon Valley clients.[44] Its employees receive an average of 95 hours of company-provided training each year. Chairman Winston Chen observed, "Technology changes so fast that we estimate 20 percent of an engineer's knowledge becomes obsolete each year. Training is an obligation we owe to our employees. If you want high growth and high quality, then training is a big part of the equation." Although the financial returns on training may be hard to calculate, most experts believe it is essential. One company that has calculated the benefit from training is Motorola. Every dollar spent on training returns $30 in productivity gains over the following three years.

Exhibit 4.3
**What Companies Are
Doing to Attract and
Retain Young Talent . . .
and What You Should Do
to Get Hired**

Here are some "best practices" that companies are using to help recruit and retain today's high-maintenance Millennials. This generation has also been termed "Generation Y" or "Echo Boom" and includes people born after 1982:

- *Don't fudge the sales pitch.* High-tech presentations and one-on-one attention may be attractive to undergrads, but the pitch had better match the experience. Today's ultraconnected students can get the lowdown on a company by spending five minutes on a social networking site.

- *Let them have a life.* Wary of their parents' 80-hour workweeks, Millennials strive for more balance, so liberal vacations are a must. They also want assurances they'll be able to use it. At KPMG, 80 percent of employees used 40 hours of paid time off in the six months through May 2006.

- *No time clocks, please.* Recent grads don't mind long hours if they can work them on their own time. Lockheed Martin allows employees to work nine-hour days and take every other Friday off.

- *Give them responsibility.* A chance to work on fulfilling projects and develop ones of their own is important to Millennials. Google urges entry-level employees to spend 20 percent of their time developing new ideas. PepsiCo allows promising young employees to manage small teams in six months.

- *Feedback and more feedback.* Career planning advice and frequent performance appraisals are keys to holding on to young hires. Lehman Brothers provides new hires with two mentors—a slightly older peer to help them get settled and a senior employee to give long-term guidance.

- *Giving back matters.* Today's altruistic young graduates expect to have opportunities for community service. Wells Fargo encourages its employees to teach financial literacy classes in the community. Accenture and Bain allow employees to consult for nonprofits.

Some advice on how to get hired (based on Fortune's "100 Best Companies to Work For"):

- **It helps to know someone.** Almost all of the "Best Companies" rely extensively on employee referrals. Principal Financial Group and many others get about 40 percent of new hires this way.

- **Do creative research.** Know more about the place and the industry than your rivals. A Google search is not viewed as a form of "creative research." Says Jay Jones, a recruiting manager for Alcon Laboratories: "Detailed research, including talking to customers, is so rare it will almost guarantee you get hired."

- **Unleash your inner storyteller.** By far the most popular interview style is what's known as behavioral, meaning that you will be asked to describe troublesome situations in past jobs and tell exactly how you handled them.

- **No lone rangers need apply.** By and large, team players are wanted. "I actually count the number of times a candidates says 'I' in an interview," says Adobe's recruiting director, Jeff Vijungco. "We'd rather hear 'we.'"

- **Be open to learning new things.** Showing passion is a must, and most of the "100 Best" pride themselves on creating "learning environments." Thus, talk about the skills you'd like to acquire or polish. Declaring that you're already the best at what you do is a turnoff.

Source: Fisher, A. 2008. How to Get Hired by a "Best" Company. *Fortune,* February 4: 96; and Gerdes, L. 2006. The Top 50 Employers for New College Grads. *BusinessWeek,* September 18: 64–81.

In addition to training and developing human capital, firms must encourage widespread involvement, monitor and track employee development, and evaluate human capital.[45]

Encouraging Widespread Involvement Developing human capital requires the active involvement of leaders at all levels. It won't be successful if it is viewed only as the responsibility of the human resources department. Each year at General Electric, 200 facilitators, 30 officers, 30 human resource executives, and many young managers actively participate in GE's orientation program at Crotonville, its training center outside New York City. Topics include global competition, winning on the global playing field, and personal examination of the new employee's core values vis-à-vis GE's values. As a senior manager once commented, "There is nothing like teaching Sunday school to force you to confront your own values."

Similarly, A. G. Lafley, Procter & Gamble's former CEO, claimed that he spent 40 percent of his time on personnel.[46] Andy Grove, who was previously Intel's CEO, required all senior people, including himself, to spend at least a week a year teaching high flyers. And Nitin Paranjpe, CEO of Hindustan Unilever, recruits people from campuses and regularly visits high-potential employees in their offices.

Transferring Knowledge Often in our lives, we need to either transfer our knowledge to someone else (a child, a junior colleague, a peer) or access accumulated bits of wisdom—someone else's tacit knowledge.[47] This is a vital aspect of developing human capital.[48] However, before we can even begin to plan such a transfer, we need to understand how our brains process incoming information. According to Dorothy A. Leonard of Harvard University:

> Our existing tacit knowledge determines how we assimilate new experiences. Without receptors—hooks on which to hang new information—we may not be able to perceive and process the information. It is like being sent boxes of documents but having no idea how they could or should be organized.

This cognitive limitation also applies to the organizational level. When GE Healthcare sets up or transfers operations, it appoints an experienced manager as the "pitcher" and a team in the receiving plant as the "catcher." These two teams work together, often over a period of years—first at the pitcher's location and then at the catcher's. To ensure a smooth transition, the pitching team needs to be sensitive to the catching team's level of experience and familiarity with GE Healthcare procedures.

Strategy Spotlight 4.2 discusses an emerging trend in organizations—reverse mentoring. Here, Internet savvy new hires mentor seasoned executives.

Monitoring Progress and Tracking Development Whether a firm uses on-site formal training, off-site training (e.g., universities), or on-the-job training, tracking individual progress—and sharing this knowledge with both the employee and key managers—becomes essential. Like many leading-edge firms, GlaxoSmithKline (GSK) places strong emphasis on broader experiences over longer time periods. Dan Phelan, senior vice president and director of human resources, explained, "We ideally follow a two-plus-two-plus-two formula in developing people for top management positions." This reflects the belief that GSK's best people should gain experience in two business units, two functional units (such as finance and marketing), and in two countries.

Evaluating Human Capital In today's competitive environment, collaboration and interdependence are vital to organizational success. Individuals must share their knowledge and work constructively to achieve collective, not just individual, goals. However, traditional systems evaluate performance from a single perspective (i.e., "top down") and generally don't address the "softer" dimensions of communications and social skills, values, beliefs, and attitudes.[49]

Time Warner's Reverse Mentoring Program

Time Warner recently developed a mentoring program that engages people on both ends of their careers. In this case, some of the company's senior executives were challenged to stay at the forefront of a rapidly evolving new-media landscape. To raise awareness of digital media, Time Warner launched Digital Reverse Mentoring—a program in which tech-savvy college students mentor senior executives on emerging digital trends and technologies such as Facebook, Twitter, and other Web 2.0 applications. Gen Y mentors meet with senior executives for

Source: Hewlett, S. A., Sherbin, L. & Sumberg, K. 2009. How Gen Y & Boomers will reshape your agenda. *Harvard Business Review*, 87(7/8): 76.

one-on-one meetings about writing blogs, posting videos on YouTube, and making imaginative use of new media. The program helps them not only to better understand how new technologies are affecting Time Warner but also to obtain fresh ideas on optimizing the firm's online presence. In addition to imparting technical skills, Gen Y mentors provide Boomer mentees with insights into the values, consumer behaviors, and communication styles of the younger generation.

Time Warner enjoys the immeasurable benefits of a more market-attuned leadership team. In a broader sense, however, programs like these pay off by proving that a company is part of a new breed of employer—one that respects educated workers' increasing desires for flexibility, personal growth, connectivity, and a chance to give back.

To address the limitations of the traditional approach, many organizations use 360-degree evaluation and feedback systems.[50] Here, superiors, direct reports, colleagues, and even internal and external customers rate a person's performance.[51] Managers rate themselves to have a personal benchmark. The 360-degree feedback system complements teamwork, employee involvement, and organizational flattening. As organizations continue to push responsibility downward, traditional top-down appraisal systems become insufficient.[52] For example, a manager who previously managed the performance of 3 supervisors might now be responsible for 10 and is less likely to have the in-depth knowledge needed to appraise and develop them adequately. Exhibit 4.4 provides a portion of GE's 360-degree system.

Evaluation systems must also ensure that a manager's success does not come at the cost of compromising the organization's core values. Such behavior generally leads to only short-term wins for both the manager and the organization. The organization typically suffers long-term losses in terms of morale, turnover, productivity, and so on. Accordingly, Merck's former chairman, Ray Gilmartin, told his employees, "If someone is achieving results but not demonstrating the core values of the company, at the expense of our people, that manager does not have much of a career here."

> **360-degree evaluation and feedback systems** superiors, direct reports, colleagues, and even external and internal customers rate a person's performance.

Retaining Human Capital

It has been said that talented employees are like "frogs in a wheelbarrow."[53] They can jump out at any time! By analogy, the organization can either try to force employees to stay in the firm or try to keep them from jumping out by creating incentives.[54] In other words, today's leaders can either provide the work environment and incentives to keep productive employees and management from wanting to bail out, or they can use legal means such as employment contracts and noncompete clauses.[55] Firms must prevent the transfer of valuable and sensitive information outside the organization. Failure to do so would be the neglect of a leader's fiduciary responsibility to shareholders. However, greater efforts should be directed at the former (e.g., good work environment and incentives), but, as we all know, the latter (e.g., employment contracts and noncompete clauses) have their place.[56]

Vision	• Has developed and communicated a clear, simple, customer-focused vision/direction for the organization.
	• Forward-thinking, stretches horizons, challenges imaginations.
	• Inspires and energizes others to commit to Vision. Captures minds. Leads by example.
	• As appropriate, updates Vision to reflect constant and accelerating change affecting the business.

Customer/Quality Focus

Integrity

Accountability/Commitment

Communication/Influence

Shared Ownership/Boundaryless

Team Builder/Empowerment

Knowledge/Expertise/Intellect

Initiative/Speed

Global Mind-Set

Source: Adapted from Slater, R. 1994. *Get Better or Get Beaten:* 152–155. Burr Ridge, IL: Irwin Professional Publishing.

Note: This evaluation system consists of 10 "characteristics"—Vision, Customer/Quality Focus, Integrity, and so on. Each of these characteristics has four "performance criteria." For illustrative purposes, the four performance criteria of "Vision" are included.

Identifying with an Organization's Mission and Values People who identify with and are more committed to the core mission and values of the organization are less likely to stray or bolt to the competition. For example, take the perspective of Steve Jobs, Apple's widely admired CEO:[57]

> When I hire somebody really senior, competence is the ante. They have to be really smart. But the real issue for me is: Are they going to fall in love with Apple? Because if they fall in love with Apple, everything else will take care of itself. They'll want to do what's best for Apple, not what's best for them, what's best for Steve, or anyone else.

"Tribal loyalty" is another key factor that links people to the organization.[58] A tribe is not the organization as a whole (unless it is very small). Rather, it is teams, communities of practice, and other groups within an organization or occupation.

Brian Hall, CEO of Values Technology in Santa Cruz, California, documented a shift in people's emotional expectations from work. From the 1950s on, a "task first" relationship—"tell me what the job is, and let's get on with it"—dominated employee attitudes. Emotions and personal life were checked at the door. In the past few years, a "relationship-first" set of values has challenged the task orientation. Hall believes that it will become dominant. Employees want to share attitudes and beliefs as well as workspace.

Challenging Work and a Stimulating Environment Arthur Schawlow, winner of the 1981 Nobel Prize in physics, was asked what made the difference between highly creative and less creative scientists. His reply: "The labor of love aspect is very important. The most successful scientists often are not the most talented.[59] But they are the ones impelled by curiosity. They've got to know what the answer is."[60] Such insights highlight the importance of intrinsic motivation: the motivation to work on something because it is exciting, satisfying, or personally challenging.[61]

One way firms keep highly mobile employees motivated and challenged is through opportunities that lower barriers to an employee's mobility within a company. For example, Shell Oil Company has created an "open sourcing" model for talent. Jobs are listed on Shell's intranet, and, with a two-month notice, employees can go to work on anything that interests them. Monsanto[62] has developed a similar approach. According to one executive:

> Because we don't have a lot of structure, people will flow toward where success and innovation are taking place. We have a free-market system where people can move, so you have an outflow of people in areas where not much progress is being made. Before, the HR function ran processes like management development and performance evaluation. Now it also facilitates this movement of people.

Financial and Nonfinancial Rewards and Incentives   Financial rewards are a vital organizational control mechanism (as we will discuss in Chapter 9). Money—whether in the form of salary, bonus, stock options, and so forth—can mean many different things to people. It might mean security, recognition, or a sense of freedom and independence.

Paying people more is seldom the most important factor in attracting and retaining human capital.[63] Most surveys show that money is not the most important reason why people take or leave jobs, and that money, in some surveys, is not even in the top 10. Consistent with these findings, Tandem Computers (part of Hewlett-Packard) typically doesn't tell people being recruited what their salaries would be. People who asked were told that their salaries were competitive. If they persisted along this line of questioning, they would not be offered a position. Why? Tandem realized a rather simple idea: People who come for money will leave for money.

Another nonfinancial reward is accommodating working families with children. Balancing demands of family and work is a problem at some point for virtually all employees.

Exhibit 4.5 describes strategies used by three leading-edge firms to retain their key employees—even during difficult economic times.

Start a Talent Agency: Yum Brands started a Talent Scout program to recruit outsiders. Selected top performers nominate at least 25 people, and they get cash when a recruit is hired. Global talent VP John Kurnick says 25 percent of the finance team's recent hires came from this program. Although it wasn't designed for retention, "it's been the most gratifying for the scout," says Kurnick, and it encourages the scout to stay with the company.

Change Up Bonus Time: Software maker Intuit moved its annual restricted stock grant up from July to February to address the economic uncertainties that the employees felt. Intuit's human resources team wanted the grant to make a big impact. Program manager Eileen Fagan claims: "It took one more worry off people's plates. It was a huge incentive for feeling good about the company."

Send Them Abroad—If It Fits: During recessionary times, global opportunities can energize top performers, says Ari Bousbib, former executive VP of United Technologies. During the downturn, he says, the company offered more expatriate assignments (for those whose family situations allowed it) as bonuses came under pressure.

Source: McGregor, J. & Dubey, R. 2010. Giving Back to Your Stars. *Fortune*. November 1: 53–54.

Exhibit 4.5
Retention Rules: How Three Companies Are Keeping Their Best during Tough Times

Enhancing Human Capital: The Role of Diversity in the Workforce

A combination of demographic trends and accelerating globalization of business has made the management of cultural differences a critical issue.[64] Workforces, which reflect demographic changes in the overall population, will be increasingly heterogeneous along dimensions such as gender, race, ethnicity, and nationality.[65] Demographic trends in the United States indicate a growth in Hispanic Americans from 6.9 million in 1960 to over 35 million in 2000, an expected increase to over 59 million by 2020 and 102 million by 2050. Similarly, the Asian-American population should grow to 20 million in 2020 from 12 million in 2000 and only 1.5 million in 1970. And the African-American population is becoming more ethnically heterogeneous. Census estimates project that in 2010 as many as 10 percent of Americans of African descent were immigrants from Africa or the Caribbean.[66]

Such demographic changes have implications not only for the labor pool but also for customer bases, which are also becoming more diverse.[67] This creates important organizational challenges and opportunities.

The effective management of diversity can enhance the social responsibility goals of an organization.[68] However, there are many other benefits as well. Six other areas where sound management of diverse workforces can improve an organization's effectiveness and competitive advantages are: (1) cost, (2) resource acquisition, (3) marketing, (4) creativity, (5) problem-solving, and (6) organizational flexibility.

- *Cost Argument.* As organizations become more diverse, firms effective in managing diversity will have a cost advantage over those that are not.
- *Resource Acquisition Argument.* Firms with excellent reputations as prospective employers for women and ethnic minorities will have an advantage in the competition for top talent. As labor pools shrink and change in composition, such advantages will become even more important.
- *Marketing Argument.* For multinational firms, the insight and cultural sensitivity that members with roots in other countries bring to marketing efforts will be very useful. A similar rationale applies to subpopulations within domestic operations.
- *Creativity Argument.* Less emphasis on conformity to norms of the past and a diversity of perspectives will improve the level of creativity.
- *Problem-Solving Argument.* Heterogeniety in decision-making and problem-solving groups typically produces better decisions because of a wider range of perspectives as well as more thorough analysis. Jim Schiro, former CEO of PriceWaterhouse Coopers, explains, "When you make a genuine commitment to diversity, you bring a greater diversity of ideas, approaches, and experiences and abilities that can be applied to client problems. After all, six people with different perspectives have a better shot at solving complex problems than sixty people who all think alike."[69]
- *Organizational Flexibility Argument.* With effective programs to enhance workplace diversity, systems become less determinant, less standardized, and therefore more fluid. Such fluidity should lead to greater flexibility to react to environmental changes. Reactions should be faster and less costly.

Consider how MTV Networks (part of Viacom) has benefited from a diverse workforce.[70]

> One cross-cultural group discovered marketing opportunities in the similarities between North American country music and Latin American music, which use many of the same instruments, feature singers with similar vocal styles, and—in the U.S. Sunbelt—appeal to much the same audience. Other groups have influenced the multicultural content of Nickelodeon's children's programming. Says Tom Freston, MTV's former CEO, "Those teams are diverse by design to generate innovation. The probability that you will get a good, original, innovative idea with that type of chemistry is simply much higher."

The Vital Role of Social Capital

>LO4.3
The key role of social capital in leveraging human capital within and across the firm.

Successful firms are well aware that the attraction, development, and retention of talent *is a necessary but not sufficient condition* for creating competitive advantages.[71] In the knowledge economy, it is not the stock of human capital that is important, but the extent to which it is combined and leveraged.[72] In a sense, developing and retaining human capital becomes less important as key players (talented professionals, in particular) take the role of "free agents" and bring with them the requisite skill in many cases. Rather, the development of social capital (that is, the friendships and working relationships among talented individuals) gains importance, because it helps tie knowledge workers to a given firm.[73] Knowledge workers often exhibit greater loyalties to their colleagues and their profession than their employing organization, which may be "an amorphous, distant, and sometimes threatening entity."[74] Thus, a firm must find ways to create "ties" among its knowledge workers.

Let's look at a hypothetical example. Two pharmaceutical firms are fortunate enough to hire Nobel Prize–winning scientists.[75] In one case, the scientist is offered a very attractive salary, outstanding facilities and equipment, and told to "go to it!" In the second case, the scientist is offered approximately the same salary, facilities, and equipment plus one additional ingredient: working in a laboratory with 10 highly skilled and enthusiastic scientists. Part of the job is to collaborate with these peers and jointly develop promising drug compounds. There is little doubt as to which scenario will lead to a higher probability of retaining the scientist. The interaction, sharing, and collaboration will create a situation in which the scientist will develop firm-specific ties and be less likely to "bolt" for a higher salary offer. Such ties are critical because knowledge-based resources tend to be more tacit in nature, as we mentioned early in this chapter. Therefore, they are much more difficult to protect against loss (i.e., the individual quitting the organization) than other types of capital, such as equipment, machinery, and land.

Another way to view this situation is in terms of the resource-based view of the firm that we discussed in Chapter 3. That is, competitive advantages tend to be harder for competitors to copy if they are based on "unique bundles" of resources.[76] So, if employees are working effectively in teams and sharing their knowledge and learning from each other, not only will they be more likely to add value to the firm, but they also will be less likely to leave the organization, because of the loyalties and social ties that they develop over time.

How Social Capital Helps Attract and Retain Talent

The importance of social ties among talented professionals creates a significant challenge (and opportunity) for organizations. In *The Wall Street Journal,* Bernard Wysocki described the increase in a type of "Pied Piper Effect," in which teams or networks of people are leaving one company for another.[77] The trend is to recruit job candidates at the crux of social relationships in organizations, particularly if they are seen as having the potential to bring with them valuable colleagues.[78] This is a process that is referred to as "hiring via personal networks." Let's look at one instance of this practice.

> Gerald Eickhoff, founder of an electronic commerce company called Third Millennium Communications, tried for 15 years to hire Michael Reene. Why? Mr. Eickhoff says that he has "these Pied Piper skills." Mr. Reene was a star at Andersen Consulting in the 1980s and at IBM in the 1990s. He built his businesses and kept turning down overtures from Mr. Eickhoff.
>
> However, in early 2000, he joined Third Millennium as chief executive officer, with a salary of just $120,000 but with a 20 percent stake in the firm. Since then, he has brought in a raft of former IBM colleagues and Andersen subordinates. One protégé from his time

at Andersen, Mary Goode, was brought on board as executive vice president. She promptly tapped her own network and brought along former colleagues.

Wysocki considers the Pied Piper effect one of the underappreciated factors in the war for talent today. This is because one of the myths of the New Economy is rampant individualism, wherein individuals find jobs on the Internet career sites and go to work for complete strangers. Perhaps, instead of Me Inc., the truth is closer to We Inc.[79]

Another example of social relationships causing human capital mobility is the emigration of talent from an organization to form start-up ventures. Microsoft is perhaps the best-known example of this phenomenon.[80] Professionals frequently leave Microsoft en masse to form venture capital and technology start-ups, called "Baby Bills," built around teams of software developers. For example, Ignition Corporation, of Bellevue, Washington, was formed by Brad Silverberg, a former Microsoft senior vice president. Eight former Microsoft executives, among others, founded the company.

Social relationships can provide an important mechanism for obtaining both resources and information from individuals and organizations outside the boundary of a firm.[81] Strategy Spotlight 4.3 describes how alumni programs for recently laid-off employees benefit both the individuals and the firm.

Social Networks: Implications for Knowledge Management and Career Success

>LO4.4
The importance of social networks in knowledge management and in promoting career success.

Managers face many challenges driven by such factors as rapid changes in globalization and technology. Leading a successful company is more than a one-person job. As Tom Malone recently put it in *The Future of Work,* "As managers, we need to shift our thinking from command and control to coordinate and cultivate—the best way to gain power is sometimes to give it away."[82] The move away from top-down bureaucratic control to more open, decentralized network models makes it more difficult for managers to understand how work is actually getting done, who is interacting with whom both within and outside the organization, and the consequences of these interactions for the long-term health of the organization.[83] In short, coordination, cultivation, and collaboration are increasingly becoming the mode of work at every level.[84]

social network analysis analysis of the pattern of social interactions among individuals.

But how can this be done? **Social network analysis** depicts the pattern of interactions among individuals and helps to diagnose effective and ineffective patterns.[85] It helps identify groups or clusters of individuals that comprise the network, individuals who link the clusters, and other network members. It helps diagnose communication patterns and, consequently, communication effectiveness.[86] Such analysis of communication patterns is helpful because the configuration of group members' social ties within and outside the group affects the extent to which members connect to individuals who:

- convey needed resources,
- have the opportunity to exchange information and support,
- have the motivation to treat each other in positive ways, and,
- have the time to develop trusting relationships that might improve the groups' effectiveness.

However, such relationships don't "just happen."[87] Developing social capital requires interdependence among group members. Social capital erodes when people in the network become independent. And increased interactions between members aid in the development and maintenance of mutual obligations in a social network.[88] Social networks such as Facebook may facilitate increased interactions between members in a social network via Internet-based communications.

Let's take a brief look at a simplified network analysis to get a grasp of the key ideas. In Exhibit 4.6, the links are used to depict informal relationships among individuals involving communication flows, personal support, and advice networks. There may be some individuals with literally no linkages, such as Fred. These individuals are typically labeled "isolates." However, most people do have some linkages with others.

To simplify, there are two primary types of mechanisms through which social capital will flow: *closure relationships* (depicted by Bill, Frank, George, and Susan) and *bridging relationships* (depicted by Mary). As we can see, in the former relationships one member is central to the communication flows in a group. In contrast, in the latter relationship, one person "bridges" or brings together groups that would have been otherwise unconnected.

Both closure and bridging relationships have important implications for the effective flow of information in organizations and for the management of knowledge. We will now briefly discuss each of these types of relationships. We will also address some of the implications that understanding social networks has for one's career success.

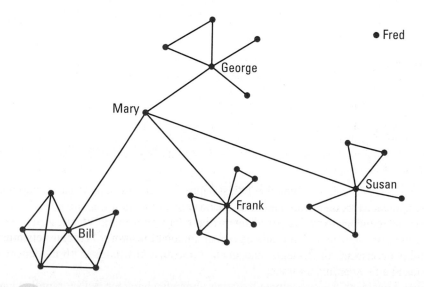

Exhibit 4.6 **A Simplified Social Network**

closure the degree to which all members of a social network have relationships (or ties) with other group members.

Closure   With **closure,** many members have relationships (or ties) with other members. As indicated in Exhibit 4.6, Bill's group would have a higher level of closure than Frank, Susan, or George's groups because more group members are connected to each other. Through closure, group members develop strong relationships with each other, high levels of trust, and greater solidarity. High levels of trust help to ensure that informal norms in the group are easily enforced and there is less "free riding." Social pressure will prevent people from withholding effort or shirking their responsibilities. In addition, people in the network are more willing to extend favors and "go the extra mile" on a colleague's behalf because they are confident that their efforts will be reciprocated by another member in their group. Another benefit of a network with closure is the high level of emotional support. This becomes particularly valuable when setbacks occur that may destroy morale or an unexpected tragedy happens that might cause the group to lose its focus. Social support helps the group to rebound from misfortune and get back on track.

But high levels of closure often come with a price. Groups that become too closed can become insular. They cut themselves off from the rest of the organization and fail to share what they are learning from people outside their group. Research shows that while managers need to encourage closure up to a point, if there is too much closure, they need to encourage people to open up their groups and infuse new ideas through bridging relationships.[89]

bridging relationships relationships in a social network that connect otherwise disconnected people.

Bridging Relationships   The closure perspective rests on an assumption that there is a high level of similarity among group members. However, members can be quite heterogeneous with regard to their positions in either the formal or informal structures of the group or the organization. Such heterogeneity exists because of, for example, vertical boundaries (different levels in the hierarchy) and horizontal boundaries (different functional areas).

Bridging relationships, in contrast to closure, stresses the importance of ties connecting people. Employees who bridge disconnected people tend to receive timely, diverse information because of their access to a wide range of heterogeneous information flows. Such bridging relationships span a number of different types of boundaries.

structural holes social gaps between groups in a social network where there are few relationships bridging the groups.

The University of Chicago's Ron Burt originally coined the term **"structural holes"** to refer to the social gap between two groups. Structural holes are common in organizations. When they occur in business, managers typically refer to them as "silos" or "stovepipes." Sales and engineering are a classic example of two groups whose members traditionally interact with their peers rather than across groups.

A study that Burt conducted at Raytheon, a $25 billion U.S. electronics company and military contractor, provides further insight into the benefits of bridging.[90]

> Burt studied several hundred managers in Raytheon's supply chain group and asked them to write down ideas to improve the company's supply chain management. Then he asked two Raytheon executives to rate the ideas. The conclusion: *The best suggestions consistently came from managers who discussed ideas outside their regular work group.*
>
> Burt found that Raytheon managers were good at thinking of ideas but bad at developing them. Too often, Burt said, the managers discussed their ideas with colleagues already in their informal discussion network. Instead, he said, they should have had discussions outside their typical contacts, particularly with an informal boss, or someone with enough power to be an ally but not an actual supervisor.

Before we address how to overcome barriers to collaboration and the implications of social network theory for managers' career success, one might ask: Which is the more valuable mechanism to develop and nurture social capital—closure or bridging relationships? As with many aspects of strategic management, the answer becomes: "It all depends." So let's look at a few contingent issues.[91]

First, consider firms in competitive environments characterized by rapidly changing technologies and markets. Such firms should bridge relationships across networks because they need a wide variety of timely sources of information. Also, innovation is facilitated if there are multiple, interdisciplinary perspectives. On the other hand, firms competing in a stable environment would typically face less unpredictability. Thus, the cohesive ties associated with network closure would help to ensure the timely and effective implementation of strategies.

A second contingent factor would be the type of business strategies that a firm may choose to follow (a topic that we address next in Chapter 5). Managers with social networks characterized by closure would be in a preferred position if their firm is following an overall low cost strategy.[92] Here, there is a need for control and coordination to implement strategies that are rather constrained by pressures to reduce costs. Alternatively, the uncertainties generally associated with differentiation strategies (i.e., creating products that are perceived by customers as unique and highly valued) would require a broad range of information sources and inputs. Social networks characterized by bridging relationships across groups would access the diverse informational sources needed to deal with more complex, multifaceted strategies.

A caveat: In both contingencies that we have discussed—competitive environment and business strategy—closure and bridging relationships across groups are necessary. Our purpose is to address where one type should be more dominant.

Developing Social Capital: Overcoming Barriers to Collaboration Social capital within a group or organization develops through repeated interactions among its members and the resulting collaboration.[93] However, collaboration does not "just happen." People don't collaborate for various reasons. Effective collaboration requires overcoming four barriers:

- The not-invented-here barrier (people aren't willing to provide help)
- The hoarding barrier (people aren't willing to provide help)
- The search barrier (people are unable to find what they are looking for)
- The transfer barrier (people are unable to work with the people they don't know well)

All four barriers need to be low before effective collaboration can take place. Each one is enough to prevent people from collaborating well. The key is to identify which barriers are present in an organization and then to devise appropriate ways to overcome them.

Different barriers require different solutions. Motivational barriers require leaders to pull levers that make people more willing to collaborate. Ability barriers mean that leaders need to pull levers that enable motivated people to collaborate throughout the organization.

To be effective, leaders can choose a mix of three levers. First, when motivation is the problem, they can use the *unification lever,* wherein they craft compelling common goals, articulate a strong value of cross-company teamwork, and encourage collaboration in order to send strong signals to lift people's sights beyond their narrow interests toward a common goal.

Second, with the *people lever,* the emphasis isn't on getting people to collaborate more. Rather, it's on getting the right people to collaborate on the right projects. This means cultivating what may be called *T-shaped management:* people who simultaneously focus on the performance of their unit (the vertical part of the T) and across boundaries (the horizontal part of the T). People become able to collaborate when needed but are disciplined enough to say no when it's not required.

Third, by using the *network lever,* leaders can build nimble interpersonal networks across the company so that employees are better able to collaborate. Interpersonal networks are more effective than formal hierarchies. However, there is a dark side to networks: When people spend more time networking than getting work done, collaboration can adversely affect results.

unification lever method for making people more willing to collaborate by crafting compelling common goals articulating a strong value of cross-company teamwork, and encouraging collaboration in order to send strong signals to lift people's sights beyond their narrow interests towards a common goal.

network lever method for making people more willing to collaborate by building nimble interpersonal networks across the company.

T-shaped management people's dual focus on the performance of their unit (the vertical part of the T) and across boundaries (the horizontal part of the T).

people lever method for making people more willing to collaborate by getting the right people to work on the right projects.

Picasso versus van Gogh: Who Was More Successful and Why?

Vincent van Gogh and Pablo Picasso are two of the most iconoclastic—and famous—artists of modern times. Paintings by both of them have fetched over $100 million. And both of them were responsible for some of the most iconic images in the art world: Van Gogh's *Self-Portrait* (the one sans the earlobe) and *Starry Night* and Picasso's *The Old Guitarist* and *Guernica*. However, there is an important difference between van Gogh and Picasso. Van Gogh died penniless. Picasso's estate was estimated at $750 million when he died in 1973. What was the difference?

Van Gogh's primary connection to the art world was through his brother. Unfortunately, this connection didn't feed directly into the money that could have turned him into a living success. In contrast, Picasso's myriad connections provided him with access to commercial riches. As noted by Gregory Berns in his book *Iconoclast: A Neuroscientist Reveals How to Think Differently,* "Picasso's wide ranging social network, which included artists, writers, and politicians, meant that he was never more than a few people away from anyone of importance in the world."

In effect, van Gogh was a loner, and the charismatic Picasso was an active member of multiple social circles. In social networking terms, van Gogh was a solitary "node" who had few connections. Picasso, on the other hand, was a "hub" who embedded himself in a vast network

● Picasso was far more financially successful during his lifetime than van Gogh largely because of his extensive social network.

that stretched across various social lines. Where Picasso smoothly navigated multiple social circles, van Gogh had to struggle just to maintain connections with even those closest to him. Van Gogh inhabited an alien world, whereas Picasso was a social magnet. And because he knew so many people, the world was at Picasso's fingertips. From his perspective, the world was smaller.

Sources: Hayashi, A. M. 2008. Why Picasso Out Earned van Gogh. *MIT Sloan Management Review*, 50(1): 11–12; and Berns, G. 2008. *A Neuroscientist Reveals How to Think Differently.* Boston, MA: Harvard Business Press.

private information information that is not available from public sources, and is usually communicated in the context of personal relationships.

public information information that is available from public sources such as the internet.

Implications for Career Success   Let's go back in time in order to illustrate the value of social networks in one's career success. Consider two of the most celebrated artists of all time: Vincent van Gogh and Pablo Picasso. Strategy Spotlight 4.4 points out why these two artists enjoyed sharply contrasting levels of success during their lifetimes.

Effective social networks provide many advantages for the firm.[94] They can play a key role in an individual's career advancement and success. One's social network potentially can provide three unique advantages: private information, access to diverse skill sets, and power.[95] Managers see these advantages at work every day but might not consider how their networks regulate them.

Private Information   We make judgments, using both public and private information. Today, public information is available from many sources, including the Internet. However, since it is so accessible, public information offers less competitive advantage than it used to.

In contrast, private information from personal contacts can offer something not found in publicly available sources, such as the release date of a new product or knowledge about what a particular interviewer looks for in candidates. Private information can give managers an edge, though it is more subjective than public information since it cannot be easily verified by independent sources, such as Dunn & Bradstreet. Consequently the value of your private information to others—and the value of others' private information to you—depends on how much trust exists in the network of relationships.

Access to Diverse Skill Sets Linus Pauling, one of only two people to win a Nobel Prize in two different areas and considered one of the towering geniuses of the 20th century, attributed his creative success not to his immense brainpower or luck but to his diverse contacts. He said, "The best way to have a good idea is to have a lot of ideas."

While expertise has become more specialized during the past 15 years, organizational, product, and marketing issues have become more interdisciplinary. This means that success is tied to the ability to transcend natural skill limitations through others. Highly diverse network relationships, therefore, can help you develop more complete, creative, and unbiased perspectives on issues. Trading information or skills with people whose experiences differ from your own, provides you with unique, exceptionally valuable resources. It is common for people in relationships to share their problems. If you know enough people, you will begin to see how the problems that another person is struggling with can be solved by the solutions being developed by others. If you can bring together problems and solutions, it will greatly benefit your career.

Power Traditionally, a manager's power was embedded in a firm's hierarchy. But, when corporate organizations became flatter, more like pancakes than pyramids, that power was repositioned in the network's brokers (people who bridged multiple networks), who could adapt to changes in the organization, develop clients, and synthesize opposing points of view. Such brokers weren't necessarily at the top of the hierarchy or experts in their fields, but they linked specialists in the firm with trustworthy and informative relationships.[96]

Most personal networks are highly clustered; that is, an individual's friends are likely to be friends with one another as well. Most corporate networks are made up of several clusters that have few links between them. Brokers are especially powerful because they connect separate clusters, thus stimulating collaboration among otherwise independent specialists.

Before moving on, Strategy Spotlight 4.5 discusses an interesting research study. It points out how women may differ from men in how they develop their social networks.

The Potential Downside of Social Capital

We'd like to close our discussion of social capital by addressing some of its limitations. First, some firms have been adversely affected by very high levels of social capital because it may breed **"groupthink"**—a tendency not to question shared beliefs.[97] Such thinking may occur in networks with high levels of closure where there is little input from people outside of the network. In effect, too many warm and fuzzy feelings among group members prevent people from rigorously challenging each other. People are discouraged from engaging in the "creative abrasion" that Dorothy Leonard of Harvard University describes as a key source of innovation.[98] Two firms that were well known for their collegiality, strong sense of employee membership, and humane treatment—Digital Equipment (now part of Hewlett-Packard) and Polaroid—suffered greatly from market misjudgments and strategic errors. The aforementioned aspects of their culture contributed to their problems.

Second, if there are deep-rooted mindsets, there would be a tendency to develop dysfunctional human resource practices. That is, the organization (or group) would continue to

groupthink a tendency in an organization for individuals not to question shared beliefs.

Developing Social Capital: Do Women and Men Differ?

Several years ago, Boris Groysberg conducted a study in which he warned managers about the risks associated with hiring star performers away from companies. His research investigated more than 1,000 star stock analysts, and he found that when one of them switches companies, not only does the star's performance plunge, but also the market value of the star's new company declines. In addition, the players don't tend to stay with their new firms very long—despite the generous pay packages that lured them in the first place. So everyone loses out.

However, when Groysberg further analyzed the data, he gained some new insights. One group of analysts maintained their stardom after changing employers: women. Unlike their male counterparts, female stars who switched firms performed just as well, in aggregate, as those who stayed put.

Why the gender discrepancy? There were two explanations. *First, the best female analysts appear to have built their franchises on portable, external relationships with clients and companies they covered—rather than on relationships within their firms.* In contrast, male analysts

Source: Groysberg, B . 2008. How Star Women Build Portable Skills. *Harvard Business Review,* 86(2): 74–81.

built up greater firm- and team-specific human capital. That is, they invested more in internal networks and unique capabilities and resources of the firms where they worked.

Second, women took greater care when assessing a prospective employer. They evaluated their options more carefully and analyzed a wider range of factors than men did before deciding to uproot themselves from a firm where they had been successful. Female star analysts, it seems, take their work environment more seriously yet rely on it less than male stars do. And they tend to look for a firm that will allow them to keep building their successful franchise their own way.

There is a clear explanation as to why the female analysts spent more time developing their external networks. Most salespeople, traders, and investment bankers are men. And men tend to spend more time with other men. Not surprisingly, the star women in the study were generally thwarted in their efforts to integrate themselves into the existing power structure. Thus, they went to greater lengths to cultivate relationships with clients and contacts at the companies they covered. Their decision to maintain such an external focus rested on four main factors: uneasy in-house relationships, poor mentorships, neglect by colleagues, and a vulnerable position in the labor market.

hire, reward, and promote like-minded people who tend to further intensify organizational inertia and erode innovation. Such homogeneity would increase over time and decrease the effectiveness of decision-making processes.

Third, the socialization processes (orientation, training, etc.) can be expensive in terms of both financial resources and managerial commitment. Such investments can represent a significant opportunity cost that should be evaluated in terms of the intended benefits. If such expenses become excessive, profitability would be adversely affected.

Finally, individuals may use the contacts they develop to pursue their own interests and agendas that may be inconsistent with the organization's goals and objectives. Thus, they may distort or selectively use information to favor their preferred courses of action or withhold information in their own self-interest to enhance their power to the detriment of the common good. Drawing on our discussion of social networks, this is particularly true in an organization that has too many bridging relationships but not enough closure relationships. In high closure groups, it is easier to watch each other to ensure that illegal or unethical acts don't occur. By contrast, bridging relationships make it easier for a person to play one group or individual off on another, with no one being the wiser.[99] We will discuss some behavioral control mechanisms in Chapter 9 (rewards, control, boundaries) that reduce such dysfunctional behaviors and actions.[100]

Using Technology to Leverage Human Capital and Knowledge

Sharing knowledge and information throughout the organization can be a means of conserving resources, developing products and services, and creating new opportunities. In this section we will discuss how technology can be used to leverage human capital and knowledge within organizations as well as with customers and suppliers beyond their boundaries.

>LO4.5
The vital role of technology in leveraging knowledge and human capital.

Using Networks to Share Information

As we all know, e-mail is an effective means of communicating a wide variety of information. It is quick, easy, and almost costless. Of course, it can become a problem when employees use it extensively for personal reasons. And we all know how fast jokes or rumors can spread within and across organizations!

Below is an example of how a CEO curbed what he felt was excessive e-mail use in his firm.[101]

> Scott Dockter, CEO of PBD Worldwide Fulfillment Services in Alpharetta, Georgia, launched "no e-mail Friday." Why? He suspected that overdependence on e-mail at PBD, which offers services such as call center management and distribution, was hurting productivity and, perhaps, sales. Accordingly, he instructed his 275 employees to pick up the phone or meet in person each Friday, and reduce e-mail use the rest of the time.
>
> That was tough to digest, especially for the younger staffers. "We discovered a lot of introverts . . . who had drifted into a pattern of communicating by e-mail," says Dockter. "However, in less than four months, the simple directive resulted in quicker problem-solving, better teamwork, and, best of all, happier customers." "Our relationship with PBD is much stronger," says Cynthia Fitzpatrick of Crown Financial Ministries. "You can't get to know someone through e-mail."

E-mail can also cause embarrassment if one is not careful. Consider the plight of a potential CEO—as recalled by Marshall Goldsmith, a well-known executive coach:[102]

> I witnessed a series of e-mails between a potential CEO and a friend inside the company. The first e-mail to the friend provided an elaborate description of "why the current CEO is an idiot." The friend sent a reply. Several rounds of e-mails followed. Then the friend sent an e-mail containing a funny joke. The potential CEO decided that the current CEO would love this joke and forwarded it to him. You can guess what happened next. The CEO scrolled down the e-mail chain and found the "idiot" message. The heir apparent was gone in a week.

E-mail can, however, be a means for top executives to communicate information efficiently. For example, Martin Sorrell, chairman of WPP Group PLC, a $2.4 billion advertising and public relations firm, is a strong believer in the use of e-mail.[103] He e-mails all of his employees once a month to discuss how the company is doing, address specific issues, and offer his perspectives on hot issues, such as new business models for the Internet. He believes that it keeps people abreast of what he is working on.

Technology can also enable much more sophisticated forms of communication in addition to knowledge sharing. Buckman Laboratories is a $505 million specialty chemicals company based in Memphis, Tennessee, with approximately 1,500 employees in over 100 countries. Buckman has successfully used its global knowledge-sharing network—known as K'Netix—to enhance its competitive advantages:[104]

> Here's an example of how the network can be applied. One of Buckman's paper customers in Michigan realized that the peroxide it was adding to remove ink from old magazines

was no longer working. A Buckman sales manager presented this problem to the knowledge network. Within two days, salespeople from Belgium and Finland identified a likely cause: Bacteria in the paper slurry was producing an enzyme that broke down the peroxide. The sales manager recommended a chemical to control the bacteria, solving the problem. You can imagine how positive the customer felt about Buckman. And with the company and the customer co-creating knowledge, a new level of trust and value can emerge.

Electronic Teams: Using Technology to Enhance Collaboration

>LO4.6
Why "electronic" or "virtual" teams are critical in combining and leveraging knowledge in organizations and how they can be made more effective.

Technology enables professionals to work as part of electronic, or virtual, teams to enhance the speed and effectiveness with which products are developed. For example, Microsoft has concentrated much of its development on **electronic teams** (or e-teams) that are networked together.[105] This helps to accelerate design and testing of new software modules that use the Windows-based framework as their central architecture. Microsoft is able to foster specialized technical expertise while sharing knowledge rapidly throughout the firm. This helps the firm learn how its new technologies can be applied rapidly to new business ventures such as cable television, broadcasting, travel services, and financial services.

What are electronic teams (or e-teams)? There are two key differences between e-teams and more traditional teams:[106]

electronic teams a team of individuals that completes tasks primarily through e-mail communication.

- E-team members either work in geographically separated work places or they may work in the same space but at different times. E-teams may have members working in different spaces and time zones, as is the case with many multinational teams.
- Most of the interactions among members of e-teams occur through electronic communication channels such as fax machines and groupware tools such as e-mail, bulletin boards, chat, and videoconferencing.

E-teams have expanded exponentially in recent years.[107] Organizations face increasingly high levels of complex and dynamic change. E-teams are also effective in helping businesses cope with global challenges. Most e-teams perform very complex tasks and most knowledge-based teams are charged with developing new products, improving organizational processes, and satisfying challenging customer problems. For example, Eastman Kodak's e-teams design new products, Hewlett Packard's e-teams solve clients' computing problems, and Sun Microsystems' (part of oracle) e-teams generate new business models.

Advantages   There are multiple advantages of e-teams.[108] In addition to the rather obvious use of technology to facilitate communications, the potential benefits parallel the other two major sections in this chapter—human capital and social capital.

First, e-teams are less restricted by the geographic constraints that are placed on face-to-face teams. Thus, e-teams have the potential to acquire a broader range of "human capital" or the skills and capacities that are necessary to complete complex assignments. So, e-team leaders can draw upon a greater pool of talent to address a wider range of problems since they are not constrained by geographic space. Once formed, e-teams can be more flexible in responding to unanticipated work challenges and opportunities because team members can be rotated out of projects when demands and contingencies alter the team's objectives.

Second, e-teams can be very effective in generating "social capital"—the quality of relationships and networks that form. Such capital is a key lubricant in work transactions and operations. Given the broader boundaries associated with e-teams, members and leaders generally have access to a wider range of social contacts than would be typically available in more traditional face-to-face teams. Such contacts are often connected to a broader scope of clients, customers, constituents, and other key stakeholders.

Challenges However, there are challenges associated with making e-teams effective. Successful action by both traditional teams and e-teams requires that:

- Members *identify* who among them can provide the most appropriate knowledge and resources, and,
- E-team leaders and key members know how to *combine* individual contributions in the most effective manner for a coordinated and appropriate response.

Group psychologists have termed such activities "identification and combination" activities and teams that fail to perform them face a "process loss."[109] Process losses prevent teams from reaching high levels of performance because of inefficient interaction dynamics among team members. Such poor dynamics require that some collective energy, time, and effort be devoted to dealing with team inefficiencies, thus diverting the team away from its objectives. For example, if a team member fails to communicate important information at critical phases of a project, other members may waste time and energy. This can lead to conflict and resentment as well as to decreased motivation to work hard to complete tasks.

The potential for process losses tends to be more prevalent in e-teams than in traditional teams because the geographical dispersion of members increases the complexity of establishing effective interaction and exchanges. Generally, teams suffer process loss because of low cohesion, low trust among members, a lack of appropriate norms or standard operating procedures, or a lack of shared understanding among team members about their tasks. With e-teams, members are more geographically or temporally dispersed, and the team becomes more susceptible to the risk factors that can create process loss. Such problems can be exacerbated when team members have less than ideal competencies and social skills. This can erode problem-solving capabilities as well as the effective functioning of the group as a social unit.

A variety of technologies, from e-mail and Internet groups to Skype (acquired by eBay in 2005) and Cisco's Umi TelePresence, have facilitated the formation and effective functioning of e-teams as well as a wide range of collaborations within companies. Strategy Spotlight 4.6 highlights Cisco's efforts to use technology to enable such communication. Such technologies greatly enhance the collaborative abilities of employees and managers within a company at a reasonable cost—despite the distances that separate them.

Codifying Knowledge for Competitive Advantage

There are two different kinds of knowledge. Tacit knowledge is embedded in personal experience and shared only with the consent and participation of the individual. Explicit (or codified) knowledge, on the other hand, is knowledge that can be documented, widely distributed, and easily replicated. One of the challenges of knowledge-intensive organizations is to capture and codify the knowledge and experience that, in effect, resides in the heads of its employees. Otherwise, they will have to constantly "reinvent the wheel," which is both expensive and inefficient. Also, the "new wheel" may not necessarily be superior to the "old wheel."[110]

Once a knowledge asset (e.g., a software code or processes) is developed and paid for, it can be reused many times at very low cost, assuming that it doesn't have to be substantially modified each time. Let's take the case of a consulting company, such as Accenture (formerly Andersen Consulting).[111] Since the knowledge of its consultants has been codified and stored in electronic repositories, it can be employed in many jobs by a huge number of consultants. Additionally, since the work has a high level of standardization (i.e., there are strong similarities across the numerous client engagements), there is a rather high ratio of consultants to partners. For example, the ratio of consultants to partners is roughly 30, which is quite high. As one might expect, there must be extensive training of the newly hired consultants for such an approach to work. The recruits are trained at Accenture's

strategy spotlight

Videoconferencing: Allowing Employees to Communicate Face-to-Face over Long Distances

Cisco Systems has recognized that collaboration is the biggest technological trend of the next decade, driving productivity gains of 5 to 10 percent per year. It has created a strong portfolio of collaboration technologies, including TelePresence; WebEx; phones that run over the Internet; devices that produce, distribute, and archive videos; and hardware that can carry, distribute, and manage communications traffic no matter the origin or destination.

Internally, the use of these technologies has helped make Cisco's workforce one of the most distributed, connected, and productive in the world. Employees have experienced—and driven—a cultural revolution of not only information-sharing, but also teamwork and transparency.

Sources: Copeland, M. V. 2010. The New Global Worker Gadget: Videophones. *Fortune*, November 15: 36; Sidhu, I. 2010. *Doing Both*. Boston: Harvard Business Press; and Baig, E. C. 2010. Umi TelePresence Brings Videoconferencing Home. *www.usatoday.com*. December 2: np.

In a recent year, for example, TelePresence usage has increased 10 times, while WebEx conferencing usage has soared by 25 times. In addition, video postings have grown by more than 11 times on the company's website.

Cisco recently launched a new videoconferencing product, Umi TelePresence, that is aimed at the consumer market. It costs $599 (for the camera, console, cables, and remote control that constitute the system) and comes with an unlimited calling plan that runs $25 a month. What makes the product more expensive is that you might have to purchase a second or third Umi for family members, simply because it takes at least "two to tango" when it comes to videoconferencing. However, corporations could also use such home systems to allow global employees to connect with headquarters during business hours. As noted by Srinath Narasimhan, CEO of Tata Communications, remote employees are loath to go to the office for a 3 A.M. call in a video "suite." However, with a home setup, these employees could stumble out of bed and into a meeting—as long as they remember to comb their hair first!

Center for Professional Education, a 150-acre campus in St. Charles, Illinois. Using the center's knowledge-management respository, the consultants work through many scenarios designed to improve business processes. In effect, the information technologies enable the consultants to be "implementers, not inventors."

Access Health, a call-in medical center, also uses technology to capture and share knowledge. When someone calls the center, a registered nurse uses the company's "clinical decision architecture" to assess the caller's symptoms, rule out possible conditions, and recommend a home remedy, doctor's visit, or trip to the emergency room. The company's knowledge repository contains algorithms of the symptoms of more than 500 illnesses. According to CEO Joseph Tallman, "We are not inventing a new way to cure disease. We are taking available knowledge and inventing processes to put it to better use." The software algorithms were very expensive to develop, but the investment has been repaid many times over. The first 300 algorithms that Access Health developed have each been used an average of 8,000 times a year. Further, the company's paying customers—insurance companies and provider groups—save money because many callers would have made expensive trips to the emergency room or the doctor's office had they not been diagnosed over the phone.

The user community can be a major source of knowledge creation for a firm. Strategy Spotlight 4.7 highlights how SAP, in an example of effective crowdsourcing, has been able to leverage the expertise and involvement of its users to develop new knowledge and transmit it to their entire user community.

Crowdsourcing: How SAP Taps Knowledge Well beyond Its Boundaries

Traditionally, organizations built and protected their knowledge stocks—proprietary resources that no one else could access. However, the more the business environment changes, the faster the value of what you know at any point in time diminishes. In today's world, success hinges on the ability to access a growing variety of knowledge flows in order to rapidly replenish the firm's knowledge stocks. For example, when an organization tries to improve cycle times in a manufacturing process, it finds far more value in problem solving shaped by the diverse experiences, perspectives, and learning of a tightly knit team (shared through knowledge flows) than in a training manual (knowledge stocks) alone.

Knowledge flows can help companies gain competitive advantage in an age of near-constant disruption. The software company SAP, for example, routinely taps the more than 1.5 million participants in its Developer Network, which extends well beyond the boundaries of the firm. Those who post questions for the network community to address will receive a response in 17 minutes, on average, and 85 percent of all questions posted to date have been rated as "resolved." By providing a virtual platform for customers, developers, system integrators, and service vendors to create and exchange knowledge, SAP has significantly increased the productivity of all the participants in its ecosystem.

The site is open to everyone, regardless of whether you are an SAP customer, partner, or newcomer who needs to work with SAP technology. The site offers technical articles, Web-based training, code samples, evaluation systems, discussion forums, and excellent blogs for community experts.

Source: Hagel, J., III., Brown, J. S., & Davison, L. 2009. The Big Shift: Measuring the Forces of Change. *Harvard Business Review,* 87(4): 87; and Anonymous. undated. SAP Developer Network. *sap.sys-con.com.* np.

crowdsourcing

We close this section with a series of questions managers should consider in determining (1) how effective their organization is in attracting, developing, and retaining human capital and (2) how effective they are in leveraging human capital through social capital and technology. These questions, included in Exhibit 4.7, summarize some of the key issues addressed in this chapter.

Protecting the Intellectual Assets of the Organization: Intellectual Property and Dynamic Capabilities

In today's dynamic and turbulent world, unpredictability and fast change dominate the business environment. Firms can use technology, attract human capital, or tap into research and design networks to get access to pretty much the same information as their competitors. So what would give firms a sustainable competitive advantage?[112] Protecting a firm's intellectual property requires a concerted effort on the part of the company. After all, employees become disgruntled and patents expire. The management of intellectual property (IP) involves, besides patents, contracts with confidentiality and noncompete clauses, copyrights, and the development of trademarks. Moreover, developing dynamic capabilities is the only avenue providing firms with the ability to reconfigure their knowledge and activities to achieve a sustainable competitive advantage.

Intellectual Property Rights

Intellectual property rights are more difficult to define and protect than property rights for physical assets (e.g., plant, equipment, and land). However, if intellectual property

>LO4.7
The challenge of protecting intellectual property and the importance of a firm's dynamic capabilities.

intellectual property rights intangible property owned by a firm in the forms of patents, copyrights, trademarks, or trade secrets.

Human Capital

Recruiting "Top-Notch" Human Capital

- Does the organization assess attitude and "general makeup" instead of focusing primarily on skills and background in selecting employees at all levels?
- How important are creativity and problem-solving ability? Are they properly considered in hiring decisions?
- Do people throughout the organization engage in effective networking activities to obtain a broad pool of worthy potential employees? Is the organization creative in such endeavors?

Enhancing Human Capital through Employee Development

- Does the development and training process inculcate an "organizationwide" perspective?
- Is there widespread involvement, including top executives, in the preparation and delivery of training and development programs?
- Is the development of human capital effectively tracked and monitored?
- Are there effective programs for succession at all levels of the organization, especially at the top-most levels?
- Does the firm effectively evaluate its human capital? Is a 360-degree evaluation used? Why? Why not?
- Are mechanisms in place to assure that a manager's success does not come at the cost of compromising the organization's core values?

Retaining the Best Employees

- Are there appropriate financial rewards to motivate employees at all levels?
- Do people throughout the organization strongly identify with the organization's mission?
- Are employees provided with a stimulating and challenging work environment that fosters professional growth?
- Are valued amenities provided (e.g., flex time, child-care facilities, telecommuting) that are appropriate given the organization's mission, strategy, and how work is accomplished?
- Is the organization continually devising strategies and mechanisms to retain top performers?

Social Capital

- Are there positive personal and professional relationships among employees?
- Is the organization benefiting (or being penalized) by hiring (or by voluntary turnover) en masse?
- Does an environment of caring and encouragement rather than competition enhance team performance?
- Do the social networks within the organization have the appropriate levels of closure and bridging relationships?
- Does the organization minimize the adverse effects of excessive social capital, such as excessive costs and "groupthink"?

Technology

- Has the organization used technologies such as e-mail and networks to develop products and services?
- Does the organization effectively use technology to transfer best practices across the organization?
- Does the organization use technology to leverage human capital and knowledge both within the boundaries of the organization and among its suppliers and customers?
- Has the organization effectively used technology to codify knowledge for competitive advantage?
- Does the organization try to retain some of the knowledge of employees when they decide to leave the firm?

Source: Adapted from Dess, G. G., & Picken, J. C. 1999. *Beyond Productivity:* 63–64. New York: AMACON.

rights are not reliably protected by the state, there will be no incentive to develop new products and services. Property rights have been enshrined in constitutions and rules of law in many countries. In the information era, though, adjustments need to be made to accommodate the new realities of knowledge. Knowledge and information are fundamentally different assets from the physical ones that property rights have been designed to protect.

The protection of intellectual rights raises unique issues, compared to physical property rights. IP is characterized by significant development costs and very low marginal costs. Indeed, it may take a substantial investment to develop a software program, an idea, or a digital music tune. Once developed, though, their reproduction and distribution cost may be almost zero, especially if the Internet is used. Effective protection of intellectual property is necessary before any investor will finance such an undertaking. Appropriation of their returns is harder to police since possession and deployment are not as readily observable. Unlike physical assets, intellectual property can be stolen by simply broadcasting it. Recall Napster and MP3 as well as the debates about counterfeit software, music CDs, and DVDs coming from developing countries such as China. Part of the problem is that using an idea does not prevent others from simultaneously using it for their own benefit, which is typically impossible with physical assets. Moreover, new ideas are frequently built on old ideas and are not easily traceable.

Strategy Spotlight 4.8 describes the many legal battles fought by a Canadian firm, Research in Motion of Waterloo, the developer of the popular BlackBerry. This example illustrates the high stakes that ride on intellectual property rights.

Countries are attempting to pass new legislation to cope with developments in new pharmaceutical compounds, stem cell research, and biotechnology. However, a firm that is faced with this challenge today cannot wait for the legislation to catch up. New technological developments, software solutions, electronic games, online services, and other products and services contribute to our economic prosperity and the creation of wealth for those entrepreneurs who have the idea first and risk bringing it to the market.

Dynamic Capabilities

Dynamic capabilities entail the capacity to build and protect a competitive advantage.[113] This rests on knowledge, assets, competencies, and complementary assets and technologies as well as the ability to sense and seize new opportunities, generate new knowledge, and reconfigure existing assets and capabilities.[114] According to David Teece, an economist at the University of California at Berkeley, dynamic capabilities are related to the entrepreneurial side of the firm and are built within a firm through its environmental and technological "sensing" apparatus, its choices of organizational form, and its collective ability to strategize. Dynamic capabilities are about the ability of an organization to challenge the conventional wisdom within its industry and market, learn and innovate, adapt to the changing world, and continuously adopt new ways to serve the evolving needs of the market.[115]

Examples of dynamic capabilities include product development, strategic decision making, alliances, and acquisitions.[116] Some firms have clearly developed internal processes and routines that make them superior in such activities. For example, 3M and Apple are ahead of their competitors in product development. Cisco Systems has made numerous acquisitions over the years. They seem to have developed the capability to identify and evaluate potential acquisition candidates and seamlessly integrate them once the acquisition is completed. Other organizations can try to copy Cisco's practices. However, Cisco's combination of the resources of the acquired companies and their reconfiguration that Cisco has already achieved places them well ahead of their competitors. As markets become

dynamic capabilities a firm's capacity to build and protect a competitive advantage, which rests on knowledge, assets, competencies, complementary assets, and technologies. Dynamic capabilities include the ability to sense and seize new opportunities, generate new knowledge, and reconfigure existing assets and capabilities.

strategy spotlight

Research in Motion, Maker of the BlackBerry, Loses an Intellectual Property Lawsuit

Research in Motion (RIM) is a Waterloo, Ontario–based company that is best known for developing the Black-Berry, a wireless device that integrates the functionalities of a cell phone with the ability to receive e-mail messages. During its brief history, it has become one of the fastest growing companies in North America. Founded by Mike Lazaridis, a former University of Waterloo student in 1984, Research in Motion was a competent but obscure technology firm until 1999 when the first BlackBerry was released. Through the development of integrated hardware, software, and services that support multiple wireless network standards, the BlackBerry has enabled RIM to grow from less than $50 million in sales revenue in 1999 to $15 billion by 2010. Even more impressive, by early 2011 the company boasted a market capitalization in excess of $30 billion. RIM's commitment to their slogan "always on, always connected" has won them a legion of dedicated followers around the globe.

Interestingly, legal challenges have been the biggest obstacles that Research in Motion has faced in the eight years since the introduction of the first BlackBerry. In 2000, NTP, a pure patent-holding company, filed suit against RIM for violation of five of its patents and petitioned the court for an injunction on the sale and support of BlackBerry devices. The case dragged on for years, and RIM felt relatively secure that no injunction would be

● Research in Motion (RIM) has faced litigation over its highly successful BlackBerry.

issued. On February 24, 2006, things dramatically changed. U.S. District Court Judge James Spencer indicated that he was inclined to grant the injunction and that his ruling was imminent. Faced with the acute risk of an unfavorable decision, RIM settled only one week later for $612.5 million. It wound up paying a fortune for rights that were dubious at best—given that all five NTP patents had already been preliminarily invalidated by the U.S. Patent and Trademark Office and that two of them then received a final rejection.

Sources: Henkel, J. & Reitzig, M. 2008. Patent Sharks. *Harvard Business Review*, 86(6): 129–133; Hesseldahl, A. 2006. RIM's Latest Patent Problem. *BusinessWeek Online*, May 2: np; Anonymous. 2006. Settlement Reached in BlackBerry Patent Case. (The Associated Press) MSNBC.Com. March 3: np; Wolk, M . 2006. RIM Pays Up, Taking "One for the Team." MSNBC.Com. March 3; and *finance.yahoo.com*.

increasingly dynamic, traditional sources of long-term competitive advantage become less relevant. In such markets, all that a firm can strive for are a series of temporary advantages. Dynamic capabilities allow a firm to create this series of temporary advantages through new resource configurations.[117]

Reflecting on Career Implications . . .

- *Human Capital:* Does your organization effectively attract, develop, and retain talent? If not, you may have fewer career opportunities to enhance your human capital at your organization. Do you take advantage of your organization's human resource programs such as tuition reimbursement, mentoring, etc.
- *Human Capital:* Does your organization value diversity? What kinds of diversity seem to be encouraged (e.g., age-based or ethnicity-based)? If not, there may be limited perspectives on strategic and operational issues and a career at this organization may be less attractive to you.
- *Social Capital:* Does your organization have effective programs to build and develop social capital such that professionals develop strong "ties" to the organization? Alternatively, is social capital so strong that you see effects occur such as "groupthink"? From your perspective, how might you better leverage social capital towards pursuing other career opportunities?
- *Technology:* Does your organization provide and effectively use technology (e.g., groupware, knowledge management systems) to help you leverage your talents and expand your knowledge base?

Summary

Firms throughout the industrial world are recognizing that the knowledge worker is the key to success in the marketplace. However, we also recognize that human capital, although vital, is still only a necessary, but not a sufficient, condition for creating value. We began the first section of the chapter by addressing the importance of human capital and how it can be attracted, developed, and retained. Then we discussed the role of social capital and technology in leveraging human capital for competitive success. We pointed out that intellectual capital—the difference between a firm's market value and its book value—has increased significantly over the past few decades. This is particularly true for firms in knowledge-intensive industries, especially where there are relatively few tangible assets, such as software development.

The second section of the chapter addressed the attraction, development, and retention of human capital. We viewed these three activities as a "three-legged stool"—that is, it is difficult for firms to be successful if they ignore or are unsuccessful in any one of these activities. Among the issues we discussed in *attracting* human capital were "hiring for attitude, training for skill" and the value of using social networks to attract human capital. In particular, it is important to attract employees who can collaborate with others, given the importance of collective efforts such as teams and task forces. With regard to *developing* human capital, we discussed the need to encourage widespread involvement throughout the organization, monitor progress and track the development of human capital, and evaluate human capital. Among the issues that are widely practiced in evaluating human capital is the 360-degree evaluation system. Employees are evaluated by their superiors, peers, direct reports, and even internal and external customers. We also addressed the value of maintaining a diverse workforce. Finally, some mechanisms for retaining human capital are employees' identification with the organization's mission and values, providing challenging work and a stimulating environment, the importance of financial and nonfinancial rewards and incentives, and providing flexibility and amenities. A key issue here is that a firm should not overemphasize financial rewards. After all, if individuals join an organization for money, they also are likely to leave for money. With money as the primary motivator, there is little chance that employees will develop firm-specific ties to keep them with the organization.

The third section of the chapter discussed the importance of social capital in leveraging human capital. Social capital refers to the network of relationships that individuals have throughout the organization as well as with customers and suppliers. Such ties can be critical in obtaining both information and resources. With regard to recruiting, for example, we saw how some firms are able to hire en masse groups of individuals who are part of social networks. Social relationships can also be very important in the effective functioning of groups. Finally, we discussed some of the potential downsides of social capital. These include the expenses that firms may bear when promoting social and working relationships among individuals as well as the potential for "groupthink," wherein individuals are reluctant to express divergent (or opposing) views on an issue because of social pressures to conform. We also introduced the concept of social networks. The relative advantages of being central in a network versus bridging multiple networks was discussed. We addressed the key role that social networks can play in both improving knowledge management and promoting career success.

The fourth section addressed the role of technology in leveraging human capital. We discussed relatively simple means of using technology, such as e-mail and networks where individuals can collaborate by way of personal computers. We provided suggestions and guidelines on how electronic teams can be effectively managed. We also addressed more sophisticated uses of technology, such as sophisticated management systems. Here knowledge can be codified and reused at very low cost, as we saw in the examples of firms in the consulting, health care, and high-technology industries.

In the last section we discussed the increasing importance of protecting a firm's intellectual property. Although traditional approaches such as patents, copyrights, and trademarks are important, the development of dynamic capabilities may be the best protection in the long run.

Summary Review Questions

1. Explain the role of knowledge in today's competitive environment.
2. Why is it important for managers to recognize the interdependence in the attraction, development, and retention of talented professionals?

3. What are some of the potential downsides for firms that engage in a "war for talent"?
4. Discuss the need for managers to use social capital in leveraging their human capital both within and across their firm.
5. Discuss the key role of technology in leveraging knowledge and human capital.

Key Terms

knowledge economy, 125
intellectual capital, 126
human capital, 126
social capital, 126
explicit knowledge, 127
tacit knowledge, 127
social network analysis, 138
360-degree evaluation and feedback systems, 133
closure, 140
bridging relationships, 140
structural holes, 140
unification lever, 141
people lever, 141
T-shaped management, 141
networth lever, 141
private information, 142
public information, 142
groupthink, 143
electronic teams, 146
intellectual property rights, 149
dynamic capabilities, 151

Experiential Exercise

Pfizer, a leading health care firm with $68 billion in revenues, is often rated as one of *Fortune*'s "Most Admired Firms." It is also considered an excellent place to work and has generated high return to shareholders. Clearly, they value their human capital. Using the Internet and/or library resources, identify some of the actions/strategies Pfizer has taken to attract, develop, and retain human capital. What are their implications?

Activity	Actions/Strategies	Implications
Attracting human capital		
Developing human capital		
Retaining human capital		

Application Questions & Exercises

1. Look up successful firms in a high-technology industry as well as two successful firms in more traditional industries such as automobile manufacturing and retailing. Compare their market values and book values. What are some implications of these differences?

2. Select a firm for which you believe its social capital— both within the firm and among its suppliers and customers—is vital to its competitive advantage. Support your arguments.

3. Choose a company with which you are familiar. What are some of the ways in which it uses technology to leverage its human capital?

4. Using the Internet, look up a company with which you are familiar. What are some of the policies and procedures that it uses to enhance the firm's human and social capital?

Ethics Questions

1. Recall an example of a firm that recently faced an ethical crisis. How do you feel the crisis and management's handling of it affected the firm's human capital and social capital?

2. Based on your experiences or what you have learned in your previous classes, are you familiar with any companies that used unethical practices to attract talented professionals? What do you feel were the short-term and long-term consequences of such practices?

References

1. Farmbrough, R. 2010. List of the largest global technology companies: Part 1. *www.wikipedia.org*. November 1: np; and Arai, H. 2000. *Intellectual Property Policies for the Twenty-First Century: The Japanese Experience in Wealth Creation*. WIPO Publication No. 834 (E). We thank Pratik Kapadia for his valued contribution.

2. Parts of this chapter draw upon some of the ideas and examples from Dess, G. G. & Picken, J. C. 1999. *Beyond productivity*. New York: AMACOM.

3. An acknowledged trend: The world economic survey. 1996. *The Economist,* September 2(8): 25–28.

4. Quinn, J. B., Anderson, P., & Finkelstein, S. 1996. Leveraging intellect. *Academy of Management Executive*, 10(3): 7–27; and *https://www.cia.gov/library/publications/the=world=factbook/geos/us.html*.

5. Hamel, G. & Prahalad, C. K. 1996. Competing in the new economy: Managing out of bounds. *Strategic Management Journal,* 17: 238.

6. Stewart, T. A. 1997. *Intellectual capital: The new wealth of organizations*. New York: Doubleday/Currency.

7. Leif Edvisson and Michael S. Malone have a similar, more detailed definition of *intellectual capital:* "the combined knowledge, skill, innovativeness, and ability to meet the task at hand." They consider intellectual capital to equal human capital plus structural capital. *Structural capital* is defined as "the hardware, software, databases, organization structure, patents, trademarks, and everything else of organizational capability that supports those employees' productivity— in a word, everything left at the office when the employees go home." Edvisson, L. & Malone, M. S. 1997. *Intellectual capital: Realizing your company's true value by finding its hidden brainpower:* 10–14. New York: HarperBusiness.

8. Stewart, T. A. 2001. Accounting gets radical. *Fortune,* April 16: 184–194.

9. Adams, S. & Kichen, S. 2008. Ben Graham then and now. *Forbes,* November 10: 56.

10. An interesting discussion of Steve Jobs's impact on Apple's valuation is in: Lashinsky, A. 2009. Steve's leave—what does it really mean? *Fortune,* February 2: 96–102.

11. Anonyous. 2007. Intel opens first high volume 45 nm microprocessor manufacturing factory. *www.intel.com*. October 25: np.

12. Thomas Stewart has suggested this formula in his book *Intellectual capital.* He provides an insightful discussion on pages 224–225, including some of the limitations of this approach to measuring intellectual capital. We recognize, of course, that during the late 1990s and in early 2000, there were some excessive market valuations of high-technology and Internet firms. For an interesting discussion of the extraordinary market valuation of Yahoo!, an Internet company, refer to Perkins, A. B. 2001. The Internet bubble encapsulated: Yahoo! *Red Herring,* April 15: 17–18.

13. Roberts, P. W. & Dowling, G. R. 2002. Corporate reputation and sustained superior financial performance. *Strategic Management Journal,* 23(12): 1077–1095.

14. For a recent study on the relationships between human capital, learning, and sustainable competitive advantage, read Hatch, N. W. & Dyer, J. H. 2005. Human capital and learning as a source of sustainable competitive advantage. *Strategic Management Journal,* 25: 1155–1178.

15. One of the seminal contributions on knowledge management is Becker, G. S. 1993. *Human capital: A theoretical and empirical analysis with special reference to education* (3rd ed.). Chicago: University of Chicago Press.

16. For an excellent overview of the topic of social capital, read Baron, R. A. 2005. Social capital. In Hitt, M. A. & Ireland, R. D. (Eds.), *The Blackwell encyclopedia of management* (2nd ed.): 224–226. Malden, MA: Blackwell.

17. For an excellent discussion of social capital and its impact on organizational performance, refer to Nahapiet, J. & Ghoshal, S. 1998. Social capital, intellectual capital, and the organizational advantage. *Academy of Management Review,* 23: 242–266.

18. An interesting discussion of how knowledge management (patents) can enhance organizational performance can be found in Bogner, W. C. & Bansal, P. 2007. Knowledge management as the basis of sustained high performance. *Journal of Management Studies,* 44(1): 165–188.

19. Polanyi, M. 1967. *The tacit dimension.* Garden City, NY: Anchor Publishing.

20. Barney, J. B. 1991. Firm resources and sustained competitive advantage. *Journal of Management,* 17: 99–120.

21. For an interesting perspective of empirical research on how knowledge can adversely affect performance, read Haas, M. R. & Hansen, M. T. 2005. When using knowledge can hurt performance: The value of organizational capabilities in a management consulting company. *Strategic Management Journal,* 26(1): 1–24.

22. New insights on managing talent are provided in: Cappelli, P. 2008. Talent management for the twenty-first century. *Harvard Business Review,* 66(3): 74–81.

23. Some of the notable books on this topic include Edvisson & Malone, op. cit.; Stewart, op. cit.; and Nonaka, I. & Takeuchi, I. 1995. *The knowledge creating company.* New York: Oxford University Press.

24. Segalla, M. & Felton, N. 2010. Find the real power in your organization. *Harvard Business Review,* 88(5): 34–35.

25. Stewart, T. A. 2000. Taking risk to the marketplace. *Fortune,* March 6: 424.

26. Insights on the Generation X's perspective on the workplace are in: Erickson, T. J. 2008. Task, not time: Profile of a Gen Y job. *Harvard Business Review,* 86(2): 19.

27. Pfeffer, J. 2010. Building sustainable organizations: The human factor. *The Academy of Management Perspectives,* 24(1): 34–45.

28. Dutton, G. 1997. Are you technologically competent? *Management Review,* November: 54–58.

29. Some workplace implications for the aging workforce are addressed in: Strack, R., Baier, J., & Fahlander, A. 2008. Managing demographic risk. *Harvard Business Review,* 66(2): 119–128.

30. For a discussion of attracting, developing, and retaining top talent, refer to Goffee, R. & Jones, G. 2007. Leading clever people. *Harvard Business Review,* 85(3): 72–89.

31. Dess & Picken, op. cit.: 34.

32. Webber, A. M. 1998. Danger: Toxic company. *Fast Company,* November: 152–161.

33. Martin, J. & Schmidt, C. 2010. How to keep your top talent. *Harvard Business Review,* 88(5): 54–61.

34. Some interesting insights on why home-grown American talent is going abroad is found in: Saffo, P. 2009. A looming American diaspora. *Harvard Business Review,* 87(2): 27.

35. Morris, B. 1997. Key to success: People, people, people. *Fortune,* October 27: 232.

36. Davenport, T. H., Harris, J. & Shapiro, J. 2010. Competing on talent analytics. *Harvard Business Review,* 88(10): 62–69.

37. Ployhart, R. E. & Moliterno, T. P. 2011. Emergence of the human capital resource: A multilevel model. *Academy of Management Review,* 36(1): 127–150.

38. For insights on management development and firm performance in several countries, refer to: Mabey, C. 2008. Management development and firm performance in Germany, Norway, Spain, and the UK. *Journal of International Business Studies,* 39(8): 1327–1342.

39. Martin, J. 1998. So, you want to work for the best. . . . *Fortune,* January 12: 77.

40. Cardin, R. 1997. Make your own Bozo Filter. *Fast Company,* October–November: 56.

41. Gallagher, L. 2011. 100 best companies to work for *money.cnn.com.* January 20: np.

42. Martin, op. cit.; Henkoff, R. 1993. Companies that train best. *Fortune,* March 22: 53–60.

43. An interesting perspective on developing new talent rapidly when they join an organization can be found in Rollag, K., Parise, S., & Cross, R. 2005. Getting new hires up to speed quickly. *MIT Sloan Management Review,* 46(2): 35–41.

44. Stewart, T. A. 1998. Gray flannel suit? moi? *Fortune,* March 18: 80–82.

45. An interesting perspective on how Cisco Systems develops its talent can be found in Chatman, J., O'Reilly, C., & Chang, V. 2005. Cisco Systems: Developing a human capital strategy. *California Management Review,* 47(2): 137–166.

46. Anonymous. 2011. Schumpeter: The tussle for talent. *The Economist.* January 8: 68.

47. This section is based on Leonard, D. A. & Swap, W. 2004. Deep smarts. *Harvard Business Review,* 82(9): 88–97.

48. Useful insights on coaching can be found in: Coutu, D. & Kauffman, C. 2009. What coaches can do for you? *Harvard Business Review,* 67(1): 91–97.

49. For an innovative perspective on the appropriateness of alternate approaches to evaluation and rewards, refer to Seijts, G. H. & Lathan, G. P. 2005. Learning versus performance goals: When should each be used? *Academy of Management Executive,* 19(1): 124–132.

50. The discussion of the 360-degree feedback system draws on the article UPS. 1997. 360-degree feedback: Coming from all sides. *Vision* (a UPS Corporation internal company publication), March: 3; Slater, R. 1994. *Get better or get beaten: Thirty-one leadership secrets from Jack Welch.* Burr Ridge, IL: Irwin; Nexon, M. 1997. General Electric: The secrets of the finest company in the world.

L'Expansion, July 23: 18–30; and Smith, D. 1996. Bold new directions for human resources. *Merck World* (internal company publication), October: 8.

51. Interesting insights on 360-degree evaluation systems are discussed in: Barwise, P. & Meehan, Sean. 2008. So you think you're a good listener. *Harvard Business Review,* 66(4): 22–23.

52. Insights into the use of 360-degree evaluation are in: Kaplan, R. E. & Kaiser, R. B. 2009. Stop overdoing your strengths. *Harvard Business Review,* 87(2): 100–103.

53. Kets de Vries, M. F. R. 1998. Charisma in action: The transformational abilities of Virgin's Richard Branson and ABB's Percy Barnevik. *Organizational Dynamics,* Winter: 20.

54. For an interesting discussion on how organizational culture has helped Zappos become number one in *Fortune's* 2009 survey of the best companies to work for, see: O'Brien, J. M. 2009. Zappos knows how to kick it. *Fortune,* February 2: 54–58.

55. We have only to consider the most celebrated case of industrial espionage in recent years, wherein José Ignacio Lopez was indicted in a German court for stealing sensitive product planning documents from his former employer, General Motors, and sharing them with his executive colleagues at Volkswagen. The lawsuit was dismissed by the German courts, but Lopez and his colleagues were investigated by the U.S. Justice Department. Also consider the recent litigation involving noncompete employment contracts and confidentiality clauses of *International Paper v. Louisiana-Pacific, Campbell Soup v. H. J. Heinz Co.,* and *PepsiCo v. Quaker Oats's Gatorade.* In addition to retaining valuable human resources and often their valuable network of customers, firms must also protect proprietary information and knowledge. For interesting insights, refer to Carley, W. M. 1998. CEO gets hard lesson in how not to keep his lieutenants. *The Wall Street Journal,* February 11: A1, A10; and Lenzner, R.

& Shook, C. 1998. Whose Rolodex is it, anyway? *Forbes,* February 23: 100–103.

56. For an insightful discussion of retention of knowledge workers in today's economy, read Davenport, T. H. 2005. *The care and feeding of the knowledge worker.* Boston, MA: Harvard Business School Press.

57. Fisher, A. 2008. America's most admired companies. *Fortune,* March 17: 74.

58. Stewart, T. A. 2001. *The wealth of knowledge.* New York: Currency.

59. For insights on fulfilling one's potential, refer to: Kaplan, R. S. 2008. Reaching your potential. *Harvard Business Review,* 66(7/8): 45–57.

60. Amabile, T. M. 1997. Motivating creativity in organizations: On doing what you love and loving what you do. *California Management Review,* Fall: 39–58.

61. For an insightful perspective on alternate types of employee–employer relationships, read Erickson, T. J. & Gratton, L. 2007. What it means to work here. *Harvard Business Review,* 85(3): 104–112.

62. Monsanto has been part of Pharmacia since 2002. *Hoover's Handbook of Am. Bus.* 2004: 562.

63. Pfeffer, J. 2001. Fighting the war for talent is hazardous to your organization's health. *Organizational Dynamics,* 29(4): 248–259.

64. Cox, T. L. 1991. The multinational organization. *Academy of Management Executive,* 5(2): 34–47. Without doubt, a great deal has been written on the topic of creating and maintaining an effective diverse workforce. Some excellent, recent books include: Harvey, C. P. & Allard, M. J. 2005. *Understanding and managing diversity: Readings, cases, and exercises.* (3rd ed.). Upper Saddle River, NJ: Pearson Prentice-Hall; Miller, F. A. & Katz, J. H. 2002. *The inclusion breakthrough: Unleashing the real power of diversity.* San Francisco: Berrett Koehler; and Williams, M. A. 2001. *The 10 lenses: Your guide to living and working in a multicultural world.* Sterling, VA: Capital Books.

65. For an interesting perspective on benefits and downsides of diversity in global consulting firms, refer to: Mors, M. L. 2010. Innovation in a global consulting firm: When the problem is too much diversity. *Strategic Management Journal,* 31(8): 841–872.

66. www.rand.org/publications/RB/ RB/5050. U. S. Census Bureau. 1970, 1980, 1990, and 2000 decennial censuses. Population projections, July 1, 2000, to July 1, 2050.

67. Hewlett, S. A. & Rashid, R. 2010. The battle for female talent in emerging markets. *Harvard Business Review,* 88(5): 101–107.

68. This section, including the six potential benefits of a diverse workforce, draws on Cox, T. H. & Blake, S. 1991. Managing cultural diversity: Implications for organizational competitiveness. *Academy of Management Executive,* 5(3): 45–56.

69. *www.pwcglobal.com/us/eng/careers/ diversity/index.html.*

70. Johansson, F. 2005. Masters of the multicultural. *Harvard Business Review,* 83(10): 18–19.

71. This discussion draws on Dess, G. G. & Lumpkin, G. T. 2001. Emerging issues in strategy process research. In Hitt, M. A., Freeman, R. E. & Harrison, J. S. (Eds.). *Handbook of strategic management:* 3–34. Malden, MA: Blackwell.

72. Wong, S.-S. & Boh, W. F. 2010. Leveraging the ties of others to build a reputation for trustworthiness among peers. *Academy of Management Journal,* 53(1): 129–148.

73. Adler, P. S. & Kwon, S. W. 2002. Social capital: Prospects for a new concept. *Academy of Management Review,* 27(1): 17–40.

74. Capelli, P. 2000. A market-driven approach to retaining talent. *Harvard Business Review,* 78(1): 103–113.

75. This hypothetical example draws on Peteraf, M. 1993. The cornerstones of competitive advantage. *Strategic Management Journal,* 14: 179–191.

76. Wernerfelt, B. 1984. A resource-based view of the firm. *Strategic Management Journal,* 5: 171–180.

77. Wysocki, B., Jr. 2000. Yet another hazard of the new economy: The Pied

Piper Effect. *The Wall Street Journal,* March 20: A1–A16.

78. Ideas on how managers can more effectively use their social network are addressed in: McGrath, C. & Zell, D. 2009. Profiles of trust: Who to turn to, and for what. *MIT Sloan Management Review,* 50(2): 75–80.

79. Ibid.

80. Buckman, R. C. 2000. Tech defectors from Microsoft resettle together. *The Wall Street Journal,* October: B1–B6.

81. An insightful discussion of the interorganizational aspects of social capital can be found in Dyer, J. H. & Singh, H. 1998. The relational view: Cooperative strategy and sources of interorganizational competitive advantage. *Academy of Management Review,* 23: 66–79.

82. A study of the relationship between social networks and performance in China is found in: Li, J. J., Poppo, L., & Zhou, K. Z. 2008. Do managerial ties in China always produce value? Competition, uncertainty, and domestic vs. foreign firms. *Strategic Management Journal,* 29(4): 383–400.

83. Aime, F., Johnson, S., Ridge, J. W. & Hill, A. D. 2010. The routine may be stable but the advantage is not: Competitive implications of key employee mobility. *Strategic Management Journal,* 31(1): 75–87.

84. Hoppe, B. 2005. Structural holes, Part one. *connectedness.blogspot. com.* January 18: np.

85. There has been a tremendous amount of theory building and empirical research in recent years in the area of social network analysis. Unquestionably, two of the major contributors to this domain have been Ronald Burt and J. S. Coleman. For excellent background discussions, refer to: Burt, R. S. 1992. *Structural holes: The social structure of competition.* Cambridge, MA: Harvard University Press; Coleman, J. S. 1990. *Foundations of social theory.* Cambridge, MA: Harvard University Press; and Coleman, J. S. 1988. Social capital in the creation of human capital. *American Journal of Sociology.* 94: S95–S120. For a more recent review and integration of current thought on

social network theory, consider: Burt, R. S. 2005. *Brokerage & closure: An introduction to social capital.* Oxford Press: New York.

86. Our discussion draws on the concepts developed by Burt, 1992, op. cit.; Coleman, 1990, op. cit.; Coleman, 1988, op. cit.; and Oh, H., Chung, M. & Labianca, G. 2004. Group social capital and group effectiveness: The role of informal socializing ties. *Academy of Management Journal,* 47(6): 860–875. We would like to thank Joe Labianca (University of Kentucky) for his helpful feedback and ideas in our discussion of social networks.

87. Arregle, J. L., Hitt, M. A., Sirmon, D. G., & Very, P. 2007. The development of organizational social capital: Attributes of family firms. *Journal of Management Studies,* 44(1): 73–95.

88. A novel perspective on social networks is in: Pentland, A. 2009. How social networks network best. *Harvard Business Review,* 87(2): 37.

89. Oh et al., op. cit.

90. Hoppe, op. cit.

91. The discussion of these two contingent factors draws on Dess, G. G. & Shaw, J. D. 2001. Voluntary turnover, social capital, and organizational performance. *Academy of Management Review,* 26(3): 446–456.

92. The business-level strategies of overall low cost and differentiation draws upon Michael E. Porter's classic work and will be discussed in more detail in Chapter 5. Source: Porter, M. E. 1985. *Competitive advantage.* Free Press: New York.

93. This section draws on: Hansen, M. T. 2009. *Collaboration: How leaders avoid the traps, create unity, and reap big results.* Boston, MA: Harvard Business Press.

94. Perspectives on how to use and develop decision networks are discussed in: Cross, R., Thomas, R. J., & Light, D. A. 2009. How "who you know" affects what you decide. *MIT Sloan Management Review,* 50(2): 35–42.

95. Our discussion of the three advantages of social networks draws on Uzzi, B. & Dunlap. S. 2005. How to

build your network. *Harvard Business Review,* 83(12): 53–60. For a recent, excellent review on the research exploring the relationship between social capital and managerial performance, read Moran, P. 2005. Structural vs. relational embeddedness: Social capital and managerial performance. *Strategic Management Journal,* 26(12): 1129–1151.

96. A perspective on personal influence is in: Christakis, N. A. 2009. The dynamics of personal influence. *Harvard Business Review,* 87(2): 31.

97. Prusak, L. & Cohen, D. 2001. How to invest in social capital. *Harvard Business Review,* 79(6): 86–93.

98. Leonard, D. & Straus, S. 1997. Putting your company's whole brain to work. *Harvard Business Review,* 75(4): 110–122.

99. For an excellent discussion of public (i.e., the organization) versus private (i.e., the individual manager) benefits of social capital, refer to Leana, C. R. & Van Buren, H. J. 1999. Organizational social capital and employment practices. *Academy of Management Review,* 24(3): 538–555.

100. The authors would like to thank Joe Labianca, University of Kentucky, and John Lin, University of Texas at Dallas, for their very helpful input in our discussion of social network theory and its practical implications.

101. Brady, D. 2006. !#?@ the e-mail. Can we talk?. *BusinessWeek,* December 4: 109.

102. Goldsmith, M. 2009. How not to lose the top job. *Harvard Business Review,* 87(1): 74.

103. Taylor, W. C. 1999. Whatever happened to globalization? *Fast Company,* December: 228–236.

104. Prahalad, C. K. & Ramaswamy, V. 2004. *The future of competition: Co-creating value with customers.* Boston: Harvard Business School Press.

105. Lei, D., Slocum, J., & Pitts, R. A. 1999. Designing organizations for competitive advantage: The power of unlearning and learning. *Organizational Dynamics,* Winter: 24–38.

106. This section draws upon Zaccaro, S. J. & Bader, P. 2002. E-Leadership and

the challenges of leading e-teams: Minimizing the bad and maximizing the good. *Organizational Dynamics,* 31(4): 377–387.

107. Kirkman, B. L., Rosen, B., Tesluk, P. E., & Gibson, C. B. 2004. The impact of team empowerment on virtual team performance: The moderating role of face-to-face interaction. *Academy of Management Journal,* 47(2): 175–192.

108. The discussion of the advantages and challenges associated with e-teams draws on Zacarro & Bader, op. cit.

109. For a recent study exploring the relationship between team empowerment, face-to-face interaction, and performance in virtual teams, read Kirkman, Rosen, Tesluk, & Gibson, op. cit.

110. For an innovative study on how firms share knowledge with competitors and the performance implications, read Spencer, J. W. 2003. Firms' knowledge sharing strategies in the global innovation system: Empirical evidence from the flat panel display industry. *Strategic Management Journal,* 24(3): 217–235.

111. The examples of Andersen Consulting and Access Health draw upon Hansen, M. T., Nohria, N., & Tierney, T. 1999. What's your strategy for managing knowledge? *Harvard Business Review,* 77(2): 106–118.

112. This discussion draws on Conley, J. G. 2005. *Intellectual capital management,* Kellogg School of Management and Schulich School of Business, York University, Toronto, KS 2003; Conley, J. G. & Szobocsan, J. 2001. Snow White shows the way. *Managing Intellectual Property,* June: 15–25; Greenspan, A. 2004. Intellectual property rights, The Federal Reserve Board, Remarks by the chairman, February 27; and Teece, D. J. 1998. Capturing value from knowledge assets, *California Management Review,* 40(3): 54–79. The authors would like to thank Professor Theo Peridis, York University, for his contribution to this section.

113. E. Danneels. 2011. Trying to become a different type of company: Dynamic capability at Smith Corona. *Strategic Management Journal,* 32(1): 1–31.

114. A study of the relationship between dynamic capabilities and related diversification is: Doving, E. & Gooderham, P. N. 2008. *Strategic Management Journal,* 29(8): 841–858.

115. A perspective on strategy in turbulent markets is in: Sull, D. 2009. How to thrive in turbulent markets. *Harvard Business Review,* 87(2): 78–88.

116. Lee, G. K. 2008. Relevance of organizational capabilities and its dynamics: What to learn from entrants' product portfolios about the determinants of entry timing. *Strategic Management Journal,* 29(12): 1257–1280.

117. Eisenhardt, K. M. & Martin, J. E. 2000. Dynamic capabilities: What are they? *Strategic Management Journal,* 21: 1105–1121.

chapter FIVE

Business-Level Strategy:

Creating and Sustaining Competitive Advantages

After reading this chapter, you should have a good understanding of:

LO5.1 The central role of competitive advantage in the study of strategic management, and the three generic strategies: overall cost leadership, differentiation, and focus.

LO5.2 How the successful attainment of generic strategies can improve a firm's relative power vis-à-vis the five forces that determine an industry's average profitability.

LO5.3 The pitfalls managers must avoid in striving to attain generic strategies.

LO5.4 How firms can effectively combine the generic strategies of overall cost leadership and differentiation.

LO5.5 What factors determine the sustainability of a firm's competitive advantage.

LO5.6 How Internet-enabled business models are being used to improve strategic positioning.

LO5.7 The importance of considering the industry life cycle to determine a firm's business-level strategy and its relative emphasis on functional area strategies and value-creating activities.

LO5.8 The need for turnaround strategies that enable a firm to reposition its competitive position in an industry.

LEARNING OBJECTIVES

How firms compete with each other and how they attain and sustain competitive advantages go to the heart of strategic management. In short, the key issue becomes: Why do some firms outperform others and enjoy such advantages over time? This subject, business-level strategy, is the focus of Chapter 5.

The first part of the chapter draws on Michael Porter's framework of generic strategies. He identifies three strategies—overall cost leadership, differentiation, and focus—that firms may apply to outperform their rivals in an industry. We begin by describing each of these strategies and providing examples of firms that have successfully attained them as a means of outperforming competitors in their industry. Next, we address how these strategies help a firm develop a favorable position vis-à-vis the "five forces," suggest some of the pitfalls that managers must avoid when pursuing these generic strategies, and discuss the conditions under which firms may effectively combine generic strategies to outperform rivals.

The second section discusses the factors that determine the sustainability of competitive advantages. Using an example from the manufacturing sector, we discuss whether or not a firm's competitive advantages may be sustained over a long period of time.

The third section addresses how competitive strategies should be revised and redeployed in light of the shifts in industry and competitive forces caused by Internet and digital strategies. Here, combination strategies are the most solid because they integrate the new capabilities with sound principles.

The fourth and final section discusses a vital consideration in the effective use of business-level strategies: industry life cycles. The four stages of the industry life cycle—introduction, growth, maturity, and decline—are indicative of an evolving management process that affects factors such as the market growth rate and the intensity of competition. Accordingly, the stages of an industry's life cycle are an important contingency that managers should take into account when making decisions concerning the optimal overall business-level strategies and the relative emphasis to place on functional capabilities and value-creating activities. At times, firms are faced with performance declines and must find ways to revitalize their competitive positions. The actions followed to do so are referred to as turnaround strategies, which may be needed at any stage of the industry life cycle. However, they occur more frequently during the maturity and decline stages.

Recently, a battle over strategy divided top management and franchise owners at KFC.[1] Many franchise owners became upset with KFC's new strategy that moved away from its Southern fried heritage and moved toward promoting grilled chicken and sandwiches. In early 2009, CEO Roger Eaton introduced grilled chicken in a move to target health-conscious consumers in today's changing society. However, many franchise owners were disappointed with this strategy. Why? What went wrong?

On January 2010, the KFC National Council and Advertising Cooperative (which represents all U.S. franchises) sued KFC to gain control of their own ad strategy. This "civil war" erupted when the company introduced grilled chicken with the slogan "Unthink KFC." To make matters worse, after a year in the market, reports stated that grilled chicken accounted for only about 16 percent of all "on the bone" chicken sold. Also, an internal survey of 642 franchisees showed almost 50 percent of the stores' grilled chicken was thrown away!

One glaring example of miscommunication regarding business strategy between management and franchise owners occurred when KFC launched a grilled chicken giveaway on *Oprah,* a wildly popular television program, in May 2009. Management told franchisees to expect a couple hundred customers to redeem online coupons at each store. However, thousands showed up expecting free grilled chicken. One franchise owner said, "The cost to the franchisee was much larger than they said," and that the promotion cost her almost $15,000! This started a continued downfall in trust between management and owners. KFC canceled the promotion, and CEO Eaton apologized to customers in an online video.

Disagreements between KFC management and franchise owners over strategy led to decreased sales and store closings. KFC's franchisees were upset with the decision to push grilled chicken and claimed that it hurts the brand. They sued KFC and now do a lot of their own advertising to promote fried chicken at their stores.

business-level strategy a strategy designed for a firm or a division of a firm that competes within a single business.

generic strategies an analysis of business strategy into basic types based on breadth of target market (industrywide versus narrow market segment) and type of competitive advantage (low cost versus uniqueness).

In order to create and sustain a competitive advantage, companies such as KFC should analyze the value chains of their customers and suppliers to see where they can add value. They should not focus only on their internal operations. By not listening to and consulting with franchise owners, KFC has ignored and angered a large part of their extended value chain. The battle over ad strategy within the company has hurt the brand and eroded KFC's competitive advantage.

Types of Competitive Advantage and Sustainability

>LO5.1

The central role of competitive advantage in the study of strategic management, and the three generic strategies: overall cost leadership, differentiation, and focus.

Michael Porter presented three generic strategies that a firm can use to overcome the five forces and achieve competitive advantage.[2] Each of Porter's generic strategies has the potential to allow a firm to outperform rivals in their industry. The first, *overall cost leadership,* is based on creating a low-cost-position. Here, a firm must manage the relationships throughout the value chain and lower costs throughout the entire chain. Second, *differentiation* requires a firm to create products and/or services that are unique and valued. Here, the primary emphasis is on "nonprice" attributes for which customers will gladly pay a premium.[3] Third, a *focus* strategy directs attention (or "focus") toward narrow product lines, buyer segments, or targeted geographic markets and they must attain advantages either through differentiation or cost leadership.[4] Whereas the overall cost leadership and differentiation strategies strive to attain advantages industrywide, focusers have a narrow target market in mind. Exhibit 5.1 illustrates these three strategies on two dimensions: competitive advantage and strategic target.

Exhibit 5.1 **Three Generic Strategies**

Source: Adapted and reprinted with the permission of The Free Press, a division of Simon & Schuster Inc. from *Competitive Strategy: Techniques for Analyzing Industries and Competitors* Michael E. Porter. Copyright © 1980, 1998 by The Free Press. All rights reserved.

Both casual observation and research support the notion that firms that identify with one or more of the forms of competitive advantage outperform those that do not.[5] There has been a rich history of strategic management research addressing this topic. One study analyzed 1,789 strategic business units and found that businesses combining multiple forms of competitive advantage (differentiation and overall cost leadership) outperformed businesses that used only a single form. The lowest performers were those that did not identify with any type of advantage. They were classified as "stuck in the middle." Results of this study are presented in Exhibit 5.2.[6]

For an example of the dangers of being "stuck in the middle," consider Coach and Tiffany—two brands in the "affordable luxury" category.[7] Such brands target middle-class customers for whom a $300 bag is a splurge. After sales and stock declines, they are migrating away from the middle—and going either higher or lower:

> In early 2008, Coach said that it would turn 40 of its nearly 300 stores into a more upscale format that will offer higher-end bags and concierge services. Tiffany, on the other hand, took

Exhibit 5.2 **Competitive Advantage and Business Performance**

Competitive Advantage					
Differentiation and Cost	Differentiation	Cost	Differentiation and Focus	Cost and Focus	Stuck in the Middle
Performance					
Return on investment (%) 35.5	32.9	30.2	17.0	23.7	17.8
Sales growth (%) 15.1	13.5	13.5	16.4	17.5	12.2
Gain in market share (%) 5.3	5.3	5.5	6.1	6.3	4.4
Sample size 123	160	100	141	86	105

the opposite tack. A new store opening in California will not sell any of its $148,000 diamond necklaces and instead focus on less expensive products like its $200-and-under silver jewelry. Claims Pat Conroy, head of Deloitte & Touche's consumer products sector: "Being in the middle is not a good place to be. You get assaulted from everyone."

overall cost leadership a firm's generic strategy based on appeal to the industrywide market using a competitive advantage based on low cost.

Overall Cost Leadership

The first generic strategy is overall cost leadership. Overall cost leadership requires a tight set of interrelated tactics that include:

- Aggressive construction of efficient-scale facilities.
- Vigorous pursuit of cost reductions from experience.
- Tight cost and overhead control.

Exhibit 5.3 Value-Chain Activities: Examples of Overall Cost Leadership

Support Activities
Firm Infrastructure
• Few management layers to reduce overhead costs.
• Standardized accounting practices to minimize personnel required.
Human Resource Management
• Minimize costs associated with employee turnover through effective policies.
• Effective orientation and training programs to maximize employee productivity.
Technology Development
• Effective use of automated technology to reduce scrappage rates.
• Expertise in process engineering to reduce manufacturing costs.
Procurement
• Effective policy guidelines to ensure low-cost raw materials (with acceptable quality levels).
• Shared purchasing operations with other business units.
Primary Activities
Inbound Logistics
• Effective layout of receiving dock operations.
Operations
• Effective use of quality control inspectors to minimize rework.
Outbound Logistics
• Effective utilization of delivery fleets
Marketing and Sales
• Purchase of media in large blocks.
• Sales force utilization is maximized by territory management.
Service
• Thorough service repair guidelines to minimize repeat maintenance calls.
• Use of single type of vehicle to minimize repair costs.

Source: Adapted from: Porter, M.E. 1985. *Competitive Advantage: Creating and Sustaining Superior Performance.* New York: Free Press.

strategy spotlight

The Experience Curve

The experience curve, developed by the Boston Consulting Group in 1968, is a way of looking at efficiencies developed through a firm's cumulative experience. In its basic form, the experience curve relates production costs to production output. As output doubles, costs decline by 10 percent to 30 percent. For example, if it costs $1 per unit to produce 100 units, the per unit cost will decline to between 70 to 90 cents as output increases to 200 units.

What factors account for this increased efficiency? First, the success of an experience curve strategy depends on the industry life cycle for the product. Early stages of a product's life cycle are typically characterized by rapid gains in technological advances in production efficiency. Most experience curve gains come early in the product life cycle.

Second, the inherent technology of the product offers opportunities for enhancement through gained experience. High-tech products give the best opportunity for gains in production efficiencies. As technology is developed, "value engineering" of innovative production processes is implemented, driving down the per unit costs of production.

Third, a product's sensitivity to price strongly affects a firm's ability to exploit the experience curve. Cutting the price of a product with high demand elasticity—where demand increases when price decreases—rapidly creates consumer purchases of the new product. By cutting prices, a firm can increase demand for its product. The increased demand in turn increases product manufacture, thus increasing the firm's experience in the manufacturing process. So by decreasing price and increasing demand, a firm gains manufacturing experience in that particular product, which drives down per unit production costs.

Fourth, the competitive landscape factors into whether or not a firm might benefit from an experience curve strategy. If other competitors are well positioned in the market,

Sources: Ghemawat, P. 1985. Building Strategy on the Experience Curve. *Harvard Business Review*, March–April: 143–149; Porter, M. E. 1996. *On Competition.* Boston: Harvard Business Review Press; and Oster, S. M. 1994. *Modern Competitive Analysis* (2nd ed.). New York: Oxford University Press.

have strong capital resources, and are known to promote their product lines aggressively to gain market share, an experience curve strategy may lead to nothing more than a price war between two or more strong competitors. But if a company is the first to market with the product and has good financial backing, an experience curve strategy may be successful.

In an article in the *Harvard Business Review,* Pankaj Ghemawat recommended answering several questions when considering an experience curve strategy.

- Does my industry exhibit a significant experience curve?
- Have I defined the industry broadly enough to take into account interrelated experience?
- What is the precise source of cost reduction?
- Can my company keep cost reductions proprietary?
- Is demand sufficiently stable to justify using the experience curve?
- Is cumulated output doubling fast enough for the experience curve to provide much strategic leverage?
- Do the returns from an experience curve strategy warrant the risks of technological obsolescence?
- Is demand price-sensitive?
- Are there well-financed competitors who are already following an experience curve strategy or are likely to adopt one if my company does?

Michael Porter suggested, however, that the experience curve is not useful in all situations. Whether or not to base strategy on the experience curve depends on what specifically causes the decline in costs. For example, if costs drop from efficient production facilities and not necessarily from experience, the experience curve is not helpful. But as Sharon Oster pointed out in her book on competitive analysis, the experience curve can help managers analyze costs when efficient learning, rather than efficient machinery, is the source of cost savings.

- Avoidance of marginal customer accounts.
- Cost minimization in all activities in the firm's value chain, such as R&D, service, sales force, and advertising.

Exhibit 5.3 draws on the value-chain concept (see Chapter 3) to provide examples of how a firm can attain an overall cost leadership strategy in its primary and support activities.

Key to an overall cost leadership strategy is the **experience curve,** which refers to how business "learns" to lower costs as it gains experience with production processes. With experience, unit costs of production decline as output increases in most industries. The experience curve concept is discussed in Strategy Spotlight 5.1 and Exhibit 5.4.

experience curve the decline in unit costs of production as cumulative output increases.

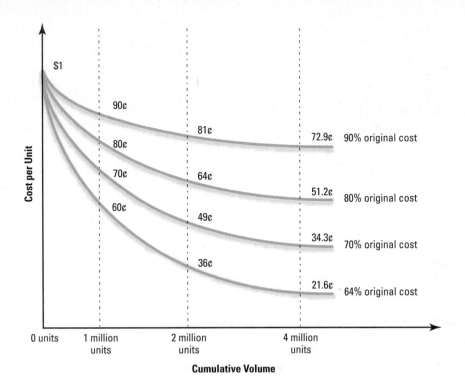

Exhibit 5.4 Comparing Experience Curve Effects

Cost per Unit

$1

90¢

80¢

81¢   72.9¢   90% original cost

70¢   64¢

60¢   51.2¢   80% original cost

49¢   34.3¢   70% original cost

36¢   21.6¢   64% original cost

0 units   1 million units   2 million units   4 million units

Cumulative Volume

---

competitive parity a firm's achievement of similarity, or being "on par," with competitors with respect to low cost, differentiation, or other strategic product characteristic.

To generate above-average performance, a firm following an overall cost leadership position must attain **competitive parity** on the basis of differentiation relative to competitors.[8] In other words, a firm achieving parity is similar to its competitors, or "on par," with respect to differentiated products.[9] Competitive parity on the basis of differentiation permits a cost leader to translate cost advantages directly into higher profits than competitors. Thus, the cost leader earns above-average returns.[10]

The failure to attain parity on the basis of differentiation can be illustrated with an example from the automobile industry—the ill-fated Yugo. Below is an excerpt from a speech by J. W. Marriott, Jr., Chairman of the Marriott Corporation:[11]

> . . . money is a big thing. But it's not the only thing. In the 1980s, a new automobile reached North America from behind the Iron Curtain. It was called the Yugo, and its main attraction was price. About $3,000 each. But the only way they caught on was as the butt of jokes. Remember the guy who told his mechanic, "I want a gas cap for my Yugo." "OK," the mechanic replied, "that sounds like a fair trade."

Yugo was offering a lousy value proposition. The cars literally fell apart before your eyes. And the lesson was simple. Price is just one component of value. No matter how good the price, the most cost-sensitive consumer won't buy a bad product.

Next, we discuss some examples of how firms enhance cost leadership position.

While other managed care providers were having a string of weak years, WellPoint, based in Thousand Oaks, California, has had a number of banner years and recently enjoyed an annual profit growth of over 42 percent to $4.8 billion over the past three years.[12] Chairman Leonard Schaeffer credits the company's focus on innovation for both expanding revenues and cutting costs. For example, WellPoint asked the Food and Drug Administration (FDA) to make the allergy drug Claritin available over the counter. Surprisingly, this may be the first time that an insurer has approached the FDA with such a request. Schaeffer claimed, "They were kind of stunned," but the FDA agreed to consider it. It was a smart move for WellPoint. If approved as an over-the-counter drug, Claritin would reduce patient

Ryanair: A Highly Effective Overall Cost Leadership Strategy

Michael O'Leary, CEO of Ryanair Holdings PLC, makes no apologies for his penny-pinching. Want to check luggage? You'll pay up to $9.50 per bag for the privilege. Expecting free drinks and snacks? You'll be disappointed. Even a bottle of water will cost you $3.40. And it is not just the passengers who are affected. Flight crews buy their own uniforms, and staff at Ryanair's Spartan Dublin Airport headquarters must supply their own pens. After a customer sued Ryanair for charging $34 for the use of a wheelchair, the company added a 63 cent "wheelchair levy" to every ticket!

Low-fare U.S. carriers have taken the opposite approach of Ryanair by adding perks such as leather seats, live television, and business class. "All of the low-cost carriers' costs have gotten a little out of control," says Tim Sieber, general manager of The Boyd Group, an Evergreen (Colorado) aviation consultant. Clearly Ryanair hasn't followed its industry peers.

Ryanair has been extremely successful. It recently became the first airline in Europe to carry more than 7 million passengers in one month. As of late 2010, the company had a market capitalization of $7.2 billion, dwarfing competitors easyJet ($2.3 billion) and Ireland's legacy airline, Aer Lingus ($612 million), but it is still a bit short of Southwest ($8.29 billion) and Delta ($8.22 billion). Over the past decade, at a time when the global airline industry collectively lost nearly $50 billion, Ryanair turned healthy net profits in 9 out of the 10 years—earning $431 million in the most recent year. In the process, O'Leary has become one of Ireland's wealthiest citizens—the value of his Ryanair shares is nearly $300 million.

What is O'Leary's secret? He thinks like a retailer and charges for every little thing. Imagine the seat as a cell

Sources: Gillete, F. 2010. The Duke of Discomfort. *Bloomberg, BusinessWeek* September 12: 58–61; Ryanair Annual Report, 2008; Capell, K. 2006. Walmart with Wings. *BusinessWeek.* November 27: 44–45; Kumar, N. 2006. Strategies to Fight Low-Cost Rivals. *Harvard Business Review,* 84(12): 104–113; and *Ryanair Annual Report,* 2006.

phone: It comes free, or nearly free, but its owner winds up spending money on all sorts of services.

However, what O'Leary loses in seat revenue he more than makes up by turning both his planes and the Ryanair website into stores brimming with irresistible goodies, even as he charges for such "perks" as priority boarding and assigned seating.

Sounds outrageous? Probably so, but the strategy is clearly working. Although its average fare is $53, compared with $92 for Southwest Airlines, Ryanair's net margins are, at 18 percent—more than double the 7 percent achieved by Southwest. Says Nick van den Brul, an aviation analyst: "Ryanair is Walmart with wings." As O'Leary says, "You want luxury? Go somewhere else."

A few other Ryanair practices include:

- Flight attendants sell digital cameras ($137.50) and iPocket MP3 players ($165).

- The seats don't recline, seat-back pockets have been removed to cut cleaning time and speed turnaround of the planes, there's no entertainment, and seat-back trays will soon carry ads.

- Ryanair sells more than 98 percent of its tickets online. Its website offers insurance, hotels, car rentals, and more—even online bingo.

O'Leary is certainly a colorful person, and he has some "creative" or downright nutty ideas. Recently, he came up with the idea of replacing the last 10 rows with a standing cabin, outfitted with handrails, much like a New York City subway car, only without the benches and panhandlers. The increased capacity, he claims, would lower fares by 20 percent to 25 percent. He says: "In no plane ever operated by Ryanair will it be all standing. You will always have the choice of paying for the seat. The argument against it is that if there's ever a crash, people will be injured. If there's ever a crash, the people in the sit-down seats will be injured, too."

---

visits to the doctor and eliminate the need for prescriptions—two reimbursable expenses for which WellPoint would otherwise be responsible.

Stephen Sanger, CEO of General Mills, recently came up with an idea that helped his firm cut costs.[13] To improve productivity, he sent technicians to watch pit crews during a NASCAR race. That experience inspired the techies to figure out how to reduce the time it takes to switch a plant line from five hours to 20 minutes. This provided an important lesson: Many interesting benchmarking examples can take place far outside of an industry. Often, process improvements involve identifying the best practices in other industries and adapting them for implementation in your own firm. After all, when firms benchmark competitors in their own industry, the end result is often copying and playing catch-up.[14]

A business that strives for a low-cost advantage must attain an absolute cost advantage relative to its rivals.[15] This is typically accomplished by offering a no-frills product or service to a broad target market using standardization to derive the greatest benefits from economies of scale and experience. However, such a strategy may fail if a firm is unable to attain parity on important dimensions of differentiation such as quick responses to customer requests for services or design changes. Strategy Spotlight 5.2 discusses Ryanair—a firm that has developed a very unique overall cost leadership strategy. One might say that it "one upped" Southwest Airlines!

>LO5.2

How the successful attainment of generic strategies can improve a firm's relative power vis-à-vis the five forces that determine an industry's average profitability.

Overall Cost Leadership: Improving Competitive Position vis-à-vis the Five Forces An overall low-cost position enables a firm to achieve above-average returns despite strong competition. It protects a firm against rivalry from competitors, because lower costs allow a firm to earn returns even if its competitors eroded their profits through intense rivalry. A low-cost position also protects firms against powerful buyers. Buyers can exert power to drive down prices only to the level of the next most efficient producer. Also, a low-cost position provides more flexibility to cope with demands from powerful suppliers for input cost increases. The factors that lead to a low-cost position also provide substantial entry barriers from economies of scale and cost advantages. Finally, a low-cost position puts the firm in a favorable position with respect to substitute products introduced by new and existing competitors.[16]

A few examples will illustrate these points. Ryanair's close attention to costs helps to protect them from buyer power and intense rivalry from competitors. Thus, they are able to drive down costs and enjoy relatively high power over their customers. By increasing productivity and lowering unit costs, General Mills (and its competitors in that industry) enjoy greater scale economies and erect higher entry barriers for others. Finally, as competitors such as WellPoint lower costs through means such as petitioning the FDA to make certain drugs available over the counter, they become less vulnerable to substitutes such as Internet-based competitors.

>LO5.3

The pitfalls managers must avoid in striving to attain generic strategies.

Potential Pitfalls of Overall Cost Leadership Strategies Potential pitfalls of overall cost leadership strategy include:

- *Too much focus on one or a few value-chain activities.* Would you consider a person to be astute if he cancelled his newspaper subscription and quit eating out to save money, but then "maxed out" several credit cards, requiring him to pay hundreds of dollars a month in interest charges? Of course not. Similarly, firms need to pay attention to all activities in the value chain.[17] Too often managers make big cuts in operating expenses, but don't question year-to-year spending on capital projects. Or managers may decide to cut selling and marketing expenses but ignore manufacturing expenses. Managers should explore *all* value-chain activities, including relationships among them, as candidates for cost reductions.

- *All rivals share a common input or raw material.* Here, firms are vulnerable to price increases in the factors of production. Since they're competing on costs, they are less able to pass on price increases, because customers can take their business to rivals who have lower prices. For example, consider manufacturing firms based in China which rely on a common input—low labor costs. Due to demographic factors, the supply of workers 16 to 24 years old has peaked and will drop by a third in the next 12 years, thanks to stringent family-planning policies that have sharply reduced China's population growth.[18] In one city, many factories are operating with vacancies of 15 to 20 percent, compelling some supervisors to cruise the streets in a desperate hiring quest during crunch times. Needless to say, there are strong demands for better working conditions and higher wages.

- *The strategy is imitated too easily.* One of the common pitfalls of a cost-leadership strategy is that a firm's strategy may consist of value-creating activities that are easy to imitate.[19] Such was the case with online brokers in recent years.[20] As of early 2001, there were about 140 online brokers, hardly symbolic of an industry where imitation is extremely difficult. But according to Henry McVey, financial services analyst at Morgan Stanley, "We think you need five to ten" online brokers.

What are some of the dynamics? First, although online brokers were geared up to handle 1.2 million trades a day, volume had shrunk to about 834,000—a 30 percent drop. Thus, competition for business intensified. Second, when the stock market is down, many investors trust their instincts less and seek professional guidance from brokerages that offer differentiated services. Eric Rajendra of A. T. Kearney, an international consulting company, claimed, "The current (online broker) model is inadequate for the pressures the industry is facing now."

- *A lack of parity on differentiation.* As noted earlier, firms striving to attain cost leadership advantages must obtain a level of parity on differentiation.[21] Firms providing online degree programs may offer low prices. However, they may not be successful unless they can offer instruction that is perceived as comparable to traditional providers. For them, parity can be achieved on differentiation dimensions such as reputation and quality and through signaling mechanisms such as accreditation agencies.

- *Erosion of cost advantages when the pricing information available to customers increases.* This is becoming a more significant challenge as the Internet dramatically increases both the quantity and volume of information available to consumers about pricing and cost structures. Life insurance firms offering whole life insurance provide an interesting example.[22] One study found that for each 10 percent increase in consumer use of the Internet, there is a corresponding reduction in insurance prices to consumers of 3 to 5 percent. Recently, the nationwide savings (or, alternatively, reduced revenues to providers) was between $115 and $125 million annually.

Differentiation

As the name implies, a **differentiation strategy** consists of creating differences in the firm's product or service offering by creating something that is perceived *industrywide* as unique and valued by customers.[23] Differentiation can take many forms:

- Prestige or brand image (Adam's Mark hotels, BMW automobiles).[24]
- Technology (Martin guitars, Marantz stereo components, North Face camping equipment).
- Innovation (Medtronic medical equipment, Apple's iPods).
- Features (Cannondale mountain bikes, Honda Goldwing motorcycles).
- Customer service (Nordstrom department stores, Sears lawn equipment retailing).
- Dealer network (Lexus automobiles, Caterpillar earthmoving equipment).

differentiation strategy a firm's generic strategy based on creating differences in the firm's product or service offering by creating something that is perceived *industrywide* as unique and valued by customers.

● Caterpillar is well known for its outstanding dealer network.

Exhibit 5.5
Value-Chain Activities: Examples of Differentiation

Support Activities

Firm Infrastructure

- Superior MIS—To integrate value-creating activities to improve quality.
- Facilities that promote firm image.
- Widely respected CEO enhances firm reputation.

Human Resource Management

- Programs to attract talented engineers and scientists.
- Provide training and incentives to ensure a strong customer service orientation.

Technology Development

- Superior material handling and sorting technology.
- Excellent applications engineering support.

Procurement

- Purchase of high-quality components to enhance product image.
- Use of most prestigious outlets.

Primary Activities

Inbound Logistics

- Superior material handling operations to minimize damage.
- Quick transfer of inputs to manufacturing process.

Operations

- Flexibility and speed in responding to changes in manufacturing specifications.
- Low defect rates to improve quality.

Outbound Logistics

- Accurate and responsive order processing.
- Effective product replenishment to reduce customer inventory.

Marketing and Sales

- Creative and innovative advertising programs.
- Fostering of personal relationship with key customers.

Service

- Rapid response to customer service requests.
- Complete inventory of replacement parts and supplies.

Source: Adapted from Porter, M.E. 1985. *Competitive Advantage: Creating and Sustaining Superior Performance.* New York: Free Press.

Exhibit 5.5 draws on the concept of the value chain as an example of how firms may differentiate themselves in primary and support activities.

Firms may differentiate themselves along several different dimensions at once.[25] For example, BMW is known for its high prestige, superior engineering, and high-quality automobiles. And Harley-Davidson differentiates on image and dealer services.[26]

Firms achieve and sustain differentiation advantages and attain above-average performance when their price premiums exceed the extra costs incurred in being unique.[27]

For example, both BMW and Harley-Davidson must increase consumer costs to offset added marketing expenses. Thus, a differentiator will always seek out ways of distinguishing itself from similar competitors to justify price premiums greater than the costs incurred by differentiating.[28] Clearly, a differentiator cannot ignore costs. After all, its premium prices would be eroded by a markedly inferior cost position. Therefore, it must attain a level of cost *parity* relative to competitors. Differentiators can do this by reducing costs in all areas that do not affect differentiation. Porsche, for example, invests heavily in engine design—an area in which its customers demand excellence—but it is less concerned and spends fewer resources in the design of the instrument panel or the arrangement of switches on the radio.[29]

Many companies successfully follow a differentiation strategy.[30] For example, FedEx's CEO and founder, Fred Smith, claims that the key to his firm's success is innovation.[31] He contends his management team didn't understand their real goal when they started the firm in 1971: "We thought that we were selling the transportation of goods; in fact, we were selling peace of mind." They now provide drivers with a handheld computer and a transmitting device so that customers can track their packages from their desktop PCs.

Lexus, a division of Toyota, provides an example of how a firm can strengthen its differentiation strategy by *achieving integration at multiple points along the value chain.*[32] Although the luxury car line was not introduced until the late 1980s, by the early 1990s the cars had already soared to the top of J. D. Power & Associates' customer satisfaction ratings.

> In the spirit of benchmarking, one of Lexus's competitors hired Custom Research Inc. (CRI), a marketing research firm, to find out why Lexus owners were so satisfied. CRI conducted a series of focus groups in which Lexus drivers eagerly offered anecdotes about the special care they experienced from their dealers. It became clear that, although Lexus was manufacturing cars with few mechanical defects, it was the extra care shown by the sales and service staff that resulted in satisfied customers. Such pampering is reflected in the feedback from one customer who claimed she never had a problem with her Lexus. However, upon further probing, she said, "Well, I suppose you could call the four times they had to replace the windshield a 'problem.' But frankly, they took care of it so well and always gave me a loaner car, so I never really considered it a problem until you mentioned it now." An insight gained in CRI's research is that perceptions of product quality (design, engineering, and manufacturing) can be strongly influenced by downstream activities in the value chain (marketing and sales, service).

Strategy Spotlight 5.3 addresses how Netflix, the successful Internet movie rental company, uses crowdsourcing to enhance its differentiation.

Differentiation: Improving Competitive Position vis-à-vis the Five Forces Differentiation provides protection against rivalry since brand loyalty lowers customer sensitivity to price and raises customer switching costs.[33] By increasing a firm's margins, differentiation also avoids the need for a low-cost position. Higher entry barriers result because of customer loyalty and the firm's ability to provide uniqueness in its products or services.[34] Differentiation also provides higher margins that enable a firm to deal with supplier power. And it reduces buyer power, because buyers lack comparable alternatives and are therefore less price sensitive.[35] Supplier power is also decreased because there is a certain amount of prestige associated with being the supplier to a producer of highly differentiated products and services. Last, differentiation enhances customer loyalty, thus reducing the threat from substitutes.[36]

Our examples illustrate these points. Lexus has enjoyed enhanced power over buyers because its top J. D. Power ranking makes buyers more willing to pay a premium price. This lessens rivalry, since buyers become less price-sensitive. The prestige associated with its brand name also lowers supplier power since margins are high. Suppliers would probably desire to be associated with prestige brands, thus lessening their incentives to drive up prices. Finally, the loyalty and "peace of mind" associated with a service provider such as FedEx makes such firms less vulnerable to rivalry or substitute products and services.

Crowdsourcing: How Netflix Boosts Its Differentiation

Netflix is well-known for its inviting online presentation and efficient distribution system. However, this highly successful movie-rental company prides itself on its capability to offer subscribers a compact list of films that they are likely to enjoy watching. And it must be working: Netflix sends 35,000 titles a day to its 7.5 million subscribers.

"Imagine that our website was a brick-and-mortar store," says Netflix vice president, James Bennett. "When people walk through the door, they see DVDs rearrange themselves. The movies that might interest them fly onto the shelves, and all the rest go to the back room."

The movies, of course, don't do the rearranging—that is done by the customers themselves, with an assist from a computer program called Cinematch, which Netflix developed in 2000. Customers are invited to rate each film they watch on a 1 to 5 scale. Cinematch analyzes these ratings, searches through 80,000 titles in inventory, and determines the list of films tailored to the taste of each of the firm's subscribers. By enticing them to rate films, Netflix achieves the latest in business innovation—getting customers to serve themselves.

Netflix is not unique in their use of so-called recommenders. Consider other online retailers such as Amazon, Apple, eBay, and Overstock. All of these rely on their customers for a helping hand in predicting what products the customers will prefer—whether the product is bedding, books, CDs, or DVDs. Customer ratings are used to rank corporate service providers as well.

For all these companies, the recommender system provides more than a chance to create an extra service. It helps them to establish a stronger connection with their customers. And studies have shown that it can substantially increase online sales.

Sources: Copeland, M.V. 2009. Tapping Tech's Beautiful Minds. *Fortune* October 12: 35–36; Libert, B. & Spector, J. 2008. *We Are Smarter Than Me*. Philadelphia: Wharton Publishing; and Howe, J. 2008. *Crowdsourcing*. New York: Crown Business.

The extent of Netflix's commitment to personalized movie recommendations was made clear in 2006 when it offered a $1 million prize to anyone who could build a system that was at least 10 percent better than Cinematch. In late 2009, it awarded the prize to a seven-person team of computer scientists, mathematicians, and statisticians who were from New Jersey, Israel, Quebec, and Austria. They built a system that was 20 percent better than Cinematch.

● Netflix generated a lot of favorable publicity with its $1 million prize competition.

Netflix has also developed another crowdsourcing feature called Friends. Here, subscribers see each other's list of films watched and compare the ratings they have awarded the films—in exchange for suggestions on other films to watch.

crowdsourcing

Potential Pitfalls of Differentiation Strategies   Potential pitfalls of a differentiation strategy include:

- *Uniqueness that is not valuable.* A differentiation strategy must provide unique bundles of products and/or services that customers value highly. It's not enough just to be "different." An example is Gibson's Dobro bass guitar. Gibson came up with a unique idea: Design and build an acoustic bass guitar with sufficient sound volume so that amplification wasn't necessary. The problem with other acoustic bass guitars was that they did not project enough volume because of the low-frequency bass notes. By adding a resonator plate on the body of the traditional acoustic bass, Gibson increased the sound volume. Gibson believed this product would serve a particular niche market—bluegrass and folk artists who played in small group "jams" with other acoustic musicians. Unfortunately, Gibson soon discovered that its targeted market was content with their existing options: an upright bass amplified with a microphone or an acoustic electric guitar. Thus, Gibson developed a unique product, but it was not perceived as valuable by its potential customers.[37]

- **Too much differentiation.** Firms may strive for quality or service that is higher than customers desire.[38] Thus, they become vulnerable to competitors who provide an appropriate level of quality at a lower price. For example, consider the expensive Mercedes-Benz S-Class, which ranges in price between $93,650 and $138,000 for the 2011 models.[39] *Consumer Reports* described it as "sumptuous," "quiet and luxurious," and a "delight to drive." The magazine also considered it to be the least reliable sedan available in the United States. According to David Champion, who runs their testing program, the problems are electronic. "The engineers have gone a little wild," he says. "They've put every bell and whistle that they think of, and sometimes they don't have the attention to detail to make these systems work." Some features include: a computer-driven suspension that reduces body roll as the vehicle whips around a corner; cruise control that automatically slows the car down if it gets too close to another car; and seats that are adjustable 14 ways and that are ventilated by a system that uses eight fans.

- **Too high a price premium.** This pitfall is quite similar to too much differentiation. Customers may desire the product, but they are repelled by the price premium. For example, Duracell (a division of Gillette) recently charged too much for batteries.[40] The firm tried to sell consumers on its superior quality products, but the mass market wasn't convinced. Why? The price differential was simply too high. At a CVS drugstore just one block from Gillette's headquarters, a four-pack of Energizer AA batteries was on sale at $2.99 compared with a Duracell four-pack at $4.59. Duracell's market share dropped 2 percent in a recent two-year period, and its profits declined over 30 percent. Clearly, the price/performance proposition Duracell offered customers was not accepted.

- **Differentiation that is easily imitated.** As we noted in Chapter 3, resources that are easily imitated cannot lead to sustainable advantages. Similarly, firms may strive for, and even attain, a differentiation strategy that is successful for a time. However, the advantages are eroded through imitation. Consider Cereality's innovative differentiation strategy of stores which offer a wide variety of cereals and toppings for around $4.00.[41] As one would expect, once their idea proved successful, competitors entered the market because much of the initial risk had already been taken. Rivals include an Iowa City restaurant named the Cereal Cabinet, the Cereal Bowl in Miami, and Bowls: A Cereal Joint in Gainesville, Florida. Says David Roth, one of Cereality's founders: "With any good business idea, you're faced with people who see you've cracked the code and who try to cash in on it."

- **Dilution of brand identification through product-line extensions.** Firms may erode their quality brand image by adding products or services with lower prices and less quality. Although this can increase short-term revenues, it may be detrimental in the long run. Consider Gucci.[42] In the 1980s Gucci wanted to capitalize on its prestigious brand name by launching an aggressive strategy of revenue growth. It added a set of lower-priced canvas goods to its product line. It also pushed goods heavily into department stores and duty-free channels and allowed its name to appear on a host of licensed items such as watches, eyeglasses, and perfumes. In the short term, this strategy worked. Sales soared. However, the strategy carried a high price. Gucci's

Overall Cost Leadership:

- Too much focus on one or a few value-chain activities.
- All rivals share a common input or raw material.
- The strategy is imitated too easily.
- A lack of parity on differentiation.
- Erosion of cost advantages when the pricing information available to customers increases.

Differentiation:

- Uniqueness that is not valuable.
- Too much differentiation.
- The price premium is too high.
- Differentiation that is easily imitated.
- Dilution of brand identification through product-line extensions.
- Perceptions of differentiation may vary between buyers and sellers.

indiscriminate approach to expanding its products and channels tarnished its sterling brand. Sales of its high-end goods (with higher profit margins) fell, causing profits to decline.

- ***Perceptions of differentiation may vary between buyers and sellers.*** The issue here is that "beauty is in the eye of the beholder." Companies must realize that although they may perceive their products and services as differentiated, their customers may view them as commodities. Indeed, in today's marketplace, many products and services have been reduced to commodities.[43] Thus, a firm could overprice its offerings and lose margins altogether if it has to lower prices to reflect market realities.

Exhibit 5.6 summarizes the pitfalls of overall cost leadership and differentiation strategies. In addressing the pitfalls associated with these two generic strategies there is one common, underlying theme. Managers must be aware of the dangers associated with concentrating so much on one strategy that they fail to attain parity on the other.

Focus

focus strategy a firm's generic strategy based on appeal to a narrow market segment within an industry.

A **focus strategy** is based on the choice of a narrow competitive scope within an industry. A firm following this strategy selects a segment or group of segments and tailors its strategy to serve them. The essence of focus is the exploitation of a particular market niche. As you might expect, narrow focus itself (like merely "being different" as a differentiator) is simply not sufficient for above-average performance.

The focus strategy, as indicated in Exhibit 5.1, has two variants. In a cost focus, a firm strives to create a cost advantage in its target segment. In a differentiation focus, a firm seeks to differentiate in its target market. Both variants of the focus strategy rely on providing better service than broad-based competitors who are trying to serve the focuser's target segment. Cost focus exploits differences in cost behavior in some segments, while differentiation focus exploits the special needs of buyers in other segments.

Let's look at examples of two firms that have successfully implemented focus strategies. Network Appliance (NA) has developed a more cost-effective way to store and distribute computer files.[44] Its larger rival, EMC, makes mainframe-style products priced over $1 million that store files and accommodate Internet traffic. NA makes devices that cost under $200,000 for particular storage jobs such as caching (temporary storage) of Internet

If You Can't Afford an Extremely Expensive Car . . . You Can Rent One

If we assume that indulgence is best experienced in moderation, it should come as no surprise that the business of renting expensive sheet metal is soaring. Ken Kerzner, managing partner of Midway Car Rental in Los Angeles, has been renting high-end cars to business travelers, wealthy tourists, and movie moguls for 41 years.

He is having one of his best years. He claims that today's recession-weary customers are looking to try

Source: Callaway, S. 2010. Hot Rides for Rent. *Fortune.* September 6: 24.

new things while avoiding the headaches and overhead of ownerships. His 2,000-vehicle fleet offers just about everything. It ranges from the Smart car ($89 a day) to the Ferrari California and Lamborghini Gallardo at $2,850 and $2,999 a day, respectively. Don't want to spring for these two super-high-end cars? You can get a Porsche Targa 4S for *only* $1,499 a day.

Kerzner does have some serious competition. Beverly Hills Rent-a-Car, with locations in Los Angeles and Las Vegas, offers an even wider range. Interested in renting the $1.7 million Bugatti Veyron with an astonishing 1,001 horse power? You can find it here.

content. Focusing on such narrow segments has certainly paid off for NA; it has posted a remarkable 20 straight quarters of revenue growth.

Paccar, an $8 billion Bellevue, Washington–based heavy-truck manufacturer, has chosen a differentiation focus strategy.[45] The firm targets one group of customers: owner-operators. These are the drivers who own their trucks and contract directly with shippers or serve as subcontractors to larger trucking companies.

Paccar has invested heavily to develop a variety of features with owner-operators in mind: luxurious sleeper cabins, plush leather seats, noise-insulated cabins, sleek exterior styling, and so forth. At Paccar's extensive network of dealers, prospective buyers use software to select among thousands of options to put their personal signature on their trucks. These customized trucks are built to order, not to stock, and are delivered in eight weeks. Not surprisingly, customers are happy to pay Paccar a 10 percent premium, and its Kenworth and Peterbilt brands are considered status symbols at truck stops.

Strategy Spotlight 5.4 illustrates that you can pay as much as you want for some products or services. Case in point: car rentals.

Focus: Improving Competitive Position vis-à-vis the Five Forces   Focus requires that a firm either have a low-cost position with its strategic target, high differentiation, or both. As we discussed with regard to cost and differentiation strategies, these positions provide defenses against each competitive force. Focus is also used to select niches that are least vulnerable to substitutes or where competitors are weakest.

Let's look at our examples to illustrate some of these points. First, Paccar experienced lower rivalry and greater bargaining power by providing products and services to a targeted market segment that was less price-sensitive. New rivals have difficulty attracting customers away from Paccar based only on lower prices. Similarly, the brand image and quality that this brand evoked heightened rivals' entry barriers. With regard to the strategy of cost focus, Network Appliances, the successful rival to EMC in the computer storage industry, was better able to absorb pricing increases from suppliers as a result of its lower cost structure, reducing supplier power.

Potential Pitfalls of Focus Strategies   Potential pitfalls of focus strategies include:

- ***Erosion of cost advantages within the narrow segment.*** The advantages of a cost focus strategy may be fleeting if the cost advantages are eroded over time. For example, Dell's pioneering direct selling model in the personal computer industry has been eroded by rivals such as Hewlett Packard as they gain experience with Dell's distribution method. Similarly, other firms have seen their profit margins drop as competitors enter their product segment.

- *Even product and service offerings that are highly focused are subject to competition from new entrants and from imitation.* Some firms adopting a focus strategy may enjoy temporary advantages because they select a small niche with few rivals. However, their advantages may be short-lived. A notable example is the multitude of dot-com firms that specialize in very narrow segments such as pet supplies, ethnic foods, and vintage automobile accessories. The entry barriers tend to be low, there is little buyer loyalty, and competition becomes intense. And since the marketing strategies and technologies employed by most rivals are largely nonproprietary, imitation is easy. Over time, revenues fall, profits margins are squeezed, and only the strongest players survive the shakeout.

- *Focusers can become too focused to satisfy buyer needs.* Some firms attempting to attain advantages through a focus strategy may have too narrow a product or service. Consider many retail firms. Hardware chains such as Ace and True Value are losing market share to rivals such as Lowe's and Home Depot that offer a full line of home and garden equipment and accessories. And given the enormous purchasing power of the national chains, it would be difficult for such specialty retailers to attain parity on costs.

>LO5.4
How firms can effectively combine the generic strategies of overall cost leadership and differentiation.

Combination Strategies: Integrating Overall Low Cost and Differentiation

Perhaps the primary benefit to firms that integrate low-cost and differentiation strategies is the difficulty for rivals to duplicate or imitate.[45] This strategy enables a firm to provide two types of value to customers: differentiated attributes (e.g., high quality, brand identification, reputation) and lower prices (because of the firm's lower costs in value-creating activities). The goal is thus to provide unique value to customers in an efficient manner.[46] Some firms are able to attain both types of advantages simultaneously.[47] For example, superior quality can lead to lower costs because of less need for rework in manufacturing, fewer warranty claims, a reduced need for customer service personnel to resolve customer complaints, and so forth. Thus, the benefits of combining advantages can be additive, instead of merely involving trade-offs. Next, we consider three approaches to combining overall low cost and differentiation.

combination strategies firms' integrations of various strategies to provide multiple types of value to customers.

Automated and Flexible Manufacturing Systems Given the advances in manufacturing technologies such as CAD/CAM (computer aided design and computer aided manufacturing) as well as information technologies, many firms have been able to manufacture unique products in relatively small quantities at lower costs—a concept known as **mass customization.**[48]

mass customization a firm's ability to manufacture unique products in small quantities at low cost.

Let's consider Andersen Windows of Bayport, Minnesota—a $3 billion manufacturer of windows for the building industry.[49] Until about 20 years ago, Andersen was a mass producer, in small batches, of a variety of standard windows. However, to meet changing customer needs, Andersen kept adding to its product line. The result was catalogs of ever-increasing size and a bewildering set of choices for both homeowners and contractors. Over a 6-year period, the number of products tripled, price quotes took several hours, and the error rate increased. This not only damaged the company's reputation, but also added to its manufacturing expenses.

To bring about a major change, Andersen developed an interactive computer version of its paper catalogs that it sold to distributors and retailers. Salespersons can now customize each window to meet the customer's needs, check the design for structural soundness, and provide a price quote. The system is virtually error free, customers get exactly what

Exhibit 5.7 Effective Uses of Flexible Production Systems

- At Nikeid.com, customers can design an athletic or casual shoe to their specifications online, selecting almost every element of the shoe from the material of the sole to the color of the shoelace.

- Eleuria sells custom perfumes. Each product is created in response to a user profile constructed from responses to a survey about habits and preferences. Eleuria then provides a sample at modest cost to verify fit.

- Lands' End offers customized shirts and pants. Consumers specify style parameters, measurements, and fabrics through the firm's website. These settings are saved so that returning users can easily order a duplicate item.

- Cannondale permits consumers to specify the parameters that define a road bike frame, including custom colors and inscriptions. The user specifies the parameters on the firm's website and then arranges for delivery through a dealer.

Source: Randall, T., Terwiesch, C. & Ulrich, K. T. 2005. Principles for User Design of Custom Products. *California Management Review,* 47(4): 68–85.

they want, and the time to develop the design and furnish a quotation has been cut by 75 percent. Each showroom computer is connected to the factory, and customers are assigned a code number that permits them to track the order. The manufacturing system has been developed to use some common finished parts, but it also allows considerable variation in the final products. Despite its huge investment, Andersen has been able to lower costs, enhance quality and variety, and improve its response time to customers.

Exhibit 5.7 provides other examples of how flexible production systems have enabled firms to successfully engage in mass customization for their customers:[50]

Exploiting the Profit Pool Concept for Competitive Advantage   A profit pool is defined as the total profits in an industry at all points along the industry's value chain.[51] Although the concept is relatively straightforward, the structure of the profit pool can be complex.[52] The potential pool of profits will be deeper in some segments of the value chain than in others, and the depths will vary within an individual segment. Segment profitability may vary widely by customer group, product category, geographic market, or distribution channel. Additionally, the pattern of profit concentration in an industry is very often different from the pattern of revenue generation.

> **profit pool** the total profits in an industry at all points along the industry's value chain.

Consider the automobile industry profit pool in Exhibit 5.8. Here we see little relationship between the generation of revenues and capturing of profits. While manufacturing generates most of the revenue, this value activity is far smaller profitwise than other value activities such as financing and extended warranty operations. So while a car manufacturer may be under tremendous pressure to produce cars efficiently, much of the profit (at least proportionately) can be captured in the aforementioned downstream operations. Thus, a carmaker would be ill-advised to focus solely on manufacturing and leave downstream operations to others through outsourcing.

Coordinating the "Extended" Value Chain by Way of Information Technology
Many firms have achieved success by integrating activities throughout the "extended value chain" by using information technology to link their own value chain with the value chains of their customers and suppliers. As noted in Chapter 3, this approach enables a firm to add value not only through its own value-creating activities, but also for its customers and suppliers.

Such a strategy often necessitates redefining the industry's value chain. A number of years ago, Walmart took a close look at its industry's value chain and decided to

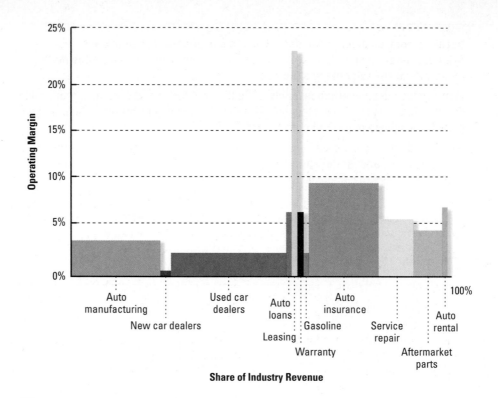

Operating Margin

25%

20%

15%

10%

5%

0%

Auto
manufacturing

New car dealers

Used car
dealers

Auto
loans

Leasing

Warranty

Gasoline

Auto
insurance

Service
repair

Aftermarket
parts

Auto
rental

100%

Share of Industry Revenue

Exhibit 5.8 The U.S. Automobile Industry's Profit Pool

Source: Reprinted by permission of *Harvard Business Review,* Exhibit from "Profit Pools: A Fresh
Look at Strategy," by O. Gadiesh and J. L. Gilbert, May–June 1999. Copyright © 1999 by the Harvard
Business School Publishing Corporation; all rights reserved.

reframe the competitive challenge.[53] Although its competitors were primarily focused on
retailing—merchandising and promotion—Walmart determined that it was not so much
in the retailing industry as in the transportation logistics and communications industries.
Here, linkages in the extended value chain became central. That became Walmart's chosen
battleground. By redefining the rules of competition that played to its strengths, Walmart
has attained competitive advantages and dominates its industry.

**Integrated Overall Low-Cost and Differentiation Strategies: Improving Com-
petitive Position vis-à-vis the Five Forces**   Firms that successfully integrate both differentiation and cost advantages create an enviable position. For example, Walmart's integration
of information systems, logistics, and transportation helps it to drive down costs and provide outstanding product selection. This dominant competitive position, serves to erect high
entry barriers to potential competitors that have neither the financial nor physical resources to
compete head-to-head. Walmart's size—over $400 billion in 2011 sales—provides the chain
with enormous bargaining power over suppliers. Its low pricing and wide selection reduce
the power of buyers (its customers), because there are relatively few competitors that can
provide a comparable cost/value proposition. This reduces the possibility of intense head-to-
head rivalry, such as protracted price wars. Finally, Walmart's overall value proposition makes
potential substitute products (e.g., Internet competitors) a less viable threat.

**Pitfalls of Integrated Overall Cost Leadership and Differentiation Strate-
gies**   The pitfalls of integrated overall cost leadership and differentiation include:

• *Firms that fail to attain both strategies may end up with neither and become "stuck
in the middle."* A key issue in strategic management is the creation of competitive

advantages that enable a firm to enjoy above-average returns. Some firms may become "stuck in the middle" if they try to attain both cost and differentiation advantages. An example that we are all familiar with would be the Big 3 U.S. automobile makers. They have been plagued by expensive "legacy costs" associated with pension and health care obligations—a central issue in 2008 federal bailout legislation. And they suffer from long-term customer perceptions of mediocre quality—inferior to their European and Japanese rivals. The troubling quality perceptions persist despite the fact that the Big 3 has attained approximate parity with their Japanese and European competitors in recent J. D. Power surveys.

- ***Underestimating the challenges and expenses associated with coordinating value-creating activities in the extended value chain.*** Integrating activities across a firm's value chain with the value chain of suppliers and customers involves a significant investment in financial and human resources. Firms must consider the expenses linked to technology investment, managerial time and commitment, and the involvement and investment required by the firm's customers and suppliers. The firm must be confident that it can generate a sufficient scale of operations and revenues to justify all associated expenses.

- ***Miscalculating sources of revenue and profit pools in the firm's industry.*** Firms may fail to accurately assess sources of revenue and profits in their value chain. This can occur for several reasons. For example, a manager may be biased due to his or her functional area background, work experiences, and educational background. If the manager's background is in engineering, he or she might perceive that proportionately greater revenue and margins were being created in manufacturing, product, and process design than a person whose background is in a "downstream" value-chain activity such as marketing and sales. Or politics could make managers "fudge" the numbers to favor their area of operations. This would make them responsible for a greater proportion of the firm's profits, thus improving their bargaining position.

A related problem is directing an overwhelming amount of managerial time, attention, and resources to value-creating activities that produce the greatest margins—to the detriment of other important, albeit less profitable, activities. For example, a car manufacturer may focus too much on downstream activities, such as warranty fulfillment and financing operations, to the detriment of differentiation and cost of the cars themselves.

Can Competitive Strategies Be Sustained? Integrating and Applying Strategic Management Concepts

>LO5.5
What factors determine the sustainability of a firm's competitive advantage.

Thus far this chapter has addressed how firms can attain competitive advantages in the marketplace. We discussed the three generic strategies—overall cost leadership, differentiation, and focus—as well as combination strategies. Next we discussed the importance of linking value-chain activities (both those within the firm and those linkages between the firm's suppliers and customers) to attain such advantages. We also showed how successful competitive strategies enable firms to strengthen their position vis-à-vis the five forces of industry competition as well as how to avoid the pitfalls associated with the strategies.

Competitive advantages are, however, often short-lived. As we discussed in the beginning of Chapter 1, the composition of the firms that constitute the Fortune 500 list has experienced significant turnover in its membership over the years—reflecting the temporary nature of competitive advantages. And recall Dell's fall from grace (Chapter 3). Here was a firm whose advantages in the marketplace seemed unassailable in the early 2000s. In fact, it was *Fortune*'s "Most Admired Firm" in 2005. However, cracks began to appear in 2007, and its competitive position has recently been severely eroded by rivals such as Hewlett-Packard. In short, Dell focused so much on operational efficiency and perfecting its "direct model" that it failed to deliver innovations that an increasingly sophisticated market demanded. Also, Dell continues to face further pricing pressures as a result of the commoditization of the personal computer industry.[54]

Clearly, "nothing is forever" when it comes to competitive advantages. Rapid changes in technology, globalization, and actions by rivals from within—as well as outside—the industry can quickly erode a firm's advantages. It is becoming increasingly important to recognize that the duration of competitive advantages is declining, especially in technology intensive industries.[55] Even in industries which are normally viewed as "low tech," the increasing use of technology has suddenly made competitive advantages less sustainable.[56] Amazon's success in book retailing at the cost of Barnes & Noble, the former industry leader, as well as Blockbuster's struggle against Netflix in the video rental industry serve to illustrate how difficult it has become for industry leaders to sustain competitive advantages that they once thought would last forever.

In this section, we will discuss some factors that help determine whether a strategy is sustainable over a long period of time. We will draw on some strategic management concepts from the first five chapters. To illustrate our points, we will look at a company, Atlas Door, which created an innovative strategy in its industry and enjoyed superior performance for several years. Our discussion of Atlas Door draws on a *Harvard Business Review* article by George Stalk, Jr.[57]. It was published some time ago (1988), which provides us the benefit of hindsight to make our points about the sustainability of competitive advantage. After all, the strategic management concepts we have been addressing in the text are quite timeless in their relevance to practice. A brief summary follows:

Atlas Door: A Case Example

Atlas Door, a U.S.-based company, has enjoyed remarkable success. It has grown at an average annual rate of 15 percent in an industry with an overall annual growth rate of less than 5 percent. Recently, its pre-tax earnings were 20 percent of sales—about five times the industry average. Atlas is debt free and by its 10th year, the company achieved the number one competitive position in its industry.

Atlas produces industrial doors—a product with almost infinite variety, involving limitless choices of width and height and material. Given the importance of product variety, inventory is almost useless in meeting customer orders. Instead, most doors can be manufactured only after the order has been placed.

How Did Atlas Door Create Its Competitive Advantages in the Marketplace? *First,* Atlas built just-in-time factories. Although simple in concept, they require extra tooling and machinery to reduce changeover times. Further, the manufacturing process must be organized by product and scheduled to start and complete with all of the parts available at the same time.

Second, Atlas reduced the time to receive and process an order. Traditionally, when customers, distributors, or salespeople called a door manufacturer with a request for price and delivery, they would have to wait more than one week for a response. In contrast, Atlas first streamlined and then automated its entire order-entry, engineering, pricing, and scheduling process. Atlas can price and schedule 95 percent of its incoming orders while the callers are still on the telephone. It can quickly engineer new special orders because it has preserved on computer the design and production data of all previous special orders—which drastically reduces the amount of reengineering necessary.

Third, Atlas tightly controlled logistics so that it always shipped only fully complete orders to construction sites. Orders require many components, and gathering all of them at the factory and making sure that they are with the correct order can be a time-consuming task. Of course, it is even more time-consuming to get the correct parts to the job site after the order has been shipped! Atlas developed a system to track the parts in production and the purchased parts for each order. This helped to ensure the arrival of all necessary parts at the shipping dock in time—a just-in-time logistics operation.

The Result?   When Atlas began operations, distributors had little interest in its product. The established distributors already carried the door line of a much larger competitor and saw little to no reason to switch suppliers except, perhaps, for a major price concession. But as a startup, Atlas was too small to compete on price alone. Instead, it positioned itself as the door supplier of last resort—the company people came to if the established supplier could not deliver or missed a key date.

Of course, with an average industry order fulfillment time of almost four months, some calls inevitably came to Atlas. And when it did get the call, Atlas commanded a higher price because of its faster delivery. Atlas not only got a higher price, but its effective integration of value-creating activities saved time and lowered costs. Thus, it enjoyed the best of both worlds.

In 10 short years, the company replaced the leading door suppliers in 80 percent of the distributors in the United States. With its strategic advantage, the company could be selective—becoming the supplier for only the strongest distributors.

Are Atlas Door's Competitive Advantages Sustainable?

We will now take both the "pro" and "con" position as to whether or not Atlas Door's competitive advantages will be sustainable for a very long time. It is important, of course, to assume that Atlas Door's strategy is unique in the industry, and the central issue becomes whether or not rivals will be able to easily imitate their strategy or create a viable substitute strategy.

"Pro" Position: The Strategy Is Highly Sustainable   Drawing on Chapter 2, it is quite evident that Atlas Door has attained a very favorable position vis-á-vis the five forces of industry competition. For example, it is able to exert power over its customers (distributors) because of its ability to deliver a quality product in a short period of time. Also, its dominance in the industry creates high entry barriers for new entrants. It is also quite evident that Atlas Door has been able to successfully integrate many value-chain activities within the firm—a fact that is integral to its just-in-time strategy. As noted in Chapter 3, such integration of activities provides a strong basis for sustainability, because rivals would have difficulty in imitating this strategy due to causal ambiguity and path dependency (i.e., it is difficult to build up in a short period of time the resources that Atlas Door has accumulated and developed as well as disentangle the causes of what the valuable resources are or how they can be re-created). Further, as noted in Chapter 4, Atlas Door benefits from the social capital that they have developed with a wide range of key stakeholders (Chapter 1) These would include customers, employees, and managers (a reasonable assumption, given how smoothly the internal operations flow and their long-term relationships with distributors). It would be very difficult for a rival to replace Atlas Door as the supplier of last resort—given the reputation that it has earned over time for "coming through in the clutch" on time-sensitive orders. Finally, we can conclude that Atlas Door has created competitive advantages in both overall low cost and differentiation (Chapter 5). Its strong linkages among value-chain activities—a requirement for its just-in-time operations—not only lowers costs but enables the company to respond quickly to customer orders. As noted in Exhibit 5.5 (page 170), many of the value-chain activities associated with a differentiation strategy reflect the element of speed or quick response.

"Con" Position: The Strategy Can Be Easily Imitated or Substituted   An argument could be made that much of Atlas Door's strategy relies on technologies that are rather well known and nonproprietary. Over time, a well-financed rival could imitate its strategy (via trial and error), achieve a tight integration among its value-creating activities, and implement a just-in-time manufacturing process. Because human capital is highly mobile (Chapter 4), a rival could hire away Atlas Door's talent, and these individuals could aid the rival in transferring Atlas Door's best practices. A new rival could also enter the industry with a large resource base, which might enable it to price its doors well under Atlas Door to build market share (but this would likely involve pricing below cost and would be a risky and nonsustainable strategy). Finally, a rival could potentially "leapfrog" the technologies and processes that Atlas Door has employed and achieve competitive superiority. With the benefit of hindsight, it could use the Internet to further speed up the linkages among its value-creating activities and the order entry processes with its customers and suppliers. (But even this could prove to be a temporary advantage, since rivals could relatively easily do the same thing.)

What Is the Verdict?   Both positions have merit. Over time, it would be rather easy to see how a new rival could achieve parity with Atlas Door—or even create a superior competitive position with new technologies or innovative processes. However, two factors make it extremely difficult for a rival to challenge Atlas Door in the short term: (1) the success that Atlas Door has enjoyed with its just-in-time scheduling and production systems—which involve the successful integration of many value-creating activities—helps the firm not only lower costs but also respond quickly to customer needs, and (2) the strong, positive reputational effects that it has earned with multiple stakeholders—especially its customers.

Finally, it is important to also understand that it is Atlas Door's ability to appropriate most of the profits generated by its competitive advantages that make it a highly successful company. As we discussed in Chapter 3, profits generated by resources can be appropriated by a number of stakeholders such as suppliers, customers, employees, or rivals. The structure of the industrial door industry makes such value appropriation difficult: the suppliers provide generic parts, no one buyer is big enough to dictate prices, the tacit nature of the knowledge makes imitation difficult, and individual employees may be easily replaceable. Still, even with the advantages that Atlas Door enjoys, they need to avoid becoming complacent or suffer the same fate as the dominant firm they replaced.

>LO5.6
How Internet-enabled business models are being used to improve strategic positioning.

How the Internet and Digital Technologies Affect the Competitive Strategies

Internet and digital technologies have swept across the economy and now have an impact on how nearly every company conducts its business. These changes have created new cost efficiencies and avenues for differentiation. However, the presence of these technologies is so widespread that it is questionable how any one firm can use them effectively in ways that genuinely set them apart from rivals. Thus, to stay competitive, firms must update their strategies to reflect the new possibilities and constraints that these phenomena represent. In this section, we address both the opportunities and the pitfalls that Internet and digital technologies offer to companies using overall cost leadership, differentiation, and focus strategies. We also briefly consider two major impacts that the Internet is having on business: lowering transaction costs and enabling mass customization.

digital technologies
information that is in numerical form, which facilitates its storage, transmission, analysis and manipulation.

Overall Cost Leadership

The Internet and digital technologies create new opportunities for firms to achieve low-cost advantages by enabling them to manage costs and achieve greater efficiencies. Managing costs, and even changing the cost structures of certain industries, is a key feature of the digital economy. Most analysts agree that the Internet's ability to lower transaction costs has transformed business. Broadly speaking, *transaction costs* refer to all the various expenses associated with conducting business. It applies not just to buy/sell transactions

Exhibit 5.9 Internet-Enabled Low-Cost Leader Strategies

- Online bidding and order processing eliminate the need for sales calls and minimize sales-force expenses.

- Online purchase orders have made many transactions paperless, thus reducing the costs of procurement and paper.

- Direct access to progress reports and the ability of customers to periodically check work in progress minimize rework.

- Collaborative design efforts using Internet technologies that link designers, materials suppliers, and manufacturers reduce the costs and speed the process of new product development.

but to the costs of interacting with every part of a firm's value chain, within and outside the firm. Think about it. Hiring new employees, meeting with customers, ordering supplies, addressing government regulations—all of these exchanges have some costs associated with them. Because business can be conducted differently on the Internet, new ways of saving money are changing the competitive landscape.

Other factors also help to lower transaction costs. The process of disintermediation (in Chapter 2) has a similar effect. Each time intermediaries are used in a transaction, additional costs are added. Removing intermediaries lowers transaction costs. The Internet reduces the costs to search for a product or service, whether it is a retail outlet (as in the case of consumers) or a trade show (as in the case of business-to-business shoppers). Not only is the need for travel eliminated but so is the need to maintain a physical address, whether it's a permanent retail location or a temporary presence at a trade show.

disintermediation the process of bypassing buyer channel intermediaries such as wholesalers, distributors, and retailers.

Exhibit 5.9 identifies several types of cost leadership strategies that are made possible by Internet and digital technologies. These cost savings are available throughout a firm's value chain, in both primary and support activities.

Potential Internet-Related Pitfalls for Low-Cost Leaders One of the biggest threats to low-cost leaders is imitation. This problem is intensified for business done on the Internet. Most of the advantages associated with contacting customers directly, and even capabilities that are software driven (e.g., customized ordering systems or real-time access to the status of work in progress), can be duplicated quickly and without threat of infringement on proprietary information. Another pitfall relates to companies that become overly enamored with using the Internet for cost-cutting and thus jeopardize customer relations or neglect other cost centers.

Differentiation

For many companies, Internet and digital technologies have enhanced their ability to build brand, offer quality products and services, and achieve other differentiation advantages.[58] Among the most striking trends are new ways to interact with consumers. In particular, the Internet has created new ways of differentiating by enabling *mass customization,* which improves the response to customer wishes.

Mass customization has changed how companies go to market and has challenged some of the tried-and-true techniques of differentiation. Traditionally, companies reached customers using high-end catalogs, the showroom floor, personal sales calls and products using prestige packaging, celebrity endorsements, and charity sponsorships. All of these avenues are still available and may still be effective, depending on a firm's competitive environment. But many customers now judge the quality and uniqueness of a product or service by their ability to be involved in its planning and design, combined with speed of delivery and reliable results. Internet and digitally based capabilities are thus changing the

Exhibit 5.10 Internet-
Enabled Differentiation
Strategies

- Personalized online access provides customers with their own "site within a site" in which their prior orders, status of current orders, and requests for future orders are processed directly on the supplier's website.
- Online access to real-time sales and service information is being used to empower the sales force and continually update R&D and technology development efforts.
- Internet-based knowledge management systems that link all parts of the organization are shortening response times and accelerating organization learning.
- Quick online responses to service requests and rapid feedback to customer surveys and product promotions are enhancing marketing efforts.

way differentiators make exceptional products and achieve superior service. Such improvements are being made at a reasonable cost, allowing firms to achieve parity on the basis of overall cost leadership.

Exhibit 5.10 identifies differentiation activities that are made possible by Internet and digital technologies. Opportunities to differentiate are available in all parts of a company's value chain—both primary and support activities.

Potential Internet-Related Pitfalls for Differentiators   Traditional differentiation strategies such as building strong brand identity and prestige pricing have been undermined by Internet-enabled capabilities such as the ability to compare product features side-by-side or bid online for competing services. The sustainability of Internet-based gains from differentiation will deteriorate if companies offer differentiating features that customers don't want or create a sense of uniqueness that customers don't value. The result can be a failed value proposition—the value companies thought they were offering, does not translate into sales.

Focus

A focus strategy targets a narrow market segment with customized products and/or services. With focus strategies, the Internet offers new avenues in which to compete because they can access markets less expensively (low cost) and provide more services and features (differentiation). Some claim that the Internet has opened up a new world of opportunities for niche players who seek to access small markets in a highly specialized fashion.[59] Niche businesses are among the most active users of digital technologies and e-business solutions. According to the ClickZ.com division of Jupitermedia Corporation, 77 percent of small businesses agree that a website is essential for small business success. Small businesses also report that the Internet has helped them grow (58 percent), made them more profitable (51 percent), and helped reduce transaction costs (49 percent).[60] Clearly niche players and small businesses are using the Internet and digital technologies to create more viable focus strategies.

Many aspects of the Internet economy favor focus strategies because niche players and small firms have been able to extend their reach and effectively compete with larger competitors. For example, niche firms have been quicker than Fortune 1000 firms to adopt blogging as a way to create a community and gather customer feedback.[61] Effective use of blogs is an example of how focusers are using the new technology to provide the kinds of advantages that have been the hallmark of a focus strategy in the past—specialized knowledge, rapid response, and strong customer service. Thus, the Internet has provided many firms that pursue focus strategies with new tools for creating competitive advantages.

Exhibit 5.11 Internet-
Enabled Focus Strategies

- Permission marketing techniques are focusing sales efforts on specific customers who opt to receive advertising notices.

- Niche portals that target specific groups are providing advertisers with access to viewers with specialized interests.

- Virtual organizing and online "officing" are being used to minimize firm infrastructure requirements.

- Procurement technologies that use Internet software to match buyers and sellers are highlighting specialized buyers and drawing attention to smaller suppliers.

Exhibit 5.11 outlines several approaches to strategic focusing that are made possible by Internet and digital technologies. Both primary and support activities can be enhanced using the kind of singlemindedness that is characteristic of a focus strategy.

Potential Internet-Related Pitfalls for Focusers A key danger for focusers using the Internet relates to correctly assessing the size of the online marketplace. Focusers can misread the scope and interests of their target markets. This can cause them to focus on segments that are too narrow to be profitable or to lose their uniqueness in overly broad niches, making them vulnerable to imitators or new entrants.

What happens when an e-business focuser tries to overextend its niche? Efforts to appeal to a broader audience by carrying additional inventory, developing additional content, or offering additional services can cause it to lose the cost advantages associated with a limited product or service offering. Conversely, when focus strategies become too narrow, the e-business may have trouble generating enough activity to justify the expense of operating the website.

Are Combination Strategies the Key to E-Business Success?

Because of the changing dynamics presented by digital and Internet-based technologies, new strategic combinations that make the best use of the competitive strategies may hold the greatest promise.[62] Many experts agree that the net effect of the digital economy is *fewer* rather than more opportunities for sustainable advantages.[63] This means strategic thinking becomes more important.

More specifically, the Internet has provided all companies with greater tools for managing costs. So it may be that cost management and control will become more important management tools. In general, this may be good if it leads to an economy that makes more efficient use of its scarce resources. However, for individual companies, it may shave critical percentage points off profit margins and create a climate that makes it impossible to survive, much less achieve sustainable above-average profits.

Many differentiation advantages are also diminished by the Internet. The ability to comparison shop—to check product reviews and inspect different choices with a few clicks of the mouse—is depriving some companies, such as auto dealers, of the unique advantages that were the hallmark of their prior success. Differentiating is still an important strategy, of course. But how firms achieve it may change, and the best approach may be to combine differentiation with other competitive strategies.

Perhaps the greatest beneficiaries are the focusers who can use the Internet to capture a niche that previously may have been inaccessible. However, because the same factors that make it possible for a small niche player to be a contender may make that same niche attractive to a big company. That is, an incumbent firm that previously thought a niche

Liberty Mutual's Electronic Invoice System: Combining Low Cost and Differentiation Advantages

Boston-based Liberty Mutual Group is a leading global insurer and the sixth largest property and casualty insurer in the United States. Its largest line of business is personal automobile insurance. Liberty Mutual has $112.2 billion in assets and $33 billion in annual revenues—ranking the firm 71st on the Fortune 500 list of the largest corporations.

In 2000, Liberty Mutual became one of the first companies to experiment with electronic invoices. It set up a pilot program with a few law firms to submit its bills through a secured website. These firms, for the most part, handle claims litigation for Liberty, defending its policyholders in lawsuits. Its success with this program convinced Liberty that it could achieve significant cost savings and also pass along differentiating features to its customers and strategic partners. Liberty now processes nearly 400,000 electronic legal-services invoices a year—70 percent of the total invoices that the firm receives.

As expected, the initial transition was quite expensive. The company invested nearly $1 million in the first four years. However, Liberty estimates that the electronic invoice program saves the company $750,000 a year in direct costs by streamlining the distribution, payment, storage, and retrieval of invoices. E-invoices enable Liberty to move from intake to payment with half the staff that it had taken to process paper invoices. The firm has also created new efficiencies by cutting costs resulting from data entry errors, late payments, and overpayments. As a relatively minor issue, Liberty saves more than $20,000 per year on postage, photocopying, archiving, and retrieval costs.

The legal invoices are organized by litigation phase or task—for example, taking a deposition or reporting a witness statement. Work is diced into tiny increments of

six minutes or less. A single invoice that covers a month of complex litigation, for example, can include well over 1,000 lines. However, by building and mining a database of law firm billing practices, Liberty is able to generate a highly granular report card about law firm activities and performance. The new knowledge generated by this system not only increases internal effectiveness but also allows Liberty to provide detailed feedback to clients and other external stakeholders.

Online invoicing has also helped speed up both processing and response time. Liberty can instantaneously see how firms deploy and bill for partners, paralegals, and other staff, how they compare with each other on rates, hours, and case outcomes; and whether, how, and how often they send duplicate invoices or charge for inappropriate services. The system also allows Liberty to instantly review all of the time billed for a particular attorney across many cases, enabling the firm to reconstruct the total time billed to Liberty during a single day. More than once they have found that attorneys have billed more than 24 hours in a day. Liberty is also able to easily expose prohibited formula billing patterns (wherein, for example, they are billed a set amount for a service instead of actual time spent). In two cases in which formula billing was used, Liberty found that there were more than $28,000 in suspected overcharges.

Liberty Mutual is in the process of developing a large database of law firms' billing practices on different types of cases. The database should eventually enable Liberty to evaluate a law firm's billing activities and compare them to the norms of all of its partner firms. With such intelligence, it will be a rather straightforward matter to rate each firm's cost effectiveness in handling certain types of cases and match firms with cases accordingly.

Liberty's decision to use electronic invoices was initially based on the potential for cost savings. But the differentiating advantages it has achieved in terms of rapid feedback, decreased response time, and a knowledge trove in databases that can be electronically mined has provided the company with a fruitful combination of Internet-based strategic advantages.

Sources: Coyle, M., & Angevine, R. 2007. Liberty Mutual Group reports fourth quarter 2006 results. February 26, *www.libertymutual.com*; Smunt, T. L., & Sutcliffe, C. L., 2004. There's Gold in Them Bills. *Harvard Business Review,* 82(9): 24–25; and *www.libertymutualgroup.com*.

market was not worth the effort may use Internet technologies to enter that segment for a lower cost than in the past. The larger firm can then bring its market power and resources to bear in a way that a smaller competitor cannot match.

A combination strategy challenges a company to carefully blend alternative strategic approaches and remain mindful of the impact of different decisions on the firm's value-creating processes and its extended value-chain activities. Strong leadership is needed to maintain a bird's-eye perspective on a company's overall approach and to coordinate the multiple dimensions of a combination strategy.

Strategy Spotlight 5.5 describes the efforts of Liberty Mutual, a company that used Internet and digital technologies to successfully combine both differentiation and overall low-cost advantages.

Industry Life Cycle Stages: Strategic Implications

The **industry life cycle** refers to the stages of introduction, growth, maturity, and decline that occur over the life of an industry. In considering the industry life cycle, it is useful to think in terms of broad product lines such as personal computers, photocopiers, or long-distance telephone service. Yet the industry life cycle concept can be explored from several levels, from the life cycle of an entire industry to the life cycle of a single variation or model of a specific product or service.

Why are industry life cycles important?[64] The emphasis on various generic strategies, functional areas, value-creating activities, and overall objectives varies over the course of an industry life cycle. Managers must become even more aware of their firm's strengths and weaknesses in many areas to attain competitive advantages. For example, firms depend on their research and development (R&D) activities in the introductory stage. R&D is the source of new products and features that everyone hopes will appeal to customers. Firms develop products and services to stimulate consumer demand. Later, during the maturity phase, the functions of the product have been defined, more competitors have entered the market, and competition is intense. Managers then place greater emphasis on production efficiencies and process (as opposed to the product) engineering in order to lower manufacturing costs. This helps to protect the firm's market position and to extend the product life cycle because the firm's lower costs can be passed on to consumers in the form of lower prices, and price-sensitive customers will find the product more appealing.

Exhibit 5.12 illustrates the four stages of the industry life cycle and how factors such as generic strategies, market growth rate, intensity of competition, and overall objectives change over time. Managers must strive to emphasize the key functional areas during each of the four stages and to attain a level of parity in all functional areas and value-creating activities. For example, although controlling production costs may be a primary concern during the maturity stage, managers should not totally ignore other functions such as marketing and R&D. If they do, they can become so focused on lowering costs that they miss market trends or fail to incorporate important product or process designs. Thus, the firm may attain low-cost products that have limited market appeal.

It is important to point out a caveat. While the life cycle idea is analogous to a living organism (i.e., birth, growth, maturity, and death), the comparison has limitations.[65] Products and services go through many cycles of innovation and renewal. Typically, only fad products have a single life cycle. Maturity stages of an industry can be "transformed" or followed by a stage of rapid growth if consumer tastes change, technological innovations take place, or new developments occur. The cereal industry is a good example. When medical research indicated that oat consumption reduced a person's cholesterol, sales of Quaker Oats increased dramatically.[66]

Strategies in the Introduction Stage

In the **introduction stage,** products are unfamiliar to consumers.[67] Market segments are not well defined, and product features are not clearly specified. The early development of an industry typically involves low sales growth, rapid technological change, operating losses, and the need for strong sources of cash to finance operations. Since there are few players and not much growth, competition tends to be limited.

---

industry life cycle
the stages of introduction, growth, maturity, and decline that typically occur over the life of an industry.

>LO5.7
The importance of considering the industry life cycle to determine a firm's business-level strategy and its relative emphasis on functional area strategies and value-creating activities.

introduction stage
the first stage of the industry life cycle, characterized by (1) new products that are not known to customers, (2) poorly defined market segments, (3) unspecified product features, (4) low sales growth, (5) rapid technological change, (6) operating losses, and (7) a need for financial support.

Exhibit 5.12 Stages of the Industry Life Cycle

Stage Factor	Introduction	Growth	Maturity	Decline
Generic strategies	Differentiation	Differentiation	Differentiation Overall cost leadership	Overall cost leadership Focus
Market growth rate	Low	Very large	Low to moderate	Negative
Number of segments	Very few	Some	Many	Few
Intensity of competition	Low	Increasing	Very intense	Changing
Emphasis on product design	Very high	High	Low to moderate	Low
Emphasis on process design	Low	Low to moderate	High	Low
Major functional area(s) of concern	Research and development	Sales and marketing	Production	General management and finance
Overall objective	Increase market awareness	Create consumer demand	Defend market share and extend product life cycles	Consolidate, maintain, harvest, or exit

Success requires an emphasis on research and development and marketing activities to enhance awareness. The challenge becomes one of (1) developing the product and finding a way to get users to try it, and (2) generating enough exposure so the product emerges as the "standard" by which all other rivals' products are evaluated.

There's an advantage to being the "first mover" in a market.[68] It led to Coca-Cola's success in becoming the first soft-drink company to build a recognizable global brand and enabled Caterpillar to get a lock on overseas sales channels and service capabilities.

However, there can also be a benefit to being a "late mover." Target carefully considered its decision to delay its Internet strategy. Compared to its competitors Walmart and Kmart, Target was definitely an industry laggard. But things certainly turned out well:[69]

By waiting, Target gained a late mover advantage. The store was able to use competitors' mistakes as its own learning curve. This saved money, and customers didn't seem to mind the wait: When Target finally opened its website, it quickly captured market share from both Kmart and Walmart Internet shoppers. Forrester Research Internet analyst Stephen Zrike commented, "There's no question, in our mind, that Target has a far better understanding of how consumers buy online."

Examples of products currently in the introductory stages of the industry life cycle include electric vehicles, solar panels, and high-definition television (HDTV).

Strategies in the Growth Stage

The **growth stage** is characterized by strong increases in sales. Such potential attracts other rivals. In the growth stage, the primary key to success is to build consumer preferences for specific brands. This requires strong brand recognition, differentiated products, and the financial resources to support a variety of value-chain activities such as marketing and sales, and research and development. Whereas marketing and sales initiatives were mainly directed at spurring *aggregate* demand—that is, demand for all such products in the introduction stage—efforts in the growth stage are directed toward stimulating *selective* demand, in which a firm's product offerings are chosen instead of a rival's.

Revenues increase at an accelerating rate because (1) new consumers are trying the product and (2) a growing proportion of satisfied consumers are making repeat purchases.[70] In general, as a product moves through its life cycle, the proportion of repeat buyers to new purchasers increases. Conversely, new products and services often fail if there are relatively few repeat purchases. For example, Alberto-Culver introduced Mr. Culver's Sparklers, which were solid air fresheners that looked like stained glass. Although the product quickly went from the introductory to the growth stage, sales collapsed. Why? Unfortunately, there were few repeat purchasers because buyers treated them as inexpensive window decorations, left them there, and felt little need to purchase new ones. Examples of products currently in the growth stage include Internet servers and personal digital assistants (e.g., Palm Pilots).

> **growth stage** the second stage of the product life cycle, characterized by (1) strong increases in sales; (2) growing competition; (3) developing brand recognition; and (4) a need for financing complementary value-chain activities such as marketing, sales, customer service, and research and development.

Strategies in the Maturity Stage

In the **maturity stage** aggregate industry demand softens. As markets become saturated, there are few new adopters. It's no longer possible to "grow around" the competition, so direct competition becomes predominant.[71] With few attractive prospects, marginal competitors exit the market. At the same time, rivalry among existing rivals intensifies because of fierce price competition at the same time that expenses associated with attracting new buyers are rising. Advantages based on efficient manufacturing operations and process engineering become more important for keeping costs low as customers become more price sensitive. It also becomes more difficult for firms to differentiate their offerings, because users have a greater understanding of products and services.

An article in *Fortune* magazine that addressed the intensity of rivalry in mature markets was aptly titled "A Game of Inches." It stated, "Battling for market share in a slowing industry can be a mighty dirty business. Just ask laundry soap archrivals Unilever and Procter & Gamble."[72] These two firms have been locked in a battle for market share since 1965. Why is the competition so intense? There is not much territory to gain and industry sales were flat. An analyst noted, "People aren't getting any dirtier." Thus, the only way to win is to take market share from the competition. To increase its share, Procter & Gamble (P&G) spends $100 million a year promoting its Tide brand on television, billboards, buses, magazines, and the Internet. But Unilever isn't standing still. Armed with an $80 million budget, it launched a soap tablet product named Wisk Dual Action Tablets. For example, it delivered samples of this product to 24 million U.S. homes in Sunday

> **maturity stage** the third stage of the product life cycle, characterized by (1) slowing demand growth, (2) saturated markets, (3) direct competition, (4) price competition, and (5) strategic emphasis on efficient operations.

Reverse and Breakaway Positioning: How to Avoid Being Held Hostage to the Life-Cycle Curve

When firms adopt a reverse or breakaway positioning strategy, there is typically no pretense about what they are trying to accomplish. In essence, they subvert convention through unconventional promotions, prices, and attributes. That becomes a large part of their appeal—a cleverly positioned product offering. Next we discuss Commerce Bank's reverse positioning and Swatch's breakaway positioning.

Commerce Bank

While most banks offer dozens of checking and savings accounts and compete by trying to offer the highest interest rates, Commerce Bank takes a totally different approach. It pays among the lowest rates in its market. Further, it offers a very limited product line—just four checking accounts, for example. One would think that such a stingy approach would seem to scare off customers. However, Commerce Bank has been very successful. Between 1999 and 2005, it expanded from 120 to 373 branches and its total assets have soared from $5.6 billion to $39 billion.

How has it been so successful? It has stripped away all of what customers expect—lots of choices and peak interest rates and it has *reverse positioned* itself as "the most convenient bank in America." It's open seven days a week, including evenings until 8 p.m. You can get a debit card while you wait. And, when it rains, an escort with an umbrella will escort you to your car. Further, the bank offers free coffee, newspapers, and most of the branches

have free coin-counting machines that customers love (in one recent week, customers fed the machines a total of $28 million in loose change). Not too surprisingly, despite the inferior rates and few choices, new customers are flocking to the bank.

Swatch

Interestingly, the name "Swatch" is often misconstrued as a contraction of the words *Swiss watch.* However, Nicholas Hayek, Chairman, affirms that the original contraction was "Second Watch"—the new watch was introduced as a new concept of watches as casual, fun, and relatively disposable accessories. And therein lies Swatch's *breakaway positioning.*

When Swatch was launched in 1983, Swiss watches were marketed as a form of jewelry. They were serious, expensive, enduring, and discreetly promoted. Once a customer purchased one, it lasted a lifetime. Swatch changed all of that by defining its watches as playful fashion accessories which were showily promoted. They inspired impulse buying—customers would often purchase half a dozen in different designs. Their price—$40 when the brand was introduced—expanded Swatch's reach beyond its default category (watches as high-end jewelry) and moved it into the fashion accessory category, where it has different customers and competitors. Swatch was the official timekeeper of the 1996, 2000, and 2004 Summer Olympics.

Today, The Swatch Group is the largest watch company in the world. It has acquired many brands over the years including Omega, Longines, Calvin Klein, and Hamilton. Revenues have grown to $5.5 billion in 2009 and net income has increased to $753 million. These figures represent compound annual increases of 11 percent and 12 percent, respectively, over a four-year period.

Sources: Moon, Y. 2005. Break Free from the Product Life Cycle. *Harvard Business Review,* 83(5): 87–94; Commerce Bancorp, Inc. *www.hoovers.com*; Swatch. *en.wikipedia.org*; and *www.commercebank.com*.

reverse positioning a break in industry tendency to continuously augment products, characteristic of the product life cycle, by offering products with fewer product attributes and lower prices.

newspapers, followed by a series of TV ads. P&G launched a counteroffensive with Tide Rapid Action Tablets ads showed in side-by-side comparisons of the two products dropped into beakers of water. In the promotion, P&G claimed that its product is superior because it dissolves faster than Unilever's product.

Although this is only one example, many product classes and industries, including consumer products such as beer, automobiles, and televisions, are in maturity.

Firms do not need to be "held hostage" to the life-cycle curve. By positioning or repositioning their products in unexpected ways, firms can change how customers mentally categorize them. Thus, firms are able to rescue products floundering in the maturity phase of their life cycles and return them to the growth phase.

Two positioning strategies that managers can use to affect consumers' mental shifts are **reverse positioning,** which strips away "sacred" product attributes while adding new ones, and **breakaway positioning,** which associates the product with a radically different category.[73] We discuss each of these positioning strategies below and then provide an example of each in Strategy Spotlight 5.6.

Reverse Positioning   This assumes that although customers may desire more than the baseline product, they don't necessarily want an endless list of features. Such companies make the creative decision to step off the augmentation treadmill and shed product attributes that the rest of the industry considers sacred. Then, once a product is returned to its baseline state, the stripped-down product adds one or more carefully selected attributes that would usually be found only in a highly augmented product. Such an unconventional combination of attributes allows the product to assume a new competitive position within the category and move backward from maturity into a growth position on the life-cycle curve.

Breakaway Positioning   As noted above, with reverse positioning, a product establishes a unique position in its category but retains a clear category membership. However, with breakaway positioning, a product escapes its category by deliberately associating with a different one. Thus, managers leverage the new category's conventions to change both how products are consumed and with whom they compete. Instead of merely seeing the breakaway product as simply an alternative to others in its category, consumers perceive it as altogether different.

When a breakaway product is successful in leaving its category and joining a new one, it is able to redefine its competition. Similar to reverse positioning, this strategy permits the product to shift backward on the life-cycle curve, moving from the rather dismal maturity phase to a thriving growth opportunity.

Strategy Spotlight 5.6 provides examples of reverse and breakaway positioning.

Strategies in the Decline Stage

Although all decisions in the phases of an industry life cycle are important, they become particularly difficult in the **decline stage.** Firms must face up to the fundamental strategic choices of either exiting or staying and attempting to consolidate their position in the industry.[74]

The decline stage occurs when industry sales and profits begin to fall. Typically, changes in the business environment are at the root of an industry or product group entering this stage.[75] Changes in consumer tastes or a technological innovation can push a product into decline. Typewriters have entered into the decline stage because of the word processing capabilities of personal computers. Compact disks have forced cassette tapes into decline in the prerecorded music industry, and digital video disks (DVDs) are replacing compact disks. About 30 years earlier, of course, cassette tapes had led to the demise of long-playing records (LPs).

Products in the decline stage often consume a large share of management time and financial resources relative to their potential worth. Sales and profits decline. Also, competitors may start drastically cutting their prices to raise cash and remain solvent. The situation is further aggravated by the liquidation of assets, including inventory, of some of the competitors that have failed. This further intensifies price competition.

In the decline stage, a firm's strategic options become dependent on the actions of rivals. If many competitors leave the market, sales and profit opportunities increase. On the other hand, prospects are limited if all competitors remain.[76] If some competitors merge, their increased market power may erode the opportunities for the remaining players. Managers must carefully monitor the actions and intentions of competitors before deciding on a course of action.

Four basic strategies are available in the decline phase: *maintaining, harvesting, exiting,* or *consolidating.*[77]

breakaway positioning a break in industry tendency to incrementally improve products along specific dimensions, characteristic of the product life cycle, by offering products that are still in the industry but that are perceived by customers as being different.

decline stage the fourth stage of the product life cycle, characterized by (1) falling sales and profits, (2) increasing price competition, and (3) industry consolidation.

- **Maintaining** refers to keeping a product going without significantly reducing marketing support, technological development, or other investments, in the hope that competitors will eventually exit the market. Many offices, for example, still use typewriters for filling out forms and other purposes that cannot be completed on a PC. In some rural areas, rotary (or dial) telephones persist because of the older technology used in central switching offices. Thus, there may still be the potential for revenues and profits.

harvesting strategy a strategy of wringing as much profit as possible out of a business in the short to medium term by reducing costs.

- **Harvesting** involves obtaining as much profit as possible and requires that costs be reduced quickly. Managers should consider the firm's value-creating activities and cut associated budgets. Value-chain activities to consider are primary (e.g., operations, sales and marketing) and support (e.g., procurement, technology development). The objective is to wring out as much profit as possible.

- **Exiting the market** involves dropping the product from a firm's portfolio. Since a residual core of consumers exist, eliminating it should be carefully considered. If the firm's exit involves product markets that affect important relationships with other product markets in the corporation's overall portfolio, an exit could have repercussions for the whole corporation. For example, it may involve the loss of valuable brand names or human capital with a broad variety of expertise in many value-creating activities such as marketing, technology, and operations.

consolidation strategy a firm's acquiring or merging with other firms in an industry in order to enhance market power and gain valuable assets.

- **Consolidation** involves one firm acquiring at a reasonable price the best of the surviving firms in an industry. This enables firms to enhance market power and acquire valuable assets. One example of a consolidation strategy took place in the defense industry in the early 1990s. As the cliché suggests, "peace broke out" at the end of the Cold War and overall U.S. defense spending levels plummeted.[78] Many companies that make up the defense industry saw more than 50 percent of their market disappear. Only one-quarter of the 120,000 companies that once supplied the Department of Defense still serve in that capacity; the others have shut down their defense business or dissolved altogether. But one key player, Lockheed Martin, became a dominant rival by pursuing an aggressive strategy of consolidation. During the 1990s, it purchased 17 independent entities, including General Dynamics' tactical aircraft and space systems divisions, GE Aerospace, Goodyear Aerospace, and Honeywell ElectroOptics. These combinations enabled Lockheed Martin to emerge as the top provider to three governmental customers: the Department of Defense, the Department of Energy, and NASA.

Examples of products currently in the decline stage of the industry life cycle include automotive spark plugs (replaced by electronic fuel ignition), videocassette recorders (replaced by digital video disk recorders), and personal computer zip drives (replaced by compact disk read-write drives). And, as we mentioned previously, compact disks are being replaced by digital video disks (DVDs).

The introduction of new technologies and associated products does not always mean that old technologies quickly fade away. Research shows that in a number of cases, old technologies actually enjoy a very profitable "last gasp."[79] Examples include mainframe computers (versus minicomputers and PCs), coronary artery bypass graft surgery (versus angioplasty), and CISC (Complex Instruction Set Computing) architecture in computer processors versus RISC (Reduced Instruction Set Computing). In each case, the advent of new technology prompted predictions of the demise of the older technology, but each of these has proved to be resilient survivors. What accounts for their continued profitability and survival?

Retreating to more defensible ground is one strategy that firms specializing in technologies threatened with rapid obsolescence have followed. For example, while angioplasty may be appropriate for relatively healthier patients with blocked arteries, sicker, higher-risk patients seem to benefit more from coronary artery bypass graft surgery. This enabled the surgeons to concentrate on the more difficult cases and improve the technology itself. The advent of television unseated the radio as the major source of entertainment from American homes. However, the radio has survived and even thrived in venues where people are also engaged in other activities, such as driving.

Using the new to improve the old is a second approach. Carburetor manufacturers have improved the fuel efficiency of their product by incorporating electronic controls that were originally developed for electronic fuel injection systems. Similarly, CISC computer chip manufacturers have adopted many features from RISC chips.

Improving the price-performance trade-off is a third approach. IBM continues to make money selling mainframes long after their obituary was written. It retooled the technology using low-cost microprocessors and cut their prices drastically. Further, it invested and updated the software, enabling them to offer clients such as banks better performance and lower costs.

Clearly, "last gasps" may not necessarily translate into longer term gains, as the experience of the integrated steel mills suggests. When the first mini-mills appeared, integrated steel mills shifted to higher margin steel, but eventually mini-mills entered even the last strongholds of the integrated steel mills.

Turnaround Strategies

A **turnaround strategy** involves reversing performance decline and reinvigorating growth toward profitability.[80] A need for turnaround may occur at any stage in the life cycle but is more likely to occur during maturity or decline.

Most turnarounds require a firm to carefully analyze the external and internal environments.[81] The external analysis leads to identification of market segments or customer groups that may still find the product attractive.[82] Internal analysis results in actions aimed at reduced costs and higher efficiency. A firm needs to undertake a mix of both internally and externally oriented actions to effect a turnaround.[83] In effect, the cliché "you can't shrink yourself to greatness" applies.

A study of 260 mature businesses in need of a turnaround identified three strategies used by successful companies.[84]

- **Asset and cost surgery.** Very often, mature firms tend to have assets that do not produce any returns. These include real estate, buildings, etc. Outright sales or sale and leaseback free up considerable cash and improve returns. Investment in new plants and equipment can be deferred. Firms in turnaround situations try to aggressively cut administrative expenses and inventories and speed up collection of receivables. Costs also can be reduced by outsourcing production of various inputs for which market prices may be cheaper than in-house production costs.

- **Selective product and market pruning.** Most mature or declining firms have many product lines that are losing money or are only marginally profitable. One strategy is to discontinue such product lines and focus all resources on a few core profitable areas. For example, in the early 1980s, faced with possible bankruptcy, Chrysler Corporation sold off all its nonautomotive businesses as well as all its production facilities abroad. Focus on the North American market and identification of a profitable niche—namely, minivans—were keys to their eventual successful turnaround.

- **Piecemeal productivity improvements.** There are many ways in which a firm can eliminate costs and improve productivity. Although individually these are small gains, they cumulate over a period of time to substantial gains. Improving business processes by reengineering them, benchmarking specific activities against industry leaders, encouraging employee input to identify excess costs, increasing capacity utilization, and improving employee productivity lead to a significant overall gain.

Software maker Intuit is a case of a quick but well-implemented turnaround strategy. After stagnating and stumbling during the dot-com boom, Intuit, which is known for

turnaround strategy a strategy that reverses a firm's decline in performance and returns it to growth and profitability.

>LO5.8
The need for turnaround strategies that enable a firm to reposition its competitive position in an industry.

Alan Mulally: Leading Ford's Extraordinary Turnaround

Shortly after Alan Mulally took over as Ford's CEO in September 2006, he organized a weekly meeting with his senior managers and asked them how things were going. Fine, fine, fine were the responses from around the table. To this, an incredulous Mulally exclaimed: "We are forecasting a $17 billion loss and no one has any problems!" Clearly, there were cultural issues at play (such as denial and executive rivalry) but also very serious strategic and financial problems as well.

What a change a few years can make! Ford's profits for 2010 were $6.6 billion and the firm has enjoyed seven straight quarters of profitability. This is quite a sharp contrast from its $14.7 billion loss in 2008—a time when high gasoline prices, bloated operations, and uncompetitive labor costs combined with the deep recession to create a perfect storm.

How did Mulally turn Ford around? It took many tough strategic decisions—involving not just company executives but Ford staff and the United Auto Workers (UAW). It involved downsizing, creating greater efficiency, improving quality, selling off the European luxury brands, and mortgaging assets to raise money. Ford's leaders and the United Auto Workers (UAW) also made transformational changes to lower the company's cost structure—a critical component to the company's long-term competitiveness.

Let's take a closer look at Mulally's strategic actions. We have to begin with the plan to undertake a dramatic refinancing of the business by raising bank loans secured against the company's assets. One of his first tasks was to finalize Ford's recovery plan and sell it to the banks. This financing enabled Ford to be the only major American automaker that avoided government-sponsored bankruptcy. And, as noted by Mulally, "The response that we received because we did not ask for the precious taxpayer's money has been tremendous." In fact, Jim Farley, head of marketing for Ford worldwide, estimates that Ford's standing on its own feet has been worth $1 billion in favorable publicity for the company and has attracted appreciative Americans into its dealers' showrooms.

Second, he decided that the firm would concentrate resources on the Ford brand and sell off the Premier Automotive Group (PAG) businesses—even if it meant taking a loss. Mulally had ridiculed the idea that top management could focus on Jaguar before breakfast, attend to Volvo or Land Rover before lunch, and then consider Ford and its Lincoln offshoot in North America in the afternoon. Accordingly, in 2007, Aston Martin was sold to private investors; Jaguar and Land Rover were sold to India's Tata Group in 2008; and a Chinese carmaker, Geely, bought Volvo in 2010. Further, the Mercury brand is being phased out.

Third, Mulally realized that in addition to fewer brands, Ford needed a much narrower range of cars, albeit higher quality ones, carrying its familiar blue oval logo in all segments of the market. At one point Ford's designers had to deal with 97 different models—that was cut to 36 and may go lower.

Fourth, along with rationalizing the product range, Mulally insisted on raising the aspiration level with regard to quality. Although Ford used to talk about claiming parity with Toyota's Camry, Mulally shifted the emphasis to trying to make each car that Ford sells "best in class." A number of new cars being created under the One Ford policy are coming from Europe. Quality has improved dramatically according to some of the industry's outside arbiters, such as J. D. Power.

Fifth, to ensure that regional stars such as the Focus could become global successes, 8 of Ford's 10 platforms (the floor pan and its underpinnings) are now global platforms. More shared platforms enables Ford to build different models more quickly and economically to account for regional tastes in cars and variations in regulations. For example, the various Fiesta-based cars may look different, but they share about two-thirds of their parts. Such actions are particularly important as Ford focuses (no pun intended) its efforts toward smaller, more fuel-efficient automobiles which traditionally have smaller margins. As noted by Lewis Booth, Ford's finance director, "Customers' tastes are converging. Fuel efficiency matters everywhere."

Sixth, Mulally had to make many painful restructuring decisions in order to match production to the number of cars that Ford could sell. Since 2006, Ford cut half of its shop-floor workforce in North America and a third of its office jobs. By the end of 2011, a total of 17 factories will have closed, and Ford's total employment will have fallen from 128,000 to 75,000. In addition, the number of dealers has been cut by a fifth. Helped by union concessions, Ford has shed about $14 billion in annual operational costs and now can compete with Japan's "transplant" factories in America.

Regarding Ford's successful transformation, Mulally cliams: "We have earned the right now to make a complete family of best-in-class vehicles right here in the United States with U.S. workers and competing with the very best in the world. That's not only good for Ford and our customers and our stakeholders but that's good for the United States of America." Without doubt, such a statement a few years ago would have been dismissed as hyperbole.

Sources: Linn, A. 2010. For Ford's Mulally, big bets are paying off. *www.msnbc.com*. October 26: nd; Anonymous. 2010. Epiphany in Dearborn. *The Economist*. December 11: 83–85; Reagan, J. Ford Motor's extraordinary turnaround. December 10: np; and *www.finance.yahoo.com*.

its Quickbook and Turbotax software, hired Stephen M. Bennett, a 22-year GE veteran, in 1999. He immediately discontinued Intuit's online finance, insurance, and bill-paying operations that were losing money. Instead, he focused on software for small businesses that employ less than 250 people. He also instituted a performance-based reward system that greatly improved employee productivity. Within a few years, Intuit was once again making substantial profits and its stock was up 42 percent.[85]

Even when an industry is in overall decline, pockets of profitability remain. These are segments with customers who are relatively price insensitive. For example, the replacement demand for vacuum tubes affords its manufacturers an opportunity to earn above normal returns although the product itself is technologically obsolete. Surprisingly, within declining industries, there may still be segments that are either stable or growing. Although fountain pens ceased to be the writing instrument of choice a long time ago, the fountain pen industry has successfully reconceptualized the product as a high margin luxury item that signals accomplishment and success. In the final analysis, every business has the potential for rejuvenation. But it takes creativity, persistence, and most of all a clear strategy to translate that potential into reality.

Strategy Spotlight 5.7 discusses Ford's remarkable turnaround under the direction of CEO Alan Mulally.

Reflecting on Career Implications . . .

- **Types of Competitive Advantage:** Always be aware of your organization's business-level strategy. What do you do to help your firm either increase differentiation or lower costs? What are some ways that your role in the firm can help realize these outcomes?
- **Combining Sources of Competitive Advantage:** Are you engaged in activities that simultaneously help your organization increase differentiation and lower costs?
- **Industry Life Cycle:** If your firm is in the mature stage of the industry life cycle, can you think of ways to enhance your firm's level of differentiation in order to make customers less price sensitive to your organization's goods and services?
- **Industry Life Cycle:** If you sense that your career is maturing (or in the decline phase!), what actions can you take to restore career growth and momentum (e.g., training, mentoring, professional networking)? Should you actively consider professional opportunities in other industries?

Summary

How and why firms outperform each other goes to the heart of strategic management. In this chapter, we identified three generic strategies and discussed how firms are able not only to attain advantages over competitors, but also to sustain such advantages over time. Why do some advantages become long-lasting while others are quickly imitated by competitors?

The three generic strategies—overall cost leadership, differentiation, and focus—form the core of this chapter. We began by providing a brief description of each

generic strategy (or competitive advantage) and furnished examples of firms that have successfully implemented these strategies. Successful generic strategies invariably enhance a firm's position vis-à-vis the five forces of that industry—a point that we stressed and illustrated with examples. However, as we pointed out, there are pitfalls to each of the generic strategies. Thus, the sustainability of a firm's advantage is always challenged because of imitation or substitution by new or existing rivals. Such competitor moves erode a firm's advantage over time.

We also discussed the viability of combining (or integrating) overall cost leadership and generic differentiation strategies. If successful, such integration can enable a firm to enjoy superior performance and improve its competitive position. However, this is challenging, and managers must be aware of the potential downside risks associated with such an initiative.

We addressed the challenges inherent in determining the sustainability of competitive advantages. Drawing on an example from a manufacturing industry, we discussed both the "pro" and "con" positions as to why competitive advantages are sustainable over a long period of time.

The way companies formulate and deploy strategies is changing because of the impact of the Internet and digital technologies in many industries. Further, Internet technologies are enabling the mass customization capabilities of greater numbers of competitors. Focus strategies are likely to increase in importance because the Internet provides highly targeted and lower-cost access to narrow or specialized markets. These strategies are not without their pitfalls, however, and firms need to understand the dangers as well as the potential benefits of Internet-based approaches.

The concept of the industry life cycle is a critical contingency that managers must take into account in striving to create and sustain competitive advantages. We identified the four stages of the industry life cycle—introduction, growth, maturity, and decline—and suggested how these stages can play a role in decisions that managers must make at the business level. These include overall strategies as well as the relative emphasis on functional areas and value—creating activities.

When a firm's performance severely erodes, turnaround strategies are needed to reverse its situation and enhance its competitive position. We have discussed three approaches—asset cost surgery, selective product and market pruning, and piecemeal productivity improvements.

Summary Review Questions

1. Explain why the concept of competitive advantage is central to the study of strategic management.
2. Briefly describe the three generic strategies—overall cost leadership, differentiation, and focus.
3. Explain the relationship between the three generic strategies and the five forces that determine the average profitability within an industry.
4. What are some of the ways in which a firm can attain a successful turnaround strategy?
5. Describe some of the pitfalls associated with each of the three generic strategies.

6. Can firms combine the generic strategies of overall cost leadership and differentiation? Why or why not?
7. Explain why the industry life cycle concept is an important factor in determining a firm's business-level strategy.

Key Terms

business-level strategy, 162
generic strategies, 162
overall cost leadership, 164
experience curve, 165
competitive parity, 166
differentiation strategy, 169
focus strategy, 174
combination strategies, 176
mass customization, 176
profit pool, 177
digital technologies, 182
disintermediation, 183
industry life cycle, 187
introduction stage, 187
growth stage, 189
maturity stage, 189
reverse positioning, 190
breakaway positioning, 191
decline stage, 191
consolidation strategy, 192
harvesting strategy, 192
turnaround strategy, 193

Experiential Exercise

What are some examples of primary and support activities that enable Nucor, a $19 billion steel manufacturer, to achieve a low-cost strategy? (Fill in table on the following page.)

Application Questions Exercises

1. Go to the Internet and look up *www.walmart.com*. How has this firm been able to combine overall cost leadership and differentiation strategies?
2. Choose a firm with which you are familiar in your local business community. Is the firm successful in following one (or more) generic strategies? Why or why not? What do you think are some of the challenges it faces in implementing these strategies in an effective manner?
3. Think of a firm that has attained a differentiation focus or cost focus strategy. Are their advantages sustainable? Why? Why not? (*Hint:* Consider its position vis-à-vis Porter's five forces.)
4. Think of a firm that successfully achieved a combination overall cost leadership and differentiation strategy. What can be learned from this example? Are these advantages sustainable? Why? Why not? (*Hint:* Consider its competitive position vis-à-vis Porter's five forces.)

Value-Chain Activity	Yes/No	How Does Nucor Create Value for the Customer?
Primary:		
Inbound logistics		
Operations		
Outbound logistics		
Marketing and sales		
Service		
Support:		
Procurement		
Technology development		
Human resource management		
General administration		

Ethics Questions

1. Can you think of a company that suffered ethical consequences as a result of an overemphasis on a cost leadership strategy? What do you think were the financial and nonfinancial implications?

2. In the introductory stage of the product life cycle, what are some of the unethical practices that managers could engage in to enhance their firm's market position? What could be some of the long-term implications of such actions?

References

1. Helm, B. 2010. At KFC, a battle among the chicken-hearted. *Bloomberg Businessweek,* August 16: 19; De Nies, Y. 2010. Kentucky fried fight. *www.abcnews.go.com.* August 17: np; and Morran, C. 2010. Squabble between KFC & franchisees over advertising goes to court. *www.consumerist.com.* September 20: np. We thank Jason Hirsch for his valued contributions.

2. For a recent perspective by Porter on competitive strategy, refer to Porter, M. E. 1996. What is strategy? *Harvard Business Review,* 74(6): 61–78.

3. For insights into how a start-up is using solar technology, see: Gimbel, B. 2009. Plastic power. *Fortune,* February 2: 34.

4. Useful insights on strategy in an economic downturn are in: Rhodes, D. & Stelter, D. 2009. Seize advantage in a downturn. *Harvard Business Review,* 87(2): 50–58.

5. Some useful ideas on maintaining competitive advantages can be found in Ma, H. & Karri, R. 2005. Leaders beware: Some sure ways to lose your

competitive advantage. *Organizational Dynamics,* 343(1): 63–76.

6. Miller, A. & Dess, G. G. 1993. Assessing Porter's model in terms of its generalizability, accuracy, and simplicity. *Journal of Management Studies,* 30(4): 553–585.

7. Cendrowski, S. 2008. Extreme retailing. *Fortune,* March 31: 14.

8. For insights on how discounting can erode a firm's performance, read: Stibel, J. M. & Delgrosso, P. 2008. Discounts can be dangerous. *Harvard Business Review,* 66(12): 31.

9. For a scholarly discussion and analysis of the concept of competitive parity, refer to Powell, T. C. 2003. Varieties of competitive parity. *Strategic Management Journal,* 24(1): 61–86.

10. Rao, A. R., Bergen, M. E., & Davis, S. 2000. How to fight a price war. *Harvard Business Review,* 78(2): 107–120.

11. Marriot, J. W. Jr. Our competitive strength: Human capital. A speech given to the Detroit Economic Club on October 2, 2000.

12. Whalen, C. J., Pascual, A. M., Lowery, T., & Muller, J. 2001. The top 25 managers. *BusinessWeek,* January 8: 63.

13. Ibid.

14. For an interesting perspective on the need for creative strategies, refer to Hamel, G. & Prahalad, C. K. 1994. *Competing for the future.* Boston: Harvard Business School Press.

15. Interesting insights on Walmart's effective cost leadership strategy are found in: Palmeri, C. 2008. Wal-Mart is up for this downturn. *BusinessWeek,* November 6: 34.

16. An interesting perspective on the dangers of price discounting is: Mohammad, R. 2011. Ditch the discounts. *Harvard Business Review,* 89 (1/2): 23–25.

17. Dholakia, U. M. 2011. Why employees can wreck promotional offers. *Harvard Business Review,* 89(1/2): 28.

18. Jacobs, A. 2010. Workers in China voting with their feet. *International Herald Tribune.* July 13: 1, 14.

19. For a perspective on the sustainability of competitive advantages, refer to

Barney, J. 1995. Looking inside for competitive advantage. *Academy of Management Executive,* 9(4): 49–61.

20. Thornton, E., 2001, Why e-brokers are broker and broker. *BusinessWeek,* January 22: 94.

21. Mohammed, R. 2011. Ditch the discounts. *Harvard Business Review,* 89(1/2): 23–25.

22. Koretz, G. 2001. E-commerce: The buyer wins. *BusinessWeek,* January 8: 30.

23. For an "ultimate" in differentiated services, consider time shares in exotic automobiles such as Lamborghinis and Bentleys. Refer to: Stead, D. 2008. My Lamborghini—today, anyway. *BusinessWeek,* January 18:17.

24. For an interesting perspective on the value of corporate brands and how they may be leveraged, refer to Aaker, D. A. 2004, *California Management Review,* 46(3): 6–18.

25. A unique perspective on differentiation strategies is: Austin, R. D. 2008. High margins and the quest for aesthetic coherence. *Harvard Business Review,* 86(1): 18–19.

26. MacMillan, I. & McGrath, R. 1997. Discovering new points of differentiation. *Harvard Business Review,* 75(4): 133–145; Wise, R. & Baumgarter, P. 1999. Beating the clock: Corporate responses to rapid change in the PC industry. *California Management Review,* 42(1): 8–36.

27. For a discussion on quality in terms of a company's software and information systems, refer to Prahalad, C. K. & Krishnan, M. S. 1999. The new meaning of quality in the information age. *Harvard Business Review,* 77(5): 109–118.

28. The role of design in achieving differentiation is addressed in: Brown, T. 2008. Design thinking. *Harvard Business Review.* 86(6): 84–92.

29. Taylor, A., III. 2001. Can you believe Porsche is putting its badge on this car? *Fortune,* February 19: 168–172.

30. Ward, S., Light, L., & Goldstine, J. 1999. What high-tech managers need to know about brands. *Harvard Business Review,* 77(4): 85–95.

31. Rosenfeld, J. 2000. Unit of one. *Fast Company,* April: 98.

32. Markides, C. 1997. Strategic innovation. *Sloan Management Review,* 38(3): 9–23.

33. Bonnabeau, E., Bodick, N., & Armstrong, R. W. 2008. A more rational approach to new-product development. *Harvard Business Review.* 66(3): 96–102.

34. Insights on Google's innovation are in: Iyer, B. & Davenport, T. H. 2008. Reverse engineering Google's innovation machine. *Harvard Business Review.* 66(4): 58–68.

35. A discussion of how a firm used technology to create product differentiation is in: Mehta, S. N. 2009. Under Armor reboots. *Fortune.* February 2: 29–33 (5)

36. Bertini, M. & Wathieu, L. 2010. How to stop customers from fixating on price. *Harvard Business Review,* 88(5): 84–91.

37. The authors would like to thank Scott Droege, a faculty member at Western Kentucky University, for providing this example.

38. Dixon, M., Freeman, K. & Toman, N. 2010. Stop trying to delight your customers. *Harvard Business Review,* 88(7/8).

39. Flint, J. 2004. Stop the nerds. *Forbes,* July 5: 80; and, Fahey, E. 2004. Over-engineering 101. *Forbes,* December 13: 62.

40. Symonds, W. C. 2000. Can Gillette regain its voltage? *BusinessWeek,* October 16: 102–104.

41. Caplan, J. 2006. In a real crunch. *Inside Business,* July: A37–A38.

42. Gadiesh, O. & Gilbert, J. L. 1998. Profit pools: A fresh look at strategy. *Harvard Business Review,* 76(3): 139–158.

43. Colvin, G. 2000. Beware: You could soon be selling soybeans. *Fortune,* November 13: 80.

44. Whalen et al., op. cit.: 63. Porter, M. E. 2008. The five competitive forces that shape strategy. *Harvard Business Review,* 86(1): 78–97; and *www.finance.yahoo.com.*

45. Hall, W. K. 1980. Survival strategies in a hostile environment, *Harvard Business Review,* 58: 75–87; on the paint and allied products industry, see Dess, G. G. & Davis, P. S. 1984. Porter's (1980) generic strategies as determinants of strategic group membership and organizational performance. *Academy of Management Journal,* 27: 467–488; for the Korean electronics industry, see Kim, L. & Lim, Y. 1988. Environment, generic strategies, and performance in a rapidly developing country: A taxonomic approach. *Academy of Management Journal,* 31: 802–827; Wright, P., Hotard, D., Kroll, M., Chan, P., & Tanner, J. 1990. Performance and multiple strategies in a firm: Evidence from the apparel industry. In Dean, B. V. & Cassidy, J. C. (Eds.). *Strategic management: Methods and studies:* 93–110. Amsterdam: Elsevier-North Holland; and Wright, P., Kroll, M., Tu, H., & Helms, M. 1991. Generic strategies and business performance: An empirical study of the screw machine products industry. *British Journal of Management,* 2: 1–9.

46. Gilmore, J. H. & Pine, B. J., II. 1997. The four faces of customization. *Harvard Business Review,* 75(1): 91–101.

47. Heracleous, L. & Wirtz, J. 2010. Singapore Airlines' balancing act. *Harvard Business Review,* 88(7/8): 145–149.

48. Gilmore & Pine, op. cit. For interesting insights on mass customization, refer to Cattani, K., Dahan, E., & Schmidt, G. 2005. Offshoring versus "spackling." *MIT Sloan Management Review,* 46(3): 6–7.

49. Goodstein, L. D. & Butz, H. E. 1998. Customer value: The linchpin of organizational change. *Organizational Dynamics,* Summer: 21–34.

50. Randall, T., Terwiesch, C., & Ulrich, K. T. 2005. Principles for user design of customized products. *California Management Review,* 47(4): 68–85.

51. Gadiesh & Gilbert, op. cit.: 139–158.

52. Insights on the profit pool concept are addressed in: Reinartz, W. & Ulaga, W. 2008. How to sell services more profitably. *Harvard Business Review,* 66(5): 90–96.

53. This example draws on Dess & Picken. 1997. op. cit.

54. A rigorous and thorough discussion of the threats faced by industries due to the commoditization of products and services and what strategic actions firm should consider is found

in: D'Aveni, R. A. 2010. *Beating the commodity trap.* Boston: Harvard Business Press.

55. For an insightful, recent discussion on the difficulties and challenges associated with creating advantages that are sustainable for any reasonable period of time and suggested strategies, refer to: D'Aveni, R. A., Dagnino, G. B. & Smith, K. G. 2010. The age of temporary advantage. *Strategic Management Journal.* 31(13): 1371–1385. This is the lead article in a special issue of this journal that provides many ideas that are useful to both academics and practicing managers. For an additional examination of declining advantage in technologically intensive industries, see: Vaaler, P. M. & McNamara, G. 2010. Are technology-intensive industries more dynamically competitive? No and yes. *Organization Science.* 21: 271–289.

56. Rita McGrath provides some interesting ideas on possible strategies for firms facing highly uncertain competitive environments: McGrath, R. G. 2011. When your business model is in trouble. *Harvard Business Review,* 89(1/2); 96–98.

57. The Atlas Door example draws on: Stalk, G., Jr. 1988. Time—the next source of competitive advantage. *Harvard Business Review,* 66(4): 41–51.

58. Edelman, D. C. 2010. Branding in the digital age. *Harvard Business Review,* 88(12): 62–69.

59. Seybold, P. 2000. Niches bring riches. *Business 2.0,* June 13: 135.

60. Greenspan, R. 2004. Net drives profits to small biz. ClickZ.com, March 25, *www.clickz.com.* Greenspan, R. 2002. Small biz benefits from Internet tools. ClickZ.com, March 28, *www.clickz.com.*

61. Burns, E. 2006. Executives slow to see value of corporate blogging. ClickZ. com, May 9, *www.clickz.com.*

62. Empirical support for the use of combination strategies in an e-business context can be found in Kim, E., Nam, D., & Stimpert, J. L. 2004. The applicability of Porter's generic strategies in the Digital Age: Assumptions, conjectures, and suggestions. *Journal of Management,* 30(5): 569–589.

63. Porter, M. E. 2001. Strategy and the Internet. *Harvard Business Review,* 79: 63–78.

64. For an interesting perspective on the influence of the product life cycle and rate of technological change on competitive strategy, refer to Lei, D. & Slocum, J. W. Jr. 2005. Strategic and organizational requirements for competitive advantage. *Academy of Management Executive,* 19(1): 31–45.

65. Dickson, P. R. 1994. *Marketing management:* 293. Fort Worth, TX: Dryden Press; Day, G. S. 1981. The product life cycle: Analysis and application. *Journal of Marketing Research,* 45: 60–67.

66. Bearden, W. O., Ingram, T. N., & LaForge, R. W. 1995. *Marketing principles and practices.* Burr Ridge, IL: Irwin.

67. MacMillan, I. C. 1985. Preemptive strategies. In Guth, W. D. (Ed.). *Handbook of business strategy:* 9-1–9-22. Boston: Warren, Gorham & Lamont; Pearce, J. A. & Robinson, R. B. 2000. *Strategic management* (7th ed.). New York: McGraw-Hill; Dickson, op. cit.: 295–296.

68. Bartlett, C. A. & Ghoshal, S. 2000. Going global: Lessons for late movers. *Harvard Business Review,* 78(2): 132–142.

69. Neuborne, E. 2000. E-tailers hit the relaunch key. *BusinessWeek,* October 17: 62.

70. Berkowitz, E. N., Kerin, R. A., & Hartley, S. W. 2000. *Marketing* (6th ed.). New York: McGraw-Hill.

71. MacMillan, op. cit.

72. Brooker, K. 2001. A game of inches. *Fortune,* February 5: 98–100.

73. Our discussion of reverse and breakaway positioning draws on Moon, Y. 2005. Break free from the product life cycle. *Harvard Business Review,* 83(5): 87–94. This article also discusses stealth positioning as a means of overcoming consumer resistance and advancing a product from the introduction to the growth phase.

74. MacMillan, op. cit.

75. Berkowitz et al., op. cit.

76. Bearden et al., op. cit.

77. The discussion of these four strategies draws on MacMillan, op. cit.; Berkowitz et al., op. cit.; and Bearden et al., op. cit.

78. Augustine, N. R. 1997. Reshaping an industry: Lockheed Martin's survival story. *Harvard Business Review,* 75(3): 83–94.

79. Snow, D. C. 2008. Beware of old technologies' last gasps. *Harvard Business Review,* January: 17–18. Lohr, S. 2008. Why old technologies are still kicking. *New York Times,* March 23: np; and McGrath, R. G. 2008. Innovation and the last gasps of dying technologies. ritamcgrath.com, March 18: np.

80. Coyne, K. P., Coyne, S. T. & Coyne, E. J. Sr. 2010. When you've got to cut costs—now. *Harvard Business Review,* 88(5): 74–83.

81. A study that draws on the resource-based view of the firm to investigate successful turnaround strategies is: Morrow, J. S., Sirmon, D. G., Hitt, M. A., & Holcomb, T. R. 2007. *Strategic Management Journal,* 28(3): 271–284.

82. For a study investigating the relationship between organizational restructuring and acquisition performance, refer to: Barkema, H. G. & Schijven, M. Toward unlocking the full potential of acquisitions: The role of organizational restructuring. *Academy of Management Journal,* 51(4): 696–722.

83. For some useful ideas on effective turnarounds and handling downsizings, refer to Marks, M. S. & De Meuse, K. P. 2005. Resizing the organization: Maximizing the gain while minimizing the pain of layoffs, divestitures and closings. *Organizational Dynamics,* 34(1): 19–36.

84. Hambrick, D. C. & Schecter, S. M. 1983. Turnaround strategies for mature industrial product business units. *Academy of Management Journal,* 26(2): 231–248.

85. Mullaney, T. J. 2002. The wizard of Intuit. *BusinessWeek,* October 28: 60–63.

Learning from Mistakes

Internet company AOL purchased the social networking firm Bebo in early 2008 for $850 million. In June 2010, it sold Bebo for the fire-sale price of $10 million. What went wrong?[1]

AOL was one of the biggest stars of the dotcom era, but its traditional business, dial-up Internet services, has steadily declined since its peak in 2001. The company tried to reinvent itself in 2008 by entering the social networking market by acquiring Bebo; the acquisition came shortly before AOL demerged from Time Warner in 2009. But in the words of Jeff Bewkes, Time Warner CEO at the time, from the get-go Bebo was seen as the "riskiest acquisition" the company made that year.

AOL's original rationale in purchasing Bebo was to tap into the phenomenon of online social networking by acquiring a presence in the rapidly growing community. The deal was part of AOL's strategy to shift from a subscription-based service for Internet connectivity to one focused on generating ad revenue by providing online media. The acquisition of Bebo pulled AOL away from their core strength of providing Internet service and placed the company in direct competition with social networking firms, such as Facebook. Unfortunately, Bebo proved to be an ineffective means of entering the online media industry.

In 2008, Bebo was a thriving, mainly European online social network community that was popular among teens, with about 40 million users. AOL's purchase of Bebo was intended to further the community's expansion into the U.S. market. Quite the opposite happened. In May of 2007, the firm had almost 9 million unique U.S. visitors, and a year later this number dropped to only 5 million unique visitors. (This was in contrast with their largest competitor in the social networking market, Facebook, who had 130.4 million unique U.S. visitors, showing continuous strong growth.)

One of the few actors that actually profited from Bebo was its founder, Michael Birch, who made $300 million from Bebo's original sale to AOL. According to Rory Cellan-Jones, BBC technology correspondent, AOL's decision to purchase Bebo was "one of the worst deals ever made in the dotcom era."

The acquisition was just one of a series of poor decisions that forced AOL to remove Randy Falco, the reigning CEO when the Bebo acquisition was made. They replaced him with Tim Armstrong, the one who divested it, in an effort to change strategies and bring the company back to profitability. According to Jim Clark, senior technology analyst at Mintel, the problems faced by AOL in integrating Bebo were a combination of paying too much in the first place as well as a lack of enough investment to make it profitable.*

* To make matters worse, in July 2010, AOL also sold ICQ instant messenger for $187.5 million, having purchased it for $400 million in 1998. The sales of Bebo and ICQ led to write-downs of $1.4 billion in the second quarter of 2010 and to a posted loss of $1.06 billion for the quarter.

>LO6.1

The reasons for the failure of many diversification efforts.

corporate-level strategy a strategy that focuses on gaining long-term revenue, profits, and market value through managing operations in multiple businesses.

AOL's experience with acquisitions is more the rule than the exception. Research shows that the vast majority of acquisitions result in value destruction rather than value creation. Many large multinational firms have also failed to effectively integrate their acquisitions, paid too high a premium for the target's common stock, or were unable to understand how the acquired firm's assets would fit with their own lines of business.[2] And, at times, top executives may not have acted in the best interests of shareholders. That is, the motive for the acquisition may have been to enhance the executives' power and prestige rather than to improve shareholder returns. At times, the only other people who may have benefited were the shareholders of the *acquired* firms—or the investment bankers who advise the acquiring firm, because they collect huge fees upfront regardless of what happens afterward![3]

Consider, for example, Pfizer's announcement on January 26, 2009, that it was acquiring Wyeth for $68 billion in cash and stock—which represented a 15 percent premium.[4] How did the market react? In rather typical fashion, Wyeth's stock went up 2 percent;

Pfizer's went down 9 percent. And, interestingly, the shares of Crucell, a Dutch biotech company, sank 10 percent after Wyeth pulled out of talks to buy it.

There have been several studies that were conducted over a variety of time periods that show how disappointing acquisitions have typically turned out. For example:

- A study evaluated the stock market reaction of 600 acquisitions over the period between 1975 and 1991. The results indicated that the acquiring firms suffered an average 4 percent drop in market value (after adjusting for market movements) in the three months following the acquisitions announcement.[5]

- In a study by Solomon Smith Barney of U.S. companies acquired since 1997 in deals for $15 billion or more, the stocks of the acquiring firms have, on average, underperformed the S&P stock index by 14 percentage points and underperformed their peer group by 4 percentage points after the deals were announced.[6]

- A study investigated 270 mergers that took place between 2000 and 2003 in multiple countries and regions. It found that after a merger, sales growth decreased by 6 percent, earnings growth dropped 9.4 percent, and market valuations declined 2.5 percent (figures are adjusted for industry trends and refer to three years pre- or postmerger).[7]

- A study that investigated 86 completed takeover bids that took place between 1993 and 2008 noted a negative return of 2 percent per month in long-term performance for the 3-year postacquisition period.[8]

Exhibit 6.1 lists some well-known examples of failed acquisitions and mergers. Recently there have been several acquisitions—often at fire sale prices—by financial services firms during the global financial crisis in 2008. For example, Bank of America bought

Exhibit 6.1
Some Well-Known M&A Blunders

Here are examples of some very expensive blunders:

- Sprint and Nextel merged in 2005. On January 31, 2008, the firm said it would take a merger-related charge of $31 billion. And, as of late-January, 2011, the stock has lost over 85 percent of its value since the merger.

- AOL paid $114 billion to acquire Time Warner in 2001. Over the next two years, AOL Time Warner lost $150 billion in market valuation.

- Conseco paid $5.8 billion to buy Green Tree, a mobile home mortgage lender, in 1998 though the company's net worth was not even $1 billion. In the next two years, Conseco lost 90 percent of its market value!

- Daimler Benz paid $36 billion to acquire Chrysler in 1998. After years of losses, it sold 80.1 percent of the unit to Cerberus Capital Management for $7.4 billion in 2007. And, as of 2009, Cerberus was trying to unload the unit.

- Quaker Oats' acquisition of the once high-flying Snapple for $1.8 billion in 1994 was followed by its divestment for $300 million three years later.

- AT&T bought computer equipment maker NCR for $7.4 billion in 1991, only to spin it off for $3.4 billion six years later.

- Sony acquired Columbia Pictures in 1989 for $4.8 billion although it had no competencies in movie production. Five years later, Sony was forced to take a $2.7 billion write-off on the acquisition.

Source: Ante, S.E. 2008. Sprint's Wake-Up Call. *Businessweek.com*. February 21: np; Gupta, P. 2008. Daimler May Sell Remaining Chrysler Stake. *www.reuters.com*, September 24: np; and Tully, S. 2006. The (Second) Worst Deal Ever. *Fortune*, October 16: 102–119.

Merrill Lynch, Wells Fargo purchased Wachovia, and JPMorgan acquired Washington Mutual. Only time will tell how well these turn out over the next few years.

Many acquisitions ultimately result in divestiture—an admission that things didn't work out as planned. In fact, some years ago, a writer for *Fortune* magazine lamented, "Studies show that 33 percent to 50 percent of acquisitions are later divested, giving corporate marriages a divorce rate roughly comparable to that of men and women."[9]

Admittedly, we have been rather pessimistic so far.[10] Clearly, many diversification efforts have worked out very well—whether through mergers and acquisitions, strategic alliances and joint ventures, or internal development. We will discuss many success stories throughout this chapter. Next, we will discuss the primary rationales for diversification.

Making Diversification Work: An Overview

>LO6.2
How managers can create value through diversification initiatives.

Clearly, not all diversification moves, including those involving mergers and acquisitions, erode performance. For example, acquisitions in the oil industry, such as British Petroleum's purchases of Amoco and Arco, are performing well as is the Exxon-Mobil merger. In the automobile industry, the Renault-Nissan alliance, under CEO Carlos Ghosn's leadership, has led to a quadrupling of its collective market capitalization—from $20.4 billion to $84.9 billion—by the end of 2006.[11] Many leading high-tech firms such as Microsoft, Cisco Systems, and Intel have dramatically enhanced their revenues, profits, and market values through a wide variety of diversification initiatives, including acquisitions, strategic alliances, and joint ventures, as well as internal development.*

So the question becomes: Why do some diversification efforts pay off and others produce poor results? This chapter addresses two related issues: (1) What businesses should a corporation compete in? and (2) How should these businesses be managed to jointly create more value than if they were freestanding units?

diversification the process of firms expanding their operations by entering new businesses.

Diversification initiatives—whether through mergers and acquisitions, strategic alliances and joint ventures, or internal development—must be justified by the creation of value for shareholders.[12] But this is not always the case.[13] Acquiring firms typically pay high premiums when they acquire a target firm. For example, in 2006 Freeport-McMoran paid a 30 percent premium to acquire Phelps Dodge in order to create the largest metals and mining concern in the U.S. In contrast, you and I, as private investors, can diversify our portfolio of stocks very cheaply. With an intensely competitive online brokerage industry, we can acquire hundreds (or thousands) of shares for a transaction fee of as little as $10.00 or less—a far cry from the 30 to 40 percent (or higher) premiums that corporations typically must pay to acquire companies.

Given the seemingly high inherent downside risks and uncertainties, one might ask: Why should companies even bother with diversification initiatives? The answer, in a word, is *synergy,* derived from the Greek word *synergos,* which means "working together." This can have two different, but not mutually exclusive, meanings.

First, a firm may diversify into *related* businesses. Here, the primary potential benefits to be derived come from *horizontal relationships;* that is, businesses sharing intangible resources (e.g., core competencies such as marketing) and tangible resources (e.g., production facilities, distribution channels).[14] Firms can also enhance their market power via

---

* Many high-tech firms, such as Motorola, IBM, Qualcomm, and Intel have also diversified through company-owned venture capital arms. Intel Capital, for example, has invested $4 billion in 1,000 companies over 15 years. Some 160 of those companies have been sold to other firms, while another 150 of them have been publicly listed. In 2006, Intel Capital's investments added $214 million to the parent company's net income. For an insightful discussion of how Apple might benefit from a venture capital initiative, refer to Hesseldahl, A. 2007. What to Do with Apple's Cash. *BusinessWeek,* March 19: 80.

pooled negotiating power and vertical integration. For example, Procter & Gamble enjoys many synergies from having businesses that share distribution resources.

Second, a corporation may diversify into *unrelated* businesses.[15] Here, the primary potential benefits are derived largely from *hierarchical relationships;* that is, value creation derived from the corporate office. Examples of the latter would include leveraging some of the support activities in the value chain that we discussed in Chapter 3, such as information systems or human resource practices. Cooper Industries has followed a successful strategy of unrelated diversification. There are few similarities in the products it makes or the industries in which it competes. However, the corporate office adds value through such activities as superb human resource practices and budgeting systems.

Please note that such benefits derived from horizontal (related diversification) and hierarchical (unrelated diversification) relationships are not mutually exclusive. Many firms that diversify into related areas benefit from information technology expertise in the corporate office. Similarly, unrelated diversifiers often benefit from the "best practices" of sister businesses even though their products, markets, and technologies may differ dramatically.

Exhibit 6.2 provides an overview of how we will address the various means by which firms create value through both related and unrelated diversification and also include a summary of some examples that we will address in this chapter.[16]

Exhibit 6.2
Creating Value through Related and Unrelated Diversification

Related Diversification: Economies of Scope

Leveraging core competencies

- 3M leverages its competencies in adhesives technologies to many industries, including automotive, construction, and telecommunications.

Sharing activities

- McKesson, a large distribution company, sells many product lines, such as pharmaceuticals and liquor, through its superwarehouses.

Related Diversification: Market Power

Pooled negotiating power

- The Times Mirror Company increases its power over customers by providing "one-stop shopping" for advertisers to reach customers through multiple media—television and newspapers—in several huge markets such as New York and Chicago.

Vertical integration

- Shaw Industries, a giant carpet manufacturer, increases its control over raw materials by producing much of its own polypropylene fiber, a key input to its manufacturing process.

Unrelated Diversification: Parenting, Restructuring, and Financial Synergies

Corporate restructuring and parenting

- The corporate office of Cooper Industries adds value to its acquired businesses by performing such activities as auditing their manufacturing operations, improving their accounting activities, and centralizing union negotiations.

Portfolio management

- Novartis, formerly Ciba-Geigy, uses portfolio management to improve many key activities, including resource allocation and reward and evaluation systems.

related diversification a firm entering a different business in which it can benefit from leveraging core competencies, sharing activities, or building market power.

economies of scope cost savings from leveraging core competencies or sharing related activities among businesses in a corporation.

>LO6.3
How corporations can use related diversification to achieve synergistic benefits through economies of scope and market power.

core competencies a firm's strategic resources that reflect the collective learning in the organization.

Related Diversification: Economies of Scope and Revenue Enhancement

Related diversification enables a firm to benefit from horizontal relationships across different businesses in the diversified corporation by leveraging core competencies and sharing activities (e.g., production and distribution facilities). This enables a corporation to benefit from economies of scope. **Economies of scope** refers to cost savings from leveraging core competencies or sharing related activities among businesses in the corporation. A firm can also enjoy greater revenues if two businesses attain higher levels of sales growth combined than either company could attain independently.

For example, a sporting goods store with one or several locations may acquire retail stores carrying other product lines. This enables it to leverage, or reuse, many of its key resources—favorable reputation, expert staff and management skills, efficient purchasing operations—the basis of its competitive advantage(s), over a larger number of stores.[17]

Leveraging Core Competencies

The concept of core competencies can be illustrated by the imagery of the diversified corporation as a tree.[18] The trunk and major limbs represent core products; the smaller branches are business units; and the leaves, flowers, and fruit are end products. The core competencies are represented by the root system, which provides nourishment, sustenance, and stability. Managers often misread the strength of competitors by looking only at their end products, just as we can fail to appreciate the strength of a tree by looking only at its leaves. Core competencies may also be viewed as the "glue" that binds existing businesses together or as the engine that fuels new business growth.

Core competencies reflect the collective learning in organizations—how to coordinate diverse production skills, integrate multiple streams of technologies, and market diverse products and services.[19] The knowledge necessary to put a radio on a chip does not in itself assure a company of the skill needed to produce a miniature radio approximately the size of a business card. To accomplish this, Casio, a giant electronic products producer, must synthesize know-how in miniaturization, microprocessor design, material science, and ultrathin precision castings. These are the same skills that it applies in its miniature card calculators, pocket TVs, and digital watches.

For a core competence to create value and provide a viable basis for synergy among the businesses in a corporation, it must meet three criteria.[20]

- *The core competence must enhance competitive advantage(s) by creating superior customer value.* Every value-chain activity has the potential to provide a viable basis for building on a core competence.[21] At Gillette, for example, scientists developed the Fusion and Mach 3 after the introduction of the tremendously successful Sensor System because of a thorough understanding of several phenomena that underlie shaving. These include the physiology of facial hair and skin, the metallurgy of blade strength and sharpness, the dynamics of a cartridge moving across skin, and the physics of a razor blade severing hair. Such innovations are possible only with

● Gillette's expertise in multiple competencies helps them develop superior shaving products.

Procter & Gamble Leverages Its Core Competence in Marketing and (Believe It or Not!) Franchising

Procter & Gamble, long dominant in detergents to wash clothes, wants to also dry clean them. The world's biggest consumer products company plans to roll out franchised Tide Dry Cleaners across America. P&G wants to put its brands to work selling services to boost U.S. revenue for its products.

Some think that their strategy could be a huge hit. For example, Andrew Cherng, founder of Panda Restaurant Group, which operates Chinese fast-food outlets in U.S. malls, plans to open around 150 Tide-branded dry cleaners over the next four years. He claims: "I wasn't around when McDonald's was taking franchisees. I'm not going to miss this one."

In 2007, the firm launched Mr. Clean Car Wash. Nine franchises are now in operation. The following year, P&G opened three test Tide Dry Cleaners in Kansas City. Having fine-tuned the concept, the firm is now going national. According to Michael Stone, P&G is moving into services

"that are virtually unbranded. One would think consumers would trust a Tide Dry Cleaners because they know P&G is behind it."

With more than 800,000 Facebook fans and legions of customers, P&G hopes that the Tide brand will draw people into franchise stores and that superior service—which includes drive-through service, 24-hour pickup, and cleaning methods it markets as environmentally safe—will keep them coming back. "The power of our brands represents disruptive innovation in these industries," claims Nathan Estruth, vice president for FutureWorks, P&G's entrepreneurial arm. "Imagine getting to start my new business with the power of Tide."

But . . . it won't be easy. Competition is fierce, and customers can be prickly: Woe to the dry cleaner that ruins a favorite suit or dress—even if it was cheaply made and decades old. Sanjiv Mehra, who headed Unilever's attempt to break into the dry-cleaning business about a decade ago, says that the key to success is in figuring out a way to do it cheaper or much better than the mom-and-pop stores that dominate the industry. At the end of the day, Unilever realized that it couldn't do either. He claims: "It comes back to, are you fundamentally changing the economics of the business?" adding that P&G's marketing muscle could turn out to be the difference. "That's where they will make a lot of money if they do it right."

Sources: Coleman-Lochner, L. & Clothier, M. 2010. P&G Puts Its Big Brands to Work in Franchises. *Bloomberg Businessweek.* September 6–12: 20; and Martin, A. 2010. Smelling an Opportunity. *www.nytimes.com.* December 8: np.

an understanding of such phenomena and the ability to combine such technologies into innovative products. Customers are willing to pay more for such technologically differentiated products.

- ***Different businesses in the corporation must be similar in at least one important way related to the core competence.*** It is not essential that the products or services themselves be similar. Rather, at least one element in the value chain must require similar skills in creating competitive advantage if the corporation is to capitalize on its core competence. At first glance you might think that cars and clothes have little in common. However, Strategy Spotlight 6.1 discusses how Procter & Gamble is leveraging its newfound competence in franchising to create a new revenue stream.

- ***The core competencies must be difficult for competitors to imitate or find substitutes for.*** As we discussed in Chapter 5, competitive advantages will not be sustainable if the competition can easily imitate or substitute them. Similarly, if the skills associated with a firm's core competencies are easily imitated or replicated, they are not a sound basis for sustainable advantages. Consider Sharp Corporation, a consumer electronics giant with 2010 revenues of $30 billion.[22] It has a set of specialized core competencies in optoelectronics technologies that are difficult to replicate and contribute to its competitive advantages in its core businesses. Its most successful technology has been liquid crystal displays (LCDs) that are critical components in nearly all of Sharp's products. Its expertise in this technology enabled Sharp to succeed in videocassette recorders (VCRs) with its innovative LCD viewfinder and led to the creation of its Wizard, a personal electronic organizer.

Steve Jobs provides insights on the importance of a firm's core competence. The Apple CEO is widely considered one of the world's most respected business leaders:[23]

> One of our biggest insights (years ago) was that we didn't want to get into any business where we didn't own or control the primary technology, because you'll get your head handed to you. We realized that for almost all future consumer electronics, the primary technology was going to be software. And we were pretty good at software. We could do the operating system software. We could write applications like iTunes on the Mac or even PC. And we could write the back-end software that runs on a cloud like iTunes. So we could write all these different kinds of software and tweed it all together and make it work seamlessly. And you ask yourself: What other companies can do that? It's a pretty short list.

Sharing Activities

As we saw above, leveraging core competencies involves transferring accumulated skills and expertise across business units in a corporation. Corporations also can achieve synergy by **sharing activities** across their business units. These include value-creating activities such as common manufacturing facilities, distribution channels, and sales forces. As we will see, sharing activities can potentially provide two primary payoffs: cost savings and revenue enhancements.

Deriving Cost Savings   Typically, this is the most common type of synergy and the easiest to estimate. Peter Shaw, head of mergers and acquisitions at the British chemical and pharmaceutical company ICI, refers to cost savings as "hard synergies" and contends that the level of certainty of their achievement is quite high. Cost savings come from many sources, including the elimination of jobs, facilities, and related expenses that are no longer needed when functions are consolidated, or from economies of scale in purchasing. Cost savings are generally highest when one company acquires another from the same industry in the same country. Shaw Industries, recently acquired by Berkshire Hathaway, is the nation's largest carpet producer. Over the years, it has dominated the competition through a strategy of acquisition which has enabled Shaw, among other things, to consolidate its manufacturing operations in a few, highly efficient plants and to lower costs through higher capacity utilization.

Sharing activities inevitably involve costs that the benefits must outweigh such as the greater coordination required to manage a shared activity. Even more important is the need to compromise on the design or performance of an activity so that it can be shared. For example, a salesperson handling the products of two business units must operate in a way that is usually not what either unit would choose if it were independent. If the compromise erodes the unit's effectiveness, then sharing may reduce rather than enhance competitive advantage.

Enhancing Revenue and Differentiation   Often an acquiring firm and its target may achieve a higher level of sales growth together than either company could on its own. Shortly after Gillette acquired Duracell, it confirmed its expectation that selling Duracell batteries through Gillette's existing channels for personal care products would increase sales, particularly internationally. Gillette sold Duracell products in 25 new markets in the first year after the acquisition and substantially increased sales in established international markets. Also, a target company's distribution channel can be used to escalate the sales of the acquiring company's product. Such was the case when Gillette acquired Parker Pen. Gillette estimated that it could gain an additional $25 million in sales of its own Waterman pens by taking advantage of Parker's distribution channels.

Firms also can enhance the effectiveness of their differentiation strategies by means of sharing activities among business units. A shared order-processing system, for example, may permit new features and services that a buyer will value. Also, sharing can reduce the cost of differentiation. For instance, a shared service network may make more advanced, remote service technology economically feasible. To illustrate the potential for enhanced differentiation through sharing, consider $7 billion VF Corporation—producer of such well-known brands as Lee, Wrangler, Vanity Fair, and Jantzen.

> VF's acquisition of Nutmeg Industries and H. H. Cutler provided it with several large customers that it didn't have before, increasing its plant utilization and productivity. But more importantly, Nutmeg designs and makes licensed apparel for sports teams and organizations, while Cutler manufactures licensed brand-name children's apparel, including Walt Disney kids' wear. Such brand labeling enhances the differentiation of VF's apparel products. According to VF President Mackey McDonald, "What we're doing is looking at value-added knitwear, taking our basic fleece from Basset-Walker [one of its divisions], embellishing it through Cutler and Nutmeg, and selling it as a value-added product." Additionally, Cutler's advanced high-speed printing technologies will enable VF to be more proactive in anticipating trends in the fashion-driven fleece market. Claims McDonald, "Rather than printing first and then trying to guess what the customer wants, we can see what's happening in the marketplace and then print it up."[24]

As a cautionary note, managers must keep in mind that sharing activities among businesses in a corporation can have a negative effect on a given business's differentiation. For example, with the merger of Chrysler and Daimler-Benz, many consumers may lower their perceptions of Mercedes's quality and prestige because they felt that common production components and processes were being used across the two divisions. And Ford's Jaguar division was adversely affected as consumers came to understand that it shared many components with its sister divisions at Ford, including Lincoln. Perhaps, it is not too surprising that both Chrysler and Jaguar were divested by their parent corporations.

Related Diversification: Market Power

We now discuss how companies achieve related diversification through **market power.** We also address the two principal means by which firms achieve synergy through market power: *pooled negotiating power* and *vertical integration.* Managers do, however, have limits on their ability to use market power for diversification, because government regulations can sometimes restrict the ability of a business to gain very large shares of a particular market. Consider GE's attempt to acquire Honeywell:

> When General Electric announced a $41 billion bid for Honeywell, the European Union stepped in. GE's market clout would have expanded significantly with the deal: GE would supply over one-half the parts needed to build several aircraft engines. The commission's concern, causing them to reject the acquisition, was that GE could use its increased market power to dominate the aircraft engine parts market and crowd out rivals.[25] Thus, while managers need to be aware of the strategic advantages of market power, they must at the same time be aware of regulations and legislation.

market power firms' abilities to profit through restricting or controlling supply to a market or coordinating with other firms to reduce investment.

Pooled Negotiating Power

Similar businesses working together or the affiliation of a business with a strong parent can strengthen an organization's bargaining position relative to suppliers and customers and enhance its position vis-à-vis competitors. Compare, for example, the position of an independent food manufacturer with the same business within Nestlé. Being part of Nestlé provides the business with significant clout—greater bargaining power with suppliers and customers—since it is part of a firm that makes large purchases from suppliers

pooled negotiating power the improvement in bargaining position relative to suppliers and customers.

and provides a wide variety of products. Access to the parent's deep pockets increases the business's strength, and the Nestlé unit enjoys greater protection from substitutes and new entrants. Not only would rivals perceive the unit as a more formidable opponent, but the unit's association with Nestlé would also provide greater visibility and improved image.

Consolidating an industry can also increase a firm's market power.[26] This is clearly an emerging trend in the multimedia industry.[27] All of these mergers and acquisitions have a common goal: to control and leverage as many news and entertainment channels as possible.

When acquiring related businesses, a firm's potential for pooled negotiating power vis-à-vis its customers and suppliers can be very enticing. However, managers must carefully evaluate how the combined businesses may affect relationships with actual and potential customers, suppliers, and competitors. For example, when PepsiCo diversified into the fast-food industry with its acquisitions of Kentucky Fried Chicken, Taco Bell, and Pizza Hut (now part of Yum! Brands), it clearly benefited from its position over these units that served as a captive market for its soft-drink products. However, many competitors, such as McDonald's, have refused to consider PepsiCo as a supplier of its own soft-drink needs because of competition with Pepsi's divisions in the fast-food industry. Simply put, McDonald's did not want to subsidize the enemy! Thus, although acquiring related businesses can enhance a corporation's bargaining power, it must be aware of the potential for retaliation.

Strategy Spotlight 6.2 discusses how 3M's actions to increase its market power led to a lawsuit (which 3M lost) by a competitor.

Vertical Integration

vertical integration an expansion or extension of the firm by integrating preceding or successive production processes.

Vertical integration occurs when a firm becomes its own supplier or distributor. That is, it represents an expansion or extension of the firm by integrating preceding or successive production processes.[28] The firm incorporates more processes toward the original source of raw materials (backward integration) or toward the ultimate consumer (forward integration). For example, a car manufacturer might supply its own parts or make its own engines to secure sources of supply or control its own system of dealerships to ensure retail outlets for its products. Similarly, an oil refinery might secure land leases and develop its own drilling capacity to ensure a constant supply of crude oil. Or it could expand into retail operations by owning or licensing gasoline stations to guarantee customers for its petroleum products.

Clearly, vertical integration can be a viable strategy for many firms. Strategy Spotlight 6.3 discusses Shaw Industries, a carpet manufacturer that has attained a dominant position in the industry via a strategy of vertical integration. Shaw has successfully implemented strategies of both forward and backward integration. Exhibit 6.3 depicts the stages of Shaw's vertical integration.

Benefits and Risks of Vertical Integration   Vertical integration is a means for an organization to reduce its dependence on suppliers or its channels of distribution to end users. However, the benefits associated with vertical integration—backward or forward—must be carefully weighed against the risks.[29]

The *benefits* of vertical integration include (1) a secure supply of raw materials or distribution channels that cannot be "held hostage" to external markets where costs can fluctuate over time, (2) protection and control over assets and services required to produce and deliver valuable products and services, (3) access to new business opportunities and new forms of technologies, and (4) simplified procurement and administrative procedures since key activities are brought inside the firm, eliminating the need to deal with a wide variety of suppliers and distributors.

Winnebago, the leader in the market for drivable recreational vehicles with a 19.3 percent market share, illustrates some of vertical integration's benefits.[30] The word

How 3M's Efforts to Increase Its Market Power Backfired

In the spring and summer of 2006, 3M found itself in court facing three class-action lawsuits launched by consumers and retailers of transparent and invisible adhesive tape (often generically known as "Scotch tape"). The suits all alleged that 3M had unlawfully bullied its way into a monopoly position in the tape market and that, as a result, consumers had been deprived of their rightful amount of choice and often paid up to 40 percent too much for their tape.

One rival that was particularly interested in these cases is LaPage's Inc. of North York, Ontario—3M's only significant competitor in the home and office adhesive tape market. LaPage's has everything to gain from court penalties against 3M's selling practices. This includes greater access to the lucrative North American market. The Canadian company started 3M's legal travails in the first place: all of the current class-action suits were initiated by LePage's.

Back in 1997, LePage's (then based in Pittsburgh) filed a complaint in the Pennsylvania District Court against 3M's practice of selling its various tape products using what was called "bundled rebates." LePage's argued that it violated the Sherman Act, the century-old U.S. legislation that limited monopoly power. 3M's bundled rebate program offered significant rebates—sometimes in the millions of dollars—to retailers as a reward for selling targeted amounts of six product lines. LePage's claimed that such selling targets were so large that retailers could only meet them by excluding competing products—in this case LePage's tape—from store shelves. For example, LePage's argued that Kmart, which had constituted 10% of LePage's sales dropped the account when 3M started offering the discount chain $1 million in rebates in return for selling more than $15 million worth of 3M products each year. Further, LePage's offered its own conspiracy theory: 3M introduced rebates not simply to grow its sales, but to eliminate LePage's—its only significant competitor.

A jury awarded LePage's $68.5 million in damages (the amount after trebling)—almost 15 percent of the 3M Consumer and Office Business unit's operating income in 2000. The Court of Appeals for the Third Circuit rejected 3M's appeal and upheld the judgment. It concluded that rebate bundling, even if above cost, may exclude equally efficient competitors from offering product (in this case, tape). In the ruling, Judge Dolores K. Sloviter wrote that "they may foreclose portions of the market to a potential competitor who does not manufacture an equally diverse group of products and who therefore cannot make a comparable offer." Therefore, the bundled rebates were judged to be an exploitation of 3M's monopoly power.

Sources: Bush, D. & Gelb, B. D. 2005. When Marketing Practices Raise Antitrust Concerns. *MIT Sloan Management Review,* 46(4): 73–81; Campbell, C. 2006. Tale of the Tape. *Canadian Business.* April 24: 39–40; and Bergstrom, B. 2003. $68M Jury Award Upheld against 3M in Antitrust Case. *The Associated Press:* March 26.

ethics

Winnebago means "big RV" to most Americans. And the firm has a sterling reputation for great quality. The firm's huge northern Iowa factories do everything from extruding aluminum for body parts to molding plastics for water and holding tanks to dashboards. Such vertical integration at the factory may appear to be outdated and expensive, but it

Exhibit 6.3 **Simplified Stages of Vertical Integration: Shaw Industries**

Vertical Integration at Shaw Industries

Shaw Industries (now part of Berkshire Hathaway) is an example of a firm that has followed a very successful strategy of vertical integration. By relentlessly pursuing both backward and forward integration, Shaw has become the dominant manufacturer of carpeting products in the United States. According to CEO Robert Shaw, "We want to be involved with as much of the process of making and selling carpets as practical. That way, we're in charge of costs." For example, Shaw acquired Amoco's polypropylene fiber manufacturing facilities in Alabama and Georgia. These new plants provide carpet fibers for internal use and for sale to other manufacturers. With this backward integration, fully one-quarter of Shaw's carpet fiber needs are now met in-house. In early 1996 Shaw began to integrate forward, acquiring seven floor-covering retailers in a move that suggested a strategy to consolidate the fragmented industry and increase its influence over retail pricing. Exhibit 6.3 provides a simplified depiction of the stages of vertical integration for Shaw Industries.

Sources: White, J. 2003. Shaw to home in on more with Georgia Tufters deal. *HFN: The Weekly Newspaper for the Home Furnishing Network,* May 5: 32; Shaw Industries. 1993, 2000. Annual reports; and Server, A. 1994. How to escape a price war. *Fortune,* June 13: 88.

guarantees excellent quality. The Recreational Vehicle Dealer Association started giving a quality award in 1996, and Winnebago has won it every year.

The *risks* of vertical integration include (1) the costs and expenses associated with increased overhead and capital expenditures to provide facilities, raw material inputs, and distribution channels inside the organization; (2) a loss of flexibility resulting from the inability to respond quickly to changes in the external environment because of the huge investments in vertical integration activities that generally cannot be easily deployed elsewhere; (3) problems associated with unbalanced capacities or unfilled demand along the value chain; and (4) additional administrative costs associated with managing a more complex set of activities. Exhibit 6.4 summarizes the benefits and risks of vertical integration.

In making vertical integration decisions, five issues should be considered.[31]

Exhibit 6.4
Benefits and Risks of Vertical Integration

Benefits
• A secure source of raw materials or distribution channels.
• Protection of and control over valuable assets.
• Access to new business opportunities.
• Simplified procurement and administrative procedures.

Risks
• Costs and expenses associated with increased overhead and capital expenditures.
• Loss of flexibility resulting from large investments.
• Problems associated with unbalanced capacities along the value chain.
• Additional administrative costs associated with managing a more complex set of activities.

1. *Is the company satisfied with the quality of the value that its present suppliers and distributors are providing?* If the performance of organizations in the vertical chain—both suppliers and distributors—is satisfactory, it may not, in general, be appropriate for a company to perform these activities themselves. Nike and Reebok have outsourced the manufacture of their shoes to countries such as China and Indonesia where labor costs are low. Since the strengths of these companies are typically in design and marketing, it would be advisable to continue to outsource production operations and continue to focus on where they can add the most value.

2. *Are there activities in the industry value chain presently being outsourced or performed independently by others that are a viable source of future profits?* Even if a firm is outsourcing value-chain activities to companies that are doing a credible job, it may be missing out on substantial profit opportunities. To illustrate, consider the automobile industry's profit pool. As you may recall from Chapter 5, there is much more potential profit in many downstream activities (e.g., leasing, warranty, insurance, and service) than in the manufacture of automobiles. Not surprisingly, carmakers such as Toyota and Honda are undertaking forward integration strategies to become bigger players in these high-profit activities.

3. *Is there a high level of stability in the demand for the organization's products?* High demand or sales volatility are not conducive to vertical integration. With the high level of fixed costs in plant and equipment as well as operating costs that accompany endeavors toward vertical integration, widely fluctuating sales demand can either strain resources (in times of high demand) or result in unused capacity (in times of low demand). The cycles of "boom and bust" in the automobile industry are a key reason why the manufacturers have increased the amount of outsourced inputs.

4. *Does the company have the necessary competencies to execute the vertical integration strategies?* As many companies would attest, successfully executing strategies of vertical integration can be very difficult. For example, Unocal, a major petroleum refiner, which once owned retail gas stations, was slow to capture the potential grocery and merchandise side of the business that might have resulted from customer traffic to its service stations. Unocal lacked the competencies to develop a separate retail organization and culture. The company eventually sold the assets and brand.

5. *Will the vertical integration initiative have potential negative impacts on the firm's stakeholders?* Managers must carefully consider the impact that vertical integration may have on existing and future customers, suppliers, and competitors. After Lockheed Martin, a dominant defense contractor, acquired Loral Corporation, an electronics supplier, for $9.1 billion, it had an unpleasant and unanticipated surprise. Loral, as a captive supplier of Lockheed, is now viewed as a rival by many of its previous customers. Thus, before Lockheed Martin can realize any net synergies from this acquisition, it must make up for the substantial business that it has lost.

Analyzing Vertical Integration: The Transaction Cost Perspective Another approach that has proved very useful in understanding vertical integration is the **transaction cost perspective.**[32] According to this perspective, every market transaction involves some *transaction costs.* First, a decision to purchase an input from an outside source leads to *search* costs (i.e., the cost to find where it is available, the level of quality, etc.). Second, there are costs associated with *negotiating.* Third, a *contract* needs to be written spelling out future possible contingencies. Fourth, parties in a contract have to *monitor* each other. Finally, if a party does not comply with the terms of the contract, there are *enforcement* costs. Transaction costs are thus the sum of search costs, negotiation costs, contracting costs, monitoring costs, and enforcement costs. These transaction costs can be avoided by internalizing the activity, in other words, by producing the input in-house.

transaction cost perspective a perspective that the choice of a transaction's governance structure, such as vertical integration or market transaction, is influenced by transaction costs, including search, negotiating, contracting, monitoring, and enforcement costs, associated with each choice.

A related problem with purchasing a specialized input from outside is the issue of *transaction-specific investments*. For example, when an automobile company needs an input specifically designed for a particular car model, the supplier may be unwilling to make the investments in plant and machinery necessary to produce that component for two reasons. First, the investment may take many years to recover but there is no guarantee the automobile company will continue to buy from them after the contract expires, typically in one year. Second, once the investment is made, the supplier has no bargaining power. That is, the buyer knows that the supplier has no option but to supply at ever-lower prices because the investments were so specific that they cannot be used to produce alternative products. In such circumstances, again, vertical integration may be the only option.

Vertical integration, however, gives rise to a different set of costs. These costs are referred to as *administrative costs*. Coordinating different stages of the value chain now internalized within the firm causes administrative costs to go up. Decisions about vertical integration are, therefore, based on a comparison of transaction costs and administrative costs. If transaction costs are lower than administrative costs, it is best to resort to market transactions and avoid vertical integration. For example, McDonald's may be the world's biggest buyer of beef, but they do not raise cattle. The market for beef has low transaction costs and requires no transaction-specific investments. On the other hand, if transaction costs are higher than administrative costs, vertical integration becomes an attractive strategy. Most automobile manufacturers produce their own engines because the market for engines involves high transaction costs and transaction-specific investments.

>LO6.4
How corporations can use unrelated diversification to attain synergistic benefits through corporate restructuring, parenting, and portfolio analysis.

Unrelated Diversification: Financial Synergies and Parenting

With unrelated diversification, unlike related diversification, few benefits are derived from *horizontal relationships*—that is, the leveraging of core competencies or the sharing of activities across business units within a corporation. Instead, potential benefits can be gained from *vertical (or hierarchical) relationships*—the creation of synergies from the interaction of the corporate office with the individual business units. There are two main sources of such synergies. First, the corporate office can contribute to "parenting" and restructuring of (often acquired) businesses. Second, the corporate office can add value by viewing the entire corporation as a family or "portfolio" of businesses and allocating resources to optimize corporate goals of profitability, cash flow, and growth. Additionally, the corporate office enhances value by establishing appropriate human resource practices and financial controls for each of its business units.

unrelated diversification a firm entering a different business that has little horizontal interaction with other businesses of a firm.

parenting advantage the positive contributions of the corporate office to a new business as a result of expertise and support provided and not as a result of substantial changes in assets, capital structure, or management.

Corporate Parenting and Restructuring

We have discussed how firms can add value through related diversification by exploring sources of synergy *across* business units. Now, we discuss how value can be created *within* business units as a result of the expertise and support provided by the corporate office.

Parenting   The positive contributions of the corporate office are called the **"parenting advantage."**[33] Many firms have successfully diversified their holdings without strong evidence of the more traditional sources of synergy (i.e., horizontally across business units). Diversified public corporations such as BTR, Emerson Electric, and Hanson and leveraged buyout firms such as Kohlberg, Kravis, Roberts & Company, and Clayton, Dublilier & Rice are a few examples.[34] These parent companies create value through management expertise. How? They improve plans and budgets and provide especially competent central functions such as legal, financial, human resource management, procurement, and the like. They also help subsidiaries make wise choices in their own acquisitions, divestitures, and new internal development decisions. Such contributions often help business units to substantially increase their revenues and profits. Consider Texas-based Cooper Industries' acquisition of Champion International, the spark plug company, as an example of corporate parenting:[35]

> Cooper applies a distinctive parenting approach designed to help its businesses improve their manufacturing performance. New acquisitions are "Cooperized"—Cooper audits their manufacturing operations; improves their cost accounting systems; makes their planning, budgeting, and human resource systems conform with its systems; and centralizes union negotiations. Excess cash is squeezed out through tighter controls and reinvested in productivity enhancements, which improve overall operating efficiency. As one manager observed, "When you get acquired by Cooper, one of the first things that happens is a truckload of policy manuals arrives at your door." Such active parenting has been effective in enhancing the competitive advantages of many kinds of manufacturing businesses.

Restructuring   **Restructuring** is another means by which the corporate office can add value to a business.[36] The central idea can be captured in the real estate phrase "buy low and sell high." Here, the corporate office tries to find either poorly performing firms with unrealized potential or firms in industries on the threshold of significant, positive change. The parent intervenes, often selling off parts of the business; changing the management; reducing payroll and unnecessary sources of expenses; changing strategies; and infusing the company with new technologies, processes, reward systems, and so forth. When the restructuring is complete, the firm can either "sell high" and capture the added value or keep the business and enjoy financial and competitive benefits.[37]

Loews Corporation, a conglomerate with $15 billion in revenues competes in such industries as oil and gas, tobacco, watches, insurance, and hotels. It provides an exemplary example of how firms can successfully "buy low and sell high" as part of their corporate strategy.[38]

> Energy accounts for 33 percent of Loews' $30 billion in total assets. In the 1980s it bought six oil tankers for only $5 million each during a sharp slide in oil prices. The downside was limited. After all these huge hulks could easily have been sold as scrap steel. However, that didn't have to happen. Eight years after Loews purchased the tankers, they sold them for $50 million each.
>
> Loews was also extremely successful with its next energy play—drilling equipment. Although wildcatting for oil is very risky, selling services to wildcatters is not, especially if the assets are bought during a down cycle. Loews did just that. It purchased 10 offshore drilling rigs for $50 million in 1989 and formed Diamond Offshore Drilling. In 1995 Loews received $338 million after taking a 30 percent piece of this operation public!

For the restructuring strategy to work, the corporate management must have both the insight to detect undervalued companies (otherwise the cost of acquisition would be too high) or businesses competing in industries with a high potential for transformation.[39] Additionally, of course, they must have the requisite skills and resources to turn the businesses around, even if they may be in new and unfamiliar industries.

Restructuring can involve changes in assets, capital structure, or management.

- *Asset restructuring* involves the sale of unproductive assets, or even whole lines of businesses, that are peripheral. In some cases, it may even involve acquisitions that strengthen the core business.
- *Capital restructuring* involves changing the debt-equity mix, or the mix between different classes of debt or equity. Although the substitution of equity with debt is more common in buyout situations, occasionally the parent may provide additional equity capital.
- *Management restructuring* typically involves changes in the composition of the top management team, organizational structure, and reporting relationships. Tight

restructuring the intervention of the corporate office in a new business that substantially changes the assets, capital structure, and/or management, including selling off parts of the business, changing the management, reducing payroll and unnecessary sources of expenses, changing strategies, and infusing the new business with new technologies, processes, and reward systems.

financial control, rewards based strictly on meeting short- to medium-term performance goals, and reduction in the number of middle-level managers are common steps in management restructuring. In some cases, parental intervention may even result in changes in strategy as well as infusion of new technologies and processes.

Hanson, plc, a British conglomerate, made numerous such acquisitions in the United States in the 1980s, often selling these firms at significant profits after a few years of successful restructuring efforts. Hanson's acquisition and subsequent restructuring of the SCM group is a classic example of the restructuring strategy. Hanson acquired SCM, a diversified manufacturer of industrial and consumer products (including Smith-Corona typewriters, Glidden paints, and Durkee Famous Foods), for $930 million in 1986 after a bitter takeover battle. In the next few months, Hanson sold SCM's paper and pulp operations for $160 million, the chemical division for $30 million, Glidden paints for $580 million, and Durkee Famous Foods for $120 million, virtually recovering the entire original investment. In addition, Hanson also sold the SCM headquarters in New York for $36 million and reduced the headquarters staff by 250. They still retained several profitable divisions, including the titanium dioxide operations and managed them with tight financial controls that led to increased returns.[40]

Exhibit 6.5 summarizes the three primary types of restructuring activities.

Portfolio Management

During the 1970s and early 1980s, several leading consulting firms developed the concept of **portfolio management** to achieve a better understanding of the competitive position of an overall portfolio (or family) of businesses, to suggest strategic alternatives for each of the businesses, and to identify priorities for the allocation of resources. Several studies have reported widespread use of these techniques among American firms.[41]

Description and Potential Benefits   The key purpose of portfolio models is to assist a firm in achieving a balanced portfolio of businesses.[42] This consists of businesses whose profitability, growth, and cash flow characteristics complement each other and adds up to a satisfactory overall corporate performance. Imbalance, for example, could be caused either by excessive cash generation with too few growth opportunities or by insufficient cash generation to fund the growth requirements in the portfolio. Monsanto, for example, used portfolio planning to restructure its portfolio, divesting low-growth commodity chemicals businesses and acquiring businesses in higher-growth industries such as biotechnology.

The Boston Consulting Group's (BCG) growth/share matrix is among the best known of these approaches.[43] In the BCG approach, each of the firm's strategic business units (SBUs) is plotted on a two-dimensional grid in which the axes are relative market share and industry growth rate. The grid is broken into four quadrants. Exhibit 6.6 depicts the BCG matrix. Following are a few clarifications:

1.   Each circle represents one of the corporation's business units. The size of the circle represents the relative size of the business unit in terms of revenues.

Exhibit 6.5
The Three Primary Types of Restructuring Activities

Asset Restructuring: The sale of unproductive assets, or even whole lines of businesses, that are peripheral.

Capital Restructuring: Changing the debt-equity mix, or the mix between different classes of debt or equity.

Management Restructuring: Changes in the composition of the top management team, organization structure, and reporting relationships.

Exhibit 6.6 The Boston Consulting Group (BCG) Portfolio Matrix

2. Relative market share, measured by the ratio of the business unit's size to that of its largest competitor, is plotted along the horizontal axis.

3. Market share is central to the BCG matrix. This is because high relative market share leads to unit cost reduction due to experience and learning curve effects and, consequently, superior competitive position.

Each of the four quadrants of the grid has different implications for the SBUs that fall into the category:

- *Stars* are SBUs competing in high-growth industries with relatively high market shares. These firms have long-term growth potential and should continue to receive substantial investment funding.

- *Question Marks* are SBUs competing in high-growth industries but having relatively weak market shares. Resources should be invested in them to enhance their competitive positions.

- *Cash Cows* are SBUs with high market shares in low-growth industries. These units have limited long-run potential but represent a source of current cash flows to fund investments in "stars" and "question marks."

- *Dogs* are SBUs with weak market shares in low-growth industries. Because they have weak positions and limited potential, most analysts recommend that they be divested.

In using portfolio strategy approaches, a corporation tries to create shareholder value in a number of ways.[44] First, portfolio analysis provides a snapshot of the businesses in a corporation's portfolio. Therefore, the corporation is in a better position to allocate resources among the business units according to prescribed criteria (e.g., use cash flows from the "cash cows" to fund promising "stars"). Second, the expertise and analytical resources in the corporate office provide guidance in determining what firms may be attractive (or unattractive) acquisitions. Third, the corporate office is able to provide financial resources to the business units on favorable terms that reflect the corporation's overall ability to raise funds. Fourth, the corporate office can provide high-quality review and coaching for the individual businesses. Fifth, portfolio analysis provides a basis for developing strategic goals and reward/evaluation systems for business managers. For example, managers of cash cows would have lower targets for revenue growth than managers of stars, but the former would have higher threshold levels of profit targets on proposed projects than the managers of star businesses. Compensation systems would also reflect such realities. Cash cows understandably would be rewarded more on the basis of cash that their businesses generate than would managers of star businesses. Similarly, managers of star businesses would be held to higher standards for revenue growth than managers of cash cow businesses.

To see how companies can benefit from portfolio approaches, consider Ciba-Geigy.

In 1994 Ciba-Geigy adopted portfolio planning approaches to help it manage its business units, which competed in a wide variety of industries, including chemicals, dyes, pharmaceuticals, crop protection, and animal health.[45] It placed each business unit in a category corresponding to the BCG matrix. The business unit's goals, compensation programs, personnel selection, and resource allocation were strongly associated with the category within which the business was placed. For example, business units classified as "cash cows" had much higher hurdles for obtaining financial resources (from the corporate office) for expansion than "question marks" since the latter were businesses for which Ciba-Geigy had high hopes for accelerated future growth and profitability. Additionally, the compensation of a business unit manager in a cash cow would be strongly associated with its success in generating cash to fund other businesses, whereas a manager of a question mark business would be rewarded on his or her ability to increase revenue growth and market share. The portfolio planning approaches appear to be working. In 2010, Ciba-Geigy's (now Novartis) revenues and net income stood at $45 billion and $8.5 billion, respectively. This represents a 110 percent increase in revenues and a most impressive 49 percent growth in net income over a six-year period.

Limitations Despite the potential benefits of portfolio models, there are also some notable downsides. First, they compare SBUs on only two dimensions, making the implicit but erroneous assumption that (1) those are the only factors that really matter and (2) every unit can be accurately compared on that basis. Second, the approach views each SBU as a stand-alone entity, ignoring common core business practices and value-creating activities that may hold promise for synergies across business units. Third, unless care is exercised, the process becomes largely mechanical, substituting an oversimplified graphical model for the important contributions of the CEO's (and other corporate managers') experience and judgment. Fourth, the reliance on "strict rules" regarding resource allocation across SBUs can be detrimental to a firm's long-term viability. For example, according to one study, over one-half of all the businesses that should have been cash users (based on the BCG matrix) were instead cash providers.[46] Finally, while colorful and easy to comprehend, the imagery of the BCG matrix can lead to some troublesome and overly simplistic prescriptions. According to one author:

The dairying analogy is appropriate (for some cash cows), so long as we resist the urge to oversimplify it. On the farm, even the best-producing cows eventually begin to dry up. The farmer's solution to this is euphemistically called "freshening" the cow: The farmer arranges a date for the cow with a bull, she has a calf, the milk begins flowing again. Cloistering the cow—isolating her from everything but the feed trough and the milking machines—assures that she will go dry.[47]

To see what can go wrong, consider Cabot Corporation.

Cabot Corporation supplies carbon black for the rubber, electronics, and plastics industries. Following the BCG matrix, Cabot moved away from its cash cow, carbon black, and diversified into stars such as ceramics and semiconductors in a seemingly overaggressive effort to create more revenue growth for the corporation. Predictably, Cabot's return on assets declined as the firm shifted away from its core competence to unrelated areas. The portfolio model failed by pointing the company in the wrong direction in an effort to spur growth—away from their core business. Recognizing its mistake, Cabot Corporation returned to its mainstay carbon black manufacturing and divested unrelated businesses. Today the company is a leader in its field with $3 billion in 2010 revenues.[48]

Exhibit 6.7 summarizes the limitations of portfolio model analysis.

Caveat: Is Risk Reduction a Viable Goal of Diversification?

One of the purposes of diversification is to reduce the risk that is inherent in a firm's variability in revenues and profits over time. That is, if a firm enters new products or markets that are affected differently by seasonal or economic cycles, its performance over time will be more stable. For example, a firm manufacturing lawn mowers may diversify into snow blowers to even out its annual sales. Or a firm manufacturing a luxury line of household furniture may introduce a lower-priced line since affluent and lower-income customers are affected differently by economic cycles.

At first glance the above reasoning may make sense, but there are some problems with it. First, a firm's stockholders can diversify their portfolios at a much lower cost than a corporation, and they don't have to worry about integrating the acquisition into their portfolio. Second, economic cycles as well as their impact on a given industry (or firm) are difficult to predict with any degree of accuracy.

Notwithstanding the above, some firms have benefited from diversification by lowering the variability (or risk) in their performance over time. Consider Emerson Electronic.[49]

> Emerson Electronic is a $21 billion manufacturer that produces a wide variety of products, including measurement devices for heavy industry, temperature controls for heating

Exhibit 6.7
Benefits and Limitations of Portfolio Models

Benefits

- The corporation is in a better position to allocate resources to businesses according to explicit criteria.
- The corporate office can provide guidance on what firms may be attractive acquisitions.
- The corporate office can provide financial resources to businesses on favorable terms (that reflect the corporation's ability to raise funds).
- The corporate office can provide high-quality review and coaching for the individual businesses.
- It provides a basis for developing strategic goals and evaluation/reward systems for businesses.

Limitations

- They are overly simplistic, consisting of only two dimensions (growth and market share).
- They view each business as separate, ignoring potential synergies across businesses.
- The process may become overly largely mechanical, minimizing the potential value of managers' judgment and experience.
- The reliance on strict rules for resource allocation across SBUs can be detrimental to a firm's long-term viability.
- The imagery (e.g., cash cows, dogs) while colorful, may lead to troublesome and overly simplistic prescriptions.

and ventilation systems, and power tools sold at Home Depot. Recently, many analysts questioned Emerson's purchase of companies that sell power systems to the volatile tele-communications industry. Why? This industry is expected to experience, at best, minimal growth. However, CEO David Farr maintained that such assets could be acquired inexpensively because of the aggregate decline in demand in this industry. Additionally, he argued that the other business units, such as the sales of valves and regulators to the now-booming oil and natural gas companies, were able to pick up the slack. Therefore, while net profits in the electrical equipment sector (Emerson's core business) sharply decreased, Emerson's overall corporate profits increased 1.7 percent.

Risk reduction in and of itself is rarely viable as a means to create shareholder value. It must be undertaken with a view of a firm's overall diversification strategy.

The Means to Achieve Diversification

>LO6.5
The various means of engaging in diversification—mergers and acquisitions, joint ventures/strategic alliances, and internal development.

We have addressed the types of diversification (e.g., related and unrelated) that a firm may undertake to achieve synergies and create value for its shareholders. Now, we address the means by which a firm can go about achieving these desired benefits.

There are three basic means. First, through acquisitions or mergers, corporations can directly acquire a firm's assets and competencies. Although the terms *mergers* and *acquisitions* are used quite interchangeably, there are some key differences. With **acquisitions,** one firm buys another either through a stock purchase, cash, or the issuance of debt.[50] **Mergers,** on the other hand, entail a combination or consolidation of two firms to form a new legal entity. Mergers are relatively rare and entail a transaction among two firms on a relatively equal basis. Despite such differences, we consider both mergers and acquisitions to be quite similar in terms of their implications for a firm's corporate-level strategy.[51]

acquisitions the incorporation of one firm into another through purchase.

Second, corporations may agree to pool the resources of other companies with their resource base, commonly known as a joint venture or strategic alliance. Although these two forms of partnerships are similar in many ways, there is an important difference. Joint ventures involve the formation of a third-party legal entity where the two (or more) firms each contribute equity, whereas strategic alliances do not.

mergers the combining of two or more firms into one new legal entity.

Third, corporations may diversify into new products, markets, and technologies through internal development. Called corporate entrepreneurship, it involves the leveraging and combining of a firm's own resources and competencies to create synergies and enhance shareholder value. We address this subject in greater length in Chapter 12.

Mergers and Acquisitions

The rate of mergers and acquisitions (M&A) had dropped off beginning in 2001. This trend was largely a result of a recession, corporate scandals, and a declining stock market. However, the situation has changed dramatically. Over the past several years, several large mergers and acquisitions were announced. These include:[52]

- Kraft's acquisition of Cadbury for $19.4 billion.
- In Bev's acquisition of Anheuser-Busch for $52 billion.
- Pfizer's acquisition of Wyeth for $68 billion.
- Mittal Steel's acquisition of Arcelor for $33 billion.
- BellSouth's acquisition of AT&T for $86.0 billion.
- Sprint's merger with Nextel for $39 billion.
- Boston Scientific's $27 billion acquisition of medical device maker Guidant.
- Procter & Gamble's purchase of Gillette for $54 billion.
- Kmart Holding Corp.'s acquisition of Sears, Roebuck & Co. for $11 billion.

Exhibit 6.8 illustrates the dramatic increase in worldwide M&A activity in the U.S. up until 2008, when the global recession began. Several factors help to explain the rapid rise between 2002 and 2007. First, there was the robust economy and the increasing corporate profits that had boosted stock prices and cash. For example, the S&P 500 stock index companies, including financial companies, had a record of over $2 trillion in cash and other short-term assets.

Second, the weak U.S. dollar made U.S. assets less expensive relative to other countries. That is, from the perspective of a foreign acquirer, compared to any other period in recent memory, U.S. companies were "cheap." For example, a Euro, which was worth only 80 cents in 1999, was worth $1.35 by mid-2007. This made U.S. companies a relative bargain for a European acquirer.

Third, stricter governance standards were requiring poorly performing CEOs and boards of directors to consider unsolicited offers. In essence, top executives and board members were less likely to be protected by antitakeover mechanisms such as greenmail, poison pills, and golden parachutes (discussed at the end of the chapter).

2009 was a bad year for M&A activities due to the global recession. However, with the economy improving in 2010, the pace picked up again. The total value for M&A activity in 2010 was $2.8 trillion—a 17 percent increase over the previous year. Further, in the United States, companies sought approval on 1,166 M&A transactions in 2010 compared to only 716 in 2009—reflecting a 63 percent increase. (U.S. merger approval is required by the Federal Trade Commission for any deal valued at $63 million or more.)[53] According to Andrew Gavil, an antitrust law professor, "Merger activity is often associated with optimism, willingness to spend cash on hand, availability of credit and general levels of economic activity," though it may also indicate how difficult the recovery has been for some businesses (that is, assets can be acquired quite cheaply).

Motives and Benefits   Growth through mergers and acquisitions has played a critical role in the success of many corporations in a wide variety of high-technology and knowledge-intensive industries. Here, market and technology changes can occur very quickly and unpredictably.[54] Speed—speed to market, speed to positioning, and speed to becoming a viable company—is critical in such industries. For example, Alex Mandl, then

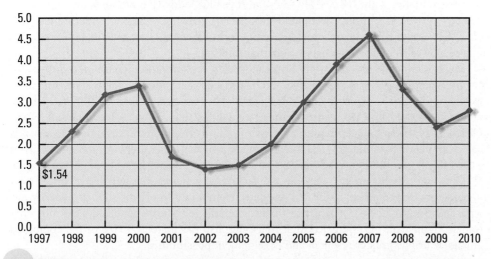

Global Value of Mergers and Acquisitions

Global mergers and acquisitions soared past their previous record and hit $4.6 trillion for the year 2007.

Exhibit 6.8 Global Value of Mergers and Acquisitions

Source: Bloomberg; Dealogic; personal communication with Meredith Leonard at Dealogic on January 27, 2009; and personal communication with Natalie Logan at Dealogic on January 27, 2011.

AT&T's president, was responsible for the acquisition of McCaw Cellular. Although many industry experts felt the price was too steep, he believed that cellular technology was a critical asset for the telecommunications business. Mandl claimed, "The plain fact is that acquiring is much faster than building."[55]

Mergers and acquisitions also can be a means of *obtaining valuable resources that can help an organization expand its product offerings and services.* For example, Cisco Systems, a dominant player in networking equipment, acquired more than 70 companies over a recent seven-year period.[56] This provides Cisco with access to the latest in networking equipment. Then it uses its excellent sales force to market the new technology to its corporate customers. Cisco also provides strong incentives to the staff of acquired companies to stay on. To realize the greatest value from its acquisitions, Cisco also has learned to integrate acquired companies efficiently and effectively.[57]

Mergers and acquisitions also can *provide the opportunity for firms to attain the three bases of synergy—leveraging core competencies, sharing activities, and building market power.* Consider Procter & Gamble's $57 billion acquisition of Gillette.[58] First, it helps Procter & Gamble to leverage its core competencies in marketing and product positioning in the area of grooming and personal care brands. For example, P&G has experience in repositioning brands such as Old Spice in this market (which recently passed Gillette's Right Guard brand to become No. 1 in the deodorant market). Gillette has very strong brands in razors and blades. Thus, P&G's marketing expertise enhances its market position. Second, there are opportunities to share value-creating activities. Gillette will benefit from P&G's stronger distribution network in developing countries where the potential growth rate for the industry's products remains higher than in the United States, Europe, or Japan. Consider the insight of A. F. Lafley, P&G's former CEO:

> When I was in Asia in the 90s, we had already gone beyond the top 500 cities in China. Today, we're way down into the rural areas. So we add three, four, five Gillette brands, and we don't even have to add a salesperson.

Third, the addition of Gillette increases P&G's market power. In recent years, the growth of powerful global retailers such as Walmart, Carrefour, and Costco has eroded much of the consumer goods industry's pricing power. A central part of P&G's recent strategy has been to focus its resources on enhancing its core brands. Today, 16 of its brands (each with revenues of over $1 billion) account for $30 billion of the firm's $51.4 billion in total revenues. Gillette, with $10.5 billion in total revenues, adds five brands which also have revenues of over $1 billion. P&G anticipates that its growing stable of "superbrands" will help it to weather the industry's tough pricing environment and enhance its power relative to large, powerful retailers such as Walmart and Target.

Merger and acquisition activity also can *lead to consolidation within an industry and can force other players to merge.*[59] In the pharmaceutical industry, the patents for many top-selling drugs are expiring and M&A activity is expected to heat up.[60] For example, many patents held by U.S. pharmaceutical companies (e.g., Pfizer's Lipitor) will expire in the next few years, which represents tens of billions of dollars in revenue. Clearly, this is an example of how the political—legal segment of the general environment (discussed in Chapter 2) can affect a corporation's strategy and performance. Although health care providers and patients are happy about the lower-cost generics that will arrive, drug firms are being pressed to make up for lost revenues. Combining top firms such as Glaxo Wellcome and SmithKline Beecham has many potential long-term benefits. They not only promise significant postmerger cost savings, but also the increased size of the combined companies brings greater research and development possibilities.

Corporations can also *enter new market segments by way of acquisitions.* Although Charles Schwab & Co. is best known for providing discount trading services for middle

America, it clearly is interested in other target markets.[61] In late 2000 Schwab surprised its rivals by paying $2.7 billion to acquire (divested in 2006) U.S. Trust Corporation, a 147-year-old financial services institution that is a top estate planner for the wealthy. However, Schwab is not ignoring its core market. The firm also purchased Cybercorp Inc., a Texas brokerage company, for $488 million. That firm offers active online traders sophisticated quotes and stock-screening tools. Exhibit 6.9 summarizes the benefits of mergers and acquisitions.

Potential Limitations   As noted in the previous section, mergers and acquisitions provide a firm with many potential benefits. However, at the same time, there are many potential drawbacks or limitations to such corporate activity.[62]

First, *the takeover premium that is paid for an acquisition typically is very high.* Two times out of three, the stock price of the acquiring company falls once the deal is made public. Since the acquiring firm often pays a 30 percent or higher premium for the target company, the acquirer must create synergies and scale economies that result in sales and market gains exceeding the premium price. Firms paying higher premiums set the performance hurdle even higher. For example, Household International paid an 82 percent premium to buy Beneficial, and Conseco paid an 83 percent premium to acquire Green Tree Financial. Historically, paying a high premium over the stock price has been a poor strategy.

Second, *competing firms often can imitate any advantages realized or copy synergies that result from the M&A.*[63] Thus, a firm can often see its advantages quickly erode. Unless the advantages are sustainable and difficult to copy, investors will not be willing to pay a high premium for the stock. Similarly, the time value of money must be factored into the stock price. M&A costs are paid up front. Conversely, firms pay for R&D, ongoing marketing, and capacity expansion over time. This stretches out the payments needed to gain new competencies. The M&A argument is that a large initial investment is worthwhile because it creates long-term advantages. However, stock analysts want to see immediate results from such a large cash outlay. If the acquired firm does not produce results quickly, investors often divest the stock, driving the price down.

Third, *managers' credibility and ego can sometimes get in the way of sound business decisions.* If the M&A does not perform as planned, managers who pushed for the deal find their reputation tarnished. This can lead them to protect their credibility by funneling more money, or escalating their commitment, into an inevitably doomed operation. Further, when a merger fails and a firm tries to unload the acquisition, they often must sell at a huge discount. These problems further compound the costs and erode the stock price.

Fourth, *there can be many cultural issues that may doom the intended benefits from M&A endeavors.* Consider, the insights of Joanne Lawrence, who played an important role in the merger between SmithKline and the Beecham Group.[64]

> The key to a strategic merger is to create a new culture. This was a mammoth challenge during the SmithKline Beecham merger. We were working at so many different cultural

---

- Obtain valuable resources that can help an organization expand its product offerings.
- Provide the opportunity for firms to attain three bases of synergy: leveraging core competencies, sharing activities, and building market power.
- Lead to consolidation within an industry and force other players to merge.
- Enter new market segments.

Exhibit 6.9
Benefits of Mergers and Acquisitions

Effectively Managing the Human Side of Acquisitions

When managing the human side of the merger and acquisition (M&A) process, firms face issues such as anxiety, employee shock, and protests. How companies manage such issues will reduce the volume of customer defections, supplier unrest, and government disapproval—as well as increase employee commitment.

In the follow-up to the P&G and Gillette merger, headhunters started targeting Gillette talent. P&G faced government disapproval and investigations in Gillette's home state of Massachusetts, as well as potential problems in India—where it intended to reduce the number of distributors. However, P&G was able to keep 90 percent of Gillette employees who were offered jobs, which is much higher than the average in M&A situations.

P&G enlisted all Gillette employees in an active effort to keep customers, suppliers, and distributors happy, even employees who would eventually be let go. Former Gillette Chairman Jim Kilts said, "A lot of people who left were going to retire and leave anyway in the short term. And I think we seeded the company with some great talent down in the organization, so time will tell." In the instances when processes used by Gillette were deemed more efficient than P&G's, they were adopted. Overall, the company achieved its cost and revenue targets from the first year following the merger.

The best may be yet to come, as the company was able to make aggressive moves in key markets such as Brazil and India. In addition, there was a growing investment and expertise in sports marketing and faster internal decision making.

Source: Kanter, R. M. 2009. Mergers That Stick. *Harvard Business Review*, 87(10): 121–125; and Neff, J. 2010. Why P&G's $57 Billion Bet on Gillette Hasn't Paid Off Big—Yet. *www.adage.com*. February 15: np.

levels, it was dizzying. We had two national cultures to blend—American and British—that compounded the challenge of selling the merger in two different markets with two different shareholder bases. There were also two different business cultures: One was very strong, scientific, and academic; the other was much more commercially oriented. And then we had to consider within both companies the individual businesses, each of which has its own little culture.

Exhibit 6.10 summarizes the limitations of mergers and acquisitions.

Strategy Spotlight 6.4 addresses the human side of M&A activity—how they may be successfully managed.

Divestment: The Other Side of the "M&A Coin"   When firms acquire other businesses, it typically generates quite a bit of "press" in business publications such as *The Wall Street Journal, BusinessWeek,* and *Fortune.* It makes for exciting news, and one thing is for sure—large acquiring firms automatically improve their standing in the Fortune 500 rankings (since it is based solely on total revenues). However, managers must also carefully consider the strategic implications of exiting businesses.

Exhibit 6.10
Limitations of Mergers and Acquisitions

- Takeover premiums paid for acquisitions are typically very high.
- Competing firms often can imitate any advantages or copy synergies that result from the merger or acquisition.
- Managers' egos sometimes get in the way of sound business decisions.
- Cultural issues may doom the intended benefits from M&A endeavors.

Why Did Tyco International Sell a Majority Stake in One of Its Businesses?

Tyco International, with $17 billion in revenues, is the world's largest maker of security systems. On November 9, 2010, Tyco announced that it had agreed to sell a majority stake in its electrical and metal products unit to buyout firm Clayton Dubilier & Rice (CD&R) for $720 million. By taking this action, it withdrew its plans to spin off the division.

The proceeds from the sale of Tyco's 51 percent stake will help the firm accelerate its share buyback program, which it had announced two months earlier. The unit, which had $1.4 billion in 2009 revenues, will operate as a standalone entity called Atkore International. It makes products such as metal-clad electrical cables and barbed razor ribbon. Tyco felt that it could profit more by selling the remaining 49 percent when markets improve.

The acquisition is very attractive to CD&R. According to Nathan K. Sleeper, a CD&R partner, "As a manufacturer and distributor of industrial products, Atkore is a leader in a market that CD&R knows very well. We look forward to working with the Atkore management team to build on the core strengths of the business—including an outstanding reputation, well-recognized brands, long-term customer relationships, and significant scale advantages—to create an even more successful independent enterprise."

Sources: Winter, C. 2010. Tyco International: Biding Time in Hope of Better Markets. *Bloomberg Businessweek*. November 15–22: 34; and Franco, T. C. 2010. Clayton, Dubilier & Rice to Acquire Tyco International's Electrical and Metal Products Business to Be Renamed Atkore International. *www.prnewswire.com*. November 9: np.

Divestments, the exit of a business from a firm's portfolio, are quite common. One study found that large, prestigious U.S. companies divested more acquisitions than they had kept.[65] Well-known divestitures in business history include (1) Novell's purchase of WordPerfect for stock valued at $1.4 billion and later sold to Corel for $124 million, and (2) Quaker Oats' unloading of the Snapple Beverage Company to Triarc for only $300 million in 1997—three years after it had bought it for $1.8 billion!

Divesting a business can accomplish many different objectives.* As the examples above demonstrate, it can be used to help a firm reverse an earlier acquisition that didn't work out as planned. Often, this is simply to help "cut their losses." Other objectives include: (1) enabling managers to focus their efforts more directly on the firm's core businesses,[66] (2) providing the firm with more resources to spend on more attractive alternatives, and (3) raising cash to help fund existing businesses. Strategy Spotlight 6.5 discusses another reason for a divestiture. Here, Tyco International sold part of one of its businesses to raise cash for its share buyback.

Divesting can enhance a firm's competitive position only to the extent that it reduces its tangible (e.g., maintenance, investments, etc.) or intangible (e.g., opportunity costs, managerial attention) costs without sacrificing a current competitive

> **divestment** the exit of a business from a firm's portfolio.

---

* Firms can divest their businesses in a number of ways. Sell-offs, spin-offs, equity carve-outs, asset sales/dissolution, and split-ups are some such modes of divestment. In a sell-off, the divesting firm privately negotiates with a third party to divest a unit/subsidiary for cash/stock. In a spin-off, a parent company distributes shares of the unit/subsidiary being divested pro-rata to its existing shareholders and a new company is formed. Equity carve-outs are similar to spin-offs except that shares in the unit/subsidiary being divested are offered to new shareholders. Dissolution involves sale of redundant assets, not necessarily as an entire unit/subsidiary as in sell-offs but a few bits at a time. A split-up, on the other hand, is an instance of divestiture where the parent company is split into two or more new companies and the parent ceases to exist. Shares in the parent company are exchanged for shares in new companies and the exact distribution varies case by case.

advantage or the seeds of future advantages.[67] To be effective, divesting requires a thorough understanding of a business unit's current ability and future potential to contribute to a firm's value creation. However, since such decisions involve a great deal of uncertainty, it is very difficult to make such evaluations. In addition, because of managerial self-interests and organizational inertia, firms often delay divestments of underperforming businesses.

Successful divestment involves establishing objective criteria for determining divestment candidates.[68] Clearly, firms should not panic and sell for a song in bad times. Private equity firms and conglomerates naturally place great emphasis on value when it comes to assessing which business units to keep. In identifying which assets to sell, the management committee of $10 billion Textron, for example, applies three tests of value to the firm's diverse portfolio—which is composed of some 12 divisions and 72 strategic business units (SBUs). For Textron to retain a business unit:

- The unit's long-term fundamentals must be sound. The team gauges this by assessing the attractiveness of each SBU's market and the unit's competitive strength within that market.
- Textron must be able to grow the unit's intrinsic value by 15 percent or more annually. The team applies this screen by carefully analyzing each SBU's business plan each year and challenging its divisional management teams to assess the value-growth potential of each business objectively.
- The unit's revenues must reach a certain threshold. Textron seeks to hold a portfolio of relevant businesses, each with at least $1 billion in revenue. Businesses that are not generating $1 billion or more in sales—and are not likely to reach this watershed within the foreseeable future—are targets for divestiture.

Strategic Alliances and Joint Ventures

strategic alliance a cooperative relationship between two or more firms.

A **strategic alliance** is a cooperative relationship between two (or more) firms.[69] Alliances may be either informal or formal—that is, involving a written contract. **Joint ventures** represent a special case of alliances, wherein two (or more) firms contribute equity to form a new legal entity.

Strategic alliances and joint ventures are assuming an increasingly prominent role in the strategy of leading firms, both large and small.[70] Such cooperative relationships have many potential advantages.[71] Among these are entering new markets, reducing manufacturing (or other) costs in the value chain, and developing and diffusing new technologies.[72]

joint ventures new entities formed within a strategic alliance in which two or more firms, the parents, contribute equity to form the new legal entity.

Entering New Markets Often a company that has a successful product or service wants to introduce it into a new market. However, it may not have the financial resources or the requisite marketing expertise because it does not understand customer needs, know how to promote the product, or have access to the proper distribution channels.[73]

The partnerships formed between Time-Warner, Inc., and three African American–owned cable companies in New York City are examples of joint ventures created to serve a domestic market. Time-Warner built a 185,000-home cable system in the city and asked the three cable companies to operate it. Time-Warner supplied the product, and the cable companies supplied the knowledge of the community and the know-how to market the cable system. Joining with the local companies enabled Time-Warner to win the acceptance of the cable customers and to benefit from an improved image in the black community.

Strategy Spotlight 6.6 discusses how a strategic alliance between two firms will help them crowdsource creative concepts.

Crowdsourcing: How a Strategic Alliance Will Benefit Both Parties

MRM Worldwide, a New York–based advertising firm, has entered into a strategic alliance with Aniboom, a "virtual" animation company. The alliance is designed to bring MRM's clients quicker and more cost-efficient animation services.

Aniboom, an Israeli company with offices in New York and San Francisco, was founded in 2006 by Uri Shinar, the former CEO of Israeli broadcaster Kesheet. It is a web-based platform that connects 8,000 animators in 70 countries around the world with clients in the TV, film, music, and video game sectors. Prospective clients submit Request for Proposals (RFPs) via the platform, and animators all over the world can respond. MRM global Chief Creative Officer Oren Frank believes that agencies are more likely to rely on this crowdsourcing approach in the future as clients seek more efficient ways of doing business.

MRM's plans are to have animators compete for work: "MRMs clients can launch a content creation competition in the Aniboom community for advertising solutions and have the community at large or a panel of judges select the top finalists and ultimate winner of the assignment. Or the competition could be private, with only the final results exhibited to the public."

Such competitions are part of a group of highly volatile trends that have become increasingly popular. They breed competition and bolster the idea that capitalism weeds out the weak links. It also becomes harder (or more unappealing) for established industries to bid on business that's sought through these methods, because costs can outweigh profits. However, there is one thing that it has done: The playing field has been leveled somewhat for new players. May the best _____ win!

Sources: Van Hoven, M. 2009. Strategic Alliances: MRM and Aniboom Team Up, Crowdsource. *www.mediabistro.com*. August 31: np; and McClellan, S. 2009. MRM, Aniboom Team Up. *www.adweek.com*. August 31: np.

Reducing Manufacturing (or Other) Costs in the Value Chain   Strategic alliances (or joint ventures) often enable firms to pool capital, value-creating activities, or facilities in order to reduce costs. For example, Molson Companies and Carling O'Keefe Breweries in Canada formed a joint venture to merge their brewing operations. Although Molson had a modern and efficient brewery in Montreal, Carling's was outdated. However, Carling had the better facilities in Toronto. In addition, Molson's Toronto brewery was located on the waterfront and had substantial real estate value. Overall, the synergies gained by using their combined facilities more efficiently added $150 million of pretax earnings during the initial year of the venture. Economies of scale were realized and facilities were better utilized.

Developing and Diffusing New Technologies   Strategic alliances also may be used to build jointly on the technological expertise of two or more companies. This may enable then to develop products technologically beyond the capability of the companies acting independently.[74]

STMicroelectronics (ST) is a high-tech company based in Geneva, Switzerland, that has thrived—largely due to the success of its strategic alliances.[75] The firm develops and manufactures computer chips for a variety of applications such as mobile phones, set-top boxes, smart cards, and flash memories. In 1995 it teamed up with Hewlett-Packard to develop powerful new processors for various digital applications that are now nearing completion. Another example was its strategic alliance with Nokia to develop a chip that would give Nokia's phones a longer battery life. Here, ST produced a chip that tripled standby time to 60 hours—a breakthough that gave Nokia a huge advantage in the marketplace.

The firm's CEO, Pasquale Pistorio, was among the first in the industry to form R&D alliances with other companies. Now ST's top 12 customers, including HP, Nokia, and Nortel, account for 45 percent of revenues. According to Pistorio, "Alliances are in our DNA." Such relationships help ST keep better-than-average growth rates, even in difficult times. That's because close partners are less likely to defect to other suppliers.

Potential Downsides   Despite their promise, many alliances and joint ventures fail to meet expectations for a variety of reasons.[76] First, without the proper partner, a firm should never consider undertaking an alliance, even for the best of reasons.[77] Each partner should bring the desired complementary strengths to the partnership. Ideally, the strengths contributed by the partners are unique; thus synergies created can be more easily sustained and defended over the longer term. The goal must be to develop synergies between the contributions of the partners, resulting in a win–win situation. Moreover, the partners must be compatible and willing to trust each other.[78] Unfortunately, often little attention is given to nurturing the close working relationships and interpersonal connections that bring together the partnering organizations.[79]

Internal Development

Firms can also diversify by means of corporate entrepreneurship and new venture development. **In today's economy, internal development is such an important means by which companies expand their businesses that we have devoted a whole chapter to it (see Chapter 12).** Sony and the Minnesota Mining & Manufacturing Co. (3M), for example, are known for their dedication to innovation, R&D, and cutting-edge technologies. For example, 3M has developed its entire corporate culture to support its ongoing policy of generating at least 25 percent of total sales from products created within the most recent four-year period. During the 1990s, 3M exceeded this goal by achieving about 30 percent of sales per year from new internally developed products.

Zingerman's, a gourmet deli, has created a new business based on their core competence in human resource management. We discuss this new internal venture in Strategy Spotlight 6.7

Compared to mergers and acquisitions, firms that engage in internal development capture the value created by their own innovative activities without having to "share the wealth" with alliance partners or face the difficulties associated with combining activities across the value chains of several firms or merging corporate cultures.[80] Also, firms can often develop new products or services at a relatively lower cost and thus rely on their own resources rather than turning to external funding.[81]

There are also potential disadvantages. It may be time consuming; thus, firms may forfeit the benefits of speed that growth through mergers or acquisitions can provide. This may be especially important among high-tech or knowledge-based organizations in fast-paced environments where being an early mover is critical. Thus, firms that choose to diversify through internal development must develop capabilities that allow them to move quickly from initial opportunity recognition to market introduction.

How Managerial Motives Can Erode Value Creation

Thus far in the chapter, we have implicitly assumed that CEOs and top executives are "rational beings"; that is, they act in the best interests of shareholders to maximize long-term shareholder value. In the real world, however, they may often act in their own self-interest. We now address some managerial motives that can serve to erode, rather than

A Gourmet Deli Firm Leverages Its Core Competence and Creates a New Business

In 1982, when Ari Weinzweig and Paul Saginaw opened Zingerman's Delicatessen in Ann Arbor, Michigan, their goal was to offer a world-class corned-beef sandwich. By 2003, Zingerman's was named "The Coolest Small Company in America" by *Inc.* magazine. Today, the Zingerman's Community of Businesses—including seven businesses—employs more than 500 people and generates annual sales of more than $35 million.

In 1994, the firm created a training arm, ZingTrain, to develop and deliver seminars on how to hire, fire, and inspire people. The program, mainly targeted at managers and small-business owners, promises "tips, tools, and techniques" to be more effective at every step—from hiring to the exit interview. At one session, the 15 participants included four managers from a pizza chain, a furniture store owner, two nonprofit executives, a co-owner of an Italian ice-cart business, and a journalist.

Source: Kanter, R. M. 2009. Mergers That Stick. *Harvard Business Review,* 87(10): 121–125; O'Brien, C. 2008. ZingTrain Keeps Retail Workers on the Right Track. *newhope360.com.* October 1: np; and *www.zingtrain.com.*

● Zingerman's, a delicatessen, leveraged its core competence in human resource management to create training programs.

During the session, the leaders drew on Zingerman's culture, discussing the "compact" in which employees take responsibility for their training's effectiveness. There were also tips for writing a great job description.

---

enhance, value creation. These include "growth for growth's sake," excessive egotism, and the creation of a wide variety of antitakeover tactics.

Growth for Growth's Sake

There are huge incentives for executives to increase the size of their firm. And these are not consistent with increasing shareholder wealth. Top managers, including the CEO, of larger firms typically enjoy more prestige, higher rankings for their firms on the Fortune 500 list (based on revenues, *not* profits), greater incomes, more job security, and so on. There is also the excitement and associated recognition of making a major acquisition. As noted by Harvard's Michael Porter, "There's a tremendous allure to mergers and acquisitions. It's the big play, the dramatic gesture. With one stroke of the pen you can add billions to size, get a front-page story, and create excitement in markets."[82]

In recent years many high-tech firms have suffered from the negative impact of their uncontrolled growth. Consider, for example, Priceline.com's ill-fated venture into an online service to offer groceries and gasoline.[83] A myriad of problems—perhaps most importantly, a lack of participation by manufacturers—caused the firm to lose more than $5 million a *week* prior to abandoning these ventures. Such initiatives are often little more than desperate moves by top managers to satisfy investor demands for accelerating revenues. Unfortunately, the increased revenues often fail to materialize into a corresponding hike in earnings.

growth for growth's sake managers' actions to grow the size of their firms not to increase long-term profitability but to serve managerial self-interest.

strategy spotlight

Cornelius Vanderbilt: Going to Great Lengths to Correct a Wrong

Cornelius Vanderbilt's legendary ruthlessness set a bar for many titans to come. Back in 1853, the commodore took his first vacation, an extended voyage to Europe aboard his yacht. He was in for a big surprise when he returned.

Source: McGregor, J. 2007. Sweet Revenge. *Business Week*, January 22: 64–70.

Two of his associates had taken the power of attorney that he had left them and sold his interest in his steamship concern, Accessory Transit Company, to themselves.

"Gentlemen," he wrote, in a classic battle cry, "you have undertaken to cheat me. I won't sue you for the law is too slow. I'll ruin you." He converted his yacht to a passenger ship to compete with them and added other vessels. He started a new line, appropriately named *Opposition*. Before long, he bought his way back in and regained control of the company.

At times, executives' overemphasis on growth can result in a plethora of ethical lapses, which can have disastrous outcomes for their companies. A good example (of bad practice) is Joseph Bernardino's leadership at Andersen Worldwide. Bernardino had a chance early on to take a hard line on ethics and quality in the wake of earlier scandals at clients such as Waste Management and Sunbeam. Instead, according to former executives, he put too much emphasis on revenue growth. Consequently, the firm's reputation quickly eroded when it audited and signed off on the highly flawed financial statements of such infamous firms as Enron, Global Crossing, and WorldCom. Bernardino ultimately resigned in disgrace in March 2002, and his firm was dissolved later that year.[84]

egotism managers' actions to shape their firms' strategies to serve their selfish interests rather than to maximize long-term shareholder value.

Egotism

A healthy ego helps make a leader confident, clearheaded, and able to cope with change. CEOs, by their very nature, are intensely competitive people in the office as well as on the tennis court or golf course. But, sometimes when pride is at stake, individuals will go to great lengths to win. Such behaviour, of course, is not a new phenomenon. We discuss the case of Cornelius Vanderbilt, one of the original Americans moguls, in Strategy Spotlight 6.8

Egos can get in the way of a "synergistic" corporate marriage. Few executives (or lower-level managers) are exempt from the potential downside of excessive egos. Consider, for example, the reflections of General Electric's former CEO Jack Welch, considered by many to be the world's most admired executive. He admitted to a regrettable decision: "My hubris got in the way in the Kidder Peabody deal. [He was referring to GE's buyout of the soon-to-be-troubled Wall Street firm.] I got wise advice from Walter Wriston and other directors who said, 'Jack, don't do this.' But I was bully enough and on a run to do it. And I got whacked right in the head."[85] In addition to poor financial results, Kidder Peabody was wracked by a widely publicized trading scandal that tarnished the reputations of both GE and Kidder Peabody. Welch ended up selling Kidder in 1994.

The business press has included many stories of how egotism and greed have infiltrated organizations.[86] Some incidents are considered rather astonishing, such as Tyco's former (and now convicted) CEO Dennis Kozlowski's well-chronicled purchase of a $6,000 shower curtain and vodka-spewing, full-size replica of Michaelangelo's David.[87]

How Antitakeover Measures May Benefit Multiple Stakeholders, Not Just Management

Antitakeover defenses represent a gray area, because management can often legitimately argue that such actions are not there solely to benefit themselves. Rather, they can benefit other stakeholders, such as employees, customers, and the community.

In the late 1980s, takeovers were very popular. The Dayton Hudson Corporation (now Target) even appealed to the Minnesota legislature to pass an antitakeover bill to help Dayton Hudson in its struggle with Hafts—the former owners of Dart, a drug store chain on the East Coast. History had shown that the Dayton Hudson management in place at the time was much better able to manage Dayton Hudson in the long run. In addition to Minnesota, many states now have laws that allow firms to take the interests of all stakeholders into account when considering a takeover bid.

In the summer of 2003, Oracle launched a hostile bid for PeopleSoft. Many charged that the tactics of Oracle CEO Larry Ellison had been unfair, and many of PeopleSoft's customers took its side, indicating that Oracle ownership would not be of benefit to them. PeopleSoft was concerned that Oracle was merely seeking to buy PeopleSoft for its lucrative base of application software and was not interested in supporting the company's products. Oracle, on the other hand, sued PeopleSoft in an attempt to have the latter's so-called poison pill takeover defense removed.

In December 2004, Oracle struck a deal to buy PeopleSoft—ending a bitter 18-month hostile takeover battle. Oracle's $10.3 billion acquisition valued the firm at $26.50 a share—an increase of 66 percent over its initial offer of $16 a share. Noted analyst John DiFucci: "This is a financial acquisition primarily. Oracle is buying PeopleSoft for its maintenance stream." And, worth noting, PeopleSoft executives, including CEO and company founder David Duffield, did not join Oracle during the conference call announcing the acquisition. Oracle dropped its suit against PeopleSoft in which the former charged that PeopleSoft's "poison pill" takeover defense should be dismissed.

On moral grounds, some antitakeover defenses are not undertaken to entrench and protect management, but often they are. When such defenses are used simply to keep management in power, they are wrong. However, when they are used to defend the long-term financial health of the company and to protect broader stakeholder interests, they will be morally permissible.

Sources: Bowie, N. E. & Werhane, P. H. 2005. *Management Ethics*. Malden, MA: Blackwell Publishing; and La Monica, P. R. 2004. Finally, Oracle to Buy PeopleSoft. *CNNMoney.com*, December 13: np.

Other well-known examples of power grabs and extraordinary consumption of compensation and perks include executives at Enron, the Rigas family who were convicted of defrauding Adelphia of roughly $1 billion, former CEO Bernie Ebbers's $408 million loan from WorldCom, and so on.

A more recent example of excess and greed was exhibited by John Thain.[88] On January 22, 2009, he was ousted as head of Merrill Lynch by Bank of America's CEO, Ken Lewis:

> Thain embarrassingly doled out $4 billion in discretionary year-end bonuses to favored employees just before Bank of America's rescue purchase of failing Merrill. The bonuses amounted to about 10 percent of Merrill's 2008 losses.

> Obviously, John Thain believed that he was entitled. When he took over ailing Merrill in early 2008, he began planning major cuts, but he also ordered that his office be redecorated. He spent $1.22 million of company funds to make it "livable," which, in part, included $87,000 for a rug, $87,000 for a pair of guest chairs, $68,000 for a 19th-century credenza, and (what really got the attention of the press) $35,000 for a "commode with legs."

antitakeover tactics managers' actions to avoid losing wealth or power as a result of a hostile takeover

He later agreed to repay the decorating costs. However, one might still ask: What kind of person treats other people's money like this? And who needs a commode that costs as much as a new Lexus? Finally, a comment by Bob O'Brien, stock editor at Barrons.com clearly applies: "The sense of entitlement that's been engendered in this group of people has clearly not been beaten out of them by the brutal performance of the financial sector over the course of the last year."

Antitakeover Tactics

Unfriendly or hostile takeovers can occur when a company's stock becomes undervalued. A competing organization can buy the outstanding stock of a takeover candidate in sufficient quantity to become a large shareholder. Then it makes a tender offer to gain full control of the company. If the shareholders accept the offer, the hostile firm buys the target company and either fires the target firm's management team or strips them of their power. Thus, antitakeover tactics are common, including greenmail, golden parachutes, and poison pills.[89]

greenmail a payment by a firm to a hostile party for the firm's stock at a premium, made when the firm's management feels that the hostile party is about to make a tender offer.

The first, **greenmail,** is an effort by the target firm to prevent an impending takeover. When a hostile firm buys a large block of outstanding target company stock and the target firm's management feels that a tender offer is impending, they offer to buy the stock back from the hostile company at a higher price than the unfriendly company paid for it. Although this often prevents a hostile takeover, the same price is not offered to preexisting shareholders. However, it protects the jobs of the target firm's management.

golden parachute a prearranged contract with managers specifying that, in the event of a hostile takeover, the target firm's managers will be paid a significant severance package.

Second, a **golden parachute** is a prearranged contract with managers specifying that, in the event of a hostile takeover, the target firm's managers will be paid a significant severance package. Although top managers lose their jobs, the golden parachute provisions protect their income.

Third, **poison pills** are used by a company to give shareholders certain rights in the event of a takeover by another firm. They are also known as shareholder rights plans.

Clearly, antitakeover tactics can often raise some interesting ethical—and legal—issues. Strategy Spotlight 6.9 addresses how antitakeover measures can benefit multiple stakeholders—not just management.

poison pill used by a company to give shareholders certain rights in the event of takeover by another firm.

Reflecting on Career Implications . . .

- *Corporate-Level Strategy:* Be aware of your firm's corporate-level strategy. Can you come up with an initiative that will create value both within and across business units?
- *Core Competencies:* What do you see as your core competencies? How can you leverage them both within your business unit as well as across other business units?
- *Sharing Infrastructures:* What infrastructure activities and resources (e.g., information systems, legal) are available in the corporate office that would help you add value for your business unit—or other business units?
- *Diversification:* From your career perspective, what actions can you take to diversify your employment risk (e.g., coursework at a local university, obtain professional certification such as a C.P.A., networking through professional affiliation, etc.)? For example, in periods of retrenchment, such actions will provide you with a greater number of career options.

Summary

A key challenge for today's managers is to create "synergy" when engaging in diversification activities. As we discussed in this chapter, corporate managers do not, in general, have a very good track record in creating value in such endeavors when it comes to mergers and acquisitions. Among the factors that serve to erode shareholder values are paying an excessive premium for the target firm, failing to integrate the activities of the newly acquired businesses into the corporate family, and undertaking diversification initiatives that are too easily imitated by the competition.

We addressed two major types of corporate-level strategy: related and unrelated diversification. With *related diversification* the corporation strives to enter into areas in which key resources and capabilities of the corporation can be shared or leveraged. Synergies come from horizontal relationships between business units. Cost savings and enhanced revenues can be derived from two major sources. First, economies of scope can be achieved from the leveraging of core competencies and the sharing of activities. Second, market power can be attained from greater, or pooled, negotiating power and from vertical integration.

When firms undergo *unrelated diversification* they enter product markets that are dissimilar to their present businesses. Thus, there is generally little opportunity to either leverage core competencies or share activities across business units. Here, synergies are created from vertical relationships between the corporate office and the individual business units. With unrelated diversification, the primary ways to create value are corporate restructuring and parenting, as well as the use of portfolio analysis techniques.

Corporations have three primary means of diversifying their product markets—mergers and acquisitions, joint ventures/strategic alliances, and internal development. There are key trade-offs associated with each of these. For example, mergers and acquisitions are typically the quickest means to enter new markets and provide the corporation with a high level of control over the acquired business. However, with the expensive premiums that often need to be paid to the shareholders of the target firm and the challenges associated with integrating acquisitions, they can also be quite expensive. Not surprisingly, many poorly performing acquisitions are subsequently divested. At times, however, divestitures can help firms refocus their efforts and generate resources. Strategic alliances and joint ventures between two or more firms, on the other hand, may be a means of reducing risk since they involve the sharing and combining of resources. But such joint initiatives also provide a firm with less control (than it would have with an acquisition) since governance is shared between two independent entities. Also, there is a limit to the potential upside for each partner because returns must be shared as well. Finally, with internal development, a firm is able to capture all of the value from its initiatives (as opposed to sharing it with a merger or alliance partner). However, diversification by means of internal development can be very time-consuming—a disadvantage that becomes even more important in fast-paced competitive environments.

Finally, some managerial behaviors may serve to erode shareholder returns. Among these are "growth for growth's sake," egotism, and antitakeover tactics. As we discussed, some of these issues—particularly antitakeover tactics—raise ethical considerations because the managers of the firm are not acting in the best interests of the shareholders.

Summary Review Questions

1. Discuss how managers can create value for their firm through diversification efforts.
2. What are some of the reasons that many diversification efforts fail to achieve desired outcomes?
3. How can companies benefit from related diversification? Unrelated diversification? What are some of the key concepts that can explain such success?
4. What are some of the important ways in which a firm can restructure a business?
5. Discuss some of the various means that firms can use to diversify. What are the pros and cons associated with each of these?
6. Discuss some of the actions that managers may engage in to erode shareholder value.

Key Terms

corporate-level
   strategy, 202
diversification, 204
related diversification, 206
economies of scope, 206
core competencies, 206
sharing activities, 208
market power, 209
pooled negotiating
   power, 209
vertical integration, 210
transaction cost
   perspective, 213

unrelated
   diversification, 214
parenting advantage, 214
restructuring, 215
portfolio
   management, 216
acquisitions, 220
mergers, 220
divestment, 225
strategic alliance, 226
joint ventures, 226
internal
   development, 228

Application Questions & Exercises

1. What were some of the largest mergers and acquisitions over the last two years? What was the rationale for these actions? Do you think they will be successful? Explain.

2. Discuss some examples from business practice in which an executive's actions appear to be in his or her self-interest rather than the corporation's well-being.

3. Discuss some of the challenges that managers must overcome in making strategic alliances successful. What are some strategic alliances with which you are familiar? Were they successful or not? Explain.

4. Use the Internet and select a company that has recently undertaken diversification into new product markets. What do you feel were some of the reasons for this

diversification (e.g., leveraging core competencies, sharing infrastructures)?

Ethics Questions

1. In recent years there has been a rash of corporate downsizing and layoffs. Do you feel that such actions raise ethical considerations? Why or why not?

2. What are some of the ethical issues that arise when managers act in a manner that is counter to their firm's best interests? What are the long-term implications for both the firms and the managers themselves?

Experiential Exercise

Time Warner (formerly AOL Time Warner) is a firm that follows a strategy of related diversification. Evaluate its success (or lack thereof) with regard to how well it has: (1) built on core competencies, (2) shared infrastructures, and (3) increased market power. (Fill answers in table below.)

Rationale for Related Diversification	Successful/Unsuccessful?	Why?
1. Build on core competencies		
2. Share infrastructures		
3. Increase market power		

References

1. Anonymous. 2010. Bebo sold by AOL after just two years. *www.bbc.co.uk*. June 17: np; Anonymous. 2010. AOL plans to sell or shut down Bebo. *www.bbc.co.uk*. April 7: np; Pimentel, B. 2008. AOL to buy Bebo for $850. *www.marketwatch.com*. October 25: np; Sarno, D. 2010. AOL posts loss but stock rises. *Los Angeles Times,* August 5: 3; Quinn, J. 2005. AOL losses top $1bn after write-downs. *The Daily Telegraph.* August 5: 3; Shearman, S. 2010. Returning to the fray. *Marketing.* October 13: 19;

Steel, E. & Worthen, B. 2010 With Bebo a no-go, AOL will unload the social site. *The Wall Street Journal,* June 17: B1; and Whitney, L. 2010. AOL sells off Bebo at last. *www.news.cnet.com.* October 25: np. We thank Ciprian Stan for his valued contribution.

2. Insights on measuring M&A performance are addressed in: Zollo, M. & Meier, D. 2008. What is M&A performance? *BusinessWeek,* 22(3): 55–77.

3. Insights on how and why firms may overpay for acquisitions are

addressed in: Malhotra, D., Ku, G., & Murnighan, J. K. 2008. When winning is everything. *Harvard Business Review,* 66(5); 78–86.

4. Pfizer deal helps lift stocks. 2009. online.wsy.com, January 26: np.

5. Dr. G. William Schwert, University of Rochester study cited in Pare, T. P. 1994. The new merger boom. *Fortune.* November 28: 96.

6. Lipin, S. & Deogun, N. 2000. Big mergers of the 1990's prove disappointing to shareholders. *The Wall Street Journal.* October 30: C1.

7. Rothenbuecher, J. & Schrottke, J. 2008. To get value from a merger, grow sales. *Harvard Business Review,* 86(5): 24–25; and Rothenbuecher, J. 2008. Personal communication, October 1.

8. Kyriazis, D. 2010. The long-term post acquisition performance of Greek acquiring firms. *International Research Journal of Finance and Economics.* 43: 69–79.

9. Pare, T. P. 1994. The new merger boom. *Fortune,* November 28: 96.

10. A discussion of the effects of director experience and acquisition performance is in: McDonald, M. L. & Westphal, J. D. 2008. What do they know? The effects of outside director acquisition experience on firm acquisition performance. *Strategic Management Journal,* 29(11): 1155–1177.

11. Ghosn, C. 2006. Inside the alliance: The win–win nature of a unique business mode. *Address to the Detroit Economic Club,* November 16.

12. For a study that investigates several predictors of corporate diversification, read: Wiersema, M. F. & Bowen, H. P. 2008. Corporate diversification: The impact of foreign competition, industry globalization, and product diversification. *Strategic Management Journal,* 29(2): 114–132.

13. Kumar, M. V. S. 2011. Are joint ventures positive sum games? The relative effects of cooperative and non-cooperative behavior. *Strategic Management Journal,* 32(1): 32–54.

14. Makri, M., Hitt, M. A., & Lane, P. J. 2010. Complementary technologies, knowledge relatedness, and invention outcomes in high technology mergers and acquisitions. *Strategic Management Journal,* 31(6): 602–628.

15. A discussion of Tyco's unrelated diversification strategy is in: Hindo, B. 2008. Solving Tyco's identity crisis. *BusinessWeek,* February 18: 62.

16. Our framework draws upon a variety of sources, including Goold, M. & Campbell, A. 1998. Desperately seeking synergy. *Harvard Business Review,* 76(5): 131–143; Porter, M. E. 1987. From advantage to corporate strategy. *Harvard Business Review,* 65(3): 43–59; and Hitt, M. A., Ireland,

R. D., & Hoskisson, R. E. 2001. *Strategic management: competitiveness and globalization* (4th ed.). Cincinnati, OH: South-Western.

17. Collis, D. J. & Montgomery, C. A. 1987. *Corporate strategy: Resources and the scope of the firm.* New York: McGraw-Hill.

18. This imagery of the corporation as a tree and related discussion draws on Prahalad, C. K. & Hamel, G. 1990. The core competence of the corporation. *Harvard Business Review,* 68(3): 79–91. Parts of this section also draw on Picken, J. C. & Dess, G. G. 1997. *Mission critical:* chap. 5. Burr Ridge, IL: Irwin Professional Publishing.

19. Graebner, M. E., Eisenhardt, K. M. & Roundy, P. T. 2010. Success and failure in technology acquisitions: Lessons for buyers and sellers. *The Academy of Management Perspectives,* 24(3): 73–92.

20. This section draws on Prahalad & Hamel, op. cit.; and Porter, op. cit.

21. A recent study that investigates the relationship between a firm's technology resources, diversification, and performance can be found in Miller, D. J. 2004. Firms' technological resources and the performance effects of diversification. A longitudinal study. *Strategic Management Journal,* 25: 1097–1119.

22. Collis & Montgomery, op. cit.

23. Fisher, A. 2008. America's most admired companies. *Fortune,* March 17: 74.

24. Henricks, M. 1994. VF seeks global brand dominance. *Apparel Industry Magazine,* August: 21–40; VF Corporation. 1993. First quarter corporate summary report. *1993 VF Annual Report.*

25. Hill, A. & Hargreaves, D. 2001. Turbulent times for GE-Honeywell deal. *Financial Times,* February 28: 26.

26. An interesting discussion of a merger in the Russian mining industry is in: Bush, J. 2008. Welding a new metals giant. *BusinessWeek,* July 14 & 21: 56.

27. Lowry, T. 2001. Media. *BusinessWeek,* January 8: 100–101.

28. This section draws on Hrebiniak, L. G. & Joyce, W. F. 1984. *Implementing*

strategy. New York: MacMillan; and Oster, S. M. 1994. *Modern competitive analysis.* New York: Oxford University Press.

29. The discussion of the benefits and costs of vertical integration draws on Hax, A. C. & Majluf, N. S. 1991. *The strategy concept and process: A pragmatic approach:* 139. Englewood Cliffs, NJ: Prentice Hall.

30. Fahey, J. 2005. Gray winds. *Forbes.* January 10: 143.

31. This discussion draws on Oster, op. cit.; and Harrigan, K. 1986. Matching vertical integration strategies to competitive conditions. *Strategic Management Journal,* 7(6): 535–556.

32. For a scholarly explanation on how transaction costs determine the boundaries of a firm, see Oliver E. Williamson's pioneering books *Markets and Hierarchies: Analysis and Antitrust Implications* (New York: Free Press, 1975) and *The Economic Institutions of Capitalism* (New York: Free Press, 1985).

33. Campbell, A., Goold, M., & Alexander, M. 1995. Corporate strategy: The quest for parenting advantage. *Harvard Business Review,* 73(2): 120–132; and Picken & Dess, op. cit.

34. Anslinger, P. A. & Copeland, T. E. 1996. Growth through acquisition: A fresh look. *Harvard Business Review,* 74(1): 126–135.

35. Campbell et al., op. cit.

36. This section draws on Porter, op. cit.; and Hambrick, D. C. 1985. Turnaround strategies. In Guth, W. D. (Ed.). *Handbook of business strategy:* 10-1–10-32. Boston: Warren, Gorham & Lamont.

37. There is an important delineation between companies that are operated for a long-term profit and those that are bought and sold for short-term gains. The latter are sometimes referred to as "holding companies" and are generally more concerned about financial issues than strategic issues.

38. Lenzner, R. 2007. High on Loews. *Forbes,* February 26: 98–102.

39. Casico. W. F. 2002. Strategies for responsible restructuring. *Academy of Management Executive,* 16(3): 80–91; and Singh, H. 1993. Challenges in

researching corporate restructuring. *Journal of Management Studies,* 30(1): 147–172.

40. Cusack, M. 1987. *Hanson Trust: A review of the company and its prospects.* London: Hoare Govett.

41. Hax & Majluf, op. cit. By 1979, 45 percent of Fortune 500 companies employed some form of portfolio analysis, according to Haspelagh, P. 1982. Portfolio planning: Uses and limits. *Harvard Busines Review,* 60: 58–73. A later study conducted in 1993 found that over 40 percent of the respondents used portfolio analysis techniques, but the level of usage was expected to increase to more than 60 percent in the near future: Rigby, D. K. 1994. Managing the management tools. *Planning Review,* September–October: 20–24.

42. Goold, M. & Luchs, K. 1993. Why diversify? Four decades of management thinking. *Academy of Management Executive,* 7(3): 7–25.

43. Other approaches include the industry attractiveness–business strength matrix developed jointly by General Electric and McKinsey and Company, the life-cycle matrix developed by Arthur D. Little, and the profitability matrix proposed by Marakon. For an extensive review, refer to Hax & Majluf, op. cit.: 182–194.

44. Porter, op. cit.: 49–52.

45. Collis, D. J. 1995. Portfolio planning at Ciba-Geigy and the Newport investment proposal. Harvard Business School Case No. 9-795-040. Novartis AG was created in 1996 by the merger of Ciba-Geigy and Sandoz.

46. Buzzell, R. D. & Gale, B. T. 1987. *The PIMS principles: Linking strategy to performance.* New York: Free Press; and Miller, A. & Dess, G. G. 1996. *Strategic management,* (2nd ed.). New York: McGraw-Hill.

47. Seeger, J. 1984. Reversing the images of BCG's growth share matrix. *Strategic Management Journal,* 5(1): 93–97.

48. Picken & Dess, op. cit.; Cabot Corporation. 2001. 10-Q filing, Securities and Exchange Commission, May 14.

49. Koudsi, S. 2001. Remedies for an economic hangover. *Fortune,* June 25: 130–139.

50. Insights on the performance of serial acquirers is found in: Laamanen, T. & Keil, T. 2008. Performance of serial acquirers: Toward an acquisition program perspective. *Strategic Management Journal,* 29(6): 663–672.

51. Some insights from Lazard's CEO on mergers and acquisitions are addressed in: Stewart, T. A. & Morse, G. 2008. Giving great advice. *Harvard Business Review,* 66(1): 106–113.

52. Coy, P., Thornton, E., Arndt, M., & Grow, B. 2005. Shake, rattle, and merge. *BusinessWeek,* January 10: 32–35; and Anonymous. 2005. Love is in the air. *Economist,* February 5: 9.

53. Silva, M. & Rovella, D. E. 2011. Intel is model to fight unfair competition, FTC chairman says. www.bloomberg.com. January 11: np.

54. For an interesting study of the relationship between mergers and a firm's product-market strategies, refer to Krisnan, R. A., Joshi, S., & Krishnan, H. 2004. The influence of mergers on firms' product-mix strategies. *Strategic Management Journal,* 25: 587–611.

55. Carey, D., moderator. 2000. A CEO roundtable on making mergers succeed. *Harvard Business Review,* 78(3): 146.

56. Shinal, J. 2001. Can Mike Volpi make Cisco sizzle again? *BusinessWeek,* February 26: 102–104; Kambil, A., Eselius, E. D., & Monteiro, K. A. 2000. Fast venturing: The quick way to start Web businesses. *Sloan Management Review,* 41(4): 55–67; and Elstrom, P. 2001. Sorry, Cisco: The old answers won't work. *BusinessWeek,* April 30: 39.

57. Like many high-tech firms during the economic slump that began in mid-2000, Cisco Systems experienced declining performance. On April 16, 2001, it announced that its revenues for the quarter closing April 30 would drop 5 percent from a year earlier—and a stunning 30 percent from the previous three months—to about $4.7 billion. Furthermore, Cisco announced that it would lay off 8,500 employees and take an enormous $2.5 billion charge to write down

inventory. By late October 2002, its stock was trading at around $10, down significantly from its 52-week high of $70. Elstrom, op. cit.: 39.

58. Coy, P., Thornton, E., Arndt, M., & Grow, B. 2005, Shake, rattle, and merge. *BusinessWeek,* January 10: 32–35; and, Anonymous. 2005. The rise of the superbrands. *Economist.* February 5: 63–65; and, Sellers, P. 2005. It was a no-brainer. *Fortune,* February 21: 96–102.

59. For a discussion of the trend toward consolidation of the steel industry and how Lakshmi Mittal is becoming a dominant player, read Reed, S. & Arndt, M. 2004. The Raja of steel. *BusinessWeek,* December 20: 50–52.

60. Barrett, A. 2001. Drugs. *BusinessWeek,* January 8: 112–113.

61. Whalen, C. J., Pascual, A. M., Lowery, T., & Muller, J. 2001. The top 25 managers. *BusinessWeek,* January 8: 63.

62. This discussion draws upon Rappaport, A. & Sirower, M. L. 1999. Stock or cash? The trade-offs for buyers and sellers in mergers and acquisitions. *Harvard Business Review,* 77(6): 147–158; and Lipin, S. & Deogun, N. 2000. Big mergers of 90s prove disappointing to shareholders. *The Wall Street Journal,* October 30: C1.

63. The downside of mergers in the airline industry is found in: Gimbel, B. 2008. Why airline mergers don't fly. *BusinessWeek,* March 17: 26.

64. Mouio, A. (Ed.). 1998. Unit of one. *Fast Company,* September: 82.

65. Porter, M. E. 1987. From competitive advantage to corporate strategy. *Harvard Business Review,* 65(3): 43.

66. The divestiture of a business which is undertaken in order to enable managers to better focus on its core business has been termed "downscoping." Refer to Hitt, M. A., Harrison, J. S., & Ireland, R. D. 2001. *Mergers and acquisitions: A guide to creating value for stakeholders.* Oxford Press: New York.

67. Sirmon, D. G., Hitt, M. A., & Ireland, R. D. 2007. Managing firm resources in dynamic environments to create value: Looking inside the black box. *Academy of Management Review,* 32(1): 273–292.

68. This discussion draws on: Mankins, M. C., Harding, D., & Weddigne, R-M. 2008. How the best divest. *Harvard Business Review,* 86(1): 92–99.

69. A study that investigates alliance performance is: Lunnan, R. & Haugland, S. A. 2008. Predicting and measuring alliance performance: A multidimensional analysis. *Strategic Management Journal,* 29(5): 545–556.

70. For scholarly perspectives on the role of learning in creating value in strategic alliances, refer to Anard, B. N. & Khanna, T. 2000. Do firms learn to create value? *Strategic Management Journal,* 12(3): 295–317; and Vermeulen, F. & Barkema, H. P. 2001. Learning through acquisitions. *Academy of Management Journal,* 44(3): 457–476.

71. For a detailed discussion of transaction cost economics in strategic alliances, read Reuer, J. J. & Arno, A. 2007. Strategic alliance contracts: Dimensions and determinants of contractual complexity. *Strategic Management Journal,* 28(3): 313–330.

72. This section draws on Hutt, M. D., Stafford, E. R., Walker, B. A., & Reingen, P. H. 2000. Case study: Defining the strategic alliance. *Sloan Management Review,* 41(2): 51–62; and Walters, B. A., Peters, S., & Dess, G. G. 1994. Strategic alliances and joint ventures: Making them work. *Business Horizons,* 4: 5–10.

73. A study that investigates strategic alliances and networks is: Tiwana, A. 2008. Do bridging ties complement strong ties? An empirical examination of alliance ambidexterity.

74. Phelps, C. 2010. A longitudinal study of the influence of alliance network structure and composition on firm exploratory innovation. *Academy of Management Journal,* 53(4): 890–913.

75. Edmondson, G. & Reinhardt, A. 2001. From niche player to Goliath. *BusinessWeek,* March 12: 94–96.

76. For an institutional theory perspective on strategic alliances, read: Dacin, M. T., Oliver, C., & Roy, J. P. 2007. The legitimacy of strategic alliances: An institutional perspective. *Strategic Management Journal,* 28(2): 169–187.

77. A study investigating factors that determine partner selection in strategic alliances is found in: Shah, R. H. & Swaminathan, V. 2008. *Strategic Management Journal,* 29(5): 471–494.

78. Arino, A. & Ring, P. S. 2010. The role of fairness in alliance formation. *Strategic Management Journal,* 31(6): 1054–1087.

79. Greve, H. R., Baum, J. A. C., Mitsuhashi, H. & Rowley, T. J. 2010. Built to last but falling apart: Cohesion, friction, and withdrawal from interfirm alliances. *Academy of Management Journal,* 53(4): 302–322.

80. For an insightful perspective on how to manage conflict between innovation and ongoing operations in an organization, read: Govindarajan, V. & Trimble, C. 2010. *The other side of innovation: Solving the execution*

Strategic Management Journal, 29(3): 251–272.

challenge. Boston, MA: Harvard Business School Press.

81. Dunlap-Hinkler, D., Kotabe, M. & Mudambi, R. 2010. A story of breakthrough versus incremental innovation: Corporate entrepreneurship in the global pharmaceutical industry. *Strategic Entrepreneurship Journal.* 4(2): 106–127.

82. Porter, op. cit.: 43–59.

83. Angwin, J. S. & Wingfield, N. 2000. How Jay Walker built WebHouse on a theory that he couldn't prove. *The Wall Street Journal,* October 16: A1, A8.

84. The fallen. 2003. *BusinessWeek,* January 13: 80–82.

85. The Jack Welch example draws upon Sellers, P. 2001. Get over yourself. *Fortune,* April 30: 76–88.

86. Li, J. & Tang, Y. 2010. CEO hubris and firm risk taking in China: The moderating role of managerial discretion. *Academy of Management Journal,* 53(1): 45–68.

87. Polek, D. 2002. The rise and fall of Dennis Kozlowski. *BusinessWeek,* December 23: 64–77.

88. John Thain and his golden commode. 2009. Editorial. Dallasnews .com, January 26: np; Task, A. 2009. Wall Street's $18.4B bonus: The sense of entitlement has not been beaten out. finance.yahoo.com, January 29: np; and Exit Thain. 2009. Newsfinancialcareers.com, January 22: np.

89. This section draws on Weston, J. F., Besley, S., & Brigham, E. F. 1996. *Essentials of managerial finance* (11th ed.): 18–20. Fort Worth, TX: Dryden Press, Harcourt Brace.

chapter SEVEN

International Strategy:

Creating Value in Global Markets

After reading this chapter, you should have a good understanding of:

LO7.1 The importance of international expansion as a viable diversification strategy.

LO7.2 The sources of national advantage; that is, why an industry in a given country is more (or less) successful than the same industry in another country.

LO7.3 The motivations (or benefits) and the risks associated with international expansion, including the emerging trend for greater offshoring and outsourcing activity.

LO7.4 The two opposing forces—cost reduction and adaptation to local markets—that firms face when entering international markets.

LO7.5 The advantages and disadvantages associated with each of the four basic strategies: international, global, multidomestic, and transnational.

LO7.6 The difference between regional companies and truly global companies.

LO7.7 The four basic types of entry strategies and the relative benefits and risks associated with each of them.

LEARNING OBJECTIVES

The global marketplace provides many opportunities for firms to increase their revenue base and their profitability. Furthermore, in today's knowledge-intensive economy, there is the potential to create advantages by leveraging firm knowledge when crossing national boundaries to do business. At the same time, however, there are pitfalls and risks that firms must avoid in order to be successful. In this chapter we will provide insights on how to be successful and create value when diversifying into global markets.

After some introductory comments on the global economy, we address the question: What explains the level of success of a given industry in a given country? To provide a framework for analysis, we draw on Michael Porter's "diamond of national advantage," in which he identified four factors that help to explain performance differences.

In the second section of the chapter, we shift our focus to the level of the firm and discuss some of the major motivations and risks associated with international expansion. Recognizing such potential benefits and risks enables managers to better assess the growth and profit potential in a given country. We also address important issues associated with a topic of growing interest in the international marketplace—offshoring and outsourcing.

Next, in the third section—the largest in this chapter—we address how firms can attain competitive advantages in the global marketplace. We discuss two opposing forces firms face when entering foreign markets: cost reduction and local adaptation. Depending on the intensity of each of these forces, they should select among four basic strategies: international, global, multidomestic, and transnational. We discuss both the strengths and limitations of each of these strategies. We also present a recent perspective which posits that even the largest multinational firms are more regional than global even today.

The final section addresses the four categories of entry strategies that firms may choose in entering foreign markets. These strategies vary along a continuum from low investment, low control (exporting) to high investment, high control (wholly owned subsidiaries and greenfield ventures). We discuss the pros and cons associated with each.

Learning from Mistakes

Carrefour is Europe's top retailer and ranks second in the world (behind Walmart). However, in late 2010, it decided to close up shop in much of Southeast Asia.[1] Its 44 stores in Thailand, 23 in Malaysia, and 2 in Singapore are up for sale. Potential buyers include Britain's Tesco, Japan's Aeon, and France's Casino.

Unfortunately, Carrefour's retreat may be ill-timed. Compared to Europe, the Southeast Asian economy is very strong. Thailand's modern retail sector is growing rapidly despite the country's political turmoil. Ditto for Malaysia. What went wrong?

Carrefour was one of the first foreign grocers to open shops in the region in the 1990s. However, Tesco, which arrived later, was far savvier in figuring out what consumers wanted. For example, when it found out that Thai shoppers traveled for miles to its "big-box" stores, it opened much smaller stores in rural towns. Carrefour, on the other hand, focused on Bangkok's big spenders and stuck to its hypermarket format. Toby Desforges, a marketing consultant, called this a "take it or leave it" approach. Unfortunately, Thai shoppers left it.

Another factor in Tesco's success in these markets was its choice of local partners. For example, in Thailand, it joined forces with CP Group, an agri-conglomerate, before going it alone. And its Malaysian partner, Sime Darby, was able to help it find properties that were suitable for its hypermarkets. Tesco also acquired eight stores in Malaysia from a rival in 2007. In contrast, Carrefour decided to go it alone in both markets and found itself boxed in by rivals.

Carrefour has operations in about 30 countries (twice as many as Tesco) and it may have overreached. In 2009, it pulled the plug on Russia—only months after opening its first store there. Tesco's outgoing chief executive, Sir Terry Leahy, felt that its rival entered emerging markets without a clear roadmap. He asserts, "Lots of retailers have begun international expansion, hit a problem, then retreated and lost market share." In the end, Carrefour ranked a distant fourth in Thailand and Malaysia; Tesco was first in both countries. Globally speaking, Carrefour still outranks Tesco in total revenues. But Tesco is more profitable.

In this chapter we discuss how firms create value and achieve competitive advantage in the global marketplace. Multinational firms are constantly faced with the dilemma of choosing between local adaptation—in product offerings, locations, advertising, and pricing—and global integration. We discuss how firms can avoid pitfalls such as those experienced by Carrefour in Southeast Asia. In addition, we address factors that can influence a nation's success in a particular industry. In our view, this is an important context in determining how well firms might eventually do when they compete beyond their nation's boundaries.

>LO7.1

The importance of international expansion as a viable diversification strategy.

The Global Economy: A Brief Overview

Managers face many opportunities and risks when they diversify abroad.[2] The trade among nations has increased dramatically in recent years and it is estimated that by 2015, the trade *across* nations will exceed the trade within nations. In a variety of industries such as semiconductors, automobiles, commercial aircraft, telecommunications, computers, and consumer electronics, it is almost impossible to survive unless firms scan the world for competitors, customers, human resources, suppliers, and technology.[3]

GE's wind energy business benefits by tapping into talent around the world. The firm has built research centers in China, Germany, India, and the U.S. "We did it," says CEO Jeffrey Immelt, "to access the best brains everywhere in the world." All four centers have played a key role in GE's development of huge 92-ton turbines:[4]

- Chinese researchers in Shanghai designed the microprocessors that control the pitch of the blade.

- Mechanical engineers from India (Bangalore) devised mathematical models to maximize the efficiency of materials in the turbine.
- Power-systems experts in the U.S. (Niskayuna, New York), which has researchers from 55 countries, do the design work.
- Technicians in Munich, Germany, have created a "smart" turbine that can calculate wind speeds and signal sensors in other turbines to produce maximum electricity.

The rise of **globalization**—meaning the rise of market capitalism around the world—has undeniably contributed to the economic boom in America's New Economy, where knowledge is the key source of competitive advantage and value creation.[5] It is estimated that it has brought phone service to about 300 million households in developing nations and a transfer of nearly $2 trillion from rich countries to poor countries through equity, bond investments, and commercial loans.[6]

There have been extremes in the effect of global capitalism on national economies and poverty levels around the world.[7] The economies of East Asia have attained rapid growth, but there has been comparatively little progress in other areas of the world.[8] For example, income in Latin America grew by only 6 percent in the past two decades when the continent was opening up to global capitalism. Average incomes in sub-Saharan Africa and the old Eastern European bloc have actually declined. The World Bank estimates that the number of people living on $1 per day has *increased* to 1.3 billion over the past decade.

Such disparities in wealth among nations raise an important question: Why do some countries and their citizens enjoy the fruits of global capitalism while others are mired in poverty? Or why do some governments make the best use of inflows of foreign investment and know-how and others do not? There are many explanations. Among these are the need of governments to have track records of business-friendly policies to attract multinationals and local entrepreneurs to train workers, invest in modern technology, and nurture local suppliers and managers. Also, it means carefully managing the broader economic factors in an economy, such as interest rates, inflation, and unemployment, as well as a good legal system that protects property rights, strong educational systems, and a society where prosperity is widely shared.

The above policies are the type that East Asia—in locations such as Hong Kong, Taiwan, South Korea, and Singapore—has employed to evolve from the sweatshop economies of the 1960s and 1970s to industrial powers today. On the other hand, many countries have moved in the other direction. For example, in Guatemala only 52.0 percent of males complete fifth grade and an astonishing 39.8 percent of the population subsists on less than $1 per day.[9] (By comparison, the corresponding numbers for South Korea are 98 percent and less than 2 percent, respectively.)

Strategy Spotlight 7.1 provides an interesting perspective on global trade—marketing to the "bottom of the pyramid."[10] This refers to the practice of a multinational firm targeting its goods and services to the nearly 5 billion poor people in the world who inhabit developing countries. Collectively, this represents a very large market with $14 trillion in purchasing power.

Next, we will address in more detail the question of why some nations and their industries are more competitive.[11] This establishes an important context or setting for the remainder of the chapter. After we discuss why some *nations and their industries* outperform others, we will be better able to address the various strategies that *firms* can take to create competitive advantage when they expand internationally.

Factors Affecting a Nation's Competitiveness

Michael Porter of Harvard University conducted a four-year study in which he and a team of 30 researchers looked at the patterns of competitive success in 10 leading trading

globalization has two meanings. One is the increase in international exchange, including trade in goods and services as well as exchange of money, ideas, and information. Two is the growing similarity of laws, rules, norms, values, and ideas across countries.

Diamond of national advantage a framework for explaining why countries foster successful multinational corporations, consisting of four factors—factor endowments; demand conditions; related and supporting industries; and firm strategy, structure, and rivalry.

Marketing to the "Bottom of the Pyramid"

Many executives wrongly believe that profitable opportunities to sell consumer goods exist only in countries where income levels are high. Even when they expand internationally, they often tend to limit their marketing to only the affluent segments within the developing countries. Such narrow conceptualizations of the market cause them to ignore the vast opportunities that exist at "the bottom of the pyramid," according to University of Michigan professor C. K. Prahalad. The *bottom of the pyramid* refers to the nearly 5 billion poor people who inhabit the developing countries. Surprisingly, they represent $14 trillion in purchasing power! And they are looking for products and services that can improve the quality of their lives such as clean energy, personal-care products, lighting, and medicines. Multinationals are missing out on growth opportunities if they ignore this vast segment of the market.

Unilever, the Anglo-Dutch maker of such brands as Dove, Lipton, and Vaseline, built a following among the world's poorest consumers by upending some of the basic rules of marketing. Instead of focusing on value for money, it shrunk packages to set a price even consumers living on $2 a day could afford. It helped people make money to buy its products. "It's not about doing good," but about tapping new markets, says Chief Executive Patrick Cescau.

Sources: Reingold, J. 2011. Can P&G Make Money in Places Where People Earn $2-A-Day? *Fortune*, January 17: 86–91; McGregor, J. 2008. The World's Most Influential Companies. *BusinessWeek*, December 22: 43–53; Miller, C. C. 2006. Easy Money. *Forbes*, November 27: 134–138; and Prahalad, C. K. 2005. *The Fortune at the Bottom of the Pyramid: Eradicating Poverty through Profits*. Philadelphia: Wharton School Publishing.

The strategy was forged about 25 years ago when Indian subsidiary Hindustan Lever (HL) found its products out of reach for millions of Indians. HL came up with a strategy to lower the price while making a profit: single-use packets for everything from shampoo to laundry detergent, costing pennies a pack. A bargain? Maybe not. But it put marquee brands within reach.

It has trained rural women to sell products to their neighbors. "What Unilever does well is get inside these communities, understand their needs, and adapt its business model accordingly," notes a professor at Barcelona's IESE Business School.

Similarly, Procter & Gamble, with $79 billion in annual revenues, has launched a skunkworks. It is staffed mostly by technical staff, rather than market researchers, to approach the $2-a-day consumer from a new perspective. Rather than try to invent products first or rely on market research alone, the group spends days or weeks in the field, visiting homes in Brazil, China, India, and elsewhere. It's the same approach the company uses in developed markets but requires much more effort, without the obvious potential payoff from consumers with disposable income. According to Robert McDonald, P&G's CEO and Chairman: "Our innovation strategy is not just diluting the top-tier product for the lower-end consumer. You have to discretely innovate for every one of those consumers on that economic curve, and if you don't do that, you'll fail."

No one is helped by viewing the poor as the wretched of the earth. Instead, they are the latest frontier of opportunity for those who can meet their needs. A vast market that is barely tapped, the bottom of the pyramid offers enormous opportunities.

---

factor endowments (national advantage) a nation's position in factors of production.

demand conditions (national advantage) the nature of home-market demand for the industry's product or service.

nations. He concluded that there are four broad attributes of nations that individually, and as a system, constitute what is termed "the diamond of national advantage." In effect, these attributes jointly determine the playing field that each nation establishes and operates for its industries. These factors are:

- *Factor endowments.* The nation's position in factors of production, such as skilled labor or infrastructure, necessary to compete in a given industry.
- *Demand conditions.* The nature of home-market demand for the industry's product or service.
- *Related and supporting industries.* The presence or absence in the nation of supplier industries and other related industries that are internationally competitive.
- *Firm strategy, structure, and rivalry.* The conditions in the nation governing how companies are created, organized, and managed, as well as the nature of domestic rivalry.

Factor Endowments[12,13]

Classical economics suggests that factors of production such as land, labor, and capital are the building blocks that create usable consumer goods and services.[14] However, companies in advanced nations seeking competitive advantage over firms in other nations *create* many of the factors of production. For example, a country or industry dependent on scientific innovation must have a skilled human resource pool to draw upon. This resource pool is not inherited; it is created through investment in industry-specific knowledge and talent. The supporting infrastructure of a country—that is, its transportation and communication systems as well as its banking system—are also critical.

>LO7.2
The sources of national advantage; that is, why an industry in a given country is more (or less) successful than the same industry in another country.

Factors of production must be developed that are industry and firm specific. In addition, the pool of resources is less important than the speed and efficiency with which these resources are deployed. Thus, firm-specific knowledge and skills created within a country that are rare, valuable, difficult to imitate, and rapidly and efficiently deployed are the factors of production that ultimately lead to a nation's competitive advantage.

For example, the island nation of Japan has little land mass, making the warehouse space needed to store inventory prohibitively expensive. But by pioneering just-in-time inventory management, Japanese companies managed to create a resource from which they gained advantage over companies in other nations that spent large sums to warehouse inventory.

Demand Conditions

Demand conditions refer to the demands that consumers place on an industry for goods and services. Consumers who demand highly specific, sophisticated products and services force firms to create innovative, advanced products and services to meet the demand. This consumer pressure presents challenges to a country's industries. But in response to these challenges, improvements to existing goods and services often result, creating conditions necessary for competitive advantage over firms in other countries.

Countries with demanding consumers drive firms in that country to meet high standards, upgrade existing products and services, and create innovative products and services. The conditions of consumer demand influence how firms view a market. This, in turn, helps a nation's industries to better anticipate future global demand conditions and proactively respond to product and service requirements.

Denmark, for instance, is known for its environmental awareness. Demand from consumers for environmentally safe products has spurred Danish manufacturers to become leaders in water pollution control equipment—products it successfully exported.

Related and Supporting Industries

Related and supporting industries enable firms to manage inputs more effectively. For example, countries with a strong supplier base benefit by adding efficiency to downstream activities. A competitive supplier base helps a firm obtain inputs using cost-effective, timely methods, thus reducing manufacturing costs. Also, close working relationships with suppliers provide the potential to develop competitive advantages through joint research and development and the ongoing exchange of knowledge.

related and supporting industries (national advantage) the presence, absence, and quality in the nation of supplier industries and other related industries that supply services, support, or technology to firms in the industry value chain.

Related industries offer similar opportunities through joint efforts among firms. In addition, related industries create the probability that new companies will enter the market, increasing competition and forcing existing firms to become more competitive through efforts such as cost control, product innovation, and novel approaches to distribution. Combined, these give the home country's industries a source of competitive advantage.

In the Italian footwear industry the supporting industries enhance national competitive advantage. In Italy, shoe manufacturers are geographically located near their suppliers. The manufacturers have ongoing interactions with leather suppliers and learn about new textures, colors, and manufacturing techniques while a shoe is still in the prototype stage. The manufacturers are able to project future demand and gear their factories for new products long before companies in other nations become aware of the new styles.

Firm Strategy, Structure, and Rivalry

firm strategy, structure, and rivalry (national advantage) the conditions in the nation governing how companies are created, organized, and managed, as well as the nature of domestic rivalry.

Rivalry is particularly intense in nations with conditions of strong consumer demand, strong supplier bases, and high new entrant potential from related industries. This competitive rivalry in turn increases the efficiency with which firms develop, market, and distribute products and services within the home country. Domestic rivalry thus provides a strong impetus for firms to innovate and find new sources of competitive advantage.

This intense rivalry forces firms to look outside their national boundaries for new markets, setting up the conditions necessary for global competitiveness. Among all the points on Porter's diamond of national advantage, domestic rivalry is perhaps the strongest indicator of global competitive success. Firms that have experienced intense domestic competition are more likely to have designed strategies and structures that allow them to successfully compete in world markets.

In the U.S., for example, intense rivalry has spurred companies such as Dell Computer to find innovative ways to produce and distribute its products. This is largely a result of competition from IBM and Hewlett-Packard.

Strategy Spotlight 7.2 discusses India's software industry. It provides an integrative example of how Porter's "diamond" can help to explain the relative degree of success of an industry in a given country. Exhibit 7.1 illustrates India's "software diamond."

Concluding Comment on Factors Affecting a Nation's Competitiveness

Porter drew his conclusions based on case histories of firms in more than 100 industries. Despite the differences in strategies employed by successful global competitors, a common theme emerged: Firms that succeeded in global markets had first succeeded in intensely competitive home markets. We can conclude that competitive advantage for global firms typically grows out of relentless, continuing improvement, and innovation.[15]

International Expansion: A Company's Motivations and Risks

>LO7.3 The motivations (or benefits) and the risks associated with international expansion, including the emerging trend for greater offshoring and outsourcing activity.

Motivations for International Expansion

Increase Market Size   There are many motivations for a company to pursue international expansion. The most obvious one is to *increase the size of potential markets* for a firm's products and services.[16] By early 2009, the world's population exceeded 6.9 billion, with the U.S. representing less than 5 percent. Exhibit 7.2 lists the population of the U.S. compared to other major markets abroad.

Many multinational firms are intensifying their efforts to market their products and services to countries such as India and China as the ranks of their middle class have increased over the past decade. These include Procter & Gamble's success in achieving a 50 percent share in China's shampoo market as well as PepsiCo's impressive inroads in the Indian soft-drink market.[17] Let's take a brief look at China's emerging middle class:[18]

multinational firms firms that manage operations in more than one country.

- China's middle class has finally attained a critical mass—between 35 million and 200 million people, depending on what definition is used. The larger number is preferred by Fan Gong, director of China's National Economic Research Institute, who fixes the lower boundary of "middle" as a family income of $10,000.

India and the Diamond of National Advantage

Consider the following facts:

- SAP, the German software company, has developed new applications for notebook PCs at its 500-engineer Bangalore facility.

- General Electric plans to invest $100 million and hire 2,600 scientists to create the world's largest research and development lab in Bangalore, India.

- Microsoft plans to invest $400 million in new research partnerships in India.

- Over one-fifth of Fortune 1000 companies outsource their software requirements to firms in India.

- Indian software exports have soared from $5.9 billion in 2000 to $23.6 billion in 2005 to a predicted $68 to $70 billion by 2012.

- For the past decade, the Indian software industry has grown at a 25 percent annual rate.

- More than 800 firms in India are involved in software services as their primary activity.

- Software and information technology firms in India employed 2.3 million people in 2010.

- The information technology industry accounted for 6 percent of India's Gross Domestic Product (GDP) in 2010—up from only 4.8 percent in 2007.

Sources: Sachitanand, R. 2010. The New Face of IT. *Business Today,* 19:62; Anonymous. 2010. Training to Lead. *www.Dqindia.com.* October 5: np; Nagaraju, B.2011. India's Software Exports Seen Up 16–18 pct.in Fy12. *www. reuters.com.* February 2: np; Ghemawat, P. & Hout, T. 2008. Tomorrow's Global Giants. *Harvard Business Review,* 86(11): 80–88; Mathur, S. K. 2007. Indian IT Industry: A Performance Analysis and a Model for Possible Adoption. *ideas.repec.org,* January 1: np; Kripalani, M. 2002. Calling Bangalore: Multinationals Are Making It a Hub for High-Tech Research *BusinessWeek,* November 25: 52–54; Kapur, D. & Ramamurti, R. 2001. India's Emerging Competitive Advantage in Services. 2001. *Academy of Management Executive,* 15(2): 20–33; World Bank. *World Development Report:* 6. New York: Oxford University Press. Reuters. 2001. Oracle in India Push, Taps Software Talent. *Washington Post Online,* July 3.

Note: Dashed lines represent weaker interactions.

Exhibit 7.1 India's Diamond in Software

Source: From Kampur D. and Ramamurti R., "India's Emerging Competition Advantage in Services," *Academy of Management Executive: The Thinking Manager's Source.* Copyright © 2001 by Academy of Management. Reproduced with permission of Academy of Management via Copyright Clearance Center.

(continued)

(continued)

What is causing such global interest in India's software services industry? Porter's diamond of national advantage helps clarify this question. See Exhibit 7.1.

First, *factor endowments* are conducive to the rise of India's software industry. Through investment in human resource development with a focus on industry-specific knowledge, India's universities and software firms have literally created this essential factor of production. For example, India produces the second largest annual output of scientists and engineers in the world, behind only the United States. In a knowledge-intensive industry such as software, development of human resources is fundamental to both domestic and global success.

Second, *demand conditions* require that software firms stay on the cutting edge of technological innovation. India has already moved toward globalization of its software industry; consumer demand conditions in developed nations such as Germany, Denmark, parts of Southeast Asia, and the United States created the consumer demand necessary to propel India's software makers toward sophisticated software solutions.*

Third, India has the *supplier base as well as the related industries* needed to drive competitive rivalry and enhance competitiveness. In particular, information technology (IT) hardware prices declined rapidly in the 1990s. Furthermore, rapid technological change in IT hardware meant that latecomers like India were not locked into older-generation technologies. Thus, both the IT hardware and software industries could "leapfrog" older technologies. In addition, relationships among knowledge workers in these IT hardware and software industries offer the social structure for ongoing knowledge exchange, promoting further enhancement of existing products. Further infrastructure improvements are occurring rapidly.

Fourth, with over 800 firms in the software services industry in India, *intense rivalry forces firms to develop competitive strategies and structures.* Although firms like TCS, Infosys, and Wipro have become large, they were quite small less than a decade ago. And dozens of small and midsized companies are aspiring to catch up. This intense rivalry is one of the primary factors driving Indian software firms to develop overseas distribution channels, as predicted by Porter's diamond of national advantage.

It is interesting to note that the cost advantage of Indian firms may be eroding. For example, TCS's engineers' compensation has soared 13 percent in 2010. Other Asian companies are trying to steal its customers, and it is working hard to better understand overseas customers. Further, IBM and Accenture are aggressively building up their Indian operations, hiring tens of thousands of sought-after Indians by paying them more, thereby lowering their costs while raising those of TCS.

---

* Although India's success cannot be explained in terms of its home market demand (according to Porter's model), the nature of the industry enables software to be transferred among different locations simultaneously by way of communications links. Thus, competitiveness of markets outside India can be enhanced without a physical presence in those markets.

- The central government's emphasis on science and technology has boosted the rapid development of higher education, which is the incubator of the middle class.
- China may be viewed as a new example of economies of scale. Many American companies already have factories in China exporting goods. Now that there is a domestic market to go along with the export market, those factories can increase their output with little additional cost. That is one reason why many foreign companies' profits in China have been so strong in recent years.

Exhibit 7.2
Populations of Selected Nations and the World

Country	February 2011 (in est. millions)
China	1,334
India	1,182
United States	312
Japan	127
Germany	82
World Total	6,877

Source: *www.geohive.com/global/pop_data2.php.*

7.3 — strategy spotlight

How Walmart Profits from Arbitrage

With sales of over $405 billion and net income of $14.8 billion, Walmart is considered one of the most successful companies in the world. In recent years, Walmart has embarked upon an ambitious international expansion agenda, opening stores in countries such as Mexico, China, Japan, and England. Walmart today has 4,122 stores outside the United States. Together they account for $100 billion in sales and $5 billion in operating income.

Walmart's above average industry profitability has been attributed to various factors, such as their superior logistics, strict control over overhead costs, and effective use of information systems. What is often lost sight of is that their "everyday low pricing" strategy cannot work successfully unless they are able to procure the thousands of items they carry in each of their stores at the lowest possible prices. This is where their expertise in arbitraging plays a critical role. In 2004, Walmart bought $18 billion worth of goods directly from China. By 2006, this had grown to $26.7 billion. If one considers indirect imports through their other suppliers as well, Walmart's total imports from China could be anywhere between $50 billion and $70 billion each year. At a conservative estimate, this represents cost savings of approximately $16 billion to $23 billion! (These savings represent how much more these goods would have likely cost Walmart had the firm purchased them from the United States.) Clearly, the core of Walmart's international strategy is not their international store expansion strategy but their pursuit of worldwide arbitrage opportunities.

Sources: 2010 Walmart Annual Report; Ghemawat, P. 2007. *Redefining Global Strategy.* Boston: Harvard Business School Press; Scott, R.E. 2007. The WalMart Effect. *epi.org,* June 26: np; and Basker, E. & Pham, V.H. 2008. WalMart as Catalyst to U.S.-China Trade. *ssrn.com;* np.

Expanding a firm's global presence also automatically increases its scale of operations, providing it with a larger revenue and asset base.[19] As we noted in Chapter 5 in discussing overall cost leadership strategies, such an increase in revenues and asset base potentially enables a firm to *attain economies of scale.* This provides multiple benefits. One advantage is the spreading of fixed costs such as R&D over a larger volume of production. Examples include the sale of Boeing's commercial aircraft and Microsoft's operating systems in many foreign countries.

Filmmaking is another industry in which international sales can help amortize huge developmental costs.[20] For example, Tom Cruise found foreign buyers for his "Valkyrie" in 2008 and the film ultimately got about 59 percent of its $200 million in ticket sales abroad. And Sylvester Stallone's latest *Rambo* opened the same year and picked up $70 million, or 62 percent of its $113 million in total ticket sales from international markets.

Take Advantage of Arbitrage *Taking advantage of arbitrage opportunities* is a second advantage of international expansion. In its simplest form, arbitrage involves buying something from where it is cheap and selling it somewhere where it commands a higher price. A big part of Walmart's success can be attributed to the company's expertise in arbitrage (see Strategy Spotlight 7.3). The possibilities for arbitrage are not necessarily confined to simple trading opportunities. It can be applied to virtually any factor of production and every stage of the value chain. For example, a firm may locate its call centers in India, its manufacturing plants in China, and its R&D in Europe, where the specific types of talented personnel may be available at the lowest possible price. In today's integrated global financial markets, a firm can borrow anywhere in the world where capital is cheap and use it to fund a project in a country where capital is expensive. Such arbitrage opportunities are even more attractive to global corporations because their larger size enables them to buy in huge volume, thus increasing their bargaining power with suppliers.

> **arbitrage opportunities** an opportunity to profit by buying and selling the same good in different markets.

Extend a Product's Life Cycle *Extending the life cycle of a product* that is in its maturity stage in a firm's home country but that has greater demand potential elsewhere is another benefit of international expansion. As we noted in Chapter 5, products (and industries) generally go through a four-stage life cycle of introduction, growth, maturity, and decline. In recent decades, U.S. soft-drink producers such as Coca-Cola and PepsiCo have aggressively pursued international markets to attain levels of growth that simply would not be available in the United States. Similarly, personal computer manufacturers such as Dell and Hewlett-Packard have sought out foreign markets to offset the growing saturation in the U.S. market.

Optimize the Location of Value-Chain Activities   *Optimizing the physical location for every activity in its value chain* is another benefit. Recall from our discussions in Chapters 3 and 5 that the value chain represents the various activities in which all firms must engage to produce products and services. They include primary activities, such as inbound logistics, operations, and marketing, as well as support activities, such as procurement, R&D, and human resource management. All firms have to make critical decisions as to where each activity will take place.[21] Optimizing the location for every activity in the value chain can yield one or more of three strategic advantages: performance enhancement, cost reduction, and risk reduction. We will now discuss each of these.

Performance Enhancement Microsoft's decision to establish a corporate research laboratory in Cambridge, England, is an example of a location decision that was guided mainly by the goal of building and sustaining world-class excellence in selected value-creating activities.[22] This strategic decision provided Microsoft with access to outstanding technical and professional talent. Location decisions can affect the quality with which any activity is performed in terms of the availability of needed talent, speed of learning, and the quality of external and internal coordination.

Cost Reduction Two location decisions founded largely on cost-reduction considerations are (1) Nike's decision to source the manufacture of athletic shoes from Asian countries such as China, Vietnam, and Indonesia, and (2) the decision of many multinational companies to set up production operations just south of the U.S.–Mexico border to access lower-cost labor. These operations are called *maquiladoras.* Such location decisions can affect the cost structure in terms of local manpower and other resources, transportation and logistics, and government incentives and the local tax structure.

Performance enhancement and cost-reduction benefits parallel the business-level strategies (discussed in Chapter 5) of differentiation and overall cost leadership. They can at times be attained simultaneously. Consider our example in the previous section on the Indian software industry. When Oracle set up a development operation in that country, the company benefited both from lower labor costs and operational expenses as well as from performance enhancements realized through the hiring of superbly talented professionals.

Risk Reduction Given the erratic swings in the exchange ratios between the U.S. dollar and the Japanese yen (in relation to each other and to other major currencies), an important basis for cost competition between Ford and Toyota has been their relative ingenuity at managing currency risks. One way for such rivals to manage currency risks has been to spread the high-cost elements of their manufacturing operations across a few select and carefully chosen locations around the world. Location decisions such as these can affect the overall risk profile of the firm with respect to currency, economic, and political risks.[23]

reverse innovation
new products developed by developed country multination firms for emerging markets that have adequate functionality at a low cost.

Explore Reverse Innovation   Finally, *exploring possibilities for reverse innovation* has become a major motivation for international expansion. Many leading companies are discovering that developing products specifically for emerging markets can pay off in a big way. In the past, multinational companies typically developed products for their rich home markets and then tried to sell them in developing countries with minor adaptations.

However, as growth slows in rich nations and demand grows rapidly in developing countries such as India and China, this approach becomes increasingly inadequate. Instead, companies like GE have committed significant resources to developing products that meet the needs of developing nations, products that deliver adequate functionality at a fraction of the cost. Interestingly, these products have subsequently found considerable success in value segments in wealthy countries as well. Hence, this process is referred to as reverse innovation, a new motivation for international expansion.

As $3,000 cars, $300 computers, and $30 mobile phones bring what were previously considered as luxuries within the reach of the middle class of emerging markets, it is important to understand the motivations and implications of reverse innovation. *First,* it is impossible to sell first-world versions of products with minor adaptations in countries where average income per person is between $1,000 and $4,000, as is the case in most developing countries. To sell in these markets, entirely new products must be designed and developed by local technical talent and manufactured with local components. *Second,* although these countries are relatively poor, they are growing rapidly. For example, the Indian and Chinese economies are growing at double digit rates, and Brazil has achieved full employment. *Third,* if the innovation does not come from first-world multinationals, there are any number of local firms that are ready to grab the market with low-cost products. *Fourth,* as the consumers and governments of many first-world countries are rediscovering the virtues of frugality and are trying to cut down expenses, these products and services originally developed for the first world may gain significant market shares in developing countries as well.

Strategy Spotlight 7.4 describes several examples of reverse innovation.

Potential Risks of International Expansion

When a company expands its international operations, it does so to increase its profits or revenues. As with any other investment, however, there are also potential risks.[24] To help companies assess the risk of entering foreign markets, rating systems have been developed to evaluate political, economic, as well as financial and credit risks.[25] *Euromoney* magazine publishes a semiannual "Country Risk Rating" that evaluates political, economic, and other risks that entrants potentially face.[26] Exhibit 7.3 depicts a sample of country risk ratings, published by the World Bank, from the 178 countries that *Euromoney* evaluates. Note that the lower the score, the higher the country's expected level of risk.[27]

Next we will discuss the four main types of risk: political risk, economic risk, currency risk, and management risk.

Political and Economic Risk   Generally speaking, the business climate in the United States is very favorable. However, some countries around the globe may be hazardous to the health of corporate initiatives because of **political risk.**[28] Forces such as social unrest, military turmoil, demonstrations, and even violent conflict and terrorism can pose serious threats.[29] Consider, for example, the ongoing tension and violence in the Middle East between Israelis and Palestinians, and the social and political unrest in Indonesia.[30] Such conditions increase the likelihood of destruction of property and disruption of operations as well as nonpayment for goods and services. Thus, countries that are viewed as high risk are less attractive for most types of business.[31]

Another source of political risk in many countries is the absence of the rule of law. The absence of rules or the lack of uniform enforcement of existing rules leads to what might often seem to be arbitrary and inconsistent decisions by government officials. This can make it difficult for foreign firms to conduct business.

Consider Libya. The country is noted for its capricious government under the leadership of its ruler, Muammar Qaddafi, who has been in power for over 40 years. Here, business people often incur significant political risks. Let's look at a few examples:[32]

political risk potential threat to a firm's operations in a country due to ineffectiveness of the domestic political system.

rule of law a characteristic of legal systems where behavior is governed by rules that are uniformly enforced.

Reverse Innovation: How Developing Countries Are Becoming Hotbeds of Innovation

GE Healthcare's largest R&D facility is surprisingly located in Bangalore, India, thousands of miles away from its home country. Here, customers can hardly afford the sky-high prices of GE's medical devices. At 50,000 square feet and employing about 1,000 researchers and engineers, this facility recently developed a portable electrocardiogram that weighs only about two pounds, runs on batteries, and can do an electrocardiogram for 20 cents! Over the next six years, GE plans to spend $3 billion to create at least 100 healthcare innovations that would significantly lower costs, improve quality, increase access, and conquer the medical devices market in developing countries. Increasingly, many developing countries are becoming hotbeds of a new type of innovation often referred to as "reverse innovation" or "frugal innovation." Let us look at a few other examples of reverse innovation by GE as well as other companies:

- In the 1990s, GE attempted to sell ultrasound machines costing about $100,000 to high-end Chinese hospital imaging centers. But these expensive, bulky devices were poorly received by Chinese customers. Responding to this failure, a local GE team developed a cheap, portable ultrasound machine using a laptop computer enhanced with a probe which sold at a price between $30,000 and $40,000. By 2007, they were able to bring the price down to just $15,000. Today, these machines have found a worldwide market—both in developing economies as well as in the United States, where ambulance squads and emergency rooms are increasingly using them. Overall, sales of medical technology are exploding in China and India. China's market is expected to grow by 15 percent a year to 2015 and reach $43 billion by 2019. India's demand is growing

at an even higher rate, 23 percent, and should top $10 billion by 2020.

- Moline, Illinois–based Deere & Co. opened a center in Pune, India, almost a decade ago with the intention to penetrate the Indian market. Many observers were skeptical about the ability of a company known for its heavy-duty farm equipment and big construction gear to succeed in a market where the majority of the farmers still used oxen-pulled plows. However, Deere saw potential and its engineers in Pune responded with four no-frills models. Though lacking first-world features like GPS and air conditioning, they were sturdy enough to handle the rigors of commercial farming. The tractors cost between $8400 and $11,600 in India. Subsequently, Deere targeted a segment of the home market that they had previously largely ignored—hobbyists as well as bargain hunters. These buyers do not care for advanced features but covet the same qualities as Indian farmers: affordability and maneuverability. Today, half of the no-frills models that Deere produces in India are exported to other countries. "These tractors are like Swiss Army knives. They get used for anything: mowing, transporting bales of hay, pushing dirt, and removing manure," claims Mike Alvin, a product manager at Deere.

- Narayana Hrudayalaya Hospital in Bangalore performs open heart surgeries at about $2000, which is a fraction of the $20,000 to $100,000 that it would cost in a U.S. hospital. How do they do it? By applying mass-production techniques pioneered by Henry Ford in the auto industry. The hospital has 1000 beds, roughly eight times the size of an American hospital, and performs 600 operations a week. The large volume allows the hospital to benefit from both economies of scale (that reduce cost) and, even more importantly, experience curve effects that improve the success rate. Today the hospital has established video and Internet links with hospitals not only in India, but in countries in Africa as well as in Malaysia. As the need to contain healthcare costs becomes more pressing in developed countries like the United States, techniques pioneered by Narayana Hrudayalaya Hospital may find acceptance in these countries.

Sources: Anonymous. 2011. Frugal healing. *The Economist.* January 22: 73–74; Immelt, J. R., Govindarajan, V., & Trimble, C. 2009. How GE Is Disrupting Itself. *Harvard Business Review,* 87 (10): 56–64; Chandran, R. 2010. Profiting from Treating India's Poor. *International Herald Tribune,* July 6: 17; Anonymous. 2010. The World Turned Upside Down. *The Economist,* April 17: 3–17; Mero, J. 2008. John Deere's Farm Team. *Fortune,* April 14: 119–124; and Anonymous. 2008. No-Frills IndianTtractors Find Favor with U.S. Farmers. *www.theindian.com,* April 29: np.

Exhibit 7.3 A Sample of International Country Risk Ratings: September 2010

Rank	Country	Overall Score (100)	Political Risk (30)	Economic Performance (30)	Infrastructure (10)	Total of Debt and Credit Indicators (20)	Access to Bank Finance/Capital Markets (10)
1	Norway	93.33	28.19	26.89	8.25	20.00	10.00
2	Switzerland	90.22	26.80	24.99	8.44	20.00	10.00
3	Sweden	88.93	28.04	22.65	8.24	20.00	10.00
4	Denmark	88.80	27.90	22.81	8.09	20.00	10.00
5	Finland	88.55	27.99	22.40	8.16	20.00	10.00
6	Luxembourg	88.27	27.54	21.71	9.03	20.00	10.00
7	Canada	88.26	27.80	22.12	8.34	20.00	10.00
8	Netherlands	88.20	27.71	22.85	7.64	20.00	10.00
9	Hong Kong	87.18	25.25	24.87	8.10	18.96	10.00
10	Australia	86.18	27.10	21.43	7.86	19.79	10.00
17	United States	82.10	26.26	17.91	7.92	20.00	10.00
36	China	72.60	17.37	22.31	6.81	17.45	8.67
110	Nigeria	37.80	11.25	12.12	5.25	2.19	7.00
120	Nicaragua	34.53	10.71	9.96	1.00	9.86	3.00
127	Iran	32.97	12.25	14.81	5.24	0.00	0.67
151	Afghanistan	20.95	8.26	8.31	3.38	0.00	1.00

Source: Country Risk September 2010: Full Results. *www.euromoney.com*.

- An Egyptian grocer spent years building a thriving business in Libya. Unfortunately, he made the mistake of going home during a holiday. Abrupt changes to visa rules meant that he could no longer return.
- The new manager of a hotel in Tripoli, an expatriate, fired some staff and switched suppliers. This prompted someone to make a telephone call. A sudden snap health inspection of the hotel revealed a few canned goods beyond their sell-by date. The manager is now in prison!
- A small Canadian oil firm, Verenex, joined the rush into Libya and struck an exciting find. Early in 2009, a Chinese company offered to buy Verenex, nearly all of whose assets are in Libya, for close to $450 million. The Libyan government blocked the sale but promised to match the price. After months of wrangling in the oil ministry, Libya's sovereign wealth fund slashed its offer to barely $300 million. Faced with further trouble if they failed to sell, Verenex shareholders reluctantly agreed.

The laws, and the enforcement of laws, associated with the protection of intellectual property rights can be a major potential **economic risk** in entering new countries.[33] Microsoft, for example, has lost billions of dollars in potential revenue through piracy of its software products in many countries, including China. Other areas of the globe, such as the former Soviet Union and some eastern European nations, have piracy problems as well.[34] Firms rich in intellectual property have encountered financial losses as imitations of their products have grown due to a lack of law enforcement of intellectual property rights.[35]

economic risk potential threat to a firm's operations in a country due to economic policies and conditions, including property rights laws and enforcement of those laws.

Counterfeiting: A Worldwide Problem

Although counterfeiting used to be a luxury goods problem, people are now trying to counterfeit items that have a wider effect on the economy, such as pharmaceuticals and computer parts. A new study by the U.S. Department of Commerce shows that fake goods have been infiltrating the army. The number of counterfeit parts in military electronics systems more than doubled between 2005 and 2008, potentially damaging high-tech weapons.

Counterfeiting can have health and safety implications as well. The World Health Organization says that up to 10 percent of medicines worldwide are counterfeit—a deadly hazard that could be costing the pharmaceutical industry $46 billion a year. "You won't die from purchasing a pair of counterfeit blue jeans or a counterfeit golf club. You can die from taking counterfeit pharmaceutical products. And there's no doubt that people have died in China from bad medicine," says John Theirault, head of global security for American pharmaceutical giant Pfizer.

The International Anti-Counterfeiting Coalition (IACC), a Washington D.C.–based nonprofit organization, estimates that the true figure for counterfeit and pirated goods is close to $600 billion and makes up about 5–7 percent of world trade. Several factors have contributed to the increase in counterfeiting in recent years. The shift of much of the world's manufacturing to countries with poor

protection of intellectual property rights has provided both technology and opportunity to make knock-offs. And the Internet and e-commerce sites like eBay have made it easier to distribute counterfeit goods. MarkMonitor, a firm that helps companies defend their brands online, estimates that sales of counterfeit goods via the Internet is about $135 billion.

The IACC provides some rather startling statistics relating to counterfeiting and its costs to business and society:

- Counterfeiting costs U.S. businesses $200 billion to $250 billion annually.

- Counterfeit merchandise is directly responsible for the loss of more than 750,000 American jobs.

- Since 1982, the global trade in illegitimate goods has increased from approximately $5.5 billion to $600 billion annually.

- U.S. companies suffer $9 billion in world trade losses due to international copyright piracy.

- Counterfeiting poses a threat to global health and safety.

The recent recession in the richer countries may have also given a boost to counterfeit goods. An anti-counterfeiting group has noticed a spike in knock-offs this recession, as consumers trade down from the real thing. Cost-cutting measures may have also made firms' supply chains more vulnerable to counterfeit parts. Lawsuits brought by companies are at an all-time high, says Kirsten Gilbert, a partner at a British law firm.

Source: Anonymous. 2010. Knock-offs Catch On. *The Economist*, March 6: 81–82; Balfour, F. 2005. Fake! *BusinessWeek*, February 7: 54–64; and Quinn, G. 2010. Counterfeiting Costs US Businesses $200 Billion Annually. *www.ipwatchdog.com*, August 30: np.

---

counterfeiting selling of trademarked goods without the consent of the trademark holder.

currency risk potential threat to a firm's operations in a country due to fluctuations in the local currency's exchange rate.

Strategy Spotlight 7.5 discusses a problem that is a severe threat to global trade—counterferting. Estimates are that counterfeiting accounts for between 5 to 7 percent of global merchandise trade—the equivalent of as much as $600 billion a year. And the potential corrosive effects include health and safety, not just economic, damage.[36]

Currency Risks Currency fluctuations can pose substantial risks. A company with operations in several countries must constantly monitor the exchange rate between its own currency and that of the host country to minimize **currency risks.** Even a small change in the exchange rate can result in a significant difference in the cost of production or net profit when doing business overseas. When the U.S. dollar appreciates against other currencies, for example, U.S. goods can be more expensive to consumers in foreign countries. At the same time, however, appreciation of the U.S. dollar can have negative implications for American companies that have branch operations overseas. The reason for this is that profits from abroad must be exchanged for dollars at a more expensive rate of exchange, reducing the amount of profit when measured in dollars. For example, consider an American firm doing business in Italy. If this firm had a 20 percent profit in euros at its Italian center of operations, this profit would be totally wiped out when converted into U.S. dollars if the euro had depreciated 20 percent against the U.S. dollar. (U.S. multinationals typically engage in sophisticated "hedging strategies" to minimize currency risk. The discussion of this is beyond the scope of this section.)

It is important to note that even when government intervention is well intended, the macroeconomic effects of such action can be very negative for multinational corporations. Such was the case in 1997 when Thailand suddenly chose to devalue its currency, the baht, after months of trying to support it at an artificially high level. This, in effect, made the baht nearly worthless compared to other currencies. And in 1998 Russia not only devalued its ruble but also elected not to honor its foreign debt obligations.

Below, we discuss how Israel's strong currency—the shekel—forced a firm to reevaluate its strategy.

> For years O.R.T. Technologies resisted moving any operations outside of Israel. However, when faced with a sharp rise in the value of the shekel, the maker of specialized software for managing gas stations froze all local hiring and decided to transfer some developmental work to Eastern Europe. Laments CEO Alex Milner, "I never thought I'd see the day when we would have to move R&D outside of Israel, but the strong shekel has forced us to do so."[37]

Management Risks **Management risks** may be considered the challenges and risks that managers face when they must respond to the inevitable differences that they encounter in foreign markets. These take a variety of forms: culture, customs, language, income levels, customer preferences, distribution systems, and so on.[38] As we will note later in the chapter, even in the case of apparently standard products, some degree of local adaptation will become necessary.[39]

Differences in cultures across countries can also pose unique challenges for managers.[40] Cultural symbols can evoke deep feelings.[41] For example, in a series of advertisements aimed at Italian vacationers, Coca-Cola executives turned the Eiffel Tower, Empire State Building, and the Tower of Pisa into the familiar Coke bottle. So far, so good. However, when the white marble columns of the Parthenon that crowns the Acropolis in Athens were turned into Coke bottles, the Greeks became outraged. Why? Greeks refer to the Acropolis as the "holy rock," and a government official said the Parthenon is an "international symbol of excellence" and that "whoever insults the Parthenon insults international culture." Coca-Cola apologized. Below are some cultural tips for conducting business in HongKong:

- Handshakes when greeting and before leaving are customary.
- After the initial handshake, business cards are presented with both hands on the card. Carefully read the card before putting it away.
- In Hong Kong, Chinese people should be addressed by their professional title (or Mr., Mrs., Miss) followed by their surname.
- Appointments should be made as far in advance as possible.
- Punctuality is very important and demonstrates respect.

management risk potential threat to a firm's operations in a country due to the problems that managers have making decisions in the context of foreign markets.

● Some of Hong Kong's customs are quite different from those of western countries.

- Negotiations in Hong Kong are normally very slow with much attention to detail. The same negotiating team should be kept throughout the proceedings.
- Tea will be served during the negotiations. Always accept and wait for the host to begin drinking before you partake.
- Be aware that "yes" may just be an indication that the person heard you rather than indicating agreement. A Hong Kong Chinese businessperson will have a difficult time saying "no" directly.

Below, we discuss a rather humorous example of how a local custom can affect operations at a manufacturing plant in Singapore.

> Larry Henderson, plant manager, and John Lichthental, manager of human resources, were faced with a rather unique problem. They were assigned by Celanese Chemical Corp. to build a plant in Singapore, and the plant was completed in July. However, according to local custom, a plant should only be christened on "lucky" days. Unfortunately, the next lucky day was not until September 3.
>
> The managers had to convince executives at Celanese's Dallas headquarters to delay the plant opening. As one might expect, it wasn't easy. But after many heated telephone conversations and flaming e-mails, the president agreed to open the new plant on a lucky day—September 3.[42]

Global Dispersion of Value Chains: Outsourcing and Offshoring

A major recent trend has been the dispersion of the value chains of multinational corporations across different countries; that is, the various activities that constitute the value chain of a firm are now spread across several countries and continents. Such dispersion of value occurs mainly through increasing offshoring and outsourcing.

A report issued by the World Trade Organization describes the production of a particular U.S. car as follows: "30 percent of the car's value goes to Korea for assembly, 17.5 percent to Japan for components and advanced technology, 7.5 percent to Germany for design, 4 percent to Taiwan and Singapore for minor parts, 2.5 percent to U.K. for advertising and marketing services, and 1.5 percent to Ireland and Barbados for data processing. This means that only 37 percent of the production value is generated in the U.S."[43] In today's economy, we are increasingly witnessing two interrelated trends: outsourcing and offshoring.

outsourcing using other firms to perform value-creating activities that were previously performed in-house.

Outsourcing occurs when a firm decides to utilize other firms to perform value-creating activities that were previously performed in-house.[44] It may be a new activity that the firm is perfectly capable of doing but chooses to have someone else perform for cost or quality reasons. Outsourcing can be to either a domestic or foreign firm.

offshoring shifting a value-creating activity from a domestic location to a foreign location.

Offshoring takes place when a firm decides to shift an activity that they were performing in a domestic location to a foreign location.[45] For example, both Microsoft and Intel now have R&D facilities in India, employing a large number of Indian scientists and engineers. Often, offshoring and outsourcing go together; that is, a firm may outsource an activity to a foreign supplier, thereby causing the work to be offshored as well.[46] Spending on offshore information technology will nearly triple between 2004 and 2010 to $60 billion, according to research firm Gartner.[47]

The recent explosion in the volume of outsourcing and offshoring is due to a variety of factors. Up until the 1960s, for most companies, the entire value chain was in one location. Further, the production took place close to where the customers were in order to keep transportation costs under control. In the case of service industries, it was generally believed that offshoring was not possible because the producer and consumer had to be present at the same place at the same time. After all, a haircut could not be performed if the barber and the client were separated!

For manufacturing industries, the rapid decline in transportation and coordination costs has enabled firms to disperse their value chains over different locations. For example, Nike's R&D takes place in the U.S., raw materials are procured from a multitude of countries, actual manufacturing takes place in China or Indonesia, advertising is produced in the U.S., and sales and service take place in practically all the countries. Each value-creating activity is performed in the location where the cost is the lowest or the quality is the best. Without finding optimal locations for each activity, Nike could not have attained its position as the world's largest shoe company.

The experience of the manufacturing sector was also repeated in the service sector by the mid-1990s. A trend that began with the outsourcing of low-level programming and data entry work to countries such as India and Ireland suddenly grew manyfold, encompassing a variety of white collar and professional activities ranging from call-centers to R&D. The cost of a long distance call from the U.S. to India has decreased from about $3 to $0.03 in the last 20 years, thereby making it possible to have call centers located in countries like India, where a combination of low labor costs and English proficiency presents an ideal mix of factor conditions.

Bangalore, India, in recent years, has emerged as a location where more and more U.S. tax returns are prepared. In India, U.S.–trained and licensed radiologists interpret chest X-rays and CT scans from U.S. hospitals for half the cost. The advantages from offshoring go beyond mere cost savings today. In many specialized occupations in science and engineering, there is a shortage of qualified professionals in developed countries, whereas countries, like India, China, and Singapore have what seems like an inexhaustible supply.[48]

For most of the 20th century, domestic companies catered to the needs of local populations. However, with the increasing homogenization of customer needs around the world and the institutionalization of free trade and investment as a global ideology (especially after the creation of the WTO), competition has become truly global. Each company has to keep its costs low in order to survive.[49] They also must find the best suppliers and the most skilled workers as well as locate each stage of the value chain in places where factor conditions are most conducive. Thus, outsourcing and offshoring are no longer mere options to consider, but an imperative for competitive survival.

While there is a compelling logic for companies to engage in offshoring, there can be many pitfalls. This has spurred many companies to outsource tech services to low-cost locations within the United States, instead of offshoring to foreign countries. We discuss this trend in Strategy Spotlight 7.6.

Achieving Competitive Advantage in Global Markets

We now discuss the two opposing forces that firms face when they expand into global markets: cost reduction and adaptation to local markets. Then we address the four basic types of international strategies that they may pursue: international, global, multidomestic, and transnational. The selection of one of these four types of strategies is largely dependent on a firm's relative pressure to address each of the two forces.

Two Opposing Pressures: Reducing Costs and Adapting to Local Markets

Many years ago, the famed marketing strategist Theodore Levitt advocated strategies that favored global products and brands. He suggested that firms should standardize all of their products and services for all of their worldwide markets. Such an approach would help a firm lower its overall costs by spreading its investments over as large a market as possible. Levitt's approach rested on three key assumptions:

>LO7.4
The two opposing forces—cost reduction and adaptation to local markets—that firms face when entering international markets.

A Small-Town Alternative to Offshoring Tech Services Work

These are great times for Cayuse Technologies, a 200-employee tech outsourcing firm. It is owned by the Confederated Tribes of the Umatilla Indian Reservation in northeast Oregon. In 2009 it had $7.7 million in revenues—seven times what it had in 2007, its first year in operation. And with its business from corporate clients like Accenture expected to soar next year, Cayuse plans to hire another 75 workers. Says Marc Benoist, the firm's general manager, "We still have capacity here at our facility, so we have plenty of room for growth."

Cayuse is one of many information technology companies in remote areas of the United States who position themselves as alternatives to offshore outsourcing. And the economics seem to make sense. On an hourly basis, these "rural outsourcers" charge much more than their overseas rivals. But when factors such as oversight and quality control of the offshore work are factored in, their rates are competitive. Their rates are also much lower than their domestic counterparts located in big cities, because they operate in areas that have lower living costs. "Their value proposition is, 'We cost less than the East or West Coast, and we're easier to deal with than India,'" says Mary Lacity, a professor at the University of Missouri at St. Louis, who studies outsourcing. Cayuse Technologies develops software, provides outsourcing of business processes, and serves as a contact for Accenture's clients, for example, processing and adjusting insurance claims. "It makes much more sense for Cayuse to perform those activities," according to Randall Willis, managing director of Accenture.

Sources: Lieber, N. 2010. 'Rural Outsourcers' vs. Bangalore. *Bloomberg Businessweek,* September 27–October 3: 52–53; Brickey, D. 2010. Rural Outsourcing Gains Favor; Cayuse Technologies as a Model. *www.eastoregonian.com,* October 13: np; and Alsever, J. 2010. Forget India, Outsource to Arkansas. *www.money.cnn.com,* July 8: np.

Consider the rationale behind Human Genome Sciences's (HGS) decision to use a rural outsourcing firm: HGS, a Rockville, Maryland biotech company with 900 employees, got bids from several outsourcers to handle the technical support for its back-office software. One of the bidders would have offshored the work to India. However, the idea of sending confidential company information overseas, outside the reach of the American intellectual property law, did not sit too well with David Evans, their IT director.

Instead, Evans hired Atlanta-based Rural Sourcing, Inc., and its team of software experts located in Jonesboro, Arkansas. HGS pays about $55 an hour for technical support from Rural Sourcing—a figure that is about 15 percent higher than the rates quoted by the Indian outsourcing firm that he considered. However, it is still about half of what it would cost for him to hire a software development firm located in the Washington, D.C., metro area.

Recently, IT research firm Gartner said in a report that while these firms make up a tiny portion of the market, they are an "attractive alternative" to offshore outsourcers because of language and other cultural factors. It is also easier for them to comply with U.S. data privacy regulations, according to the report.

Without a doubt, rural outsourcers won't replace the offshorers. After all, India has outsourcing revenues of about $50 billion, and that number is expected to triple by 2020, according to estimates by McKinsey & Company and an Indian trade group. In contrast, the rural outsourcing market is estimated to be less than $100 million. However, Lacity believes that this segment has growth potential—in part because of the efforts by federal policymakers to seek ways of creating jobs and as government outsourcing contracts increasingly require work to be done in the United States.

1. Customer needs and interests are becoming increasingly homogeneous worldwide.
2. People around the world are willing to sacrifice preferences in product features, functions, design, and the like for lower prices at high quality.
3. Substantial economies of scale in production and marketing can be achieved through supplying global markets.[50]

However, there is ample evidence to refute these assumptions.[51] Regarding the first assumption—the increasing worldwide homogeneity of customer needs and interests—consider the number of product markets, ranging from watches and handbags to soft drinks and fast foods. Companies have identified global customer segments and developed global products and brands targeted to those segments. Also, many other companies adapt lines to idiosyncratic country preferences and develop local brands targeted to local market segments. For example, Nestlé's line of pizzas marketed in the United Kingdom includes cheese with ham and pineapple topping on a French bread crust. Similarly, Coca-Cola in Japan markets Georgia (a tonic drink) as well as Classic Coke and Hi-C.

Consider the second assumption—the sacrifice of product attributes for lower prices. While there is invariably a price-sensitive segment in many product markets, there is no indication that this is increasing. In contrast, in many product and service markets—ranging from watches, personal computers, and household appliances, to banking and insurance—there is a growing interest in multiple product features, product quality, and service.

Finally, the third assumption is that significant economies of scale in production and marketing could be achieved for global products and services. Although standardization may lower manufacturing costs, such a perspective does not consider three critical and interrelated points. First, as we discussed in Chapter 5, technological developments in flexible factory automation enable economies of scale to be attained at lower levels of output and do not require production of a single standardized product. Second, the cost of production is only one component, and often not the critical one, in determining the total cost of a product. Third, a firm's strategy should not be product-driven. It should also consider other activities in the firm's value chain, such as marketing, sales, and distribution.

Based on the above, we would have a hard time arguing that it is wise to develop the same product or service for all markets throughout the world. While there are some exceptions, such as Harley-Davidson motorcycles and some of Coca-Cola's soft-drink products, managers must also strive to tailor their products to the culture of the country in which they are attempting to do business. Few would argue that "one size fits all" generally applies.

The opposing pressures that managers face place conflicting demands on firms as they strive to be competitive.[52] On the one hand, competitive pressures require that firms do what they can to *lower unit costs* so that consumers will not perceive their product and service offerings as too expensive. This may lead them to consider locating manufacturing facilities where labor costs are low and developing products that are highly standardized across multiple countries.

In addition to responding to pressures to lower costs, managers also must strive to be *responsive to local pressures* in order to tailor their products to the demand of the local market in which they do business. This requires differentiating their offerings and strategies from country to country to reflect consumer tastes and preferences and making changes to reflect differences in distribution channels, human resource practices, and governmental regulations. However, since the strategies and tactics to differentiate products and services to local markets can involve additional expenses, a firm's costs will tend to rise.

The two opposing pressures result in four different basic strategies that companies can use to compete in the global marketplace: international, global, multidomestic, and transnational. The strategy that a firm selects depends on the degree of pressure that it is facing for cost reductions and the importance of adapting to local markets. Exhibit 7.4 shows the conditions under which each of these strategies would be most appropriate.

It is important to note that we consider these four strategies to be "basic" or "pure"; that is, in practice, all firms will tend to have some elements of each strategy.

International Strategy

There are a small number of industries in which pressures for both local adaptation and lowering costs are rather low. An extreme example of such an industry is the "orphan" drug industry. These are medicines for diseases that are severe but affect only a small number of people. Diseases such as the Gaucher disease and Fabry disease fit into this category. Companies such as Genzyme and Oxford GlycoSciences are active in this segment of the drug

>LO7.5
The advantages and disadvantages associated with each of the four basic strategies: international, global, multidomestic, and transnational.

international strategy a strategy based on firms' diffusion and adaptation of the parent companies' knowledge and expertise to foreign markets, used in industries where the pressures for both local adaptation and lowering costs are low.

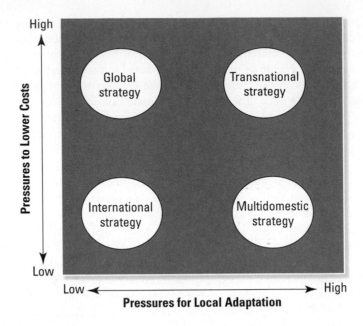

Exhibit 7.4 Opposing Pressures and Four Strategies

industry. There is virtually no need to adapt their products to the local markets. And the pressures to reduce costs are low; even though only a few thousand patients are affected, the revenues and margins are significant, because patients are charged up to $100,000 per year. Legislation has made this industry even more attractive. The 1983 Orphan Drug Act provides various tax credits and exclusive marketing rights for any drug developed to treat a disease that afflicts fewer than 200,000 patients. Since 1983, more than 280 orphan drugs have been licensed and used to treat 14 million patients.[53]

An international strategy is based on diffusion and adaptation of the parent company's knowledge and expertise to foreign markets. Country units are allowed to make some minor adaptations to products and ideas coming from the head office, but they have far less independence and autonomy compared to multidomestic companies. The primary goal of the strategy is worldwide exploitation of the parent firm's knowledge and capabilities. All sources of core competencies are centralized.

The majority of large U.S. multinationals pursued the international strategy in the decades following World War II. These companies centralized R&D and product development but established manufacturing facilities as well as marketing organizations abroad. Companies such as McDonald's and Kellogg are examples of firms following such a strategy. Although these companies do make some local adaptations, they are of a very limited nature. With increasing pressures to reduce costs due to global competition, especially from low-cost countries, opportunities to successfully employ international strategy are becoming more limited. This strategy is most suitable in situations where a firm has distinctive competencies that local companies in foreign markets lack.

Risks and Challenges   Below, are some of the risks and challenges associated with an international strategy.

- Different activities in the value chain typically have different optimal locations. That is, R&D may be optimally located in a country with an abundant supply of scientists and engineers, whereas assembly may be better conducted in a low-cost location.

Nike, for example, designs its shoes in the United States, but all the manufacturing is done in countries like China or Thailand. The international strategy, with its tendency to concentrate most of its activities in one location, fails to take advantage of the benefits of an optimally distributed value chain.

- The lack of local responsiveness may result in the alienation of local customers. Worse still, the firm's inability to be receptive to new ideas and innovation from its foreign subsidiaries may lead to missed opportunities.

Exhibit 7.5 summarizes the strengths and weaknesses of international strategies in the global marketplace.

Global Strategy

As indicated in Exhibit 7.4, a firm whose emphasis is on lowering costs tends to follow a global strategy. Competitive strategy is centralized and controlled to a large extent by the corporate office. Since the primary emphasis is on controlling costs, the corporate office strives to achieve a strong level of coordination and integration across the various businesses.[54] Firms following a global strategy strive to offer standardized products and services as well as to locate manufacturing, R&D, and marketing activities in only a few locations.[55]

A global strategy emphasizes economies of scale due to the standardization of products and services, and the centralization of operations in a few locations. As such, one advantage may be that innovations that come about through efforts of either a business unit or the corporate office can be transferred more easily to other locations. Although costs may be lower, the firm following a global strategy may, in general, have to forgo opportunities for revenue growth since it does not invest extensive resources in adapting product offerings from one market to another.

A global strategy is most appropriate when there are strong pressures for reducing costs and comparatively weak pressures for adaptation to local markets. Economies of scale becomes an important consideration.[56] Advantages to increased volume may come from larger production plants or runs as well as from more efficient logistics and distribution networks. Worldwide volume is also especially important in supporting high levels of investment in research and development. As we would expect, many industries requiring high levels of R&D, such as pharmaceuticals, semiconductors, and jet aircraft, follow global strategies.

Another advantage of a global strategy is that it can enable a firm to create a standard level of quality throughout the world. Let's look at what Tom Siebel, former chairman of Siebel Systems (now part of Oracle), the $2 billion developer of e-business application software, has to say about global standardization.

> Our customers—global companies like IBM, Zurich Financial Services, and Citicorp—expect the same high level of service and quality, and the same licensing policies, no matter where we do business with them around the world. Our human resources and legal

global strategy a strategy based on firms' centralization and control by the corporate office, with the primary emphasis on controlling costs, and used in industries where the pressure for local adaptation is low and the pressure for lowering costs is high.

Strengths	Limitations
• Leverage and diffusion of a parent firm's knowledge and core competencies. • Lower costs because of less need to tailor products and services.	• Limited ability to adapt to local markets. • Inability to take advantage of new ideas and innovations occurring in local markets.

Exhibit 7.5
Strengths and Limitations of International Strategies in the Global Marketplace

departments help us create policies that respect local cultures and requirements worldwide, while at the same time maintaining the highest standards. We have one brand, one image, one set of corporate colors, and one set of messages, across every place on the planet. An organization needs central quality control to avoid surprises.[57]

Risks and Challenges There are, of course, some risks associated with a global strategy.[58]

- A firm can enjoy scale economies only by concentrating scale-sensitive resources and activities in one or few locations. Such concentration, however, becomes a "double-edged sword." For example, if a firm has only one manufacturing facility, it must export its output (e.g., components, subsystems, or finished products) to other markets, some of which may be a great distance from the operation. Thus, decisions about locating facilities must weigh the potential benefits from concentrating operations in a single location against the higher transportation and tariff costs that result from such concentration.
- The geographic concentration of any activity may also tend to isolate that activity from the targeted markets. Such isolation may be risky since it may hamper the facility's ability to quickly respond to changes in market conditions and needs.
- Concentrating an activity in a single location also makes the rest of the firm dependent on that location. Such dependency implies that, unless the location has world-class competencies, the firm's competitive position can be eroded if problems arise. A European Ford executive, reflecting on the firm's concentration of activities during a global integration program in the mid-1990s, lamented, "Now if you misjudge the market, you are wrong in 15 countries rather than only one."

Many firms have learned through experience that products that work in one market may not be well received in other markets. Strategy Spotlight 7.7 describes the very different receptions that Pura, a cleaner-burning gasoline from Shell, received in Thailand and the Netherlands.

Exhibit 7.6 summarizes the strengths and weaknesses of global strategies.

Multidomestic Strategy

According to Exhibit 7.4, a firm whose emphasis is on differentiating its product and service offerings to adapt to local markets follows a multidomestic strategy.[59] Decisions evolving from a multidomestic strategy tend to be decentralized to permit the firm to tailor its products and respond rapidly to changes in demand. This enables a firm to expand its market and to charge different prices in different markets. For firms following this strategy, differences in language, culture, income levels, customer preferences, and distribution systems are only a few of the many factors that must be considered. Even in the case of relatively standardized products, at least some level of local adaptation is often necessary. Consider, for example, Honda motorcycles.

> While Honda uses a common basic technology, it must develop different types of motorcycles for different regions of the world. For example, North Americans primarily use motorcycles for leisure and sports; thus aggressive looks and high horsepower are key. Southeast Asians provide a counterpoint. Here, motorcycles are a basic means of transportation. Thus, they require low cost and ease of maintenance. And in Australia and New Zealand, shepherds use motorcycles to herd sheep. Therefore, they demand low-speed torque, rather than high speed and horsepower.[60]

In addition to the products themselves, how they are packaged must sometimes be adapted to local market conditions. Some consumers in developing countries are likely to have packaging preferences very different from Western consumers. For example, single-serve packets, or sachets, are very popular in India.[61] They permit consumers to purchase

multidomestic strategy a strategy based on firms' differentiating their products and services to adapt to local markets, used in industries where the pressure for local adaptation is high and the pressure for lowering costs is low.

Why Shell's Innovative Gasoline Product Backfired in Holland

Not every consumer wants eco-friendly goods, and relatively few will pay more for them. However, every day more customers are including environmental factors in their buying decisions. But what "sells" in one place might not in another.

Consider, for example, Shell Oil's (part of the Royal Dutch/Shell Group) experience in marketing Pura, a new, cleaner-burning gasoline in two very different countries. According to Mark Weintraub, Shell's director of sustainable development strategy, the firm used a "sustainable development lens" to identify a need for cleaner fuels in Thailand. As is the case in much of Asia, the combination of dense cities and high traffic volume was damaging air quality in Bangkok and elsewhere. A cleaner-burning fuel such as Pura, which produced less sulfur and other harmful emissions, seemed like a winner.

In an example of superior eco-design, Shell developed just such a fuel by converting natural gas to a zero-sulfur liquid and then mixing it with regular diesel. Shell

Source: Esty, D. C., & Winston, A. S. 2009. *Green to Gold*. Hoboken, NJ: Wiley; Peckham, J. 2002. Shell Spots "Premium Diesel" Opportunity for GTL Blend. *Diesel Fuel News*. February 4: np; and *www.showa-shell.co.jp*.

touted the blend as providing "more complete combustion to reduce smoke emissions and restore lost engine performance." Shell-Thailand Chairman Khun Vajrabhaya claimed, "Motorists should experience better performance of their vehicles within 2–3 tank-fulls of Shell Pura diesel. From our road tests on diesel-engine vehicles in both Thailand and the U.K., black smoke was satisfactorily reduced." Even though Shell charged a 7.5 cent a gallon premium, Pura gained market share and sales have been very strong. In short, the launch was a complete success.

Shell assumed that it could use the same pitch when it rolled out Pura in other countries. However, the launch in the Netherlands fell flat. Why? Shell later realized that emphasizing how cleaner-burning fuel protects a car's engine was not resonating in Holland. The message was more important in Thailand, where people are much more concerned about gasoline quality and the effect of impurities on engine performance and quality of life.

Clearly, the "green pitch" never went over well in Holland—even though the country is full of customers who say that they will buy green. It is just that the need to clean the local city air is not as pressing a concern as it is in Asia. Eventually, Shell relaunched Pura in Holland under the name V-Power and marketed it by stressing enhanced engine power.

---

only what they need, experiment with new products, and conserve cash. Products as varied as detergents, shampoos, pickles, and cough syrup are sold in sachets in India. It is estimated that they make up 20 to 30 percent of the total sold in their categories. In China, sachets are spreading as a marketing device for such items as shampoos. This reminds us of the importance of considering all activities in a firm's value chain (discussed in Chapters 3 and 5) in determining where local adaptations may be required.

Cultural differences may also require a firm to adapt its personnel practices when it expands internationally.[62] For example, some facets of Walmart stores have been easily

Strengths	Limitations
• Strong integration across various businesses.	• Limited ability to adapt to local markets.
• Standardization leads to higher economies of scale, which lowers costs.	• Concentration of activities may increase dependence on a single facility.
• Helps create uniform standards of quality throughout the world.	• Single locations may lead to higher tariffs and transportation costs.

Exhibit 7.6
Strengths and Limitations of Global Strategies

Dealing with Bribery Abroad

Most multinational firms experience difficult dilemmas when it comes to the question of adapting rules and guidelines, both formal and informal, while operating in foreign countries. A case in point is the Foreign Corrupt Practices Act of 1977, which makes it illegal for U.S. companies to bribe foreign officials to gain business or facilitate approvals and permissions. Unfortunately, in many parts of the world, bribery is a way of life, with large payoffs to government officials and politicians the norm to win government contracts. At a lower level, goods won't clear customs unless routine illegal, but well-accepted, payments, are made to officials. What is an American company to do in such situations?

Intel follows a strict rule-based definition of bribery as "a thing of value given to someone with the intent of obtaining favorable treatment from the recipient." The company strictly prohibits payments to expedite a shipment through customs if the payment did not "follow applicable rules and regulations, and if the agent gives money or payment in kind to a government official for personal benefit." Texas Instruments, on the other hand, follows a middle approach. They require employees to "exercise good judgment" in questionable circumstances "by avoiding activities that could create even the appearance that our decisions could be compromised." And Analog Devices has set up a policy manager as a consultant to overseas operations. The policy manager does not make decisions for country managers. Instead, the policy manager helps country managers think through the issues and provides information on how the corporate office has handled similar situations in the past.

Source: Begley, T. M., & Boyd, D. P. 2003. The Need for a Corporate Global Mind-Set. *MIT Sloan Management Review,* Winter: 25–32.

"exported" to foreign operations, while others have required some modifications.[63] When the retailer entered the German market in 1997, it took along the company "cheer"—Give me a W! Give me an A! Give me an L! Who's Number One? The Customer!—which suited German employees. However, Walmart's 10-Foot Rule, which requires employees to greet any customer within a 10-foot radius, was not so well received in Germany, where employees and shoppers alike weren't comfortable with the custom.

Strategy Spotlight 7.8 describes how U.S. multinationals have adapted to the problem of bribery in various countries while adhering to strict federal laws on corrupt practices abroad.

Risks and Challenges   As you might expect, there are some risks associated with a multidomestic strategy. Among these are the following:

- Typically, local adaptation of products and services will increase a company's cost structure. In many industries, competition is so intense that most firms can ill afford any competitive disadvantages on the dimension of cost. A key challenge of managers is to determine the trade-off between local adaptation and its cost structure. For example, cost considerations led Procter & Gamble to standardize its diaper design across all European

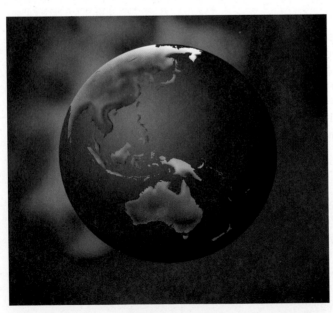

● Australia is geographically distant from the United States. However, it is much closer when other dimensions are considered, such as income levels, language, culture, and political/legal systems.

markets. This was done despite research data indicating that Italian mothers, unlike those in other countries, preferred diapers that covered the baby's navel. Later, however, P&G recognized that this feature was critical to these mothers, so the company decided to incorporate this feature for the Italian market despite its adverse cost implications.

- At times, local adaptations, even when well intentioned, may backfire. When the American restaurant chain TGI Fridays entered the South Korean market, it purposely incorporated many local dishes, such as kimchi (hot, spicy cabbage), in its menu. This responsiveness, however, was not well received. Company analysis of the weak market acceptance indicated that Korean customers anticipated a visit to TGI Fridays as a visit to America. Thus, finding Korean dishes was inconsistent with their expectations.

- The optimal degree of local adaptation evolves over time. In many industry segments, a variety of factors, such as the influence of global media, greater international travel, and declining income disparities across countries, may lead to increasing global standardization. On the other hand, in other industry segments, especially where the product or service can be delivered over the Internet (such as music), the need for even greater customization and local adaptation may increase over time. Firms must recalibrate the need for local adaptation on an ongoing basis; excessive adaptation extracts a price as surely as underadaptation.

Some films and TV programs may cross country boundaries rather successfully, while others are less successful. Let's consider an effort by Disney that fell far short:

Remember *The Alamo,* not the nineteenth-century battle between Mexican forces and Texas rebels, but the 2004 movie? The film definitely met the big-budget criterion—it cost Disney nearly $100 million. It did not generate strong box-office receipts in English. But what was surprising was Disney's attempt to create crossover appeal to Latinos. These efforts included more balanced treatment of Anglos versus Mexicans, prominently featuring Tejano folk heroes in the film, and running a separate Spanish-language marketing effort. But such efforts were doomed to fail. Why? According to one authority, the Alamo is "such an open wound among American Hispanics."[64]

Exhibit 7.7 summarizes the strengths and limitations of multidomestic strategies.

Transnational Strategy

A *transnational strategy* strives to optimize the trade-offs associated with efficiency, local adaptation, and learning.[65] It seeks efficiency not for its own sake, but as a means to achieve global competitiveness.[66] It recognizes the importance of local responsiveness but as a tool for flexibility in international operations.[67] Innovations are regarded as an outcome of a larger process of organizational learning that includes the contributions of everyone in the firm.[68] Also, a core tenet of the transnational model is that a firm's assets and capabilities

transnational strategy a strategy based on firms' optimizing the trade-offs associated with efficiency, local adaptation, and learning, used in industries where the pressures for both local adaptation and lowering costs are high.

Strengths	Limitations
• Ability to adapt products and services to local market conditions.	• Decreased ability to realize cost savings through scale economies.
• Ability to detect potential opportunities for attractive niches in a given market, enhancing revenue.	• Greater difficulty in transferring knowledge across countries.
	• May lead to "overadaptation" as conditions change.

Exhibit 7.7
Strengths and Limitations of Multidomestic Strategies

are dispersed according to the most beneficial location for each activity. Thus, managers avoid the tendency to either concentrate activities in a central location (a global strategy) or disperse them across many locations to enhance adaptation (a multidomestic strategy). Peter Brabeck, Chairman of Nestlé, the giant food company, provides such a perspective.

> We believe strongly that there isn't a so-called global consumer, at least not when it comes to food and beverages. People have local tastes based on their unique cultures and traditions—a good candy bar in Brazil is not the same as a good candy bar in China. Therefore, decision making needs to be pushed down as low as possible in the organization, out close to the markets. Otherwise, how can you make good brand decisions? That said, decentralization has its limits. If you are too decentralized, you can become too complicated—you get too much complexity in your production system. The closer we come to the consumer, in branding, pricing, communication, and product adaptation, the more we decentralize. The more we are dealing with production, logistics, and supply-chain management, the more centralized decision making becomes. After all, we want to leverage Nestlé's size, not be hampered by it.[69]

The Nestlé example illustrates a common approach in determining whether or not to centralize or decentralize a value-chain activity. Typically, primary activities that are "downstream" (e.g., marketing and sales, and service), or closer to the customer, tend to require more decentralization in order to adapt to local market conditions. On the other hand, primary activities that are "upstream" (e.g., logistics and operations), or further away from the customer, tend to be centralized. This is because there is less need for adapting these activities to local markets and the firm can benefit from economies of scale. Additionally, many support activities, such as information systems and procurement, tend to be centralized in order to increase the potential for economies of scale.

A central philosophy of the transnational organization is enhanced adaptation to all competitive situations as well as flexibility by capitalizing on communication and knowledge flows throughout the organization.[70] A principal characteristic is the integration of unique contributions of all units into worldwide operations. Thus, a joint innovation by headquarters and by one of the overseas units can lead potentially to the development of relatively standardized and yet flexible products and services that are suitable for multiple markets.

Asea Brown Boveri (ABB) is a firm that successfully follows a transnational strategy. ABB, with its home bases in Sweden and Switzerland, illustrates the trend toward cross-national mergers that lead firms to consider multiple headquarters in the future. It is managed as a flexible network of units, and one of management's main functions is the facilitation of information and knowledge flows between units. ABB's subsidiaries have complete responsibility for product categories on a worldwide basis. Such a transnational strategy enables ABB to benefit from access to new markets and the opportunity to utilize and develop resources wherever they may be located.

Risks and Challenges   As with the other strategies, there are some unique risks and challenges associated with a transnational strategy.

- *The choice of a seemingly optimal location cannot guarantee that the quality and cost of factor inputs (i.e., labor, materials) will be optimal.* Managers must ensure that the relative advantage of a location is actually realized, not squandered because of weaknesses in productivity and the quality of internal operations. Ford Motor Co., for example, has benefited from having some of its manufacturing operations in Mexico. While some have argued that the benefits of lower wage rates will be partly offset by lower productivity, this does not always have to be the case. Since unemployment in Mexico is higher than in the United States, Ford can be more selective in its hiring practices for its Mexican operations. And, given the lower turnover among its Mexican employees, Ford can justify a high level of investment in training and development. Thus, the net result can be not only lower wage rates but also higher productivity than in the United States.

- *Although knowledge transfer can be a key source of competitive advantage, it does not take place "automatically."* For knowledge transfer to take place from one subsidiary to another, it is important for the source of the knowledge, the target units, and the corporate headquarters to recognize the potential value of such unique know-how. Given that there can be significant geographic, linguistic, and cultural distances that typically separate subsidiaries, the potential for knowledge transfer can become very difficult to realize. Firms must create mechanisms to systematically and routinely uncover the opportunities for knowledge transfer.

Exhibit 7.8 summarizes the relative advantages and disadvantages of transnational strategies.

Global or Regional? A Second Look at Globalization

>LO7.6
The difference between regional companies and truly global companies.

Thus far, we have suggested four possible strategies from which a firm must choose once it has decided to compete in the global marketplace. In recent years, many writers have asserted that the process of globalization has caused national borders to become increasingly irrelevant.[71] However, some scholars have recently questioned this perspective, and they have argued that it is unwise for companies to rush into full scale globalization.[72]

Before answering questions about the extent of firms' globalization, let's try to clarify what "globalization" means. Traditionally, a firm's globalization is measured in terms of its foreign sales as a percentage of total sales. However, this measure can be misleading. For example, consider a U.S. firm that has expanded its activities into Canada. Clearly, this initiative is qualitatively different from achieving the same sales volume in a distant country such as China. Similarly, if a Malaysian firm expands into Singapore or a German firm starts selling its products in Austria, this would represent an expansion into a geographically adjacent country. Such nearby countries would often share many common characteristics in terms of language, culture, infrastructure, and customer preferences. In other words, this is more a case of regionalization than globalization.

Extensive analysis of the distribution data of sales across different countries and regions led Alan Rugman and Alain Verbeke to conclude that there is a stronger case to be made in favor of regionalization than globalization. According to their study, a company would have to have at least 20 percent of its sales in each of the three major economic regions—North America, Europe, and Asia—to be considered a global firm. However, they found that only nine of the world's 500 largest firms met this standard! Even when they relaxed the criterion to 20 percent of sales each in at least two of the three regions, the number only increased to 25. *Thus, most companies are regional or, at best, biregional—not global—even today.* Exhibit 7.9 provides a listing of the large firms that met each of these two criteria.

regionalization
increasing international exchange of goods, services, money, people, ideas, and information; and the increasing similarity of culture, laws, rules, and norms within a region such as Europe, North America, or Asia.

Strengths	Limitations
• Ability to attain economies of scale.	• Unique challenges in determining optimal locations of activities to ensure cost and quality.
• Ability to adapt to local markets.	
• Ability to locate activities in optimal locations.	• Unique managerial challenges in fostering knowledge transfer.
• Ability to increase knowledge flows and learning.	

Exhibit 7.8
Strengths and Limitations of Transnational Strategies

Firms with at least 20 percent sales in Asia, Europe, and North America each but with less than 50 percent sales in any one region:

IBM	Nokia	Coca-Cola
Sony	Intel	Flextronics
Philips	Canon	LVMH

Firms with at least 20 percent sales in at least two of the three regions (Asia, Europe, North America) but with less than 50 percent sales in any one region:

BP Amoco	Alstom	Michelin
Toyota	Aventis	Kodak
Nissan	Daigeo	Electrolux
Unilever	Sun Microsystems	BAE
Motorola	Bridgestone	Alcan
GlaxoSmithKline	Roche	L'Oreal
EADS	3M	Lafarge
Bayer	Skanska	
Ericsson	McDonald's	

Firms with at least 50 percent of their sales in one of the three regions—other than their home region:

Daimler Chrysler	Santander	Sodexho Alliance
ING Group	Delhaize "Le Lion"	Manpower
Royal Ahold	Astra Zeneca	Wolseley
Honda	News Corporation	

Sources: Peng, M.W. 2010. *Global Strategy* 2nd ed. Mason, OH: Thomson Southwestern; and Rugman, A.M., & Verbeke, A. 2004. A Perspective on Regional and Global Strategies of Multinational Enterprises. *Journal of International Business Studies,* 35: 3–18.

In a world of instant communication, rapid transportation, and governments that are increasingly willing to open up their markets to trade and investment, why are so few firms "global"? The most obvious answer is that distance still matters. After all, it is easier to do business in a neighboring country than in a far away country, all else being equal. Distance, in the final analysis, may be viewed as a concept with many dimensions, not just a measure of geographical distance. For example, both Canada and Mexico are the same distance from the U.S. However, U.S. companies find it easier to expand operations into Canada than into Mexico. Why? Canada and the U.S. share many commonalities in terms of language, culture, economic development, legal and political systems, and infrastructure development. Thus, if we view distance as having many dimensions, the U.S. and Canada are very close, whereas there is greater distance between the U.S. and Mexico. Similarly, when we look at what we might call the "true" distance between the U.S. and China, the effects of geographic distance are multiplied by distance in terms of culture, language, religion, and legal and political systems between the two countries. On the other hand, although U.S. and Australia are geographically distant, the "true" distance is somewhat less when one considers distance along the other dimensions.

Another reason for regional expansion is the rise of the trading blocs. The European Union originally started in the 1950s as a regional trading bloc. However, recently it has

trading blocs groups of countries agreeing to increase trade between them by lowering trade barries.

achieved a large degree of economic and political integration in terms of common currency and common standards that many thought infeasible, if not impossible, only 20 years ago. The resulting economic benefits have led other regions also to consider similar moves. For example, the North American Free Trade Agreement (NAFTA) has the eventual abolition of all barriers to the free movement of goods and services among Canada, the U.S., and Mexico as its goal. Other regional trading blocks include MERCOSUR (consisting of Argentina, Brazil, Paraguay, and Uruguay) and the Association of Southeast Asian Nations (ASEAN) (consisting of about a dozen Southeast Asian countries).

Regional economic integration has progressed at a faster pace than global economic integration and the trade and investment patterns of the largest companies reflect this reality. After all, regions represent the outcomes of centuries of political and cultural history that results not only in commonalities but also mutual affinity. For example, stretching from Algeria and Morocco in the West to Oman and Yemen in the East, more than 30 countries share the Arabic language and the Muslim religion, making these countries a natural regional bloc. Similarly, the countries of South and Central America share the Spanish language (except Brazil), Catholic religion, and a shared history of Spanish colonialism. No wonder firms find it easier and less risky to expand within their region than to other regions.

Entry Modes of International Expansion

>LO7.7
The four basic types of entry strategies and the relative benefits and risks associated with each of them.

A firm has many options available to it when it decides to expand into international markets. Given the challenges associated with such entry, many firms first start on a small scale and then increase their level of investment and risk as they gain greater experience with the overseas market in question.[73]

Exhibit 7.10 illustrates a wide variety of modes of foreign entry, including exporting, licensing, franchising, joint ventures, strategic alliances, and wholly owned subsidiaries.[74] As the exhibit indicates, the various types of entry form a continuum ranging from exporting (low investment and risk, low control) to a wholly owned subsidiary (high investment and risk, high control).[75]

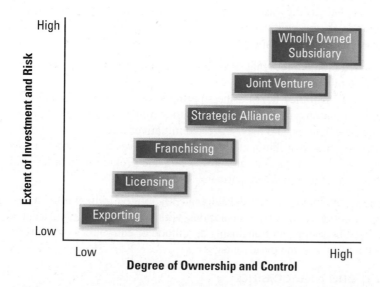

Exhibit 7.10 Entry Modes for International Expansion

There can be frustrations and setbacks as a firm evolves its international entry strategy from exporting to more expensive types, including wholly owned subsidiaries. For example, according to the CEO of a large U.S. specialty chemical company:

> In the end, we always do a better job with our own subsidiaries; sales improve, and we have greater control over the business. But we still need local distributors for entry, and we are still searching for strategies to get us through the transitions without battles over control and performance.[76]

Exporting

Exporting consists of producing goods in one country to sell in another.[77] This entry strategy enables a firm to invest the least amount of resources in terms of its product, its organization, and its overall corporate strategy. Many host countries dislike this entry strategy because it provides less local employment than other modes of entry.[78]

Multinationals often stumble onto a stepwise strategy for penetrating markets, beginning with the exporting of products. This often results in a series of unplanned actions to increase sales revenues. As the pattern recurs with entries into subsequent markets, this approach, named a "beachhead strategy," often becomes official policy.[79]

Benefits   Such an approach definitely has its advantages. After all, firms start from scratch in sales and distribution when they enter new markets. Because many foreign markets are nationally regulated and dominated by networks of local intermediaries, firms need to partner with local distributors to benefit from their valuable expertise and knowledge of their own markets. Multinationals, after all, recognize that they cannot master local business practices, meet regulatory requirements, hire and manage local personnel, or gain access to potential customers without some form of local partnership.

Multinationals also want to minimize their own risk. They do this by hiring local distributors and investing very little in the undertaking. In essence, the firm gives up control of strategic marketing decisions to the local partners—much more control than they would be willing to give up in their home market.

Risks and Limitations   Exporting is a relatively inexpensive way to enter foreign markets. However, it can still have significant downsides. In a study of 250 instances in which multinational firms used local distributors to implement their exporting entry strategy, the results were dismal. In the vast majority of the cases, the distributors were bought (to increase control) by the multinational firm or fired. In contrast, successful distributors shared two common characteristics:

- They carried product lines that complemented, rather than competed with, the multinational's products.
- They behaved as if they were business partners with the multinationals. They shared market information with the corporations, they initiated projects with distributors in neighboring countries, and they suggested initiatives in their own or nearby markets. Additionally, these distributors took on risk themselves by investing in areas such as training, information systems, and advertising and promotion in order to increase the business of their multinational partners.

The key point is the importance of developing collaborative, win–win relationships.

To ensure more control over operations without incurring significant risks, many firms have used licensing and franchising as a mode of entry. Let's now discuss these and their relative advantages and disadvantages.

Licensing and Franchising

Licensing and franchising are both forms of contractual arrangements. **Licensing** enables a company to receive a royalty or fee in exchange for the right to use its trademark, patent, trade secret, or other valuable item of intellectual property.[80]

Franchising contracts generally include a broader range of factors in an operation and have a longer time period during which the agreement is in effect. Franchising remains a primary form of American business. According to a recent survey, more than 400 U.S. franchisers have international exposure.[81] This is greater than the combined totals of the next four largest franchiser home countries—France, the United Kingdom, Mexico, and Austria.

Benefits In international markets, an advantage of licensing is that the firm granting a license incurs little risk, since it does not have to invest any significant resources into the country itself. In turn, the licensee (the firm receiving the license) gains access to the trademark, patent, and so on, and is able to potentially create competitive advantages. In many cases, the country also benefits from the product being manufactured locally. For example, Yoplait yogurt is licensed by General Mills from Sodima, a French cooperative, for sale in the United States. The logos of college and professional athletic teams in the United States are another source of trademarks that generate significant royalty income domestically and internationally.

Franchising has the advantage of limiting the risk exposure that a firm has in overseas markets. At the same time, the firm is able to expand the revenue base of the company.

> **franchising** a contractual arrangement in which a company receives a royalty or fee in exchange for the right to use its intellectual property; it usually involves a longer time period than licensing and includes other factors, such as monitoring of operations, training, and advertising.

Risks and Limitations The licensor gives up control of its product and forgoes potential revenues and profits. Furthermore, the licensee may eventually become so familiar with the patent and trade secrets that it may become a competitor; that is, the licensee may make some modifications to the product and manufacture and sell it independently of the licensor without having to pay a royalty fee. This potential situation is aggravated in countries that have relatively weak laws to protect intellectual property. Additionally, if the licensee selected by the multinational firm turns out to be a poor choice, the brand name and reputation of the product may be tarnished.[82]

With franchising, the multinational firm receives only a portion of the revenues, in the form of franchise fees. Had the firm set up the operation itself (e.g., a restaurant through direct investment), it would have had the entire revenue to itself.

Companies often desire a closer collaboration with other firms in order to increase revenue, reduce costs, and enhance their learning—often through the diffusion of technology. To achieve such objectives, they enter into strategic alliances or joint ventures, two entry modes we will discuss next.

Strategic Alliances and Joint Ventures

Joint ventures and strategic alliances have recently become increasingly popular.[83] These two forms of partnership differ in that joint ventures entail the creation of a third-party legal entity, whereas strategic alliances do not. In addition, strategic alliances generally focus on initiatives that are smaller in scope than joint ventures.[84]

Benefits As we discussed in Chapter 6, these strategies have been effective in helping firms increase revenues and reduce costs as well as enhance learning and diffuse technologies.[85] These partnerships enable firms to share the risks as well as the potential revenues and profits. Also, by gaining exposure to new sources of knowledge and technologies, such partnerships can help firms develop core competencies that can lead to competitive advantages in the marketplace.[86] Finally, entering into partnerships with host country firms can provide very useful information on local market tastes, competitive conditions, legal matters, and cultural nuances.[87]

Strategic alliances can be between firms in totally different industries. Strategy Spotlight 7.9 discusses a collaboration between the Italian automaker Lamborghini and Callaway, the U.S. golf equipment manufacturer.

Lamborghini and Callaway Form a High-Tech Alliance

Lamborghini's Sesto Elemento concept car was the hit at the 2010 Paris Auto Show. It would not seem to have much in common with Callaway's new Diablo Octane and Octane Tour drivers. However, both are made using an ingenious new material called Forged Composite that the companies developed together. The material is much stronger than titanium but weighs only one-third as much.

The partnership between Lamborghini and Callaway began in 2008. Researchers from the two companies met at a materials science conference and found that they had much in common. Says Callaway's CEO George Fellows, "The collaboration has been great. The DNA of both companies, pushing for a technological edge in performance-oriented consumer products, is very similar." In short, both firms are engaged in developing lighter and stronger composite materials for their products. And most would agree that the markets that they serve are dissimilar enough to make full cooperation feasible.

Source: Newport, J. P. 2010. Drive the Ball Like It's a Lamborghini, Maybe. *Wall Street Journal.* November 13–14: A14; *www.callaway.com*; and Anonymous. 2010. Automobili Lamborghini and Callaway Golf Form Strategic Partnership. *autonewscast.com*, September 30: np.

Let's look at how each company has benefited from their joint development of Forged Composite.

The weight-savings in Callaway's new drivers, which deploy Forged Composite only in the crowns (the bottom half of the clubheads is still made of titanium), is only 10 grams. Although 10 grams might seem insignificant, such weight loss up top gives designers much more flexibility in how they distribute mass around the bottom. This helps to create more desirable ball flight characteristics and improve forgiveness on off-center hits.

For Lamborghini, Forged Composite enhances a car's power-to weight ratio and acceleration capability. To illustrate, the Sesto Elemento can accelerate from zero to 60 miles per hour in an astonishing 2.5 seconds. This is almost a full second faster than the Italian automaker's speed champ—the $240,000 Superleggera. The difference is entirely due to weight, in part because both cars use the same 570-horsepower, four-wheel-drivetrain. But by building the chassis almost entirely of Forged Composite, engineers were able to reduce the curb weight by nearly a third—to an anorexic 2,072 pounds. "The power-to-weight ratio is more like a motorcycle's," claims Lamborghini's CEO Stephan Winkelmann. After further testing, he expects Forged Composite to begin working its way into production within a few years.

Risks and Limitations Managers must be aware of the risks associated with strategic alliances and joint ventures and how they can be minimized.[88] First, there needs to be a clearly defined strategy that is strongly supported by the organizations that are party to the partnership. Otherwise, the firms may work at cross-purposes and not achieve any of their goals. Second, and closely allied to the first issue, there must be a clear understanding of capabilities and resources that will be central to the partnership. Without such clarification, there will be fewer opportunities for learning and developing competencies that could lead to competitive advantages. Third, trust is a vital element. Phasing in the relationship between alliance partners permits them to get to know each other better and develop trust. Without trust, one party may take advantage of the other by, for example, withholding its fair share of resources and gaining access to privileged information through unethical (or illegal) means. Fourth, cultural issues that can potentially lead to conflict and dysfunctional behaviors need to be addressed. An organization's culture is the set of values, beliefs, and attitudes that influence the behavior and goals of its employees.[89] Thus, recognizing cultural differences as well as striving to develop elements of a "common culture" for the partnership is vital. Without a unifying culture, it will become difficult to combine and leverage resources that are increasingly important in knowledge-intensive organizations (discussed in Chapter 4).[90]

Finally, the success of a firm's alliance should not be left to chance.[91] To improve their odds of success, many companies have carefully documented alliance-management knowledge by creating guidelines and manuals to help them manage specific aspects of the entire alliance life cycle (e.g., partner selection and alliance negotiation and contracting). For example, Lotus Corp. (part of IBM) created what it calls its "35 rules of thumb" to manage each phase of an alliance from formation to termination. Hewlett-Packard developed 60 different tools and templates, which it placed in a 300-page manual for guiding decision making. The manual included such tools as a template for making the business case for an alliance, a partner evaluation form, a negotiation template outlining the roles and responsibilities of different departments, a list of the ways to measure alliance performance, and an alliance termination checklist.

When a firm desires the highest level of control, it develops wholly owned subsidiaries. Although wholly owned subsidiaries can generate the greatest returns, they also have the highest levels of investment and risk. We will now discuss them.

Wholly Owned Subsidiaries

A **wholly owned subsidiary** is a business in which a multinational company owns 100 percent of the stock. Two ways a firm can establish a wholly owned subsidiary are to (1) acquire an existing company in the home country or (2) develop a totally new operation (often referred to as a "greenfield venture").

wholly owned subsidiary a business in which a multinational company owns 100 percent of the stock.

Benefits   Establishing a wholly owned subsidiary is the most expensive and risky of the various entry modes. However, it can also yield the highest returns. In addition, it provides the multinational company with the greatest degree of control of all activities, including manufacturing, marketing, distribution, and technology development.[92]

Wholly owned subsidiaries are most appropriate where a firm already has the appropriate knowledge and capabilities that it can leverage rather easily through multiple locations. Examples range from restaurants to semiconductor manufacturers. To lower costs, for example, Intel Corporation builds semiconductor plants throughout the world—all of which use virtually the same blueprint. Knowledge can be further leveraged by hiring managers and professionals from the firm's home country, often through hiring talent from competitors.

Risks and Limitations   As noted, wholly owned subsidiaries are typically the most expensive and risky entry mode. With franchising, joint ventures, or strategic alliances, the risk is shared with the firm's partners. With wholly owned subsidiaries, the entire risk is assumed by the parent company. The risks associated with doing business in a new country (e.g., political, cultural, and legal) can be lessened by hiring local talent.

For example, Wendy's avoided committing two blunders in Germany by hiring locals to its advertising staff.[93] In one case, the firm wanted to promote its "old-fashioned" qualities. However, a literal translation would have resulted in the company promoting itself as "outdated." In another situation, Wendy's wanted to emphasize that its hamburgers could be prepared 256 ways. The problem? The German word that Wendy's wanted to use for "ways" usually meant "highways" or "roads." Although such errors may sometimes be entertaining to the public, it is certainly preferable to catch these mistakes before they confuse the consumer or embarrass the company.

We have addressed entry strategies as a progression from exporting through the creation of wholly owned subsidiaries. However, we must point out that many firms do not follow such an evolutionary approach. For example, because of political and regulatory reasons, Pepsi entered India through a joint venture with two Indian firms in 1998. As discussed in Strategy Spotlight 7.10, this provided Pepsi with a first-mover advantage within the Indian market, where it remains well ahead of its archrival, Coca-Cola.

Pepsi's First-Mover Advantage in India Has Paid Off

Pepsi (pronounced "Pay-psee") became a common synonym for cola in India's most widely spoken language after having the market to itself in the early 1990s. PepsiCo's linguistic advantage translates into higher sales for its namesake product. Although Atlanta-based Coke has larger total beverage sales in India because it owns several non-cola drink brands, Pepsi's 4.5 percent of the soft drink market outshines Coke's 2.6 percent, according to Euromonitor. That's a notable exception to much of the rest of the world, where Coke's cola soundly beats its main rival.

What explains Pepsi's success in India? Coke pulled out of the market in 1977 after new government regulations forced it to partner with an Indian company and share the drink's secret formula. In contrast, Pepsi formed a joint venture in 1988 with two Indian companies and introduced products under the Lehar brand. (Lehar Pepsi was introduced in 1990.) Coke then re-entered the market in 1993 after Indian regulations were changed to permit foreign brands to operate without Indian partners.

Coke's time out of India cost it dearly. "Pepsi got here sooner, and got to India just as it was starting to engage with the West and with Western products," said Lalita Desai, a linguist at Jadavpur University who studies how English words enter Indian languages. "And with no real international competition, 'Pepsi' became the catch-all for anything that was bottled, fizzy, and from abroad."

PepsiCo has also been very successful in promoting water conservation in India. Its Indian operation became the first of its global units (and probably the only one in the beverage industry) to conserve and replenish more water that it consumed in 2009. Its rival, Coca Cola, on the other hand, is facing a serious situation in India as it has been fined Rs 216 crore ($4.7 million) as compensation for groundwater pollution and depletion.

Today, PepsiCo is the fourth largest consumer products company in India. The firm also has invested more than $1 billion in India, created direct and indirect employment to 150,000 people in the country, and has 13 company-owned bottling plants, according to its website.

Source: Srivastava, M. 2010. For India's Consumers, Pepsi Is the Real Thing. *Bloomberg Businessweek.* September 20–26: 26–27; Bhushan, R. 2010. Pepsi India Touches Eco Watershed, First Unit to Achieve Positive Water Balance. *www.indiatimes.com.* May 27: np; and *www.pepsicoindia.*

Reflecting on Career Implications . . .

- *International Strategy:* Be aware of your organization's international strategy. What percentage of the total firm activity is international? What skills are needed to enhance your company's international efforts? How can you get more involved in your organization's international strategy? For your career, what conditions in your home country might cause you to seek careers abroad?
- *Outsourcing and Offshoring:* What activities in your organization can/should be outsourced or offshored? Be aware that you are competing in the global marketplace for employment and professional advancement. Continually take inventory of your talents, skills, and competencies.
- *International Career Opportunities:* Work assignments in other countries can often provide a career boost. Be proactive in pursuing promising career opportunities in other countries. Anticipate how such opportunities will advance your short- and long-term career aspirations.
- *Management Risks:* Develop cultural sensitivity. This applies, of course, to individuals from different cultures in your home-based organization as well as in your overseas experience.

Summary

We live in a highly interconnected global community where many of the best opportunities for growth and profitability lie beyond the boundaries of a company's home country. Along with the opportunities, of course, there are many risks associated with diversification into global markets.

The first section of the chapter addressed the factors that determine a nation's competitiveness in a particular industry. The framework was developed by Professor Michael Porter of Harvard University and was based on a four-year study that explored the competitive success of 10 leading trading nations. The four factors, collectively termed the "diamond of national advantage," were factor conditions, demand characteristics, related and supporting industries, and firm strategy, structure, and rivalry.

The discussion of Porter's "diamond" helped, in essence, to set the broader context for exploring competitive advantage at the firm level. In the second section, we discussed the primary motivations and the potential risks associated with international expansion. The primary motivations included increasing the size of the potential market for the firm's products and services, achieving economies of scale, extending the life cycle of the firm's products, and optimizing the location for every activity in the value chain. On the other hand, the key risks included political and economic risks, currency risks, and management risks. Management risks are the challenges associated with responding to the inevitable differences that exist across countries such as customs, culture, language, customer preferences, and distribution systems. We also addressed some of the managerial challenges and opportunities associated with offshoring and outsourcing.

Next, we addressed how firms can go about attaining competitive advantage in global markets. We began by discussing the two opposing forces—cost reduction and adaptation to local markets—that managers must contend with when entering global markets. The relative importance of these two factors plays a major part in determining which of the four basic types of strategies to select: international, global, multidomestic, or transnational. The chapter covered the benefits and risks associated with each type of strategy. We also presented a recent perspective by Alan Rugman who argues that despite all the talk of globalization, most of the large multinationals are regional or at best biregional (in terms of geographical diversification of sales) rather than global.

The final section discussed the four types of entry strategies that managers may undertake when entering international markets. The key trade-off in each of these strategies is the level of investment or risk versus the level of control. In order of their progressively greater investment/risk and control, the strategies range from exporting to licensing and franchising, to strategic alliances and joint ventures, to wholly owned subsidiaries. The relative benefits and risks associated with each of these strategies were addressed.

Summary Review Questions

1. What are some of the advantages and disadvantages associated with a firm's expansion into international markets?

2. What are the four factors described in Porter's diamond of national advantage? How do the four factors explain why some industries in a given country are more successful than others?

3. Explain the two opposing forces—cost reduction and adaptation to local markets—that firms must deal with when they go global.

4. There are four basic strategies—international, global, multidomestic, and transnational. What are the advantages and disadvantages associated with each?

5. What is the basis of Alan Rugman's argument that most multinationals are still more regional than global? What factors inhibit firms from becoming truly global?

6. Describe the basic entry strategies that firms have available when they enter international markets. What are the relative advantages and disadvantages of each?

Key Terms

globalization, 241
diamond of national advantage, 241
factor endowments (national advantage), 242
related and supporting industries (national advantage), 243
firm strategy, structure, and rivalry (national advantage), 244
multinational firms, 244
arbitrage opportunities, 247
reverse innovation, 248
political risk, 249
rule of law, 249
economic risk, 251
counterfeiting, 252
currency risk, 252
management risk, 253
outsourcing, 254
offshoring, 254
international strategy, 257
global strategy, 259
multidomestic strategy, 260
transnational strategy, 263
regionalization, 265
trading blocs, 266
exporting, 268
licensing, 268
franchising, 269
wholly owned subsidiary, 271

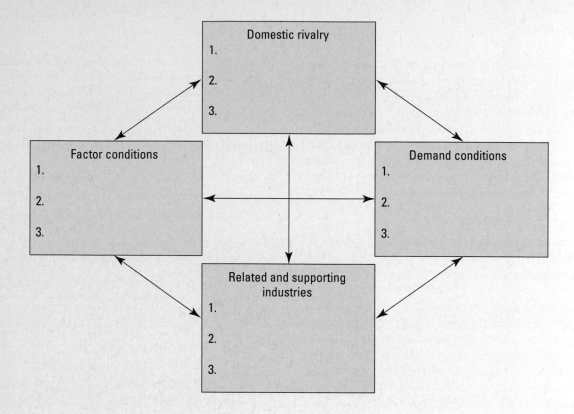

Domestic rivalry
1.
2.
3.

Factor conditions
1.
2.
3.

Demand conditions
1.
2.
3.

Related and supporting industries
1.
2.
3.

Experiential Exercise

The United States is considered a world leader in the motion picture industry. Using Porter's diamond framework for national competitiveness, explain the success of this industry.

Application Questions & Exercises

1. Data on the "competitiveness of nations" can be found at *www.imd.ch/wcy/ranking/*. This website provides a ranking on a 331 criteria for 59 countries. How might Porter's diamond of national advantage help to explain the rankings for some of these countries for certain industries that interest you?

2. The Internet has lowered the entry barriers for smaller firms that wish to diversify into international markets. Why is this so? Provide an example.

3. Many firms fail when they enter into strategic alliances with firms that link up with companies based in other countries. What are some reasons for this failure? Provide an example.

4. Many large U.S.–based management consulting companies such as McKinsey and Company and the BCG Group have been very successful in the international marketplace. How can Porter's diamond explain their success?

Ethics Questions

1. Over the past few decades, many American firms have relocated most or all of their operations from the United States to countries such as Mexico and China that pay lower wages. What are some of the ethical issues that such actions may raise?

2. Business practices and customs vary throughout the world. What are some of the ethical issues concerning payments that must be made in a foreign country to obtain business opportunities?

References

1. Anonymous. 2010. Exit Carrefour. *The Economist.* September 23: 77; Thomas, D. & Fuse, T. 2010. Retailers jump in for Carrefour SE Asia assets. *www.reuters.com.* September 1: np; and Chan, C. 2010. Carrefour said to list Tesco, Casino as potential unit buyers. *www.businessweek.com.* September 9: np.

2. For a recent discussion on globalization by one of international business's most respected authors, read Ohmae, K. 2005. *The next global stage: Challenges and opportunities in our borderless world.* Philadelphia: Wharton School Publishing.

3. Our discussion of globalization draws upon Engardio, P. & Belton, C. 2000. Global capitalism: Can it be made to work better? *BusinessWeek,* November 6: 72–98.

4. Sellers, P. 2005. Blowing in the wind. *Fortune,* July 25: 63.

5. An interesting and balanced discussion on the merits of multinationals to the U.S. economy is found in: Mandel, M. 2008. Multinationals: Are they good for America? *BusinessWeek,* March 10: 41–64.

6. Engardio & Belton, op. cit.

7. For insightful perspectives on strategy in emerging economies, refer to the article entitled: Strategy research in emerging economies: Challenging the conventional wisdom in the January 2005 issue of *Journal of Management Studies,* 42(1).

8. Black, J. S. & Morrison, A. J. 2010. A cautionary tale for emerging market giants. *Harvard Business Review,* 88(9): 99–105.

9. The above discussion draws on Clifford, M. L., Engardio, P., Malkin, E., Roberts, D., & Echikson, W. 2000. Up the ladder. *BusinessWeek,* November 6: 78–84.

10. A recent discussion of the "bottom of the pyramid" is: Akula, V. 2008. Business basics at the bottom of the pyramid. *Harvard Business Review,* 86(6): 53–59.

11. Some insights into how winners are evolving in emerging markets are addressed in: Ghemawat, P. & Hout, T. 2008. Tomorrow's global giants:

Not the usual suspects. *Harvard Business Review,* 66(11): 80–88.

12. For another interesting discussion on a country perspective, refer to Makino, S. 1999. MITI Minister Kaora Yosano on reviving Japan's competitive advantages. *Academy of Management Executive,* 13(4): 8–28.

13. The following discussion draws heavily upon Porter, M. E. 1990. The competitive advantage of nations. *Harvard Business Review,* March–April: 73–93.

14. Landes, D. S. 1998. *The wealth and poverty of nations.* New York: W. W. Norton.

15. A recent study that investigates the relationship between international diversification and firm performance is Lu, J. W. & Beamish, P. W. 2004. International diversification and firm performance: The s-curve hypothesis. *Academy of Management Journal,* 47(4): 598–609.

16. Part of our discussion of the motivations and risks of international expansion draws upon Gregg, F. M. 1999. International strategy. In Helms, M. M. (Ed.). *Encyclopedia of management:* 434–438. Detroit: Gale Group.

17. These two examples are discussed, respectively, in Dawar, N. & Frost, T. 1999. Competing with giants: Survival strategies for local companies in emerging markets. *Harvard Business Review,* 77(2): 119–129; and Prahalad, C. K. & Lieberthal, K. 1998. The end of corporate imperialism. *Harvard Business Review,* 76(4): 68–79.

18. Meredith, R. 2004. Middle kingdom, middle class. *Forbes,* November 15: 188–192; and Anonymous. 2004. Middle class becomes rising power in China. *www.Chinadaily.com.* November 6.

19. Eyring, M. J., Johnson, M. W. & Nair, H. 2011. New business models in emerging markets. *Harvard Business Review,* 89 (1/2): 88–98.

20. Cieply, M. & Barnes, B. 2010. After rants, skepticism over Gibson bankability grows in non-U.S. markets. *International Herald Tribune,* July 23: 1.

21. This discussion draws upon Gupta, A. K. & Govindarajan, V. 2001. Converting global presence into global competitive advantage. *Academy of Management Executive,* 15(2): 45–56.

22. Stross, R. E. 1997. Mr. Gates builds his brain trust. *Fortune,* December 8: 84–98.

23. For a good summary of the benefits and risks of international expansion, refer to Bartlett, C. A. & Ghoshal, S. 1987. Managing across borders: New strategic responses. *Sloan Management Review,* 28(5): 45–53; and Brown, R. H. 1994. *Competing to win in a global economy.* Washington, DC: U.S. Department of Commerce.

24. For an interesting insight into rivalry in global markets, refer to MacMillan, I. C., van Putten, A. B., & McGrath, R. G. 2003. Global gamesmanship. *Harvard Business Review,* 81(5): 62–73.

25. It is important for firms to spread their foreign operations and outsourcing relationships with a broad, well-balanced mix of regions and countries to reduce risk and increase potential reward. For example, refer to Vestring, T., Rouse, T., & Reinert, U. 2005. Hedge your offshoring bets. *MIT Sloan Management Review,* 46(3): 27–29.

26. An interesting discussion of risks faced by Lukoil, Russia's largest oil firm is in: Gimbel, B. 2009. Russia's king of crude. *Fortune,* February 2: 88–92.

27. Some insights on how Africa has improved as a potential source of investment is in: Collier, P. & Warnholz, J-L. 2009. Now's the time to invest in Africa. *Harvard Business Review,* 87(2): 23.

28. For a discussion of some of the challenges associated with government corruption regarding entry strategies in foreign markets, read Rodriguez, P., Uhlenbruck, K., & Eden, L. 2005. Government corruption and entry strategies of multinationals. *Academy of Management Review,* 30(2): 383–396.

29. For a discussion of the political risks in China for United States companies,

refer to Garten, J. E. 1998. Opening the doors for business in China. *Harvard Business Review,* 76(3): 167–175.

30. Shari, M. 2001. Is a holy war brewing in Indonesia? *BusinessWeek,* October 15: 62.

31. Insights on how forensic economics can be used to investigate crimes and wrongdoing are in: Fisman, R. 2009. The rise of forensic economics. *Harvard Business Review,* 87(2): 26.

32. Anonymous. 2010. Libya: Why it is still stuck. *The Economist,* April 10: 49.

33. For an interesting perspective on the relationship between diversification and the development of a nation's institutional environment, read Chakrabarti, A., Singh, K., & Mahmood, I. 2007. Diversification and performance: Evidence from East Asian firms. *Strategic Management Journal,* 28(2): 101–120.

34. A study looking into corruption and foreign direct investment is: Brouthers, L. E., Gao, Y., & McNicol, J. P. 2008. *Strategic Management Journal,* 29(6): 673–680.

35. Gikkas, N. S. 1996. International licensing of intellectual property: The promise and the peril. *Journal of Technology Law & Policy,* 1(1): 1–26.

36. Insights into bribery in the international context are addressed in: Martin, K. D., Cullen, J. B., Johnson, J. L., & Parboteeah, P. 2008. Deciding to bribe: A cross-level analysis of firm and home country influences on bribery activity. *Academy of Management Journal,* 50(6): 1401–1422.

37. Sandler, N. 2008. Israel: Attack of the super-shekel. *BusinessWeek,* Februrary 25: 38.

38. For an excellent theoretical discussion of how cultural factors can affect knowledge transfer across national boundaries, refer to Bhagat, R. S., Kedia, B. L., Harveston, P. D., & Triandis, H. C. 2002. Cultural variations in the cross-border transfer of organizational knowledge: An integrative framework. *Academy of Management Review,* 27(2): 204–221.

39. An interesting discussion on how local companies compete effectively with large multinationals is in: Bhatacharya, A. K. & Michael, D. C.

2008. *Harvard Business Review,* 66(3): 84–95.

40. To gain insights on the role of national and regional cultures on knowledge management models and frameworks, read Pauleen, D. J. & Murphy, P. 2005. In praise of cultural bias. *MIT Sloan Management Review,* 46(2): 21–22.

41. Berkowitz, E. N. 2000. *Marketing* (6th ed.). New York: McGraw-Hill.

42. Harvey, M. & Buckley, M. R. 2002. Assessing the "conventional wisdoms" of management for the 21st century organization. *Organization Dynamics,* 30 (4): 368–378.

43. World Trade Organization. *Annual Report 1998.* Geneva: World Trade Organization.

44. Lei, D. 2005. Outsourcing. In Hitt, M. A. & Ireland, R. D. (Eds.). *The Blackwell encyclopedia of management.* Entrepreneurship: 196–199. Malden, MA: Blackwell.

45. Future trends in offshoring are addressed in: Manning, S., Massini, S., & Lewin, A. Y. 2008. A dynamic perspective on next-generation offshoring: The global sourcing of science and engineering talent. *Academy of Management Perspectives,* 22(3): 35–54.

46. An interesting perspective on the controversial issue regarding the offshoring of airplane maintenance is in: Smith, G. & Bachman, J. 2008. Flying in for a tune-up overseas. *Business Week.* April 21: 26–27.

47. Dolan, K.A. 2006. Offshoring the offshorers. *Forbes.* April 17: 74–78.

48. The discussion above draws from Colvin, J. 2004. Think your job can't be sent to India? Just watch. *Fortune,* December 13: 80; Schwartz, N. D. 2004. Down and out in white collar America. *Fortune,* June 23: 321–325; Hagel, J. 2004. Outsourcing is not just about cost cutting. *The Wall Street Journal,* March 18: A3.

49. Insightful perspectives on the outsourcing of decision making are addressed in: Davenport, T. H. & Iyer, B. 2009. Should you outsource your brain? *Harvard Business Review.* 87 (2): 38. (7)

50. Levitt, T. 1983. The globalization of markets. *Harvard Business Review,* 61(3): 92–102.

51. Our discussion of these assumptions draws upon Douglas, S. P. & Wind, Y. 1987. The myth of globalization. *Columbia Journal of World Business,* Winter: 19–29.

52. Ghoshal, S. 1987. Global strategy: An organizing framework. *Strategic Management Journal,* 8: 425–440.

53. Huber, P. 2009. Who pays for a cancer drug? *Forbes,* January 12: 72.

54. For insights on global branding, refer to Aaker, D. A. & Joachimsthaler, E. 1999. The lure of global branding. *Harvard Business Review,* 77(6): 137–146.

55. For an interesting perspective on how small firms can compete in their home markets, refer to Dawar & Frost, op. cit.: 119–129.

56. Hout, T., Porter, M. E., & Rudden, E. 1982. How global companies win out. *Harvard Business Review,* 60(5): 98–107.

57. Fryer, B. 2001. Tom Siebel of Siebel Systems: High tech the old-fashioned way. *Harvard Business Review,* 79(3): 118–130.

58. The risks that are discussed for the global, multidomestic, and transnational strategies draw upon Gupta & Govindarajan, op. cit.

59. A discussion on how McDonald's adapts its products to overseas markets is in: Gumbel, P. 2008. Big Mac's local flavor. *Fortune,* May 5: 115–121.

60. Sigiura, H. 1990. How Honda localizes its global strategy. *Sloan Management Review,* 31: 77–82.

61. Prahalad & Lieberthal, op. cit.: 68–79. Their article also discusses how firms may have to reconsider their brand management, costs of market building, product design, and approaches to capital efficiency when entering foreign markets.

62. Hofstede, G. 1980. *Culture's consequences: International differences in work-related values.* Beverly Hills, CA: Sage; Hofstede, G. 1993. Cultural constraints in management theories. *Academy of Management Executive,* 7(1): 81–94; Kogut, B. & Singh, H. 1988. The effect of national culture on the choice of entry mode. *Journal of International Business Studies,* 19: 411–432; and

Usinier, J. C. 1996. *Marketing across cultures.* London: Prentice Hall.

63. McCune, J. C. 1999. Exporting corporate culture. *Management Review,* December: 53–56.

64. Ghemawat, P. 2007. *Redefining global strategy.* Boston: Harvard School Press.

65. Prahalad, C. K. & Doz, Y. L. 1987. *The multinational mission: Balancing local demands and global vision.* New York: Free Press.

66. For an insightful discussion on knowledge flows in multinational corporations, refer to: Yang, Q., Mudambi, R., & Meyer, K. E. 2008. Conventional and reverse knowledge flows in multinational corporations. *Journal of Management,* 34(5): 882–902.

67. Kidd, J. B. & Teramoto, Y. 1995. The learning organization: The case of Japanese RHQs in Europe. *Management International Review,* 35 (Special Issue): 39–56.

68. Gupta, A. K. & Govindarajan, V. 2000. Knowledge flows within multinational corporations. *Strategic Management Journal,* 21(4): 473–496.

69. Wetlaufer, S. 2001. The business case against revolution: An interview with Nestlé's Peter Brabeck. *Harvard Business Review,* 79(2): 112–121.

70. Nobel, R. & Birkinshaw, J. 1998. Innovation in multinational corporations: Control and communication patterns in international R&D operations. *Strategic Management Journal,* 19(5): 461–478.

71. Chan, C. M., Makino, S., & Isobe, T. 2010. Does subnational region matter? Foreign affiliate performance in the United States and China. *Strategic Management Journal,* 31 (11): 1226–1243.

72. This section draws upon Ghemawat, P. 2005. Regional strategies for global leadership. *Harvard Business Review.* 84(12): 98–108; Ghemawat, P. 2006. Apocalypse now? *Harvard Business Review.* 84(12): 32; Ghemawat, P. 2001. Distance still matters: The hard reality of global expansion. *Harvard Business Review,* 79(8): 137–147; Peng, M.W. 2006. *Global strategy:* 387. Mason, OH: Thomson Southwestern; and Rugman, A. M. & Verbeke, A. 2004. A perspective on regional and global strategies of multinational enterprises. *Journal of International Business Studies.* 35: 3–18.

73. For a rigorous analysis of performance implications of entry strategies, refer to Zahra, S. A., Ireland, R. D., & Hitt, M. A. 2000. International expansion by new venture firms: International diversity, modes of entry, technological learning, and performance. *Academy of Management Journal,* 43(6): 925–950.

74. Li, J. T. 1995. Foreign entry and survival: The effects of strategic choices on performance in international markets. *Strategic Management Journal,* 16: 333–351.

75. For a discussion of how home-country environments can affect diversification strategies, refer to Wan, W. P. & Hoskisson, R. E. 2003. Home country environments, corporate diversification strategies, and firm performance. *Academy of Management Journal,* 46(1): 27–45.

76. Arnold, D. 2000. Seven rules of international distribution. *Harvard Business Review,* 78(6): 131–137.

77. Sharma, A. 1998. Mode of entry and ex-post performance. *Strategic Management Journal,* 19(9): 879–900.

78. This section draws upon Arnold, op. cit.: 131–137; and Berkowitz, op. cit.

79. Salomon, R. & Jin, B. 2010. Do leading or lagging firms learn more from exporting? *Strategic Management Journal,* 31(6): 1088–1113.

80. Kline, D. 2003. Strategic licensing. *MIT Sloan Management Review,* 44(3): 89–93.

81. Martin, J. 1999. Franchising in the Middle East. *Management Review.* June: 38–42.

82. Arnold, op. cit.; and Berkowitz, op. cit.

83. An in-depth case study of alliance dynamics is found in: Faems, D., Janssens, M., Madhok, A., & Van Looy, B. 2008. Toward an integrative perspective on alliance governance: Connecting contract design, trust dynamics, and contract application. *Academy of Management Journal,* 51(6): 1053–1078.

84. Knowledge transfer in international joint ventures is addressed in: Inkpen, A. 2008. Knowledge transfer and international joint ventures. *Strategic Management Journal,* 29(4): 447–453.

85. Wen, S. H. & Chuang, C.-M. 2010. To teach or to compete? A strategic dilemma of knowledge owners in international alliances. *Asia Pacific Journal of Management,* 27(4): 697–726.

86. Manufacturer–supplier relationships can be very effective in global industries such as automobile manufacturing. Refer to Kotabe, M., Martin, X., & Domoto, H. 2003. Gaining from vertical partnerships: Knowledge transfer, relationship duration, and supplier performance improvement in the U.S. and Japanese automotive industries. *Strategic Management Journal,* 24(4): 293–316.

87. For a good discussion, refer to Merchant, H. & Schendel, D. 2000. How do international joint ventures create shareholder value? *Strategic Management Journal,* 21(7): 723–738.

88. This discussion draws upon Walters, B. A., Peters, S., & Dess, G. G. 1994. Strategic alliances and joint ventures: Making them work. *Business Horizons,* 37(4): 5–11.

89. Some insights on partnering in the global area are discussed in: MacCormack, A. & Forbath, T. 2008. *Harvard Business Review,* 66(1): 24, 26.

90. For a rigorous discussion of the importance of information access in international joint ventures, refer to Reuer, J. J. & Koza, M. P. 2000. Asymmetric information and joint venture performance: Theory and evidence for domestic and international joint ventures. *Strategic Management Journal,* 21(1): 81–88.

91. Dyer, J. H., Kale, P., & Singh, H. 2001. How to make strategic alliances work. *MIT Sloan Management Review,* 42(4): 37–43.

92. For a discussion of some of the challenges in managing subsidiaries, refer to O'Donnell, S. W. 2000. Managing foreign subsidiaries: Agents of headquarters, or an independent network? *Strategic Management Journal,* 21(5): 525–548.

93. Ricks, D. 2006. *Blunders in international business* (4th ed.). Malden, MA: Blackwell Publishing.

Entrepreneurial Strategy and Competitive Dynamics

After reading this chapter, you should have a good understanding of:

LO8.1 The role of new ventures and small businesses in the U.S. economy.

LO8.2 The role of opportunities, resources, and entrepreneurs in successfully pursuing new ventures.

LO8.3 Three types of entry strategies—pioneering, imitative, and adaptive—commonly used to launch a new venture.

LO8.4 How the generic strategies of overall cost leadership, differentiation, and focus are used by new ventures and small businesses.

LO8.5 How competitive actions, such as the entry of new competitors into a marketplace, may launch a cycle of actions and reactions among close competitors.

LO8.6 The components of competitive dynamics analysis—new competitive action, threat analysis, motivation and capability to respond, types of competitive actions, and likelihood of competitive reaction.

LEARNING OBJECTIVES

New technologies, shifting social and demographic trends, and sudden changes in the business environment create opportunities for entrepreneurship. New ventures, which often emerge under such conditions, face unique strategic challenges if they are going to survive and grow. Young and small businesses, which are a major engine of growth in the U.S. economy because of their role in job creation and innovation, must rely on sound strategic principles to be successful.

This chapter addresses how new ventures and entrepreneurial firms can achieve competitive advantages. It also examines how entrepreneurial activity influences a firm's strategic priorities and intensifies the rivalry among an industry's close competitors.

In the first section, we discuss the role of opportunity recognition in the process of new venture creation. Three factors that are important in determining whether a value-creating opportunity should be pursued are highlighted—the nature of the opportunity, the resources available to undertake it, and the characteristics of the entrepreneur(s) pursuing it.

The second section addresses three different types of new entry strategies—pioneering, imitative, and adaptive. Then, the generic strategies (discussed in Chapter 5) as well as combination strategies are addressed in terms of how they apply to new ventures and entrepreneurial firms. Additionally, some of the pitfalls associated with each of these strategic approaches are presented.

In section three, we explain how new entrants and other competitors often set off a series of actions and reactions that affect the competitive dynamics of an industry. In determining how to react to a competitive action, firms must analyze whether they are seriously threatened by the action, how important it is for them to respond, and what resources they can muster to mount a response. They must also determine what type of action is appropriate—strategic or tactical—and whether their close competitors are likely to counterattack. Taken together, these actions often have a strong impact on the strategic choices and overall profitability of an industry ●.

▰▰▰ Learning from Mistakes

The wildly successful eBay concept allowed individuals to sell to the world.[1] Not surprisingly, the business of intermediating such sales quickly took off. It was even portrayed in the movie *The 40-Year-Old Virgin*. iSold It was one of the champions of this model and quickly gained popularity, as it made eBay access easier for people who did not want the hassle of researching prices, posting online, and collecting money. The company began in December 2003 by helping customers sell their unwanted stuff on eBay—basically acting as an intermediary and charging a percentage of the sales price. More recently, however, the company stopped selling franchises and is retracting many of the franchises already sold, because of financial losses. How did the company go from a top franchise pick by *Entrepreneur* magazine in 2006 to the firm in full retreat that we see today?

In 2005 the idea of a store helping customers sell their unwanted things on eBay was very popular, resulting in 7,000 of these types of stores opening around the United States. In June 2006, *Entrepreneur* magazine named iSold It "Hotter than hot" and ranked the firm 30th among other fastest-growing franchises. What is more, in 2007 iSold It earned the top spot in *Entrepreneur*'s new franchise rankings, listing a start-up cost of $105,000 per location! At the time, it seemed that selling other people's stuff online and collecting a fee had endless potential.

The firm researched the potential sale price, wrote the product description, posted the ads on eBay, monitored the auction, responded to any e-mails, collected the proceeds from the sale, and finally mailed the purchaser the product. The firm did not guarantee that the product would sell and had selection standards about what they tried to sell—they have to put in the same amount of effort whether the product sells for $75 or $1,000. If the advertised product did not sell, the firm still paid eBay's listing fee.

iSold It's founders realized that the firm was growing at a rate above their capabilities, so they stepped aside and hired outside help. In 2004 Ken Sully, a former vice president of Mail Boxes Etc., came on board as the new CEO. Ken standardized the firm's operations and made it possible for a store to be installed and set up in 48 hours. iSold It's founders saw no end in sight for the firm's growth, stating in 2006, "We've created this brick-and-mortar interface to the Internet" and stating that their firm was in a position to capitalize on the growth of Internet trade. In fact, by June 2006 the firm had already sold 800 franchises.

Although iSold It knew that people could sell their own merchandise online, they overestimated their willingness to pay an intermediary 20–30 percent of the sales price for the convenience of listing their products and collecting the money. *Entrepreneur* magazine in January 2010 called the eBay drop-off store concept "ridiculous," as customers quickly learned how to sell their stuff by themselves. With low barriers to entry in this industry, many copycat firms quickly entered the market. In early 2007, iSold It stopped selling new franchises and is quickly losing the ones they sold.

By offering a service tied to the rapid growth of eBay, iSold It seemed to have identified an attractive opportunity. But the start-up's failure shows what can go wrong when—even though a good opportunity, sufficient resources, and an experienced entrepreneurial team are brought together—a business opportunity disappears as quickly as it appeared.

The iSold It case illustrates how important it is for new entrepreneurial entrants—whether they are start-ups or incumbents—to think and act strategically. Even with a strong resource base and good track record, entrepreneurs are unlikely to succeed if their business ideas are easily imitated or substituted for.

In this chapter we address entrepreneurial strategies. The previous three chapters have focused primarily on the business-level, corporate-level, and international strategies of incumbent firms. Here we ask: What about the strategies of those entering into a market or industry for the first time? Whether it's a fast-growing start-up such as iSold It or an existing company seeking growth opportunities, new entrants need effective strategies.

Companies wishing to launch new ventures must also be aware that, consistent with the five forces model in Chapter 2, new entrants are a threat to existing firms in an industry. Entry into a new market arena is intensely competitive from the perspective of incumbents in that arena. Therefore, new entrants can nearly always expect a competitive response from other companies in the industry it is entering. Knowledge of the competitive dynamics that are at work in the business environment is an aspect of entrepreneurial new entry that will be addressed later in this chapter.

Before moving on, it is important to highlight the role that entrepreneurial start-ups and small business play in entrepreneurial value creation. Young and small firms are responsible for more innovations and more new job creation than any other type of business.[2] Strategy Spotlight 8.1 addresses some of the reasons why small business and entrepreneurship are viewed favorably in the United States.

>LO8.1
The role of new ventures and small businesses in the U.S. economy.

Recognizing Entrepreneurial Opportunities

Defined broadly, **entrepreneurship** refers to new value creation. Even though entrepreneurial activity is usually associated with start-up companies, new value can be created in many different contexts including:

- Start-up ventures
- Major corporations
- Family-owned businesses
- Non-profit organizations
- Established institutions

entrepreneurship
the creation of new value by an existing organization or new venture that involves the assumption of risk.

For an entrepreneurial venture to create new value, three factors must be present—an entrepreneurial opportunity, the resources to pursue the opportunity, and an entrepreneur or entrepreneurial team willing and able to undertake the opportunity.[3] The entrepreneurial strategy that an organization uses will depend on these three factors. Thus, beyond merely identifying a venture concept, the opportunity recognition process also involves organizing the key people and resources that are needed to go forward. Exhibit 8.3 depicts the three factors that are needed to successfully proceed—opportunity, resources, and entrepreneur(s). In the sections that follow, we address each of these factors.

>LO8.2
The role of opportunities, resources, and entrepreneurs in successfully pursuing new ventures.

Entrepreneurial Opportunities

The starting point for any new venture is the presence of an entrepreneurial opportunity. Where do opportunities come from? For new business start-ups, opportunities come from many sources—current or past work experiences, hobbies that grow into businesses or lead to inventions, suggestions by friends or family, or a chance event that makes an entrepreneur aware of an unmet need. For established firms, new business opportunities come from the needs of existing customers, suggestions by suppliers, or technological developments that lead to new advances.[4] For all firms, there is a major, overarching factor behind all viable opportunities that emerge in the business landscape: change. Change creates opportunities. Entrepreneurial firms make the most of changes brought about by new technology, sociocultural trends, and shifts in consumer demand.

How do changes in the external environment lead to new business creation? They spark creative new ideas and innovation. Businesspeople often have ideas for entrepreneurial ventures. However, not all such ideas are good ideas—that is, viable business opportunities. To determine which ideas are strong enough to become new ventures, entrepreneurs

The Contribution of Small Businesses to the U.S. Economy

In the late 1970s, MIT professor David Birch launched a study to explore the sources of business growth. "I wasn't really looking for anything in particular," says Birch. But the findings surprised him: Small businesses create the most jobs. Since then, Birch and others have shown that it's not just big companies that power the economy. Small business and entrepreneurship have become a major component of new job creation.

Here are the facts:

- In the United States, there are approximately 5.9 million companies with fewer than 100 employees. Another 88,586 companies have 100 to 500 employees. In addition, approximately 17.0 million individuals are nonemployer sole proprietors.

- Small businesses create the majority of new jobs. According to recent data, small business created 65 percent of U.S. net new jobs in a recent 17-year period. A small percentage of the fastest growing entrepreneurial firms (5 to 15 percent) account for a majority of the new jobs created.

Sources: Small Business Administration. 2009. *The Small Business Economy.* Washington, DC: U.S. Government Printing Office; Small Business Administration. 2010. Small Business by the Numbers. *SBA Office of Advocacy,* June, *www.sba.gov/advo/; Inc.* 2001. Small Business 2001: Where We Are Now? May 29: 18–19; Minniti, M., & Bygrave, W. D. 2004. *Global Entrepreneurship Monitor—National Entrepreneurship Assessment: United States of America 2004, Executive Report.* Kansas City, MO: Kauffman Center for Entrepreneurial Leadership; and *Fortune.* 2001. The Heroes: A Portfolio. October 4: 74.

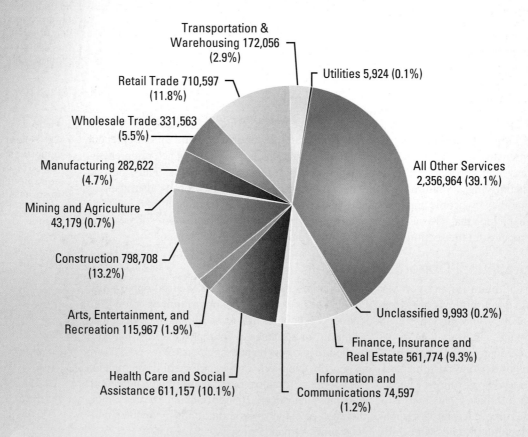

Transportation & Warehousing 172,056 (2.9%)
Utilities 5,924 (0.1%)
Retail Trade 710,597 (11.8%)
Wholesale Trade 331,563 (5.5%)
Manufacturing 282,622 (4.7%)
Mining and Agriculture 43,179 (0.7%)
All Other Services 2,356,964 (39.1%)
Construction 798,708 (13.2%)
Arts, Entertainment, and Recreation 115,967 (1.9%)
Unclassified 9,993 (0.2%)
Finance, Insurance and Real Estate 561,774 (9.3%)
Health Care and Social Assistance 611,157 (10.1%)
Information and Communications 74,597 (1.2%)

Exhibit 8.1 All U.S. Small Companies by Industry*

* Businesses with 500 or fewer employees in 2007.

Source: Small Business Administration's Office of Advocacy, based on data provided by the U.S. Census Bureau, statistics of U.S. businesses.

(continued)

(continued)

- Small businesses (fewer than 500 employees) employ more than half of the private sector workforce (59.9 million in 2007) and account for more than 50 percent of nonfarm private gross domestic product (GDP).

- Small firms produce 13 to 14 times more patents per employee than large patenting firms and employ 39 percent of high-tech workers (such as scientists and engineers). In addition, smaller entrepreneurial firms account for 55 percent of all innovations.

- Small businesses make up 97.5 percent of all U.S. exporters and accounted for 31 percent of known U.S. export value in 2008.

Exhibit 8.1 shows the number of small businesses in the United States and how they are distributed through different sectors of the economy.

There are also many types of small businesses. Exhibit 8.2 identifies three major categories that are often small and generally considered to be entrepreneurial—franchises, family businesses, and home-based businesses.

Type	Characteristics
Family Businesses	*Definition:* A family business, broadly defined, is a privately held firm in which family members have some degree of control over the strategic direction of the firm and intend for the business to remain within the family. *Scope:* According to the Family Firm Institute (FFI), family-owned businesses that meet the broad definition above comprise 80 to 90 percent of all business enterprises in the U.S., including 30 to 35 percent of the Fortune 500 companies. Further, 64 percent of the U.S. Gross Domestic Product (GDP) is generated by family-owned businesses.
Franchises	*Definition:* A franchise exists when a company that already has a successful product or service (franchisor) contracts with another business to be a dealer (franchisee) by using the franchisor's name, trademark and business system in exchange for a fee. The most common type is the Business Format Franchise in which the franchisor provides a complete plan, or format, for managing the business. *Scope:* According to the International Franchise Association (IFA), franchises were the cause of $863 billion in annual output in the U.S. in 2010. There are over 900,000 franchise establishments employing more than 9.5 million people.
Home-Based Businesses	*Definition:* A home-based business, also referred to as SOHO (Small Office/Home Office) consists of companies with 20 or fewer employees, including the self-employed, freelancers, telecommuters, or other independent professionals working from a home-based setting. *Scope:* According to the National Association of Home-Based Businesses (NAHBB), approximately 20 million businesses are home-based. The U.S. Commerce Department estimates that more than half of all small businesses are home-based.

Sources: *www.ffi.org*; *www.franchise.org*; and *www.workingsolo.com*.

Exhibit 8.2 Types of Entrepreneurial Ventures

Exhibit 8.3 **Opportunity Analysis Framework**

Sources: Based on Timmons, J. A. & Spinelli, S. 2004.
New Venture Creation (6th ed.). New York: McGraw-Hill/
Irwin; and Bygrave, W. D. 1997. The Entrepreneurial
Process. In W. D. Bygrave (Ed.), *The Portable MBA in
Entrepreneurship* (2nd ed.). New York: Wiley.

opportunity recognition the process of discovering and evaluating changes in the business environment, such as a new technology, sociocultural trends, or shifts in consumer demand, that can be exploited.

must go through a process of identifying, selecting, and developing potential opportunities. This is the process of **opportunity recognition.**[5]

Opportunity recognition refers to more than just the "Eureka!" feeling that people sometimes experience at the moment they identify a new idea. Although such insights are often very important, the opportunity recognition process involves two phases of activity—discovery and evaluation—that lead to viable new venture opportunities.[6]

The discovery phase refers to the process of becoming aware of a new business concept.[7] Many entrepreneurs report that their idea for a new venture occurred to them in an instant, as a sort of "Aha!" experience—that is, they had some insight or epiphany, often based on their prior knowledge, that gave them an idea for a new business. The discovery of new opportunities is often spontaneous and unexpected. For example, Howard Schultz, CEO of Starbucks, was in Milan, Italy, when he suddenly realized that the coffee-and-conversation café model that was common in Europe would work in the U.S. as well. According to Schultz, he didn't need to do research to find out if Americans would pay $3 for a cup of coffee—he just *knew.* Starbucks was just a small business at the time but Schultz began literally shaking with excitement about growing it into a bigger business.[8] Strategy Spotlight 8.2 tells how three entrepreneurs in the struggling city of Detroit identified their business opportunities.

Opportunity discovery also may occur as the result of a deliberate search for new venture opportunities or creative solutions to business problems. Viable opportunities often emerge only after a concerted effort. It is very similar to a creative process, which may be unstructured and "chaotic" at first but eventually leads to a practical solution or business innovation. To stimulate the discovery of new opportunities, companies often encourage creativity, out-of-the-box thinking, and brainstorming.

Opportunity evaluation, which occurs after an opportunity has been identified, involves analyzing an opportunity to determine whether it is viable and strong enough to be developed into a full-fledged new venture. Ideas developed by new-product groups or in brainstorming sessions are tested by various methods, including talking to potential target customers and discussing operational requirements with production or logistics managers. A technique known as feasibility analysis is used to evaluate these and other critical

Entrepreneurial Vision to Revitalize Detroit

Detroit is the poorest major city in America. With an unemployment rate of 26 percent and a declining population, it would seem to be a nearly impossible place to start a new business. But challenging economic times are often the trigger for entrepreneurs to pursue their vision. Half the corporations listed on the *Fortune* 500 in 2010 were founded during challenging economic times, according to Dane Stangler, a senior analyst at the Kauffman Foundation. Individually and with the help of others, a range of entrepreneurs is striving to rejuvenate Detroit and realize their visions. Some of their businesses are the result of "Aha!" moments in which they envisioned bold new opportunities. Others are more modest traditional business ideas, but they all aim both to enrich the firms' founders and to improve the economic climate and the community of Detroit.

Daniel Gizaw, Founder of Danotek Motion Technologies

Rural Ethiopia is far from Detroit in more ways than one. Daniel Gizaw has taken the long journey from working on his father's farm in Ethiopia to founding a firm that produces products for the green energy business. He began by leaving home to study electrical engineering in Poland and Germany and later was part of the team designing the EV1, General Motor's first electric car. In order to follow his desire to pursue bold innovations and to exploit growing markets, he founded Danotek Motion Technologies, a firm that builds highly efficient turbines for the wind energy market as well as components for electric vehicles. To achieve his vision, he has recruited former colleagues, gotten support from Automation Alley (a consortium of business and government partners to improve the economic conditions of southeastern Michigan), and received governmental tax breaks to foster business growth. His firm plans to grow its business rapidly, keeping all its manufacturing in the greater Detroit area, as they create over 350 new jobs. Daniel's advice to would-be entrepreneurs is clear, "Don't limit yourself to the sector you are in. Look into growing industries and ask, 'What can I offer?'"

Glenn Oliver, Founder of H2bid.com

Though he is an attorney by training and never ran a business prior to starting H2bid, Glenn Oliver inherited an entrepreneurial interest from his grandfather, who owned an appliance repair and installation business. Living in a state that is surrounded by the Great Lakes and having served as a member of the Detroit Water and Sewerage Board of Commissioners, Oliver appreciated the value of water as a critical resource needed for economic development. Fresh water is a commodity increasingly demanded around the globe. Oliver saw opportunity here and has created H2bid.com, a marketplace where contractors and suppliers can bid on water supply projects around the world. While he thinks the business will be profitable, he also believes his start-up will benefit the Detroit area. As he concludes, "Entrepreneurship is the largest creator of wealth." Others in the area are noting the potential with this business. Oliver received recognition as a "Champion of the New Economy," an award sponsored by *DBusiness,* WJR radio, and Junior Achievement to recognize people whose businesses are helping to diversify Michigan's economy.

John Hantz, Founder of Hantz Farms

When many people drive through Detroit, they see a landscape of abandoned homes, empty commercial buildings, and vacant land. John Hantz sees opportunity. Already a successful entrepreneur, having founded Hantz Financial Services, a firm with 20 offices, 500 employees, and over $1.3 billion in assets under management, Hantz now has a new entrepreneurial vision. His vision grew out of his commuting across Detroit from his home to his office. Seeing all of the unused land and abandoned homes, he realized that he had to find a way to change the supply and demand relationship for land in Detroit. He sees urban farming as a partial solution to this issue. The farms he envisions are not the old style of farms growing crops in rows in large, open-air plots worked with large tractors. Instead, he plans to build compost-heated greenhouses and use hydroponic and aeroponic growing systems that don't rely on soil to grow crops. He is drawing on up to $30 million of his own financial resources to start the project and has tapped into expertise in the region, hiring Mike Score, an agricultural expert from Michigan State University to serve as president of the firm. He sees an economic opportunity here but also a chance to revitalize the area. His plan is to build small, visually attractive 300 to 1,000 acre farms or "pods" all across Detroit which will be surrounded by frontage property that could be developed for housing or commercial activity. Thus, he sees the farms as a way to reduce the supply of unused land while also stoking demand for redeveloped land surrounding the farms.

Although these businesses span a wide range of industries, they demonstrate that entrepreneurial vision often arises out an individual's experiences and can encompass both a business idea as well as a vehicle with which to improve conditions in a larger community.

Sources: Sohail, F. 2010. Alternative Energy: Creating Non-exportable Jobs. *Forbes.com*, June 30: np; Easton, N. 2010. If You Can Remake Yourself Here. *Fortune*, November 1: 59–63; Gray, S. 2010. Where Entrepreneurs Need Nerves of Steel. *Fortune*, October 18: 63–66; Saulny, S. 2010. Detroit Entrepreneurs Opt to Look Up. *The New York Times*, January 10: A18; Anonymous. 2010. Champions of the New Economy, *dBusiness*, May/June: np; Whitford, D. 2010. Can Farming Save Detroit? *Fortune*, January 18: 78–84.

success factors. This type of analysis often leads to the decision that a new venture project should be discontinued. If the venture concept continues to seem viable, a more formal business plan may be developed.[9]

Among the most important factors to evaluate is the market potential for the product or service. Established firms tend to operate in established markets. They have to adjust to market trends and to shifts in consumer demand, of course, but they usually have a customer base for which they are already filling a marketplace need. New ventures, in contrast, must first determine whether a market exists for the product or service they are contemplating. Thus, a critical element of opportunity recognition is assessing to what extent the opportunity is viable *in the marketplace.*

For an opportunity to be viable, it needs to have four qualities.[10]

- *Attractive.* The opportunity must be attractive in the marketplace; that is, there must be market demand for the new product or service.
- *Achievable.* The opportunity must be practical and physically possible.
- *Durable.* The opportunity must be attractive long enough for the development and deployment to be successful; that is, the window of opportunity must be open long enough for it to be worthwhile.
- *Value creating.* The opportunity must be potentially profitable; that is, the benefits must surpass the cost of development by a significant margin.

If a new business concept meets these criteria, two other factors must be considered before the opportunity is launched as a business: the resources available to undertake it, and the characteristics of the entrepreneur(s) pursuing it. In the next section, we address the issue of entrepreneurial resources; following that, we address the importance of entrepreneurial leaders and teams. But first, consider the opportunities that have been created by the recent surge in interest in environmental sustainability. Strategy Spotlight 8.3 discusses how an entrepreneurial firm is working to develop and sell a line of biodegradable plastics.

Entrepreneurial Resources

As Exhibit 8.3 indicates, resources are an essential component of a successful entrepreneurial launch. For start-ups, the most important resource is usually money because a new firm typically has to expend substantial sums just to start the business. However, financial resources are not the only kind of resource a new venture needs. Human capital and social capital are also important. Many firms also rely on government resources to help them thrive.[11]

Financial Resources   Hand-in-hand with the importance of markets (and marketing) to new-venture creation, entrepreneurial firms must also have financing. In fact, the level of available financing is often a strong determinant of how the business is launched and its eventual success. Cash finances are, of course, highly important. But access to capital, such as a line of credit or favorable payment terms with a supplier, can also help a new venture succeed.

The types of financial resources that may be needed depend on two factors: the stage of venture development and the scale of the venture.[12] Entrepreneurial firms that are starting from scratch—start-ups—are at the earliest stage of development. Most start-ups also begin on a relatively small scale. The funding available to young and small firms tends to be quite limited. In fact, the majority of new firms are low-budget start-ups launched with personal savings and the contributions of family and friends.[13] Among firms included in the *Entrepreneur* list of the 100 fastest-growing new businesses in a recent year, 61 percent reported that their start-up funds came from personal savings.[14]

strategy spotlight

Green Plastics

Despite an increasing emphasis on recycling, only 7 percent of the plastic used by Americans is currently recycled. The remainder goes into landfills or ends up in lakes and oceans, where the plastic poisons fish that consume it. One vivid place to find the consequences of plastic use is in the middle of the ocean over a thousand miles off the California coast. It is the Great Pacific Garbage Patch, a collection of mostly plastic trash that has been estimated to be up to twice the size of France, formed as ocean currents pull plastic trash from coastal areas.

How do we reduce our reliance on nonbiodegradable plastics that clog our landfills and oceans? Metabolix, a small firm based in Cambridge, Massachusetts, is stepping up with an innovative solution—environmentally friendly biodegradable plastics. Plastic is typically made from petroleum, and the products made from petroleum-based plastic can take hundreds of years to decompose in landfills. Metabolix has developed a process to make plastics out of plant materials—the first 100 percent bioplastic product that is both biodegradable and durable enough to stand up to heat and use. The firm uses a genetically engineered microbe that consumes the sugar in corn, producing a plastic molecule called PHA. Plastic products made from PHA will decompose in water or soil in a few months. The products are so pure that consumers can toss them into their backyard compost piles and use the resulting mulch in their vegetable gardens or around their fruit trees.

To manufacture and sell the product, Metabolix has created a joint venture, Telles, with agribusiness giant Archer Daniels Midland (ADM). They sell the biodegradable plastic for around $2.50 a pound, about twice the cost of typical, petroleum-based plastic. Since they can't compete head to head on price with other plastics and want to maximize the ecological benefits of their product, Metabolix and ADM have initially focused on getting their plastic used in products that would not normally be recycled. Instead of trying to get their plastic, Mirel, used in plastic bottles, they have aimed their sales toward plastic gift cards, bags, forks and knives, container lids, and disposable pens. For example, one of the first products to use Mirel is a biodegradable Paper Mate pen. One of the benefits is that the pen uses so little plastic that the use of the higher cost bioplastic has a minimal effect on the overall cost of the pen.

Metabolix is aiming to improve the cost efficiency of their product to be able to compete with other plastics by developing genetically engineered nonfood crops, such as switchgrass and oilseeds, that will produce the PHA polymer within the plant and require less processing to extract into usable plastics. Their goal is to grow 160 million tons of plastic-producing plants to produce 15 million tons of bioplastic per year. This will reduce the need for petroleum and landfill space and, hopefully, begin to reduce the size of the Great Pacific Garbage Patch.

Sources: Dumaine, B. 2010. Feel-Good Plastic. *Fortune*, May 3: 36; Ziegler, J. 2009. Metabolix Defies Skeptics with Plastic from Plants. *Bloomberg*, May 7: np; Anonymous. 2010. Metabolix: FDA Clears Bioplastic for Use with Food. *BusinessWeek Online*, May 12: np; Anonymous. 2009. Drowning in Plastic: The Great Pacific Garbage Patch Is Twice the Size of France. *telegraph.co.uk*, April 24: np.

environmental sustainability

Although bank financing, public financing, and venture capital are important sources of small business finance, these types of financial support are typically available only after a company has started to conduct business and generate sales. Even "angel" investors—private individuals who provide equity investments for seed capital during the early stages of a new venture—favor companies that already have a winning business model and dominance in a market niche.[15] According to Cal Simmons, coauthor of *Every Business Needs an Angel*, "I would much rather talk to an entrepreneur who has already put his money and his effort into proving the concept."[16] Peer-to-peer lending is a rapidly increasing Internet-based source of funding for entrepreneurs. Strategy Spotlight 8.4 discusses Prosper.com, a peer-to-peer lending website that uses social affiliation to bring together entrepreneurs and potential lenders.

angel investors private individuals who provide equity investments for seed capital during the early stages of a new venture.

Prosper.com: Using the Power of the Social Group to Fund Entrepreneurs

Start-up entrepreneurs may need only a small amount of money to launch their ventures. However, if they have limited personal resources, they may never be able to turn their business ideas into operating enterprises. With lower credit limits and higher interest rates on credit cards and tougher standards for borrowers seeking bank loans, entrepreneurs are increasingly turning to other sources for seed capital. To fill this need, a new breed of lender has emerged online: peer-to-peer (P2P) lenders. This form of lending has taken off and was projected to involve over $5.8 billion in lending in 2010 according to the research firm Celent.

With P2P lending, borrowers seeking loans post descriptions of their business concepts, including the amount of funding they are seeking and personal information, such as their credit rating. Lenders, who are looking for opportunities to lend their money and make a decent return but who also often find satisfaction from helping out entrepreneurs, review business proposals and the borrowers' background information before making lending decisions. Depending on the rules of each P2P website, lenders either make a loan to borrowers at a preset interest rate or participate in an auction to "win" the opportunity to lend to the borrower. On the auction sites, lenders willing to lend at the lowest interest rates fund a borrower. Since the loans are unsecured, lenders are encouraged to spread their funds around, making small loans to a number of borrowers. As a result, a number of lenders typically provide small amounts of money that collectively meet the borrowing needs of an individual borrower.

One of the largest P2P lending websites is Prosper. com. Launched in 2006, Prosper reports that investors lending through their website have provided over $214 million in loans to entrepreneurs and that they have over one million members. The root idea for Prosper.com came from the experience of Lyna Lam, the wife of Prosper's founder Chris Larsen. Lyna's family came to the United States as refugees from Vietnam in the early 1980s. Once they settled in San Jose, California, they joined a Vietnamese Hui group, a group of individuals who make contributions to create a pool of money that one of the members can borrow to start or grow a business. Lyna Lam's family used money from the Hui to start a landscaping business.

Chris saw the group structure as a key strength of the Hui. Hui groups tend to be successful because members of the group offer advice to each other but also feel strong social pressure from the group to work hard to repay the money borrowed from the group. This addresses one of the key weaknesses of P2P lending—the lack of trust that someone the lender doesn't know and never interacted with directly will repay the loan. Like most other P2P lending sites, Prosper collects factual information on the borrower and the business idea, runs a credit check on the borrower, and offers them scores that range from AA (the best rating) to HR (high risk) or NC (no credit history). But they also give borrowers the opportunity to join a group. These groups are created and organized by a leader and bring together borrowers that share a common interest or identity, such as nationality, educational affiliation, religion, type of business, or hobby. Members of successful groups, those that have a strong repayment record, can attract more favorable interest terms from lenders. Thus, the group offers positive peer pressure to members to repay their loans. Members don't want to lose face by defaulting on their loan and tarnishing the group's reputation, resulting in financial consequences for all borrowers in the group. The group leader can also provide advice to the borrower and is rewarded when members of the group repay their loans. The system appears to work well, as 92 percent of loans were being repaid on schedule as of February 2010 according to Prosper.com's statistics.

Sources: Libert, B. & Spector, J. 2008. *How to Unleash the Power of Crowds in Your Business.* Philadelphia: Wharton School Publishing: 104–106; Dishman, L. 2009. Peer-to-Peer Lending Explained: Brother, Can You Spare $100? *Fast Company,* November 11: np; *www.prosper.com*; *www.wikipedia. org*; and *www.oneviet.com*.

crowdsourcing

Once a venture has established itself as a going concern, other sources of financing become readily available. Banks, for example, are more likely to provide later-stage financing to companies with a track record of sales or other cash-generating activity. Start-ups that involve large capital investments or extensive development costs—such as manufacturing or engineering firms trying to commercialize an innovative product—may have high cash requirements soon after they are founded. Others need financing only when they are on the brink of rapid growth. To obtain such funding, entrepreneurial firms often seek venture capital.

Venture capital is a form of private equity financing through which entrepreneurs raise money by selling shares in the new venture. In contrast to angel investors, who invest their own money, venture capital companies are organized to place the funds of private investors into lucrative business opportunities. Venture capitalists nearly always have high performance expectations from the companies they invest in, but they also provide important managerial advice and links to key contacts in an industry.[17]

venture capitalists
companies organized to place their investors' finds in lucrative business opportunities.

Despite the importance of venture capital to many fast-growing firms, the majority of external funding for young and small firms comes from informal sources such as family and friends. Based on a Kaufmann Foundation survey of entrepreneurial firms, Exhibit 8.4 identifies the source of funding used by start-up businesses and by ongoing firms that are five years old. The survey shows that most start-up funding, about 70 percent, comes from either equity investments by the entrepreneur and the entrepreneur's family and friends or personal loans taken out by the entrepreneur. After five years of operation, the largest source of funding is from loans taken out by the business. At both stages, 5 percent or less of the funding comes from outside investors, such as angel investors or venture capitalists. In fact, very few firms ever receive venture-capital investments—only 7 of 2606 firms in the Kaufmann study received money from outside investors. But when they do, these firms receive a substantial level of investment—over $1 million on average in the survey—because they tend to be the firms that are the most innovative and have the greatest growth potential. Regardless of their source, financial resources are essential for entrepreneurial ventures.[18]

Human Capital   Bankers, venture capitalists, and angel investors agree that the most important asset an entrepreneurial firm can have is strong and skilled management.[19] According to Stephen Gaal, founding member of Walnut Venture Associates, venture investors do not invest in businesses; instead "We invest in people . . . very smart people with very high integrity." Managers need to have a strong base of experience and extensive domain knowledge, as well as an ability to make rapid decisions and change direction as shifting circumstances may require. In the case of start-ups, more is better. New ventures that are started by teams of three, four, or five entrepreneurs are more likely to succeed in the long run than are ventures launched by "lone wolf" entrepreneurs.[20]

Exhibit 8.4
Sources of Capital for Start-Up Firms

	Capital Invested in Their First Year	Percentage of Capital Invested in Their First Year	Capital Invested in Their Fifth Year	Percentage of Capital Invested in Their Fifth Year
Insider equity	$33,034	41.1	$13,914	17.9
Investor equity	$4,108	5.1	$3,108	4.0
Personal debt of owners	$23,353	29.1	$21,754	28.0
Business debt	$19,867	24.7	$39,009	50.1
Total average capital invested	$80,362		$77,785	

Source: From Robb, A., Reedy, E. J., Ballou, J., DesRoches, D., Potter, F., & Zhao, A. 2010. An Overview of the Kauffman Firm Survey. Reproduced with permission from the Ewing Marion Kauffman Foundation.

Social Capital   New ventures founded by entrepreneurs who have extensive social contacts are more likely to succeed than are ventures started without the support of a social network.[21] Even though a venture may be new, if the founders have contacts who will vouch for them, they gain exposure and build legitimacy faster.[22] This support can come from several sources: prior jobs, industry organizations, and local business groups such as the chamber of commerce. These contacts can all contribute to a growing network that provides support for the entrepreneurial firm. Janina Pawlowski, co-founder of the online lending company E-Loan, attributes part of her success to the strong advisors she persuaded to serve on her board of directors, including Tim Koogle, former CEO of Yahoo![23]

Strategic alliances represent a type of social capital that can be especially important to young and small firms.[24] Strategy Spotlight 8.5 presents a few examples of alliances and some potential pitfalls of using alliances.[25]

Government Resources   In the U.S., the federal government provides support for entrepreneurial firms in two key arenas—financing and government contracting. The Small Business Administration (SBA) has several loan guarantee programs designed to support the growth and development of entrepreneurial firms. The government itself does not typically lend money but underwrites loans made by banks to small businesses, thus reducing the risk associated with lending to firms with unproven records. The SBA also offers training, counseling, and support services through its local offices and Small Business Development Centers.[26] State and local governments also have hundreds of programs to provide funding, contracts, and other support for new ventures and small businesses. These programs are often designed to grow the economy of a region, as seen with Danotek Motion Technologies in Strategy Spotlight 8.2.

Another key area of support is in government contracting. Programs sponsored by the SBA and other government agencies ensure that small businesses have the opportunity to bid on contracts to provide goods and services to the government. Although working with the government sometimes has its drawbacks in terms of issues of regulation and time-consuming decision making, programs to support small businesses and entrepreneurial activity constitute an important resource for entrepreneurial firms.

Entrepreneurial Leadership

entrepreneurial leadership
leadership appropriate for new ventures that requires courage, belief in ones convictions, and the energy to work hard even in difficult circumstances; and embody vision, dedication and drive, and commit to excellence.

Whether a venture is launched by an individual entrepreneur or an entrepreneurial team, effective leadership is needed. Launching a new venture requires a special kind of leadership.[27] It involves courage, belief in one's convictions, and the energy to work hard even in difficult circumstances. Yet these are the very challenges that motivate most business owners. Entrepreneurs put themselves to the test and get their satisfaction from acting independently, overcoming obstacles, and thriving financially. To do so, they must embody three characteristics of leadership—vision, dedication and drive, and commitment to excellence—and pass these on to all those who work with them:

- *Vision.* This may be an entrepreneur's most important asset. Entrepreneurs envision realities that do not yet exist. But without a vision, most entrepreneurs would never even get their venture off the ground. With vision, entrepreneurs are able to exercise a kind of transformational leadership that creates something new and, in some way, changes the world. Just having a vision, however, is not enough. To develop support, get financial backing, and attract employees, entrepreneurial leaders must share their vision with others.

- *Dedication and drive.* Dedication and drive are reflected in hard work. Drive involves internal motivation; dedication calls for an intellectual commitment that keeps an entrepreneur going even in the face of bad news or poor luck. They both require patience, stamina, and a willingness to work long hours. However, a business built on the heroic efforts of one person may suffer in the long run. That's why the

strategy spotlight

Strategic Alliances: A Key Entrepreneurial Resource

Strategic alliances provide a key avenue for growth by entrepreneurial firms. By partnering with other companies, young or small firms can expand or give the appearance of entering numerous markets and/or handling a range of operations. Here are several types of alliances that have been used to extend or strengthen entrepreneurial firms:

Technology Alliances

Tech-savvy entrepreneurial firms often benefit from forming alliances with older incumbents. The alliance allows the larger firm to enhance its technological capabilities and expands the revenue and reach of the smaller firm.

Manufacturing Alliances

The use of outsourcing and other manufacturing alliances by small firms has grown dramatically in recent years. Internet-enabled capabilities such as collaborating online about delivery and design specifications has greatly simplified doing business, even with foreign manufacturers.

Retail Alliances

Licensing agreements allow one company to sell the products and services of another in different markets, including overseas. Specialty products—the types sometimes made by entrepreneurial firms—often seem more exotic when sold in another country.

According to the National Federation of Independent Business (NFIB), nearly two-thirds of small businesses currently hold or have held some type of alliance. Strategic alliances among entrepreneurial firms can take many different forms. Exhibit 8.5 shows the different types of partnering that small businesses and small manufacturers in the NFIB study often use.

Although such alliances often sound good, there are also potential pitfalls. Lack of oversight and control is one danger of partnering with foreign firms. Problems with product quality, timely delivery, and receiving payments can also sour an alliance relationship if it is not carefully managed. With technology alliances, there is a risk that big firms may take advantage of the technological know-how of their entrepreneurial partners. However, even with these potential problems, strategic alliances provide a good means for entrepreneurial firms to develop and grow.

Sources: Copeland, M. V. & Tilin, A. 2005. Get Someone to Build It. *Business 2.0,* 6(5): 88–90 Misner, I. 2008. Use Small Actions to Get Big Results. *Entrepreneur. www.entrepreneur.com*, December 3. Monahan, J. 2005. All Systems Grow. *Entrepreneur,* March: 78–82; Prince, C. J. 2005. Foreign Affairs. *Entrepreneur,* March: 56; and, Weaver, K. M. & Dickson, P. 2004. Strategic Alliances. In W. J. Dennis, Jr. (Ed.), *NFIB National Small Business Poll.* Washington, DC: National Federation of Independent Business.

Type of Alliance and/or Long-Term Agreement*	Small Manufacturers	Small Businesses
Licensing	20.0%	32.5%
Export/Import	14.4%	7.3%
Franchise	5.0%	5.3%
Marketing	18.0%	25.2%
Distribution	20.1%	20.5%
Production	26.5%	11.3%
Product/Services R&D	12.2%	12.6%
Process R&D	6.7%	5.3%
Purchaser/Supplier	23.5%	13.9%
Outside Contracting	23.2%	28.5%

Source: From Weaver, K. M. & Dickson, P. 2004. Strategic Alliances. In W. J. Dennis, Jr. (Ed.), *NFIB National Small Business Poll.* Washington, DC: National Federation of Independent Business. Reprinted with permission.

* Columns add to over 100 percent because firms may use multiple alliances.

Exhibit 8.5   Use of Strategic Alliances by Small Businesses and Small Manufacturers dedicated entrepreneur's enthusiasm is also important—like a magnet, it attracts others to the business to help with the work.[28]

- **_Commitment to excellence._** Excellence requires entrepreneurs to commit to knowing the customer, providing quality goods and services, paying attention to details, and continuously learning. Entrepreneurs who achieve excellence are sensitive to how these factors work together. However, entrepreneurs may flounder if they think they are the only ones who can create excellent results. The most successful, by contrast, often report that they owe their success to hiring people smarter than themselves.

In his book *Good to Great,* Jim Collins makes another important point about entrepreneurial leadership: Ventures built on the charisma of a single person may have trouble growing "from good to great" once that person leaves.[29] Thus, the leadership that is needed to build a great organization is usually exercised by a team of dedicated people working together rather than a single leader. Another aspect of this team approach is attracting team members who fit with the company's culture, goals, and work ethic. Thus, for a venture's leadership to be a valuable resource and not a liability it must be cohesive in its vision, drive and dedication, and commitment to excellence.

Once an opportunity has been recognized, and an entrepreneurial team and resources have been assembled, a new venture must craft a strategy. Prior chapters have addressed the strategies of incumbent firms. In the next section, we highlight the types of strategies and strategic considerations faced by new entrants.

Entrepreneurial Strategy

entrepreneurial strategy a strategy that enables a skilled and dedicated entrepreneur, with a viable opportunity and access to sufficient resources, to successfully launch a new venture.

Successfully creating new ventures requires several ingredients. As indicated in Exhibit 8.3, three factors are necessary—a viable opportunity, sufficient resources, and a skilled and dedicated entrepreneur or entrepreneurial team. Once these elements are in place, the new venture needs a strategy. In this section, we consider several different strategic factors that are unique to new ventures and also how the generic strategies introduced in Chapter 5 can be applied to entrepreneurial firms. We also indicate how combination strategies might benefit entrepreneurial firms and address the potential pitfalls associated with launching new venture strategies.

To be successful, new ventures must evaluate industry conditions, the competitive environment, and market opportunities in order to position themselves strategically. However, a traditional strategic analysis may have to be altered somewhat to fit the entrepreneurial situation. For example, five-forces analysis (as discussed in Chapter 2) is typically used by established firms. It can also be applied to the analysis of new ventures to assess the impact of industry and competitive forces. But you may ask: How does a new entrant evaluate the threat of other new entrants?

First, the new entrant needs to examine barriers to entry. If the barriers are too high, the potential entrant may decide not to enter or to gather more resources before attempting to do so. Compared to an older firm with an established reputation and available resources, the barriers to entry may be insurmountable for an entrepreneurial start-up. Therefore, understanding the force of these barriers is critical in making a decision to launch.

A second factor that may be especially important to a young venture is the threat of retaliation by incumbents. In many cases, entrepreneurial ventures *are* the new entrants that pose a threat to incumbent firms. Therefore, in applying the five-forces model to new ventures, the threat of retaliation by established firms needs to be considered.

Part of any decision about what opportunity to pursue is a consideration of how a new entrant will actually enter a new market. The concept of entry strategies provides a useful means of addressing the types of choices that new ventures have.

Entry Strategies

One of the most challenging aspects of launching a new venture is finding a way to begin doing business that quickly generates cash flow, builds credibility, attracts good employees, and overcomes the liability of newness. The idea of an entry strategy or "entry wedge" describes several approaches that firms may take to get a foothold in a market.[30] Several factors will affect this decision.

- Is the product/service high-tech or low-tech?
- What resources are available for the initial launch?
- What are the industry and competitive conditions?
- What is the overall market potential?
- Does the venture founder prefer to control the business or to grow it?

In some respects, any type of entry into a market for the first time may be considered entrepreneurial. But the entry strategy will vary depending on how risky and innovative the new business concept is.[31] New-entry strategies typically fall into one of three categories—pioneering new entry, imitative new entry, or adaptive new entry.[32]

Pioneering New Entry   New entrants with a radical new product or highly innovative service may change the way business is conducted in an industry. This kind of breakthrough—creating new ways to solve old problems or meeting customers' needs in a unique new way—is referred to as a **pioneering new entry.** If the product or service is unique enough, a pioneering new entrant may actually have little direct competition. The first personal computer was a pioneering product; there had never been anything quite like it and it revolutionized computing. The first Internet browser provided a type of pioneering service. These breakthroughs created whole new industries and changed the competitive landscape. And breakthrough innovations continue to inspire pioneering entrepreneurial efforts. Strategy Spotlight 8.6 discusses Pandora, a firm that pioneered a new way to broadcast music.

The pitfalls associated with a pioneering new entry are numerous. For one thing, there is a strong risk that the product or service will not be accepted by consumers. The history of entrepreneurship is littered with new ideas that never got off the launching pad. Take, for example, Smell-O-Vision, an invention designed to pump odors into movie theatres from the projection room at preestablished moments in a film. It was tried only once (for the film *Scent of a Mystery*) before it was declared a major flop. Innovative? Definitely. But hardly a good idea at the time.[33]

A pioneering new entry is disruptive to the status quo of an industry. It is likely based on a technological breakthrough. If it is successful, other competitors will rush in to copy it. This can create issues of sustainability for an entrepreneurial firm, especially if a larger company with greater resources introduces a similar product. For a new entrant to sustain its pioneering advantage, it may be necessary to protect its intellectual property, advertise heavily to build brand recognition, form alliances with businesses that will adopt its products or services, and offer exceptional customer service.

Imitative New Entry   Whereas pioneers are often inventors or tinkerers with new technology, imitators usually have a strong marketing orientation. They look for opportunities to capitalize on proven market successes. An **imitative new entry** strategy is used by entrepreneurs who see products or business concepts that have been successful in one market niche or physical locale and introduce the same basic product or service in another segment of the market.

Sometimes the key to success with an imitative strategy is to fill a market space where the need had previously been filled inadequately. Entrepreneurs are also prompted to be imitators when they realize that they have the resources or skills to do a job better than an existing competitor. This can actually be a serious problem for entrepreneurial start-ups if the imitator is an established company. Consider the example of Tesla Motors. Founded in

pioneering new entry a firm's entry into an industry with a radical new product or highly innovative service that changes the way business is conducted.

imitative new entry a firm's entry into an industry with products or services that capitalize on proven market successes and that usually has a strong marketing orientation.

Pandora Rocks the Music Business

Whether the music was transmitted over FM radio signals, streamed over the web, or from a satellite, the musical choices radio listeners had were fairly standardized until Pandora arrived. Radio stations determined their play list based on a combination of interest evident in music sales and listener surveys along with the format of their stations. Listeners in a given market could decide if they wanted to listen to a top 40, adult contemporary, country, or classic rock station, but they couldn't custom design a station to meet their eclectic musical tastes.

Tim Westergren completely changed the radio business when he created Pandora. In 1999 he developed the Music Genome Project—a system that analyzes music for its underlying traits, including melody, rhythm, lyrics, instrumentation, and many other traits. Each song is measured on approximately 400 musical "genes" and given a vector or list of attributes. The vectors of multiple songs can be compared to assess the "distance" between the two songs. Using the Music Genome Project, Westergren launched Pandora in 2000. Users input bands or songs

they like, and Pandora creates a customized station that plays music that meets the users' tastes. Users can then tweak the station by giving input on whether or not they like the songs Pandora plays for them.

Pandora radically changes the radio business in multiple ways. First, users create their own customized stations. Second, users can access their personal radio stations wherever they go through any Internet-connected device. Third, the playing of songs is driven by their musical traits, not how popular a band is. If an unsigned garage band has musical traits similar to Pearl Jam, their music will get play on a user's Pearl Jam station. This offers great exposure to aspiring musicians not available on commercial radio. It also offers an avenue for record labels to get exposure for newly signed bands that don't yet get air play on traditional radio.

Pandora has grown in 10 years from a boldly new idea to become the largest "radio" station in the world, with 65 million registered users. The next move is to dominate the location where Americans do most of their radio listening—their cars. Ford began offering a voice-activated Pandora system in their cars in early 2011. Other manufacturers are following suit. Pioneer is selling car stereos that support Pandora. In gaining control of music in cars, Pandora continues to rock the music business.

Sources: Copeland, M. V. 2010. Pandora's Founder Rocks the Music Business. *Fortune*, July 5: 27–28; Levy, A. 2010. Pandora's Next Frontier: Your Wheels. *BusinessWeek.com*, October 14: np; and *www.pandora.com*.

2003, Tesla designs and manufactures electric cars. The average cost of a gallon of gasoline was about $1.50 when Tesla was incorporated, and the demand for alternative-fuel cars was not strong. Thus, they initially faced limited competition in this niche of the automotive market. However, by the time their first Tesla Roadster was ready for sale in 2008, rising gasoline prices and concerns about auto emissions had dramatically increased interest in electric cars. Tesla's success in winning design awards and car orders increased the profile of the firm and, more generally, electric cars. The major automakers are responding with their own models in this market. The Chevy Volt and Nissan Leaf both came on the market in 2010. Ford will launch an electric version of the Ford Focus in 2011. Other major auto manufacturers are following suit. While Tesla's original vehicle is a high-performance car that faces no direct competition, their goal was to expand into the mainstream market with an electric-powered sedan. With the fast response by major competitors, it is not clear that Tesla will be able to continue to grow their business.[34]

Adaptive New Entry   Most new entrants use a strategy somewhere between "pure" imitation and "pure" pioneering. That is, they offer a product or service that is somewhat new and sufficiently different to create new value for customers and capture market share. Such firms are adaptive in the sense that they are aware of marketplace conditions and conceive entry strategies to capitalize on current trends.

According to business creativity coach Tom Monahan, "Every new idea is merely a spin of an old idea. [Knowing that] takes the pressure off from thinking [you] have to be totally creative. You don't. Sometimes it's one slight twist to an old idea that makes all the difference."[35] An **adaptive new entry** approach does not involve "reinventing the wheel," nor is it merely imitative either. It involves taking an existing idea and adapting it to a particular situation. Exhibit 8.6 presents examples of four young companies that successfully modified or adapted existing products to create new value.

There are several pitfalls that might limit the success of an adaptive new entrant. First, the value proposition must be perceived as unique. Unless potential customers believe a new product or service does a superior job of meeting their needs, they will have little motivation to try it. Second, there is nothing to prevent a close competitor from mimicking the new firm's adaptation as a way to hold on to its customers. Third, once an adaptive entrant achieves initial success, the challenge is to keep the idea fresh. If the attractive features of the new business are copied, the entrepreneurial firm must find ways to adapt and improve the product or service offering.

Considering these choices, an entrepreneur or entrepreneurial team might ask, Which new entry strategy is best? The choice depends on many competitive, financial, and marketplace considerations. Nevertheless, research indicates that the greatest opportunities may stem from being willing to enter new markets rather than seeking growth only in existing markets. A recent study found that companies that ventured into arenas that were new to the world or new to the company earned total profits of 61 percent. In contrast, companies that made only incremental improvements, such as extending an existing product line, grew total profits by only 39 percent.[36]

> **adaptive new entry** a firm's entry into an industry by offering a product or service that is somewhat new and sufficiently different to create value for customers by capitalizing on current market trends.

Exhibit 8.6   **Examples of Adaptive New Entrants**

Company Name	Product	Adaptation	Result
Under Armour, Inc. Founded in 1995	Undershirts and other athletic gear	Used moisture-wicking fabric to create better gear for sweaty sports.	Under Armour has 3,000 employees and 2010 sales in excess of $850 million.
Mint.com Founded in 2005	Comprehensive online money management	Created software that tells users what they are spending by aggregating financial information from online bank and credit card accounts.	Mint has over 4 million users and is tracking $200 billion in transactions.
Plum Organics Founded in 2005	Organic frozen baby food	Made convenient line of baby food using organic ingredients.	Added to Whole Foods product offering in 2006 and Babies 'R' Us in 2009.
Spanx Founded in 2000	Footless pantyhose and other undergarments for women	Combined nylon and Lycra® to create a new type of undergarment that is comfortable and eliminates panty lines.	Now produces over 200 products sold in 3,000 stores to over 6 million customers.

Sources: Bryan, M. 2007. Spanx Me, Baby! www.observer.com, December 10, np.; Carey, J. 2006. Perspiration Inspiration. *BusinessWeek,* June 5: 64; Palanjian, A. 2008. A Planner Plumbs for a Niche. www.wsj.com, September 30, np.; Worrell, D. 2008. Making Mint. *Entrepreneur,* September: 55; www.mint.com; www.spanx.com; www.underarmour.com; and Buss, D. 2010. The Mothers of Invention. *The Wall Street Journal,* February 8: R7.

These findings led W. Chan Kim and Renee Mauborgne in their new book *Blue Ocean Strategy* to conclude that companies that are willing to venture into market spaces where there is little or no competition—labeled "blue oceans"—will outperform those firms that limit growth to incremental improvements in competitively crowded industries—labeled "red oceans." Companies that identify and pursue blue ocean strategies follow somewhat different rules than those that are "bloodied" by the competitive practices in red oceans. Consider the following elements of a blue ocean strategy:

- ***Create uncontested market space.*** By seeking opportunities where they are not threatened by existing competitors, blue ocean firms can focus on customers rather than on competition.
- ***Make the competition irrelevant.*** Rather than using the competition as a benchmark, blue ocean firms cross industry boundaries to offer new and different products and services.
- ***Create and capture new demand.*** Rather than fighting over existing demand, blue ocean companies seek opportunities in uncharted territory.
- ***Break the value/cost trade-off.*** Blue ocean firms reject the idea that a trade-off between value and cost is inevitable and instead seek opportunities in areas that benefit both their cost structure and their value proposition to customers.
- ***Pursue differentiation and low cost simultaneously.*** By integrating the range of a firm's utility, price, and cost activities, blue ocean companies align their whole system to create sustainable strategies.

The essence of blue ocean strategy is not just to find an uncontested market, but to create one. Some blue oceans arise because new technologies create new possibilities, such as eBay's online auction business. Yet technological innovation is not a defining feature of a blue ocean strategy. Most blue oceans are created from within red oceans by companies that push beyond the existing industry boundaries. Any of the new entry strategies described earlier could be used to pursue a blue ocean strategy. Consider the example of Cirque du Soleil, which created a new market for circus entertainment by making traditional circus acts more like theatrical productions:

> By altering the industry boundaries that traditionally defined the circus concept, Cirque du Soleil created a new type of circus experience. Since the days of Ringling Bros. and Barnum & Bailey, the circus had consisted of animal acts, star performers, and Bozo-like clowns. Cirque questioned this formula and researched what audiences really wanted. It found that interest in animal acts was declining, in part because of public concerns over the treatment of circus animals. Because managing animals—and the celebrity trainers who performed with them—was costly, Cirque eliminated them.
>
> Instead, Cirque focused on three elements of the traditional circus tent event that still captivated audiences: acrobatic acts, clowns, and the tent itself. Elegant acrobatics became a central feature of its performances, and clown humor became more sophisticated and less slapstick. Cirque also preserved the image of the tent by creating exotic facades that captured the symbolic elements of the traditional tent. Finally, rather than displaying three different acts simultaneously, as in the classic three-ring circus, Cirque offers multiple productions with theatrical story lines, giving audiences a reason to go to the circus more often. Each production has a different theme and its own original musical score.
>
> Cirque's efforts to redefine the circus concept have paid off. Since 1984, Cirque's productions have been seen by over 90 million people in some 200 cities around the world.[37]

Once created, a blue ocean strategy is difficult to imitate. If customers flock to blue ocean creators, firms rapidly achieve economies of scale, learning advantages, and synergies across their organizational systems. Body Shop, for example chartered new territory by refusing to focus solely on beauty products. Traditional competitors such as Estee

Lauder and L'Oreal, whose brands are based on promises of eternal youth and beauty, found it difficult to imitate this approach without repudiating their current images.

These factors suggest that blue ocean strategies provide an avenue by which firms can pursue an entrepreneurial new entry. Such strategies are not without risks, however. A new entrant must decide not only the best way to enter into business but also what type of strategic positioning will work best as the business goes forward. Those strategic choices can be informed by the guidelines suggested for the generic strategies. We turn to that subject next.

Generic Strategies

>LO8.4
How the generic strategies of overall cost leadership, differentiation, and focus are used by new ventures and small businesses.

Typically, a new entrant begins with a single business model that is equivalent in scope to a business-level strategy (Chapter 5). In this section we address how overall low cost, differentiation, and focus strategies can be used to achieve competitive advantages.

Overall Cost Leadership   One of the ways entrepreneurial firms achieve success is by doing more with less. By holding down costs or making more efficient use of resources than larger competitors, new ventures are often able to offer lower prices and still be profitable. Thus, under the right circumstances, a low-cost leader strategy is a viable alternative for some new ventures. The way most companies achieve low-cost leadership, however, is typically different for young or small firms.

Recall from Chapter 5 that three of the features of a low-cost approach included operating at a large enough scale to spread costs over many units of production (economies of scale), making substantial capital investments in order to increase scale economies, and using knowledge gained from experience to make cost-saving improvements. These elements of a cost-leadership strategy may be unavailable to new ventures. Because new ventures are typically small, they usually don't have high economies of scale relative to competitors. Because they are usually cash strapped, they can't make large capital investments to increase their scale advantages. And because many are young, they often don't have a wealth of accumulated experience to draw on to achieve cost reductions.

Given these constraints, how can new ventures successfully deploy cost-leader strategies? Compared to large firms, new ventures often have simple organizational structures that make decision making both easier and faster. The smaller size also helps young firms change more quickly when upgrades in technology or feedback from the marketplace indicate that improvements are needed. They are also able to make decisions at the time they are founded that help them deal with the issue of controlling costs. For example, they may source materials from a supplier that provides them more cheaply or set up manufacturing facilities in another country where labor costs are especially low. Thus, new firms have several avenues for achieving low cost leadership. Strategy Spotlight 8.7 highlights the success of Vizio, Inc., a new entrant with an overall cost leadership strategy. Whatever methods young firms use to achieve a low-cost advantage, this has always been a way that entrepreneurial firms take business away from incumbents—by offering a comparable product or service at a lower price.

Differentiation   Both pioneering and adaptive entry strategies involve some degree of differentiation. That is, the new entry is based on being able to offer a differentiated value proposition. In the case of pioneers, the new venture is attempting to do something strikingly different, either by using a new technology or deploying resources in a way that radically alters the way business is conducted. Often, entrepreneurs do both.

Amazon founder Jeff Bezos set out to use Internet technology to revolutionize the way books are sold. He garnered the ire of other booksellers and the attention of the public by making bold claims about being the "earth's largest bookseller." As a bookseller, Bezos was not doing anything that had not been done before. But two key differentiating

strategy spotlight

Low-Cost Imitator Vizio, Inc., Takes Off

The popularity of flat-panel TVs has grown rapidly since they were first introduced in the late 1990s—by 2012, it is estimated 85 percent of U.S households will have one. When first introduced, major manufacturers such as Samsung, Sony, and Matsushita (maker of Panasonic) made heavy investments in R&D in a competition for technological leadership. As a result, the early flat-panel TVs were expensive. Even as technological advances drove prices down, the TVs were growing larger and flatter, and they continued to command premium prices. By 2002, 50-inch plasma TVs were still selling for $8,000–$10,000. But by then, panel technology had also become somewhat commoditized. That's when William Wang, a former marketer of computer monitors, realized he could use existing technologies to create a high quality TV. Wang discovered he could keep operations lean and outsource everything from tech support to R&D, so he founded Vizio, Inc.

In January 2003, Wang pitched Costco Wholesale Corp. on a 46-inch flat-panel plasma TV for $3,800—half the price of the competition. Although Costco executives laughed when Wang said he wanted to become the next

Sony, they decided to give him a chance. By March 2003, the TVs were being offered in over 300 of Costco's U.S. warehouse stores. Today, Vizio is one of Costco's largest suppliers of TVs.

Vizio's success is due not only to enlightened imitation and low-cost operations, but also to Wang's unique approach to financing growth. Although he initially mortgaged his home and borrowed from family and friends, when he needed additional funding, he targeted the manufacturing partners who were supplying him parts. In 2004, Taiwan-based contract manufacturer AmTran Technology Co. purchased an 8 percent stake in Vizio for $1 million; today, AmTran owns 23 percent of Vizio and supplies over 80 percent of its TVs. "Unlike many PC companies who try to make their money by squeezing the vendor," says Wang, "we try to work with our vendor."

Although Vizio has a long way to go to be the next Sony, it has made remarkable progress. Vizio shipped 19.9 percent of the LCD TVs sold in the third quarter of 2010, leading the number two firm, Samsung, which had 17.7 percent of the market. Vizio expected to sell 6 million TVs in 2010, generating over $2.5 billion in sales. Vizio is now turning its attention to smaller electronic devices. Vizio recently announced it will introduce a line of cellphones and tablet computers. In extending its low-cost business model to these markets, it is taking one more step to being a full-range competitor to Sony, Samsung, and other major consumer electronics firms.

Sources: Lawton, C., Kane, Y. I., & Dean, J. 2008. U.S. Upstart Takes on TV Giants in Price War. *www.wsj.com*, April 15, np.; Taub, E. A. 2008. Flat-Panel TV Prices Plummet. *www.nytimes.com*, December 2, np.; Wilson, S. 2008. Picture It. *Entrepreneur,* July: 43; *www.wikipedia.com*; Kane, Y.I. 2011. Vizio Extends Battle Plan. *Wall Street Journal,* January 3: B3; and Edwards, C. 2010. How Vizio Beat Sony in High-def TV. *Bloomberg Businessweek,* April 26: 51–52. www.keloland.com

features—doing it on the Internet and offering extraordinary customer service—have made Amazon a differentiated success.

There are several factors that make it more difficult for new ventures to be successful as differentiators. For one thing, the strategy is generally thought to be expensive to enact. Differentiation is often associated with strong brand identity, and establishing a brand is usually considered to be expensive because of the cost of advertising and promotion, paid endorsements, exceptional customer service, etc. Differentiation successes are sometimes built on superior innovation or use of technology. These are also factors where it may be challenging for young firms to excel relative to established competitors.

Nevertheless all of these areas—innovation, technology, customer service, distinctive branding—are also arenas where new ventures have sometimes made a name for themselves even though they must operate with limited resources and experience. To be successful, according to Garry Ridge, CEO of the WD-40 Company, "You need to have a great product, make the end user aware of it, and make it easy to buy."[38] It sounds simple, but it is a difficult challenge for new ventures with differentiation strategies.

Focus   Focus strategies are often associated with small businesses because there is a natural fit between the narrow scope of the strategy and the small size of the firm. A focus strategy may include elements of differentiation and overall cost leadership, as well as combinations of these approaches. But to be successful within a market niche, the key strategic requirement is to stay focused. Here's why:

Despite all the attention given to fast-growing new industries, most start-ups enter industries that are mature.[39] In mature industries, growth in demand tends to be slow and there are often many competitors. Therefore, if a start-up wants to get a piece of the action, it often has to take business away from an existing competitor. If a start-up enters a market with a broad or aggressive strategy, it is likely to evoke retaliation from a more powerful competitor. Young firms can often succeed best by finding a market niche where they can get a foothold and make small advances that erode the position of existing competitors.[40] From this position, they can build a name for themselves and grow.

Consider, for example, the "Miniature Editions" line of books launched by Running Press, a small Philadelphia publisher. The books are palm-sized minibooks positioned at bookstore cash registers as point-of-sale impulse items costing about $4.95. Beginning with just 10 titles in 1993, Running Press grew rapidly and within 10 years had sold over 20 million copies. Even though these books represent just a tiny fraction of total sales in the $23 billion publishing industry, they have been a mainstay for Running Press.[41] As the Running Press example indicates, many new ventures are successful even though their share of the market is quite small.

Combination Strategies

One of the best ways for young and small businesses to achieve success is by pursuing combination strategies. By combining the best features of low-cost, differentiation, and focus strategies, new ventures can often achieve something truly distinctive.

Entrepreneurial firms are often in a strong position to offer a combination strategy because they have the flexibility to approach situations uniquely. For example, holding down expenses can be difficult for big firms because each layer of bureaucracy adds to the cost of doing business across the boundaries of a large organization.[42]

A similar argument could be made about entrepreneurial firms that differentiate. Large firms often find it difficult to offer highly specialized products or superior customer services. Entrepreneurial firms, by contrast, can often create high-value products and services through their unique differentiating efforts. Strategy Spotlight 8.8 shows how two entrepreneurs found a recipt to sell a common product line to a niche market while both cutting costs and offering a high service level.

For nearly all new entrants, one of the major dangers is that a large firm with more resources will copy what they are doing. Well-established incumbents that observe the success of a new entrant's product or service will copy it and use their market power to overwhelm the smaller firm. The threat may be lessened for firms that use combination strategies. Because of the flexibility of entrepreneurial firms, they can often enact combination strategies in ways that the large firms cannot copy. This makes the new entrant's strategies much more sustainable.

Perhaps more threatening than large competitors are close competitors, because they have similar structural features that help them adjust quickly and be flexible in decision making. Here again, a carefully crafted and executed combination strategy may be the best way for an entrepreneurial firm to thrive in a competitive environment. Nevertheless, competition among rivals is a key determinant of new venture success. To address this, we turn next to the topic of competitive dynamics.

>LO8.5
How competitive actions, such as the entry of new competitors into a marketplace, may launch a cycle of actions and reactions among close competitors.

Competitive Dynamics

New entry into markets, whether by start-ups or by incumbent firms, nearly always threatens existing competitors. This is true in part because, except in very new markets, nearly

Diapers.com—Combining Focus, Low Cost, and Differentiation

Focusing on the needs of families with infants and toddlers, Marc Lore and Vinit Bharara turned a simple idea into a business worth $540 million in a matter of six years. Founded in January 2005, Diapers.com began by selling diapers out of a garage in Long Island, New York. Their business grew rapidly in geographic reach, products sold, and sales. But the firm's success relied on their ability to simultaneously focus on a particular market segment, offer a higher level of service, and maintain efficiency in operations. They now have a 30,000 square foot headquarters, over 500 employees, and over 600,000 square feet in warehouse space. In November 2010, at about the same time that they shipped their 500 millionth diaper, Diapers.com agreed to be acquired by Amazon.com for over a half billion dollars.

Diapers.com attracts customers by offering a high service level to busy parents who don't have the time to run out to Costco every time they need diapers and related baby care items. Over 70 percent of Diapers.com sales are to women, the majority of whom are in the 25–34 age range. Diapers.com sells 25,000 products, but they are high-use products for baby care, such as diapers, wipes, shampoo, and formula. In focusing on this limited range of products, Diapers.com is able to differentiate itself by offering a high level of service. Their website is simpler to navigate than broad Internet retailers. If customers need the help of knowledgeable customer service agents, Diapers.com has a staff of 85 agents to handle their inquiries. Meeting the needs of their customers, whom they refer to as Moms, is key. As co-founder Marc Lore commented, "The concept is just if Mom calls and there's an issue, do whatever is necessary to make her happy and really wow her." Diapers.com also delivers quickly, with nearly 75 percent of their shipments being overnight deliveries and free shipping for any order over $49. This has resulted in a loyal set of customers whose word-of-mouth advertising draws in new customers to the firm. Their focus allows the firm to be extremely efficient. Their advertising is focused in magazines targeted toward parents. Operationally, they have developed sophisticated algorithms to maintain the minimum inventory needed to insure they can fill customer orders 95 percent of the time and have a highly automated warehouse that relies on robots manufactured by Kiva Systems to quickly and efficiently fill orders. They also rely on a computer algorithm to pick out the smallest box possible for an order to minimize shipping costs. They also use different shipping firms to ship to different regions, finding the lowest cost firm for that area. By meeting the needs of a narrow set of customers with a high service level and efficiency-oriented processes and resources, Diapers.com has excelled in a competitive, low-margin business.

Sources: Fowler, G. A. & Byron, L. 2010. Corporate News: Amazon to Buy Diapers.com Site. *The Wall Street Journal*, November 8: B4; Urstadt, B. 2010. Diapers vs. Goliath: Can Two Guys from Jersey Outsell Amazon? *Bloomberg Businessweek*, October 11: 62–68. Birchall, J. 2010. Amazon Aims to Woo Women with Quidsi Acquisition. *Financial Times*, November 9: 23; and Tiku, N. 2009. The Way I Work: Marc Lore of Diapers.com. *Inc. com*, September 1: np.

every market need is already being met, either directly or indirectly, by existing firms. As a result, the competitive actions of a new entrant are very likely to provoke a competitive response from companies that feel threatened. This, in turn, is likely to evoke a reaction to the response. As a result, a competitive dynamic—action and response—begins among the firms competing for the same customers in a given marketplace.

Competitive dynamics—intense rivalry among similar competitors—has the potential to alter a company's strategy. New entrants may be forced to change their strategies or develop new ones to survive competitive challenges by incumbent rivals. New entry is among the most common reasons why a cycle of competitive actions and reactions gets started. It might also occur because of threatening actions among existing competitors, such as aggressive cost cutting. Thus, studying competitive dynamics helps explain why strategies evolve and reveals how, why, and when to respond to the actions of close competitors. Exhibit 8.7 identifies the factors that competitors need to consider when determining how to respond to a competitive act.

competitive dynamics intense rivalry, involving actions and responses, among similar competitors vying for the same customers in a marketplace.

Exhibit 8.7 **Model of Competitive Dynamics**

Sources: Adapted from Chen, M. J. 1996. Competitor Analysis and Interfirm Rivalry: Toward a Theoretical Integration. *Academy of Management Review,* 21(1): 100–134; Ketchen, D. J., Snow, C. C., & Hoover, V. L. 2004. Research on competitive dynamics: Recent Accomplishments and Future Challenges. *Journal of Management,* 30(6): 779–804; and Smith, K. G., Ferrier, W. J., & Grimm, C. M. 2001. King of the Hill: Dethroning the Industry Leader. *Academy of Management Executive,* 15(2): 59–70.

New Competitive Action

Entry into a market by a new competitor is a good starting point to begin describing the cycle of actions and responses characteristic of a competitive dynamic process.[43] However, new entry is only one type of competitive action. Price cutting, imitating successful products, or expanding production capacity are other examples of competitive acts that might provoke competitors to react.

Why do companies launch new competitive actions? There are several reasons:

- Improve market position
- Capitalize on growing demand
- Expand production capacity
- Provide an innovative new solution
- Obtain first mover advantages

Underlying all of these reasons is a desire to strengthen financial outcomes, capture some of the extraordinary profits that industry leaders enjoy, and grow the business. Some companies are also motivated to launch competitive challenges because they want to build their reputation for innovativeness or efficiency. For example, Southwest Airlines, once an upstart airline with only a few routes, has become phenomenally successful and an industry leader. For years it went virtually unchallenged. But Southwest's costs have crept up, and now start-up airlines such as JetBlue are challenging the industry leader with their own low-cost strategies.[44] This is indicative of the competitive dynamic cycle. As former Intel Chairman Andy Grove stated, "Business success contains the seeds of its own destruction. The more successful you are, the more people want a chunk of your business and then another chunk and then another until there is nothing left."[45]

When a company enters into a market for the first time, it is an attack on existing competitors. As indicated earlier in the chapter, any of the entry strategies can be used to take competitive action. But competitive attacks come from many sources besides new entrants. Some of the most intense competition is among incumbent rivals intent on gaining strategic advantages. "Winners in business play rough and don't apologize for it," according to Boston Consulting Group authors George Stalk, Jr. and Rob Lachenauer in

> **>LO8.6**
> The components of competitive dynamics analysis—new competitive action, threat analysis, motivation and capability to respond, types of competitive actions, and likelihood of competitive reaction.

new competitive action acts that might provoke competitors to react, such as new market entry, price cutting, imitating successful products, and expanding production capacity.

their book *Hardball: Are You Playing to Play or Playing to Win?*[46] Exhibit 8.8 outlines their five strategies.

The likelihood that a competitor will launch an attack depends on many factors.[47] In the remaining sections, we discuss factors such as competitor analysis, market conditions, types of strategic actions, and the resource endowments and capabilities companies need to take competitive action.

Threat Analysis

Prior to actually observing a competitive action, companies may need to become aware of potential competitive threats. That is, companies need to have a keen sense of who their closest competitors are and the kinds of competitive actions they might be planning.[48] This may require some environmental scanning and monitoring of the sort described in Chapter 2. Awareness of the threats posed by industry rivals allows a firm to understand what type of competitive response, if any, may be necessary.

For example, Netflix founder and CEO Reed Hastings has faced numerous competitive threats since launching the online movie rental company in 1997. According to Hastings, however, not all potential threats need to be taken seriously:

> We have to recognize that now there are tens and maybe hundreds of start-ups who think that they are going to eat Netflix's lunch. The challenge for a management team is to figure out which are real threats and which aren't. . . . It's conventional to say, "only the paranoid survive" but that's not true. The paranoid die because the paranoid take all threats as serious and get very distracted.
>
> There are markets that aren't going to get very big, and then there are markets that are going to get big, but they're not directly in our path. In the first camp we have small companies like Movielink—a well-run company but not an attractive model for consumers, sort of a $4-download to watch a movie. We correctly guessed when it launched four years ago that this was not a threat and didn't react to it.
>
> The other case I brought up is markets that are going to be very large markets, but we're just not the natural leader. Advertising supported online video, whether that's at CBS. com or You Tube—great market, kind of next door to us. But we don't do advertising-supported video, we do subscription, so it would be a huge competence expansion for us. And it's not a threat to movies.

Being aware of competitors and cognizant of whatever threats they might pose is the first step in assessing the level of competitive threat. Once a new competitive action becomes apparent, companies must determine how threatening it is to their business. Competitive dynamics are likely to be most intense among companies that are competing for the same customers or who have highly similar sets of resources.[49] Two factors are used to assess whether or not companies are close competitors:

- **Market commonality**—Whether or not competitors are vying for the same customers and how many markets they share in common. For example, aircraft manufacturers Boeing and Airbus have a high degree of market commonality because they make very similar products and have many buyers in common.
- **Resource similarity**—The degree to which rivals draw on the same types of resources to compete. For example, the home pages of Google and Yahoo! may look very different, but behind the scenes, they both rely on the talent pool of high-caliber software engineers to create the cutting-edge innovations that help them compete.

When any two firms have both a high degree of market commonality and highly similar resource bases, a stronger competitive threat is present. Such a threat, however, may not lead to competitive action. On the one hand, a market rival may be hesitant to attack a company that it shares a high degree of market commonality with because it could lead to

Exhibit 8.8 Five "Hardball" Strategies

Strategy	Description	Examples
Devastate rivals' profit sanctuaries	Not all business segments generate the same level of profits for a company. Through focused attacks on a rival's most profitable segments, a company can generate maximum leverage with relatively smaller-scale attacks. Recognize, however, that companies closely guard the information needed to determine just what their profit sanctuaries are.	In 2005, Walmart began offering low-priced extended warranties on home electronics after learning that its rivals such as Best Buy derived most of their profits from extended warranties.
Plagiarize with pride	Just because a close competitor comes up with an idea first does not mean it cannot be successfully imitated. Second movers, in fact, can see how customers respond, make improvements, and launch a better version without all the market development costs. Successful imitation is harder than it may appear and requires the imitating firm to keep its ego in check.	Blockbuster copied the online DVD rental strategy of its rival Netflix. Not only does Blockbuster continue to struggle even after this imitation, but also Netflix sued Blockbuster for patent violations.
Deceive the competition	A good gambit sends the competition off in the wrong direction. This may cause the rivals to miss strategic shifts, spend money pursuing dead ends, or slow their responses. Any of these outcomes support the deceiving firms' competitive advantage. Companies must be sure not to cross ethical lines during these actions.	Boeing spent several years touting its plans for a new high-speed airliner. After it became clear the customer valued efficiency over speed, Boeing quietly shifted its focus. When Boeing announced its new 7e7 (now 787) Dreamliner, its competitor, Airbus Industries, was surprised and caught without an adequate response, which helped the 787 set new sales records.
Unleash massive and overwhelming force	While many hardball strategies are subtle and indirect, this one is not. This is a full-frontal attack where a firm commits significant resources to a major campaign to weaken rivals' positions in certain markets. Firms must be sure they have the mass and stamina required to win before they declare war against a rival.	Southwest Airlines took on US Airways in Baltimore and drove US Airways' market share from over 50 percent to 10 percent. Southwest followed this up by flying to Philadelphia and Pittsburgh as well— additional key markets for US Airways.
Raise competitors' costs	If a company has superior insight into the complex cost and profit structure of the industry, it can compete in a way that steers its rivals into relatively higher cost/lower profit arenas. This strategy uses deception to make the rivals think they are winning, when in fact they are not. Again, companies using this strategy must be confident that they understand the industry better than their rivals.	Ecolab, a company that sells cleaning supplies to businesses, encouraged a leading competitor, Diversity, to adopt a strategy to go after the low-volume, high-margin customers. What Ecolab knew that Diversity didn't is that the high servicing costs involved with this segment make the segment unprofitable—a situation Ecolab assured by bidding high enough to lose the contracts to Diversity but low enough to ensure the business lost money for Diversity.

Sources: Berner, R. 2005. Watch Out, Best Buy and Circuit City. *BusinessWeek,* November 10; Halkias, M. 2006. Blockbuster Strikes Back at Netflix Suit. *Dallas Morning News,* June 14; McCartney, S. 2007. Southwest Makes Inroads at Hubs. *The Wall Street Journal,* May 1, D3; Stalk, G. Jr. 2006. Curveball Strategies to Fool the Competition. *Harvard Business Review,* 84(9): 114–121; and Stalk, Jr., G. & Lachenauer, R. 2004. *Hardball: Are You Playing to Play or Playing to Win?* Cambridge, MA: Harvard Business School Press. Reprinted by permission of Harvard Business School Press from G. Stalk, Jr. and R. Lachenauer. Copyright 2004 by the Harvard Business School Publishing Corporation; all rights reserved.

an intense battle. On the other hand, once attacked, rivals with high market commonality will be much more motivated to launch a competitive response. This is especially true in cases where the shared market is an important part of a company's overall business.

How strong a response an attacked rival can mount will be determined by their strategic resource endowments. In general, the same set of conditions holds true with regard to resource similarity. Companies that have highly similar resource bases will be hesitant to launch an initial attack but pose a serious threat if required to mount a competitive response.[50] Greater strategic resources increase a firm's capability to respond.

Motivation and Capability to Respond

Once attacked, competitors are faced with deciding how to respond. Before deciding, however, they need to evaluate not only how they will respond, but also their reasons for responding and their capability to respond. Companies need to be clear about what problems a competitive response is expected to address and what types of problems it might create.[51] There are several factors to consider.

First, how serious is the impact of the competitive attack to which they are responding? For example, a large company with a strong reputation that is challenged by a small or unknown company may elect to simply keep an eye on the new competitor rather than quickly react or overreact. Part of the story of online retailer Amazon's early success is attributed to Barnes & Noble's overreaction to Amazon's claim that it was "earth's biggest bookstore." Because Barnes & Noble was already using the phrase "world's largest bookstore," it sued Amazon, but lost. The confrontation made it to the front pages of *The Wall Street Journal* and Amazon was on its way to becoming a household name.[52]

Companies planning to respond to a competitive challenge must also understand their motivation for responding. What is the intent of the competitive response? Is it merely to blunt the attack of the competitor or is it an opportunity to enhance its competitive position? Sometimes the most a company can hope for is to minimize the damage caused by a competitive action.

A company that seeks to improve its competitive advantage may be motivated to launch an attack rather than merely respond to one. Strategy Spotlight 8.9 highlights how *The Wall Street Journal* saw an opportunity to improve its position by attaching a weakened *New York Times*. A company must also assess its capability to respond. What strategic resources can be deployed to fend off a competitive attack? Does the company have an array of internal strengths it can draw on, or is it operating from a position of weakness?

Consider, the role of firm age and size in calculating a company's ability to respond. Most entrepreneurial new ventures start out small. The smaller size makes them more nimble compared to large firms so they can respond quickly to competitive attacks. Because they are not well-known, start-ups also have the advantage of the element of surprise in how and when they attack. Innovative uses of technology, for example, allow small firms to deploy resources in unique ways.

Because they are young, however, start-ups may not have the financial resources needed to follow through with a competitive response.[53] In contrast, older and larger firms may have more resources and a repertoire of competitive techniques they can use in a counterattack. Large firms, however, tend to be slower to respond. Older firms tend to be predictable in their responses because they often lose touch with the competitive environment and rely on strategies and actions that have worked in the past.

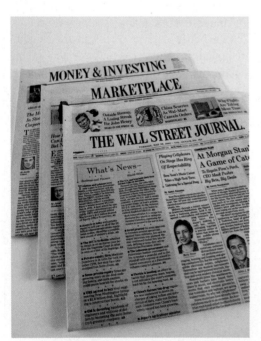

● *The Wall Street Journal* and *The New York Times* are engaged in an intense rivalry for market share.

The Wall Street Journal Challenges *The New York Times*

The newspaper business is an increasingly tough market. Circulation and advertising rates are dropping as news consumers move from traditional newspaper providers to online news services. In this difficult environment, newspapers both have increased motivation to take business from their remaining traditional competitors and reduced capability to respond to competitive attacks. These competing factors have resulted in an interesting competitive action in New York City. *The Wall Street Journal* (*WSJ*), a newspaper that has emphasized business and investing news since its inception in 1889, is taking on *The New York Times* (*Times*), a traditional city newspaper. The *WSJ* launched its Greater New York Edition in April 2010 to increase its base of affluent subscribers and female readers in the New York region, the core readers of the *Times*.

Why the *Times*, and why now? The *WSJ* has high motivation to act now. News Corp. purchased the *WSJ* in 2007 and brought with it an aggressive attitude that called for change at the *WSJ*. Rupert Murdoch, the chairman of News Corp., specifically stated at the time that he wanted to see the *WSJ* compete more directly with the *Times*. They are also motivated to act since the customers they are striving to attract make the *WSJ* more attractive to luxury product and service advertisers in the New York

area. Their new edition has signed on luxury advertisers Saks Fifth Avenue, Bloomingdales, Cathay Pacific Airlines, Broadway's *Jersey Boys* musical, and the American Ballet Theatre. They also have the capability to act because the *WSJ* is one of the few traditional news providers with a growing number of readers. They also have the backing of News Corp., a major global media firm. Thus, they have the financial resources necessary to launch and sustain a competitive action against the *Times*.

But it is a different situation at the *Times*. While motivated to respond to the *WSJ*'s attack, they have limited resources to mount a major competitive response. They have experienced a significant decline in subscriptions, with the number of subscribers falling 8.5 percent in March 2010 compared to one year earlier. This has reduced the advertising rates they are able to charge. Also, the *Times* has limited cash resources. They are so strapped for cash that they were forced to borrow $250 million from Mexican industrialist Carlos Slim in 2009 at a 14 percent interest rate. When the *WSJ* launched their Greater New York Edition, the *Times* only had $36.5 million in cash on their balance sheet—not much of a war chest to take on News Corp. For Rupert Murdoch, the *Times*'s struggles are a signal to attack and an opportunity to cripple and potentially destroy *The New York Times*. As media investment expert Richard Dorfman stated, "This could be a money-losing venture for the *Journal*, but a potential big winner for Rupert if he's able to throw the *Times* over the edge of the abyss."

Other local papers should be wary. There are reports that, if successful with their Greater New York Edition, *The Wall Street Journal* will consider launching similar ventures in other major markets, including San Francisco, Los Angeles, and Washington, D.C.

Sources: Anonymous. 2010. Is the *Times* Ready for a Newspaper War? *Bloomberg Businessweek*, April 26: 30–31; Bensinger, G. 2010. *Wall Street Journal* Circulation Gains as New Edition Debuts. *Bloomberg Businessweek*, April 26: np; Anonymous. 2010. *Wall Street Journal* Considers Other Local Markets if NY Edition a Success. *Mediabuyerplanner.com*, April 18: np; and Sreenivasan, S. 2010. The *Wall Street Journal*'s Local Edition Launches. *Dnainfo.com*, April 26: np.

Other resources may also play a role in whether a company is equipped to retaliate. For example, one avenue of counterattack may be launching product enhancements or new product/service innovations. For that approach to be successful, it requires a company to have both the intellectual capital to put forward viable innovations and the teamwork skills to prepare a new product or service and get it to market. Resources such as cross-functional teams and the social capital that makes teamwork production effective and efficient represent the type of human capital resources that enhance a company's capability to respond.

Types of Competitive Actions

Once an organization determines whether it is willing and able to launch a competitive action, it must determine what type of action is appropriate. The actions taken will be determined by both its resource capabilities and its motivation for responding. There are also marketplace considerations. What types of actions are likely to be most effective given a company's internal strengths and weaknesses as well as market conditions?

AMD and Intel: The Multiple Dimensions of Competitive Dynamics

Few business battles are as intense or as intensely reported as the one between chipmakers Intel and Advanced Micro Devices (AMD). These two firms have fought an intense competitive battle for over two decades. They started out on a much different footing. They were both founded in the late 1960s in Silicon Valley and were partners in their early years. But their history changed in 1986 after Intel cancelled a licensing agreement with AMD to manufacture microprocessors and refused to turn over technical details. Since that time, Intel has dominated the microprocessor market with approximately 80 percent market share but has regularly faced competitive initiatives from AMD and has as regularly taken competitive initiatives against AMD. As Intel Executive Vice President Sean Maloney stated, "We intend to energetically compete for every single microprocessor opportunity."

Their battle points out how highly competitive firms can take their competitive attacks to multiple battlefields. They have fought product design battles. Time and time again, they have aimed to pioneer new generations of chips. They fought over who would launch the first 64-bit processors. They competed in introducing multiple-core chips. They competed in producing low-energy chips for laptops and notebooks. Currently, they are racing to launch chips that integrate graphics chip capabilities into the microprocessor. They have fought to build relationships with customers. According to governmental regulators, Intel locked in Dell and other PC manufacturers as exclusive customers by offering them rebates to use only Intel microprocessors. AMD fought back and won business supplying chips to Dell in 2006 and for Lenovo notebooks in 2009. They have developed aggressive marketing campaigns to promote their products. They have acquired other firms to pull in new technology to gain an advantage. For example, AMD bought ATI Technologies to gain access to graphics chip technology that they have integrated with the CPU in their latest generation of chips, the Fusion. They have fought legal battles. Both firms have sued each other over the right to technologies. Intel finally settled a multiyear legal battle with AMD for $1.25 billion in 2009.

This competitive battle shows how a long-standing competitive battle between firms can include a range of tactical and strategic actions as firms act to improve their own competitive position and unsettle the competitive position of their rival. This battle also demonstrates the potential benefits of high industry rivalry for consumers. The rivalry between AMD and Intel has led to tremendous improvements in microprocessor capabilities with declining prices over time. And there is no end in sight for these two pitched rivals.

Sources: Fortt, J. 2010. Intel vs. AMD Gets Interesting Again. *CNNmoney.com,* May 12: np; Clark, D. 2010. AMD Starts Shipping New Breed of Chips. *The Wall Street Journal,* November 10: B7; Vance, A. 2010. Dell's Trouble Kicking the Intel Habit. *New York Times,* July 23; Parloff, R. 2010. What the Dell Settlement Means for Intel. *Fortune.com,* July 27: np; and *www.wikipedia.org.*

---

strategic actions major commitments of distinctive and specific resources to strategic initiatives.

tactical actions refinements or extensions of strategies usually involving minor resource commitments.

Two broadly defined types of competitive action include strategic actions and tactical actions. **Strategic actions** represent major commitments of distinctive and specific resources. Examples include launching a breakthrough innovation, building a new production facility, or merging with another company. Such actions require significant planning and resources and, once initiated, are difficult to reverse.

Tactical actions include refinements or extensions of strategies. Examples of tactical actions include cutting prices, improving gaps in service, or strengthening marketing efforts. Such actions typically draw on general resources and can be implemented quickly. Exhibit 8.9 identifies several types of strategic and tactical competitive actions, and Strategy Spotlight 8.10 shows the range of actions that can occur in a rivalrous relationship.

Some competitive actions take the form of frontal assaults, that is, actions aimed directly at taking business from another company or capitalizing on industry weaknesses. This can be especially effective when firms use a low-cost strategy. The airline industry provides a good example of this head-on approach. When Southwest Airlines began its no-frills, no-meals, strategy in the late-1960s, it represented a direct assault on the major carriers of the day. In Europe, Ryanair has similarly directly challenged the traditional carriers with an overall cost leadership strategy.

Exhibit 8.9 Strategic and Tactical Competitive Actions

	Actions	Examples
Strategic Actions	• Entering new markets	• Make geographical expansions • Expand into neglected markets • Target rivals' markets • Target new demographics
	• New product introductions	• Imitate rivals' products • Address gaps in quality • Leverage new technologies • Leverage brand name with related products • Protect innovation with patents
	• Changing production capacity	• Create overcapacity • Tie up raw materials sources • Tie up preferred suppliers and distributors • Stimulate demand by limiting capacity
	• Mergers/Alliances	• Acquire/partner with competitors to reduce competition • Tie up key suppliers through alliances • Obtain new technology/intellectual property • Facilitate new market entry
Tactical Actions	• Price cutting (or increases)	• Maintain low price dominance • Offer discounts and rebates • Offer incentives (e.g., frequent flyer miles) • Enhance offering to move upscale
	• Product/service enhancements	• Address gaps in service • Expand warranties • Make incremetal product improvements
	• Increased marketing efforts	• Use guerilla marketing • Conduct selective attacks • Change product packaging • Use new marketing channels
	• New distribution channels	• Access suppliers directly • Access customers directly • Develop multiple points of contact with customers • Expand Internet presence

Sources: Chen, M. J. & Hambrick, D. 1995. Speed, Stealth, and Selective Attack: How Small Firms Differ from Large Firms in Competitive Behavior. *Academy of Management Journal,* 38: 453–482; Davies, M. 1992. Sales Promotions as a Competitive Strategy. *Management Decision,* 30(7): 5–10; Ferrier, W., Smith, K., & Grimm, C. 1999. The Role of Competitive Action in Market Share Erosion and Industry Dethronement: A Study of Industry Leaders and Challengers. *Academy of Management Journal,* 42(4): 372–388; and Garda, R. A. 1991. Use Tactical Pricing to Uncover Hidden Profits. *Journal of Business Strategy,* 12(5): 17–23.

Guerilla offensives and selective attacks provide an alternative for firms with fewer resources.[54] These draw attention to products or services by creating buzz or generating enough shock value to get some free publicity. TOMS shoes has found a way to generate interest in its products without a large advertising budget to match Nike. Their policy of donating one pair of shoes to those in need for every pair of shoes purchased by customers has generated a lot of buzz on the internet.[55] Over 700,000 people have given a "like" rating on TOMS's Facebook page.

● Intel and AMD have had a fierce rivalry over the years.

The policy has a real impact as well, with over 1,000,000 shoes donated as of September 2010.[56]

Some companies limit their competitive response to defensive actions. Such actions rarely improve a company's competitive advantage, but a credible defensive action can lower the risk of being attacked and deter new entry. This may be especially effective during periods such as an industry shake-up, when pricing levels or future demand for a product line become highly uncertain. At such times, tactics such as lowering prices on products that are easily duplicated, buying up the available supply of goods or raw materials, or negotiating exclusive agreements with buyers and/or suppliers can insulate a company from a more serious attack.

Several of the factors discussed earlier in the chapter, such as types of entry strategies and the use of cost leadership versus differentiation strategies, can guide the decision about what types of competitive actions to take. Before launching a given strategy, however, assessing the likely response of competitors is a vital step.[57]

Likelihood of Competitive Reaction

The final step before initiating a competitive response is to evaluate what a competitor's reaction is likely to be. The logic of competitive dynamics suggests that once competitive actions are initiated, it is likely they will be met with competitive responses.[58] The last step before mounting an attack is to evaluate how competitors are likely to respond. Evaluating potential competitive reactions helps companies plan for future counterattacks. It may also lead to a decision to hold off—that is, not to take any competitive action at all because of the possibility that a misguided or poorly planned response will generate a devastating competitive reaction.

How a competitor is likely to respond will depend on three factors: market dependence, competitor's resources, and the reputation of the firm that initiates the action (actor's reputation). The implications of each of these is described briefly in the following sections.

market dependence degree of concentration of a firm's business in a particular industry.

Market Dependence   If a company has a high concentration of its business in a particular industry, it has more at stake because it must depend on that industry's market for its sales. Single-industry businesses or those where one industry dominates are more likely to mount a competitive response. Young and small firms with a high degree of market dependence may be limited in how they respond due to resource constraints. JetBlue, itself an aggressive competitor, is unable to match some of the perks its bigger rivals can offer, such as first-class seats or international travel benefits.

Competitor's Resources   Previously, we examined the internal resource endowments that a company must evaluate when assessing its capability to respond. Here, it is the competitor's resources that need to be considered. For example, a small firm may be unable to mount a serious attack due to lack of resources. Also, as we saw in Strategy Spotlight 8.9, a large but poorly performing firm may lack the resources to respond to an attack. As a result, it is more likely to react to tactical actions such as incentive pricing or enhanced service offerings because they are less costly to attack than large-scale strategic actions. In contrast, a firm with financial "deep pockets" may be able to mount and sustain a costly counterattack.

Actor's Reputation   Whether a company should respond to a competitive challenge will also depend on who launched the attack against it. Compared to relatively smaller firms with less market power, competitors are more likely to respond to competitive moves by market leaders. Another consideration is how successful prior attacks have been. For example, price-cutting by the big automakers usually has the desired result—increased sales to price-sensitive buyers—at least in the short run. Given that history, when GM offers discounts or incentives, rivals Ford and Chrysler cannot afford to ignore the challenge and quickly follow suit.

Choosing Not to React: Forbearance and Co-opetition

The above discussion suggests that there may be many circumstances in which the best reaction is no reaction at all. This is known as **forbearance**—refraining from reacting at all as well as holding back from initiating an attack. The decision of whether a firm should respond or show forbearance is not always clear. In Strategy Spotlight 8.11, we see the NFL and the UFL facing such a decision.

Related to forbearance is the concept of **co-opetition.** This is a term that was coined by network software company Novell's founder and former CEO Raymond Noorda to suggest that companies often benefit most from a combination of competing and cooperating.[59] Close competitors that differentiate themselves in the eyes of consumers may work together behind the scenes to achieve industrywide efficiencies.[60] For example, breweries in Sweden cooperate in recycling used bottles but still compete for customers on the basis of taste and variety. As long as the benefits of cooperating are enjoyed by all participants in a co-opetition system, the practice can aid companies in avoiding intense and damaging competition.[61]

Despite the potential benefits of co-opetition, companies need to guard against cooperating to such a great extent that their actions are perceived as collusion, a practice that has legal ramifications in the United States. Recently, Dell and other PC manufacturers have faced scrutiny due to their possible collusion with Intel.

Once a company has evaluated a competitor's likelihood of responding to a competitive challenge, it can decide what type of action is most appropriate. Competitive actions can take many forms: the entry of a start-up into a market for the first time, an attack by a lower-ranked incumbent on an industry leader, or the launch of a breakthrough innovation that disrupts the industry structure. Such actions forever change the competitive dynamics of a marketplace. Thus, the cycle of actions and reactions that occur in business every day is a vital aspect of entrepreneurial strategy that leads to continual new value creation and the ongoing advancement of economic well-being.

> **forbearance** a firm's choice of not reacting to a rival's new competitive action.

> **co-opetition** a firm's strategy of both cooperating and competing with rival firms.

Reflecting on Career Implications . . .

- *Opportunity Recognition:* What ideas for new business activities are actively discussed in your work environment? Could you apply the four characteristics of an opportunity to determine whether they are viable opportunities?
- *Entrepreneurial New Entry:* Are there opportunities to launch new products or services that might add value to the organization? What are the best ways for you to bring these opportunities to the attention of key managers? Or, might this provide an opportunity for you to launch your own entrepreneurial venture?
- *Entrepreneurial Strategy:* Does your organization face competition from new ventures? If so, how are those young firms competing: Low cost? Differentiation? Focus? What could you do to help your company to address those competitive challenges?
- *Competitive Dynamics:* Is your organization "on the offense" with its close competitors or "playing defense"? What types of strategic and/or tactical actions have been taken by your close rivals recently to gain competitive advantages?

The UFL and the NFL: Cooperate or Compete?

If we look at the success and failure of professional football leagues from the past, the future for the United Football League (UFL) would not appear to be promising. Since the merger of the NFL with the AFL in the 1960s, several leagues trying to build a position in the American football market have failed. In the 1970s, it was the World Football League that rose and fell in a few years. In the 1980s, it was the United States Football league that followed the same pattern. In the 1990s, the Canadian Football League tried expanding south of the border, only to quickly retreat back north. The XFL lasted only a single year in 2001. Only the unique Arena Football League has lasted more than a few years, but its history has still been bumpy. The league went through bankruptcy in 2008 only to return in 2010.

The UFL is a new upstart football league trying to carve out a position in the professional football market. Unlike the Arena Football League, the UFL is playing a version of football that is almost identical to the NFL and plays during the traditional fall football season. The league began play in 2009 with four teams, expanded to five teams in 2010, and will play with either six or eight teams in 2011.

However, it is unclear at this point to what degree the UFL will compete with the NFL, and it is also unclear whether the NFL will act in a way to push the UFL out of the market or show forbearance and let them stay in the game. The UFL appears to be taking actions to avoid a direct confrontation with the NFL. They have placed their franchises in cities, such as Las Vegas, Omaha, and Orlando, that

currently do not have NFL franchises. They also have not tried to compete with the NFL for players. They have made no effort to sign active NFL players. Instead, their rosters are a combination of former NFL players, such as JaMarcus Russell, hoping to revive their NFL careers and young players hoping to make an impression and move up to the NFL. However, the league appears reluctant to position themselves simply as a minor or developmental league for the NFL. They require the NFL to pay a $150,000 transfer fee to allow a UFL player to sign with an NFL team, limiting the willingness of NFL teams to sign UFL players. Also, they are looking to expand into markets that the NFL also sees as desirable. The UFL has announced an expansion into the Los Angeles market in either 2011 or 2012, but the NFL is working with potential owners interested in moving an NFL franchise into the LA market as well. The intentions of the NFL are also unclear. The NFL has not taken any direct actions against the UFL. But the NFL has also not pursued a cooperative relationship with the upstart league. According to ESPN, the UFL offered the NFL the opportunity to buy part of the league and set up consistent rules for players to move from one league to the other, but the NFL did not agree to make the investment. It may be that the NFL is focused on their unsettled labor contract with the players' union and, as a result, doesn't have the motivation to act either cooperatively or competitively with the UFL at this point in time.

Given the history of prior football leagues, the ability of the UFL to find a position where they don't directly compete with the NFL for ticket buyers, players, or TV placement would appear to be key to their viability. Thus, figuring out how to appear similar enough to the NFL to attract fans while also different enough to not trigger a competitive reaction by the NFL should be a primary factor driving the UFL's actions.

Sources: Mortensen, C. 2010. UFL Puts 30 Percent Offer on NFL's Table. *ESPN.com*, March 19: np; Cohan, W. D. 2010. Football's New Game in Town. *Fortune*, October 18: 111–112; and *www.wikipedia.org*.

Summary

New ventures and entrepreneurial firms that capitalize on marketplace opportunities make an important contribution to the U.S. economy. They are leaders in terms of implementing new technologies and introducing innovative products and services. Yet entrepreneurial firms face unique challenges if they are going to survive and grow.

To successfully launch new ventures or implement new technologies, three factors must be present: an entrepreneurial opportunity, the resources to pursue the opportunity, and an entrepreneur or entrepreneurial team willing and able to undertake the venture. Firms must develop a strong ability to recognize viable opportunities.

Opportunity recognition is a process of determining which venture ideas are, in fact, promising business opportunities.

In addition to strong opportunities, entrepreneurial firms need resources and entrepreneurial leadership to thrive. The resources that start-ups need include financial resources as well as human and social capital. Many firms also benefit from government programs that support new venture development and growth. New ventures thrive best when they are led by founders or owners who have vision, drive and dedication, and a commitment to excellence.

Once the necessary opportunities, resources, and entrepreneur skills are in place, new ventures still face numerous strategic challenges. Decisions about the strategic positioning of new entrants can benefit from conducting strategic analyses and evaluating the requirements of niche markets. Entry strategies used by new ventures take several forms, including pioneering new entry, imitative new entry, and adaptive new entry. Entrepreneurial firms can benefit from using overall low cost, differentiation, and focus strategies although each of these approaches has pitfalls that are unique to young and small firms. Entrepreneurial firms are also in a strong position to benefit from combination strategies.

The entry of a new company into a competitive arena is like a competitive attack on incumbents in that arena. Such actions often provoke a competitive response, which may, in turn, trigger a reaction to the response. As a result, a competitive dynamic—action and response—begins among close competitors. In deciding whether to attack or counterattack, companies must analyze the seriousness of the competitive threat, their ability to mount a competitive response, and the type of action—strategic or tactical—that the situation requires. At times, competitors find it is better not to respond at all or to find avenues to cooperate with, rather than challenge, close competitors.

Summary Review Questions

1. Explain how the combination of opportunities, resources, and entrepreneurs helps determine the character and strategic direction of an entrepreneurial firm.
2. What is the difference between discovery and evaluation in the process of opportunity recognition? Give an example of each.
3. Describe the three characteristics of entrepreneurial leadership: vision, dedication and drive, and commitment to excellence.

4. Briefly describe the three types of entrepreneurial entry strategies: pioneering, imitative, and adaptive.
5. Explain why entrepreneurial firms are often in a strong position to use combination strategies.
6. What does the term *competitive dynamics* mean?
7. Explain the difference between strategic actions and tactical actions and provide examples of each.

Key Terms

entrepreneurship, 281	competitive dynamics, 300
opportunity recognition, 284	new competitive action, 301
angel investors, 287	threat analysis, 302
venture capitalists, 289	market commonality, 302
entrepreneurial leadership, 290	resource similarity, 302
entrepreneurial strategy, 292	strategic actions, 306
pioneering new entry, 293	tactical actions, 306
	market dependence, 308
imitative new entry, 293	forbearance, 309
adaptive new entry, 295	co-opetition, 309

Applications Questions & Answers

1. E-Loan and Lending Tree are two entrepreneurial firms that offer lending services over the Internet. Evaluate the features of these two companies and, for each company:
   a. Evaluate their characteristics and assess the extent to which they are comparable in terms of market commonality and resource similarity.
   b. Based on your analysis, what strategic and/or tactical actions might these companies take to improve their competitive position? Could E-Loan and Lending Tree improve their performance more through co-opetition rather than competition? Explain your rationale.
2. Using the Internet, research the Small Business Administration's website (*www.sba.gov*). What different types of financing are available to small firms? Besides financing, what other programs are available to support the growth and development of small businesses?
3. Think of an entrepreneurial firm that has been successfully launched in the last 10 years. What kind of entry strategy did it use—pioneering, imitative, or adaptive? Since the firm's initial entry, how has

Company	Market Commonality	Resource Similarity
E-Loan		
Lending Tree		

Company	Strategic Actions	Tectical Actions
E-Loan		
Lending Tree		

it used or combined overall low-cost, differentiation and/or focus strategies?

4. Select an entrepreneurial firm you are familiar with in your local community. Research the company and discuss how it has positioned itself relative to its close competitors. Does it have a unique strategic advantage? Disadvantage? Explain.

Ethics Questions

1. Imitation strategies are based on the idea of copying another firm's idea and using it for your own purposes. Is this unethical or simply a smart business practice? Discuss the ethical implications of this practice (if any).

2. Intense competition such as price wars are an accepted practice in the United States, but cooperation between companies has legal ramifications because of antitrust laws. Should price wars that drive small businesses or new entrants out of business be illegal? What ethical considerations are raised (if any)?

References

1. Anonymous. 2006. 2006 Fastest-growing franchise rankings. *Entrepreneur.* http://entrepreneur.com, October 2010: np; Anonymous, 2007. Rising stars. *Entrepreneur.* http://entrepreneur.com, October 2010: np; Edersheim Kalb, P. 2009 Cranky consumer: Hiring middlemen to sell stuff on eBay. *Wall Street Journal,* January 29: D2; Ohngren, K.

2010. Kaboom! A look back at the wacky franchise ideas that exploded (and imploded) in an instant. Meet you at the eBay store. *Entrepreneur,* January 38(1): 120–124; and Wilson, S. 2006. Hotter than hot. *Entrepreneur,* June 34(6): 72–81; April 35(4): 108–111. We thank Ciprian Stan for his valued contribution.

2. Small Business Administration. 2004. *The small business economy* Washington, D.C.: U.S. Government Printing Office.

3. Timmons, J. A. & Spinelli, S. 2004. *New venture creation* (6th ed.). New York: McGraw-Hill/Irwin; and Bygrave, W. D. 1997. The entrepreneurial process. In W. D. Bygrave

(Ed.), *The portable MBA in entrepreneurship,* 2nd ed. New York: Wiley.

4. Fromartz, S. 1998. How to get your first great idea. *Inc. Magazine,* April 1: 91–94; and, Vesper, K. H. 1990. *New venture strategies,* 2nd ed. Englewood Cliffs, NJ: Prentice-Hall.

5. For an interesting perspective on the nature of the opportunity recognition process, see Baron, R. A. 2006. Opportunity recognition as pattern recognition: How entrepreneurs "connect the dots" to identify new business opportunities. *Academy of Management Perspectives,* February: 104–119.

6. Gaglio, C. M. 1997. Opportunity identification: Review, critique and suggested research directions. In J. A. Katz, ed. *Advances in entrepreneurship, firm emergence and growth,* vol. 3. Greenwich, CT: JAI Press: 139–202; Lumpkin, G. T., Hills, G. E., & Shrader, R. C. 2004. Opportunity recognition. In Harold L. Welsch, (Ed.), *Entrepreneurship: The road ahead,* pp. 73–90. London: Routledge; and Long, W. & McMullan, W. E. 1984. Mapping the new venture opportunity identification process. *Frontiers of entrepreneurship research, 1984.* Wellesley, MA: Babson College: 567–90.

7. For an interesting discussion of different aspects of opportunity discovery, see Shepherd, D. A. & De Tienne, D. R. 2005. Prior knowledge, potential financial reward, and opportunity identification. *Entrepreneurship theory & practice,* 29(1): 91–112; and Gaglio, C. M. 2004. The role of mental simulations and counterfactual thinking in the opportunity identification process. *Entrepreneurship theory & practice,* 28(6): 533–552.

8. Stewart, T. A. 2002. How to think with your gut. *Business 2.0,* November: 99–104.

9. For more on the opportunity recognition process, see Smith, B. R., Matthews, C. H., & Schenkel, M. T. 2009. Differences in entrepreneurial opportunities: The role of tacitness and codification in opportunity identification. *Journal of Small Business Management,* 47(1): 38–57.

10. Timmons, J. A. 1997. Opportunity recognition. In W. D. Bygrave, ed.

The portable MBA in entrepreneurship, 2nd ed. New York: John Wiley: 26–54.

11. Social networking is also proving to be an increasingly important type of entrepreneurial resource. For an interesting discussion, see Aldrich, H. E. & Kim, P. H. 2007. Small worlds, infinite possibilities? How social networks affect entrepreneurial team formation and search. *Strategic Entrepreneurship Journal,* 1(1): 147–166.

12. Bhide, A. V. 2000. *The origin and evolution of new businesses.* New York: Oxford University Press.

13. Small Business 2001: Where are we now? 2001. *Inc. Magazine,* May 29: 18–19; and Zacharakis, A. L., Bygrave, W. D., & Shepherd, D. A. 2000. *Global entrepreneurship monitor—National entrepreneurship assessment: United States of America 2000 Executive Report.* Kansas City, MO: Kauffman Center for Entrepreneurial Leadership.

14. Cooper, S. 2003. Cash cows. *Entrepreneur,* June: 36.

15. Seglin, J. L. 1998. What angels want. *Inc. Magazine,* 20(7): 43–44.

16. Torres, N. L. 2002. Playing an angel. *Entrepreneur,* May: 130–138.

17. For an interesting discussion of how venture capital practices vary across different sectors of the economy, see Gaba, V. & Meyer, A. D. 2008. Crossing the organizational species barrier: How venture capital practices infiltrated the information technology sector. *Academy of Management Journal,* 51(5): 391–412.

18. For more on how different forms of organizing entrepreneurial firms as well as different stages of new firm growth and development affect financing, see Cassar, G. 2004. The financing of business start-ups. *Journal of Business Venturing,* 19(2): 261–283.

19. Kroll, M., Walters, B., & Wright, P. 2010. The impact of insider control and environment on post-IPO performance. *Academy of Management Journal,* 53: 693–725.

20. Eisenhardt, K. M. & Schoonhoven, C. B. 1990. Organizational growth: Linking founding team, strategy,

environment, and growth among U.S. semiconductor ventures, 1978–1988. *Administrative Science Quarterly,* 35: 504–529.

21. Dubini, P. & Aldrich, H. 1991. Personal and extended networks are central to the entrepreneurship process. *Journal of Business Venturing,* 6(5): 305–333.

22. For more on the role of social contacts in helping young firms build legitimacy, see Chrisman, J. J. & McMullan, W. E. 2004. Outside assistance as a knowledge resource for new venture survival. *Journal of Small Business Management,* 42(3): 229–244.

23. Vogel, C. 2000. Janina Pawlowski. *Working woman,* June: 70.

24. For a recent perspective on entrepreneurship and strategic alliances, see Rothaermel, F. T. & Deeds, D. L. 2006. Alliance types, alliance experience and alliance management capability in high-technology ventures. *Journal of Business Venturing,* 21(4): 429–460; and Lu, J. W. & Beamish, P. W. 2006. Partnering strategies and performance of SMEs' international joint ventures. *Journal of Business Venturing,* 21(4): 461–486.

25. For more on the role of alliances in creating competitive advantages, see Wiklund, J. & Shepherd, D. A. 2009. The effectiveness of alliances and acquisitions: The role of resource combination activities. *Entrepreneurship Theory & Practice,* 33(1): 193–212.

26. For more information, go to the Small Business Administration website at *www.sba.gov.*

27. Simsek, Z., Heavey, C., & Veiga, J. 2009. The Impact of CEO core self-evaluations on entrepreneurial orientation. *Strategic Management Journal,* 31: 110–119.

28. For an interesting study of the role of passion in entrepreneurial success, see Chen, X-P., Yao, X., & Kotha, S. 2009 Entrepreneur passion and preparedness in business plan presentations: A persuasion analysis of venture capitalists' funding decisions. *Academy of Management Journal,* 52(1): 101–120.

29. Collins, J. 2001. *Good to great.* New York: HarperCollins.

30. The idea of entry wedges was discussed by Vesper, K. 1990. *New venture*

strategies (2nd ed.). Englewood Cliffs, NJ: Prentice-Hall; and Drucker, P. F. 1985. *Innovation and entrepreneurship.* New York: HarperBusiness.

31. See Dowell, G. & Swaminathan, A. 2006. Entry timing, exploration, and firm survival in the early U.S. bicycle industry. *Strategic Management Journal,* 27: 1159–1182, for a recent study of the timing of entrepreneurial new entry.

32. Dunlap-Hinkler, D., Kotabe, M., & Mudambi, R. 2010. A story of breakthrough vs. incremental innovation: Corporate entrepreneurship in the global pharmaceutical industry. *Strategic Entrepreneurship Journal,* 4: 106–127.

33. Maiello, M. 2002. They almost changed the world. *Forbes,* December 22: 217–220.

34. Wilson, R. 2010. 7 electric cars you'll be able to buy very soon. *The Huffington Post,* November 17: np.

35. Williams, G. 2002. Looks like rain. *Entrepreneur,* September: 104–111.

36. Pedroza, G. M. 2002. Tech tutors. *Entrepreneur,* September: 120.

37. Kim, W. C., and Mauborgne, R. 2004. Blue ocean strategy. *Harvard Business Review,* October: 76–84; and *www.cirquedusoleil.com.*

38. Romanelli, E. 1989. Environments and strategies of organization start-up: Effects on early survival. *Administrative Science Quarterly,* 34(3): 369–87.

39. Wallace, B. 2000. Brothers. *Philadelphia Magazine,* April: 66–75.

40. Buchanan, L. 2003. The innovation factor: A field guide to innovation. *Forbes,* April 21, *www.forbes.com.*

41. Kim, W. C. & Mauborgne, R. 2005. *Blue ocean strategy.* Boston: Harvard Business School Press.

42. For more on how unique organizational combinations can contribute to competitive advantages of entrepreneurial firms, see Steffens, P., Davidsson, P., & Fitzsimmons, J. Performance configurations over times: Implications for growth- and profit-oriented strategies. *Entrepreneurship Theory & Practice,* 33(1): 125–148.

43. Smith, K. G., Ferrier, W. J., & Grimm, C. M. 2001. King of the hill: Dethroning the industry leader. *Academy of Management Executive,* 15(2): 59–70.

44. Kumar, N. 2006. Strategies to fight low-cost rivals. *Harvard Business Review,* December: 104–112.

45. Grove, A. 1999. *Only the paranoid survive: How to exploit the crises points that challenge every company.* New York: Random House.

46. Stalk, Jr., G. & Lachenauer, R. 2004. *Hardball: Are you playing to play or playing to win?* Cambridge, MA: Harvard Business School Press.

47. Chen, M. J., Lin, H. C, & Michel, J. G. 2010. Navigating in a hypercompetitive environment: The roles of action aggressiveness and TMT integration. *Strategic Management Journal,* 31: 1410–1430.

48. Peteraf, M. A. & Bergen, M. A. 2003. Scanning competitive landscapes: A market-based and resource-based framework. *Strategic Management Journal,* 24: 1027–1045.

49. Chen, M. J. 1996. Competitor analysis and interfirm rivalry: Toward a theoretical integration. *Academy of Management Review,* 21(1): 100–134.

50. Chen, 1996, op.cit.

51. Chen, M. J., Su, K. H, & Tsai, W. 2007. Competitive tension: The awareness-motivation-capability perspective. *Academy of Management Journal,* 50(1): 101–118.

52. St. John, W. 1999. Barnes & Noble's Epiphany. *Wired, www.wired.com,* June.

53. Souder, D. & Shaver, J. M. 2010. Constraints and incentives for making long horizon corporate investments. *Strategic Management Journal,* 31: 1316–1336.

54. Chen, M. J. & Hambrick, D. 1995. Speed, stealth, and selective attack: How small firms differ from large firms in competitive behavior. *Academy of Management Journal,* 38: 453–482.

55. Fenner, L. 2009. TOMS shoes donates one pair of shoes for every pair purchased. *America.gov,* October 19: np.

56. *www.facebook.com/tomsshoes.*

57. For a discussion of how the strategic actions of Apple Computer contribute to changes in the competitive dynamics in both the cellular phone and music industries, see Burgelman, R. A. & Grove, A. S. 2008. Cross-boundary disruptors: Powerful interindustry entrepreneurial change agents. *Strategic Entrepreneurship Journal,* 1(1): 315–327,

58. Smith, K. G., Ferrier, W. J., & Ndofor, H. 2001. Competitive dynamics research: Critique and future directions. In M. A. Hitt, R. E. Freeman, & J. S. Harrison (Eds.), *The Blackwell handbook of strategic management,* pp. 315–361. Oxford, UK: Blackwell.

59. Gee, P. 2000. Co-opetition: The new market milieu. *Journal of Healthcare Management,* 45: 359–363.

60. Ketchen, D. J., Snow, C. C., & Hoover, V. L. 2004. Research on competitive dynamics: Recent accomplishments and future challenges. *Journal of Management,* 30(6): 779–804.

61. Khanna, T., Gulati, R., & Nohria, N. 2000. The economic modeling of strategy process: Clean models and dirty hands. *Strategic Management Journal,* 21: 781–790.

Learning from Mistakes

Chesapeake Energy had a terrible year in 2008. Its net income dropped about 50 percent from the previous year and its stock plummeted from 39 to 17 during the year—a loss of 56 percent.[1] Its board of directors, however, fared much better than its shareholders. In fact, its directors were among the highest paid corporate directors in 2008. For example, one of the eight "independent" directors, 80-year-old Breene Kerr, received $784,687 in total compensation. He's considered independent only because he is not a member of Chesapeake's management, but he just happens to be the cousin of the CEO, Aubrey McClendon. The other directors did almost as well, receiving an average of about $670,000 each. Let's take a look and see what possible reasons there may be for why the directors have been compensated so well.

CEO Aubrey McClendon aggressively bought Chesapeake's stock in July 2008, mostly on margin, at prices as high as $72 a share. Unfortunately, the stock began to sharply drop. In September, margin calls forced McClendon to sell almost all of his position at a price between $13.60 and $24 a share, depleting his net worth.

The board rushed to the rescue! It promptly awarded McClendon a $75 million "special bonus" for 2008. As if such enormous (and undeserved) compensation were not sufficient, the board felt it necessary to justify another use of corporate funds. In December 2008, the company purchased McClendon's extensive collection of antique historic maps of the American Southwest for $12.1 million.

But that is not all. At a cost of $3.5 million, the company became a founding sponsor of the Oklahoma City Thunder, a National Basketball Association franchise owned and operated by The Professional Basketball Club, LLC ("PBC"). McClendon had a 19.2 percent equity interest in the franchise.

The company's compensation committee did provide a rationale for McClendon's huge bonus: it stressed the board's wish to keep him as CEO. And McClendon reciprocated when asked why Chesapeake pays its directors so much, "We have a very large and complex company and we value our directors' time."

---

strategic control the process of monitoring and correcting a firm's strategy and performance.

We first explore two central aspects of **strategic control:**[2] (1) *informational control,* which is the ability to respond effectively to environmental change, and (2) *behavioral control,* which is the appropriate balance and alignment among a firm's culture, rewards, and boundaries. In the final section of this chapter, we focus on strategic control from a much broader perspective—what is referred to as *corporate governance.*[3] Here, we direct our attention to the need for a firm's shareholders (the owners) and their elected representatives (the board of directors) to ensure that the firm's executives (the management team) strive to fulfill their fiduciary duty of maximizing long-term shareholder value. As we just saw in the Chesapeake Energy example, clearly there was a breakdown in corporate governance. This gave the CEO seemingly unlimited power at the expense of the shareholders.

>LO9.1

The value of effective strategic control systems in strategy implementation.

Ensuring Informational Control: Responding Effectively to Environmental Change

We discuss two broad types of control systems: "traditional" and "contemporary." As both general and competitive environments become more unpredictable and complex, the need for contemporary systems increases.

A Traditional Approach to Strategic Control

The **traditional approach to strategic control** is sequential: (1) strategies are formulated and top management sets goals, (2) strategies are implemented, and (3) performance is measured against the predetermined goal set, as illustrated in Exhibit 9.1.

Control is based on a feedback loop from performance measurement to strategy formulation. This process typically involves lengthy time lags, often tied to a firm's annual planning cycle. Such traditional control systems, termed "single-loop" learning by Harvard's Chris Argyris, simply compare actual performance to a predetermined goal.[4] They are most appropriate when the environment is stable and relatively simple, goals and objectives can be measured with a high level of certainty, and there is little need for complex measures of performance. Sales quotas, operating budgets, production schedules, and similar quantitative control mechanisms are typical. The appropriateness of the business strategy or standards of performance is seldom questioned.[5]

James Brian Quinn of Dartmouth College has argued that grand designs with precise and carefully integrated plans seldom work.[6] Rather, most strategic change proceeds incrementally—one step at a time. Leaders should introduce some sense of direction, some logic in incremental steps.[7] Similarly, McGill University's Henry Mintzberg has written about leaders "crafting" a strategy.[8] Drawing on the parallel between the potter at her wheel and the strategist, Mintzberg pointed out that the potter begins work with some general idea of the artifact she wishes to create, but the details of design—even possibilities for a different design—emerge as the work progresses. For businesses facing complex and turbulent business environments, the craftsperson's method helps us deal with the uncertainty about how a design will work out in practice and allows for a creative element.

Mintzberg's argument, like Quinn's, questions the value of rigid planning and goal-setting processes. Fixed strategic goals also become dysfunctional for firms competing in highly unpredictable competitive environments. Strategies need to change frequently and opportunistically. An inflexible commitment to predetermined goals and milestones can prevent the very adaptability that is required of a good strategy.

Even organizations that have been extremely successful in the past can become complacent or fail to adapt their goals and strategies to the new conditions. An example of such a firm is General Motors (GM). For many decades, it was the leading firm in the automotive industry. As recently as 2006, it was recognized by Morgan Stanley as the top car producer. However, GM suffered from many underlying problems that were aggravated by the recent worldwide recession, which eroded demand for automobiles. In Strategy Spotlight 9.1, we address what may be considered one of their key underlying problems—a lack of informational control.

A Contemporary Approach to Strategic Control

Adapting to and anticipating both internal and external environmental change is an integral part of strategic control. The relationships between strategy formulation, implementation, and control are highly interactive, as suggested by Exhibit 9.2. It also illustrates two different types of strategic control: informational control and behavioral control. **Informational control** is primarily concerned with whether or not the organization is "doing the right

```
Formulate      →    Implement      →    Strategic
strategies          strategies           control
```

Exhibit 9.1 Traditional Approach to Strategic Control

---

traditional approach to strategic control a sequential method of organizational control in which (1) strategies are formulated and top management sets goals, (2) strategies are implemented, and (3) performance is measured against the predetermined goal set.

>LO9.2
The key difference between "traditional" and "contemporary" control systems.

>LO9.3
The imperative for "contemporary" control systems in today's complex and rapidly changing competitive and general environments.

informational control a method of organizational control in which a firm gathers and analyzes information from the internal and external environment in order to obtain the best fit between the organization's goals and strategies and the strategic environment.

What Did General Motors Do Wrong?

General Motors (GM), which was founded in 1908, had been ruling the automotive industry for more than half a century. GM provided a broad range of vehicles, reflecting the company's promise to offer "a car for every purse and purpose." As recently as 2007, their stock was trading above $40 a share. And then just few months after celebrating its 100th anniversary in 2008, GM filed for bankruptcy. On May 29, 2009, GM's stock closed at 75 cents a share, which was a historic low for the company. The government funded a $50 billion bailout to save GM and took a 60 percent ownership stake in the company when they exited bankruptcy in 2010.

GM's market dominance grew out of its abilities to mass manufacture, market, and distribute cars for all customer types. While their advantage initially was based on automotive design and manufacturing prowess, over time, GM became rigid and lost its feel for reading the American car market that it helped create. They were not manufacturing competitive vehicles and increasingly relied on volume and the profits from financing auto sales for their success. At the same time, GM faced increasing competition from Japanese automakers, but they were slow to respond to this competitive entry due to their bureaucratic culture and complacency driven by the profitability of their financing operations. The Japanese competitors developed competencies to design world-class vehicles and produced them more efficiently than GM. As a result, they lured away many of GM's customers. GM's management failed to respond to changes in customer needs and automotive technologies as well as the evolving competitive landscape.

GM did have vast numbers of loyal buyers, but lost many of them through a series of strategic and cultural missteps. Trying to balance the competing needs of seven major brands, GM often resorted to a practice (sarcastically) called "launch and leave"—spending billions upfront to bring vehicles to market, but then failing to keep supporting them with sustained advertising. They also failed to differentiate the brands. Originally, each brand was designed to meet the needs of a different customer segment. However, GM's brand identities became muddled as they sold essentially the same car for different brands. According to Jim Wangers, a retired advertising

● A 1957 Cadillac—a successful product that reflects General Motors' glory days.

executive, "Nobody gave any respect to this thing called image because it wasn't in the business plan. It was all about, 'When is this going to earn a profit?'"

Faced with a declining market position, GM executives did not address the need for changes. Instead, they fell prey to two common biases. First, they exhibited *attribution bias.* When their performance started to fall, they attributed their struggles to outside forces, such as the weak Japanese yen, unfair trade practices, and higher costs from their unionized workers. In short, they became expert at the art of explaining away their problems, attributing blame to everyone but themselves. Second, they exhibited *confirmation bias*—the tendency of managers to filter out information that does not match up with their preconceived notions. GM rewarded people who followed the old way of doing things, and those who challenged that thinking were marginalized—causing them to lose opportunities for promotion. So the smart thing for those seeking promotion within GM was to praise the CEO's wisdom and carry out his orders. This confirmation bias syndrome kept GM from viewing the threat from Japanese automakers as significant, contributed to its decision to pull its electric car off the market, and more recently led it to ignore the effect of higher gas prices and a collapse in credit markets on consumers' willingness to buy profitable gas guzzlers like the Hummer or tricked-out Escalades and SUVs. In falling prey to these biases, GM's management failed to recognize the need for change in response to changes in the market, in technology, and in customers' demands.

Sources: Maynard, M. 2009. After Many Stumbles, the Fall of a Giant. *The New York Times.* June 1: A1; Smith, A. 2009. GM Stock Falls below $1. *money. cnn.com.* May 29: np; Maynard, M. 2009. After 93 Years, GM Shares Go Out on a Low Note. *dealbook.nytimes.com.* May 29: np; Holstein, W. J. 2009. Who's to Blame for GM's Bankruptcy? *www.businessweek.com.* June 1: np; and Cohan, P. 2009. After 101 Years, Why GM Failed. *www.dailyfinance.com.* May 31: np.

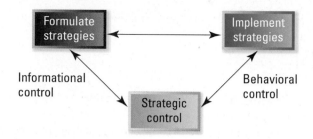

Exhibit 9.2 Contemporary Approach to Strategic Control

things." **Behavioral control,** on the other hand, asks if the organization is "doing things right" in the implementation of its strategy. Both the informational and behavioral components of strategic control are necessary, but not sufficient, conditions for success. What good is a well-conceived strategy that cannot be implemented? Or what use is an energetic and committed workforce if it is focused on the wrong strategic target?

John Weston is the former CEO of ADP Corporation, the largest payroll and tax-filing processor in the world. He captures the essence of contemporary control systems.

> At ADP, 39 plus 1 adds up to more than 40 plus 0. The 40-plus-0 employee is the harried worker who at 40 hours a week just tries to keep up with what's in the "in" basket. . . . Because he works with his head down, he takes zero hours to think about what he's doing, why he's doing it, and how he's doing it. . . . On the other hand, the 39-plus-1 employee takes at least 1 of those 40 hours to think about what he's doing and why he's doing it. That's why the other 39 hours are far more productive.[9]

Informational control deals with the internal environment as well as the external strategic context. It addresses the assumptions and premises that provide the foundation for an organization's strategy. Do the organization's goals and strategies still "fit" within the context of the current strategic environment? Depending on the type of business, such assumptions may relate to changes in technology, customer tastes, government regulation, and industry competition.

This involves two key issues. First, managers must scan and monitor the external environment, as we discussed in Chapter 2. Also, conditions can change in the internal environment of the firm, as we discussed in Chapter 3, requiring changes in the strategic direction of the firm. These may include, for example, the resignation of key executives or delays in the completion of major production facilities.

In the contemporary approach, information control is part of an ongoing process of organizational learning that continuously updates and challenges the assumptions that underlie the organization's strategy. In such "double-loop" learning, the organization's assumptions, premises, goals, and strategies are continuously monitored, tested, and reviewed. The benefits of continuous monitoring are evident—time lags are dramatically shortened, changes in the competitive environment are detected earlier, and the organization's ability to respond with speed and flexibility is enhanced.

Contemporary control systems must have four characteristics to be effective.[10]

1. Focus on constantly changing information that has potential strategic importance.
2. The information is important enough to demand frequent and regular attention from all levels of the organization.
3. The data and information generated are best interpreted and discussed in face-to-face meetings.
4. The control system is a key catalyst for an ongoing debate about underlying data, assumptions, and action plans.

An executive's decision to use the control system interactively—in other words, to invest the time and attention to review and evaluate new information—sends a clear signal

behavioral control a method of organizational control in which a firm influences the actions of employees through culture, rewards, and boundaries.

Google's Interactive Control System

Google has tried typical hierarchical control systems typically found in large firms. However, the firm reverted to its interactive control system within weeks. All of Google's roughly 5,000 product developers work in teams of three engineers. Larger projects simply assemble several teams of three workers. Within teams, there is a rotating "über-tech leader" depending on the project. Engineers tend to work in more than one team and do not need permission to switch teams. According to Shona Brown, VP for operations, "If at all possible, we want people to commit to things rather than be assigned to things." At Google "employees don't need a lot of signoffs to try something new, but they won't get much in the way of resources until they've accumulated some positive user feedback."

Google's executives regularly review projects with project leaders and analyze data about projects. Google uses some of its own web page ranking technology in the review of software and other business projects. Using their own employees as mini test markets, managers often solicit employee opinions and analyze usage patterns of new product features and technologies. This interactive control of corporate information allows Google to make faster decisions about its business, including:

- Compare performance of customer usage and feedback among all components of the Google business in real time.

- Quickly discover shortfalls before major problems arise.

Sources: Hamel, G. 2007. Break Free. *Fortune,* October 1, 156(7): 119–126; Iyer, B. and Davenport, T. 2008. Reverse Engineering Google's Innovation Machine. *Harvard Business Review,* April: 59–68; Pham, A. 2008. Google to End Virtual World, Lively, Launched by the Internet Giant Less Than Five Months Ago. *Los Angeles Times,* November 21: C3; and Helft, M. 2009. Google Ends Sale of Ads in Papers after 2 Years. *New York Times,* January 21: B3.

- Become aware of unexpected successes that have often led to innovations.

- Discontinue failing products and services in a timely manner to save the company money.

These manager meetings return significant rewards for Google. Innovations that have been implemented as a result of high information control include:

- Gmail, an e-mail system that utilizes Google's core search features to help users organize and find e-mail messages easily.

- Google News, a computer-generated news site that aggregates headlines from more than 4,500 English-language news sources worldwide, groups similar stories together, and displays them according to each reader's personalized interests.

- Google AdSense, a service that matches ads to a website's content and audience and operates on a revenue-sharing business model.

Google managers are able to quickly analyze user feedback and revenue data to discontinue projects that are not working out as originally intended. This information control allows managers to reallocate resources to more promising projects in a timely manner.

- Google Lively, a virtual world simulation, was launched and shut down after five months in 2008 after management determined that the service was not competitive.

- Google Print Ads, Google's automated method of selling ads through auctions to the newspaper industry, was terminated in early 2009 when managers analyzed the data and determined that the revenue stream was negligible compared to the costs of the program.

---

to the organization about what is important. The dialogue and debate that emerge from such an interactive process can often lead to new strategies and innovations. Strategy Spotlight 9.2 discusses how executives at Google use an interactive control process.

>LO9.4

The benefits of having the proper balance among the three levers of behavioral control: culture, rewards and incentives, and boundaries.

Attaining Behavioral Control: Balancing Culture, Rewards, and Boundaries

Behavioral control is focused on implementation—doing things right. Effectively implementing strategy requires manipulating three key control "levers": culture, rewards, and boundaries (see Exhibit 9.3). There are two compelling reasons for an increased emphasis on culture and rewards in a system of behavioral controls.[11]

First, the competitive environment is increasingly complex and unpredictable, demanding both flexibility and quick response to its challenges. As firms simultaneously downsize and face the need for increased coordination across organizational boundaries, a control system based primarily on rigid strategies, rules, and regulations is dysfunctional. The use of rewards and culture to align individual and organizational goals becomes increasingly important.

Second, the implicit long-term contract between the organization and its key employees has been eroded.[12] Today's younger managers have been conditioned to see themselves as "free agents" and view a career as a series of opportunistic challenges. As managers are advised to "specialize, market yourself, and have work, if not a job," the importance of culture and rewards in building organizational loyalty claims greater importance.

Each of the three levers—culture, rewards, and boundaries—must work in a balanced and consistent manner. Let's consider the role of each.

Building a Strong and Effective Culture

Organizational culture is a system of shared values (what is important) and beliefs (how things work) that shape a company's people, organizational structures, and control systems to produce behavioral norms (the way we do things around here).[13] How important is culture? Very. Over the years, numerous best sellers, such as *Theory Z, Corporate Cultures, In Search of Excellence,* and *Good to Great,*[14] have emphasized the powerful influence of culture on what goes on within organizations and how they perform.

Collins and Porras argued in *Built to Last* that the key factor in sustained exceptional performance is a cultlike culture.[15] You can't touch it or write it down, but it's there in every organization; its influence is pervasive; it can work for you or against you.[16] Effective leaders understand its importance and strive to shape and use it as one of their important levers of strategic control.[17]

organizational culture a system of shared values and beliefs that shape a company's people, organizational structures, and control systems to produce behavioral norms.

The Role of Culture Culture wears many different hats, each woven from the fabric of those values that sustain the organization's primary source of competitive advantage. Some examples are:

- Federal Express and Southwest Airlines focus on customer service.
- Lexus (a division of Toyota) and Hewlett-Packard emphasize product quality.
- Newell Rubbermaid and 3M place a high value on innovation.
- Nucor (steel) and Emerson Electric are concerned, above all, with operational efficiency.

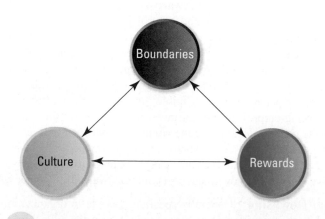

Exhibit 9.3 **Essential Elements of Behavioral Control**

Culture sets implicit boundaries—unwritten standards of acceptable behavior—in dress, ethical matters, and the way an organization conducts its business.[18] By creating a framework of shared values, culture encourages individual identification with the organization and its objectives. Culture acts as a means of reducing monitoring costs.[19]

Sustaining an Effective Culture   Powerful organizational cultures just don't happen overnight, and they don't remain in place without a strong commitment—both in terms of words and deeds—by leaders throughout the organization.[20] A viable and productive organizational culture can be strengthened and sustained. However, it cannot be "built" or "assembled"; instead, it must be cultivated, encouraged, and "fertilized."[21]

Storytelling is one way effective cultures are maintained. Many are familiar with the story of how Art Fry's failure to develop a strong adhesive led to 3M's enormously successful Post-it Notes. Perhaps less familiar is the story of Francis G. Okie.[22] In 1922 Okie came up with the idea of selling sandpaper to men as a replacement for razor blades. The idea obviously didn't pan out, but Okie was allowed to remain at 3M. Interestingly, the technology developed by Okie led 3M to develop its first blockbuster product: a waterproof sandpaper that became a staple of the automobile industry. Such stories foster the importance of risk taking, experimentation, freedom to fail, and innovation—all vital elements of 3M's culture.

Rallies or "pep talks" by top executives also serve to reinforce a firm's culture. The late Sam Walton was known for his pep rallies at local Walmart stores. Four times a year, the founders of Home Depot—former CEO Bernard Marcus and Arthur Blank—used to don orange aprons and stage Breakfast with Bernie and Arthur, a 6:30 a.m. pep rally, broadcast live over the firm's closed-circuit TV network to most of its 45,000 employees.[23]

Southwest Airlines' "Culture Committee" is a unique vehicle designed to perpetuate the company's highly successful culture. The following excerpt from an internal company publication describes its objectives:

> The goal of the Committee is simple—to ensure that our unique Corporate Culture stays alive. . . . Culture Committee members represent all regions and departments across our system and they are selected based upon their exemplary display of the "Positively Outrageous Service" that won us the first-ever Triple Crown; their continual exhibition of the "Southwest Spirit" to our Customers and to their fellow workers; and their high energy level, boundless enthusiasm, unique creativity, and constant demonstration of teamwork and love for their fellow workers.[24]

Motivating with Rewards and Incentives

Reward and incentive systems represent a powerful means of influencing an organization's culture, focusing efforts on high-priority tasks, and motivating individual and collective task performance.[25] Just as culture deals with influencing beliefs, behaviors, and attitudes of people within an organization, the **reward system**—by specifying who gets rewarded and why—is an effective motivator and control mechanism.[26] Consider how Starbucks uses its stock option plan as an incentive to motivate its employees.[27] By introducing a stock option plan called "bean stock" to managers, baristas, and other employees, Starbucks has turned every employee into a partner. Starbucks' managers began referring to all employees as *partners,* an appropriate title because all staff, including part-timers working at least 20 hours per week, were eligible for stock options after six months with the company. By turning employees into partners, Starbucks gave them a chance to share in the success of the company and make the connection between their contributions and the company's market value very clear. There was a pronounced effect on the attitudes and performance of employees because of the bean stock program. They began coming up with many innovative ideas about how to cut costs, increase sales, and create value.

The Potential Downside   Generally speaking, people in organizations act rationally, each motivated by their personal best interest.[28] However, the collective sum of individual

reward system
policies that specify who gets rewarded and why.

behaviors of an organization's employees does not always result in what is best for the organization; individual rationality is no guarantee of organizational rationality.

As corporations grow and evolve, they often develop different business units with multiple reward systems. They may differ based on industry contexts, business situations, stage of product life cycles, and so on. Subcultures within organizations may reflect differences among functional areas, products, services, and divisions. To the extent that reward systems reinforce such behavioral norms, attitudes, and belief systems, cohesiveness is reduced; important information is hoarded rather than shared, individuals begin working at cross-purposes, and they lose sight of overall goals.

Such conflicts are commonplace in many organizations. For example, sales and marketing personnel promise unrealistically quick delivery times to bring in business, much to the dismay of operations and logistics; overengineering by R&D creates headaches for manufacturing; and so on. Conflicts also arise across divisions when divisional profits become a key compensation criterion. As ill will and anger escalate, personal relationships and performance may suffer.

Creating Effective Reward and Incentive Programs   To be effective, incentive and reward systems need to reinforce basic core values, enhance cohesion and commitment to goals and objectives, and meet with the organization's overall mission and purpose.[29]

At General Mills, to ensure a manager's interest in the overall performance of his or her unit, half of a manager's annual bonus is linked to business-unit results and half to individual performance.[30] For example, if a manager simply matches a rival manufacturer's performance, his or her salary is roughly 5 percent lower. However, if a manager's product ranks in the industry's top 10 percent in earnings growth and return on capital, the manager's total pay can rise to nearly 30 percent beyond the industry norm.

Effective reward and incentive systems share a number of common characteristics.[31] (see Exhibit 9.4). The perception that a plan is "fair and equitable" is critically important. The firm must have the flexibility to respond to changing requirements as its direction and objectives change. In recent years many companies have begun to place more emphasis on growth. Emerson Electric has shifted its emphasis from cost cutting to growth. To ensure that changes take hold, the management compensation formula has been changed from a largely bottom-line focus to one that emphasizes growth, new products, acquisitions, and international expansion. Discussions about profits are handled separately, and a culture of risk taking is encouraged.[32]

Setting Boundaries and Constraints

In an ideal world, a strong culture and effective rewards should be sufficient to ensure that all individuals and subunits work toward the common goals and objectives of the whole organization.[33] However, this is not usually the case. Counterproductive behavior can arise because of motivated self-interest, lack of a clear understanding of goals and objectives, or outright malfeasance. **Boundaries and constraints** can serve many useful purposes for organizations, including:

boundaries and constraints rules that specify behaviors that are acceptable and unacceptable.

- Objectives are clear, well understood, and broadly accepted.
- Rewards are clearly linked to performance and desired behaviors.
- Performance measures are clear and highly visible.
- Feedback is prompt, clear, and unambiguous.
- The compensation "system" is perceived as fair and equitable.
- The structure is flexible; it can adapt to changing circumstances.

Exhibit 9.4
Characteristics of Effective Reward and Evaluation Systems

- Focusing individual efforts on strategic priorities.
- Providing short-term objectives and action plans to channel efforts.
- Improving efficiency and effectiveness.
- Minimizing improper and unethical conduct.

Focusing Efforts on Strategic Priorities   Boundaries and constraints play a valuable role in focusing a company's strategic priorities. A well-known example of a strategic boundary is Jack Welch's (former CEO of General Electric) demand that any business in the corporate portfolio be ranked first or second in its industry. Similarly, Eli Lilly has reduced its research efforts to five broad areas of disease, down from eight or nine a decade ago.[34] This concentration of effort and resources provides the firm with greater strategic focus and the potential for stronger competitive advantages in the remaining areas.

Norman Augustine, Lockheed Martin's former chairman, provided four criteria for selecting candidates for diversification into "closely related" businesses.[35] They must (1) be high tech, (2) be systems-oriented, (3) deal with large customers (either corporations or government) as opposed to consumers, and (4) be in growth businesses. Augustine said, "We have found that if we can meet most of those standards, then we can move into adjacent markets and grow."

Boundaries also have a place in the nonprofit sector. For example, a British relief organization uses a system to monitor strategic boundaries by maintaining a list of companies whose contributions it will neither solicit nor accept. Such boundaries are essential for maintaining legitimacy with existing and potential benefactors.

Providing Short-Term Objectives and Action Plans   In Chapter 1 we discussed the importance of a firm having a vision, mission, and strategic objectives that are internally consistent and that provide strategic direction. In addition, short-term objectives and action plans provide similar benefits. That is, they represent boundaries that help to allocate resources in an optimal manner and to channel the efforts of employees at all levels throughout the organization.[36] To be effective, short-term objectives must have several attributes. They should:

- Be specific and measurable.
- Include a specific time horizon for their attainment.
- Be achievable, yet challenging enough to motivate managers who must strive to accomplish them.

Research has found that performance is enhanced when individuals are encouraged to attain specific, difficult, yet achievable, goals (as opposed to vague "do your best" goals).[37]

Short-term objectives must provide proper direction and also provide enough flexibility for the firm to keep pace with and anticipate changes in the external environment, new government regulations, a competitor introducing a substitute product, or changes in consumer taste. Unexpected events within a firm may require a firm to make important adjustments in both strategic and short-term objectives. The emergence of new industries can have a drastic effect on the demand for products and services in more traditional industries.

Action plans are critical to the implementation of chosen strategies. Unless action plans are specific, there may be little assurance that managers have thought through all of the resource requirements for implementing their strategies. In addition, unless plans are specific, managers may not understand what needs to be implemented or have a clear time frame for completion. This is essential for the scheduling of key activities that must be implemented. Finally, individual managers must be held accountable for the implementation. This helps to provide the necessary motivation and "sense of ownership" to implement action plans on a timely basis. Strategy Spotlight 9.3 illustrates how action

Developing Meaningful Action Plans: Aircraft Interior Products, Inc.

MSA Aircraft Interior Products, Inc., is a manufacturing firm based in San Antonio, Texas, that was founded in 1983 by Mike Spraggins and Robert Plenge. The firm fulfills a small but highly profitable niche in the aviation industry with two key products. The Accordia line consists of patented, lightweight, self-contained window-shade assemblies. MSA's interior cabin shells are state-of-the-art assemblies that include window panels, side panels, headliners, and suspension system structures. MSA's products have been installed on a variety of aircraft, such as the Gulfstream series; the Cessna Citation; and Boeing's 727, 737, 757, and 707.

Much of MSA's success can be attributed to carefully articulated action plans consistent with the firm's mission and objectives. During the past five years, MSA has increased its sales at an annual rate of 15 to 18 percent. It has also succeeded in adding many prestigious companies to its customer base. Below are excerpts from MSA's mission statement and objectives as well as the action plans to achieve a 20 percent annual increase in sales.

Mission Statement

- Be recognized as an innovative and reliable supplier of quality interior products for the high-end, personalized transportation segments of the aviation, marine, and automotive industries.

- Design, develop, and manufacture interior fixtures and components that provide exceptional value to

the customer through the development of innovative designs in a manner that permits decorative design flexibility while retaining the superior functionality, reliability, and maintainability of well-engineered, factory-produced products.

- Grow, be profitable, and provide a fair return, commensurate with the degree of risk, for owners and stockholders.

Objectives

1. Achieve sustained and profitable growth over the next three years:

   - 20 percent annual growth in revenues
   - 12 percent pretax profit margins
   - 18 percent return on shareholder's equity

2. Expand the company's revenues through the development and introduction of two or more new products capable of generating revenues in excess of $8 million a year by 2014.

3. Continue to aggressively expand market opportunities and applications for the Accordia line of window-shade assemblies, with the objective of sustaining or exceeding a 20 percent annual growth rate for at least the next three years.

Exhibit 9.5 details an "Action Plan" for Objective 3.

MSA's action plans are supported by detailed month-by-month budgets and strong financial incentives for its executives. Budgets are prepared by each individual department and include all revenue and cost items. Managers are motivated by their participation in a profit-sharing program, and the firm's two founders each receive a bonus equal to three percent of total sales.

Source: For purposes of confidentiality, some of the information presented in this spotlight has been disguised. We would like to thank company management and Joseph Picken, consultant, for providing us with the information used in this application.

	Description	Primary Responsibility	Target Date
1.	Develop and implement 2010 marketing plan, including specific plans for addressing Falcon 20 retrofit programs and expanded sales of cabin shells.	R. H. Plenge (V.P. Marketing)	December 15, 2011
2.	Negotiate new supplier agreement with Gulfstream Aerospace.	M. Spraggins (President)	March 1, 2012
3.	Continue and complete the development of the UltraSlim window and have a fully tested and documented design ready for production at a manufacturing cost of less than $900 per unit.	D. R. Pearson (V.P. Operations)	June 15, 2012
4.	Develop a window design suitable for L-1011 and similar wide-body aircraft and have a fully tested and documented design ready for production at a manufacturing cost comparable to the current Boeing window.	D. R. Pearson (V.P. Operations)	September 15, 2012

Exhibit 9.5   Action Plan for Objective Number 3

plans fit into the mission statement and objectives of a small manufacturer of aircraft interior components. Exhibit 9.5 provides details of an action plan to fulfill one of the firm's objectives.

Improving Operational Efficiency and Effectiveness Rule-based controls are most appropriate in organizations with the following characteristics:

- Environments are stable and predictable.
- Employees are largely unskilled and interchangeable.
- Consistency in product and service is critical.
- The risk of malfeasance is extremely high (e.g., in banking or casino operations).[38]

McDonald's Corp. has extensive rules and regulations that regulate the operation of its franchises.[39] Its policy manual states, "Cooks must turn, never flip, hamburgers. If they haven't been purchased, Big Macs must be discarded in 10 minutes after being cooked and French fries in 7 minutes. Cashiers must make eye contact with and smile at every customer."

Guidelines can also be effective in setting spending limits and the range of discretion for employees and managers, such as the $2,500 limit that hotelier Ritz-Carlton uses to empower employees to placate dissatisfied customers. Regulations also can be initiated to improve the use of an employee's time at work.[40] Computer Associates restricts the use of e-mail during the hours of 10 a.m. to noon and 2 p.m. to 4 p.m. each day.[41]

Minimizing Improper and Unethical Conduct Guidelines can be useful in specifying proper relationships with a company's customers and suppliers.[42] Many companies have explicit rules regarding commercial practices, including the prohibition of any form of payment, bribe, or kickback. Cadbury Schweppes has followed a simple but effective step in controlling the use of bribes by specifying that all payments, no matter how unusual, are recorded on the company's books. Its former chairman, Sir Adrian Cadbury, contended that such a practice causes managers to pause and consider whether a payment is simply a bribe or a necessary and standard cost of doing business.[43]

Regulations backed up with strong sanctions can also help an organization avoid conducting business in an unethical manner. After the passing of the Sarbanes-Oxley Act (which provides for stiffer penalties for financial reporting misdeeds), many chief financial officers (CFOs) have taken steps to ensure ethical behavior in the preparation of financial statements. For example, Home Depot's CFO, Carol B. Tome, strengthened the firm's code of ethics and developed stricter guidelines. Now all 25 of her subordinates must sign personal statements that all of their financial statements are correct—just as she and her CEO, have to do now.[44]

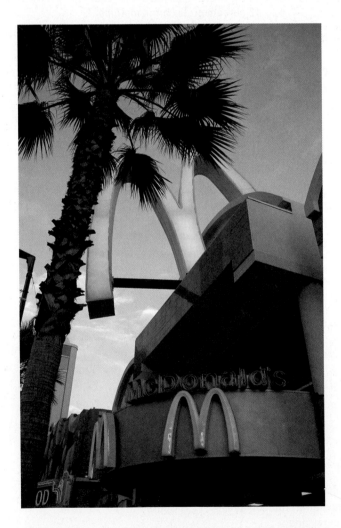

● McDonald's relies on extensive rules and regulations to maintain efficient operations at its restaurants.

Behavioral Control in Organizations: Situational Factors

Here, the focus is on ensuring that the behavior of individuals at all levels of an organization is directed toward achieving organizational goals and objectives. The three fundamental types of control are culture, rewards and incentives, and boundaries and constraints. An organization may pursue one or a combination of them on the basis of a variety of internal and external factors.

Not all organizations place the same emphasis on each type of control.[45] In high-technology firms engaged in basic research, members may work under high levels of autonomy. An individual's performance is generally quite difficult to measure accurately because of the long lead times involved in R&D activities. Thus, internalized norms and values become very important.

When the measurement of an individual's output or performance is quite straightforward, control depends primarily on granting or withholding rewards. Frequently, a sales manager's compensation is in the form of a commission and bonus tied directly to his or her sales volume, which is relatively easy to determine. Here, behavior is influenced more strongly by the attractiveness of the compensation than by the norms and values implicit in the organization's culture. The measurability of output precludes the need for an elaborate system of rules to control behavior.[46]

Control in bureaucratic organizations is dependent on members following a highly formalized set of rules and regulations. Most activities are routine and the desired behavior can be specified in a detailed manner because there is generally little need for innovative or creative activity. Managing an assembly plant requires strict adherence to many rules as well as exacting sequences of assembly operations. In the public sector, the Department of Motor Vehicles in most states must follow clearly prescribed procedures when issuing or renewing driver licenses.

Exhibit 9.6 provides alternate approaches to behavioral control and some of the situational factors associated with them.

Evolving from Boundaries to Rewards and Culture

In most environments, organizations should strive to provide a system of rewards and incentives, coupled with a culture strong enough that boundaries become internalized. This reduces the need for external controls such as rules and regulations.

First, hire the right people—individuals who already identify with the organization's dominant values and have attributes consistent with them. We addressed this issue in Chapter 4; recall the "Bozo Filter" developed by Cooper Software (pages 129–130). Microsoft's David Pritchard is well aware of the consequences of failing to hire properly.

Exhibit 9.6
Organizational Control: Alternative Approaches

Approach	Some Situational Factors
Culture: A system of unwritten rules that forms an internalized influence over behavior.	• Often found in professional organizations. • Associated with high autonomy. • Norms are the basis for behavior.
Rules: Written and explicit guidelines that provide external constraints on behavior.	• Associated with standardized output. • Tasks are generally repetitive and routine. • Little need for innovation or creative activity.
Rewards: The use of performance-based incentive systems to motivate.	• Measurement of output and performance is rather straightforward. • Most appropriate in organizations pursuing unrelated diversification strategies. • Rewards may be used to reinforce other means of control.

If I hire a bunch of bozos, it will hurt us, because it takes time to get rid of them. They start infiltrating the organization and then they themselves start hiring people of lower quality. At Microsoft, we are always looking for people who are better than we are.

Second, training plays a key role. For example, in elite military units such as the Green Berets and Navy SEALs, the training regimen so thoroughly internalizes the culture that individuals, in effect, lose their identity. The group becomes the overriding concern and focal point of their energies. At firms such as FedEx, training not only builds skills, but also plays a significant role in building a strong culture on the foundation of each organization's dominant values.

Third, managerial role models are vital. Andy Grove, former CEO and co-founder of Intel, didn't need (or want) a large number of bureaucratic rules to determine who is responsible for what, who is supposed to talk to whom, and who gets to fly first class (no one does). He encouraged openness by not having many of the trappings of success—he worked in a cubicle like all the other professionals. Can you imagine any new manager asking whether or not he can fly first class? Grove's personal example eliminated such a need.

Fourth, reward systems must be clearly aligned with the organizational goals and objectives. Where do you think rules and regulations are more important in controlling behavior—Home Depot, with its generous bonus and stock option plan, or Walmart, which does not provide the same level of rewards and incentives?

The Role of Corporate Governance

>LO9.5
The three key participants in corporate governance: shareholders, management (led by the CEO), and the board of directors.

We now address the issue of strategic control in a broader perspective, typically referred to as "corporate governance." Here we focus on the need for both shareholders (the owners of the corporation) and their elected representatives, the board of directors, to actively ensure that management fulfills its overriding purpose of increasing long-term shareholder value.[47]

Robert Monks and Nell Minow, two leading scholars in **corporate governance,** define it as "the relationship among various participants in determining the direction and performance of corporations. The primary participants are (1) the shareholders, (2) the management (led by the CEO), and (3) the board of directors."* Our discussion will center on how corporations can succeed (or fail) in aligning managerial motives with the interests of the shareholders and their elected representatives, the board of directors.[48] As you will recall from Chapter 1, we discussed the important role of boards of directors and provided some examples of effective and ineffective boards.[49]

corporate governance the relationship among various participants in determining the direction and performance of corporations. The primary participants are (1) the shareholders, (2) the management, and (3) the board of directors.

Good corporate governance plays an important role in the investment decisions of major institutions, and a premium is often reflected in the price of securities of companies that practice it. The corporate governance premium is larger for firms in countries with sound corporate governance practices compared to countries with weaker corporate governance standards.[50]

Sound governance practices often lead to superior financial performance. However, this is not always the case. For example, practices such as independent directors (directors who are not part of the firm's management) and stock options are generally assumed to result in

---

*Management cannot ignore the demands of other important firm stakeholders such as creditors, suppliers, customers, employees, and government regulators. At times of financial duress, powerful creditors can exert strong and legitimate pressures on managerial decisions. In general, however, the attention to stakeholders other than the owners of the corporation must be addressed in a manner that is still consistent with maximizing long-term shareholder returns. For a seminal discussion on stakeholder management, refer to Freeman, R. E. 1984. *Strategic Management: A Stakeholder Approach.* Boston: Pitman.

The Relationship between Recommended Corporate Governance Practices and Firm Performance

A significant amount of research has examined the effect of corporate governance on firm performance. Some research has shown that implementing good corporate governance structures yields superior financial performance. Other research has not found a positive relationship between governance and performance. Results of a few of these studies are summarized below.

1. *A positive correlation between corporate governance and different measures of corporate performance.* Recent studies show that there is a strong positive correlation between effective corporate governance and different indicators of corporate performance such as growth, profitability, and customer satisfaction. Over a recent three-year period, the average return of large capitalized firms with the best governance practices was more than five times higher than the performance of firms in the bottom corporate governance quartile.

Sources: Dalton, D. R., Daily, C. M., Ellstrand, A. E., & Johnson, J. L., 1998. Meta-analytic reviews of board composition, leadership structure, and financial performance. *Strategic Management Journal,* 19(3): 269–290; Sanders, W. G. & Hambrick, D. C. 2007. Swinging for the fences: The effects of CEO stock options on company risk-taking and performance. *Academy of Management Journal,* 50(5): 1055–1078; Harris, J. & Bromiley, P. 2007. Incentives to cheat: The influence of executive compensation and firm performance on financial misrepresentation. *Organization Science,* 18(3): 350–367; Bauwhede, H. V. 2009. On the relation between corporate governance compliance and operating performance. *Accounting and Business Research.* 39(5): 497–513; Gill, A. 2001. Credit Lyonnais Securities (Asia). *Corporate governance in emerging markets: Saints and sinners,* April; and Low, C. K. 2002. *Corporate governance: An Asia-Pacific critique.* Hong Kong: Sweet & Maxwell Asia.

2. *Compliance with international best practices leads to superior performance.* Studies of European companies show that greater compliance with international corporate governance best practices concerning board structure and function has significant and positive relationships with return on assets (ROA). In 10 of 11 Asian and Latin American markets, companies in the top corporate governance quartile for their respective regions averaged 10 percent greater return on capital employed (ROCE) than their peers. In a study of 12 emerging markets, companies in the lowest corporate governance quartile had a much lower ROCE than their peers.

3. *Many recommended corporate governance practices do not have a positive relationship with firm performance.* In contrast to these studies, there is also a body of research suggesting that corporate governance practices do not have a positive influence on firm performance. With corporate boards, there is no evidence that including more external directors on the board of directors of U.S. corporations has led to substantially higher firm performance. Also, giving more stock options to CEOs to align their interests with stakeholders may lead them to take high-risk bets in firm investments that have a low probability to improve firm performance. Rather than making good decisions, CEOs may "swing for the fences" with these high-risk investments. Additionally, motivating CEOs with large numbers of stock options appears to increase the likelihood of unethical accounting violations by the firm as the CEO tries to increase the firm's stock price.

ethics

better performance. But in many cases, independent directors may not have the necessary expertise or involvement, and the granting of stock options to the CEO may lead to decisions and actions calculated to prop up share price only in the short term. Strategy Spotlight 9.4 presents some research evidence on governance practices and firm performance.

At the same time, few topics in the business press are generating as much interest (and disdain!) as corporate governance.

Some recent notable examples of flawed corporate governance include:[51]

- Satyam Computer Services, a leading Indian outsourcing company that serves more than a third of the Fortune 500 companies, significantly inflated its earnings and assets for years. The chairman, Ramalinga Raju, resigned and admitted he had cooked the books. Mr. Raju said he had overstated cash on hand by $1 billion and inflated profits and revenues in the September 2008 quarter. Satyam shares sank 78 percent, and the benchmark Sensex index lost 7.3 percent that day (January 7, 2009).

- Former Brocade CEO Gregory Reyes was sentenced to 21 months in prison and fined $15 million for his involvement in backdating stock option grants. Mr. Reyes was the first executive to go on trial and be convicted over the improper dating of stock-option awards, which dozens of companies have acknowledged since the practice came to light (January 17, 2008).
- In October 2010, Angelo Mozilo, the co-founder of Countrywide Financial, agreed to pay $67.5 million to the Securities and Exchange Commission (SEC) to settle fraud charges. He was charged with deceiving the home loan company's investors while reaping a personal windfall. He was accused of hiding risks about Countrywide's loan portfolio as the real estate market soured. Former Countrywide President David Sambol and former Chief Financial Officer Eric Sieracki were also charged with fraud, as they failed to disclose the true state of Countrywide's deteriorating mortgage portfolio. The SEC accused Mozilo of insider trading, alleging that he sold millions of dollars worth of Countrywide stock after he knew the company was doomed.
- Bernard L. Madoff, a former stock broker, investment advisor, and nonexecutive chairman of the NASDAQ stock market, was sentenced to 150 years of prison in June 2009 for a massive Ponzi scheme that defrauded thousands of investors of billions of dollars. Mr. Madoff pleaded guilty to 11 felony counts and admitted to managing the largest Ponzi scheme in history and concealing it from federal authorities and investors for more than a decade.

Because of the many lapses in corporate governance, we can see the benefits associated with effective practices.[52] However, corporate managers may behave in their own self-interest, often to the detriment of shareholders. Next we address the implications of the separation of ownership and management in the modern corporation, and some mechanisms that can be used to ensure consistency (or alignment) between the interests of shareholders and those of the managers to minimize potential conflicts.

The Modern Corporation:
The Separation of Owners (Shareholders) and Management

Some of the proposed definitions for a *corporation* include:

- "The business corporation is an instrument through which capital is assembled for the activities of producing and distributing goods and services and making investments. Accordingly, a basic premise of corporation law is that a business corporation should have as its objective the conduct of such activities with a view to enhancing the corporation's profit and the gains of the corporation's owners, that is, the shareholders." (Melvin Aron Eisenberg, *The Structure of Corporation Law*)
- "A body of persons granted a charter legally recognizing them as a separate entity having its own rights, privileges, and liabilities distinct from those of its members." (*American Heritage Dictionary*)
- "An ingenious device for obtaining individual profit without individual responsibility." (Ambrose Bierce, *The Devil's Dictionary*)[53]

corporation a mechanism created to allow different parties to contribute capital, expertise, and labor for the maximum benefit of each party.

All of these definitions have some validity and each one reflects a key feature of the corporate form of business organization—its ability to draw resources from a variety of groups and establish and maintain its own persona that is separate from all of them. As Henry Ford once said, "A great business is really too big to be human."

Simply put, a **corporation** is a mechanism created to allow different parties to contribute capital, expertise, and labor for the maximum benefit of each party.[54] The shareholders (investors) are able to participate in the profits of the enterprise without taking direct responsibility for the operations. The management can run the company without the responsibility of personally providing the funds. The shareholders have limited liability as well as rather limited involvement in the company's affairs. However, they reserve the right to elect directors who have the fiduciary obligation to protect their interests.

Over 70 years ago, Columbia University professors Adolf Berle and Gardiner C. Means addressed the divergence of the interests of the owners of the corporation from the professional managers who are hired to run it. They warned that widely dispersed ownership "released management from the overriding requirement that it serve stockholders." The separation of ownership from management has given rise to a set of ideas called "agency theory." Central to agency theory is the relationship between two primary players—the *principals* who are the owners of the firm (stockholders) and the *agents,* who are the people paid by principals to perform a job on their behalf (management). The stockholders elect and are represented by a board of directors that has a fiduciary responsibility to ensure that management acts in the best interests of stockholders to ensure long-term financial returns for the firm.

Agency theory is concerned with resolving two problems that can occur in agency relationships.[55] *The first is the agency problem that arises (1) when the goals of the principals and agents conflict, and (2) when it is difficult or expensive for the principal to verify what the agent is actually doing.*[56] The board of directors would be unable to confirm that the managers were actually acting in the shareholders' interests because managers are "insiders" with regard to the businesses they operate and thus are better informed than the principals. Thus, managers may act "opportunistically" in pursuing their own interests—to the detriment of the corporation.[57] Managers may spend corporate funds on expensive perquisites (e.g., company jets and expensive art), devote time and resources to pet projects (initiatives in which they have a personal interest but that have limited market potential), engage in power struggles (where they may fight over resources for their own betterment and to the detriment of the firm), and negate (or sabotage) attractive merger offers because they may result in increased employment risk.[58]

The second issue is the problem of risk sharing. This arises when the principal and the agent have different attitudes and preferences toward risk. The executives in a firm may favor additional diversification initiatives because, by their very nature, they increase the size of the firm and thus the level of executive compensation.[59] At the same time, such diversification initiatives may erode shareholder value because they fail to achieve some synergies that we discussed in Chapter 6 (e.g., building on core competencies, sharing activities, or enhancing market power). Agents (executives) may have a stronger preference toward diversification than shareholders because it reduces their personal level of risk from potential loss of employment. Executives who have large holdings of stock in their firms were more likely to have diversification strategies that were more consistent with shareholder interests—increasing long-term returns.[60]

At times, top-level managers engage in actions that reflect their self-interest rather than the interests of shareholders. We provide two examples below:[61]

- Micky M. Arison is chief executive of Carnival, the big cruise line. He is also chief executive and owner of the Miami Heat of the National Basketball Association. Carnival paid the Heat $675,000 for sponsorship, advertising, and season tickets. Although that may be a rather small sum—given Carnival's $2.2 billion in net income for the period—we could still ask whether the money would have been spent on something else if Arison didn't own the team.
- Alliance Semiconductor CEO N. Damodar Reddy has committed $20 million to Solar Ventures, a venture capital company run by his brother, C. N. Reddy. Other unnamed insiders purchased undisclosed stakes in Solar. However, Alliance won't disclose whether its CEO is one of them. To date, it has invested $12.5 million in

agency theory a theory of the relationship between principals and their agents, with emphasis on two problems: (1) the conflicting goals of principals and agents, along with the difficulty of principals to monitor the agents, and (2) the different attitudes and preferences toward risk of principals and agents.

Solar. Beth Young, senior research associate of the Corporate Library poses an interesting question: "Is Reddy using shareholder capital just to keep afloat his brother's fund and the insiders' investment?"

Governance Mechanisms: Aligning the Interests of Owners and Managers

>LO9.6
The role of corporate governance mechanisms in ensuring that the interests of managers are aligned with those of shareholders from both the United States and international perspectives.

As noted above, a key characteristic of the modern corporation is the separation of ownership from control. To minimize the potential for managers to act in their own self-interest, or "opportunistically," the owners can implement some governance mechanisms.[62] First, there are two primary means of monitoring the behavior of managers. These include (1) a committed and involved *board of directors* that acts in the best interests of the shareholders to create long-term value and (2) *shareholder activism,* wherein the owners view themselves as share*owners* instead of share*holders* and become actively engaged in the governance of the corporation. Finally, there are managerial incentives, sometimes called "contract-based outcomes," which consist of *reward and compensation agreements.* Here the goal is to carefully craft managerial incentive packages to align the interests of management with those of the stockholders.[63]

We close this section with a brief discussion of one of the most controversial issues in corporate governance—duality. Here, the question becomes: Should the CEO also be chairman of the board of directors? In many Fortune 500 firms, the same individual serves in both roles. However, in recent years, we have seen a trend toward separating these two positions. The key issue is what implications CEO duality has for firm governance and performance.

board of directors a group that has a fiduciary duty to ensure that the company is run consistently with the long-term interests of the owners, or shareholders, of a corporation and that acts as an intermediary between the shareholders and management.

A Committed and Involved Board of Directors   The **board of directors** acts as a fulcrum between the owners and controllers of a corporation. They are the intermediaries who provide a balance between a small group of key managers in the firm based at the corporate headquarters and a sometimes vast group of shareholders.[64] In the United States, the law imposes on the board a strict and absolute fiduciary duty to ensure that a company is run consistent with the long-term interests of the owners—the shareholders. The reality, as we have seen, is somewhat more ambiguous.[65]

The Business Roundtable, representing the largest U.S. corporations, describes the duties of the board as follows:

1. Select, regularly evaluate, and, if necessary, replace the CEO. Determine management compensation. Review succession planning.
2. Review and, where appropriate, approve the financial objectives, major strategies, and plans of the corporation.
3. Provide advice and counsel to top management.
4. Select and recommend to shareholders for election an appropriate slate of candidates for the board of directors; evaluate board processes and performance.
5. Review the adequacy of the systems to comply with all applicable laws/regulations.[66]

Given these principles, what makes for a good board of directors?[67] According to the Business Roundtable, the most important quality is a board of directors who are active, critical participants in determining a company's strategies.[68] That does not mean board members should micromanage or circumvent the CEO. Rather, they should provide strong oversight going beyond simply approving the CEO's plans. A board's primary responsibilities are to ensure that strategic plans undergo rigorous scrutiny, evaluate managers against high performance standards, and take control of the succession process.[69]

Although boards in the past were often dismissed as CEO's rubber stamps, increasingly they are playing a more active role by forcing out CEOs who cannot deliver on performance.[70] According to the consulting firm Booz Allen Hamilton, the rate of CEO departures for performance reasons more than tripled, from 1.3 percent to 4.2 percent, between 1995 and 2002.[71] And today's CEOs are not immune to termination. In September 2010, Jonathan Klein, the president of the CNN/U.S. cable channel, was fired because CNN's ratings had suffered.[72] Don Blankenship, CEO of coal mining giant Massey Energy, resigned in December 2010 after a deadly explosion in Massey's Upper Big Branch mine in West Virginia, a mine that had received numerous citations for safety violations in the last few years. The blast was the worst mining disaster in the United States in 40 years and resulted in criminal as well as civil investigations and lawsuits. Tony Hayward, CEO of oil and energy company British Petroleum (BP), was forced to step down in October 2010 after the Deepwater Horizon oil spill in the Gulf of Mexico led to an environmental disaster and a $20 billion recovery fund financed by BP.

Interestingly, CEO turnover declined during the recent financial crisis—going from 12.7 percent in 2007 to only 9.4 percent in 2010. One likely reason: Boards were reluctant to change leadership during the recession, concerned that if a CEO departed, investors might think that the company was coming unglued. However, with the economy recovering, Peter Crist, chairman of an executive search firm, predicts a return to double-digit turnover at big companies. He says, "We are going into a 24-month cycle of CEO volatility." "Deliver or depart" will clearly become a stronger message from boards.

Increasing CEO turnover could, however, pose a major problem for many organizations. Why? It appears that boards of directors are not typically engaged in effective succession planning. For example, only 35 percent of 1,318 executives surveyed by Korn/Ferry International in December 2010 said their companies had a succession plan. And 61 percent of respondents to a survey (conducted by Heidrick & Struggles and Stanford University's Rock Center for Corporate Governance) claimed their companies had *no* viable internal candidates.

Another key component of top-ranked boards is director independence.[73] Governance experts believe that a majority of directors should be free of all ties to either the CEO or the company.[74] That means a minimum of "insiders" (past or present members of the management team) should serve on the board, and that directors and their firms should be barred from doing consulting, legal, or other work for the company.[75] Interlocking directorships—in which CEOs and other top managers serve on each other's boards—are not desirable. But perhaps the best guarantee that directors act in the best interests of shareholders is the simplest: Most good companies now insist that directors own significant stock in the company they oversee.[76]

Such guidelines are not always followed. At times, the practices of the boards of directors are the antithesis of such guidelines. Consider the Walt Disney Co. Over a five-year period, former CEO Michael Eisner pocketed an astonishing $531 million. He likely had very little resistance from his board of directors:

> Many investors view the Disney board as an anachronism. Among Disney's 16 directors is Eisner's personal attorney—who for several years was chairman of the company's compensation committee! There was also the architect who designed Eisner's Aspen home and his parents' apartment. Joining them are the principal of an elementary school once attended by his children and the president of a university to which Eisner donated $1 million. The board also includes the actor Sidney Poitier, seven current and former Disney executives, and an attorney who does business with Disney. Moreover, most of the outside directors own little or no Disney stock. "It is an egregiously bad board—a train wreck waiting to happen," warns Michael L. Useem, a management professor at the University of Pennsylvania's Wharton School.[77]

This example also shows that "outside directors" are only beneficial to strong corporate governance if they are vigilant in carrying out their responsibilities.[78] As humorously suggested by Warren Buffett, founder and chairman of Berkshire Hathaway: "The ratcheting up of compensation has been obscene. . . . There is a tendency to put cocker spaniels on compensation committees, not Doberman pinschers."[79]

Many firms do have exemplary board practices. Below we list some of the excellent practices at Intel Corp., the world's largest semiconductor chip manufacturer, with $35 billion in revenues:[80]

- ***Mix of inside and outside directors.*** The board believes that there should be a majority of independent directors on the board. However, the board is willing to have members of management, in addition to the CEO, as directors.
- ***Board presentations and access to employees.*** The board encourages management to schedule managers to be present at meetings who: (1) can provide additional insight into the items being discussed because of personal involvement in these areas, or (2) have future potential that management believes should be given exposure to the board.
- ***Formal evaluation of officers.*** The Compensation Committee conducts, and reviews with the outside directors, an annual evaluation to help determine the salary and executive bonus of all officers, including the chief executive officer.

Exhibit 9.7 shows how boards of directors can improve their practices.

Shareholder Activism   As a practical matter, there are so many owners of the largest American corporations that it makes little sense to refer to them as "owners" in the sense of

Exhibit 9.7 Best Practice Ideas: The New Rules for Directors

Issue	Suggestion
Pay	**Know the Math**
Companies will disclose full details of CEO payouts. Activist investors are already drawing up hit lists of companies where CEO paychecks are out of line with performance.	Before okaying any financial package, directors must make sure they can explain the numbers. They need to adopt the mindset of an activist investor and ask: What's the harshest criticism someone could make about this package?
Strategy	**Make It a Priority**
Boards have been so focused on compliance that duties like strategy and leadership oversight too often get ignored. Only 59 percent of directors in a recent study rated their board favorably on setting strategy	To avoid spending too much time on compliance issues, move strategy up to the beginning of the meeting. Annual one-, two- or three-day offsite meetings on strategy alone are becoming standard for good boards.
Financials	**Put in the Time**
Although 95 percent of directors in the recent study said they were doing a good job of monitoring financials, the number of earnings restatements hit a new high in 2006, after breaking records in 2004 and 2005.	Even nonfinancial board members need to monitor the numbers and keep a close eye on cash flows. Audit committee members should prepare to spend 300 hours a year on committee responsibilities.
Crisis Management	**Dig in**
Some 120 companies are under scrutiny for options backdating, and the 100 largest companies have replaced 56 CEOs in the past five years—nearly double the terminations in the prior five years.	The increased scrutiny on boards means that a perfunctory review will not suffice if a scandal strikes. Directors can no longer afford to defer to management in a crisis. They must roll up their sleeves and move into watchdog mode.

Source: From No Byrnes and J. Sassen, "Board of Hard Knocks," *BusinessWeek,* January 22, 2007, pp. 36–39. Used with permission of *Bloomberg BusinessWeek.* copyright © 2007. All rights reserved.

individuals becoming informed and involved in corporate affairs.[81] However, even an individual shareholder has several rights, including (1) the right to sell the stock, (2) the right to vote the proxy (which includes the election of board members), (3) the right to bring suit for damages if the corporation's directors or managers fail to meet their obligations, (4) the right to certain information from the company, and (5) certain residual rights following the company's liquidation (or its filing for reorganization under bankruptcy laws), once creditors and other claimants are paid off.[82]

Collectively, shareholders have the power to direct the course of corporations.[83] This may involve acts such as being party to shareholder action suits and demanding that key issues be brought up for proxy votes at annual board meetings.[84] The power of shareholders has intensified in recent years because of the increasing influence of large institutional investors such as mutual funds (e.g., T. Rowe Price and Fidelity Investments) and retirement systems such as TIAA-CREF (for university faculty members and school administrative staff).[85] Institutional investors hold approximately 50 percent of all listed corporate stock in the United States.[86]

Shareholder activism refers to actions by large shareholders, both institutions and individuals, to protect their interests when they feel that managerial actions diverge from shareholder value maximization.

Many institutional investors are aggressive in protecting and enhancing their investments. They are shifting from traders to owners. They are assuming the role of permanent shareholders and rigorously analyzing issues of corporate governance. In the process they are reinventing systems of corporate monitoring and accountability.[87]

Consider the proactive behavior of CalPERS, the California Public Employees' Retirement System, which manages over $200 billion in assets and is the third largest pension fund in the world. Every year CalPERS reviews the performance of U.S. companies in its stock portfolio and identifies those that are among the lowest long-term relative performers and have governance structures that do not ensure full accountability to company owners. This generates a long list of companies, each of which may potentially be publicly identified as a CalPERS "Focus Company"—corporations to which CalPERS directs specific suggested governance reforms. CalPERS meets with the directors of each of these companies to discuss performance and governance issues. The CalPERS Focus List contains those companies that continue to merit public and market attention at the end of the process.

The 2009 CalPERS Focus List named four companies for poor economic and governance practices: *Eli Lilly* of Indianapolis, Indiana; *Hill-Rom Holdings* of Batesville, Indiana; *Hospitality Properties Trust* of Newton, Massachusetts; and *IMS Health* of Norwalk, Connecticut.[88] In addition to the four firms performing below their peer group for the past five years, CalPERS has expressed the following specific concerns about these firms:

- Eli Lilly, the big drug manufacturer, continues to deny shareowners any opportunity to amend bylaws.
- Hill-Rom Holdings, a medical technology provider, refuses to remove its staggered board structure and to allow shareowners to amend its bylaws.
- Hospitality Properties Trust, a real estate investment fund in hotels and trade centers, refuses to terminate its "classified" board, where directors serve staggered terms rather than standing for election each year.
- IMS Health, a provider of intelligence to the pharmaceutical and health care industries, denies the right of shareowners to call a special meeting or act by written consent and to adopt annual nonbinding advisory votes on executive compensation practices.

While appearing punitive to company management, such aggressive activism has paid significant returns for CalPERS (and other stockholders of the "Focused" companies). A Wilshire Associates study of the "CalPERS Effect" of corporate governance examined the performance of 62 targets over a five-year period: while the stock of these companies

shareholder activism actions by large shareholders to protect their interests when they feel that managerial actions of a corporation diverge from shareholder value maximization.

trailed the Standard & Poor's Index by 89 percent in the five-year period before CalPERS acted, the same stocks outperformed the index by 23 percent in the following five years, adding approximately $150 million annually in additional returns to the fund.

Perhaps no discussion of shareholder activism would be complete without mention of Carl Icahn, a famed activist with a personal net worth of about $13 billion:

> The bogeyman I am now chasing is the structure of American corporations, which permit managements and boards to rule arbitrarily and too often receive egregious compensation even after doing a subpar job. Yet they remain accountable to no one.[89]

Managerial Rewards and Incentives   As we discussed earlier in the chapter, incentive systems must be designed to help a company achieve its goals.[90] From the perspective of governance, one of the most critical roles of the board of directors is to create incentives that align the interests of the CEO and top executives with the interests of owners of the corporation—long-term shareholder returns.[91] Shareholders rely on CEOs to adopt policies and strategies that maximize the value of their shares.[92] A combination of three basic policies may create the right monetary incentives for CEOs to maximize the value of their companies:[93]

1. Boards can require that the CEOs become substantial owners of company stock.
2. Salaries, bonuses, and stock options can be structured so as to provide rewards for superior performance and penalties for poor performance.
3. Threat of dismissal for poor performance can be a realistic outcome.

In recent years the granting of stock options has enabled top executives of publicly held corporations to earn enormous levels of compensation. In 2007, the average CEO in the Standard & Poor's 500 stock index took home 433 times the pay of the average worker—up from 40 times the average in 1980. The counterargument, that the ratio is down from the 514 multiple in 2000, doesn't get much traction.[94] It has been estimated that there could be as many as 50 or more companies with CEO pay packages over $150 million.[95]

Many boards have awarded huge option grants despite poor executive performance, and others have made performance goals easier to reach. In 2002 nearly 200 companies swapped or repriced options—all to enrich wealthy executives who are already among the country's richest people. However, stock options can be a valuable governance mechanism to align the CEO's interests with those of the shareholders. The extraordinarily high level of compensation can, at times, be grounded in sound governance principles.[96] For example, Howard Solomon, CEO of Forest Laboratories, received total compensation of $148.5 million in 2001.[97] This represented $823,000 in salary, $400,000 in bonus, and $147.3 million in stock options that were exercised. However, shareholders also did well, receiving gains of 40 percent. The firm has enjoyed spectacular growth over the past ten years, and Solomon has been CEO since 1977. Thus, huge income is attributed largely to gains that have built up over many years. As stated by compensation committee member Dan Goldwasser, "If a CEO is delivering substantial increases in shareholder value, . . . it's only appropriate that he be rewarded for it."

However, the "pay for performance" principle doesn't always hold.[98] In addition to the granting of stock options, boards of directors are often failing to fulfill their fiduciary responsibilities to shareholders when they lower the performance targets that executives need to meet in order to receive millions of dollars. At Ford, for example, its "profit" goal for 2007 was to *lose* $4.9 billion. Ford beat the target, however, and lost *only* $3.9 billion. CEO Alan Mulally was rewarded $12 million in compensation, including a $7 million bonus for exceeding the profit goal. Ford's stock price fell 10 percent in 2007.

TIAA-CREF has provided several principles of corporate governance with regard to executive compensation (see Exhibit 9.8).[99] These include the importance of aligning the rewards of all employees—rank and file as well as executives—to the long-term performance of the corporation; general guidelines on the role of cash compensation, stock, and "fringe benefits"; and the mission of a corporation's compensation committee.[100]

Stock-based compensation plans are a critical element of most compensation programs and can provide opportunities for managers whose efforts contribute to the creation of shareholder wealth. In evaluating the suitability of these plans, considerations of reasonableness, scale, linkage to performance, and fairness to shareholders and all employees also apply. TIAA-CREF, the largest pension system in the world, has set forth the following guidelines for stock-based compensation. Proper stock-based plans should:

- Allow for creation of executive wealth that is reasonable in view of the creation of shareholder wealth. Management should not prosper through stock while share-holders suffer.

- Have measurable and predictable outcomes that are directly linked to the company's performance.

- Be market oriented, within levels of comparability for similar positions in companies of similar size and business focus.

- Be straightforward and clearly described so that investors and employees can understand them.

- Be fully disclosed to the investing public and be approved by shareholders.

Source: *www.tiaa-cref.org/pubs.*

CEO Duality: Is It Good or Bad?

CEO duality is one of the most controversial issues in corporate governance. It refers to the dual leadership structure where the CEO acts simultaneously as the chair of the board of directors.[101] Scholars, consultants, and executives who are interested in determining the best way to manage a corporation are divided on the issue of the roles and responsibilities of a CEO. Two schools of thought represent the alternative positions:

Unity of Command   Advocates of the unity of command perspective believe when one person holds both roles, he or she is able to act more efficiently and effectively. CEO duality provides firms with a clear focus on both objectives and operations as well as eliminates confusion and conflict between the CEO and the chairman. Thus, it enables smoother, more effective strategic decision making. Holding dual roles as CEO/chairman creates unity across a company's managers and board of directors and ulti-mately allows the CEO to serve the shareholders even better. Having leadership focused in a single individual also enhances a firm's responsiveness and ability to secure critical resources. This perspective maintains that separating the two jobs—that of a CEO and that of the chairperson of the board of directors—may produce all types of undesir-able consequences. CEOs may find it harder to make quick decisions. Ego-driven chief executives and chairmen may squabble over who is ultimately in charge. The shortage of first-class business talent may mean that bosses find themselves second-guessed by peo-ple who know little about the business.[102] Companies like Coca-Cola, JPMorgan Chase, and Time Warner have refused to divide the CEO's and chairman's jobs and support this duality structure.

Agency Theory   Supporters of agency theory argue that the positions of CEO and chairman should be separate. The case for separation is based on the simple principle of the separation of power. How can boards discharge their basic duty—monitoring the boss—if the boss is chairing its meetings and setting its agenda? How can a board act as a safeguard against corruption or incompetence when the possible source of that corruption and incompetence is sitting at the head of the table? CEO duality can create a conflict of interest that could negatively affect the interests of the shareholders.

Duality also complicates the issue of CEO succession. In some cases, a CEO/chairman may choose to retire as CEO but keep his or her role as the chairman. Although this splits up the roles, which appeases an agency perspective, it nonetheless puts the new CEO in a difficult position. The chairman is bound to question some of the new changes put in place, and the board as a whole might take sides with the chairman they trust and with whom they have a history. This conflict of interest would make it difficult for the new CEO to institute any changes, as the power and influence would still remain with the former CEO.[103]

Duality also serves to reinforce popular doubts about the legitimacy of the system as a whole and evokes images of bosses writing their own performance reviews and setting their own salaries. One of the first things that some of America's troubled banks, including Citigroup, Washington Mutual, Wachovia, and Wells Fargo, did when the financial crisis hit in 2007–2008 was to separate the two jobs. Firms like Siebel Systems, Disney, Oracle, and Microsoft have also decided to divide the roles between CEO and the chairman and eliminate duality.

The increasing pressures for effective corporate governance have led to a sharp decline in duality. Firms now routinely separate the jobs of chairman and chief executive. For example, in 2009, fewer than 12 percent of incoming CEOs were also made chairman—compared with 48 percent in 2002.

These same pressures have led to other changes in corporate governance practices. For example, the New York Stock Exchange and NASDAQ have demanded that companies should have a majority of independent directors. Also, CEOs are held accountable for their performance and tossed out if they fail to perform, with the average length of tenure dropping from 8.1 years in 2000 to 6.3 years in 2009. Finally, more than 90 percent of S&P 500 companies with CEOs who also serve as chairman of the board have appointed "lead" or "presiding" directors to act as a counterweight to a combined chairman and chief executive.

External Governance Control Mechanisms

Thus far, we've discussed internal governance mechanisms. Internal controls, however, are not always enough to ensure good governance. The separation of ownership and control that we discussed earlier requires multiple control mechanisms, some internal and some external, to ensure that managerial actions lead to shareholder value maximization. Further, society-at-large wants some assurance that this goal is met without harming other stakeholder groups. Now we discuss several **external governance control mechanisms** that have developed in most modern economies. These include the market for corporate control, auditors, governmental regulatory bodies, banks and analysts, media, and public activists.

external governance control mechanisms methods that ensure that managerial actions lead to shareholder value maximization and do not harm other stakeholder groups that are outside the control of the corporate governance system.

The Market for Corporate Control   Let us assume for a moment that internal control mechanisms in a company are failing. This means that the board is ineffective in monitoring managers and is not exercising the oversight required of them and that shareholders are passive and are not taking any actions to monitor or discipline managers. Under these circumstances managers may behave opportunistically.[104] Opportunistic behavior can take many forms. First, they can *shirk* their responsibilities. Shirking means that managers fail to exert themselves fully, as is required of them. Second, they can engage in *on the job consumption*. Examples of on the job consumption include private jets, club memberships, expensive artwork in the offices, and so on. Each of these represents consumption by managers that does not in any way increase shareholder value. Instead, they actually diminish shareholder value. Third, managers may engage in *excessive product-market diversification*.[105] As we discussed in Chapter 6, such diversification serves to reduce only the employment risk of the managers rather than the financial risk of the shareholders, who can more cheaply diversify their risk by owning a portfolio of investments. Is there any external mechanism to stop managers from shirking, consumption on the job, and excessive diversification?

The **market for corporate control** is one external mechanism that provides at least some partial solution to the problems described. If internal control mechanisms fail and the management is behaving opportunistically, the likely response of most shareholders will be to sell their stock rather than engage in activism.[106] As more stockholders vote with their feet, the value of the stock begins to decline. As the decline continues, at some point the market value of the firm becomes less than the book value. A corporate raider can take over the company for a price less than the book value of the assets of the company. The first thing that the raider may do on assuming control over the company will be to fire the underperforming management. The risk of being acquired by a hostile raider is often referred to as the **takeover constraint.** The takeover constraint deters management from engaging in opportunistic behavior.[107]

market for corporate control an external control mechanism in which shareholders dissatisfied with a firm's management sell their shares.

Although in theory the takeover constraint is supposed to limit managerial opportunism, in recent years its effectiveness has become diluted as a result of a number of defense tactics adopted by incumbent management (see Chapter 6). Foremost among them are poison pills, greenmail, and golden parachutes. Poison pills are provisions adopted by the company to reduce its worth to the acquirer. An example would be payment of a huge one-time dividend, typically financed by debt. Greenmail involves buying back the stock from the acquirer, usually at an attractive premium. Golden parachutes are employment contracts that cause the company to pay lucrative severance packages to top managers fired as a result of a takeover, often running to several million dollars.

takeover constraint the risk to management of the firm being acquired by a hostile raider.

Auditors   Even when there are stringent disclosure requirements, there is no guarantee that the information disclosed will be accurate. Managers may deliberately disclose false information or withhold negative financial information as well as use accounting methods that distort results based on highly subjective interpretations. Therefore, all accounting statements are required to be audited and certified to be accurate by external auditors. These auditing firms are independent organizations staffed by certified professionals who verify the firm's books of accounts. Audits can unearth financial irregularities and ensure that financial reporting by the firm conforms to standard accounting practices.

Recent developments leading to the bankruptcy of firms such as Enron and World-Com and a spate of earnings restatements raise questions about the failure of the auditing firms to act as effective external control mechanisms. Why did an auditing firm like Arthur Andersen, with decades of good reputation in the auditing profession at stake, fail to raise red flags about accounting irregularities? First, auditors are appointed by the firm being audited. The desire to continue that business relationship sometimes makes them overlook financial irregularities. Second, most auditing firms also do consulting work and often have lucrative consulting contracts with the firms that they audit. Understandably, some of them tend not to ask too many difficult questions, because they fear jeopardizing the consulting business, which is often more profitable than the auditing work.

The recent restatement of earnings by Xerox is an example of the lack of independence of auditing firms. The SEC filed a lawsuit against KPMG, the world's third largest accounting firm, in January 2003 for allowing Xerox to inflate its revenues by $3 billion between 1997 and 2000. Of the $82 million that Xerox paid KPMG during those four years, only $26 million was for auditing. The rest was for consulting services. When one of the auditors objected to Xerox's practice of booking revenues for equipment leases earlier than it should have, Xerox asked KPMG to replace him. It did.[108]

Banks and Analysts   Commercial and investment banks have lent money to corporations and therefore have to ensure that the borrowing firm's finances are in order and that the loan covenants are being followed. Stock analysts conduct ongoing in-depth studies of the firms that they follow and make recommendations to their clients to buy, hold, or sell. Their rewards and reputation depend on the quality of these recommendations. Their access to information, knowledge of the industry and the firm, and the insights they gain from interactions with the management of the company enable them to alert the investing community of both positive and negative developments relating to a company.

It is generally observed that analyst recommendations are often more optimistic than warranted by facts. "Sell" recommendations tend to be exceptions rather than the norm. Many analysts failed to grasp the gravity of the problems surrounding failed companies such as Enron and Global Crossing till the very end. Part of the explanation may lie in the fact that most analysts work for firms that also have investment banking relationships with the companies they follow. Negative recommendations by analysts can displease the management, who may decide to take their investment banking business to a rival firm. Otherwise independent and competent analysts may be pressured to overlook negative information or tone down their criticism. A recent settlement between the Securities and Exchange Commission and the New York State Attorney General with 10 banks requires them to pay $1.4 billion in penalties and to fund independent research for investors.[109]

Regulatory Bodies   The extent of government regulation is often a function of the type of industry. Banks, utilities, and pharmaceuticals are subject to more regulatory oversight because of their importance to society. Public corporations are subject to more regulatory requirements than private corporations.[110]

All public corporations are required to disclose a substantial amount of financial information by bodies such as the Securities and Exchange Commission. These include quarterly and annual filings of financial performance, stock trading by insiders, and details of executive compensation packages. There are two primary reasons behind such requirements. First, markets can operate efficiently only when the investing public has faith in the market system. In the absence of disclosure requirements, the average investor suffers from a lack of reliable information and therefore may completely stay away from the capital market. This will negatively impact an economy's ability to grow. Second, disclosure of information such as insider trading protects the small investor to some extent from the negative consequences of information asymmetry. The insiders and large investors typically have more information than the small investor and can therefore use that information to buy or sell before the information becomes public knowledge.

The failure of a variety of external control mechanisms led the U.S. Congress to pass the Sarbanes-Oxley Act in 2002. This act calls for many stringent measures that would ensure better governance of U.S. corporations. Some of these measures include:[111]

- *Auditors* are barred from certain types of nonaudit work. They are not allowed to destroy records for five years. Lead partners auditing a client should be changed at least every five years.
- *CEOs* and *CFOs* must fully reveal off-balance-sheet finances and vouch for the accuracy of the information revealed.
- *Executives* must promptly reveal the sale of shares in firms they manage and are not allowed to sell when other employees cannot.
- *Corporate lawyers* must report to senior managers any violations of securities law lower down.

Strategy Spotlight 9.5 addresses one of the increased expenses that many companies now face in complying with the Sarbanes-Oxley Act—higher compensation for more involved and committed directors.

Media and Public Activists   The press is not usually recognized as an external control mechanism in the literature on corporate governance. There is no denying that in all developed capitalist economies, the financial press and media play an important indirect role in monitoring the management of public corporations. In the United States, business magazines such as *Bloomberg Businessweek* and *Fortune,* financial newspapers such as

The Impact of the 2002 Sarbanes-Oxley Act on Corporate Directors

The cost of outside directors has been rising. Not only are well-qualified directors in short supply but also the Sarbanes-Oxley Act has increased the demands of the job. According to compensation consultants Pearl Meyer & Partners, the typical director of a large corporation earned $216,000 in 2009, up from $129,667 in 2003. For some, total compensation, including cash payments, stock grants, and other perks, has climbed above seven figures. Even during the recession of 2008–2009, corporate directors' paychecks seemed to be soaring. For example, in 2008 Anthony P. Terracciano made $4.8 million as the chairman of student loan giant SLM and Jack P. Randall made $1.5 million from XTO Energy, an oil and natural gas producing company.

Directors can thank the Sarbanes-Oxley Act for the continuing generosity. The Act was created to protect shareholders by restricting the power of corporate executives. In the past, many boards had become little more than rubber stamps for everything from merger strategy to executive compensation. This led to disaster in cases such as Enron, WorldCom, and Tyco. Sarbanes-Oxley and other regulatory efforts sought to protect shareholders by empowering directors and making them more accountable.

Following the Sarbanes-Oxley Act, there were several years of 20 percent to 30 percent annual increases as director compensation rose to reflect the new realities of expanded responsibilities for directors as well as the increased demand for directors who met independence rules. The pay increases came at a time when the supply of new directors was declining due to the additional risks—real or perceived—of serving as a director.

One consequence of Sarbanes-Oxley is that many directors work harder. A decade ago a typical director attended four board meetings a year and spent about 100 hours a year on board tasks, according to the National Association of Corporate Directors. Now, directors attend an average of six board meetings a year, spend an average of 225 hours a year on board duties, and convene at other times for committee meetings. In fact, corporate directors can log as many as 400 hours a year when corporations are financially distressed or reorganizing.

Sources: Byrnes, N. 2010. The Gold-Plated Boardroom. *Bloomberg Businessweek.* February 22: 72–73; and Hilburn, W. 2010. Trends in Director Compensation. *www.businessweek.com.* October 19: np.

The Wall Street Journal and *Investors Business Daily,* as well as television networks like Financial News Network and CNBC are constantly reporting on companies. Public perceptions about a company's financial prospects and the quality of its management are greatly influenced by the media. Food Lion's reputation was sullied when ABC's *Prime Time Live* in 1992 charged the company with employee exploitation, false package dating, and unsanitary meat handling practices. Bethany McLean of *Fortune* magazine is often credited as the first to raise questions about Enron's long-term financial viability.[112]

Similarly, consumer groups and activist individuals often take a crusading role in exposing corporate malfeasance.[113] Well-known examples include Ralph Nader and Erin Brockovich, who played important roles in bringing to light the safety issues related to GM's Corvair and environmental pollution issues concerning Pacific Gas and Electric Company, respectively. Ralph Nader has created over 30 watchdog groups, including:[114]

- *Aviation Consumer Action Project.* Works to propose new rules to prevent flight delays, impose penalties for deceiving passengers about problems, and push for higher compensation for lost luggage.
- *Center for Auto Safety.* Helps consumers find plaintiff lawyers and agitate for vehicle recalls, increased highway safety standards, and lemon laws.
- *Center for Study of Responsive Law.* This is Nader's headquarters. Home of a consumer project on technology, this group sponsored seminars on Microsoft remedies and pushed for tougher Internet privacy rules. It also took on the drug industry over costs.
- *Pension Rights Center.* This center helped employees of IBM, General Electric, and other companies to organize themselves against cash-balance pension plans.

strategy spotlight

Two Examples of Powerful External Control Mechanisms

McDonald's

After years of fending off and ignoring critics, McDonald's has begun working with them. In 1999, People for the Ethical Treatment of Animals (PETA) launched its "McCruelty" campaign asking the company to take steps to alleviate the suffering of animals killed for its restaurants. Since then, PETA has switched tactics and is cooperating with the burger chain to modernize the company's animal welfare standards and make further improvements. Following pressure from PETA, McDonald's used its influence to force egg suppliers to improve the living conditions of hens and cease debeaking them. PETA has publicly lauded the company for its efforts. Recently, McDonald's also has required beef and pork processors to improve their handling of livestock prior to slaughter. The company conducts regular audits of the packing plants to determine whether the animals are being treated humanely and will suspend purchases from slaughterhouses that don't meet the company's standards. The company's overall image appears to have improved. According to the global consulting firm Reputation Institute, McDonald's score, on a scale of 100, has climbed 8 points to 63 since 2007—a dramatic improvement.

Sources: Kiley, D. & Helm, B. 2009. The Great Trust Offensive. *Bloomberg Businessweek*, September 28: 38–42; Brasher, P. 2010. McDonald's Orders Improvements in Treatment of Hens. *abcnews.com*, August 23: np; Glover, K. 2009. PETA vs. McDonald's: The Nicest Way to Kill a Chicken. *www.bnet.com*. February 20: np; *www.mccruelty.com*; Greenhouse, S. 2010. Pressured, Nike to Help Workers in Honduras. *The New York Times*, July 27: B1; Padgett, T. 2010. Just Pay It: Nike Creates Fund for Honduran Workers. *www.time.com*, July 27: np; and Bustillo, M. 2010. Nike to Pay Some $2 Million to Workers Fired by Subcontractors. *www.online.wsj.com*, July 26: np.

Nike

In January 2009, 1,800 laborers lost their jobs in Honduras when two local factories that made shirts for the U.S. sports-apparel giant Nike suddenly closed their doors and did not pay workers the $2 million in severance and other unemployment benefits they were due by law. Following pressure from U.S. universities and student groups, Nike announced that it was setting up a $1.5 million "workers' relief fund" to assist the workers. Nike also agreed to provide vocational training and finance health coverage for workers laid off by the two subcontractors.

The relief fund from Nike came after pressure by groups such as the Worker Rights Consortium, which informed Nike customers of the treatment of the workers. The Worker Rights Consortium also convinced scores of U.S. universities whose athletic programs and campus shops buy Nike shoes and clothes to threaten cancellation of those lucrative contracts unless Nike did something to address the plight of the Honduran workers. Another labor watchdog, United Students Against Sweatshops, staged demonstrations outside Nike shops while chanting "Just Pay It," a play on Nike's commercial slogan, "Just Do It." The University of Wisconsin cancelled its licensing agreement with the company over the matter and other schools, including Cornell University and the University of Washington, indicated they were thinking of following suit. The agreement is the latest involving overseas apparel factories in which an image-conscious brand like Nike responded to campaigns led by college students, who often pressure universities to stand up to producers of college-logo apparel when workers' rights are threatened.

As we have noted above, some public activists and watchdog groups can exert a strong force on organizations and influence decisions that they may make. Strategy Spotlight 9.6 provides two examples of this phenomenon.

Corporate Governance: An International Perspective

The topic of corporate governance has long been dominated by agency theory and based on the explicit assumption of the separation of ownership and control.[115] The central conflicts are principal–agent conflicts between shareholders and management. However, such an underlying assumption seldom applies outside of the United States and the United Kingdom. This is particularly true in emerging economies and continental Europe. Here, there is often concentrated ownership, along with extensive family ownership and control, business group structures, and weak legal protection for minority shareholders. Serious conflicts tend to exist between two classes of principals: controlling shareholders and minority shareholders. Such conflicts can be called **principal–principal (PP) conflicts,** as opposed to *principal–agent* conflicts (see Exhibits 9.9 and 9.10).

Strong family control is one of the leading indicators of concentrated ownership. In East Asia (excluding China), approximately 57 percent of the corporations have board chairmen and CEOs from the controlling families. In continental Europe, this number is 68 percent. A very common practice is the appointment of family members as board chairmen, CEOs, and other top executives. This happens because the families are controlling (not necessarily majority) shareholders. In 2003, 30-year-old James Murdoch was appointed CEO of British Sky Broadcasting (BSkyB), Europe's largest satellite broadcaster. There was very vocal resistance by minority shareholders. Why was he appointed in the first place? James's father just happened to be Rupert Murdoch, who controlled 35 percent of BSkyB and chaired the board. Clearly, this is a case of a PP conflict.

In general, three conditions must be met for PP conflicts to occur:

- A dominant owner or group of owners who have interests that are distinct from minority shareholders.
- Motivation for the controlling shareholders to exercise their dominant positions to their advantage.
- Few formal (such as legislation or regulatory bodies) or informal constraints that would discourage or prevent the controlling shareholders from exploiting their advantageous positions.

principal–principal conflicts conflicts between two classes of principals— controlling shareholders and minority shareholders— within the context of a corporate governance system.

	Principal–Agent Conflicts	Principal–Principal Conflicts
Goal Incongruence	Between shareholders and professional managers who own a relatively small portion of the firm's equity.	Between controlling shareholders and minority shareholders.
Ownership Pattern	Dispersed—5%–20% is considered "concentrated ownership."	Concentrated—Often greater than 50% of equity is controlled by controlling shareholders.
Manifestations	Strategies that benefit entrenched managers at the expense of shareholders in general (e.g., shirking, pet projects, excessive compensation, and empire building).	Strategies that benefit controlling shareholders at the expense of minority shareholders (e.g., minority shareholder expropriation, nepotism, and cronyism).
Institutional Protection of Minority Shareholders	Formal constraints (e.g., judicial reviews and courts) set an upper boundary on potential expropriation by majority shareholders. Informal norms generally adhere to shareholder wealth maximization.	Formal institutional protection is often lacking, corrupted, or un-enforced. Informal norms are typically in favor of the interests of controlling shareholders ahead of those of minority investors.

Exhibit 9.9
Traditional Principal–Agent Conflicts versus Principal–Principal Conflicts: How They Differ along Dimensions

Source: Adapted from Young, M., Peng, M. W., Ahlstrom, D., & Bruton, G. 2002. Governing the Corporation in Emerging Economies: A Principal–Principal Perspective. *Academy of Management Best Papers Proceedings,* Denver.

Exhibit 9.10 Principal–Agent Conflicts and Principal–Principal Conflicts: A Diagram

Source: Young, M. N., Peng, M. W., Ahlstrom, D., Bruton, G. D., & Jiang, 2008. Principal–Principal Conflicts in Corporate Governance. *Journal of Management Studies* 45(1):196–220; and Peng, M. V. 2006. *Global Strategy.* Cincinnati: Thomson South-Western. We are very appreciative of the helpful comments of Mike Young of Hong Kong Baptist University and Mike Peng of the University of Texas at Dallas.

expropriation of minority shareholders activities that enrich the controlling shareholders at the expense of the minority shareholders.

business groups a set of firms that, though legally independent, are bound together by a constellation of formal and informal ties and are accustomed to taking coordinated action.

The result is often that family managers, who represent (or actually are) the controlling shareholders, engage in **expropriation of minority shareholders,** which is defined as activities that enrich the controlling shareholders at the expense of minority shareholders. What is their motive? After all, controlling shareholders have incentives to maintain firm value. But controlling shareholders may take actions that decrease aggregate firm performance if their personal gains from expropriation exceed their personal losses from their firm's lowered performance.

Another ubiquitous feature of corporate life outside of the United States and United Kingdom are *business groups* such as the keiretsus of Japan and the chaebols of South Korea. This is particularly dominant in emerging economies. A **business group** is "a set of firms that, though legally independent, are bound together by a constellation of formal and informal ties and are accustomed to taking coordinated action."[116] Business groups are especially common in emerging economies, and they differ from other organizational forms in that they are communities of firms without clear boundaries.

Business groups have many advantages that can enhance the value of a firm. They often facilitate technology transfer or intergroup capital allocation that otherwise might be impossible because of inadequate institutional infrastructure such as excellent financial services firms. On the other hand, informal ties—such as cross-holdings, board interlocks, and coordinated actions—can often result in intragroup activities and transactions, often at very favorable terms to member firms. Expropriation can be legally done through *related transactions,* which can occur when controlling owners sell firm assets to another firm they own at below market prices or spin off the most profitable part of a public firm and merge it with another of their private firms.

Strategy Spotlight 9.7 provides examples from Latin America of effective corporate governance.

Effective and Ineffective Corporate Governance among "Multilatinas"

Latin-owned companies, such as Mexico's Cemex, Argentina's Arcor, and Brazil's Embraer, have been successful in their home markets against U.S. and European competitors. Several of these companies have become "multilatinas," pursuing a strategy of regional and international expansion. Recently, 82 percent of merger and acquisition deals in Latin America were originated by Latin companies. However, while the rise of these Latin firms is promising, it is not enough to ensure they will be competitive globally against large industrialized multinational firms. Access to international capital markets necessary for the "multilatinas" to grow has created a need for a new openness in corporate governance and transparency for these firms.

There are three components emerging-market multinational firms need to implement to succeed:

Sources: Pigorini, P., Ramos, A., & de Souza, I. 2008. Pitting Latin Multinationals against Established Giants. *Strategy + Business,* November 4: *www.strategy-business.com/media/file/leading_ideas-20081104.pdf*; Martinez, J., Esperanca, J., & de la Torre, J. 2005. Organizational Change among Emerging Latin American Firms: From "Multilatinas" to Multinationals. *Management Research,* 3(3): 173–188; Krauss, C. 2007. Latin American Companies Make Big U.S. Gains. *New York Times,* May 2: *www.nytimes.com/2007/05/02/-business/worldbusiness/02latin.html*.

- **Shareholder rights.** Minority shareholders must be protected through clear and fair dividend distribution and fair valuation in the event of mergers and acquisitions.
- **Compliance.** The audit committee of the board must be empowered to evaluate the financial statements of the firm and interact with both internal and external auditors.
- **Board and management composition.** Because many multilatinas are still in the process of building effective governance systems, it is important that the board members and top managers have credible professional backgrounds and experience.

These firms need to set up the right board and manager dynamics both to improve access to capital and to implement international management. Many multilatinas were or still are family-owned firms. Boards of these firms tend to be filled with members who have a strong loyalty to the controlling family, but not necessarily exposure to global strategic initiatives and strategies. Many of these firms still use centralized information control systems. In order to grow, some firms may have to consider giving local country managers more authority to make decisions.

Reflecting on Career Implications . . .

- *Behavioral Control:* What sources of behavioral control does your organization employ? In general, too much emphasis on rules and regulations may stifle initiative and be detrimental to your career opportunities.
- *Rewards and Incentives:* Is your organization's reward structure fair and equitable? Does it effectively reward outstanding performance? If not, there may be a long-term erosion of morale which may have long-term adverse career implications for you.
- *Culture:* Consider the type of organization culture that would provide the best work environment for your career goals. How does your organization's culture deviate from this concept? Does your organization have a strong and effective culture? If so, professionals are more likely to develop strong "firm specific" ties, which further enhances collaboration.
- *Corporate Governance:* Does your organization practice effective corporate governance? Such practices will enhance a firm's culture and it will be easier to attract top talent. Operating within governance guidelines is usually a strong indicator of organizational citizenship which, in turn, should be good for your career prospects.

Summary

For firms to be successful, they must practice effective strategic control and corporate governance. Without such controls, the firm will not be able to achieve competitive advantages and outperform rivals in the marketplace.

We began the chapter with the key role of informational control. We contrasted two types of control systems: what we termed "traditional" and "contemporary" information control systems. Whereas traditional control systems may have their place in placid, simple competitive environments, there are fewer of those in today's economy. Instead, we advocated the contemporary approach wherein the internal and external environment are constantly monitored so that when surprises emerge, the firm can modify its strategies, goals, and objectives.

Behavioral controls are also a vital part of effective control systems. We argued that firms must develop the proper balance between culture, rewards and incentives, and boundaries and constraints. Where there are strong and positive cultures and rewards, employees tend to internalize the organization's strategies and objectives. This permits a firm to spend fewer resources on monitoring behavior, and assures the firm that the efforts and initiatives of employees are more consistent with the overall objectives of the organization.

In the final section of this chapter, we addressed corporate governance, which can be defined as the relationship between various participants in determining the direction and performance of the corporation. The primary participants include shareholders, management (led by the chief executive officer), and the board of directors. We reviewed studies that indicated a consistent relationship between effective corporate governance and financial performance. There are also several internal and external control mechanisms that can serve to align managerial interests and shareholder interests. The internal mechanisms include a committed and involved board of directors, shareholder activism, and effective managerial incentives and rewards. The external mechanisms include the market for corporate control, banks and analysts, regulators, the media, and public activists. We also addressed corporate governance from both a United States and an international perspective.

Summary Review Questions

1. Why are effective strategic control systems so important in today's economy?
2. What are the main advantages of "contemporary" control systems over "traditional" control systems? What are the main differences between these two systems?
3. Why is it important to have a balance between the three elements of behavioral control—culture; rewards and incentives; and, boundaries?
4. Discuss the relationship between types of organizations and their primary means of behavioral control.
5. Boundaries become less important as a firm develops a strong culture and reward system. Explain.
6. Why is it important to avoid a "one best way" mentality concerning control systems? What are the consequences of applying the same type of control system to all types of environments?
7. What is the role of effective corporate governance in improving a firm's performance? What are some of the key governance mechanisms that are used to ensure that managerial and shareholder interests are aligned?
8. Define principal–principal (PP) conflicts. What are the implications for corporate governance?

Key Terms

strategic control, 318
traditional approach to strategic control, 319
informational control, 319
behavioral control, 321
organizational culture, 323
reward system, 324
boundaries and constraints, 325
corporate governance, 330
corporation, 332
agency theory, 333
board of directors, 334
shareholder activism, 337
external governance control mechanisms, 340
market for corporate control, 341
takeover constraint, 341
principal–principal conflicts, 345
expropriation of minority shareholders, 346
business groups, 346

Experiential Exercise

McDonald's Corporation, the world's largest fast-food restaurant chain, with 2010 revenues of $24 billion, has recently been on a "roll." Its shareholder value has more than doubled between February 2006 and February 2011. Using the Internet or library sources, evaluate the quality of the corporation in terms of management, the board of directors, and shareholder activism. Are the issues you list favorable or unfavorable for sound corporate governance?

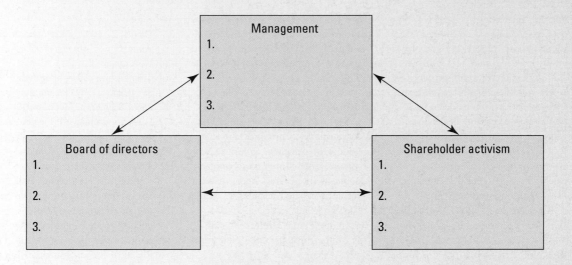

Management
1.
2.
3.

Board of directors
1.
2.
3.

Shareholder activism
1.
2.
3.

Application Questions & Exercises

1. The problems of many firms may be attributed to a "traditional" control system that failed to continuously monitor the environment and make necessary changes in their strategy and objectives. What companies are you familiar with that responded appropriately (or inappropriately) to environmental change?

2. How can a strong, positive culture enhance a firm's competitive advantage? How can a weak, negative culture erode competitive advantages? Explain and provide examples.

3. Use the Internet to research a firm that has an excellent culture and/or reward and incentive system. What are this firm's main financial and nonfinancial benefits?

4. Using the Internet, go to the website of a large, publicly held corporation in which you are interested. What evidence do you see of effective (or ineffective) corporate governance?

Ethics Questions

1. Strong cultures can have powerful effects on employee behavior. How does this create inadvertent control mechanisms? That is, are strong cultures an ethical way to control behavior?

2. Rules and regulations can help reduce unethical behavior in organizations. To be effective, however, what other systems, mechanisms, and processes are necessary?

References

1. Loomis, C. J. 2010. Directors: Feeding at the trough. *Fortune,* January 18: 20; Schonberger, J. 2009. Why you should care about corporate governance, *www.fool.com.* November 10: np; Hood, H. J. 2009. *Chesapeake Energy Corporation* Schedule 14A; and *www.sec.gov.* November 10: np. We thank Zia Shakir for his valued contributions.

2. This chapter draws upon Picken, J. C. & Dess, G. G. 1997. *Mission critical.* Burr Ridge, IL: Irwin Professional Publishing.

3. For a unique perspective on governance, refer to: Carmeli, A. & Markman, G. D. 2011. Capture, governance, and resilience: Strategy implications from the history of Rome. *Strategic Management Journal,* 32(3):332–341.

4. Argyris, C. 1977. Double-loop learning in organizations. *Harvard Business Review,* 55: 115–125.

5. Simons, R. 1995. Control in an age of empowerment. *Harvard Business Review,* 73: 80–88. This chapter draws on this source in the discussion of informational control.

6. Goold, M. & Quinn, J. B. 1990. The paradox of strategic controls. *Strategic Management Journal,* 11: 43–57.

7. Quinn, J. B. 1980. *Strategies for change.* Homewood, IL: Richard D. Irwin.

8. Mintzberg, H. 1987. Crafting strategy. *Harvard Business Review,* 65: 66–75.

9. Weston, J. S. 1992. Soft stuff matters. *Financial Executive,* July–August: 52–53.

10. This discussion of control systems draws upon Simons, op. cit.

11. Ryan, M. K., Haslam, S. A., & Renneboog, L. D. R. 2011. Who gets the carrot and who gets the stick? Evidence of gender discrimination in executive remuneration. *Strategic Management Journal,* 32(3): 301–321.

12. For an interesting perspective on this issue and how a downturn in the economy can reduce the tendency toward "free agency" by managers and professionals, refer to Morris, B. 2001. White collar blues. *Fortune,* July 23: 98–110.

13. For a colorful example of behavioral control in an organization, see: Beller, P. C. 2009. Activision's unlikely hero. *Forbes.* February 2: 52–58.

14. Ouchi, W. 1981. *Theory Z.* Reading, MA: Addison-Wesley; Deal, T. E. & Kennedy, A. A. 1982. *Corporate cultures.* Reading, MA: Addison-Wesley; Peters, T. J. & Waterman, R. H. 1982. *In search of excellence.* New York: Random House; Collins, J. 2001. *Good to great.* New York: HarperCollins.

15. Collins, J. C. & Porras, J. I. 1994. *Built to last: Successful habits of visionary companies.* New York: Harper Business.

16. Lee, J. & Miller, D. 1999. People matter: Commitment to employees, strategy, and performance in Korean firms. *Strategic Management Journal,* 6: 579–594.

17. For an insightful discussion of IKEA's unique culture, see Kling, K. & Goteman, I. 2003. IKEA CEO Anders Dahlvig on international growth and IKEA's unique corporate culture and brand identity. *Academy of Management Executive,* 17(1): 31–37.

18. For a discussion of how professionals inculcate values, refer to Uhl-Bien, M. & Graen, G. B. 1998. Individual self-management: Analysis of professionals' self-managing activities in functional and cross-functional work teams. *Academy of Management Journal,* 41(3): 340–350.

19. A perspective on how antisocial behavior can erode a firm's culture can be found in Robinson, S. L. & O'Leary-Kelly, A. M. 1998. Monkey see, monkey do: The influence of work groups on the antisocial behavior of employees. *Academy of Management Journal,* 41(6): 658–672.

20. An interesting perspective on organizational culture is in: Mehta, S. N. 2009. UnderArmour reboots. *Fortune,* February 2: 29–33.

21. For insights on social pressure as a means for control, refer to: Goldstein, N. J. 2009. Harnessing social pressure. *Harvard Business Review,* 87(2): 25.

22. Mitchell, R. 1989. Masters of innovation. *BusinessWeek,* April 10: 58–63.

23. Sellers, P. 1993. Companies that serve you best. *Fortune,* May 31: 88.

24. Southwest Airlines Culture Committee. 1993. *Luv Lines* (company publication), March–April: 17–18; for an interesting perspective on the "downside" of strong "cultlike" organizational cultures, refer to Arnott, D. A. 2000. *Corporate cults.* New York: AMACOM.

25. Kerr, J. & Slocum, J. W., Jr. 1987. Managing corporate culture through reward systems. *Academy of Management Executive,* 1(2): 99–107.

26. For a unique perspective on leader challenges in managing wealthy professionals, refer to Wetlaufer, S. 2000. Who wants to manage a millionaire? *Harvard Business Review,* 78(4): 53–60.

27. *www.starbucks.com*; Wood, Z. 2010. Starbucks' staff set to get free shares in incentive schemes. *www.guardian.co.uk*; December 19: np; and Hammers, M. 2003. Starbucks is pleasing employees and pouring profits. *Workforce Management.* October: 58–59.

28. These next two subsections draw upon Dess, G. G. & Picken, J. C. 1997. *Beyond productivity.* New York: AMACOM.

29. For a discussion of the benefits of stock options as executive compensation, refer to Hall, B. J. 2000. What you need to know about stock options. *Harvard Business Review,* 78(2): 121–129.

30. Tully, S. 1993. Your paycheck gets exciting. *Fortune,* November 13: 89.

31. Carter, N. M. & Silva, C. 2010. Why men still get more promotions than women. *Harvard Business Review,* 88(9): 80–86.

32. Zellner, W., Hof, R. D., Brandt, R., Baker, S., & Greising, D. 1995. Go-go goliaths. *BusinessWeek,* February 13: 64–70.

33. This section draws on Dess & Picken, op. cit.: chap. 5.

34. Simons, op. cit.

35. Davis, E. 1997. Interview: Norman Augustine. *Management Review,* November: 11.

36. This section draws upon Dess, G. G. & Miller, A. 1993. *Strategic management.* New York: McGraw-Hill.

37. For a good review of the goal-setting literature, refer to Locke, E. A. & Latham, G. P. 1990. *A theory of goal setting and task performance.* Englewood Cliffs, NJ: Prentice Hall.

38. For an interesting perspective on the use of rules and regulations that is counter to this industry's (software) norms, refer to Fryer, B. 2001. Tom Siebel of Siebel Systems: High tech the old fashioned way. *Harvard Business Review,* 79(3): 118–130.

39. Thompson, A. A. Jr. & Strickland, A. J., III. 1998. *Strategic management: Concepts and cases* (10th ed.): 313. New York: McGraw-Hill.

40. Ibid.

41. Teitelbaum, R. 1997. Tough guys finish first. *Fortune,* July 21: 82–84.

42. Weaver, G. R., Trevino, L. K., & Cochran, P. L. 1999. Corporate ethics programs as control systems: Influences of executive commitment and environmental factors. *Academy of Management Journal,* 42(1): 41–57.

43. Cadbury, S. A. 1987. Ethical managers make their own rules. *Harvard Business Review,* 65: 3, 69–73.

44. Weber, J. 2003. CFOs on the hot seat. *BusinessWeek,* March 17: 66–70.

45. William Ouchi has written extensively about the use of clan control (which is viewed as an alternate to bureaucratic or market control). Here, a powerful culture results in people aligning their individual interests with those of the firm. Refer to Ouchi, op. cit. This section also draws on Hall, R. H. 2002. *Organizations: Structures, processes, and outcomes* (8th ed.). Upper Saddle River, NJ: Prentice Hall.

46. Poundstone, W. 2003. *How would you move Mount Fuji?* New York: Little, Brown and company, page 59.

47. Interesting insights on corporate governance are in: Kroll, M., Walters, B. A., & Wright, P. 2008. Board vigilance, director experience, and

corporate outcomes. *Strategic Management Journal,* 29(4): 363–382.

48. For a brief review of some central issues in corporate governance research, see: Hambrick, D. C., Werder, A. V., & Zajac, E. J. 2008. New directions in corporate governance research. *Organization Science,* 19(3): 381–385.

49. Monks, R. & Minow, N. 2001. *Corporate governance* (2nd ed.). Malden, MA: Blackwell.

50. Pound, J. 1995. The promise of the governed corporation. *Harvard Business Review,* 73(2): 89–98.

51. Maurer, H. & Linblad, C. 2009. Scandal at Satyam. *BusinessWeek,* January 19: 8; Scheck, J. & Stecklow, S. 2008. Brocade ex-CEO gets 21 months in prison. *The Wall Street Journal,* January 17: A3; Levine, D. & Graybow, M. 2010. Mozilo to pay millions in Countrywide settlement. *finance. yahoo.com.* October 15: np; Ellis, B. 2010. Countrywide's Mozilo to pay $67.5 million settlement. *cnnmoney. com.* October 15: np; Frank, R., Efrati, A., Lucchetti, A. & Bray, C. 2009. Madoff jailed after admitting epic scam. *The Wall Street Journal.* March 13: A1; and Henriques, D. B. 2009. Madoff is sentenced to 150 years for Ponzi scheme. *www. nytimes.com.* June 29: np.

52. Corporate governance and social networks are discussed in: McDonald, M. L., Khanna, P., & Westphal, J. D. 2008. *Academy of Management Journal.* 51(3): 453–475.

53. This discussion draws upon Monks & Minow, op. cit.

54. For an interesting perspective on the politicization of the corporation, read: Palazzo, G. & Scherer, A. G. 2008. Corporate social responsibility, democracy, and the politicization of the corporation. *Academy of Management Review,* 33(3): 773–774.

55. Eisenhardt, K. M. 1989. Agency theory: An assessment and review. *Academy of Management Review,* 14(1): 57–74. Some of the seminal contributions to agency theory include Jensen, M. & Meckling, W. 1976. Theory of the firm: Managerial behavior, agency costs, and ownership

structure. *Journal of Financial Economics,* 3: 305–360; Fama, E. & Jensen, M. 1983. Separation of ownership and control. *Journal of Law and Economics,* 26: 301, 325; and Fama, E. 1980. Agency problems and the theory of the firm. *Journal of Political Economy,* 88: 288–307.

56. Nyberg, A. J., Fulmer, I. S., Gerhart, B. & Carpenter, M. 2010. Agency theory revisited: CEO return and shareholder interest alignment. *Academy of Management Journal,* 53(5): 1029–1049.

57. Managers may also engage in "shirking"—that is, reducing or withholding their efforts. See, for example, Kidwell, R. E., Jr. & Bennett, N. 1993. Employee propensity to withhold effort: A conceptual model to intersect three avenues of research. *Academy of Management Review,* 18(3): 429–456.

58. For an interesting perspective on agency and clarification of many related concepts and terms, visit *www.encycogov.com.*

59. The relationship between corporate ownership structure and export intensity in Chinese firms is discussed in: Filatotchev, I., Stephan, J., & Jindra, B. 2008. Ownership structure, strategic controls and export intensity of foreign-invested firms in transition economies. *Journal of International Business,* 39(7): 1133–1148.

60. Argawal, A. & Mandelker, G. 1987. Managerial incentives and corporate investment and financing decisions. *Journal of Finance,* 42: 823–837.

61. The Carnival and Alliance Semiconductor examples draw upon: MacDonald, E. 2004. Crony capitalism. *Forbes,* June 21: 140–146.

62. For an insightful, recent discussion of the academic research on corporate governance, and in particular the role of boards of directors, refer to Chatterjee, S. & Harrison, J. S. 2001. Corporate governance. In Hitt, M. A., Freeman, R. E., & Harrison, J. S. (Eds.). *Handbook of strategic management:* 543–563. Malden, MA: Blackwell.

63. For an interesting theoretical discussion on corporate governance in

Russia, see: McCarthy, D. J. & Puffer, S. M. 2008. Interpreting the ethicality of corporate governance decisions in Russia: Utilizing integrative social contracts theory to evaluate the relevance of agency theory norms. *Academy of Management Review,* 33(1): 11–31.

64. Haynes, K. T. & Hillman, A. 2010. The effect of board capital and CEO power on strategic change. *Strategic Management Journal,* 31(110): 1145–1163.

65. This opening discussion draws on Monks & Minow, op. cit. 164, 169; see also Pound, op. cit.

66. Business Roundtable. 1990. *Corporate governance and American competitiveness,* March: 7.

67. The director role in acquisition performance is addressed in: Westphal, J. D. & Graebner, M. E. 2008. What do they know? The effects of outside director acquisition experience on firm acquisition performance. *Strategic Management Journal,* 29(11): 1155–1178.

68. Byrne, J. A., Grover, R., & Melcher, R. A. 1997. The best and worst boards. *BusinessWeek,* November 26: 35–47. The three key roles of boards of directors are monitoring the actions of executives, providing advice, and providing links to the external environment to provide resources. See Johnson, J. L., Daily, C. M., & Ellstrand, A. E. 1996. Boards of directors: A review and research agenda. *Academy of Management Review,* 37: 409–438.

69. Pozen, R. C. 2010. The case for professional boards. *Harvard Business Review,* 88(12): 50–58.

70. The role of outside directors is discussed in: Lester, R. H., Hillman, A., Zardkoohi, A., & Cannella, A. A. Jr. 2008. Former government officials as outside directors: The role of human and social capital. *Academy of Management Journal,* 51(5): 999–1013.

71. McGeehan, P. 2003. More chief executives shown the door, study says. *New York Times,* May 12: C2.

72. The examples in this paragraph draw upon Helyar, J. & Hymowitz,

C. 2011. The recession is gone, and the CEO could be next. *Bloomberg Businessweek.* Februrary 7–February 13: 24–26; Stelter, B. 2010. Jonathan Klein to leave CNN. *mediadecoder. blogs.nytimes.com.* September 24: np; Silver, A. 2010. Milestones. *TIME Magazine.* December 20: 28; *www. bp.com* and Mouawad, J. & Krauss, C. 2010. BP is expected to replace Hayward as chief with American. *The New York Times.* July 26: A1.

73. For an analysis of the effects of outside directors' compensation on acquisition decisions, refer to Deutsch, T., Keil, T., & Laamanen, T. 2007. Decision making in acquisitions: The effect of outside directors' compensation on acquisition patterns. *Journal of Management,* 33(1): 30–56.

74. Director interlocks are addressed in: Kang, E. 2008. Director interlocks and spillover effects of reputational penalties from financial reporting fraud. *Academy of Management Journal,* 51(3): 537–556.

75. There are benefits, of course, to having some insiders on the board of directors. Inside directors would be more aware of the firm's strategies. Additionally, outsiders may rely too often on financial performance indicators because of information asymmetries. For an interesting discussion, see Baysinger, B. D. & Hoskisson, R. E. 1990. The composition of boards of directors and strategic control: Effects on corporate strategy. *Academy of Management Review,* 15: 72–87.

76. Hambrick, D. C. & Jackson, E. M. 2000. Outside directors with a stake: The linchpin in improving governance. *California Management Review,* 42(4): 108–127.

77. Ibid.

78. Disney has begun to make many changes to improve its corporate governance, such as assigning only independent directors to important board committees, restricting directors from serving on more than three boards, and appointing a lead director who can convene the board without approval by the CEO. In recent years, the Disney Co. has shown up on some "best" board lists. In addition Eisner has recently relinquished the chairman position.

79. Talk show. 2002. *BusinessWeek,* September 30: 14.

80. Ward, R. D. 2000. *Improving corporate boards.* New York: Wiley.

81. A discussion on the shareholder approval process in executive compensation is presented in: Brandes, P., Goranova, M., & Hall, S. 2008. Navigating shareholder influence: Compensation plans and the shareholder approval process. *Academy of Management Perspectives,* 22(1): 41–57.

82. Monks and Minow, op. cit.: 93.

83. A discussion of the factors that lead to shareholder activism is found in Ryan, L. V. & Schneider, M. 2002. The antecedents of institutional investor activism. *Academy of Management Review,* 27(4): 554–573.

84. For an insightful discussion of investor activism, refer to David, P., Bloom, M., & Hillman, A. 2007. Investor activism, managerial responsiveness, and corporate social performance. *Strategic Management Journal,* 28(1): 91–100.

85. There is strong research support for the idea that the presence of large block shareholders is associated with value-maximizing decisions. For example, refer to Johnson, R. A., Hoskisson, R. E., & Hitt, M. A. 1993. Board of director involvement in restructuring: The effects of board versus managerial controls and characteristics. *Strategic Management Journal,* 14: 33–50.

86. For a discussion of institutional activism and its link to CEO compensation, refer to: Chowdhury, S. D. & Wang, E. Z. 2009. Institutional activism types and CEO compensation. *Journal of Management,* 35(1): 5–36.

87. For an interesting perspective on the impact of institutional ownership on a firm's innovation strategies, see Hoskisson, R. E., Hitt, M. A., Johnson, R. A., & Grossman, W. 2002. *Academy of Management Journal,* 45(4): 697–716.

88. *www.calpers.ca.gov;*

89. Icahn, C. 2007. Icahn: On activist investors and private equity run wild. *BusinessWeek,* March 12: 21–22. For an interesting perspective on Carl Icahn's transition (?) from corporate raider to shareholder activist, read Grover, R. 2007. Just don't call him a raider. *BusinessWeek,* March 5: 68–69. The quote in the text is part of Icahn's response to the article by R. Grover.

90. For a study of the relationship between ownership and diversification, refer to Goranova, M., Alessandri, T. M., Brandes, P., & Dharwadkar, R. 2007. Managerial ownership and corporate diversification: A longitudinal view, *Strategic Management Journal,* 28(3): 211–226.

91. Jensen, M. C. & Murphy, K. J. 1990. CEO incentives—It's not how much you pay, but how. *Harvard Business Review,* 68(3): 138–149.

92. For a perspective on the relative advantages and disadvantages of "duality"—that is, one individual serving as both Chief Executive Office and Chairman of the Board, see Lorsch, J. W. & Zelleke, A. 2005. Should the CEO be the chairman? *MIT Sloan Management Review,* 46(2): 71–74.

93. A discussion of knowledge sharing is addressed in: Fey, C. F. & Furu, P. 2008. Top management incentive compensation and knowledge sharing in multinational corporations. *Strategic Management Journal,* 29(12): 1301–1324.

94. Sasseen, J. 2007. A better look at the boss's pay. *BusinessWeek,* February 26: 44–45; and Weinberg, N., Maiello, M., & Randall, D. 2008. Paying for failure. *Forbes,* May 19: 114, 116.

95. Byrnes, N. & Sasseen, J. 2007. Board of hard knocks. *BusinessWeek,* January 22: 36–39.

96. Research has found that executive compensation is more closely aligned with firm performance in companies with compensation committees and boards dominated by outside directors. See, for example, Conyon, M. J. & Peck, S. I. 1998. Board control, remuneration committees, and top management compensation. *Academy of Management Journal,* 41: 146–157.

97. Lavelle, L., Jespersen, F. F., & Arndt, M. 2002. Executive pay. *Business-Week,* April 15: 66–72.

98. A perspective on whether or not CEOs are overpaid is provided in: Kaplan, S. N. 2008. Are U.S. CEOs overpaid: A response to Bogle and Walsh, J. P. *Academy of Management Perspectives.* 22(3): 28–34.

99. *www.tiaa-cref.org/pubs.*

100. Some insights on CEO compensation—and the importance of ethics—are addressed in: Heineman, B. W. Jr. 2008. The fatal flaw in pay for performance. *Harvard Business Review.* 86(6): 31, 34.

101. Chahine, S. & Tohme, N. S. 2009. Is CEO duality always negative? An exploration of CEO duality and ownership structure in the Arab IPO context. *Corporate Governance: An International Review.* 17(2): 123–141; and McGrath, J. 2009. How CEOs work. *HowStuffWorks.com.* January 28: np.

102. Anonymous. 2009. Someone to watch over them. *The Economist.* October 17: 78; Anonymous. 2004. Splitting up the roles of CEO and Chairman: Reform or red herring? *Knowledge@Wharton.* June 2: np; and Kim, J. 2010. Shareholders reject split of CEO and chairman jobs at JPMorgan. *FierceFinance.com.* May 18: np.

103. Tuggle, C. S., Sirmon, D. G., Reutzel, C. R. & Bierman, L. 2010. Commanding board of director attention: Investigating how organizational performance and CEO duality affect board members' attention to monitoring. *Strategic Management Journal.* 31: 946–968; Weinberg, N. 2010. No more lapdogs. *Forbes.* May 10: 34–36; and Anonymous. 2010. Corporate constitutions. *The Economist.* October 30: 74.

104. Such opportunistic behavior is common in all principal-agent relationships. For a description of agency problems, especially in the context of the relationship between shareholders and managers, see Jensen, M. C. & Meckling, W. H. 1976. Theory of the firm: Managerial behavior, agency costs, and ownership structure. *Journal of Financial Economics,* 3: 305–360.

105. Hoskisson, R. E. & Turk, T. A. 1990. Corporate restructuring: Governance and control limits of the internal market. *Academy of Management Review,* 15: 459–477.

106. For an insightful perspective on the market for corporate control and how it is influenced by knowledge intensity, see Coff, R. 2003. Bidding wars over R&D-intensive firms: Knowledge, opportunism, and the market for corporate control. *Academy of Management Journal,* 46(1): 74–85.

107. Walsh, J. P. & Kosnik, R. D. 1993. Corporate raiders and their disciplinary role in the market for corporate control. *Academy of Management Journal,* 36: 671–700.

108. Gunning for KPMG. 2003. *Economist,* February 1: 63.

109. Timmons, H. 2003. Investment banks: Who will foot their bill? *BusinessWeek,* March 3: 116.

110. The role of regulatory bodies in the banking industry is addressed in: Bhide, A. 2009. Why bankers got so reckless. *BusinessWeek,* February 9: 30–31.

111. Wishy-washy: The SEC pulls its punches on corporate-governance rules. 2003. *Economist,* February 1: 60.

112. McLean, B. 2001. Is Enron overpriced? *Fortune,* March 5: 122–125.

113. Swartz, J. 2010. Timberland's CEO on standing up to 65,000 angry activists. *Harvard Business Review,* 88 (9): 39–43.

114. Bernstein, A. 2000. Too much corporate power. *BusinessWeek,* September 11: 35–37.

115. This section draws upon Young, M. N., Peng, M. W., Ahlstrom, D., Bruton, G. D., & Jiang, Y. 2005. Principal–principal conflicts in corporate governance (un-published manuscript); and, Peng, M. W. 2006. *Globalstrategy.* Cincinnati: Thomson South-Western. We appreciate the helpful comments of Mike Young of Hong Kong Baptist University and Mike Peng of the University of Texas at Dallas.

116. Khanna, T. & Rivkin, J. 2001. Estimating the performance effects of business groups in emerging markets. *Strategic Management Journal,* 22: 45–74.

chapter TEN

Creating Effective Organizational Designs

After reading this chapter, you should have a good understanding of:

LO10.1 The growth patterns of major corporations and the relationship between a firm's strategy and its structure.

LO10.2 Each of the traditional types of organizational structure: simple, functional, divisional, and matrix.

LO10.3 The implications of a firm's international operations for organizational structure.

LO10.4 Why there is no "one best way" to design strategic reward and evaluation systems, and the important contingent roles of business- and corporate-level strategies.

LO10.5 The different types of boundaryless organizations—barrier-free, modular, and virtual—and their relative advantages and disadvantages.

LO10.6 The need for creating ambidextrous organizational designs that enable firms to explore new opportunities and effectively integrate existing operations.

LEARNING OBJECTIVES

To implement strategies successfully, firms must have appropriate organizational designs. These include the processes and integrating mechanisms necessary to ensure that boundaries among internal activities and external parties, such as suppliers, customers, and alliance partners, are flexible and permeable. A firm's performance will suffer if its managers don't carefully consider both of these organizational design attributes.

In the first section, we begin by discussing the growth patterns of large corporations to address the important relationships between the strategy that a firm follows and its corresponding structure. For example, as firms diversify into related product-market areas, they change their structure from functional to divisional. We then address the different types of traditional structures—simple, functional, divisional, and matrix—and their relative advantages and disadvantages. We close with a discussion of the implications of a firm's international operations for the structure of its organization.

The second section takes the perspective that there is no "one best way" to design an organization's strategic reward and evaluation system. Here we address two important contingencies: business- and corporate-level strategy. For example, when strategies require a great deal of collaboration, as well as resource and information sharing, there must be incentives and cultures that encourage and reward such initiatives.

The third section discusses the concept of the "boundaryless" organization. We do *not* argue that organizations should have no internal and external boundaries. Instead, we suggest that in rapidly changing and unpredictable environments, organizations must strive to make their internal and external boundaries both flexible and permeable. We suggest three different types of boundaryless organizations: barrier-free, modular, and virtual.

The fourth section focuses on the need for managers to recognize that they typically face two opposing challenges: (1) being proactive in taking advantage of new opportunities and (2) ensuring the effective coordination and integration of existing operations. This suggests the need for ambidextrous organizations; that is, firms that can both be efficient in how they manage existing assets and competencies and take advantage of opportunities in rapidly changing and unpredictable environments—conditions that are becoming more pronounced in today's global markets. ●

Learning from Mistakes

In mid-July 2010, Hong Kong's travel industry was reeling from a wild rant by a commission-based tour guide which was unfortunately captured on video.[1] The video went viral on the Internet and hit television screens across the mainland. More than a dozen television stations picked up the online video and played it constantly over a two-day period. What happened?

The seven-minute clip featured a female guide (nicknamed Ah Zhen) berating a group of mainland visitors and threatening to lock them out of their hotel rooms because they did not spend much at a jewelry store. In effect, this provided a shocking view of what Hong Kong can offer visitors. It followed a series of complaints about visitors being strong-armed by tour guides to go shopping and spend their money.

Ah Zhen is heard scolding the tourists in fluent Mandarin after they boarded their bus. "Don't tell me you don't need to shop," she said. "So later you are going to say you don't need to eat? I will lock you out of your hotel rooms. It's okay for you to stay poor at home, but when you travel outside, don't be like this. In this world there is no such thing as a free lunch."

She went on to talk about how the visitors found money for their airfares and then chides them: "We don't do this for charity. Let me be responsible for charity. I donated 10,500 yuan ($1,500) for Sichuan earthquake victims." She then pointed to shops offering top-quality goods, before adding, "Why did you bother to come to Hong Kong?" She lamented that the group did not look good compared with another group of tourists, who spent HKD137,000 ($17,000). "For a group of 24 people you only just spent HKD13,000 ($2,100). How can you just walk out of the shop like that?"

"It's you who owe me here, not me owing you," the guide continued. "I provided you with food and accommodations, but you people will not give. If you don't repay the debt in this life, you will have to repay it in your next life." She added, "Tonight I will lock all hotel room doors, because you don't need accommodations."

The clip sparked an outcry on the Internet. Some people said that they would no longer dare visit Hong Kong. Travel Industry Council Chairman Michael Wu Siu-ying said he had asked for the names of the travel agency and the tour agent from Guangdong, so that the council could take action.

When contacted, the tour guide became defensive and extremely vocal about mainland tourists condemning tour guides for forcing them to make purchases. "We don't force them to buy. When they sign up for the tour group, they should act responsibly.. . . You can see how much the tour group fees are.. . . You sign up for such a group, then you must do whatever is required. It is that simple. We did not force them to buy anything. We can't force them." She also said, "When they come, they know what they are doing. How much do they pay in fees? How many days are they staying?"

She further said, "Everybody has to earn a living. . . . I did this for the sake of surviving, just like you calling me in order for you to survive. . . . I have to eat. It is very normal for me to tell them about making purchases." Clearly, she was not happy about the media "hyping trivia" so that fewer mainland tour groups are coming. She also threatened the reporter not to write about her. "I will come and hold you accountable. I don't think there is anything wrong with what I did."

The government has given the Travel Industry Council three months to develop concrete measures to address the deteriorating image of Hong Kong as a tourist destination amid anger at the treatment of mainland tourists by commission-hungry guides. The council has set up a special task force to look into the issue.

One person's action has caused a chain reaction and tarnished the image of Hong Kong. One of the pitfalls of outsourcing is that the firm has less control. When companies outsource key activities, an inherent risk is that the quality of the performance of the contractors is not up to the standards of the firm. Further, at times, there are differences in cultural norms and insufficient training in place to ensure that contract employees adhere to standards and expectations.

One of the central concepts in this chapter is the importance of boundaryless organizations. Successful organizations create permeable boundaries among the internal activities as well as between the organization and its external customers, suppliers, and alliance partners. We introduced this idea in Chapter 3 in our discussion of the value-chain concept, which consisted of several primary (e.g., inbound logistics, marketing and sales) and support activities (e.g., procurement, human resource management). There are a number of possible benefits to outsourcing activities as part of becoming an effective boundaryless organization. However, outsourcing can also create challenges. As in the case of the tour operator in Hong Kong, the firm lost a certain amount of control by using independent contractors to provide services. Clearly, the outsourced tour guide was more focused on her personal financial incentives than the welfare of the travel firm or the tourists.

Today's managers are faced with two ongoing and vital activities in structuring and designing their organizations.[2] First, they must decide on the most appropriate type of organizational structure. Second, they need to assess what mechanisms, processes, and techniques are most helpful in enhancing the permeability of both internal and external boundaries.

Traditional Forms of Organizational Structure

Organizational structure refers to the formalized patterns of interactions that link a firm's tasks, technologies, and people.[3] Structures help to ensure that resources are used effectively in accomplishing an organization's mission. Structure provides a means of balancing two conflicting forces: a need for the division of tasks into meaningful groupings and the need to integrate such groupings in order to ensure efficiency and effectiveness.[4] Structure identifies the executive, managerial, and administrative organization of a firm and indicates responsibilities and hierarchical relationships. It also influences the flow of information as well as the context and nature of human interactions.[5]

> **organizational structure** the formalized patterns of interactions that link a firm's tasks, technologies, and people.

Most organizations begin very small and either die or remain small. Those that survive and prosper embark on strategies designed to increase the overall scope of operations and enable them to enter new product-market domains. Such growth places additional pressure on executives to control and coordinate the firm's increasing size and diversity. The most appropriate type of structure depends on the nature and magnitude of growth.

Patterns of Growth of Large Corporations: Strategy-Structure Relationships

A firm's strategy and structure change as it increases in size, diversifies into new product markets, and expands its geographic scope.[6] Exhibit 10.1 illustrates common growth patterns of firms.

> **>LO10.1**
> The growth patterns of major corporations and the relationship between a firm's strategy and its structure.

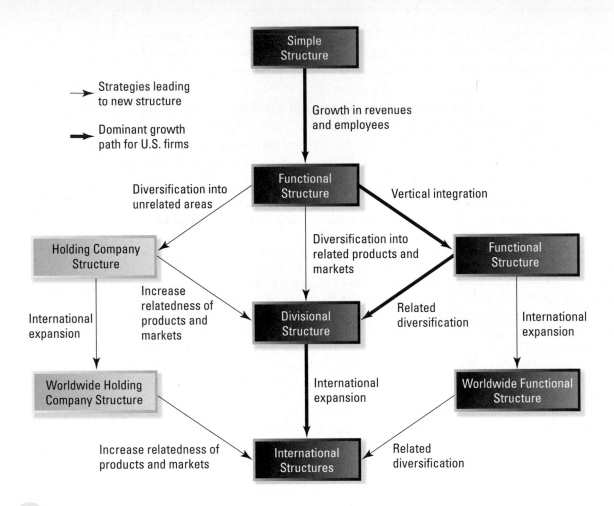

Exhibit 10.1   **Dominant Growth Patterns of Large Corporations**

Source: Adapted from J. R. Galbraith and R. K. Kazanjian. *Strategy Implementation: Structure, Systems and Process,* 2nd ed. Copyright © 1986.

A new firm with a *simple structure* typically increases its sales revenue and volume of outputs over time. It may also engage in some vertical integration to secure sources of supply (backward integration) as well as channels of distribution (forward integration). The simple-structure firm then implements a *functional structure* to concentrate efforts on both increasing efficiency and enhancing its operations and products. This structure enables the firm to group its operations into either functions, departments, or geographic areas. As its initial markets mature, a firm looks beyond its present products and markets for possible expansion.

A strategy of related diversification requires a need to reorganize around product lines or geographic markets. This leads to a *divisional structure.* As the business expands in terms of sales revenues, and domestic growth opportunities become somewhat limited, a firm may seek opportunities in international markets. A firm has a wide variety of structures to choose from. These include *international division, geographic area, worldwide product division, worldwide functional,* and *worldwide matrix.* Deciding upon the most appropriate structure when a firm has international operations depends on three primary factors: the extent of international expansion, type of strategy (global, multidomestic, or transnational), and the degree of product diversity.[7]

Some firms may find it advantageous to diversify into several product lines rather than focus their efforts on strengthening distributor and supplier relationships through vertical integration. They would organize themselves according to product lines by implementing a divisional structure. Also, some firms may choose to move into unrelated product areas, typically by acquiring existing businesses. Frequently, their rationale is that acquiring assets and competencies is more economical or expedient than developing them internally. Such an unrelated, or conglomerate, strategy requires relatively little integration across businesses and sharing of resources. Thus, a *holding company structure* becomes appropriate. There are many other growth patterns, but these are the most common.*

Now we will discuss some of the most common types of organizational structures—simple, functional, divisional (including two variants: *strategic business unit* and *holding company*), and matrix and their advantages and disadvantages. We will close the section with a discussion of the structural implications when a firm expands its operations into international markets.[8]

Simple Structure

The **simple organizational structure** is the oldest, and most common, organizational form. Most organizations are very small and have a single or very narrow product line in which the owner-manager (or top executive) makes most of the decisions. The owner-manager controls all activities, and the staff serves as an extension of the top executive.

Advantages The simple structure is highly informal and the coordination of tasks is accomplished by direct supervision. Decision making is highly centralized, there is little specialization of tasks, few rules and regulations, and an informal evaluation and reward system. Although the owner-manager is intimately involved in almost all phases of the business, a manager is often employed to oversee day-to-day operations.

Disadvantages   A simple structure may foster creativity and individualism since there are generally few rules and regulations. However, such "informality" may lead to problems. Employees may not clearly understand their responsibilities, which can lead to conflict and confusion. Employees may take advantage of the lack of regulations, act in their own self-interest, which can erode motivation and satisfaction and lead to the possible misuse of organizational resources. Small organizations have flat structures that limit opportunities for upward mobility. Without the potential for future advancement, recruiting and retaining talent may become very difficult.

Functional Structure

When an organization is small (15 employees or less), it is not necessary to have a variety of formal arrangements and groupings of activities. However, as firms grow, excessive demands may be placed on the owner-manager in order to obtain and process all of the information necessary to run the business. Chances are the owner will not be skilled in all specialties (e.g., accounting, engineering, production, marketing). Thus, he or she will need to hire specialists in the various functional areas. Such growth in the overall scope and complexity of the business necessitates a **functional organizational structure** wherein the major functions of the firm are grouped internally. The coordination and integration of the functional areas becomes one of the most important responsibilities of the chief executive of the firm (see Exhibit 10.2).

---

* The lowering of transaction costs and globalization have led to some changes in the common historical patterns that we have discussed. Some firms are, in effect, bypassing the vertical integration stage. Instead, they focus on core competencies and outsource other value-creation activities. Also, even relatively young firms are going global early in their history because of lower communication and transportation costs. For an interesting perspective on global start-ups, see McDougall, P. P. & Oviatt, B. M. 1996. New Venture Internationalization, Strategic Change and Performance: A Follow-Up Study. *Journal of Business Venturing,* 11: 23–40; and McDougall, P. P. & Oviatt, B. M. (Eds.). 2000. The Special Research Forum on International Entrepreneurship. *Academy of Management Journal,* October: 902–1003.

Chief Executive Officer or President

| Manager Production | Manager Engineering | Manager Marketing | Manager R&D | Manager Personnel | Manager Accounting |

Lower-level managers, specialists, and operating personnel

Exhibit 10.2 Functional Organizational Structure

Functional structures are generally found in organizations in which there is a single or closely related product or service, high production volume, and some vertical integration. Initially, firms tend to expand the overall scope of their operations by penetrating existing markets, introducing similar products in additional markets, or increasing the level of vertical integration. Such expansion activities clearly increase the scope and complexity of the operations. The functional structure provides for a high level of centralization that helps to ensure integration and control over the related product-market activities or multiple primary activities (from inbound logistics to operations to marketing, sales, and service) in the value chain (addressed in Chapters 3 and 4). Strategy Spotlight 10.1 provides an example of an effective functional organization structure—Parkdale Mills.

Advantages   By bringing together specialists into functional departments, a firm is able to enhance its coordination and control within each of the functional areas. Decision making in the firm will be centralized at the top of the organization. This enhances the organizational-level (as opposed to functional area) perspective across the various functions in the organization. In addition, the functional structure provides for a more efficient use of managerial and technical talent since functional area expertise is pooled in a single department (e.g., marketing) instead of being spread across a variety of product-market areas. Finally, career paths and professional development in specialized areas are facilitated.

Disadvantages   The differences in values and orientations among functional areas may impede communication and coordination. Edgar Schein of MIT has argued that shared assumptions, often based on similar backgrounds and experiences of members, form around functional units in an organization. This leads to what are often called "stove pipes" or "silos," in which departments view themselves as isolated, self-contained units with little need for interaction and coordination with other departments. This erodes communication because functional groups may have not only different goals but also differing meanings of words and concepts. According to Schein:

> The word "marketing" will mean product development to the engineer, studying customers through market research to the product manager, merchandising to the salesperson, and constant change in design to the manufacturing manager. When they try to work together, they will often attribute disagreements to personalities and fail to notice the deeper, shared assumptions that color how each function thinks.[9]

Such narrow functional orientations also may lead to short-term thinking based largely upon what is best for the functional area, not the entire organization. In a manufacturing firm, sales may want to offer a wide range of customized products to appeal to the firm's

Parkdale Mills: A Successful Functional Organizational Structure

For more than 80 years, Parkdale Mills, with approximately $1 billion in revenues, has been the industry leader in the production of cotton and cotton blend yarns. Their expertise comes by concentrating on a single product line, perfecting processes, and welcoming innovation. According to CEO Andy Warlick, "I think we've probably spent more than any two competitors combined on new equipment and robotics. We do this because we have to compete in a global market where a lot of the competition has a lower wage structure and gets subsidies that we don't receive, so we really have to focus on consistency and cost control." Yarn making is generally considered to be a commodity business, and Parkdale is the industry's low-cost producer.

Tasks are highly standardized and authority is centralized with Duke Kimbrell, founder and chairman, and CEO Andy Warlick. The firm operates a bare-bones staff with a small staff of top executives. Kimbrell and Warlick are considered shrewd about the cotton market, technology, customer loyalty, and incentive pay.

Sources: Stewart, C. 2003. The Perfect Yarn. The Manufacturer.com, July 31; *www.parkdalemills.com*; Berman, P. 1987. The Fast Track Isn't Always the Best Track. *Forbes*, November 2: 60–64; and personal communication with Duke Kimbrell, March 11, 2005.

customers; R&D may overdesign products and components to achieve technical elegance; and manufacturing may favor no-frills products that can be produced at low cost by means of long production runs. Functional structures may overburden the top executives in the firm because conflicts have a tendency to be "pushed up" to the top of the organization since there are no managers who are responsible for the specific product lines. Functional structures make it difficult to establish uniform performance standards across the entire organization. It may be relatively easy to evaluate production managers on the basis of production volume and cost control, but establishing performance measures for engineering, R&D, and accounting become more problematic.

Divisional Structure

The **divisional organizational structure** (sometimes called the multidivisional structure or M-Form) is organized around products, projects, or markets. Each of the divisions, in turn, includes its own functional specialists who are typically organized into departments.[10] A divisional structure encompasses a set of relatively autonomous units governed by a central corporate office. The operating divisions are relatively independent and consist of products and services that are different from those of the other divisions.[11] Operational decision making in a large business places excessive demands on the firm's top management. In order to attend to broader, longer-term organizational issues, top-level managers must delegate decision making to lower-level managers. Divisional executives play a key role: they help to determine the product-market and financial objectives for the division as well as their division's contribution to overall corporate performance.[12] The rewards are based largely on measures of financial performance such as net income and revenue. Exhibit 10.3 illustrates a divisional structure.

divisional organizational structure an organizational form in which products, projects, or product markets are grouped internally.

General Motors was among the earliest firms to adopt the divisional organizational structure.[13] In the 1920s the company formed five major product divisions (Cadillac, Buick, Oldsmobile, Pontiac, and Chevrolet) as well as several industrial divisions. Since then, many firms have discovered that as they diversified into new product-market activities, functional structures—with their emphasis on single functional departments—were unable to manage the increased complexity of the entire business.

Advantages By creating separate divisions to manage individual product markets, there is a separation of strategic and operating control. Divisional managers can focus

Exhibit 10.3 Divisional Organizational Structure

their efforts on improving operations in the product markets for which they are responsible, and corporate officers can devote their time to overall strategic issues for the entire corporation. The focus on a division's products and markets—by the divisional executives—provides the corporation with an enhanced ability to respond quickly to important changes. Since there are functional departments within each division of the corporation, the problems associated with sharing resources across functional departments are minimized. Because there are multiple levels of general managers (executives responsible for integrating and coordinating all functional areas), the development of general management talent is enhanced.

Disadvantages   It can be very expensive; there can be increased costs due to the duplication of personnel, operations, and investment since each division must staff multiple functional departments. There also can be dysfunctional competition among divisions since each division tends to become concerned solely about its own operations. Divisional managers are often evaluated on common measures such as return on assets and sales growth. If goals are conflicting, there can be a sense of a "zero-sum" game that would discourage sharing ideas and resources among the divisions for the common good of the corporation. Ghoshal and Bartlett, two leading strategy scholars, note:

> As their label clearly warns, divisions divide. The divisional model fragmented companies' resources; it created vertical communication channels that insulated business units and prevented them from sharing their strengths with one another. Consequently, the whole of the corporation was often less than the sum of its parts.[14]

With many divisions providing different products and services, there is the chance that differences in image and quality may occur across divisions. One division may offer no-frills products of lower quality that may erode the brand reputation of another division that has top quality, highly differentiated offerings. Since each division is evaluated in terms of financial measures such as return on investment and revenue growth, there is often an urge to focus on short-term performance. If corporate management uses quarterly profits as the

Why Sun Microsystems Experienced Major Problems When It Changed Its Organizational Structure

In general, organizational structures don't fail; managers fail at implementing them correctly. For example, in the 1990s, Sun Microsystems (acquired by Oracle in 2010) undertook a major corporate reorganization and changed from a functional structure to a divisional structure. At the time, the rationale seemed quite logical: Management wanted to create miniature Suns to provide autonomy, which would help restore the entrepreneurial spirit of the firm's start-up days.

Separate divisions were created for high-end servers, desktop computers, printers, software, services, and so on. In total, there were nine divisions. Such a configuration led them to call the structure "Sun and the nine planets." However, things certainly didn't work out as planned!

Within a few years, Sun discovered the problems associated with this new structure. Management discovered that they wound up with nine different compensation plans, nine IT systems, nine sales forces calling on the same customers, and so on. In essence, they had nine of everything and, not surprisingly, escalating overhead expenses. As noted by Larry Hambly, Sun's chief quality officer and president of its customer service division, "The planets placed too much visibility on each entity." This resulted in the sales forces competing with each other, while people who were supposed to give customer service passed the buck. Lamented Hambly, "There was too much of, 'I don't know; that is somebody else's problem.'" In addition, it became almost impossible to move talent from one division to the next. As one would expect, Sun soon abandoned this highly autonomous structure and moved back to one similar to what it previously had.

Does this mean that autonomous divisional structures don't work? Of course not. Such a structure works well at diversified firms such as United Technologies and General Electric. Sun simply failed to implement the structure best suited to its particular situation.

Sources: Galbraith, J. 2009. *Designing Matrix Organizations That Actually Work.* San Francisco: Jossey-Bass; Southwick, K. *High Noon: The Inside Story of Scott McNealy and the Rise of Sun Microsystems.* Hoboken, NJ: Wiley; and Shankland, S. 2010. Oracle Buys Sun, Becomes Hardware Company. *www.news.cnet.com.* January 27: np.

key performance indicator, divisional management may tend to put significant emphasis on "making the numbers" and minimizing activities, such as advertising, maintenance, and capital investments, which would detract from short-term performance measures.

When firms change their organization's structure, things don't always work out as planned. In Strategy Spotlight 10.2 we give one example—the problems that Sun Mircosystems faced when the firm changed from a functional structure to a divisional structure.

We'll discuss two variations of the divisional form: the strategic business unit (SBU) and holding company structures.

Strategic Business Unit (SBU) Structure   Highly diversified corporations such as ConAgra, a $12 billion food producer, may consist of dozens of different divisions.[15] If ConAgra were to use a purely divisional structure, it would be nearly impossible for the corporate office to plan and coordinate activities, because the span of control would be too large. To attain synergies, ConAgra has put its diverse businesses into three primary SBUs: food service (restaurants), retail (grocery stores), and agricultural products.

With an **SBU structure,** divisions with similar products, markets, and/or technologies are grouped into homogeneous units to achieve some synergies. These include those discussed in Chapter 6 for related diversification, such as leveraging core competencies, sharing infrastructures, and market power. Generally the more related businesses are within a corporation, the fewer SBUs will be required. Each of the SBUs in the corporation operates as a profit center.

> **strategic business unit (SBU) structure** an organizational form in which products, projects, or product market divisions are grouped into homogeneous units.

Advantages   The SBU structure makes the task of planning and control by the corporate office more manageable. Also, with greater decentralization of authority, individual businesses can react more quickly to important changes in the environment than if all divisions had to report directly to the corporate office.

Disadvantages Since the divisions are grouped into SBUs, it may become difficult to achieve synergies across SBUs. If divisions in different SBUs have potential sources of synergy, it may become difficult for them to be realized. The additional level of management increases the number of personnel and overhead expenses, while the additional hierarchical level removes the corporate office further from the individual divisions. The corporate office may become unaware of key developments that could have a major impact on the corporation.

holding company structure an organizational form that is a variation of the divisional organizational structure in which the divisions have a high degree of autonomy both from other divisions and from corporate headquarters.

Holding Company Structure   The **holding company structure** (sometimes referred to as a *conglomerate*) is also a variation of the divisional structure. Whereas the SBU structure is often used when similarities exist between the individual businesses (or divisions), the holding company structure is appropriate when the businesses in a corporation's portfolio do not have much in common. Thus, the potential for synergies is limited.

Holding company structures are most appropriate for firms with a strategy of unrelated diversification. Companies such as Hanson Trust, ITT, and the CP group of Thailand have used holding company structure to implement their unrelated diversification strategies. Since there are few similarities across the businesses, the corporate offices in these companies provide a great deal of autonomy to operating divisions and rely on financial controls and incentive programs to obtain high levels of performance from the individual businesses. Corporate staffs at these firms tend to be small because of their limited involvement in the overall operation of their various businesses.[16]

Advantages The holding company structure has the cost savings associated with fewer personnel and the lower overhead resulting from a small corporate office and fewer hierarchical levels. The autonomy of the holding company structure increases the motivational level of divisional executives and enables them to respond quickly to market opportunities and threats.

Disadvantages There is an inherent lack of control and dependence that corporate-level executives have on divisional executives. Major problems could arise if key divisional executives leave the firm, because the corporate office has very little "bench strength"—additional managerial talent ready to quickly fill key positions. If problems arise in a division, it may become very difficult to turn around individual businesses because of limited staff support in the corporate office.

Matrix Structure

matrix organizational structure an organizational form in which there are multiple lines of authority and some individuals report to at least two managers.

One approach that tries to overcome the inadequacies inherent in the other structures is the **matrix organizational structure.** It is a combination of the functional and divisional structures. Most commonly, functional departments are combined with product groups on a project basis. For example, a product group may want to develop a new addition to its line; for this project, it obtains personnel from functional departments such as marketing, production, and engineering. These personnel work under the manager of the product group for the duration of the project, which can vary from a few weeks to an open-ended period of time. The individuals who work in a matrix organization become responsible to two managers: the project manager and the manager of their functional area. Exhibit 10.4 illustrates a matrix structure.

Some large multinational corporations rely on a matrix structure to combine product groups and geographical units. Product managers have global responsibility for the development, manufacturing, and distribution of their own line, while managers of geographical regions have responsibility for the profitability of the businesses in their regions. In the mid-1990s, Caterpillar, Inc., implemented this type of structure.

Exhibit 10.4 Matrix Organizational Structure

Advantages   The matrix structure facilitates the use of specialized personnel, equipment, and facilities. Instead of duplicating functions, as would be the case in a divisional structure based on products, the resources are shared. Individuals with high expertise can divide their time among multiple projects. Such resource sharing and collaboration enable a firm to use resources more efficiently and to respond more quickly and effectively to changes in the competitive environment. The flexibility inherent in a matrix structure provides professionals with a broader range of responsibility. Such experience enables them to develop their skills and competencies.

Disadvantages   The dual-reporting structures can result in uncertainty and lead to intense power struggles and conflict over the allocation of personnel and other resources. Working relationships become more complicated. This may result in excessive reliance on group processes and teamwork, along with a diffusion of responsibility, which in turn may erode timely decision making.

Let's look at Procter & Gamble (P&G) to see some of the disadvantages associated with a matrix structure:

> After 50 years with a divisional structure, P&G went to a matrix structure in 1987. In this structure, they had product categories, such as soaps and detergents, on one dimension and functional managers on the other dimension. Within each product category, country managers reported to regional managers who then reported to product managers. The structure became complex to manage, with 13 layers of management and significant power struggles as the functional managers developed their own strategic agendas that often were at odds with the product managers' agendas. After seeing their growth rate decline from 8.5 percent in the 1980s to 2.6 percent in the late 1990s, P&G scrapped the matrix structure to go to a global product structure with three major product categories to offer unity in direction and more responsive decision making.[17]

Exhibit 10.5 Functional, Divisional, and Matrix Organizational Structures: Advantages and Disadvantages

Functional Structure

Advantages	Disadvantages
• Pooling of specialists enhances coordination and control.	• Differences in functional area orientation impede communication and coordination.
• Centralized decision making enhances an organizational perspective across functions.	• Tendency for specialists to develop short-term perspective and narrow functional orientation.
• Efficient use of managerial and technical talent.	• Functional area conflicts may overburden top-level decision makers.
• Facilitates career paths and professional development in specialized areas.	• Difficult to establish uniform performance standards.

Divisional Structure

Advantages	Disadvantages
• Increases strategic and operational control, permitting corporate-level executives to address strategic issues.	• Increased costs incurred through duplication of personnel, operations, and investment.
• Quick response to environmental changes.	• Dysfunctional competition among divisions may detract from overall corporate performance.
• Increases focus on products and markets.	• Difficult to maintain uniform corporate image.
• Minimizes problems associated with sharing resources across functional areas.	• Overemphasis on short-term performance.
• Facilitates development of general managers.	

Matrix Structure

Advantages	Disadvantages
• Increases market responsiveness through collaboration and synergies among professional colleagues.	• Dual-reporting relationships can result in uncertainty regarding accountability.
• Allows more efficient utilization of resources.	• Intense power struggles may lead to increased levels of conflict.
• Improves flexibility, coordination, and communication.	• Working relationships may be more complicated and human resources duplicated
• Increases professional development through a broader range of responsibility.	• Excessive reliance on group processes and teamwork may impede timely decision making.

Exhibit 10.5 briefly summarizes the advantages and disadvantages of the functional, divisional, and matrix organizational structures.

>LO10.3
The implications of a firm's international operations for organizational structure.

International Operations: Implications for Organizational Structure

Today's managers must maintain an international outlook on their firm's businesses and competitive strategies. In the global marketplace, managers must ensure consistency between their strategies (at the business, corporate, and international levels) and the structure of their organization. As firms expand into foreign markets, they generally follow a pattern of change in structure that parallels the changes in their strategies.[18] Three major contingencies that influence the chosen structure are (1) the type of strategy that is driving a firm's foreign operations, (2) product diversity, and (3) the extent to which a firm is dependent on foreign sales.[19]

As international operations become an important part of a firm's overall operations, managers must make changes that are consistent with their firm's structure. The primary types of structures used to manage a firm's international operations are:[20]

- International division
- Geographic-area division
- Worldwide functional
- Worldwide product division
- Worldwide matrix

Multidomestic strategies are driven by political and cultural imperatives requiring managers within each country to respond to local conditions. The structures consistent with such a strategic orientation are the **international division** and **geographic-area division structures.** Here local managers are provided with a high level of autonomy to manage their operations within the constraints and demands of their geographic market. As a firm's foreign sales increase as a percentage of its total sales, it will likely change from an international division to a geographic-area division structure. And, as a firm's product and/or market diversity becomes large, it is likely to benefit from a **worldwide matrix structure.**

Global strategies are driven by economic pressures that require managers to view operations in different geographic areas to be managed for overall efficiency. The structures consistent with the efficiency perspective are the *worldwide functional* and *worldwide product division s*tructures. Here, division managers view the marketplace as homogeneous and devote relatively little attention to local market, political, and economic factors. The choice between these two types of structures is guided largely by the extent of product diversity. Firms with relatively low levels of product diversity may opt for a worldwide product division structure. However, if significant product–market diversity results from highly unrelated international acquisitions, a worldwide holding company structure should be implemented. Such firms have very little commonality among products, markets, or technologies, and have little need for integration.

Global Start-Ups: A New Phenomenon

International expansion occurs rather late for most corporations, typically after possibilities of domestic growth are exhausted. Increasingly, we are seeing two interrelated phenomena. First, many firms now expand internationally relatively early in their history. Second, some firms are "born global"—that is, from the very beginning, many start-ups are global in their activities. For example, Logitech Inc., a leading producer of personal computer accessories, was global from day one. Founded in 1982 by a Swiss national and two Italians, the company was headquartered both in California and Switzerland. R&D and manufacturing were also conducted in both locations and, subsequently, in Taiwan and Ireland.[21]

The success of companies such as Logitech challenges the conventional wisdom that a company must first build up assets, internal processes, and experience before venturing into faraway lands. It also raises a number of questions: What exactly is a global start-up? Under what conditions should a company start out as a global start-up? What does it take to succeed as a global start-up?

A **global start-up** has been defined as a business organization that, from inception, seeks to derive significant competitive advantage from the use of resources and the sale of outputs in multiple countries. Right from the beginning, it uses in-puts from around the world and sells its products and services to customers around the world. Geographical boundaries of nation-states are irrelevant for a global start-up.

---

international division structure an organizational form in which international operations are in a separate, autonomous division. Most domestic operations are kept in other parts of the organization.

geographic-area division structure a type of divisional organizational structure in which operations in geographical regions are grouped internally.

worldwide matrix structure a type of matrix organizational structure that has one line of authority for geographic-area divisions and another line of authority for worldwide product divisions.

worldwide functional structure a functional structure in which all departments have worldwide reponsibilities.

worldwide product division structure a product division structure in which all divisions have worldwide responsibilities.

global start-up a business organization that, from inception, seeks to derive significant advantage from the use of resources and the sale of outputs in multiple countries.

There is no reason for every start-up to be global. Being global necessarily involves higher communication, coordination, and transportation costs. Therefore, it is important to identify the circumstances under which going global from the beginning is advantageous.[22] First, if the required human resources are globally dispersed, going global may be the best way to access those resources. For example, Italians are masters in fine leather and Europeans in ergonomics. Second, in many cases foreign financing may be easier to obtain and more suitable. Traditionally, U.S. venture capitalists have shown greater willingness to bear risk, but they have shorter time horizons in their expectations for return. If a U.S. start-up is looking for patient capital, it may be better off looking overseas. Third, the target customers in many specialized industries are located in other parts of the world. Fourth, in many industries a gradual move from domestic markets to foreign markets is no longer possible because, if a product is successful, foreign competitors may immediately imitate it. Therefore, pre-emptive entry into foreign markets may be the only option. Finally, because of high up-front development costs, a global market is often necessary to recover the costs. This is particularly true for start-ups from smaller nations that do not have access to large domestic markets.

Successful management of a global start-up presents many challenges. Communication and coordination across time zones and cultures are always problematic. Since most global start-ups have far less resources than well-established corporations, one key for success is to internalize few activities and outsource the rest. Managers of such firms must have considerable prior international experience so that they can successfully handle the inevitable communication problems and cultural conflicts. Another key for success is to keep the communication and coordination costs low. The only way to achieve this is by creating less costly administrative mechanisms. The boundaryless organizational designs that we discuss in the next section are particularly suitable for global start-ups because of their flexibility and low cost.

Strategy Spotlight 10.3 discusses three global start-ups.

How an Organization's Structure Can Influence Strategy Formulation

Discussions of the relationship between strategy and structure usually strongly imply that structure follows strategy. The strategy that a firm chooses (e.g., related diversification) dictates such structural elements as the division of tasks, the need for integration of activities, and authority relationships within the organization. However, an existing structure can influence strategy formulation. Once a firm's structure is in place, it is very difficult and expensive to change.[23] Executives may not be able to modify their duties and responsibilities greatly, or may not welcome the disruption associated with a transfer to a new location. There are costs associated with hiring, training, and replacing executive, managerial, and operating personnel. Strategy cannot be formulated without considering structural elements.

An organization's structure can also have an important influence on how it competes in the marketplace. It can also strongly influence a firm's strategy, day-to-day operations, and performance.[24] We discussed Brinker International's move to a divisional structure in order to organize its restaurant groups into different units to focus on market niches. This new structure should enable the firm to adapt to change more rapidly and innovate more effectively with the various restaurant brands. Brinker's management did not feel that they were as effective with their previous functional organizational structure.

>LO10.4

Why there is no "one best way" to design strategic reward and evaluation systems, and the important contingent roles of business- and corporate-level strategies.

Linking Strategic Reward and Evaluation Systems to Business-Level and Corporate-Level Strategies

The effective use of reward and evaluation systems can play a critical role in motivating managers to conform to organizational strategies, achieve performance targets, and

Global on Day One

Conventional wisdom would suggest that a firm "get it right" in its home market before venturing abroad. Once established in the home market, a firm could consider the relatively risky move of selling in other countries. However, many new firms are turning conventional wisdom on its head.

More and more start-ups are being born global for two basic reasons. One reason is defensive: to be competitive, many new businesses need to globalize some parts of their business to control costs, access customers, or tap employees from day one. While this might seem an obviously logical choice, until recently many venture capital firms required companies to build locally first, gain a track record, and then branch out. The other reason firms are born global is offensive; many entrepreneurs find that new business opportunities span multiple countries. Going after opportunities in several countries simultaneously from the start can sometimes give firms the operating scope they need to thrive.

Going global is not without significant challenges. Coping with distance in terms of physical, time zone, and cultural dimensions is perhaps a larger hurdle for smaller organizations to tackle. However, start-ups that can articulate a global purpose tend to do better than those with weaker goal orientation toward a global strategy. The following three examples are of start-ups that thought global from day one:

- In 2008, Actavis Pharmaceuticals' revenues were over $2 billion. Robert Wessman took control of this

Sources: Isenberg, D. J. 2008. The Global Entrepreneur. *Harvard Business Review*, December: 107–111; Copeland, M. V. 2004. The Start-Up Oasis. *Business 2.0*, August: 46–48.; Brown, E. 2004. Global Start-Up. *Forbes*, November 29: 150–161.

small generic pharmaceutical maker in his native Iceland in 1999. Within weeks of taking over, he realized that to succeed in the generics market, a player had to globalize its core functions, including manufacturing and R&D. Actavis has since entered 60 countries to gain scale and develop a larger portfolio of drugs. By 2009 the company had 650 products on the market and 400 more in development.

- Baradok Pridor, 38, and Yonatan Aumann, 42, Israeli founders of ClearForest, developed an innovative software product—a program that can analyze unstructured electronic data, such as a webpage or a video clip, as if it were already in a spreadsheet or database. Instead of waiting for customers to show up, right from the beginning, they started sending their engineers to make presentations to potential clients around the world. Today, the company's customers include Dow Chemical, Thomson Financial, and the FBI! They have raised $33 million so far in three rounds of venture financing. Interestingly, the headquarters of the 83-person company is in Boston!

- HyperRoll, an Israeli company that makes software for analyzing massive databases, has raised $28 million in venture funding. Referring to the firm's hiring practices, Yossi Matias, founder of HyperRoll, says, "We build the strongest team possible, unconstrained by locality, affinity, or culture. It requires every employee to accept and support a multicultural environment." Although the firm is essentially an Israeli start-up, he even banned the use of Hebrew in the office to facilitate greater integration between the American and Israeli employees.

reduce the gap between organizational and individual goals. In contrast, reward systems, if improperly designed, can lead to behaviors that either are detrimental to organizational performance or can lower morale and cause employee dissatisfaction.

As we will see in this section, there is no "one best way" to design reward and evaluation systems. Instead, it is contingent on many factors. Two of the most important factors are a firm's business-level strategy (see Chapter 5) and its corporate-level strategy (see Chapter 6).

Business-Level Strategy: Reward and Evaluation Systems

In Chapter 5 we discussed two approaches that firms may take to secure competitive advantages: overall cost leadership and differentiation.[25] As we might expect, implementing these strategies requires fundamentally different organizational arrangements, approaches to control, and reward and incentive systems.

Overall Cost Leadership This strategy requires that product lines remain rather stable and that innovations deal mostly with production processes. Given the emphasis on efficiency, costly changes even in production processes tend to be rare. Since products are quite standardized and change rather infrequently, procedures can be developed to divide work into its basic components—those that are routine, standardized, and ideal for semiskilled and unskilled employees. As such, firms competing on the basis of cost must implement tight cost controls, frequent and comprehensive reports to monitor the costs associated with outputs, and highly structured tasks and responsibilities. Incentives tend to be based on explicit financial targets since innovation and creativity are expensive and might tend to erode competitive advantages.

Nucor a highly successful steel producer with $16 billion in revenues, competes primarily on the basis of cost and has a reward and incentive system that is largely based on financial outputs and financial measures.[26] Nucor uses four incentive compensation systems that correspond to the levels of management.

1. *Production incentive program.* Groups of 20 to 40 people are paid a weekly bonus based on either anticipated product time or tonnage produced. Each shift and production line is in a separate bonus group.
2. *Department managers.* Bonuses are based on divisional performance, primarily measured by return on assets.
3. *Employees not directly involved in production.* These include engineers, accountants, secretaries, receptionists, and others. Bonuses are based on two factors: divisional and corporate return on assets.
4. *Senior incentive programs.* Salaries are lower than comparable companies, but a significant portion of total compensation is based on return on stockholder equity. A portion of pretax earnings is placed in a pool and divided among officers as bonuses that are part cash and part stock.

The culture at Nucor reflects its reward and incentive system. Since incentive compensation can account for more than half of their paychecks, employees become nearly obsessed with productivity and apply a lot of pressure on each other. Ken Iverson, a former CEO, recalled an instance in which one employee arrived at work in sunglasses instead of safety glasses, preventing the team from doing any work. Furious, the other workers chased him around the plant with a piece of angle iron!

Differentiation This strategy involves the development of innovative products and services that require experts who can identify the crucial elements of intricate, creative designs and marketing decisions. Highly trained professionals such as scientists and engineers are essential for devising, assessing, implementing and continually changing complex product designs. This also requires extensive collaboration and cooperation among specialists and functional managers from different areas within a firm. They must evaluate and implement a new design, constantly bearing in mind marketing, financial, production, and engineering considerations.

Given the need for cooperation and coordination in many functional areas, it becomes difficult to evaluate individuals using set quantitative criteria. It also is difficult to measure specific outcomes of such efforts and attribute outcomes to specific individuals. More behavioral measures (how effectively employees collaborate and share information) and intangible incentives and rewards become necessary to support a strong culture and to motivate employees. Consider 3M, a highly innovative company whose core value is innovation.

> Rewards are tied closely to risk-taking and innovation-oriented behavior. Managers are not penalized for product failures. Instead, those same people are encouraged to work on another project that borrows from their shared experience and insight. A culture of creativity and "thinking out of the box" is reinforced by their well-known "15 percent rule," which

permits employees to set aside 15 percent of their work time to pursue personal research interests. And a familiar 3M homily, "Thou shall not kill new ideas for products," is known as the 11th commandment. It is the source of countless stories, including one that tells how L. D. DeSimone (3M's former CEO) tried five times (and failed) to kill the project that yielded the 3M blockbuster product, Thinsulate.[27]

Corporate-Level Strategy: Reward and Evaluation Systems

In Chapter 6 we discussed two broad types of diversification strategies: related and unrelated. The type of diversification strategy that a firm follows has important implications for the type of reward and evaluation systems that it should use.

Sharp Corporation, a $34 billion Japanese consumer electronics giant follows a strategy of *related* diversification.[28] Its most successful technology has been liquid crystal displays (LCDs) that are critical components in nearly all of the firm's products. With their expertise in this area, they are moving into high-end displays for cellular telephones, handheld computers, and digital computers.[29]

Given the need to leverage such technologies across multiple product lines, Sharp needs reward and evaluation systems that foster coordination and sharing. It must focus more on individuals' behavior rather than on short-term financial outcomes. Promotion is a powerful incentive, and it is generally based on seniority and subtle skills exhibited over time, such as teamwork and communication. It helps to ensure that the company's reward system will not reward short-term self-interested orientations.

Like many Japanese companies, Sharp's culture reinforces the view that the firm is a family whose members should cooperate for the greater good. With the policy of lifetime employment, turnover is low. This encourages employees to pursue what is best for the entire company. Such an outlook lessens the inevitable conflict over sharing important resources such as R&D knowledge.

In contrast to Sharp, Hanson PLC (a British conglomerate) followed a strategy of unrelated diversification for most of its history. At one time it owned as many as 150 operating companies in areas such as tobacco, footwear, building products, brewing, and food. There were limited product similarities across businesses and therefore little need for sharing of resources and knowledge across divisional boundaries. James Hanson and Gordon White, founders of the company, actually did not permit any sharing of resources between operating companies even if it was feasible!

Their reward and evaluation system placed such heavy emphasis on individual accountability that they viewed resource sharing, with its potential for mutual blaming, unacceptable. The operating managers had more than 60 percent of their compensation tied to annual financial performance of their subsidiaries. All decision making was decentralized so that subsidiary managers could be held responsible for the return on capital they employed. However, there was one area in which they had to obtain approval from the corporate office. No subsidiary manager was allowed to incur a capital expenditure greater than $3,000 without permission from the corporate office. Hanson managed to be successful with a very small corporate office because of its decentralized structure, tight financial controls, and an incentive system that motivated managers to meet financial goals. Gordon White was proud of claiming that he had never visited any of the operating companies that were part of the Hanson empire.[30]

The key issue becomes the need for *in*dependence versus *inter*dependence. With cost leadership strategies and unrelated diversification, there tends to be less need for interdependence. The reward and evaluation systems focus more on the use of financial indicators because unit costs, profits, and revenues can be rather easily attributed to a given business unit or division.

In contrast, firms that follow related diversification strategies have intense needs for tight interdependencies among the functional areas and business units. Sharing of resources, including raw materials, R&D knowledge, marketing information, and so on, is critical to organizational success. It is more important to achieve synergies with value-creating activities and business units than with cost leadership or unrelated strategies. Reward and evaluation systems tend to incorporate more behavioral indicators.

Although Exhibit 10.6 suggests guidelines on how an organization should match its strategies to its evaluation and reward systems, all organizations must have combinations of both financial and behavioral rewards. Both overall cost leadership and unrelated diversification strategies require a need for collaboration and the sharing of best practices across both value-creating activities and business units. General Electric has developed many integrating mechanisms to enhance sharing "best practices" across what would appear to be rather unrelated businesses such as jet engines, appliances, and network television. For both differentiation and related diversification strategies, financial indicators such as revenue growth and profitability should not be overlooked at both the business-unit and corporate levels.

>LO10.5
The different types of boundaryless organizations—barrier-free, modular, and virtual—and their relative advantages and disadvantages.

Boundaryless Organizational Designs

The term *boundaryless* may bring to mind a chaotic organizational reality in which "anything goes." This is not the case. As Jack Welch, GE's former CEO, has suggested, boundaryless does not imply that all internal and external boundaries vanish completely, but that they become more open and permeable.[31] Strategy Spotlight 10.4 discusses four types of boundaries.

We are not suggesting that **boundaryless organizational designs** replace the traditional forms of organizational structure, but they should complement them. Sharp Corp. has implemented a functional structure to attain economies of scale with its applied research and manufacturing skills. However, to bring about this key objective, Sharp has relied on several integrating mechanisms and processes:

> To prevent functional groups from becoming vertical chimneys that obstruct product development, Sharp's product managers have responsibility—but not authority—for coordinating the entire set of value-chain activities. And the company convenes enormous numbers of cross-unit and corporate committees to ensure that shared activities, including the corporate R&D unit and sales forces, are optimally configured and allocated among the different product lines. Sharp invests in such time-intensive coordination to minimize the inevitable conflicts that arise when units share important activities.[32]

boundaryless organizational designs organizations in which the boundaries, including vertical, horizontal, external, and geographic boundaries, are permeable.

We will discuss three approaches to making boundaries more permeable, that help to facilitate the widespread sharing of knowledge and information across both the internal and external boundaries of the organization. The *barrier-free* type involves making all organizational boundaries—internal and external—more permeable. Teams are a central building block for implementing the boundaryless organization. The *modular* and *virtual* types of organizations focus on the need to create seamless relationships

Exhibit 10.6
Summary of Relationships between Reward and Evaluation Systems and Business-Level and Corporate-Level Strategies

Level of Strategy	Types of Strategy	Need for Interdependence	Primary Type of Reward and Evaluation System
Business-level	Overall cost leadership	Low	Financial
Business-level	Differentiation	High	Behavioral
Corporate-level	Related diversification	High	Behavioral
Corporate-level	Unrelated diversification	Low	Financial

Boundary Types

There are primarily four types of boundaries that place limits on organizations. In today's dynamic business environment, different types of boundaries are needed to foster high degrees of interaction with outside influences and varying levels of permeability.

1. *Vertical boundaries between levels in the organization's hierarchy.* SmithKline Beecham asks employees at different hierarchical levels to brainstorm ideas for managing clinical trial data. The ideas are incorporated into action plans that significantly cut the new product approval time of its pharmaceuticals. This would not have been possible if the barriers between levels of individuals in the organization had been too high.

2. *Horizontal boundaries between functional areas.* Fidelity Investments makes the functional barriers

more porous and flexible among divisions, such as marketing, operations, and customer service, in order to offer customers a more integrated experience when conducting business with the company. Customers can take their questions to one person, reducing the chance that customers will "get the run-around" from employees who feel customer service is not their responsibility. At Fidelity, customer service is everyone's business, regardless of functional area.

3. *External boundaries between the firm and its customers, suppliers, and regulators.* GE Lighting, by working closely with retailers, functions throughout the value chain as a single operation. This allows GE to track point-of-sale purchases, giving it better control over inventory management.

4. *Geographic boundaries between locations, cultures, and markets.* The global nature of today's business environment spurred PricewaterhouseCoopers to use a global groupware system. This allows the company to instantly connect to its 26 worldwide offices.

Source: Ashkenas, R. 1997. The organization's New Clothes. In Hesselbein, F., Goldsmith, M., and Beckhard, R. (Eds.). *The Organization of the Future:* 104–106. San Francisco: Jossey Bass.

---

with external organizations such as customers or suppliers. While the modular type emphasizes the outsourcing of noncore activities, the virtual (or network) organization focuses on alliances among independent entities formed to exploit specific market opportunities.

The Barrier-Free Organization

The "boundary" mind-set is ingrained deeply into bureaucracies. It is evidenced by such clichés as "That's not my job," "I'm here from corporate to help," or endless battles over transfer pricing. In the traditional company, boundaries are clearly delineated in the design of an organization's structure. Their basic advantage is that the roles of managers and employees are simple, clear, well-defined, and long-lived. A major shortcoming was pointed out to the authors during an interview with a high-tech executive: "Structure tends to be divisive; it leads to territorial fights."

Such structures are being replaced by fluid, ambiguous, and deliberately ill-defined tasks and roles. Just because work roles are no longer clearly defined, however, does not mean that differences in skills, authority, and talent disappear. A **barrier-free organization** enables a firm to bridge real differences in culture, function, and goals to find common ground that facilitates information sharing and other forms of cooperative behavior. Eliminating the multiple boundaries that stifle productivity and innovation can enhance the potential of the entire organization.

Creating Permeable Internal Boundaries   For barrier-free organizations to work effectively, the level of trust and shared interests among all parts of the organization must be raised.[33] The organization needs to develop among its employees the skill level needed

> **barrier-free organization** an organizational design in which firms bridge real differences in culture, function, and goals to find common ground that facilitates information sharing and other forms of cooperative behavior.

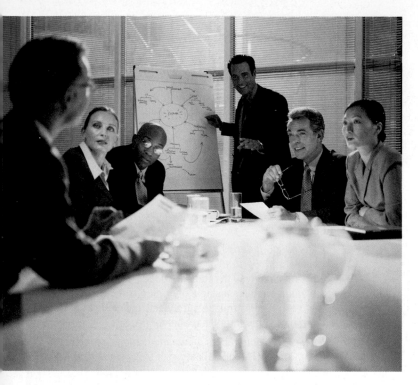

to work in a more democratic organization. Barrier-free organizations also require a shift in the organization's philosophy from executive to organizational development, and from investments in high-potential individuals to investments in leveraging the talents of all individuals.

Teams can be an important aspect of barrier-free structures.[34] Jeffrey Pfeffer, author of several insightful books, including *The Human Equation,* suggests that teams have three primary advantages.[35] First, teams substitute peer-based control for hierarchical control of work activities. Employees control themselves, reducing the time and energy management needs to devote to control. Second, teams frequently develop more creative solutions to problems because they encourage the sharing of the tacit knowledge held by individuals.[36] Brainstorming, or group problem solving, involves the pooling of ideas and expertise to enhance the chances that at least one group member will think of a way to solve the problems at hand. Third, by substituting peer control for hierarchical control, teams permit the removal of layers of hierarchy and absorption of administrative tasks previously performed by specialists. This avoids the costs of having people whose sole job is to watch the people who watch other people do the work.

● Teams frequently develop more creative solutions to problems because they can share each individual's knowledge.

Effective barrier-free organizations must go beyond achieving close integration and coordination within divisions in a corporation. Research on multidivisional organizations has stressed the importance of interdivisional coordination and resource sharing.[37] This requires interdivisional task forces and committees, reward and incentive systems that emphasize interdivisional cooperation, and common training programs.

Frank Carruba (former head of Hewlett-Packard's labs) found that the difference between mediocre teams and good teams was generally varying levels of motivation and talent.[38] But what explained the difference between good teams and truly superior teams? The key difference—and this explained a 40 percent overall difference in performance—was the way members treated each other: the degree to which they believed in one another and created an atmosphere of encouragement rather than competition. Vision, talent, and motivation could carry a team only so far. What clearly stood out in the "super" teams were higher levels of authenticity and caring, which allowed the full synergy of their individual talents, motivation, and vision.

Developing Effective Relationships with External Constituencies   In barrier-free organizations, managers must also create flexible, porous organizational boundaries and establish communication flows and mutually beneficial relationships with internal (e.g., employees) and external (e.g., customers) constituencies.[39] Michael Dell, founder and CEO of Dell Computer, is a strong believer in fostering close relationships with his customers:

> We're not going to be just your PC vendor anymore. We're going to be your IT department for PCs. Boeing, for example, has 100,000 Dell PCs, and we have 30 people that live at

The Business Roundtable: A Forum for Sharing Best Environmental Sustainability Practices

The Business Roundtable is a group of chief executive officers of major U.S. corporations that was created to promote probusiness public policy. It was formed in 1972 through the merger of three existing organizations: The March Group, the Construction Users Anti-Inflation Roundtable, and the Labor Law Study Committee. The group has been called President Obama's "closest ally in the business community."

The Business Roundtable became the first broad-based business group to agree on the need to address climate change through collective action, and it remains committed to limiting greenhouse gas emissions and setting the United States on a more sustainable path. The organization considers that threats to water quality and quantity, rising greenhouse gas emissions, and the risk of climate change—along with increasing energy prices and growing demand—are of great concern.

Its recent report, "Enhancing Our Commitment to a Sustainable Future 2010" provides best practices and metrics from Business Roundtable member companies that represent nearly all sectors of the economy with $6 trillion in annual revenues. CEOs from Walmart, FedEx, PepsiCo, Whirlpool and Verizon are among the 97 executives from leading U.S. companies that shared some of their best sustainability initiatives in this report. These companies are committed to reducing emissions, increasing energy efficiency, and developing more sustainable business practices.

Let's look, for example, at some of Walmart's initiatives. The firm's CEO, Mike Duke, says it is working with

suppliers, partners, and consumers to drive its sustainability program. It has helped establish the Sustainability Consortium to drive metrics for measuring the environmental effects of consumer products across their life cycle. The retailer also helped lead the creation of a Sustainable Product Index to provide product information to consumers about the environmental impact of the products they purchase.

There are many ways in which Walmart has increased the energy efficiency of its operations:

- It has 30 facilities in California and Hawaii with solar power installations, and it is purchasing 226 million kilowatt hours (kWh) of wind energy annually in Texas.

- It has an agreement in Japan to buy 1 million kWh of clean, renewable energy per year.

- Its trucking fleet in the United Kingdom has cut greenhouse gas emissions (GHG) by 40 percent through the use of new technology, consolidated supplier deliveries, and increased use of rail transportation.

Walmart has also significantly removed GHG emissions from the products that they sell:

- In February 2009, Walmart committed to eliminating 20 million metric tons of GHG emissions from the life cycle of the products they sell worldwide by 2015.

- In 2007, Walmart launched a pilot program to cut supply-chain emissions. Through this program, DVD suppliers reduced packaging and cut more than 28,000 metric tons of GHG.

- Walmart has sold more than 350 million compact fluorescent light bulbs in the United States alone. The firm estimates that during the life of these bulbs, its customers will save more than $13 billion and avoid producing more than 65 million metric tons of GHG emissions.

Sources: Anonymous. 2010. Leading CEOs Share Best Sustainability Practices. *www.environmentalleader.com*, April 26: np; Hopkins, M. No date. Sustainable Growth. *www.businessroundtable*, np; Castellani, J. J. 2010. Enhancing our commitment to a sustainable future report. *www.businessroundtable.org*, March 31: np; and Business Roundtable. *www.en.wikipedia.org*.

Boeing, and if you look at the things we're doing for them or for other customers, we don't look like a supplier, we look more like Boeing's PC department. We become intimately involved in planning their PC needs and the configuration of their network.

It's not that we make these decisions by ourselves. They're certainly using their own people to get the best answer for the company. But the people working on PCs together, from both Dell and Boeing, understand the needs in a very intimate way. They're right there living it and breathing it, as opposed to the typical vendor who says, "Here are your computers. See you later."[40]

Barrier-free organizations create successful relationships between both internal and external constituencies, but there is one additional constituency—competitors—with whom some organizations have benefited as they developed cooperative relationships. After years of seeing its empty trucks return from warehouses back to production facilities after deliveries, General Mills teamed up with 16 of its competitors. They formed an e-commerce business to help the firms find carriers with empty cargo trailers to piggyback freight loads to distributors near the production facilities.[41] This increases revenue for all network members and reduces fuel costs.

By joining and actively participating in the Business Roundtable—an organization consisting of CEOs of leading U.S. corporations—Walmart has been able to learn about cutting-edge sustainable initiatives of other major firms. This free flow of information has enabled Walmart to undertake a number of steps that increased the energy efficiency of its operations. These are described in Strategy Spotlight 10.5

Risks, Challenges, and Potential Downsides   Many firms find that creating and managing a barrier-free organization can be frustrating.[42] Puritan-Bennett Corporation, a manufacturer of respiratory equipment, found that its product development time more than doubled after it adopted team management. Roger J. Dolida, director of R&D, attributed this failure to a lack of top management commitment, high turnover among team members, and infrequent meetings. Often, managers trained in rigid hierarchies find it difficult to make the transition to the more democratic, participative style that teamwork requires.

Christopher Barnes, a consultant with PricewaterhouseCoopers, previously worked as an industrial engineer for Challenger Electrical Distribution (a subsidiary of Westinghouse, now part of CBS) at a plant which produced circuit-breaker boxes. His assignment was to lead a team of workers from the plant's troubled final-assembly operation with the mission: "Make things better." That vague notion set the team up for failure. After a year of futility, the team was disbanded. In retrospect, Barnes identified several reasons for the debacle: (1) limited personal credibility—he was viewed as an "outsider"; (2) a lack of commitment to the team—everyone involved was forced to be on the team; (3) poor communications—nobody was told why the team was important; (4) limited autonomy—line managers refused to give up control over team members; and (5) misaligned incentives—the culture rewarded individual performance over team performance. Barnes's experience has implications for all types of teams, whether they are composed of managerial, professional, clerical, or production personnel.[43] The pros and cons of barrier-free structures are summarized in Exhibit 10.7.

Exhibit 10.7
Pros and Cons of Barrier-Free Structures

Pros	Cons
• Leverages the talents of all employees.	• Difficult to overcome political and authority boundaries inside and outside the organization.
• Enhances cooperation, coordination, and information sharing among functions, divisions, SBUs, and external constituencies.	• Lacks strong leadership and common vision, which can lead to coordination problems.
• Enables a quicker response to market changes through a single-goal focus.	• Time-consuming and difficult-to-manage democratic processes.
• Can lead to coordinated win–win initiatives with key suppliers, customers, and alliance partners.	• Lacks high levels of trust, which can impede performance.

The Modular Organization

As Charles Handy, author of *The Age of Unreason,* has noted:

> While it may be convenient to have everyone around all the time, having all of your work-force's time at your command is an extravagant way of marshaling the necessary resources. It is cheaper to keep them outside the organization . . . and to buy their services when you need them.[44]

The **modular organization** outsources nonvital functions, tapping into the knowledge and expertise of "best in class" suppliers, but retains strategic control. Outsiders may be used to manufacture parts, handle logistics, or perform accounting activities.[45] The value chain can be used to identify the key primary and support activities performed by a firm to create value: Which activities do we keep "in-house" and which activities do we outsource to suppliers?[46] The organization becomes a central hub surrounded by networks of outside suppliers and specialists and parts can be added or taken away. Both manufacturing and service units may be modular.[47]

Apparel is an industry in which the modular type has been widely adopted. Nike and Reebok, for example, concentrate on their strengths: designing and marketing high-tech, fashionable footwear. Nike has few production facilities and Reebok owns no plants. These two companies contract virtually all their footwear production to suppliers in China, Vietnam, and other countries with low-cost labor. Avoiding large investments in fixed assets helps them derive large profits on minor sales increases. Nike and Reebok can keep pace with changing tastes in the marketplace because their suppliers have become expert at rapidly retooling to produce new products.[48]

In a modular company, outsourcing the non-core functions offers three advantages.

1. A firm can decrease overall costs, stimulate new product development by hiring suppliers with superior talent to that of in-house personnel, avoid idle capacity, reduce inventories, and avoid being locked into a particular technology.

2. A company can focus scarce resources on the areas where it holds a competitive advantage. These benefits can translate into more funding for R&D hiring the best engineers, and providing continuous training for sales and service staff.

3. An organization can tap into the knowledge and expertise of its specialized supply-chain partners, adding critical skills and accelerating organizational learning.[49]

The modular type enables a company to leverage relatively small amounts of capital and a small management team to achieve seemingly unattainable strategic objectives.[50] Certain preconditions are necessary before the modular approach can be successful. First, the company must work closely with suppliers to ensure that the interests of each party are being fulfilled. Companies need to find loyal, reliable vendors who can be trusted with trade secrets. They also need assurances that suppliers will dedicate their financial, physical, and human resources to satisfy strategic objectives such as lowering costs or being first to market.

modular organization an organization in which nonvital functions are outsourced, which uses the knowledge and expertise of outside suppliers while retaining strategic control.

● Nike is one of many athletic shoe companies that have outsourced most of its production to low-cost-labor countries such as Indonesia and Vietnam.

Video Games: Microsoft's Outsourcing Strategy

The convergence of Hollywood and Silicon Valley has led to the explosive growth of the worldwide video game industry, with revenues of $66.5 billion. In fact, it has recently overtaken the movie industry's box office receipts. While broadcast TV audiences dwindle and movie attendance stagnates, gaming is emerging as the newest and perhaps the strongest pillar in the media world. So it's no surprise that film studios, media giants, game creators, and Japanese electronics companies are all battling to win the "Game Wars."

Microsoft has dominated the market for computer software with its Windows operating system and its Office and Explorer application software. Seeing the growth in the gaming market, the company diversified into the video game industry with the Xbox and its successor, the Xbox 360. Microsoft faces tough competition from Sony Corp.'s PlayStation 3 and Nintendo Co.'s Wii in the video game industry. However, Microsoft's Xbox 360 beat Wii and PlayStation 3 in sales in the month of February 2010 to become the best-selling video game console in the United States for the first time in more than two years. Microsoft extended their advantage in November 2010 by introducing Kinect, the first motion-sensing system that doesn't require a remote.

Microsoft has a sophisticated approach to outsourcing video game software and hardware. On the software front, since the developmental phase of Xbox

360 in early 2003, Microsoft has reached out to developers by organizing events for the developers to recruit support for the system. Instead of limiting access to video game development software to those with big projects, big budgets, and the backing of the big game labels, Microsoft delivered the necessary tools of game development to hobbyists, students, indie developers, and studios alike. Knowing full well that great game ideas are brewing in the minds of students everywhere, Microsoft has targeted students at colleges, universities, and high schools as game developers. This practice helped bring creative game ideas to life while nurturing game development talent, a collaboration that benefited the entire industry.

For manufacturing the hardware of Xbox 360, Microsoft partnered with companies like Flextronics, Wistron, and Celestica, who produce the game system in their plants in China. According to Jim Sacherman, vice president of business development at Flextronics, "Our goal is to act as a true partner, not just a contractor." The firm showed a willingness to be a team player by collaborating with Microsoft on all aspects of the manufacturing and design process. From the beginning, Microsoft and Flextronics worked together to outline each company's roles and responsibilities and to ensure that all parties knew what was expected of them in all anticipated scenarios. The relationship between Microsoft and Flextronics quickly became a successful hybrid of the two most traditional outsourcing arrangements: Microsoft never turned over complete responsibility to Flextronics or passively waited to hear about progress. Neither did it act as a typical employer, dictating tasks and keeping Flextronics in the dark about its long-term plans for the product. Instead, the two companies worked together collaboratively from the beginning.

Sources: *www.microsoft.com*; Alpeyev, P. & Satariano, A. 2010. Microsoft's Xbox Sales Beat Wii, PS3 in February on "BioShock." *www.businessweek.com*, March 11: np; Grover, R., Edwards, C., Rowley, I., & Moon, I. 2005. Game Wars. *BusinessWeek*, February 28: 35–40; Radd, D. 2005. Xbox 360 Manufacturers Revealed. *www.businessweek.com*, August 16: np; Anonymous. 2002. Outsourcing Xbox Manufacturing: Microsoft Shows the Way for Successful Outsourcing Relationships. *www.goliath.ecnext.com*, np.

Second, the modular company must be sure that it selects the proper competencies to keep in-house. For Nike and Reebok, the core competencies are design and marketing, not shoe manufacturing; for Honda, the core competence is engine technology. An organization must avoid outsourcing components that may compromise its long-term competitive advantages.

Strategic Risks of Outsourcing   The main strategic concerns are (1) loss of critical skills or developing the wrong skills, (2) loss of cross-functional skills, and (3) loss of control over a supplier.[51]

Too much outsourcing can result in a firm "giving away" too much skill and control.[52] Outsourcing relieves companies of the requirement to maintain skill levels needed to manufacture essential components.[53] At one time, semiconductor chips seemed like a simple technology to outsource, but they have now become a critical component of a wide variety of products. Companies that have outsourced the manufacture of these chips run the risk of losing the ability to manufacture them as the technology escalates. They become more dependent upon their suppliers.

Cross-functional skills refer to the skills acquired through the interaction of individuals in various departments within a company.[54] Such interaction assists a department in solving problems as employees interface with others across functional units. However, if a firm outsources key functional responsibilities, such as manufacturing, communication across departments can become more difficult. A firm and its employees must now integrate their activities with a new, outside supplier.

The outsourced products may give suppliers too much power over the manufacturer. Suppliers that are key to a manufacturer's success can, in essence, hold the manufacturer "hostage." Nike manages this potential problem by sending full-time "product expatriates" to work at the plants of its suppliers. Also, Nike often brings top members of supplier management and technical teams to its headquarters. This way, Nike keeps close tabs on the pulse of new developments, builds rapport and trust with suppliers, and develops long-term relationships with suppliers to prevent hostage situations.

Strategy Spotlight 10.6 discusses Microsoft's effective outsourcing strategy for its video games. Exhibit 10.8 summarizes the pros and cons of modular structures.[55]

The Virtual Organization

In contrast to the "self-reliant" thinking that guided traditional organizational designs, the strategic challenge today has become doing more with less and looking outside the firm for opportunities and solutions to problems. The virtual organization provides a new means of leveraging resources and exploiting opportunities.[56]

The **virtual organization** can be viewed as a continually evolving network of independent companies—suppliers, customers, even competitors—linked together to share skills, costs, and access to one another's markets.[57] The members of a virtual organization, by pooling and sharing the knowledge and expertise of each of the component organizations, simultaneously "know" more and can "do" more than any one member of the group

virtual organization a continually evolving network of independent companies that are linked together to share skills, costs, and access to one another's markets.

Pros	Cons
• Directs a firm's managerial and technical talent to the most critical activities.	• Inhibits common vision through reliance on outsiders.
• Maintains full strategic control over most critical activities—core competencies.	• Diminishes future competitive advantages if critical technologies or other competencies are outsourced.
• Achieves "best in class" performance at each link in the value chain.	• Increases the difficulty of bringing back into the firm activities that now add value due to market shifts
• Leverages core competencies by outsourcing with smaller capital commitment.	• Leads to an erosion of cross-functional skills.
• Encourages information sharing and accelerates organizational learning.	• Decreases operational control and potential loss of control over a supplier.

Exhibit 10.8 Pros and Cons of Modular Structures

could do alone. By working closely together, each gains in the long run from individual and organizational learning.[58] The term *virtual,* meaning "being in effect but not actually so," is commonly used in the computer industry. A computer's ability to appear to have more storage capacity than it really possesses is called virtual memory. Similarly, by assembling resources from a variety of entities, a virtual organization may seem to have more capabilities than it really possesses.[59]

The virtual organization is a grouping of units from different organizations that have joined in an alliance to exploit complementary skills in pursuing common strategic objectives. A case in point is Lockheed Martin's use of specialized coalitions between and among three entities—the company, academia, and government—to enhance competitiveness. According to former CEO Norman Augustine:

> The underlying beauty of this approach is that it forces us to reach outward. No matter what your size, you have to look broadly for new ideas, new approaches, new products. Lockheed Martin used this approach in a surprising manner when it set out during the height of the Cold War to make stealth aircraft and missiles. The technical idea came from research done at the Institute of Radio Engineering in Moscow in the 1960s that was published, and publicized, quite openly in the academic media.
>
> Despite the great contrasts among government, academia and private business, we have found ways to work together that have produced very positive results, not the least of which is our ability to compete on a global scale.[60]

Virtual organizations need not be permanent and participating firms may be involved in multiple alliances. Virtual organizations may involve different firms performing complementary value activities, or different firms involved jointly in the same value activities, such as production, R&D, and distribution. The percentage of activities that are jointly performed with partners may vary significantly from alliance to alliance.[61]

How does the virtual type of structure differ from the modular type? Unlike the modular type, in which the focal firm maintains full strategic control, the virtual organization is characterized by participating firms that give up part of their control and accept interdependent destinies. Participating firms pursue a collective strategy that enables them to cope with uncertainty through cooperative efforts. The benefit is that, just as virtual memory increases storage capacity, the virtual organizations enhance the capacity or competitive advantage of participating firms. Strategy Spotlight 10.7 addresses the variety of collaborative relationships in the biotechnology industry.

Each company that links up with others to create a virtual organization contributes only what it considers its core competencies. It will mix and match what it does best with the best of other firms by identifying its critical capabilities and the necessary links to other capabilities.[62]

Challenges and Risks   Such alliances often fail to meet expectations: The alliance between IBM and Microsoft soured in early 1991 when Microsoft began shipping Windows in direct competition to OS/2, which they jointly developed. The runaway success of Windows frustrated IBM's ability to set an industry standard. In retaliation, IBM entered into an alliance with Microsoft's archrival, Novell, to develop network software to compete with Microsoft's LAN Manager.

The virtual organization demands that managers build relationships with other companies, negotiate win–win deals for all parties find the right partners with compatible goals and values, and provide the right balance of freedom and control. Information systems must be designed and integrated to facilitate communication with current and potential partners.

Managers must be clear about the strategic objectives while forming alliances. Some objectives are time bound, and those alliances need to be dissolved once the

How Eli Lilly Used the Collaborative Power of Internet-Based Collaboration to Foster Innovation

The e.Lilly division of pharmaceutical giant Eli Lilly was among the first to harness the collaborative power of the Internet when it launched Innocentive in 2001. Innocentive is the first online, incentive-based scientific network created specifically for the global research and development community. Innocentive's online platform enabled world-class scientists and R&D-based companies to collaborate to attain innovative solutions to complex challenges.

Innocentive offers "seeker companies" the opportunity to increase their R&D potential by posting challenges without violating their confidentiality and intellectual property interests. Seeker companies might be looking for a chemical to be used in art restoration, for example, or the efficient synthesis of butane tetracarboxylic acid. David Bradin, a patent attorney from Seattle, was recently paid $4,000 for his tetracarboxylic acid formula. And Procter & Gamble claims that Innocentive has increased its share of its new products originating outside the company from 20 to 35 percent.

Often individuals outside of the seeker company find the best solutions to the company's problem. By using Innocentive to post their problems, companies do not have to admit publicly that they need help, yet they get access to a much broader range of ideas than can be generated inside the firm. Within firms, even those firms hiring the best and brightest scientists and engineers, ideas are tossed around by the same few people over and over. This situation can create a narrowing of the possible solutions to a problem (i.e., groupthink can occur) rather than searching over the broadest range of ideas. Anne Goldberg, technical knowledge manager at Solvay Pharmaceuticals, said, "The benefits [of Innocentive] are mainly in the simultaneous access to a lot of different scientific backgrounds that could bring new perspectives on sometimes old problems."

Sources: Libert, B. & Spector, J. 2008. *We Are Smarter Than Me.* Wharton School Publishing, Philadelphia; Lakhani, K. & Jeppesen, L. 2007. Getting Unusual Suspects to Solve R&D Puzzles. *Harvard Business Review,* 85(5): 30–32; Caldwell, T. 2007. R&D Finds Answers in the Crowd. *Information World Review,* 236: 8.

crowdsourcing

objective is fulfilled. Some alliances may have relatively long-term objectives and will need to be clearly monitored and nurtured to produce mutual commitment and avoid bitter fights for control. The highly dynamic personal computer industry is characterized by multiple temporary alliances among hardware, operating systems, and software producers.[63] But alliances in the more stable automobile industry, such as those involving Nissan and Volkswagen have long-term objectives and tend to be relatively stable.

The virtual organization is a logical culmination of joint-venture strategies of the past. Shared risks, costs, and rewards are the facts of life in a virtual organization.[64] When virtual organizations are formed, they involve tremendous challenges for strategic planning. As with the modular corporation, it is essential to identify core competencies. However, for virtual structures to be successful, a strategic plan is also needed to determine the effectiveness of combining core competencies.

The strategic plan must address the diminished operational control and overwhelming need for trust and common vision among the partners. This new structure may be appropriate for firms whose strategies require merging technologies (e.g., computing and communication) or for firms exploiting shrinking product life cycles that require simultaneous entry into multiple geographical markets. It may be effective for firms that desire to be quick to the market with a new product or service. The recent profusion of alliances among airlines was primarily motivated by the need to provide seamless travel demanded by the full-fare paying business traveler. Exhibit 10.9 summarizes the advantages and disadvantages.

Exhibit 10.9

Pros and Cons of Virtual Structures

Pros	Cons
• Enables the sharing of costs and skills. • Enhances access to global markets. • Increases market responsiveness. • Creates a "best of everything" organization since each partner brings core competencies to the alliance. • Encourages both individual and organizational knowledge sharing and accelerates organizational learning.	• Harder to determine where one company ends and another begins, due to close interdependencies among players. • Leads to potential loss of operational control among partners. • Results in loss of strategic control over emerging technology. • Requires new and difficult-to-acquire managerial skills.

Source: Miles, R. E., & Snow, C. C. 1986. Organizations: New Concepts for New Forms. *California Management Review,* Spring: 62–73; Miles & Snow. 1999. Causes of Failure in Network Organizations. *California Management Review,* Summer: 53–72; and Bahrami, H. 1991. The Emerging Flexible Organization: Perspectives from Silicon Valley. *California Management Review,* Summer: 33–52.

Boundaryless Organizations: Making Them Work

Designing an organization that simultaneously supports the requirements of an organization's strategy, is consistent with the demands of the environment, and can be effectively implemented by the people around the manager is a tall order for any manager.[65] The most effective solution is usually a combination of organizational types. That is, a firm may outsource many parts of its value chain to reduce costs and increase quality, engage simultaneously in multiple alliances to take advantage of technological developments or penetrate new markets, and break down barriers within the organization to enhance flexibility.

When an organization faces external pressures, resource scarcity, and declining performance, it tends to become more internally focused, rather than directing its efforts toward managing and enhancing relationships with existing and potential external stakeholders. This may be the most opportune time for managers to carefully analyze their value-chain activities and evaluate the potential for adopting elements of modular, virtual, and barrier-free organizational types.

Achieving the coordination and integration necessary to maximize the potential of an organization's human capital involves much more than just creating a new structure. Techniques and processes to ensure the coordination and integration of an organization's key value-chain activities are critical. Teams are key building blocks of the new organizational forms, and teamwork requires new and flexible approaches to coordination and integration.

Managers trained in rigid hierarchies may find it difficult to make the transition to the more democratic, participative style that teamwork requires. As Douglas K. Smith, co-author of *The Wisdom of Teams,* pointed out, "A completely diverse group must agree on a goal, put the notion of individual accountability aside and figure out how to work with each other. Most of all, they must learn that if the team fails, it's everyone's fault."[66] Within the framework of an appropriate organizational design, managers must select a mix and balance of tools and techniques to facilitate the effective coordination and integration of key activities. Some of the factors that must be considered include:

- Common culture and shared values.
- Horizontal organizational structures.
- Horizontal systems and processes.
- Communications and information technologies.
- Human resource practices.

Common Culture and Shared Values   Shared goals, mutual objectives, and a high degree of trust are essential to the success of boundaryless organizations. In the fluid and flexible environments of the new organizational architectures, common cultures, shared values, and carefully aligned incentives are often less expensive to implement and are often a more effective means of strategic control than rules, boundaries, and formal procedures.

Horizontal Organizational Structures   These structures, which group similar or related business units under common management control, facilitate sharing resources and infrastructures to exploit synergies among operating units and help to create a sense of common purpose. Consistency in training and the development of similar structures across business units facilitates job rotation and cross training and enhances understanding of common problems and opportunities. Cross-functional teams and inter-divisional commit- tees and task groups represent important opportunities to improve understanding and foster cooperation among operating units.

Horizontal Systems and Processes   Organizational systems, policies, and proce- dures are the traditional mechanisms for achieving integration among functional units. Existing policies and procedures often do little more than institutionalize the barriers that exist from years of managing within the framework of the traditional model. Begin- ning with an understanding of basic business processes in the context of "a collection of activities that takes one or more kinds of input and creates an output that is of value to the customer," Michael Hammer and James Champy's 1993 best-selling *Reengineering the Corporation* outlined a methodology for redesigning internal systems and procedures that has been embraced by many organizations.[67] Successful reengineering lowers costs, reduces inventories and cycle times, improves quality, speeds response times, and enhances organizational flexibility. Others advocate similar benefits through the reduction of cycle times, total quality management, and the like.

Communications and Information Technologies (IT)   The effective use of IT can play an important role in bridging gaps and breaking down barriers between organizations. Electronic mail and videoconferencing can improve lateral communications across long distances and multiple time zones and circumvent many of the barriers of the traditional model. IT can be a powerful ally in the redesign and streamlining of internal business processes and in improving coordination and integration between suppliers and customers. Internet technologies have eliminated the paperwork in many buyer–supplier relationships, enabling cooperating organizations to reduce inventories, shorten delivery cycles, and reduce operating costs. IT must be viewed more as a prime component of an organization's overall strategy than simply in terms of administrative support.

Human Resource Practices   Change always involves and affects the human dimen- sion of organizations. The attraction, development, and retention of human capital are vital to value creation. As boundaryless structures are implemented, processes are reengineered, and organizations become increasingly dependent on sophisticated ITs, the skills of work- ers and managers alike must be upgraded to realize the full benefits.

Strategy Spotlight 10.8 discusses Procter & Gamble's successful introduction of Crest Whitestrips. This example shows how P&G's tools and techniques, such as communities of practice, information technology, and human resource practices, help to achieve effective collaboration and integration across the firm's different business units.

Creating Ambidextrous Organizational Designs

In Chapter 1, we introduced the concept of "ambidexterity," which incorporates two contra- dictory challenges faced by today's managers.[68] First, managers must explore new oppor- tunities and adjust to volatile markets in order to avoid complacency. They must ensure

Crest's Whitestrips: An Example of How P&G Creates and Derives Benefits from a Boundaryless Organization

Given its breadth of products—soaps, diapers, tooth-paste, potato chips, lotions, detergent—Procter & Gamble (P&G) has an enormous pool of resources it can integrate in various ways to launch exciting new products. For example, the company created a new category, teeth-whitening systems, with Crest Whitestrips. Teeth whitening done at a dentist's office can brighten one's smile in as little as one visit, but it can cost hundreds of dollars. On the other hand, over-the-counter home whitening kits like Crest Whitestrips cost far less and are nearly equally effective.

Whitestrip was created through a combined effort of product developers from three different units in P&G. People at the oral-care division provided teeth-whitening

expertise; experts from the fabric and home-care division supplied bleach expertise; and scientists at corporate research and development provided a novel film technol-ogy. Three separate units, by collaborating and combining their technologies, succeeded in developing an affordable product to brighten smiles and, according to the website, bring "greater success in work and love." With $300 mil-lion in annual retail sales, the launch of the Whitestrips product has been a big success for P&G, one that would not have been possible without the firm's collaborative ability.

Such collaborations are the outcome of well-established organizational mechanisms. P&G has created more than 20 communities of practice, with 8,000 partici-pants. Each group comprises volunteers from different parts of the company and focuses on an area of expertise (fragrance, packaging, polymer chemistry, skin science, and so on). The groups solve specific problems that are brought to them, and they meet to share best practices. The company also has posted an "ask me" feature on its intranet, where employees can describe a business prob-lem, which is directed to those people with appropriate expertise. At a more fundamental level, P&G promotes from within and rotates people across countries and business units. As a result, its employees build powerful cross-unit networks.

Sources: Hansen, M. T. 2009. *Collaboration: How Leaders Avoid the Traps, Create Unity, and Reap Big Results.* Boston: Harvard Business Press, 24–25; Anonymous. 2004. At P&G, It's 360-Degree Innovation. *www.businessweek.com*, October 11: np; *www.whitestrips.com*; Anonymous. 2009. The Price of a Whiter, Brighter Smile. *www.washingtonpost.com*, July 21: np; Hansen, M. T. & Birkinshaw, J. 2007. The Innovation Value Chain. *Harvard Business Review,* June: 85(6): 121–130.

adaptibility
managers' exploration of new opportunities and adjustment to volatile markets in order to avoid complacency.

alignment
managers' clear sense of how value is being created in the short term and how activities are integrated and properly coordinated.

that they maintain *adaptability* and remain proactive in expanding and/or modifying their product–market scope to anticipate and satisfy market conditions. Such competencies are especially challenging when change is rapid and unpredictable.

Second, managers must also effectively exploit the value of their existing assets and competencies. They need to have *alignment,* which is a clear sense of how value is being created in the short term and how activities are integrated and properly coordinated. Firms that achieve both adaptability and alignment are considered *ambidextrous organizations—* aligned and efficient in how they manage today's business but flexible enough to changes in the environment so that they will prosper tomorrow.

Handling such opposing demands is difficult because there will always be some degree of conflict. Firms often suffer when they place too strong a priority on either adapt-ability or alignment. If it places too much focus on adaptability, the firm will suffer low profitability in the short term. If managers direct their efforts primarily at alignment, they will likely miss out on promising business opportunities.

Ambidextrous Organizations: Key Design Attributes

A recent study by Charles O'Reilly and Michael Tushman[69] provides some insights into how some firms were able to create successful **ambidextrous organizational designs.** They investigated companies that attempted to simultaneously pursue modest, incremental innovations as well as more dramatic, breakthrough innovations. The team investigated 35 attempts to launch breakthrough innovations undertaken by 15 business units in nine different industries. They studied the organizational designs and the processes, systems, and cultures associated with the breakthrough projects as well as their impact on the operations and performance of the traditional businesses.

ambidextrous organizational designs organizational designs that attempt to simultaneously pursue modest, incremental innovations as well as more dramatic, breakthrough innovations.

Companies structured their breakthrough projects in one of four primary ways:

- Seven were carried out within existing *functional organizational structures.* The projects were completely integrated into the regular organizational and management structure.
- Nine were organized as *cross-functional teams.* The groups operated within the established organization but outside of the existing management structure.
- Four were organized as *unsupported teams.* Here, they became independent units set up outside the established organization and management hierarchy.
- Fifteen were conducted within *ambidextrous organizations.* Here, the breakthrough efforts were organized within structurally independent units, each having its own processes, structures, and cultures. However, they were integrated into the existing senior management structure.

The performance results of the 35 initiatives were tracked along two dimensions:

- Their success in creating desired innovations was measured by either the actual commercial results of the new product or the application of practical market or technical learning.
- The performance of the existing business was evaluated.

The study found that the organizational structure and management practices employed had a direct and significant impact on the performance of both the breakthrough initiative and the traditional business. The ambidextrous organizational designs were more effective than the other three designs on both dimensions: launching breakthrough products or services (i.e., adaptation) and improving the performance of the existing business (i.e., alignment).

Why Was the Ambidextrous Organization the Most Effective Structure?

The study found that there were many factors. A clear and compelling vision, consistently communicated by the company's senior management team was critical in building the ambidextrous designs. The structure enabled cross-fertilization while avoiding cross-contamination. The tight coordination and integration at the managerial levels enabled the newer units to share important resources from the traditional units such as cash, talent, and expertise. Such sharing was encouraged and facilitated by effective reward systems that emphasized overall company goals. The organizational separation ensured that the new units' distinctive processes, structures, and cultures were not overwhelmed by the forces of "business as usual." The established units were shielded from the distractions of launching new businesses, and they continued to focus all of their attention and energy on refining their operations, enhancing their products, and serving their customers.

Reflecting on Career Implications . . .

- *Strategy–Structure:* Is there an effective "fit" between your organization's strategy and its structure? If not, there may be inconsistencies in how you are evaluated which often leads to role ambiguity and confusion. A poor fit could also affect communication among departments as well as across the organization's hierarchy.
- *Matrix Structure:* If your organization employs elements of a matrix structure (e.g., dual reporting relationships), are there effective structural supporting elements (e.g., culture and rewards)? If not, there could be a high level of dysfunctional conflict among managers.
- *The "Fit" between Rewards and Incentives and "Levels of Strategy" (Business- and Corporate-Level):* What metrics are used to evaluate the performance of your work unit? Are there strictly financial measures of success or are you also rewarded for achieving competitive advantages (through effective innovation, organizational learning, or other activities that increase knowledge but may be costly in the short run)?
- *Boundaryless Organizational Designs:* Does your firm have structural mechanisms (e.g., culture, human resource practices) that facilitate sharing of information across boundaries? If so, you should be better able to enhance your human capital by leveraging your talents and competencies.

Summary

Successful organizations must ensure that they have the proper type of organizational structure. Furthermore, they must ensure that their firms incorporate the necessary integration and processes so that the internal and external boundaries of their firms are flexible and permeable. Such a need is increasingly important as the environments of firms become more complex, rapidly changing, and unpredictable.

In the first section of the chapter, we discussed the growth patterns of large corporations. Although most organizations remain small or die, some firms continue to grow in terms of revenues, vertical integration, and diversity of products and services. In addition, their geographical scope may increase to include international operations. We traced the dominant pattern of growth, which evolves from a simple structure to a functional structure as a firm grows in terms of size and increases its level of vertical integration. After a firm expands into related products and services, its structure changes from a functional to a divisional form of organization. Finally, when the firm enters international markets, its structure again changes to accommodate the change in strategy.

We also addressed the different types of organizational structure—simple, functional, divisional (including two variations—strategic business unit and holding company), and matrix—as well as their relative advantages and disadvantages. We closed the section with a discussion of the implications for structure when a firm enters international markets. The three primary factors to take into account when determining the appropriate structure are type of international strategy, product diversity, and the extent to which a firm is dependent on foreign sales.

In the second section, we took a contingency approach to the design of reward and evaluation systems. That is, we argued that there is no one best way to design such systems; rather, it is dependent on a variety of factors. The two that we discussed are business- and corporate-level strategies. With an overall cost leadership strategy and unrelated diversification, it is appropriate to rely primarily on cultures and reward systems that emphasize the production outcomes of the organization, because it is rather easy to quantify such indicators. In contrast, differentiation strategies and related diversification require cultures and incentive systems that encourage and reward creativity initiatives as well as the cooperation among professionals in many different functional areas. Here it becomes more difficult to measure accurately each individual's contribution, and more subjective indicators become essential.

The third section of the chapter introduced the concept of the boundaryless organization. We did not suggest that the concept of the boundaryless organization replaces the traditional forms of organizational structure. Rather, it should complement them. This is necessary to cope with the increasing complexity and change in the competitive environment. We addressed three types of boundaryless organizations. The barrier-free type focuses on the need for the internal and external boundaries of a firm to be more flexible and permeable. The modular type emphasizes the strategic outsourcing of noncore activities. The virtual type centers on the strategic benefits of alliances and the forming of network organizations. We discussed both the advantages and disadvantages of each type of boundaryless organization as well as suggested some techniques and processes that are necessary to successfully implement them. These are common culture and values, horizontal organizational structures, horizontal systems and processes, communications and information technologies, and human resource practices.

The final section addresses the need for managers to develop ambidextrous organizations. In today's rapidly changing global environment, managers must be responsive and proactive in order to take advantage of new opportunities. At the same time, they must effectively integrate and coordinate existing operations. Such requirements call for organizational designs that establish project teams that are structurally independent units, with each having its own processes, structures, and cultures. But, at the same time, each unit needs to be effectively integrated into the existing management hierarchy.

Summary Review Questions

1. Why is it important for managers to carefully consider the type of organizational structure that they use to implement their strategies?
2. Briefly trace the dominant growth pattern of major corporations from simple structure to functional structure to divisional structure. Discuss the relationship between a firm's strategy and its structure.
3. What are the relative advantages and disadvantages of the types of organizational structure—simple, functional, divisional, matrix—discussed in the chapter?

4. When a firm expands its operations into foreign markets, what are the three most important factors to take into account in deciding what type of structure is most appropriate? What are the types of international structures discussed in the text and what are the relationships between strategy and structure?
5. Briefly describe the three different types of boundaryless organizations: barrier-free, modular, and virtual.
6. What are some of the key attributes of effective groups? Ineffective groups?
7. What are the advantages and disadvantages of the three types of boundaryless organizations: barrier-free, modular, and virtual?
8. When are ambidextrous organizational designs necessary? What are some of their key attributes?

Key Terms

organizational structure, 357
simple organizational structure, 359
functional organizational structure, 359
divisional organizational structure, 361
strategic business unit (SBU) structure, 363
holding company structure, 364
matrix organizational structure, 364
international division structure, 367
geographic-area division structure, 367
worldwide matrix structure, 367
worldwide functional structure, 367
worldwide product division structure, 367
global start-up, 367
boundaryless organizational designs, 372,
barrier-free organization, 373
modular organization, 377
virtual organization, 379
horizontal organizational structures, 383
adaptability, 384
alignment, 384
ambidextrous organizational designs, 385

Experiential Exercise

Many firms have recently moved toward a modular structure. For example, they have increasingly outsourced many of their information technology (IT) activities. Identify three such organizations. Using secondary sources, evaluate (1) the firm's rationale for IT outsourcing and (2) the implications for performance.

Firm	Rationale	Implication(s) for Performance
1.		
2.		
3.		

Application Questions & Exercises

1. Select an organization that competes in an industry in which you are particularly interested. Go on the Internet and determine what type of organizational structure this organization has. In your view, is it consistent with the strategy that it has chosen to implement? Why? Why not?

2. Choose an article from *Businessweek, Fortune, Forbes, Fast Company,* or any other well-known publication that deals with a corporation that has undergone a significant change in its strategic direction. What are the implications for the structure of this organization?

3. Go on the Internet and look up some of the public statements or speeches of an executive in a major corporation about a significant initiative such as entering into a joint venture or launching a new product line. What do you feel are the implications for making the internal and external barriers of the firm more flexible and permeable? Does the executive discuss processes, procedures, integrating mechanisms, or cultural issues that should serve this purpose? Or are other issues discussed that enable a firm to become more boundaryless?

4. Look up a recent article in the publications listed in question 2 above that addresses a firm's involvement in outsourcing (modular organization) or in strategic alliance or network organizations (virtual organization). Was the firm successful or unsuccessful in this endeavor? Why? Why not?

Ethics Questions

1. If a firm has a divisional structure and places extreme pressures on its divisional executives to meet short-term profitability goals (e.g., quarterly income), could this raise some ethical considerations? Why? Why not?

2. If a firm enters into a strategic alliance but does not exercise appropriate behavioral control of its employees (in terms of culture, rewards and incentives, and boundaries—as discussed in Chapter 9) that are involved in the alliance, what ethical issues could arise? What could be the potential long-term and short-term downside for the firm?

References

1. Eng, D. 2010. Free tour, new steps to mend HK image. *South China Morning Post,* July 17: A2; Carothers, C. 2010. Hong Kong: Don't shop? Don't come. blogs.wsj.com, November 10: np; and Xinhua, J. 2010. Authority issues travel advisory on trip to Hong Kong. *china.org.cn,* November 10: np. We thank Zia Shakir for his valued contributions.

2. For a unique perspective on organization design, see: Rao, R. 2010. What 17th century pirates can teach us about job design. *Harvard Business Review,* 88(10): 44.

3. This introductory discussion draws upon Hall, R. H. 2002. *Organizations: Structures, processes, and outcomes* (8th ed.). Upper Saddle River, NJ: Prentice Hall; and Duncan, R. E. 1979. What is the right organization structure? Decision-tree analysis provides the right answer. *Organizational Dynamics,* 7(3): 59–80. For an insightful discussion of strategy-structure relationships in the organization theory and strategic management literatures, refer to Keats, B. & O'Neill, H. M. 2001. Organization structure: Looking

through a strategy lens. In Hitt, M. A., Freeman, R. E., & Harrison, J. S. 2001. *The Blackwell handbook of strategic management:* 520–542. Malden, MA: Blackwell.

4. Gratton, L. 2011. The end of the middle manager. *Harvard Business Review,* 89(1/2): 36.

5. An interesting discussion on the role of organizational design in strategy execution is in: Neilson, G. L., Martin, K. L., & Powers, E. 2009. The secrets to successful strategy execution. *Harvard Business Review,* 87(2): 60–70.

6. This discussion draws upon Chandler, A. D. 1962. *Strategy and structure.* Cambridge, MA: MIT Press; Galbraith J. R. & Kazanjian, R. K. 1986. *Strategy implementation: The role of structure and process.* St. Paul, MN: West Publishing; and Scott, B. R. 1971. Stages of corporate development. Intercollegiate Case Clearing House, 9-371-294, BP 998. Harvard Business School.

7. Our discussion of the different types of organizational structures draws on a variety of sources, including Galbraith & Kazanjian, op. cit.; Hrebiniak, L. G. & Joyce, W. F. 1984. *Implementing strategy.* New York: Macmillan; Distelzweig, H. 2000. Organizational structure. In Helms, M. M. (Ed.). *Encyclopedia of management:* 692–699. Farmington Hills, MI: Gale; and Dess, G. G. & Miller, A. 1993. *Strategic management.* New York: McGraw-Hill.

8. A discussion of an innovative organizational design is in: Garvin, D. A. & Levesque, L. C. 2009. The multiunit enterprise. *Harvard Business Review,* 87(2): 106–117.

9. Schein, E. H. 1996. Three cultures of management: The key to organizational learning. *Sloan Management Review,* 38(1): 9–20.

10. Insights on governance implications for multidivisional forms are in: Verbeke, A. & Kenworthy, T. P. 2008. Multidivisional vs. metanational governance. *Journal of International Business,* 39(6): 940–956.

11. Martin, J. A. & Eisenhardt, K. 2010. Rewiring: Cross-business-unit collaborations in multibusiness organizations. *Academy of Management Journal,* 53(2): 265–301.

12. For a discussion of performance implications, refer to Hoskisson, R. E. 1987. Multidivisional structure and performance: The contingency of diversification strategy. *Academy of Management Journal,* 29: 625–644.

13. For a thorough and seminal discussion of the evolution toward the divisional form of organizational structure in the United States, refer to Chandler, op. cit. A rigorous empirical study of the strategy and structure relationship is found in Rumelt, R. P. 1974. *Strategy, structure, and economic performance.* Cambridge, MA: Harvard Business School Press.

14. Ghoshal S. & Bartlett, C. A. 1995. Changing the role of management: Beyond structure to processes. *Harvard Business Review,* 73(1): 88.

15. Koppel, B. 2000. Synergy in ketchup? *Forbes,* February 7: 68–69; and Hitt, M. A., Ireland, R. D., & Hoskisson, R. E. 2001. *Strategic management: Competitiveness and globalization* (4th ed.). Cincinnati, OH: Southwestern Publishing.

16. Pitts, R. A. 1977. Strategies and structures for diversification. *Academy of Management Journal,* 20(2): 197–208.

17. Andersen, M. M., Froholdt, M., Poulfelt, F. 2010. *Return on strategy: How to achieve it.* New York: Routledge.

18. Haas, M. R. 2010. The double-edged swords of autonomy and external knowledge: Analyzing team effectiveness in a multinational organization. *Academy of Management Journal,* 53(5): 989–1008.

19. Daniels, J. D., Pitts, R. A., & Tretter, M. J. 1984. Strategy and structure of U.S. multinationals: An exploratory study. *Academy of Management Journal,* 27(2): 292–307.

20. Habib, M. M. & Victor, B. 1991. Strategy, structure, and performance of U.S. manufacturing and service MNCs: A comparative analysis. *Strategic Management Journal,* 12(8): 589–606.

21. Our discussion of global start-ups draws from Oviatt, B. M. & McDougall, P. P. 2005. The internationalization of entrepreneurship. *Journal of International Business Studies,* 36(1): 2–8; Oviatt, B. M. & McDougall, P. P. 1994. Toward a theory of international new ventures. *Journal of International Business Studies,* 25(1): 45–64; and Oviatt, B. M. & McDougall, P. P. 1995. Global start-ups: Entrepreneurs on a worldwide stage. *Academy of Management Executive,* 9(2): 30–43.

22. Some useful guidelines for global start-ups are provided in Kuemmerle, W. 2005. The entrepreneur's path for global expansion. *MIT Sloan Management Review,* 46(2): 42–50.

23. See, for example, Miller, D. & Friesen, P. H. 1980. Momentum and revolution in organizational structure. *Administrative Science Quarterly,* 13: 65–91.

24. Many authors have argued that a firm's structure can influence its strategy and performance. These include Amburgey, T. L. & Dacin, T. 1995. As the left foot follows the right? The dynamics of strategic and structural change. *Academy of Management Journal,* 37: 1427–1452; Dawn, K. & Amburgey, T. L. 1991. Organizational inertia and momentum: A dynamic model of strategic change. *Academy of Management Journal,* 34: 591–612; Fredrickson, J. W. 1986. The strategic decision process and organization structure. *Academy of Management Review,* 11: 280–297; Hall, D. J. & Saias, M. A. 1980. Strategy follows structure! *Strategic Management Journal,* 1: 149–164; and Burgelman, R. A. 1983. A model of the interaction of strategic behavior, corporate context, and the concept of strategy. *Academy of Management Review,* 8: 61–70.

25. This discussion of generic strategies and their relationship to organizational control draws upon Porter, M. E. 1980. *Competitive strategy.* New York: Free Press; and Miller, D. 1988. Relating Porter's business strategies to environment and structure: Analysis and performance implications. *Academy of Management Journal,* 31(2): 280–308.

26. Rodengen, J. L. 1997. *The legend of Nucor Corporation.* Fort Lauderdale, FL: Write Stuff Enterprises.

27. The 3M example draws upon *Blueprints for service quality.* 1994. New York: American Management Association; personal communication

with Katerine Hagmeier, program manager, external communications, 3M Corporation, March 26, 1998; Lei, D., Slocum, J. W., & Pitts, R. A. 1999. Designing organizations for competitive advantage: The power of unlearning and learning. *Organizational Dynamics,* 27(3): 24–38; and Graham, A. B. & Pizzo, V. G. 1996. A question of balance: Case studies in strategic knowledge management. *European Management Journal,* 14(4): 338–346.

28. The Sharp Corporation and Hanson plc examples are based on Collis, D. J. & Montgomery, C. A. 1998. Creating corporate advantage. *Harvard Business Review,* 76(3): 70–83.

29. Kunii, I. 2002. Japanese companies' survival skills. *BusinessWeek,* November 18: 18.

30. White, G. 1988. How I turned $3,000 into $10 billion. *Fortune,* November 7: 80–89. After the death of the founders, the Hanson plc conglomerate was found to be too unwieldy and was broken up into several separate, publicly traded corporations. For more on its more limited current scope of operations, see www.hansonplc.com.

31. An interesting discussion on how the Internet has affected the boundaries of firms can be found in Afuah, A. 2003. Redefining firm boundaries in the face of the Internet: Are firms really shrinking? *Academy of Management Review,* 28(1): 34–53.

32. Collis & Montgomery, op. cit.

33. Govindarajan, V. G. & Trimble, C. 2010. Stop the innovation wars. *Harvard Business Review,* 88(7/8): 76–83.

34. For a discussion of the role of coaching on developing high performance teams, refer to Kets de Vries, M. F. R. 2005. Leadership group coaching in action: The zen of creating high performance teams. *Academy of Management Executive,* 19(1): 77–89.

35. Pfeffer, J. 1998. *The human equation: Building profits by putting people first.* Cambridge, MA: Harvard Business School Press.

36. For a discussion on how functional area diversity affects performance, see Bunderson, J. S. & Sutcliffe, K.

M. 2002. *Academy of Management Journal,* 45(5): 875–893.

37. See, for example, Hoskisson, R. E., Hill, C. W. L., & Kim, H. 1993. The multidivisional structure: Organizational fossil or source of value? *Journal of Management,* 19(2): 269–298.

38. Pottruck, D. A. 1997. Speech delivered by the co-CEO of Charles Schwab Co., Inc., to the Retail Leadership Meeting, San Francisco, CA, January 30; and Miller, W. 1999. Building the ultimate resource. *Management Review,* January: 42–45.

39. Public-private partnerships are addressed in: Engardio, P. 2009. State capitalism. *BusinessWeek,* February 9: 38–43.

40. Magretta, J. 1998. The power of virtual integration: An interview with Dell Computer's Michael Dell. *Harvard Business Review,* 76(2): 75.

41. Forster, J. 2001. Networking for cash. *BusinessWeek,* January 8: 129.

42. Dess, G. G., Rasheed, A. M. A., McLaughlin, K. J., & Priem, R. 1995. The new corporate architecture. *Academy of Management Executive,* 9(3): 7–20.

43. Barnes, C. 1998. A fatal case. *Fast Company,* February–March: 173.

44. Handy, C. 1989. *The age of unreason.* Boston: Harvard Business School Press; Ramstead, E. 1997. APC maker's low-tech formula: Start with the box. *The Wall Street Journal,* December 29: B1; Mussberg, W. 1997. Thin screen PCs are looking good but still fall flat. *The Wall Street Journal,* January 2: 9; Brown, E. 1997. Monorail: Low cost PCs. *Fortune,* July 7: 106–108; and Young, M. 1996. Ex-Compaq executives start new company. *Computer Reseller News,* November 11: 181.

45. An original discussion on how open-sourcing could help the Big 3 automobile companies is in: Jarvis, J. 2009. How the Google model could help Detroit. *BusinessWeek,* February 9: 32–36.

46. For a discussion of some of the downsides of outsourcing, refer to Rossetti, C. & Choi, T. Y. 2005. On the dark side of strategic sourcing: Experiences from the aerospace industry.

Academy of Management Executive, 19(1): 46–60.

47. Tully, S. 1993. The modular corporation. *Fortune,* February 8: 196.

48. Offshoring in manufacturing firms is addressed in: Coucke, K. & Sleuwaegen, L. 2008. Offshoring as a survival strategy: Evidence from manufacturing firms in Belgium. *Journal of International Business Studies,* 39(8): 1261–1277.

49. Quinn, J. B. 1992. *Intelligent enterprise: A knowledge and service based paradigm for industry.* New York: Free Press.

50. For an insightful perspective on outsourcing and its role in developing capabilities, read Gottfredson, M., Puryear, R., & Phillips, C. 2005. Strategic sourcing: From periphery to the core. *Harvard Business Review,* 83(4): 132–139.

51. This discussion draws upon Quinn, J. B. & Hilmer, F. C. 1994. Strategic outsourcing. *Sloan Management Review,* 35(4): 43–55.

52. Reitzig, M. & Wagner, S. 2010. The hidden costs of outsourcing: Evidence from patent data. *Strategic Management Journal.* 31(11): 1183–1201.

53. Insights on outsourcing and private branding can be found in: Cehn, S-F. S. 2009. A transaction cost rationale for private branding and its implications for the choice of domestic vs. offshore outsourcing. *Journal of International Business Strategy,* 40(1): 156–175.

54. For an insightful perspective on the use of outsourcing for decision analysis, read: Davenport, T. H. & Iyer, B. 2009. Should you outsource your brain? *Harvard Business Review,* 87(2): 38.

55. See also Stuckey, J. & White, D. 1993. When and when not to vertically integrate. *Sloan Management Review,* Spring: 71–81; Harrar, G. 1993. Outsource tales. *Forbes ASAP,* June 7: 37–39, 42; and Davis, E. W. 1992. Global outsourcing: Have U.S. managers thrown the baby out with the bath water? *Business Horizons,* July–August: 58–64.

56. For a discussion of knowledge creation through alliances, refer to

To compete in the global marketplace, organizations need to have strong and effective leadership. This involves the active process of both creating and implementing proper strategies. In this chapter we address key activities in which leaders throughout the organization must be involved to be successful in creating and sustaining competitive advantages.

In the first section, we provide a brief overview of the three key leadership activities. These are (1) setting a direction, (2) designing the organization, and (3) nurturing a culture committed to excellence and ethical behavior. Each of these activities is "necessary but not sufficient"; that is, to be effective, leaders must give proper attention to each of them.

Section two addresses practices and capabilities that enable executives to be effective as leaders. To be successful in a complex business environment, leaders must perform a variety of functions and exhibit key strengths. We focus on three capabilities that effective leaders often exhibit—integrative thinking, overcoming barriers to change, and the effective use of power.

The third section discusses the vital role of emotional intelligence (EI) in effective strategic leadership. EI refers to an individual's capacity for recognizing his or her emotions and those of others. It consists of five components: self-awareness, self-regulation, motivation, empathy, and social skills. We also address potential downsides or drawbacks that may result from the ineffective use of EI.

Next we address the important role of a leader in creating a learning organization. Here, leaders must strive to harness the individual and collective talents of individuals throughout the entire organization. Creating a learning organization is particularly important in today's competitive environment, which is increasingly unpredictable, dynamic, and interdependent. The key elements of a learning organization are inspiring and motivating people with a mission or purpose, empowering employees at all levels, accumulating and sharing internal and external information, and challenging the status quo to enable creativity.

The final section discusses a leader's challenge in creating and maintaining an ethical organization. There are many benefits of having an ethical organization. It can provide financial benefits, enhance human capital, and help to ensure positive relationships with suppliers, customers, society at large and governmental agencies. By contrast failure to operate ethically leading to an ethical crisis can be very costly for many reasons. We address four key elements of an ethical organization: role models, corporate credos and codes of conduct, reward and evaluation systems, and policies and procedures.

Inkpen, A. C. 1996. Creating knowledge through collaboration. *California Management Review*, 39(1): 123–140; and Mowery, D. C., Oxley, J. E., & Silverman, B. S. 1996. Strategic alliances and interfirm knowledge transfer. *Strategic Management Journal*, 17 (Special Issue, Winter): 77–92.

57. Doz, Y. & Hamel, G. 1998. *Alliance advantage: The art of creating value through partnering*. Boston: Harvard Business School Press.

58. DeSanctis, G., Glass, J. T., & Ensing, I. M. 2002. Organizational designs for R&D. *Academy of Management Executive*, 16(3): 55–66.

59. Barringer, B. R. & Harrison, J. S. 2000. Walking a tightrope: Creating value through interorganizational alliances. *Journal of Management*, 26: 367–403.

60. Davis, E. 1997. Interview: Norman Augustine. *Management Review*, November: 14.

61. One contemporary example of virtual organizations is R&D consortia. For an insightful discussion, refer to Sakaibara, M. 2002. Formation of R&D consortia: Industry and company effects. *Strategic Management Journal*, 23(11): 1033–1050.

62. Bartness, A. & Cerny, K. 1993. Building competitive advantage through a global network of capabilities. *California Management Review*, Winter: 78–103. For an insightful historical discussion of the usefulness of alliances in the computer industry, see Moore, J. F. 1993. Predators and prey: A new ecology of competition. *Harvard Business Review*, 71(3): 75–86.

63. See Lorange, P. & Roos, J. 1991. Why some strategic alliances succeed and others fail. *Journal of Business Strategy*, January–February: 25–30; and Slowinski, G. 1992. The human touch in strategic alliances. *Mergers and Acquisitions*, July–August: 44–47. A compelling argument for strategic alliances is provided by Ohmae, K. 1989. The global logic of strategic alliances. *Harvard Business Review*, 67(2): 143–154.

64. Some of the downsides of alliances are discussed in Das, T. K. & Teng, B. S. 2000. Instabilities of strategic alliances: An internal tensions perspective. *Organization Science*, 11: 77–106.

65. This section draws upon Dess, G. G. & Picken, J. C. 1997. *Mission critical*. Burr Ridge, IL: Irwin Professional Publishing.

66. Katzenbach, J. R. & Smith, D. K. 1994. *The wisdom of teams: Creating the high performance organization*. New York: HarperBusiness.

67. Hammer, M. & Champy, J. 1993. *Reengineering the corporation: A manifesto for business revolution*. New York: HarperCollins.

68. This section draws on Birkinshaw, J. & Gibson, C. 2004. Building ambidexterity into an organization. *MIT Sloan Management Review*, 45(4): 47–55; and Gibson, C. B. & Birkinshaw, J. 2004. The antecedents, consequences, and mediating role of organizational ambidexterity. *Academy of Management Journal*, 47(2): 209–226. Robert Duncan is generally credited with being the first to coin the term "ambidextrous organizations" in his article entitled: Designing dual structures for innovation. In Kilmann, R. H., Pondy, L. R., & Slevin, D. (Eds.). 1976. *The management of organizations*, vol. 1: 167–188. For a seminal academic discussion of the concept of exploration and exploitation, which parallels adaptation and alignment, refer to: March, J. G. 1991. Exploration and exploitation in organizational learning. *Organization Science*, 2: 71–86.

69. This section is based on O'Reilly, C. A. & Tushman, M. L. 2004. The ambidextrous organization. *Harvard Business Review*, 82(4): 74–81.

chapter **ELEVEN**

Strategic Leadership:

Creating a Learning Organization and an Ethical Organization

After reading this chapter, you should have a good understanding of:

LO11.1   The three key interdependent activities in which all successful leaders must be continually engaged.

LO11.2   Three elements of effective leadership: integrative thinking, overcoming barriers to change, and the effective use of power.

LO11.3   The crucial role of emotional intelligence (EI) in successful leadership as well as its potential drawbacks.

LO11.4   The value of creating and maintaining a learning organization in today's global marketplace.

LO11.5   The leader's role in establishing an ethical organization.

LO11.6   The difference between integrity-based and compliance-based approaches to organizational ethics.

LO11.7   Several key elements that organizations must have to become an ethical organization.

LEARNING OBJECTIVES

▓▓▓ Learning from Mistakes

Duke Energy appeared to be doing the right thing by investing in clean-coal technology. Through a state-of-the-art power plant, Duke Energy would convert coal to flammable gas, a move approved by state regulators, who allowed the firm to pass some of the costs on to consumers. The firm's CEO, Jim Rogers, had even been profiled by the *New York Times* in 2008 as a "green coal baron," who constantly lobbied for a national price on carbon output, seeking to move out of low-tech coal plants to cleaner, more expensive coal plants. Yet in December 2010, the firm was rocked by an ethics scandal caused by e-mail exchanges between some of its executives and state regulators who oversaw its operations, and who decided what rates the utility could charge its customers. What went wrong?[1]

An ethics investigation led to several resignations. These included James Turner (one of Duke Energy's top executives) and two other executives as well as a prominent Indiana state regulator. The press obtained several e-mail exchanges between the four men, relating to alcohol, cars, their wives, and the open mocking of state ethical standards. While the investigation focused on the e-mail exchanges, the main concern was the relationship between Duke and state regulators, raising the question of a possible revolving door between the two entities. The improper relationship between Duke and regulators might have been foreseeable, considering that most big players at Duke had at one point worked for the Indiana government and that the head of Indiana's utility commission had been a lawyer for a local utility acquired by Duke.

While working for Duke, Turner was the second highest paid executive in 2009, totaling $4.3 million in compensation. Even following his resignation, he received a severance and retirement package worth more than $10 million. Turner had frequent e-mail exchanges with the head of Indiana's Utility Regulatory Commission, David Hardy, at times trading up to 10 messages a day. The men frequently ridiculed state ethics rules that were enacted to prevent state-regulated utilities from exerting undue influence on their regulators. In an e-mail, Turner wondered whether the "ethics police would have a cow" if he was visited at his weekend home by a top state regulator. In another published e-mail, Hardy brags about relaxing by the pool in the morning and inquiring about a good breakfast wine, and in reply Turner wrote, "Does anyone know if a desire to 'bitch slap a chairman' violates any state's hate crime laws?" Other e-mails addressed the hiring process of Scott Storm and Mike Reed, as they sought and then obtained jobs with Duke, with Hardy, their former boss, constantly demanding reports on the hiring process and inquiring whether he should try to influence Duke's CEO's decision.

The relationship with state regulators is an important one for Duke, as it invests heavily in the state in an attempt to position itself to prosper in the age of climate politics by investing in a first-of-its-kind clean-coal power plant. Duke received approval from a state commission to raise its rates for Indiana customers by approximately 16 percent, passing on to them costs of almost $2.9 billion when the plant is completed in 2012. Considering that the firm is $1 billion over its previous budget estimates, critics point out that there are cheaper ways to produce energy to meet the state's needs. Some of the matters related to the approval of the clean-coal plant had been overseen by Scott Storm, who was hired by Duke in September 2010.

Storm was a lawyer who had, until then, worked for the Indiana Utility Regulatory Commission as an administrative law judge, as their top legal officer. In that position he had worked on several Duke cases, but there was no indication that he had provided special treatment to the firm. He received an ethics waiver from a state panel to forgo a one-year cooling-off period after leaving state service prior to accepting employment with a company that he had helped regulate. This decision outraged consumer advocates and finally led to the firing of the commission's head, Hardy, by the governor of Indiana and to the reopening of the decision regarding Duke. Both Storm and the Duke executive that hired him, Mike Reed, resigned from the company. Reed had taken the position at Duke as its president for Indiana 16 months after he had himself been the executive director of the Indiana Utility Regulatory Commission. Even after leaving Duke, Storm faced a state ethics panel hearing claiming that he did not recuse himself from cases related to Duke while considering employment with the company.

In response, Duke has drafted new employment guidelines to ensure that they only hire from "regulatory and oversight groups" with no prior affairs related to Duke Energy. However, this seems to be too little, too late.

Clearly, many of the decisions and actions of Duke Energy's top executives were not in the best interests of the firm and its shareholders and were not consistent with norms of ethical behavior. In contrast, effective leaders play an important and often pivotal role in creating and implementing strategies.

This chapter provides insights into the role of strategic leadership in managing, adapting, and coping in the face of increased environmental complexity and uncertainty. First, we define leadership and its components. Then, we identify three elements of leadership that contribute to success—integrative thinking, overcoming barriers to change, and the effective use of power. The third section focuses on emotional intelligence, a trait that is increasingly acknowledged to be critical to successful leadership. Next, we emphasize the importance of developing a learning organization and how leaders can help their firms learn and proactively adapt in the face of accelerating change. Here, we focus on empowerment wherein employees and managers throughout an organization develop a sense of self-determination, competence, meaning, and impact that is centrally important to learning. Finally, we address the leader's role in building an ethical organization and the elements of an ethical culture that contribute to firm effectiveness.

Leadership: Three Interdependent Activities

In today's chaotic world, few would argue against the need for leadership, but how do we go about encouraging it? Is it enough to merely keep an organization afloat, or is it essential to make steady progress toward some well-defined objective? We believe custodial management is not leadership. Leadership is proactive, goal-oriented, and focused on the creation and implementation of a creative vision. **Leadership** is the process of transforming organizations from what they are to what the leader would have them become. This definition implies a lot: *dissatisfaction* with the status quo, a *vision* of what should be, and a *process* for bringing about change. An insurance company executive shared the following insight: "I lead by the Noah Principle: It's all right to know when it's going to rain, but, by God, you had better build the ark."

leadership the process of transforming organizations from what they are to what the leader would have them become.

Doing the right thing is becoming increasingly important. Many industries are declining; the global village is becoming increasingly complex, interconnected, and unpredictable; and product and market life cycles are becoming increasingly compressed. When asked to describe the life cycle of his company's products, the CEO of a supplier of computer components replied, "Seven months from cradle to grave—and that includes three months to design the product and get it into production!" Richard D'Aveni, author of *Hypercompetition,* argued that in a world where all dimensions of competition appear to be compressed in time and heightened in complexity, *sustainable* competitive advantages are no longer possible.

Despite the importance of doing the "right thing," leaders must also be concerned about "doing things right." Charan and Colvin strongly believe that execution, that is, the implementation of strategy, is also essential to success.

> Mastering execution turns out to be the odds-on best way for a CEO to keep his job. So what's the right way to think about that sexier obsession, strategy? It's vitally important—obviously. The problem is that our age's fascination feeds the mistaken belief that developing exactly the right strategy will enable a company to rocket past competitors. In reality, that's less than half the battle.[2]

>LO11.1

The three key interdependent activities in which all successful leaders must be continually engaged.

Thus, leaders are change agents whose success is measured by how effectively they formulate *and* implement a strategic vision and mission.[3]

Many authors contend that successful leaders must recognize three interdependent activities that must be continually reassessed for organizations to succeed. As shown in Exhibit 11.1, these are: (1) setting a direction, (2) designing the organization, and (3) nurturing a culture dedicated to excellence and ethical behavior.[4]

The interdependent nature of these three activities is self-evident. Consider an organization with a great mission and a superb organizational structure, but a culture that implicitly encourages shirking and unethical behavior. Or one with a sound direction and strong culture, but counterproductive teams and a "zero-sum" reward system that leads to the dysfunctional situation in which one party's gain is viewed as another party's loss, and collaboration and sharing are severely hampered. Clearly, such combinations would be ineffective.

A new approach on leadership highlights the importance of being "ambicultural," which emphasizes taking the best elements of the philosophies and practices from multiple cultures while avoiding their negative aspects. Such an approach can be highly effective in performing the three leadership activities in today's increasingly global economy.

Exhibit 11.1 Three Interdependent Leadership Activities

Julie Gilbert Sets a New Direction for Best Buy

Julie Gilbert is evidence that significant and creative change can be brought about by people who do not happen to be at the very top of an organization. As a senior VP at retailer Best Buy from 2000 to early 2009, she saw a looming crisis in the firm's failure to profit from the greater involvement of women in the male-oriented world of consumer electronics. Women were becoming more influential in purchasing decisions, directly and indirectly. But capitalizing on this trend would require something beyond a smart marketing plan. It would demand a change in the company's orientation.

Getting an organization to adapt to changes in the environment is not easy. You need to confront loyalty to legacy practices and understand that your desire to change them makes you a target of attack. Gilbert believed that instead of simply selling technology products to mostly male customers, Best Buy needed to appeal to women by reflecting the increasing integration of consumer electronics into family life. So Gilbert headed up an initiative to establish in-store boutiques that sold home theater systems along with coordinated furniture and accessories. Stores set up living-room displays to showcase not just electronics but also the entertainment environment. Salespeople were trained to interact with the previously ignored female customers who came in with men to look at systems.

Source: Heifetz, R., Grashow, A. & Linsky, M. 2009. Leadership in a (Permanent) Crisis. *Harvard Business Review,* 87 (7/8): 62–69; and Bustillo, M. & Lloyd, M. 2010. Best Buy Tests New Appeals to Women. *www.wsj.com,* June 16: np.

Gilbert says that championing this approach subjected her to some nasty criticism from managers who viewed Best Buy as a retailer of technology *products,* not experiences. However, focusing on the female purchaser when a man and a woman walked into the store—making eye contact and greeting her, asking about her favorite movies, and demonstrating them on the systems—often resulted in the couple's purchasing a higher-end product than they had originally considered. According to Gilbert, returns and exchanges of purchases made by couples were 60 percent lower than those made by men. With the rethinking of traditional practices, Best Buy's home theater business flourished, growing from two pilot in-store boutiques in mid-2004 to more than 350 five years later.

Such success does not appear to just happen by chance at Best Buy. Consider:

- Best Buy is empowering female workers and consulting teenage girls to suggest new ways to sell to women. The move reflects that women are becoming the most coveted customers in some of the hottest areas of electronic retailing in stores—smart phones and other mobile services.

- Executives say that the best insights on expanding the female customer base come from the company's "Women Leadership Forums," a loose-knit group of female workers and customers that meet around the country. The groups helped increase appliance sales, for example, by suggesting that showrooms be redesigned to resemble kitchens.

Often, failure of today's organizations can be attributed to a lack of equal consideration of these three activities. The imagery of a three-legged stool is instructive: It will collapse if one leg is missing or broken. Let's briefly look at each of these activities as well as the value of an ambicultural approach to leadership.

Setting a Direction

A holistic understanding of an organization's stakeholders requires an ability to scan the environment to develop a knowledge of all of the company's stakeholders and other salient environmental trends and events. Managers must integrate this knowledge into a vision of what the organization could become.[5] It necessitates the capacity to solve increasingly complex problems, become proactive in approach, and develop viable strategic options. A strategic vision provides many benefits: a clear future direction; a framework for the organization's mission and goals; and enhanced employee communication, participation, and commitment.

setting a direction
a strategic leadership activity of strategy analysis and strategy formulation.

At times the creative process involves what the CEO of Yokogawa, GE's Japanese partner in the Medical Systems business, called "bullet train" thinking.[6] That is, if you want to increase the speed by 10 miles per hour, you look for incremental advances. However, if you want to double the speed, you've got to think "out of the box" (e.g., widen the track, change the overall suspension system). Leaders need more creative solutions than just keeping the same train with a few minor tweaks. Instead, they must come up with more revolutionary visions.

The experience of Julie Gilbert, VP of electronics retailer Best Buy, in changing the orientation of the company to attract more female shoppers is an excellent example of how leaders can overcome resistance and set new directions for their organizations. Strategy Spotlight 11.1 describes her initiatives.

Designing the Organization

designing the organization a strategic leadership activity of building structures, teams, systems, and organizational processes that facilitate the implementation of the leader's vision and strategies.

At times, almost all leaders have difficulty implementing their vision and strategies.[7] Such problems may stem from a variety of sources:

- Lack of understanding of responsibility and accountability among managers.
- Reward systems that do not motivate individuals (or collectives such as groups and divisions) toward desired organizational goals.
- Inadequate or inappropriate budgeting and control systems.
- Insufficient mechanisms to integrate activities across the organization.

Successful leaders are actively involved in building structures, teams, systems, and organizational processes that facilitate the implementation of their vision and strategies. We discussed the necessity for consistency between business-level and corporate-level strategies and organizational control in Chapter 9. Without appropriately structuring organizational activities, a firm would generally be unable to attain an overall low-cost advantage by closely monitoring its costs through detailed and formalized cost and financial control procedures. With regard to corporate-level strategy, a related diversification strategy would necessitate reward systems that emphasize behavioral measures, whereas an unrelated strategy should rely more on financial (or objective) indicators of performance.

These examples illustrate the important role of leadership in creating systems and structures to achieve desired ends. As Jim Collins says about the importance of designing the organization, "Along with figuring out what the company stands for and pushing it to understand what it's really good at, building mechanisms is the CEO's role—the leader as architect."[8]

Nurturing an Excellent and Ethical Culture

excellent and ethical organizational culture an organizational culture focused on core competencies and high ethical standards.

Organizational culture can be an effective means of organizational control.[9] Leaders play a key role in changing, developing, and sustaining an organization's culture. Consider a Chinese firm, Huawei, a highly successful producer of communication network solutions and services.[10] In 2009, it achieved revenues of $21.8 billion and net profits of $2.7 billion. Its strong culture can be attributed to its founder, Ren Zhengfei, and his background in the People's Liberation Army. It is a culture which eliminates individualism and promotes collectivism and the idea of hunting in packs. It is the "wolf culture" of Huawei:

> The culture of Huawei is built on a sense of patriotism, with Mr. Zhengfei frequently citing Mao Zedong's thoughts in his speeches and internal publications such as the employee magazine "Huawei People." Sales teams are referred to as "Market Guerrillas," and battlefield tactics, such as "occupy rural areas first to surround cities," are used internally. In addition to Mao Zedong, Mr. Zhengfei has urged his employees to look to the Japanese and Germans for inspiration on how to conduct themselves. This is exemplified by the words written in a letter to new hires that states, "I hope you abandon the mentality of achieving

IKEA's Founder: "Low Prices—But Not at Any Price"

IKEA's founder, Ingvar Kamprad, although believed to be one of the world's top 10 richest men, is leading his company by example. He flies coach, drives an aging Volvo, and stays in cheap hotels when traveling. Early in his career, Kamprad recognized that promoting a double standard between him and his employees would be detrimental to the health and wealth of the entire company. He contends, "It's a question of good leadership."

His money-pinching habits are thus exemplified and reinforced in the company he founded. As an example of his thriftiness: upon seeing some small pencils in a pile of debris on the floor, Kamprad sent the store manager to recover the pencils, even though their value was less than a penny.

Even though the company is usually tight-fisted, when it comes to environmental issues, IKEA spends millions of dollars in sorting and recycling the various types of plastic, metal, and wood used in packaging its products. Clearly, taking the time to sort the various materials entails significant costs and slows down the replenishment process. However, the processes are considered highly relevant to the firm's spirit of leadership. It is worth mentioning that

Source: Esty, D. C. & Winston, A. S. 2009. *Green to Gold. Hoboken*, NJ: Wiley; and Carmichael, E. undated. Lesson #2: The Best Leadership Is by Example. *www.evancarmichael.com*, np.

● IKEA is well-known for its inexpensive but stylish furniture as well as its concern for the environment.

none of these steps are a regulatory requirement, but are voluntary.

An explanation for IKEA's actions can be found in the company's slogan that is often observed in its offices: "Low prices—but not at any price." For IKEA this is not just another slogan but is reflected in its employees' everyday actions.

quick results, learn from the Japanese down-to-earth attitude and the German's spirit of being scrupulous to every detail."

The notion of "wolf culture" stems from the fact that Huawei workers are encouraged to learn from the behavior of wolves, which have a keen sense of smell, are aggressive, and, most important of all, hunt in packs. It is this collective and aggressive spirit that is the center of the Huawei culture. Combining the behavior of wolves with military-style training has been instrumental in building the culture of the company, which, in turn, is widely thought to be instrumental in the company's success.

In sharp contrast, leaders can also have a very detrimental effect on a firm's culture and ethics. Imagine the negative impact that Todd Berman's illegal activities have had on a firm that he cofounded—New York's private equity firm Chartwell Investments.[11] He stole more than $3.6 million from the firm and its investors. Berman pleaded guilty to fraud charges brought by the Justice Department. For 18 months he misled Chartwell's investors concerning the financial condition of one of the firm's portfolio companies by falsely claiming it needed to borrow funds to meet operating expenses. Instead, Berman transferred the money to his personal bank account, along with fees paid by portfolio companies.

Clearly, a leader's behavior and values can make a strong impact on an organization—for good or for bad. Strategy Spotlight 11.2 provides a positive example. It discusses how the values and behavior of Ingvar Kamprad, founder of Swedish furniture retailer IKEA, have resulted in a culture of frugality and environmental consciousness within the company.

Managers and top executives must accept personal responsibility for developing and strengthening ethical behavior throughout the organization. They must consistently demonstrate that such behavior is central to the vision and mission of the organization. Several elements must be present and reinforced for a firm to become highly ethical, including role models, corporate credos and codes of conduct, reward and evaluation systems, and policies and procedures. Given the importance of these elements, we address them in detail in the last section of this chapter.

The Ambicultural Approach: A Key to Successfully Fulfilling the Three Leadership Activities

Highly successful leaders don't rely strictly on one philosophy and its associated set of business practices and apply them to every decision they face. Rather, they endeavor to merge the best from different approaches. For example, leaders can benefit by taking the best of different philosophies and business practices while avoiding the negatives. This is called an "ambicultural" perspective on leadership.[12] For example, a company can try to combine the best of Chinese and Western practices to create a truly ambicultural organization.

Each society has particular strengths and weaknesses as they apply to business practice. The challenge for managers is to utilize the thinking and orientations of both cultures in order to understand, identify with, and benefit from each of them. And we will see that it has important implications for setting an organization's direction, designing structures and processes, as well as instilling a strong culture.

Stan Shih, the legendary founder of the Acer Group, personifies the ambicultural perspective on leadership. Acer is the second-largest computer maker in the world, with revenues for the firm and its sister businesses, BenQ and Winstron, totaling $52 billion. Shih's overall orientation might be best described as a long-term view that values benefits not only for all company stakeholders but the entire global community.[13]

His major influence from the Chinese culture is a patient, holistic, community-driven orientation. From the Western perspective, he has taken a more decentralized and empowering management philosophy. At the same time, he has striven to avoid the mistrust, secrecy, and authoritarian paternalism that have sometimes characterized Eastern practices, and to avoid the short-term, bottom-line-driven focus and grandiosity of some Western companies.

Let's take a closer look at some Western practices that Shih has avoided and some that he has adopted. Most of all, he has avoided short-termism and narrow individualism and its corresponding intolerant, money-driven, up-or-out culture. His concern has never been with short-term profits or kill-or-be-killed competitive reasoning. He has avoided corporate cultures that lavishly reward the very few at the expense of the many. Nor has he focused exclusively on owners at the expense of other stakeholders or society as a whole. In these respects, he has much in common with enduring great Western family businesses.

At the same time, Shih has not universally ignored or dismissed aspects of American or Western management. He has been a strong proponent of decentralization, flat structures, and employee discretion. He has been quick to give up power to the next generations, and he has appreciated the value of brands, branding, and globalization. Unlike most Chinese firms, Acer did not pursue a typical cost-driven strategy or focus on low-end manufacturing. Theirs was more of a Western approach to branding and selling higher-end products. However, Shih did take note of the mistake of so many Western firms of outsourcing too many functions and thereby letting the outsourcers move up the value chain and steal their business. Acer kept total control of the value chain by employing different companies belonging to the same corporate group.

Elements of Effective Leadership

The demands on leaders in today's business environment require them to perform a variety of functions. The success of their organizations often depends on how they as individuals meet challenges and deliver on promises. What practices and skills are needed to get the job done effectively? In this section, we focus on three capabilities that are marks of successful leadership—integrative thinking, overcoming barriers to change, and the effective use of power. Then, in the next section, we will examine an important human trait that helps leaders be more effective—emotional intelligence.

Integrative Thinking

The challenges facing today's leaders require them to confront a host of opposing forces. As the previous section indicated, maintaining consistency across a company's culture, vision, and organizational design can be difficult, especially if the three activities are out of alignment.

How does a leader make good strategic decisions in the face of multiple contingencies and diverse opportunities? A recent study by Roger L. Martin reveals that executives who have a capability known as "integrative thinking" are among the most effective leaders. In his book *The Opposable Mind,* Martin contends that people who can consider two conflicting ideas simultaneously, without dismissing one of the ideas or becoming discouraged about reconciling them, often make the best problem solvers because of their ability to creatively synthesize the opposing thoughts. In explaining the source of his title, Martin quotes F. Scott Fitzgerald, who observed, "The test of a first-rate intelligence is the ability to hold two opposing ideas in mind at the same time and still retain the ability to function. One should, for example, be able to see that things are hopeless yet be determined to make them otherwise."[14]

In contrast to conventional thinking, which tends to focus on making choices between competing ideas from a limited set of alternatives, integrative thinking is the process by which people reconcile opposing thoughts to identify creative solutions that provide them with more options and new alternatives. Exhibit 11.2 outlines the four stages of the integrative thinking and deciding process. Martin uses the admittedly simple example of deciding where to go on vacation to illustrate the stages:

> **integrative thinking** a process of reconciling opposing thoughts by generating new alternatives and creative solutions rather than rejecting one thought in favor of another.

- *Salience*—Take stock of what features of the decision you consider relevant and important. For example: Where will you go? What will you see? Where will you stay? What will it cost? Is it safe? Other features may be less important, but try to think of everything that may matter.
- *Causality*—Make a mental map of the causal relationships between the features, that is, how the various features are related to one another. For example, is it worth it to invite friends to share expenses? Will an exotic destination be less safe?
- *Architecture*—Use the mental map to arrange a sequence of decisions that will lead to a specific outcome. For example, will you make the hotel and flight arrangements first, or focus on which sightseeing tours are available? No particular decision path is right or wrong, but considering multiple options simultaneously may lead to a better decision.
- *Resolution*—Make your selection. For example, choose which destination, which flight, and so forth. You final resolution is linked to how you evaluated the first three stages; if you are dissatisfied with your choices, the dotted arrows in the diagram (Exhibit 11.2) suggest you can go back through the process and revisit your assumptions.

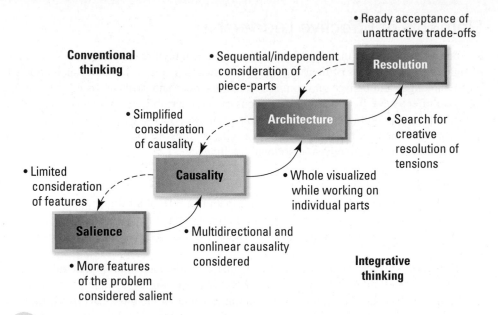

Conventional
thinking

- Ready acceptance of
  unattractive trade-offs

- Sequential/independent
  consideration of
  piece-parts

Resolution

- Simplified
  consideration
  of causality

Architecture

- Search for
  creative
  resolution of
  tensions

- Limited
  consideration
  of features

Causality

- Whole visualized
  while working on
  individual parts

Salience

- Multidirectional and
  nonlinear causality
  considered

Integrative
thinking

- More features
  of the problem
  considered salient

Exhibit 11.2 **Integrative Thinking: The Process of Thinking and Deciding**

Source: Reprinted by permission of Harvard Business School Press from R. L. Martin. *The Opposable Mind*, 2007. Copyright 2007 by the Harvard Business School Publishing Corporation; all rights reserved.

Applied to business, an integrative thinking approach enables decision makers to consider situations not as forced trade-offs—either decrease costs or invest more; either satisfy shareholders or please the community—but as a method for synthesizing opposing ideas into a creative solution. The key is to think in terms of "both-and" rather than "either-or." "Integrative thinking," says Martin, "shows us that there's a way to integrate the advantages of one solution without canceling out the advantages of an alternative solution."

Although Martin found that integrative thinking comes naturally to some people, he also believes it can be taught. But it may be difficult to learn, in part because it requires people to *un*learn old patterns and become aware of how they think. For executives willing to take a deep look at their habits of thought, integrative thinking can be developed into a valuable skill. Strategy Spotlight 11.3 tells how Red Hat Inc. cofounder Bob Young made his company a market leader by using integrative thinking to resolve a major problem in the domain of open-source software.

Overcoming Barriers to Change

What are the **barriers to change** that leaders often encounter, and how can they best bring about organizational change?[15] After all, people generally have some level of choice about how strongly they support or resist a leader's change initiatives. Why is there often so much resistance? Organizations at all levels are prone to inertia and are slow to learn, adapt, and change because:

1. Many people have **vested interests in the status quo.** People tend to be risk averse and resistant to change. There is a broad stream of research on "escalation," wherein certain individuals continue to throw "good money at bad decisions" despite negative performance feedback.[16]

2. There are **systemic barriers.** The design of the organization's structure, information processing, reporting relationships, and so forth impede the proper flow and evaluation of information. A bureaucratic structure with multiple layers, onerous

---

barriers to change characteristics of individuals and organizations that prevent a leader from transforming an organization.

>LO11.2
Three elements of effective leadership: integrative thinking, overcoming barriers to change, and the effective use of power.

vested intrest in the status quo a barrier to change that stems from people's risk aversion.

systemic barriers barriers to change that stem from an organizational design that impedes the proper flow and evaluation of information.

Integrative Thinking at Red Hat, Inc.

How can a software developer make money giving away free software? That was the dilemma Red Hat founder Bob Young was facing during the early days of the open-source software movement. A Finnish developer named Linus Torvalds, using freely available UNIX software, had developed an operating system dubbed "Linux" that was being widely circulated in the freeware community. The software was intended specifically as an alternative to the pricey proprietary systems sold by Microsoft and Oracle. To use proprietary software, corporations had to pay hefty installation fees and were required to call Microsoft or Oracle engineers to fix it when anything went wrong. In Young's view it was a flawed and unsustainable business model.

But the free model was flawed as well. Although several companies had sprung up to help companies use Linux, there were few opportunities to profit from using it. As Young said, "You couldn't make any money selling [the Linux] operating system because all this stuff was free, and if you started to charge money for it, someone else would come in and price it lower. It was a commodity in the truest sense of the word." To complicate matters, hundreds of developers were part of the software community that was constantly modifying and debugging Linux—at a rate equivalent to three updates per day. As a result, systems administrators at corporations that tried to adopt the software spent so much time keeping track of updates that they didn't enjoy the savings they expected from using free software.

Source: Martin, R. L. 2007. *The Opposable Mind*. Boston: Harvard Business School Press; and *www.finance.yahoo.com*.

Young saw the appeal of both approaches but also realized a new model was needed. While contemplating the dilemma, he realized a salient feature that others had overlooked—because most major corporations have to live with software decisions for at least ten years, they will nearly always choose to do business with the industry leader. Young realized he had to position Red Hat as the top provider of Linux software. To do that, he proposed a radical solution: provide the authoritative version of Linux and deliver it in a new way—as a download rather than on CD. He hired programmers to create a download-able version—still free—and promised, in essence, to maintain its quality (for a fee, of course) by dealing with all the open-source programmers who were continually suggesting changes. In the process, he created a product companies could trust and then profited by establishing ongoing service relationships with customers. Red Hat's version of Linux became the de facto standard. By 2000, Linux was installed in 25 percent of server operating systems worldwide and Red Hat had captured over 50 percent of the global market for Linux systems.

By recognizing that a synthesis of two flawed business models could provide the best of both worlds, Young exhibited the traits of integrative thinking. He pinpointed the causal relationships between the salient features of the marketplace and Red Hat's path to prosperity. He then crafted an approach that integrated aspects of the two existing approaches into a new alternative. By resolving to provide a free downloadable version, Young also took responsibility for creating his own path to success. The pay-off was substantial: when Red Hat went public in 1999, Young became a billionaire on the first day of trading. And by February 2011 Red Hat had over $850 million in annual revenues and a market capitalization of nearly $9 billion.

---

requirements for documentation, and rigid rules and procedures will often "inoculate" the organization against change.

3. **Behavioral barriers** cause managers to look at issues from a biased or limited perspective due to their education, training, work experiences, and so forth. Consider an incident shared by David Lieberman, marketing director at GVO, an innovation consulting firm:

   A company's creative type had come up with a great idea for a new product. Nearly everybody loved it. However, it was shot down by a high-ranking manufacturing representative who exploded: "A new color? Do you have any idea of the spare-parts problem that it will create?" This was not a dimwit exasperated at having to build a few storage racks at the warehouse. He'd been hearing for years about cost cutting, lean inventories, and "focus." Lieberman's comment: "Good concepts, but not always good for innovation."

behavioral barriers barriers to change associated with the tendency for managers to look at issues from a biased or limited perspective based on their prior education and experience.

political barriers barriers to change related to conflicts arising from power relationships.

personal time constraints a barrier to change that stems from people's not having sufficient time for strategic thinking and reflection.

4. **Political barriers** refer to conflicts arising from power relationships. This can be the outcome of a myriad of symptoms such as vested interests, refusal to share information, conflicts over resources, conflicts between departments and divisions, and petty interpersonal differences.

5. **Personal time constraints** bring to mind the old saying about "not having enough time to drain the swamp when you are up to your neck in alligators." Gresham's law of planning states that operational decisions will drive out the time necessary for strategic thinking and reflection. This tendency is accentuated in organizations experiencing severe price competition or retrenchment wherein managers and employees are spread rather thin.

Leaders must draw on a range of personal skills as well as organizational mechanisms to move their organizations forward in the face of such barriers. Integrative thinking provides one avenue by equipping leaders with an ability to consider creative alternatives to the kind of resistance and doubt that cause many barriers. Two factors mentioned earlier—building a learning organization and ethical organization—provide the kind of climate within which a leader can advance the organization's aims and make progress toward its goals.

One of the most important tools a leader has for overcoming barriers to change is their personal and organizational power. On the one hand, good leaders must be on guard not to abuse power. On the other hand, successful leadership requires the measured exercise of power. We turn to that topic next.

The Effective Use of Power

power a leader's ability to get things done in a way he or she wants them to be done.

Successful leadership requires effective use of power in overcoming barriers to change.[17] As humorously noted by Mark Twain, "I'm all for progress. It's change I object to." **Power** refers to a leader's ability to get things done in a way he or she wants them to be done. It is the ability to influence other people's behavior, to persuade them to do things that they otherwise would not do, and to overcome resistance and opposition to changing direction. Effective exercise of power is essential for successful leadership.[18]

A leader derives his or her power from several sources or bases. The simplest way to understand the bases of power is by classifying them as organizational and personal, as shown in Exhibit 11.3.

organizational bases of power a formal management position that is the basis of a leader's power.

Organizational bases of power refer to the power that a person wields because of holding a formal management position.[19] These include legitimate power, reward power, coercive power, and information power. *Legitimate power* is derived from organizationally conferred decision-making authority and is exercised by virtue of a manager's position in the organization. *Reward power* depends on the ability of the leader or manager to confer rewards for positive behaviors or outcomes. *Coercive power* is the power a manager exercises over employees using fear of punishment for errors of omission or commission. *Information power* arises from a manager's access, control, and distribution of information that is not freely available to everyone in an organization.

personal bases of power a leader's personality characteristics and behavior that are the basis of the leader's power.

A leader might also be able to influence subordinates because of his or her personality characteristics and behavior. These would be considered the **personal bases of power,** including referent power and expert power. The source of *referent power* is a subordinate's identification with the leader. A leader's personal attributes or charisma might influence subordinates and make them devoted to that leader. The source of *expert power* is the leader's expertise and knowledge in a particular field. The leader is the expert on whom subordinates depend for information that they need to do their jobs successfully.

Exhibit 11.3 A Leader's Bases of Power

Successful leaders use the different bases of power, and often a combination of them, as appropriate to meet the demands of a situation, such as the nature of the task, the personality characteristics of the subordinates, the urgency of the issue, and other factors.[20] Leaders must recognize that persuasion and developing consensus are often essential, but so is pressing for action. At some point stragglers must be prodded into line.[21] Peter Georgescu, who recently retired as CEO of Young & Rubicam (an advertising and media subsidiary of the UK-based WPP Group), summarized a leader's dilemma brilliantly (and humorously), "I have knee pads and a .45. I get down and beg a lot, but I shoot people too."[22]

Strategy Spotlight 11.4 addresses some of the subtleties of power. It focuses on William Bratton, Chief of the Los Angeles Police Department, who has enjoyed a very successful career in law enforcement.

Emotional Intelligence: A Key Leadership Trait

> **>LO11.3**
> The crucial role of emotional intelligence (EI) in successful leadership as well as its potential drawbacks.

In the previous sections, we discussed skills and activities of strategic leadership. The focus was on "what leaders do and how they do it." Now, the issue becomes "who leaders *are*," that is, what leadership traits are the most important. Clearly, these two issues are related, because successful leaders possess the valuable traits that enable them to perform effectively in order to create value for their organization.[23]

There has been a vast amount of literature on the successful traits of leaders.[24] These traits include integrity, maturity, energy, judgment, motivation, intelligence, expertise, and so on. For simplicity, these traits may be grouped into three broad sets of capabilities:

- Purely technical skills (like accounting or operations research).
- Cognitive abilities (like analytical reasoning or quantitative analysis).
- Emotional intelligence (like self-management and managing relationships).

William Bratton: Using Multiple Bases of Power

William Bratton, Chief of the Los Angeles Police Department has an enviable track record in turning around police departments in crime-ridden cities. First, while running the police division of Massachusetts Bay Transit Authority (MBTA) in Boston, then as police commissioner of New York in the mid-1990s, and with Los Angeles from 2002 to late 2009, Chief Bratton is credited with reducing crime and improving police morale in record time. An analysis of his success at each of these organizations reveals similar patterns both in terms of the problems he faced and the many ways in which he used the different bases of power to engineer a rapid turnaround.

In Boston, New York, and Los Angeles, Chief Bratton faced similar hurdles: organizations wedded to the status quo, limited resources, demotivated staffs, and opposition from powerful vested interests. But he does not give up in the face of these seemingly insurmountable problems. He is persuasive in calls for change, capable of mobilizing the commitment of key players, silencing vocal naysayers, and building rapport with superiors and subordinates while building bridges with external constituencies.

Chief Bratton's persuasion tactics are unconventional, yet effective. When he was running the MBTA police, the Transit Authority decided to buy small squad cars, which are cheaper to buy and to run, but inadequate for the police officer's task. Instead of arguing, Bratton invited the general manager for a tour of the city. He rode with the general manager in exactly the same type of car that was ordered for ordinary officers, and drove over every pothole on the road. He moved the seats forward so that the general manager could feel how little leg room was there. And he put on his belt, cuffs, and gun so that the general manager could understand how limited the space was. After two hours in the cramped car, the gen-

eral manager was ready to change the order and get more suitable cars for the officers!

Another tactic Bratton used effectively was insisting on community meetings between police officers and citizens. This went against the long-standing practice of detachment between police and community to decrease the chances of corruption. The result was that his department had a better understanding of public concerns and rearranged their priorities, which in turn led to better community relations. For internal communications, he relied mainly on professionally produced videos instead of long, boring memos.

Chief Bratton also shows a remarkable talent for building political bridges and silencing naysayers. As he was introducing his zero-tolerance policing approach that aggressively targets "quality of life" crimes such as panhandling, drunkenness, and prostitution, opposition came from the city's courts, which feared being inundated by a large number of small-crimes cases. Bratton enlisted the support of Rudolph Giuliani, the mayor of New York, who had considerable influence over the district attorneys, the courts, and the city jail. He also took the case to the *New York Times* and managed to get the issue of zero-tolerance on the front pages of the newspaper. The courts were left with no alternative but to cooperate.

To a great extent, Bratton's success can be attributed to his understanding of the subtleties of power, including persuasion, motivation, coalition building, empathy for subordinates, and a focus on goals.

Let's take a quick look at his success during his tenure as Los Angeles's chief of police. Crime dropped significantly: violent crimes were down 53 percent; property crimes were down 33 percent, and gang-related crimes were cut by 34 percent. Connie Rice, a prominent civil-rights lawyer, feels that Bratton's biggest achievement was turning the LAPD's old "warrior culture" into "policing as something not done to people but with people." She says, "Little old ladies who used to shake their head when the cops came around are now calling them about somebody doing crack." This is quite a strong endorsement coming from someone who *The Economist* says "spent much of her career suing the Los Angeles Police Department."

Sources: Exit Bratton. 2009. *The Economist*, October 31:42; Chan Kim, W. & Renee Mauborgne, R. 2003. Tipping Point Leadership. *Harvard Business Review*, 81(4): 60–69; and McCarthy, T. 2004. The Gang Buster. *Time*, January 19: 56–58.

"Emotional intelligence (EI)" has become popular in both the literature and management practice in recent years.[25] *Harvard Business Review* articles published in 1998 and 2000 by psychologist/journalist Daniel Goleman, who is most closely associated with the concept, have become *HBR*'s most highly requested reprint articles. And two of Goleman's recent books, *Emotional Intelligence* and *Working with Emotional Intelligence,* were both on the *New York Times*'s best-seller lists. Goleman defines **emotional intelligence** as the capacity for recognizing one's own emotions and those of others.[26]

Recent studies of successful managers have found that effective leaders consistently have a high level of EI.[27] Findings indicate that EI is a better predictor of life success (economic well-being, satisfaction with life, friendship, family life), including occupational attainments, than IQ. Such evidence has been extrapolated to the catchy phrase: "IQ gets you hired, but EQ (Emotional Quotient) gets you promoted." Human resource managers believe this statement to be true, even for highly technical jobs such as those of scientists and engineers.

This is not to say that IQ and technical skills are irrelevant, but they become "threshold capabilities." They are the necessary requirements for attaining higher-level managerial positions. EI, on the other hand, is essential for leadership success. Without it, Goleman claims, a manager can have excellent training, an incisive analytical mind, and many smart ideas but will still not be a great leader.

Exhibit 11.4 identifies the five components of EI: self-awareness, self-regulation, motivation, empathy, and social skill.

> **emotional intelligence (EI)**
> an individual's capacity for recognizing his or her own emotions and those of others, including the five components of self-awareness, self-regulation, motivation, empathy, and social skills.

Exhibit 11.4   The Five Components of Emotional Intelligence at Work

	Definition	Hallmarks
Self-management skills:		
Self-awareness	• The ability to recognize and understand your moods, emotions, and drives, as well as their effect on others.	• Self-confidence • Realistic self-assessment • Self-deprecating sense of humor
Self-regulation	• The ability to control or redirect disruptive impulses and moods. • The propensity to suspend judgment—to think before acting.	• Trustworthiness and integrity • Comfort with ambiguity • Openness to change
Motivation	• A passion to work for reasons that go beyond money or status. • A propensity to pursue goals with energy and persistence.	• Strong drive to achieve • Optimism, even in the face of failure • Organizational commitment
Managing relationships:		
Empathy	• The ability to understand the emotional makeup of other people. • Skill in treating people according to their emotional reactions.	• Expertise in building and retaining talent • Cross-cultural sensitivity • Service to clients and customers
Social skill	• Proficiency in managing relationships and building networks. • An ability to find common ground and build rapport.	• Effectiveness in leading change • Persuasiveness • Expertise in building and leading teams

Source: Reprinted by permission of *Harvard Business Review*. Exhibit from "What Makes a Leader," by D. Goleman, January 2004. Copyright © 2004 by the Harvard Business School Publishing Corporation; all rights reserved.

Self-Awareness

Self-awareness is the first component of EI and brings to mind that Delphic oracle who gave the advice "know thyself" thousands of years ago. Self-awareness involves a person having a deep understanding of his or her emotions, strengths, weaknesses, and drives. People with strong self-awareness are neither overly critical nor unrealistically optimistic. Instead, they are honest with themselves and others.

People generally admire and respect candor. Leaders are constantly required to make judgment calls that require a candid assessment of capabilities—their own and those of others. People who assess themselves honestly (i.e., self-aware people) are well suited to do the same for the organizations they run.[28]

Self-Regulation

Biological impulses drive our emotions. Although we cannot do away with them, we can strive to manage them. Self-regulation, which is akin to an ongoing inner conversation, frees us from being prisoners of our feelings.[29] People engaged in such conversation feel bad moods and emotional impulses just as everyone else does. However, they find ways to control them and even channel them in useful ways.

Self-regulated people are able to create an environment of trust and fairness where political behavior and infighting are sharply reduced and productivity tends to be high. People who have mastered their emotions are better able to bring about and implement change in an organization. When a new initiative is announced, they are less likely to panic; they are able to suspend judgment, seek out information, and listen to executives explain the new program.

Motivation

Successful executives are driven to achieve beyond expectations—their own and everyone else's. Although many people are driven by external factors, such as money and prestige, those with leadership potential are driven by a deeply embedded desire to achieve for the sake of achievement.

Motivated people show a passion for the work itself, such as seeking out creative challenges, a love of learning, and taking pride in a job well done. They also have a high level of energy to do things better as well as a restlessness with the status quo. They are eager to explore new approaches to their work.

Empathy

Empathy is probably the most easily recognized component of EI. Empathy means thoughtfully considering an employee's feelings, along with other factors, in the process of making intelligent decisions. Empathy is particularly important in today's business environment for at least three reasons: the increasing use of teams, the rapid pace of globalization, and the growing need to retain talent.[30]

When leading a team, a manager is often charged with arriving at a consensus—often in the face of a high level of emotions. Empathy enables a manager to sense and understand the viewpoints of everyone around the table.

Globalization typically involves cross-cultural dialogue that can easily lead to miscues. Empathetic people are attuned to the subtleties of body language; they can hear the message beneath the words being spoken. They have a deep understanding of the existence and importance of cultural and ethnic differences.

Empathy also plays a key role in retaining talent. Human capital is particularly important to a firm in the knowledge economy when it comes to creating advantages that are sustainable. Leaders need empathy to develop and keep top talent, because when high performers leave, they take their tacit knowledge with them.

Social Skill

While the first three components of EI are all self-management skills, the last two—empathy and social skill—concern a person's ability to manage relationships with others. Social skill may be viewed as friendliness with a purpose: moving people in the direction you desire, whether that's agreement on a new marketing strategy or enthusiasm about a new product.

Socially skilled people tend to have a wide circle of acquaintances as well as a knack for finding common ground and building rapport. They recognize that nothing gets done alone, and they have a network in place when the time for action comes.

Social skill can be viewed as the culmination of the other dimensions of EI. People will be effective at managing relationships when they can understand and control their own emotions and empathize with others' feelings. Motivation also contributes to social skill. People who are driven to achieve tend to be optimistic, even when confronted with setbacks. And when people are upbeat, their "glow" is cast upon conversations and other social encounters. They are popular, and for good reason.

Carol Bartz, CEO of Yahoo!, provides some insights on the importance of emotional intelligence in successfully leading an organization:[31]

> When asked what she had learned over her years leading corporations, Bartz said one mistake was "letting people who didn't fit the culture stay too long because they seemed like such a superstar. . . . You hire for talent but fire for fit."
>
> About hiring, Bartz said, "I have to make it through dinner—without two bottles of wine. And if I can't make it through dinner, then I know I can't work with that person." She added that the dinner test often brought out whether the candidate had the right energy level and personality for her organization.
>
> On changing company culture: "Pick your battles. Changing culture can become like arguing with a teenager, and if you fight over everything—one of you is dead by the end of it."
>
> In a surprising comment, Bartz said she stopped the practice of annual reviews at Yahoo! "Development happens every day. Just like athletes work on their skills every day, managers work on their skills every day."

Emotional Intelligence: Some Potential Drawbacks and Cautionary Notes

Many great leaders have great reserves of empathy, interpersonal astuteness, awareness of their own feelings, and an awareness of their impact on others.[32] More importantly, they know how to apply these capabilities judiciously as best benefits the situation. Having some minimum level of EI will help a person be effective as a leader as long as it is channeled appropriately. However, if a person has a high level of these capabilities it may become "too much of a good thing" if he or she is allowed to drive inappropriate behaviors. Some additional potential drawbacks of EI can be gleaned by considering the flip side of its benefits.

Effective Leaders Have Empathy for Others However, they also must be able to make the "tough decisions." Leaders must be able to appeal to logic and reason and acknowledge others' feelings so that people feel the decisions are correct. However, it is easy to overidentify with others or confuse empathy with sympathy. This can make it more difficult to make the tough decisions.

Effective Leaders Are Astute Judges of People A danger is that leaders may become judgmental and overly critical about the shortcomings they perceive in others. They are likely to dismiss other people's insights, making them feel undervalued.

Effective Leaders Are Passionate about What They Do, and They Show It

This doesn't mean that they are always cheerleaders. Rather, they may express their passion as persistence in pursuing an objective or a relentless focus on a valued principle. However, there is a fine line between being excited about something and letting your passion close your mind to other possibilities or cause you to ignore realities that others may see.

Effective Leaders Create Personal Connections with Their People

Most effective leaders take time to engage employees individually and in groups, listening to their ideas, suggestions and concerns, and responding in ways that make people feel that their ideas are respected and appreciated. However, if the leader makes too many unannounced visits, it may create a culture of fear and micromanagement. Clearly, striking a correct balance is essential.

From a moral standpoint, emotional leadership is neither good nor bad. On the one hand, emotional leaders can be altruistic, focused on the general welfare of the company and its employees, and highly principled. On the other hand, they can be manipulative, selfish, and dishonest. For example, if a person is using leadership solely to gain power, that is not leadership at all.[33] Rather, they are using their EI to grasp what people want and pander to those desires in order to gain authority and influence. After all, easy answers sell.

Next, we turn to guidelines for developing a "learning organization." In today's competitive environment, the old saying that "a chain is only as strong as the weakest link" applies more than ever before. To learn and adapt proactively, firms need "eyes, ears, and brains" throughout all parts of the organization. One person, or a small group of individuals, can no longer think and learn for the entire entity.

>LO11.4
The value of creating and maintaining a learning organization in today's global marketplace.

Developing a Learning Organization

Charles Handy, author of *The Age of Unreason* and *The Age of Paradox* and one of today's most respected business visionaries, shared an amusing story several years ago:

> The other day, a courier could not find my family's remote cottage. He called his base on his radio, and the base called us to ask directions. He was just around the corner, but his base managed to omit a vital part of the directions. So he called them again, and they called us again. Then the courier repeated the cycle a third time to ask whether we had a dangerous dog. When he eventually arrived, we asked whether it would not have been simpler and less aggravating to everyone if he had called us directly from the roadside telephone booth where he had been parked. "I can't do that," he said, "because they won't refund any money I spend." "But it's only pennies!" I exclaimed. "I know," he said, "but that only shows how little they trust us!"[34]

At first glance, it would appear that the story epitomizes the lack of empowerment and trust granted to the hapless courier: Don't ask questions! Do as you're told![35] However, implicit in this scenario is also the message that learning, information sharing, adaptation, decision making, and so on are *not* shared throughout the organization. In contrast, leading-edge organizations recognize the importance of having everyone involved in the process of actively learning and adapting. As noted by today's leading expert on learning organizations, MIT's Peter Senge, the days when Henry Ford, Alfred Sloan, and Tom Watson *"learned **for** the organization"* are gone.

> In an increasingly dynamic, interdependent, and unpredictable world, it is simply no longer possible for anyone to "figure it all out at the top." The old model, "the top thinks and the local acts," must now give way to integrating thinking and acting at all levels. While the challenge is great, so is the potential payoff. "The person who figures out how to harness the collective genius of the people in his or her organization," according to former Citibank CEO Walter Wriston, "is going to blow the competition away."[36]

Exhibit 11.5 Key Elements of a Learning Organization

These are the five key elements of a learning organization. Each of these items should be viewed as *necessary, but not sufficient.* That is, successful learning organizations need all five elements.

1. Inspiring and motivating people with a mission or purpose.

2. Empowering employees at all levels.

3. Accumulating and sharing internal knowledge.

4. Gathering and integrating external information.

5. Challenging the status quo and enabling creativity.

Learning and change typically involve the ongoing questioning of an organization's status quo or method of procedure. This means that all individuals throughout the organization must be reflective.[37] Many organizations get so caught up in carrying out their day-to-day work that they rarely, if ever, stop to think objectively about themselves and their businesses. They often fail to ask the probing questions that might lead them to call into question their basic assumptions, to refresh their strategies, or to reengineer their work processes. According to Michael Hammer and Steven Stanton, the pioneer consultants who touched off the reengineering movement:

> Reflection entails awareness of self, of competitors, of customers. It means thinking without preconception. It means questioning cherished assumptions and replacing them with new approaches. It is the only way in which a winning company can maintain its leadership position, by which a company with great assets can ensure that they continue to be well deployed.[38]

To adapt to change, foster creativity, and remain competitive, leaders must build learning organizations. Exhibit 11.5 lists the five elements of a learning organization.

Inspiring and Motivating People with a Mission or Purpose

Successful **learning organizations** create a proactive, creative approach to the unknown, actively solicit the involvement of employees at all levels, and enable all employees to use their intelligence and apply their imagination. Higher-level skills are required of everyone, not just those at the top.[39] A learning environment involves organizationwide commitment to change, an action orientation, and applicable tools and methods.[40] It must be viewed by everyone as a guiding philosophy and not simply as another change program.

A critical requirement of all learning organizations is that everyone feels and supports a compelling purpose. In the words of William O'Brien, CEO of Hanover Insurance, "Before there can be meaningful participation, people must share certain values and pictures about where we are trying to go. We discovered that people have a real need to feel that they're part of an enabling mission."[41] Such a perspective is consistent with an intensive study by Kouzes and Posner, authors of *The Leadership Challenge.*[42] They recently analyzed data from nearly one million respondents who were leaders at various levels in many organizations throughout the world. A major finding was that what leaders struggle with most is communicating an image of the future that draws others in, that is, it speaks to what others see and feel. To illustrate:

> Buddy Blanton, a principal program manager at Rockwell Collins, learned this lesson firsthand. He asked his team for feedback on his leadership, and the vast majority of it was positive. However, he got some strong advice from his team about how he could be more effective in inspiring a shared vision. "You would benefit by helping us, as a team, to

learning organizations organizations that create a proactive, creative approach to the unknown, characterized by (1) inspiring and motivating people with a mission and purpose, (2) empowering employees at all levels, (3) accumulating and sharing internal knowledge, (4) gathering and integrating external information, and (5) challenging the status quo and enabling creativity.

understand how you go to your vision. We want to walk with you while you create the goals and vision, so we all get to the end of the vision together."[43]

Inspiring and motivating people with a mission or purpose is a necessary but not sufficient condition for developing an organization that can learn and adapt to a rapidly changing, complex, and interconnected environment.

Empowering Employees at All Levels

"The great leader is a great servant," asserted Ken Melrose, CEO of Toro Company and author of *Making the Grass Greener on Your Side*.[44] A manager's role becomes one of creating an environment where employees can achieve their potential as they help move the organization toward its goals. Instead of viewing themselves as resource controllers and power brokers, leaders must envision themselves as flexible resources willing to assume numerous roles as coaches, information providers, teachers, decision makers, facilitators, supporters, or listeners, depending on the needs of their employees.[45]

The central key to empowerment is effective leadership. Empowerment can't occur in a leadership vacuum. According to Melrose, "You best lead by serving the needs of your people. You don't do their jobs for them; you enable them to learn and progress on the job." Robert Quinn and Gretchen Spreitzer made an interesting point about two diametrically opposite perspectives on empowerment—top-down and bottom-up.[46]

In the top-down perspective, empowerment is about delegation and accountability—senior management has developed a clear vision and has communicated specific plans to the rest of the organization.[47] This strategy for empowerment encompasses the following:

- Start at the top.
- Clarify the organization's mission, vision, and values.
- Clearly specify the tasks, roles, and rewards for employees.
- Delegate responsibility.
- Hold people accountable for results.

By contrast, the bottom-up view looks at empowerment as concerned with risk taking, growth, and change. It involves trusting people to "do the right thing" and having a tolerance for failure. It encourages employees to act with a sense of ownership and typically "ask for forgiveness rather than permission." Here the salient elements of empowerment are:

- Start at the bottom by understanding the needs of employees.
- Teach employees self-management skills and model desired behavior.
- Build teams to encourage cooperative behavior.
- Encourage intelligent risk taking.
- Trust people to perform.

These two perspectives draw a sharp contrast in assumptions that people make about trust and control. Quinn and Spreitzer recently shared these contrasting views of empowerment with a senior management team. After an initial heavy silence, someone from the first group voiced a concern about the second group's perspective, "We can't afford loose cannons around here." A person in the second group retorted, "When was the last time you saw a cannon of any kind around here?"

Many leading-edge organizations are moving in the direction of the second perspective—recognizing the need for trust, cultural control, and expertise at all levels instead of the extensive and cumbersome rules and regulations inherent in hierarchical control.[48] Some have argued that too often organizations fall prey to the "heroes-and-drones syndrome," wherein the value of those in powerful positions is exalted and the value of those who fail to achieve top rank is diminished. Such an attitude is implicit in phrases

A Hospital's Unique Approach to Empowerment

Beth Israel Deaconess is a medical center formed by the merger of two Harvard teaching hospitals. Early in 2009, it was facing a projected $20 million annual loss after several years of profitability. CEO Paul Levy held a meeting to discuss layoffs.

He expressed concern that cutbacks would affect low-wage employees, such as housekeepers, and he floated what he thought would be an unpopular idea: protecting some of those low-paying jobs by reducing the salary and benefits of higher-paid employees—including many sitting in the auditorium. To his surprise, the room erupted in applause!

His candid request for help led to countless suggestions for cost savings. This included an offer by the 13 medical department heads to save 10 jobs through personal donations totaling $350,000. In addition, the plan for reducing layoffs included a combination of delayed raises and a temporary reduction in benefits. Such efforts ultimately reduced the number of planned layoffs by 75 percent.

In the end, the low-wage workers were really taken care of. They were exempt from the salary cuts and even received 3 percent raises.

Sources: Heifetz, R., Grashow, A., & Linsky, M. 2009. Leadership in a (Permanent) Crisis. *Harvard Business Review,* 87(4): 67; and Cooney, E. 2009. Beth Israel Pares Its Plan for Layoffs. *www.bostonglobe.com,* March 25: np.

such as "Lead, follow, or get out of the way" or, even less appealing, "Unless you're the lead horse, the view never changes." Few will ever reach the top hierarchical positions in organizations, but in the information economy, the strongest organizations are those that effectively use the talents of all the players on the team.

Empowering individuals by soliciting their input helps an organization to enjoy better employee morale. It also may help to create a culture of shared sacrifice, which may be critical during difficult economic times, as described in Strategy Spotlight 11.5.

Accumulating and Sharing Internal Knowledge

Effective organizations must also *redistribute information, knowledge* (skills to act on the information), and *rewards.*[49] A company might give frontline employees the power to act as "customer advocates," doing whatever is necessary to satisfy customers. The company needs to disseminate information by sharing customer expectations and feedback as well as financial information. The employees must know about the goals of the business as well as how key value-creating activities in the organization are related to each other. Finally, organizations should allocate rewards on how effectively employees use information, knowledge, and power to improve customer service quality and the company's overall performance.[50]

Let's take a look at Whole Foods Market, Inc., the largest natural foods grocer in the United States.[51] An important benefit of the sharing of internal information at Whole Foods becomes the active process of *internal benchmarking.* Competition is intense at Whole Foods. Teams compete against their own goals for sales, growth, and productivity; they compete against different teams in their stores; and they compete against similar teams at different stores and regions. There is an elaborate system of peer reviews through which teams benchmark each other. The "Store Tour" is the most intense. On a periodic schedule, each Whole Foods store is toured by a group of as many as 40 visitors from another region. Lateral learning—discovering what your colleagues are doing right and carrying those practices into your organization—has become a driving force at Whole Foods.

In addition to enhancing the sharing of company information both up and down as well as across the organization, leaders also have to develop means to tap into some of the more informal sources of internal information. In a recent survey of presidents, CEOs, board members, and top executives in a variety of nonprofit organizations, respondents were asked what differentiated the successful candidates for promotion. The consensus: The executive was seen as a person who listens. According to Peter Meyer, the author of the study, "The value of listening is clear: You cannot succeed in running a company if you do not hear what your people, customers, and suppliers are telling you. . . . Listening and understanding well are key to making good decisions."[52]

Gathering and Integrating External Information

Recognizing opportunities, as well as threats, in the external environment is vital to a firm's success. As organizations *and* environments become more complex and evolve rapidly, it is far more critical for employees and managers to become more aware of environmental trends and events—both general and industry-specific—and more knowledgeable about their firm's competitors and customers. Next, we will discuss some ideas on how to do it.

First, the Internet has dramatically accelerated the speed with which anyone can track down useful information or locate people who might have useful information. Prior to the Net, locating someone who used to work at a company—always a good source of information—was quite a challenge. However, today people post their résumés on the web; they participate in discussion groups and talk openly about where they work.

Marc Friedman, manager of market research at $1 billion Andrew Corporation, a fast-growing manufacturer of wireless communications products provides an example of effective Internet use.[53] One of Friedman's preferred sites to visit is Corptech's website, which provides information on 45,000 high-tech companies and more than 170,000 executives. One of his firm's product lines consisted of antennae for air-traffic control systems. He got a request to provide a country-by-country breakdown of upgrade plans for various airports. He knew nothing about air-traffic control at the time. However, he found a site on the Internet for the International Civil Aviation Organization. Fortunately, it had a great deal of useful data, including several research companies working in his area of interest.

Second, company employees at all levels can use "garden variety" traditional sources to acquire external information. Much can be gleaned by reading trade and professional journals, books, and popular business magazines. Other venues for gathering external information include membership in professional or trade organizations, attendance at meetings and conventions, and networking among colleagues inside and outside of your industry. Intel's Andy Grove gathers information from people like DreamWorks SKG's Steven Spielberg and Tele-Communications Inc.'s John Malone.[54] He believes that such interaction provides insights into how to make personal computers more entertaining and better at communicating. Internally, Grove spends time with the young engineers who run Intel Architecture labs, an Oregon-based facility that Grove hopes will become the de facto R&D lab for the entire PC industry.

Third, benchmarking can be a useful means of employing external information. Here managers seek out the best examples of a particular practice as part of an ongoing effort to improve the corresponding practice in their own organization.[55] There are two primary types of benchmarking. *Competitive benchmarking* restricts the search for best practices to competitors, while *functional benchmarking* endeavors to determine best practices regardless of industry. Industry-specific standards (e.g., response times required to repair power outages in the electric utility industry) are typically best handled through competitive benchmarking, whereas more generic processes (e.g., answering 1-800 calls) lend themselves to functional benchmarking because the function is essentially the same in any industry.

benchmarking
managers seeking out best examples of a particular practice as part of an ongoing effort to improve the corresponding practice in their own organization.

competitive benchmarking
benchmarking where the examples are drawn from competitors in the industry.

functional benchmarking
benchmarking where the examples are drawn from any organization, even those outside the industry.

Ford Motor Company used benchmarking to study Mazda's accounts payable operations.[56] Its initial goal of a 20 percent cut in its 500-employee accounts payable staff was ratcheted up to 75 percent—and met. Ford found that staff spent most of their time trying to match conflicting data in a mass of paper, including purchase orders, invoices, and receipts. Following Mazda's example, Ford created an "invoiceless system" in which invoices no longer trigger payments to suppliers. The receipt does the job.

Fourth, focus directly on customers for information. For example, William McKnight, head of 3M's Chicago sales office, required that salesmen of abrasives products talk directly to the workers in the shop to find out what they needed, instead of calling on only front-office executives.[57] This was very innovative at the time—1909! But it illustrates the need to get to the end user of a product or service. (McKnight went on to become 3M's president from 1929 to 1949 and chairman from 1949 to 1969.) More recently, James Taylor, senior vice president for global marketing at Gateway 2000, discussed the value of customer input in reducing response time, a critical success factor in the PC industry.

> We talk to 100,000 people a day—people calling to order a computer, shopping around, looking for tech support. Our website gets 1.1 million hits per day. The time it takes for an idea to enter this organization, get processed, and then go to customers for feedback is down to minutes. We've designed the company around speed and feedback.[58]

Challenging the Status Quo and Enabling Creativity

Earlier in this chapter we discussed some of the barriers that leaders face when trying to bring about change in an organization: vested interests in the status quo, systemic barriers, behavioral barriers, political barriers, and personal time constraints. For a firm to become a learning organization, it must overcome such barriers in order to foster creativity and enable it to permeate the firm. This becomes quite a challenge if the firm is entrenched in a status quo mentality.

Perhaps the best way to challenge the status quo is for the leader to forcefully create a sense of urgency. For example, when Tom Kasten was vice president of Levi Strauss, he had a direct approach to initiating change.

> You create a compelling picture of the risks of *not* changing. We let our people hear directly from customers. We videotaped interviews with customers and played excerpts. One big customer said, "We trust many of your competitors implicitly. We sample their deliveries. We open *all* Levi's deliveries." Another said, "Your lead times are the worst. If you weren't Levi's, you'd be gone." It was powerful. I wish we had done more of it.[59]

Such initiative, if sincere and credible, establishes a shared mission and the need for major transformations. It can channel energies to bring about both change and creative endeavors.

Establishing a "culture of dissent" can be another effective means of questioning the status quo and serving as a spur toward creativity. Here norms are established whereby dissenters can openly question a superior's perspective without fear of retaliation or retribution. Consider the perspective of Steven Balmer, Microsoft's CEO.

> Bill [Gates] brings to the company the idea that conflict can be a good thing. . . . Bill knows it's important to avoid that gentle civility that keeps you from getting to the heart of an issue quickly. He likes it when anyone, even a junior employee, challenges him, and you know he respects you when he starts shouting back.[60]

Motorola has gone a step further and institutionalized its culture of dissent.[61] By filing a "minority report," an employee can go above his or her immediate supervisor's head and officially lodge a different point of view on a business decision. According to former CEO George Fisher, "I'd call it a healthy spirit of discontent and a freedom by and large to express your discontent around here or to disagree with whoever it is in the company, me or anybody else."

Closely related to the culture of dissent is the fostering of a culture that encourages risk taking. "If you're not making mistakes, you're not taking risks, and that means you're not going anywhere," claimed John Holt, coauthor of *Celebrate Your Mistakes*.[62] "The key is to make errors faster than the competition, so you have more chances to learn and win."

Companies that cultivate cultures of experimentation and curiosity make sure that *failure* is not, in essence, an obscene word. They encourage mistakes as a key part of their competitive advantage. This philosophy was shared by Stan Shih, CEO of Acer, a Taiwan-based computer company. If a manager at Acer took an intelligent risk and made a mistake—even a costly one—Shih wrote off the loss as tuition payment for the manager's education. Such a culture must permeate the entire organization. As a high-tech executive told us during an interview: "Every person has a freedom to fail."

Exhibit 11.6 has insights on how organizations can both embrace risk and learn from failure.

Exhibit 11.6 Best Practices: Learning from Failures

It's innovation's great paradox: Success—that is, true breakthroughs—usually comes through failure. Here are some ideas on how to help your team get comfortable with taking risks and learning from mistakes:

- **Formalize Forums for Failure**
  To keep failures and the valuable lessons they offer from getting swept under the rug, *carve out time for reflection.* GE recently began sharing lessons from failures by bringing together managers whose "Imagination Breakthrough" efforts are put on the shelf.

- **Move the Goalposts**
  Innovation requires flexibility in meeting goals, since early predictions are often little more than educated guesses. Intuit's Scott Cook even suggests that teams developing new products ignore forecasts in the early days. "For every one of our failures, we had spreadsheets that looked awesome," he says.

- **Share Personal Stories**
  If employees hear leaders discussing their own failures, *they'll feel more comfortable talking about their own.* But it's not just the CEO's job. Front-line leaders are even more important, says Harvard Business School professor Amy Edmondson. "That person needs to be inviting, curious, and the first to say: 'I made a mistake.'"

- **Bring in Outsiders**
  Outsiders can *help neutralize the emotions and biases that prop up a flop.* Customers can be the most valuable. After its DNA chip failed, Corning brought pharmaceutical companies in early to test its new drug-discovery technology, Epic.

- **Prove Yourself Wrong, Not Right**
  Development teams tend to look for supporting, rather than countervailing, evidence. "You have to reframe what you're seeking in the early days," says Innosight's Scott Anthony. *"You're not really seeking proof that you have the right answer.* It's more about testing to prove yourself wrong."

- **Celebrate Smart Failures**
  Managers should design performance-management systems that reward risk taking and foster a long-term view. But they should also *celebrate failures that teach something new,* energizing people to try again and offering them closure.

Source: From J. McGregor, "How Failure Breeds Success,". *Bloombarg BusinessWeek*, July 10, 2006, pp. 42–52. used with permission of *Bloombery BusinessWeek*. Copyright © 2006. All rights reserved.

Creating an Ethical Organization

>LO11.5
The leader's role in establishing an ethical organization.

Ethics may be defined as a system of right and wrong.[63] Ethics assists individuals in deciding when an act is moral or immoral, socially desirable or not. The sources for an individual's ethics include religious beliefs, national and ethnic heritage, family practices, community standards, educational experiences, and friends and neighbors. Business ethics is the application of ethical standards to commercial enterprise.

Individual Ethics versus Organizational Ethics

Many leaders think of ethics as a question of personal scruples, a confidential matter between employees and their consciences. Such leaders are quick to describe any wrongdoing as an isolated incident, the work of a rogue employee. They assume the company should not bear any responsibility for individual misdeeds. In their view, ethics has nothing to do with leadership.

ethics a system of right and wrong that assists individuals in deciding when an act is moral or immoral and/or socially desirable or not.

Ethics has everything to do with leadership. Seldom does the character flaw of a lone actor completely explain corporate misconduct. Instead, unethical business practices typically involve the tacit, if not explicit, cooperation of others and reflect the values, attitudes, and behavior patterns that define an organization's operating culture. Ethics is as much an organizational as a personal issue. Leaders who fail to provide proper leadership to institute proper systems and controls that facilitate ethical conduct share responsibility with those who conceive, execute, and knowingly benefit from corporate misdeeds.[64]

The **ethical orientation** of a leader is a key factor in promoting ethical behavior. Ethical leaders must take personal, ethical responsibility for their actions and decision making. Leaders who exhibit high ethical standards become role models for others and raise an organization's overall level of ethical behavior. Ethical behavior must start with the leader before the employees can be expected to perform accordingly.

organizational ethics the values, attitudes, and behavioral patterns that define an organization's operating culture and that determine what an organization holds as acceptable behavior.

There has been a growing interest in corporate ethical performance. Some reasons for this trend may be the increasing lack of confidence regarding corporate activities, the growing emphasis on quality of life issues, and a spate of recent corporate scandals. Without a strong ethical culture, the chance of ethical crises occurring is enhanced. Ethical crises can be very expensive—both in terms of financial costs and in the erosion of human capital and overall firm reputation. Merely adhering to the minimum regulatory standards may not be enough to remain competitive in a world that is becoming more socially conscious. Strategy Spotlight 11.6 highlights potential ethical problems at utility companies that are trying to capitalize on consumers' desire to participate in efforts to curb global warming.

ethical orientation the practices that firms use to promote an ethical business culture, including ethical role models, corporate credos and codes of conduct, ethically-based reward and evaluation systems, and consistently enforced ethical policies and procedures.

The past several years have been characterized by numerous examples of unethical and illegal behavior by many top-level corporate executives. These include executives of firms such as Enron, Tyco, WorldCom, Inc., Adelphia, and Healthsouth Corp., who were all forced to resign and are facing (or have been convicted of) criminal charges. Perhaps the most glaring example is Bernie Madoff, whose Ponzi scheme, which unraveled in 2008, defrauded investors of $50 billion in assets they had set aside for retirement and charitable donations.

The ethical organization is characterized by a conception of ethical values and integrity as a driving force of the enterprise.[65] Ethical values shape the search for opportunities, the design of organizational systems, and the decision-making process used by individuals and groups. They provide a common frame of reference that serves as a unifying force across different functions, lines of business, and employee groups. Organizational ethics helps to define what a company is and what it stands for.

There are many potential benefits of an ethical organization, but they are often indirect. Research has found somewhat inconsistent results concerning the overall relationship between ethical performance and measures of financial performance.[66] However, positive

Green Energy: Real or Just a Marketing Ploy?

Many consumers want to "go green" and are looking for opportunities to do so. Utility companies that provide heat and electricity are one of the most obvious places to turn, because they often use fossil fuels that could be saved through energy conservation or replaced by using alternative energy sources. In fact, some consumers are willing to pay a premium to contribute to environmental sustainability efforts if paying a little more will help curb global warming. Knowing this, many power companies in the United States have developed alternative energy programs and appealed to customers to help pay for them.

Unfortunately, many of the power companies that are offering eco-friendly options are falling short on delivering on them. Some utilities have simply gotten off to a slow start or found it difficult to profitably offer alternative power. Others, however, are suspected of committing a new type of fraud—"greenwashing." This refers to companies that make unsubstantiated claims about how environmentally friendly their products or services really are. In the case of many power companies, their claims of "green power" are empty promises. Instead of actually generating additional renewable energy, most of the premiums are going for marketing costs. "They are preying on people's goodwill," says Stephen Smith, executive director of the Southern Alliance for Clean Energy, an advocacy group in Knoxville, Tennessee.

Exhibit 11.7 shows what three power companies offered and how the money was actually spent. Unfortunately, utilities that spend only a fraction of voluntary energy premiums on renewable energy are becoming more rather than less common. It will likely be up to consumers or Public Service Commissions to hold the utilities to a higher ethical standard—either by making power companies' advertising more truthful or, better still, by insisting that they deliver on their renewable energy promises. Either way, the idea of defrauding customers who are trying to "do the right thing" makes the utilities' unethical decision even more dishonorable.

 environmental sustainability

Sources: Elgin, B. & Holden, D. 2008. Green Power: Buyers Beware. *Business-Week*, September 29: 68–70; and *www.cleanenergy.org.*

Exhibit 11.7 How "Green" Utilities Actually Used Customer Payments

Company/Program	What Customers Were Told	What Really Happened
Duke Energy of Indiana GoGreen Power	Pay a green energy premium and a specified amount of electricity will be obtained from renewable sources.	Less than 18 percent of voluntary customer contributions in a recent year went to renewable energy development.
Alliant Energy of Iowa Second Nature™	"Support the growth of earth-friendly 'green power' created by wind and biomass."	More than 56 percent of expenditures went to marketing and administrative costs, not green energy development.
Georgia Power Green Energy®	Paying the premium "is equivalent to planting 125 trees or not driving 2,000 miles" and will "help bring more renewable power to Georgia."	Customers pay an annual $54 premium, but green energy is actually cheaper to provide than electricity from conventional sources.

Sources: Elgin, B. & Holden, D. 2008. Green Power: Buyers Beware. *BusinessWeek*, September 29: 68–70; *www.alliantenergy.com; www.duke-energy.com;* and *www.georgiapower.com.*

relationships have generally been found between ethical performance and strong organizational culture, increased employee efforts, lower turnover, higher organizational commitment, and enhanced social responsibility.

The advantages of a strong ethical orientation can have a positive effect on employee commitment and motivation to excel. This is particularly important in today's knowledge-intensive organizations, where human capital is critical in creating value and competitive advantages. Positive, constructive relationships among individuals (i.e., social capital) are vital in leveraging human capital and other resources in an organization. Drawing on the concept of stakeholder management, an ethically sound organization can also strengthen its bonds among its suppliers, customers, and governmental agencies.

Integrity-Based versus Compliance-Based Approaches to Organizational Ethics

>LO11.6
The difference between integrity-based and compliance-based approaches to organizational ethics.

Before discussing the key elements of an ethical organization, one must understand the links between organizational integrity and the personal integrity of an organization's members.[67] There cannot be high-integrity organizations without high-integrity individuals. However, individual integrity is rarely self-sustaining. Even good people can lose their bearings when faced with pressures, temptations, and heightened performance expectations in the absence of organizational support systems and ethical boundaries. Organizational integrity rests on a concept of purpose, responsibility, and ideals for an organization as a whole. An important responsibility of leadership is to create this ethical framework and develop the organizational capabilities to make it operational.[68]

Lynn Paine, an ethics scholar at Harvard, identifies two approaches: the compliance-based approach and the integrity-based approach. (See Exhibit 11.8 for a comparison of compliance-based and integrity-based strategies.) Faced with the prospect of litigation, several organizations reactively implement **compliance-based ethics programs.** Such programs are typically designed by a corporate counsel with the goal of preventing, detecting, and punishing legal violations. But being ethical is much more than being legal, and an integrity-based approach addresses the issue of ethics in a more comprehensive manner.

compliance-based ethics programs programs for building ethical organizations that have the goal of preventing, detecting, and punishing legal violations.

Exhibit 11.8 Approaches to Ethics Management

Characteristics	Compliance-Based Approach	Integrity-Based Approach
Ethos	Conformity with externally imposed standards	Self-governance according to chosen standards
Objective	Prevent criminal misconduct	Enable responsible conduct
Leadership	Lawyer-driven	Management-driven with aid of lawyers, HR, and others
Methods	Education, reduced discretion, auditing and controls, penalties	Education, leadership, accountability, organizational systems and decision processes, auditing and controls, penalties
Behavioral Assumptions	Autonomous beings guided by material self-interest	Social beings guided by material self-interest, values, ideals, peers

Source: Reprinted by permission of *Harvard Business Review*. Exhibit from "Managing Organizational Integrity," by L. S. Paine. Copyright © 1994 by the Harvard Business School Publishing Corporation; all rights reserved.

integrity-based ethics programs programs for building ethical organizations that combine a concern for law with an emphasis on managerial responsibility for ethical behavior, including (1) enabling ethical conduct; (2) examining the organization's and members' core guiding values, thoughts, and actions; and (3) defining the responsibilities and aspirations that constitute an organization's ethical compass.

Integrity-based ethics programs combine a concern for law with an emphasis on managerial responsibility for ethical behavior. It is broader, deeper, and more demanding than a legal compliance initiative. It is broader in that it seeks to enable responsible conduct. It is deeper in that it cuts to the ethos and operating systems of an organization and its members, their core guiding values, thoughts, and actions. It is more demanding because it requires an active effort to define the responsibilities that constitute an organization's ethical compass. Most importantly, organizational ethics is seen as the responsibility of management.

A corporate counsel may play a role in designing and implementing integrity strategies, but it is managers at all levels and across all functions that are involved in the process. Once integrated into the day-to-day operations, such strategies can prevent damaging ethical lapses, while tapping into powerful human impulses for moral thought and action. Ethics becomes the governing ethos of an organization and not burdensome constraints. Here is an example of an organization that goes beyond mere compliance to laws in building an ethical organization:

> In teaching ethics to its employees, Texas Instruments, the $14 billion chip and electronics manufacturer, asks them to run an issue through the following steps: Is it legal? Is it consistent with the company's stated values? Will the employee feel bad doing it? What will the public think if the action is reported in the press? Does the employee think it is wrong? If the employees are not sure of the ethicality of the issue, they are encouraged to ask someone until they are clear about it. In the process, employees can approach high-level personnel and even the company's lawyers. At TI, the question of ethics goes much beyond merely being legal. It is no surprise, that this company is a benchmark for corporate ethics and has been a recipient of three ethics awards: the David C. Lincoln Award for Ethics and Excellence in Business, American Business Ethics Award, and Bentley College Center for Business Ethics Award.[69]

Compliance-based approaches are externally motivated—that is, based on the fear of punishment for doing something unlawful. On the other hand, integrity-based approaches are driven by a personal and organizational commitment to ethical behavior.

A firm must have several key elements to become a highly ethical organization:

>LO11.7
Several key elements that organizations must have to become an ethical organization.

- Role models.
- Corporate credos and codes of conduct.
- Reward and evaluation systems.
- Policies and procedures.

These elements are highly interrelated. Reward structures and policies will be useless if leaders are not sound role models. That is, leaders who implicitly say, "Do as I say, not as I do," will quickly have their credibility eroded and such actions will sabotage other elements that are essential to building an ethical organization.

Role Models

For good or for bad, leaders are role models in their organizations. Leaders must "walk the talk"; they must be consistent in their words and deeds. The values as well as the character of leaders become transparent to an organization's employees through their behaviors. When leaders do not believe in the ethical standards that they are trying to inspire, they will not be effective as good role models. Being an effective leader often includes taking responsibility for ethical lapses within the organization—even though the executives themselves are not directly involved. Consider the perspective of Dennis Bakke, CEO of AES, the $14 billion global electricity company based in Arlington, Virginia.

> There was a major breach (in 1992) of the AES values. Nine members of the water treatment team in Oklahoma lied to the EPA about water quality at the plant. There was no environmental damage, but they lied about the test results. A new, young chemist at the plant discovered it, told a team leader, and we then were notified. Now, you could argue that the people who lied were responsible and were accountable, but the senior management team also took responsibility by taking pay cuts. My reduction was about 30 percent.[70]

Elements of a Corporate Code

Corporate codes are not simply useful for conveying organizational norms and policies, but they also serve to legitimize an organization in the eyes of others. In the United States, federal guidelines advise judges, when determining how to sentence a company convicted of a crime, to consider whether it had a written code and was out of compliance with its own ethical guidelines. The United Nations and countries around the world have endorsed codes as a way to promote corporate social responsibility. As such, a code provides an increasingly important corporate social contract that signals a company's willingness to act ethically.

For employees, codes of conduct serve four key purposes:

Sources: Paine, L., Deshpande, R., Margolis, J. D., & Bettcher, K. E. 2005. Up to Code: Does Your Company's Conduct Meet World Class Standards? *Harvard Business Review*, 82(12): 122–126; and Stone, A. 2004. Putting Teeth in Corporate Ethics Codes. *www.businessweek.com*, February 19.

1. Help employees from diverse backgrounds work more effectively across cultural backgrounds.

2. Provide a reference point for decision making.

3. Help attract individuals who want to work for a business that embraces high standards.

4. Help a company to manage risk by reducing the likelihood of damaging misconduct.

With recent scandals on Wall Street, many corporations are trying to put more teeth into their codes of conduct. Nasdaq now requires that listed companies distribute a code to all employees. German software giant SAP's code informs employees that violations of the code "can result in consequences that affect employment, and could possibly lead to external investigation, civil law proceedings, or criminal charges." Clearly, codes of conduct are an important part of maintaining an ethical organization.

Such action enhances the loyalty and commitment of employees throughout the organization. Many would believe that it would have been much easier (and personally less expensive!) for Bakke and his management team to merely take strong punitive action against the nine individuals who were acting contrary to the behavior expected in AES's ethical culture. However, by taking responsibility for the misdeeds, the top executives—through their highly visible action—made it clear that responsibility and penalties for ethical lapses go well beyond the "guilty" parties. Such courageous behavior by leaders helps to strengthen an organization's ethical environment.

Corporate Credos and Codes of Conduct

Corporate credos and codes of conduct are mechanisms that provide statements of norms and beliefs as well as guidelines for decision making. They provide employees with a clear understanding of the organization's policies and ethical position. Such guidelines also provide the basis for employees to refuse to commit unethical acts and help to make them aware of issues before they are faced with the situation. For such codes to be truly effective, organization members must be aware of them and what behavioral guidelines they contain.[71] Strategy Spotlight 11.7 identifies four key reasons why codes of conduct support organizational efforts to maintain a safe and ethical workplace.

> **corporate credo** a statement of the beliefs typically held by managers in a corporation.

Large corporations are not the only ones to develop and use codes of conduct. Consider the example of Wetherill Associates (WAI), a small, privately held supplier of electrical parts to the automotive market.

> Rather than a conventional code of conduct, WAI has a Quality Assurance Manual—a combination of philosophy text, conduct guide, technical manual, and company profile—that describes the company's commitment to honesty, ethical action, and integrity. WAI doesn't have a corporate ethics officer, because the company's corporate ethics officer is

Exhibit 11.9

Johnson & Johnson's Credo

We believe our first responsibility is to the doctors, nurses and patients, to mothers and fathers and all others who use our products and services. In meeting their needs everything we do must be of high quality. We must constantly strive to reduce our costs in order to maintain reasonable prices. Customers' orders must be serviced promptly and accurately. Our suppliers and distributors must have an opportunity to make a fair profit.

We are responsible to our employees, the men and women who work with us throughout the world. Everyone must be considered as an individual. We must respect their dignity and recognize their merit. They must have a sense of security in their jobs. Compensation must be fair and adequate, and working conditions clean, orderly, and safe. We must be mindful of ways to help our employees fulfill their family responsibilities. Employees must feel free to make suggestions and complaints. There must be equal opportunity for employment, development, and advancement for those qualified. We must provide competent management, and their actions must be just and ethical.

We are responsible to the communities in which we live and work and to the world community as well. We must be good citizens—support good works and charities and bear our fair share of taxes. We must encourage civic improvements and better health and education. We must maintain in good order the property we are privileged to use, protecting the environment and natural resources

Our final responsibility is to our stockholders. Business must make a sound profit. We must experiment with new ideas. Research must be carried on, innovative programs developed, and mistakes paid for. New equipment must be purchased, new facilities provided, and new products launched. Reserves must be created to provide for adverse times. When we operate according to these principles, the stockholders should realize a fair return.

Source: Reprinted with permission of Johnson & Johnson Co.

Marie Bothe, WAI's CEO. She sees her main function as keeping the 350-employee company on the path of ethical behavior and looking for opportunities to help the community. She delegates the "technical" aspects of the business—marketing, finance, personnel, and operations—to other members of the organization.[72]

Perhaps the best-known credo is that of Johnson & Johnson (J&J). It is reprinted in Exhibit 11.9. The credo stresses honesty, integrity, superior products, and putting people before profits. What distinguishes the J&J credo from others is the amount of energy the company's top managers devote to ensuring that employees live by its precepts:

Over a recent three-year period, Johnson & Johnson undertook a massive effort to assure that its original credo, already decades old, was still valid. More than 1,200 managers attended two-day seminars in groups of 25, with explicit instructions to challenge the credo. The president or CEO of the firm presided over each session. The company came out of the process believing that its original document was still valid. However, the questioning process continues. Such "challenge meetings" are still replicated every other year for all new managers. These efforts force J&J to question, internalize, and then implement its credo. Such investments have paid off handsomely many times—most notably in 1982, when eight people died from swallowing capsules of Tylenol, one of its flagship products, that someone had laced with cyanide. Leaders such as James Burke, who without hesitation made an across-the-board recall of the product even though it affected only a limited number of untraceable units, send a strong message throughout the firm.

Reward and Evaluation Systems

It is entirely possible for a highly ethical leader to preside over an organization that commits several unethical acts. How? A flaw in the organization's reward structure may inadvertently cause individuals to act in an inappropriate manner if rewards are seen as being distributed on the basis of outcomes rather than the means by which goals and objectives are achieved.[73]

Consider the example of Sears, Roebuck & Co.'s automotive operations. Here, unethical behavior, rooted in a faulty reward system, took place primarily at the operations level: its automobile repair facilities.[74]

> In 1992 Sears was flooded with complaints about its automotive service business. Consumers and attorneys general in more than 40 states accused the firm of misleading customers and selling them unnecessary parts and services, from brake jobs to front-end alignments.

> In the face of declining revenues and eroding market share, Sears's management had attempted to spur the performance of its auto centers by introducing new goals and incentives for mechanics. Automotive service advisers were given product-specific quotas for a variety of parts and repairs. Failure to meet the quotas could lead to transfers and reduced hours. Many employees spoke of "pressure, pressure, pressure" to bring in sales.

> Not too surprisingly, the judgment of many employees suffered. In essence, employees were left to chart their own course, given the lack of management guidance and customer ignorance.

The bottom line: In settling the spate of lawsuits, Sears offered coupons to customers who had purchased certain auto services over the most recent two-year period. The total cost of the settlement, including potential customer refunds, was estimated to be $60 million. The cost in terms of damaged reputation? Difficult to assess, but certainly not trivial.

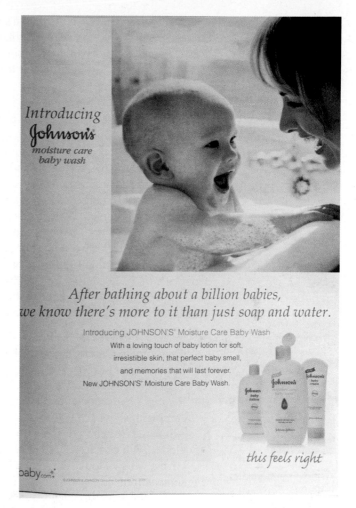

Introducing
Johnson's
*moisture care
baby wash*

*After bathing about a billion babies,
we know there's more to it than just soap and water.*

Introducing JOHNSON'S® Moisture Care Baby Wash
With a loving touch of baby lotion for soft,
irresistible skin, that perfect baby smell,
and memories that will last forever.
New JOHNSON'S® Moisture Care Baby Wash.

this feels right

baby.com®

● Johnson & Johnson is well-known for its credo, which stresses honesty, integrity, superior products, and putting people before profits.

This example makes two points. First, inappropriate reward systems may cause individuals at all levels throughout an organization to commit unethical acts that they might not otherwise commit. Second, the penalties in terms of damage to reputations, human capital erosion, and financial loss—in the short run and long run—are typically much higher than any gains that could be obtained through such unethical behavior.

Many companies have developed reward and evaluation systems that evaluate whether a manager is acting in an ethical manner. For example, Raytheon, a $20 billion defense contractor, incorporates the following items in its "Leadership Assessment Instrument":[75]

- Maintains unequivocal commitment to honesty, truth, and ethics in every facet of behavior.
- Conforms with the letter and intent of company policies while working to affect any necessary policy changes.
- Actions are consistent with words; follows through on commitments; readily admits mistakes.
- Is trusted and inspires others to be trusted.

As noted by Dan Burnham, Raytheon's former CEO: "What do we look for in a leadership candidate with respect to integrity? What we're really looking for are people who have developed an inner gyroscope of ethical principles. We look for people for whom ethical thinking is part of what they do—no different from 'strategic thinking' or 'tactical thinking.'"

Policies and Procedures

Many situations that a firm faces have regular, identifiable patterns. Leaders tend to handle such routine by establishing a policy or procedure to be followed that can be applied uniformly to each occurrence. Such guidelines can be useful in specifying the proper relationships with a firm's customers and suppliers. For example, Levi Strauss has developed stringent global sourcing guidelines and Chemical Bank (part of J. P. Morgan Chase Bank) has a policy of forbidding any review that would determine if suppliers are Chemical customers when the bank awards contracts.

Carefully developed policies and procedures guide behavior so that all employees will be encouraged to behave in an ethical manner. However, they must be reinforced with effective communication, enforcement, and monitoring, as well as sound corporate governance practices. In addition, the Sarbanes-Oxley Act of 2002 provides considerable legal protection to employees of publicly traded companies who report unethical or illegal practices. Provisions in the Act coauthored by Senator Grassley include:[76]

- Make it unlawful to "discharge, demote, suspend, threaten, harass, or in any manner discriminate against 'a whistleblower.'"
- Establish criminal penalties of up to 10 years in jail for executives who retaliate against whistleblowers.
- Require board audit committees to establish procedures for hearing whistleblower complaints.
- Allow the Secretary of Labor to order a company to rehire a terminated whistleblower with no court hearings whatsoever.
- Give a whistleblower the right to a jury trial, bypassing months or years of cumbersome administrative hearings.

Reflecting on Career Implications . . .

- **Strategic Leadership:** Do managers in your firm effectively set the direction; design the organization; and, instill a culture committed to excellence and ethical behavior? If you are in a position of leadership, do you practice all of these three elements effectively?
- **Power:** What sources of power do managers in your organization use? For example, if there is an overemphasis on organizational sources of power (e.g., position power); there could be negative implications for creativity, morale and turnover among professionals. How much power do you have? What is the basis of it? How might it be used to both advance your career goals and benefit the firm?
- **Emotional Intelligence:** Do leaders of your firm have sufficient levels of EI? Alternatively, are there excessive levels of EI present that have negative implications for your organization? Is your level of EI sufficient to allow you to have effective interpersonal and judgment skills in order to enhance your career success?
- **Learning Organization:** Does your firm effectively practice all five elements of the learning organization? If one or more elements are absent, adaptability and change will be compromised. What can you do to enhance any of the elements that might be lacking?
- **Ethics:** Does your organization practice a compliance-based or integrity-based ethical culture? Integrity-based cultures can enhance your personal growth. In addition, such cultures foster greater loyalty and commitment among all employees.

Summary

Strategic leadership is vital in ensuring that strategies are formulated and implemented in an effective manner. Leaders must play a central role in performing three critical and interdependent activities: setting the direction, designing the organization, and nurturing a culture committed to excellence and ethical behavior. If leaders ignore or are ineffective at performing any one of the three, the organization will not be very successful. We also identified three elements of leadership that contribute to success—integrative thinking, overcoming barriers to change, and the effective use of power.

For leaders to effectively fulfill their activities, emotional intelligence (EI) is very important. Five elements that contribute to EI are self-awareness, self-regulation, motivation, empathy, and social skill. The first three elements pertain to self-management skills, whereas the last two are associated with a person's ability to manage relationships with others. We also addressed some of the potential drawbacks from the ineffective use of EI. These include the dysfunctional use of power as well as a tendency to become overly empathetic, which may result in unreasonably lowered performance expectations.

Leaders must also play a central role in creating a learning organization. Gone are the days when the top-level managers "think" and everyone else in the organization "does." With the rapidly changing, unpredictable, and complex competitive environments that characterize most industries, leaders must engage everyone in the ideas and energies of people throughout the organization. Great ideas can come from anywhere in the organization—from the executive suite to the factory floor. The five elements that we discussed as central to a learning organization are inspiring and motivating people with a mission or purpose, empowering people at all levels throughout the organization, accumulating and sharing internal knowledge, gathering external information, and challenging the status quo to stimulate creativity.

In the final section of the chapter, we addressed a leader's central role in instilling ethical behavior in the organization. We discussed the enormous costs that firms face when ethical crises arise—costs in terms of financial and reputational loss as well as the erosion of human capital and relationships with suppliers, customers, society at large, and governmental agencies. And, as we would expect, the benefits of having a strong ethical organization are also numerous. We contrasted compliance-based and integrity-based approaches to organizational ethics. Compliance-based approaches are largely externally motivated; that is, they are motivated by the fear of punishment for doing something that is unlawful. Integrity-based approaches, on the other hand, are driven by a personal and organizational commitment to ethical behavior. We also addressed the four key elements of an ethical organization: role models, corporate credos and codes of conduct, reward and evaluation systems, and policies and procedures.

Summary Review Questions

1. Three key activities—setting a direction, designing the organization, and nurturing a culture and ethics—are all part of what effective leaders do on a regular basis. Explain how these three activities are interrelated.

2. Define emotional intelligence (EI). What are the key elements of EI? Why is EI so important to successful strategic leadership? Address potential "downsides."

3. The knowledge a firm possesses can be a source of competitive advantage. Describe ways that a firm can continuously learn to maintain its competitive position.

4. How can the five central elements of "learning organizations" be incorporated into global companies?

5. What are the benefits to firms and their shareholders of conducting business in an ethical manner?

6. Firms that fail to behave in an ethical manner can incur high costs. What are these costs and what is their source?

7. What are the most important differences between an "integrity organization" and a "compliance organization" in a firm's approach to organizational ethics?

8. What are some of the important mechanisms for promoting ethics in a firm?

Key Terms

leadership,   395
setting a direction,   397
designing the
  organization,   398
excellent and ethical
  organizational
  culture,   398
integrative thinking,   401
barriers to change,   402
vested intrest in
  the status quo,   402
systemic barriers,   402
behavioral barriers,   403
political barriers,   404
power,   404
organizational bases of
  power,   404
personal bases of
  power,   404
personal time
  constraints,   404

emotional intelligence
  (EI),   407
learning
  organizations,   411
benchmarking,   414
competitive
  benchmarking,   414
functional
  benchmaking,   414
ethics,   417
organizational
  ethics,   417
ethical
  orientation,   417
compliance-based
  ethics programs,   419
integrity-based
  ethics programs,   420
corporate credo,   421

Experiential Exercise

Select two well-known business leaders—one you admire and one you do not. Evaluate each of them on the five characteristics of emotional intelligence.

Emotional Intelligence Characteristics	Admired Leader	Leader Not Admired
Self-awareness		
Self-regulation		
Motivation		
Empathy		
Social skills		

Application Questions & Exercises

1. Identify two CEOs whose leadership you admire. What is it about their skills, attributes, and effective use of power that causes you to admire them?

2. Founders have an important role in developing their organization's culture and values. At times, their influence persists for many years. Identify and describe two organizations in which the cultures and values established by the founder(s) continue to flourish. You may find research on the Internet helpful in answering these questions.

3. Some leaders place a great emphasis on developing superior human capital. In what ways does this help a firm to develop and sustain competitive advantages?

4. In this chapter we discussed the five elements of a "learning organization." Select a firm with which you are familiar and discuss whether or not it epitomizes some (or all) of these elements.

Ethics Questions

1. Sometimes organizations must go outside the firm to hire talent, thus bypassing employees already working for the firm. Are there conditions under which this might raise ethical considerations?

2. Ethical crises can occur in virtually any organization. Describe some of the systems, procedures, and processes that can help to prevent such crises.

References

1. Smith, R. 2010. Another Duke exit amid inquiry. *Wall Street Journal,* December 7: B3; Smith R. 2010. Corporate news: Indiana panel finds Duke wasn't favored. *Wall Street Journal,* December 9: B4; O'Malley, C. 2010. Scandal rocks IURC, Duke. *Indianapolis Business Journal,* December 27: 13A; Jenkins, H. W. 2010. A fine clean coal mess. *Wall Street Journal,* December 15: A19; Anonymous. 2010. Top Duke executive who resigned after ethics flap gets $10 million severance retirement deal. *Associated Press Newswires,* December 10, 11: 11; Henderson, B. 2010. Duke Energy executive resigns over e-mails. *The Herald,* December 7: 11. We thank Ciprian Stan for his valued contribution.

2. Charan, R. & Colvin, G. 1999. Why CEOs fail. *Fortune,* June 21: 68–78.

3. Yukl, G. 2008. How leaders influence organizational effectiveness. *Leadership Quarterly,* 19(6): 708–722.

4. These three activities and our discussion draw from Kotter, J. P. 1990. What leaders really do. *Harvard Business Review,* 68(3): 103–111; Pearson, A. E. 1990. Six basics for general managers. *Harvard Business Review,* 67(4): 94–101; and Covey, S. R. 1996. Three roles of the leader in the new paradigm. In *The leader of the future:* 149–160. Hesselbein, F., Goldsmith, M., & Beckhard, R. (Eds.). San Francisco: Jossey-Bass.

Some of the discussion of each of the three leadership activity concepts draws on Dess, G. G. & Miller, A. 1993. *Strategic management:* 320–325. New York: McGraw-Hill.

5. García-Morales, V. J., Lloréns-Montes, F. J., & Verdú-Jover, A. J. 2008. The effects of transformational leadership on organizational performance through knowledge and innovation. *British Journal of Management,* 19(4): 299–319.

6. Day, C., Jr. & LaBarre, P. 1994. GE: Just your average everyday $60 billion family grocery store. *Industry Week,* May 2: 13–18.

7. Martin, R. 2010. The execution trap. *Harvard Business Review,* 88(7/8): 64–71.

8. Collins, J. 1997. What comes next? *Inc. Magazine.* October: 34–45.

9. Hsieh, T. 2010. Zappos's CEO on going to extremes for customers. *Harvard Business Review,* 88(7/8): 41–44.

10. Andersen, M. M., Froholdt, M. & Poulfelt, F. 2010. *Return on strategy.* New York: Routledge; and 2009 Huawei Annual Report.

11. Anonymous. 2006. Looking out for number one. *BusinessWeek,* October 30: 66.

12. This section draws on: Chen, M.-J. & Miller, D. 2010. West meets East: Toward an ambicultural approach to management. *Academy of Management Perspectives,* 24(4): 17–24.

13. For an interesting, in-depth interview with Stan Shih, read: Lin, H.-C. & Hou, S. T. 2010. Managerial lessons from the East: An interview with Acer's Stan Shih. *Academy of Management Perspectives,* 24(4): 6–16.

14. Evans, R. 2007. The either/or dilemma. *www.ft.com,* December 19; and Martin, R. L. 2007. *The opposable mind.* Boston: Harvard Business School Press.

15. Schaffer, R. H. 2010. Mistakes leaders keep making. *Harvard Business Review,* 88(9): 86–91.

16. For insightful perspectives on escalation, refer to Brockner, J. 1992. The escalation of commitment to a failing course of action. *Academy of Management Review,* 17(1): 39–61; and Staw, B. M. 1976. Knee-deep in the big muddy: A study of commitment to a chosen course of action. *Organizational Behavior and Human Decision Processes,* 16: 27–44. The discussion of systemic, behavioral, and political barriers draws on Lorange, P. & Murphy, D. 1984. Considerations in implementing strategic control. *Journal of Business Strategy,* 5: 27–35. In a similar vein, Noel M. Tichy has addressed three types of resistance to change in the context of General Electric: technical resistance, political resistance, and cultural resistance. See Tichy, N. M. 1993. Revolutionize your company. *Fortune,* December 13: 114–118. Examples draw from O'Reilly, B. 1997. The secrets of America's most admired corporations: New ideas and new products. *Fortune,* March 3: 60–64.

17. This section draws on Champoux, J. E. 2000. *Organizational behavior: Essential tenets for a new millennium.* London: South-Western; and The mature use of power in organizations. 2003. *RHR International-Executive Insights,* May 29, *12.19.168.197/ execinsights/8-3.htm.*

18. An insightful perspective on the role of power and politics in organizations is provided in Ciampa, K. 2005. Almost ready: How leaders move up. *Harvard Business Review,* 83(1): 46–53.

19. Pfeffer, J. 2010. Power play. *Harvard Business Review,* 88(7/8): 84–92.

20. Westphal, J. D., & Graebner, M. E. 2010. A matter of appearances: How corporate leaders manage the impressions of financial analysts about the conduct of their boards. *Academy of Management Journal,* 53(4): 15–44.

21. A discussion of the importance of persuasion in bringing about change can be found in Garvin, D. A. & Roberto, M. A. 2005. Change through persuasion. *Harvard Business Review,* 83(4): 104–113.

22. Lorsch, J. W. & Tierney, T. J. 2002. *Aligning the stars: How to succeed when professionals drive results.* Boston: Harvard Business School Press.

23. Some consider EI to be a "trait," that is, an attribute that is stable over time. However, many authors, including Daniel Goleman, have argued that it can be developed through motivation, extended practice, and feedback. For example, in D. Goleman, 1998, What makes a leader? *Harvard Business Review,* 76(5): 97, Goleman addresses this issue in a sidebar: "Can emotional intelligence be learned?"

24. For a review of this literature, see Daft, R. 1999. *Leadership: Theory and practice.* Fort Worth, TX: Dryden Press.

25. This section draws on Luthans, F. 2002. Positive organizational behavior: Developing and managing psychological strengths. *Academy of Management Executive,* 16(1): 57–72; and Goleman, D. 1998. What makes a leader? *Harvard Business Review,* 76(6): 92–105.

26. EI has its roots in the concept of "social intelligence" that was first identified by E. L. Thorndike in 1920 (Intelligence and its uses. *Harper's Magazine,* 140: 227–235). Psychologists have been uncovering other intelligences for some time now and have grouped them into such clusters as abstract intelligence (the ability to understand and manipulate verbal and mathematical symbols), concrete intelligence (the ability to understand and manipulate objects), and social intelligence (the ability to understand and relate to people). See Ruisel, I. 1992. Social intelligence: Conception and methodological problems. *Studia Psychologica,* 34(4–5): 281–296. Refer to *trochim.human.cornell.edu/ gallery.*

27. See, for example, Luthans, op. cit.; Mayer, J. D., Salvoney, P., & Caruso, D. 2000. Models of emotional intelligence. In Sternberg, R. J. (Ed.). *Handbook of intelligence.* Cambridge, UK: Cambridge University Press; and Cameron, K. 1999. Developing emotional intelligence at the Weatherhead School of Management. *Strategy: The Magazine of the Weatherhead School of Management,* Winter: 2–3.

28. Tate, B. 2008. A longitudinal study of the relationships among self-monitoring, authentic leadership, and perceptions of leadership. *Journal of Leadership & Organizational Studies,* 15(1): 16–29.

29. Moss, S. A., Dowling, N., & Callanan, J. 2009. Towards an integrated model of leadership and self-regulation. *Leadership Quarterly,* 20(2): 162–176.

30. An insightful perspective on leadership, which involves discovering, developing and celebrating what is unique about each individual, is found in Buckingham, M. 2005. What great managers do. *Harvard Business Review,* 83(3): 70–79.

31. Redefining leadership. 2010. *Foster Business,* Fall: 8.

32. This section draws upon Klemp. G. 2005. *Emotional intelligence and leadership: What really matters.* Cambria Consulting, Inc., *www. cambriaconsulting.com.*

33. Heifetz, R. 2004. Question authority. *Harvard Business Review,* 82(1): 37.

34. Handy, C. 1995. Trust and the virtual organization. *Harvard Business Review,* 73(3): 40–50.

35. This section draws upon Dess, G. G. & Picken, J. C. 1999. *Beyond productivity.* New York: AMACOM. The elements of the learning organization in this section are consistent with the work of Dorothy Leonard-Barton. See, for example, Leonard-Barton, D. 1992. The factory as a learning laboratory. *Sloan Management Review,* 11: 23–38.

36. Senge, P. M. 1990. The leader's new work: Building learning organizations. *Sloan Management Review,* 32(1): 7–23.

37. Bernoff, J. & Schandler, T. 2010. Empowered. *Harvard Business Review,* 88(7/8): 94–101.

38. Hammer, M. & Stanton, S. A. 1997. The power of reflection. *Fortune,* November 24: 291–296.

39. Hannah, S. T. & Lester, P. B. 2009. A multilevel approach to building and leading learning organizations. *Leadership Quarterly,* 20(1): 34–48.

40. For some guidance on how to effectively bring about change in organizations, refer to Wall, S. J. 2005. The protean organization: Learning to love change. *Organizational Dynamics,* 34(1): 37–46.

41. Covey, S. R. 1989. *The seven habits of highly effective people: Powerful lessons in personal change.* New York: Simon & Schuster.

42. Kouzes, J. M. & Posner, B. Z. 2009. To lead, create a shared vision. *Harvard Business Review,* 87(1): 20–21.

43. Kouzes and Posner, op. cit.

44. Melrose, K. 1995. *Making the grass greener on your side: A CEO's journey to leading by servicing.* San Francisco: Barrett-Koehler.

45. Tekleab, A. G., Sims Jr., H. P., Yun, S., Tesluk, P. E., & Cox, J. 2008. Are we on the same page? Effects of self-awareness of empowering and transformational leadership. *Journal of Leadership & Organizational Studies,* 14(3): 185–201.

46. Quinn, R. C. & Spreitzer, G. M. 1997. The road to empowerment: Seven questions every leader should consider. *Organizational Dynamics,* 25: 37–49.

47. For an interesting perspective on top-down approaches to leadership, see Pellegrini, E. K. & Scandura, T. A. 2008. Paternalistic leadership: A review and agenda for future research. *Journal of Management,* 34(3): 566–593.

48. Helgesen, S. 1996. Leading from the grass roots. In *Leader of the future:* 19–24 Hesselbein et al.

49. Bowen, D. E. & Lawler, E. E.,III. 1995. Empowering service employees. *Sloan Management Review,* 37: 73–84.

50. Easterby-Smith, M. & Prieto, I. M. 2008. Dynamic capabilities and knowledge management: An integrative role for learning? *British Journal of Management,* 19(3): 235–249.

51. Schafer, S. 1997. Battling a labor shortage? It's all in your imagination. *Inc.,* August: 24.

52. Meyer, P. 1998. So you want the president's job . . . *Business Horizons,* January–February: 2–8.

53. Imperato, G. 1998. Competitive intelligence: Get smart! *Fast Company,* May: 268–279.

54. Novicki, C. 1998. The best brains in business. *Fast Company,* April: 125.

55. The introductory discussion of benchmarking draws on Miller, A. 1998. *Strategic management:* 142–143. New York: McGraw-Hill.

56. Port, O. & Smith, G. 1992. Beg, borrow—and benchmark. *BusinessWeek,* November 30: 74–75.

57. Main, J. 1992. How to steal the best ideas around. *Fortune,* October 19: 102–106.

58. Taylor, J. T. 1997. What happens after what comes next? *Fast Company,* December–January: 84–85.

59. Sheff, D. 1996. Levi's changes everything. *Fast Company,* June–July: 65–74.

60. Isaacson, W. 1997. In search of the real Bill Gates. *Time,* January 13: 44–57.

61. Baatz, E. B. 1993. Motorola's secret weapon. *Electronic Business,* April: 51–53.

62. Holt, J. W. 1996. *Celebrate your mistakes.* New York: McGraw-Hill.

63. This opening discussion draws upon Conley, J. H. 2000. Ethics in business. In Helms, M. M. (Ed.). *Encyclopedia of management* (4th ed.): 281–285; Farmington Hills, MI: Gale Group; Paine, L. S. 1994. Managing for organizational integrity. *Harvard Business Review,* 72(2): 106–117; and Carlson, D. S. & Perrewe, P. L. 1995. Institutionalization of organizational ethics through transformational leadership. *Journal of Business Ethics,* 14: 829–838.

64. Pinto, J., Leana, C. R., & Pil, F. K. 2008. Corrupt organizations or organizations of corrupt individuals? Two types of organization-level corruption. *Academy of Management Review,* 33(3): 685–709.

65. Soule, E. 2002. Managerial moral strategies—in search of a few good principles. *Academy of Management Review,* 27(1): 114–124.

66. Carlson & Perrewe, op. cit.

67. This discussion is based upon Paine. Managing for organizational integrity; Paine, L. S. 1997. *Cases in leadership, ethics, and organizational integrity: A Strategic approach.* Burr Ridge, IL: Irwin; and Fontrodona, J. 2002. Business ethics across the Atlantic. Business Ethics Direct, *www.ethicsa.org/ BED_art_fontrodone.html.*

68. For more on operationalizing capabilities to sustain an ethical framework, see Largay III, J. A. & Zhang, R. 2008. Do CEOs worry about being fired when making investment decisions. *Academy of Management Perspectives,* 22(1): 60–61.

69. See *www.ti.com/corp/docs/company/ citizen/ethics/benchmark.shtml;* and *www.ti.com/corp/docs/company/ citizen/ethics/quicktest.shtml.*

70. Wetlaufer, S. 1999. Organizing for empowerment: An interview with AES's Roger Sant and Dennis Bakke. *Harvard Business Review,* 77(1): 110–126.

71. For an insightful, academic perspective on the impact of ethics codes on executive decision making, refer to Stevens, J. M., Steensma, H. K., Harrison, D. A., & Cochran, P. S. 2005. Symbolic or substantive document? The influence of ethics code on financial executives' decisions. *Strategic Management Journal,* 26(2): 181–195.

72. Paine. Managing for organizational integrity.

73. For a recent study on the effects of goal setting on unethical behavior, read Schweitzer, M. E., Ordonez, L., & Douma, B. 2004. Goal setting as a motivator of unethical behavior. *Academy of Management Journal,* 47(3): 422–432.

74. Paine. Managing for organizational integrity.

75. Fulmer, R. M. 2004. The challenge of ethical leadership. *Organizational Dynamics,* 33 (3): 307–317.

76. *www.sarbanes-oxley.com.*

TWELVE

Managing Innovation and Fostering Corporate Entrepreneurship

After reading this chapter, you should have a good understanding of:

LO12.1 The importance of implementing strategies and practices that foster innovation.

LO12.2 The challenges and pitfalls of managing corporate innovation processes.

LO12.3 How corporations use new venture teams, business incubators, and product champions to create an internal environment and culture that promote entrepreneurial development.

LO12.4 How corporate entrepreneurship achieves both financial goals and strategic goals.

LO12.5 The benefits and potential drawbacks of real options analysis in making resource deployment decisions in corporate entrepreneurship contexts.

LO12.6 How an entrepreneurial orientation can enhance a firm's efforts to develop promising corporate venture initiatives.

LEARNING OBJECTIVES

To remain competitive, established firms must continually seek out opportunities for growth and new methods for strategically renewing their performance. Changes in customer needs, new technologies, and shifts in the competitive landscape require that companies continually innovate and initiate corporate ventures in order to compete effectively. This chapter addresses how entrepreneurial activities can be an avenue for achieving competitive advantages.

In the first section, we address the importance of innovation in identifying venture opportunities and strategic renewal. Innovations can take many forms, including radical breakthroughs, incremental improvements, and disruptive innovations. Innovations often create new markets, update products or services, and help renew organizational processes. We discuss how firms can successfully manage the innovation process. Impediments and challenges to effective innovation are discussed, and examples of good innovation practices are presented.

We discuss the unique role of corporate entrepreneurship in the strategic management process in the second section. Here we highlight two types of activities corporations use to remain competitive—focused and dispersed. New venture groups and business incubators are often used to focus a firm's entrepreneurial activities. In other corporations, the entrepreneurial spirit is dispersed throughout the organization and gives rise to product champions and other autonomous strategic behaviors that organizational members engage in to foster internal corporate venturing. We also discuss the benefits and potential drawbacks of real options analysis in making decisions about which venture activities merit additional investment and which should be abandoned.

In the final section we describe how a firm's entrepreneurial orientation can contribute to its growth and renewal as well as enhance the methods and processes strategic managers use to recognize opportunities and develop initiatives for internal growth and development. The chapter also evaluates the pitfalls that firms may encounter when implementing entrepreneurial strategies. ●

In April 2006, *Bloomberg Businessweek* described HTC as "the hottest tech outfit you never heard of," but oh how the times have changed.[1]

Founded in 1997 as a contract manufacturer, the company has long been the world's top maker of mobile handsets using Microsoft's Windows Mobile operating system. HTC has several strategic partnerships, including partners such as Intel, Texas Instruments, and Qualcomm. HTC is known for its innovation and is consistently highly ranked by insiders and consumers alike. It is constantly broadening the range of devices it offers—introducing devices to support specific applications that meet the increasingly diverse needs of its customers and partners. Currently *Bloomberg Businessweek* lists HTC as number 47 of the Most Innovative Companies. HTC Chief Executive Peter Chou says, "Innovation is not a one-time job—innovation is a journey. . . . Hardware innovation is less than half the battle," when it comes to the handheld market.

Let's take a look at what happens when corporate entrepreneurship fails to add value through innovation.

HTC paired its proprietary intuitive user interface, Sense, with Windows Mobile version 6.5, Microsoft's mobile operating system, to create the HD2 Smartphone available through T-Mobile. It features a luxurious 4.3-inch touch screen, Qualcomm Snapdragon processor (the same one that powers Google's Nexus One), 5-megapixel camera with flash, and all in sleek design that fits in a shirt pocket! Just one catch, Microsoft's operating system is soon to be obsolete, and its new Windows Mobile 7 is not backward compatible. Bottom line: Consumers are spending $199 on two-year contracts with T-Mobile to have a phone that won't work! What went wrong?

Although Microsoft was one of the first to recognize the power of handhelds, it struggled to look past its ideas of a handheld computer to a more intuitive smartphone. This allowed Microsoft to slip in the market as it attempted to perfect its software. Microsoft—as first mover—was the market leader. However, Blackberry followed and took over the corporate market, while Apple's iPhone ruled the consumer market. In three months, Microsoft smartphone subscribers slipped down to 15.7 percent of the smartphone market by January 2010, according to comScore. HTC has a long history of pairing with Microsoft to innovate in the handheld market. Unfortunately, this partnership of corporate entrepreneurs could not overcome the poor mix of Microsoft's baffling software with HTC's elegant hardware. All of this reinforces the fact that, according to *Bloomberg Businessweek,* "even innovative companies can be hobbled by suppliers peddling out-of-date technology."

>LO12.1

The importance of implementing strategies and practices that foster innovation.

Managing change is one of the most important functions performed by strategic leaders. There are two major avenues through which companies can expand or improve their business—innovation and corporate entrepreneurship. These two activities go hand-in-hand because they both have similar aims. The first is strategic renewal. Innovations help an organization stay fresh and reinvent itself as conditions in the business environment change. This is why managing innovation is such an important strategic implementation issue. The second is the pursuit of venture opportunities. Innovative breakthroughs, as well as new product concepts, evolving technologies, and shifting demand, create opportunities for corporate venturing. In this chapter we will explore these topics—how change and innovation can stimulate strategic renewal and foster corporate entrepreneurship.

Managing Innovation

One of the most important sources of growth opportunities is innovation. **Innovation** involves using new knowledge to transform organizational processes or create commercially viable products and services. The sources of new knowledge may include the latest technology, the results of experiments, creative insights, or competitive information. However it comes about, innovation occurs when new combinations of ideas and information bring about positive change.

The emphasis on newness is a key point. For example, for a patent application to have any chance of success, one of the most important attributes it must possess is novelty. You can't patent an idea that has been copied. This is a central idea. In fact, the root of the word *innovation* is the Latin *novus,* which means new. Innovation involves introducing or changing to something new.[2]

Among the most important sources of new ideas is new technology. Technology creates new possibilities. Technology provides the raw material that firms use to make innovative products and services. But technology is not the only source of innovations. There can be innovations in human resources, firm infrastructure, marketing, service, or in many other value-adding areas that have little to do with anything "high-tech." Strategy Spotlight 12.1 highlights a simple but effective innovation by Dutch Boy paints. As the Dutch Boy example suggests, innovation can take many forms.

> **innovation** the use of new knowledge to transform organizational processes or create commercially viable products and services.

Types of Innovation

Although innovations are not always high-tech, changes in technology can be an important source of change and growth. When an innovation is based on a sweeping new technology, it often has a more far-reaching impact. Sometimes even a small innovation can add value and create competitive advantages. Innovation can and should occur throughout an organization—in every department and all aspects of the value chain.

One distinction that is often used when discussing innovation is between process innovation and product innovation.[3] *Product innovation* refers to efforts to create product designs and applications of technology to develop new products for end users. Recall from Chapter 5 how generic strategies were typically different depending on the stage of the industry life cycle. Product innovations tend to be more common during the earlier stages of an industry's life cycle. Product innovations are also commonly associated with a differentiation strategy. Firms that differentiate by providing customers with new products or services that offer unique features or quality enhancements often engage in product innovation.

> **product innovation** efforts to create product designs and applications of technology to develop new products for end users.

Process innovation, by contrast, is typically associated with improving the efficiency of an organizational process, especially manufacturing systems and operations. By drawing on new technologies and an organization's accumulated experience (Chapter 5), firms can often improve materials utilization, shorten cycle time, and increase quality. Process innovations are more likely to occur in the later stages of an industry's life cycle as companies seek ways to remain viable in markets where demand has flattened out and competition is more intense. As a result, process innovations are often associated with overall cost leader strategies, because the aim of many process improvements is to lower the costs of operations.

> **process innovation** efforts to improve the efficiency of organizational processes, especially manufacturing systems and operations.

Another way to view the impact of an innovation is in terms of its degree of innovativeness, which falls somewhere on a continuum that extends from incremental to radical.[4]

- *Radical innovations* produce fundamental changes by evoking major departures from existing practices. These breakthrough innovations usually occur because of technological change. They tend to be highly disruptive and can transform a company or even revolutionize a whole industry. They may lead to products or processes that can be patented, giving a firm a strong competitive advantage. Examples include

> **radical innovation** an innovation that fundamentally changes existing practices.

Dutch Boy's Simple Paint Can Innovation

Sometimes a simple change can make a vast improvement in a product. Any painter knows that getting the paint can open and pouring out paint without drips are two of the challenges of painting. Dutch Boy addressed this issue by developing a twist and pour paint container. The all-plastic container has a large, easy-to-use twist-off top and a handle on the side. The result was a consumer-friendly product that made painting easier and less messy. The handle also reduces the need for a paint stirring stick since you can mix the paint by shaking the container. Even though Dutch Boy's innovation was simple, nontechnological, and had nothing to do with the core product, the launch of the new packaging led to articles in 30 national consumer magazines and 60 major newspapers as well as a story on *Good Morning America*. The Twist and Pour can was also named "Product of the Year" by *USA Today, Bloomberg Businessweek,* and *Better Homes & Gardens.* It was also named a winner of the 2011 Good Housekeeping VIP Awards, which commemorate the most innovative products from the past decade.

Sources: 11 Innovative Products from the Past Decade. 2011 *The Good Housekeeping Research Institute; www.fallscommunications.com.*

electricity, the telephone, the transistor, desktop computers, fiber optics, artificial intelligence, and genetically engineered drugs.

incremental innovation an innovation that enhances existing practices or makes small improvements in products and processes.

- ***Incremental innovations*** enhance existing practices or make small improvements in products and processes. They may represent evolutionary applications within existing paradigms of earlier, more radical innovations. Because they often sustain a company by extending or expanding its product line or manufacturing skills, incremental innovations can be a source of competitive advantage by providing new capabilities that minimize expenses or speed productivity. Examples include frozen food, sports drinks, steel-belted radial tires, electronic bookkeeping, shatterproof glass, and digital telephones.

Some innovations are highly radical; others are only slightly incremental. But most innovations fall somewhere between these two extremes (see Exhibit 12.1).

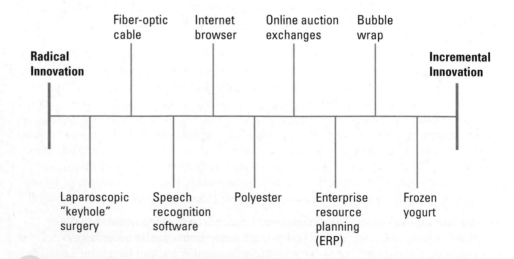

Exhibit 12.1 Continuum of Radical and Incremental Innovations

Harvard Business School Professor Clayton M. Christensen identified another useful approach to characterize types of innovations.[5] Christensen draws a distinction between sustaining and disruptive innovations. *Sustaining innovations* are those that extend sales in an existing market, usually by enabling new products or services to be sold at higher margins. Such innovations may include either incremental or radical innovations. For example, the Internet was a breakthrough technology that transformed retail selling. But rather than disrupting the activities of catalog companies such as Lands' End and L.L. Bean, the Internet energized their existing business by extending their reach and making their operations more efficient.

By contrast, *disruptive innovations* are those that overturn markets by providing an altogether new approach to meeting customer needs. The features of a disruptive innovation make it somewhat counterintuitive. Disruptive innovations:

- Are technologically simpler and less sophisticated than currently available products or services.
- Appeal to less demanding customers who are seeking more convenient, less expensive solutions.
- Take time to take effect and only become disruptive once they have taken root in a new market or low-end part of an existing market.

Christensen cites Walmart and Southwest Airlines as two disruptive examples. Walmart started with a single store, Southwest with a few flights. But because they both represented major departures from existing practices and tapped into unmet needs, they steadily grew into ventures that appealed to a new category of customers and eventually overturned the status quo. "Instead of sustaining the trajectory of improvement that has been established in a market," says Christensen, a disruptive innovation "disrupts it and redefines it by bringing to the market something that is simpler."[6]

The Linux operating system provides a more recent example. When it first became available, few systems administrators used the open-source operating system even though it was free. However, problems with more expensive proprietary operating systems, such as Microsoft Windows, have made Linux increasingly popular. By 2008, the majority of Internet hosting companies and supercomputer operating systems were Linux-based. In addition to being relatively more convenient to use, it is supported by a community of developers.

Seeing the unmet needs of others can also trigger the development of potentially disruptive innovations. One innovator, Dean Kaman, has seen the need for clean water across the globe as a situation crying out for a disruptive innovation. Strategic Spotlight 12.2 describes an innovative product he sees as the solution for the one billion people who don't have access to clean drinking water.

Innovation is a force in both the external environment (technology, competition) and also a factor affecting a firm's internal choices (generic strategy, value-adding activities).[7] Nevertheless, innovation can be quite difficult for some firms to manage, especially those that have become comfortable with the status quo.

Challenges of Innovation

Innovation is essential to sustaining competitive advantages. Recall from Chapter 3 that one of the four elements of the Balanced Scorecard is the innovation and learning perspective. The extent and success of a company's innovation efforts are indicators of its overall performance. As management guru Peter Drucker warned, "An established company which, in an age demanding innovation, is not capable of innovation is doomed to decline and extinction."[8] In today's competitive environment, most firms have only one choice: "Innovate or die."

>LO12.2
The challenges and pitfalls of managing corporate innovation processes.

A Disruptive Innovation: The Slingshot and Affordable Clean Water

Over one billion people have no access to clean water in their homes. Dean Kamen sees this as both a moral dilemma and a business opportunity. Kamen has made innovation his calling. He has had successes, such as developing a pump that improved the delivery of drugs to cancer patients and insulin to diabetics. He also has had notable failures, such as the Segway scooter, which was designed to change how people commute in major cities but, instead, became one of the most overhyped product failures in business history. Now he has focused his attention on clean water.

Providing clean drinking water has been a major point of emphasis for governments and nongovernmental organizations (NGOs) trying to improve living conditions in developing countries. The World Health Organization (WHO) identified universal access to clean water as one of its Millenium Development Goals, goals it aims to reach by 2015. While two-thirds of the earth's surface is covered with water, only 1 percent of this water is safe to drink. To increase the amount of clean, drinkable water, governments and NGOs have invested billions of dollars in major public water projects to take available water from rivers, lakes, and oceans and treat it to provide drinkable water. Still, with all of these efforts, 20 percent of the world's population lives without clean water.

Kamen decided to address this issue by developing a water purification system that is simple, portable, and affordable. Engineers at DEKA Research, Kamen's engineering and design firm, have developed a small water purification system, called the Slingshot. This system has the potential to radically change the method of bringing clean water to developing areas. Rather than relying on major, multimillion dollar water projects, this is a low-cost system (about $2,000 each) that could produce 250 gallons of drinkable water each day, enough water for approximately 100 people or the number of people in a small village. The Slingshot is about the size of a dormitory refrigerator and borrows from a desalination process used to generate drinking water on naval ships. Using a vapor compression distillation process, the system heats water through multiple cycles. This process removes minerals, heavy metals, and other contaminants by evaporating the water away from the contaminants. It also kills bacteria and viruses through pasteurization of the water. It is also a small user of energy, only requiring about the same energy as a coffee maker.

Still, DEKA faces a major challenge bringing this technology to market. To get the cost of the machines down to the $2,000 target, Kamen needs to build scaled facilities to mass manufacture the Slingshot. But how can he build demand for the product? It is hard for Kamen and his backers to tap into governmental investment programs for water to generate sales for his product. Most investment money for clean water is already geared to major projects. Also, it is difficult to generate orders from the potential users. While the target cost for the Slingshot is low by our standards, the cost is still out of reach for many of the potential users, since $2,000 is more than the inhabitants of many small villages can afford, with individual incomes often below $500 a year in the target markets. Kamen has identified a different potential path to build the demand he needs to mass manufacture the product. He is now pitching the benefits of the Slingshot to major corporations, like Coca-Cola, and small business owners, such as the proprietors of bars and restaurants or small manufacturers in areas without clean water. His aim is to build demand from these commercial customers to allow him to build the scale of operations needed to produce the Slingshot at the target cost of $2,000 and to demonstrate the value of the Slingshot to the WHO and others who he hopes would see it as a tool to meet the goal of providing clean water to all.

Sources: Copeland, M. V. 2010. Dean Kamen (Still) Wants to Save the World. *Fortune*, May 3: 61–62; Nasr, S. L. 2009. How the Slingshot Water Purifier Works. *HowStuffWorks.com*, July 27: np;. Segway Creator Unveils His Next Invention, a Magic Water Purifier. 2008. *www.hubpages.com*: np.

environmental sustainability

As with change, however, firms are often resistant to innovation. Only those companies that actively pursue innovation, even though it is often difficult and uncertain, will get a payoff from their innovation efforts. But managing innovation is challenging.[9] As former Pfizer chairman and CEO William Steere puts it: "In some ways, managing innovation is analogous to breaking in a spirited horse. You are never sure of success until you achieve your goal. In the meantime, everyone takes a few lumps."[10]

What is it that makes innovation so difficult? The uncertainty about outcomes is one factor. Companies are often reluctant to invest time and resources into activities with an unknown future. Another factor is that the innovation process involves so many choices. These choices present five dilemmas that companies must wrestle with when pursuing innovation.[11]

- **Seeds versus Weeds.** Most companies have an abundance of innovative ideas. They must decide which of these is most likely to bear fruit—the "Seeds"—and which should be cast aside—the "Weeds." This is complicated by the fact that some innovation projects require a considerable level of investment before a firm can fully evaluate whether they are worth pursuing. Firms need a mechanism with which they can choose among various innovation projects.

- **Experience versus Initiative.** Companies must decide who will lead an innovation project. Senior managers may have experience and credibility but tend to be more risk averse. Midlevel employees, who may be the innovators themselves, may have more enthusiasm because they can see firsthand how an innovation would address specific problems. Firms need to support and reward organizational members who bring new ideas to light.

- **Internal versus External Staffing.** Innovation projects need competent staffs to succeed. People drawn from inside the company may have greater social capital and know the organization's culture and routines. But this knowledge may actually inhibit them from thinking outside the box. Staffing innovation projects with external personnel requires that project managers justify the hiring and spend time recruiting, training, and relationship building. Firms need to streamline and support the process of staffing innovation efforts.

- **Building Capabilities versus Collaborating.** Innovation projects often require new sets of skills. Firms can seek help from other departments and/or partner with other companies that bring resources and experience as well as share costs of development. However, such arrangements can create dependencies and inhibit internal skills development. Further, struggles over who contributed the most or how the benefits of the project are to be allocated may arise. Firms need a mechanism for forging links with outside parties to the innovation process.

- **Incremental versus Preemptive Launch.** Companies must manage the timing and scale of new innovation projects. An incremental launch is less risky because it requires fewer resources and serves as a market test. But a launch that is too tentative can undermine the project's credibility. It also opens the door for a competitive response. A large-scale launch requires more resources, but it can effectively preempt a competitive response. Firms need to make funding and management arrangements that allow for projects to hit the ground running and be responsive to market feedback.

These dilemmas highlight why the innovation process can be daunting even for highly successful firms. Next, we consider five steps that firms can take to improve the innovation process within the firm.[12]

Cultivating Innovation Skills

Some firms, such as Apple, Google, and Amazon, regularly produce innovative products and services, while other firms struggle to generate new, marketable products. What separates these innovative firms from the rest of the pack? Jeff Dyer, Hal Gregersen, and Clayton Christensen argue it is the Innovative DNA of the leaders of these firms.[13] The leaders of these firms have exhibited "discovery skills" that allow them to see the potential in innovations and to move the organization forward in leveraging the value of those innovations.[14] These leaders spend 50 percent more time on these discovery activities than the leaders of less innovative firms. To improve their innovative processes, firms need to cultivate the innovation skills of their managers.

The key attribute that firms need to develop in their managers in order to improve their innovative potential is creative intelligence. Creative intelligence is driven by a core skill of associating—the ability to see patterns in data and integrating different questions, information, and insights—and four patterns of action: questioning, observing, experimenting, and networking. As managers practice the four patterns of action, they will begin to develop the skill of association. Dyer and his colleagues offer the following illustration to demonstrate that individuals using these skills are going to develop more-creative, higher-potential innovations.

> Imagine that you have an identical twin, endowed with the same brains and natural talents that you have. You're both given one week to come up with a creative new business-venture idea. During that week, you come up with ideas alone in your room. In contrast, your twin (1) talks with 10 people—including an engineer, a musician, a stay-at-home dad, and a designer—about the venture, (2) visits three innovative start-ups to observe what they do, (3) samples five "new to the market" products, (4) shows a prototype he's built to five people, and (5) asks the questions "What if I tried this?" and "Why do you do that?" at least 10 times each day during these networking, observing, and experimenting activities. Who do you bet will come up with the more innovative (and doable) ideas?

The point is that by questioning, observing, experimenting, and networking as part of the innovative process, managers will both make better innovation decisions now but, more importantly, start to build the innovative DNA needed to be more successful innovators in the future. As they get into the practice of these habits, decision makers will see opportunities and be more creative as they associate information from different parts of their life, different people they come in contact with, and different parts of their organizations. The ability to innovate is not hard-wired into our brains at birth. Research suggests that only one-third of our ability to think creatively is genetic. The other two-thirds is developed over time. Neuroscience research indicates that the brain is "plastic," meaning it changes over time due to experiences. As managers build up the ability to ask creative questions, develop a wealth of experiences from diverse settings, and link together insights from different arenas of their lives, their brains will follow suit and will build the ability to easily see situations creatively and draw upon a wide range of experiences and knowledge to identify creative solutions. The five traits of the effective innovator are described and examples of each trait are presented in Exhibit 12.2.

Defining the Scope of Innovation

Firms must have a means to focus their innovation efforts. By defining the "strategic envelope"—the scope of a firm's innovation efforts—firms ensure that their innovation efforts are not wasted on projects that are outside the firm's domain of interest. Strategic enveloping defines the range of acceptable projects. As Alistair Corbett, an innovation expert with the global consulting firm Bain & Company, said, "One man's radical innovation is another man's incremental innovation."[15] A strategic envelope creates a firm-specific view of innovation that defines how a firm can create new knowledge and learn from an innovation initiative even if the project fails. It also gives direction to a firm's innovation efforts, which helps separate seeds from weeds and builds internal capabilities.

strategic envelope a firm-specific view of innovation that defines how a firm can create new knowledge and learn from an innovation initiative even if the project fails.

One way to determine which projects to work on is to focus on a common technology. Then, innovation efforts across the firm can aim at developing skills and expertise in a given technical area. Another potential focus is on a market theme. Consider how DuPont responded to a growing concern for environmentally sensitive products:

> In the early 1990s, DuPont sought to use its knowledge of plastics to identify products to meet a growing market demand for biodegradable products. It conducted numerous experiments with a biodegradable polyester resin it named Biomax. By trying different applications and formulations demanded by potential customers, the company was finally able to create a product that could be produced economically and had market appeal. DuPont has continued to extend the Biomax brand and now produces a large line of environmentally sensitive plastics.[16]

Exhibit 12.2 The Innovator's DNA

Trait	Description	Example
Associating	Innovators have the ability to connect seemingly unrelated questions, problems, and ideas from different fields. This allows them to creatively see opportunities that others miss.	Pierre Omidyar saw the opportunity that led to eBay when he linked three items: (1) a personal fascination with creating more efficient markets, (2) his fiancee's desire to locate hard to find collectible Pez dispensers, and (3) the ineffectiveness of local classified ads in locating such items.
Questioning	Innovators constantly ask questions that challenge common wisdom. Rather than accept the status quo, they ask "Why not?" or "What if?" This gets others around them to challenge the assumptions that limit the possible range of actions the firm can take.	After witnessing the emergence of eBay and Amazon, Marc Benioff questioned why computer software was still sold in boxes rather than leased with a subscription and downloaded through the Internet. This was the genesis of Salesforce.com, a firm with over $1.3 billion in sales in 2010.
Observing	Discovery-driven executives produce innovative business ideas by observing regular behavior of individuals, especially customers and potential customers. Such observations often identify challenges customers face and previously unidentified opportunities.	From watching his wife struggle to keep track of the family's finances, Intuit founder Scott Cook identified the need for easy-to-use financial software that provided a single place for managing bills, bank accounts, and investments.
Experimenting	Thomas Edison once said, "I haven't failed. I've simply found 10,000 ways that do not work." Innovators regularly experiment with new possibilities, accepting that many of their ideas will fail. Experimentation can include new jobs, living in different countries, and new ideas for their businesses.	Founders Larry Page and Sergey Brin provide time and resources for Google employees to experiment. Some, such as the Android cell phone platform, have been big winners. Others, such as the Orkut and Buzz social networking systems, have failed. But Google will continue to experiment with new products and services.
Networking	Innovators develop broad personal networks. They use this diverse set of individuals to find and test radical ideas. This can be done by developing a diverse set of friends. It can also be done by attending idea conferences where individuals from a broad set of backgrounds come together to share their perspectives and ideas, such as the Technology, Entertainment, and Design (TED) Conference or the Aspen Ideas Festival.	Michael Lazaridis got the idea for a wireless e-mail device that led him to found Research in Motion from a conference he attended. At the conference, a speaker was discussing a wireless system Coca-Cola was using that allowed vending machines to send a signal when they needed refilling. Lazaridis saw the opportunity to use the same concept with e-mail communications, and the idea for the Blackberry was hatched.

Source: Reprinted by permission of Harvard Business Review. Exhibit from "The Innovator's DNA," by J. H. Dyer, H. G. Gregerson and C. M. Christensen. Copyright 2009 by The Harvard Business School Publishing Corporation; all rights reserved.

Staffing for Innovation Success at Air Products

When it comes to implementing its innovation efforts, Air Products and Chemicals, Inc. (APCI) recognizes the importance of staffing for achieving success. Air Products is a global manufacturer of industrial gases, chemicals, and related equipment. Headquartered in Allentown, Pennsylvania, Air Products has annual sales of $10 billion, manufacturing facilities in over 30 countries, and 22,000 employees worldwide. The company has a strong reputation for effectively embedding innovation into its culture through its unique employee engagement processes.

Ron Pierantozzi, a 30-year veteran of the company and its director of innovation and new product development, says, "Innovation is about discipline. . . . It

requires a different type of training, different tools and new approaches to experimentation." To enact this philosophy, Pierantozzi begins with his people. He recruits people with diverse backgrounds and a wide range of expertise including engineers, entrepreneurs, and government officials. It is made clear to those on his innovation teams that they will return to mainstream operations after four years—a fact that most consider a plus since working in the innovation unit usually provides a career boost. He also assures players that there is no stigma associated with a failed venture because experimentation is highly valued.

Innovation teams are created to manage the company's intellectual assets and determine which technologies have the most potential value. A key benefit of this approach has been to more effectively leverage its human resources to achieve innovative outcomes without increasing its R&D expenses. These efforts resulted in an innovation award from APQC (formerly known as the American Productivity and Quality Center) which recognizes companies for exemplary practices that increase productivity.

Sources: Chesbrough, H. 2007. Why Bad Things Happen to Good Technology. *The Wall Street Journal:* April 28–29, R11; Leavitt, P. 2005. Delivering the Difference: Business Process Management at APCI. *APQC, www.apqc.com;* McGrath, R. G. & Keil, T. 2007. The Value Captor's Process: Getting the Most Out of Your New Business Ventures. *Harvard Business Review,* May: 128–136; and *www.apci.com.*

To choose partners, firms need to ask what competencies they are looking for and what the innovation partner will contribute.[25] These might include knowledge of markets, technology expertise, or contacts with key players in an industry. Innovation partnerships also typically need to specify how the rewards of the innovation will be shared and who will own the intellectual property that is developed.[26]

Innovation efforts that involve multiple partners and the speed and ease with which partners can network and collaborate are changing the way innovation is conducted.[27] Strategy Spotlight 12.4 outlines how IBM is using crowdsourcing technologies to foster collaboration between employees, customers, suppliers, and other stakeholders to enhance its innovation efforts.

Successful innovation involves a companywide commitment because the results of innovation affect every part of the organization. Innovation also requires an entrepreneurial spirit and skill set to be effective. Few companies have a more exemplary reputation than W. L. Gore. Exhibit 12.3 highlights the policies that help make Gore an innovation leader. One of the most important ways that companies improve and grow is when innovation is put to the task of creating new corporate ventures.

corporate entrepreneurship
the creation of new value for a corporation, through investments that create either new sources of competitive advantage or renewal of the value proposition.

Corporate Entrepreneurship

Corporate entrepreneurship (CE) has two primary aims: the pursuit of new venture opportunities and strategic renewal.[28] The innovation process keeps firms alert by exposing them to new technologies, making them aware of marketplace trends, and helping them

Crowdsourcing: IBM's Innovation Jam

IBM is one of the best known corporations in the world, but their CEO, Samuel Palmisano, saw a major challenge for the firm. Though IBM had great ability to do basic scientific research and owned the rights to over 40,000 patents, they had struggled to translate their patented knowledge into marketable products. Also, they had built a reputation with investors as a firm with incremental product development, not the reputation needed in dynamic technological markets. Palmisano saw crowdsourcing as a means to move IBM forward in a bold way.

In 2006, IBM hosted an Innovation Jam, an open event that involved 150,000 IBM employees, family members, business partners, clients, and university researchers. The jam took place over two 72-hour sessions. Participants from over 100 countries jammed for 24 hours a day over three days. The discussions were organized around 25 technologies in six broad categories. While the jam discussions were rich in content, it was a challenge for IBM to pull meaningful data from them. The 24-hour format meant that no single moderator could follow any discussion, and the volume of posts to the discussion threads left IBM with a huge amount of data to wade through. The discussions yielded 46,000 potential business ideas. To make sense of the data, IBM organized the discussion threads using sophisticated text analysis software and had a team of 50 managers read through the organized data. Using data from the first session, the managers identified 31 "big ideas." They further explored these 31 ideas in the second jam session. IBM then used another set of 50 global managers to review the discussions from the jam. Teams of managers focused on related groups of ideas, such as health care and the environment.

IBM's managers saw the jam as serving three purposes. First, it gave individuals both inside and outside IBM who already had big ideas a forum in which to share their vision with top managers. Second, it gave individuals with smaller ideas a venue to link up with others with related ideas, resulting in larger major initiatives. For example, individuals who had ideas about better local weather forecasting, sensing devices for water utilities, and long-term climate forecasting came together to create "Predictive Water Management," a comprehensive solution for water authorities to manage their resources, a business solution no one at IBM had thought of before the jam. Third, the global structure of the jam allowed IBM, early on, to see how employees, partners, and customers from different regions had different goals and concerns about possible new businesses. For example, what customers wanted from systems to manage health care records varied greatly across regions.

Based on the jam sessions, IBM launched 10 new businesses using $100 million in funding. One, the Intelligent Transportation System, a system that gathers, manages, and disseminates real-time information about metropolitan transportation systems to optimize traffic flow, has been sold to transportation authorities in Sweden, the UK, Singapore, Dubai, and Australia. Another, Intelligent Utility Networks, became a core product in IBM's public utility business. A third, Big Green, became part of the largest initiative in IBM's history, a billion-dollar project on better managing energy and other resources.

Sources: Bjelland, O. M. & Wood, R. C. 2008. An Inside View of IBM's Innovation Jam. *Sloan Management Review.* Fall: 32–40; Hempel, J. 2006. Big Blue Brainstorm. *BusinessWeek,* August 7: 70; Takahashi, D. 2008. IBM's Innovation Jam 2008 Shows How Far Crowdsourcing Has Come. *Businessweek.com,* October 9: np.

crowdsourcing

---

evaluate new possibilities. CE uses the fruits of the innovation process to help firms build new sources of competitive advantage and renew their value propositions. Just as the innovation process helps firms to make positive improvements, corporate entrepreneurship helps firms identify opportunities and launch new ventures. Strategy Spotlight 12.5 outlines how Cisco is being entrepreneurial by expanding into new, growing product segments.

Corporate new venture creation was labeled "intrapreneuring" by Gifford Pinchot because it refers to building entrepreneurial businesses within existing corporations.[29] However, to engage in corporate entrepreneurship that yields above-average returns and

Exhibit 12.3
W. L. Gore's New Rules
for Fostering Innovation

Rule	Implications
The power of small teams	Gore believes that small teams promote familiarity and autonomy. Even its manufacturing plants are capped at just 200 people. That way everyone can get to know one another on a first-name basis and work together with minimal rules. This also helps to cultivate "an environment where creativity can flourish," according to CEO Chuck Carroll.
No ranks, no titles, no bosses	Because Gore believes in maximizing individual potential, employees, dubbed "associates," decide for themselves what new commitments to take on. Associates have "sponsors," rather than bosses, and there are no standardized job descriptions or categories. Everyone is supposed to take on a unique role. Committees of co-workers evaluate each team member's contribution and decide on compensation.
Take the long view	Although impatient about the status quo, Gore exhibits great patience with the time—often years, sometimes decades—it takes to nurture and develop breakthrough products and bring them to market.
Make time for face time	Gore avoids the traditional hierarchical chain of command, opting instead for a team-based environment that fosters personal initiative. Gore also discourages memos and e-mail and promotes direct, person-to-person communication among all associates—anyone in the company can talk to anyone else.
Lead by leading	Associates are encouraged to spend about 10 percent of their time pursuing speculative new ideas. Anyone is free to champion products, as long as they have the passion and ideas to attract followers. Many of Gore's breakthroughs started with one person acting on his or her own initiative and developed as colleagues helped in their spare time.
Celebrate failure	When a project doesn't work out and the team decides to kill it, they celebrate just as they would if it had been a success—with some beer and maybe a glass of champagne. Rather than condemning failure, Gore figures that celebrating it encourages experimentation and risk taking.

Source: Deutschman, A. 2004. The Fabric of Creativity. *Fast Company,* 89: 54–62; Levering, R. & Moskowitz, M. 2006. The 100 Best Companies to Work For. *Fortune, www.fortune.com,* January; and *www.gore.com.*

contributes to sustainable advantages, it must be done effectively. In this section we will examine the sources of entrepreneurial activity within established firms and the methods large corporations use to stimulate entrepreneurial behavior.

In a typical corporation, what determines how entrepreneurial projects will be pursued? That depends on many factors, including:

- Corporate culture.
- Leadership.

Cisco Looks to Video to Spur Demand

Cisco produces both hardware and software used to manage network and communication systems. Cisco, which was founded in San Francisco in 1984, began by manufacturing routers to manage Internet communications. It has expanded from its original market position in computer routers by acquiring firms that make network switches, Voice over Internet Protocol (VOIP) systems, home networking equipment, and other information technology products and services. Today, Cisco dominates the market for Internet protocol-based networking equipment and provides routers and switches used to direct data, voice, and video traffic. Cisco has had a nice run over the last 10 years, with sales growing from $19 billion in 2001 to $40 billion in 2010 and net income growing from $2.7 billion to $7.8 billion over the same period.

Even with this success, Cisco is not one to rest on its laurels. Managers at Cisco retain an entrepreneurial orientation and look to expand their product portfolio to meet where the market is going. A few years ago, Cisco introduced Teleprescence, an Internet-based videoconference technology. This has been a winning product during the recent recessionary years, since many corporations have turned to videoconferencing as a means to host meetings without the travel expense of bringing employees together. From this experience, John Chambers, the firm's CEO, began to believe that the Internet's primary payload going forward will be video and has placed a big bet on Internet video.

As the Internet moves toward being primarily a video-based medium, communications hardware and software to manage video traffic will be valued resources, because HD video takes about 50 times as much Internet bandwidth as audio data. To meet the challenge of this new Internet era, Cisco has developed a technology, called Medianet, that facilitates the flow of video media across all devices transferring, delivering, or receiving Internet-based videos. For example, a smartphone could tell a Medianet-enabled network the phone's screen size and connection speed. The network would then tailor how it delivered the media to the phone to optimize the transfer and to use the network hardware as efficiently as possible.

Sources: Fortt, J. 2010. Cisco's Online Video Gamble. *Fortune*, November 1: 43; Lawson, S. 2008. Cisco Plays Up Video for Business, Carriers. *IDG News Service*, September 16: np; *www.hoovers.com; www.cisco.com*.

● Cisco Systems is developing its Internet-based video media products.

Cisco's ultimate objective with this new product is to extend its dominance in the network business. As Cisco develops systems that increase the use of Internet-based video, it stokes up demand for its core products. Telecommunication service providers and corporations will need to ramp up their investment in network gear to meet the growing demand for Internet video. These firms will likely to turn to Cisco to purchase Medianet-enabled network gear as they expand their network systems. As Robert Hagerty, the former CEO of Polycom, a competitor of Cisco, commented, Cisco's "real motivation is to sell more routers and switches on the enterprise side." In line with this, Procter & Gamble has expanded its purchasing of Cisco's network equipment as it has worked to double its network capacity in 2010 in anticipation of greater video traffic. Thus, Cisco's entrepreneurial entry into the Internet-video business has fostered growth in the value of its core markets.

- Structural features that guide and constrain action.
- Organizational systems that foster learning and manage rewards.

All of the factors that influence the strategy implementation process will also shape how corporations engage in internal venturing.

Other factors will also affect how entrepreneurial ventures will be pursued.

- The use of teams in strategic decision making.
- Whether the company is product or service oriented.
- Whether its innovation efforts are aimed at product or process improvements.
- The extent to which it is high-tech or low-tech.

Because these factors are different in every organization, some companies may be more involved than others in identifying and developing new venture opportunities.[30] These factors will also influence the nature of the CE process.

Successful CE typically requires firms to reach beyond their current operations and markets in the pursuit of new opportunities. It is often the breakthrough opportunities that provide the greatest returns. Such strategies are not without risks, however. In the sections that follow, we will address some of the strategic choice and implementation issues that influence the success or failure of CE activities.

Two distinct approaches to corporate venturing are found among firms that pursue entrepreneurial aims. The first is *focused* corporate venturing, in which CE activities are isolated from a firm's existing operations and worked on by independent work units. The second approach is *dispersed,* in which all parts of the organization and every organization member are engaged in intrapreneurial activities.

Focused Approaches to Corporate Entrepreneurship

Firms using a focused approach typically separate the corporate venturing activity from the other ongoing operations of the firm. CE is usually the domain of autonomous work groups that pursue entrepreneurial aims independent of the rest of the firm. The advantage of this approach is that it frees entrepreneurial team members to think and act without the constraints imposed by existing organizational norms and routines. This independence is often necessary for the kind of open-minded creativity that leads to strategic breakthroughs. The disadvantage is that, because of their isolation from the corporate mainstream, the work groups that concentrate on internal ventures may fail to obtain the resources or support needed to carry an entrepreneurial project through to completion. Two forms—new venture groups (NVGs) and business incubators—are among the most common types of focused approaches.

New Venture Groups (NVGs) Corporations often form NVGs whose goal is to identify, evaluate, and cultivate venture opportunities. These groups typically function as semi-autonomous units with little formal structure. The **new venture group** may simply be a committee that reports to the president on potential new ventures. Or it may be organized as a corporate division with its own staff and budget. The aims of the NVG may be open-ended in terms of what ventures it may consider. Alternatively, some corporations use them to promote concentrated effort on a specific problem. In both cases, they usually have a substantial amount of freedom to take risks and a supply of resources to do it with.[31]

NVGs usually have a larger mandate than a typical R&D department. Their involvement extends beyond innovation and experimentation to coordinating with other corporate divisions, identifying potential venture partners, gathering resources, and actually launching the venture. Strategy Spotlight 12.6 shows how WD-40 has used an NVG to improve its CE efforts.

>LO12.3
How corporations use new venture teams, business incubators, and product champions to create an internal environment and culture that promote entrepreneurial development.

focused approches to corporate entrepreneurship corporate entrepreneurship in which the venturing entity is seperated from the other ongoing operations of the firm.

new venture group a group of individuals, or a division within a corporation, that identifies, evaluates, and cultivates venture opportunities.

Using Team Tomorrow to Grow WD-40

When a hinge squeaks, most people reach for a can of WD-40. The iconic lubricant in the blue cans has been around for over 50 years and commands a 70 percent market share in the spray lubricant business. Garry Ridge, the CEO of WD-40, quips that "more people use WD-40 every day than use dental floss." Still, Ridge wanted the firm to look forward, searching for growth opportunities. Historically, WD-40's marketing team was responsible for new product development, but this typically involved minor product changes or new packaging for existing products.

Knowing the incremental focus of the current structure and wanting to get WD-40 focused on bolder new product opportunities, Ridge created a multifunctional team, dubbed Team Tomorrow, to manage its global CE efforts. This team includes members from marketing, research, supply chain, purchasing, and distribution. To head the team, Ridge tapped an experienced executive, Graham Milner, who thought globally and had a marketing

Sources: Ferrarini, E. 2010. WD-40 Company CEO Talks about Rebuilding an Innovative Brand and Taking It Global. *Enterprise Leadership*, February 27: np; Bounds, G. 2006. WD-40 CEO Repackages a Core Product. *Pittsburgh Post Gazette*, May 23: np; Govindarajan, V. & Trimble, D. 2010. Stop the Innovation Wars. *Harvard Business Review*, July–August: 76–83; *www.intheboardroom.com*.

background. There was some resistance from the marketing staff, because they lost power in the new product-development process. Ridge overcame this in a number of ways. He was active in forming the team, got involved during times of conflict between Team Tomorrow and other groups in the organization, and carried around an early prototype of the team's first product, the No Mess Pen, to show how interested he was in the new product. His involvement signaled the importance of the team to WD-40. By placing a marketing executive in charge of Team Tomorrow, he signaled the importance of marketing to the organization. Milner and the other team leader, Stephanie Barry, worked collaboratively with the head of marketing, instituted an open-door policy, and shared information with marketing. Collectively, these actions broke down resistance to Team Tomorrow.

Ridge also gave the team a bold goal. He charged the team to create new products that would generate $100 million in sales per year from products developed and launched within the previous three years. As of 2010, the team had created products that generate $165 million in sales. Ridge also sees a large change in the rest of the firm as a result of this effort. He sees the firm's employees as being members of a "tribe" and the organization as a "living learning laboratory."

Business Incubators   The term *incubator* was originally used to describe a device in which eggs are hatched. **Business incubators** are designed to "hatch" new businesses. They are a type of corporate NVG with a somewhat more specialized purpose—to support and nurture fledgling entrepreneurial ventures until they can thrive on their own as stand-alone businesses. Corporations use incubators as a way to grow businesses identified by the NVG. Although they often receive support from many parts of the corporation, they still operate independently until they are strong enough to go it alone. Depending on the type of business, they are either integrated into an existing corporate division or continue to operate as a subsidiary of the parent firm.

Incubators typically provide some or all of the following five functions.[32]

> **business incubator**
> a corporate new venture group that supports and nurtures fledgling entrepreneurial ventures until they can thrive on their own as stand-alone businesses.

- *Funding.* Includes capital investments as well as in-kind investments and loans.
- *Physical space.* Incubators in which several start-ups share space often provide fertile ground for new ideas and collaboration.
- *Business services.* Along with office space, young ventures need basic services and infrastructure; may include anything from phone systems and computer networks to public relations and personnel management.
- *Mentoring.* Senior executives and skilled technical personnel often provide coaching and experience-based advice.

- *Networking.* Contact with other parts of the firm and external resources such as suppliers, industry experts, and potential customers facilitates problem solving and knowledge sharing.

The risks associated with incubating ventures should not be overlooked. Companies have at times spent millions on new ideas with very little to show for it. Major corporations such as Lucent, British Airways, and Hewlett-Packard deactivated their incubators and scaled back new venture portfolios after experiencing major declines in value during recent financial downturns.[33]

To encourage entrepreneurship, corporations sometimes need to do more than create independent work groups or venture incubators to generate new enterprises. In some firms, the entrepreneurial spirit is spread throughout the organization.

Dispersed Approaches to Corporate Entrepreneurship

The second type of CE is dispersed. For some companies, a dedication to the principles and practices of entrepreneurship is spread throughout the organization. One advantage of this approach is that organizational members don't have to be reminded to think entrepreneurially or be willing to change. The ability to change is considered to be a core capability. This leads to a second advantage: Because of the firm's entrepreneurial reputation, stakeholders such as vendors, customers, or alliance partners can bring new ideas or venture opportunities to anyone in the organization and expect them to be well-received. Such opportunities make it possible for the firm to stay ahead of the competition. However, there are disadvantages as well. Firms that are overzealous about CE sometimes feel they must change for the sake of change, causing them to lose vital competencies or spend heavily on R&D and innovation to the detriment of the bottom line. Two related aspects of dispersed entrepreneurship include entrepreneurial cultures that have an overarching commitment to CE activities and the use of product champions in promoting entrepreneurial behaviors.

Entrepreneurial Culture   In some large corporations, the corporate culture embodies the spirit of entrepreneurship. A culture of entrepreneurship is one in which the search for venture opportunities permeates every part of the organization. The key to creating value successfully is viewing every value-chain activity as a source of competitive advantage. The effect of CE on a firm's strategic success is strongest when it animates all parts of an organization. It is found in companies where the strategic leaders and the culture together generate a strong impetus to innovate, take risks, and seek out new venture opportunities.[34]

In companies with an entrepreneurial culture, everyone in the organization is attuned to opportunities to help create new businesses. Many such firms use a top-down approach to stimulate entrepreneurial activity. The top leaders of the organization support programs and incentives that foster a climate of entrepreneurship. Many of the best ideas for new corporate ventures, however, come from the bottom up. Here's what Martin Sorrell, CEO of the WPP Group, a London-based global communication services group, says about drawing on the talents of lower-level employees:

> The people at the so-called bottom of an organization know more about what's going on than the people at the top. The people in the trenches are the ones in the best position to make critical decisions. It's up to the leaders to give those people the freedom and the resources they need.[35]

An entrepreneurial culture is one in which change and renewal are on everybody's mind. Sony, 3M, Intel, and Cisco are among the corporations best known for their corporate venturing activities. Many fast-growing young corporations also attribute much of their success to an entrepreneurial culture. But other successful firms struggle in their efforts to remain entrepreneurial. Strategy Spotlight 12.7 describes Microsoft's struggles with its CE efforts.

dispersed approaches to corporate entrepreneurship
corporate entrepreunership in which a dedication to the principles and policies of entrepreunership is spread throughout the organization.

entrepreneurial culture
corpotate culture in which change and renewal are a constant focus of attention.

Microsoft's Struggles with Corporate Entrepreneurship

Microsoft generated $62 billion in sales and nearly $19 billion in profits in 2010 and dominates the market for PC operating system and office suite application software, yet its stock languishes at a price lower than it was 10 years ago. Why is this the case? Investors have little confidence that Microsoft will produce blockbuster products that will replace its core PC software products as the information technology market moves into the post-PC phase.

It isn't that Microsoft has failed to generate innovative ideas. The firm spends $9 billion a year on R&D. Over 10 years ago, engineers at Microsoft developed a tablet PC and an e-book system, two of the hottest technology products today. They also pioneered Web-TV. But they failed to turn these pioneering efforts into marketable products. In other markets, they have not pioneered, but have seen limited success with products they've designed to meet emerging challengers. The Zune music player was supposed to challenge the iPod but was a flop in the market. Recently, they introduced the Kin One and Kin Two, smartphones with flashy designs and social networking capabilities, but they pulled the phones from the market within two months. The Xbox 360 has arguably been Microsoft's most successful product launch designed to take on a pioneering rival, but even there, the firm is competitive but not dominating the market.

With all of its resources, why has Microsoft struggled to translate its innovations into market successes? Let's

look at three reasons that have been talked about in the business press.

First, the dominance of the Windows and Office software has made it difficult to launch new products. Developers of new products have, at times, had to justify how their new product fit into the core Microsoft product line. Dick Brass, a former VP at Microsoft, states, "The company routinely manages to frustrate the efforts of its visionary leaders." For example, when Brass and his team developed an innovative technology to display text on a screen, called ClearType, engineers in the Windows group hampered the product by falsely arguing it had bugs and wouldn't display some colors properly. Others in the firm stated they would support the technology only if they could control it. In the end, it took 10 years to get ClearType integrated into Windows.

Second, Microsoft has a difficult time attracting the top software designers. The firm is not seen as a hip place to work. It is seen by developers as too bureaucratic. And their flat stock price makes it hard to entice top designers with promises of wealth from rising stock options—a common compensation element for technology talent.

Third, great innovations are increasingly the output of collaborative, open-source design, but Microsoft is reluctant to fully embrace the open-source development model. They developed a system where start-up firms can sign onto a program to gain access to free Microsoft software and provide development ideas to Microsoft and have signed up 35,000 firms, but its system is still more bureaucratic than those of its competitors. As one entrepreneur commented about working with Microsoft, "We got introduced to Microsoft through our investors. They don't do this for just anybody." As a result, Microsoft has lost those "anybodies" as development partners and future customers.

Sources: Vance, A. 2010. At Top of Business but Just Not Cool. *International Herald Tribune*, July 6: 2; Clarke, G. 2010. Inside Microsoft's Innovation Crisis. *Theregister.co.uk*, February 5: np; Brass, D. 2010. Microsoft's Creative Destruction. *NYTimes.com*, February 4: np.

Product Champions CE does not always involve making large investments in start-ups or establishing incubators to spawn new divisions. Often, innovative ideas emerge in the normal course of business and are brought forth and become part of the way of doing business. Entrepreneurial champions are often needed to take charge of internally generated ventures. **Product** (or project) **champions** are those individuals working within a corporation who bring entrepreneurial ideas forward, identify what kind of market exists for the product or service, find resources to support the venture, and promote the venture concept to upper management.[36]

When lower-level employees identify a product idea or novel solution, they will take it to their supervisor or someone in authority. A new idea that is generated in a technology lab may be introduced to others by its inventor. If the idea has merit, it gains support

> **product champion**
> an individual working within a corporation who brings entrepreneurial ideas forward, identifies what kind of market exists for the product or service, finds resources to support the venture, and promotes the venture concept to upper management.

>LO12.5

The benefits and potential drawbacks of real options analysis in making resource deployment decisions in corporate entrepreneurship contexts.

real options analysis an investment analysis tool that looks at an investment or activity as a series of sequential steps, and for each step the investor has the option of (a) investing additional funds to grow or accelerate, (b) delaying, (c) shrinking the scale of, or (d) abandoning the activity.

Real Options Analysis: A Useful Tool

One way firms can minimize failure and avoid losses from pursuing faulty ideas is to apply the logic of real options. **Real options analysis** (ROA) is an investment analysis tool from the field of finance. It has been slowly, but increasingly, adopted by consultants and executives to support strategic decision making in firms. What does ROA consist of and how can it be appropriately applied to the investments required to initiate strategic decisions? To understand *real* options it is first necessary to have a basic understanding of what *options* are.

Options exist when the owner of the option has the right but not the obligation to engage in certain types of transactions. The most common are stock options. A stock option grants the holder the right to buy (call option) or sell (put option) shares of the stock at a fixed price (strike price) at some time in the future.[50] The investment to be made immediately is small, whereas the investment to be made in the future is generally larger. An option to buy a rapidly rising stock currently priced at $50 might cost as little as $.50.[51] Owners of such a stock option have limited their losses to $.50 per share, while the upside potential is unlimited. This aspect of options is attractive, because options offer the prospect of high gains with relatively small up-front investments that represent limited losses.

The phrase "real options" applies to situations where options theory and valuation techniques are applied to real assets or physical things as opposed to financial assets. Applied to entrepreneurship, real options suggest a path that companies can use to manage the uncertainty associated with launching new ventures. Some of the most common applications of real options are with property and insurance. A real estate option grants the holder the right to buy or sell a piece of property at an established price some time in the future. The actual market price of the property may rise above the established (or strike) price—or the market value may sink below the strike price. If the price of the property goes up, the owner of the option is likely to buy it. If the market value of the property drops below the strike price, the option holder is unlikely to execute the purchase. In the latter circumstance, the option holder has limited his or her loss to the cost of the option, but during the life of the option retains the right to participate in whatever the upside potential might be.

Applications of Real Options Analysis to Strategic Decisions

The concept of options can also be applied to strategic decisions where management has flexibility. Situations arise where management must decide whether to invest additional funds to grow or accelerate the activity, perhaps delay in order to learn more, shrink the scale of the activity, or even abandon it. Decisions to invest in new ventures or other business activities such as R&D, motion pictures, exploration and production of oil wells, and the opening and closing of copper mines often have this flexibility.[52] Important issues to note are:

- ROA is appropriate to use when investments can be staged; a smaller investment up front can be followed by subsequent investments. Real options can be applied to an investment decision that gives the company the right, but not the obligation, to make follow-on investments.
- Strategic decision makers have "tollgates," or key points at which they can decide whether to continue, delay, or abandon the project. Executives have flexibility. There are opportunities to make other go or no-go decisions associated with each phase.
- It is expected that there will be increased knowledge about outcomes at the time of the next investment and that additional knowledge will help inform the decision makers about whether to make additional investments (i.e., whether the option is in the money or out of the money).

Many strategic decisions have the characteristic of containing a series of options. The phenomenon is called "embedded options," a series of investments in which at each stage of the investment there is a go/no–go decision. Consider the real options logic that Johnson Controls, a maker of car seats, instrument panels, and interior control systems uses to advance or eliminate entrepreneurial ideas.[53] Johnson options each new innovative idea by making a small investment in it. To decide whether to exercise an option, the idea must continue to prove itself at each stage of development. Here's how Jim Geschke, vice president and general manager of electronics integration at Johnson, describes the process:

> Think of Johnson as an innovation machine. The front end has a robust series of gates that each idea must pass through. Early on, we'll have many ideas and spend a little money on each of them. As they get more fleshed out, the ideas go through a gate where a go or no-go decision is made. A lot of ideas get filtered out, so there are far fewer items, and the spending on each goes up. . . . Several months later each idea will face another gate. If it passes, that means it's a serious idea that we are going to develop. Then the spending goes way up, and the number of ideas goes way down. By the time you reach the final gate, you need to have a credible business case in order to be accepted. At a certain point in the development process, we take our idea to customers and ask them what they think. Sometimes they say, "That's a terrible idea. Forget it." Other times they say, "That's fabulous. I want a million of them."

This process of evaluating ideas by separating winning ideas from losing ones in a way that keeps investments low has helped Johnson Controls grow its revenues to over $34 billion a year. Using real options logic to advance the development process is a key way that firms reduce uncertainty and minimize innovation-related failures.[54]

Potential Pitfalls of Real Options Analysis

Despite the many benefits that can be gained from using ROA, managers must be aware of its potential limitations or pitfalls. Below we will address three major issues.[55]

Agency Theory and the Back-Solver Dilemma Let's assume that companies adopting a real-options perspective invest heavily in training and that their people understand how to effectively estimate variance—the amount of dispersion or range that is estimated for potential outcomes. Such training can help them use ROA. However, it does not solve another inherent problem: managers may have an incentive and the know-how to "game the system." Most electronic spreadsheets permit users to simply back-solve any formula; that is, you can type in the answer you want and ask what values are needed in a formula to get that answer. If managers know that a certain option value must be met in order for the proposal to get approved, they can back-solve the model to find a variance estimate needed to arrive at the answer that upper management desires.

Agency problems are typically inherent in investment decisions. They may occur when the managers of a firm are separated from its owners—when managers act as "agents" rather than "principals" (owners). A manager may have something to gain by not acting in the owner's best interests, or the interests of managers and owners are not co-aligned. Agency theory suggests that as managerial and owner interests diverge, managers will follow the path of their own self-interests. Sometimes this is to secure better compensation: Managers who propose projects may believe that if their projects are approved, they stand a much better chance of getting promoted. So while managers have an incentive to propose projects that *should* be successful, they also have an incentive to propose projects that *might* be successful. And because of the subjectivity involved in formally modeling a real option, managers may have an incentive to choose variance values that increase the likelihood of approval.

Managerial Conceit: Overconfidence and the Illusion of Control Often, poor decisions are the result of such traps as biases, blind spots, and other human frailties. Much of this literature falls under the concept of **managerial conceit.**[56]

First, managerial conceit occurs when decision makers who have made successful choices in the past come to believe that they possess superior expertise for managing uncertainty. They believe that their abilities can reduce the risks inherent in decision making to a much greater extent than they actually can. Such managers are more likely to shift

back-solver dilemma problem with investment decisions in which managers scheme to have a project meet investment approval criteria, even though the investment may not enhance firm value.

managerial conceit biases, blind spots, and other human frailties that lead to poor managerial decisions.

away from analysis to trusting their own judgment. In the case of real options, they can simply declare that any given decision is a real option and proceed as before. If asked to formally model their decision, they are more likely to employ variance estimates that support their viewpoint.

Second, employing the real-options perspective can encourage decision makers toward a bias for action. Such a bias may lead to carelessness. Managerial conceit is as much a problem (if not more so) for small decisions as for big ones. Why? The cost to write the first stage of an option is much smaller than the cost of full commitment, and managers pay less attention to small decisions than to large ones. Because real options are designed to minimize potential losses while preserving potential gains, any problems that arise are likely to be smaller at first, causing less concern for the manager. Managerial conceit could suggest that managers will assume that those problems are the easiest to solve and control—a concern referred to as the illusion of control. Managers may fail to respond appropriately because they overlook the problem or believe that since it is small, they can easily resolve it. Thus, managers may approach each real-option decision with less care and diligence than if they had made a full commitment to a larger investment.

escalation of commitment the tendency for managers to irrationally stick with an investment, even one that is broken down into a sequential series of decisions, when investment criteria are not be met.

Managerial Conceit: Irrational Escalation of Commitment   A strength of a real options perspective is also one of its Achilles heels. Both real options and decisions involving escalation of commitment require specific environments with sequential decisions.[57] As the escalation-of-commitment literature indicates, simply separating a decision into multiple parts does not guarantee that decisions made will turn out well. This condition is potentially present whenever the exercise decision retains some uncertainty, which most still do. The decision to abandon also has strong psychological factors associated with it that affect the ability of managers to make correct exercise decisions.[58]

An option to exit requires reversing an initial decision made by someone in the organization. Organizations typically encourage managers to "own their decisions" in order to motivate them. As managers invest themselves in their decision, it proves harder for them to lose face by reversing course. For managers making the decision, it feels as if they made the wrong decision in the first place, even if it was initially a good decision. The more specific the manager's human capital becomes, the harder it is to transfer it to other organizations. Hence, there is a greater likelihood that managers will stick around and try to make an existing decision work. They are more likely to continue an existing project even if it should perhaps be ended.[59]

Despite the potential pitfalls of a real options approach, many of the strategic decisions that product champions and top managers must make are enhanced when decision makers have an entrepreneurial mind-set.

>LO12.6

How an entrepreneurial orientation can enhance a firm's efforts to develop promising corporate venture initiatives.

Entrepreneurial Orientation

entrepreneurial orientation the strategy-making practices that businesses use in identifying and launching new ventures, consisting of autonomy, innovativeness, proactiveness, competitive aggressiveness, and risk taking.

Firms that want to engage in successful CE need to have an entrepreneurial orientation (EO).[60] EO refers to the strategy-making practices that businesses use in identifying and launching corporate ventures. It represents a frame of mind and a perspective toward entrepreneurship that is reflected in a firm's ongoing processes and corporate culture.[61]

An EO has five dimensions that permeate the decision-making styles and practices of the firm's members: autonomy, innovativeness, proactiveness, competitive aggressiveness, and risk taking. These factors work together to enhance a firm's entrepreneurial performance. But even those firms that are strong in only a few aspects of EO can be very successful.[62] Exhibit 12.4 summarizes the dimensions of **entrepreneurial orientation.** Below, we discuss the five dimensions of EO and how they have been used to enhance internal venture development.

Exhibit 12.4
**Dimensions of
Entrepreneurial
Orientation**

Dimension	Definition
Autonomy	Independent action by an individual or team aimed at bringing forth a business concept or vision and carrying it through to completion.
Innovativeness	A willingness to introduce novelty through experimentation and creative processes aimed at developing new products and services as well as new processes.
Proactiveness	A forward-looking perspective characteristic of a market-place leader that has the foresight to seize opportunities in anticipation of future demand.
Competitive aggressiveness	An intense effort to outperform industry rivals characterized by a combative posture or an aggressive response aimed at improving position or overcoming a threat in a competitive marketplace.
Risk taking	Making decisions and taking action without certain knowledge of probable outcomes; some undertakings may also involve making substantial resource commitments in the process of venturing forward.

Sources: Dess, G. G. & Lumpkin, G. T. 2005. The Role of Entrepreneurial Orientation in Stimulating Effective Corporate Entrepreneurship. *Academy of Management Executive,* 19(1): 147–156; Covin, J. G. & Slevin, D. P. 1991. A Conceptual Model of Entrepreneurship as Firm Behavior. *Entrepreneurship Theory & Practice,* Fall: 7–25; Lumpkin, G. T. and Dess, G. G. 1996. Clarifying the Entrepreneurial Orientation Construct and Linking It to Performance. *Academy of Management Review,* 21: 135–172; Miller, D. 1983. The Correlates of Entrepreneurship in Three Types of Firms. *Management Science,* 29: 770–791.

Autonomy

Autonomy refers to a willingness to act independently in order to carry forward an entrepreneurial vision or opportunity. It applies to both individuals and teams that operate outside an organization's existing norms and strategies. In the context of corporate entrepreneurship, autonomous work units are often used to leverage existing strengths in new arenas, identify opportunities that are beyond the organization's current capabilities, and encourage development of new ventures or improved business practices.[63]

The need for autonomy may apply to either dispersed or focused entrepreneurial efforts. Because of the emphasis on venture projects that are being developed outside of the normal flow of business, a focused approach suggests a working environment that is relatively autonomous. But autonomy may also be important in an organization where entrepreneurship is part of the corporate culture. Everything from the methods of group interaction to the firm's reward system must make organizational members feel as if they can think freely about venture opportunities, take time to investigate them, and act without fear of condemnation. This implies a respect for the autonomy of each individual and an openness to the independent thinking that goes into championing a corporate venture idea. Thus, autonomy represents a type of empowerment (see Chapter 11) that is directed at identifying and leveraging entrepreneurial opportunities. Exhibit 12.5 identifies two techniques that organizations often use to promote autonomy.

autonomy
independent action by an individual or team aimed at bringing forth a business concept or vision and carrying it through to completion.

even when their benefits are unclear. However, in today's climate of rapid change, effectively producing, assimilating, and exploiting innovations can be an important avenue for achieving competitive advantages. Interest in global warming and other ecological concerns has led many corporations to focus their innovativeness efforts on solving environmental problems. Strategy Spotlight 12.8 describes how Best Buy is using entrepreneurial thinking and innovative practices to deliver socially responsible solutions.

As our earlier discussion of CE indicated, many corporations owe their success to an active program of innovation-based corporate venturing.[66] Exhibit 12.6 highlights two of the methods companies can use to enhance their competitive position through innovativeness.

Innovativeness can be a source of great progress and strong corporate growth, but there are also major pitfalls for firms that invest in innovation. Expenditures on R&D aimed at identifying new products or processes can be a waste of resources if the effort does not yield results. Another danger is related to the competitive climate. Even if a company innovates a new capability or successfully applies a technological breakthrough, another company may develop a similar innovation or find a use for it that is more profitable. Finally R&D and other innovation efforts are among the first to be cut back during an economic downturn.

Even though innovativeness is an important means of internal corporate venturing, it also involves major risks, because investments in innovations may not pay off. For strategic managers of entrepreneurial firms, successfully developing and adopting innovations can generate competitive advantages and provide a major source of growth for the firm.

proactiveness a forward-looking perspective characteristic of a marketplace leader that has the foresight to seize opportunities in anticipation of future demand.

Proactiveness

Proactiveness refers to a firm's efforts to seize new opportunities. Proactive organizations monitor trends, identify the future needs of existing customers, and anticipate changes

Exhibit 12.6 Innovativeness Techniques

Innovativeness		
Technique	**Description/Purpose**	**Example**
Foster creativity and experimentation	Companies that support idea exploration and allow employees to express themselves creatively enhance innovation outcomes.	To tap into its reserves of innovative talent, Royal Dutch/Shell created "GameChanger" to help employees develop promising ideas. The process provides funding up to $600,000 for would-be entrepreneurs to pursue innovative projects and conduct experiments.
Invest in new technology, R&D, and continuous improvement	The latest technologies often provide sources of new competitive advantages. To extract value from a new technology, companies must invest in it.	Dell Computer Corporation's new OptiPlex manufacturing system revolutionized the traditional assembly line. Hundreds of custom-built computers can be made in an eight-hour shift using state of the art automation techniques that have increased productivity per person by 160 percent.

Sources: Breen, B. 2004. Living in Dell Time. *Fast Company*, November: 88–92: Hammonds, K. H. 2002. Size Is Not a Strategy. *Fast Company*, August: 78–83; Perman, S. 2001. Automate or Die. *eCompanyNow.com*, July; Dell, M. 1999. *Direct from Dell*. New York: HarperBusiness; and Watson, R. 2006. Expand Your Innovation Horizons. *Fast Company*, www.fastcompany.com, May.

in demand or emerging problems that can lead to new venture opportunities. Proactiveness involves not only recognizing changes but also being willing to act on those insights ahead of the competition.[67] Strategic managers who practice proactiveness have their eye on the future in a search for new possibilities for growth and development. Such a forward-looking perspective is important for companies that seek to be industry leaders. Many proactive firms seek out ways not only to be future oriented but also to change the very nature of competition in their industry.

Proactiveness puts competitors in the position of having to respond to successful initiatives. The benefit gained by firms that are the first to enter new markets, establish brand identity, implement administrative techniques, or adopt new operating technologies in an industry is called first mover advantage.[68]

First movers usually have several advantages. First, industry pioneers, especially in new industries, often capture unusually high profits because there are no competitors to drive prices down. Second, first movers that establish brand recognition are usually able to retain their image and hold on to the market share gains they earned by being first. Sometimes these benefits also accrue to other early movers in an industry, but, generally speaking, first movers have an advantage that can be sustained until firms enter the maturity phase of an industry's life cycle.[69]

First movers are not always successful. The customers of companies that introduce novel products or embrace breakthrough technologies may be reluctant to commit to a new way of doing things. In his book *Crossing the Chasm,* Geoffrey A. Moore noted that most firms seek evolution, not revolution, in their operations. This makes it difficult for a first mover to sell promising new technologies.[70]

Even with these caveats, however, companies that are first movers can enhance their competitive position. Exhibit 12.7 illustrates two methods firms can use to act proactively.

Exhibit 12.7 Proactiveness Techniques

Proactiveness		
Technique	**Description/Purpose**	**Example**
Introduce new products or technological capabilities ahead of the competition.	Being a first mover provides companies with an ability to shape the playing field and shift competitive advantages in their favor.	Sony's mission states, "We should always be the pioneers with our products—out front leading the market." This philosophy has made Sony technologically strong with industry-leading products such as the PlayStation and Vaio laptop computers.
Continuously seek out new product or service offerings.	Firms that provide new resources or sources of supply can benefit from a proactive stance.	Costco seized a chance to leverage its success as a warehouse club that sells premium brands when it introduced Costco Home Stores. The home stores are usually located near its warehouse stores and its rapid inventory turnover gives it a cost advantage of 15 to 25 percent over close competitors such as Bassett Furniture and the Bombay Company.

Sources: Bryce, D. J. & Dyer, J. H. 2007. Strategies to Crack Well-Guarded Markets. *Harvard Business Review,* May: 84–92; Collins, J. C. & Porras, J. I. 1997. *Built to Last.* New York: HarperBusiness; Robinson, D. 2005. Sony Pushes Reliability in Vaio Laptops. *IT Week, www.itweek.co.uk*, October 12; and *www.sony.com*.

Being an industry leader does not always lead to competitive advantages. Some firms that have launched pioneering new products or staked their reputation on new brands have failed to get the hoped-for payoff. Coca-Cola and PepsiCo invested $75 million to launch sodas that would capitalize on the low-carb diet trend. But with half the carbohydrates taken out, neither *C2*, Coke's entry, nor *Pepsi Edge* tasted very good. The two new brands combined never achieved more than one percent market share. PepsiCo halted production in 2005 and Coca-Cola followed suit in 2007.[71] Such missteps are indicative of the dangers of trying to proactively anticipate demand. Another danger for opportunity-seeking companies is that they will take their proactiveness efforts too far. For example, Porsche has tried to extend its brand images outside of the automotive arena. While some efforts have worked, such as Porsche-designed T-shirts and sunglasses, other efforts have failed, such as the Porsche-branded golf clubs.

Careful monitoring and scanning of the environment, as well as extensive feasibility research, are needed for a proactive strategy to lead to competitive advantages. Firms that do it well usually have substantial growth and internal development to show for it. Many of them have been able to sustain the advantages of proactiveness for years.

Competitive Aggressiveness

competitive aggressiveness an intense effort to outperform industry rivals characterized by a combative posture or an aggressive response aimed at improving position or overcoming a threat in a competitive marketplace.

Competitive aggressiveness refers to a firm's efforts to outperform its industry rivals. Companies with an aggressive orientation are willing to "do battle" with competitors. They might slash prices and sacrifice profitability to gain market share or spend aggressively to obtain manufacturing capacity. As an avenue of firm development and growth, competitive aggressiveness may involve being very assertive in leveraging the results of other entrepreneurial activities such as innovativeness or proactiveness.

Competitive aggressiveness is directed toward competitors. The SWOT analysis discussed in Chapters 2 and 3 provides a useful way to distinguish between these different approaches to CE. Proactiveness, as we saw in the last section, is a response to opportunities—the O in SWOT. Competitive aggressiveness, by contrast, is a response to threats—the T in SWOT. A competitively aggressive posture is important for firms that seek to enter new markets in the face of intense rivalry.

Strategic managers can use competitive aggressiveness to combat industry trends that threaten their survival or market position. Sometimes firms need to be forceful in defending the competitive position that has made them an industry leader. Firms often need to be aggressive to ensure their advantage by capitalizing on new technologies or serving new market needs. Exhibit 12.8 suggests two of the ways competitively aggressive firms enhance their entrepreneurial position.

Another practice companies use to overcome the competition is to make preannouncements of new products or technologies. This type of signaling is aimed not only at potential customers but also at competitors to see how they will react or to discourage them from launching similar initiatives. Sometimes the preannouncements are made just to scare off competitors, an action that has potential ethical implications.

Competitive aggressiveness may not always lead to competitive advantages. Some companies (or their CEOs) have severely damaged their reputations by being overly aggressive. Although it continues to be a dominant player, Microsoft's highly aggressive profile makes it the subject of scorn by some businesses and individuals. Efforts to find viable replacements for the Microsoft products have helped fuel interest in alternative options provided by Google, Apple, and the open-source software movement.[72]

Competitive aggressiveness is a strategy that is best used in moderation. Companies that aggressively establish their competitive position and vigorously exploit opportunities to achieve profitability may, over the long run, be better able to sustain their competitive advantages if their goal is to defeat, rather than decimate, their competitors.

Exhibit 12.8   Competitive Aggressiveness Techniques

Competitive Aggressiveness		
Technique	**Description/Purpose**	**Example**
Enter markets with drastically lower prices.	Narrow operating margins make companies vulnerable to extended price competition.	Using open-source software, California-based Zimbra, Inc. has become a leader in messaging and collaboration software. Its product costs about one-third less than its direct competitor Microsoft Exchange. Zimbra now has over 60 million users.
Find successful business models and copy them.	As long as a practice is not protected by intellectual property laws, it's probably okay to imitate it. Finding solutions to existing problems is generally quicker and cheaper than inventing them.	Best Practices LLC is a North Carolina consulting group that seeks out best practices and then repackages and resells them. With annual revenues in excess of $8 million, Best Practices has become a leader in continuous improvement and benchmarking strategies.

Sources: Guth, R. A. 2006. Trolling the Web for Free Labor, Software Upstarts Are New Force. *The Wall Street Journal,* November 12: 1; Mochari, I. 2001. Steal This Strategy. *Inc.,* July: 62–67; *www.best-in-class.com*; and *www.zimbra.com*.

Risk Taking

Risk taking refers to a firm's willingness to seize a venture opportunity even though it does not know whether the venture will be successful—to act boldly without knowing the consequences. To be successful through corporate entrepreneurship, firms usually have to take on riskier alternatives, even if it means forgoing the methods or products that have worked in the past. To obtain high financial returns, firms take such risks as assuming high levels of debt, committing large amounts of firm resources, introducing new products into new markets, and investing in unexplored technologies.

All of the approaches to internal development that we have discussed are potentially risky. Whether they are being aggressive, proactive, or innovative, firms on the path of CE must act without knowing how their actions will turn out. Before launching their strategies, corporate entrepreneurs must know their firm's appetite for risk.[73]

Three types of risk that organizations and their executives face are business risk, financial risk, and personal risk:

- *Business risk taking* involves venturing into the unknown without knowing the probability of success. This is the risk associated with entering untested markets or committing to unproven technologies.
- *Financial risk taking* requires that a company borrow heavily or commit a large portion of its resources in order to grow. In this context, risk is used to refer to the risk/return trade-off that is familiar in financial analysis.
- *Personal risk taking* refers to the risks that an executive assumes in taking a stand in favor of a strategic course of action. Executives who take such risks stand to influence the course of their whole company, and their decisions also can have significant implications for their careers.

risk taking making decisions and taking action without certain knowledge of probable outcomes. Some undertakings may also involve making substantial resource commitments in the process of venturing forward.

Exhibit 12.9 **Risk-Taking Techniques**

Risk Taking		
Technique	**Description/Purpose**	**Example**
Research and assess risk factors to minimize uncertainty	Companies that "do their homework"—that is, carefully evaluate the implications of bold actions—reduce the likelihood of failure.	Graybar Electric Co. took a risk when it invested $144 million to revamp its distribution system. It consolidated 231 small centers into 16 supply warehouses and installed the latest communications network. Graybar is now considered a leader in facility redesign and its sales have increased steadily since the consolidation, topping $5 billion in sales in a recent year.
Use techniques that have worked in other domains	Risky methods that other companies have tried may provide an avenue for advancing company goals.	Autobytel.com, one of the first companies to sell cars online, decided on an approach that worked well for others—advertising during the Super Bowl. It was the first dot-com ever to do so and its $1.2 million 30-second ad paid off well by generating weeks of free publicity and favorable business press.

Sources: Anonymous. 2006. Graybar Offers Data Center Redesign Seminars. *Cabling Installation and Maintenance, www.cim.pennnet.com*, September 1; Keenan, F. & Mullaney, T. J. 2001. Clicking at Graybar. *BusinessWeek,* June 18: 132–34; Weintraub, A. 2001. Make or break for Autobytel. *BusinessWeek e.biz,* July 9: EB30–EB32; *www.autobytel.com*; and *www.graybar.com.*

Even though risk taking involves taking chances, it is not gambling. The best-run companies investigate the consequences of various opportunities and create scenarios of likely outcomes. A key to managing entrepreneurial risks is to evaluate new venture opportunities thoroughly enough to reduce the uncertainty surrounding them. Exhibit 12.9 indicates two methods companies can use to strengthen their competitive position through risk taking.

Risk taking, by its nature, involves potential dangers and pitfalls. Only carefully managed risk is likely to lead to competitive advantages. Actions that are taken without sufficient forethought, research, and planning may prove to be very costly. Therefore, strategic managers must always remain mindful of potential risks. In his book *Innovation and Entrepreneurship,* Peter Drucker argued that successful entrepreneurs are typically not risk takers. Instead, they take steps to minimize risks by carefully understanding them. That is how they avoid focusing on risk and remain focused on opportunity.[74] Risk taking is a good place to close this chapter on corporate entrepreneurship. Companies that choose to grow through internal corporate venturing must remember that entrepreneurship always involves embracing what is new and uncertain.

Reflecting on Career Implications . . .

- *Innovation:* Look around at the types of innovations being pursued by your company. Do they tend to be incremental or radical? Product-related or process-related? What new types of innovations might benefit your organization? How can you add value to such innovations?
- *Managing Innovation:* How might your organization's chances of a successful innovation increase through collaboration with innovation partners? Your ability to collaborate with individuals from other departments and firms will make you more receptive to and capable of innovation initiatives and enhance your career opportunities.
- *Corporate Entrepreneurship:* Do you consider the company you work for to be entrepreneurial? If not, what actions might you take to enhance its entrepreneurial spirit? If so, what have been the keys to its entrepreneurial success? Can these practices be repeated to achieve future successes?
- *Entrepreneurial Orientation:* Consider the five dimensions of entrepreneurial orientation. Is your organization especially strong at any of these? Especially weak? What are the career implications of your company's entrepreneurial strengths or weaknesses?

Summary

To remain competitive in today's economy, established firms must find new avenues for development and growth. This chapter has addressed how innovation and corporate entrepreneurship can be a means of internal venture creation and strategic renewal, and how an entrepreneurial orientation can help corporations enhance their competitive position.

Innovation is one of the primary means by which corporations grow and strengthen their strategic position. Innovations can take several forms, ranging from radical breakthrough innovations to incremental improvement innovations. Innovations are often used to update products and services or for improving organizational processes. Managing the innovation process is often challenging, because it involves a great deal of uncertainty and there are many choices to be made about the extent and type of innovations to pursue. By cultivating innovation skills, defining the scope of innovation, managing the pace of innovation, staffing to capture value from innovation, and collaborating with innovation partners, firms can more effectively manage the innovation process.

We also discussed the role of corporate entrepreneurship in venture development and strategic renewal. Corporations usually take either a focused or dispersed approach to corporate venturing. Firms with a focused approach usually separate the corporate venturing activity from the ongoing operations of the firm in order to foster independent thinking and encourage entrepreneurial team members to think and act without the constraints imposed by the corporation. In corporations where venturing activities are dispersed, a culture of entrepreneurship permeates all parts of the company in order to induce strategic behaviors by all organizational members. In measuring the success of corporate venturing activities, both financial and strategic objectives should be considered. Real options analysis is often used to make better quality decisions in uncertain entrepreneurial situations. However, a real options approach has potential drawbacks.

Most entrepreneurial firms need to have an entrepreneurial orientation: the methods, practices, and decision-making styles that strategic managers use to act entrepreneurially. Five dimensions of entrepreneurial orientation are found in firms that pursue corporate venture strategies. Autonomy, innovativeness, proactiveness, competitive aggressiveness, and risk taking each make a unique contribution to the pursuit of new opportunities. When deployed effectively, the methods and practices of an entrepreneurial orientation can be used to engage successfully in corporate entrepreneurship and new venture creation. However, strategic managers must remain mindful of the pitfalls associated with each of these approaches.

Summary Review Questions

1. What is meant by the concept of a continuum of radical and incremental innovations?

2. What are the dilemmas that organizations face when deciding what innovation projects to pursue? What steps can organizations take to effectively manage the innovation process?

3. What is the difference between focused and dispersed approaches to corporate entrepreneurship?

4. How are business incubators used to foster internal corporate venturing?

5. What is the role of the product champion in bringing a new product or service into existence in a corporation? How can companies use product champions to enhance their venture development efforts?

6. Explain the difference between proactiveness and competitive aggressiveness in terms of achieving and sustaining competitive advantage.

7. Describe how the entrepreneurial orientation (EO) dimensions of innovativeness, proactiveness, and risk taking can be combined to create competitive advantages for entrepreneurial firms.

Key Terms

innovation, 433
radical innovation, 433
product innovation, 433
process innovation, 433
incremental
    innovation, 434
strategic envelope, 438
corporate
    entrepreneurship, 442
new venture group, 446
focused approaches
    to corporate
    entrepreneurship, 446
business incubator, 447
dispersed approaches
    to corporate
    entrepreneurship, 448
entrepreneurial
    culture, 448

product champion, 449
exit champion, 451
real options
    analysis, 452
back-solver
    dilemma, 453
managerial
    conceit, 453
entrepreneurial
    orientation, 454
escalation of
    commitment, 454
autonomy, 455
innovativeness, 456
proactiveness, 458
competitive
    aggressiveness, 460
risk taking, 461

Entrepreneurial Orientation	Company A	Company B
Autonomy		
Innovativeness		
Proactiveness		
Competitive Aggressiveness		
Risk Taking		

Experiential Exercise

Select two different major corporations from two different industries (you might use Fortune 500 companies to make your selection). Compare and contrast these organizations in terms of their entrepreneurial orientation.

Based on Your Comparison:

1. How is the corporation's entrepreneurial orientation reflected in its strategy?

2. Which corporation would you say has the stronger entrepreneurial orientation?

3. Is the corporation with the stronger entrepreneurial orientation also stronger in terms of financial performance?

Application Questions & Exercises

1. Select a firm known for its corporate entrepreneurship activities. Research the company and discuss how it has positioned itself relative to its close competitors.

Does it have a unique strategic advantage? Disadvantage? Explain.

2. Explain the difference between product innovations and process innovations. Provide examples of firms that have recently introduced each type of innovation. What are the types of innovations related to the strategies of each firm?

3. Using the Internet, select a company that is listed on the NASDAQ or New York Stock Exchange. Research the extent to which the company has an entrepreneurial culture. Does the company use product champions? Does it have a corporate venture capital fund? Do you believe its entrepreneurial efforts are sufficient to generate sustainable advantages?

4. How can an established firm use an entrepreneurial orientation to enhance its overall strategic position? Provide examples.

Ethics Questions

1. Innovation activities are often aimed at making a discovery or commercializing a technology ahead of the competition. What are some of the unethical practices that companies could engage in during the innovation process? What are the potential long-term consequences of such actions?

2. Discuss the ethical implications of using entrepreneurial policies and practices to pursue corporate social responsibility goals. Are these efforts authentic and genuine or just an attempt to attract more customers?

References

1. HTC. 2010. About HTC. *HTC.com*, np; Einhorn, M. and Arndt, B. 2010. The 50 most innovative companies. *Bloomberg Businessweek*, April 25: 34–40; and Jaroslovsky, R. 2010. HTC's elegant dead-end phone. *Bloomberg Businessweek*, April 25: 42. We thank Kimberly Kentfield for her valued contributions.

2. For an interesting discussion, see Johannessen, J. A., Olsen, B., & Lumpkin, G. T. 2001. Innovation as newness: What is new, how new, and new to whom? *European Journal of Innovation Management*, 4(1): 20–31.

3. The discussion of product and process innovation is based on Roberts, E. B. (Ed.). 2002. *Innovation: Driving product, process, and market change*. San Francisco: Jossey-Bass; Hayes, R. & Wheelwright, S. 1985. Competing through manufacturing. *Harvard Business Review*, 63(1): 99–109; and Hayes, R. & Wheelwright, S. 1979. Dynamics of product–process life cycles. *Harvard Business Review*, 57(2): 127–136.

4. The discussion of radical and incremental innovations draws from Leifer, R., McDermott, C. M., Colarelli, G., O'Connor, G. C., Peters, L. S., Rice, M. P., & Veryzer, R. W. 2000. *Radical innovation: How mature companies can outsmart upstarts*. Boston: Harvard Business School Press; Damanpour, F. 1996. Organizational complexity and innovation: Developing and testing multiple contingency models. *Management Science*, 42(5): 693–716; and Hage, J. 1980. *Theories of organizations*. New York: Wiley.

5. Christensen, C. M. & Raynor, M. E. 2003. *The innovator's solution*. Boston: Harvard Business School Press.

6. Dressner, H. 2004. The Gartner Fellows interview: Clayton M. Christensen. *www.gartner.com*, April 26.

7. For another perspective on how different types of innovation affect organizational choices, see Wolter, C. & Veloso, F. M. 2008. The effects of innovation on vertical structure: Perspectives on transactions costs and competences. *Academy of Management Review*, 33(3): 586–605.

8. Drucker, P. F. 1985. *Innovation and entrepreneurship: 2000* New York: Harper & Row.

9. Birkinshaw, J., Hamel, G., & Mol, M. J. 2008. Management innovation. *Academy of Management Review*, 33(4): 825–845.

10. Steere, W. C., Jr. & Niblack, J. 1997. Pfizer, Inc. In Kanter, R. M., Kao, J., & Wiersema, F. (Eds.), *Innovation: Breakthrough thinking at 3M, DuPont, GE, Pfizer, and Rubbermaid*: 123–145. New York: HarperCollins.

11. Morrissey, C. A. 2000. Managing innovation through corporate venturing. *Graziadio Business Report*, Spring, gbr.pepperdine.edu; and Sharma, A. 1999. Central dilemmas of managing innovation in large firms. *California Management Review*, 41(3): 147–164.

12. Sharma, op. cit.

13. Dyer, J. H., Gregerson, H. B., & Christensen, C. M. 2009. The innovator's DNA. *Harvard Business Review*, December: 61-67.

14. Eggers, J. P., & Kaplan, S. 2009. Cognition and renewal: Comparing CEO and organizational effects on incumbent adaptation to technical change. *Organization Science*, 20: 461–477.

15. Canabou, C. 2003. Fast ideas for slow times. *Fast Company*, May: 52.

16. Biodegradable Products Institute. 2003. "Compostable Logo" of the Biodegradable Products Institute gains momentum with approval of DuPont Biomax resin, *www.bpiworld.org*, June 12; Leifer et al., op. cit.

17. For more on defining the scope of innovation, see Valikangas, L. & Gibbert, M. 2005. Boundary-setting strategies for escaping innovation traps. *MIT Sloan Management Review*, 46(3): 58–65.

18. Leifer et al., op. cit.

19. Bhide, A. V. 2000. *The origin and evolution of new businesses*. New York: Oxford University Press; Brown, S. L. & Eisenhardt, K. M. 1998. *Competing on the edge: Strategy as structured chaos*. Cambridge, MA: Harvard Business School Press.

20. Caulfield, B. 2003. Why techies don't get Six Sigma. *Business 2.0*, June: 90.

21. McGrath, R. G. & Keil, T. 2007. The value captor's process: Getting

Why Analyze Strategic Management Cases?

>LO13.1

How strategic case analysis is used to simulate real-world experiences.

It is often said that the key to finding good answers is to ask good questions. Strategic managers and business leaders are required to evaluate options, make choices, and find solutions to the challenges they face every day. To do so, they must learn to ask the right questions. The study of strategic management poses the same challenge. The process of analyzing, decision making, and implementing strategic actions raises many good questions.

- Why do some firms succeed and others fail?
- Why are some companies higher performers than others?
- What information is needed in the strategic planning process?
- How do competing values and beliefs affect strategic decision making?
- What skills and capabilities are needed to implement a strategy effectively?

How does a student of strategic management answer these questions? By strategic case analysis. **Case analysis** simulates the real-world experience that strategic managers and company leaders face as they try to determine how best to run their companies. It places students in the middle of an actual situation and challenges them to figure out what to do.[1]

case analysis a method of learning complex strategic management concepts—such as environmental analysis, the process of decision making, and implementing strategic actions—through placing students in the middle of an actual situation and challenging them to figure out what to do.

Asking the right questions is just the beginning of case analysis. In the previous chapters we have discussed issues and challenges that managers face and provided analytical frameworks for understanding the situation. But once the analysis is complete, decisions have to be made. Case analysis forces you to choose among different options and set forth a plan of action based on your choices. But even then the job is not done. Strategic case analysis also requires that you address how you will implement the plan and the implications of choosing one course of action over another.

A strategic management case is a detailed description of a challenging situation faced by an organization.[2] It usually includes a chronology of events and extensive support materials, such as financial statements, product lists, and transcripts of interviews with employees. Although names or locations are sometimes changed to provide anonymity, cases usually report the facts of a situation as authentically as possible.

One of the main reasons to analyze strategic management cases is to develop an ability to evaluate business situations critically. In case analysis, memorizing key terms and conceptual frameworks is not enough. To analyze a case, it is important that you go beyond textbook prescriptions and quick answers. It requires you to look deeply into the information that is provided and root out the essential issues and causes of a company's problems.

>LO13.2

How analyzing strategic management cases can help develop the ability to differentiate, speculate, and integrate when evaluating complex business problems.

The types of skills that are required to prepare an effective strategic case analysis can benefit you in actual business situations. Case analysis adds to the overall learning experience by helping you acquire or improve skills that may not be taught in a typical lecture course. Three capabilities that can be learned by conducting case analysis are especially useful to strategic managers—the ability to differentiate, speculate, and integrate.[3] Here's how case analysis can enhance those skills.

1. **Differentiate.** Effective strategic management requires that many different elements of a situation be evaluated at once. This is also true in case analysis. When analyzing cases, it is important to isolate critical facts, evaluate whether assumptions are useful or faulty, and distinguish between good and bad information. Differentiating between the factors that are influencing the situation presented by a case is necessary for making a good analysis. Strategic management also involves understanding that problems are often complex and multilayered. This applies to case analysis as well. Ask whether the case deals with operational, business-level, or corporate issues. Do the problems stem from weaknesses in the internal value chain or threats in

the external environment? Dig deep. Being too quick to accept the easiest or least controversial answer will usually fail to get to the heart of the problem.

2. *Speculate.* Strategic managers need to be able to use their imagination to envision an explanation or solution that might not readily be apparent. The same is true with case analysis. Being able to imagine different scenarios or contemplate the outcome of a decision can aid the analysis. Managers also have to deal with uncertainty since most decisions are made without complete knowledge of the circumstances. This is also true in case analysis. Case materials often seem to be missing data or the information provided is contradictory. The ability to speculate about details that are unknown or the consequences of an action can be helpful.

3. *Integrate.* Strategy involves looking at the big picture and having an organization-wide perspective. Strategic case analysis is no different. Even though the chapters in this textbook divide the material into various topics that may apply to different parts of an organization, all of this information must be integrated into one set of recommendations that will affect the whole company. A strategic manager needs to comprehend how all the factors that influence the organization will interact. This also applies to case analysis. Changes made in one part of the organization affect other parts. Thus, a holistic perspective that integrates the impact of various decisions and environmental influences on all parts of the organization is needed.

In business, these three activities sometimes "compete" with each other for your attention. For example, some decision makers may have a natural ability to differentiate among elements of a problem but are not able to integrate them very well. Others have enough innate creativity to imagine solutions or fill in the blanks when information is missing. But they may have a difficult time when faced with hard numbers or cold facts. Even so, each of these skills is important. The mark of a good strategic manager is the ability to simultaneously make distinctions and envision the whole, and to imagine a future scenario while staying focused on the present. Thus, another reason to conduct case analysis is

to help you develop and exercise your ability to differentiate, speculate, and integrate.

Case analysis takes the student through the whole cycle of activity that a manager would face. Beyond the textbook descriptions of concepts and examples, case analysis asks you to "walk a mile in the shoes" of the strategic decision maker and learn to evaluate situations critically. Executives and owners must make decisions every day with limited information and a swirl of business activity going on around them. Consider the example of Sapient Health Network, an Internet start-up that had to undergo some analysis and problem solving just to survive. Strategy Spotlight 13.1 describes how this company transformed itself after a serious self-examination during a time of crisis.

As you can see from the experience of Sapient Health Network, businesses are often faced with immediate challenges that threaten their lives. The Sapient case illustrates how the strategic management process helped it survive. First, the company realistically assessed the environment, evaluated the marketplace, and analyzed its resources. Then it made tough decisions, which included shifting its market focus, hiring and firing, and redeploying its assets. Finally, it took action. The result was not only firm survival, but also a quick turnaround leading to rapid success.

How to Conduct a Case Analysis

>LO13.3
The steps involved in conducting a strategic management case analysis.

The process of analyzing strategic management cases involves several steps. In this section we will review the mechanics of preparing a case analysis. Before beginning, there are two things to keep in mind that will clarify your understanding of the process and make the results of the process more meaningful.

Analysis, Decision Making, and Change at Sapient Health Network

Sapient Health Network (SHN) had gotten off to a good start. CEO Jim Kean and his two cofounders had raised $5 million in investor capital to launch their vision: an Internet-based health care information subscription service. The idea was to create an Internet community for people suffering from chronic diseases. It would provide members with expert information, resources, a message board, and chat rooms so that people suffering from the same ailments could provide each other with information and support. "Who would be more voracious consumers of information than people who are faced with life-changing, life-threatening illnesses?" thought Bill Kelly, one of SHN's cofounders. Initial market research and beta tests had supported that view.

During the beta tests, however, the service had been offered for free. The troubles began when SHN tried to convert its trial subscribers into paying ones. Fewer than 5 percent signed on, far less than the 15 percent the company had projected. Sapient hired a vice president of marketing who launched an aggressive promotion, but after three months of campaigning SHN still had only 500 members. SHN was now burning through $400,000 per month, with little revenue to show for it.

At that point, according to SHN board member Susan Clymer, "there was a lot of scrambling around trying to figure out how we could wring value out of what we'd already accomplished." One thing SHN had created was

an expert software system which had two components: an "intelligent profile engine" (IPE) and an "intelligent query engine" (IQE). SHN used this system to collect detailed information from its subscribers.

SHN was sure that the expert system was its biggest selling point. But how could they use it? Then the founders remembered that the original business plan had suggested there might be a market for aggregate data about patient populations gathered from the website. Could they turn the business around by selling patient data? To analyze the possibility, Kean tried out the idea on the market research arm of a huge East Coast health care conglomerate. The officials were intrigued. SHN realized that its expert system could become a market research tool.

Once the analysis was completed, the founders made the decision: They would still create Internet communities for chronically ill patients, but the service would be free. And they would transform SHN from a company that processed subscriptions to one that sold market research.

Finally, they enacted the changes. Some of it was painful, including laying off 18 employees. Instead, SHN needed more health care industry expertise. It even hired an interim CEO, Craig Davenport, a 25-year veteran of the industry, to steer the company in its new direction. Finally, SHN had to communicate a new message to its members. It began by reimbursing the $10,000 of subscription fees they had paid.

All of this paid off dramatically in a matter of just two years. Revenues jumped to $1.9 million and early in the third year, SHN was purchased by WebMD. Less than a year after that, WebMD merged with Healtheon. The combined company still operates a thriving office out of SHN's original location in Portland, Oregon.

Sources: Ferguson, S. 2007. Health Care Gets a Better IT Prescription. *Baseline, www.baselinemag.com*, May 24. Brenneman, K. 2000. Healtheon/WebMD's Local Office Is Thriving. *Business Journal of Portland,* June 2; Raths, D. 1998. Reversal of Fortune. *Inc. Technology,* 2: 52–62.

First, unless you prepare for a case discussion, there is little you can gain from the discussion and even less that you can offer. Effective strategic managers don't enter into problem-solving situations without doing some homework—investigating the situation, analyzing and researching possible solutions, and sometimes gathering the advice of others. Good problem solving often requires that decision makers be immersed in the facts, options, and implications surrounding the problem. In case analysis, this means reading and thoroughly comprehending the case materials before trying to make an analysis.

The second point is related to the first. To get the most out of a case analysis you must place yourself "inside" the case—that is, think like an actual participant in the case situation. However, there are several positions you can take. These are discussed in the following paragraphs:

- *Strategic decision maker.* This is the position of the senior executive responsible for resolving the situation described in the case. It may be the CEO, the business owner, or a strategic manager in a key executive position.

- **Board of directors.** Since the board of directors represents the owners of a corporation, it has a responsibility to step in when a management crisis threatens the company. As a board member, you may be in a unique position to solve problems.
- **Outside consultant.** Either the board or top management may decide to bring in outsiders. Consultants often have an advantage because they can look at a situation objectively. But they also may be at a disadvantage since they have no power to enforce changes.

Before beginning the analysis, it may be helpful to envision yourself assuming one of these roles. Then, as you study and analyze the case materials, you can make a diagnosis and recommend solutions in a way that is consistent with your position. Try different perspectives. You may find that your view of the situation changes depending on the role you play. As an outside consultant, for example, it may be easy for you to conclude that certain individuals should be replaced in order to solve a problem presented in the case. However, if you take the role of the CEO who knows the individuals and the challenges they have been facing, you may be reluctant to fire them and will seek another solution instead.

The idea of assuming a particular role is similar to the real world in various ways. In your career, you may work in an organization where outside accountants, bankers, lawyers, or other professionals are advising you about how to resolve business situations or improve your practices. Their perspective will be different from yours but it is useful to understand things from their point of view. Conversely, you may work as a member of the audit team of an accounting firm or the loan committee of a bank. In those situations, it would be helpful if you understood the situation from the perspective of the business leader who must weigh your views against all the other advice that he or she receives. Case analysis can help develop an ability to appreciate such multiple perspectives.

One of the most challenging roles to play in business is as a business founder or owner. For small businesses or entrepreneurial start-ups, the founder may wear all hats at once—key decision maker, primary stockholder, and CEO. Hiring an outside consultant may not be an option. However, the issues faced by young firms and established firms are often not that different, especially when it comes to formulating a plan of action. Business plans that entrepreneurial firms use to raise money or propose a business expansion typically revolve around a few key issues that must be addressed no matter what the size or age of the business. Strategy Spotlight 13.2 reviews business planning issues that are most important to consider when evaluating any case, especially from the perspective of the business founder or owner.

Next we will review five steps to follow when conducting a strategic management case analysis: becoming familiar with the material, identifying the problems, analyzing the strategic issues using the tools and insights of strategic management, proposing alternative solutions, and making recommendations.[4]

Become Familiar with the Material

Written cases often include a lot of material. They may be complex and include detailed financials or long passages. Even so, to understand a case and its implications, you must become familiar with its content. Sometimes key information is not immediately apparent. It may be contained in the footnotes to an exhibit or an interview with a lower-level employee. In other cases the important points may be difficult to grasp because the subject matter is so unfamiliar. When you approach a strategic case try the following technique to enhance comprehension:

- Read quickly through the case one time to get an overall sense of the material.
- Use the initial read-through to assess possible links to strategic concepts.
- Read through the case again, in depth. Make written notes as you read.

Using a Business Plan Framework to Analyze Strategic Cases

Established businesses often have to change what they are doing in order to improve their competitive position or sometimes simply to survive. To make the changes effectively, businesses usually need a plan. Business plans are no longer just for entrepreneurs. The kind of market analysis, decision making, and action planning that is considered standard practice among new ventures can also benefit going concerns that want to make changes, seize an opportunity, or head in a new direction.

The best business plans, however, are not those loaded with decades of month-by-month financial projections or that depend on rigid adherence to a schedule of events that is impossible to predict. The good ones are focused on four factors that are critical to new-venture success. These same factors are important in case analysis as well because they get to the heart of many of the problems found in strategic cases.

1. *The People.* "When I receive a business plan, I always read the résumé section first," says Harvard Professor William Sahlman. The people questions that are critically important to investors include: What are their skills? How much experience do they have? What is their reputation? Have they worked together as a team? These same questions also may be used in case analysis to evaluate the role of individuals in the strategic case.

2. *The Opportunity.* Business opportunities come in many forms. They are not limited to new ventures.

Sources: Wasserman, E. 2003. A Simple Plan. *MBA Jungle,* February: 50–55; DeKluyver, C. A. 2000. *Strategic Thinking: An Executive Perspective.* Upper Saddle River, NJ: Prentice Hall; and Sahlman, W. A. 1997. How to Write a Great Business Plan. *Harvard Business Review,* 75(4): 98–108.

The chance to enter new markets, introduce new products, or merge with a competitor provides many of the challenges that are found in strategic management cases. What are the consequences of such actions? Will the proposed changes affect the firm's business concept? What factors might stand in the way of success? The same issues are also present in most strategic cases.

3. *The Context.* Things happen in contexts that cannot be controlled by a firm's managers. This is particularly true of the general environment where social trends, economic changes, or events such as the September 11, 2001, terrorist attacks can change business overnight. When evaluating strategic cases, ask: Is the company aware of the impact of context on the business? What will it do if the context changes? Can it influence the context in a way that favors the company?

4. *Risk and Reward.* With a new venture, the entrepreneurs and investors take the risks and get the rewards. In strategic cases, the risks and rewards often extend to many other stakeholders, such as employees, customers, and suppliers. When analyzing a case, ask: Are the managers making choices that will pay off in the future? Are the rewards evenly distributed? Will some stakeholders be put at risk if the situation in the case changes? What if the situation remains the same? Could that be even riskier?

Whether a business is growing or shrinking, large or small, industrial or service oriented, the issues of people, opportunities, context, and risks and rewards will have a large impact on its performance. Therefore, you should always consider these four factors when evaluating strategic management cases.

- Evaluate how strategic concepts might inform key decisions or suggest alternative solutions.
- After formulating an initial recommendation, thumb through the case again quickly to help assess the consequences of the actions you propose.

Identify Problems

When conducting case analysis, one of your most important tasks is to identify the problem. Earlier we noted that one of the main reasons to conduct case analysis was to find solutions. But you cannot find a solution unless you know the problem. Another saying you may have heard is, "A good diagnosis is half the cure." In other words, once you have determined what the problem is, you are well on your way to identifying a reasonable solution.

Some cases have more than one problem. But the problems are usually related. For a hypothetical example, consider the following: Company A was losing customers to a new competitor. Upon analysis, it was determined that the competitor had a 50 percent faster delivery time even though its product was of lower quality. The managers of company A could not understand why customers would settle for an inferior product. It turns out that no one was marketing to company A's customers that its product was superior. A second problem was that falling sales resulted in cuts in company A's sales force. Thus, there were two related problems: inferior delivery technology and insufficient sales effort.

When trying to determine the problem, avoid getting hung up on symptoms. Zero in on the problem. For example, in the company A example above, the symptom was losing customers. But the problems were an underfunded, understaffed sales force combined with an outdated delivery technology. Try to see beyond the immediate symptoms to the more fundamental problems.

case symptoms
observable and concrete information in a case analysis that indicates an undesirable state of affairs.

Another tip when preparing a case analysis is to articulate the problem.[5] Writing down a problem statement gives you a reference point to turn to as you proceed through the case analysis. This is important because the process of formulating strategies or evaluating implementation methods may lead you away from the initial problem. Make sure your recommendation actually addresses the problems you have identified.

case problems
inferred causes of case symptoms.

One more thing about identifying problems: Sometimes problems are not apparent until *after* you do the analysis. In some cases the problem will be presented plainly, perhaps in the opening paragraph or on the last page of the case. But in other cases the problem does not emerge until after the issues in the case have been analyzed. We turn next to the subject of strategic case analysis.

Conduct Strategic Analyses

This textbook has presented numerous analytical tools (e.g., five-forces analysis and value-chain analysis), contingency frameworks (e.g., when to use related rather than unrelated diversification strategies), and other techniques that can be used to evaluate strategic situations. The previous 12 chapters have addressed practices that are common in strategic management, but only so much can be learned by studying the practices and concepts. The best way to understand these methods is to apply them by conducting analyses of specific cases.

The first step is to determine which strategic issues are involved. Is there a problem in the company's competitive environment? Or is it an internal problem? If it is internal, does it have to do with organizational structure? Strategic controls? Uses of technology? Or perhaps the company has overworked its employees or underutilized its intellectual capital. Has the company mishandled a merger? Chosen the wrong diversification strategy? Botched a new product introduction? Each of these issues is linked to one or more of the concepts discussed earlier in the text. Determine what strategic issues are associated with the problems you have identified. Remember also that most real-life case situations involve issues that are highly interrelated. Even in cases where there is only one major problem, the strategic processes required to solve it may involve several parts of the organization.

Once you have identified the issues that apply to the case, conduct the analysis. For example, you may need to conduct a five-forces analysis or dissect the company's competitive strategy. Perhaps you need to evaluate whether its resources are rare, valuable, difficult to imitate, or difficult to substitute. Financial analysis may be needed to assess the company's economic prospects. Perhaps the international entry mode needs to be reevaluated because of changing conditions in the host country. Employee empowerment techniques may need to be improved to enhance organizational learning. Whatever the case, all the strategic concepts introduced in the text include insights for assessing their effectiveness. Determining how well a company is doing these things is central to the case analysis process.

Financial ratio analysis is one of the primary tools used to conduct case analysis. Appendix 1 to Chapter 13 includes a discussion and examples of the financial ratios that are often used to evaluate a company's performance and financial well-being. Exhibit 13.1 provides a summary of the financial ratios presented in Appendix 1 to this chapter.

In this part of the overall strategic analysis process, it is also important to test your own assumptions about the case.[6] First, what assumptions are you making about the case materials? It may be that you have interpreted the case content differently than your team members or classmates. Being clear about these assumptions will be important in determining how to analyze the case. Second, what assumptions have you made about the best way to resolve the problems? Ask yourself why you have chosen one type of analysis over another. This process of assumption checking can also help determine if you have gotten to the heart of the problem or are still just dealing with symptoms.

Exhibit 13.1   Summary of Financial Ratio Analysis Techniques

Ratio	What It Measures
Short-term solvency, or liquidity, ratios:	
Current ratio	Ability to use assets to pay off liabilities.
Quick ratio	Ability to use liquid assets to pay off liabilities quickly.
Cash ratio	Ability to pay off liabilities with cash on hand.
Long-term solvency, or financial leverage, ratios:	
Total debt ratio	How much of a company's total assets are financed by debt.
Debt-equity ratio	Compares how much a company is financed by debt with how much it is financed by equity.
Equity multiplier	How much debt is being used to finance assets.
Times interest earned ratio	How well a company has its interest obligations covered.
Cash coverage ratio	A company's ability to generate cash from operations.
Asset utilization, or turnover, ratios:	
Inventory turnover	How many times each year a company sells its entire inventory.
Days' sales in inventory	How many days on average inventory is on hand before it is sold.
Receivables turnover	How frequently each year a company collects on its credit sales.
Days' sales in receivables	How many days on average it takes to collect on credit sales (average collection period).
Total asset turnover	How much of sales is generated for every dollar in assets.
Capital intensity	The dollar investment in assets needed to generate $1 in sales.
Profitability ratios:	
Profit margin	How much profit is generated by every dollar of sales.
Return on assets (ROA)	How effectively assets are being used to generate a return.
Return on equity (ROE)	How effectively amounts invested in the business by its owners are being used to generate a return.
Market value ratios:	
Price-earnings ratio	How much investors are willing to pay per dollar of current earnings.
Market-to-book ratio	Compares market value of the company's investments to the cost of those investments.

As mentioned earlier, sometimes the critical diagnosis in a case can only be made after the analysis is conducted. However, by the end of this stage in the process, you should know the problems and have completed a thorough analysis of them. You can now move to the next step: finding solutions.

Propose Alternative Solutions

It is important to remember that in strategic management case analysis, there is rarely one right answer or one best way. Even when members of a class or a team agree on what the problem is, they may not agree upon how to solve the problem. Therefore, it is helpful to consider several different solutions.

After conducting strategic analysis and identifying the problem, develop a list of options. What are the possible solutions? What are the alternatives? First, generate a list of all the options you can think of without prejudging any one of them. Remember that not all cases call for dramatic decisions or sweeping changes. Some companies just need to make small adjustments. In fact, "Do nothing" may be a reasonable alternative in some cases. Although that is rare, it might be useful to consider what will happen if the company does nothing. This point illustrates the purpose of developing alternatives: to evaluate what will happen if a company chooses one solution over another.

Thus, during this step of a case analysis, you will evaluate choices and the implications of those choices. One aspect of any business that is likely to be highlighted in this part of the analysis is strategy implementation. Ask how the choices made will be implemented. It may be that what seems like an obvious choice for solving a problem creates an even bigger problem when implemented. But remember also that no strategy or strategic "fix" is going to work if it cannot be implemented. Once a list of alternatives is generated, ask:

- Can the company afford it? How will it affect the bottom line?
- Is the solution likely to evoke a competitive response?
- Will employees throughout the company accept the changes? What impact will the solution have on morale?
- How will the decision affect other stakeholders? Will customers, suppliers, and others buy into it?
- How does this solution fit with the company's vision, mission, and objectives?
- Will the culture or values of the company be changed by the solution? Is it a positive change?

The point of this step in the case analysis process is to find a solution that both solves the problem and is realistic. A consideration of the implications of various alternative solutions will generally lead you to a final recommendation that is more thoughtful and complete.

Make Recommendations

The basic aim of case analysis is to find solutions. Your analysis is not complete until you have recommended a course of action. In this step the task is to make a set of recommendations that your analysis supports. Describe exactly what needs to be done. Explain why this course of action will solve the problem. The recommendation should also include suggestions for how best to implement the proposed solution because the recommended actions and their implications for the performance and future of the firm are interrelated.

Recall that the solution you propose must solve the problem you identified. This point cannot be overemphasized; too often students make recommendations that treat only symptoms or fail to tackle the central problems in the case. Make a logical argument that shows how the problem led to the analysis and the analysis led to the recommendations you are proposing. Remember, an analysis is not an end in itself; it is useful only if it leads to a solution.

The actions you propose should describe the very next steps that the company needs to take. Don't say, for example, "If the company does more market research, then I would recommend the following course of action. . . ." Instead, make conducting the research part of your recommendation. Taking the example a step further, if you also want to suggest subsequent actions that may be different *depending* on the outcome of the market research, that's OK. But don't make your initial recommendation conditional on actions the company may or may not take.

In summary, case analysis can be a very rewarding process but, as you might imagine, it can also be frustrating and challenging. If you will follow the steps described above, you will address the different elements of a thorough analysis. This approach can give your analysis a solid footing. Then, even if there are differences of opinion about how to interpret the facts, analyze the situation, or solve the problems, you can feel confident that you have not missed any important steps in finding the best course of action.

Students are often asked to prepare oral presentations of the information in a case and their analysis of the best remedies. This is frequently assigned as a group project. Or you may be called upon in class to present your ideas about the circumstances or solutions for a case the class is discussing. Exhibit 13.2 provides some tips for preparing an oral case presentation.

How to Get the Most from Case Analysis

>LO13.4
How to get the most out of case analysis.

One of the reasons case analysis is so enriching as a learning tool is that it draws on many resources and skills besides just what is in the textbook. This is especially true in the study of strategy. Why? Because strategic management itself is a highly integrative task that draws on many areas of specialization at several levels, from the individual to the whole of society. Therefore, to get the most out of case analysis, expand your horizons beyond the concepts in this text and seek insights from your own reservoir of knowledge. Here are some tips for how to do that.[7]

- *Keep an open mind.* Like any good discussion, a case analysis discussion often evokes strong opinions and high emotions. But it's the variety of perspectives that makes case analysis so valuable: Many viewpoints usually lead to a more complete analysis. Therefore, avoid letting an emotional response to another person's style or opinion keep you from hearing what he or she has to say. Once you evaluate what is said, you may disagree with it or dismiss it as faulty. But unless you keep an open mind in the first place, you may miss the importance of the other person's contribution. Also, people often place a higher value on the opinions of those they consider to be good listeners.
- *Take a stand for what you believe.* Although it is vital to keep an open mind, it is also important to state your views proactively. Don't try to figure out what your friends or the instructor wants to hear. Analyze the case from the perspective of your own background and belief system. For example, perhaps you feel that a decision is unethical or that the managers in a case have misinterpreted the facts. Don't be afraid to assert that in the discussion. For one thing, when a person takes a strong stand, it often encourages others to evaluate the issues more closely. This can lead to a more thorough investigation and a more meaningful class discussion.
- *Draw on your personal experience.* You may have experiences from work or as a customer that shed light on some of the issues in a case. Even though one of the purposes of case analysis is to apply the analytical tools from this text, you may be able to add to the discussion by drawing on your outside experiences and background. Of course, you need to guard against carrying that to extremes. In other words, don't think that your perspective is the only viewpoint that matters! Simply recognize that

Exhibit 13.2 **Preparing an Oral Case Presentation**

Rule	Description
Organize your thoughts.	Begin by becoming familiar with the material. If you are working with a team, compare notes about the key points of the case and share insights that other team members may have gleaned from tables and exhibits. Then make an outline. This is one of the best ways to organize the flow and content of the presentation.
Emphasize strategic analysis.	The purpose of case analysis is to diagnose problems and find solutions. In the process, you may need to unravel the case material as presented and reconfigure it in a fashion that can be more effectively analyzed. Present the material in a way that lends itself to analysis—don't simply restate what is in the case. This involves three major categories with the following emphasis:

	Background/Problem Statement	10–20%
	Strategic Analysis/Options	60–75%
	Recommendations/Action Plan	10–20%

	As you can see, the emphasis of your presentation should be on analysis. This will probably require you to reorganize the material so that the tools of strategic analysis can be applied.
Be logical and consistent.	A presentation that is rambling and hard to follow may confuse the listener and fail to evoke a good discussion. Present your arguments and explanations in a logical sequence. Support your claims with facts. Include financial analysis where appropriate. Be sure that the solutions you recommend address the problems you have identified.
Defend your position.	Usually an oral presentation is followed by a class discussion. Anticipate what others might disagree with and be prepared to defend your views. This means being aware of the choices you made and the implications of your recommendations. Be clear about your assumptions. Be able to expand on your analysis.
Share presentation responsibilities.	Strategic management case analyses are often conducted by teams. Each member of the team should have a clear role in the oral presentation, preferably a speaking role. It's also important to coordinate the different parts of the presentation into a logical, smooth-flowing whole. How well a team works together is usually very apparent during an oral presentation.

firsthand experience usually represents a welcome contribution to the overall quality of case discussions.

- ***Participate and persuade.*** Have you heard the phrase, "Vote early . . . and often"? Among loyal members of certain political parties, it has become rather a joke. Why? Because a democratic system is built on the concept of one person, one vote. Even though some voters may want to vote often enough to get their candidate elected, it is against the law. Not so in a case discussion. People who are persuasive and speak their mind can often influence the views of others. But to do so, you have to be prepared and convincing. Being persuasive is more than being loud or long-winded. It involves understanding all sides of an argument and being able to overcome objections to your own point of view. These efforts can make a case discussion more lively. And they parallel what happens in the real world; in business, people frequently share their opinions and attempt to persuade others to see things their way.

- *Be concise and to the point.* In the previous point, we encouraged you to speak up and "sell" your ideas to others in a case discussion. But you must be clear about what you are selling. Make your arguments in a way that is explicit and direct. Zero in on the most important points. Be brief. Don't try to make a lot of points at once by jumping around between topics. Avoid trying to explain the whole case situation at once. Remember, other students usually resent classmates who go on and on, take up a lot of "airtime," or repeat themselves unnecessarily. The best way to avoid this is to stay focused and be specific.

- *Think out of the box.* It's OK to be a little provocative; sometimes that is the consequence of taking a stand on issues. But it may be equally important to be imaginative and creative when making a recommendation or determining how to implement a solution. Albert Einstein once stated, "Imagination is more important than knowledge." The reason is that managing strategically requires more than memorizing concepts. Strategic management insights must be applied to each case differently—just knowing the principles is not enough. Imagination and out-of-the-box thinking help to apply strategic knowledge in novel and unique ways.

- *Learn from the insights of others.* Before you make up your mind about a case, hear what other students have to say. Get a second opinion, and a third, and so forth. Of course, in a situation where you have to put your analysis in writing, you may not be able to learn from others ahead of time. But in a case discussion, observe how various students attack the issues and engage in problem solving. Such observation skills also may be a key to finding answers within the case. For example, people tend to believe authority figures, so they would place a higher value on what a company president says. In some cases, however, the statements of middle managers may represent a point of view that is even more helpful for finding a solution to the problems presented by the case.

- *Apply insights from other case analyses.* Throughout the text, we have used examples of actual businesses to illustrate strategy concepts. The aim has been to show you how firms think about and deal with business problems. During the course, you may be asked to conduct several case analyses as part of the learning experience. Once you have performed a few case analyses, you will see how the concepts from the text apply in real-life business situations. Incorporate the insights learned from the text examples and your own previous case discussions into each new case that you analyze.

- *Critically analyze your own performance.* Performance appraisals are a standard part of many workplace situations. They are used to determine promotions, raises, and work assignments. In some organizations, everyone from the top executive down is subject to such reviews. Even in situations where the owner or CEO is not evaluated by others, they often find it useful to ask themselves regularly, Am I being effective? The same can be applied to your performance in a case analysis situation. Ask yourself, Were my comments insightful? Did I make a good contribution? How might I improve next time? Use the same criteria on yourself that you use to evaluate others. What grade would you give yourself? This technique will not only make you more fair in your assessment of others but also will indicate how your own performance can improve.

- *Conduct outside research.* Many times, you can enhance your understanding of a case situation by investigating sources outside the case materials. For example, you may want to study an industry more closely or research a company's close competitors. Recent moves such as mergers and acquisitions or product introductions may be reported in the business press. The company itself may provide useful information on its website or in its annual reports. Such information can usually spur additional discussion and enrich the case analysis. (*Caution:* It is best to check with your instructor in advance to be sure this kind of additional research is encouraged. Bringing in outside research may conflict with the instructor's learning objectives.)

Several of the points suggested above for how to get the most out of case analysis apply only to an open discussion of a case, like that in a classroom setting. Exhibit 13.3 provides some additional guidelines for preparing a written case analysis.

Using Conflict-Inducing Decision-Making Techniques in Case Analysis

>LO13.5
How conflict-inducing discussion techniques can lead to better decisions.

Next we address some techniques often used to improve case analyses that involve the constructive use of conflict. In the classroom—as well as in the business world—you will

Exhibit 13.3 Preparing a Written Case Analysis

Rule	Description
Be thorough.	Many of the ideas presented in Exhibit 13.2 about oral presentations also apply to written case analysis. However, a written analysis typically has to be more complete. This means writing out the problem statement and articulating assumptions. It is also important to provide support for your arguments and reference case materials or other facts more specifically.
Coordinate team efforts.	Written cases are often prepared by small groups. Within a group, just as in a class discussion, you may disagree about the diagnosis or the recommended plan of action. This can be healthy if it leads to a richer understanding of the case material. But before committing your ideas to writing, make sure you have coordinated your responses. Don't prepare a written analysis that appears contradictory or looks like a patchwork of disconnected thoughts.
Avoid restating the obvious.	There is no reason to restate material that everyone is familiar with already, namely, the case content. It is too easy for students to use up space in a written analysis with a recapitulation of the details of the case—this accomplishes very little. Stay focused on the key points. Only restate the information that is most central to your analysis.
Present information graphically.	Tables, graphs, and other exhibits are usually one of the best ways to present factual material that supports your arguments. For example, financial calculations such as break-even analysis, sensitivity analysis, or return on investment are best presented graphically. Even qualitative information such as product lists or rosters of employees can be summarized effectively and viewed quickly by using a table or graph.
Exercise quality control.	When presenting a case analysis in writing, it is especially important to use good grammar, avoid misspelling words, and eliminate typos and other visual distractions. Mistakes that can be glossed over in an oral presentation or class discussion are often highlighted when they appear in writing. Make your written presentation appear as professional as possible. Don't let the appearance of your written case keep the reader from recognizing the importance and quality of your analysis.

frequently be analyzing cases or solving problems in groups. While the word *conflict* often has a negative connotation (e.g., rude behavior, personal affronts), it can be very helpful in arriving at better solutions to cases. It can provide an effective means for new insights as well as for rigorously questioning and analyzing assumptions and strategic alternatives. In fact, if you don't have constructive conflict, you may only get consensus. When this happens, decisions tend to be based on compromise rather than collaboration.

In your organizational behavior classes, you probably learned the concept of "groupthink."[8] Groupthink, a term coined by Irving Janis after he conducted numerous studies on executive decision making, is a condition in which group members strive to reach agreement or consensus without realistically considering other viable alternatives. In effect, group norms bolster morale at the expense of critical thinking and decision making is impaired.[9]

Many of us have probably been "victims" of groupthink at one time or another in our life. We may be confronted with situations when social pressure, politics, or "not wanting to stand out" may prevent us from voicing our concerns about a chosen course of action. Nevertheless, decision making in groups is a common practice in the management of many businesses. Most companies, especially large ones, rely on input from various top managers to provide valuable information and experience from their specialty area as well as their unique perspectives. Chapter 11 emphasized the importance of empowering individuals at all levels to participate in decision-making processes. In terms of this course, case analysis involves a type of decision making that is often conducted in groups. Strategy Spotlight 13.3 provides guidelines for making team-based approaches to case analysis more effective.

● Effectively working in teams is a critical skill— both in the classroom and in business organizations.

Clearly, understanding how to work in groups and the potential problems associated with group decision processes can benefit the case analysis process. Therefore, let's first look at some of the symptoms of groupthink and suggest ways of preventing it. Then, we will suggest some conflict-inducing decision-making techniques—devil's advocacy and dialectical inquiry—that can help to prevent groupthink and lead to better decisions.

Symptoms of Groupthink and How to Prevent It

Irving Janis identified several symptoms of groupthink, including:

- *An illusion of invulnerability.* This reassures people about possible dangers and leads to overoptimism and failure to heed warnings of danger.
- *A belief in the inherent morality of the group.* Because individuals think that what they are doing is right, they tend to ignore ethical or moral consequences of their decisions.
- *Stereotyped views of members of opposing groups.* Members of other groups are viewed as weak or not intelligent.
- *The application of pressure to members who express doubts about the group's shared illusions or question the validity of arguments proposed.*
- *The practice of self-censorship.* Members keep silent about their opposing views and downplay to themselves the value of their perspectives.

Making Case Analysis Teams More Effective

Working in teams can be very challenging. Not all team members have the same skills, interests, or motivations. Some team members just want to get the work done. Others see teams as an opportunity to socialize. Occasionally, there are team members who think they should be in charge and make all the decisions; other teams have freeloaders—team members who don't want to do anything except get credit for the team's work.

One consequence of these various styles is that team meetings can become time wasters. Disagreements about how to proceed, how to share the work, or what to do at the next meeting tend to slow down teams and impede progress toward the goal. While the dynamics of case analysis teams are likely to always be challenging depending on the personalities involved, one thing nearly all members realize is that, ultimately, the team's work must be completed. Most team members also aim to do the highest quality work possible. The following guidelines provide some useful insights about how to get the work of a team done more effectively.

Spend More Time Together

One of the factors that prevents teams from doing a good job with case analysis is their failure to put in the necessary time. Unless teams really tackle the issues surrounding case analysis—both the issues in the case itself and organizing how the work is to be conducted—the end result will probably be lacking because decisions that are made too quickly are unlikely to get to the heart of the problem(s) in the case. "Meetings should be a precious resource, but they're treated like a necessary evil," says Kenneth Sole, a consultant who specializes in organizational behavior. As a result, teams that care more about finishing the analysis than getting the analysis right often make poor decisions.

Therefore, expect to have a few meetings that run long, especially at the beginning of the project when the work is being organized and the issues in the case are being sorted out, and again at the end when the team must coordinate the components of the case analysis that will be presented. Without spending this kind of time together, it is doubtful that the analysis will be comprehensive and the presentation is likely to be choppy and incomplete.

Make a Focused and Disciplined Agenda

To complete tasks and avoid wasting time, meetings need to have a clear purpose. To accomplish this at Roche, the Swiss drug and diagnostic product maker, CEO Franz Humer implemented a "decision agenda." The agenda focuses only on Roche's highest value issues and discussions are limited to these major topics. In terms of case analysis, the major topics include sorting out the issues of the case, linking elements of the case to the strategic issues presented in class or the text, and assigning roles to various team members. Such objectives help keep team members on track.

Agendas also can be used to address issues such as the time line for accomplishing work. Otherwise the purpose of meetings may only be to manage the "crisis" of getting the case analysis finished on time. One solution is to assign a team member to manage the agenda. That person could make sure the team stays focused on the tasks at hand and remains mindful of time constraints. Another role could be to link the team's efforts to the steps presented in Exhibits 13.2 and Exhibit 13.3 on how to prepare a case analysis.

Pay More Attention to Strategy

Teams often waste time by focusing on unimportant aspects of a case. These may include details that are interesting but irrelevant or operational issues rather than strategic issues. It is true that useful clues to the issues in the case are sometimes embedded in the conversations of key managers or the trends evident in a financial statement. But once such insights are discovered, teams need to focus on the underlying strategic problems in the case. To solve such problems, major corporations such as Cadbury Schweppes and Boeing hold meetings just to generate strategic alternatives for solving their problems. This gives managers time to consider the implications of various courses of action. Separate meetings are held to evaluate alternatives, make strategic decisions, and approve an action plan.

Once the strategic solutions or "course corrections" are identified—as is common in most cases assigned—the operational implications and details of implementation will flow from the strategic decisions that companies make. Therefore, focusing primarily on strategic issues will provide teams with insights for making recommendations that are based on a deeper understanding of the issues in the case.

Produce Real Decisions

Too often, meetings are about discussing rather than deciding. Teams often spend a lot of time talking without reaching any conclusions. As Raymond Sanchez, CEO of Florida-based Security Mortgage Group, says, meetings are often used to "rehash the hash that's already been hashed." To be efficient and productive, team meetings

(continued)

need to be about more than just information sharing and group input. For example, an initial meeting may result in the team realizing that it needs to study the case in greater depth and examine links to strategic issues more carefully. Once more analysis is conducted, the team needs to reach a consensus so that the decisions that are made will last once the meeting is over. Lasting decisions are more actionable because it frees team members to take the next steps.

One technique for making progress in this way is recapping each meeting with a five-minute synthesis report. According to Pamela Schindler, director of the

Center for Applied Management at Wittenberg University, it's important to think through the implications of the meeting before ending it. "The real joy of synthesis," says Schindler, "is realizing how many meetings you won't need."

Not only are these guidelines useful for helping teams finish their work, but they can also help resolve some of the difficulties that teams often face. By involving every team member, using a meeting agenda, and focusing on the strategic issues that are critical to nearly every case, the discussion is limited and the criteria for making decisions become clearer. This allows the task to dominate rather than any one personality. And if the team finishes its work faster, this frees up time to focus on other projects or put the finishing touches on a case analysis presentation.

Sources: Mankins, M. C. 2004. Stop Wasting Valuable Time. *Harvard Business Review,* September: 58–65; and Sauer, P. J. 2004. Escape from Meeting Hell. *Inc. Magazine,* May, *www.inc.com.*

- *An illusion of unanimity.* People assume that judgments expressed by members are shared by all.
- *The appointment of mindguards.* People sometimes appoint themselves as mindguards to protect the group from adverse information that might break the climate of consensus (or agreement).

Clearly, groupthink is an undesirable and negative phenomenon that can lead to poor decisions. Irving Janis considers it to be a key contributor to such faulty decisions as the failure to prepare for the attack on Pearl Harbor, the escalation of the Vietnam conflict, and the failure to prepare for the consequences of the Iraqi invasion. Many of the same sorts of flawed decision making occur in business organizations—as we discussed above with the EDS example. Janis has provided several suggestions for preventing groupthink that can be used as valuable guides in decision making and problem solving:

- Leaders must encourage group members to address their concerns and objectives.
- When higher-level managers assign a problem for a group to solve, they should adopt an impartial stance and not mention their preferences.
- Before a group reaches its final decision, the leader should encourage members to discuss their deliberations with trusted associates and then report the perspectives back to the group.
- The group should invite outside experts and encourage them to challenge the group's viewpoints and positions.
- The group should divide into subgroups, meet at various times under different chairpersons, and then get together to resolve differences.
- After reaching a preliminary agreement, the group should hold a "second chance" meeting which provides members a forum to express any remaining concerns and rethink the issue prior to making a final decision.

Using Conflict to Improve Decision Making

In addition to the above suggestions, the effective use of conflict can be a means of improving decision making. Although conflict can have negative outcomes, such as ill will, anger, tension, and lowered motivation, both leaders and group members must strive to assure that it is managed properly and used in a constructive manner.

Two conflict-inducing decision-making approaches that have become quite popular are *devil's advocacy* and *dialectical inquiry.* Both approaches incorporate conflict into the decision-making process through formalized debate. A group charged with making a decision or solving a problem is divided into two subgroups and each will be involved in the analysis and solution.

Devil's Advocacy   With the devil's advocate approach, one of the groups (or individuals) acts as a critic to the plan. The devil's advocate tries to come up with problems with the proposed alternative and suggest reasons why it should not be adopted. The role of the devil's advocate is to create dissonance. This ensures that the group will take a hard look at its original proposal or alternative. By having a group (or individual) assigned the role of devil's advocate, it becomes clear that such an adversarial stance is legitimized. It brings out criticisms that might otherwise not be made.

Some authors have suggested that the use of a devil's advocate can be very helpful in helping boards of directors to ensure that decisions are addressed comprehensively and to avoid groupthink.[10] And Charles Elson, a director of Sunbeam Corporation, has argued that:

> Devil's advocates are terrific in any situation because they help you to figure a decision's numerous implications. . . . The better you think out the implications prior to making the decision, the better the decision ultimately turns out to be. That's why a devil's advocate is always a great person, irritating sometimes, but a great person.

As one might expect, there can be some potential problems with using the devil's advocate approach. If one's views are constantly criticized, one may become demoralized. Thus, that person may come up with "safe solutions" in order to minimize embarrassment or personal risk and become less subject to criticism. Additionally, even if the devil's advocate is successful with finding problems with the proposed course of action, there may be no new ideas or counterproposals to take its place. Thus, the approach sometimes may simply focus on what is wrong without suggesting other ideas.

Dialectical Inquiry   Dialectical inquiry attempts to accomplish the goals of the devil's advocate in a more constructive manner. It is a technique whereby a problem is approached from two alternative points of view. The idea is that out of a critique of the opposing perspectives—a thesis and an antithesis—a creative synthesis will occur. Dialectical inquiry involves the following steps:

1. Identify a proposal and the information that was used to derive it.
2. State the underlying assumptions of the proposal.
3. Identify a counterplan (antithesis) that is believed to be feasible, politically viable, and generally credible. However, it rests on assumptions that are opposite to the original proposal.
4. Engage in a debate in which individuals favoring each plan provide their arguments and support.
5. Identify a synthesis which, hopefully, includes the best components of each alternative.

There are some potential downsides associated with dialectical inquiry. It can be quite time consuming and involve a good deal of training. Further, it may result in a series of compromises between the initial proposal and the counterplan. In cases where the original proposal was the best approach, this would be unfortunate.

● Conflict-inducing decision-making techniques, such as devil's advocacy, can be very effective.

devil's advocacy a method of introducing conflict into a decision-making process by having specific individuals or groups act as a critic to an analysis or planned solution.

dialectical inquiry a method of introducing conflict into a decision-making process by devising different proposals that are feasible, politically viable, and credible, but rely on different assumptions; and debating the merits of each.

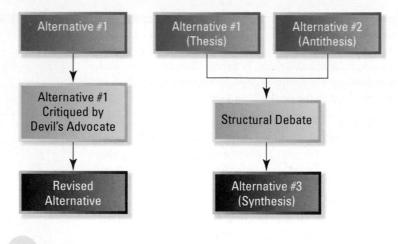

Exhibit 13.4 Two Conflict-Inducing Decision-Making Processes

Despite some possible limitations associated with these conflict-inducing decision-making techniques, they have many benefits. Both techniques force debate about underlying assumptions, data, and recommendations between subgroups. Such debate tends to prevent the uncritical acceptance of a plan that may seem to be satisfactory after a cursory analysis. The approach serves to tap the knowledge and perspectives of group members and continues until group members agree on both assumptions and recommended actions. Given that both approaches serve to use, rather than minimize or suppress, conflict, higher quality decisions should result. Exhibit 13.4 briefly summarizes these techniques.

Following the Analysis-Decision-Action Cycle in Case Analysis

In Chapter 1 we defined strategic management as the analysis, decisions, and actions that organizations undertake to create and sustain competitive advantages. It is no accident that we chose that sequence of words because it corresponds to the sequence of events that typically occurs in the strategic management process. In case analysis, as in the real world, this cycle of events can provide a useful framework. First, an analysis of the case in terms of the business environment and current events is needed. To make such an analysis, the case background must be considered. Next, based on that analysis, decisions must be made. This may involve formulating a strategy, choosing between difficult options, moving forward aggressively, or retreating from a bad situation. There are many possible decisions, depending on the case situation. Finally, action is required. Once decisions are made and plans are set, the action begins. The recommended action steps and the consequences of implementing these actions are the final stage.

>LO13.6
How to use the strategic insights and material from each of the 12 previous chapters in the text to analyze issues posed by strategic management cases.

Each of the previous 12 chapters of this book includes techniques and information that may be useful in a case analysis. However, not all of the issues presented will be important in every case. As noted earlier, one of the challenges of case analysis is to identify the most critical points and sort through material that may be ambiguous or unimportant.

In this section we draw on the material presented in each of the 12 chapters to show how it informs the case analysis process. The ideas are linked sequentially and in terms of an overarching strategic perspective. One of your jobs when conducting case analysis is to see how the parts of a case fit together and how the insights from the study of strategy can help you understand the case situation.

1. ***Analyzing organizational goals and objectives.*** A company's vision, mission, and objectives keep organization members focused on a common purpose. They also influence how an organization deploys its resources, relates to its stakeholders, and matches its short-term objectives with its long-term goals. The goals may even impact how a company formulates and implements strategies. When exploring issues of goals and objectives, you might ask:

   - Has the company developed short-term objectives that are inconsistent with its long-term mission? If so, how can management realign its vision, mission, and objectives?

   - Has the company considered all of its stakeholders equally in making critical decisions? If not, should the views of all stakeholders be treated the same or are some stakeholders more important than others?

   - Is the company being faced with an issue that conflicts with one of its long-standing policies? If so, how should it compare its existing policies to the potential new situation?

2. ***Analyzing the external environment.*** The business environment has two components. The general environment consists of demographic, sociocultural, political/legal, technological, economic, and global conditions. The competitive environment includes rivals, suppliers, customers, and other factors that may directly affect a company's success. Strategic managers must monitor the environment to identify opportunities and threats that may have an impact on performance. When investigating a firm's external environment, you might ask:

   - Does the company follow trends and events in the general environment? If not, how can these influences be made part of the company's strategic analysis process?

   - Is the company effectively scanning and monitoring the competitive environment? If so, how is it using the competitive intelligence it is gathering to enhance its competitive advantage?

   - Has the company correctly analyzed the impact of the competitive forces in its industry on profitability? If so, how can it improve its competitive position relative to these forces?

3. ***Analyzing the internal environment.*** A firm's internal environment consists of its resources and other value-adding capabilities. Value-chain analysis and a resource-based approach to analysis can be used to identify a company's strengths and weaknesses and determine how they are contributing to its competitive advantages. Evaluating firm performance can also help make meaningful comparisons with competitors. When researching a company's internal analysis, you might ask:

   - Does the company know how the various components of its value chain are adding value to the firm? If not, what internal analysis is needed to determine its strengths and weakness?

   - Has the company accurately analyzed the source and vitality of its resources? If so, is it deploying its resources in a way that contributes to competitive advantages?

   - Is the company's financial performance as good as or better than that of its close competitors? If so, has it balanced its financial success with the performance criteria of other stakeholders such as customers and employees?

4. ***Assessing a firm's intellectual assets.*** Human capital is a major resource in today's knowledge economy. As a result, attracting, developing, and retaining talented workers is a key strategic challenge. Other assets such as patents and trademarks are also critical. How companies leverage their intellectual assets through social networks and strategic alliances, and how technology is used to manage knowledge may be a major

influence on a firm's competitive advantage. When analyzing a firm's intellectual assets, you might ask:

- Does the company have underutilized human capital? If so, what steps are needed to develop and leverage its intellectual assets?
- Is the company missing opportunities to forge strategic alliances? If so, how can it use its social capital to network more effectively?
- Has the company developed knowledge-management systems that capture what it learns? If not, what technologies can it employ to retain new knowledge?

5. *Formulating business-level strategies.* Firms use the competitive strategies of differentiation, focus, and overall cost leadership as a basis for overcoming the five competitive forces and developing sustainable competitive advantages. Combinations of these strategies may work best in some competitive environments. Additionally, an industry's life cycle is an important contingency that may affect a company's choice of business-level strategies. When assessing business-level strategies, you might ask:

- Has the company chosen the correct competitive strategy given its industry environment and competitive situation? If not, how should it use its strengths and resources to improve its performance?
- Does the company use combination strategies effectively? If so, what capabilities can it cultivate to further enhance profitability?
- Is the company using a strategy that is appropriate for the industry life cycle in which it is competing? If not, how can it realign itself to match its efforts to the current stage of industry growth?

6. *Formulating corporate-level strategies.* Large firms often own and manage portfolios of businesses. Corporate strategies address methods for achieving synergies among these businesses. Related and unrelated diversification techniques are alternative approaches to deciding which business should be added to or removed from a portfolio. Companies can diversify by means of mergers, acquisitions, joint ventures, strategic alliances, and internal development. When analyzing corporate-level strategies, you might ask:

- Is the company competing in the right businesses given the opportunities and threats that are present in the environment? If not, how can it realign its diversification strategy to achieve competitive advantages?
- Is the corporation managing its portfolio of businesses in a way that creates synergies among the businesses? If so, what additional business should it consider adding to its portfolio?
- Are the motives of the top corporate executives who are pushing diversification strategies appropriate? If not, what action can be taken to curb their activities or align them with the best interests of all stakeholders?

7. *Formulating international-level strategies.* Foreign markets provide both opportunities and potential dangers for companies that want to expand globally. To decide which entry strategy is most appropriate, companies have to evaluate the trade-offs between two factors that firms face when entering foreign markets: cost reduction and local adaptation. To achieve competitive advantages, firms will typically choose one of three strategies: global, multidomestic, or transnational. When evaluating international-level strategies, you might ask:

- Is the company's entry into an international marketplace threatened by the actions of local competitors? If so, how can cultural differences be minimized to give the firm a better chance of succeeding?
- Has the company made the appropriate choices between cost reduction and local adaptation to foreign markets? If not, how can it adjust its strategy to achieve competitive advantages?

- Can the company improve its effectiveness by embracing one international strategy over another? If so, how should it choose between a global, multidomestic, or transnational strategy?

8. *Formulating entrepreneurial strategies.* New ventures add jobs and create new wealth. To do so, they must identify opportunities that will be viable in the marketplace as well as gather resources and assemble an entrepreneurial team to enact the opportunity. New entrants often evoke a strong competitive response from incumbent firms in a given marketplace. When examining the role of strategic thinking on the success of entrepreneurial ventures and the role of competitive dynamics, you might ask:

   - Is the company engaged in an ongoing process of opportunity recognition? If not, how can it enhance its ability to recognize opportunities?
   - Do the entrepreneurs who are launching new ventures have vision, dedication and drive, and a commitment to excellence? If so, how have these affected the performance and dedication of other employees involved in the venture?
   - Have strategic principles been used in the process of developing strategies to pursue the entrepreneurial opportunity? If not, how can the venture apply tools such as five-forces analysis and value-chain analysis to improve its competitive position and performance?

9. *Achieving effective strategic control.* Strategic controls enable a firm to implement strategies effectively. Informational controls involve comparing performance to stated goals and scanning, monitoring, and being responsive to the environment. Behavioral controls emerge from a company's culture, reward systems, and organizational boundaries. When assessing the impact of strategic controls on implementation, you might ask:

   - Is the company employing the appropriate informational control systems? If not, how can it implement a more interactive approach to enhance learning and minimize response times?
   - Does the company have a strong and effective culture? If not, what steps can it take to align its values and rewards system with its goals and objectives?
   - Has the company implemented control systems that match its strategies? If so, what additional steps can be taken to improve performance?

10. *Creating effective organizational designs.* Organizational designs that align with competitive strategies can enhance performance. As companies grow and change, their structures must also evolve to meet new demands. In today's economy, firm boundaries must be flexible and permeable to facilitate smoother interactions with external parties such as customers, suppliers, and alliance partners. New forms of organizing are becoming more common. When evaluating the role of organizational structure on strategy implementation, you might ask:

    - Has the company implemented organizational structures that are suited to the type of business it is in? If not, how can it alter the design in ways that enhance its competitiveness?
    - Is the company employing boundaryless organizational designs where appropriate? If so, how are senior managers maintaining control of lower-level employees?
    - Does the company use outsourcing to achieve the best possible results? If not, what criteria should it use to decide which functions can be outsourced?

11. *Creating a learning organization and an ethical organization.* Strong leadership is essential for achieving competitive advantages. Two leadership roles are especially important. The first is creating a learning organization by harnessing talent and encouraging the development of new knowledge. Second, leaders play a vital role in

motivating employees to excellence and inspiring ethical behavior. When exploring the impact of effective strategic leadership, you might ask:

- Do company leaders promote excellence as part of the overall culture? If so, how has this influenced the performance of the firm and the individuals in it?
- Is the company committed to being a learning organization? If not, what can it do to capitalize on the individual and collective talents of organizational members?
- Have company leaders exhibited an ethical attitude in their own behavior? If not, how has their behavior influenced the actions of other employees?

12. *Fostering corporate entrepreneurship.* Many firms continually seek new growth opportunities and avenues for strategic renewal. In some corporations, autonomous work units such as business incubators and new-venture groups are used to focus corporate venturing activities. In other corporate settings, product champions and other firm members provide companies with the impetus to expand into new areas. When investigating the impact of entrepreneurship on strategic effectiveness, you might ask:

- Has the company resolved the dilemmas associated with managing innovation? If so, is it effectively defining and pacing its innovation efforts?
- Has the company developed autonomous work units that have the freedom to bring forth new product ideas? If so, has it used product champions to implement new venture initiatives?
- Does the company have an entrepreneurial orientation? If not, what can it do to encourage entrepreneurial attitudes in the strategic behavior of its organizational members?

Summary

Strategic management case analysis provides an effective method of learning how companies analyze problems, make decisions, and resolve challenges. Strategic cases include detailed accounts of actual business situations. The purpose of analyzing such cases is to gain exposure to a wide variety of organizational and managerial situations. By putting yourself in the place of a strategic decision maker, you can gain an appreciation of the difficulty and complexity of many strategic situations. In the process you can learn how to ask good strategic questions and enhance your analytical skills. Presenting case analyses can also help develop oral and written communication skills.

In this chapter we have discussed the importance of strategic case analysis and described the five steps involved in conducting a case analysis: becoming familiar

with the material, identifying problems, analyzing strategic issues, proposing alternative solutions, and making recommendations. We have also discussed how to get the most from case analysis. Finally, we have described how the case analysis process follows the analysis-decision-action cycle of strategic management and outlined issues and questions that are associated with each of the previous 12 chapters of the text.

Key Terms

case analysis, 470
case symptoms, 475
case problems, 475
financial ratio
    analysis, 476

devil's
    advocacy, 485
dialectical
    inquiry, 485

References

1. The material in this chapter is based on several sources, including Barnes, L. A., Nelson, A. J., & Christensen, C. R. 1994. *Teaching and the case method: Text, cases and readings.* Boston: Harvard Business School Press; Guth, W. D. 1985. Central concepts of business unit and corporate strategy. In W. D. Guth (Ed.). *Handbook of business strategy:* 1–9. Boston: Warren, Gorham & Lamont; Lundberg, C. C., & Enz, C. 1993. A framework for student case preparation. *Case Research Journal,* 13 (Summer): 129–140; and Ronstadt, R. 1980. *The art of case analysis: A guide to the diagnosis of business situations.* Dover, MA: Lord Publishing.

2 Edge, A. G. & Coleman, D. R. 1986. *The guide to case analysis and reporting* (3rd ed.). Honolulu, HI: System Logistics.

3. Morris, E. 1987. Vision and strategy: A focus for the future. *Journal of Business Strategy* 8: 51–58.

4. This section is based on Lundberg & Enz, op. cit., and Ronstadt, op. cit.

5. The importance of problem definition was emphasized in Mintzberg, H., Raisinghani, D. & Theoret, A. 1976. The structure of "unstructured" decision processes. *Administrative Science Quarterly,* 21(2): 246–275.

6. Drucker, P. F. 1994. The theory of the business. *Harvard Business Review,* 72(5): 95–104.

7. This section draws on Edge & Coleman, op. cit.

8. Irving Janis is credited with coining the term *groupthink,* and he applied it primarily to fiascos in government (such as the Bay of Pigs incident in 1961). Refer to Janis, I. L. 1982. *Victims of groupthink* (2nd ed.). Boston: Houghton Mifflin.

9. Much of our discussion is based upon Finkelstein, S. & Mooney, A. C. 2003. Not the usual suspects: How to use board process to make boards better. *Academy of Management Executive,* 17(2): 101–113; Schweiger, D. M., Sandberg, W. R., & Rechner, P. L. 1989. Experiential effects of dialectical inquiry, devil's advocacy, and consensus approaches to strategic decision making. *Academy of Management Journal,* 32(4): 745–772; and Aldag, R. J. & Stearns, T. M. 1987. *Management.* Cincinnati: South-Western Publishing.

10. Finkelstein and Mooney, op. cit.

APPENDIX 1 TO CHAPTER 13

Financial Ratio Analysis*

Standard Financial Statements

One obvious thing we might want to do with a company's financial statements is to compare them to those of other, similar companies. We would immediately have a problem, however. It's almost impossible to directly compare the financial statements for two companies because of differences in size.

For example, Oracle and IBM are obviously serious rivals in the computer software market, but IBM is much larger (in terms of assets), so it is difficult to compare them directly. For that matter, it's difficult to even compare financial statements from different points in time for the same company if the company's size has changed. The size problem is compounded if we try to compare IBM and, say, SAP (of Germany). If SAP's financial statements are denominated in German marks, then we have a size *and* a currency difference.

To start making comparisons, one obvious thing we might try to do is to somehow standardize the financial statements. One very common and useful way of doing this is to work with percentages instead of total dollars. The resulting financial statements are called *common-size statements.* We consider these next.

Common-Size Balance Sheets

For easy reference, Prufrock Corporation's 2010 and 2011 balance sheets are provided in Exhibit 13A.1. Using these, we construct common-size balance sheets by expressing each item as a percentage of total assets. Prufrock's 2010 and 2011 common-size balance sheets are shown in Exhibit 13A.2.

---

*This entire Appendix is adapted from Rows, S. A., Westerfield, R. W., & Jordan, B. D. 1999. *Essentials of Corporate Finance* (2nd ed.). chap. 3. New York: McGraw-Hill.

	2010	2011
Assets		
Current assets		
Cash	$ 84	$ 98
Accounts receivable	165	188
Inventory	393	422
Total	$ 642	$ 708
Fixed assets		
Net plant and equipment	$2,731	$2,880
Total assets	$3,373	$3,588
Liabilities and Owners' Equity		
Current liabilities		
Accounts payable	$ 312	$ 344
Notes payable	231	196
Total	$ 543	$ 540
Long-term debt	$ 531	$ 457
Owners' equity		
Common stock and paid-in surplus	$ 500	$ 550
Retained earnings	1,799	2,041
Total	$2,299	$2,591
Total liabilities and owners' equity	$3,373	$3,588

Notice that some of the totals don't check exactly because of rounding errors. Also notice that the total change has to be zero since the beginning and ending numbers must add up to 100 percent.

In this form, financial statements are relatively easy to read and compare. For example, just looking at the two balance sheets for Prufrock, we see that current assets were 19.7 percent of total assets in 2011, up from 19.1 percent in 2010. Current liabilities declined from 16.0 percent to 15.1 percent of total liabilities and equity over that same time. Similarly, total equity rose from 68.1 percent of total liabilities and equity to 72.2 percent.

Overall, Prufrock's liquidity, as measured by current assets compared to current liabilities, increased over the year. Simultaneously, Prufrock's indebtedness diminished as a percentage of total assets. We might be tempted to conclude that the balance sheet has grown "stronger."

Common-Size Income Statements

A useful way of standardizing the income statement, shown in Exhibit 13A.3, is to express each item as a percentage of total sales, as illustrated for Prufrock in Exhibit 13A.4.

This income statement tells us what happens to each dollar in sales. For Prufrock, interest expense eats up $.061 out of every sales dollar and taxes take another $.081. When all is said and done, $.157 of each dollar flows through to the bottom line (net income), and that amount is split into $.105 retained in the business and $.052 paid out in dividends.

	2010	2011	Change
Assets			
Current assets			
Cash	2.5%	2.7%	+ .2%
Accounts receivable	4.9	5.2	+ .3
Inventory	11.7	11.8	+ .1
Total	19.1	19.7	+ .6
Fixed assets			
Net plant and equipment	80.9	80.3	− .6
Total assets	100.0%	100.0%	.0%
Liabilities and Owners' Equity			
Current liabilities			
Accounts payable	9.2%	9.6%	+ .4%
Notes payable	6.8	5.5	−1.3
Total	16.0	15.1	− .9
Long-term debt	15.7	12.7	−3.0
Owners' equity			
Common stock and paid-in surplus	14.8	15.3	+ .5
Retained earnings	53.3	56.9	+3.6
Total	68.1	72.2	+4.1
Total liabilities and owners' equities	100.0%	100.0%	.0%

Exhibit 13A.2
Prufrock Corporation
Common-Size Balance Sheets as of December 31, 2010 and 2011 (%)

Note: Numbers may not add up to 100.0% due to rounding.

These percentages are very useful in comparisons. For example, a relevant figure is the cost percentage. For Prufrock, $.582 of each $1.00 in sales goes to pay for goods sold. It would be interesting to compute the same percentage for Prufrock's main competitors to see how Prufrock stacks up in terms of cost control.

Ratio Analysis

Another way of avoiding the problems involved in comparing companies of different sizes is to calculate and compare *financial ratios*. Such ratios are ways of comparing and investigating the relationships between different pieces of financial information. We cover some of the more common ratios next, but there are many others that we don't touch on.

One problem with ratios is that different people and different sources frequently don't compute them in exactly the same way, and this leads to much confusion. The specific definitions we use here may or may not be the same as others you have seen or will see elsewhere. If you ever use ratios as a tool for analysis, you should be careful to document how you calculate each one, and, if you are comparing your numbers to those of another source, be sure you know how its numbers are computed.

For each of the ratios we discuss, several questions come to mind:

1. How is it computed?
2. What is it intended to measure, and why might we be interested?
3. What is the unit of measurement?

Exhibit 13A.3

Prufrock Corporation

2011 Income Statement
($ in millions)

Sales	$2,311
Cost of goods sold	1,344
Depreciation	276
Earnings before interest and taxes	$ 691
Interest paid	141
Taxable income	$ 550
Taxes (34%)	187
Net income	$ 363
Dividends	$121
Addition to retained earnings	242

Exhibit 13A.4

Prufrock Corporation

2011 Common-Size
Income Statement (%)

Sales	100.0%
Cost of goods sold	58.2
Depreciation	11.9
Earnings before interest and taxes	29.9
Interest paid	6.1
Taxable income	23.8
Taxes (34%)	8.1
Net income	15.7%
Dividends	5.2%
Addition to retained earnings	10.5

4. What might a high or low value be telling us? How might such values be misleading?
5. How could this measure be improved?

Financial ratios are traditionally grouped into the following categories:

1. Short-term solvency, or liquidity, ratios.
2. Long-term solvency, or financial leverage, ratios.
3. Asset management, or turnover, ratios.
4. Profitability ratios.
5. Market value ratios.

We will consider each of these in turn. In calculating these numbers for Prufrock, we will use the ending balance sheet (2011) figures unless we explicitly say otherwise. The numbers for the various ratios come from the income statement and the balance sheet.

Short-Term Solvency, or Liquidity, Measures

As the name suggests, short-term solvency ratios as a group are intended to provide information about a firm's liquidity, and these ratios are sometimes called *liquidity measures*. The primary concern is the firm's ability to pay its bills over the short run without undue stress. Consequently, these ratios focus on current assets and current liabilities.

For obvious reasons, liquidity ratios are particularly interesting to short-term creditors. Since financial managers are constantly working with banks and other short-term lenders, an understanding of these ratios is essential.

One advantage of looking at current assets and liabilities is that their book values and market values are likely to be similar. Often (though not always), these assets and liabilities just don't live long enough for the two to get seriously out of step. On the other hand, like any type of near cash, current assets and liabilities can and do change fairly rapidly, so today's amounts may not be a reliable guide to the future.

Current Ratio   One of the best-known and most widely used ratios is the *current ratio*. As you might guess, the current ratio is defined as:

$$\text{Current ratio} = \frac{\text{Current assets}}{\text{Current liabilities}}$$

For Prufrock, the 2011 current ratio is:

$$\text{Current ratio} = \frac{\$708}{\$540} = 1.31 \text{ times}$$

Because current assets and liabilities are, in principle, converted to cash over the following 12 months, the current ratio is a measure of short-term liquidity. The unit of measurement is either dollars or times. So, we could say Prufrock has $1.31 in current assets for every $1 in current liabilities, or we could say Prufrock has its current liabilities covered 1.31 times over.

To a creditor, particularly a short-term creditor such as a supplier, the higher the current ratio, the better. To the firm, a high current ratio indicates liquidity, but it also may indicate an inefficient use of cash and other short-term assets. Absent some extraordinary circumstances, we would expect to see a current ratio of at least 1, because a current ratio of less than 1 would mean that net working capital (current assets less current liabilities) is negative. This would be unusual in a healthy firm, at least for most types of businesses.

The current ratio, like any ratio, is affected by various types of transactions. For example, suppose the firm borrows over the long term to raise money. The short-run effect would be an increase in cash from the issue proceeds and an increase in long-term debt. Current liabilities would not be affected, so the current ratio would rise.

Finally, note that an apparently low current ratio may not be a bad sign for a company with a large reserve of untapped borrowing power.

Quick (or Acid-Test) Ratio   Inventory is often the least liquid current asset. It's also the one for which the book values are least reliable as measures of market value, since the quality of the inventory isn't considered. Some of the inventory may later turn out to be damaged, obsolete, or lost.

More to the point, relatively large inventories are often a sign of short-term trouble. The firm may have overestimated sales and overbought or overproduced as a result. In this case, the firm may have a substantial portion of its liquidity tied up in slow-moving inventory.

To further evaluate liquidity, the *quick,* or *acid-test, ratio* is computed just like the current ratio, except inventory is omitted:

$$\text{Quick ratio} = \frac{\text{Current assets} - \text{Inventory}}{\text{Current liabilities}}$$

Notice that using cash to buy inventory does not affect the current ratio, but it reduces the quick ratio. Again, the idea is that inventory is relatively illiquid compared to cash.

For Prufrock, this ratio in 2011 was:

$$\text{Quick ratio} = \frac{\$708 - 422}{\$540} = .53 \text{ times}$$

The quick ratio here tells a somewhat different story than the current ratio, because inventory accounts for more than half of Prufrock's current assets. To exaggerate the point, if this inventory consisted of, say, unsold nuclear power plants, then this would be a cause for concern.

Cash Ratio   A very short-term creditor might be interested in the *cash ratio:*

$$\text{Cash ratio} = \frac{\text{Cash}}{\text{Current liabilities}}$$

You can verify that this works out to be .18 times for Prufrock.

Long-Term Solvency Measures

Long-term solvency ratios are intended to address the firm's long-run ability to meet its obligations, or, more generally, its financial leverage. These ratios are sometimes called *financial leverage ratios* or just *leverage ratios.* We consider three commonly used measures and some variations.

Total Debt Ratio   The *total debt ratio* takes into account all debts of all maturities to all creditors. It can be defined in several ways, the easiest of which is:

$$\text{Total debt ratio} = \frac{\text{Total assets} - \text{Total equity}}{\text{Total assets}}$$

$$= \frac{\$3,588 - 2,591}{\$3,588} = .28 \text{ times}$$

In this case, an analyst might say that Prufrock uses 28 percent debt.[1] Whether this is high or low or whether it even makes any difference depends on whether or not capital structure matters.

Prufrock has \$.28 in debt for every \$1 in assets. Therefore, there is \$.72 in equity (\$1 − .28) for every \$.28 in debt. With this in mind, we can define two useful variations on the total debt ratio, the *debt-equity ratio* and the *equity multiplier:*

$$\text{Debt-equity ratio} = \text{Total debt/Total equity}$$
$$= \$.28/\$.72 = .39 \text{ times}$$
$$\text{Equity multiplier} = \text{Total assets/Total equity}$$
$$= \$1/\$.72 = 1.39 \text{ times}$$

The fact that the equity multiplier is 1 plus the debt-equity ratio is not a coincidence:

$$\text{Equity multiplier} = \text{Total assets/Total equity} = \$1/\$.72 = 1.39$$
$$= (\text{Total equity} + \text{Total debt})/\text{Total equity}$$
$$= 1 + \text{Debt-equity ratio} = 1.39 \text{ times}$$

The thing to notice here is that given any one of these three ratios, you can immediately calculate the other two, so they all say exactly the same thing.

Times Interest Earned   Another common measure of long-term solvency is the *times interest earned* (TIE) *ratio.* Once again, there are several possible (and common) definitions, but we'll stick with the most traditional:

$$\text{Times interest earned ratio} = \frac{\text{EBIT}}{\text{Interest}}$$

$$= \frac{\$691}{\$141} = 4.9 \text{ times}$$

As the name suggests, this ratio measures how well a company has its interest obligations covered, and it is often called the interest coverage ratio. For Prufrock, the interest bill is covered 4.9 times over.

Cash Coverage   A problem with the TIE ratio is that it is based on earnings before interest and taxes (EBIT), which is not really a measure of cash available to pay interest. The reason is that

---

[1] Total equity here includes preferred stock, if there is any. An equivalent numerator in this ratio would be (Current liabilities + Long-term debt).

depreciation, a noncash expense, has been deducted. Since interest is most definitely a cash outflow (to creditors), one way to define the *cash coverage ratio* is:

$$\text{Cash coverage ratio} = \frac{\text{EBIT} + \text{Depreciation}}{\text{Interest}}$$

$$= \frac{\$691 + 276}{\$141} = \frac{\$967}{\$141} = 6.9 \text{ times}$$

The numerator here, EBIT plus depreciation, is often abbreviated EBDIT (earnings before depreciation, interest, and taxes). It is a basic measure of the firm's ability to generate cash from operations, and it is frequently used as a measure of cash flow available to meet financial obligations.

Asset Management, or Turnover, Measures

We next turn our attention to the efficiency with which Prufrock uses its assets. The measures in this section are sometimes called *asset utilization ratios.* The specific ratios we discuss can all be interpreted as measures of turnover. What they are intended to describe is how efficiently, or intensively, a firm uses its assets to generate sales. We first look at two important current assets: inventory and receivables.

Inventory Turnover and Days' Sales in Inventory   During the year, Prufrock had a cost of goods sold of $1,344. Inventory at the end of the year was $422. With these numbers, *inventory turnover* can be calculated as:

$$\text{Inventory turnover} = \frac{\text{Cost of goods sold}}{\text{Inventory}}$$

$$= \frac{\$1,344}{\$422} = 3.2 \text{ times}$$

In a sense, we sold off, or turned over, the entire inventory 3.2 times. As long as we are not running out of stock and thereby forgoing sales, the higher this ratio is, the more efficiently we are managing inventory.

If we know that we turned our inventory over 3.2 times during the year, then we can immediately figure out how long it took us to turn it over on average. The result is the average *days' sales in inventory:*

$$\text{Days' sales in inventory} = \frac{365 \text{ days}}{\text{Inventory turnover}}$$

$$= \frac{365}{3.2} = 114 \text{ days}$$

This tells us that, on average, inventory sits 114 days before it is sold. Alternatively, assuming we used the most recent inventory and cost figures, it will take about 114 days to work off our current inventory.

For example, we frequently hear things like "Majestic Motors has a 60 days' supply of cars." This means that, at current daily sales, it would take 60 days to deplete the available inventory. We could also say that Majestic has 60 days of sales in inventory.

Receivables Turnover and Days' Sales in Receivables   Our inventory measures give some indication of how fast we can sell products. We now look at how fast we collect on those sales. The *receivables turnover* is defined in the same way as inventory turnover:

$$\text{Receivables turnover} = \frac{\text{Sales}}{\text{Accounts receivable}}$$

$$= \frac{\$2,311}{\$188} = 12.3 \text{ times}$$

Loosely speaking, we collected our outstanding credit accounts and reloaned the money 12.3 times during the year.[2]

This ratio makes more sense if we convert it to days, so the *days' sales in receivables* is:

$$\text{Days' sales in receivables} = \frac{365 \text{ days}}{\text{Receivables turnover}}$$

$$= \frac{365}{12.3} = 30 \text{ days}$$

Therefore, on average, we collect on our credit sales in 30 days. For obvious reasons, this ratio is very frequently called the *average collection period* (ACP).

Also note that if we are using the most recent figures, we can also say that we have 30 days' worth of sales currently uncollected.

Total Asset Turnover   Moving away from specific accounts like inventory or receivables, we can consider an important "big picture" ratio, the *total asset turnover ratio.* As the name suggests, total asset turnover is:

$$\text{Total asset turnover} = \frac{\text{Sales}}{\text{Total assets}}$$

$$= \frac{\$2,311}{\$3,588} = .64 \text{ times}$$

In other words, for every dollar in assets, we generated $.64 in sales.

A closely related ratio, the *capital intensity ratio,* is simply the reciprocal of (i.e., 1 divided by) total asset turnover. It can be interpreted as the dollar investment in assets needed to generate $1 in sales. High values correspond to capital intensive industries (e.g., public utilities). For Prufrock, total asset turnover is .64, so, if we flip this over, we get that capital intensity is $1/.64 = $1.56. That is, it takes Prufrock $1.56 in assets to create $1 in sales.

Profitability Measures

The three measures we discuss in this section are probably the best known and most widely used of all financial ratios. In one form or another, they are intended to measure how efficiently the firm uses its assets and how efficiently the firm manages its operations. The focus in this group is on the bottom line, net income.

Profit Margin   Companies pay a great deal of attention to their *profit margin:*

$$\text{Profit margin} = \frac{\text{Net income}}{\text{Sales}}$$

$$= \frac{\$363}{\$2,311} = 15.7\%$$

This tells us that Prufrock, in an accounting sense, generates a little less than 16 cents in profit for every dollar in sales.

All other things being equal, a relatively high profit margin is obviously desirable. This situation corresponds to low expense ratios relative to sales. However, we hasten to add that other things are often not equal.

For example, lowering our sales price will usually increase unit volume, but will normally cause profit margins to shrink. Total profit (or, more importantly, operating cash flow) may go up or down; so the fact that margins are smaller isn't necessarily bad. After all, isn't it possible that, as the saying goes, "Our prices are so low that we lose money on everything we sell, but we make it up in volume!"[3]

---

[2] Here we have implicitly assumed that all sales are credit sales. If they were not, then we would simply use total credit sales in these calculations, not total sales.

[3] No, it's not; margins can be small, but they do need to be positive!

Return on Assets   *Return on assets* (ROA) is a measure of profit per dollar of assets. It can be defined several ways, but the most common is:

$$\text{Return on assets} = \frac{\text{Net income}}{\text{Total assets}}$$

$$= \frac{\$363}{\$3,588} = 10.12\%$$

Return on Equity   *Return on equity* (ROE) is a measure of how the stockholders fared during the year. Since benefiting shareholders is our goal, ROE is, in an accounting sense, the true bottom-line measure of performance. ROE is usually measured as:

$$\text{Return on equity} = \frac{\text{Net income}}{\text{Total equity}}$$

$$= \frac{\$363}{\$2,591} = 14\%$$

For every dollar in equity, therefore, Prufrock generated 14 cents in profit, but, again, this is only correct in accounting terms.

Because ROA and ROE are such commonly cited numbers, we stress that it is important to remember they are accounting rates of return. For this reason, these measures should properly be called *return on book assets* and *return on book equity*. In addition, ROE is sometimes called *return on net worth*. Whatever it's called, it would be inappropriate to compare the results to, for example, an interest rate observed in the financial markets.

The fact that ROE exceeds ROA reflects Prufrock's use of financial leverage. We will examine the relationship between these two measures in more detail below.

Market Value Measures

Our final group of measures is based, in part, on information not necessarily contained in financial statements—the market price per share of the stock. Obviously, these measures can only be calculated directly for publicly traded companies.

We assume that Prufrock has 33 million shares outstanding and the stock sold for $88 per share at the end of the year. If we recall that Prufrock's net income was $363 million, then we can calculate that its earnings per share were:

$$\text{EPS} = \frac{\text{Net income}}{\text{Shares outstanding}} = \frac{\$363}{33} = \$11$$

Price-Earnings Ratio   The first of our market value measures, the *price-earnings,* or PE, *ratio* (or multiple), is defined as:

$$\text{PE ratio} = \frac{\text{Price per share}}{\text{Earnings per share}}$$

$$= \frac{\$88}{\$11} = 8 \text{ times}$$

In the vernacular, we would say that Prufrock shares sell for eight times earnings, or we might say that Prufrock shares have, or "carry," a PE multiple of 8.

Since the PE ratio measures how much investors are willing to pay per dollar of current earnings, higher PEs are often taken to mean that the firm has significant prospects for future growth. Of course, if a firm had no or almost no earnings, its PE would probably be quite large; so, as always, be careful when interpreting this ratio.

Market-to-Book Ratio A second commonly quoted measure is the *market-to-book ratio:*

$$\text{Market-to-book ratio} = \frac{\text{Market value per share}}{\text{Book value per share}}$$

$$= \frac{\$88}{(\$2{,}591/33)} = \frac{\$88}{\$78.5} = 1.12 \text{ times}$$

Notice that book value per share is total equity (not just common stock) divided by the number of shares outstanding.

Since book value per share is an accounting number, it reflects historical costs. In a loose sense, the market-to-book ratio therefore compares the market value of the firm's investments to their cost. A value less than 1 could mean that the firm has not been successful overall in creating value for its stockholders.

Conclusion

This completes our definition of some common ratios. Exhibit 13A.5 summarizes the ratios we've discussed.

I. Short-term solvency, or liquidity, ratios

$$\text{Current ratio} = \frac{\text{Current assets}}{\text{Current liabilities}}$$

$$\text{Quick ratio} = \frac{\text{Current assets} - \text{Inventory}}{\text{Current liabilities}}$$

$$\text{Cash ratio} = \frac{\text{Cash}}{\text{Current liabilities}}$$

II. Long-term solvency, or financial leverage, ratios

$$\text{Total debt ratio} = \frac{\text{Total assets} - \text{Total equity}}{\text{Total assets}}$$

$$\text{Debt-equity ratio} = \text{Total debt/Total equity}$$

$$\text{Equity multiplier} = \text{Total assets/Total equity}$$

$$\text{Times interest earned ratio} = \frac{\text{EBIT}}{\text{Interest}}$$

$$\text{Cash coverage ratio} = \frac{\text{EBIT} + \text{Depreciation}}{\text{Interest}}$$

III. Asset utilization, or turnover, ratios

$$\text{Inventory turnover} = \frac{\text{Cost of goods sold}}{\text{Inventory}}$$

$$\text{Days' sales in inventory} = \frac{365 \text{ days}}{\text{Inventory turnover}}$$

$$\text{Receivables turnover} = \frac{\text{Sales}}{\text{Accounts receivable}}$$

$$\text{Days' sales in receivables} = \frac{365 \text{ days}}{\text{Receivables turnover}}$$

$$\text{Total asset turnover} = \frac{\text{Sales}}{\text{Total assets}}$$

$$\text{Capital intensity} = \frac{\text{Total assets}}{\text{Sales}}$$

IV. Profitability ratios

$$\text{Profit margin} = \frac{\text{Net income}}{\text{Sales}}$$

$$\text{Return on assets (ROA)} = \frac{\text{Net income}}{\text{Total assets}}$$

$$\text{Return on equity (ROE)} = \frac{\text{Net income}}{\text{Total equity}}$$

$$\text{ROE} = \frac{\text{Net income}}{\text{Sales}} \times \frac{\text{Sales}}{\text{Assets}} \times \frac{\text{Assets}}{\text{Equity}}$$

V. Market value ratios

$$\text{Price-earnings ratio} = \frac{\text{Price per share}}{\text{Earnings per share}}$$

$$\text{Market-to-book ratio} = \frac{\text{Market value per share}}{\text{Book value per share}}$$

Exhibit 13A.5 A Summary of Five Types of Financial Ratios

Sources of Company and Industry Information*

In order for business executives to make the best decisions when developing corporate strategy, it is critical for them to be knowledgeable about their competitors and about the industries in which they compete. The process used by corporations to learn as much as possible about competitors is often called "competitive intelligence." This appendix provides an overview of important and widely available sources of information that may be useful in conducting basic competitive intelligence. Much information of this nature is available in libraries in article databases, business reference books, and on websites. This list will recommend a variety of them. Ask a librarian for assistance, because library collections and resources vary.

The information sources are organized into 10 categories:

Competitive Intelligence

Public or Private—Subsidiary or Division—U.S. or Foreign?

Annual Report Collections—Public Companies

Guides and Tutorials

SEC Filings/EDGAR—Company Disclosure Reports

Company Rankings

Business Websites

Strategic and Competitive Analysis—Information Sources

Sources for Industry Research and Analysis

Search Engines

Competitive Intelligence

Students and other researchers who want to learn more about the value and process of competitive intelligence should see four recent books on this subject.

Mike Biere. *The New Era of Enterprise Business Intelligence: Using Analytics to Achieve a Global Competitive Advantage.* Upper Saddle River, NJ: IBM Press/Pearson, 2011.

Seena Sharp. *Competitive Intelligence Advantage: How to Minimize Risk, Avoid Surprises, and Grow Your Business in a Changing World.* Hoboken, NJ: Wiley, 2009.

T. J. Waters. *Hyperformance: Using Competitive Intelligence for Better Strategy and Execution.* San Francisco: Jossey-Bass, 2010.

Benjamin Gilad. *Early Warning: Using Competitive Intelligence to Anticipate Market Shifts, Control Risk, and Create Powerful Strategies.* New York: American Management Association, 2004.

Public or Private—Subsidiary or Division—U.S. or Foreign?

Companies traded on stock exchanges in the United States are required to file a variety of reports that disclose information about the company. This begins the process that produces a wealth of data on public companies and at the same time distinguishes them from private companies, which often lack available data. Similarly, financial data of subsidiaries and divisions are typically filed in a

---

* This information was compiled by Ruthie Brock and Carol Byrne, Business Librarians at The University of Texas at Arlington. We greatly appreciate their valuable contribution.

consolidated financial statement by the parent company, rather than treated independently, thus limiting the kind of data available on them. On the other hand, foreign companies that trade on U.S. stock exchanges are required to file 20F reports, similar to the 10-K for U.S. companies, the most comprehensive of the required reports. The following directories provide brief facts about companies, including whether they are public or private, subsidiary or division, U.S. or foreign.

Corporate Directory of U.S. Public Companies. San Mateo, CA: Walker's Research, LLC, 2010.
The *Corporate Directory* provides company profiles of more than 9,000 publicly traded companies in the United States, including foreign companies trading on the U.S. exchanges (ADRs). Some libraries may subscribe to an alternative online version at *www.walkersresearch.com*.

Corporate Affiliations. New Providence, NJ: LexisNexis, 2010.
This 8-volume directory features brief profiles of major U.S. and foreign corporations, both public and private, as well as their subsidiaries, divisions, and affiliates. The directory also indicates hierarchies of corporate relationships. An online version of the directory allows retrieval of a list of companies that meet specific criteria. Results can be downloaded to a spreadsheet. The online version requires a subscription, available in some libraries.

ReferenceUSA. Omaha, NE: Infogroup.Inc.
ReferenceUSA is an online directory of more than 14 million businesses located in the United States. One of the unique features is that it includes public and private companies, both large and small. Custom and Guided search tabs are available. Also, results can be analyzed using Quick, the data summary feature, which allows for a snapshot of how the industry breaks down by size, geographic location, etc. Other subscription options are available using the ReferenceUSA interface and may be available in some libraries.

Ward's Business Directory of U.S. Private and Public Companies. Farmington Hills, MI: Gale CENGAGE Learning, 2010. 8 vols.
Ward's Business Directory lists brief profiles on more than 112,000 public and private companies and indicates whether they are public or private, a subsidiary or division. Two volumes of the set are arranged using the Standard Industrial Classifications (SIC) and the North American Industry Classification System (NAICS) and feature company rankings within industries. Some libraries may offer this business directory as part of a database called *Gale Directory Library.*

Finding Public Company Information

Most companies have their annual report to shareholders and other financial reports available on their corporate website. Note that some companies use a variation of their company name in their Web address, such as Procter & Gamble: *www.pg.com*. A few "aggregators" have also conveniently provided an accumulation of links to many reports of U.S. and international corporations or include a PDF document as part of their database, although these generally do not attempt to be comprehensive.

The Public Register Online. Woodstock Valley, CT: Bay Tact Corp.
Public Register Online includes over 5,000 public company shareholder annual reports and 10-K filings for online viewing. Links are provided to reports on individual companies' websites, official filings from the Securities and Exchange Commission website, stock information from the NYSE Euronext exchange, or some combination of these sources. A link is also provided on this website for ordering personal copies of hard copy annual reports.
http://www.annualreportservice.com/

Mergent Online. New York: Mergent, Inc.
Mergent Online is a database that provides company reports and financial statements for both U.S. and foreign public companies. Mergent's database has up to 25 years of quarterly and annual financial data that can be downloaded into a spreadsheet for analysis across time or across companies. Students should check with a librarian to determine the availability of this database at their college or university library.
http://mergentonline.com

Guides & Tutorials for Researching Companies and Industries

Researching Companies Online. Debbie Flanagan. Fort Lauderdale, FL
This site provides a step-by-step process for finding free company and industry information on the web.
www.learnwebskills.com/company/

Guide to Financial Statements and *How to Read Annual Reports.* Armonk, NY: IBM
These two educational guides, located on IBM's website, provide basic information on how to read and make sense of financial statements and other information in 10-K and shareholder annual reports for companies in general, not IBM specifically.
www.ibm.com/investor/help/guide/introduction.wss
www.ibm.com/investor/help/reports/introduction.wss

EDGAR Full-Text Search Frequently Asked Questions (FAQ). Washington DC: U.S. Securities and Exchange Commission
The capability to search full-text SEC filings (popularly known as EDGAR filings), was vastly improved when the SEC launched its new search form in late 2006. Features are explained at the FAQ page.
www.sec.gov/edgar/searchedgar/edgarfulltextfaq.htm

Locating Company Information. Tutorial. William and Joan Schreyer Business Library, Penn State University, University Park, PA
Created by librarians at Penn State, this outstanding tutorial provides suggestions for online and print resources for company information. Click on "how to" links for each item to view a brief instruction vignette.
www.libraries.psu.edu/psul/researchguides/business.html

Ten Steps to Industry Intelligence. Industry Tutorial. George A. Smathers Libraries, University of Florida, Gainesville, FL
Provides a step-by-step approach for finding information about industries, with embedded links to recommended sources.
http://businesslibrary.uflib.ufl.edu/industryresearch

SEC Filings/EDGAR—Company Disclosure Reports

SEC Filings are the various reports that publicly traded companies must file with the Securities and Exchange Commission to disclose information about their corporation. These are often referred to as "EDGAR" filings, an acronym for the Electronic Data Gathering, Analysis and Retrieval System. Some websites and commercial databases improve access to these reports by offering additional retrieval features not available on the official (*www.sec.gov*) website.

EDGAR Database Full-Text Search. U.S. Securities and Exchange Commission (SEC), Washington, DC
10-K reports and other required corporate documents are made available in the SEC's EDGAR database within 24 hours after being filed. Annual reports, on the other hand, are typically sent directly to shareholders and are not required as part of EDGAR by the SEC, although some companies voluntarily include them. Both 10-Ks and shareholder's annual reports are considered basic sources of company research. The SEC offers a search interface for full-text searching of the content and exhibits of EDGAR SEC filings. The advanced search is recommended to locate "hard-to-find" information within documents filed by corporations and their competitors. Searches for specific types of reports or certain industries can also be performed.
http://searchwww.sec.gov/EDGARFSClient/jsp/EDGAR_MainAccess.jsp

LexisNexis Academic—SEC Filings & Reports. Bethesda, MD: LexisNexis.
Company Securities Exchange Commission filings and reports are available through a database called LexisNexis Academic. These reports and filings can be retrieved by company name, industry code, or ticker symbol for a particular time period or by a specific report. Proxy, 10-Ks, prospectus, and registration filings are also available.

Mergent Online—EDGAR Search. New York: Mergent, Inc.

As an alternative to *sec.gov,* the Securities and Exchange Commission website, it is possible to use the *Mergent Online* database to search for official company filings. Check to be sure if your library subscribes to the *Mergent Online* database. Select the "Filings" tab and then click on the "EDGAR Search" link. Next, Mergent's Government Filings search allows searching by company name, ticker, CIK (Central Index Key) number, or industry SIC number. The search can be limited by date and by type of SEC filing. The URL below should also work if your library subscribes to the Mergent Online database.

http://www.mergentonline.com/filingsearch.php?type=edgar&criteriatype=findall& submitvalues

Company Rankings

Fortune 500. New York: Time Inc.

The *Fortune 500* list and other company rankings are published in the printed edition of *Fortune* magazine and are also available online.

http://money.cnn.com/magazines/fortune/fortune500/2008/full_list/index.html

Forbes Global 2000. Forbes, Inc.

The companies listed on The Forbes Global 2000 are the biggest and most powerful in the world.

http://www.forbes.com/lists

Ward's Business Directory of U.S. Private and Public Companies. Farmington Hills, MI: Gale CENGAGE Learning, 2008, 8 vols.

Ward's Business Directory is one of the few directories to rank both public and private companies together by sales within an industry, using both the Standard Industrial Classification system (in vol. 5 only) and the North American Industry Classification System (in vol. 8 only). With this information, it is easy to spot who the big "players" are in a particular product or industry category. Market share within an industry group can be calculated by determining what percentage a company's sales figure is of the total given by Ward's for that industry group. Some libraries may offer this business directory as part of a database called *Gale Directory Library.*

Business Websites

Big Charts. San Francisco: MarketWatch, Inc.

BigCharts is a comprehensive and easy-to-use investment research website, providing access to professional-level research tools such as interactive charts, current and historical quotes, industry analysis, and intraday stock screeners, as well as market news and commentary. MarketWatch operates this website, a service of Dow Jones & Company. Supported by site sponsors, it is free to self-directed investors.

http://bigcharts.marketwatch.com/

GlobalEdge. East Lansing, MI: Michigan State University

GlobalEdge is a web portal providing a significant amount of information about international business, countries around the globe, the U.S. states, industries, and news.

http://globaledge.msu.edu/

Hoover's Online. Hoover's, Inc., Short Hills, NJ: Dun & Bradstreet Corp.

Hoover's includes a limited amount of free information on companies and industries. The subscribers' edition provides more in-depth information, especially for competitors and industries.

www.hoovers.com/free

Yahoo Finance. Sunnyvale, CA: Yahoo! Inc.

This website links to information on U.S. markets, world markets, data sources, finance references, investment editorials, financial news, and other helpful websites.

http://finance.yahoo.com

Strategic and Competitive Analysis—Information Sources

Analyzing a company can take the form of examining its internal and external environment. In the process, it is useful to identify the company's strengths, weaknesses, opportunities and threats (SWOT). Sources for this kind of analysis are varied, but perhaps the best would be to locate articles from *The Wall Street Journal,* business magazines and industry trade publications. Publications such as these can be found in the following databases available at many public and academic libraries. When using a database that is structured to allow it, try searching the company name combined with one or more keywords, such as "IBM and competition" or "Microsoft and lawsuits" or "AMR and fuel costs" to retrieve articles relating to the external environment.

ABI/Inform Complete. Ann Arbor, MI: ProQuest LLC
ABI/Inform Complete provides abstracts and full-text articles covering management, law, taxation, human resources, and company and industry information from more than 5,400 business and management journals. *ABI/Inform* includes market condition reports, corporate strategies, case studies, executive profiles, and global industry conditions.

Business & Company Resource Center. Farmington Hills, MI: Gale CENGAGE Learning
Business & Company Resource Center provides company and industry intelligence for a selection of public and private companies. Company profiles include parent-subsidiary relationships, industry rankings, products and brands, investment reports, industry statistics, and financial ratios. A selection of full-text investment reports and SWOT analysis reports are also available.

Business Source Complete. Ipswich, MA: EBSCO Publishing
Business Source Complete is a full-text database with over 3,800 scholarly business journals covering management, economics, finance, accounting, international business, and more. The database also includes detailed company profiles for the world's 10,000 largest companies, as well as selected country economic reports provided by the Economist Intelligence Unit (EIU). The database includes case studies, investment and market research reports, SWOT analyses, and more. *Business Source Complete* contains over 1,850 peer-reviewed business journals.

Investext Research Reports. Detroit, MI: Thomson Reuters Corp.
Investext Research Reports offer full-text analytical reports on more than 65,000 companies worldwide. The research reports are excellent sources for strategic and financial profiles of a company and its competitors and of industry trends. Developed by a global roster of brokerage, investment banking, and research firms, these full-text investment reports include a wealth of current and historical information useful for evaluating a company or industry over time.

International Directory of Company Histories. Detroit, MI: St. James Press, 1988–present. 120 volumes to date.
This directory covers more than 11,000 multinational companies, and the series is still adding volumes. Each company history is approximately three to five pages in length and provides a summary of the company's mission, goals, and ideals, followed by company milestones, principal subsidiaries, and competitors. Strategic decisions made during the company's period of existence are usually noted. This series covers public and private companies and nonprofit entities. Entry information includes a company's legal name, headquarters information, URL, incorporation date, ticker symbol, stock exchange, sales figures, and the primary North American Industry Classification System (NAICS) code. Further reading selections complete the entry information. Volume 59 to current date, is available electronically in the Gale Virtual Reference Library database from Gale CENCAGE Learning.

LexisNexis Academic. Bethesda, MD: LexisNexis
The "business" category in *LexisNexis Academic* provides access to timely business articles from newspapers, magazines, journals, wires, and broadcast transcripts. Other information available in this section includes detailed company financials, company comparisons, and database industry and market information for over 25 industries. The Company Dossier research tool allows a researcher to compare up to five companies' financial statements at one time with download capabilities.

The Wall Street Journal. New York: Dow Jones & Co.

This respected business newspaper is available in searchable full-text from 1984 to the present in the *Factiva* database. The "News Pages" link provides access to current articles and issues of *The Wall Street Journal.* Dow Jones, publisher of the print version of the *Wall Street Journal,* also has an online subscription available at wsj.com. Some libraries provide access to *The Wall Street Journal* through the ProQuest Newspapers database.

Sources for Industry Research and Analysis

Factiva. New York: Dow Jones & Co.

The *Factiva* database has several options for researching an industry. One would be to search the database for articles in the business magazines and industry trade publications. A second option in *Factiva* would be to search in the Companies/Markets category for company/industry comparison reports.

Mergent Online. New York: Mergent Inc.

Mergent Online is a searchable database of over 60,000 global public companies. The database offers worldwide industry reports, U.S. and global competitors, and executive biographical information. *Mergent*'s Basic Search option permits searching by primary industry codes (either SIC or NAICS). Once the search is executed, companies in that industry should be listed. A comparison or standard peer group analysis can be created to analyze companies in the same industry on various criteria. The Advanced Search allows the user to search a wider range of financial and textual information. Results, including ratios for a company and its competitors, can be downloaded to a spreadsheet.

North American Industry Classification System (NAICS)

The North American Industry Classification System has officially replaced the Standard Industrial Classification (SIC) as the numerical structure used to define and analyze industries, although some publications and databases offer both classification systems. The NAICS codes are used in Canada, the United States, and Mexico. In the United States, the NAICS codes are used to conduct an Economic Census every five years providing a snapshot of the U.S. economy at a given moment in time.

NAICS: *www.census.gov/eos/www/naics/*

Economic Census: *www.census.gov/econ/census07/*

NetAdvantage. New York: Standard & Poor's

The database includes company, financial, and investment information as well as the well-known publication called *Industry Surveys.* Each industry report includes information on the current environment, industry trends, key industry ratios and statistics, and comparative company financial analysis. Available in HTML, PDF, or Excel formats.

Search Engines

Google. Mountain View, CA: Google, Inc.

Recognized for its advanced technology, quality of results, and simplicity, the search engine Google is highly recommended by librarians and other expert Web surfers.

www.google.com

Dogpile. Bellevue, WA: InfoSpace, Inc.

Dogpile is a metasearch engine that searches and compiles the most relevant results from more than 12 individual search engines.

http://www.dogpile.com/

Cases

Case 3   The Skeleton in the Corporate Closet*

"David," Donna Cooper exclaimed. "You won't believe it, but these look like love letters! And look, they're from when he was in the service!"

David Fisher, the corporate archivist for GPC Incorporated, hastened toward the young woman sprawled on his dusty floor but cheerily holding aloft a packet of yellowed envelopes. Unaccustomed to so much commotion in this room, he was still trying to process what had just happened. A moment ago, he'd been giving Miss Cooper, the writer hired to pen GPC's 75th anniversary book, a tour of his admittedly cluttered storeroom. Following at some distance, she'd chosen another path through the debris, only to reach an impasse. He'd glanced back just in time to see her give a shove to—of all things—the founder's writing desk. The brittle wooden legs, now in their 100th year at least, could hardly have been expected to scoot across the rough cement swirls of the basement floor. One had snapped immediately, the desk had toppled, and Miss Cooper had followed the whole wreck down.

Which was when, even through the air of the old storeroom, semiopaque with suspended dust, and even despite the early-stage cataract in his left eye, David spotted something that made his historian's heart leap. The back of the desk, now splintered, had mysteriously yielded a drawer, one he had never discovered in his years of puttering around it. Visible inside were some papers. Following his wondering gaze, the infuriating, wonderful Miss Cooper had spied, and snatched out, the treasure.

A Bittersweet Discovery

She was right, of course. They were letters composed to a sweetheart by Hudson Parker after he'd shipped out with Company K, the 137th U.S. Infantry unit made up of recruits from Kansas and Missouri. The first was dated August 6, 1917—a full decade before he'd founded General Parkelite Company. David took quick note of the addressee: Mary Beatrice White. Not a name he'd heard before. Clearly this romance preceded Virginia, the woman Hud had married. David was faintly scandalized to realize that old Hud had squirreled away these letters, no doubt unbeknownst to his wife. At the same time, he was touched at the thought of an unforgotten first love. And although his first instinct would usually have been to don cotton gloves and carry the letters into better light, he instead cleared a bit of floor space near Miss Cooper and sat. There was an undeniable charm in having this young woman eagerly extract letters from envelopes and read them aloud.

"My dearest Mary," she recited. "It began raining here this morning, and it is still at it. No drill today, so I will have time to write a letter or two." Impatient to find something juicier, she scanned the rest of the letter before handing it over. "Oh, look, David, how he signs it: 'With best of love to my own little girl.'" David accepted the letter and pushed his glasses down on his nose to peer over them. As always, he took a moment to appreciate the superior penmanship of an earlier age. Then his trained eye went to work on the page, drilling for facts that could be cataloged and cross-referenced with other accounts of the founder's war years. Donna, meanwhile, merrily called out other quaint snippets.

A half-hour passed in this way before David's joints, chilled by the bare floor, started to protest, and he suggested a change of venue. "Yeah," said Donna. "It's pretty musty in here, isn't it?" But as David took a moment to prop up the damaged desk and replace its drawer, Donna pulled another paper from an envelope. "Oh, this is the kind of thing you'll like," she noted, unfolding what looked, curiously, like drafting paper. She thrust it toward him and promptly launched into the accompanying letter. "You will recall from my last letter that we expect to see action this week, Mary darling. Enclosed is a document I hardly expect you to find interesting but entreat you to keep safe till my return." Indeed, it didn't interest Donna, so she rose to her feet and briskly dusted her skirt. "Honestly, David, I don't know how you work in here. My eyes are beginning to burn." But when she turned toward him, she was dismayed to see him staring at the paper he was clutching, his own eyes filling with tears.

Our Founder, a Thief?

A day passed before David appeared at the door of Jill Pierce, the communications VP who was his boss, and asked for a meeting at her convenience. Masking her surprise (in her seven years as his superior, she couldn't recall his ever initiating contact), she invited him in on the spot. Soon she was holding the letter herself and listening to David explain its import. Shockingly, it proved that the formula for Parkelite—the miracle plastic that was the company's first patent and its bread and butter for two full decades—had been someone else's innovation, not Hud Parker's. Not to put too fine a point on it, GPC's revered founder was a thief.

David filled in the parts of the story she didn't know. Of course, she needed no reminder of what Parkelite was. Although it had long since been superseded by better materials, it had been a huge technological advance in its day. A dense synthetic polymer, it could be molded or extruded and had the advantage of not changing shape after being mixed and heated. Most important, it wasn't flammable like earlier celluloid plastics. Manufacturers had used it to make things like engine parts, radio boxes, switches—even costume jewelry and inexpensive dinnerware. At the height of its popularity, General Parkelite was producing some 200,000 tons of the stuff per year.

What Jill had never heard was that in 1938, a lawsuit had been brought against Hud Parker and General Parkelite by the father of Karl Gintz, claiming that his son had been the true, sole inventor of Parkelite. Hud and Karl had studied chemistry together at Princeton, David explained, and had been star pupils who had egged each other on. But as well as being competitors, they were close friends, even to the extent that when war broke out in Europe, they enlisted together. Both dreamed of becoming pilots in the Army's Signal Corps, and both easily made the grade. They were transferred to the 94th Pursuit Group and posted to France. But in August 1918—just a week, Jill noted with a shiver, prior to the postmark on the envelope she held—Karl had been killed in maneuvers when the wing of his French-built trainer had collapsed. David pointed out that the formulas and diagrams neatly lettered on the graph paper were clearly the genesis of Parkelite, which Hud Parker had patented in 1920. Just as clearly, they were the work of Karl Gintz. "This is the document," David concluded, "that would have allowed the Gintz family to win its case."

Unprepared for the Worst

Jill had kept her composure while David was in her office, but as soon as he left, she opened her desk drawer, fished out a bottle of liquid antacid, and took a slug. David's chief concern seemed to be who would tell Hap—that is, Hudson Parker III, GPC's longtime CEO and the grandson of the founder. But that was the least of her worries. Clearly, this was a potential PR disaster, and her mind raced through the various ways it might play out. In honor of GPC's 75th anniversary, she'd introduced a heavy dose of nostalgia into this year's advertising. Hud Parker's image was splashed everywhere, along with the tag line, "He started it all." More like he *stole* it all, Jill thought bitterly, then felt guilty that such a remark would even occur to her. What a contrast to the pride she'd felt last summer when some focus groups she'd observed had come up with words like "trusted," "straight shooting," and "dependable" to describe the GPC brand. This was a catastrophe. And with all the extra planning that the special anniversary promotions required, she was already working flat out.

On her way to the CEO's office that afternoon, she lost her nerve at least three times. The fourth time, she even had Hap's doorway in sight, only to detour to the elevator lobby instead. She had a sudden determination to go down to the archives and urge David to destroy the incriminating paper and forget about it. But the fantasy died quickly as she recalled his haggard look in her office that morning. He'd already struggled with whether he could do that, she now realized, and decided he couldn't. She stopped short of hitting the down button and turned back toward the corner office.

History in the Remaking

Three days later, it was Hap Parker who was deciding what to do with the unwelcome news and 80-year-old graph paper now in his possession.

He'd been shocked, of course, and indeed had lost an entire weekend working through the implications on a purely personal level. On Saturday morning, he'd driven the two hours to the lakeside cottage where he'd spent summer days with his grandfather half a century before. He sat cross-legged on the dock, looked across the glittering water, then put his face in his hands and wept. First for his grandfather, who regardless of this incident didn't deserve to be impugned. The Parkelite patent, after all, was only a formula. It still took a great man to build a great company—and he had. And he had hardly coasted on that initial success. Instead, he'd infused the whole organization with the importance and excitement of constant innovation. It was his continuing attention to R&D that had led to General Parkelite's next generation of products, which, along with those of competitors, had made Parkelite obsolete. He'd won the respect of business leaders—indeed, of his country. He was a World War I ace, for God's sake! And a fair-dealing businessman, philanthropist, and community leader. A compassionate employer, certainly. And a dear grandfather, revered no less by his grandchildren for his tendency to dote on them.

This line of thought led Hap directly to self-pity. For neither did he, who had always held himself to the highest standard—with his grandfather's example as his North Star—deserve to have his name smeared. What was that line from Exodus about the sins of the fathers? He struggled to retrieve a long-forgotten catechism. Something about being visited on even the third and fourth generations. And now a fresh horror occurred to him: How much would Chip suffer, and even little Teddy, if this became known?

If. Had he really allowed himself to think "if"? He meant "when."

Reputation—or Reparation?

By Monday, Hap's thoughts were back with GPC and its employees, shareholders, and customers. He was listening to Newland Lowell, GPC's legal counsel, weigh in on the matter. No doubt about it, Newland was sharp. He'd come up with angles on this thing Hap hadn't anticipated.

As soon as he'd pressed the door shut behind him, in fact, Newland had broken into an improbable grin. "I know you're upset, Hap, so I'm going to get to the bottom line first," he said. "We haven't been able to turn up an heir to Karl Gintz." When he got no reaction, he hastened to pull out his other notes. "So. Let's take this from the top."

Newland first outlined a carefully reasoned argument that the letter, had it been introduced at trial long ago, would not necessarily have changed the verdict. The jury, he managed to persuade Hap, was fundamentally sympathetic to Hud Parker and not a little suspicious of Gintz's family. "If there's one thing I've learned," Newland said, "it's that jurors vote with their hearts and then find the legal hook to hang their emotions on." Besides, there would have been no proof that Karl hadn't meant to give the intellectual property to his friend and fellow soldier. "After all, no one else in his family was a chemist. They wouldn't have been able to make heads or tails of his notes. How do we know it wasn't his intent to let your grandfather take it forward? Maybe they were collaborating on it."

"But, Newland," Hap interjected. "If that had been the case, why wouldn't Hud have simply said so?"

"We're talking about a court case," Lowell reminded him. "His legal counsel would never have let him say that."

Hap fell silent again and let Newland continue to lay out his next argument: that there was no way of knowing when the letters Hud had sent to Mary Beatrice White had come back into his possession. It could have been years after the court case. "Not to mention," Newland added, "that if he needed this paper to fudge his own documentation for the patent, then why was it still in that envelope? Isn't it conceivable that the innovation was essentially your grandfather's but that Karl had taken careful notes on it to study and perhaps improve upon?"

Believing his arguments were carrying the day, Newland finally plunged into his last set of notes. These were legal strategies for "containing the discovery"—in essence placing a gag order on the few people in the organization who knew the truth. But Hap had already begun to chafe at what were sounding increasingly like elaborate rationalizations, and this was a bridge too far. He stood up from his desk and nodded to Newland. "Thank you, that's as much as I care to hear this afternoon."

Newland Lowell had known Hap Parker long enough not to mistake his tone, courteous though it might have seemed to others. He sighed as he swept his files back into his briefcase and rose from his chair. "Look, Hap. I'll be straight with you. I know you have a strong sense of what's ethical here. But you also have an organization to take care of. Your employees will be better off, not to mention your shareholders—hell, the *world* is better off if Hud Parker remains a hero. Don't be overly fastidious about this."

Doing the Right Thing

Packing up for the day, Hap had made up his mind. It was absurd that a company whose culture was all about honesty and integrity would tolerate a lie at its core. Maybe there was no one deserving of reparations out there, but surely the company deserved to pay some. He'd find some heir, somewhere.

He wasn't 20 yards down the hall, though, before he encountered a group of three GPC managers, two of them quite new to the company and the other a veteran. As he approached, he overheard the veteran, whose back was to Hap, saying patiently to one of the others, "Well, but, of course, Kevin, that just wouldn't be right." Then, catching sight of Hap, he fell into step with him, hoping to sound out the boss on some other matter.

Just out of earshot, Hap tilted his head back toward where the three had been standing and asked, "What was that about?" The manager explained that Kevin had proposed a marketing idea that seemed a little, well, not exactly underhanded, but. . . . The kid had come to GPC from a competitor with a certain industry reputation. "You know, people there learn to work all the angles and do a lot of things with a wink," he shrugged. "Don't worry, though. He wasn't comfortable there—that's why we got him."

"So you think he's got the potential to be a GPC'er?" Hap pressed.

"Well, that's the great thing about a strong culture, isn't it, Hap? It rubs off. He'll soon pick up on how things are done around here."

The unintended irony of those words made Hap queasy. Suddenly, he couldn't imagine damaging the strong belief in GPC held by this decent man and his 8,000 coworkers. Maybe Newland was right, he thought, and he was being too narrow in his ethics—even self-indulgent.

Was it possible for the right thing to be a lie?

Case 4   The Best-Laid Incentive Plans*

Hiram Phillips finished tying his bow tie and glanced in the mirror. Frowning, he tugged on the left side, then caught sight of his watch in the mirror. Time to get going. Moments later, he was down the stairs, whistling cheerfully and heading toward the coffeemaker.

"You're in a good mood," his wife said, looking up from the newspaper and smiling. "What's that tune? 'Accentuate the Positive'?"

"Well done!" Hiram called out. "You know, I do believe you're picking up some pop culture in spite of yourself." It was a running joke with them. She was a classically trained cellist and on the board of the local symphony. He was the one with the Sinatra and Bing Crosby albums and the taste for standards. "You're getting better at naming that tune."

"Or else you're getting better at whistling." She looked over her reading glasses and met his eye. They let a beat pass before they said in unison: "Naaah." Then, with a wink, Hiram shrugged on his trench coat, grabbed his travel mug, and went out the door.

Fat and Happy

It was true. Hiram Phillips, CFO and chief administrative officer of Rainbarrel Products, a diversified consumer-durables manufacturer, was in a particularly good mood. He was heading into a breakfast meeting that would bring nothing but good news. Sally Hamilton and Frank Ormondy from Felding & Company would no doubt already be at the office when he arrived and would have with them the all-important numbers—the statistics that would demonstrate the positive results of the performance management system he'd put in place a year ago. Hiram had already seen many of the figures in bits and pieces. He'd retained the consultants to establish baselines on the metrics he wanted to watch and had seen various interim reports from them since. But today's meeting would be the impressive summation capping off a year's worth of effort. Merging into the congestion of Route 45, he thought about the upbeat presentation he would spend the rest of the morning preparing for tomorrow's meeting of the corporate executive council.

It was obvious enough what his introduction should be. He would start at the beginning—or, anyway, his own

Harvard Business Review's cases, which are fictional, present common managerial dilemmas and offer concrete solutions from experts.

* Steven Kerr is the chief learning officer at Goldman Sachs in New York. Prior to joining Goldman Sachs in 2001, he spent seven years as the chief learning officer and head of leadership development at General Electric. He was responsible for GE's leadership development center at Crotonville.

beginning at Rainbarrel Products a year ago. At the time, the company had just come off a couple of awful quarters. It wasn't alone. The sudden slowdown in consumer spending, after a decade-long boom, had taken the whole industry by surprise. But what had quickly become clear was that Rainbarrel was adjusting to the new reality far less rapidly than its biggest competitors.

Keith Randall, CEO of Rainbarrel, was known for being an inspiring leader who focused on innovation. Even outside the industry, he had a name as a marketing visionary. But over the course of the ten-year economic boom, he had allowed his organization to become a little lax.

Take corporate budgeting. Hiram still smiled when he recalled his first day of interviews with Rainbarrel's executives. It immediately became obvious that the place had no budget integrity whatsoever. One unit head had said outright, "Look, none of us fights very hard at budget time, because after three or four months, nobody looks at the budget anyway." Barely concealing his shock, Hiram asked how that could be; what did they look at, then? The answer was that they operated according to one simple rule: "If it's a good idea, we say yes to it. If it's a bad idea, we say no."

"And what happens," Hiram had pressed, "when you run out of money halfway through the year?" The fellow rubbed his chin and took a moment to think before answering. "I guess we've always run out of good ideas before we've run out of money." Unbelievable!

"Fat and happy" was how Hiram characterized Rainbarrel in a conversation with the headhunter who had recruited him. Of course, he wouldn't use those words in the CEC meeting. That would sound too disparaging. In fact, he'd quickly fallen in love with Rainbarrel and the opportunities it presented. Here was a company that had the potential for greatness but that was held back by a lack of discipline. It was like a racehorse that had the potential to be a Secretariat but lacked a structured training regimen. Or a Ferrari engine that needed the touch of an expert mechanic to get it back in trim. In other words, the only thing Rainbarrel was missing was what someone like Hiram Phillips could bring to the table. The allure was irresistible; this was the assignment that would define his career. And now, a year later, he was ready to declare a turnaround.

Lean and Mean

Sure enough, as Hiram steered toward the entrance to the parking garage, he saw Sally and Frank in a visitor parking space, pulling their bulky file bags out of the trunk of Sally's sedan. He caught up to them at the security checkpoint in the lobby and took a heavy satchel from Sally's hand.

Moments later, they were at a conference table, each of them poring over a copy of the consultants' spiral-bound report. "This is great," Hiram said. "I can hand this out just as it is. But what I want to do while you're here is to really nail down what the highlights are. I have the floor for 40 minutes, but I guess I'd better leave ten for questions. There's no way I can plow through all of this."

"If I were you," Sally advised, "I would lead off with the best numbers. I mean, none of them are bad. You hit practically every target. But some of these, where you even exceeded the stretch goal. . . ."

Hiram glanced at the line Sally was underscoring with her fingernail. It was an impressive achievement: a reduction in labor costs. This had been one of the first moves he'd made, and he'd tried to do it gently. He'd come up with the idea of identifying the bottom quartile of performers throughout the company and offering them fairly generous buyout packages. But when that hadn't attracted enough takers, he'd gone the surer route. He'd imposed an across-the-board headcount reduction of 10% on all the units. In that round, the affected people were given no financial assistance beyond the normal severance.

"It made a big difference," he nodded. "But it wasn't exactly the world's most popular move." Hiram was well aware that a certain segment of the Rainbarrel workforce currently referred to him as "Fire 'em." He pointed to another number on the spreadsheet. "Now, that one tells a happier story: lower costs as a result of higher productivity."

"And better customer service to boot," Frank chimed in. They were talking about the transformation of Rainbarrel's call center—where phone representatives took orders and handled questions and complaints from both trade and retail customers. The spreadsheet indicated a dramatic uptick in productivity: The number of calls each service rep was handling per day had gone up 50%. A year earlier, reps were spending up to six minutes per call, whereas now the average was less than four minutes. "I guess you decided to go for that new automated switching system?" Frank asked.

"No!" Hiram answered. "That's the beauty of it. We got that improvement without any capital investment. You know what we did? We just announced the new targets, let everyone know we were going to monitor them, and put the names of the worst offenders on a great big 'wall of shame' right outside the cafeteria. Never underestimate the power of peer pressure!"

Sally, meanwhile, was already circling another banner achievement: an increase in on-time shipments. "You should talk about this, given that it's something that wasn't even being watched before you came."

It was true. As much as Rainbarrel liked to emphasize customer service in its values and mission statement, no reliable metric had been in place to track it. And getting a metric in place hadn't been as straightforward as it might've seemed—people had haggled about what constituted "on time" and even what constituted "shipped." Finally, Hiram had put his foot down and insisted on the most objective of measures. On time meant when the goods were promised to ship. And nothing was counted as shipped till it left company property. Period. "And once again," Hiram announced, "not a dollar of capital expenditure. I simply let people know that, from now on, if they made commitments and didn't keep them, we'd have their number."

"Seems to have done the trick," Sally observed. "The percentage of goods shipped by promise date has gone up steadily for the last six months. It's now at 92%."

Scanning the report, Hiram noticed another huge percentage gain, but he couldn't recall what the acronym stood for. "What's this? Looks like a good one: a 50% cost reduction?"

Sally studied the item. "Oh, that. It's a pretty small change, actually. Remember we separated out the commissions on sales to employees?" It came back to Hiram immediately. Rainbarrel had a policy that allowed current and retired employees to buy products at a substantial discount. But the salespeople who served them earned commissions based on the full retail value, not the actual price paid. So, in effect, employee purchases were jacking up the commission expenses. Hiram had created a new policy in which the commission reflected the actual purchase price. On its own, the change didn't amount to a lot, but it reminded Hiram of a larger point he wanted to make in his presentation: the importance of straightforward rules—and rewards—in driving superior performance.

"I know you guys don't have impact data for me, but I'm definitely going to talk about the changes to the commission structure and sales incentives. There's no question they must be making a difference."

"Right," Sally nodded. "A classic case of 'keep it simple,' isn't it?" She turned to Frank to explain. "The old way they calculated commissions was by using this really complicated formula that factored in, I can't remember, at least five different things."

"Including sales, I hope?" Frank smirked.

"I'm still not sure!" Hiram answered. "No, seriously, sales were the most important single variable, but they also mixed in all kinds of targets around mentoring, prospecting new clients, even keeping the account information current. It was all way too subjective, and salespeople were getting very mixed signals. I just clarified the message so they don't have to wonder what they're getting paid for. Same with the sales contests. It's simple now: If you sell the most product in a given quarter, you win."

With Sally and Frank nodding enthusiastically, Hiram again looked down at the report. Row after row of numbers attested to Rainbarrel's improved performance. It wouldn't be easy to choose the rest of the highlights, but what a problem to have! He invited the consultants to weigh in again and leaned back to bask in the superlatives. And his smile grew wider.

Cause for Concern

The next morning, a well-rested Hiram Phillips strode into the building, flashed his ID badge at Charlie, the guard, and joined the throng in the lobby. In the crowd waiting for the elevator, he recognized two young women from Rainbarrel, lattes in hand and headphones around their necks. One was grimacing melodramatically as she turned to her friend. "I'm so dreading getting to my desk," she said. "Right when I was leaving last night, an e-mail showed up from the buyer at Sullivan. I just know it's going to be some big, hairy problem to sort out. I couldn't bring myself to open it, with the day I'd had. But I'm going to be sweating it today trying to respond by five o'clock. I can't rack up any more late responses, or my bonus is seriously history."

Her friend had slung her backpack onto the floor and was rooting through it, barely listening. But she glanced up to set her friend straight in the most casual way. "No, see, all they check is whether you responded to an e-mail within 24 hours of opening it. So that's the key. Just don't open it. You know, till you've got time to deal with it."

Then a belltone announced the arrival of the elevator, and they were gone.

More Cause for Concern

An hour later, Keith Randall was calling to order the quarterly meeting of the corporate executive council. First, he said, the group would hear the results of the annual employee survey, courtesy of human resources VP Lew Hart. Next would come a demonstration by the chief marketing officer of a practice the CEO hoped to incorporate into all future meetings. It was a "quick market intelligence," or QMI, scan, engaging a few of Rainbarrel's valued customers in a prearranged—but not predigested—conference call, to collect raw data on customer service concerns and ideas. "And finally," Keith concluded, "Hiram's going to give us some very good news about cost reductions and operating efficiencies, all due to the changes he's designed and implemented this past year."

Hiram nodded to acknowledge the compliment. He heard little of the next ten minutes' proceedings, thinking instead about how he should phrase certain points for maximum effect. Lew Hart had lost him in the first moments of his presentation on the "people survey" by beginning with an overview of "purpose, methodology, and historical trends." Deadly.

It was the phrase "mindlessly counting patents" that finally turned Hiram's attention back to his colleague. Lew, it seemed, was now into the "findings" section of his remarks. Hiram pieced together that he was reporting on an unprecedented level of negativity in the responses from Rainbarrel's R&D department and was quoting the complaints people had scribbled on their surveys. "Another one put it this way," Lew said. "We're now highly focused on who's getting the most patents, who's getting the most copyrights, who's submitting the most grant proposals, etc. But are we more creative? It's not that simple."

"You know," Rainbarrel's chief counsel noted, "I have thought lately that we're filing for a lot of patents for products that will never be commercially viable."

"But the thing that's really got these guys frustrated seems to be their 'Innovation X' project," Lew continued. "They're all saying it's the best thing since sliced bread, a generational leap on the product line, but they're getting no uptake."

Eyes in the room turned to the products division president, who promptly threw up his hands. "What can I say, gang? We never expected that breakthrough to happen in this fiscal year. It's not in the budget to bring it to market."

Lew Hart silenced the rising voices, reminding the group he had more findings to share. Unfortunately, it didn't get much better. Both current and retired employees were complaining about being treated poorly by sales personnel when they sought to place orders or obtain information about company products. There was a lot of residual unhappiness about the layoffs, and not simply because those who remained had more work to do. Some people had noted that, because the reduction was based on headcount, not costs, managers had tended to fire low-level people, crippling the company without saving much money. And because the reduction was across the board, the highest performing departments had been forced to lay off some of the company's best employees. Others had heard about inequities in the severance deals: "As far as I can tell, we gave our lowest performers a better package than our good ones," he quoted one employee as saying.

And then there was a chorus of complaints from the sales organization. "No role models." "No mentoring." "No chance to pick the veterans' brains." "No knowledge sharing about accounts." More than ever, salespeople were dissatisfied with their territories and clamoring for the more affluent, high-volume districts. "It didn't help that all the sales-contest winners this year were from places like Scarsdale, Shaker Heights, and Beverly Hills," a salesperson was quoted as saying. Lew concluded with a promise to look further into the apparent decline in morale to determine whether it was an aberration.

The Ugly Truth

But if the group thought the mood would improve in the meeting's next segment—the QMI chat with the folks at longtime customer Brenton Brothers—they soon found out otherwise. Booming out of the speakerphone in the middle of the table came the Southern-tinged voices of Billy Brenton and three of his employees representing various parts of his organization.

"What's up with your shipping department?" Billy called out. "My people are telling me it's taking forever to get the stock replenished."

Hiram sat up straight, then leaned toward the speakerphone. "Excuse me, Mr. Brenton. This is Hiram Phillips—I don't believe we've met. But are you saying we are not shipping by our promise date?"

A cough—or was it a guffaw?—came back across the wire. "Well, son. Let me tell you about that. First of all, what y'all promise is not always what we are saying we require—and what we believe we deserve. Annie, isn't that right?"

"Yes, Mr. Brenton," said the buyer. "In some cases, I've been told to take a late date or otherwise forgo the purchase. That becomes the promise date, I guess, but it's not the date I asked for."

I was there, it's true. But I still found my job frustrating. Every proposed acquisition or new initiative of any substance had to be approved by people at headquarters who were far removed from our business. And whenever corporate profits flagged, the response was mindless across-the-board cost cutting that took little account of individual divisions' performance.

So when I was offered the opportunity to head up a small but profitable machine-tool maker in southern Ohio, I jumped at the chance.

Sunflower Tableau

I still remember driving to work my first day at Paragon Tool five years ago. Winding through the Ohio countryside, I saw a stand of sunflowers growing in a rocky patch of soil next to a barn. "Now *there's* a symbol for us," I thought, "a commonplace but hardy plant that quickly grows above its neighbors, often in fairly tough conditions." I was confident that Paragon—a solid, unexceptional business operating in an extremely difficult industry and economic environment—had the potential to grow with similarly glorious results.

For one thing, Paragon was relatively healthy. The company was built around a line of high-end machines—used by manufacturers of aerospace engines, among others—that continued to enjoy fairly good margins, despite the battering that the machine-tool industry as a whole had taken over the previous decade and a half. Still, the market for our product was essentially stagnant. Foreign competition was beginning to take its toll. And we continued to face brutal cyclical economic swings.

I quickly launched a number of initiatives designed to spur revenue growth. With some aggressive pricing, we increased sales and gained share in our core market, driving out a number of our new foreign rivals. We expanded our product line and our customer base by modifying our flagship product for use in a number of other industries. We also made a string of acquisitions in the industrial signage and electronic-labeling field, aiming to leverage the relationships we had with our machine-tool customers. No question, these moves put real pressure on our margins. Along with the price cuts and the debt we took on to make the acquisitions, we had to invest in new manufacturing equipment and a larger sales force. But we were laying the foundation for what I hoped would be a highly profitable future. The board and the senior management team, including Littlefield, seemed to share my view.

Indeed, the CFO and I had developed a rapport, despite our differing business instincts. Early on in our working relationship, this sixth-generation Yankee started in with the kidding about my alma mater. "Is that how they taught you to think about it at Rutgers?" he'd say if I was brainstorming and came up with some crazy idea. "Because at *Wharton,* they taught us. . . ." I'd just laugh and then tell whoever else was in the room how proud we were that Littlefield had been a cheerleader for the Penn

football team—like that was his biggest scholarly accomplishment. One time he "let it slip" that in fact he was Phi Beta Kappa, and we all just groaned. I said, "Give it up, Littlefield. You may have been Phi Beta Kappa, but, despite those letters on your gold pin, you'll never out-*Greek* me." To tell the truth, our skills are complementary, and between us we manage to do a pretty good job for the company.

As Paragon grew, so did the sense of excitement and urgency among our managers—indeed, among the entire workforce. People who once had been merely content to work at Paragon now couldn't wait to tackle the next challenge. And that excitement spread throughout the small Ohio town where we are based. When I'd go with my wife to a party or speak at the local Rotary Club or even stop to buy gas, people would show a genuine interest in the company and our latest doings—it helped that we always mentioned the job-creation impact when announcing new initiatives. There's no doubt it stoked my ego to be one of the bigger fish in the local pond. But even more important for me was the sense that this was business at its best, providing people with a justified sense of well-being about the present and confidence in the future.

Anyway, my point here is that we've grown fast since I arrived, but we still have a long way to go. I've come to think that the real key to our future is in the company's services division. We currently offer our customers the option to buy a standard service contract, under which we provide periodic machine maintenance and respond to service calls. But we've been developing technology and software, similar to MonitoRobotics', that would allow us to respond immediately if a machine at a customer's site goes down. The division currently accounts for less than 10% of our revenue and, because of the cost of developing the new technology, it's struggling to turn a profit.

But I can see in the services division the seeds of a business that will ultimately transform us from a manufacturing company into a high-tech company. Such a transformation, requiring an overhaul of our culture and capabilities, won't be easy. And it will surely require significant additional investments. But the potential upside is huge, with the promise of sales and profit growth that could make our current single-digit gains seem trivial by comparison. Besides, what choice do we have? A number of our competitors have already spotted these opportunities and have begun moving ahead with them. If we don't ramp up quickly, we might well miss out on the action altogether.

A Company in Play

Just over a month ago, I was sitting at my desk preparing a presentation for the handful of analysts who cover our company. Until recently, most of them have had only good things to say about all our growth moves. But last quarter, when we again reported a year-on-year drop in earnings, a few of them started asking pointed questions about our

Case 6   American International Group and the Bonus Fiasco*

After two decades of rapid growth and expansion in an environment of very little regulatory oversight and unbounded optimism about the power of the markets to create limitless wealth, the U.S. financial system came crashing down in the second half of 2008. What started as a sudden decline in housing prices after years of speculative growth very soon snowballed into a full-fledged financial crisis. Major banking companies such as Citicorp and Bank of America found their equity base wiped out by loan losses. Investment banking firms such as Merrill Lynch and Bear Stearns, which operate largely outside the regulatory framework of the Federal Reserve, were in even bigger trouble because they were highly leveraged. Fearing a complete financial meltdown, Henry Paulson, secretary of the Treasury in the Bush administration, announced a bailout package of $750 billion on September 16, 2008, to restore confidence in the banks and to jump-start the credit markets.

What exactly does the government do in a bailout? A bailout can take many forms. For example, the government can buy stock in a troubled institution, thus shoring up its equity base.

The very fact that the government has an equity stake may be taken as an implicit government guarantee by creditors, suppliers, and clients because concerns about solvency and ability to stay in business are assuaged. Alternatively, the government can extend a loan to the institution, to be paid back when the company becomes profitable again. Another approach is for the government to buy preferred stock in the company. In this case the government is entitled to a fair return on the investment. Finally, the government can buy distressed assets of the institution, thereby helping it to clean up its balance sheet. Irrespective of the form of the bailout, all bailouts represent a temporary or, in some cases, long-term commitment of public money to private companies.

As the economic crisis gathered momentum and the credit markets came to a standstill in the fall of 2008, it became clear that banks were not the only institutions in trouble. American International Group (AIG), one of the largest and most respected insurance companies in the world, found itself in even bigger financial distress in September 2008 when the rating agencies suddenly lowered its credit rating. Not only did this cause the cost of borrowing to go up for AIG, but it also triggered the requirement that the company post collateral with its counterparties. Unable to do so, AIG approached the

government for a bailout. In the next few months, the government pumped an astounding $85 billion into AIG alone to prevent it from going bankrupt. Insurance companies are generally supposed to be risk-averse and prudent. How did AIG get into such a big mess?

The primary culprit for the problems of AIG was a somewhat exotic financial product called credit default swaps (CDSs). In simple terms, these swaps represented an insurance cover to holders of mortgage-backed securities: If the value of the securities went down, AIG would make good the losses suffered by the owners. In good times, when real estate prices were climbing steadily each year, the CDSs were pure profits for AIG. Emboldened by what it perceived as negligible risk and motivated by the prospect of ever-increasing profits, AIG sold hundreds of billions of dollars' worth of these instruments. Although insurance is a business regulated by the states, these products were outside the range of regulation.

Right from the beginning, there was considerable controversy about whether the government should try to bail out any failing firm in a market economy. Even those who were not ideologically opposed to the bailout were skeptical whether the government efforts would be enough to save the company. There were also concerns about how the company would spend the bailout money.

Immediately after the first bailout was announced, AIG attracted considerable negative press when it was reported that AIG executives attended a lavish retreat in California that featured spa treatments, banquets, and golf outings. Total tab: $444,000. Immediately thereafter, AP reported that AIG executives spent $86,000 on a luxurious English hunting trip.[1] This was only days after the Fed had extended a $37.8 billion loan on top of the $85 billion mentioned earlier. The company's response: "We regret that this event was not canceled."[2]

In March 2009, it was disclosed that AIG had paid $218 million in bonus payments to employees of the financial services division, the very division that was responsible for issuing the credit default swaps that got the firm into trouble. Overall, 418 managers were the beneficiaries of these "retention" bonuses, although 53 of them were no longer with the company! The highest bonus was $6.4 million. Six managers received more than $4 million each, and 51 people received between $1 million and $2 million.

The announcement of these bonuses sparked instant outrage among the public. President Barack Obama accused the company of "recklessness and greed." Noting that AIG had "received substantial sums" of federal aid, the president announced that he was asking Treasury Secretary Timothy Geithner "to use that leverage and pursue every legal avenue to block these bonuses and make the American taxpayers whole."[3] Andrew Cuomo, New York State's attorney general, threatened to subpoena the executives and engage in a "name and shame" campaign

* This case was prepared by Professor Abdul A. Rasheed of the University of Texas at Arlington, Graduate Student Brian Pinkham, and Professor Gregory G. Dess of the University of Texas at Dallas. This case was based solely on library research and was developed for class discussion rather than to illustrate either effective or ineffective handling of an administrative situation. Copyright © 2009 Abdul A. Rasheed and Gregory G. Dess.

---

investments and when they could be expected to bear fruit. As I was giving some thought to how I'd answer their questions in the upcoming meeting, the phone rang. It was our investment banker, Jed Nixon.

"Nicky, I think we should talk," he said. I could tell from the sound of his voice he was on to something big, and then he told me what it was: "MonitoRobotics is in play."

We both did some calendar juggling and managed to get together for lunch the very next day at Jed's office in Cincinnati. The rumor was that one of our direct competitors, Bellows & Samson, was about to launch a hostile takeover bid for MonitoRobotics. As it happened, we had just started a conversation with MonitoRobotics' management a few months before, about collaborating on remote servicing technology for machine tools. But Jed's call had had its intended effect, changing my thinking about the company: Why not acquire it ourselves?

Although MonitoRobotics' technology was designed to detect and report operating failures in robotics equipment, managers there had told us when we met that adapting it for use on other industrial machinery was feasible. Indeed, MonitoRobotics had recently licensed the technology to a company that planned to modify it for use on complex assembly lines that experienced frequent breakdowns. Our engineers had confirmed that a version could be developed for our machines—though in their initial assessment they hadn't been exactly sure how long this would take.

Still, the potential benefits of acquiring MonitoRobotics seemed numerous. It would give us a powerful presence in a fast-growing business while preempting a competitor from staking a claim there. Whatever the time lag in adapting MonitoRobotics' technology for use with our products, we would almost certainly be able to offer our customers this valuable troubleshooting service more quickly than if we continued to develop the technology ourselves. And though our products were different, MonitoRobotics and Paragon potentially served many of the same manufacturing customers. "Think of the cross-selling opportunities," Jed said, as he took a bite of his sandwich. The greatest opportunity, though, lay in the possibility that MonitoRobotics' software technology would become the standard means for machine tools—and ultimately a variety of industrial machines—to communicate their service needs to the people who serviced them and to other machines that might be affected by their shutdown.

This was a fairly speculative train of thought. But a MonitoRobotics acquisition had for me the earmarks of a breakthrough opportunity for Paragon. And our earlier conversations with its management team had been cordial, suggesting the company might welcome a friendly offer from us to counter Bellows & Samson's hostile bid. Of course, even if we were able to get MonitoRobotics at a fair price, an acquisition of this size would further

delay our return to the margins and profit growth we had known in the past. And that, I knew, wouldn't sit well with everyone.

Management Dissension

The day after my meeting with Jed, I called together members of our senior management team. There was a barely suppressed gasp when I mentioned the potential acquisition, particularly given its size. "Boy, that would be a lot to digest with everything we've got on our plate right now," said Joe McCollum, our senior VP of marketing. "It also might represent the chance of a lifetime," countered Rosemary Witkowski, head of the services division. Then Littlefield spoke up. His skepticism wasn't surprising.

"I was just running a few simple numbers on what the MonitoRobotics acquisition might mean to our bottom line," he said. "Besides the costs associated with the acquisition itself, we'd be looking at some significant expenses in the near term, including accelerated software research, hiring and training, and even brand development." He pointed out that these costs would put further pressure on our earnings, just as our profits were struggling to recover from earlier growth-related investments.

Littlefield did concede that a bold acquisition like this might be just the sort of growth move that would appeal to some of our analysts—and might even prompt a few more securities firms to cover us. But he insisted that if our earnings didn't start bouncing back soon, Wall Street was going to pillory us. Then he dropped his bombshell: "I frankly think this is an opportunity to consider getting out of the services business altogether. Eliminating the continued losses that we've been experiencing there would allow us to begin realizing the profit growth that we can expect from the investments we've made in our still-healthy machine-tool business."

Littlefield argued that, whether we acquired MonitoRobotics or not, it wasn't clear we'd be able to dominate the machine-tool services market because a number of our competitors were already flocking there. Furthermore, the market might not be worth fighting over: Many of our customers were struggling with profitability themselves and might not be willing or able to buy our add-on services. "Last one in, turn out the lights" was the phrase Littlefield used to describe the rush to dominate a profitless market.

As soon as she had a chance, Rosemary shot back in defense of her operation. "This is the one area we're in that has significant growth potential," she said. "And we've already sunk an incredible amount of money into developing this software. I can't believe you'd throw all of that investment out the window." But a number of heads nodded when Littlefield argued that we'd recoup much of that investment if we sold the money-losing business.

Several days later, I polled the members of the senior management team and found them split on the issue of the acquisition. And, to be honest, I was beginning to doubt myself on this. I respected Littlefield's financial savvy. And no one had yet raised the issue of whether Paragon, a traditional manufacturing company, had the management capabilities to run what was essentially a software start-up. We decided to hire two highly regarded consulting firms to do quick analyses of the proposed MonitoRobotics acquisition.

The Sunflowers' Successor

Today, the consultants came back to us with conflicting reports. One highlighted the market potential of Monito-Robotics' technology, noting that we might be too far behind to develop similar technology on our own. The other focused on the difficulties both of integrating the company's technology with ours and of adapting it to equipment beyond the robotics field.

So as I drove home tonight, the dilemma seemed no closer to being resolved. In many ways, I am persuaded by the cautionary message of Littlefield's number crunching. At the same time, I firmly believe the pros and cons of such a complex decision can't be precisely quantified; sometimes you just have to go with your instincts—which in my case favor growth. As I turned the issue over in my head, I looked out the car window, half-consciously seeking inspired insight. Sure enough, there was the barn where the sunflowers had been growing five years before. But the bright yellow blossoms, highlighted by the red timbers of the barn, were gone. Instead, a carpet of green kudzu was growing up the side of the increasingly dilapidated building. This fast-growing vine, which already had ravaged much of the South, was now spreading, uncontrolled and unproductive, into southern Ohio.

My mind started to drift and the image of kudzu—a more sinister symbol of growth than the sunflower—began to merge with thoughts of my father, who had died of lung cancer two years before, and my mother, who these days spends most of her time managing her investments. Suddenly, my parents' favorite phrases came to mind. It occurred to me that kudzu was now becoming as American as Mom and apple pie. Even so, its dense foliage certainly seemed like a place where, if you weren't careful, you could easily misplace your shirt.

Should Paragon Tool further its growth ambitions by trying to acquire MonitoRobotics?

---

by making the list of bonus recipients public.[4] The House even passed a bill that effectively imposed a punitive 90 percent tax on the bonuses.[5]

At the same time, there were others who felt that the payments represented contractual obligations and therefore populist sentiments should not be allowed to violate the sanctity of contracts. Many of the employees felt that they had every right to receive the payments they were promised and worked for. Their feelings were best expressed in the following resignation letter sent by Jake DeSantis, an executive vice president of the American International Group's financial products unit, to Edward M. Liddy, the chief executive of AIG.

Dear Mr. Liddy:

It is with deep regret that I submit my notice of resignation from A.I.G. Financial Products. I hope you take the time to read this entire letter. Before describing the details of my decision, I want to offer some context:

I am proud of everything I have done for the commodity and equity divisions of A.I.G.-F.P. I was in no way involved in—or responsible for—the credit default swap transactions that have hamstrung A.I.G. Nor were more than a handful of the 400 current employees of A.I.G.-F.P. Most of those responsible have left the company and have conspicuously escaped the public outrage.

After 12 months of hard work dismantling the company—during which A.I.G. reassured us many times we would be rewarded in March 2009—we in the financial products unit have been betrayed by A.I.G. and are being unfairly persecuted by elected officials. In response to this, I will now leave the company and donate my entire post-tax retention payment to those suffering from the global economic downturn. My intent is to keep none of the money myself.

I take this action after 11 years of dedicated, honorable service to A.I.G. I can no longer effectively perform my duties in this dysfunctional environment, nor am I being paid to do so. Like you, I was asked to work for an annual salary of $1, and I agreed out of a sense of duty to the company and to the public officials who have come to its aid. Having now been let down by both, I can no longer justify spending 10, 12, 14 hours a day away from my family for the benefit of those who have let me down.

You and I have never met or spoken to each other, so I'd like to tell you about myself. I was raised by schoolteachers working multiple jobs in a world of closing steel mills. My hard work earned me acceptance to M.I.T., and the institute's generous financial aid enabled me to attend. I had fulfilled my American dream.

I started at this company in 1998 as an equity trader, became the head of equity and commodity trading and, a couple of years before A.I.G.'s meltdown last September, was named the head of business development for commodities. Over this period the equity and commodity

---

units were consistently profitable—in most years generating net profits of well over $100 million. Most recently, during the dismantling of A.I.G.-F.P., I was an integral player in the pending sale of its well-regarded commodity index business to UBS. As you know, business unit sales like this are crucial to A.I.G.'s effort to repay the American taxpayer.

The profitability of the businesses with which I was associated clearly supported my compensation. I never received any pay resulting from the credit default swaps that are now losing so much money. I did, however, like many others here, lose a significant portion of my life savings in the form of deferred compensation invested in the capital of A.I.G.-F.P. because of those losses. In this way I have personally suffered from this controversial activity—directly as well as indirectly with the rest of the taxpayers.

I have the utmost respect for the civic duty that you are now performing at A.I.G. You are as blameless for these credit default swap losses as I am. You answered your country's call and you are taking a tremendous beating for it.

But you also are aware that most of the employees of your financial products unit had nothing to do with the large losses. And I am disappointed and frustrated over your lack of support for us. I and many others in the unit feel betrayed that you failed to stand up for us in the face of untrue and unfair accusations from certain members of Congress last Wednesday and from the press over our retention payments, and that you didn't defend us against the baseless and reckless comments made by the attorneys general of New York and Connecticut.

My guess is that in October, when you learned of these retention contracts, you realized that the employees of the financial products unit needed some incentive to stay and that the contracts, being both ethical and useful, should be left to stand. That's probably why A.I.G. management assured us on three occasions during that month that the company would "live up to its commitment" to honor the contract guarantees.

That may be why you decided to accelerate by three months more than a quarter of the amounts due under the contracts. That action signified to us your support, and was hardly something that one would do if he truly found the contracts "distasteful."

That may also be why you authorized the balance of the payments on March 13.

At no time during the past six months that you have been leading A.I.G. did you ask us to revise, renegotiate or break these contracts—until several hours before your appearance last week before Congress.

I think your initial decision to honor the contracts was both ethical and financially astute, but it seems to have been politically unwise. It's now apparent that especially difficult for nonprofits such as United Way to maintain trust, because their products and services did not easily lend themselves to traditional quality assessment and performance review; and once that trust was broken, it was difficult to get it back.

Responding to this, United Way Worldwide's CEO, Brian Gallagher, formally initiated a shift in strategy. Responding to the environment, Gallagher established new membership standards to enhance the level of accountability and transparency in United Way affiliates' operations, rebranded United Way as doing "what matters" in the communities it served, and updated the "standards of excellence," providing a description of benchmark standards and best practices to better reflect the organization's strategic shift from its traditional role as strictly a fund-raiser to a new mission focused on identifying and addressing the long-term needs of communities.

These initiatives required that United Way affiliates buy into the change effort, because the power of the parent organization was limited to removing the affiliate from United Way membership if it didn't comply. As a nonprofit organization, it was imperative for United Way Worldwide to get the necessary support at the local level in order to achieve its stated organizational goals. Would Gallagher's various strategies be successfully implemented? Was the shift in strategy sufficient to ensure the continued viability of the United Way, or was its very mission perhaps no longer relevant?

Overview and History of the United Way of America

United Way was founded in 1887 as the Charity Organizations Society of Denver, raising $21,700 for 22 local agencies in its second year of operation. In 1913 this model was expanded to become a "Community Chest" in Cleveland, and in 1918 a dozen fund-raising federations met in Chicago to form the American Association for Community Organizations. From 1919 to 1929, over 350 Community Chests were created, and by 1948 more than 1,000 communities had these United Way Community Chests in operation. In 1973 the partnership between United Way and the National Football League began, with the goal to increase public awareness of social-service issues facing the country. Through the partnership, United Way public service announcements featured volunteer NFL players, coaches, and owners, and NFL players supported their local United Ways through personal appearances, special programs, and membership on United Way governing boards.

In 1974 United Ways in America and Canada raised $1,038,995,000, marking the first time in history that an annual campaign of a single organization raised more than $1 billion. In that same year, United Way International was formed to help nations around the world create United Way–type organizations. The 1981–1985 and 1997–1998 campaigns generated the greatest percentage increase in revenues. Amounts raised since 1999 generally failed to keep up with the rate of inflation, although a $10.5 million gift from Bill and Melinda Gates and a $50 million donation by Bank of America in 1999 made that year a good one (see Exhibit 1).[7]

The United Way was essentially a financial intermediary, providing fund-raising activities, primarily through donor organizations' employee payroll deductions, and then distributing those funds to agencies that could actually deliver services to clients in the target community. The parent organization, United Way Worldwide, serviced the local United Way chapters, who performed the bulk of the fund-raising. Although

Exhibit 1   **United Way Campaign History**

	Amount Raised in Current $					Amount Raised in Constant $		
		Change		Average Annual CPI*	Inflation Rate		Change	
Year	$, Billions	$, Millions	%	(1982–1984, 100)	%	$, Billions	$, Millions	%
1971	0.813		3.3	40.5	4.4	2.0072		-1.0
1972	0.858	45.2	5.6	41.8	3.2	2.0529	45.7	2.3
1973	0.916	58.3	6.8	44.4	6.2	2.0640	11.1	0.5
1974	0.979	62.4	6.8	49.3	11.0	1.9854	-78.6	-3.8
1975	1.023	44.1	4.5	53.8	9.1	1.9013	-84.1	-4.2
1976	1.104	81.4	8.0	56.9	5.8	1.9408	39.5	2.1
1977	1.205	100.5	9.1	60.6	6.5	1.9881	47.3	2.4
1978	1.318	112.9	9.4	65.2	7.6	2.0210	32.9	1.7

(continued)

you either misunderstood the agreements that you had made—tacit or otherwise—with the Federal Reserve, the Treasury, various members of Congress and Attorney General Andrew Cuomo of New York, or were not strong enough to withstand the shifting political winds.

You've now asked the current employees of A.I.G.-F.P. to repay these earnings. As you can imagine, there has been a tremendous amount of serious thought and heated discussion about how we should respond to this breach of trust.

As most of us have done nothing wrong, guilt is not a motivation to surrender our earnings. We have worked 12 long months under these contracts and now deserve to be paid as promised. None of us should be cheated of our payments any more than a plumber should be cheated after he has fixed the pipes but a careless electrician causes a fire that burns down the house.

Many of the employees have, in the past six months, turned down job offers from more stable employers, based on A.I.G.'s assurances that the contracts would be honored. They are now angry about having been misled by A.I.G.'s promises and are not inclined to return the money as a favor to you.

The only real motivation that anyone at A.I.G.-F.P. now has is fear. Mr. Cuomo has threatened to "name and shame," and his counterpart in Connecticut, Richard Blumenthal, has made similar threats—even though attorneys general are supposed to stand for due process, to conduct trials in courts and not the press.

So what am I to do? There's no easy answer. I know that because of hard work I have benefited more than most during the economic boom and have saved enough that my family is unlikely to suffer devastating losses during the current bust. Some might argue that members of my profession have been overpaid, and I wouldn't disagree.

That is why I have decided to donate 100 percent of the effective after-tax proceeds of my retention payment directly to organizations that are helping people who are suffering from the global downturn. This is not a tax-deduction gimmick; I simply believe that I at least deserve to dictate how my earnings are spent, and do not want to see them disappear back into the obscurity of A.I.G.'s or the federal government's budget. Our earnings have caused such a distraction for so many from the more pressing issues our country faces, and I would like to see my share of it benefit those truly in need.

On March 16 I received a payment from A.I.G. amounting to $742,006.40, after taxes. In light of the uncertainty over the ultimate taxation and legal status of this payment, the actual amount I donate may be less—in fact, it may end up being far less if the recent House bill raising the tax on the retention payments to 90 percent stands. Once all the money is donated, you will immediately receive a list of all recipients.

This choice is right for me. I wish others at A.I.G.-F.P. luck finding peace with their difficult decision, and only hope their judgment is not clouded by fear.

Mr. Liddy, I wish you success in your commitment to return the money extended by the American government, and luck with the continued unwinding of the company's diverse businesses—especially those remaining credit default swaps. I'll continue over the short term to help make sure no balls are dropped, but after what's happened this past week I can't remain much longer—there is too much bad blood. I'm not sure how you will greet my resignation, but at least Attorney General Blumenthal should be relieved that I'll leave under my own power and will not need to be "shoved out the door."

Sincerely,

Jake DeSantis

Liddy was clearly in an unwinnable situation. On the one hand, the politicians and the press were pillorying him for authorizing lavish bonuses while the company was essentially on welfare payments from the taxpayer. On the other hand, his own employees were upset at him that he was pandering to the politicians by describing these contractual payments as "distasteful."

Endnotes

1. AIG executives spent thousands during hunting trip. Associated Press, October 17, 2008, *http://ap.google.com/article/ALeqM5g3InVeHoYnmXZnM2ACXSgjG0nIQD93R68VO0*.
2. A. Taylor. AIG execs' retreat after bailout angers lawmakers. Associated Press, October 11, 2008, *http://thecoffeedesk.com/news/index.php/archives/76kers*.
3. T. Raum. Obama: AIG can't justify "outrage" of exec bonuses with taxpayer money keeping company afloat. Associated Press, March 16, 2009, *http://finance.yahoo.com/news/Frank-assails-bonuses-paid-to-apf-14646988.html*.
4. Cuomo issues subpoena to AIG on credit derivatives data. March 27, 2009, *www.rttnews.com/Content/BreakingNews.aspx?Node=B1&Id=895234%20&Category=Breaking%20News*.
5. J. D. McKinnon and A. Jones. Laws may not hinder effort to tax AIG bonuses. *Wall Street Journal*, March 18, 2009, *http://online.wsj.com/article/SB123742691757579925.html*.

In January 2011, United Way CEO Brian Gallagher participated in a panel discussion at the World Economic Forum in Davos, Switzerland. The topic was corporate norms, and Gallagher was there to encourage worldwide involvement by companies in corporate social responsibility aimed at building strong, sustainable communities. This direct appeal to worldwide corporate leaders came after a disappointing trend: In 2010 America's wealthiest individuals gave less to charity than they had since 2000; and in 2009, some of the biggest U.S. charities saw donations fall by 11 percent, the worst decline in 20 years.[1] United Way Worldwide had reported a 5 percent decline in contributions, while demand for services increased. This continued trend—reduction in giving, increase in need—had prompted United Way to change strategy. On July 1, 2009, United Way of America (UWA) changed its name to United Way Worldwide (UWW) and merged with United Way International (UWI). UWW also initiated a 10-year program, "Live United," focused less on distribution of funds and more on advancing the common good by addressing underlying causes of problems in the core areas of education, financial stability, and health. Would this be a way to get donors reenergized and create real change in the communities United Way served?

UWW provided support for over 1,800 local United Way members or affiliates operating in 46 countries. These local organizations relied on their respective parents for resources such as leadership education, public policy advocacy, marketing support, and standards for ethical governance and financial reporting. United Ways worldwide were part of a federation of nonprofits formed by caring people to serve the needs of their communities. According to UWW's website, "We advance the common good by focusing on improving education, helping people achieve financial stability, and promoting healthy lives, and by mobilizing millions of people to give, advocate, and volunteer to improve the conditions in which they live." United Way raised and distributed funds to the most effective local service providers; built alliances and coordinated volunteer support among charities, businesses, and other entities; and acted as best-practice models of management and financial accountability—but this last item had become a source of problems. With three high-profile ethical scandals since 1995 at both the national and local level, the United Way brand had to combat an erosion of trust, at the same time that it was dealing with an increasingly competitive and changing environment for charitable contributors.

Even after over 120 years of solid financial performance and steady growth, since the year 2000 United Way had seemingly reached a plateau of fund-raising in the United States. Certainly, there were options for growth from international members and from the energy and direction of nationwide objectives stated by United Way of America (education about and implementation of the national 2-1-1 phone network; the early childhood educational initiatives Success by 6 and Born Learning; encouragement of nationwide voluntarism through the Lend a Hand public service announcements funded by a donation from the NFL; and the Assets for Family Success economic self-sufficiency program for working families). Yet charitable donations still had not topped the inflation-adjusted peak-year campaign of 1989.[2]

In addition, in 2011 veteran fundraisers on all fronts were citing challenges, such as competition for donations, difficulty recruiting and keeping qualified fundraisers, difficulty raising money for general operating costs, and a growing focus on large gifts from very wealthy individuals, which, when publicized, could reduce the motivation for smaller donors to contribute (small donors might think, "If someone like Bill Gates is providing funds, why do they need my dollars?").[3] From the donors' perspective, the opportunities for both individuals and businesses to engage in charitable giving had expanded, with over 40 percent of new nonprofits appearing since 2000.[4] Many of these, especially those supporting disaster relief in the wake of 9/11 and Hurricane Katrina, had a single-issue focus that had the potential for creating a close bond with the donor. This meant that some individuals might have bypassed organizations such as the United Way, believing that they had support targets that were too broad, preferring, instead, to specify exactly where donations should go. (Such a donor might think, "If I'm giving, I want to make sure my money is going where I want it to go, to the cause I want to support").

Even prior to 9/11, American donors had expressed concern about their ability to access information regarding how their donations were going to be used, what percentage of the charity's spending went toward actual current programs, how their privacy was going to be protected when giving via the Internet, and whether the charity met voluntary standards of conduct.[5] It didn't help that many nonprofits, including United Way of America, suffered widely publicized scandals over misappropriation of funds. Organizations that serve community or broader social needs must continually be perceived as legitimate, as acting in an appropriate and desirable way within "some socially constructed set of norms, values, beliefs and definitions"[6] in order to receive needed donations. It was

* By Professor Pauline Assenza of Berkeley College, Professor Alan B. Eisner of Pace University, and graduate student Luz Barrera of Pace University. This case is based upon public documents and was developed for class discussion rather than to illustrate either effective or ineffective handling of the situation. This research was supported in part by the Wilson Center for Social Entrepreneurship, Pace University. Copyright © 2011 Pauline Assenza & Alan B. Eisner.

Exhibit 1   United Way Campaign History (continued)

| | Amount Raised in Current $ | | | Average Annual CPI* (1982–1984, 100) | Inflation Rate % | Amount Raised in Constant $ | | |
| | | Change | | | | | Change | |
Year	$, Billions	$, Millions	%			$, Billions	$, Millions	%
1979	1.424	105.8	8.0	72.6	11.3	1.9607	-60.3	-3.0
1980	1.526	102.5	7.2	82.4	13.5	1.8519	-108.8	-5.5
1981	1.680	154.0	10.1	90.9	10.3	1.8482	-3.8	-0.2
1982	1.780	100.0	6.0	96.5	6.2	1.8446	-3.6	-0.2
1983	1.950	170.0	9.6	99.6	3.2	1.9578	113.3	6.1
1984	2.145	195.0	10.0	103.9	4.3	2.0645	106.7	5.4
1985	2.330	185.0	8.6	107.6	3.6	2.1654	100.9	4.9
1986	2.440	110.0	4.7	109.6	1.9	2.2263	60.8	2.8
1987	2.600	160.0	6.6	113.6	3.6	2.2887	62.5	2.8
1988	2.780	180.0	6.9	118.3	4.1	2.3500	61.2	2.7
1989	2.980	200.0	7.2	124.0	4.8	2.4032	53.3	2.3
1990	3.110	130.0	4.4	130.7	5.4	2.3795	-23.7	-1.0
1991	3.170	60.0	1.9	136.2	4.2	2.3275	-52.0	-2.2
1992	3.040	-130.0	-4.1	140.3	3.0	2.1668	-160.7	-6.9
1993	3.047	7.0	0.2	144.5	3.0	2.1087	-58.1	-2.7
1994	3.078	31.0	1.0	148.2	2.6	2.0769	-31.7	-1.5
1995	3.148	70.0	2.3	152.4	2.8	2.0656	-11.3	-0.5
1996	3.248	100.0	3.2	156.9	3.0	2.0701	4.5	0.2
1997	3.402	154.0	4.7	160.5	2.3	2.1196	49.5	2.4
1998	3.577	175.0	5.1	163.0	1.6	2.1945	74.9	3.5
1999	3.769	192.0	5.4	166.6	2.2	2.2623	67.8	3.1
2000	3.912	143.0	3.8	172.2	3.4	2.2718	9.5	0.4
2001	3.949	37.0	0.9	177.1	2.8	2.2298	-42.0	-1.8
2002	3.709	-240.0	-6.1	179.9	1.6	2.0617	-168.1	-7.5
2003	3.591	-118.0	-3.2	184.0	2.3	1.9516	-110.1	-5.3
2004	3.606	15.0	0.4	190.9	2.7	1.9089	-42.7	-2.2
2005	4.048	442.0	12.3	197.1	3.2	2.054	14.5	7.6
2006	4.143	95.0	2.3	202.8	3.4	2.043	-1.1	-.05
2007	4.236	93.0	2.2	211.1	3.2	2.007	-3.6	-1.8
2008	4.023	-213.0	-5.3	209.6	2.9	1.919	-8.7	-4.3
2009	3.840	-183.0	-4.8	213.9	3.9	1.795	-12.4	-6.5

* CPI is annualized rate for a calendar year.
Source: United Way of America, Research Services.

there were other sources of revenue, including individual donations and government grants, around 70 percent of donations came from employees in local businesses; of the employee contributions, 75 percent were considered unrestricted dollars that the local United Ways could put to use to address critical needs in their respective communities.

The parent organization, United Way Worldwide (UWW), was supported primarily by local United Way member organizations that paid annual membership fees based on an agreed-on formula, 1 percent of their communitywide campaign contributions. Trademark members, United Way member organizations raising less than $100,000, paid a fee of 0.3 percent of their total contributions. In addition to membership support, individual and corporate sponsorship, and federal grants, other sources for funds for the national umbrella organization were conferences, program service fees, promotional material sales, investment income, rental income, and service income (see Exhibits 2 and 3).

United Way was a system that operated as a federation—a network of local affiliates that shared a mission, a brand, and a program model, but were legally independent from one another and from the national office. Historically, United Way had been the loosest of federations, with almost all power residing at the local level. Each United Way chapter member was not only independent, but also separately incorporated and governed by a local volunteer board. Through communitywide campaigns, each local United Way, utilizing a network of local volunteers, raised funds to support a great variety of health and human services organizations.

Over the years, as United Way's local chapters grew bigger and more prosperous, they began to consider themselves more autonomous—gatekeepers, allocators, and managers of the local public trust—and began to question whether the seal of approval bestowed by United Way affiliation was worth it in light of the declining financial rewards. Therefore, some United Way agencies considered forming their own member-oriented, self-governing federations.

Current Competition and Challenges

By 2011 the charitable-giving industry had fragmented into tiny, single-focus agencies (some of them probably fraudulent) that could be both competitors and recipients of United Way programs. In addition, because United Way's traditional function had been to parcel out the contributions it received to local charities, donors had begun to question the need for an organization that essentially just processed money. (A donor might ask, "Why not just give directly to the charity of my choice?") The perception was that the administrative function of United Way and other blanket charities just added an additional level of overhead to organizational costs, with a smaller portion of the original donation actually reaching the intended target.

In addition, donors were increasingly supporting specific causes, and therefore were more attracted to

Exhibit 2 Give.org Charity Report for United Way America, 2009

Governance:
Chief Executive: Brian A. Gallagher, President and CEO
Compensation: $1,037,410*
Chair of the Board: John J. Dooner, Jr.
Chair's Profession/Business Affiliation: McCann Worldgroup
Board Size: 12
Paid Staff Size: 225

Uses of Funds as Percentage of Total Expenses for Year Ended December 31, 2009:
Fund Raising: 1.0%
Administrative: 10.0%
Programs: 89.0%

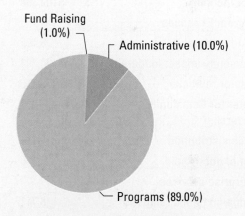

*January 1, 2008, to December 31, 2008, compensation includes annual salary and, if applicable, benefit plans, expense accounts, and other allowances.

Source: BBB Wise Giving Alliance at Give.org.

alternative recipient organizations, those possibly more responsive to the idea of community based on gender, race, or sexual orientation, among other socially driven issues.[8] A spokesperson for the American Cancer Society remarked, "Today a person might have an interest in prostate cancer, because his father died of it, or breast cancer, because it is a social issue as well as a health issue. We have to remember that an organization's mission is at least as important to supporters as its integrity." This meant that "donor-advised funds, which allow people to create grant-making accounts and recommend which charities get the money" were becoming increasingly popular.[9] This did not mean that the traditional and venerable organizations like

Exhibit 3 United Way of America Consolidated Financial Statements (in thousands)

For Year Ended	Dec. 31, 2009	Dec. 31, 2008	Dec. 31, 2007	Dec. 31, 2006
Source of Funds				
Contributions	$51,992	$38,017	$14,224	$15,477
Membership support (net)	29,202	29,900	29,364	28,978
Campaign efforts (net)	53,525	59,100	81,799	7,717
Promotional material sales	3,764	5,968	6,038	6,575
Transaction fees	—	—	4,626	3,307
Conferences	1,816	2,810	2,851	2,622
Program service fees	1,072	1,512	689	942
Investment income	342	1,851	2,121	1,667
Rental and service income	—	—	338	405
Miscellaneous and other	671	1,551	846	425
Total Income	**$102,358**	**$102,103**	**$78,463**	**$68,115**
Program Expenses				
Brand leadership	8,195	$8,478	$8,672	$7,880
Community impact leadership	20,794	19,867	6,389	5,031
Investor relations	39,010	44,458	6,363	6,639
Center for Community Leadership	—	—	6,133	6,519
Funds distribution	—	—	20,826	6,056
Cost of goods sold	2,880	4,096	2,956	3,266
Enterprise services		—	1,514	2,281
Campaign public relations	8,711	12,864	1,493	388
Selling expenses	—	—	1,271	325
Public policy	1,056	12,864	9,242	24,715
Total Program Expenses:	**$80,646**	**$90,841**	**$64,859**	**$63,100**
Total income	$102,358	$102,103	$78,463	$68,115
Program expenses	80,646	90,841	73,822	63,100
Fund-raising expenses	1,003	1,055	533	577
Administrative expenses	8,827	12,517	8,535	9,934
Total expenses	$90,476	$104,413	$73,822	$73,611
Income in excess of expenses	11,882	(2,310)	4,641	(5,496)
Beginning net assets	37,906	42,220	20,608	25,968
Changes in net assets	7,463	(4,534)	(2,939)	(5,076)
Ending net assets	$45,369	$37,906	$17,669	$20,609
Total liabilities	$56,426	$89,440	$90,169	$76,908
Total assets	$101,795	$127,346	$107,838	$97,516

Source: United Way of America, *http://national.unitedway.org/about/form990.cfm*.

United Way, the Red Cross, the Salvation Army, and the American Cancer Society were necessarily in trouble; it just meant that they were perhaps in need of some strategic adjustment (see Exhibit 4).

The partnership between United Way and the disaster relief organizations, such as the Red Cross, the Salvation Army, Boys & Girls Clubs, and Catholic Charities, was still a strong and viable one, but increasingly all these national charities needed to understand the need for a diversified revenue stream. In a video interview with UWW's Brian Gallagher, *Forbes* asked about what had changed. Gallagher noted that 55 percent of donations still came from employees in the workplace and corporate contributions from companies such as UPS, Microsoft, and IBM, and that the relationship with the NFL was still a powerful one, with 50 percent of volunteers being recruited through the NFL campaign. He mentioned that online participation was growing and that individual donations averaged $200 per year per individual. These donations included contributions coming increasingly from women and people of color, which accounted for $75 million from all United Way chapters in 2005.[10]

Entering 2011 with the donor community becoming increasingly diverse and the societal problems increasingly challenging, charitable nonprofits needed to engage in ongoing assessment of the relevance of their respective missions. This was not a new problem. In 1999 Michael Porter and Mark Kramer considered the strategic challenges facing nonprofits. Noting that the number of charitable foundations in the United States had doubled in the two decades since the 1970s, they also believed that these philanthropic organizations were not devoting enough effort to measuring their results and to figuring out how to create the most value for society with the resources they had at their disposal. This value could have been created by selecting the appropriate grantees, signaling other donors of appropriately chosen charities, improving the performance of grant recipients, and advancing the state of knowledge and practice. However, many philanthropic organizations lacked a strategic focus; their resources were scattered across too many fields, and their staffs were spread too thin, servicing too many small grants. One suggestion was that they engage in more performance assessment and unique positioning with unique activities aimed specifically at creating value; however, this would require most nonprofits to also assess the effectiveness of their governance systems.[11]

Scandals and Governance

Echoing the plateau in the charitable-giving community, the year 2002 was bad for corporate scandals: Enron, ImClone, WorldCom, and Tyco all hit the headlines with examples of corporate greed and misappropriation of both funds and public trust. Given these types of wrongdoing in publicly held organizations, the tolerance of the general population for similar activities in nonprofits was increasingly eroded, especially given the nature of the relationship—one based on donor trust.

The first major scandal at United Way had occurred 10 years earlier, in 1992, when William Aramony, president and CEO of United Way of America, and two other UWA executives were convicted of fraud, conspiracy, and

Exhibit 4 **Top 10 U.S. Charities, 2009**

Name	Total Contribution ($, billions)	Net Increase/Decrease from 2008 (%)
United Way Worldwide	$3.84	-4.5
Salvation Army	1.72	-8.4
Catholic Charities	1.28	66.0*
AmeriCares Foundation	1.19	18.1*
Feed the Children	1.19	1.2
Food for the Poor	1.08	-27.6
Fidelity Charitable Gift Fund	.953	-40.3
American Cancer Society	.898	-11.0
World Vision	.871	4.5
The Y (formerly YMCA)	.775	-17.2

* For Catholic Charities and AmeriCares, the contributions were mostly donated goods, food, and medicine, not money.
Source: *Chronicle of Philanthropy.*

money laundering in a scheme that siphoned around $1 million from the organization. This event was perceived as a turning point in public perceptions of charitable organizations and was blamed for the first drop in United Way donations since World War II.[12]

In 2001, the United Way of the National Capital Area—the Washington, D.C., chapter and the second-largest local United Way member in the country in donations—was in the news, again because of fraud. CEO Oral Suer took more than $500,000 from the charity to pay for personal expenses, annual leave, and an early pension payout he was not entitled to. Other employees took additional money for personal use, with the total fraud amounting to $1.6 million. Then, in 2002, new United Way National Capital Area CEO Norman O. Taylor was asked to resign over misstated revenues and questionable overhead and credit card charges. In 2003 the CFO of the Michigan Capital Area United Way, Jacqueline Allen-MacGregor, was imprisoned for the theft of $1.9 million from the charity, which she had used to purchase racehorses for her personal farm. Also in 2003, Pipeline Inc., a spin-off from the California Bay Area United Way that was created to collect contributions, was investigated for losing $18 million when the financial records did not accurately reflect the amount owed the charity.[13] In 2006 a former CEO of the United Way of New York City was investigated for diverting organizational assets valued at $227,000 for his own personal use.[14]

To be fair, United Way was not the only high-profile charity to experience these kinds of problems. After 9/11 and Katrina, the American Red Cross had come under scrutiny for misdirection of disaster funds. In addition, the bookkeeper at Easter Seals of Iowa had stolen $230,000, the former president and seven others at Goodwill Industries of California embezzled $26 million, the financial administrator of the American Heart Association of New Jersey was convicted of a theft of $186,000, and an executive at Goodwill Industries of Michigan was found guilty of stealing $750,000 from the agency over a 23-year period.[15] What could be done to curtail this disturbing trend?

The United Way of America's board during the Aramony scandal contained many Fortune 500 CEOs who were, according to Aramony, fully informed about his compensation and perquisites.[16] Yet it appeared they still failed to exercise appropriate oversight, as did the boards at the D.C. and Michigan chapters. Finding committed and knowledgeable board members was critical to United Way's continued success. Given the federation model, each local chapter had its own board, recruited from community members who had not only fund-raising skills but also relationships with local leaders, politicians, or even regulators. Many local United Ways wanted to distance themselves from the scandals at UWA and other high-profile chapters, and therefore they tried to stress local leadership and board autonomy. Serving on such a board required a commitment to the community and to the goals of the local United Way.

However, regardless of the degree of well-intentioned communication and disclosure, sometimes the goals of board members could have been in conflict. A 2004 survey by McKinsey & Company of executives and directors at 32 of *Worth* magazine's top 100 nonprofit performers found that many nonprofit boards had recurring problems, one of which was consensus over mission and goals: "Only 46 percent of the directors we surveyed thought that other directors on their boards could both summarize the mission of the organizations they serve and present a vision of where those organizations hope to be in five years' time." In addition, for an organization such as United Way, the goals of the diverse stakeholders, both donors and recipients, may have differed widely. This lack of consensus, coupled with the difficulty of measuring and evaluating performance, meant that nonprofit boards in general needed to practice serious self-scrutiny: "The time when nonprofit boards were populated by wealthy do-gooders who just raised money, hired CEOs, and reaffirmed board policy is over."[17]

In 2006 more than 1.8 million nonprofit organizations in the United States controlled upward of $2.5 trillion in assets, received revenues of $1.25 trillion, and were increasingly relied upon to help address both gaps in federal, state, and local governments' support after natural and manmade disasters, and the lingering effects of society's general ills. Given the degree to which the public trust had been violated after nonprofits were found to be acting irresponsibly, the Senate Finance Committee was considering "tax-exempt reform containing provisions similar to those found in the Sarbanes-Oxley Act."[18] The 2008 scandal surrounding the Association of Community Organizations for Reform Now (ACORN), although focused on voter registration fraud, brought attention in Washington once again to the question of nonprofit legitimacy.[19]

This demand for greater accountability was not new. Nonprofits had sometimes been notoriously ineffective at accomplishing their social missions, inefficient at getting maximum return on the money they raised due to high administration costs, and willing to take on too much risk, either through inexperience or ignorance. Sometimes because of lax oversight procedures, individuals in control of the nonprofits were willing to engage in outright fraud, acquiring excessive benefits for themselves. These problems were enhanced due to nonprofits' failure to provide extensive analysis, disclosure, and dissemination of relevant performance information and due to the lack of sanctions.[20] If nonprofit organizations would not police themselves, watchdog agencies would create external standards and provide public feedback, sometimes to the detriment of the organization under scrutiny (see Exhibit 5).[21]

Gallagher's Strategic Response

In 2006 United Way of America CEO Brian Gallagher was invited by the U.S. Senate Finance Committee to participate in a roundtable discussion on needed reforms in nonprofit boards and governance. He was prepared to provide specific commentary. Since accepting the CEO position in

Exhibit 5　Watchdog Agencies—Information Resources for Nonprofits

- American Institute of Philanthropy
  www.charitywatch.org
- Better Business Bureau Wise Giving Alliance
  www.give.org
- Board Source
  www.boardsource.org
- Charity Navigator
  www.charitynavigator.org
- Governance Matters
  www.governancematters.com
- Guidestar
  www.guidestar.org
- Independent Sector
  www.independentsector.org
- Internet Nonprofit Center
  www.nonprofits.org

- IRS Exempt Organizations
  www.irs.gov/charities
- National Association of Attorneys General
  www.naag.org
- National Association of State Charity Officials
  www.nasconet.org
- National Council of Nonprofits
  www.councilofnonprofits.org
- New York State Attorney General
  www.charitiesnys.com
- OMB Watch
  www.ombwatch.org

Network for Good
- Standards for Excellence Institute
  www.standardsforexcellenceinstitute.org

2001, Gallagher had been working to promote a change in the United Way strategy, including a change in mission, the creation of standards of performance excellence, and a requirement that local members certify their adherence to the membership standards.

Regarding the mission of United Way, Gallagher had worked to change the focus from fund-raising to community impact—from "How much money did we raise?" to "How much impact did we have on our community?" In his initial statement to the Senate committee, Gallagher said:

> The ultimate measure of success is whether family violence rates have gone down and whether there is more affordable housing. And fund-raising is [just] part of making that happen. When you are asking people to contribute, you're asking for an investment in your mission. And like a for-profit business, you are then accountable to your investors, not just for keeping good books, but for creating value and offering a concrete return. For those of us in human development, that means efforts that lead to measurable improvements in people's lives. In other words, the organizations that produce the greatest results should grow and be rewarded. Those that do not should be forced to change or go out of business. The American public doesn't give us money just because our operations are clean. Why they really give us money is because they want to make a difference.[22]

As a result of the new mission, UWW required local affiliates to provide the national headquarters with annual financial reports and to embrace the revised standards of excellence developed by more than 200 United Way employees, volunteers, and consultants. Of interest is the fact that these standards were not mandatory but were presented as guidelines, giving chapters suggestions for how they might revise their local strategies. The standards urged the affiliates to identify community problems, raise money to solve them, and demonstrate measurable progress toward their goals by adopting a code of ethics that included an annual independent financial audit. The hope was that by adopting these guidelines, the chapters would be able to provide tangible proof to donors, especially wealthy contributors, that the United Way chapters and the charities they support were making a difference (see Exhibit 6).[23]

Local United Ways faced a continual challenge, with inevitable tension between the diverse constituencies they served: Were their primary "customers" the donors who contribute needed funds or the agencies who were the recipients of these charitable donations? Or should the local United Way act as a networking institution, providing mechanisms for discussion of local problems and community-service needs? Or, going even further, should it act as an activist organization, leading the way with comprehensive community planning, advocating major public policy, and redistributing resources as needed? Kirsten Gronbjerg, of the Center on Philanthropy, Indiana University, stated, "The activist role is very difficult for United Ways to play, because they need to satisfy diverse constituency groups and therefore avoid conflict. As they become more donor driven institutions, they will be less able to take an activist approach just when such an approach is sorely needed."[24]

In addition, the local United Ways needed to maintain their internal consensus, providing a coherent and inspiring vision for their mainly volunteer workforce,

Exhibit 6   United Way New Standards of Excellence

Standards of Excellence, a comprehensive description of benchmark standards and best practices. Developed in conjunction United Way executives, staff, and volunteers throughout the country, the standards are designed to enhance the effectiveness of the 1,350 United Way affiliates.

- **Introduction to the Standards of Excellence.** Spanning more than 100 pages, the new standards provide highly detailed descriptions regarding five key areas of operation.

- **Community Engagement and Vision.** Working with formal and informal leaders to develop a shared vision and goals for a community, including the identification of priority issues affecting the overall well-being of its citizens.

- **Impact Strategies, Resources, and Results.** Creating "impact strategies" that address the root causes and barriers of a community's priority issues; mobilizing essential assets such as people, knowledge, relationships, technology, and money; effectively implementing impact strategies; and evaluating the effectiveness of impact strategies in fostering continuous improvement.

- **Relationship Building and Brand Management.** Developing, maintaining, and growing relationships with individuals and organizations in order to attract and sustain essential assets.

- **Organizational Leadership and Governance.** Garnering trust, legitimacy, and support of the United Way in local communities through leadership and overall management.

- **Operations.** Providing efficient and cost-effective systems, policies, and processes that enable the fulfillment of the United Way's mission, while ensuring the highest levels of transparency and accountability.

Source: United Way of America, *http://liveunited.org/*

while managing potential conflicts and sharing resources with other United Way chapters in their geographical areas. The problem of potentially scarce resources and the fact that traditional donor organizations were either consolidating their physical operations or leaving an area meant that the traditional broad base of business and industry was shrinking. This and other factors prompted the consolidation of several United Ways into more regional organizations. This movement meant potential savings and operational efficiencies from sharing marketing, financial management, and information technology functions.[25] However, it also meant a possible diffusion of mission over a larger community, with a potential loss of focus, and more challenges for communicating this mission and marketing services to a more diverse donor and recipient base. In 2009, twenty-one nonprofit groups in the Washington, D.C., area suspended their memberships in United Way and joined a new group, Community1st. These groups were lured away from United Way by a promise of "lower overhead costs, easily customized fund-raising campaigns, and fewer restrictions on where donors' money is directed".[26]

The ongoing issues faced by United Way in its 120-year history had remained constant. Consider this: During the holiday season, "when local United Way drives take place almost everywhere, likely as not questions will arise about what United Way is up to, how well it is doing what it claims to do, and for that matter, whether United Way is the best way for you to do your charitable giving."[27] This statement was written in 1977, yet it could still apply in 2011. Concerns about United Way seemed timeless, and Brian Gallagher was only one in a long line of CEOs determined to answer the critics once and for all.

Endnotes

1. Riley, C. 2011. America's wealthy turn less charitable, *CNN Money,* February 6, *money.cnn.com/2011/02/06/news/ economy/charity_gifts/index.htm*; Zongker, B. 2010. Top charities see decrease in donations, Associated Press, October 18, *www.tulsaworld.com*

2. Barrett, W. P. 2006. United Way's new way. Forbes.com, January 16, *www.forces.com*

3. Barton, N. & Hall, H. 2006. A year of big gains. *Chronicle of Philanthropy,* October 26, *philanthropy.com/ article/A-Year-of-Big-Gains/54908/.*

4. Barrett, op. cit.

5. Executive Summary of the Donor Expectations Survey, conducted by Princeton Survey Research Associates in the Spring of 2001, as reported by Give.org BBB Wise Giving Alliance, *www.give.org.*

6. Suchman, M. 1995. Managing legitimacy: Strategic and institutional approaches. *Academy of Management Review,* 20, 571–610.

7. From the United Way website, liveunited.org.
8. Graddy-Gamel, A. 2007. Review of Contesting community: The transformation of workplace charity, by Emily Barman (2006: Stanford University Press). *Philanthropy News Digest,* February 27, *foundationcenter.org/pnd/offtheshelf/ots_print.jhtml?id=171600045.*
9. Barton & Hall, op. cit.
10. Charitable giving diversifies. 2006. Forbes Video Report, December 13, *www.forbes.com*
11. Porter, M. E., & Kramer, M. R. 1999. Philanthropy's new agenda: Creating value. *Harvard Business Review,* 77(6): 121–130.
12. United Way ex-head sentenced to 7 years in prison for fraud. 1995. *New York Times,* June 23, B2.
13. Gibelman, M., & Gelman, S. R. 2004. A loss of credibility: Patterns of wrongdoing among nongovernmental organizations. *International Journal of Voluntary and Nonprofit Organizations,* 15(4): 355–381. This article provides a content analysis of worldwide NGO scandals from 2001–2004. Although the United States is overrepresented, it is certainly not alone in the world for incidents of wrongdoing.
14. Investigation finds former United Way of NYC CEO improperly diverted funds. 2006. *Philanthropy News Digest,* April 17, *foundationcenter.org/pnd/news/story_print.jhtml?id=140000004.*
15. Gibelman & Gelman, op. cit.
16. Sinclair, M. 2002. William Aramony is back on the streets. *NonProfit Times,* March 1.
17. Jansen, P., & Kilpatrick, A. 2004. The dynamic nonprofit board. *McKinsey Quarterly,* 2: 72–81.
18. Kelley, C., & Anderson, S. 2006. Advising nonprofit organizations. *CPA Journal,* 76(8): 20–26.
19. McRay, G. 2009. Bad Seeds—Why the ACORN scandal matters to other nonprofits, Foundation Group, September 16, *www.501c3.org/blog/acorn-scandel-matters-to-nonprofits/.*
20. Herzlinger, R. 1996. Can public trust in nonprofits and governments be restored? *Harvard Business Review,* March–April: 97–107.
21. Gibelman, & Gelman, op. cit.
22. Gallagher, B. 2005. Statement of Brian A. Gallagher, President and CEO United Way of America before United States Senate Committee on Finance, April 5, p. 1, liveunited.org.
23. Blum, D. E. 2005. Held to a new standard. *Chronicle of Philanthropy,* 17 (13).
24. United Way system at the crossroads: Valuable lessons from the United Way of Chicago. 2002. Snapshots: Research Highlights from the Nonprofit Sector Research Fund, The Aspen Institute, November/December, no. 26.
25. Gosier, C. 2007. 3 chapters of United Way to combine. Knight Ridder Tribune Business News, February 23.
26. Greenwell, M. 2009. 21 regional nonprofits withdraw from United Way, *Washington Post,* April 29, *www.washingtonpost.com/wp-dyn/content/article/2009/04/28/AR2009042803701.html.*
27. United Way: Are the criticisms fair? 1977. *Changing Times,* October: 29.

Case 8 General Motors*

When figures for new vehicle sales were released for January 2011, General Motors led the industry with a market share of 21.8 percent (see Exhibits 1 to 3). The firm had not achieved such a level of sales in more than two years. These gains served to reassure the executives at GM that consumers were being drawn back to their cars after they had pulled out of their recent bankruptcy. The rise in market share was particularly impressive because the firm had cut back to only four U.S. brands, trimmed its workforce, slashed production capacity, and retained only about two-thirds of its dealer network.

Some analysts expressed concern that GM's sales increase was the product of more discounting, a practice that it had been working to reduce. Although officials at the firm acknowledged that incentives had been $300 higher in January than in December, they insisted

that they were not resurrecting their bad habits. "We're not going to return to the days of driving production with incentives," said Don Johnson, vice president for U.S. sales operations. "We know that is not going to be a recipe for success for us."[1]

In fact, GM is hoping that its new lineup of cars, including the much-publicized Chevy Volt, a plug-in electric car, will help to rebuild the company as it tries to shrug off its brief fling with bankruptcy during 2009 (see Exhibit 4). The bankruptcy was forced upon GM by the government, as it tried to push the car company to undertake drastic steps to cut costs in return for providing $50 million in emergency funding. The intervention by the government also led the company to make major changes in its top management and board of directors. This included the resignation of G. Richard Wagoner, who had racked up staggering losses of money and market share since taking over the firm in 2000. GM's stock fell from a value of around $70 in early 2000 to just below $4 by the end of 2008.

Since Wagoner was forced out, GM has been headed by three different individuals. Frederick A. Henderson

*This case was developed by Professor Jamal Shamsie, Michigan State University, with the assistance of Professor Alan B. Eisner, Pace University. Material has been drawn from published sources to be used for class discussion. Copyright © 2011 Jamal Shamsie and Alan B. Eisner.

Exhibit 1 Income Statement (in thousands of dollars)

	Period Ending	
	Dec. 31, 2010	Dec. 31, 2009
Total Revenue	135,592,000	104,589,000)
Cost of revenue	118,944,000	112,195,000
Gross Profit	16,648,000	(7,606,000)
Operating expenses:		
Selling general and administrative	11,564,000	13,417,000
Operating Income or Loss	5,084,000	(21,023,000)
Income from continuing operations:		
Total other income/expenses net	1,751,000	129,638,000
Earnings before interest and taxes	6,639,000	109,804,000
Interest expense	1,098,000	6,122,000
Income before tax	5,541,000	103,682,000
Income tax expense	672,000	(2,166,000)
Minority interest	(331,000)	(396,000)
Net income from continuing operations	6,172,000	104,821,000
Net Income	6,172,000	104,821,000

Source: GM.

Exhibit 2 **Balance Sheets** (in thousands of dollars)

	Period Ending	
	Dec. 31, 2010	Dec. 31, 2009
Assets		
Current Assets:		
Cash and cash equivalents	22,301,000	36,596,000
Short-term investments	5,555,000	134,000
Net receivables	10,504,000	9,295,000
Inventory	12,125,000	10,107,000
Other current assets	2,568,000	3,115,000
Total Current Assets	**53,053,000**	**59,247,000**
Long-term investments	8,197,000	—
Property plant and equipment	19,235,000	19,217,000
Goodwill	31,778,000	30,672,000
Intangible assets	11,882,000	14,547,000
Other assets	14,445,000	12,048,000
Deferred long-term asset charges	308,000	564,000
Total Assets	**138,898,000**	**136,295,000**
Liabilities		
Current Liabilities:		
Accounts payable	45,541,000	41,859,000
Short/current long-term debt	1,616,000	10,221,000
Other current liabilities	—	355,000
Total Current Liabilities	**47,157,000**	**52,435,000**
Long-term debt	9,142,000	5,562,000
Other liabilities	31,587,000	36,064,000
Deferred long-term liability charges	13,021,000	13,279,000
Minority interest	979,000	708,000
Total Liabilities	**102,718,000**	**108,048,000**
Stockholders' Equity		
Misc. stocks options warrants	—	6,998,000
Preferred stock	10,391,000	—
Common stock	15,000	15,000
Retained earnings	266,000	(4,394,000)
Capital surplus	24,257,000	24,040,000
Other stockholder equity	1,251,000	1,588,000
Total Stockholder Equity	**36,180,000**	**21,249,000**
Net Tangible Assets	**(7,480,000)**	**(23,970,000)**

Source: GM.

Exhibit 3   **Market Shares**

U.S.		GLOBAL	
2010	18.2%	2010	11.4%
2009	19.1	2009	11.6
2008	21.0	2008	12.5
2006	24.2	2006	13.5
2004	27.2	2004	14.3
2002	28.3	2002	15.0
2000	29.0	2000	15.2
1990	35.0	1990	16.5

Source: GM.

was moved up from his position of president and chief operating officer to become the chief executive on an interim basis. But he was replaced months later by Edward E. Whitacre, Jr., who had been the head of the newly

Exhibit 4   **Vehicle Sales** (All figures are in thousands of units)

	Six Months Ending June 30, 2010	Six Months Ending June 30, 2009
United States		
Chevrolet	782	597
GMC	152	118
Buick	70	47
Cadillac	65	49
Europe		
Opel/Vauxhall	608	645
Chevrolet	232	216
Rest of World*		
Chevrolet	898	671
Buick	254	196
Wuling	637	493
Holden	73	59
GM Daewoo	60	47
Worldwide	**4,152**	**3,555**

* Excludes Canada and Mexico.
Source: GM.

appointed board of directors. Whitacre stated that he would stay only long enough to guide the firm through its difficult period of transition. Finally, in September 2010, Daniel F. Ackerson, another board member, was appointed to run the firm for the longer term.

Under each of these heads, GM continued to make drastic and long overdue changes in all aspects of its operations. As a result of these changes, the firm claims that it can break even if it sells two million cars in the United States, half the level that it needed for breakeven three years ago. As it began to show signs of recovery, GM finally offered shares in the new company, in one of the nation's largest initial stock offerings. Because of the level of interest from buyers, the firm was able to raise the price of these to $33 a share from its initial estimate of $26 to $29 a share.

Pushed into Bankruptcy

Even though he failed to turn GM around, Wagoner had made progress in tearing down the boundaries between the firm's freewheeling fiefdoms operating around the world. For most of its history, the firm had been run as a collaboration of relatively autonomous geographical divisions that rarely worked with each other. In 1994 there were 27 different units within GM that were developing their own cars, making it difficult to achieve economies of scale. Wagoner had managed to restructure GM's four different geographical units in order to get them to collaborate with each other on designing, manufacturing, and marketing cars.

Wagoner faced an even bigger challenge in dealing with the high costs that made GM's cars much more expensive to build than those of its foreign-based competitors. He carried out three major restructurings, eliminating dozens of plants and tens of thousands of jobs and jettisoning hundreds of dealers. Wagoner even managed to deal with the lavish health and retirement benefits that GM had accorded to its workers in response to a prolonged strike by the United Automobile Workers during 1970. He was finally able to persuade employees and retirees to pay for part of the firm's escalating health-care-related costs. In 2007 Wagoner negotiated with the union to create a health-care trust, called a voluntary employees' beneficiary association, which would take over the responsibility for these costs.

In spite of these efforts, GM announced a loss of $30.9 billion dollars for 2008, amounting to a staggering $50 a share. The firm had not managed to post a profit since 2004, running up cumulative losses of over $82 billion between 2005 and 2009. Wagoner eventually began to run short of funds and turned to the U.S. government for loans in order to survive. In March 2009, the Obama administration finally demanded his resignation in return for further support. "It's a pretty unceremonious ending," said John Cesesa, an industry analyst, of Wagoner's downfall. "GM lost its way in the 70's, but the company didn't know it until 20 years late. The hole was much deeper than he realized when he became C.E.O."[2]

Wagoner was replaced by Frederick A. Henderson on an interim basis as chief executive of GM. Henderson had taken the position of chief financial officer in 2006 and had been moved up to president and chief operating officer in 2008. Under Henderson, the firm was asked to negotiate with bondholders and the union for further concessions in order to reduce its bloated cost structure. Unable to reach any agreement, the firm announced in late July 2009 that it must seek Chapter 11 bankruptcy protection.

Under the terms of the bankruptcy protection, GM was able to wipe out a big chunk of its debt, reducing this from over $46 billion before the filing to around $17 billion afterward, saving about $1 billion a year in interest payments. Bondholders were forced to exchange their debt for stock at about 10 cents of equity for every dollar owed by the firm. The union agreed to accept stock to finance half of its $20 billion health care fund. The U.S. government agreed to invest another $30 billion into the firm, in addition to the $20 billion it had already contributed, in exchange for 61 percent of the stock in the new GM. Commenting on the moves taken by the government to create a new firm out of the ashes of the old one, the firm's vice chairman, Robert Lutz, stated, "Their number one goal is to make us successful."[3]

Striving to Create Changes

As soon as Henderson took over, he began to shake up the ranks of GM's senior management. But even more changes were made after the firm made its bankruptcy filing, which was tied to additional funding from the U.S. government. The board of directors was reconstituted in July 2009 with eight new members joining five from the old guard, under the leadership of Edward E. Whitacre, Jr. One of the newly appointed board members remarked that 12 of the 13 members were either automobile industry rookies or new to their jobs. Even Whitacre, a six-foot, four-inch Texan, was a former telecom executive who was responsible for turning a broken Baby Bell into the resurgent AT&T.

Under Whitacre's direction, Henderson began a push to cut layers of bureaucracy, slashing its executive ranks by a third and giving broad, new responsibilities to a cadre of younger managers. The new board was determined to address problems that had been laid bare by the task force assigned by the government to investigate GM in early 2009. They had been particularly astonished by the emphasis on past glories and the commitment to the status quo they had found to be widespread among the firm's management ranks. "Those values were driven from the top on down," said Rob Kleinbaum, a former GM executive and consultant. "And anybody inside who protested that attitude was buried."[4]

In order to speed up the change, GM's board of directors fired Henderson from his post on December 1, 2009, less than five months after he had taken over. Although he had made some progress in turning around the firm's operations, the board was skeptical that a person so strongly tied to the firm's past mistakes could bring a fresh approach that could help to reverse its decades-long slide. "While momentum has been building over the past several months, all involved agree that more changes need to be made," said Whitacre, who was selected to take over from Henderson.[5]

Within three months of taking charge, Whitacre had eased out 4 other executives, reassigned 20 more and brought in 7 outsiders to fill top jobs. Several changes were made to the individuals who managed the marketing and sales of the various GM divisions. The tide also swept out solid performers allied with the old regime, such as Vice Chairman Bob Lutz, who had overseen the development of several GM vehicles, such as the Chevy Malibu and the Cadillac CTS, that were beginning to sell well. "In the past," said Lutz, "GM was accused of not enough change. You have to find the balance between the pace of change and trauma to the organization."[6]

But Whitacre was determined to make the changes, especially in the caliber of the management team, which he deemed to be essential in turning GM around. Wagoner relied on as many as a dozen metrics to evaluate his executives and rarely failed any of them on their performance. Whitacre decided to cut his performance criteria down to six: market share, revenue, operating profit, cash flow, product quality, and customer satisfaction. Above all, he believed that GM could only be rebuilt if his managers were able to make decisions quickly and correct mistakes even faster. "We're all in this together," he reassured workers at a GM factory in Kansas, where he walked the assembly line, stopping to shake hands with workers.[7]

Focusing on Fewer Brands

For years, GM built its position of dominance by offering cars that were designed for different customers by separate divisions. Each of these divisions came to represent a distinct nameplate or brand. Its extensive brand lineup had long been GM's primary weapon in beating back both domestic and foreign rivals. But as the firm's market share began to decline, it became difficult to design and market cars under several brands. In order to cut costs, GM began to share designs and parts across divisions, leading to some loss of distinctiveness between the different brands.

Analysts had been questioning for many years GM's decision to stick with as many as eight U.S. brands, with the recent addition of Hummer. In particular, Saab, Pontiac, Hummer, and Saturn had been struggling to attract customers for many years. The firm had been forced to dump large numbers of these cars at discount rates to car rental firms, corporate fleet buyers, and GM's own employees. As a result of these practices, the firm revealed that Saturn, Saab, and Hummer had run up considerable losses since 2003. Wagoner did finally wind down the Oldsmobile division soon after he took over. But the estimated $1 billion that GM had to spend to settle with its dealers made him reluctant to close other divisions.

The decision to carry so many brands placed considerable strain on GM's efforts to revamp its product line on a regular basis. However, Wagoner only agreed to cut out four of its brands—Pontiac, Saturn, Saab, and Hummer—when it was forced to turn to the U.S. government for funding to stay afloat. A. Andrew Shapiro, an analyst, believes that GM should have started to think seriously about cutting back on its car divisions during the 1980s. By then, a number of new brands had been successfully introduced into the U.S. market, including Japanese luxury brands such as Lexus, Acura, and Infiniti and Korean mass-market brands such as Hyundai and Kia. But GM actually added more brands until Wagoner finally decided to phase out Oldsmobile by 2004. "There are always short-term reasons for not doing something," explained Shapiro.[8]

Of the four brands that GM finally decided to close down or spin off, Saturn had once held the most promise. The division was started in 1985 as a completely separate car company that would attract customers away from Toyota and Honda. Saturns featured dent-resistant plastic bodies, its dealers promised friendly, no-haggling sales, and customers were invited to an annual "homecoming" cookout at the Saturn plant in Spring Hill, Tennessee. But GM executives decided in the mid-1990s to divert funds away from Saturn in order to support the firm's other sagging brands. The firm did not add any new vehicles to the Saturn lineup for five years, despite pleas from dealers.

GM had also decided to sell its European brands and even lined up a buyer for its Opel division. However, it changed its mind shortly after emerging from bankruptcy, stating that it would retain and reorganize the division itself. The firm claimed that these brands, with their expertise in small-car technology, would be crucial to the future of the firm, both in the U.S. and in emerging markets. "Without Opel, there was a gaping hole in G.M.'s strategy," according to Michael Tyndall, an auto specialist at Nomura International.[9]

Revamping Product Development

Under Wagoner, GM had been trying to get all of its functional areas to work together more closely throughout the product-development process. In the past, even if a bold design made it off the drawing board, it had little chance of surviving as it was handed over to marketing, then passed to engineering, and finally sent to manufacturing. Analysts recall the rollout of the much-anticipated Pontiac Aztec, which would eventually be regarded as a vehicle whose design appealed to few consumers. Since then, there has been a concentrated effort to wean the GM culture away from a focus on engineering processes. GM has pushed designers to get more involved with the development process and for engineers to find ways to stick with the original car design.

Whitacre pushed for GM to roll out new models faster by making changes to its cumbersome decision-making process. By mid-2009, Thomas Stephens, the new head of product development, and Jon Lauckner, the new head of global product planning, had managed to scrap the old system for vehicle reviews. Under the old system, any product decisions would be reviewed by as many as 70 executives, often taking two months for a decision to wind its way through regional forums, then to a global committee, and finally to the all-powerful automotive products board.

To replace this, Lauckner came up with a new system that funneled all product decisions to weekly meetings run by Whitacre and Stevens, leading to much faster decisions. At the same time, it also encouraged people to raise concerns during the development process and to take steps to hold back a new model in order to make changes that could improve its chances of success. Stephens held meetings called "pride builders" with his staff to increase the commitment to build better cars. "I don't even want to talk about what was good enough anymore," said Stephens. "You can't win with good enough."[10]

Furthermore, GM refocused its efforts on developing smaller and more fuel-efficient cars to lure back consumers who had given up on it. The firm had shifted its emphasis to SUVs in large part because of its relative lack of success with smaller cars. Going back to the late 1980s, the firm introduced a family of midsized cars that it had spent six years to develop. But the Chevrolet Lumina, Pontiac Grand Prix, Oldsmobile Cutlass, and Buick Regal were plagued with high manufacturing costs, quality problems, and safety concerns and did not attract many buyers. It hopes to do better with its new lineup of smaller cars that include the Chevy Cruze, Buick Verano, and Chevy Aveo (see Exhibit 5).

Lauckner and Stevens are also trying to broaden the appeal of GM cars to younger buyers. Buick, once the bastion of large sedans marketed to consumers older than 60 years of age, is getting a decidedly youthful makeover with the new LaCrosse and the Enclave SUV. The Chevrolet Equinox crossover vehicle has been a best seller, and a sharply restyled version of the Cadillac SRX is winning raves from some consumers, even as its angular appearance polarizes others. But the firm has high hopes for other models that it is planning to introduce, such as a small rear-wheel drive luxury Cadillac that is referred to the "BMW fighter" because it is expected to compete with the German carmaker's 3 Series sedan.

Firing on All Cylinders?

A week before its initial public offering, GM reported its largest quarterly profit in 11 years, showing that the slimmed-down automaker no longer needed huge sales to generate significant earnings. The firm said it earned $2 billion in the third quarter of 2010, nearly equaling its profit for the first half of the year. For the nine months from January to September, GM earned $4.2 billion, setting it on course to record a full-year profit for the first time since 2004. Even though it reported a small loss in Europe, the firm earned $2.1 billion in North America, the region that had been responsible for most of its losses in recent years.

GM is also pleased with the response of consumers in the United States to its new cars. New models, including

Exhibit 5   New Car Models

2010
- Chevrolet Equinox
- Chevrolet Cruze
- Chevy Volt
- Buick Regal
- Buick Lacrosse
- Cadillac SRX
- Cadillac CTS
- GMC Terrain

2011
- Chevy Aveo
- Chevy Spark
- Chevrolet Camaro
- Chevrolet Orlando
- Buick Verano

2012
- Chevy Malibu
- Cadillac XTS

Source: *Fortune*, May 3, 2010.

redesigned versions of the Buick LaCrosse sedan and Chevrolet Equinox crossover vehicle, have been well received by critics and consumers, to the point that the firm has struggled to keep up with demand. Sales of a critical new car, the Chevrolet Cruze, have also been brisk. But everyone at GM is focused on the new Chevrolet Volt, a plug-in hybrid car that represents the firm's future direction. It was rolled out in December, but its sales will be expanded gradually as dealers receive training to sell and service the new offering.

A few months before its initial public offering, GM also bought a financing company, AmericaCredit, for $3.5 billion so that it could increase sales by expanding the pool of consumers who could get financing to lease or purchase its cars. The acquisition gives GM a captive financing arm for the first time since 2007, when it sold control of GMAC Financial Services. According to Whitacre, "Our dealers have been telling us that not having an in-house finance arm hurt our ability to finance certain loans and leases."[11]

Akerson feels confident that GM has already begun to make many of the changes that are needed to make it profitable over the longer term. He is particularly pleased with the response to the firm's initial public offering, which allowed it to raise the price of its shares. As a result of this stock offering, the Treasury Department was able to reduce its stake to 26 percent from nearly 61 percent, allowing the automaker to discard its label of "Government Motors." At the same time, analysts have noted that GM still has problems to overcome with its lineup of cars Fewer than a dozen, or only about a third of its models, were recommended in a recent *Consumer Reports* survey. "We know we have much more work to do," said Akerson in a recent conference call with analysts and reporters.[12]

Endnotes

1. Bunkley, N. 2011. Sales of larger vehicles bring automakers an upbeat start for 2011. *New York Times,* February 2: B3.
2. Maynard, M. 2009. The steadfast optimist who oversaw G.M.'s long decline. *New York Times,* March 30: B8.
3. Sanger, D. E., Zeleny, J., & Vlasic, B. 2009. G.M. heads to bankruptcy protection as government steps in. *New York Times,* June 1: A12.
4. Vlasic, B. 2009. Culture shock: G.M. struggles to shed a legendry bureaucracy. *New York Times,* November 13: B4.
5. Vlasic, B. 2009. G.M. shakeout signals bid to speed its recovery. *International Herald Tribune,* December 3: 17.
6. Welch, D. 2009. Ed Whitacre's battle to save GM from itself. *Bloomberg Businessweek,* May 3: 50.
7. Ibid.: 55.
8. Maynard, M. 2009. A painful departure for some G.M. brands. *New York Times,* February 18: B4.
9. Schwartz, N. D., & Jolly, D. 2009. G.M. decision to keep Opel rankles some Europeans. *New York Times,* November 5: B7.
10. Vlasic. B. 2009. Culture shock.
11. Bunkley, N. 2010. G.M. spends $3.5 billion for lender to subprime. *New York Times,* July 23: B3.
12. Bunkley, N. 2010. G.M., days away from stock offering, posts its biggest profit in 11 years. *New York Times,* November 11: B4.

Case 9   Heineken*

In January 2011, Dutch brewer Heineken announced the acquisition of five breweries in Nigeria as part of its plan to expand in one of the world's fastest growing beer markets and Africa's second largest. The purchase will raise the firm's market share to approximately 68 percent, giving it a substantial lead over its competitors. Nigeria's beer market has grown at an annual rate of about 9 percent over the past 10 years, and growing sales in the country have provided a dominant share of Heineken's profits in Africa.

The move came on the heels of the acquisition of a Mexican brewer, FEMSA Cervesa, for about $5.4 billion in 2010. The deal made the firm a stronger, more competitive player in the Latin American beer market, which has also become one of the most profitable and fastest growing markets in the world. It allowed the firm to add FEMSA's beer brands, such as *Dos Equis, Sol,* and *Tecate,* to its already vast array of offerings. Heineken had already been distributing these beers in the United States, under license from the Mexican brewery, to cater to the growing Hispanic segment of the population.

However, the firm made its most high-profile recent acquisition in 2008 when it bought Scottish-based brewer Scottish & Newcastle, the brewer of well-known brands such as *Newcastle Brown Ale* and *Kronenbourg 1664.* Although the purchase had been made in partnership with Carlsberg, Heineken was able to gain control of the Scottish & Newcastle operations in several crucial European markets, such as the United Kingdom, Ireland, Portugal, Finland, and Belgium, further solidifying Heineken's position as the leading brewer in Europe. But the Dutch-based firm also took over the Scottish brewer's ventures in far-flung places such as the United States and India.

These decisions to acquire brewers that operate in different parts of the world have been part of a series of changes that the Dutch brewer has been making to raise its stature in the various markets and to respond to changes that are occurring in the global market for beer. Beer consumption has been declining in key markets as a result of tougher drunk-driving laws and a growing appreciation for wine. At the same time, the beer industry has become ever more competitive, as the largest brewers have been expanding across the globe through acquisitions of smaller regional and national players (see Exhibits 1 and 2).

The need for change was clearly reflected in the appointment in October 2005 of Jean-Francois van Boxmeer as Heineken's first non-Dutch CEO. He was brought in to replace Thorny Ruys, who had decided to resign 18 months ahead of schedule because of his failure to show much improvement in the company's performance. Prior to the appointment of Ruys in 2002, Heineken had been run by three generations of Heineken ancestors, whose portraits still adorn the dark-paneled office of the CEO in its Amsterdam headquarters. Like Ruys, van Boxmeer faces the challenge of preserving the firm's family-driven traditions while trying to deal with threats that have never been faced before.

Confronting a Globalizing Industry

Heineken was one of the pioneers of an international strategy, using cross-border deals to expand its distribution of its *Heineken, Amstel,* and 170 other beer brands in more than 150 countries around the globe. For years, it has been picking up small brewers from several countries to add more brands and to get better access to new markets. From its roots on the outskirts of Amsterdam, the firm has evolved into one of the world's largest brewers, operating more than 125 breweries in over 70 countries in the world, claiming a little more than 8 percent of the worldwide market for beer (see Exhibits 3 and 4).

In fact, the firm's flagship *Heineken* brand ranked second only to *Budweiser* in a global brand survey jointly undertaken by *BusinessWeek* and Interbrand a couple of years ago. This premier brand has achieved worldwide recognition, according to Kevin Baker, director of alcoholic

Exhibit 1   **Income Statements** (in millions of euros)

	2010	2009	2008	2007	2006
Revenue	16,133	14,701	14,319	12,564	11,829
EBIT	2,476	1,757	1,080	1,528	1,832
Net Profit	1,436	1,018	347	807	1,211
Dividend	438	318	210	343	294

Source: Heineken.

Exhibit 2   **Balance Sheets** (in millions of euros)

	2010	2009	2008	2007	2006
Assets	26,549	20,180	20,563	12,968	12,997
Liabilities	16,321	14,533	15,811	7,022	7,477
Equity	10,228	5,647	4,752	5,946	5,520

Source: Heineken.

* This case was developed by Professor Jamal Shamsie, Michigan State University, with the assistance of Professor Alan B. Eisner, Pace University. Material has been drawn from published sources to be used for class discussion. Copyright © 2011 Jamal Shamsie and Alan B. Eisner.

Exhibit 3 Geographical Breakdown of Sales
(in millions of euros)

	2009	2008	2007
Western Europe	8,432	7,661	5,450
Central & Eastern Europe	3,200	3,687	3,686
Americas	1,541	1,566	2,043
Africa & Middle East	1,817	1,774	1,416
Asia Pacific	305	279	597

Source: Heineken.

Exhibit 4 Heineken Brands: Significant Heineken Brands in Various Markets

United States	Heineken, Amstel Light, Paulaner*, Moretti
Netherlands	Heineken, Amstel, Lingen's Blond, Murphy's Irish Red
France	Heineken, Amstel, Buckler[†], Desperados[‡]
Italy	Heineken, Amstel, Birra Moretti
Spain	Heineken, Amstel, Cruzcampo, Buckler
Poland	Heineken, Krolewskie, Kujawiak, Zywiec
China	Heineken, Tiger, Reeb[§]
Singapore	Heineken, Tiger, Anchor, Baron's
Kazakhstan	Heineken, Amstel, Tian Shan
Egypt	Heineken, Birell, Meister, Fayrouz[†]
Israel	Heineken, Maccabee, Gold Star§
Nigeria	Heineken, Amstel Malta, Maltina, Gulder
Panama	Heineken, Soberana, Crystal, Panama

*Wheat beer.
[†]Nonalcoholic beer.
[‡]Tequila-flavored beer.
[§]Minority interest.

beverages at British market researcher Canadean Ltd. A U.S. wholesaler recently asked a group of marketing students to identify an assortment of beer bottles that had been stripped of their labels. The stubby green *Heineken*

container was the only one that incited instant recognition among the group.

But the beer industry has been undergoing significant change due to a furious wave of consolidation. Most of the bigger brewers have begun to acquire or merge with their competitors in foreign markets in order to become global players. Over the past decade, South African Breweries Plc acquired U.S.-based Miller Brewing to become a major global brewer. U.S.-based Coors linked with Canada-based Molson in 2005, with their combined operations allowing it to rise to a leading position among the world's biggest brewers. More recently, Belgium's Interbrew, Brazil's AmBev, and U.S.-based Anheuser-Busch have all merged to become the largest global brewer, with operations across most of the continents (see Exhibit 5).

Many brewers have also expanded their operations without the use of such acquisitions. For example, Anheuser-Busch had bought equity stakes and struck partnership deals with Mexico's Grupo Modelo, China's Tsingtao, and Chile's CCU. Such cross-border deals have provided significant benefits to the brewing giants. To begin with, it has given them ownership of local brands that has propelled them into a dominant position in various markets around the world. Beyond this, acquisitions of foreign brewers can provide a firm with manufacturing and distribution capabilities that they could use to develop a few global brands. "The era of global brands is coming," said Alan Clark, Budapest-based managing director of SABMiller Europe.[1]

Anheuser-Busch InBev is now planning to include *Budweiser* in its existing efforts to develop *Stella Artois, Brahma,* and *Becks* as global flagship brands. Each of these brands originated in a different location, with *Budweiser* coming from the United States, *Stella Artois* from Belgium, *Brahma* from Brazil, and *Becks* from Germany. Similarly, the newly formed SABMiller has been attempting to develop the Czech brand *Pilsner Urquell* into a global brand. Exports of this pilsner have doubled since SAB acquired it in 1999. John Brock, the CEO of InBev, commented, "Global brands sell at significantly higher prices, and the margins are much better than with local beers."[2]

Wrestling with Change

Although the management of Heineken has moved away from the family for the first time, they have been well aware of the long-standing and well-established family traditions that would be difficult to change. Even with the appointment of non-family-members to manage the firm, a little over half of the shares of Heineken are still owned by a holding company that is controlled by the family. With the death of Freddy Heineken, the last family member to head the Dutch brewer, control has passed to his only child and heir, Charlene de Carvalho, who has insisted on having a say in all of the major decisions.

But the family members were behind some of the changes that were announced at the time of van Boxmeer's

Exhibit 5 Leading Brewers

Brewer	Location	2009 Sales (millions of US dollars)
Anheuser-Busch InBev	Leuven, Belgium	36,758
SABMiller	London, UK	26,350
Heineken	Amsterdam, Netherlands	21,061
Kirin Holdings Co.	Tokyo, Japan	19,695
Asahi	Tokyo, Japan	15,824
FEMSA	Monterrey, Mexico	11,435
Carlsberg	Copenhagen, Denmark	11,400
Grupo Modelo	Mexico City, Mexico	6,257
Foster's Group	Melbourne, Australia	3,826
Sapporo Holdings Ltd.	Tokyo, Japan	3,613

Source: *Beverage World.*

appointment, changes that would support the company's next phase of growth as a global organization. As part of the plan, dubbed Fit 2 Fight, the executive board was cut down from five members to three, all of whom are relatively young. Along with van Boxmeer, the board is made up of the firm's chief operating officer and chief financial officer. Later, this board was further cut down to two members. The change is expected to assist the firm in thinking about the steps that it needs to take to win over younger customers across different markets whose tastes are still developing.

Heineken has also created management positions that would be responsible for five different operating regions and nine different functional areas. These positions were created to more clearly define different spheres of responsibility. Van Boxmeer argues that the new structure also provides incentives for people to be accountable for their performance: "There is more pressure for results, for achievement."[3] He claims the new structure has already encouraged more risk taking and boosted the level of energy within the firm.

The executive committee of Heineken was also cut down from 36 to 13 members in order to speed up the decision-making process. Besides the three members of the executive board, this management group consists of the managers who are responsible for the five different operating regions and six of the key functional areas. Van Boxmeer hopes that the reduction in the size of this group will allow the firm to combat the cumbersome consensus culture that has made it difficult for Heineken to respond swiftly to various challenges even as its industry has been experiencing considerable change.

Finally, all of the activities of Heineken have been overseen by a supervisory board, which currently consists of 10 members. Individuals that make up this board are drawn from different countries and cover a wide range of expertise and experience. They set up policies for the firm to use in making major decisions in its overall operations. Members of the supervisory board are rotated on a regular basis.

Maintaining a Premium Position

For decades, Heineken has been able to rely upon the success of its flagship *Heineken* brand, which has enjoyed a leading position among premium beers in many markets around the world. It had been the best-selling imported beer in the United States for several decades, giving it a steady source of revenues and profits from the world's biggest market. But by the late 1990s, *Heineken* had lost its 65-year-old leadership among imported beers in the United States to Grupo Modelo's *Corona*. The Mexican beer has been able to reach out to the growing population of Hispanic Americans, who represent one of the fastest-growing segments of beer drinkers.

Furthermore, the firm was also concerned that *Heineken* was being perceived as an obsolete brand by many young drinkers. John A. Quelch, a professor at Harvard Business School who has studied the beer industry, said of Heineken, "It's in danger of becoming a tired, reliable, but unexciting brand."[4] The firm has therefore been working hard to increase awareness of their flagship brand among younger drinkers. As part of a global campaign for Heineken, the company launched a video called *The Entrance*, which premiered on the firm's Facebook fan page at the end of 2010 and then become a major success on YouTube. The average age of the Heineken drinker has been reduced from about 40 in the mid-1990s to about 30 as a result of such efforts.

The firm has recently introduced a light beer, *Heineken Premium Light,* to target the growing market for such beers in the United States. In 2010 Heineken also began to roll out a new design for the *Heineken* bottle that will be used across all 170 countries where it is sold. The firm has also introduced *Heineken* in other new forms of packaging. It has achieved some success with a portable draught beer system called DraughtKeg. About 20 glasses of beer can be dispensed from this mini keg. A BeerTender system, which keeps kegs fresh for several weeks once they have been tapped, also continues to grow in sales.

At the same time, Heineken has also been pushing other brands that would reduce its reliance on its core *Heineken* brand. It has already achieved considerable success with *Amstel Light,* which has become the leading imported light beer in the United States and has been selling well in many other countries. But many of the other brands that it carries are strong local brands that it has added through its string of acquisitions of smaller breweries around the globe. It has managed to develop a relatively small but loyal base of consumers by promoting some of these as specialty brands, such as *Murphy's Irish Red* and *Moretti.*

Finally, Heineken has been stepping up its marketing to Hispanics, who account for one-quarter of U.S. sales. It obtained a license from FEMSA Cervesa to market and distribute its popular brands, which include *Tecate* and *Dos Equis* within the United States. Benj Steinman, publisher and editor of the *Beer Marketer's Insight* newsletter claims that the deal will give a tremendous boost to Heineken. "This gives Heineken a commanding share of the U.S. import business and . . . gives them a bigger presence in the Southwest . . . and better access to Hispanic consumers," he stated.[5] In 2010 the firm decided to acquire the Mexican firm, allowing Heineken to add their brands to its growing portfolio of beers.

Above all, Heineken wants to maintain its leadership in the premium beer industry, which represents the most profitable segment of the beer business. In this category, the firm's brands face competition in the United States from domestic beers such as Anheuser's *Budweiser Select* and imported beers such as InBev's *Stella Artois.* Although premium brews often have slightly higher alcohol content than standard beers, they are developed through a more exclusive positioning of the brand. This allows the firm to charge a higher price for these brands. A six-pack of *Heineken,* for example, costs $10, versus around $7 for a six-pack of *Budweiser.* Furthermore, Just-drinks.com, a London-based online research service, estimates that the market for premium beer will expand considerably to $230 billion by 2012.

Building a Global Presence

Van Boxmeer is well aware of the need for Heineken to use its brands to build upon its existing stature across global markets. In spite of its formidable presence in markets around the world, Heineken has failed to match the recent moves of formidable competitors such as Belgium's InBev and the UK's SABMiller, which have grown significantly through mega-acquisitions. In large part, it is assumed that the firm has been reluctant to make such acquisitions because of the dilution of family control.

For many years, Heineken had limited itself to snapping up small national brewers, such as Italy's Moretti and Spain's Cruzcampo, that have provided it with small but profitable avenues for growth. In 1996, for example, Heineken acquired Fischer, a small French brewer whose *Desperados* brand has been quite successful in niche markets. Similarly, *Paulaner,* a wheat beer that the firm picked up in Germany a few years ago, has been making inroads into the U.S. market.

But as other brewers began reaching out to make acquisitions all over the globe, Heineken was running the risk of falling behind its more aggressive rivals. To deal with this growing challenge, the firm broke out of its play-it-safe corporate culture to make a few big deals. In 2003 Heineken spent $2.1 billion to acquire BBAG, a family-owned company based in Linz, Austria. Because of BBAG's extensive presence in Central Europe, Heineken has become the biggest beer maker in seven countries across Eastern Europe. The more recent acquisition of Scottish & Newcastle similarly reinforced the firm's dominance in Western Europe.

At the same time, Heineken has made major acquisitions in other parts of the world. Its recent acquisitions in Nigeria and Mexico have allowed it to build its position in these growing markets. The firm has also made an aggressive push into Russia with the acquisition of mid-sized brewing concerns. Through several acquisitions since 2002, Russia has become one of Heineken's largest markets by volume. Heineken now ranks as the third-largest brewer in Russia, behind Sweden's Baltic Beverages Holding and Anheuser-Busch InBev.

Rene Hooft Graafland, the company's chief financial officer, has stated that Heineken will continue to participate in the consolidation of the $460 billion global retail beer industry by targeting many different markets around the world. During the last decade, the firm has also added several labels to Heineken's shelf, pouncing on brewers in far-flung places like Belarus, Panama, Egypt, and Kazakhstan. In Egypt, Ruys bought a majority stake in Al Ahram Beverages Co. and hopes to use the Cairo-based brewer's fruit-flavored, nonalcoholic malts as an avenue into other Muslim countries.

A Break from the Past?

The recent acquisitions in different parts of the world—Africa, Latin America, and Europe—represent an important step in Heineken's quest to build upon its existing global stature. In fact, most analysts expect that van Boxmeer and his team will make efforts to continue to build Heineken into a powerful global competitor. Without providing any specific details, Graafland, the firm's CFO, did make it clear that the firm's management would take initiatives that would drive long-term growth. In his own words, "We are positive that the momentum in the company and trends will continue."[6]

Upon taking over the helm of Heineken, van Boxmeer announced that he would have to work on the company's culture in order to accelerate the speed of decision making. This led many people both inside and outside the firm to expect that the new management would try to break loose from the conservative style that has resulted from the family's tight control. Instead, the affable 46-year-old Belgian has indicated that he would be focusing on changes to the firm's decision-making process rather than making any drastic shifts in its existing culture.

Van Boxmeer's devotion to the firm is quite evident. Heineken's first non-Dutch CEO spent 20 years working his way up within the firm. Even his cufflinks are silver miniatures of a Heineken bottle top and opener. "We are in the logical flow of history," he recently explained. "Every time you have a new leader you have a new kind of vision. It is not radically different, because you are defined by what your company is and what your brands are."[7]

Furthermore, van Boxmeer seems quite comfortable working with the family-controlled structure. "Since 1952 history has proved it is the right concept," he stated about the current ownership structure. "The whole business about family restraint on us is absolutely untrue. Without its spirit and guidance, the company would not have been able to build a world leader."[8]

Endnotes

1. Ewing, J., & Khermouch, G. 2003. Waking up Heineken. *BusinessWeek,* September 8: 68.
2. Tomlinson, R. 2004. The new king of beers. *Fortune,* October 18: 238.
3. Bickerton, I., & Wiggins, J. 2006. Change is brewing at Heineken. *Financial Times,* May 9: 12.
4. Ewing & Khermouch. 2003: 69.
5. Kaplan, A. 2004. Border crossings. *Beverage World,* July 15: 6.
6. Williams, C. C. 2006. Heineken's seeing green. *Barron's,* September 18: 19.
7. Bickerton & Wiggins. 2006: 12.
8. Ibid.

Case 10   McDonald's*

McDonald's announced in January 2011 that its earnings for the fourth quarter in the previous year rose 2.1 percent in spite of a slowdown in December due to severe weather in the United States and Europe (see Exhibits 1 and 2). The fast-food giant's same-store sales rose 5 percent globally and 4.4 percent in the United Stated from the same period in the prior year. McDonald's attributed these fourth-quarter gains to its increasingly diverse menu as well as its longer store operating hours.

Part of McDonald's growth has come from introducing specialty beverages that are offered in its McCafés. During 2010, the firm began to offer ice-cold frappés and fruit smoothies, which have been quite successful. Expanding into pricier drinks has helped boost the average spent by each customer and lured them to its outlets for snacks during slower parts of the day. McDonald's president and chief operating officer, Don Thompson,

recently told analysts that sales of frappés and smoothies have been "blowing away the high-end projections."[1] In addition, the introduction of espresso-based drinks has made coffee 5 percent of total sales, double what it was in 2006.

On the whole, however, analysts have attributed the continued success of McDonald's to the "Plan to Win," which was first outlined by James R. Cantalupo in 2003 after overexpansion caused the chain to lose focus. The core of the plan was to increase sales at existing locations by improving the menu, refurbishing the outlets, and extending hours. The firm also began to add snacks and drinks, two of the few areas where restaurant sales are still growing. "We do so well because our strategies have been so well planned out," said the firm's CEO, Jim Skinner, in a recent interview.[2]

McDonald's is aware that it is facing a rapidly fragmenting market, where consumers are looking for much healthier and even more exotic foods. Many analysts therefore believe that the chain must continue to work on its turnaround strategy in order to meet these challenges. But they acknowledge that the firm has pushed hard to

*This case was developed by Professor Jamal Shamsie, Michigan State University, with the assistance of Professor Alan B. Eisner, Pace University. Material has been drawn from published sources to be used for class discussion. Copyright © 2011 Jamal Shamsie and Alan B. Eisner.

Exhibit 1   Income Statement (in thousands of dollars)

	Period Ending		
	Dec. 31, 2010	Dec. 31, 2009	Dec. 31, 2008
Total Revenue	24,074,600	22,744,700	23,522,400
Cost of Revenue	14,437,300	13,952,900	14,883,200
Gross Profit	9,637,300	8,791,800	8,639,200
Operating Expenses:			
Selling, General, and Administrative	2,135,100	2,011,900	2,355,500
Nonrecurring	29,100	(61,100)	(48,500)
Operating Income or Loss	7,473,100	6,841,000	6,332,200
Income from continuing operations:			
Total other income/expenses net	(21,900)	119,200	237,700
Earnings before interest and taxes	7,451,200	6,960,200	6,680,600
Interest expense	450,900	473,200	522,600
Income before tax	7,000,300	6,487,000	6,158,000
Income tax expense	2,054,000	1,936,000	1,844,800
Net income from continuing operations	4,946,300	4,551,000	4,313,200
Net Income	4,946,300	4,551,000	4,313,200
Net Income Applicable to Common Shares	4,946,300	4,551,000	4,313,200

Source: McDonald's.

Exhibit 2 Balance Sheets (in thousands of dollars)

	Period Ending		
	Dec 31, 2010	Dec 31, 2009	Dec 31, 2008
Assets			
Current Assets:			
Cash and cash equivalents	2,387,000	1,796,000	2,063,400
Net receivables	1,179,100	1,060,400	931,200
Inventory	109,900	106,200	111,500
Other current assets	692,500	453,700	411,500
Total Current Assets	**4,368,500**	**3,416,300**	**3,517,600**
Long-term investments	1,335,300	1,212,700	1,222,300
Property plant and equipment	22,060,600	21,531,500	20,254,500
Goodwill	2,586,100	2,425,200	2,237,400
Other assets	1,624,700	1,639,200	1,229,700
Total Assets	**31,975,200**	**30,224,900**	**28,461,500**
Liabilities			
Current Liabilities:			
Accounts payable	2,916,400	2,970,600	2,506,100
Short/current long-term debt	8,300	18,100	31,800
Total Current Liabilities	**2,924,700**	**2,988,700**	**2,537,900**
Long-term debt	11,497,000	10,560,300	10,186,000
Other liabilities	1,586,900	1,363,100	1,410,100
Deferred long-term liability charges	1,332,400	1,278,900	944,900
Total Liabilities	**17,341,000**	**16,191,000**	**15,078,900**
Stockholders' Equity			
Common stock	16,600	16,600	16,600
Retained earnings	33,811,700	31,270,800	28,953,900
Treasury stock	(25,143,400)	(22,854,800)	(20,289,400)
Capital surplus	5,196,400	4,853,900	4,600,200
Other stockholder equity	752,900	747,400	101,300
Total Stockholder Equity	**14,634,200**	**14,033,900**	**13,382,600**
Net Tangible Assets	**12,048,100**	**11,608,700**	**11,145,200**

Source: McDonald's.

transform itself and they are encouraged by the results that it has achieved over the last eight years. "They have experienced a comeback the likes of which has been pretty unprecedented," said Bob Golden, executive vice president of Technomic, a food-service consultancy. "When restaurants start to slide, it really takes a lot to turn them around."[3]

At the same time, Skinner has been monitoring pricing in order to make sure the menu stays affordable without hurting its profit margins. Even as it continues to wrestle with cost increases, McDonald's has maintained the pricing on its Dollar Menu, which generates almost 15 percent of total sales. In December 2008, McDonald's did decide to replace its $1 double cheeseburger with the McDouble, a similar burger that is less expensive to make because it has less cheese. Steven Kron, an analyst with Goldman Sachs, emphasized the attractiveness of the firm's affordable Dollar Menu: "When people are seeking value, these guys have a very powerful component."[4]

Experiencing a Downward Spiral

Since it was founded more than 50 years ago, McDonald's has been defining the fast-food business. It provided millions of Americans their first jobs even as it changed their eating habits. It rose from a single outlet in a nondescript Chicago suburb to become one of the largest chains of outlets spread around the globe. But it gradually began to run into various problems, which began to slow down its sales growth (see Exhibit 3).

This decline could be attributed in large part to a drop in McDonald's once-vaunted service and quality since its expansion in the 1990s, when headquarters stopped grading franchises for cleanliness, speed, and service. By the end of the decade, the chain ran into more problems because of the tighter labor market. McDonald's began to cut back on training as it struggled hard to find new recruits, leading to a dramatic fall-off in the skills of its employees. According to a 2002 survey by market researcher Global Growth Group, McDonald's came in third in average service time behind Wendy's and sandwich shop Chick-fil-A Inc.

McDonald's also began to fail consistently with its new product introductions, such as the low-fat McLean Deluxe and Arch Deluxe burgers, both of which were meant to appeal to adults. It did no better with its attempts to diversify beyond burgers, often because of problems with the product development process. Consultant Michael Seid, who manages a franchise consulting firm, pointed out that McDonald's offered a pizza that didn't fit through the drive-through window and salad shakers that were packed so tightly that dressing couldn't flow through them.

In 1998, after McDonald's posted its first-ever decline in annual earnings, CEO Michael R. Quinlan was forced out and replaced by Jack M. Greenberg, a 16-year veteran of the firm. Greenberg did try to cut back on McDonald's expansion as he tried to deal with some of the growing problems. But his efforts to deal with the decline of McDonald's were slowed down by his acquisition of other fast food chains such as Chipotle Mexican Grill and Boston Market.

On December 5, 2002, after watching McDonald's stock slide 60 percent in three years, the board ousted Greenberg. He had lasted little more than two years. His short tenure had been marked by the introduction of 40 new menu items, none of which caught on big, and the purchase of a handful of nonburger chains, none of which helped the firm to sell more burgers. Indeed, his critics say that, by trying so many different things and executing them poorly, Greenberg allowed the burger business to continue with its decline. According to Los Angeles franchisee Reggie Webb, "We would have been better off trying fewer things and making them work."[5]

Pinning Hopes on a New Leader

By the beginning of 2003, consumer surveys were indicating that McDonald's was headed for serious trouble. Measures for the service and quality of the chain were continuing to fall, dropping far behind those of its rivals. To deal with its deteriorating performance, the firm brought back retired Vice Chairman James R. Cantalupo, 59, who had overseen McDonald's successful international expansion in the 1980s and 1990s. Cantalupo, who had retired only a year earlier, was perceived to be the only candidate with the necessary qualifications, despite shareholder sentiment for an outsider. The board felt that it needed someone who knew the company well and could move quickly to turn things around.

Cantalupo realized that McDonald's often tended to miss the mark on delivering the critical aspects of consistent, fast, and friendly service and an all-around enjoyable experience for the whole family. He understood that its franchisees and employees alike needed to be inspired as well as retrained on their role in putting the smile back into McDonald's experience. When Cantalupo and his team laid out their turnaround plan in 2003, they stressed getting the basics of service and quality right, in part by reinstituting a tough "up or out" grading system that would kick out underperforming franchisees. "We have to rebuild the foundation. It's fruitless to add growth if the foundation is weak," said Cantalupo.[6]

To begin with, Cantalupo cut back on the opening of new outlets, focusing instead on generating more sales from its existing outlets. He shifted the firm's emphasis to obtaining most of its revenue growth from an increase in sales in the over 30,000 outlets that were already operating around the world (see Exhibits 4 through 6). In part, McDonalds tried to draw more customers by introducing new products. The chain has had a positive response to its increased emphasis on healthier foods, led by a revamped line of fancier salads. The revamped menu was promoted through a new worldwide ad slogan, "I'm loving it," which was delivered by pop idol Justin Timberlake through a set of MTV-style commercials.

But the biggest success for the firm came in the form of the McGriddles breakfast sandwich, which was launched nationwide in June 2003. The popular new offering consisted of a couple of syrup-drenched pancakes, stamped with the Golden Arches, which acted as the top and bottom of a sandwich to hold eggs, cheese, sausage, and bacon in three different combinations. McDonald's has estimated that the new breakfast addition has been bringing in about one million new customers every day.

With his efforts largely directed at a turnaround strategy for McDonald's, Cantalupo decided to divest the nonburger chains that his predecessor had acquired. Collectively lumped under the Partner Brands, these have consisted of Chipotle Mexican Grill and Boston Market. The

Exhibit 3   McDonald's Milestones

1948	Brothers Richard and Maurice McDonald open the first restaurant in San Bernadino, California, that sells hamburgers, fries, and milk shakes.
1955	Ray A. Kroc, 52, opens his first McDonald's in Des Plaines, Illinois. Kroc, a distributor of milk-shake mixers, figures he can sell a bundle of them if he franchises the McDonald's business and installs his mixers in the new stores.
1961	Six years later, Kroc buys out the McDonald brothers for $2.7 million.
1963	Ronald McDonald makes his debut as corporate spokesclown using future NBC-TV weatherman Willard Scott. During the year, the company also sells its 1 billionth burger.
1965	McDonald's stock goes public at $22.50 a share. It will split 12 times in the next 35 years.
1967	The first McDonald's restaurant outside the United States opens in Richmond, British Columbia. Today there are 31,108 McDonald's in 118 countries.
1968	The Big Mac, the first extension of McDonald's basic burger, makes its debut and is an immediate hit.
1972	McDonald's switches to the frozen variety for its successful french fries.
1974	Fred L. Turner succeeds Kroc as CEO. In the midst of a recession, the minimum wage rises to $2 per hour, a big cost increase for McDonald's, which is built around a model of young, low-wage workers.
1975	The first drive-through window is opened in Sierra Vista, Arizona.
1979	McDonald's responds to the needs of working women by introducing Happy Meals. A burger, some fries, a soda, and a toy give working moms a break.
1987	Michael R. Quinlan becomes chief executive.
1991	Responding to the public's desire for healthier foods, McDonald's introduces the low-fat McLean Deluxe burger. It flops and is withdrawn from the market. Over the next few years, the chain will stumble several times trying to spruce up its menu.
1992	The company sells its 90 billionth burger—and stops counting.
1996	In order to attract more adult customers, the company launches its Arch Deluxe, a "grownup" burger with an idiosyncratic taste. Like the low-fat burger, it also falls flat.
1997	McDonald's launches Campaign 55, which cuts the cost of a Big Mac to $0.55. It is a response to discounting by Burger King and Taco Bell. The move, which prefigures similar price wars in 2002, is widely considered a failure.
1998	Jack M. Greenberg becomes McDonald's fourth chief executive. A 16-year company veteran, he vows to spruce up the restaurants and their menu.
1999	For the first time, sales from international operations outstrip domestic revenues. In search of other concepts, the company acquires Aroma Cafe, Chipotle, Donatos, and, later, Boston Market.
2000	McDonald's sales in the United States peak at an average of $1.6 million annually per restaurant, a figure that has not changed since. It is, however, still more than at any other fast-food chain.
2001	Subway surpasses McDonald's as the fast-food chain with the most U.S. outlets. At the end of the year, it had 13,247 stores, 148 more than McDonald's.
2002	McDonald's posts its first-ever quarterly loss, of $343.8 million. The stock drops to around $13.50, down 40 percent from five years earlier.
2003	James R. Cantalupo returns to McDonald's in January as CEO. He immediately pulls back from the company's 10–15 percent forecast for per-share earnings growth.
2004	Charles H. Bell takes over the firm after the sudden death of Cantalupo. He states that he will continue with the strategies that have been developed by his predecessor.
2005	Jim Skinner takes over as CEO after Bell announces retirement for health reasons.
2006	McDonald's launches specialty beverages, including coffee-based drinks.
2008	Ralph Alvarez elected to McDonald's board of directors.
2009	Chief Operating Officer Ralph Alvarez retires.
2010	Don Thompson is elected president and COO.

Source: McDonald's.

purpose of these acquisitions had been to find new growth and to offer the best franchises new expansion opportunities. But these acquired businesses had not fueled much growth and had actually posted considerable losses in recent years.

Striving for Healthier Offerings

When Jim Skinner took over the reins of McDonald's in late 2004, he expressed his commitment to Cantalupo's plans to pursue various avenues for growth. But Skinner felt that one of his top priorities was to deal with the growing concerns about the unhealthy image of McDonald's, given the rise of obesity in the United States. These concerns were highlighted in the popular documentary *Super Size Me,* made by Morgan Spurlock. Spurlock vividly displayed the health risks that were posed by a steady diet of food from the fast-food chain. With a rise in awareness of the high fat content of most of the products offered by McDonald's, the firm was also beginning to face lawsuits from some of its loyal customers.

In response to the growing health concerns, one of the first steps taken by McDonald's was to phase out supersizing by the end of 2004. The supersizing option allowed customers to get a larger order of french fries and a bigger soft drink by paying a little extra. McDonald's has begun

Exhibit 4   Number of Outlets

	2010	2009	2008	2007	2006
Company owned	6,399	6,262	6,502	6,906	8,166
Franchised	26,338	26,216	25,465	20,505	18,685
Affiliated	3,574	4,036	4,137	3,966	4,195
Total	32,737	32,478	31,967	31,377	31,046

Source: McDonald's.

Exhibit 5   Distribution of Outlets

	2010	2009	2008	2007	2006
U.S.	14,027	13,980	13,918	13,862	13,774
Europe	6,969	6,785	6,628	6,480	6,403
Asia Pacific	8,424	8,488	8,255	7,938	7,822
Americas*	3,317	3,225	3,166	3,097	3,047

* Canada & Latin America.
Source: McDonald's.

Exhibit 6   Breakdown of Revenues (in millions of dollars)

	2010	2009	2008	2007	2006
U.S.	8,116	7,043	8,078	7,906	7,464
Europe	9,569	9,273	9,923	8,926	7,638
Asia Pacific	5,065	4,337	4,231	3,599	3,053
Americas*	1,328	1,190	1,290	2,356	2,740

*Canada & Latin America.
Source: McDonald's.

providing nutrition information on the packaging of its products. The information is easy to read and tells customers about the calories, fat, protein, carbohydrates, and sodium that are in each product. Finally, McDonald's has also removed the artery-clogging trans fatty acids from the oil that it uses to make its french fries.

But Skinner was also trying to push out more offerings that were likely to be perceived by customers to be healthier. McDonald's has continued to build upon its chicken offerings with products such as Chicken Selects. It has also placed a great deal of emphasis upon its new salad offerings. Although the firm had failed to attract many customers in the past with its salads, McDonald's carried out extensive experiments and tests with its new premium versions. It chose higher quality ingredients, from a variety of lettuces and tasty cherry tomatoes to sharper cheeses and better cuts of meat. It offered a choice of *Newman's Own* dressings, a well-known higher-end brand.

McDonald's has also been trying to include more fruits and vegetables in its well-known and popular Happy Meals. In many locations, the firm is offering apple slices called Apple Dippers in place of french fries in the children's Happy Meal. The addition of fruits and vegetables has raised the firm's operating costs, because these are more expensive to ship and store because of their more perishable nature. But Skinner believes that the firm had to push more heavily on fruits and salads. "Salads have changed the way people think of our brand," said Wade Thoma, vice president for menu development in the United States. "It tells people that we are very serious about offering things people feel comfortable eating."[7]

The current rollout of new beverages, highlighted by new coffee-based drinks, represents the chain's biggest menu expansion in almost three decades. Under a plan to add a McCafé section to all of its nearly 14,000 U.S. outlets, McDonald's has been offering lattes, cappuccinos, ice-blended frappés, and fruit-based smoothies to its customers. "In many cases, they're now coming for the beverage, whereas before they were coming for the meal," said Lee Renz, the firm's vice president who is responsible for the rollout.[8]

Revamping the Outlets

As part of its turnaround strategy, McDonald's has also been selling off the outlets that it owned. More than 75 percent of its outlets are now in the hands of franchisees and other affiliates. Skinner is now working with the franchisees to address the look and feel of many of the chain's aging stores. Without any changes to their décor, the firm is likely to be left behind by other more savvy fast-food and drink retailers. The firm is in the midst of pushing harder to refurbish—or reimage—all of its outlets around the world. "People eat with their eyes first," said president and COO Don Thompson. "If you have a restaurant that is appealing, contemporary, and relevant both from the street and interior, the food tastes better."[9]

The reimaging concept was first tried in France in 1996 by Dennis Hennequin, now president of McDonald's Europe, who felt that the effort was essential to revive the firm's sagging sales. "We were hip 15 years ago, but I think we lost that," he said.[10] McDonald's is now applying the reimaging concept to its outlets around the world, with a budget of more than half of its total annual capital expenditures. In the United States, the changes cost an average of $150,000 per restaurant, a cost that is shared with the franchisees when the outlet is not company owned.

One of the prototype interiors being tested out by McDonald's has curved counters with surfaces painted in bright colors. In one corner, a touch-activated screen allows customers to punch in orders without queuing. The interiors can feature armchairs and sofas, modern lighting, large television screens, and even wireless Internet access. The firm is also trying to develop new features for its drive-through customers, which account for 65 percent of all transactions in the United States. They include music aimed at queuing vehicles and a wall of windows on the drive-through side of the restaurant, allowing customers to see meals being prepared from their cars.

The chain has even been developing McCafés inside its outlets next to the usual fast-food counter. The McCafé concept originated in Australia in 1993 and has been rolled out in many restaurants around the world. McDonald's has just begun to introduce the concept to the United States as it refurbishes many of its existing outlets. In fact, part of the refurbishment has focused on installing a specialty beverage platform across all U.S. outlets. The cost of installing this equipment is running at about $100,000 per outlet, with McDonald's subsidizing part of this expense.

Eventually, all McCafés will offer espresso-based coffee, gourmet coffee blends, fresh baked muffins, and high-end desserts. Customers will be able to consume these while they relax in soft leather chairs listening to jazz, big band, or blues music. Commenting on this significant expansion of offerings, Marty Brochstein, executive editor of *The Licensing Letter,* said, "McDonald's wants to be seen as a lifestyle brand, not just a place to go to have a burger."[11]

A New and Improved McDonalds?

Even though Skinner's efforts to transform McDonald's have led to improvements in its sales and profits, there are questions about the future of the fast-food chain. The firm is trying out a variety of strategies to increase its appeal to different segments of the market. Through adopting a mix of outlet décor and menu items, McDonald's is trying to target young adults, teenagers, children, and families. In so doing, it must ensure that it does not alienate any one of these groups in its efforts to reach out to the other. Its new marketing campaign, anchored around the catchy phrase "I'm loving it," takes on different forms in order to target each of the groups that it is seeking.

Larry Light, the head of global marketing at McDonald's since 2002, insists that the firm has to exploit its brand through pushing it in many different directions. The brand can be positioned differently in different locations, at different times of the day, and to target different customer segments. In large urban centers, McDonald's can target young adults for breakfast with its gourmet coffee, egg sandwiches, and fat-free muffins. Light explains the adoption of such a multiformat strategy: "The days of mass-media marketing are over."[12]

Nevertheless, the expansion of the menu beyond the staple of burgers and fries does raise some fundamental questions. Most significantly, it is not clear just how far McDonald's can stretch its brand while keeping all of its outlets under the traditional symbol of its golden arches. Chief financial officer Paull acknowledged that burgers continue to be the main draw for McDonald's: "There is no question that we make more money from selling hamburgers and cheeseburgers."[13]

Above all, Skinner is convinced that McDonald's must do whatever it can to make sure that it keeps its established customer base from bolting to the growing number of competitors, such as the California-based In-N-Out chain. The long-term success of the firm may well depend on its ability to compete with rival burger chains. "The burger category has great strength," added David C. Novak, chairman and CEO of Yum! Brands, parent of KFC and Taco Bell. "That's America's food. People love hamburgers."[14]

Endnotes

1. Jargon. J. & Ziobro, P. 2010. McDonald's cup runs over. *Wall Street Journal,* August 10: B8.
2. Adamy, J. 2009. McDonald's to expand, posting strong results. *Wall Street Journal,* January 27: B1.
3. Buckley, N. 2004. McDonald's shares survive resignation. *Financial Times,* November 24: 18.
4. Adamy. 2009.
5. Gogoi, P. & Arndt, M. 2003. Hamburger hell. *BusinessWeek,* March 3: 106.
6. Ibid.: 105.
7. Warner, M. 2005. You want any fruit with that Big Mac? *New York Times,* February 20: 8.

8. Adamy, J. 2008. McDonald's coffee strategy is tough sell. *Wall Street Journal,* October 27:. B3.

9. Paynter, B. 2010. Super style me. *Fast Company,* October: 107.

10. Grant, J. 2006. McDonald's to revamp UK outlets. *Financial Times,* February 2: 14

11. Horovitz, B. 2003. McDonald's ventures beyond burgers to duds, toys. *USA Today,* November 14: 6B.

12. Big Mac's makeover. 2004. *Economist,* October 16: 65.

13. Big Mac's makeover. 2004: 64.

14. Gogoi & Arndt. 2003: 108.

Case 11   World Wrestling Entertainment*

On January 28, 2011, World Wrestling Entertainment announced that its Hall of Famer "Stone Cold" Steve Austin would host the reality series *WWE Tough Enough* on the USA network. Steve Austin has captivated audiences around the world with his magnetic presence and bold, yet charming nature. He has an immense and devoted fan base and is considered one of the most popular WWE Superstars of all time. Austin was inducted into the WWE Hall of Fame in 2009. "I am very excited about the opportunity to work with my old friends at WWE on *WWE Tough Enough,*" said Austin.[1]

The show, which is based on one that ran a few years ago on MTV, features a group of individuals looking for a shot to become the next Superstar or Diva. Austin mentors the diverse group of men and women who live, train, eat, and sleep under one roof in a house in Simi Valley, California. Each week, the contestants battle it out in a series of unique challenges designed to test for such characteristics as showmanship, creativity, athleticism, and desire, just to name a few. The finalist will be awarded a contract with WWE.

* This case was developed by Professor Jamal Shamsie, Michigan State University, with the assistance of Professor Alan B. Eisner, Pace University. Material has been drawn from published sources to be used for class discussion. Copyright © 2011 Jamal Shamsie and Alan B. Eisner.

The deal for the new reality series clearly indicates that WWE has moved out of a slump that it had endured between 2001 and 2005. During the 1990s, WWE's potent mix of shaved, pierced, and pumped-up muscled hunks; buxom, scantily-clad, and sometimes cosmetically enhanced beauties; and body-bashing clashes of good versus evil had resulted in an empire that claimed over 35 million fans. Furthermore, the vast majority of these fans were males between the ages of 12 and 34, the demographic segment that makes most advertisers drool.

Just when it looked like everything was going well, WWE hit a rough patch. The firm's failure with a football league during 2001, which folded after just one season, was followed by a drop in revenues from its core wrestling businesses. WWE was struggling with its efforts to build new wrestling stars and to introduce new characters into its shows. Some of its most valuable younger viewers were also turning to new reality-based shows on television such as *Survivor, Fear Factor,* and *Jackass.*

Since 2005, however, WWE has been winning fans back around the world. It has been rebuilding its fan base through live shows, television programming, consumer products, and Internet sales (see Exhibits 1 and 2). In fact, the firm was recently named as one of the top 200

Exhibit 1   Income Statements (in millions of dollars)

Period End Date Period Length	12/31/2010 12 Months	12/31/2009 12 Months	12/31/2008 12 Months	12/31/2007 12 Months	12/31/2006 8 Months
Total Revenue	477.66	475.16	526.46	485.66	262.94
Cost of Revenue	274.30	255.85	311.78	298.77	157.09
Gross Profit	203.36	219.31	214.67	186.89	105.84
Selling, General, Administrative Expenses	109.39	127.76	131.30	109.13	61.04
Research & Development	0.00	0.00	0.00	0.00	0.00
Depreciation, Amortization	11.71	14.42	13.08	9.32	5.56
Operating Income	82.26	77.13	70.29	68.43	39.24
Other, Net	−2.11	−0.42	−6.38	−0.52	0.88
Income before Tax	81.94	79.43	69.36	76.47	46.15
Income Tax	28.49	29.13	23.94	24.34	14.53
Income after Tax	53.45	50.30	45.42	52.14	31.62
Net Income before Extra Items	53.45	50.30	45.42	52.14	31.62
Total Extraordinary Items	0.00	0.00	0.00	0.00	0.00
Net Income	53.45	50.30	45.42	52.14	31.62

Source: *moneycentral.msn.com* and WWE.

Exhibit 2   **Balance Sheets** (in millions of dollars, except per-share items)

	Period Ending				
	12/31/2010	12/31/2009	12/31/2008	12/31/2007	12/31/2006
Assets					
Current Assets:					
Cash and Short-Term Investments	166.95	208.22	177.34	266.35	248.16
Total Receivables, Net	52.05	62.73	60.13	56.60	52.11
Total Inventory	2.09	2.18	4.96	4.72	3.05
Prepaid Expenses	38.31	21.72	37.60	20.05	13.33
Other Current Assets	0.00	0.00	0.00	0.00	0.47
Total Current Assets	259.40	294.86	280.03	347.72	317.12
Property/Plant/Equipment, Net	79.74	84.38	92.37	77.77	67.97
Intangibles, Net	0.13	0.28	1.18	2.30	3.33
Long-Term Investments	15.04	22.37	22.30	0.00	0.00
Notes Receivable, Long-Term	0.00	0.00	0.00	0.00	0.00
Other Long-Term Assets	61.42	38.74	33.53	42.26	64.86
Total Assets	415.73	440.62	429.41	470.06	453.29
Liabilities and Shareholders' Equity					
Current Liabilities:					
Accounts Payable	18.44	21.28	18.33	21.95	14.91
Accrued Expenses	24.48	35.16	27.12	30.68	25.54
Current Portion of Long-Term Debt/ Capital Leases	1.17	1.08	1.00	0.93	0.86
Other Current Liabilities	28.32	14.60	11.88	18.01	20.47
Total Current Liabilities	72.41	72.13	58.33	71.57	61.77
Long-Term Debt	1.62	2.79	3.87	4.88	5.80
Deferred Income Tax	15.07	17.15	7.23	10.23	0.00
Other Liabilities	9.88	11.53	0.00	0.00	0.00
Total Liabilities	98.98	103.60	69.44	86.68	67.57
Shareholders' Equity:					
Common Stock	0.74	0.73	0.73	0.72	0.71
Additional Paid-In Capital	336.59	326.01	317.11	301.33	286.99
Retained Earnings (Accumulated Deficit)	−23.73	7.90	40.97	78.44	97.35
Other Equity, Total	3.14	2.38	1.17	2.89	0.67
Total Equity	316.75	337.02	359.97	383.38	385.71
Total Liabilities & Shareholders' Equity	415.73	440.62	429.41	470.06	453.29
Total Common Shares Outstanding	73.92	73.46	72.29	71.79	71.00

Source: *moneycentral.msn.com* and WWE.

Best Small Companies by *Forbes* magazine. WWE has been turning pro wrestling into a perpetual road show that makes millions of fans pass through turnstiles worldwide. Its three television programs, *Raw, Smackdown,* and *WWE Superstars,* have become the leading shows among male viewers on the nights that they are broadcast. Finally, WWE has been signing pacts with dozens of licensees to sell DVDs, video games, toys, and trading cards (see Exhibits 3 to 5). "We continue to see the distribution of our creative content through various emerging channels," stated Linda McMahon, who just stepped down as WWE's president and CEO[2].

Developing a Wrestling Empire

Most of the success of the WWE can be attributed to the persistent efforts of Vince McMahon. He was a self-described juvenile delinquent who went to military school as a teenager to avoid being sent to a reformatory institution. Around 1970, Vince joined his father's wrestling company, which operated in northeastern cities such as New York, Philadelphia, and Washington, DC. He did on-air commentary, developed scripts, and otherwise promoted wrestling matches. Vince bought the wrestling firm from his father in 1982, eventually renaming it World Wrestling Federation. At that time, wrestling was managed by regional fiefdoms, and everyone avoided encroaching on anyone else's territory. Vince began to change all that by paying local television stations around the country to broadcast his matches. His aggressive pursuit of audiences across the country gradually squeezed out most of the other rivals. "I banked on the fact that they were behind the times, and they were," said Vince.[3]

Soon after, Vince broke another taboo by admitting to the public that wrestling matches were scripted. Although he had made this admission in order to avoid the scrutiny of state athletic commissions, wrestling fans appreciated the honesty. The WWF began to draw in more fans through the elaborate story lines and the captivating characters of its wrestling matches. The firm turned wrestlers such as Hulk Hogan and Andre the Giant into mainstream icons of pop culture. By the late 1980s, the WWF's *Raw Is War* had become a top-rated show on cable, and the firm had also begun to offer pay-per-view shows.

Vince faced his most formidable competition after 1988, when Ted Turner bought out World Championship Wrestling, one of the few major rivals that was still

Exhibit 3   **Breakdown of Net Revenues** (all figures in millions of dollars)

	Period Ending			
	Dec. 31, 2010	Dec. 31, 2009	Dec. 31, 2008	Dec. 31, 2007
Live & televised entertainment	331.80	335.00	331.50	316.80
Consumer products	97.40	99.70	135.70	118.10
Digital media	28.90	32.80	34.80	34.80
WWE Studios	19.60	7.70	24.50	16.00
TOTAL	477.70	475.20	526.50	485.70

Source: WWE.

Exhibit 4   **Breakdown of Operating Income** (all figures in millions of dollars)

	Period Ending			
	Dec. 31, 2010	Dec. 31, 2009	Dec. 31, 2008	Dec. 31, 2007
Live & televised entertainment	119.20	124.70	92.40	100.20
Consumer products	50.00	52.70	76.50	68.60
Digital media	5.00	5.80	6.20	6.30
WWE Studios	(1.80)	2.20	7.20	(14.80)

Source: WWE.

Exhibit 5 **Percentage Breakdown of Net Revenues** (all figures in millions of dollars)

	Period Ending			
	Dec. 31, 2010	Dec. 31, 2009	Dec. 31, 2008	Dec. 31, 2007
Live & Televised Entertainment				
Live Events	22%	23%	20%	20%
Venue Merchandise Sales	4%	4%	4%	4%
Television	27%	24%	19%	19%
Pay Per View	15%	17%	17%	20%
Video on Demand	1%	1%	2%	1%
Consumer Products				
Licensing	11%	9%	11%	10%
Home Video	7%	8%	11%	11%
Magazine Publishing	2%	3%	3%	4%
Digital Media				
WWE.com	3%	4%	3%	3%
WWEShop	3%	3%	4%	4%
WWE Studios				
Filmed Entertainment	4%	2%	5%	3%

Source: WWE.

operating. He spent millions luring away WWF stars such as Hulk Hogan and Macho Man Randy Savage. He used these stars to launch a show on his own TNT channel to go up against WWF's major show, *Raw Is War.* Although Turner's new show caused a temporary dip in the ratings for WWF's shows, Vince fought back with pumped-up scripts, mouthy muscle-men, and lycra-clad women. "Ted Turner decided to come after me and all of my talent," growled Vince, "and now he's where he should be . . ."[4]

In 2001 Vince was finally able to acquire WCW from Turner's parent firm, AOL Time Warner, for a bargain price of $5 million. Because of the manner in which he eliminated most of his rivals, Vince has earned a reputation for being as aggressive and ambitious as any character in the ring. Paul MacArthur, publisher of *Wrestling Perspective,* an industry newsletter praised his accomplishments: "McMahon understands the wrestling business better than anyone else. He's considered by most in the business to be brilliant."[5]

In 2002 WWF was also hit by a ruling by a British court that their original WWF acronym belonged to the World Wildlife Fund. The firm had to undergo a major branding transition, changing its well-known name and triple logo from WWF to WWE. Although the change in name has been costly, it is not clear that this will hurt the firm in the long run. "Their product is really the entertainment. It's the stars. It's the bodies," said Larry McNaughton, managing director and principal of CoreBrand, a branding consultancy.[6] Linda McMahon stated that the new name might actually be beneficial for the firm. "Our new name puts the emphasis on the 'E' for entertainment," she commented.[7]

Creating a Script for Success

Since taking over the firm, Vince began to change the entire focus of the wrestling shows. He looked to television soap operas for enhancing the entertainment value of his live events. Vince reduced the amount of actual wrestling and replaced it with wacky yet somewhat compelling story lines. He began to develop interesting characters and create compelling story lines by employing techniques that were similar to those being used by many successful television shows. There was a great deal of reliance on the "good versus evil" or the "settling the score" themes in the development of the plots for his wrestling matches. The plots and subplots ended up providing viewers with a mix of romance, sex, sports, comedy, and violence against a backdrop of pyrotechnics.

Over time, the scripts for the matches became tighter, with increasingly intricate story lines, plots, and dialogue. All the details of every match were worked out well in advance, leaving the wrestlers themselves to decide only the manner in which they would dispatch their opponents to the mat. Vince's use of characters was well thought out, and he began to refer to his wrestlers as "athletic performers" who were selected on the basis of their acting ability in addition to their physical stamina.

Vince also ensured that his firm owned the rights to the characters that were played by his wrestlers. This would allow him to continue to exploit the characters that he developed for his television shows, even after the wrestler that played that character had left his firm. By now, Vince holds the rights to many characters that have become familiar to audiences around the world.

By the late 1990s Vince had two weekly shows on television. Besides the original flagship program on the USA cable channel, WWE had added a *Smackdown!* show on the UPN broadcast channel. He developed a continuous story line using the same characters so that his audience would be driven to both the shows. But the acquisition of the WCW resulted in a significant increase in the number of wrestling stars under contract. Trying to incorporate more than 150 characters into the story lines for WWE's shows proved to be a challenging task. At the same time, the move of *Raw* to the Spike TV channel resulted in a loss of viewers.

In October 2005, WWE signed a new agreement with NBC that moved *Raw* back to its USA channel. WWE's other show, *Smackdown,* is now carried by the Syfy channel, which has been climbing in the charts. Its newest show, *WWE Superstars,* is featured on WGN America, Tribune Broadcasting's national superstation. All of these programs have done well in ratings, particularly for male viewers, because of the growth in popularity of a new breed of characters, such as John Cena and Chris Benoit. WWE also licenses local stations in 145 countries around the world to carry its various television shows in 30 different languages.

Managing a Road Show

A typical work week for the WWE can be grueling for the McMahons, for the talent, and for the crew. The organization is now putting on almost 300 live shows a year, requiring everyone to be on the road most days of the week. The touring crew includes over 200 crew members, including stage hands. All of WWE's live events, including those that are used for its two long-standing weekly shows, *Raw* and *Smackdown!,* as well as the newer ones, are held in different cities. Consequently, the crew is always packing up a dozen 18-wheelers and driving hundreds of miles to get from one performance to the other. Because there are no repeats of any WWE shows, the live performances must be held all year round.

In fact, the live shows form the core of all of WWE's businesses (see Exhibit 6). They give the firm a big advantage in the entertainment world. Most of the crowd show up wearing WWE merchandise and scream throughout the show. Vince and his crew pay special attention to the response of the audience to different parts of the show. The

script for each performance is not set until the day of the show, and sometimes changes are even made in the middle of a show. Vince boasted, "We're in contact with the public more than any entertainment company in the world."[8]

Although the live shows usually fill up, the tickets and the merchandise sold at these shows do not manage to cover the cost of the production. But these live performances become a source for all the other revenue streams. To begin with, they provide content for nine hours of original television programming as well as for the growing list of pay-per-view and video-on-demand programming. But the shows also create strong demand for WWE merchandise, ranging from video games and toys to magazines and home videos.

Much of the footage from these live shows is also being used on the WWE website, which is the growth engine for its new digital media business. As of 2010, the website was attracting 12.7 million unique global visitors each month. The firm even produces a show, *WWE NXT,* exclusively for the website. But it also serves to promote the various offerings of the firm and carries many segments from its various other television programs.

All of these operations have been managed not only by Vince, but also by others in his family. While the slick and highly toned Vince could be regarded as the creative muscle behind the growing sports entertainment empire, his wife Linda had been quietly managing its day-to-day operation. Throughout its existence, she helped to balance the books, do the deals, and handle the details that were necessary for the growth and development of the WWE franchise. Their son and daughter have also been involved with various activities. However, Linda left in 2009 to pursue a political career.

Pursuing New Opportunities

In 1999, shortly after going public, WWF launched an eight-team football league called the XFL. Promising full competitive sport, unlike the heavily-scripted wrestling matches, Vince tried to make the XFL a faster-paced, more fan-friendly form of football than the NFL's brand. Vince was able to partner with NBC, which was looking for a lower-priced alternative to the NFL televised games. The XFL kicked off with great fanfare in February 2001. Although the games drew good attendance, television ratings dropped steeply after the first week. The football venture was folded after just one season, resulting in a $57 million loss for WWF. Both Vince and Linda insist that the venture could have paid off if it had been given enough time. Vince commented, "I think our pals at the NFL went out of their way to make sure this was not a successful venture."[9]

Since then, the firm has tried to seek growth opportunities that are driven by its core wrestling business. With more characters at their disposal and different characters being used in each of their shows, WWE has been ramping up the number of live shows, including more in overseas locations. By 2009 the firm was staging almost 70 shows

Exhibit.6   Wrestlemania's Classic Bouts

Andre the Giant vs. Hulk Hogan

WrestleMania III, March 29, 1987

- **The Lowdown:** A record crowd of 93,173 witnessed Andre the Giant, undefeated for 15 years, versus Hulk Hogan, wrestling's golden boy.
- **The Payoff:** Hogan body-slammed the 500-pound Giant, becoming the sport's biggest star and jump-starting wrestling's first big boom.

The Rock vs. Stone Cold Steve Austin

WrestleMania X-7, April 1, 2001

- **The Lowdown:** The two biggest stars of wrestling's modern era went toe-to-toe in the culmination of a two-year-long feud.
- **The Payoff:** Good-guy Austin aligned with "evil" WWE owner Vince McMahon and decimated the Rock to win the title in front of a shocked crowd.

Hulk Hogan vs. The Ultimate Warrior

WrestleMania VI, April 1, 1990

- **The Lowdown:** The most divisive feud ever – fan favorite Hulk Hogan defended his title against up-and-coming phenom the Ultimate Warrior.
- **The Payoff:** Half the crowd went into cardiac arrest (the other half were in tears) when Hogan missed his patented leg drop and the Warrior won.

Bret Hart vs. Shawn Michaels

WrestleMania XII, March 31, 1996

- **The Lowdown:** Two men who didn't like each other outside the ring locked up in a 60-minute Iron Man match for the title.
- **The Payoff:** After an hour, neither man had scored a pinfall. Finally, Michaels, aka the Heartbreak Kid, pinned Hart in overtime to win the belt.

Kurt Angle vs. Brock Lesnar

WrestleMania XIX, March 30, 2003

- **The Lowdown:** Olympic medalist Angle squared off against former NCAA wrestling champ Lesnar in a punishing bout.
- **The Payoff:** The 295-pound Lesnar landed on his head after attempting a high-flying attack. But he recovered to pin Angle and capture the championship.

Source: *TV Guide.*

in locations around the world. These shows have also helped to boost the worldwide revenues that the firm is able to generate from its merchandise, videos, and DVDs. The company has opened offices in six cities around the world to manage its overseas operations. "While it is based in America, the themes are worldwide: sibling rivalry, jealousy. We have had no pushback on the fact it was an American product," said Linda.[10]

There has also been considerable excitement generated by the launch of WWE 24/7, a subscriber video-on-demand service. The new service allows the firm to distribute for a fee thousands of content hours consisting of highlights from old shows as well as exclusive new programming. Since its launch, WWE 24/7 has shown considerable growth by bringing in new audiences for its programming.

WWE is also pushing into a new area of digital media, building upon its e-commerce website that offers broadband and mobile services. The site offers a broad range of content and wide range of merchandise. But the firm has barely tapped into the online ad market, with digital media revenue accounting for around 7 percent of its total revenue. "The real value creation and growth will come from monetizing the presence on the Internet, where the company has a fanatic and loyal fan base," said Bobby Melnick, general partner with Terrier Partners, a New York money management firm that owns WWE stock.[11]

Finally, WWE has also become involved with movie production using its wrestling stars, releasing a few films over the past eight years. Recent releases included Steve Austin's *The Condemned* and John Cena's *Legendary*. Though the films generated a small amount of revenue in theaters, Linda believes that their movies will earn a small profit from home video markets, distribution on premium channels, and offerings on pay-per-view.

Reclaiming the Championship?

Although WWE may find it challenging to keep building on its already formidable fan base, there is no question that it continues to generate a lot of excitement. Their shows continue to generate strong ratings. One of WWE's television producers believes that the return of *Tough Enough* has been one of the most talked about topics among television insiders. And their live shows always manage to fill up the arenas. "They have the most excited fans that have come through our doors," said the director of sales and marketing at one of the arenas that holds WWE matches. "They make signs, dress up and cheer constantly."[12]

The interest in wrestling is most evident each year with the frenzy that is created by Wrestlemania, the annual pop culture extravaganza that began at New York's Madison Square Garden in 1985. Since then, it has become an almost weeklong celebration of everything wrestling. No wrestler becomes a true star until their performance is featured at WrestleMania, and any true fan must make the pilgrimage at least once in their life. Linda points to the continued popularity of this event to reject any suggestion that the fortunes of WWE may be driven by a fad that is unlikely to last.

More recently, Vince's wrestling empire is facing a challenge from mixed martial arts, a growing form of combat sport that combines kickboxing and grappling. Because of its similarity to wrestling, this new combat sport is expected to pull away some of WWE's fans. Although MMA started in Japan and Brazil, Ultimate Fighting Championship and International Fight League are promoting it as a new type of spectator sport in the United States. But Dana White, president of U.F.C. said, "People have been trying to count the W.W.E. out for years. They are a powerhouse."[13]

In fact, WWE has begun to tone down its sex and violence during recent years in order to expand their audience by making their shows more family friendly. They no longer use fake prop blood and have toned down the use of abusive language in order to get a rating of TV-PG for their television programming. By making such changes, Vince continues to find new ways to exploit wrestling as a form of mass entertainment. In response to critics who question the value of wrestling matches whose outcomes are rigged, James F. Byrne, senior vice president for marketing stated, "Wrestling is 100 percent entertainment. There's no such thing as fake entertainment."[14]

Those who understand don't need an explanation. Those who need an explanation will never understand.

—Marty, a 19-year-old wrestling addict, quoted in *Fortune,* October 6, 2000.

Endnotes

1. WWE hall of famer Steve Austin hosts USA's Tough Enough. 2011. PR Newswire, January 28.
2. WWE. 2005. World Wrestling Entertainment, Inc. reports Q3 results. Press Release, February 23.
3. McLean, B. 2000. Inside the world's weirdest family business. *Fortune,* October 16: 298.
4. Bradley, D. 2000. Wrestling's real grudge match. *Business-Week,* January 24: 164.
5. Mooradian, D. 2001. WWF gets a grip after acquisition. *Amusement Business,* June 4: 20.
6. Oestricher, D. & Steinberg, B. 2002. WW . . . E it is, after fight for F nets new name. *Wall Street Journal,* May 7: B2.
7. Finnigan, D. 2002. Down but not out, WWE is using a rebranding effort to gain strength. *Brandweek,* June 3: 12.
8. McLean. 2000: 304.
9. Bradley, D. 2004. Rousing itself off the mat? *Business-Week,* February 2: 73.
10. Masters, B. 2008. Wrestling's bottom line is no soap opera. *Financial Times,* August 25: 15.
11. La Monica, P. R. 2007. Wrestling's "Trump" card. CNN Money.com, March 30.
12. Ball, B. 2011. The face of the WWE. McClatchy-Tribune Business News, January 13.
13. SchneidermanR. M. 2008. Better days, and even the candidates are coming to WWE. *New York Times,* April 28: B3.
14. Wyatt, E. 1999. Pro wrestling tries to pin down a share value. *New York Times,* August 4: C11.

Case 12 Yahoo!*

More than two years after the board of Yahoo hired Carol A. Bartz as chief executive to apply a little shock therapy to the ailing Web portal, the firm appears to be still suffering from many of the same symptoms. Its revenues and profits remain relatively stagnant, its market share has remained low, and there still continues to be a shortage of innovation (see Exhibits 1 and 2). Most analysts feel that her turnaround plan has failed to generate any significant results so far, prompting skepticism that she may not have been well suited for the job. "She's been there long enough that you have to question her ability to have the impact that's needed," said Lou A. Kerner, an analyst with Wedbush Securities.[1]

* This case was developed by Professor Jamal Shamsie, Michigan State University, with the assistance of Professor Alan B. Eisner, Pace University. Material has been drawn from published sources to be used for class discussion. Copyright © 2011 Jamal Shamsie and Alan B. Eisner.

Bartz has long warned that reviving Yahoo would take some time. Shortly after she took charge in January 2009, Bartz had warned that she would be trying to reverse a slide that has been years in the making, one that analysts say was caused by a slow decision-making process that allowed new competitors to capitalize on the various emerging trends among Internet users. During her two years at the head of Yahoo, Bartz has made substantial changes to the organization, including a shuffling of top executives. She has also tried to refocus the firm on its strengths in content areas such as news, sports, and finance and on other popular services, such as e-mail and instant messaging.

Many other forms of services which were no longer considered to be central to the firm's strategy, such as personals, job listings, and real estate have been outsourced and are now largely handled by third parties. By far, Bartz's biggest move has been handing over its search

Exhibit 1 **Yahoo! Income Statement** (in thousands of U.S. dollars)

	Period Ending		
	Dec. 31, 2010	Dec. 31, 2009	Dec. 31, 2008
Total Revenue	6,324,651	6,460,315	7,208,502
Cost of Revenue	2,627,545	2,871,746	3,023,362
Gross Profit	3,697,106	3,588,569	4,185,140
Operating Expenses:			
Research Development	1,082,176	1,210,168	1,221,787
Selling General and Administrative	1,752,823	1,825,702	2,268,449
Nonrecurring	57,957	126,901	594,391
Others	31,626	39,106	87,550
Total Operating Expenses	2,924,582	3,201,877	4,172,177
Operating Income or Loss	772,524	386,692	12,963
Income from Continuing Operations:			
Total Other Income/Expenses Net	297,869	187,528	82,838
Earnings before Interest and Taxes	1,070,393	574,220	95,801
Income before Tax	1,070,393	574,220	95,801
Income Tax Expense	221,523	219,321	262,717
Minority Interest	(12,965)	(7,297)	(5,765)
Net Income from Continuing Operations	1,231,663	597,992	424,298
Net Income	**1,231,663**	**597,992**	**424,298**

Source: Yahoo!.

Exhibit 2 Yahoo! **Balance Sheet** (in thousands of U.S. dollars)

	Period Ending		
	Dec. 31, 2010	Dec. 31, 2009	Dec. 31, 2008
Assets			
Current Assets:			
Cash and Cash Equivalents	1,526,427	1,275,430	2,292,296
Short-Term Investments	1,357,661	2,015,655	1,159,691
Net Receivables	1,028,900	1,003,362	1,203,581
Other Current Assets	432,560	300,325	89,930
Total Current Assets	**4,345,548**	**4,594,772**	**4,745,498**
Long-Term Investments	4,756,483	4,723,207	3,372,488
Property Plant and Equipment	1,653,422	1,426,862	1,536,181
Goodwill	3,681,645	3,640,373	3,440,889
Intangible Assets	255,870	355,883	485,860
Other Assets	235,136	194,933	72,111
Deferred Long-Term Asset Charges	—	—	36,821
Total Assets	**14,928,104**	**14,936,030**	**13,689,848**
Liabilities			
Current Liabilities:			
Accounts Payable	1,371,216	1,306,584	1,073,469
Other Current Liabilities	254,656	411,144	631,546
Total Current Liabilities	**1,625,872**	**1,717,728**	**1,705,015**
Long-Term Debt	142,799	83,021	77,062
Other Liabilities	—	—	352,275
Deferred Long-Term Liability Charges	563,023	616,645	286,535
Minority Interest	38,281	25,316	18,019
Total Liabilities	**2,369,975**	**2,442,710**	**2,438,906**
Stockholders' Equity			
Common Stock	1,306	1,410	1,595
Retained Earnings	1,942,656	1,599,638	4,848,162
Treasury Stock	—	(117,331)	(5,267,484)
Capital Surplus	10,109,913	10,640,367	11,548,393
Other Stockholder Equity	504,254	369,236	120,276
Total Stockholder Equity	**12,558,129**	**12,493,320**	**11,250,942**
Net Tangible Assets	**8,620,614**	**8,497,064**	**7,324,193**

Source: Yahoo!.

engine and related advertising to Microsoft, its one-time search nemesis. The agreement allows Yahoo to forgo the cost of maintaining search infrastructure while still collecting most of the revenue from the partnership. The firm can now focus on display advertising—banners and other graphical ads—where it remains the industry leader.

In spite of all of these moves, Yahoo's financial results for the third quarter of 2010 showed only slight gains. Despite having an enormous audience of 630 million unique monthly visitors, making it the most visited Web site in the world, users are spending less time on the site. This stands in stark contrast to the traffic that is being generated by Google and Facebook, both of which continue to make big gains. "They're treading water right now," said Jordan Rohan, an analyst with Stifel, Nicolaus & Company.[2]

Bartz has acknowledged that much work needs to be done to restore Yahoo to its former glory, but she maintains that firm is showing signs of improvement or at least stability. "First you walk, then you run, then you fly," she said in a conference call with securities analysts.[3] Larry L. Cornett, a former Yahoo search executive, said that he was encouraged by the early stages of Yahoo's turnaround but that Bartz needed to clearly lay out what the company stands for. "Maybe there's some conversations internally, but from the outside, there isn't a crystal-clear definition of what Yahoo means," he explained.[4]

Dealing with a Slump

After a period of strong growth in the late 1990s, Yahoo saw a steep fall in revenues and profits as advertisers cut back on their spending after the dot-com bust. Under Tim Koogle, Yahoo had developed as a web portal that relied heavily on advertising revenues for profits. He had been confident that advertisers would continue to pay in order to reach the younger and technologically savvy surfers that would use his portal. As advertising revenues dropped off sharply, leading to a steep decline in the firm's stock price, Koogle was replaced in April 2001 by Terry Semel, an experienced Hollywood media executive who had once controlled Warner Brothers.

Semel realized that he had to entice traditional advertisers back to his site. He made an all-out push to court advertising agencies that Yahoo had pushed away with its arrogance during the years before the bust. He also tried to attract back the business of big advertisers such as General Motors, Procter & Gamble, and Coca-Cola by using technology that allowed the website to move beyond static banner advertising, offering eye-catching animation, videos, and other rich-media formats. As advertisers gradually decided to spend again on online advertising after the slump, Yahoo managed to draw many of them back to its site, leading to a dramatic increase in its advertising revenues.

But Semel did not want Yahoo to rely primarily on advertising for its revenues. He began to push for other sources of revenue by making acquisitions that would allow his site to offer more premium services that consumers would be willing to pay for. One of the first of these was the buyout of HotJobs.com in 2002, which moved the firm into the online job-hunting business. Semel followed up with the acquisition of online music service Musicmatch Inc., hoping to bring more subscribers into the Yahoo fold. Over the next few years, the firm continued to add to its growing range of services by acquiring firms such as Flickr, a photo-sharing site, and Del.icio.us, a bookmark-sharing site.

By making such smart deals, Semel was able to build Yahoo into a site that could offer surfers many different services, with several of them requiring the customer to pay a small fee. The idea has been to coax Web surfers to spend hard cash on everything from digital music and online games to job listings and premium e-mail accounts with loads of extra storage. Semel hoped that the contribution from such paid services would continue to rise over the next few years, allowing the firm to rely less heavily on advertising. In his own words, "We planted a lot of seeds . . . and some are beginning to grow."[5]

Semel's biggest moves, however, were tied to his efforts to strengthen Yahoo's position in the search area. Yahoo had been using Google to provide these services, but with Google's growing strengths in this area, Semel decided further develop Yahoo's own search engine. In 2002 he purchased Inktomi, a strong contender in search engines with whom Yahoo had also worked in the past (see Exhibit 3). A year later, Yahoo also bought Overture Services, a company that specialized in identifying and ranking the popularity of websites and in helping advertisers find the best sites to advertise on. Finally, Semel spent millions of dollars on further improving its search advertising system in order to stem the continual loss of search-related advertising revenues to Google (see Exhibit 4).

Creating a Theme Park

With the expansion of services, Semel envisioned building Yahoo into a digital Disneyland, a souped-up theme park for the Internet Age. The idea was that web surfers logging on to Yahoo's site, like customers squeezing through the turnstiles in Anaheim, should find themselves in a self-contained world full of irresistible offerings. Instead of Yahoo being an impartial tour guide to the Web, it should be able to entice surfers to stay inside its walls as long as possible. In order to make such a concept work, Semel believed that the firm should establish strong links between its various sites that would allow its consumers to move effortlessly from one of them to another.

This vision for Yahoo represented a drastic change from the model that had been developed by its original founders. The firm had let managers push for their own pet projects, resulting in an assortment of offerings that operated relatively independently. No one had thought about developing the portal as a whole, much less how the various bits and pieces could work together. Under these conditions, executives fought hard to obtain sufficient support

Exhibit 3 Yahoo!'s Significant Milestones

1994	David Filo and Jerry Yang start the company as "Jerry's guide to the World Wide Web," later renaming it Yahoo!.
1996	Yahoo! goes public, raising $338 million. Filo and Yang ask Tim Koogle, an experienced ex-Motorola executive with an engineering background, to be the new CEO.
1999	Yahoo! begins to make major acquisitions, including GeoCities, the third most visited website at the time.
2001	Koogle departs because of a sharp drop in the firm's stock price as a result of declining advertising revenue. Yang asks Terry Semel to take over the firm.
2001	Yahoo! acquires more firms, such as HotJobs, a leading Internet job-hunting and placement company.
2002	Yahoo! buys Inktomi, a search-engine leader.
2003	Yahoo! buys Overture Services, a company that specializes in web-search advertising.
2005	Yahoo! acquires Flickr, a photo-sharing site and announces that it will link several sites together to create a social-networking group.
2007	Semel is pushed out because of a decline in performance. Yang takes over as CEO of the firm.
2009	Yang steps down and Carol Bartz is appointed as the new CEO. Bartz concludes a major deal with Microsoft to cede control of Yahoo!'s search business.

Source: Yahoo!.

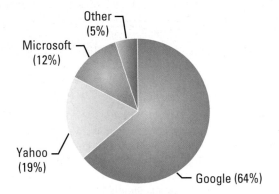

Exhibit 4 Share of U.S. Internet Searches: Monthly Estimates, January–July 2010

Source: comScore Networks.

for the particular services that each of them had developed. "Managers would beg, borrow, and steal from the network to help their own properties," said Greg Coleman, Yahoo's executive vice president for media and sales.[6]

Semel had been pushing to stitch it all together. He demanded that Yahoo's myriad of offerings, from e-mail accounts to stock quotes to job listings, interact with each other. Semel called this concept "network optimization" and regarded this as a key goal for his firm. In order to ensure that the various efforts that were being made by managers were tied to each other more closely, he moved swiftly to replace its freewheeling culture with a more deliberate sense of order.

Semel began to pursue this stronger integration by chopping the 44 business units that he had inherited down to only 5. He also made it clear that every initiative proposed by any of the units was expected not only to make money but also to feed Yahoo's other businesses. Consequently, Semel pushed Yahoo away from its earlier emphasis on long brainstorming sessions and initiatives driven by hunches. Instead, he demanded that managers make formal presentations of their new ideas in weekly meetings of a group called the Product Council, with nine managers from all corners of the company. The responsibility of the group was to make sure all new projects bring benefits to Yahoo's existing businesses.

In spite of Semel's efforts to tightly control the growth of Yahoo into new areas, the push to develop a digital theme park has led some analysts to question whether the firm has spread itself too thin. Even some people inside Yahoo began to question its goal of providing a broad range of services that can attract an audience that can be sold to advertisers. In a scathing internal memo written in the fall of 2006, Brad Garlinghouse, a senior Yahoo vice president, compared Yahoo's strategy to indiscriminately spreading peanut butter across the

Internet. "We lack a focused, cohesive vision for our company," he stated in the memo. "We want to do everything and be everything—to everyone. We've known this for years, talked about it incessantly, but done nothing to fundamentally address it."[7]

Searching for a Direction

Garlinghouse's memo was intended to push Yahoo into establishing a clearer vision for the firm to pursue. He had believed that a stronger focus on specific goals would result in more specific responsibilities for individuals and units and speedier decision making for the firm. He had realized that Yahoo's attempts to offer a wide variety of services had led to a proliferation of new executive hires, which eventually contributed to a growth of conflict between various business units. This had made it difficult to move swiftly to make critical decisions, such as making key partnerships and acquisitions to keep up with the changing competitive landscape. The once high-flying Internet pioneer was losing online advertising revenues to search engines such as Google and social networking sites such as Facebook (see Exhibit 5).

Shareholder dissatisfaction with Yahoo's financial performance finally led to the resignation of Semel in July 2007. The firm turned to Jerry Yang, one of its cofounders, who had been serving as "Chief Yahoo!" to improve earnings and profits. When he took over, Yang promised that he would move quickly to come up with a new sweeping plan for Yahoo after a 100-day review of every aspect of its operations. As part of this plan, Yang announced a three-pronged new direction for Yahoo. He wanted his site to be the premier starting point for consumers on the web, to be a top choice for marketers seeking to place ads on sites across the Web, and to open Yahoo's technology infrastructure to third-party programmers and publishers. Yang was clearly aware that these goals would require time and investments, but he was upbeat about his firm's progress. "We are seeing early signs of success as a result of this clear new focus," he announced soon after he took charge.[8]

Although these changes were welcomed, analysts were not sure that Yang could move quickly enough before competitors gain more ground and before investors lost patience. "They have six to nine months to prove their initiatives are working," said Mark Mahaney of Citigroup

Smith Barney.[9] These concerns were echoed by Jeffrey Lindsay, an analyst with Sanford C. Bernstein. "I have a lot of respect for Jerry Yang," he commented six months after Yang had taken charge. "But so far his changes have been slow and incremental instead of quick and bold. To move at such a slow pace in the Internet market is risky."[10]

It was clear that the many problems that Yahoo was facing would pose a considerable challenge for Yang. In particular, there were questions about the firm's decision to invest in its own search engine rather than forging a partnership with Google. Similarly, the firm failed to clinch some crucial deals, including one with Facebook, one of the hottest social networking websites. Rob Sanderson, an analyst at American Technology Research, warned that the firm was at a critical juncture. "They're relevant, and hold their audience pretty well, but the investor and media perception is that Yahoo is another AOL—a once-great company in decline," he explained.[11]

One of the biggest challenges faced by Yang was the offer made by Microsoft in early 2008 to buy Yahoo for $33 a share, or approximately $47.5 billion. Yang refused to sell his company for less than $37 a share, although the shares had been trading for around $20. Shareholders were upset, because they stood to lose about $20 billion by the rejection of Microsoft's offer. "I don't think anything Yahoo puts out there is going to be comparable with what Microsoft was offering" said Darren Chervitz, comanager of the Jacob Internet Fund, which owned about 150,000 shares of Yahoo.[12]

Scrambling for a Focus

Less than a year and a half after he had assumed control, Yang decided to give up his role as CEO and revert to being the Chief Yahoo!, the strategy position that he had held before. After an extensive search, the board appointed Carol Bartz as the new head of the firm. Bartz had been in charge of Autodesk, a computer-aided software design firm for 14 years before stepping down recently. She was expected to develop a stronger focus for a firm that was perceived to have been drifting, especially during Yang's turbulent leadership. Analysts were generally positive about her appointment, although many suggested that she lacked online media experience.

Bartz was expected to move quickly to reassure investors who were angry with Yahoo's board for refusing to accept Microsoft's bid for the firm. Shortly after she took over, Bartz moved to overhaul the company's top executive ranks, consolidating several positions and creating others in an attempt to make the company more efficient. She combined the firm's technology and product groups into one unit and created a customer advocacy group to better incorporate customer feedback. The changes were intended to speed up decision making within the company by making it "a lot faster on its feet," Bartz wrote in a Yahoo public blog. But Ross Sandler, an analyst with RBC Capital Markets, said the restructuring was more promising because it clarified responsibilities. "There has been

---

Exhibit 5   Number of U.S. visitors: Monthly Estimates, January–July 2010

Google	149 million
Yahoo!	136 million
Facebook	126 million
Microsoft	58 million

Source: comScore Networks.

confusion at the top for so long," he said. "This should solve that problem."[13]

By July, Bartz had reached an agreement to hand over its search operations to Microsoft, which had invested heavily in relaunching its search engine and renamed it Bing. The terms of the 10-year agreement gave Microsoft access to search technologies that Yahoo had helped to pioneer and develop. Yahoo would transfer many of its talented engineers to Microsoft and lay off 400 employees who ran the search operations. In return, Yahoo would receive 88 percent of the search-related ad revenue for the first five years of the deal, much higher than is standard in the industry.

Reactions to the deal have been mixed. Some Yahoo shareholders have expressed concerns that the company will lose its valuable search experience, which would be difficult to recover from. "It feels kind of like a stab in the chest," said Chervitz. "It certainly feels like Yahoo is giving away their strong and hard-fought share of the search market for really a modest price. My sense is that Yahoo will regret making this move."[14]

But Bartz insists that the firm could no longer continue to match the level of investment Google and Microsoft have been making in searching, one of the web's most lucrative and technically complex businesses. "This deal allows Yahoo to invest in what we should be investing in for the future—audience properties, display advertising, and the mobile Internet experience," Bartz said in an interview soon after the deal had been finalized. "Our vision is to be at the center of people's lives online."[15]

Waiting for a Turnaround?

Even though progress has been slow, Bartz has managed to refocus Yahoo on areas such as news, sports, and finance, where it has considerable strengths. While she has moved the firm away from other activities she considered to be peripheral, Bartz has invested heavily in content over the last year, hiring dozens of editorial employees and buying Associated Content, a freelance news site, to enhance local news coverage. She also claims to have made progress with revamping the technology behind the web portal that should make it possible to introduce new services more quickly in the future. At the same time, Bartz has managed to achieve an improvement in Yahoo's profit margins due to her aggressive moves to cut costs wherever possible.

In spite of these achievements, some investors are losing patience and have begun to demand that Yahoo's board replace Bartz although her contract does not run out until 2012. Besides the slow growth in revenues and profits, they point to the continual turnover among executives at the firm. Three top managers have stepped down over the past couple of months, creating a perception of continuing turmoil and uncertainty. Even with this turnover, Blake Irving, recently hired as the firm's product chief, claimed that employees are not feeling demoralized or

rudderless. "What ends up getting picked up on more are the departures than the new people coming in," he said.[16]

The news that some private equity firms are considering a bid to buy Yahoo has created more pressures for Bartz. These efforts are preliminary, however, as the equity firms are speaking with AOL and the News Corporation about teaming up on a deal. Salim Ismail, a former Yahoo executive who is now executive director of Singularity University, said that Yahoo should convert from a publicly traded company to a private one to escape the pressure of quarterly earnings reports. According to Ismail, this will free up the firm to take the steps needed to abolish the complex organizational structure that is slowing decision making and reducing innovation. "They're putting on a Band-Aid when what they really need is major surgery."[17]

Though concerns continue to surface about the future of Yahoo, many people still think that the firm just needs some time to find a new direction. Peter Thiel, a prominent Silicon Valley investor, maintains that Yahoo should not make any drastic moves. In particular, he believes that more big acquisitions would be misguided, especially if they prevent the firm from gradually focusing on what it does best. Paul Gunning, chief of a digital advertising agency, also claims that, despite some problems that need to be resolved, Yahoo has remained a great place for marketers to reach consumers. "We're bullish on them," he said.[18]

Endnotes

1. Kopytoff, V. G. 2010. Even under new captain, Yahoo seems adrift. *New York Times,* October 18: B4.
2. Kopytoff, V. G. 2010. Yahoo profit rises, but revenue is flat. *New York Times,* October 20: B2.
3. Ibid.
4. Kopytoff. 2010. Even under new captain.
5. Elgin, B. & Grover, R. 2003. Yahoo!: Act two. *BusinessWeek,* June 2: 72.
6. Ibid.: 74.
7. Ackerman, E. 2007. Can 'Chief Yahoo' Yang make it work this time as CEO? Knight Ridder Tribune Business News. June 24: 1.
8. Helft, M. 2008. Yahoo to cut 1,000 jobs, and warns on growth. *New York Times,* January 30: C3.
9. Swartz, J. 2008. Yahoo encounters a fork in road toward its future. *USA Today,* January 28: 2B.
10. Ibid.
11. Ibid.
12. Helft, M. 2008. Yahoo celebrates (for now). *New York Times,* May 5: C1.
13. Vascellaro, J. E. 2009. Bartz remakes Yahoo's top ranks. *Wall Street Journal,* February 27: B3.
14. Lohr, S. 2009. Linked up. Now what? *New York Times,* July 30: B7.
15. Ibid.
16. Kopytoff. 2010. Even under new captain.
17. Ibid.
18. Ibid.

Case 13 QVC*

On January 12, 2011, QVC announced that it had once again secured a top 10 spot in the annual NRF Foundation/ American Express Customers' Choice survey. The survey asked more than 9,000 shoppers to identify the leading retailers who provide the best customer service. "The QVC team is thrilled to be recognized as one of the 10 best customer service retailers in the country for the third year in a row," said Dan McDermott, QVC's senior vice president of customer services.[1] The NRF ranking represents only one of a number of customer service honors QVC received in recent weeks.

Since it was launched in 1986, QVC has rapidly grown to become the largest television shopping network. Although it entered the market a couple of years after rival Home Shopping Network, the channel has managed to build a leading position. By 2010, its reach had extended to over 98 million households. It regularly ships over 175 million packages annually to customers around the world, resulting in almost $7.8 million in sales (see Exhibits 1 and 2). It sells to customers who watch its shows across the United States, UK, Germany, Japan, and, since 2010, also in Italy (see Exhibit 3).

The success of QVC is largely driven by its popular television home-shopping shows that feature a wide variety of eye-catching products, many of which are unique to the channel. It organizes product searches in cities all over the United States in order to continuously find new offerings that can be pitched at customers. During these events, the firm has to screen hundreds of products to select those that it will offer. In one of its recent searches, QVC had to evaluate the appeal of products such as nail clippers that catch clippings, bicycle seats built for bigger bottoms, and novelty items shaped like coffins.

Thousands of entrepreneurs have used QVC's product searches over the years to try and sell their products on the popular home-shopping channel. A chance to display their offerings to QVC's national TV audience can transform a one-person operation into a multibillion-dollar business. "The vendors who are our success stories for this past decade have done over $1 billion in sales on QVC over the past ten years," said Marilyn Montross, the channel's director of vendor relations.[2]

But QVC is also trying to entice new customers by battling a perception that direct-response TV retailers sell just hokey, flimsy, or kitschy goods. Its jewelry selection features prestigious brands such as Tacori, which is worn by TV stars. It offers clothing from couture designers such as Marc Bouwer, who has made clothing for Angelina Jolie and Halle Berry. And it has recently added exclusive products from reality stars such as Kim Kardashian and Rachel Zoe. Such vendors have introduced thousands to QVC, often through social media like Facebook and Twitter. "Rachel Zoe brings so many new customers it's staggering," said CEO Michael George.[3]

Pursuing a Leading Position

QVC was founded by Joseph Segel in June 1986 and began broadcasting by November of the same year. In early 1986, Segel had tuned in to the Home Shopping Network, which had been launched two years earlier. He had not been particularly impressed with the crude programming and the down-market products of the firm. But Segel was convinced that another televised shopping network would have the potential to attract a large enough client base. He also felt that such an enterprise should be able to produce significant profits, because the operating expenses for a shopping network could be kept relatively low.

Over the next few months, Segel raised $30 million in start-up capital, hired several seasoned television executives, and launched his own shopping network. Operating out of headquarters that were located in West Chester, Pennsylvania, QVC offered 24-hour-a-day, seven-day-a-week television home shopping to consumers at home. By the end of its first year of operation, QVC had managed to extend its reach to 13 million homes by satellite and cable systems. 700,000 viewers had already become customers, resulting in the shipping of 3 million orders. Its sales had already topped $100 million, and the firm was actually able to show a small profit.

Exhibit 1   QVC Annual Sales

Year	Sales
2010	7.8 billion
2009	7.4 billion
2008	7.3 billion
2007	7.4 billion
2006	7.1 billion
2004	5.7 billion
2001	3.8 billion
1998	2.4 billion
1995	1.6 billion
1992	0.9 billion
1989	0.2 billion

Source: QVC; Liberty Media.

* This case was developed by Professor Jamal Shamsie, Michigan State University, with the assistance of Professor Alan B. Eisner, Pace University. Material has been drawn from published sources to be used for class discussion. Copyright © 2011 Jamal Shamsie and Alan B. Eisner.

Exhibit 2 QVC Income Statement (in millions of U.S. dollars)

| | Years Ended December 31 | | | |
	2010	2009	2008	2007
Net Revenue	$7,807	$7,352	$7,303	$7,397
Cost of Sales	(5,006)	(4,748)	(4,719)	(4,682)
Gross Profit	2,801	2,604	2,584	2,715
Operating Expenses*	(715)	(684)	(703)	(616)
S, G & A Expenses	(415)	(364)	(379)	(447)
Operating Cash Flow	1,671	1,556	1,502	1,652
Stock Compensation	(18)	(16)	(15)	(22)
Depreciation & Amortization[†]	(523)	(526)	(531)	(516)
Operating Income	$1,130	$1,014	$956	$1,114

* Operating expenses consist of commissions and license fees, order processing and customer service, credit card processing fees and provision for doubtful accounts.
[†] Depreciation & amortization includes amortization of intangible assets recorded in connection with the purchase of QVC by Liberty Media.

Source: Liberty Media; QVC.

Exhibit 3 Geographical Breakdown of QVC Revenue Sources (in millions of U.S. dollars)

| | Years Ended December 31 | | | |
	2010	2009	2008	2007
United States	$5,235	$4,965	$4,911	$5,208
UK	599	578	660	707
Germany	956	942	954	870
Japan	1,015	867	778	612
Italy	2	—	—	—

Source: Liberty Media; QVC.

Segel attributed the instant success of his company to the potential offered by television shopping. "Television's combination of sight, sound and motion is the best way to sell a product. It is more effective than presenting a product in print or just putting the product on a store shelf," he stated. "The cost-efficiency comes from the cable distribution system. It is far more economical than direct mail, print advertising, or traditional retail store distribution."[4]

In the fall of 1988, Segel acquired the manufacturing facilities, proprietary technology, and trademark rights of the Diamonique Corporation, which produced a wide range of simulated gemstones and jewelry that could be sold on QVC's shows. Over the next couple of years, Segel expanded QVC by acquiring its competitors, such as the Cable Value Network Shopping channel.

By 1993, QVC had overtaken Home Shopping Network to become the leading televised shopping channel in terms of sales and profits. Its reach extended to over 80 percent of all cable homes and to 3 million satellite dishes. Segel retired during the same year, passing control of the company to Barry Diller. Since then, QVC's sales have continued to grow at a substantial rate. As a result, it has consistently widened the gap between its sales and those of Home Shopping Network, which has remained its closest competitor.

Striving for Retailing Excellence

Over the years, QVC had managed to establish itself as the world's preeminent virtual shopping mall that never closes. Its televised shopping channel has become a place where customers around the world can, and do, shop at any hour at the rate of more than five customers per second. It sells a wide variety of products, using a combination of description and demonstration by live program hosts. QVC is extremely selective in choosing its hosts, screening as many as 3,000 applicants annually in order to pick three. New hosts are trained for at least six months before they are allowed to get on a show. In addition, most of the products are offered on regularly scheduled shows, each of which is focused on a particular type of product and a well-defined market. Each of these shows typically

Exhibit 4   **Sample of QVC Programming**

Time	Monday	Tuesday	Wednesday	Thursday	Friday	Saturday	Sunday
12:00 a.m.	Barbara Bixby Jewelry	Company's Coming Reed/Barton	Kathy Van Zeeland Accessories	Victor Costa Occasion	Gifts of Style	Bose Sound Innovation	Kitchen Aid
2:00 a.m.	Tignanello Handbags	Dennis Basso Boutique	T3 Hair Care	Tacori for Epiphany Jewelry	Late Night Gifts	Linea by Louis Dell'Olio	Ecclissi Watches
5:00 a.m.	Savings by Jeanne Bice	Steel by Design Jewelry	Chaz Dean Hair and Body Care	Boyds Bears and Friends	Arte d'Argento Silver	Gold Jewelry Special	Practical Kitchen Aid
9:00 a.m.	Barbara Bixby Jewelry	Slatkin & Co. Home Accessories	Mary Beth Accessories	Susan Graver Style	Denim & Company	AM Style	Great Gifts by Kitchen Aid
12:00 noon	Q Check Gifts	Q Check Gifts	Q Check Gifts	Q Check Gifts	Q Check Gifts	Judith Ripka Collection	Gifts from David's Kitchen
3:00 p.m.	Barbara Bixby Jewelry	Dennis Basso Boutique	Bags and Shoes	Great Gifts	Gifts of Style	QVC Beauty Exclusives	Gifts from David's Kitchen
6:00 p.m.	NFL Shop	Enjoyable Entertaining Reed/Barton	Kathy Van Zeeland Accessories	Philosophy Beauty	Great Gifts	Gifts for Mom	From Dell
8:00 p.m.	PM Style	Kitchen Gifts Reed/Barton	NARS Cosmetics	Northern Nights Bedding	What's in my beauty bag?	Saturday Night Beauty	From Dell
10:00 p.m.	Tignanello Handbags	Tuesday Night Gifts Reed/Barton	Designer Couple	Tacori for Epiphany Jewelry	Gem Fest Special	Temptation Presentable Ovenware	Nintendo featuring Wii

Source: QVC.

lasts for one hour and is based on a theme such as *Now You're Cooking* or *Cleaning Solutions* (see Exhibit 4).

QVC frequently entices celebrities, such as clothing designers or book authors, to appear live on special program segments in order to sell their own products. In order to prepare them to succeed, celebrities are given training on how to best pitch their offerings. On some occasions, customers are able to call in and have on-air conversations with program hosts and visiting celebrities. Celebrities are therefore often schooled in QVC's "backyard-fence" style, which means conversing with viewers the way they would chat with a friendly neighbor. "They're just so down-home, so it's like they're right in your living room demonstrating," said a long-time QVC customer.[5]

In spite of the folksy presentation, the sales are minutely managed. Behind the scenes, a producer scans nine television and computer screens to track sales of each featured item. "We track new orders per minute in increments of six seconds; we can look backward in time and see what it was that drove that spike," said Doug Rose, who oversees programming and marketing.[6] Hosts and guests are prompted to make adjustments in their pitch that might increase sales. A beauty designer was recently asked to rub an eyeliner on her hand, which immediately led to a surge of new orders.

QVC's themed programs are telecast live 24 hours a day, seven days a week to millions of households worldwide. The shopping channel transmits its programming from its central production facilities in Pennsylvania through uplinks to a satellite. The representatives who staff QVC's four call centers, which handled more than 180 million calls last year, are well trained to take orders.

Of all the orders placed with QVC, more than 90 percent are shipped within 48 hours from one of their distribution centers. The distribution centers have a combined floor space of 4.6 million square feet, which is equivalent to the size of 103 football fields. Finally, everyone at QVC works hard to make sure that every item works as it should before it is shipped and that its packaging will protect it during the shipping process. "Nothing ships unless it is quality-inspected first," said Paul Day, the logistics manager for QVC. "Since our product is going business-to-consumer, there's no way to fix or change a product-related problem."[7]

Searching for Profitable Products

More than 100 experienced, informed buyers comb the world on a regular basis to search for new products to launch on QVC. The shopping channel concentrates on unique products that can be demonstrated on live television. Furthermore, the price of these products must be high enough for viewers to justify the additional shipping and handling charge. Over the course of a typical year, QVC carries more than 60,000 products. As many as 2,000 items are typically offered in any given week, of which about 15 percent are new products for the network. QVC's suppliers range from some of the world's biggest companies to small entrepreneurial enterprises.

All new products must, however, pass stringent tests that are carried out by QVC's in-house Quality Assurance Lab. In many cases, this inspection process is carried out manually by the firm's employees. Only 15 percent of the products pass the firm's rigorous quality inspection on first try, and as many as a third are never offered to the public because they fail altogether. In addition, Jeffrey Rayport, author of a book on customer service, states that "QVC staff look for a product that is complex enough—or interesting enough—that the host can talk about it on air."[8]

About a third of QVC's sales come from broadly available national brands. The firm has been able to build trust among its customers in large part through offering these well-known brands. QVC also relies upon promotional campaigns with a variety of existing firms for another third of its sales. It has made deals with firms ranging from Dell, Target, and Bath & Body Works for special limited-time promotional offerings. But QVC has been most successful with products that are exclusively sold on QVC or not readily available through other distribution channels. Although such products account for another third of its sales, the firm has been able to earn higher margins with these proprietary products, many of which come from firms that are either start-ups or new entrants into the U.S. market.

Most vendors are attracted to QVC because they reap higher profits selling through their channel than they would make by selling through physical stores. Stores typically require vendors to help to train or pay the sales force and participate in periodic sales where prices are discounted. QVC rarely sells products at discount prices. Maureen Kelly, founder of Tarte Cosmetics, said she typically makes more from an eight-minute segment on QVC than she used to make in a month at a high-end department store.

Apart from searching for exclusive products, QVC has been also been trying to move away from some product categories, such as home appliances and electronic gadgets, which offer lower margins. It has been gradually expanding into many new product categories that have higher margins, such as cosmetics, apparel, food, and toys. Several of these new categories have also displayed the strongest rates of growth in sales for the shopping channel over the past couple of years.

Expanding upon the Customer Base

Since its start-up, QVC's shopping channel has managed to gradually penetrate almost all of the cable television and broadcast satellite homes in the United States. But only about 10 percent of the households that it reaches have actually bought anything from the network. However, QVC has developed a large customer base, many of whom make as many as 10 purchases in a year. QVC devotees readily call in to the live segments to offer product testimonials, are up on the personal lives of their favorite program hosts, and generally view the channel as entertaining. "As weird as it may sound, for people who love the network, it's good company," said Rayport.[9]

QVC is also hoping to attract new customers on the basis of the reasonably strong reputation that surveys indicate that it has established among a large majority of its current buyers. By its initials alone, QVC had promised that it would deliver Quality, Value, and Convenience to its viewers. More than three-quarters of the shopping channel's customers have given it a score of 7 out of 7 for trustworthiness. This has led most of its customers to recommend it to their friends.

QVC has also benefited from the growing percentage of women entering the workforce, resulting in a significant increase in dual-income families. Although the firm's current customer base does span several socioeconomic groups, it is led by young professional families who have above average disposable income. They also enjoy various forms of "thrill-seeking" activities and rank shopping relatively higher as a leisure activity when compared to the typical consumer.

The firm is also trying to increase sales by making it easier for customers to buy its products by adding features such as an interactive service that would allow them to purchase whatever QVC is offering on its shopping channel with a single click of a remote. QVC also provides a credit program to allow customers to pay for goods over a period of several months. Everything it sells is also backed by a 30-day unconditional money-back guarantee. Furthermore, QVC does not impose any hidden charges, such as a "restocking fee," for any returned merchandise. These policies help the home shopping channel to attract customers for products that they can view but are not able to either touch or feel.

Regular technological developments may, in fact, allow QVC to continue to offer much-higher-margin products to both existing and new markets. Rose claims that interactivity in all aspects of the firm's business, including its television shopping channel, will only become more pronounced in the future, making it easier for customers to act on what they see. QVC believes that it still has a lot of room to grow, since almost 90 percent of its audience has not purchased anything from the network.

Positioning for Future Growth

In 1995 QVC launched its own retail website to complement its television home-shopping channel. The website has provided the firm access to more than 100 million households in the United States that have Internet connections. Initially, the site offered more detailed information about QVC offerings. Since then, it has branched out to develop its own customer base by featuring many products that have not been recently shown on its television channel. Over the last few years, QVC has been fine-tuning its website by offering mobile phone, interactive-television, and iPad apps.

By 2010, QVC.com, a once-negligible part of the QVC empire, accounted for about a third of the firm's domestic revenue. CEO Michael George recently stated that 60 percent of QVC's new customers in the United States buy on the Internet or on mobile devices. "The online business is becoming such a crucial part of the business for QVC," remarked Douglas Anmuth, an analyst at Barclay's Capital.[10]

Furthermore, QVC.com is now more profitable than QVC's television operation. It needs fewer call-center workers, and while QVC must share profits with cable companies on TV orders, it does not have to pay them on online orders for products that have not been featured on the air for 24 hours. But online shoppers tend to be more interested in the best price than in staying loyal to brands like QVC.

For many of its loyal consumers, however, nothing will ever replace the shopping on television. The website does not offer the hybrid of talk show and sales pitch that attracts audiences to the QVC shopping channel. Online shoppers also miss out on the interaction between hosts and shoppers and the continuous feedback about the time that they may have to order before an item is sold out. "You know, on Sundays I might find a program on Lifetime Movie Network, but whatever I'm watching, if it's not QVC, when the commercial comes on I'll flip it back to QVC," said one loyal QVC fan. "I'm just stuck on them."[11]

Endnotes

1. QVC continues to be recognized for exceptional customer service. 2011. PR Newswire, January 12.
2. Feldstein, M. J. 2005. Investors, entrepreneurs vie for QVC appearance. Knight Ridder Tribune Business News, February 11: 1.
3. Clifford, S. 2010. Can QVC translate its pitch online? *New York Times,* November 21: B7.
4. QVC annual report, 1987–1988.
5. Clifford. 2010.
6. Ibid.
7. Gilligan, E. 2004. The show must go on. *Journal of Commerce,* April 12: 1.
8. Petrecca, L. 2008. QVC shops for ideas for future sales. *USA Today,* May 5: 2B. *http://www.usatoday.com/community/tags/reporter.aspx?id=384.*
9. Ibid.
10. Clifford. 2010.
11. Ibid.

Case 14   Johnson & Johnson*

On January 26, 2011, health care conglomerate Johnson & Johnson announced that earnings had declined in the fourth quarter of the previous year and lowered its estimates for its earnings for 2010. The firm claimed that the weaker results could be attributed to the depressed economy and to a string of product recalls. Sales figures do indicate that Johnson & Johnson has clearly been hurt by 17 recalls since September 2009, covering several over-the-counter medicines, a batch of contact lenses, and some hip replacements (see Exhibits 1 and 2).

The most serious problems have surfaced at McNeil Consumer Healthcare, which has had to recall many of its products, including one for an estimated 136 million bottles of children's Tylenol, Motrin, Benadryl, and Zyrtec—the biggest children's drug recall of all time—that were potentially contaminated with dark particles.

* This case was developed by Professor Jamal Shamsie, Michigan State University, with the assistance of Professor Alan B. Eisner, Pace University. Material has been drawn from published sources to be used for class discussion. Copyright © 2011 Jamal Shamsie and Alan B. Eisner.

Johnson & Johnson has been excoriated by the Food and Drug Administration for failing to catch McNeil's quality problems. The agency slapped one of McNeil's plants with a scalding inspection report, causing the company to close down the factory until 2011.

In response to these problems, Johnson & Johnson recently announced that it intended to revamp its quality controls, creating a single framework for its consumer, pharmaceutical, and medical-device divisions. Ajit Shetty, the corporate vice president responsible for supply-chain operations, will oversee the new system, reporting directly to William C. Weldon, the firm's chief executive. The company said it also planned to appoint chief quality officers for each of its three major divisions.

The decision to create a more centralized form of quality control was a difficult one for Weldon. The firm has relied heavily on acquisitions to grow over the years, resulting in a collection of as many as 250 different operating companies that are spread over 60 countries. Johnson & Johnson has been committed to providing each of these

Exhibit 1   Income Statement (in thousands of dollars)

	Period Ending		
	Jan. 2, 2011	Jan. 3, 2010	Dec. 28, 2008
Total Revenue	61,587,000	61,897,000	63,747,000
Cost of Revenue	18,792,000	18,447,000	18,511,000
Gross Profit	42,795,000	43,450,000	45,236,000
Operating Expenses:			
Research & development	6,844,000	6,986,000	7,577,000
Selling, general, and administrative	19,424,000	19,801,000	21,490,000
Nonrecurring	—	1,073,000	181,000
Operating Income or Loss	16,527,000	15,590,000	15,988,000
Income from Continuing Operations:			
Total other income/expenses net	875,000	616,000	1,376,000
Earnings before interest and taxes	17,402,000	16,206,000	17,364,000
Interest expense	455,000	451,000	435,000
Income before tax	16,947,000	15,755,000	16,929,000
Income tax expense	3,613,000	3,489,000	3,980,000
Net Income from Continuing Operations	13,334,000	12,266,000	12,949,000
Net Income	13,334,000	12,266,000	12,949,000

Source: J&J.

Exhibit 2 Balance Sheet (in thousands of dollars)

	Period Ending		
	Jan. 2, 2011	Jan. 3, 2010	Dec. 28, 2008
Assets			
Current Assets:			
Cash and cash equivalents	19,355,000	15,810,000	10,768,000
Short-term investments	8,303,000	3,615,000	2,041,000
Net receivables	11,998,000	12,439,000	13,149,000
Inventory	5,378,000	5,180,000	5,052,000
Other current assets	2,273,000	2,497,000	3,367,000
Total Current Assets	**47,307,000**	**39,541,000**	**34,377,000**
Long-Term Investments	–	–	4,000
Property, Plant, and Equipment	14,553,000	14,759,000	14,365,000
Goodwill	15,294,000	14,862,000	13,719,000
Intangible Assets	16,716,000	16,323,000	13,976,000
Other Assets	3,942,000	3,690,000	2,630,000
Deferred Long-Term Asset Charges	5,096,000	5,507,000	5,841,000
Total Assets	**102,908,000**	**94,682,000**	**84,912,000**
Liabilities			
Current Liabilities:			
Accounts payable	15,455,000	15,413,000	17,120,000
Short/Current long-term debt	7,617,000	6,318,000	3,732,000
Total Current Liabilities	**23,072,000**	**21,731,000**	**20,852,000**
Long-Term Debt	15,243,000	14,992,000	8,120,000
Other Liabilities	6,567,000	5,947,000	11,997,000
Deferred Long-Term Liability Charges	1,447,000	1,424,000	1,432,000
Total Liabilities	**46,329,000**	**44,094,000**	**42,401,000**
Stockholders' Equity			
Common Stock	3,120,000	3,120,000	3,120,000
Retained Earnings	77,773,000	70,306,000	63,379,000
Treasury Stock	(20,783,000)	(19,780,000)	(19,033,000)
Other Stockholder Equity	(3,531,000)	(3,058,000)	(4,955,000)
Total Stockholder Equity	**56,579,000**	**50,588,000**	**42,511,000**
Net Tangible Assets	**24,569,000**	**19,403,000**	**14,816,000**

Source: J&J.

units as much autonomy as possible in order to preserve an entrepreneurial culture throughout the organization. "The company really operates more like a mutual fund than anything else," commented Pat Dorsey, director of equity research at Morningstar.[1]

In spite of the benefits that Johnson & Johnson may derive from such an arrangement, Weldon had already been thinking about taking steps to be more actively involved with its far-flung business units. He recently told investors that he has been particularly concerned about pushing for more internal growth: "We'll come at it from a variety of different ways, to accelerate top- and bottom-line growth."[2] Given the scope of the businesses that J&J manages, he believes that the best opportunities may come from increased collaboration between its different units. But even as he has been pushing for some form of stronger direction for its units, Weldon does not want to threaten the strong entrepreneurial spirit that has been the basis of much of its success. The concerns over quality control have pushed the firm to try to find a more effective method of running its businesses without stripping them of their relative autonomy.

Cultivating Entrepreneurship

Johnson & Johnson has relied heavily upon acquisitions to enter into and expand into a wide range of businesses that fall broadly under the category of health care. Over the last decade alone, the firm has spent nearly $50 billion on 70 different purchases. Since 2008, J&J has made eight acquisitions, including the $1.1 billion acquisition of Mentor Corporation, a leading supplier of products for the global aesthetic market. The acquisition allowed the firm to make a substantial move into the growing field of cosmetic drugs and devices. "It's a natural extension of where J&J would want to go," said Michael Weinstein, an analyst who specializes in the medical sector for JPMorgan Chase.[3]

As it has grown, Johnson & Johnson has developed into an astonishingly complex enterprise, made up of over 250 different businesses that have been broken down into three different divisions. The most widely known of these is the division that makes consumer products such as *Johnson & Johnson* baby care products, *Band-Aid* adhesive strips, and *Visine* eye drops. The division grew substantially after J&J acquired the consumer-health unit of Pfizer in 2006 for $16.6 billion, the biggest in its 120-year-old history. The acquisition allowed the firm to add to its lineup well-known products such as *Listerine* mouthwash and *Benadryl* allergy medicine.

But Johnson & Johnson has reaped far more sales and profits from its other two divisions. Its pharmaceuticals division sells several blockbuster drugs, such as anemia drug *Procit* and schizophrenia drug *Risperdal*. Its medical devices division is responsible for best-selling products such as *Depuy* orthopedic joint replacements and *Cyper* coronary stents. These two divisions tend to generate operating profit margins of around 30 percent, almost double those generated by the consumer business.

To a large extent, however, Johnson & Johnson's success across its three divisions and many different businesses has hinged on its unique structure and culture. Most of its far-flung business units were acquired because of the potential demonstrated by some promising new products in its pipeline. Each of these units was therefore granted near-total autonomy to develop and expand upon their best-selling products (see Exhibit 3). That independence has fostered an entrepreneurial attitude that has kept J&J intensely competitive as others around it have faltered. The relative autonomy that is accorded to the business units has

(a) Pharmaceuticals

(b) Medical Devices

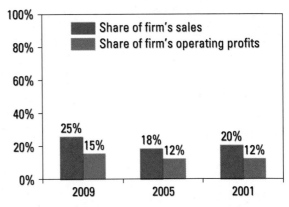

(c) Consumer Products

Exhibit 3 Segment Information Johnson & Johnson is made up of over 250 different companies. These individual companies have been assigned to three different divisions.
Source: J&J.

also provided the firm with the ability to respond swiftly to emerging opportunities.

Johnson & Johnson has been quite proud of the considerable freedom that it has given to its different

Exhibit 4   Key Brands

Pharmaceuticals

RISPERDAL for schizophrenia

PROCRIT for anemia

REMICADE for rheumatoid arthritis

TOPAMIX for epilepsy

DURAGESIC for chronic pain

DOXIL for ovarian cancer

HALDOL for psychosis

NATRECOR for heart failure

ELMIRON for bladder pain

Medical Devices

DEPUY orthopedic joint reconstruction products

CORDIS CYPHER stents

ETHICON surgery products

LIFESCAN diabetic testing products

VERIDEX diagnostic devices

ANIMAS insulin pumps

ACUVUE contact lenses

Consumer Products

BAND AID bandages

JOHNSON & JOHNSON baby care products

NEUTROGENA skin and hair care products

LISTERINE oral health care

TYLENOL pain killers

ROLAIDS antacids

BENADRYL allergy medications

BENGAY pain relief ointments

TUCK'S hemorrhoidal ointments

VISINE eye drops

ROGAINE hair regrowth treatments

STAYFREE women's health products

SPLENDA sweeteners

Source: J&J.

decentralization makes for relatively high overhead costs, none of the executives that have run J&J, Weldon included, has ever thought that this was too high a price to pay. "J&J is a huge company, but you didn't feel like you were in a big company," recalled a scientist who used to work there.[4]

Restructuring for Synergies

In spite of the benefits that Johnson & Johnson has derived from giving its various enterprises considerable autonomy, there have been growing concerns that they can no longer be allowed to operate in near isolation. Weldon has begun to realize that J&J is in a strong position to exploit new opportunities by drawing on the diverse skills of its various business units across the three divisions. He is well aware that his firm can benefit from the combination of its knowledge in drugs, devices, and diagnostics, because few companies can match its reach and strength in these basic areas.

Indeed, Johnson & Johnson has top-notch products in each of the areas in which it operates (see Exhibit 4). It has been spending heavily on research and development for many years, taking its position among the world's top spenders (see Exhibit 5). It currently spends about 12 percent of its sales, or almost $7 billion, on about 9,000 scientists working in research laboratories around the world. This allows each of the three divisions to continually introduce promising new products. Its pharmaceutical division, for example, is currently working on a drug to prevent strokes and one to treat prostrate cancer.

Weldon believes, however, that Johnson & Johnson can profit from this convergence by finding ways to make its fiercely independent businesses to work together. In his own words, "There is a convergence that will allow us to do things we haven't done before."[5] Through pushing the various far-flung units of the firm to pool their resources, Weldon believes that the firm could become one of the few that may actually be able to attain that often-promised, rarely delivered idea of synergy.

Even as Weldon has supported the efforts underway at each of its divisions, he has also pushed for all of its units

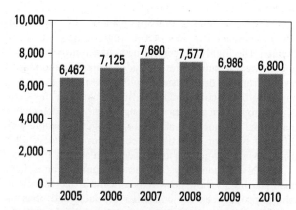

Exhibit 5   Research Expenditures (in millions of dollars)

Source: J&J.

business units to develop and execute their own strategies. Besides developing their strategies, these units have also been allowed to work with their own resources. Many of the businesses even have their own finance and human resources departments. While this degree of to work with each other to address different health problems. He has appointed one of J&J's rising stars, Nicholas Valeriani, to head a new Office of Strategy and Growth that will attempt to get business units to work together on promising new opportunities. "It's a recognition that there's a way to treat disease that's not in silos," Weldon stated, referring to J&J's largely independent businesses.[6]

Such a push for communication and coordination would allow Johnson & Johnson to develop the synergy that Weldon was seeking. But any effort to get the different business units to collaborate must not quash the entrepreneurial spirit that has spearheaded most of the growth of the firm to date. Jerry Caccott, managing director of consulting firm Strategic Decisions Group, emphasized that cultivating those alliances "would be challenging in any organization, but particularly in an organization that has been so successful because of its decentralized culture."[7]

Benefiting from Collaboration

Weldon, like every other leader in the company's history, has worked his way up through the ranks. His long tenure within the firm has turned him into a true believer in the Johnson & Johnson system. He certainly does not want to undermine the entrepreneurial spirit that has resulted from the autonomy that has been given to each of the businesses. Consequently, even though Weldon may talk incessantly about synergy and convergence, he has been cautious in the actual steps he has taken to push J&J's units to collaborate with each other.

For the most part, Weldon has confined himself to taking steps to foster better communication and more frequent collaboration among Johnson & Johnson's disparate operations. "They are the experts who know the marketplace, know the hospitals," he once said of the people who work in the firm's various business units.[8] Besides the appointment of Valeriani, he has worked with James T. Lenehan, vice chairman and president of J&J, to set up groups that draw people from across the firm to focus their efforts on specific diseases. Each of the groups has been reporting every six months on potential strategies and projects.

Perhaps the most promising result of this new collaborative approach has been J&J's drug-coated stent, called *Cypher.* The highly successful new addition to the firm's lineup was a result of the efforts of teams that combined people from the drug business with others from the device business. They collaborated on manufacturing the stent, which props open arteries after angioplasty. Weldon claims that if J&J had not been able to bring together people with different types of expertise, it could not have developed the stent without getting assistance from outside the firm.

Even the company's fabled consumer brands have been starting to show growth as a result of increased collaboration between the consumer products and pharmaceutical divisions. Its new liquid *Band-Aid* is based on a material used in a wound-closing product sold by one of J&J's hospital-supply businesses. And J&J has used its prescription antifungal treatment, *Nizoral,* to develop a dandruff shampoo. In fact, products that have developed in large part out of such a form of cross-fertilization have allowed the firm's consumer business to experience considerable internal growth.

Some of the projects that Johnson & Johnson is currently working on could produce even more significant results. Researchers working on genomic studies in the firm's labs were building a massive database using gene patterns that correlate to a certain disease or to someone's likely response to a particular drug. Weldon encouraged them to share this data with the various business units. As a result, the diagnostics team has been working on a test that the researchers in the pharmaceutical division could use to predict which patients would benefit from an experimental cancer therapy.

Dealing with Setbacks

Even as Johnson & Johnson has been trying to get more involved with the efforts of its business units, it has run into problems with quality control with several over-the-counter drugs that are made by McNeil Consumer Healthcare. Since 2008, FDA inspectors have found significant violations of manufacturing standards at two McNeil plants, leading to the temporary closure of one of these. These problems have forced the firm to make several recalls of some of its best-selling products. Weldon admitted that problems had surfaced, but he insisted that these were confined to McNeil. In a recent interview he stated: "This is one of the most difficult situations I've ever had to personally deal with. It hits at the core of who J&J is. Our first responsibility is to the people who use our products. We've let them down."[9]

Quality problems have arisen before, but they were usually fixed on a regular basis. Analysts suggest that the problems at McNeil may have been exacerbated in 2006 when J&J decided to combine it with the newly acquired consumer health care unit from Pfizer. The firm believed that it could achieve $500 to $600 million in annual savings by merging the two units. After the merger, McNeil was also transferred from the heavily regulated pharmaceutical division to the marketing-driven consumer-products division, headed by Colleen Goggins. Because these consumer executives lacked pharmaceutical experience, they demanded several changes at McNeil that led to a reduced emphasis on quality control.

Weldon is well aware of the threat faced by Johnson & Johnson as a result of its problems with quality. He is especially concerned about the allegation by the FDA that the firm initially tried to hide the problems that it found with Motrin in 2009, hiring a contractor to quietly go from store to store, buying all of the packets off the shelves. McNeil's conduct surrounding the recalls has led to an inquiry by both the House Committee on Oversight and Investigations and by the FDA's office of criminal investigations.

Various changes are underway at McNeil to resolve these quality issues. Goggins was pushed out of her post as senior executive in charge of all consumer businesses. Weldon has allocated more than $100 million to upgrade McNeil's plants and equipment, appoint new manufacturing executives, and hire a third-party consulting firm to improve procedures and systems. Bonnie Jacobs, a McNeil spokeswoman, wrote in a recent e-mail, "We will invest the necessary resources and make whatever changes are needed to do so, and we will take the time to do it right."[10]

The problems at McNeil, coupled with the recalls of contact lenses and hip replacements, have led Johnson & Johnson to make changes to its corporate oversight of its supply chain and manufacturing. In August 2010 the firm appointed Shetty, a longtime executive, to oversee a new systems of companywide quality control that involves a single framework for quality across all of the operating units and a new reporting system. The need for these changes was highlighted by Erik Gordon, a professor at the Ross School of Business at the University of Michigan, "Nothing is more valuable to Johnson & Johnson than the brand bond of trust with consumers."[11]

Is There a Cure Ahead?

Weldon realizes that the recalls have presented additional challenges for Johnson & Johnson, which is already facing a tougher economic environment. Sales of its various consumer products, such as *Tylenol, Benadryl* and *Rolaids,* showed a substantial decline over the last six months of 2010. Weldon has been working hard to reassure analysts, investors, and consumers that it was already dealing with its quality problems. But Les Funtleyder, who invests in health stocks for his investment firm, said, "These problems are accumulating. At some point investors are going to start to question J&J's management."[12]

But the firm's diversified portfolio of products spread across various areas of heath care have helped it to weather the problems that it has encountered. In particular, Johnson & Johnson has managed to offset its loss of sales in over-the-counter medications with relatively strong sales from pharmaceuticals and devices. "With interests spread out all over the health-care industry, J&J does not live or die by any one product," remarked Herman Saftlas, a pharmaceutical analyst for Standard & Poor's.[13]

Moving forward, Weldon is hoping to strike a balance between direction and freedom for Johnson & Johnson's business units as he pushes to get the firm to start to grow again. Until the first quarter of 2009, the firm had managed to increase its earnings, adjusted for special items, for 94 consecutive quarters. Weldon believes that he can resume Johnson & Johnson's record growth only by pushing its businesses to work more closely together than they have ever done in the past. The firm can tap into many more opportunities when it brings together the various skills that it has developed across different divisions.

At the same time, Weldon has become acutely aware of the problems that can arise when the corporate managers push the business units to become more effective or efficient. To a large extent, the quality problems at McNeil can be attributed to the decision by J&J to merge it with the consumer health care unit that it had acquired from Pfizer. The larger merged unit was then moved away from the pharmaceutical division and subjected to more centralized control within the consumer division. As a result of all of these efforts to wring more profits out of McNeil, the firm had to resort to a string of recalls that have tarnished the image of J&J.

Above all, Weldon knows that much of Johnson & Johnson's success has resulted from the relative autonomy that it has granted to each of its business units. Even as he strives to push for more control and direction, he does not want to threaten the entrepreneurial spirit that has served his firm so well. But it is clear that he has to rethink the process by which his firm manages its diversified portfolio of companies to ensure that there are no further threats to its reputation. "This is a company that was purer than Caesar's wife. This was the gold standard, and all of a sudden it just seems like things are breaking down," said William Trombetta, a professor of pharmaceutical marketing at Saint Joseph's University in Philadephia.[14]

Endnotes

1. Wang, S. S., & Rundle, R. L. 2008. J&J to acquire breast-implant maker. *Wall Street Journal,* December 2: B1.
2. Barrett, A. 2003. Staying on top. *BusinessWeek,* May 5: 61
3. Bowe, C. 2006. J&J reveals its Guidant motive. *Financial Times,* January 25: 17.
4. Loftus, P., & Wang, S. S. 2009. J&J sales show health care feels the pinch. *Wall Street Journal,* January 21: B1.
5. Johnson, A. 2007. J&J's consumer play paces growth. *Wall Street Journal,* January 24: A3.
6. Preston, H. H. 2005. Drug giant provides a model of consistency. *Herald Tribune,* March 12–13: 12.
7. Barrett. 2003: 62.
8. Johnson, A. 2007. J&J realigns managers, revamps units. *Wall Street Journal,* November 16: A10.
9. Barrett. 2003: 62.
10. Singer, N., & Abelson, R. 2011. Can Johnson & Johnson get its act together? *New York Times,* January 16: B4.
11. Ibid.
12. Singer, N., & Abelson, R. 2010. After recall of drugs, a congressional spotlight on J.&J.'s chief. *New York Times,* September 29: B4.
13. Bennett, J. 2008. J&J: A balm for your portfolio. *Barron's,* October 27: 39.
14. Singer, N. 2010. Hip implants are recalled by J&J unit. *New York Times,* August 27: B1.

Case 15   Samsung Electronics*

In January 2011, Samsung Electronics reported a record net profit in the previous year, well above the previous record that had been set in 2004 (see Exhibits 1 and 2). Although the electronics giant derives considerable revenue from basic components, such as semiconductors and computer monitors, it has been transforming itself into a game-changing technology company. Looking at opportunities in the mobile Internet and digital media areas, Samsung CEO Gee-Sung Choi recently said, "Amid such a rapidly evolving business environment, creativity that moves ahead of changes is required to sustain growth."[1]

Along these lines, Samsung had recently released the latest symbol of its creative ambition, the Galaxy Tab, a 7-inch tablet computer that runs on Google's Android operating system. Months earlier, the firm had released Galaxy S, a smartphone marketed in the United States as

AT&T's Captivate, T-Mobile's Vibrant, Verizon Wireless's Fascinate, and Sprint's Epic 4G. It sold over 7 million units worldwide in the six months after it was launched. Park Kang-ho, an analyst at Daishin Securities, commented, "Samsung's Galaxy lines are the only major competitors to Apple's iPhone and iPad at the moment, while the other companies are still struggling to come up with a competitive device to take on Apple."[2]

Furthermore, Samsung has insisted that its Galaxy products have several distinct features that clearly make them superior, and any resemblance to Apple's offerings resulted from similarities in the evolution of smartphones and tablet computers. Minhyoul Lee, art director in Samsung's mobile communications division, said that the Galaxy S and the Galaxy Tab were byproducts of years of research and experience. "Galaxy didn't just fall from the sky," he recently commented.[3]

In fact, the strategy of swiftly pursuing the next big thing has been paying off handsomely for Samsung. A few years ago, the market value of Samsung had risen above $100 billion, making it one of only four Asian companies

* This case was developed by Professor Jamal Shamsie, Michigan State University, with the assistance of Professor Alan B. Eisner, Pace University. Material has been drawn from published sources to be used for class discussion. Copyright © 2011 Jamal Shamsie and Alan B. Eisner.

Exhibit 1   Income Statement (in billions of KRW)

	Years Ending December 31				
	2010*	2009	2008	2007	2006
Net Sales	154,630	138,994	121,294	98,508	85,426
Gross Profit	51,960	40,049	31,532	27,627	25,779
Operating Profit	17,300	11,578	6,031	8,973	9,008
Net Income	16,150	9,649	5,525	7,421	7,926

*Estimate.
Source: Samsung.

Exhibit 2   Balance Sheet (in billions of KRW)

	Years Ending December 31				
	2010*	2009	2008	2007	2006
Total Assets	134,290	118,281	105,301	93,375	81,366
Total Liabilities	44,940	45,227	47,186	37,404	33,426
Total Shareholders Equity	89,350	73,054	58,117	55,972	47,940

*Estimate.
Source: Samsung.

to move above that mark. Based in Suwon, South Korea, the firm moved past well-known rivals such as Sony, Nokia, and Motorola on the basis of its revolutionary products. Its feature-jammed gadgets have racked up numerous design awards, allowing the firm to make its way to the top of consumer-brand awareness surveys. "They are beginning to make the transition to where their products are setting the market pace," said Charles Golvin, a technology analyst at Forrester Research.[4]

Among the changes that Samsung has been making to emphasize a new focus for the firm, analysts have paid particular attention to the recent appointment of Choi Gee Sung as the firm's CEO. Choi's appointment signifies a break from the firm's tradition of picking top managers with backgrounds in engineering. Referring to the shift away from its heavy emphasis on technology, Kang Shin Woo, chief investment officer at fund manager Korea Investment Trust Management, said, "Samsung's benchmark is shifting from Japanese companies to innovators like Apple."[5]

Discarding a Failing Strategy

The transformation of Samsung into a premier brand could be attributed to the ceaseless efforts of Yun Jong Yong, who was appointed to the position of president and CEO in 1996. When Yun took charge, Samsung was still making most of its profits from lower-priced appliances that consumers were likely to pick up if they could not afford a higher-priced brand such as Sony or Mitsubishi. It had also become an established low-cost supplier of various components to such larger and better-known manufacturers around the world.

Although the firm was making profits, Yun was concerned about the future prospects of a firm that was relying on a strategy of competing on price with products that were based on technologies that had been developed by other firms. The success of this strategy was tied to the ability of Samsung to continually scout for locations that would allow it to keep its manufacturing costs down. At the same time, it would need to keep generating sufficient orders to maintain a high volume of production. In particular, he was concerned about the growing competition that the firm was likely to face from the many low-cost producers that were springing up in other countries such as China.

Yun's concerns were well founded. Within a year of his takeover, Samsung was facing serious financial problems that threatened its very survival. The company was left with huge debt as an economic crisis engulfed most of Asia in 1997, leading to a drop in demand and a crash in the prices of many electronic goods. In the face of such a deteriorating environment, Samsung continued to push for maintaining its production and sales records even as much of its output was ending up unsold in warehouses.

By July 1998, Samsung Electronics was losing millions of dollars each month. "If we continued, we would have gone belly-up within three or four years," Yun recalled.[6] He knew that he had to make some drastic moves in order to turn things around. Yun locked himself in a hotel room for a whole day with nine other senior managers to try and find a way out. They all wrote resignation letters and pledged to resign if they failed.

After much deliberation, Yun and his management team decided to take several steps to try and push Samsung out of its precarious financial position. To begin with, they decided to lay off about 30,000 employees, representing well over a third of its entire workforce. They also closed down many of Samsung's factories for two months so that they could get rid of its large inventory. Finally, they sold off about $2 billion worth of businesses, like pagers and electric coffeemakers, that were perceived to be of marginal significance for the firm's future.

Developing a Premium Brand

Having managed to stem the losses, Yun decided to move Samsung away from its strategy of competition based largely on the lower price of its offerings. Consequently, he began to push the firm to develop its own products rather than to copy those that other firms had developed (see Exhibit 3). In particular, Yun placed considerable emphasis on developing products that would impress consumers with their attractive designs and their advanced technology. By focusing on such products, Yun hoped that he could convert Samsung into a premium brand that would allow them to charge higher prices.

In order to achieve this, Yun had to reorient the firm and help it to develop new capabilities. He recruited new managers and engineers, many of whom had developed considerable experience in the United States. Once they had been recruited, Yun got them into shape by putting them through a four-week boot camp that consisted of martial drills at the crack of dawn and mountain hikes that would last all day. To create incentives for this new talent, Yun discarded Samsung's rigid seniority-based system and replaced it with a merit-based system for advancement.

As a result of these efforts, Samsung began to launch an array of products that were designed to make a big impression on consumers. These included the largest flat-panel televisions, cell phones with a variety of features such as cameras and PDAs, ever-thinner notebook computers, and speedier and richer semiconductors (see Exhibit 4). The firm calls them "wow products," and they are designed to elevate Samsung in the same way the Trinitron television and the Walkman had helped to plant Sony in the minds of consumers

A large part of the success of Samsung's products can be tied to their efforts to focus on the specific needs of prospective customers. An executive of Best Buy recently stated that Samsung regularly gets information from retailers about the new features that customers want to see in their electronic devices. This close link with retailers helped Samsung to come up with some of their best-selling products over the years. According to Graeme Bateman, head of research for Japanese investment bank Nomura Securities, "Samsung is no longer making poor equivalents of Sony products. It is making things people want."[7]

Exhibit 3   Revenue Breakdown (in trillions of KRW)

		Years Ending December 31	
	Year	Sales	Profits
Semiconductors	2010*	37.64	10.11
Includes DRAMS, SRAMS,& NAND flash chips	2009	26.81	2.06
	2008	20.21	0.00
	2007	22.30	2.30
Telecommunications	2010*	41.20	4.30
Includes digital phones & handsets	2009	37.59	4.09
	2008	33.71	2.98
	2007	23.80	2.80
Digital Media	2010*	57.26	0.49
Includes plasma & projection displays & televisions	2009	51.26	3.06
	2008	41.14	0.39
	2007	26.50	1.10
LCD	2010*	29.92	1.99
Includes panels for desktop & laptop computers	2009	25.84	1.71
	2008	14.89	2.35
	2007	17.10	2.10
Digital Appliances	2010*	—	—
Includes "intelligent" refrigerators, microwave ovens, & air conditioners	2009	—	—
	2008	1.83	0.03
	2007	6.90	0.20

*Estimate.
Source: Samsung.

Finally, to help Samsung change its image among consumers, Yun hired a marketing whiz, Eric Kim, who has worked hard to create a more upscale image of the firm and its products. Kim moved Samsung's advertising away from 55 different advertising agencies around the world and placed it with one firm, Madison Avenues's Foote, Cone & Belding Worldwide, in order to create a consistent global brand image for its products. He also began to pull Samsung out of big discount chains like Walmart and Kmart and place more of its products into more upscale specialty stores such as Best Buy and Circuit City.

Pushing for New Products

Yun also took many steps to speed up Samsung's new-product development process. He was well aware that Samsung will be able to maintain the higher margins only as long as his firm is able to keep introducing new products into the market well ahead of its established rivals. Samsung managers who have worked for big competitors say they have to go through far fewer layers of bureaucracy than they had to in the past to win approval for new products, budgets, and marketing plans, speeding up their ability to seize opportunities.

Apart from reducing the bureaucratic obstacles, Yun made heavy investments into key technologies, ranging from semiconductors to LCD displays, that could allow it to push out a wide variety of revolutionary digital products. Samsung has continuously invested more than any of its rivals on its research and development, raising its R&D budget during the past couple of years to almost 9 percent of its revenue. In 2010 its level of spending on research and development had risen to $7.2 billion.

Exhibit 4 **Global Market Ranking, 2009**

Product Category	Market Rank
Memory chips	1
Computer monitors	1
LCD panels	1
LCD TVs	1
Plasma TVs	1
DVD-VCR combos	1
Projection TVs	2
DVD players	2
MP3 players	2
Laser printers	2
Mobile phones	2
Microwave ovens	3
Camcorders	3
Digital cameras	3

Source: Samsung.

It has a large force of designers and engineers working in 17 research centers located all around the world (see Exhibit 5).

Yun also forced Samsung's own units to compete with outsiders in order to speed up the process for developing innovative new products. In the liquid-crystal-display business, for example, Samsung bought half of its color filters from Sumitomo Chemical Company of Japan and sourced the other half internally, pitting the two teams against each other. "They really press these departments to compete," said Sumitomo President Hiromasa Yonekura.[8] As a result of these steps, Samsung claims that it has been able to reduce the time that it takes to go from new product

Exhibit 5 **Designers Employed**

2008	600
2006	550
2004	470
2002	310
2000	210
1998	170

Source: Samsung

concept to rollout to as little as five months, compared to over a year that it used to take the firm about a decade ago.

In large part, this has resulted from the effort of the firm's top managers, engineers, and designers who work relentlessly in the five-story VIP center nestled amid the firm's industrial complex in Suwon. They work day and night in the center, which includes dormitories and showers for brief rests to work out any problems that may hold back a product launch. The progress that is made by teams that pursue new-product designs in the VIP center makes it possible for Samsung to reduce complexity in the early stages of the design cycle. This allows the firm to get its products to move quickly to manufacturing with minimal problems and at the lowest possible cost. In turn, this can lead to a faster market launch of a product that is more likely to be more innovative than all others. Kyunghan Jung, a senior manager of the center, explained, "Seventy to eighty percent of quality, cost and delivery time is determined in the initial stages of product development."[9]

The speedier development process has allowed Samsung to introduce the first voice-activated phones, handsets with MP3 players, and digital camera phones that send photos over global system for mobile communications networks. As an example of the firm's speed and agility, Charles Golvin of Forrester Research talked about its ability to create four different industrial designs of its Galaxy S smartphone for four varying wirelesss network types around the world and deliver them simultaneously. "They've had a long history of responding to market trends with a lot of alacrity," he remarked.[10]

Designing for the Digital Home

Yun was hoping that Samsung's advances in digital technologies would increase its chances of dominating the digital home. He believed that his firm was in a better position to benefit from the day that all home appliances, from handheld computers to intelligent refrigerators, will be linked to each other and adapt to the personal needs of consumers. In particular, Samsung appears to be well placed to take advantage of its capabilities to design and manufacture a wide array of products that straddle traditional technology categories. "We have to combine computers, consumer electronics and communications as Koreans mix their rice with vegetables and meats," said Dae Je Chin, the head of Samsung's digital media division.[11]

Yun worked closely with Chin to summon engineers and designers from across the firm to mix wireless, semiconductor, and computer expertise in order to pursue its vision of dominating the digital home. One such product from the firm was NEXiO, a combined cell phone and handheld computer. The device has a five-inch screen, large enough for a user to run a spreadsheet or to browse the Web. Another new offering was a refrigerator called Zipel that has a 15-inch flat-panel touch screen tucked into the door. The display can be used to surf the Internet and to send or receive e-mail.

In developing these products, Samsung has begun to place a lot of emphasis on the role of design in making its products irresistible in an increasingly competitive marketplace. Since 2000, the firm has opened or expanded design centers in San Francisco, London, Tokyo, Los Angeles, and Shanghai (see Exhibit 6). Inside these centers, designers observe the way that consumers actually use various products. They may watch from behind a one-way mirror how consumers stuff a refrigerator with bagfuls of groceries. Samsung also began to send its growing group of designers to various locations to spend a few months at fashion houses, furniture designers, and cosmetic specialists to stay current with trends in other industries.

Furthermore, Samsung created the post of chief design officer to make sure that designers can get their ideas to top managers. A successful rear-projection television was developed by a designer who pitched it to one of the heads of television production. Engineers are pushed to find ways to work with the designs that are presented to them. As a result of these efforts, Samsung has earned numerous citations at top design contests in the United States, Europe, and Asia. After winning 46 awards at a recent U.S. consumer-electronics show, D.J. Oh, CEO of Samsung Electronics America, said, "Samsung strives to consistently lead the consumer electronics industry in product design and engineering innovation."[12]

Samsung has been relying on the attractiveness of its products to make them the centerpiece of a digital home. In a showroom in the lobby of its headquarters in Seoul, the firm shows off many of its latest offerings, ranging from tablet computers to digital cameras. Visitors can put on goggles to watch characters jump out on 3-D televisions or shuffle their feet on an interactive LED floor. Roger Entner, a wireless industry analyst at Neilson, said about Samsung's efforts, "With its resources and experience, it's trying to capitalize on the emergence of smart connected devices. The question is, 'Can they be a cutting-edge trendsetter like Apple?'"[13]

Creating a Sustainable Model?

Samsung CEO Choi recently launched a 10-year Vision 2020 corporate goal for Samsung to join the ranks of the top 10 global companies by achieving $400 billion in sales.

Exhibit 6   **Samsung Milestones**

1969	Samsung Electronics established as maker of televisions with technology borrowed from Sanyo.
1977	Samsung introduces its first color television.
1981	Samsung begins to focus on undercutting Japanese rivals with me-too products, with little emphasis on design.
1988	Samsung launches first mobile phone.
1993	Samsung begins to reinvent the firm through design.
1994	Samsung hires design consultancy IDEO to help develop computer monitors.
1995	Samsung sets up in-house design school, the Innovative Design Lab of Samsung.
1996	Yun Jong Yong takes over as CEO; he declares "Year of Design Revolution," stressing that designers should lead in product planning.
1998	Asian financial crisis dents Samsung's ambitions, forcing it to cut design staff by 28 percent.
2000	Samsung once again focuses on design, and CEO Yun Jong Yong calls for design-led management.
2001	Yun initiates quarterly design meetings for top executives and opens design labs in Los Angeles and London.
2002	Samsung's "usability laboratory" inaugurated in downtown Seoul.
2004	Market value of Samsung rises above $100 billion.
2008	Lee Yoon Woo takes over as CEO from Yun.
2009	Samsung is set to announce its first loss since 2000; firm announces major reorganization.
2010	Gee Sung Choi takes over as CEO.

Source: Samsung.

It already exceeds Hewlett-Packard as the largest technology company in the world by revenue. In order to achieve its long-term goals, Samsung has reorganized its divisions to focus more strongly on 8 different businesses: including visual display, IT solutions, digital appliances, mobile communications, telecommunication systems, digital imaging, semiconductors, and LCDs.

Samsung has also been investing heavily to expand its manufacturing capacity for memory chips and liquid crystal displays. It is already a market leader in each of these, but it is ramping up production to respond to increased demand, particularly for ultrathin screens for smart phones. Samsung's spending in 2010 exceeded the combined investments of Intel, IBM, and Sony, according to Bloomberg data. The firm has backed up these investments with the acquisition of a couple of firms to move into more display screens for mobile devices and to push further into medical equipment.

At the same time, Samsung has consistently refused to consider branching out like Sony or Apple into music, movies, and games. It has decided against such a move even though subscription-to-content can provide a firm with additional sources of revenue. Instead, Samsung has chosen to collaborate with various content and software providers, such as Microsoft and Time Warner. Even some of Apple's best-known products were designed with the help of components from Samsung.

Choi appears to be well aware of the challenges that lie ahead for Samsung. The life cycle of most electronics products can be brutally short, with prices tending to drop sharply over time. The profitability of a hardware firm rests on its ability to keep developing products to address new opportunities. At the same time, it must keep seeking ways to reduce its costs in order to be competitive with lower-margin products.

Critics have pointed out that Samsung is still searching for a product that would be comparable to Apple's iPod or Sony's Walkman. But the firm claims that if it keeps pushing, some of its products will end up being viewed as revolutionary. "It's critical for Samsung that the new leadership keep investing in new technologies and equipment," said Chang In Whan, chief executive at fund manager KTB Asset Management.[14]

Endnotes

1. Yu, R. 2010. Samsung cranks up creativity. *USA Today,* November 16: 4B.
2. Jung-a, S. 2011. Samsung looks to close gap with Apple. *Financial Times Online,* January 29.
3. Yu. 2010.
4. Ibid.
5. Ihlwan, M. 2009. Samsung Electronics: Same CEO, new leadership team. *BusinessWeek Online,* January 19.
6. Gibney Jr., F. 2002. Samsung moves upmarket. *Time.* March 25: 49.
7. Edwards, C., Ihlwan, M., & Engardio, P. 2003. The Samsung way. *BusinessWeek,* June 16: 60.
8. Lewis, P. 2005. A perpetual crisis machine. *Fortune,* September 19: 65.
9. Edwards, Ihlwan, & Engardio. 2003: 61.
10. Yu. 2010.
11. Rocks, D. & Ihlwan, M. 2004. Samsung design. *BusinessWeek,* December 6: 90.
12. Samsung Electronics gets 46 CES Innovations Awards for 2009. 2008. *Wireless News,* November 24.
13. Yu. 2010.
14. Ihlwan. 2009.

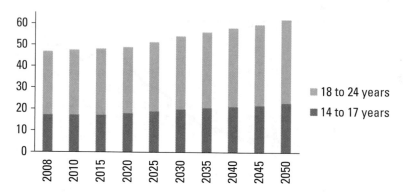

Exhibit 5 Population Trend among 14–17 and 18–24 Age Groups (millions)

Source: U.S. Census.

movie per month. Profits are driven by the studios' ability to satisfy this fickle audience. In 2008 two films targeting the core market and based on two successful comic book characters met with widely different fates.[4] Paramount's successful *Iron Man* was produced for $140 and grossed $318 million at the domestic box office. Warner Brothers' *Speed Racer*, produced for $20 million less and released the following weekend was a flop, grossing just $44 million.

Demographic trends are not favorable either. The U.S. population will increase 17 percent by 2025, an increase of 54 million people. But the number of 12–24-year-olds is expected to increase only 9 percent, just 4 million more potential viewers. Based on current theaters and screens, this is an increase of under 700 additional viewers per theater, roughly 100 per screen.

Distribution Distributors are the intermediaries between the studios and exhibitors. Distribution entails all steps following a film's artistic completion, including marketing, logistics, and administration. Exhibitors negotiate a percentage of gross by the studio or purchase rights to films and then profit from the box-office receipts. Distributors select and market films to exhibitors, seeking to maximize potential attendees. Distributors coordinate the manufacture and distribution of the film to exhibitors. They also handle collections, audits of attendees, and other administrative tasks. There are over 300 active distributors, but much is done by a few major firms, including divisions of studios. Pixar, for example, coproduced *Finding Nemo* with Disney, and distribution was done by Disney's Buena Vista.

Exhibition Studios have historically sought full vertical integration through theater ownership, allowing greater control over audiences and capturing exhibition profits. A common practice was for the studios to use their theater ownership to reduce competition by not showing pictures produced by rivals. This ended in 1948 with the Supreme

Court's ruling against the studios in *United States v. Paramount Pictures*. Theaters were soon divested, leaving studios and exhibitors to negotiate film access and rental.

Theaters are classified according to the number of screens at one location (see Exhibit 1). Single-screen theaters were the standard from the introduction of film through the 1980s. They have since rapidly declined in number, replaced by theater complexes. These include miniplexes (2–7 screens), multiplexes (8–15 screens), and megaplexes, (16 or more screens). The number of theaters decreased more than 20 percent between 2000 and 2010, but the number of screens increased because of the growth in megaplexes. Over 10 percent of the theaters are now megaplexes, and the number of screens is at a historical high of 39,717.[5] Many analysts argue the industry has overbuilt, and too many theaters and screens exist to make the business profitable.

The Lead Actors

Declining ticket sales and the increased costs associated with developing megaplexes began a wave of consolidation among exhibitors. Four companies now dominate: Regal, AMC, Cinemark, and Carmike. These companies, operating 1,383 theaters in the country (just 23 percent), control 43 percent of screens. This market share provides these exhibitors with negotiating power for access to films, prices for films and concessions, and greater access to revenues from national advertisers.

There is little differentiation in the offerings of the major theater exhibitors—prices within markets differ little, the same movies are shown at the same times, and the food and services are nearly identical. Competition between theaters often comes down to distance from home, convenience of parking, and proximity to restaurants. Innovations by one theater chain are quickly adopted by others. The chains serve different geographic markets and do so in different ways.[6] Regal focuses on midsized markets using multiplexes and megaplexes. In

Exhibit 6 Market Share of Film Production, 2000–2010

Distributor	2010				2005				2000			
	Rank	Market Share	Total Gross	# Movies	Rank	Market Share	Total Gross	# Movies	Rank	Market Share	Total Gross	# Movies
Warner Bros.	1	18.2%	$1,924	27	1	15.6%	$1,377	19	3	11.9%	$905	22
Paramount	2	16.2%	$1,715	15	6	9.4%	$832	12	4	10.4%	$791	12
20th Century Fox	3	14.0%	$1,482	17	2	15.3%	$1,354	18	6	9.5%	$723	13
Disney/Buena Vista	4	13.8%	$1,456	14	4	10.4%	$922	17	1	15.5%	$1,176	21
Sony/Columbia	5	12.1%	$1,283	18	5	10.4%	$918	24	7	9.0%	$682	29
Universal	6	8.3%	$882	15	3	11.4%	$1,010	19	2	14.1%	$1,069	13
Total for leading 6		82.6%	$8,742	106		72.5%	$6,413	109		70.4%	$5,346	110
Industry Total			$10,565	529			$8,840	547			$7,661	478
As % of Industry		82.7%		20.0%		72.5%		19.9%		69.8%		23.0%

Source: Adapted from *BoxOfficeMojo.com*.

2009 Regal's average ticket price of $8.15 was the highest among the leaders. AMC concentrates on urban areas with megaplexes and concentrates on the large population centers such as those in California, Florida, and Texas. Cinemark serves smaller markets, operating as the sole theater chain in over 80 percent of its markets. Cinemark's average ticket price of $5.46 was the lowest of the majors. Carmike concentrates on small to midsized markets, targeting populations of less than 100,000 that have few other entertainment options. Carmike's average ticket price in 2009 was $6.56, but at $3.21, their average concession revenue per patron is the highest among the majors.

The different approach of the companies is reflected in the cost of fixed assets per screens. These costs result from decisions made on how to serve customers, such as the level of technology and finish of the theater—digital projection and marble floors cost more than traditional projectors and a carpeted lobby.[7] Despite multi- and megaplex facilities, Regal's cost per screen is the highest, at $430,000. Carmike, the rural operator, has the lowest, at just $206,000. Cinemark is in the middle, at $367,000. Costs for AMC are expected to be near or exceed that of Regal.

The Business of Exhibition

There are three primary sources of revenue for exhibitors: concessions, advertising, and box-office receipts. Managers have low discretion; their ability to influence revenues and expenses is limited. Operating margins among exhibitors average a slim 10 percent. This is before significant expenses such as facility and labor costs. The result is marginal or negative net income. Overall, the business of exhibitors is best described as loss leadership on movies: the firms make money selling concessions and selling ads that are shown to patrons who are drawn by the movie.

Concessions   Moviegoers frequently lament the high prices for concessions. In 2009 concessions averaged 30 percent of exhibitor revenues. Direct costs are less than 15 percent of selling price, making concessions the largest source of exhibitor profit. These are influenced by three factors: attendance, pricing, and material costs. The most important is attendance: more attendees equals more concession sales. Per patron sales are influenced by prices—a common moviegoer complaint is high concession prices. The $3.75 price point for the large soda is not accidental, but the result of market research and profit maximization calculation. Costs are influenced by purchase volume with larger chains able to negotiate better prices on everything from popcorn and soda pop to cups and napkins.

Advertising   Exhibitors also generate revenue through preshow advertising. Though this constitutes just 5 percent of revenues, it is highly profitable. Mintel reports that advertising revenues among exhibitors are expected to increase at an annual rate of 10 percent over the coming decade despite audience disapproval.[8] Balancing the revenues from ads with audience tolerance is an ongoing struggle for exhibitors, though not a new one. In the early 1970s one industry executive argued ,"It is not a policy of our corporation to use commercial advertising for income on our screen. We are selling the public one item—a particular motion picture—and to use the screen for other purposes detracts from this item."[9]

Box-Office Revenues   Ticket sales constitute two-thirds of exhibition business revenues but yield little or no profit. Historically, the power imbalance between studios and exhibitors yielded rental contracts returning as much as 90 percent of box-office revenue to the studios during the initial weeks of a film's release. The split is now closer to 55/45 for large chains. Still, it is common for an exhibitor's portion of ticket revenues to not fully cover the operational costs. The record-setting revenues at the box office have been the result of increases in ticket prices that have flowed back to the studios and help cover exhibitors' facilities and debt load.

From 2005 to 2009 ticket price increases average 3.8 percent per year (see Exhibit 7).[10] While these increases set records, an even greater opportunity materialized for 3D. Prior to 2009, a $1 to $2 "surcharge" was installed to cover glasses, license fees paid to 3D equipment providers, and to studios in higher rental rates. Following the success of *Avatar,* exhibitors saw an opportunity to use the surcharge as an alternative to ticket price increases. The 3D premium now reaches $3 to $5; for IMAX it is $4 to $7. Price increases in March 2010 by AMC, Regal, and Cinemark averaged 8.3 percent nationally on 3D movies, rising from $13.60 to $14.73.[11] In some markets, 3D prices jumped 20 percent.[12]

Recent increases in exhibitor revenues are attributed almost entirely to 3D. In 2005 the box office for 3D was just $40 million. In 2009 it was $1.14 billion, 11 percent of all revenues. From 2008 to 2009, 3D receipts grew 375 percent while revenues for non-3D grew under one percent.[13] This may actually under represent the actual demand for 3D as rapid expansion in the number of 3D films produced created a bottleneck for the 3D screen space.[14] Longer runs on 3D screens will likely increase the proportion of revenues from 3D. However, Paul Dergarabedian of *Hollywood.com* cautions that the ticket price increases are not sustainable. "It's what we call a recession-resistant business. Times get tough and people go to the movies because it's the one thing they see as a relative bargain. The minute they cease to see it that way, it's not good for the industry."[15]

AMC may have, intentionally or not, stumbled onto a price cap when several of their New York theaters hit $20 per ticket for "Shrek" in IMAX 3D at several locations. Amidst a public outcry and unwanted media attention, the chain apologized, citing a pricing error, and reduced prices to $17 and $19. This situation suggests there is indeed a cap on moviegoers' willingness to pay for even this most extreme viewing experience. The backlash may make it

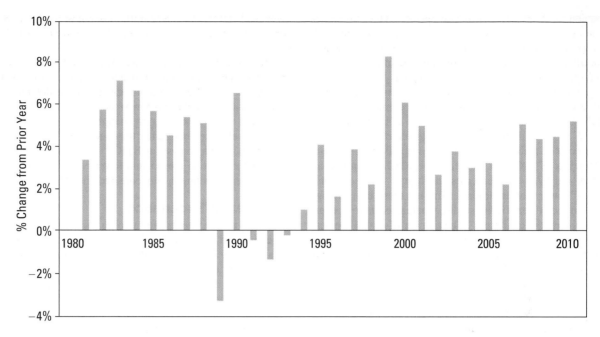

Exhibit 7 **Change in Average Ticket Price, 1980–2010**

Source: Adapted from *BoxOfficeMojo.com* and Motion Picture Association of America data.

difficult to raise prices in the near future. Any cap on ticket prices is a serious cause for concern for exhibitors, as it has been the primary way to increase revenues.

The evidence is mixed that 3D is having a positive impact on exhibitors' bottom lines. This suggests either that the benefits are yet to accrue to exhibitors or are being appropriated by studios. The National Association of Theater Owners (NATO) estimates the savings of digital over film as $1 billion annually from lower production costs, master reels and prints, elimination of shipping, and so on.[16] They argue that these cost savings will largely accrue to distributors.

By all accounts, revenues per admission have increased, but these are split with studios. At Regal, for example, film rental and advertising costs as a percentage of revenues dropped slightly, to 53.3 percent from 54.2 percent for the second quarter of 2010 compared to the same period in 2009. Similarly, Carmike's exhibition costs declined slightly as a percentage of revenue, from 57.6 percent to 56.8 percent, but other theater operating costs grew from 59.6 percent to 62.9 percent of admissions revenue. In each of these cases, the data reflect substantial increases in ticket prices and 3D surcharges begun in spring 2010. This suggests studios are appropriating a large portion of the revenue increases.

At Regal, this holds true for operating profits, as a percentage of revenues, which decreased from 12.2 percent in the second quarter of 2009 to 9.0 percent in 2010. For Carmike, the net effect was operating income declining significantly, from 8.8 percent of total revenue to

4.1 percent. The overall picture appears similar for Cinemark. Operating income as a percentage of revenues for the second quarter of 2010 declined from same period 2009 levels, dropping from 14.6 percent to 14.4 percent. While limited to just the first comparative quarter when most price increases and surcharges went into effect, these trends suggest that, despite substantial investments in digital and 3D, exhibitors may not be able to capitalize on them.

Overall, the exhibitor has limited control over both revenues and profits. Box-office receipts are the bulk of revenues but yield few profits. Attendance allows for profitable sales of concessions and advertisements, but there are significant caps on the volume of concession sales per person and selling prices seem to have reached a maximum. Advertising remains an attractive avenue for revenues and profits, but audiences loathe it.

The Process of Exhibition

The fundamentals of film exhibition changed little from when motion pictures were introduced until the late 1990s. Historically, each theater received a shipment of physical canisters containing a "release print" from the distributor. Making these prints requires $20,000–$30,000 in up-front costs and $1,000–$1,500 for each print. Thus, a modern major motion picture opening on 2,500 screens simultaneously requires $2.50–$3.75 million in print costs. This is borne by the studios but paid for by movie attendees. Each release print is actually several reels of 35 mm film that are manually loaded onto projector reels, sequenced, and retailed for $29 per diagonal inch of set size. This is expected to decrease to $22 within five years.[29] Consumers, however, are actually spending more on every television, consistently electing to purchase larger sets to achieve a better viewing experience. Sharp, a leading manufacturer of televisions, predicts that by 2015 the average screen will reach 60 inches.[30]

Large-screen televisions, DVD players, and audio and speaker components are commonly packaged as low-cost home theaters. The average DVD player now costs just $72,[31] and high-definition DVD players are beginning to penetrate the market. Retail price wars during the 2008 Christmas season led to HD Blu-Ray players dropping below $200. These home-theater systems offer a movie experience that rivals many theaters, all for $1,000—$2,000. Says Mike Gabriel, Sharp's head of marketing and communications, "People can now expect a home cinema experience from their TV. Technology that was once associated with the rich and famous is now accessible to homes across the country."[32]

Content Expansion   Sales of DVDs have aided the expansion of home theaters and profited the studios. DVD sales have been a primary source of studio profits for more than a decade but recently fell precipitously, down 13.3 percent in 2009 on top of an 8.4 percent decline in 2008.[33] At $8.5 billion, 2009's DVD sales equaled 2001 levels; total revenues from DVD sales dropped below that of box-office receipts in the United States for the first time since 2000.[34] This decline in DVD sales is due in part to the expanded availability of rentals and pay-per-view, and is at least partially attributable to the studios.

Rentals also serve this market. Netflix grew revenues 85 percent from 2006 to 2009, and it is actively expanding into online streaming. Coinstar's Redbox had over 12,000 rental kiosks offering $1 per night rentals through partnerships with McDonald's (which is also an investor in the company), Walmart, Walgreen's, and other retailers even *before* adding kiosks to half of 7-Eleven's national locations.[35]

Studios are responding by trying to spur DVD and pay-per-view fees through shorter release windows, actions seemingly incompatible and inconsistent with the drive to increase theater attendance. In 2000 the average window between theatrical release and DVD sales was 5 months, 16 days. In 2009, it was 4 months, 11 days, a 20 percent reduction.[36] Studios are eager to accelerate DVD revenue streams and capitalize on initial marketing expenditures. Arguing in favor of a reduced window, Bob Iger, CEO of Disney said, "The problem with waiting these days is that we're dealing with a much more competitive marketplace than ever before—there are more choices that people have."[37] Theaters may fear complete disintermediation.

The accelerated DVD release of *Alice in Wonderland* in the United States (just 88 days after opening and while the film remained in theaters) created great concern among film exhibitors. Exhibitors fear that shorter windows deter attendance (see Exhibit 9). U.S. theater owners and major Hollywood studios reached an agreement wherein the studios will be able to release one or two movies each year on an accelerated schedule, cutting a month off of the traditional 4-month DVD release window.[38] The *Wall Street Journal* reports, "Theaters have benefited recently from a boom in box-office receipts, even as studios have suffered from a steep decline in DVD sales. Adjusting the windows is an attempt to maintain the health of both camps, which depend on one another."[39]

Hollywood is also seeking to expand direct-to-viewer delivery, avoiding the DVD and capturing revenues directly. Studios won regulatory approval to temporarily block analog outputs on viewers' electronics during pay-per-view movies. While controls for digital outputs are features that are built in with modern electronics, viewers with analog equipment could record pay-per-view movies if the regulatory block failed. Studios considered this loophole a security issue. Allowing temporary blockage paves the way for studios to pursue short release windows, offering "premium" pay-per-view opportunities prior to DVD release.

Overall, studios are increasingly seeking to overcome their own lost profits through increased DVD sales and alternative channels to serve the home audience directly. Both are detrimental to exhibitors.

Recession Effects   Beyond the previous attendance drivers mentioned, there is a more ominous one: recession. There has been a longstanding effect between economic recession and depression and movie attendance: as the economy declines, attendance increases. As early as 1911, one observer described movies as a "door of escape, for a few cents, from the realities of life."[40] During the depression of the 1930s, movie theaters were described as "an acre of seats in a garden of dreams."[41] The recession of 2008 saw rapid increases in gas prices, a stock market decline, and significant layoffs. One summer movie patron commented, "There's not a whole lot you can do for $10 anymore."[42]

The recession of 2008 saw attendance increase 10–15 percent over 2007. The air-conditioned comfort of a dark theater and the latest Hollywood release offered a break not just from the summer heat but from reality. "It's escapism, absolutely. It's probably a subconscious thing, and people don't realize it. But there's just so much going on, with people trying to pay their mortgages and get by. It's an escape for a couple of hours."[43] However, attendance for 2008 overall was down 4.1 percent. The MPAA routinely touts movies as bargain entertainment. Four tickets to a movie costs under $27, compared to $141 for an amusement park or $261for a pro football game.[44] This comparison, however, may no longer be relevant, as the true substitute may be a home theater and an existing cable subscription.

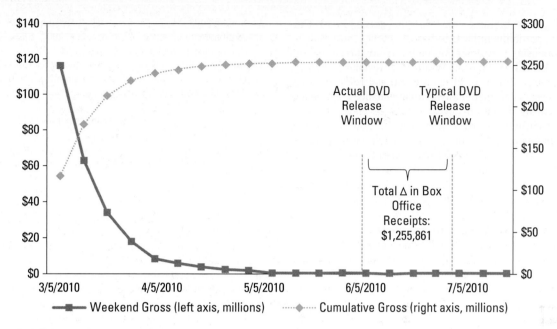

Exhibit 9 *Alice in Wonderland:* **Weekly Domestic Box Office Gross**

Source: Author estimates and data from *BoxOfficeMojo.com*

Possible Alternative Business Models

Under a studio-based film-exhibition model, unchanged since the 1930s, exhibitors have just two alternative revenue streams: advertising and concessions. Both appear limited in opportunities for increasing revenues and profits.

Advertising, while increasing, threatens to alienate customers. While a 2007 Arbitron survey indicated 63 percent of those 12 and older report they "do not mind the ads they put on before the movie begins,"[45] other viewers loathe them. Even the industry struggles with the issue. Bob Pisano, president of the MPAA, calls increased advertising or higher concession prices "mutually assured destruction" for both exhibitors and the studios. They "try moviegoers' patience," he argues, "leading them to stay home and rent or, worse, illegally download a film."[46]

While ticket prices quadrupled, per-capita spending on concessions just doubled since the 1970s.[47] Theater chains have expanded food offerings, some to the point of rivaling mall food courts. The National Association of Theater Owners (NATO) estimates that over 400 theaters now have on-site restaurant or bar service. These theaters appear at odds with the primary demographic market for movies. While the average moviegoer is the teen to twenty-something, these theaters seek 35- to 50-year-olds. AMC is experimenting with an in-theater food model to serve this market. Gold Class Cinemas adds a service approach with 40-seat theaters more akin to club lounges than auditoriums and offers full food and wine service. Tickets,

$20–$25 per person, are purchased not from a ticket booth but from a concierge. Food sales average near $20 per person. Some also offer valet parking and child care to lure customers.[48] Rob Goldberg, Gold Class's COO, explains that this is part of the appeal: "We don't get the teenage crowd."[49]

Keeping patrons coming to the theater and increased profitability may require a dramatic change for exhibitors. The investment in digital distribution and projection increase both visual quality and operational flexibility, serving as a classic "enabling technology" opening the door for alternative content. New York Metropolitan Opera's *Live in HD* is an alternative-content leader, now entering its fifth season. The series offers opera to audiences where it may not be available locally. Featuring 12 performances on Saturday afternoons, the series is broadcast to more than 500 HD-equipped theaters. Exhibitors continue to experiment with alternative content, mostly for individual sporting events, where exhibitors must compete directly with home viewing. Says Jeremy Devine, marketing VP for a Dallas-based theater chain showing the NBA All-Star game, "I don't care how good your buddy's system is, this is a 52-foot screen. And it's in 3D."[50]

Despite the potential for alternative content, virtually all admissions continue to be for studio movies. The evidence suggests continued problems with profitability under this studio-dominated model. The surge in revenues from 3D does not appear to be increasing profitability.

While exhibitors are, with the exception of Cinemark, predominantly U.S.-based, studios are increasingly focusing their attention on the international market, where growth is highest. While U.S. revenues grew 20 percent from 2005 to 2009, international revenues grew 35 percent.[51] Internationally, both attendance and receipts are growing.[52] Studios' proportional revenues are also further shifting toward international. In 2005 box-office receipts totaled $23 billion, with $14 billion (60 percent) from international. By 2009 that increased to two-thirds, on $30 billion total.[53] There appear to be opportunities to increase revenues from increased attendance and ticket price increases. In India, for example, last year's 3.3 billion attendees paid an average of just $0.50.[54] In just that market at current growth rates, the annual volume increase in attendance equals total current U.S. annual admissions.[55] Among leading U.S. exhibitors, Cinemark has the largest international presence, with 130 theaters (1,066 screens) in Mexico and seven Central and South American countries.

Raising the Exhibition Curtain in 2011 and Beyond

Despite a continuing recession, the end of the 2010 season saw an alarming statistic: summer admissions declined 3 percent from 2009 levels, resulting in a decline in both admissions and revenues. The increased costs of going to the theater may be causing audiences to be more selective in the movies they see at the theater. Perhaps the escapism of the movies is bumping into a reality of empty wallets. Higher prices are "a very dangerous situation for the movie industry," says Paul Dergarabedian, box-office analyst for *Hollywood.com*. "When is too much too much? The demand has been huge, but theater owners should not just think that they can charge whatever they want, because there is a point when people will literally just stop coming because they can't afford it."[56] Others explain the decline as a lack of content. Even with expectedly high revenues from big-budget movies, no sleeper hits emerged.

Fitch Ratings summarized the long-term situation: "Revenues and profitability of movie theatres could be increasingly challenged by factors that are largely out of managements' control. . . . The significant degree of operating leverage means that cash flow can be meaningfully affected by moderate top-line declines. These factors and financial policy decisions will remain the main drivers of credit quality over the longer term."[57]

What can exhibitors do to improve their performance? To reverse the downward trends in attendance? To improve their profitability at a time when the studios, relying on the box office more than ever, are increasingly looking internationally?

Endnotes

1. Motion Picture Association of America. 2009. *Entertainment Industry Market Statistics, 2009.*

2. Mintel. 2008. *Movie Theaters—US—February 2008.*

3. Motion Picture Association of America. 2007. *Entertainment Industry Market Statistics, 2007.*

4. All data on these two films are from *BoxOfficeMojo.com.*

5. Developed by author from: Motion Picture Association of America. 2009. *Entertainment Industry Market Statistics, 2009.*

6. Data on the firms, screen sizes, and locations are from company websites and SEC filings.

7. All data are from SEC filings, based on net property, plant, and equipment reported in 2007 balance sheets and the number of screens.

8. Mintel. 2008. *Movie Theaters—US—February 2008.* Performance–Cinema Advertising.

9. Durwood, S. H. 2002. The exhibitors (1972). In Waller, G. A. (Ed.), *Moviegoing in America: A Sourcebook in the History of Film Exhibition*, pp. 279–281 (Malden, MA: Blackwell).

10. Developed by author from: Motion Picture Association of America. 2009. *Entertainment Industry Market Statistics, 2009.*

11. Reuters. 2010. U.S. movie ticket sales strong despite price hike. *Reuters News,* April 6.

12. Schuker, L. A. E., & Smith, E. 2010. Higher prices make box-office debut. *Wall Street Journal,* March 25: B1, B5.

13. Motion Picture Association of America. 2009. *Theatrical Market Statistics, 2009.*

14. Ibid.

15. Muther, C. 2010. Prices for 3-D movies flyaway with "Dragon." *Boston Globe,* March 25: B1.

16. National Association of Theater Owners. 2010. Talking points: Digital cinema. *www.natoonline.org.*

17. International 3D Society. 2010. 3D movie fans expand box office says International 3D Society study.

18. Schuker, L. A. E. 2010. A 2-D 'Eclipse' stakes its claim in 3-D world. *Wall Street Journal,* July 6: B1, B2.

19. *The Economist.* 2010. The box office strikes back. *The Economist,* May 6.

20. Mintel. 2008. *Movie Theaters—US—February 2008.* Reasons to go to movies over watching a DVD.

21. Mintel. 2008. *Movie Theaters—US—February 2008.* Reasons why attendance is not higher.

22. Kelly, K., Orwall, B., & Sanders, P. 2005. The multiplex under siege. *Wall Street Journal,* December 24: P1.

23. Blog comment on CinemaTreasures.org. Over the past ten years, the movie theater experience has . . . *cinematreasures.org/polls/22/.*

24. Incident reported in: Goldstein, P. 2005. Now playing: A glut of ads. *Los Angeles Times,* July 12: E-1. *articles. latimes.com/2005/jul/12/entertainment/et-goldstein12.*

25. *Sramanamitra.com.* 2008. Designs of the week: The movie theater experience. November 23. *www.sramanamitra.com/2008/11/23/designs-of-the-week-the-movie-theater-experience/.*

26. DuBravac. 2007. DuBravac, S. G. (2007). The U.S. Television Set Market. Business Economics: The Journal of the National Association for Business Economics, 42(3), 52–59.

27. Ibid.
28. Ibid.
29. Keefe, B. 2008. Prices on flat-screen TVs expected to keep falling. *Atlanta Journal-Constitution,* March 15.
30. *TechDigest.* 2008. Average TV size up to 60-inch by 2015 says Sharp. *TechDigest,* January. *www.techdigest. tv/2008/01/average_tv_size.html.*
31. Motion Picture Association of America. 2007. *Entertainment Industry Market Statistics, 2007.*
32. *TechDigest.* 2008. Average TV size up to 60-inch.
33. National Association of Theater Owners. 2009. ShoWest 2010 Talking Points. *www.natoonline.org.*
34. Shuker, L. A. E., & Smith, E. 2010. Hollywood eyes shortcut to TV. *Wall Street Journal,* May 22.
35. *Business Wire.* 2009. Convenient entertainment; 7-Eleven rolls out Redbox $1 per night new release DVD rentals. *Business Wire.* January 5.
36. National Association of Theater Owners. 2010. Average Video Announcement and Video Release Windows.
37. Smith, E., & Schuker, L. A. E. 2010. Studios unlock DVD release dates. *Wall Street Journal,* February 12.
38. Ibid.
39. Ibid.
40. Vorse, M. H. 2002. Some picture show audiences (1911). In Waller, *Moviegoing in America,* pp. 50–53 .
41. Fuller, K. H. 2002. "You can have the strand in your own town": The struggle between urban and small-town exhibition in the picture palace era. In Waller, *Moviegoing in America,* pp. 88–98.
42. Woestendiek, J., & Kaltenbach, C. 2008. $10 is small price for a big escape: Movie box office figures are flourishing despite, or because of, economic worries. *Baltimore Sun,* July 8.
43. Ibid.
44. Motion Picture Association of America. 2007. *Entertainment Industry Market Statistics, 2007.*
45. Brodesser-Akner, C. 2008. What popcorn prices mean for movies; Ethanol and rising costs of paper eat into sales that subsidize tickets. *Advertising Age,* May 19.
46. Ibid.
47. Ibid.
48. Russell, J. 2009. Winning ticket? Cinemas hope high-end services pack 'em in. *Los Angeles Business Journal,* November 2.
49. Ruggless, R. 2009. Dinner and a movie: One hot ticket for operators. *Nation's Restaurant News,* 43(41).
50. Moore, M. T. 2009. Moving beyond movies. *USA Today,* February 9: 3A.
51. Motion Picture Association of America. 2009. *Theatrical Market Statistics, 2009.*
52. *The Economist.* 2010. The box office strikes back. *The Economist,* May 6.
53. Ibid.
54. Thakur, A. 2009. India dominates world of films. *Times of India,* July 29.
55. Ibid.
56. Wood, D. B., & Goodale, G. 2010. Want to see a 3D movie? Ticket prices go up 20 percent. *Christian Science Monitor,* March 26.
57. *Business Wire.* 2009. Fitch: High debt levels reduce flexibility for U.S. movie exhibitors in 2009. *Business Wire,* January 27.

	2009 Circulation				
Magazine	**Copies**	**Change from 2008**	**Revenue**	**Publisher**	**Comments**
Parenting	2,172,492	5.7%	$37.2M	Bonnier Corp.	Private. Swedish owned; also publishes *Field & Stream, Popular Science*.
Family Fun	2,157,829	17.4%	$28.5M	Disney Publishing Worldwide	Public. Targets families with children 12 and under: cooking, crafts, family activities.
Glamour	1,830,360	9.3%	$59.1M	Conde Nast Publications	Private. Also publishes *Vogue, GQ, The New Yorker*.
Birds & Blooms	1,726,023	15.5%	$34.8M	RDA	Private.
Every Day with Rachael Ray	1,429,275	4.2%	$48.3M	RDA	Private.
Country	1,235,534	5.2%	$23.6M	RDA	Private.
Reminisce	1,185,791	5.2%	NA	RDA	Private.
Women's Health	1,139,110	32.5%	$34.5M	Rodale	See above.
Family Handyman	1,106,457	0.4%	$27.5M	RDA	Private.

Note: In the list, *Better Homes & Gardens* through *Taste of Home* were among the 14 top-ranked U.S. magazines in 2009.

Source: From 2009 circulation data reported by Audit Bureau of Circulation (ABC), at *www.magazine.org/consumer_marketing/circ_trends/index.aspx*.

diversifying both products and geography . . . with a depth and breadth of content that is one of its biggest strengths. How to leverage that digitally is one of our first initiatives," she said.[10] Berner also believed that the addition of the Weekly Reader and Time Life product lines would provide more opportunities for growth, since now RDA would have "one of the largest music collections in the world."[11]

One of Berner's first acts was to restructure the company, reorganizing how the brands were marketed to consumers and advertisers by breaking them out of their corporate silos and grouping them by subject matter, such as food and entertaining. To aid in this, Berner recruited many of her former executives at Conde Nast/Fairchild Publications. Media observers commented that perhaps the new team was needed in order to market the brands more aggressively.[12] Commentators on publishing

industry mergers and acquisitions noted, "Companies that are valued the highest in the market are brands that are surrounded by multiple forms of media in good market positions that provide their readers and their advertisers with a comprehensive environment to interact."[13] Ripplewood's stated strategic approach was "to enhance the value of the businesses it acquires through a combination of strategic, operational, and financial actions."[14] However, at the time, analysts once again had cause to question RDA's long-term viability: "It's a fabulous brand, but its equity is eroding daily. . . . Reader's Digest could fade into history if they don't make drastic changes."[15]

CEO Berner had instituted several changes to the RDA lineup, including divesting businesses, reconfiguring the RDA web presence, redesigning the flagship magazine, continuing global expansion, and launching new magazines and other nonpublishing products. However, her program to "launch growth initiatives, reduce costs and transform the company culture" had not yet worked in the face of reduced consumer spending and a drop in magazine advertising worldwide.[16] The return to private status in 2007 was intended to give RDA breathing room out of the public eye, but the economic climate at the time was not favorable for many industries, publishing included. RDA's situation was not helped by the circumstances of its leveraged buyout: the Ripplewood deal had included the assumption of RDA's $776.3 million debt load, with a $1.31 billion term loan and $300 million of revolving credit, of which $206 million was still outstanding at the end of 2008.[17] In January 2009 Berner announced a plan to cut 280 employees worldwide, about 8 percent of its global workforce, leaving RDA with about 3,220 full-time employees. RDA would also ask U.S. workers to take unpaid leave in 2009 and 2010 and suspend its matching contributions to 401(k) retirement plans.[18] The hope was that this "recession plan" would allow RDA to meet the coming debt obligations, but it owed creditors $2.1 billion, and its interest payments alone in 2008 were over $160 million.[19]

This debt level became unsustainable in 2009, and RDA reached an agreement with its senior secured lenders to exchange a substantial portion of the company's $1.6 billion in senior secured debt for equity. This action paved the way for the Chapter 11 petition and subsequently reduced the company's total debt by 75 percent, from approximately $2.2 billion to $550 million.[20] RDA successfully emerged from Chapter 11 in February 2010 "with a significantly improved capital structure," $525 million in exit financing, access to an additional $50 of revolving credit, a B1 Corporate Family Rating from Moody's, and a B rating from Standard & Poor's. At that time CEO Berner said, "The new company is committed to maximizing value creation. . . . We expect that the industry and competitive environment will continue to be demanding, but we have the right team, the right model and relevant brands that engage today's consumer."[21]

Reader's Digest Association Business Mix

As of 2011, The Reader's Digest Association Inc. was a global multibrand media and marketing company that educated, entertained, and connected audiences around the world. The company used its editorial and content-delivery skills to serve multiple communities. With offices in 44 countries, it marketed books, magazines, music, videos, educational products, and other products, reaching 130 million households in 78 countries. It published 90 magazines, including 50 editions of *Reader's Digest,* the world's largest-circulation magazine; operated 83 branded websites; and sold approximately 40 million books and music and video products across the world yearly. *Reader's Digest,* the flagship magazine, reached more readers with household incomes over $100,000 than *Fortune, The Wall Street Journal, Bloomberg Businessweek,* and *Inc.*

combined.[22] In 2006 the Young & Rubicam Brand Asset Valuator study had named Reader's Digest as one of the strongest publishing brands in the United States.[23] As of 2011, total global circulation for all of RDA's magazines was approximately 34 million. Its global headquarters were in New York City.

In 2011 the company was organized around these primary business segments: *Reader's Digest United States* (formerly Reader's Digest North America), which included the *Reader's Digest,* and Lifestyle Communities (Food & Entertaining, Home & Garden, and Do-It-Yourself); *Reader's Digest International,* comprising RD Europe, RD Asia Pacific & Latin America, and RD Canada; and *Lifestyle & Entertainment Direct,* a global direct-marketing business selling an array of products, including Time Life products under license, primarily through DRTV. The company also includes the Weekly Reader Publishing Group. (See Exhibit 2). Although *Reader's Digest* magazine was the oldest and most recognizable product, many of the newer ventures maintained the vision and mission first articulated by founders DeWitt and Lila Wallace in 1922. There were total revenues of $1,714.0 million in 2010 produced from these affinity segments. (See Exhibit 3a and 3b).

At the end of 2010, revenue from these segments had yielded $1,714.0 million, down from $2,101.6 million in 2009, and was distributed as noted in Exhibit 3. The operating income, balance sheet, and cash flow numbers reflected the financial restructuring event. (See Exhibits 4–6.)

The History of Reader's Digest

DeWitt and Lila Wallace founded The Reader's Digest Association in 1921 to publish *Reader's Digest,* a magazine with condensed articles that were intended to provide lasting interest and enduring significance, to "inform, enrich, entertain, and inspire" its readers.[24] The first 5,000 copies were printed, and 1,599 were delivered to subscribers by mail. In 1929 *Reader's Digest* began selling at newsstands, and the circulation grew to 62,000. By 1935 circulation had passed the 1 million mark. By 1945 the magazine had editions circulated in 16 countries and by 1970 had expanded into 13 more.

As of 1955 RDA had also expanded into the worldwide publishing of condensed books, recorded music, and direct mail sweepstakes and accepted its first advertising, but it did not carry liquor ads until 1978 and never carried cigarette ads. In 1963 RDA founded QSP Inc., a school and youth-group fundraising organization. In 1985 RDA pioneered the use of computers in direct-mail marketing with the opening of a $15 million data center at its global headquarters in Pleasantville, New York, and in 1990 The Reader's Digest Association Inc. became a public company, trading on the New York Stock Exchange. In 1996 the *Reader's Digest* website was launched, and by 2000 the magazine was available in 13 countries in Eastern Europe.

Regarding the company's strategic direction, in 1997 the magazine was redesigned by moving the table of

Exhibit 2   **Business Segments**

Reader's Digest Community

Reader's Digest Community is the home of all Reader's Digest–branded businesses, including magazines, websites, digital newsletters, mobile applications, special-interest publications, books, music, and videos.

Brands	Available as			
	Print	Mobile	Web	E-commerce
Reader's Digest	X	X	X	X
Reader's Digest Large Print	X			
Reader's Digest Best You Website (Rework of *Best Health,* launched in 2009. Targets women 35 + with healthy lifestyle tips)			X	
Reader's Digest Select Editions (Books that each contain four novels, specially edited for quick reading. Formerly known as "condensed" books.)	X			

Lifestyle Communities

Lifestyle Communities is the multimedia provider of choice for food, entertaining, and home-and-garden communities.

Food & Entertaining Affinity

RDA is the largest food publisher in the United States, with magazine circulation of approximately 6.6 million, reaching an estimated 29 million readers.

Brands	Available as			
	Print	Mobile	Web	E-commerce
Allrecipes.com (For people to share recipes; leading social-networking food website in U.S.; versions in 22 other countries.)	X	X	X	X
Everyday with Rachael Ray (Launched in 2005; featuring the popular author & TV personality.)	X	X	X	X
Taste of Home (World's #1 food and entertaining magazine.)	X		X	X
Taste of Home Healthy Cooking (User-generated content; advice from doctors and nutritionists.)	X		X	X
Taste of Home Simple & Delicious (User-generated content; cooking & shopping tips.)	X		X	X

Home & Garden/Do-It-Yourself Affinity

Publishes leading magazines, sells home-and-garden–related bookazines, books, catalog merchandise, and travel tours; embraces a dual audience of hands-on consumers, both men and women, who enjoy the do-it-yourself lifestyle.

(*continued*)

Exhibit 2 **Business Segments** (*continued*)

Brands	Available as			
	Print	**Mobile**	**Web**	**E-commerce**
Birds & Blooms (#1 gardening and birding magazine in North America; 60% of content is reader generated.)	X		X	X
Country (Insider's view of rural North America; 60% of content is reader generated.)	X		X	X
Country Woman (Celebrates passion for home, family, community, cooking.)	X		X	X
The Family Handyman (Rated "most useful" publication in America.)	X	X	X	X
Farm & Ranch Living (How-to tips, stories from farmers & ranchers; 90% reader-generated content.)	X		X	X
FreshHOME (Design-it-yourself approach to decorating and lifestyle.)	X		X	
Reminisce (Celebrates America's stories with readers' own personal memories, photos, family recipes; 85% reader-generated content.)	X		X	X

Weekly Reader

Educational materials in digital and print formats. Inspires, informs, and engages students from preschool through high school. Weekly Reader's unique digital products and 11 classroom magazines reach more than 6 million students and have won well over 100 awards for educational excellence.

Brands	Available as			
	Print	**Mobile**	**Web**	**E-commerce**
Weekly Reader Magazine	X		X	

International Direct Marketing

Segments market products and services that address lifestyle needs across multiple communities, including health, cooking, gardening, travel, and hints and tips, among others.

Europe

Brands	Available as			
	Print	**Mobile**	**Web**	**E-commerce**
Reader's Digest Europe (In 22 countries, UK to Russia.)	X	X	X	X
Daheim in Deutschland (Beautiful sights & reader contributions from Germany.)	X		X	X
Das Beste (Catalogs; products for family, home, garden, health, & leisure.)	X		X	X

(*continued*)

Exhibit 2   **Business Segments** (*continued*)

Europe

Brands	Print	Mobile	Web	E-commerce
Meidan Suomi (#1 leisure magazine in Finland.)	X			
Mes Meilleures Recettes (Recipes contributed by French cooks; offers high-quality kitchen utensils.)	X		X	
Paprika (Recipes, kitchen tips, and ideas for Hungarian readers; complements the Hungarian TV show.)	X			
Polska Wita (For people seeking inspiration for short weekend trips and holidays in Poland.)	X		X	
Receptar (#1 do-it-yourself magazine in the Czech Republic.)	X		X	

Asia Pacific/Latin America

Brands	Print	Mobile	Web	E-commerce
Reader's Digest APLA (19 countries, Taiwan through India; Argentina through Mexico.)	X		X	X
Handyman (Australia's only true do-it-yourself magazine.)	X		X	X
HealthSmart (Health & lifestyle advice for Australians.)	X		X	X
MyShopToday (Online store in Australia, New Zealand, South Africa, & Asia; products include books, magazines, home entertainment, jewelry, & gifts. Customers can also enter Reader's Digest Sweepstakes. Launched in October 2010.)			X	X

Canada

Brands	Print	Mobile	Web	E-commerce
Reader's Digest Canada (In English & French.)	X		X	X
Best Health (For women; healthy-living tips.)	X		X	X
Our Canada (Canadians share interests and passions, pride in being Canadian; reader-generated content.)	X		X	X
Plaisirs Sante (French-language, online extension of Best Health.)			X	

(*continued*)

Exhibit 2   Business Segments (*continued*)

Lifestyle & Entertainment Direct

The Lifestyle & Entertainment Direct segment is a direct-marketing business that sells a diverse array of products, primarily through Direct Retail TV. Products include music compilations and video products sold under the Time Life brand, licensed from Time Warner Inc. and Time Inc., new music content released on the Saguaro Road label, as well as fitness and other products released as the Direct Entertainment Media Group.

Brands	Available as			
	Print	Mobile	Web	E-commerce
Direct Entertainment Media Group (Fitness and other products sold through infomercials, direct mail, Internet, and direct sales.)			X	X
Saguaro Road (Proprietary recording label, featuring gospel & bluegrass.)			X	X
Time Life (Books, music, and videos.)			X	X

Exhibit 3a   Reportable Segment and Product Results: Revenue (unaudited, in millions of U.S. dollars)

	Twelve Months Ended	
	12/31/2010*	12/31/2009 (Predecessor)
Branded Communities		
United States segment:		
Reader's Digest Community	$ 207.1	$ 259.5
Lifestyle Communities	432.0	434.0
Total United States segment	639.1	693.5
Other segment: Weekly Reader	26.2	30.5
Total branded communities	$ 665.3	$ 724.0
Direct Marketing		
Europe segment, excluding RDA UK	594.1	677.5
RDA UK (deconsolidated in 2010)**	13.3	109.7
Asia Pacific & Latin America segment	260.2	266.5
Canada segment	103.0	112.7
Lifestyle & Entertainment Direct segment	192.2	231.8
Total direct marketing	$ 1,162.8	$ 1,398.2
Total segment revenue	**$ 1,828.1**	**$ 2,122.2**
Intercompany eliminations	(5.8)	(8.5)
Fair-value adjustments	(108.3)	(12.1)
Total revenue	$ 1,714.0	$ 2,101.6

* 2010 numbers include the period between January 1 and February 19; thereafter, the company emerged from Chapter 11. 2009 is considered a "predecessor" to this event.

** RDA fully relinquished ownership of its operations in the United Kingdom to British private equity firm Better Capital in April 2010.

*** *Contribution margin* is defined as revenue less product, distribution, editorial, and marketing expenses, excluding fair-value adjustments and results from the deconsolidated UK operations.

Source: From RDA Q4 earnings press release, March 3, 2011.

Exhibit 3b **Summary of Revenue and Approximated Margins by Product: RDA Holding Co., without UK****
(in millions of U.S. dollars)

	Twelve Months Ended	
	12/31/2010*	12/31/2009 (Predecessor)
Revenue by Product		
Music and videos	$ 295	$ 347
Magazine advertising/circulation	699	745
Books	582	649
Nonpublished products & services	233	263
Total	$ 1,809	$ 2,004
Fair-value adjustments & UK	(95)	98
Reported revenue	$ 1,714	$ 2,102
Approximated Contribution Margins by Product***		
Music and videos	$ 81	$ 82
Magazine advertising/circulation	221	204
Books	136	152
Nonpublished products & services	$ 78	$ 88
Total	$ 516	$ 526

* 2010 numbers include the period between January 1 and February 19; thereafter, the company emerged from Chapter 11. 2009 is considered a "predecessor" to this event.

** RDA fully relinquished ownership of its operations in the United Kingdom to British private equity firm Better Capital in April 2010.

*** *Contribution margin* is defined as revenue less product, distribution, editorial, and marketing expenses, excluding fair-value adjustments and results from the deconsolidated UK operations.

Source: From RDA Q4 earnings press release, March 3, 2011.

contents inside, and new CEO Thomas Ryder redesigned the corporate structure to focus on five basic, growing consumer interests: home, health, family, finance, and faith. He sold some assets, including part of RDA's art collection and real estate holdings. Some warehouse jobs were also moved outside the company, and several hundred employees were laid off. Ryder also acquired Books Are Fun (BAF) Ltd. in 1999 to increase distribution channels for existing products and add new nonpublishing products.

In 2000 Ryder purchased Reiman Publications LLC for $760 million. Reiman's publications were almost wholly consumer-content driven, and included *Taste of Home,* one of the best-selling food magazines in North America. This acquisition helped RDA reduce reliance on sweepstakes magazine sales. In 2003 RDA launched ChangeOne, a web-based weight-loss program. RDA also reorganized once again into the three divisions of Reader's Digest North America, Reader's Digest International, and Consumer Business Services. In November 2004, RDA sold the original Reader's Digest Chappaqua property, including the Georgian mansion built by the Wallaces in 1939.

In 2005 RDA launched *Everyday with Rachael Ray,* featuring that popular author and TV personality. RDA also continued to expand its reach beyond publishing. They acquired AllRecipes.com, a food website intended to connect cooks across the United States. And they created *Taste of Home Entertaining,* an entertaining and party-planning business meant to extend the Taste of Home brand, which included the food magazine, cooking schools, and a best-selling cookbook. However, even with all the restructuring and expansion activity, RDA financials had not seen any appreciable change in revenue since 2002, and profits, especially from the Consumer Business Services (QSP and BAF), had continued to decline. In March 2007 RDA became a private company again after its acquisition by Ripplewood Holdings.

Exhibit 4 Operating Revenue, Income Statement (unaudited, in millions)

	12/31/2010*	12/31/2009 (Predecessor)	6/30/2008**	6/30/2007**
		Twelve Months Ended		
Revenue	**$1,714**	**$ 2,101.6**	**$2,786.4**	**$2,691.1**
Product, distribution and editorial expenses	751.5	914.2	1,223.4	1,245.1
Promotion, marketing and administrative expenses	929.2	1,044.5	1,568.2	1,544.0
Impairment of assets	42.8	1,050.0	307.2	—
Other operating items, net	55.3	14.3	25.0	49.0
Operating Loss	**(68.4)**	**(921.4)**	**(337.4)**	**(147.0)**
Interest expense	62.6	144.2	—	—
(Gain) loss on deconsolidation of subsidiary	47.3	—	—	—
Other (income) expense, net	7.3	13.8	169.1	160.1
Loss before reorganization items, income taxes, and discontinued operations	**(182)**	**(1,079.4)**	**—**	**—**
Reorganization items	(1,906.6)	58.2	—	—
(Loss) income before income taxes and discontinued operations	**(1,724.6)**	**(1,137.6)**	**(506.5)**	**(307.1)**
Income tax (benefit) expense	(5.4)	(55.7)	4.5	45.0
(Loss) income from continuing operations before discontinued operations	**1,730**	**(1,081.9)**	**(502.0)**	**(262.1)**
Income (loss) from discontinued operations, net of taxes	34	(43.1)	—	—
Net (loss) income	**$1,764**	**$(1,125.0)**	**$ (502.0)**	**$ (262.1)**

* 2010 numbers include the period between January 1 and February 19; thereafter, the company emerged from Chapter 11. 2009 is considered a "predecessor" to this event.

** Unaudited, after acquisition. Filing date changed in 2009 to December. Information is provided for comparison purposes only.

Source: From RDA company records.

Where to Go Next?

In 2007 new RDA CEO Mary Berner began by restructuring RDA once again, changing to the affinity-based focus in the United States (RD Community, Food & Entertaining, Home & Garden, and Do-It-Yourself), and clearly separating the international business from the United States activities. Berner also continued RDA's international expansion with the launch of *Health Smart* magazine in Australia and *Our Beautiful Poland* (*Nasza Piekna Polska*) in Poland (since transitioned to *Polska Wita*). In 2008 this expansion was continued: *Reader's Digest* magazine was launched in Turkey, the People's Republic of China, and Serbia, and *Best Health* was launched in Canada.

In 2008, in an attempt to reduce costs and streamline the product line, Berner sold the fundraising business QSP Inc. to subsidiaries of Time Inc. for a purchase price of $110 million, sold the home-party-planning business Taste of Home Entertaining, and sold the principal operating assets of display merchandiser Books Are Fun (BAF) to Imagine Nation Books for $16.8 billion. Then, in 2009, from the Weekly Reader Publishing Group, RDA sold off Gareth Stevens, the library publishing division, and World Almanac Education Library, the library wholesaling division. This ended Thomas Ryder's experiment in diversifying out of the publishing business, and it left the School & Educational Services business segment with only WRC

Exhibit 5 **Consolidated Balance Sheet** (unaudited, in millions)

	Twelve Months Ended	
	12/31/2010*	12/31/2009 (Predecessor)
Assets		
Current Assets:		
Cash and cash equivalents	$ 169.4	$ 297.4
Restricted cash	4.5	8.8
Accounts receivable, net	237.2	253.9
Inventories	62.5	89.4
Prepaid & deferred promotion costs	33.5	35.5
Prepaid expenses & other current assets	122.0	150.0
Assets held for sale	7.4	19.0
Total Current Assets	**$ 636.5**	**$ 854.0**
Property, plant, & equipment, net	63.7	59.4
Restricted cash	8.4	19.1
Goodwill	672.4	862.0
Other tangible assets, net	451.4	343.3
Prepaid pension assets	166.0	158.0
Other noncurrent assets	30.4	53.1
Total Assets	**$ 2,028.8**	**$ 2,348.9**
Liabilities & Stockholders' Equity (Deficit)		
Current Liabilities:		
Short-term debt	$ —	$ 255.3
Accounts payable	167.6	174.4
Accrued expenses	135.7	149.6
Income taxes payable	7.8	23.1
Unearned revenue	269.7	366.6
Other current liabilities	32.4	12.5
Liabilities held for sale	—	21.5
Total Current Liabilities	**$ 613.2**	**$ 1,003.0**
Long-term debt	510.7	—
Unearned revenue	9.3	146.3
Accrued pension	5.7	42.3
Postretirement & postemployment benefits other than pensions	12.9	16.0
Other noncurrent liabilities	199.4	185.7
Liabilities subject to compromise	—	2,673.6
Total Liabilities	**$ 1,436.2**	**$ 4,067.0**

(*continued*)

Exhibit 5   Consolidated Balance Sheet (unaudited, in millions) (*continued*)

	Twelve Months Ended	
	12/31/2010*	12/31/2009 (Predecessor)
Predecessor Company common stock	—	59.7
Paid-in capital, including warrants	597.6	671.3
Accumulated deficit	(29.6)	(2,305.9)
Accumulated other comprehensive income (loss)	24.6	(143.2)
Total Stockholders' Equity (Deficit)	**592.6**	**(1,718.1)**
Total Liabilities & Stockholders' Equity (Deficit)	**$ 2,028.8**	**$ 2,348.9**

* 2010 numbers include the period between January 1 and February 19; thereafter, the company emerged from Chapter 11. 2009 is considered a "predecessor" to this event.

Source: From RDA company records.

Exhibit 6   Consolidated Statement of Cash Flows (unaudited, in millions)

	Twelve Months Ended	
	12/31/2010*	12/31/2009 (Predecessor)
Cash flow from operating activities:		
Net (loss) income	$ 1,764.0	$ (1,125.0)
Adjustments to reconcile net (loss) income to operating cash flows:		
(Income) loss from discontinued operations	34.0	43.1
Depreciation & amortization	68.1	52.4
(Benefit) provision for deferred income taxes	(10.3)	(74.6)
Amortization of bond discount	1.4	—
Amortization of debt issuance costs	10.2	12.5
(Gain) loss on deconsolidation of subsidiary	47.3	—
Noncash loss in financing foreign exchange	6.3	—
Impairment of assets	42.8	1,050.0
Gain on settlement of prepetition liabilities	(1,765.1)	—
Loss on derivatives	—	19.4
Reevaluation of assets & liabilities in fresh-start accounting	(163.1)	—
Stock-based compensation expense	7.9	2.0
Net (gain) loss on sales of long-term assets	(1.0)	(2.1)
Changes in assets & liabilities, net of effects of dispositions:		
Restricted cash	14.8	(19.0)
Accounts receivable, net	3.7	40.9
		(*continued*)

	Twelve Months Ended	
	12/31/2010*	12/31/2009 (Predecessor)
Inventories	23.6	18.6
Prepaid & deferred promotion costs	(0.2)	4.2
Other assets	6.5	1.6
Unearned revenue	45.0	(43.5)
Income taxes	(17.7)	(12.0)
Accounts payable & accrued expenses	(115.6)	105.5
Other liabilities	1.6	(51.0)
Net change in cash due to continuing operating activities	**$ (63.8)**	**$ 23.0**
Net change in cash due to discontinued operating activities	0.4	1.8
Net change in cash due to operating activities	**$ (63.4)**	**$ 24.8**
Cash flows from investing activities:		
Capital expenditures	(24.1)	(10.2)
Purchase of intangible assets	(0.4)	(0.2)
Proceeds from sale of business	30.8	—
Proceeds from sales of assets	1.8	1.2
Loss of cash due to subsidiary deconsolidation	(16.5)	—
Proceeds from life insurance settlements	—	12.5
Proceeds from note receivables	7.5	9.3
Net change in cash due to continuing investing activities	**$ 7.8**	**$ 12.6**
Net change in cash due to discontinued investing activities	—	0.1
Net change in cash due to investing activities	**$ 7.8**	**$ 12.7**
Cash flows from financing activities:		
Proceeds from borrowings	509.3	89.9
Debt payments	(555.3)	(9.5)
Short-term borrowings, net	—	129.7
Cash paid for financing fees	(21.0)	(12.6)
Net change in cash due to financing activities	**$ (67.0)**	**$ 197.5**
Effect of exchange rate changes on cash & cash equivalents	3.3	(0.3)
Net change in cash & cash equivalents	128.0	234.7
Cash & cash equivalents at beginning of period	567.0	62.7
Cash & cash equivalents at end of period	**$ 439.0**	**$ 297.4**
Supplemental Information:		
Cash paid for interest	$ 44.4	$ 72.5
Cash paid for income taxes	$ 9.7	$ 3.7

* 2010 numbers include the period between January 1 and February 19; thereafter, the company emerged from Chapter 11. 2009 is considered a "predecessor" to this event.

Source: From RDA company records.

Media product lines *Weekly Reader* and *Compass Learning* (subsequently sold to Marlin Equity Partners in 2010).

The editorial philosophy of the Reiman publications, making extensive use of reader-generated content, was pushed to all the affinities, resulting in 85 percent of the Home & Entertaining, and 50 percent of the Home & Garden content being contributed by readers. RDA believed that, in addition to reducing editorial costs, utilizing a significant amount of reader-generated, community-oriented content created a bond with its customers, generating strong renewal rates, and was a unique differentiator in the print world as well as a popular trend in the online world.

Supporting the customer-centered approach, since RDA sold magazine subscriptions, books, music, and video products principally through direct mail, RDA had a policy where customers could return any book or home entertainment product for a full refund of the amount paid. RDA believed that this policy was essential to RDA's reputation and therefore generated a greater number of orders. Also appealing to readers, although most magazine publishers traditionally generated more than 50 percent of revenue from advertising, RDA advertising had historically represented a significantly smaller percentage of its total magazine revenue. For instance, approximately 92 percent of total international fiscal 2009 revenue for *Reader's Digest* was generated by circulation revenue (subscription, newsstand, and other retail sales) and only 8 percent by advertising revenue. This small amount of advertising reduced the "clutter" in the magazine. However, in a move to increase revenue in the publishing area, Berner decided to begin promoting and accepting advertising in Reiman magazines.

In 2008 Berner had redesigned the *Reader's Digest* magazine logo, layout, and website and initiated a redefinition of RDA's mission. The logo redesign was met by conflicting response from long-time readers: "old cover—comforting and familiar; new cover—cold and cluttered."[25] The original mission statement that had guided the company since its founding in 1921 was "We create products that inform, entertain and inspire people of all ages and cultures around the world." Berner's new mission was meant to focus the company around a "new RDA" that created "communities around branded content that can be consumed by customers when, where and how they want it." The mission read: "We are a global multi-brand and marketing company that educates, entertains and connects audiences around the world. We are dedicated to providing our customers with the inspiration, ideas and tools that *simplify* and *enrich* their lives." The new vision was to "create the world's largest multiplatform communities based on branded content."[26]

Berner also began developing a "global digital repository of all content, which will facilitate and expedite access to content and permit use of it across multiple platforms and channels."[27] In fiscal 2008 RDA saw "double digit growth in digital revenue driven by advertising and consumer transactions."[28] This underscored the necessity for continuing to increase web traffic to all RDA Internet locations. The commitment to interactive media was underscored by the creation of a position in early 2009, President, Global RDA Interactive, with responsibility for all of RDA's digital activities. This position was charged with leading RDA's "efforts to expand digital media and marketing globally, including e-commerce and other revenue-generating initiatives."[29] By the fall of 2009, this focus on "digital development" had soared, with allrecipes.com achieving the number 1 market position as the largest food website in the United States, and Taste of Home realizing a 61 percent growth for its website in the first quarter of 2009, compared to an average growth rate for magazine websites of 7.2 percent for the same time period, according to Nielsen.[30]

Also in 2009, RDA launched *Fresh Home* and *Best You* magazines, both reworked from RDA international magazines. RDA also embarked on an alliance with pastor Rick Warren, launching *Purpose Driven Connection.* These new ventures prompted one analyst to comment that, instead of launching new magazines into an uncertain economic environment, could RDA have "plowed these resources into paying its own debt"?[31] But others were cautiously positive, especially about the global appeal of Rick Warren's *Purpose Driven Connection* message. The product was conceived as a magazine plus a DVD and companion guide, a multimedia curriculum for the members of Evangelical small groups that could facilitate spiritual discussion. Alyce Alston, RDA president for the Health & Wellness affinity, which had responsibility for this launch, pointed out that "if we touched just 1% of Evangelicals in America, that's 900,000 members."[32] However, this new venture was short-lived. The magazine ceased print publication after only four issues. Severing his connection with RDA in late 2009, Pastor Warren said, "Our biggest discovery was learning that people prefer reading our content online rather than in print, because it is more convenient and accessible. . . . And, from our viewpoint, an online magazine allows us to minister to people internationally; provide more content and features than we could fit in a print magazine; create interaction and two-way dialogue; and offer it for free."[33]

This transition of Rick Warren's print magazine to a fully digital format was indicative of the direction of all print media in 2010. RDA was fully aware of this, and CEO Berner had established what seemed to be appropriate initiatives. After exiting Chapter 11, Berner said, "With the restructuring complete, RDA is focusing on driving top-line growth and transformation of its business through its affinity marketing model, which builds communities of like-minded consumers around its brands, reaching them in person, print, and online."[34]

The intent seemed to be to transform the company from a direct mail–driven business to a multichannel direct marketing–driven business. This was planned to happen by growing advertising revenue in most areas, both digital and print, and by accelerating the "global digital transformation." RDA was making a clear push toward "acquiring and selling to customers digitally" and had made a quiet but significant investment in the DRTV segment, especially the Direct Entertainment Media Group's launch of infomercial products like the AB Circle Pro in 2009. This fitness product, designed to "trim your entire core," appears to have been a success, affecting 1.5 million people worldwide.[35] In addition to the growth strategies, RDA planned to continue an "aggressive alignment" of cost of revenues, through reducing overhead, outsourcing, and eliminating businesses or product lines that have "limited upside".[36]

As its long history indicated, RDA had had its ups and downs. It appeared once again that *Reader's Digest,* the fixture of the American newsstand, might be facing an inevitable decline. The unfortunate timing of the private equity leveraged buyout might have finally created the ultimate risk factor. In the 2008 annual report, RDA had noted that "there can be no assurances that our businesses will generate sufficient cash flows from operations to fund our day-to-day operations, and, more importantly, our debt service obligations . . . a decline in our operating results or available cash could cause us to experience difficulties in complying with covenants contained in our financing agreements, which could result in our bankruptcy or liquidation."[37] And, in fact, this was what happened. Mary Berner had expressed optimism going into 2011, with her push toward growth through increased advertising, digital content, and infomercial marketing of products that had nothing to do with the old Reader's Digest. Was there anything she could do to truly resurrect this company?

Endnotes

1. Reader's Digest Association Inc. (RDA). 2011. RDA Holding Co. announces results for the fourth quarter and twelve months ended December 31, 2010. May 16. *phx.corporate-ir.net/phoenix.zhtml?c=71092&p=irol-irhome.*

2. According to RDA published 10K filings, the highest revenues came in 1995 and 1996.

3. Angeletti, N., & Oliva, A. 2004. *Magazines that make history.* Gainesville: University Press of Florida.

4. Horwitz, J. 2009. Reader's indigestion. *TheBigMoney. com,* March 23. *tbm.thebigmoney.com/articles/impressions/2009/03/20/readers-indigestion.*

5. Standard & Poor's. 2009. Reader's Digest Assn. Inc. rating cut to "CCC" from "B-"; Outlook negative, February 19; Moody's Investors Service. 2009. Moody's downgrades Reader's Digest's CFR and PDR to Caa3; Approximately $2.1 billion of debt affected, February 20; from the Reader's Digest 8K SEC filing of February 23, 2009.

6. RDA. 2009. Reader's Digest Association files for voluntary pre-arranged chapter 11 as part of previously announced restructuring plan; DA's non-U.S. operations are not part of filing; Company secures $150 million new money DIP financing facility that is convertible to exit financing upon emergence. RDA.com, August 24. *www.rda.com/investor-relations/press-releases.*

7. Kinsman, M. 2011. Consumer magazine circulation falls 1.2 percent in second half 2010; Newsstand sales drop more than 7 percent. *FolioMag,* February 7. *www.foliomag.com/2011/consumer-magazine-circulation-falls-1-2-percent-second-half-2010.*

8. RDA 2006 annual report.

9. Ali, R. 2006. Reader's Digest to be sold for $1.6 billion to private equity; Online still small but growing part. *Paid-Content.org,* November 16. *www.paidcontent.org/entry/readers-digest-sold-16-billion-to-private-equity-online-still-small-but-gro.*

10. Mediabistro.com. 2007. So what do you do, Mary Berner? Mediabistro.com, March 7. *www.mediabistro.com/articles/cache/a9542.asp.*

11. Kelly, K. J. 2007. Berner to help Digest. *New York Post,* March 3. *www.nypost.com/seven/03032007/business/berner_to_help_digest_business_keith_j__kelly.htm.*

12. Flamm, M. 2007. New chief lures Conde Nast allies as she plots overhaul of old-line publisher. *Crain's New York Business,* May 14: 3.

13. Steinmetz, M. 2007. M&A boomtown: How long will it last? *Publishing Executive,* February 1. *www.pubexec.com/story/story.bsp?sid=47357&var=story.*

14. Ripplewood Holdings announces. 2007. RDA, 2007. Ripplewood Holdings announces completion of historic transaction to acquire Reader's Digest Association; Mary Berner appointed President and CEO. March 2, 2007, http://phx.corporate-ir.net/phoenix.zhtml?c=71092&p=irol-newsArticle&ID=969809&highlight=

15. Flamm. 2007.

16. RDA economic "recession plan" to include job eliminations. 2009. January 28. RDA, 2009. RDA economic 'recession plan' to include job eliminations, January 28, 2009, http://phx.corporate-ir.net/phoenix.zhtml?c=71092&p=irol-newsArticle&ID=1254733&highlight=

17. Savitz, E. 2009. Reader's Digest: Bankruptcy candidate du jour. Barrons.com, March 4. *blogs.barrons.com/techtraderdaily/2009/03/04/readers-digest-bankruptcy-candidate-du-jour/.*

18. Ibid.

19. Horwitz. 2009.

20. RDA. 2009. Reader's Digest Association announces nearly 80 percent of secured lenders agree to support debt-for-equity restructuring plan. RDA.com, August 20. *www.rda.com/investor-relations/press-releases.*

21. RDA. 2010. Reader's Digest Association completes financial restructuring emerges as a stronger, more competitive global company; Poised to build on multi-platform affinity model of powerful brands; Announces new board of directors. February 22. *www.rda.com/investor-relations/press-releases.*

22. Statement available at *www.rda.com/our-brands/branded_communities.*

23. Reader's Digest 10K annual report, June 30, 2008: 27.

24. Information in this section is from: Reader's Digest website "timeline" at *www.rd.com;* Canning, P. 1996. *American dreamers: The Wallaces and Reader's Digest.* New York: Simon & Schuster; and *syracuseuniversitypress.syr.edu/encyclopedia/entries/readers-digest.html.*

25. *Brand New.* 2007. Reading that's hard to digest. *Brand New* blog, December 12. *www.underconsideration.com/brand-new/archives/reading_thats_hard_to_digest.php.*

26. RDA. 2009. Q2 fiscal 2009 update (Reader's Digest Association PowerPoint presentation). February 26.

27. Reader's Digest 10K annual report. 2008. June 30: 27.

28. Ibid.

29. RDA. 2009. Lara Bashkoff named president, Global RDA Interactive for the Reader's Digest Association, Inc. February2.phx.corporate-ir.net/phoenix.zhtml?c=71092&p=irol-newsArticle&ID=1254738&highlight=.

30. RDA. 2009. Reader's Digest Association announces new appointments for Lora Gier, Renee Jordan and Amber Dunn in the newly formed U.S. Affinities; New affinity will accelerate growth and efficiency across advertising sales and digital development areas. RDA. com, September 17. *www.rda.com/investor-relations/press-releases.*

31. Bissonnette, Z. 2009. Reader's Digest launches three new magazines. *Blogging Stocks,* March 3. *www.bloggingstocks.com/2009/03/03/readers-digest-launches-three-new-magazines/.*

32. Sullivan, A. 2009. Rick Warren's magazine: A publishing leap of faith. *Time,* March 10. *www.time.com/time/nation/article/0,8599,1884038,00.html.*

33. Warren, R. 2009. From message delivered by Rick Warren in late 2009 via the now-defunct web link legacy.rd.com/offer/purposedriven/index.html.

34. RDA. 2010. Reader's Digest Association completes financial restructuring.

35. Moulton Logistics. 2009. Moulton Logistics takes on Ab Circle, completes fast track direct-to-consumer market launch; With four weeks to mobilize, DEMG and Moulton Logistics partner on the Ab Circle program, shipping 300,000 units in 90 days. MoultonLogistics.com, September 9. *www.moultonlogistics.com/PR/090909.html.*

36. RDA. 2010. RDA Holding Co. 3rd quarter 2010 earnings call, for the three months ending 9/30/2010. Transcribed November 4, 2010, from *www.rda.com/investor-relations/company-reports.*

37. Reader's Digest 10K. 2008.

Case 18   One Ford

*The Shape of Ford Motor Company to Come?**

Going into 2011, Ford analysts were forecasting slow but steady growth, with sales "the best since Lehman Brothers went out of business in the second half of 2008."[1] Ford had already posted 2010 sales that made it the world's top-earning automaker.[2] This was good news indeed. In 2008 Ford had faced the most challenging times of its history. Low sales had been hurting the company for years, and macroeconomic issues such as a weak economy, volatile financial markets, and lack of liquidity in the market had added complications for the already troubled firm. Despite joining GM and Chrysler in 2009 to request emergency loans from Washington to avoid filing for bankruptcy, and therefore further disrupting the U.S. economy, Ford did not have to use its portion of the bailout. Instead, Ford would tap credit lines it had the foresight to establish before credit markets dried up in order to bolster its cash position. CEO Alan Mulally had been the one to convince the company to do this—Ford had avoided bankruptcy "because it borrowed $23 billion in late 2006, after Mulally arrived from Boeing Co. and before credit markets froze. The automaker put up all major assets, including the Ford logo, as collateral in what Mulally called 'the world's largest home-equity loan' to build a cash cushion to withstand losses while developing new models."[3] How had Mulally acquired the credibility to make this risky call?

In January 2009, the struggling automaker had posted a full-year net loss of $14.6 billion for 2008, the largest single-year loss in the company's history.[4] Attempts at restructuring Ford had been underway for years. Former CEO Jacques Nasser emphasized acquisitions to reshape Ford, but day-to-day business activities were ignored in the process. When Nasser left in October 2001, Bill Ford, great-grandson of company founder Henry Ford, took over and emphasized innovation as a core strategy to reshape Ford. In an attempt to stem the downward slide at Ford, and perhaps to jump-start a turnaround, Bill Ford had recruited Alan Mulally, who was elected as president and chief executive officer of Ford on September 5, 2006. Mulally, former head of commercial airplanes at Boeing, was expected to steer the struggling automaker out of the problems of falling market share and serious financial losses. Mulally emphasized his vision of "One Ford" to reshape the company and committed to remain "on track for both [Ford's] overall and North American Automotive pre-tax results to be breakeven or profitable in 2011."[5] But could Mulally do it? The answer, so far, appears to be yes (see Exhibit 1).

Why Did Ford Invite In an Outsider?

The Ford empire had been around for over a century, and the company had not gone outside its ranks for a top executive since hiring Ernest Breech away from General Motors Corporation in 1946 (see Exhibit 2).[6] Since taking the CEO position in 2001, Bill Ford had tried several times to find a qualified successor, "going after such industry luminaries as Renault-Nissan CEO Carlos Ghosn and DaimlerChrysler chairman Dieter Zetsche."[7] Now Mulally had been selected and was expected to accomplish "nothing less than undoing a strongly entrenched management system put into place by Henry Ford II almost 40 years ago"—a system of regional fiefdoms around the world that had sapped the company's ability to compete in today's global industry and one that Chairman Bill Ford couldn't or wouldn't unwind.[8]

It had become more common to hire a CEO from outside the family or board. According to Joseph Bower from Harvard Business School, around one-third of the time at S&P 500 firms, and around 40 percent of the time at companies that were struggling with problems in operations or financial distress, an outsider was appointed as CEO. The reason might be to get a fresh point of view or to get the support of the board. "Results suggest that forced turnover followed by outsider succession, on average, improves firm performance."[9] Bill Ford claimed that to undertake major changes in Ford's dysfunctional culture, an outsider was more qualified than even the most proficient auto industry insider.[10]

An outsider CEO might also help restore faith in Ford management among investors, who had been discontented with the Ford family's high dividends and extravagant lifestyle. The Ford family controlled about 40 percent of the company's voting shares through their ownership of all its class-B stock and holdings of common stock. The class-B family shares had almost the same market value as that of the common stock, but the voting rights of the family shares were exceptionally high by industry standards. The dividend stream had been an annuity, which over the years had enabled various family members to own a football team, fund museums and philanthropic causes, and even promote the Hare Krishna movement. Given that the company was experiencing serious financial problems, these activities had raised stockholder dissent, as the annual retained earnings in the past had been dissipated as dividends instead of reinvested in firm operations or acquisitions to increase the net value of the firm (see Exhibits 3 and 4).

* This case study was prepared by Professor Helaine J. Korn of Baruch College, City University of New York; Professor Naga Lakshmi Damaraju of the Indian School of Business; and Professor Alan B. Eisner of Pace University. The purpose of the case is to stimulate class discussion rather than to illustrate effective or ineffective handling of a business situation. Copyright © 2011 Alan B. Eisner.

Exhibit 1 **Ford Motor Company and Subsidiaries: Income Statements** (in millions, except per-share amounts; year-end December 31)

	2010	2009	2008	2007
Sales and revenues				
Automotive sales	$ 119,280	$ 103,868	$ 129,166	$ 154,379
Financial Services revenues	9,674	12,415	17,111	18,076
Total sales and revenues	128,954	116,283	146,277	172,455
Costs and expenses				
Automotive cost of sales	104,451	98,866	127,103	142,587
Selling, administrative and other expenses	11,909	13,029	21,430	21,169
Goodwill impairment	—	—	—	2,400
Interest expense	6,152	6,790	9,682	10,927
Financial Services provision for credit and insurance losses	(216)	1,030	1,874	668
Total costs and expenses	122,296	119,715	160,089	177,751
Automotive interest income and other non-operating income/(expense), net	(362)	5,284	(755)	1,161
Financial Services other income/(loss), net	315	552	—	—
Equity in net income/(loss) of affiliated companies	538	195	163	389
Income/(Loss) before income taxes	7,149	2,599	(14,404)	(3,746)
Provision for/(Benefit from) income taxes	592	(113)	63	(1,294)
Income/(Loss) before minority interests	—	—	(14,467)	(2,452)
Minority interests in net income/(loss) of subsidiaries	—	—	214	312
Income/(Loss) from continuing operations	6,557	2,712	(14,681)	(2,764)
Income/(Loss) from discontinued operations	—	5	9	41
Net Income/(loss)	6,557	2,717	$ (14,672)	$ (2,723)
Less: Income/(Loss) attributable to noncontrolling interests	(4)	5	—	—
Net Income/(loss) attributable to Ford Motor Company	6,561	2,717	—	—
Average number of shares of Common and Class-B Stock outstanding	3,449	2,992	2,273	1,979
Amounts per share of common and class-B stock				
Basic income/(loss)				
Income/(Loss) from continuing operations	$ 1.90	$ 0.91	$ (6.46)	$ (1.40)
Income/(Loss) from discontinued operations	—	—	—	0.02
Net income/(loss)	$ 1.90	$ 0.91	$ (6.46)	$ (1.38)

(*continued*)

	2010	2009	2008	2007
Diluted Income/(loss)				
Income/(Loss) from continuing operations	$ 1.66	$ 0.86	$ (6.46)	$ (1.40)
Income/(Loss) from discontinued operations	$ 1.66	$ 0.86	—	0.02
Net income/(loss)			$ (6.46)	$ (1.38)
Cash dividends	—	—	$ —	$ —

Source: Ford Motor Company 10K filings.

Exhibit 2 Ford Family Tree

Note: Family tree includes descendants of Henry Ford who worked at Ford Motor Co. and their children.

*Ford Family members who have worked at Ford Motor Co.

Source: Benson Ford Research Center; WSJ research.

Exhibit 3   **Ford Motor Company and Subsidiaries: Sector Balance Sheets** (in millions)

	December 31, 2010	December 31, 2009	December 31, 2008
Assets			
Automotive			
Cash and cash equivalents	$ 6,301	$ 9,762	$ 6,377
Marketable securities	14,207	15,169	9,296
Loaned securities	—	—	—
Total cash, marketable and loaned securities	20,508	24,931	15,673
Receivables, less allowances	3,992	3,378	3,464
Inventories	5,917	5,041	8,618
Deferred income taxes	359	479	302
Net investment in operating leases	1,282	2,208	
Other current assets	610	688	4,032
Current receivable from Financial Services	1,700	2,568	2,035
Total current assets	34,368	39,293	34,124
Equity in net assets of affiliated companies	2,441	2,246	1,069
Net property	23,027	22,455	28,352
Deferred income taxes	2,468	5,660	7,204
Goodwill and other net intangible assets	102	165	1,584
Assets of discontinued/held-for-sale operations	—	7,618	—
Other assets	2,019	1,681	1,512
Non-current receivable from Financial Services	181	—	—
Total Automotive assets	64,606	79,118	73,845
Financial Services			
Cash and cash equivalents	8,504	11,132	15,672
Marketable securities	6,759	6,864	8,607
Finance receivables, net	73,265	79,705	96,101
Net investment in operating leases	10,393	15,062	23,120
Retained interest in sold receivables	—	—	92
Equity in net assets of affiliated companies	128	121	523
Goodwill and other net intangible assets	—	—	9
Assets of discontinued/held-for-sale operations	—	—	198
Other assets	4,221	6,228	7,345
Total Financial Services assets	103,270	119,112	151,667
Intersector elimination	(2,083)	(3,224)	(2,535)
Total assets	$ 165,793	$ 195,006	$ 222,977

(*continued*)

	December 31, 2010	December 31, 2009	December 31, 2008
Liabilities and stockholders' equity Automotive			
Trade payables	$ 13,466	$ 11,607	$ 10,635
Other payables	1,544	1,458	2,167
Accrued liabilites and deferred revenue	17,065	18,138	32,395
Deferred income taxes	392	3,091	2,790
Debt payable within one year	2,049	1,638	1,191
Total current liabilities	34,516	35,932	49,178
Long-term debt	17,028	31,972	24,655
Other liabilities	23,016	23,132	24,815
Deferred income taxes	344	561	614
Liabilities of discontinued/held-for-sale operations	—	5,321	—
Total Automotive liabilities	74,904	96,918	99,262
Financial Services			
Payables	1,352	1,236	1,970
Debt	85,112	98,671	128,842
Deferred income taxes	1,505	1,735	3,280
Other liabilities and deferred income	3,764	4,884	6,184
Liabilities of discontinued/held-for-sale operations	—	—	55
Payable to Automotive	1,881	2,568	2,035
Total Financial Services liabilities	93,614	109,094	142,366
Minority interests	—	—	1,195
Intersector elimination	(2,083)	(3,224)	—
Total Liabilities	166,453	202,788	—
Stockholders' equity			
Capital stock			
Common Stock, par value $0.01 per share (2,341 million shares issued of 6 billion authorized)	—	—	23
Class-B Stock, par value $0.01 per share (71 million shares issued of 530 million authorized)	1	1	1
Capital in excess of par value of stock	20,803	16,786	9,076
Accumulated other comprehensive income/(loss)	(14,313)	(10,864)	(10,085)
Treasury stock	(163)	(177)	(181)
Retained earnings/(Accumulated deficit)	(7,038)	(13,599)	(16,145)
Total equity/(deficit) attributable to Ford Motor Company	(673)	(7,820)	(17,311)
Equity/(Deficit) attributable to noncontrolling interests	31	38	—
Total equity/(Deficit)	(642)	(7,782)	—
Intersector elimination	—	—	(2,535)
Total liabilities and stockholders' equity	$ 165,793	$ 195,006	$ 222,977

Source: Ford Motor Company 10K filings.

Exhibit 4 **Ford Motor Company and Subsidiaries: Sector Statements of Cash Flows** (in millions, year-end December 31)

	2010		2009		2008	
	Automotive	**Financial Services**	**Automotive**	**Financial Services**	**Automotive**	**Financial Services**
Cash flows from operating activities of continuing operations						
Net cash flows from operating activities	$ 6,363	$ 3,798	$ 2,874	$ 5,805	$ (12,440)	$ 9,107
Cash flows from investing activities of continuing operations						
Capital expenditures	(4,066)	(26)	(4,043)	(16)	(6,620)	(76)
Acquisitions of retail and other finance receivables and operating leases	—	(28,811)	—	(26,392)	—	(44,562)
Collections of retail and other finance receivables and operating leases	—	37,757	—	40,013	—	42,479
Net (increase)/decrease in wholesale receivables	—	(46)	—	5,542	—	2,736
Purchases of securities	(53,614)	(46,782)	(52,293)	(27,555)	(41,347)	(23,831)
Sales and maturities of securities	54,857	46,866	6,420	28,326	43,617	18,429
Settlements of derivatives	(196)	159	(76)	554	1,157	1,376
Proceeds from sales of retail and other finance receivables and operating leases	—	—	—	911	—	—
Proceeds from sale of businesses	1,318	—	8	374	3,156	3,698
Cash paid for acquisitions	—	—	—	—	(13)	—
Transfer of cash balances upon disposition of discontinued/held-for-sale operations	(456)	—	—	—	(928)	—
Receipt of cash from purchase of Bordeaux	94	—	—	—	—	—
Cash change due to deconsolidation of joint ventures	—	—	(343)	—	—	—
Investing activity to/from Financial Services	2,455	—	76	—	9	—
Other	185	85	(707)	321	40	276
Net cash (used in)/Provided by investing activities	577	9,256	(10,958)	22,078	(929)	525

(*continued*)

Exhibit 4 Ford Motor Company and Subsidiaries: Sector Statements of Cash Flows (in millions, year-end December 31) (*continued*)

	2010		2009		2008	
	Automotive	**Financial Services**	**Automotive**	**Financial Services**	**Automotive**	**Financial Services**
Cash flows from financing activities of continuing operations						
Sales of Common Stock	1,339	—	2,450	—	756	—
Purchases of Common Stock	—	—	—	—	—	—
Changes in short-term debt	391	(2,145)	281	(6,162)	104	(5,224)
Proceeds from issuance of other debt	2,648	28,173	14,730	31,263	203	41,960
Principal payments on other debt	(9,144)	(38,935)	(2,941)	(56,508)	(594)	(45,281)
Financing activity to/from Automotive	—	(2,455)	—	(76)	—	(9)
Other	292	(192)	(395)	(601)	(252)	(352)
Net cash (used in)/provided by financing activities	(10,476)	(15,554)	11,551	(32,084)	217	(8,906)
Effect of exchange rate changes on cash	75	(128)	163	291	(309)	(499)
Net change in intersector receivables/payables and other liabilities	—	—	—	(630)	(840)	840
Net increase/(decrease) in cash and cash equivalents	$ (3,461)	$ (2,628)	$ 3,630	$ (4,540)	(14,301)	1,067
Cash and cash equivalents at January 1	$ 9,762	$11,132	$ 6,132	$ 15,672	$ 20,678	$ 14,605
Net increase/(decrease) in cash and cash equivalents	(3,461)	(2,628)	3,630	(4,540)	(14,301)	1,067
Cash and cash equivalents at December 31	$ 6,301	$ 8,504	$ 9,762	$ 11,132	$ 6,377	$ 15,672

Source: Ford Motor Company 10K filings.

Mulally—The Savior

Alan Mulally came from a metal-bending business that, like automaking, was influenced by global competition, had a unionized workforce, and was subject to complex regulations and rapidly changing technologies.[11] Although he was not an auto guy, he had a proven record in an industry that faced issues similar to those faced by the automobile industry, and a lot of his expertise and management techniques were highly transferable. In his own words,

"Everybody says, well, I'm not a car guy, so you couldn't make a contribution here. But I'm a product (guy) and I'm a designer."[12]

Prior to joining Ford, Mulally served as executive vice president of the Boeing Company and as president and chief executive officer of Boeing Commercial Airplanes. In those roles, he was responsible for all the Boeing Company's commercial airplane programs and related services.[13] The advanced 777 aircraft, which Mulally led the development of in the early 1990s, became the most popular twin-engine jet in its class and was a testimony to Mulally's product and technology ingenuity. Under his leadership, Boeing regained its market leadership from its major European competitor, Airbus. The appointment of Mulally at Ford was seen by the market as a move to utilize his experience and success in managing manufacturing and assembly lines to help shape the future of Ford.

Bill Ford praised Mulally as "an outstanding leader and a man of great character." He noted that Mulally appeared to have applied many of the lessons from Ford's success in developing the Taurus to Boeing's creation of the revolutionary Boeing 777 airliner. "Clearly, the challenges Boeing faced in recent years have many parallels to our own," said Bill Ford about Mulally's appropriateness for the top position at Ford. In his e-mail to Ford employees announcing the appointment of Mulally, Bill Ford wrote, "Alan has deep experience in customer satisfaction, manufacturing, supplier relations and labor relations, all of which have applications to the challenges of Ford. He also has the personality and team-building skills that will help guide our Company in the right direction."[14]

Nonetheless, when Mulally took over the steering wheel, Ford was already poised to make significant structural changes as the company announced details of its accelerated "Way Forward" plan. Moreover, the company seemed to indicate that Mulally's appointment would not change the timelines and decisions associated with the restructuring actions, according to analyst Himanshu Patel of J. P. Morgan. This indicated that, in spite of the appointment of Mulally as CEO, much of the decision making still remained with Bill Ford, who said he would remain "extremely active" in the business.

What Changes Did Mulally Make?

In his effort to point Ford in the right direction, Mulally flew to Japan in January 2007 to meet with top executives of Ford's toughest competitor, Toyota, to seek their advice.[15] This was a huge break from the Ford tradition, and only an outsider CEO would have had the courage and imagination to openly try to learn from foreign competitors.

Mulally had set his own priorities for fixing Ford: "At the top of the list, I would put dealing with reality." The newly elected CEO signaled that "the bigger-is-better worldview that has defined Ford for decades was being replaced with a new approach: Less is More."[16] Ford needed to pay more attention to cutting costs and transforming the way it did business than to traditional measurements such as market share.[17] The vision was to have a smaller and more profitable Ford.

Mulally's cutback plan built on the 14 plant closures and 30,000-plus job cuts announced by Ford in January 2007. Ford's new plan added two more North American plants to the closure list and exceeded the targeted $5 billion in cost cuts by the end of 2008,[18] but it pushed back a target for North American profitability by one year to

2009 and then again to 2011.[19] The company targeted seven vehicle manufacturing sites for closure. At the same time, it also planned to increase the plant utilization and production levels in each production unit, while focusing more on smaller, more fuel-efficient vehicles. The overall strategy was to use restructuring as a tool to obtain operating profitability at lower volume and create a mix of products that better appealed to the market.

By 2011, Ford had closed or sold a quarter of its plants and cut its global workforce by more than a third. It also slashed labor and health-care costs, plowing the money back into the design of some well-received new products, like the Ford Fusion sedan and Ford Edge crossover. This put Ford in a better position to compete when General Motors and Chrysler filed for bankruptcy in 2009 and Toyota announced a major recall of its vehicles for "unintended acceleration" problems.[20] Ford's sales grew at double the rate of the rest of the industry in 2010, but entering 2011 its rivals' problems seemed to be in the rearview mirror, and General Motors, especially, was on the rebound.

Mulally had also refocused the company on the Ford brand when he announced a formal review of Volvo in July 2007 as the first step to putting the division up for sale. Volvo had been acquired eight years earlier to be part of the Premier Automotive Group of Ford, along with Jaguar, Aston Martin, and Land Rover.[21] However, Volvo's primary selling point of superior safety had been challenged as other manufacturers made advances in safety technologies in their own brands. Ford was also reviewing bids for Jaguar and Land Rover, both of which had lost money in four out of the five previous years. Mulally said that the "real opportunity going forward is to integrate and leverage our Ford assets around the world" and decide on the best mix of brands in the company's portfolio.[22]

The "best mix of brands" appeared to have been established going into 2011. Ford had sold Jaguar and Land Rover to Tata Motors of India in 2008, Aston Martin having been sold to a British private equity group in 2007. Volvo was sold to Chinese manufacturer Geely Automotive in August 2010, and Ford discontinued the Mercury brand at the end of 2010. Ford also had had an equity interest in Mazda Motor Corporation, which it reduced substantially in 2010, retaining only a 3.5 percent share of ownership. This left the company with only the Ford and Lincoln brands, but the Lincoln offerings had struggled against Cadillac and other rivals for the luxury car market. Mulally acknowledged that this needed fixing, and forecasted a date of 2013 for real changes in the Lincoln lineup.[23]

Since his appointment, Mulally had made some additional structural and procedural changes in the company. For instance, instead of discussing business plans monthly or semiannually as they used to do at Ford, executives now met with Mulally weekly. The in-depth sessions were a contrast to executives' previous efforts to explain away bad news, said Donat R. Leclair, Ford's chief financial officer.

"The difference I see now is that we're actually committed to hitting the numbers. Before, it was a culture of trying to explain why we were off the plan. The more eloquently you could explain why you were off the plan, the more easy it was to change the plan."[24]

Mulally also did some senior executive reorganization at Ford, and many of the newly appointed executives reported to him directly, including a global head of product development. In addition, the head of worldwide purchasing, the chief of quality and advanced manufacturing, the head of information technology, the chief technical officer, and the leaders of Ford's European division, its Asia, Pacific, and Africa units, and its Americas unit all reported directly to him.[25]

A Shift toward Smaller and More Fuel-Efficient Cars?

The global economic downturn and financial crisis had a significant impact on global sales volumes in the auto industry, which had declined by over 30 percent going into 2009.[26] It was possible that the once-profitable business of manufacturing and selling trucks and SUVs had changed. Oil prices had been persistently increasing over the last few years. This had caused a shift in consumer's car-buying habits, reducing the demand for large vehicles. And that was not all: The diminished demand for SUVs resulted in a situation in which leased cars returned at the end of the lease period were being sold for much less than their residual values. Adjusting these residual values to their fair values contributed to the losses.[27] Brenda Hines, spokeswoman for Ford Credit, said that "about 85 percent of the impaired vehicles were trucks and SUVs."[28]

However, by 2011 the new car and light truck market was headed for double-digit gains. Paul Taylor, chief economist of the National Automobile Dealers Association, believed that this increase was due to several factors—increased choices from manufacturers, with many of these being hybrid or electric vehicles; higher gas prices increasing demand for these fuel-efficient models; available credit at historically low interest rates; and a rising stock market that would boost luxury car sales.[29] In addition, truck sales were forecast to increase in 2011 because

"new U.S. tax laws allowed for businesses to get tax breaks on capital purchases for trucks like the Ford F-series."[30] See Exhibit 5 for vehicle sales figures in the U.S. market.

The core strategy at Ford centered around a change in products, shifting to smaller and more fuel-efficient cars. Ford would import European-made small vehicles, the European Focus and Fiesta, into North America. It also planned to convert three truck-manufacturing plants to small-car production.[31] The Ford and Lincoln lines would be upgraded, emphasizing fuel-economy improvement and the introduction of hybrid cars. By the end of 2010, two-thirds of spending would be on cars and crossovers—up from one-half in 2009.[32] In all, in 2010 Ford had launched 24 new or redesigned Ford or Lincoln vehicles in markets around the world.

In 2009 the first applications of Ford's EcoBoost engines were introduced. EcoBoost used direct-injection technology for up to 20 percent better fuel economy, up to 15 percent fewer CO_2 emissions, and superior driving performance. The goal was to offer this engine on more than 90 percent of the North American–manufactured cars by the end of 2012.[33] And in 2011 Ford planned to launch the Focus Electric vehicle in North America, with the crossover C-Max Energi plug-in vehicle and the C-Max Hybrid coming in 2012.

Globalizing the Ford Brand

In the auto industry it was common practice that different regions cooperated, and companies basically sold the same cars around the world. This was not the case at Ford. Since it had set up its European operations, Ford Europe and Ford North America had gone separate ways. Moreover, due to Ford Europe's relative success while Ford North America was faltering, Ford Europe was reluctant to cooperate with changes that would bring the two into greater alignment. Nonetheless, Mulally was committed to making this happen.[34]

Under the One Ford vision, Mulally intended to globalize the Ford brand, meaning that all Ford vehicles competing in global segments would be the same in North America, Europe, and Asia.[35] The company was looking for a reduction of complexity, and thus costs, in the purchasing and manufacturing processes. The idea was to

Exhibit 5 Vehicle Sales by Segment, Comparison 2011–2009

	February 2011	February 2010	% Change from February 2010	January 2009	% Change from January 2008
Passenger cars	490,994	398,818	+23.1%	315,863	−36.3%
Light-duty trucks	502,393	381,447	+31.7%	341,113	−37.8%
Total light vehicles	993,387	780,265	+27.3%	656,976	

Source: MotorIntelligence.com.

deliver more vehicles worldwide from fewer platforms and to maximize the use of common parts and systems. Ford was uniquely positioned to take advantage of its scale, global products, and brand to respond to the changing marketplace.[36] "We grew up regionally, Toyota grew up globally, essentially, and so we are going to try to use the best of those worlds going forward,"[37] said Mulally.

About the Ford Motor Company

Ford Motor had been struggling ever since 1999, when profits had reached a remarkable $7.2 billion ($5.86 per share) and pretax income was $11 billion. At that time people even speculated that Ford would soon overtake General Motors as the world's number-one automobile manufacturer.[38] But soon Toyota, through its innovative technology, management philosophy of continuous improvement, and cost arbitrage due to its presence in multiple geographic locations, overtook the giants—GM and Ford. Compounding this were Ford's internal organizational problems and a failed diversification strategy led by Jacques Nasser, the CEO at that time. Ford's market share began to drop—from 25 percent in 1999 to 15.5 percent in 2011,[39] with major blows to market share in the light-vehicle segment. However, market share had risen in 2009 and 2010, the first consecutive gains since 1992 to 1993, and in 2010, going into 2011, Ford had claimed the second spot in the U.S. market, just behind GM and ahead of Toyota (see Exhibits 6 and 7).

As further evidence of struggle, Ford's stock prices had decreased significantly over the last decade. While the stock traded at close to $60 in February 1999, prices in 2008 dropped as low as $1.43. Although they had rebounded to reach $18.70 during 2010, the financial results for 2010's fourth quarter disappointed investors, and the stock fell more than 13 percent to $16.27 in January 2011. Mulally admitted he could have done a better job communicating with the stockholders. Even though Ford had reported the long-awaited profit in 2010, investors were not expecting the 80 percent drop in the fourth quarter, which was explained as due to an unexpected loss in Europe and a necessary adjustment to fund the launch of new products like the Ford Focus and Explorer sport-utility vehicle.[40]

In 2006 Chevrolet had outsold Ford for the first time since 1986 in the sport-utility vehicle market. At that time, despite an extensive mechanical update, the much-improved Ford Explorer, which had been the world's best-selling sport-utility vehicle, fell behind the dated Chevy TrailBlazer in sales. It did not help that the new Explorer looked just like the model it replaced. The long-neglected Ford Ranger, which had been the top-selling small pickup,

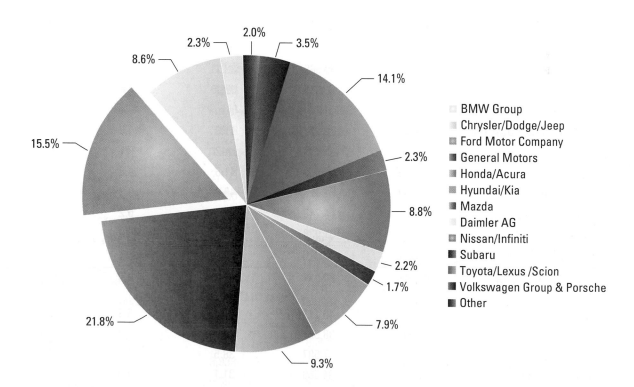

Exhibit 6 **U.S. Market Share by Brand, January 2011**

Source: www.goodcarbadcar.net/2011/02/new-vehicle-market-share-by-brand-in_02.html.

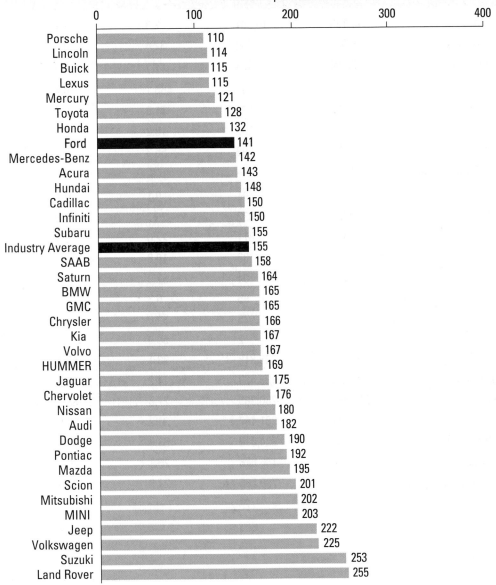

J.D. Power and Associates
2010 Vehicle Dependability Study[SM] **(VDS)**

2010 Nameplate Ranking

Problems per 100 Vehicles

Nameplate	Value
Porsche	110
Lincoln	114
Buick	115
Lexus	115
Mercury	121
Toyota	128
Honda	132
Ford	141
Mercedes-Benz	142
Acura	143
Hundai	148
Cadillac	150
Infiniti	150
Subaru	155
Industry Average	155
SAAB	158
Saturn	164
BMW	165
GMC	165
Chrysler	166
Kia	167
Volvo	167
HUMMER	169
Jaguar	175
Chervolet	176
Nissan	180
Audi	182
Dodge	190
Pontiac	192
Mazda	195
Scion	201
Mitsubishi	202
MINI	203
Jeep	222
Volkswagen	225
Suzuki	253
Land Rover	255

Exhibit 8 Vehicle Dependability Rankings, 2010

Note: Isuzu is included in the study but not ranked due to small sample size.

Source: J.D. Power and Associates. 2010. 2010 Vehicle Dependability Study. *www.jdpower.com/news/pressrelease.aspx?ID=2010034.*

Exhibit 9   **Best-Selling Cars in America, 2010**

Vehicle Rank	2010 Sales*	Change vs. 2009	MSRP	Fuel Economy	Comments
1. Ford F-150	38,541	+21.1%	$22,415 to $51,140	N/A	"Sweeping changes" will make more efficient engines available going into 2011.
2. Chevy Silverado	25,619	+11.1%	$20,850 to $41,775	20 mpg Hwy/15 mpg City	"Works hard to live up to its reputation as the 'strongest, most dependable and longest lasting truck on the road.'"
3. Toyota Camry	20,737	−27.4%	$19,720 to $29,370	33 mpg Hwy/22 mpg City	Although under recall for sticky accelerator pedals, "continues its reputation of safety, reliability, space, and power."
4. Nissan Altima	18,372	+13.7%	$19,900 to $30,100	32 mpg Hwy/23 mpg City	"Combines performance and an attractive exterior."
5. Honda CR-V	18,263	+25.4%	$21,695 to $27,895	28 mpg Hwy/21 mpg City	"Compact crossover SUV that delivers a balance of style, versatility, and comfort, along with a high level of safety technology."
6. Dodge Ram 1500	18,206	+78.3%	$20,610 to $41,585	20 mpg Hwy/14 mpg City	"Big power from a choice of engines, making it ideal for work and play."
7. Ford Fusion	18,412	+22.8%	$19,720 to $28,645	29 mpg Hwy/22 mpg City	"Attractive and purposeful . . . Has something for everyone . . . Top choice among midsize sedans."
8. Honda Accord	16,795	−3.9%	$21,180 to $29,730	33 mpg Hwy/23 mpg City	Honda's largest car. Has enhanced safety features.
9. Honda Civic	16,562	+16.3%	$15,605 to $25,490	34 mpg Hwy/26 mpg City	"One of the most reliable and popular economy compact cars in its class. For years it has set the standard for quality and performance."
10. Toyota Corolla	16,202	−29.1%	$15,450 to $18,960	35 mpg Hwy/26 mpg City	Although under recall for sticky accelerator pedals, "among the best of the compact sedans: reliable and economical yet refined and comfortable."
11. Chevrolet Equinox	15,387	+53.8%	$22,615 to $29,970	32 mpg Hwy/22 mpg City	"Competitively priced mid-sized SUV that offers exceptional versatility, distinctive design and high efficiency."

(*continued*)

Exhibit 9   Best-Selling Cars in America, 2010 (*continued*)

Vehicle Rank	2010 Sales*	Change vs. 2009	MSRP	Fuel Economy	Comments
12. Ford Escape	14,937	−5.5%	$21,060 to $27,380	28 mpg Hwy/23 mpg City	"Impressive list of features. A mid-size sport-utility vehicle with credentials that make it equally suited to urban commutes or weekend off-road outings."
13. Chevrolet Impala	14,693	+13.8%	$24,390 to $29,930	29 mpg Hwy/18 mpg City	"Comfortable and convenient full-size front-wheel drive sedan, practical and enjoyable to drive."
14. Hyundai Sonata	14,031	+64.4%	$19,195 to $27,045	35 mpg Hwy/24 mpg City	"All new sedan that has an established reputation for being well built and excellent value for the money."
15. Ford Focus	13,030	+22.5%	$16,640 to $19,670	35 mpg Hwy/25 mpg City	"Small, economical, and fun compact car. Features an available SYNC system that allows the driver to synchronize mobile electronic devices such as mp3 players and cell phones."

Source: AOL Autos. *autos.aol.com/gallery/best-selling-cars/*.

*Sales figures are from one month's sales. All models are reported as of November 2010 except the Ford F-150, which is from June 2010.

convincing consumers to believe in their quality is equally as important," said David Sargent, vice president of global vehicle research at J.D. Power and Associates. "It takes considerable time to positively change consumer perceptions of quality and dependability—sometimes a decade or more—so it is vital for manufacturers to continually improve quality and also to convince consumers of these gains."[42]

The company had also experienced serious financial problems. Ford's turnaround plan aimed to cut $5 billion in costs by the end of 2008 by slashing 10,000 white-collar workers and offering buyouts to all of its 75,000 unionized employees. The loss, including restructuring costs, was Ford's largest quarterly loss since the first quarter of 1992, when the company lost $6.7 billion due mainly to accounting changes. "Ford and the entire auto industry faced an extraordinary slowdown in all major global markets in the fourth quarter that clearly had an impact on our results,"[43] commented Mulally in 2008.

However, going into 2011, Mulally appeared to have reached his goal, the highest net income in more than 10 years. As he said, "Our 2010 results exceeded our expectations, accelerating our transition from fixing the business fundamentals to delivering profitable growth for all. We are investing in an unprecedented amount of products, technology and growth in all regions of the world."[44]

Automobile Industry in the United States

The automotive industry in the United States was a highly competitive, cyclical business. The number of cars and trucks sold to retail buyers, or "industry demand," varied substantially from year to year depending on "general economic situations, the cost of purchasing and operating cars and trucks, the availability of credit and fuel." Because cars and trucks were durable items, consumers could wait to replace them, and the length of new vehicle ownership had been increasing an average of 3.7 percent annually prior to the economic and auto industry meltdown in late 2008, and since then had climbed more than 14 percent by mid-2010, with "no signs of slowing down."[45]

Competition in the United States had intensified since the 1980s, when Japanese carmakers began gaining a foothold in the market. To counter the problem of being viewed as foreign, Japanese companies had set up production facilities in the United States and thus gained acceptance from American consumers. Production quality and lean production were judged to be the major weapons that Japanese carmakers used to gain an advantage over American carmakers. "The Toyota Motor Company of Japan issued a 2007 forecast that would make it first in global sales, ahead of General Motors, which has been the world's biggest auto company since 1931."[46] For American consumers, Toyota vehicles had been "a better value proposition" than Detroit's products, said Mulally, who was the first Detroit leader who readily said he was an avid student of Toyota.[47] However, even Toyota's sales were hurt by the weakened economy, and the Japanese carmaker had cut its annual profit forecast by half in November 2008.[48] Toyota's sales further suffered after the string of "unintended acceleration" events in 2009 forced a recall of nearly 2.2 million of its vehicles.

While there was a glut in the U.S. automobile market, the markets of Asia, Central and South America, and Central and Eastern Europe all showed increasing promise for automobiles, and the automobile industry entered into an era of "global motorization."

Challenges Mulally Faced

Mulally had been faced with a lot of challenges. He had considerable experience dealing with manufacturing and labor relations issues, but he did not have much background in finance. Given the cash drain at Ford due to restructuring costs and product development, and the B+ junk credit rating of Ford bonds, cash was crucial to keep the company afloat, and Mulally's abilities would continue to be tested.[49]

Mulally's fearlessness was well suited to pushing through projects at Boeing, but its suitability to Ford's culture remained to be seen. Like every new leader, he had to move with confidence in his early days, but as an industry outsider, he would have to take care to avoid violating long-standing industry norms.[50] Regarding his approach to culture change, one observer noted, "Mulally's approach to management and communication hasn't been seen before in the halls of Ford, which have historically been the atmosphere of a kingdom with competing dukes."[51] Mulally encountered conflict between his management style and the old "Ford way," but this didn't deter him from making changes.

One significant thing Mulally did was to break down the global structure in which Ford Europe, Ford Asia, Ford North America, Ford Australia, and Ford South America had long created redundancies of efforts, products, engineering platforms, engines, and the like as a way of perpetuating each division's independence.[52] The geographical segments were reconfigured into Ford North America, Latin America (including Mexico), Europe, and Asia/Pacific/Africa. In 2010 Mulally further consolidated top leadership to cover the major operations—the Americas, Europe, Asia/Pacific/Africa—and appointed leaders for global manufacturing and labor, and for global marketing sales and service.

However, these restructuring events also had their drawbacks. Unable to accept the Mulally management approach, some senior executives left Ford. The international chief of the company, Mark A. Schulz, was one of them. "He had decided to retire after working for more than three decades at the company. Mr. Schulz was just one of a string of senior executives to leave after Mulally took over. Ford's second-ranking North American executive, its North American manufacturing chief and its chief of staff also all announced their departures after Mulally's hiring."[53] Ford had lost some of its most experienced leaders because of the outsider CEO.

Another potentially serious clash could still occur with the United Auto Workers union, which was due to negotiate a new contract with Ford in late 2011.

Ford's U.S. factory workers had turned down a 2009 agreement that would have frozen entry-level wages and limited their ability to strike. With an eye on Ford's newly healthy profits, during upcoming contract negotiations, workers also might demand that the company give back some of the wage cuts they agreed to in their last contract. Ford had made a peace offering to its 40,600 U.S. factory workers in January 2011, announcing that they would get $5,000 profit-sharing payments that year. It was the first time Ford had handed out those checks since 1999.[54]

But this might not have been enough to soothe some union leaders, especially since Ford had also awarded more than $100 million in stock to senior executives, including both Alan Mulally and Bill Ford.

Despite his rich experience and proven success in turning around the manufacturing operations at Boeing, Mulally had had trouble being accepted as an auto guy. Just after Mulally started, "He had to ask what the name of the auto industry's lobby group is (Alliance of Automobile Manufacturers) and what NADA stands for (National Automobile Dealers Assn.)."[55] He had to learn the business and its unique terms on the fly. Speaking the auto language was still critical for an outsider CEO to be accepted in a giant company such as Ford, which had a long and distinct tradition of promoting insider leaders. Nonetheless, both Bill Ford and Mulally himself had had confidence that Mulally's years of experience running a big manufacturer and his technical background had prepared him for the challenges facing Ford.[56]

Looking Ahead

Going into 2011, among many in the business community, Alan Mulally had the popularity of a rock star. One major investor, a fund manager at a company that owned 100,000 Ford common and 100,000 preferred shares commented, "Ford is building better cars, they're more fuel-efficient and they've really focused on quality since Alan Mulally came in. He's just making this company a money machine."[57]

No small part of Ford's forecasted success going beyond 2011 was due to Mulally's emphasis on technology—not so much the technology involved in car engineering, but the link between the car and the consumer via built-in communications and voice control. Mulally saw the automobile as "the all-time mobile device," with Ford as the "automobile 'app' of choice."[58] In his keynote speech at the Consumer Electronics Show (CES) in 2011, Mulally not only introduced the Focus Electric vehicle but demonstrated the features of the MyFord Mobile app. This communications application would allow Focus Electric drivers to use their smart phones to interact with the car's systems, as well as play music on voice command and read tweets to drivers.

It was telling that Mulally was the only automobile CEO to be headlined as a keynote speaker at CES, three years in a row. Presenting to the crowd, including representatives from Sony, Microsoft, Cisco, RIM, and other tech giants, Mulally was successfully jumping Ford ahead of GM's OnStar telecommunications business. OnStar, launched in 1966, had failed to press its "first-mover advantage," remaining tied to only selected GM vehicles and lacking the interconnectivity of even Ford's SYNC product.[59] Jim Farley, Ford group vice president of marketing and communications, pointed out, "Eighty percent of our vehicles in 2011 will be offered with Sync, and of the vehicles offered with Sync the take rate is 80 percent. MyFord Touch is very similar. More than 90 percent of the Explorers we've sold so far have the MyFord system installed. I've never seen in my experience a $400 option that differentiates a brand as much as Sync has."[60]

Alan Mulally appeared to have done what seemed almost impossible coming in as an auto outsider—in four years he had taken Ford from near bankruptcy to a global leadership position. In 2010 *Fortune* gave him the rank of the number two Business Person of the Year (Reed Hastings of Netflix got the number one spot due to his company's stock performance), but the popular vote gave the top spot to Mulally. As *Fortune* writer Alex Taylor III said, "There isn't much glamour in what Alan Mulally does, toiling in America's Rustbelt. . . . Other CEOs with younger companies in fast-growing industries have posted flashier numbers. But it's hard not to be wowed by the turnaround skills required to revive a 107-year-old manufacturer in America's heartland."[61] 65-year-old Mulally hadn't yet said when he might retire but did say the new structure at Ford was "training a solid group of potential leaders."[62] Now, could Mulally not only sustain the momentum, but groom his successor?

Endnotes

1. Naughton, K. 2010. Ford says U.S. auto sales running at a 12 million pace. *Bloomberg Businessweek,* December 20. www.businessweek.com/news/2010-12-20/ford-says-u-s-auto-sales-running-at-a-12-million-pace.html.
2. Trudell, C. 2010. Ford leads automaker profits; GM tops Toyota amid record sales. *Bloomberg Businessweek,* November 11. www.businessweek.com/news/2010-11-11/ford-leads-automaker-profits-gm-tops-toyota-amid-record-sales.html.
3. Vlasic, B. 2009. After record loss, Ford will tap lines of credit to bolster cash. *New York Times,* January 30: B3; Naughton, K. 2011. Ford "money machine" may report best year since 2000. *Bloomberg Businessweek,* January 27. www.businessweek.com/news/2011-01-27/ford-money-machine-may-report-best-year-since-2000.html.
4. Vlasic. 2009. After record loss, Ford will tap lines of credit.
5. Ford Motor Company. 2009. Ford reports 4th quarter 2008 net loss of $5.9 billion; Gained market share in U.S., Europe, achieved cost target. January 29. media.ford.com/images/10031/4Qfinancials.pdf.
6. Knowles, F. 2006. Boeing exec flies the coop: Ford hires Mulally to turn things. *Chicago Sun-Times,* September 6.
7. Welch, D., Kiley, D. & Holmes, S. 2006. Alan Mulally: A plan to make Ford fly. *BusinessWeek.*
8. Kiley, D. 2007. Mulally: Ford's most important new model. *BusinessWeek Online,* January 9. www.businessweek.com.
9. Rakesh, K. 1998. The changing of the guard: Causes, process and consequences of CEO turnover.
10. Berfield, S. 2006. The best leaders. *BusinessWeek Online,* December 18. www.businessweek.com.
11. Levin, D. 2006. Mulally's hire by Ford may be too late. *Bloomberg.com.*
12. Crain, K. 2006. Mulally wants fewer platforms, fewer dealers. *New York Times,* November 20.
13. **Biography: Alan Mulally, ford motor company newsroom.** Ford Motor Company. media.ford.com/article_display.cfm?article_id=24203.
14. Ibid.
15. Maynard, M. 2007. Ford chief sees small as virtue and necessity. *New York Times,* January 25. www.nytimes.com.
16. Ibid.
17. Maynard, M. 2006. Ford expects to fall soon to no. 3 spot. *New York Times,* December 21. www.nytimes.com.
18. Ford Motor Company. 2009. Ford reports 4th quarter 2008. media.ford.com/images/10031/4Qfinancials.pdf.
19. Stoll, J. 2006. Ford looks to reshape business model, executive says. *Dow Jones Newswires,* September 18.
20. Durbin, D.-A., & Krisher, T. 2011. Ford stock falls after company misses expectations. Associated Press, January 28. www.businessweek.com/ap/financialnews/archives/March2011/D9L1JHCO1.htm.
21. Maynard, M. 2007. Ford seeks a future by going backward. *New York Times,* July 17: C1.
22. Bunkley, N., & Maynard, M. 2007. Ford breaks string of losing quarters, but says respite will be brief. *New York Times,* July 27: C3.
23. Durbin & Krisher. 2011. Ford stock falls.
24. Maynard. 2007. Ford chief sees small as virtue and necessity.
25. Bloomberg News. 2006. Ford reorganizes executives. *New York Times,* December 15. www.nytimes.com.
26. Ford Motor Company. 2009. Ford reports 4th quarter 2008. media.ford.com/images/10031/4Qfinancials.pdf.
27. Ingrassia, P. 2008. Can America's auto makers survive? *Wall Street Journal Europe.* August 8: 13.

28. Vlasik, B., & Bunkley, N. 2008. At Ford, end of era takes a toll. *New York Times,* July 27: C1.
29. National Automobile Dealers Association. 2011. Press Release: Top 5 factors that will boost auto sales in 2011. January 7. *www.inautonews.com/ nada-prediction-2011-us-auto-sales-to-raise-113-pct.*
30. Woodall, B. 2011. Ford sees pickups as harbinger for 2011 sales. *Reuters.com,* January 10. *www.reuters.com/article/ 2011/01/10/us-autoshow-ford-farley- idUSTRE7093WI20110110.*
31. Praet, N. V. 2008. US$8.7B loss turns Ford. *Financial Post,* July 25.
32. Ford Motor Company. 2008. Ford accelerates transfor- mation plan with small car offensive, manufacturing realignment. July 24. *media.ford.com/article_display. cfm?article_id=28660.*
33. Ibid.
34. Taylor III, A. 2008. Can this car save Ford? *Fortune,* May 5.
35. Ford Motor Company. 2009. Ford reports 4th quarter 2008. *media.ford.com/images/10031/4Qfinancials.pdf.*
36. Ford Motor Company. 2008. Ford accelerates trans- formation plan. *media.ford.com/article_display. cfm?article_id=28660.*
37. Pope, B. 2008. That's why they call it earnings. *WARD'S DealerBusiness,* January.
38. Autodata Corp.
39. *MotorIntelligence.com. www.motorintelligence.com.*
40. Durbin & Krisher. 2011. 2011. Ford stock falls.
41. Valdes-Dapena, P. 2008. Autos: 2008 winners and losers. *CNNMoney.com,* January.
42. J.D. Power and Associates. 2010. 2010 U.S. Vehicle Dependability Study. March 18. *www.jdpower.com/news/ pressrelease.aspx?ID=2010034.*
43. Ford Motor Company. 2009. Ford reports 4th quarter 2008. *media.ford.com/images/10031/4Qfinancials.pdf.*
44. Ford Motor Company. 2011. Ford reports 2010 full year net income of $6.6 billion; fourth quarter net income of $190 million. January 28. *corporate.ford.com/ news-center/news/press-releases/press-releases-detail/ pr-ford-reports-2010-full-year-net-33916.*
45. Polk. 2010. Consumers continuing to hold onto vehicles longer, according to Polk. November 3. *www.polk.com/ company/news/consumers_continuing_to_hold_onto_ vehicles_longer_according_to_polk.*
46. Maynard, M., & Fackler, M. 2006. Toyota is poised to supplant GM as world's largest carmaker. *New York Times,* December 22. *www.nytimes.com.*
47. Ibid.
48. Fackler, M. 2008. Wary of global downturn, Toyota cuts profit forecast by more than half. *New York Times,* November 4. *www.nytimes.com.*
49. Welch, Kiley, & Holmes. 2006. Alan Mulally.
50. Ibid.
51. Kiley. 2007. Mulally.
52. Kiley, D. 2007. The record year Ford hopes to shake off. *BusinessWeek Online,* January 26. *www.businessweek. com.*
53. Bloomberg News. 2006. Ford reorganizes executives.
54. Durbin & Krisher. 2011. Ford stock falls.
55. Kiley. 2007. Mulally.
56. Maynard. 2007. Ford chief sees small as virtue and necessity.
57. Naughton. 2011. Ford "money machine."
58. Henry, J. 2011. Ford's Mulally gets warm reception at CES. *Autoweek,* January 7. *www.autoweek.com/ article/20110107/CARNEWS/110109928.*
59. Brauer, K. 2011. Q&A: Mulally Lieutenants Execute "One Ford" Globally. *AutoObserver,* February 17. *www.autoob- server.com/2011/02/qa-mulally-lieutenants-execute-one- ford-globally.html.*
60. Welch, D. 2011. GM pushes hard with OnStar. *Bloomberg Businessweek,* March 10. *www.businessweek.com/ magazine/content/11_12/b4220019742521_page_2.htm.*
61. Taylor III, A. 2010. 2010 businessperson of the year. *For- tune,* November. *money.cnn.com/galleries/2010/news/com- panies/1011/gallery.business_person_year.fortune/ 3.html.*
62. Associated Press. 2011. Ford says culture change has led to success. March. *www.businessweek.com/ap/financialnews/ archives/March2011/D9KKK32O1.htm.*

Case 19   FreshDirect

*Is It Really Fresh?**

With a bold promise on its website entry page, FreshDirect claimed, "Our food is fresh, our customers are spoiled. . . . Order on the web today and get next-day delivery of the best food at the best price, exactly the way you want it, with 100 percent satisfaction guaranteed."[1] However, recently many consumers have questioned the freshness of the food delivered by FreshDirect. Since online shopping does not give the chance for customers to feel and choose the products themselves, they must rely completely on FreshDirect to select the food for them. This notion has not appealed to some customers.

Operating out of its production center in Long Island City, Queens, FreshDirect offers online grocery shopping and delivery service to more than 300 zip codes in Manhattan, Queens, Brooklyn, Nassau County, Riverdale, Westchester, select areas of Staten Island, New Jersey, and parts of Connecticut. FreshDirect also offers pickup service at its Long Island City facility, as well as corporate service to selected delivery zones in Manhattan and summer delivery service to the Hamptons on Long Island. When it was launched in July 2001 by Joseph Fedele and Jason Ackerman, FreshDirect pronounced to the New York area that it was "the new way to shop for food." This was a bold statement given that the previous decade had witnessed the demise of numerous other online grocery ventures. However, the creators of FreshDirect were confident in the success of their business because their entire operation had been designed to deliver one simple promise to grocery shoppers: "higher quality at lower prices."

While this promise was an extremely common tagline used within and outside the grocery business, FreshDirect had integrated numerous components into its system to give real meaning to these words. Without a retail location, FreshDirect didn't have to pay expensive rent for a retail space. To offer the highest quality products to its customers, FreshDirect had created a state-of-the-art production center and staffed it with expert personnel. The 300,000-square-foot production facility located in Long Island City was composed of 12 separate temperature zones, ensuring that each piece of food was kept at its optimal temperature for ripening or preservation—kept colder and cleaner than in any retail environment.

Further quality management was achieved by an SAP manufacturing software system that controlled every detail of the facility's operations. All of the thermometers, scales, and conveyor belts within the facility were connected to a central command center. Each specific setting was programmed into the system by an expert from the corresponding department, including everything from the ideal temperature for ripening a cantaloupe to the amount of flour that went into French bread. The system was also equipped with a monitoring alarm that alerted staff to any deviation from the programmed settings.

Another quality control element that had been made an integral part of the FreshDirect facility was an extremely high standard for cleanliness, health, and safety. The facility itself was kept immaculately clean, and all food-preparation areas and equipment were bathed in antiseptic foam at the end of each day. Incoming and outgoing food was tested in FreshDirect's in-house laboratory, which ensured that the facility adhered to USDA guidelines and the Hazard Analysis and Critical Control Point food safety system and that all food passing through FreshDirect met the company's high safety standards.[2]

System efficiency had been the key to FreshDirect's ability to offer its high-quality products at such low prices. FreshDirect's biggest operational design component for reducing costs had been the complete elimination of the middleman. Instead of going through an intermediary, both fresh and dry products were ordered from individual growers and producers and shipped directly to FreshDirect's production center, where FreshDirect's expert staff prepared them for purchase. In addition, FreshDirect did not accept any slotting allowances.[3] This unique relationship with growers and producers allowed FreshDirect to enjoy reduced purchase prices from its suppliers, enabling it to pass even greater savings on to its customers.

Each department of the facility, including the coffee roaster, butcher, and bakery, was staffed by carefully selected experts, enabling FreshDirect to offer premium fresh coffees (roasted on site), pastries and breads (baked on site), deli, cheese, meats (roast beef dry-aged on site), and seafood. Perishable produce was FreshDirect's specialty—by buying locally as much as possible and using the best sources of the season, it was able to bring food the shortest distance from farms, dairies, and fisheries to the customer's table.

FreshDirect catered to the tastes of its Manhattan clientele by offering a full line of heat-and-serve meals prepared in the FreshDirect kitchen by New York executive chef Michael Stark (formerly of Tribeca Grill) and his team. Partnering with Chef Terrance Brennan of New York's French-Mediterranean restaurant Picholine, FreshDirect also sold "restaurant-worthy" four-minute meals. Made from raw ingredients delivered in a "steam valve system" package, these complete meals were not frozen but were delivered ready to finish cooking in a microwave.

* This case was prepared by Professor Alan B. Eisner of Pace University as a basis for class discussion rather than to illustrate either effective or ineffective handling of an administrative situation. Thanks to graduate students Rohit R. Phadtare and Shruti Shrestha for research assistance. Copyright © 2011 Alan B. Eisner.

The proximity of FreshDirect's processing facility to its Manhattan customer base was also a critical factor in its cost-effective operational design. The processing center's location in Long Island City put approximately 4 million people within a 10-mile radius of the FreshDirect facility, allowing the firm to deliver a large number of orders in a short amount of time.[4] Further, cost controls had been implemented through FreshDirect's order and delivery protocols. Products in each individual order were packed in boxes, separated by type of item (meat, seafood, and produce packed together; dairy, deli, cheese, coffee, and tea packed together; grocery, specialty and nonrefrigerated products packed together), and placed on a computerized conveyor system to be sorted, assembled, and packed into a refrigerated truck for delivery.

As of 2011, orders had to be a minimum of $30, with a delivery charge between $5.49 and $6.79 per order, depending on the order dollar amount and delivery location. Delivery was made by one of FreshDirect's own trucks and was available only during a prearranged two-hour window from 6:30 a.m. to 11:30 p.m. from Sunday to Friday and from 6:30 a.m. to 10 p.m. on Saturday.

Competing with other online grocers, specialty gourmet/gourmand stores in Manhattan, and high-end chain supermarkets like Whole Foods, Trader Joe's, and Fairway, FreshDirect was trying to woo the sophisticated New Yorker with an offer of quality, delivered door-to-door, at a price more attractive than others in the neighborhood. Operating in the black for the first time in 2005,[5] by choosing to remain a private company and expanding gradually, FreshDirect's owners hoped to turn a daily profit, steadily recovering the estimated $60 million start-up costs, silencing critics, and winning converts.[6]

Founding Partners

FreshDirect was launched in July 2001. Cofounder and former chief executive officer Joseph Fedele was able to bring a wealth of experience in New York City's food industry to FreshDirect. In 1993 he cofounded Fairway Uptown, a 35,000-foot supermarket located on West 133 Street in Harlem. Many critics originally questioned the success of a store in that location, but Fairway's low prices and quality selection of produce and meats made it a hit with neighborhood residents, as well as many downtown and suburban commuters.

Vice Chairman and Chief Financial Officer Jason Ackerman had gained exposure to the grocery industry as an investment banker with Donaldson Lufkin & Jenrette, where he specialized in supermarket mergers and acquisitions. Fedele and Ackerman first explored the idea of starting a large chain of fresh-food stores, but they realized maintaining a high degree of quality would be impossible with a large enterprise. As an alternative, they elected to pursue a business that incorporated online shopping with central distribution. Using the failure of Webvan, the

dot-com delivery service that ran through $830 million in five years of rapid expansion, as their example of what not to do, Fedele and Ackerman planned to start slow, use off-the-shelf software and an automated delivery system, and pay attention to details such as forming relationships with key suppliers and micromanaging quality control.[7]

FreshDirect acquired the bulk of its $100 million investment from several private sources, with a small contribution coming from the State of New York. By locating FreshDirect's distribution center within the state border and promising to create at least 300 new permanent, full-time, private-sector jobs in the state, FreshDirect became eligible for a $500,000 training grant from the Empire State Development Jobs Now Program. As its name implied, the purpose of the Jobs Now program was to create new, immediate job opportunities for New Yorkers.

CEO Successions

Although the press was mostly positive about FreshDirect's opportunities, growth and operational challenges remained. In the words of an ex-senior executive of FreshDirect, "The major problem seems to be constant change in Senior Management. I think they are now on their 4th CEO."[8] Actually, the company is currently on its fifth CEO in eight years of operation. FreshDirect cofounder Joseph Fedele had remained CEO until January 2004, when cofounder Jason Ackerman succeeded him in that position. Since then, FreshDirect has experienced multiple CEO changes. Jason Ackerman stayed as CEO of FreshDirect for a little over seven months, until Dean Furbush succeeded him in that position in September 2004. Ackerman remained vice chairman and chief financial officer. The tenure of Dean Furbush lasted a little over two years. Steve Michaelson, president since 2004, replaced Furbush as the CEO of FreshDirect in early 2007.[9] In 2008 Michaelson left for another firm, and FreshDirect's chairman of the board, Richard Braddock, expanded his role in the firm and took over as CEO. Braddock said, "I chose to increase my involvement with the company because I love the business and I think it has great growth potential." Braddock previously worked at private equity firm MidOcean Partners and travel services retailer Priceline.com, where he also served as chairman and CEO.[10]

Business Plan

While business started out relatively slow, FreshDirect had hoped to capture around 5 percent of the New York City grocery market. The company was originally slated for availability citywide by the end of 2002. However, to maintain its superior service and product quality, FreshDirect had chosen to slowly expand its service area. By the spring of 2011, FreshDirect had delivery available to selected zip codes and neighborhoods throughout Manhattan and as far away as Westchester, Connecticut, New Jersey, and the Hamptons on Long Island (in the summer only).

The company had employed a relatively low-cost marketing approach, which originally consisted mainly of billboards, public relations, and word of mouth to promote its products and services. FreshDirect hired Trumpet, an ad agency that promoted FreshDirect as a better way to shop by emphasizing the problems associated with traditional grocery shopping. For example, one commercial stressed the unsanitary conditions in a supermarket by showing a grocery shopper bending over a barrel of olives as she sneezed, getting an olive stuck in her nose, and then blowing it back into the barrel. The advertisement ended with the question "Where's your food been?" Another ad showed a checkout clerk morph into an armed robber, demand money from the customer, and then morph back into a friendly checkout clerk once the money was received. The ad urged viewers to "stop getting robbed at the grocery store."[11] As of 2011, FreshDirect enlisted celebrity endorsements from New York City personalities such as film director Spike Lee, actress Cynthia Nixon, former mayor Ed Koch, supermodel Paulina Porizkova, and chef Bobby Flay.[12] Recently the company planned to change its marketing strategy by launching a new testimonial-based campaign using actual customers, rather than celebrities. FreshDirect was number 70 in the Internet Retailer Top 500 Guide. In 2010 the company claimed revenue of more than $250 million, an increase of $20 million from the previous year and had grown its customer base in the range of 20 percent to 25 percent.[13]

Operating Strategy

FreshDirect's operating strategy had employed a make-to-order philosophy, eliminating the middleman in order to create an efficient supply chain.[14] By focusing its energy on providing produce, meat, seafood, baked goods, and coffees that were made to the customer's specific order, FreshDirect offered its customers an alternative to the standardized cuts and choices available at most brick-and-mortar grocery stores. This strategy had created a business model that was unique within the grocery business community. A typical grocery store carried about 25,000 packaged goods, which accounted for around 50 percent of its sales, and about 2,200 perishable products, which accounted for the other 50 percent of sales. In contrast, FreshDirect offered around 5,000 perishable products, accounting for about 75 percent of its sales, but only around 3,000 packaged goods, which comprised the remaining 25 percent of sales.[15]

While this stocking pattern enabled a greater array of fresh foods, it limited the number of brands and available sizes of packaged goods, such as cereal, crackers, and laundry detergent. However, FreshDirect believed customers would accept a more limited packaged-good selection in order to get lower prices, as evidenced in the success of wholesale grocery stores, which offered bulk sales of limited items. Jason Ackerman identified the ideal FreshDirect customers as those who bought their bulk staples from Costco on a monthly basis and bought everything else from FreshDirect on a weekly basis.[16]

FreshDirect's Website

FreshDirect's website not only offered an abundance of products to choose from but also provided a broad spectrum of information on the food that was sold and the manner in which it was sold (see Exhibit 1). Web surfers could take a pictorial tour of the FreshDirect facility; get background information on the experts who managed each department; get nutritional information on food items; compare produce or cheese based on taste, price, and usage; specify the thickness of meat or seafood orders and opt for one of several marinades or rubs (see Exhibit 2); search for the right kind of coffee based on taste preferences; and read nutritional information for a variety of fully prepared meals. A large selection of recipes was available depending on the items chosen.

For example, if you wanted to purchase chicken, you were first asked to choose from breasts and cutlets, cubes and strips, ground, legs and thighs, specialty parts, split and quartered, whole, or wings. Once your selection was made—let's says you chose breasts and cutlets—you were given further options based on your preference for skin, bone, and thickness. The final selection step offered you a choice of rubs and marinades, including teriyaki, sweet and sour, garlic rosemary, poultry seasoning, lemon herb rub, and salt-and-pepper rub. Throughout, the pages offered nutritional profiles of each cut of meat as well as tips for preparation and storage.

FreshDirect employed several different delivery models. Customers within the city were attracted to the FreshDirect service because it eliminated the need to carry groceries for possibly a substantial distance from the closest grocery store or to deal with trying to park a car near their apartment to unload their purchases. Orders made by customers within the city were delivered directly to their homes by a FreshDirect truck during a prearranged two-hour delivery window.

Suburban customers were served in a slightly different manner. Many suburban customers worked at corporations in the tristate area that could arrange for depot drop-off in the office parking lot, creating a central delivery station. FreshDirect would send a refrigerated truck, large enough to hold 500 orders, to these key spots during designated periods of time. Suburbanites could then exit their office building, go to their cars, swing by the FreshDirect truck, pick up their order, and head home. FreshDirect could also provide delivery to the parking lot of football or concert events to provide for tailgate or picnic needs. In addition to providing delivery, FreshDirect allowed customers to pick

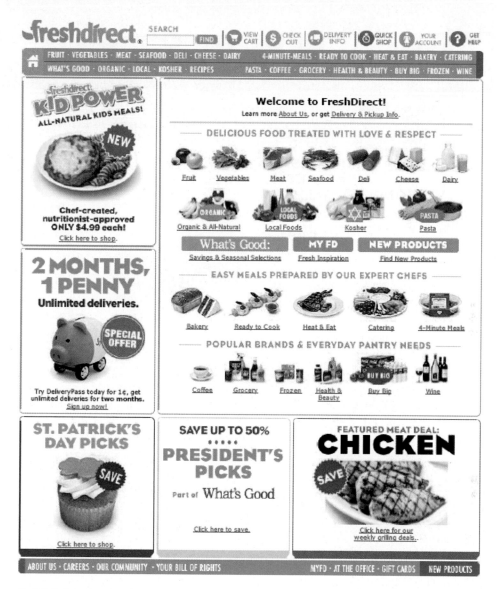

Exhibit 1 FreshDirect Website

up their orders directly from the processing center. Orders were ready at the pickup desk five to ten minutes after they were called in.

Business customers in Manhattan could also order for delivery at the office. Chef-prepared breakfast and luncheon catering platters and restaurant-quality individual meals were available for business meetings and upscale events. FreshDirect provided dedicated corporate account managers and customer service representatives for corporate clients; however, FreshDirect only provided delivery, not set-up and platter-arrangement services. The corporate delivery minimum order was $50, and delivery costs were $14.99 (see Exhibit 3).

The Retail Grocery Industry

In the United States in 2009, according to the U.S. Department of Commerce, supermarket chains made almost $556 billion in sales. The typical supermarket store carried an average of 48,750 items, averaged just around 46,235 square feet in size, and averaged just over $18 million in sales annually.[17] The top-10 supermarket chains in the United States commanded a large amount of the total grocery industry business (see Exhibit 4).

The supermarket business had traditionally been a low-margin business with net profits of only 1 to 2 percent of revenues. Store profits depended heavily on creating a high volume of customer traffic and rapid inventory turnover,

Exhibit 2 **Example of FreshDirect Seafood Selection**

especially for perishables such as produce and fresh meat. Competitors had to operate efficiently to make money, so tight control of labor costs and product spoilage was essential. Online grocery retailers, like FreshDirect—because of the flexibility of information control, automated order fulfillment, and reduced real estate costs—could potentially have operating margins of up to 10 percent, rather than the 3 to 4 percent of traditional supermarkets.[18] Because capital investment costs were modest—involving mainly the construction of distribution centers and stores—it was not unusual for supermarket chains to realize 15 to 20 percent returns on invested capital.

The Online Grocery Segment

Total online grocery shopping sales were estimated to be about $8.4 billion in 2010. However, this number accounts for less than 2 percent of total grocery sales. Online grocery shopping had been slow to catch on, and industry newcomers had encountered high start-up and operating costs. Sales volumes and profit margins remained too small to cover the high costs. The problem, according to industry analysts, was that consumers had been largely disappointed in the service, selection, and prices they had gotten from industry members. This, coupled with the extensive investment needed in warehousing, fulfillment, and inventory control, meant that the "pure play" e-grocery business models were risky. There was a belief that better success would come from traditional grocery retailers that chose to venture online.[19]

However, some analysts expected online grocery sales to grow at a rapid pace as companies improved their service and selection, personal computer penetration of households rose, and consumers became more accustomed to making purchases online.[20] An article in *Computer Bits*

SEARCH [_____] FIND | VIEW CART | CHECK OUT | DELIVERY INFO | QUICK SHOP | YOUR ACCOUNT | GET HELP

FRUIT · VEGETABLES · MEAT · SEAFOOD · DELI · CHEESE · DAIRY   4-MINUTE-MEALS · READY TO COOK · HEAT & EAT · BAKERY · CATERING
WHAT'S GOOD · ORGANIC · LOCAL · KOSHER · RECIPES   PASTA · COFFEE · GROCERY · HEALTH & BEAUTY · BUY BIG · FROZEN · WINE

DELIVERY & PICKUP INFO | Home Delivery   Pickup at FreshDirect
Corporate Delivery   Available Delivery Stops

ABOUT FRESHDIRECT AT THE OFFICE

FreshDirect At The Office delivers convenience and value to thousands of New York offices. Keep the corporate fridge and pantry stocked with a great selection of high-quality food and popular brands at everyday low prices.

One online store. One click. One delivery — it's the easiest thing you'll do all week.

Our terrific selection of specially tailored products and offerings include:

- Saving time with one-stop shopping for all your office needs
- Saving money with our competitive pricing — **up to 35% less than most vendors** — on popular snacks, beverages, paper goods and more
- Exceptional corporate customer service and a freshness guarantee
- The convenience of easy online ordering and next-day delivery
- Chef-prepared catering platters perfect for business meetings and office parties
- Delicious restaurant-quality individual meals

We deliver as soon as the next day, each weekday from 8 a.m. to 5 p.m. When you check out, just select the timeslot that's most convenient for you.

Office Delivery Areas
FreshDirect At The Office is available in Manhattan and now in parts of Westchester, southern Fairfield County in Connecticut and Essex and Union Counties in New Jersey. To see our current corporate delivery zones, click here. **If you're interested but not yet in a delivery zone, let us know.**

Office Delivery Fees
The minimum order is $50. Delivery costs just $14.99. You are under no obligation to tip but have the option of providing a nominal tip if you feel that you've received exceptional service.

Handled With Extra Care
Fresh foods need extra care in handling, and we do all the right things to make sure your food gets to you in top shape. After we prepare everything to fill your order, our trained packers carefully assemble it in sturdy boxes. We put the boxes straight into our own FreshDirect refrigerator/freezer trucks, keeping everything cool and dry until it reaches you.

FRESHDIRECT AT THE OFFICE DELIVERY AREA*

CORPORATE DELIVERY ZONES*

Exhibit 3 **FreshDirect at the Office**

examined the customer base for online grocers, looking specifically at the types of consumers who would be likely to shop online and the kinds of home computer systems that were required for online shopping. An Andersen Consulting report identified six major types of online shoppers (see Exhibit 5), and Braddock predicted that online grocery sales could account for as much as 20 percent or more of total grocery sales within next 10 years.[21] A MARC Group study concluded, "Consumers who buy groceries online are likely to be more loyal to their electronic supermarkets, spend more per store 'visit,' and take greater advantage of coupons and premiums than traditional customers."[22] By 2014, online grocery sales have been estimated to reach a value of $13.5 billion.[23]

One of the problems with online grocery shopping was that consumers were extremely price sensitive when it came to buying groceries, and the prices of many online grocers were above those at supermarkets. Shoppers, in many cases, were unwilling to pay extra to online grocers for the convenience of home delivery. Consumer price sensitivity meant that online grocers had to achieve a cost structure that would allow them to (1) price competitively, (2) cover the cost of selecting items in the store and delivering individual grocery orders, and (3) have sufficient margins to earn attractive returns on their investment. Some analysts estimated that to be successful, online grocers had to do 10 times the volume of a traditional grocer.[24]

Exhibit 4   Top-10 North American Food Retailers

Supermarket Chain	Stores	2010 Sales ($ billions)	Comments
Walmart Super Centers	4,721	$311.0	Includes Sam's Clubs
Kroger	3,624	81.1	Includes jewelry, 5% of total sales.
Costco Wholesale Corp.	540	77.9	Groceries were 72% of total sales.
Safeway	1,712	−41.0	Based in California.
Supervalu	2,349	−37.9	Licenses 876 Save-A-Lots.
Loblaw Cos.	1,029		Stop & Shop, Giant Foods.
Publix Super Markets	1,032	25.1	Based in Florida.
Ahold USA	645	23.4	Based in the Netherlands.
C&S Wholesale Grocers	0	19.4	Supplies products to above.
Delhaize America	1,605	18.8	Food Lion, Hannaford Bros.

Source: *Supermarket News*. 2011. *supermarketnews.com/profiles/top75/2011/*.

Exhibit 5   Types of Online Shoppers and Their Propensity to Be Attracted to Online Grocery Shopping

Types of Online Shoppers	Comments
Traditional shoppers	Might be older technology-avoiders or simply shoppers who like to sniff-test their own produce and eyeball the meat selection.
Responsible shoppers	Feed off the satisfaction of accomplishing this persistent to-do item.
Time Starved	Find the extra costs associated with delivery fees or other markups a small price to pay for saving time.
New technologists	Use the latest technology for any and every activity they can, because they can.
Necessity users	Have physical or circumstantial challenges that make grocery shopping difficult; likely to be the most loyal group of shoppers.
Avoiders	Dislike the grocery shopping experience for a variety of reasons.

Source: Andersen Consulting.

Potential Competitors in the Online Grocery Segment

When online grocers started appearing within the industry, many established brick-and-mortar grocers began offering online shopping in an attempt to maintain and expand their customer base. Two basic models were used for online order fulfillment: (1) to pick items from the shelves of existing stores within the grocer's chain, and (2) to build special warehouses dedicated to online orders. The demand for home delivery of groceries had been increasing, but in many market areas the demand had not yet reached a level that would justify the high cost of warehouses dedicated to fulfilling online orders.[25]

Safeway began an ambitious online grocery venture by establishing GroceryWorks, an online shopping system that included a series of warehouses dedicated to filling online orders. Unfavorable returns forced Safeway to reevaluate its system, and it eventually chose to form a partnership with Tesco, a UK-based grocer. Tesco filled its online orders from the shelves of local stores in close proximity to the customer's home. Safeway and Tesco worked together on GroceryWorks in

Portland, Oregon, where they received a positive initial response from customers.[26]

The craze over health food had created room in the grocery industry for organic food suppliers to enter as an attractive substitute to traditional groceries. When asked what kept him up at night, FreshDirect's former CEO Dean Furbush said that Whole Foods or Trader Joe's moving into a FreshDirect neighborhood was his biggest threat, as that hurt FreshDirect the most.

Whole Foods, the Austin, Texas–based supermarket chain with the organic health food focus, had already threatened FreshDirect's sales in Manhattan. Trader Joe's, another specialty food retailer, was also opening a store in downtown Union Square, prime territory for FreshDirect.[27] Although commentators believed there was enough room for all, including the street farm markets, FreshDirect focused on organic foods to respond to the threats of Whole Foods and other specialty food stores.[28] With the shift among some customers to paying attention to local, sometimes organic, suppliers, FreshDirect highlighted its support of and partnership with the local companies that provided produce, poultry, fish, cheese, milk, eggs, and specialties such as wine (Exhibit 6). However, its efforts have been inconsistent in that area. For example, in order to facilitate shoppers and checkout operators to distinguish between organic and nonorganic produce, FreshDirect wraps organics in plastic, which in itself is not organic. FreshDirect chairman Jeff Turner recognized that such an approach seemed incongruous.[29]

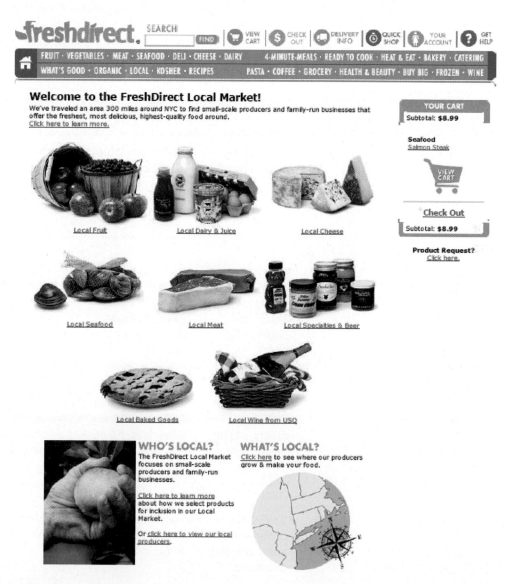

Exhibit 6 FreshDirect Local Market Offerings

Rivals in the NYC Online Grocery Segment

YourGrocer.com

FreshDirect's most geographically significant competitor in the online grocery industry was YourGrocer.com (see Exhibits 7–10). YourGrocer was launched in New York City in 1998 with the goal of being the leading online grocery service for the New York metropolitan area. By November 2001 the company ran out of money and was forced to shut down. In the spring of 2002 new capital resources were found, and the company reopened for business. However, the second time around, YourGrocer's approach was a little different.

YourGrocer was created with a bulk-buying strategy, believing that customers would order large, economical quantities of goods from the website and the company would make home deliveries in company trucks. During YourGrocer's first life, the ambitious business plan covered a large service area and included the acquisition of another online grocery company, NYCGrocery. com.[30] But the business plan was modified in the second life. The company reduced the size of its staff, got rid of warehouses, decided to rent instead of owning its delivery vans, and scaled down its delivery routes.[31] Nassau County and New Jersey were eliminated from the service area, leaving only Manhattan, the Bronx, Brooklyn, Queens, Rockland, Westchester County, and Fairfield County (Connecticut).

YourGrocer offered a limited selection of items that could be purchased only in bulk. Deliveries were made in varied time slots, depending on the customer's location in the New York area. There was a $75 minimum order with a $9.95 delivery charge (see Exhibits 9 and 10).

Exhibit 7   Profiles of Selected Online Grocers, 2011

Name	Minimum Area Covered	Delivery Order	Delivery Charge	Method	Specialization
FreshDirect	Manhattan, Queens, Brooklyn, Nassau County, Riverdale, Westchester, New Jersey	$50	$4.99–$9.99, depending on order size and destination; tipping optional	Trucks; available weekdays 2 p.m.– 11:30 p.m. and all day on weekends	• Mostly perishables: fresh produce, meats, baked goods. • Low prices because there is no middleman.
YourGrocer	Manhattan, Bronx, Westchester, Greenwich, Brooklyn, Queens, Rockland	$75	$9.95 for orders > $75; $14.95 for orders < $75	Rented vans; available select days and times, depending on location	• Bulk orders of packaged goods.
Peapod	Chicago, Boston, D.C., Long Island, Connecticut, New Jersey, Rhode Island	$60	$6.95 for orders > $100; $9.95 for orders < $100; tipping optional	Trucks; available 7 a.m.–1 p.m. and 3:30 p.m.–10 p.m. weekdays, 7 a.m.–1 p.m. weekends	• Partner with Giant Foods and Stop & Shop; items picked from shelves of local warehouses near customer's home.
NetGrocer	Lower 48 states, D.C., special service to Alaska, Hawaii, APO/FPO	None	$9.99–$624.99, depending on order size and destination	FedEx; order delivered within 3–7 business days	• Mostly nonperishables.

Source: Company websites.

Exhibit 8   Comparison of Prices for Selected Online Grocers

Grocery Item	Prices			
	FreshDirect	YourGrocer	Peapod	NetGrocer
Tide laundry detergent	$17.29/100 oz.	$24.39/170 oz ($14.31/100 oz.)	$15.29/100 oz.	$22.39/100 oz.
Wish-Bone Italian dressing	$2.29/8 oz.	$5.20/36 oz. ($1.15/8 oz.)	$1.28/8 oz.	$2.29/8 oz.
Cheerios	$4.19/14 oz.	$6.89/37 oz. ($2.60/14 oz.)	$3.79/14 oz.	$5.49/14 oz.
Ragu spaghetti sauce	$2.69/26 oz.	$3.26/45 oz. ($1.88/26 oz.)	$2.50/26 oz.	$2.65/26 oz.
Granny Smith apples	$2.99/4 pack (no per-lb. price)	$7.39/5 lb.bag ($1.48/lb.)	$0.50/each	$0.45/oz

Source: Company websites.

Exhibit 9   **Yourgrocer.com Website**

Exhibit 10 **YourGrocer's Service Focus**

New YourGrocer focuses on providing *three benefits* that families in the area most value:

1. **Easy ordering** over the Internet or on the phone to save hours of thankless shopping. You can use your last order as a starting point to save even more time.

2. **Delivery** right to the home or office, which eliminates the burden of lifting and transporting heavy and bulky items each month.

3. **Significant savings** with everyday low prices—not short-duration specials—which reduce what you pay for stock-up groceries and household supplies on average by 25% to 30% below local supermarkets.

Source: *www.yourgrocer.com.*

Peapod

Founded in 1989 by brothers Andrew and Thomas Parkinson, Peapod (see Exhibits 11 and 12) was an early pioneer in e-commerce, inventing an online home-shopping service for grocery items years ahead of the commercial emergence of the Internet. With its tagline "Smart Shopping for Busy People," the company began providing consumers with a home-shopping experience in the early 1990s, going so far as to install modems in customer homes to provide an online connection.

From its founding in 1989 until 1998, the company's business model involved filling customer orders by forming alliances with traditional grocery retailers. The company chose a retail partner in each geographic area where it operated and used the partner's local network of retail stores to pick and pack orders for delivery to customers. Peapod personnel would cruise the aisles of a partner's stores, selecting the items each customer ordered, pack and load them into Peapod vehicles, and then deliver them to customers at prearranged times. Peapod charged customers a fee for its service and collected fees from its retail supply partners for using their products in its online service. Over the next several years, Peapod built delivery capabilities in eight market areas: Chicago; Columbus, Ohio; Boston; San Francisco/San Jose; Houston, Dallas, and Austin, Texas; and Long Island, New York.

In 1997, faced with mounting losses despite growing revenues, Peapod management shifted to a new

Exhibit 11 **Peapod Website**

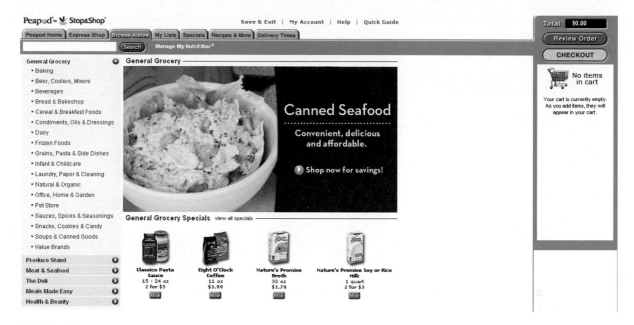

Exhibit 12 Peapod Product Selection

order-fulfillment business model utilizing a local company-owned and -operated central distribution warehouse to store, pick, and pack customer orders for delivery. By mid-1999 the company had opened new distribution centers in three of the eight markets it served—Chicago, Long Island, and Boston—and a fourth distribution center was under construction in San Francisco.

In the late spring of 2000, Peapod created a partnership with Royal Ahold, an international food provider based in the Netherlands. At the time, Ahold operated five supermarket companies in the United States: Stop & Shop, Tops Market, Giant-Landover, Giant-Carlisle, and BI-LO. In September 2000 Peapod acquired Streamline.com Inc.'s operations in Chicago and the Washington, D.C., markets and announced that it planned to exit its markets in Columbus, Ohio, and Houston, Dallas, and Austin, Texas. All of these moves were made as a part of Peapod's strategic plan for growth and future profitability. Under Peapod's initial partnership agreement with Ahold, Peapod was to continue as a stand-alone company, with Ahold supplying Peapod's goods, services, and fast-pick fulfillment centers. However, in July 2001 Ahold acquired all the outstanding shares of Peapod and merged Peapod into one of Ahold's subsidiaries.

Peapod provided online shopping and delivery service in many metropolitan areas, including Chicago, Boston, Rhode Island, Connecticut, New Jersey, Long Island, and Washington, D.C. Peapod employed a centralized distribution model in every market. As of 2011, Peapod has extended its delivery services to Baltimore, Maryland, Virginia, Indiana, and southeastern Wisconsin. In large

markets, orders are picked, packed, loaded, and delivered from a freestanding centralized fulfillment center; in smaller markets, Peapod established fast-pick centralized fulfillment centers adjacent to the facilities of retail partners.[32] Peapod's proprietary transportation routing system ensures on-time delivery and efficient truck and driver utilization.

NetGrocer

NetGrocer.com was founded in 1996 and advertised itself as the first online grocer to sell nonperishable items nationwide (see Exhibits 13 and 14). NetGrocer served all 48 continental U.S. states and the District of Columbia and had special service to Alaska, Hawaii, APO, and FPO destinations. All customer orders were filled in its single 120,000-square-foot warehouse in North Brunswick, New Jersey. Orders were shipped by Federal Express and were guaranteed to reach any part of NetGrocer's service area within three to seven days.

NetGrocer offered its customers a large selection of brand-name and specialty nonperishable items that were difficult to find in a local supermarket. The key customer segment for NetGrocer's services were busy families, urban dwellers, special-needs groups (e.g., dieters, diabetics), and senior citizens. Customers purportedly enjoyed the benefits of convenient online shopping from home 24 hours a day, access to thousands of products, and delivery of their orders directly to their homes. Manufacturers also benefited from NetGrocer, as they were able to distribute their products nationwide, rapidly, and easily.

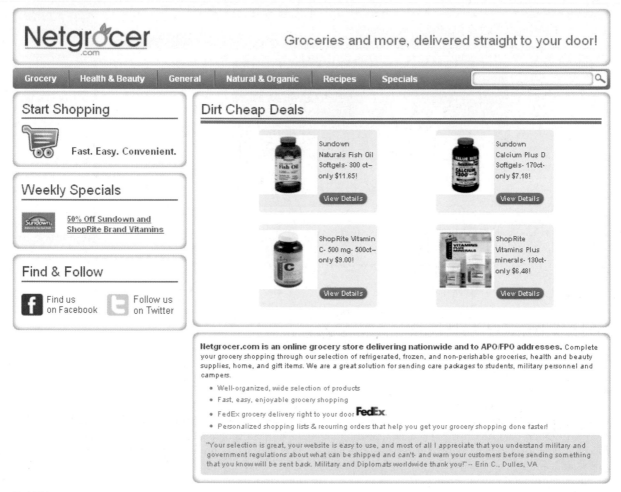

Exhibit 13 Netgrocer.com Website

Most Recent Challenges

As the online grocery retailing business continued to mature, all players needed to pay attention to customer perception. Online retailing giant, Amazon.com had entered the dry-goods grocery delivery business, posing a threat to other online retailers because of its existing loyal customer base and legendary customer service. Creating a grocery section in 2006, Amazon offered over 10,000 nonperishable items, including "long-time staples, from Kellogg's to Jiffy Pop."[33] The selection of dry goods rather than perishables meant Amazon, unlike FreshDirect and Peapod, didn't have to worry about delivery costs on time- and climate-sensitive items. However, even Amazon suffered grocery delivery failures, from out-of-stock problems to delivery glitches and website technical outages. Online grocery retailers needed to "serve their online customers just like they would serve the customers who come into their physical stores."[34]

Even though FreshDirect had been able to woo local New Yorkers, gaining a Fast Company "Local Hero" award,

the company had to absorb "hundreds of thousands of dollars in parking tickets to get its customers its orders within the delivery window."[35] And in 2007 New York City government proposed a congestion charge for traffic entering Manhattan, adding to FreshDirect's delivery expenses. The rising cost of fuel was also a potential threat, even though FreshDirect included a fuel surcharge on orders, based on the average retail price of gasoline.[36] These expenses, coupled with penalties accrued from parking violations, might have put significant pressure on FreshDirect's ability to achieve its target profit levels.

Environmental concerns also started to creep in as a major issue for FreshDirect. First, because of the conveyor packing system at the processing facility, FreshDirect was forced to use lots of cardboard boxes to deliver the groceries: Produce came in one box, dry goods in another, and a single tube of toothpaste in its separate cardboard delivery container. Although FreshDirect had transitioned to the use of 100 percent postconsumer recycled paper,[37] the reusability of the cardboard boxes was limited and the

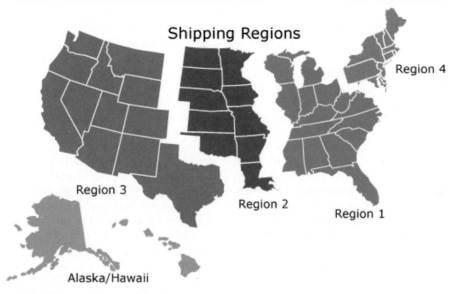

Order Total Brackets	Region 3 Rates	Region 2 Rates	Region 1 Rates	Region 4 Rates
$0 - 24.99	$9.99	$9.99	$9.99	$9.99
$25 - 49.99	$15.99	$14.99	$9.99	
$50.- 74.99	$23.99	$20.99	$14.99	
$75 - 99.99	$29.99	$27.99	$16.99	
$100 - 124.99	$35.99	$31.99	$20.99	
$125 - 149.99	$41.99	$39.99	$26.99	
$150 - 199.99	$63.99	$59.99	$31.99	
$200 - 299.99	$92.99	$83.99	$49.99	$29.99
$300 - 499.99	$116.99	$110.99	$59.99	$39.99
$500 - 749.99	$218.99	$211.99	$119.99	$49.99
$750 - 999.99	$319.99	$312.99	$179.99	$59.99
$1000+**	$624.99	$613.99	$401.99	$199.99

Alaska & Hawaii shipping charges are based on the weight of your order and are now $25.00 for up to the first 5lbs. and $2.00 for each additional pound.

Exhibit 14 Netgrocer Shipping Charges

general public was increasingly becoming aware that their tax dollars were used to "collect and dispose of the huge stacks of cardboards that FreshDirect's customers leave in the trash."[38] As one environmentally conscious consumer observed, "I was baffled by the number of boxes they used to pack things. Groceries worth $40 came in five boxes. And after I unpacked, I had to discard the boxes. There was no system of returning them to FreshDirect to be recycled."[39]

A second issue that environmentally conscious consumers became concerned about was the additional exhaust fumes that FreshDirect trucks contributed to the urban atmosphere.[40] Third, FreshDirect trucks double-parked in busy city streets had only made the traffic congestion problems worse. "It's probably no exaggeration to say that FreshDirect has built its financial success on its ability to fob off its social and environmental costs on the city as a whole."[41] Lastly, some city dwellers even expressed concern about FreshDirect's adverse effect on the overall makeup of their neighborhoods: "It is not just the impact they have on congestion, pollution, space, etc., but their very adverse impact on the best of businesses in neighborhoods that they can undersell because of their externalized costs. It is these small businesses, farmers markets and local grocery stores, that FreshDirect undercuts, that are some of the best businesses for supporting and preserving our walkable, diverse and safe neighborhoods."[42]

FreshDirect served only selected neighborhoods within New York City. As the neighborhood selection process was highly arbitrary, many people who lived in neighborhoods that FreshDirect did not serve had started to accuse the company of discrimination. As one customer put it, "FreshDirect is the most convenient way to shop for groceries in NYC . . . unless you live in a Public Housing building—they won't deliver to you!"[43] Others echoed similar concerns in terms of FreshDirect's decision to not serve specific neighborhoods: "These are neighborhoods that FreshDirect deems underserved, or in plain terms . . . not worth the bother."[44]

Some of the recent challenges FreshDirect faced were union related. FreshDirect's 500 truck drivers recently joined Local 348 of the United Food and Commercial Workers Union. Some of the reasons cited by the workers for this move were that "they made us work 12 and 14 hours a day, then . . . when some of us refused we were suspended for three days without pay." Also, the workers complained that the wages were pretty low as compared to wages at other grocery chains in New York. According to the workers, the initial beginning salaries at FreshDirect were just higher than $7, with the average per-hour pay being around $8.50. Workers also claimed that the health benefit premiums were high and not easily affordable. A firm spokesman replied to these complaints that "we have incredibly generous benefits that are more than competitive."[45]

Just a few days before Christmas in December 2007, FreshDirect asked its 900 plant workers to provide legal papers proving their immigration status.[46] As a result, many workers left immediately, some of whom had been associated with FreshDirect for 5 to 6 years.[47] Surprisingly, the majority of the workforce rejected the proposal of unionizing (around 80 percent voting against unionization). However, the number of workers voting was only 530, not 900, because so many employees had left the company after the immigration-status audit was announced.[48] FreshDirect was successful in suppressing the union revolt, but remaining workers were demoralized and the company's image was tainted among its customers.[49]

Aside from the labor challenges, FreshDirect was working hard to woo its customers. FreshDirect started a line of four-minute meals. These fresh meals were packed in microwavable containers, and, as the name implies, they could be ready to eat after four minutes in a microwave oven.

FreshDirect had teamed up with some well-known Manhattan restaurants and chefs to introduce the four-minute meal concept. The lineup included Rosa Mexicano for Mexican cuisine,[50] chef Floyd Cardoz's Tabla for Indian cuisine,[51] chef Tina Bourbeau's Presto Italiano line of Italian cuisine, and several others. Another promotion was FreshDirect's "Valentine's Dinner for Two," which allowed customers to "prepare an easy and romantic restaurant-quality meal for a special someone in the comfort of their own homes." The menu had a variety of options, including appetizers, desserts, entrées, wines, champagnes, and so on. This menu came in the price range of $69 to $99, and the meal needed less than 20 minutes of cooking time.[52]

FreshDirect expanded its delivery options with a fixed-price unlimited-delivery program in addition to the standard per-delivery fee program, which cost $5.49 to $6.79 depending on location. The unlimited-delivery program gave customers an unlimited number of deliveries for a set fee of $59 for six months or $99 per year.[53] FreshDirect also reduced its minimum order to $30 from $50 in late 2008. Another innovation was the company's online customer-created shopping list. Customers could create and save their own shopping lists, such as a weekly list, mother-in-law list, and party list. In addition, the company offered its own tailored lists, such as Simple Suppers, Pantry Basics, Top 20 Most Popular FreshDirect Items, Healthy Snacks, and Entertaining Essentials, to help customers create lists of their own.[54]

Neither labor strife nor economic downturn had stopped FreshDirect's growth. Looking into the future, there was speculation that FreshDirect might want to "seek public funding to underwrite growth possibilities."[55] Since Whole Foods Market's acquisition of Wild Oats Markets, analysts felt that some private players in the New York market, such as FreshDirect, might consider pursuing investment capital through an initial public offering.

Another major issue for FreshDirect was their customers' concerns about how fresh the produce and meats really were. One of the biggest obstacles to the growth of online ordering of groceries had been the inability to view and touch food, particularly fresh produce and meat. Online customers couldn't pick up and thump a melon or peel back the leaves on a head of Romaine lettuce to check for freshness the same way they could in the grocery store. FreshDirect received numerous inputs from consumers which basically stated, "I can't see, touch and smell the products. I have to rely on you." This lack of control over identifying the freshness of the food caused major concerns for the customers. The company recognized the problem and spun this negative aspect of online shopping into a positive one by creating a food-quality rating system. Consumer feedback jump-started a new way of doing business for FreshDirect.[56]

In order to accommodate online food shoppers who wanted more product detail, FreshDirect created its own food-quality rating system to resolve this challenge. The company introduced a Daily Produce Rating System that ranked the quality of fruits and vegetables available for delivery the next day. The five-star rating system gives shoppers "a foolproof way to ensure that the ripest fruits and crunchiest veggies are consistently delivered to their doorsteps," as advertised in the company's website. The Daily Produce Rating System is based on a daily inspection of all produce in stock by a quality assurance team.

Rating criteria include taste, color, firmness, and ripeness. Rankings are based on an easy ratings scale:[57]

- five stars signify "never better, the best we've seen";
- four stars indicate "great/delicious";
- three stars mean "good/reliably decent";
- two stars indicate "average/inconsistent quality/generally OK"; and
- one star signals "below average/expect wide inconsistency in quality/probably out of season."

Results are updated each morning on FreshDirect's website to let customers know which fruits and veggies are the best bets for deliveries to be received on the following day. FreshDirect also offers the same five-star rating service for seafood, and some 50 percent to 70 percent of its customers have used the feature.[58] The system aims to simulate the in-store shopping experience, allowing the grocers to showcase their best stuff and customers to decide what looks good. "Not everyone is an expert on the seasonality of a fruit or vegetable, so this system takes the guesswork out of choosing the best available items," said FreshDirect chief marketing officer Steve Druckman. "Each of the buyers and managers who rate the produce have years on the job, so they have great expertise. I am not aware of any other online or conventional grocer that's developing a system such as this."

However, the strategy came with a big risk: to gain customers' trust, FreshDirect would have to acknowledge that not every item it stocked was picture perfect every day. Not everyone at the company was enthusiastic about the idea. Many feared backlash from the consumers about FreshDirect's products not always being top quality. "Was it scary? Yeah!" recalled Glenn Walsh, the produce manager. "I thought it was insane in the beginning."[59]

Despite the risk, the company claims that the rating system has changed consumer buying patterns. Around 70 percent of customers have said they purchased something they wouldn't have if it wasn't for the rating system. Druckman asserted, "One hundred percent of customers changed buying patterns. The rating system works. If we put something out like black seedless grapes or golden pineapples with four stars, we'll sell twice as many of those because of their rating than otherwise."[60]

Rick Braddock also decided to upgrade FreshDirect's website, using the company's internal database to profile customers and serve a customized online experience. For example, the site's software could now analyze order patterns, reminding customers of their favorite products and suggesting other items they might like, a marketing tool that had worked well for Netflix and Amazon. In addition, the database recognizes whether a visiting customer is a new, infrequent, lapsed, or loyal customer—and serves appropriate messages and ads.

It remains to be seen whether FreshDirect can survive all the changes. Given that only 2 percent of all purchases are made online, FreshDirect still has a long way to go.

Endnotes

1. *www.freshdirect.com/site_access/site_access.jsp.*
2. Dubbs, D. 2003. Catch of the day. *Multichannel Merchant,* July 1. *multichannelmerchant.com/opsandfulfillment/orders/fulfillment_catch_day.*
3. A "slotting allowance" is defined by the American Marketing Association as "1. (retailing definition) A fee paid by a vendor for space in a retail store. 2. (sales promotion definition) The fee a manufacturer pays to a retailer in order to get distribution for a new product. It covers the costs of making room for the product in the warehouse and on the store shelf, reprogramming the computer system to recognize the product's UPC code, and including the product in the retailer's inventory system." *www.marketingpower.com/mg-dictionary-view2910.php.*
4. Laseter, T., et al. What FreshDirect learned from Dell. *Strategy Business,* 30 (Spring). *www.strategy-business.com/press/16635507/8202.*
5. Schoenberger, C. R. 2006. Will work with food. *Forbes,* September 18. *members.forbes.com/global/2006/0918/041.html.*
6. Smith, C. 2004. Splat: The supermarket battle between Fairway, FreshDirect and Whole Foods. *New York: The Magazine,* May 24. *nymag.com/nymetro/food/industry/n_10421.*
7. Dignan, L. 2004 FreshDirect: Ready to deliver. *Baseline: The Project Management Center,* February 17. *www.baselinemag.com/print_article2/0,1217,a=119342,00.asp.*
8. *Chelsea-Wide Blogs.* 2006. *chelsea.clickyourblock.com/bb/-archive/index.php?t-128.html.*
9. *Supermarket News.* 2007. Michaelson named CEO at FreshDirect; Furbush resigns. January 9. *supermarketnews.com/retail_financial/-michaelson_named_ceo_at_freshdirect_furbush_resigns_337/index.html.*
10. *InternetRetailer.com.* 2008. FreshDirect's chairman hopes to deliver the goods in bigger role. July 14.
11. Elliot, S. 2003. A "fresh" and "direct" approach. *New York Times,* February 11.
12. Bosman, J. 2006. FreshDirect emphasizes its New York flavor. *New York Times,* January 31. *www.nytimes.com/2006/01/31/business/media/31adco.html?ex=1182657600&en=14d9c9f5d468064f&ei=5070.*
13. Bruno, K. 2010. Inside FreshDirect's expansion. *Forbes,* June 29. *www.forbes.com/2010/06/29/freshdirect-online-grocery-braddock-cmo-network-grocery.html.*
14. Laseter. 2003. What FreshDirect learned from Dell.
15. Ibid.
16. Ibid.
17. Food Market Institute. *Supermarket Facts: Industry Overview 2006. www.fmi.org/facts_figs/superfact.htm.*
18. Leonhardt, D. 2006. Filling pantries without a middleman. *New York Times,* November 22. *www.nytimes.com/2006/11/22/-business/22leonhardt.html?pagewanted=1&ei=5070&en=102ea06150518b7a&ex=1182657600.*
19. Kempiak, M., & Fox, M. A. 2002. Online grocery shopping: Consumer motives, concerns and business models. *First Monday,* vol. 7, no. 9. *www.firstmonday.org/issues/issue7_9/kempiak.*

20. Machlis, S. 1998. Filling up grocery carts online. *Computerworld,* July 27: 4.

21. Hamstra, M. 2010. FreshDirect CEO predicts online gains in next decade. *Supermarketnews,* March 1. *supermarketnews.com/retail_financial/ freshdirect-ceo-projects-online-gains-0301.*

22. Woods, B. 1998. America Online goes grocery shopping for e-commerce bargains. *Computer News,* August 10: 42.

23. Brook-Carter, C. 2010. Focus: UK, US central to online grocery sales growth. *Just-food,* February 23. *www. just-food.com/analysis/uk-us-central-to-online-grocery-sales-growth_id109940.aspx.*

24. Fisher, L. M. 1999. Online grocer is setting up delivery system for $1 billion. *New York Times,* July 10: 1.

25. *Frontline Solutions.* 2002. Online supermarkets keep it simple. Vol. 3, no. 2: 46–49.

26. Ibid.

27. Smerd, J. 2005. Specialty foods stores will go head-to-head at Union Square. *New York Sun,* March 4. *www.nysun.com/ article/10058?page_no=1.*

28. *Progressive Grocer.* 2005. NYC's FreshDirect launches street fight against Whole Foods. March 3. *www. allbusiness.com/retail-trade/food-stores/4258105-1.html.*

29. *New Zealand Herald.* 2007. We don't have time to waste. February 3.

30. Joyce, E. 2002. YourGrocer.com wants to come back. *ECommerce,* May 15. *ecommerce.internet.com/news/news/-article/0,10375_1122671,00.html.*

31. Fickenscher, L. 2002. Bouncing back from cyber limbo: Resurgence of failed dot coms after downsizing. *Crain's New York Business,* June 24.

32. Peapod Inc. Corporate fact sheet. *www.peapod.com/corpinfo/peapodFacts.pdf.*

33. Regan, K. 2006. Amazon dips toe into online grocery business. *E-Commerce Times,* June 15. *www.ecommercetimes. com/-story/51136.html.*

34. Hamstra, M. 2007. Online stores may need to bone up on their execution. *Supermarket News,* January 29. *supermarketnews.com/viewpoints/-online-stores-bone-up-execution/ index.html.*

35. Danigelis, A. 2006. Customers' first local hero: FreshDirect. *Fast Company,* September. *www.fastcompany.com/ customer/-2006/articles/local-fresh-direct.html.*

36. See *www.freshdirect.com/about/index.jsp* and click on FAQs.

37. *Supermarket News.* 2007. FreshDirect transitions to eco-friendly boxes. May 11. *supermarketnews.com/fresh_ market/-freshdirect_eco_friendly/index.html.*

38. *StreetsBlog.* 2006. FreshDirect builds a grocery empire on free street space. November 22. *www.streetsblog.org/2006/11/22/ fresh-direct-builds-a-grocery-empire-on-free-street-space.*

39. Wadia, A. S. 2007. Is FreshDirect good for you? *Metroblogging NYC,* January 30. *nyc.metblogs.com/ archives/-2007/01/is_freshdirect.html.*

40. *StreetsBlog.* 2006. FreshDirect builds a grocery empire on free street space.

41. Ibid.

42. Ibid.

43. Rodriguez, N. 2007. FreshDirect.com discriminates! *Metroblogging NYC,* February 7. *nyc.metblogs.com/ archives/-2007/01/is_freshdirect.phtml.*

44. Wadia. 2007. Is FreshDirect good for you?

45. FreshDirect takes heat, workers try to unionize. *Daily News* (New York), September 28, 2007. *www.nydailynews.com/ news/2007/09/28/2007-09-28_freshdirect_takes_heat_ workers_try_to_un.html.*

46. Lauinger, J. Workers say FreshDirect bosses pressing them to reject union vote. *Daily News* (New York), December 21, 2007. *www.nydailynews.com/ny_local/ queens/2007/12/21/2007-12-21_workers_say_freshdirect_ bosses_pressing_-4.html*

47. Lauinger, J. FreshDirect axes immigrant workers. *Daily News* (New York), December 12, 2007. *www.nydailynews. com/news/2007/12/12/2007-12-12_freshdirect_axes_immigrant_workers.html*

48. Lee, T. In wake of recent manpower loss, FreshDirect workers vote 'No Union'. *New York Times,* December 24, 2007. *www.nytimes.com/2007/12/24/nyregion/24fresh.html?scp= 12&sq=freshdirect&st=cse*

49. Fickenscher, L. 2008. *Crain's New York Business,* January 14.

50. ProgressiveGrocer.com. 2007. April 18.

51. *ProgressiveGrocer.com.* 2008. February 28.

52. *ProgressiveGrocer.com.* 2007. February 7; and 2008. February 5.

53. *Supermarket News.* October 20, 2008.

54. *ProgressiveGrocer.com.* October 19, 2007.

55. Merrefield, D. 2007. How different companies approach the growth challenge. *Supermarket News,* February 5. *supermarketnews.com/viewpoints/how-different-companies-approach-growth-challenge/index.html.*

56. McConnon. 2009. The Issue: FreshDirect focuses on customer service. *Bloomberg Businessweek,* July 1.

57. FreshDirect. About our daily produce rating system. *www. freshdirect.com/brandpop.jsp?brandId=fd_ratings.*

58. Cohan, P. 2010. Growth matters: FreshDirect nudges its way to profits. *Dailyfinance,* March 23. *www.dailyfinance. com/story/company-news/growth-matters-freshdirect-nudges-its-way-to-profits/19372267/.*

59. Bruder, J. 2010. At FreshDirect, reinvention after a crisis. *New York Times.* August 12: B9.

60. *Perishable Pundit.* 2009. New York's FreshDirect succeeds when most online grocers have failed. May 22. *www.perishablepundit.com/index.php?date=05/22/09&pundit=2*

Case 20   Apple Inc.

Taking a Bite Out of the Competition*

In January 2011 came the news that Apple's visionary leader and CEO, Steve Jobs, would be taking yet another medical leave of absence. He did not say when he would return or why he was leaving, but the hints were ominous. The announcement prompted speculation of the return of pancreatic cancer, which was the cause of previous medical leaves by Jobs. In a letter to his 50,000 employees, Jobs handed off daily control of the company to Apple's chief operating officer, Timothy D. Cook. He referred to his management team's plans for 2011 and sounded an unusual emotional note: "I love Apple so much and hope to be back as soon as I can."[1]

For shareholders, the announcement of Jobs taking another medical leave was troubling news. Apple Inc. shares

* This case was prepared by Professor Alan B. Eisner of Pace University and Professor Pauline Assenza of Berkeley College. This case was solely based on library research and was developed for class discussion rather than to illustrate either effective or ineffective handling of an administrative situation. Copyright © 2011 Alan B. Eisner.

dipped, and investors voiced their concerns for the future of the world's largest technology firm. It posed yet again the unavoidable question that now loomed over 35-year-old Apple: What happens to a modern company whose innovations and inspirations are so closely tied to the vision of one leader when that leader's influence is in decline?[2]

The company tried to downplay the impact of his departure. It tried to bury the news by announcing it on January 17, the Martin Luther King holiday in the United States, and then by presenting blowout financial results the next day. During a call with stock-market analysts, Cook said, "We feel very confident about the future of the company." Apple had every reason to be confident.[3] In the 2011 first quarter, Apple reported $26.7 billion in revenue, up 70 percent from a year before (see Exhibits 1 and 2).[4] Although Apple may have mapped product plans for 2012 and beyond, analysts believed that without Jobs' stubbornness and obsession about process and product details, Apple would never be the same.

Exhibit 1   Apple Sales

Product Net Sales	2010 (in millions)	Change	2009 (in millions)	Change	2008 (in millions)
Desktops	$ 6,201	43%	$ 4,324	(23)%	$ 5,622
Portables	11,278	18	9,535	9	8,732
iPod	8,274	2	8,091	(12)	9,153
Music	4,948	23	4,036	21	3,340
iPhone*	25,179	93	13,033	93	6,742
iPad†	4,958	N/A	—	N/A	—
Peripherals	1,814	23	1,475	13	1,694
Software, services	2,573	7	2,411	9	2,208
Total net sales	$ 65,225	52%	$ 42,905	14%	$ 37,491
Cost of sales	39,541		25,683		24,294
Gross margin	$ 25,684		$ 17,222		$ 13,197
Gross margin %	39.4		40.1		35.2
Research and development	$ 1,782		$ 1,333		$ 1,109
Percent of net sales	2.7%		3.1%		3.0%
Selling, general, and administrative	$ 5,517		$ 4,149		$ 3,761
Percent of net sales	8.5%		9.7%		10.0%

(continued)

Exhibit 1 Apple Sales *(continued)*

	2010 (in millions)	Change	2009 (in millions)	Change	2008 (in millions)
Product Net Sales					
Total operating expenses	$ 7,299		$ 5,482		$ 4,870
Net income‡	$ 14,013		$ 8,235		$ 6,119
Region Net Sales					
Americas	$ 24,498	29%	$ 18,981	15%	$ 16,552
Europe	18,692	58	11,810	28	9,233
Japan	3,981	75	2,279	32	1,728
Retail	9,798	47	6,656	(9)	7,292
Asia-Pacific	8,256	160	3,179	18	2,686

*iPhone sales derived from handset sales, carrier agreements, and Apple-branded and third-party iPhone accessories.

†iPad sales include revenue recognized from iPad sales, services, and Apple-branded and third-party iPad accessories.

‡Net income reflects other income and expense, plus provision for income taxes.

Source: Apple 10K SEC filing.

Exhibit 2 Apple First Quarter 2011 Sales

	1st Quarter 2011 (in millions)	1st Quarter 2010 (in millions)	Percentage Change
Product Net Sales			
Desktops	$ 1,731	$ 1,692	2%
Portables	3,699	2,758	34
iPod	3,425	3,391	1
Music	1,431	1,164	23
iPhone*	10,468	5,578	88
iPad†	4,608	N/A	—
Peripherals	593	469	26
Software, services	786	631	25
Total net sales	**$ 26,741**	**$ 15,683**	**71%**
Region Net Sales			
Americas	$ 9,218	$ 6,092	51%
Europe	7,256	5,024	44
Japan	1,433	783	83
Retail	3,847	1,971	95
Asia-Pacific	4,987	1,813	175

*iPhone sales derived from handset sales, carrier agreements, and Apple-branded and third-party iPhone accessories.

†iPad sales include revenue recognized from iPad sales, services, and Apple-branded and third-party iPad accessories.

Source: Apple 10Q SEC filing.

Apple, at the top of *BusinessWeek*'s Most Innovative Companies list since 2004,[5] had distinguished itself by excelling over the years not only in product innovation but also in revenue and margins (since 2006 Apple had consistently reported gross margins of around 30 percent). Founded as a computer company in 1976 and known initially for its intuitive adaptation of the "graphical user interface" or GUI (via the first mouse and the first onscreen "windows"),[6] Apple had dropped the word *computer* from its corporate name in 2007. Apple Inc. in 2010 was known for having top-selling products not only in desktop (iMac) and notebook (MacBook) personal computers but also in portable digital music players (iPod), online music services (iTunes), mobile communication devices (iPhone), digital consumer entertainment (Apple TV), handheld devices able to download third-party applications, including games (iPod Touch via the App Store), and, recently, tablet computers (iPad) (see Exhibit 3).

Exhibit 3   **Apple Innovation Time Line**

Date	Product	Events
1976	Apple I	Steve Jobs, Steve Wozniak, and Ronald Wayne found Apple Computer.
1977	Apple II	Apple logo first used.
1979	Apple II +	Apple employs 250 people; the first personal computer spreadsheet software, VisiCalc, is written by Dan Bricklin on an Apple II.
1980	Apple III	Apple goes public with 4.6 million shares; IBM personal computer announced.
1983	Lisa	John Sculley becomes CEO.
1984	Mac 128K, Apple IIc	Super Bowl ad introduces the Mac desktop computer.
1985		**Jobs resigns** and forms NeXT Software; Windows 1.01 released.
1986	Mac Plus	Jobs establishes Pixar.
1987	Mac II, Mac SE	Apple sues Microsoft over GUI.
1989	Mac Portable	Apple sued by Xerox over GUI.
1990	Mac LC	Apple listed on Tokyo Stock Exchange.
1991	Powerbook 100, System 7	System 7 operating-system upgrade released, the first Mac OS to support PowerPC–based computers.
1993	Newton Message Pad (one of the first PDAs)	Sculley resigns; Spindler becomes CEO; PowerBook sales reach 1 million units.
1996		Spindler is out; Amelio becomes CEO; Apple acquires NeXT Software, with Jobs as adviser.
1997		Amelio is out; **Jobs returns** as interim CEO; online retail Apple Store opened.
1998	iMac	iMac colorful design introduced, including USB interface; Newton scrapped.
1999	iMovie, Final Cut Pro video editing software	iBook (part of Powerbook line) becomes best-selling retail notebook in October; Apple has 11% share of notebook market.
2000	G4Cube	**Jobs becomes permanent CEO.**
2001	iPod, OS X	First retail store opens, in Virginia.
2002	iMac G4	Apple releases iLife software suite.
2003	iTunes	Apple reaches 25 million iTunes downloads.
2004	iMac G5	**Jobs undergoes successful surgery for pancreatic cancer.**
2005	iPod Nano, iPod Shuffle, Mac Mini	First video iPod released; video downloads available from iTunes.

(*continued*)

Exhibit 3 Apple Innovation Time Line *(continued)*

Date	Product	Events
2006	MacBook Pro	Apple computers use Intel's Core Duo CPU and can run Windows software; iWork software competes with Microsoft Office.
2007	iPhone, Apple TV, iPod Touch	Apple Computer changes name to Apple Inc.; Microsoft Vista released.
2008	iPhone 3G, MacBook Air	App Store launched for third-party applications for iPhone and iPod Touch and brings in $1million in one day.
2009	17-inch MacBook Pro, iLife, iWork '09	iTunes Plus provides DRM-free music, with variable pricing; **Jobs takes medical leave.**
2010	iPad, iPhone 4	iPhone 4 provides FaceTime feature.
2011	iPad2	iPhone available on Verizon Wireless; **Jobs takes medical leave again.**

Source: *Apple.com*; Fried, I. 2009. Celebrating three decades of Apple. *CNET News,* Special issue: Apple turns 30, March 28. *news.cnet. com/2009-1041-6053869.html*; and *Wikipedia.* Apple Inc. *en.wikipedia.org/wiki/Apple_inc.*

Although most of those innovations occurred after 1998, when Apple was under Steve Jobs's leadership, there was a 12-year period in which Jobs was not in charge. The company's ongoing stated strategy had been to leverage "its unique ability to design and develop its own operations system, hardware, application software, and services to provide its customers new products and solutions with superior ease-of-use, seamless integration and innovative industrial design."[7] This strategy required not only product design and marketing expertise but also scrupulous attention to operational details. Given Apple's global growth in multiple product categories, and the associated complexity in strategic execution, would the potential loss of one man be sufficient to prevent the company from sustaining its competitive advantage? Was Steve Jobs essential to Apple's success?

Company Background

Founder Steve Jobs

Apple Computer was founded in Mountain View, California, on April 1, 1976, by Steve Jobs and Steve Wozniak. Jobs was the visionary and marketer, Wozniak was the technical genius, and A. C. "Mike" Markkula Jr., who had joined the team several months earlier, was the businessman. Jobs set the mission of empowering individuals, one person–one computer, and doing so with elegance of design and fierce attention to detail. In 1977 the first version of the Apple II became the first computer ordinary people could use right out of the box, and its instant success in the home market caused a computing revolution, essentially creating the personal computer industry. By 1980 Apple was the industry leader and went public in December of that year.

In 1983 Wozniak left the firm and Jobs hired John Sculley away from PepsiCo to take the role of CEO at Apple, citing the need for someone to spearhead marketing and operations while Jobs worked on technology. The result of Jobs's creative focus on personal computing was the Macintosh. Introduced in 1984, with the now-famous Super Bowl television ad based on George Orwell's novel,[8] the Macintosh was a breakthrough in terms of elegant design and ease of use. Its ability to handle large graphic files quickly made it a favorite with graphic designers, but it had slow performance and limited compatible software was available, so the product was unable to significantly help Apple's failing bottom line. In addition, Jobs had given Bill Gates at Microsoft some Macintosh prototypes to use to develop software, and in 1985 Microsoft subsequently came out with the Windows operating system, a version of GUI for use on IBM PCs.

Steve Jobs's famous volatility led to his resignation from Apple in 1985. Jobs then founded NeXT Computer; the NeXT Cube computer proved too costly for the business to become commercially profitable, but its technological contributions could not be ignored. In 1997 then Apple CEO Gilbert Amelio bought out NeXT, hoping to use its Rhapsody, a version of the NeXTStep operating system, to jump-start the Mac OS development, and Jobs was brought back as a part-time adviser.

Under CEOs Sculley, Spindler, and Amelio

John Sculley tried to take advantage of Apple's unique capabilities. Because of this, Macintosh computers were easy to use, with seamless integration (the original plug-and-play) and reliable performance. This premium performance meant Apple could charge a premium price. However, with the price of IBM compatibles dropping, and Apple's costs, especially R&D, way above industry averages (in 1990 Apple spent 9 percent of sales on R&D, compared to

5 percent at Compaq and 1 percent at many manufacturers of IBM clones),[9] this was not a sustainable scenario.

All Sculley's innovative efforts were not enough to substantially improve Apple's bottom line, and he was replaced as CEO in 1993 by company president Michael Spindler. Spindler continued the focus on innovation, producing the PowerMac, based on the PowerPC microprocessor, in 1994. Even though this combination produced a significant price-performance edge over both previous Macs and Intel-based machines, the IBM clones continued to undercut Apple's prices. Spindler's response was to allow other companies to manufacture Mac clones, a strategy that ultimately led to clones stealing 20 percent of Macintosh unit sales.

Gilbert Amelio, an Apple director and former semiconductor turnaround expert, was asked to reverse the company's financial direction. Amelio intended to reposition Apple as a premium brand, but his extensive reorganizations and cost-cutting strategies couldn't prevent Apple's stock price from slipping to a new low. However, Amelio's decision to stop work on a brand-new operating system and try to jump-start development by using NeXTStep brought Steve Jobs back to Apple in 1997.

Steve Jobs's Return

One of Jobs's first strategies on his return was to strengthen Apple's relationships with third-party software developers, including Microsoft. In 1997 Jobs announced an alliance with Microsoft that would allow for the creation of a Mac version of the popular Microsoft Office software. He also made a concerted effort to woo other developers, such as Adobe, to continue to produce Mac-compatible programs.

In late October 2001, Apple released its first major noncomputer product, the iPod. This device was an MP3 music player that packed up to 1,000 CD-quality songs into an ultraportable, 6.5-ounce design: "With iPod, Apple has invented a whole new category of digital music player that lets you put your entire music collection in your pocket and listen to it wherever you go," said Steve Jobs. "With iPod, listening to music will never be the same again."[10]

This prediction became even truer in 2002, when Apple introduced an iPod that would download from Windows—its first product that didn't require a Macintosh computer and thus opened up the Apple "magic" to everyone. In 2003 all iPod products were sold with a Windows version of iTunes, making it even easier to use the device regardless of computer platform.

In April 2003, Apple opened the online iTunes Music Store to everyone. This software, downloadable on any computer platform, sold individual songs through the iTunes application for 99 cents each. When announced, the iTunes Music Store already had the backing of five major record labels and a catalog of 200,000 songs. Later that year, the iTunes Music Store was selling roughly 500,000 songs a day. In 2003 the iPod was the only portable digital player that could play music purchased from iTunes, and this intended exclusivity helped both products become dominant.

After 30 years of carving a niche for itself as the premier provider of technology solutions for graphic artists, Web designers, and educators, Apple appeared to be reinventing itself as a digital entertainment company, moving beyond the personal computer industry. The announcement in 2007 of the iPhone, a product incorporating a wireless phone, a music and video player, and a mobile Internet browsing device, meant Apple was also competing in the cell phone/smartphone industry.

In 2011 Apple expanded the iPhone to operate on the Verizon network along with AT&T's network. The company introduced the iPod Touch, a portable media player and Wi-Fi Internet device that allowed users to purchase and download music directly from iTunes without a computer. Apple also opened the App Store. Users could now purchase applications written by third-party developers specifically for the iPhone and iPod Touch. These applications included games, prompting analysts to wonder whether Apple was now becoming a competitor in the gaming market.

Apple was becoming a diversified digital entertainment corporation (see Exhibit 4). Analysts had already believed Apple had "changed the rules of the game for three industries—PCs, consumer electronics, and music . . . and appears to have nothing to fear from major rivals."[11] On top of steady sales increases of its computers sales and of the iPod/iTunes, the added categories of iPhone and iPad were showing substantial growth. Apple was now taking bites out of the competition on all fronts (see Exhibit 5).

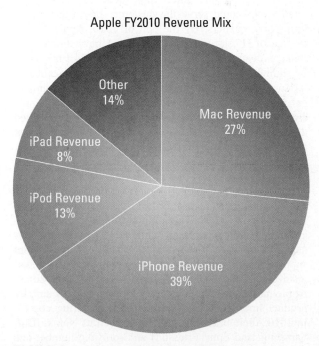

Apple FY2010 Revenue Mix

- Other 14%
- Mac Revenue 27%
- iPad Revenue 8%
- iPod Revenue 13%
- iPhone Revenue 39%

Exhibit 4 **Apple Product Sales, 2010**

Exhibit 5 Apple's Product Lines and Major Competitors

Product Category	Apple Products	Major Competitors
Computers	iMac, Mac Pro, Mac mini, MacBook, MacBook Pro, MacBook Air	HP, Dell, Toshiba in the laptop, Acer in the netbook form factor
Portable music/media players	iPod Shuffle, iPod Nano, iPod Classic, iPod Touch	Creative Zen, SanDisk Sansa, Archos, Microsoft Zune
Smartphones	iPhone	Nokia, RIM, Samsung, LG, Sony Ericsson, HTC
Music/media downloads	iTunes, the App Store	Amazon, MySpace
Handheld gaming devices	iPod Touch, iPhone	Nintendo, Sony
Software*	Safari web browser QuickTime	Microsoft IE, Mozilla Firefox, Google Chrome Windows Media Player, RealNetworks
Home theater downloads	Apple TV	Possibly Tivo
Tablet computers	iPad	Samsung Galaxy Tab

*Includes only the software that is sold separately to use on either Windows or Mac computers.

Apple's Operations

Maintaining a competitive edge required more than innovative product design. Operational execution was also important. For instance, while trying to market its increasingly diverse product line, Apple believed that its own retail stores could serve the customer better than could third-party retailers. By the end of 2010, Apple had an average of 317 stores open, including 84 international locations, with average store revenue of about $34.1 million.[12] In addition to the "Genius Bars" Apple had installed in its own retail stores, Apple also invested in programs to enhance reseller sales, including the placement of Apple employees and knowledgeable contractors at selected third-party reseller locations. The company explained that it "believes providing direct contact with its targeted customers is an efficient way to demonstrate the advantages of its . . . products over those of its competitors."[13]

In further operational matters, regarding a head-to-head competition against Dell in the computer market, for instance, Steve Jobs was quick to point out that market share wasn't everything. While Dell's perceived dominance might have been partly the result of its efficient supply-chain management, Apple had outperformed Dell in inventory and other metrics since 2001.[14] In addition, Apple had the best margins, partly because of its simpler product line, leading to cheaper manufacturing costs.[15] In 2010 Apple beat Dell and HP (as well as Nokia, IBM, Samsung, and Sony Ericsson) and took the number-one spot on AMR Research's Supply Chain Top 25.[16]

Regarding suppliers of components for Apple's diverse products, Apple had entered into certain multiyear agreements with suppliers of key components, including microprocessors, NAND flash memory, dynamic random access memory (DRAM), and LCD displays. Some of these long-term supplier-agreement partners included Hynix Semiconductor, Intel Corporation, Micron Technology, Samsung Electronics, and Toshiba Corporation. Also, in addition to using its own manufacturing facilities in Ireland, Apple had been outsourcing manufacturing and final assembly of iMacs, iPods, and iPhones to partners in Asia, paying close attention to scheduling and quality issues.

Supply chain and product design and manufacturing efficiencies were not the only measures of potential competitive superiority. Apple had also historically paid attention to research and development, increasing its R&D investment year after year. In 2010, Apple spent $1.8 billion on R&D, an increase from $1.3 billion in the previous year.[17] Among its current rivals, Apple's R&D investment was beaten only by Microsoft, Hewlett-Packard, and Google.[18]

Status of Apple's Business Units in 2011
The Apple Computer Business

In the computer market, Apple had always refused to compete on price, relying instead on its reliability, design elegance, ease of use, and integrated features to win customers. Some analysts believed Apple had the opportunity to steal PC market share as long as its system was compatible, and no longer exclusively proprietary, and offered upgrades at a reasonable cost.[19] But the real opportunity for increased market share was the Intel-based iMac desktop and the MacBook/MacBook Pro portable, both using the Intel Core Duo processor. The only part of the computer system not designed and manufactured by Apple was this processor and the memory.

In October 2010 Apple introduced a newer, lighter, redesigned version of the MacBook Air, the "world's thinnest notebook." The new MacBook Air combined features of the iPad with the notebook.[20] Although the design was considered "revolutionary," the stripped-down product did not have an optical drive except as a separate external purchase, had limited connectivity with only one USB port, and had a battery that was not user-replaceable. Even so, with its aluminum construction, it was perceived to be sturdy and much easier to carry than other full-size notebooks and therefore most appropriate for travelers in Wi-Fi hotspot areas.[21]

The continuing push to convert customers to the Macintosh computing products saw Apple sell 4.13 million Mac computers, both desktops and laptops, worldwide during the first quarter of 2011, an increase of almost 23 percent over the same quarter in the previous year.[22] Sales of Apple computers in the United States did see a decline over the previous quarter, but not as much as the yearly domestic shipments of HP (down 6.1 percent) and Dell (down 6 percent). According to market analysis done by Gartner, the Mac's domestic market share grew from 7.4 to 9.7 percent, putting it in fifth place overall in Gartner's survey of PC vendor units shipped in 4Q2010 (see Exhibit 6).[23]

The Personal Digital Entertainment Devices: iPod

Although many analysts felt the MP3 player market was oversaturated, Apple introduced the iPod Touch in 2007, intending it to be "an iPhone without the phone," a portable media player and Wi-Fi Internet device without the AT&T phone bill.[24] The iPod Touch borrowed most of its features from the iPhone, including the finger-touch interface, but it remained mainly an iPod, with a larger viewing area for videos. Apple released the fourth-generation iPod Touch in September 2010, with upgraded features like an HD camcorder, front-facing camera, integrated microphone, FaceTime video calling, Retina Display, gyroscope sensor, and a slimmer, lighter design. It was deemed the best iPod yet, offering all the fun of the iPhone experience without a carrier contract or monthly bill.[25]

Apple reported selling 19.45 million iPod units during the first quarter of 2011, a decline of 7 percent over the same period in the previous year.[26] Even with the decline in iPod sales, Apple was still leading well over its rivals. The research by NPD group in 2010 claimed that iPod had a 76 percent share of the MP3 player market in the United States, while Microsoft's Zune had only a 1 percent share.[27]

Mobile Communication Devices: iPhone

In 2007 further competition came from the blurring of lines between the digital music player and other consumer electronic devices: The telecom players wanted to join the digital music market. While others may have seen the computer as central to the future of digital music, the telecom companies thought the mobile phone could become a center of this emerging world. Apple's entry, the new iPhone device, combined an Internet-enabled smartphone and video iPod. The iPhone allowed users to access all iPod content and play music and video content purchased from iTunes. Apple made an exclusive arrangement with AT&T's Cingular Wireless network to provide cellular service.

The iPhone debuted with a 4-GB model for $499 and an 8-GB model for $599, and estimates from component manufacturers suggested it would cost between $230 and $265 to make, yielding Apple's preferred gross margin of

Exhibit 6 Domestic PC Market Share, Fourth Quarter 2010

Company	4Q10 Shipments	4Q10 Market Share (%)	4Q09 Shipments	4Q09 Market Share (%)	4Q10–4Q09 Growth (%)
Hewlett-Packard	5,596,608	29.3	5,951,547	29.1	−6.0
Dell	4,210,000	22.1	4,483,074	21.9	−6.1
Acer	2,120,853	11.1	3,048,552	14.9	−30.4
Toshiba	1,968,000	10.3	1,719,700	8.4	14.4
Apple	1,860,000	9.7	1,503,900	7.4	23.7
Others	3,325,955	17.4	3,727,142	18.2	−10.8
Total	**19,081,416**	**100.0**	**20,433,915**	**100.0**	−6.6

Note: Data include desk-based PCs and mobile PCs (notebooks and netbooks) but not media tablets such as iPad.

Source: Gartner. 2011. January.

about 50 percent.[28] This would allow room for price adjustments based on component or customer demand. The smartphone market in 2007 was estimated at 10 percent of all mobile phone sales, or 100 million devices a year. Steve Jobs said he "would like to see the iPhone represent 1 percent of all mobile phone sales by the end of 2008."[29] This proved to be a conservative estimate.

In July 2008 Apple began selling the iPhone 3G, the second-generation of the iPhone product. The 3G service upgrade accompanied expanded worldwide distribution, through carrier relationships in over 70 countries. Either because of the increased access or because of Apple's marketing push, 6.9 million iPhone 3Gs were sold in the first quarter of its availability, compared to "6.1 million first-generation iPhone units sold in the prior five quarters combined."[30] As one analyst commented, "When Steve Jobs first introduced the iPhone in 2007, he pointed out that the market for cell phones worldwide was far greater than the market for any other type of consumer electronic device."[31] Worldwide demand for the iPhone was growing: The iPhone was launched in Saudi Arabia and the UAE through Mobily and Etisalat, and got 25,000 subscribers in the first few hours of its availability.[32] Now it appeared that Jobs was correct. He had forecast a 1 percent market share of the cell phone market and by 2010 had achieved 2.9 percent (see Exhibit 7).

Going into 2009, it appeared that the cell phone landscape was changing yet again, with smartphones becoming the device of choice for most manufacturers—smartphones with multiple features, including cameras. New cell phones with megapixel cameras debuted at

Exhibit 7 **Worldwide Market Share—Cell Phones, 2010**

Manufacturer	Market Share 2010	Market Share 2009
Nokia	28.9%	36.4%
Samsung	17.6	19.5
LG	7.1	10.1
Research in Motion	3.0	2.8
Apple	2.9	2.1
Sony Ericsson	2.6	4.5
Motorola	2.4	4.8
ZTE	1.8	1.3
HTC	1.5	0.9
Huawei	1.5	1.1
Others	30.6	16.5

Source: Gartner. 2011. February.

Barcelona's 2009 Mobile World Congress from Sony Ericsson and Samsung: "What's behind the megapixel marathon? It's no secret that the iPhone's camera is one of its weakest points. Seems to me the competition is looking for vulnerabilities and has identified imaging capability as something they can deliver that the iPhone so far hasn't."[33] Along with Sony Ericsson and Samsung, other cell phone makers, LG and Taiwanese manufacturer High Tech Computers (HTC), offered new phones with touch screens in an attempt to compete with the iPhone.[34]

Part of the popularity of the iPhone during the 2008 holiday season was explained by analysts as being the result of the highly prolific output of third-party software developers. These applications were available via Apple's App Store, where they could be downloaded to the iPhone, either increasing its capability or allowing users to play games and otherwise entertain themselves. This prompted these analysts to wonder whether gaming companies such as Nintendo and Sony would have to pay attention to Apple as a competitor in the gaming market. The analysts quoted one iPhone customer who said he had sold his Sony PSP and might get rid of his Nintendo DS, because in "the short amount of time I've had the iPhone, I've played more games on that than on my PSP and DS combined."[35] Regarding additional upgrades to the iPhone, or to other products in the smartphone group, CEO Steve Jobs agreed that Apple's iPhone business "had become too big to ignore."

iPhone 4

In the beginning of June 2010, Apple introduced the new iPhone 4, which claimed to be the thinnest smartphone with the newest version of Apple's most advanced mobile operating system. "iPhone 4 is the biggest leap since the original iPhone," said Steve Jobs. "FaceTime video calling sets a new standard for mobile communication, and our new Retina display is the highest resolution display ever in a phone, with text looking like it does on a fine printed page. We have been dreaming about both of these breakthroughs for decades."[36] The video call did not use up the AT&T minutes, which made the FaceTime feature very marketable. The speed of the operating system was apparent in every app being launched, the form factor of the phone is super thin and incredibly solid, and Apple boasted a 44 percent increase in battery life compared to the iPhone 3G. The iPhone 4's 16-GB and 32-GB models received preorders for more than 600,000, which was the largest number of preorders Apple has ever taken in a single day. Apple had sold over 1.7 million of its iPhone 4 within just three days after its launch, making it the most successful product launch in Apple's history.[37]

However, iPhone 4 came with its own share of controversies. Despite the rapid sales, soon there were lots of complaints from customers about the iPhone 4 dropping calls. Apparently the phone could lose reception if a palm or a finger blocked the device's lower left corner. This hot topic of an iPhone 4 problem created a huge web uproar, earning its own moniker: "Antenna-gate."[38] When Steve

Jobs was asked about the reception problem, his reply to the customers was: "Just avoid holding it that way or simply use one of the cases." *Consumer Reports* refused to recommend the iPhone 4 and recommended duct tape as a solution. Apple and Jobs were heavily criticized for their less than impressive handling of the issue. Jobs appeared visibly annoyed at the whole "antenna-gate" affair and said, "This has been blown so out of proportion—it's incredible" as he paced back and forth across a stage. But he also stressed customer satisfaction as a priority and offered a free phone case to help prevent the reception problem.[39] Bloomberg reported that Jobs knew about the issue before the phone was released, alleging that management had been told about it by Apple's antenna expert, Ruben Caballero. Though Jobs described the story as "a crock," Apple had suggested as early as June 2010 that users buy a case or avoid touching the lower left corner, indicating they likely knew something was up.[40]

On July 2, 2010, Apple issued a statement saying that it had found a mistake in the formula for calculating signal strength. Jobs called a press conference where he admitted there was a mistake and said that the company would issue a free software update that incorporated the correct formula. Although the "antenna-gate" problem created a lot of buzz and criticism on the Internet, it did not seem to diminish Apple's sales in any way.[41] Apple disclosed strong results for the second quarter of 2010 that exceeded analysts' expectations. "Let me be very clear on this," COO Tim Cook said during Apple's call with analysts. "We are selling every unit we can make." He informed the analysts that U.S. schools had managed to spend a record amount on Macs despite struggling with plummeting budgets. It seemed like the antenna problem had not affected Apple's reputation in a strong way, as the demand for Apple's devices and services remained as high as ever.[42]

In February 2011 Apple released the iPhone 4 in the Verizon network in addition to the (formerly exclusive) AT&T network. The move was expected to give Apple an important new source of sales in its biggest market for the iPhone and help it compete with rival Google Inc., which had made inroads with its Android operating system to develop high-end smartphones. Analysts predicted that Verizon could sell up to 13 million iPhones in 2011.[43]

However, analysts believed that the idea of Apple transforming the smartphone industry as it had the MP3 player market might require that Apple broaden its market even more. New offerings might include cell phone products that could compete with the new netbook PCs: a portable book reader to compete with Amazon's new Kindle reader, a portable movie player, and even a low-cost, entry-level phone—and all should provide services and add-ons through the App Store so that "average users can clearly see that there are enough high-quality services on offer to justify spending $30 per month [for a] mobile broadband subscription."[44]

Tablet Computer: iPad

In April 2010 Apple released the iPad, a tablet computer, as a platform for audio-visual media, including books, periodicals, movies, music, games, and web content. More than 300,000 iPads were scooped up by eager tech consumers during the device's first day on store shelves. By the first quarter of 2011, Apple had sold around 15 million iPads around the world. The price ranged from $499 to $829, with the costlier models having more memory and/or 3G, and it worked on the AT&T network. Weighing only 1.5 pounds, this lightweight, portable, and touch-screen device was seen as a gigantic iPod Touch.[45]

Considering that previous tablet computers had failed to catch on in the mass market, Apple made a bold move by introducing the iPad. Since its release, some users have criticized the iPad for a lack of features such as a physical keyboard, a webcam, USB ports, flash support, and its inability to multitask, share files, and print. However, features like the sleek design, accurate touch screen, iBooks, photo and e-mail apps, and fast and easy-to-navigate software have made the iPad popular in business, education, and the entertainment industry. A survey by a research company showed that iPad usage in office workplaces was linked to the goals of increased employee productivity, reduced paperwork, and increased revenue. The research firm estimated that the mobile-office application market in North America may reach $6.85 billion in 2015, up from an estimated $1.76 billion in 2010.[46] Selected by *Time* magazine as one of the 50 Best Inventions of the Year 2010, the iPad has been labeled by critics as simply a new category of gadget.[47]

Up until September 2010, Apple iPads accounted for 95 percent of tablet computer sales, according to research firm Strategy Analytics. By the end of 2010, that figure had fallen to 75 percent. The loss of share was due to the arrival of new tablet devices, mainly based on Google's open-source Android system. Other platforms had also begun to appear, including Microsoft's Windows 7 and HP's WebOS.[48]

In March 2011 Apple released the iPad 2, a slimmer, lighter, and faster device than its predecessor, complete with cameras both on the front and rear. It was made available on both the AT&T and Verizon networks at the same price as the original iPad.

The Software Market

Although Apple has always created innovative hardware, software development was also an important goal, with implications for long-term sales growth. Software was increasingly becoming Apple's core strength.[49] The premier piece of Apple software is the operating system. OS X allowed Apple to develop software applications such as Final Cut Pro, a video-editing program for professionals' digital camcorders, and the simplified version for regular consumers, called iMovie. The iLife software package provided five integrated applications, allowing the computer to become a home studio: iMovie; iDVD, for recording photos, movies, and music onto DVDs; iPhoto, for touching up digital photos; GarageBand, for making and mixing personally created music; and the iTunes digital music jukebox. Also available is iWork, containing a PowerPoint-type program called Keynote and a word-processor/page-layout program called Pages. Both iLife and iWork underwent major upgrades in 2009, further increasing their respective abilities to compete with Microsoft applications.

Apple's Web browser, Safari, was upgraded in 2009 to further compete with Windows Internet Explorer, Mozilla Firefox, and the new entrant, Chrome from Google. Apple announced, "Safari 4 is the world's fastest and most innovative browser,"[50] but analysts were quick to point out that Google's Chrome, which debuted six months earlier, was perhaps the first to take the browser interface in a new direction. One commentator called Chrome "a wake-up call for the Safari UI guys. . . . It's not that any particular feature of Chrome is so wonderful, or even that the sum of those features puts Safari back on its heels in the browser wars. It's the idea that someone other than Apple has taken such clear leadership in this area. Google Chrome makes Safari's user interface look conservative; it makes Apple look timid. And when it comes to innovation, overall daring counts for a lot more than individual successes or failures on the long-term graph."[51] Reviews of Apple's Safari upgrade noted, "Whether or not the individual features of Chrome inspired Apple, it's clear that Apple isn't going to let Google have the lead in browser innovation without a fight. And the more innovation that happens, the better it will be for users of Web browsers—which at this point is pretty much everybody with a computer!"[52]

Operating Systems

Further opportunity for software development came from the Mac's new ability to run Windows. This meant that software such as iWorks could now convert Microsoft Office files to run on a Mac. In the past, third-party software developers such as Adobe always had to make a sometimes risky decision to create Mac OS versions of their popular products. Now that the Macs were using Intel Core Duo chips, much more versatility and cross-platform compatibility made it more profitable to design and develop for the Mac market.

An additional opportunity for operating-system competition opened up in 2007 with the introduction of the "netbook" category of portable computers. Smaller and cheaper than a regular laptop or notebook, these machines didn't have the computing power to run the full version of either Windows XP or Mac OS X, so most manufacturers used the Linux operating system.[53] Microsoft announced in late 2008 that its new operating system, Windows 7, the replacement for Vista, would be capable of running on a netbook. However, according to CEO Steve Jobs, Apple did not have any plans for producing a netbook product.[54] Because the Apple operating system, designed to run only on Apple computers, was not available for independent sale, the new Windows operating system might gain traction in another computing category once again.

iTunes

Arguably, Apple's most innovative software product was iTunes, a free downloadable software program for consumers running on either newer Mac or Windows operating systems. It was bundled with all Mac computers and iPods and connected with the iTunes Music Store for purchasing digital music and movie files that could be played by iPods and the iPhone and by iTunes on PCs.

Although the volume was there, iTunes had not necessarily been a profitable venture. Out of the 99 cents Apple charged for a song, about 65 cents went to the music label; 25 cents went for distribution costs, including credit card charges, servers, and bandwidth; and the balance went to marketing, promotion, and the amortized cost of developing the iTunes software.[55]

Several competitors had tried to compete with the iTunes service. RealNetworks's Rhapsody subscription service, Yahoo MusicMatch, and AOL music downloads all had competed for the remaining market share, using the potentially buggy Microsoft Windows Media format.[56] Even though one commentator had said in 2004 that "ultimately someone will build a piece of software that matches iTunes,"[57] as of 2011 the only serious competition was from Amazon and My Space.

Making it potentially worse for Apple's competitors, music artists overwhelmingly supported Apple, because, as Jobs reported, "almost every song and CD is made on a Mac, it's recorded on a Mac, it's mixed on a Mac. The artwork's done on a Mac. Almost every artist I've met has an iPod, and most of the music execs now have iPods. And one of the reasons Apple was able to do what we did was because we are perceived by the music industry as the most creative technology company."[58]

Steve Jobs had negotiated a deal with the Big Five record companies (Sony Music Entertainment, BMG, EMI, Universal, and Warner) to sell songs on iTunes. Jobs asked the music labels to stop requiring that digital music distributors such as iTunes use copyright protection. By taking the lead in this, Apple could potentially come out ahead of the game again: If copyright protection was not required, iTunes songs could be played on non-iPod music players, and music purchased on other services could be played on the iPod. In what might have been perceived as a PR ploy, Jobs said that allowing music to be sold online without digital rights management (DRM) technology would "create a truly interoperable music marketplace—one that Apple would embrace 'wholeheartedly.'"[59]

Four major music labels—Universal Music Group, Sony BMG, Warner Music Group, and EMI, along with thousands of independent labels, offered their music in iTunes Plus, Apple's DRM-free format with higher-quality 256 kbps ACC encoding for audio quality virtually indistinguishable from the original recordings."[60] This made iTunes, with its 10 million DRM-free tracks, "the largest music store library on Earth."[61] In addition, iPhone 3G customers could download music directly onto their phone for the same price as downloading to their computer, the price having changed to include three price points, $0.69, $0.99, or $1.29, depending on what the music labels charged Apple. This tiered pricing was supposedly adopted in response to potential competition from other download sites such as Amazon and MySpace, although analysts pointed out that the music labels had previously demanded variable pricing and that Apple needed this cooperation from the content providers.[62]

As of 2010 the iTunes Store had sold over 10 billion songs, and analysts projected that by 2012 it could "well account for a staggering 28 percent of *all* music sold worldwide."[63] The iTunes store continued to dominate the U.S. market for online movies in 2010, accounting for $248.3 million, or 64.5 percent of total consumer spending on movie electronic sell-through and Internet video on demand.[64]

The App Store

In March 2008, Apple announced that it was releasing the iPhone software development kit (SDK), allowing developers to create applications for the iPhone and iPod Touch and sell these third-party applications via the Apple App Store. The App Store was made available on version 7.7 of iTunes, and it was directly available from the iPhone and iPod Touch products. This opened the window for another group of Apple customers, the application developers, to collaborate with Apple. Developers could purchase the iPhone Developer Program from Apple for $99, create either free or commercial applications for the iPhone and iPod Touch, and then submit these applications to be sold in the App Store. Developers would be paid 70 percent of the download fee iPhone or iPod Touch customers paid to the App Store, and Apple would get 30 percent of the revenue. The applications ranged from simple audio files that were available for free (e.g., ringtones), to straightforward programs that sold for 99 cents (e.g., a program that turned the iPhone into a simple voice recorder), to full-featured applications that retailed for up to $69.99 (e.g., Fore-Flight Mobile, which allowed pilots to get weather and airport information).

As of March 2011, over 10 billion apps had been downloaded from the App Store. The revolutionary App Store offered more than 350,000 apps in 20 different categories to users worldwide.[64] The success of this distribution channel for smartphone add-ons had Microsoft and other manufacturers, such as Nokia and Blackberry maker Research in Motion, rushing to open their own mobile software stores, hoping to follow Apple's "runaway success"[65] in yet another category.

The Future of Apple

Although Steve Jobs was credited with Apple's ability to innovate and to appeal especially to a certain type of consumer (Jobs estimated Apple's market share in the creative-professional marketplace as over 50 percent),[66] Jobs himself credited his people:

> We hire people who want to make the best things in the world . . . our primary goal is to make the world's best PCs—not to be the biggest or the richest. We have a second goal, which is to always make a profit—both to make some money but also so we can keep making those great products. . . . [Regarding the systemization of innovation,] the system is that there is no system. That doesn't mean we don't have process. Apple is a very disciplined company, and we have great processes. But that's not what it's about. Process makes you more efficient . . . but innovation . . . comes from saying no to 1,000 things to make sure we don't get on the wrong track or try to do too much. We're always thinking about new markets we could enter, but it's only by saying no that you can concentrate on the things that are really important.[67]

Jobs, according to the portrait laid out in countless biographies and articles over the years, is a control freak with a compulsive attention to detail. He routinely sent products back to the lab, killed them in their crib, demanded new features, or euthanized old ones, all while keeping Apple's attention narrowly focused on just a few products with the potential for high returns. Jobs' obsession with process and detail even filtered down to how he rolled out products. Besides exhaustively rehearsing his own presentations, he often insisted that executives from partner companies submit to a week or more of dry runs—and has been known to bounce executives at the last minute if they showed signs of nerves that could spoil a Jobs keynote.[68]

When Jobs announced he was taking another medical leave, the lingering question on everyone's mind was obvious: Who will steer the ship when, inevitably, Jobs is gone? Most analysts were enthusiastic about the talents of Tim Cook, who was widely viewed as Apple's next chief executive if and when Jobs permanently stepped aside. Cook was an operations genius, keen-minded, demanding, and adept at cutting costs while delivering complex products on time and coping with staggering growth targets. He was also monastic and incredibly devoted to Apple. He had oversight of sales, customer support, and logistics—which meant much of the company already reported to him. During Jobs' previous two absences, Cook steadied the corporate ship so capably that in 2010 he was rewarded with $59 million in salary and stock. Still, during those past medical leaves, Jobs had remained involved in all major strategic decisions, Apple says. In that respect, Tim Cook was untested as a potential CEO.[69] Critics claimed that he was a good temporary replacement, but lacked dynamism and creative vision.[70]

The rest of Jobs' team was filled with star role players but not accomplished generalists.

- Jonathan Ive, Apple's design chief, was one of the award-winning brains behind nearly all of Apple's iconic computing and mobile products, was a highly accomplished presenter and speaker, and was known as a perfectionist. However, he lacked overall business expertise and credibility with Wall Street. Although he lacked the industrial and technical training to replace his boss, critics believed he could be a powerful cochair.[71]
- Marketing chief Philip W. Schiller was credited with some of the smart moves that placed iMacs, iPods, and iPhones as the chic devices to own in the public's eye. He was known as loyal and effective but wasn't considered a tech visionary. He did not have a dynamic public presence, and some saw him as a bad CEO—probably better suited at staying where he was, to support any future new CEO and ensure consistency.
- Scott Forstall, Apple's software chief, was credited with the successful industry-defining iOS interface of the iPhone and iPad. He was a smooth public speaker, had notable attention to detail, possessed the right kind of technical knowledge and dynamism, and had become an increasingly important figure in key Apple product decisions. But he had little experience minting new hardware.
- Ron Johnson, the head of retail operations, had helped turn Apple into one of the world's most profitable chains, but he was a retailer, not a technologist.[72]

Some outsiders feared that Jobs alone could stir this mix of talent. The unavoidable fact was that lots of people could manage the company. But only Steve Jobs could have had the visionary spirit—and risk tolerance—to turn Apple into a mobile phone company.

Apple had no shortage of talent within the company, but people needed to get to know them in order to prove Apple as a brand, not a person. More than just demonstrating that there was a capable team to take charge in Jobs's absence, however, Apple could also mitigate concerns by demonstrating that many of the company's values that Jobs represented would continue in his absence: true passion for innovation, design excellence, and almost unstoppable momentum around new product development.[73]

In the short term, the current team of Apple might actually outperform in the absence of its stubborn mentor. Without Jobs' obstinacy at the negotiating table and unrelenting dedication to simplicity, it's possible Apple could have avoided its rare mistakes, such as waiting too long to move the iPhone to Verizon (which gave momentum to phones powered by Google's Android operating system) and blocking Adobe's popular Flash video format on the iPad. An Apple without Jobs might one day even allow the iTunes media store to appear on devices such as HDTVs made by the likes of Sony and Samsung. Or perhaps Apple could introduce a stripped-down version of the iPhone to compete with lower-cost handsets. These moves would likely horrify Jobs; he would see them as muddying the user experience and diluting the Apple brand. Yet they would also make some business sense. Even without Jobs at the wheels, Apple could still deliver satisfying returns for shareholders. It could continue to press its gains in PC and mobile market share around the world, and it could build a sizable business selling to corporations.[74]

All this was speculative, of course, given the uncertainties about Jobs' health. The fallout could be short term. People may admire CEOs, but ultimately it's the brand they buy. Critics claim that while the shareholders may be concerned, the Apple brand will ultimately prove to be more than just one man—no matter how influential that man was. Whatever happens, the spirit of Steve Jobs will live on within Apple, and when it finally has to, Apple will carry on without him.[75]

Endnotes

1. Stone, B., & Burrows, P. 2011. The Essence of Apple. *Bloomberg Businessweek,* January 24–30.
2. Ibid.
3. *Newsweek.* 2011. Facing a Jobs-Less Apple. *www.newsweek.com/2011/01/23/facing-a-jobs-less-apple.html.*
4. Apple Inc. 2010. 2010 annual report, 10-K filing. Available at *www.apple.com/investor.*
5. See BusinessWeek.com. 2008. Innovative companies: The methodology. April 17. *www.businessweek.com/magazine/content/08_17/b4081062882948.htm.*
6. Apple was the first firm to have commercial success selling GUI systems, but Xerox developed the first systems in 1973. Xerox PARC researchers built a single-user computer called the Alto that featured a bit-mapped display and a mouse and the world's first what-you-see-is-what-you-get (WYSIWYG) editor. From *www.parc.xerox.com/about/history/default.html.*
7. Apple Inc. 2008. 2008 annual report, 10-K filing. Available at *www.apple.com/investor.*
8. January 24, 2009, was the 25th anniversary of the Macintosh, unveiled by Apple in the "Big Brother" Super Bowl ad in 1984. Watch via YouTube: *www.youtube.com/watch?v=OYecfV3ubP8.* See also the 1983 Apple keynote speech by a young Steve Jobs, introducing this ad: *www.youtube.com/watch?v=lSiQA6KKyJo.*
9. See Mank, D. A., & Nystrom, H. E. 2000. The relationship between R&D spending and shareholder returns in the computer industry. *Engineering Management Society, Proceedings of the 2000 IEEE.* 501–504.
10. Apple Inc. 2001. Ultra-portable MP3 music player puts 1,000 songs in your pocket. October 23. *www.apple.com/pr/library/2001/oct/23ipod.html.*
11. Schlender, B. 2005. How big can Apple get? *Fortune,* February 21. *money.cnn.com/magazines/fortune/-fortune_archive/2005/02/21/8251769/index.htm.*
12. Apple Inc. 2010. 2010 annual report.

13. Apple Inc. 2008. 2008 annual report.
14. Burrows, P. 2004. The seed of Apple's innovation. *BusinessWeek Online,* October 12. www.businessweek.com/bwdaily/dnflash/oct2004/nf20041012_4018_db083.htm.
15. Fox, F. 2008. Mac Pro beats HP and Dell at their own game: Price. lowendmac.com, May 16. lowendmac.com/ed/fox/08ff/mac-pro-vs-dell-hp.html.
16. AMR Research. 2008. AMR Research supply chain top 25, 2008. www.amrresearch.com/supplychaintop25.
17. Apple Inc. 2010. 2010 annual report.
18. Hertzberg, R. 2008. Top 50 technology R&D spenders. *CIO Zone.* www.ciozone.com/index.php/Editorial-Research/Top-50-Technology-R&D-Spenders/50-Biggest-R.html.
19. StealingShare.com. 2006. Growing market share—branding in the computer industry 2006. www.stealingshare.com/content/1137644625875.htm.
20. Bloomberg.com. 2010. Apple's Steve Jobs to introduce updated Macintosh-line operating system. October 20. www.bloomberg.com/news/2010-10-20/apple-s-steve-jobs-to-introduce-updated-macintosh-line-operating-system.html.
21. *CNET Review.* 2008. Apple MacBook Air (80GB). January 25. reviews.cnet.com/laptops/apple-macbook-air-80gb/4505-3121_7-32818756.html.
22. Apple Inc. 2011. Apple's first quarter results, 2011.
23. *MacWorld Middle East.* 2011. Apple shipments up in US: Market share boosted. January 14. www.macworldme.net/2011/01/14/apple-shipments-up-in-us-market-share-boosted/.
24. Elmer-DeWitt, P. 2008. Apple challenges Sony and Nintendo. *Apple 2.0—Blogs,* December 13. apple20.blogs.fortune.cnn.com/2008/12/13/apple-challenges-sony-and-nintendo.
25. TechGeeze.com. 2010. iPod Touch review (4th Generation). September 8. www.techgeeze.com/2010/09/ipod-touch-review-4th-generation.html.
26. Apple Inc. 2011. Apple's first quarter results, 2011.
27. AbdulRehman.net. 2010. iPod gains 76 percent of mp3 player market in US while Zune is a failure with just 1 percent share after 4 years. July 14. www.abdulrehman.net/ipod-gains-76-percent-of-mp3-player-market-in-us-while-zune-is-a-failure-with-just-1-percent-share-after-4-years/.
28. Hesseldahl, A. 2007. What the iPhone will cost to make. *BusinessWeek Online,* January 18. www.businessweek.com/technology/content/jan2007/tc20070118_961148.htm.
29. Ogren, E. 2007. Ballmer says iPhone won't succeed. Has Windows Mobile? *InformationWeek,* May 1. www.informationweek.com/blog/main/archives/2007/05/ballmer_says_ip.html.
30. Apple Inc. 2008. Apple reports fourth-quarter results. October 21. www.apple.com/pr/library/2008/10/21results.html.
31. *Edible Apple.* 2009. iPhone reaches 1% market share in worldwide cellphone market. February 1. www.edibleapple.com/iphone-reaches-1-market-share-in-worldwide-cell-phone-market.
32. Sambridge, A. 2009. 25,000 Saudi iPhone subscribers within hours of launch. *ArabianBusiness.com,* February 23. www.arabianbusiness.com/547625-25000-saudi-iphone-subscribers-within-hours-of-launch.
33. Arar, Y. 2009. Sony Ericsson, Samsung duke it out for megapixel supremacy. *PC World,* February 15. www.pcworld.com/article/159579/article.html?tk=nl_cxanws.
34. Arar, Y. 2009. Next-gen cell phone stars shine in Barcelona. *PC World,* February 17. www.pcworld.com/article/159659-6/nextgen_cell_phone_stars_shine_in_barcelona.html.
35. Wingfield, N., & Lawton, C. 2008. Apple's iPhone faces off with the game champs. *Wall Street Journal: Personal Technology,* November 12. online.wsj.com/article/SB122644912858819085.html.
36. Apple Inc. 2010. www.apple.com/pr/library/2010/06/07iphone.html.
37. Apple Inc. 2010. www.apple.com/pr/library/2010/06/28iphone.html.
38. *Furniture/Today.* 2010. Editorial: Jobs shows how to fix a mistake. July 26.
39. Sorensen, C. 2010. Steve Jobs finally loses his cool. *Maclean's,* 123, no. 29/30 (August 2): 60.
40. Gallagher, M. 2010. Apple's Bumper Solution. *Red Herring,* July 22: 4.
41. Palenchar, J. 2010. Apple profits despite iPhone 4 controversy. *Twice,* 25, no. 16 (August 2).
42. Burrows, P., & Dye, C. 2010. They still believe in Steve. *Bloomberg Businessweek.* July 26 (no. 4189): 34–36.
43. Thompson, A. 2011. Verizon to sell iPhone Feb. 10, ending AT&T exclusive. *Bloomberg Businessweek,* January 11. www.businessweek.com/news/2011-01-11/verizon-to-sell-iphone-feb-10-ending-at-t-exclusive.html.
44. Wingfield, N., & Lawton, C. 2008. Apple's iPhone faces off with the game champs. *Wall Street Journal: Personal Technology,* November 12 online.wsj.com/article/SB122644912858819085.html.
45. Pogue, D. 2010. Looking at the iPad from two angles. *New York Times.* March 31. www.nytimes.com/2010/04/01/technology/personaltech/01pogue.html?_r=1&pagewanted=all&partner=rss&emc=rss.
46. King, R. 2010. MicroStrategy's corporate apps boost productivity. *Bloomberg Businessweek,* November 1. www.businessweek.com/technology/content/nov2010/tc2010111_549315.htm.
47. McCracken, H. 2010. iPad. *Time,* November 11. www.time.com/time/specials/packages/article/0,28804,2029497_2030652,00.html.
48. Cellan-Jones, R. 2011. iPad 2 tablet launched by Apple's Steve Jobs. *BBC News,* March 2. www.bbc.co.uk/news/technology-12620077.
49. Schlender. 2005. How big can Apple get?
50. Apple Inc. 2009. Apple announces Safari 4—the world's fastest and most innovative browser. February 24. www.apple.com/pr/library/2009/02/24safari.html.
51. Siracusa, J. 2008. Straight out of Compton: Google Chrome as a paragon of ambition, if not necessarily execution. *ars technica,* September 2. arstechnica.com/staff/fatbits/2008/09/straight-out-of-compton.ars.
52. Snell, J. 2009. Google Chrome: A wake-up call for Safari. *PC World,* February 24. www.pcworld.com/businesscenter/

instructions or performed preflight tricks such as popping out of overhead bins).[6] Southwest was the first major airline to introduce ticketless travel and one of the first to put up a website and offer online booking.[7] It operated a single aircraft type, the Boeing 737, that kept its training costs low and personnel utilization high, as having only one type of plane offered great flexibility in personnel deployment. Starting with three Boeing 737s in 1971, the company fleet grew to 548 Boeing 737 aircraft providing service to 69 cities in 35 states throughout the United States by the end of 2010 (see Exhibits 1, 2, and 3).[8]

The SWA Leadership and Culture

There are many stories about Herb Kelleher's flamboyant style as CEO. He smoked cigars, loved Wild Turkey whiskey, was often seen dressed up as Elvis Presley, and publicly arm-wrestled and defeated a rival company CEO to settle a dispute over an advertisement slogan.[9] Kelleher truly believed that business could and should be fun—at too many companies, people put on masks when they came into the office. At work, people were not themselves and would be overly serious, which explained why most business encounters were bland and impersonal. Therefore,

Exhibit 1 * **Financial and Operating Data for Southwest Airlines, 2006–2010** (year-end December 31)

	2010	2009	2008	2007	2006
Financial Data (in millions, except per-share amounts)					
Operating revenues	12,104	10,350	11,023	9,861	9,086
Operating expenses	11,116	10,088	10,574	9,070	8,152
Operating income	988	262	449	791	934
Other expenses (income), net	243	98	171	−267	144
Income before taxes	745	164	278	1,058	790
Provision for income taxes	286	65	100	413	291
Net income	459	99	178	645	499
Net income per share, basic	0.62	0.13	0.24	0.85	0.63
Net income per share, diluted	0.61	0.13	0.24	0.84	0.61
Cash dividends per common share	0.018	0.018	0.018	0.018	0.018
Total assets at period-end	15,463	14,269	14,308	16,772	13,460
Long-term obligations at period-end	2,875	3,325	3,498	2,050	1,567
Stockholders' equity at period-end	6,237	5,454	4,953	6,941	6,449
Operating Data					
Revenue passengers carried	88,191,322	86,310,229	88,529,234	88,713,472	83,814,823
Enplaned passengers	114,213,010	101,338,228	101,920,598	101,910,809	96,276,907
Revenue passenger-miles (RPMs) (000s)	78,046,967	74,456,710	73,491,687	72,318,812	67,691,289
Available seat-miles (ASMs) (000s)	98,437,092	98,001,550	103,271,343	99,635,967	92,663,023
Load factor	79.3%	76.0%	71.20%	72.60%	73.10%

(*continued*)

Exhibit 1 * Financial and Operating Data for Southwest Airlines, 2006–2010 (year-end December 31) (continued)

Operating Data					
Average length of passenger haul (miles)	885	863	830	815	808
Average aircraft stage length (miles)	648	639	636	629	622
Trips flown	1,114,451	1,125,111	1,191,151	1,160,699	1,092,331
Average passenger fare	$130.27	$114.61	$119.16	$106.6	$104.4
Passenger revenue yield per RPM	14.72¢	13.29¢	14.35¢	13.08¢	12.93¢
Operating revenue yield per ASM	12.30¢	10.56¢	10.67¢	9.9¢	9.81¢
Operating expenses per ASM	11.29¢	10.29¢	10.24¢	9.1¢	8.8¢
Fuel costs per gallon (average)	$2.51	$2.12	$2.44	$1.7	$1.53
Fuel consumed, in gallons (millions)	1,437	1,428	1,511	1,489	1,389
Full-time equivalent employees at period-end	34,901	34,726	35,499	34,378	32,664
Size of fleet at period-end	548	537	537	520	481

* Refer to the appendix at the end of this case for a glossary of the terms used in this table.

Source: Southwest Airlines. SEC filings, Form 10-K, *www.sec.gov*.

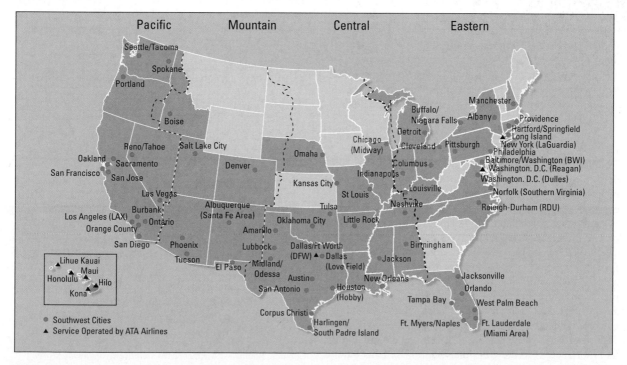

Exhibit 2 Cities Served by Southwest Airlines

Source: Printed with permission from Southwest Airlines, *www.southwest.com/about_swa/routemap.html*.

Year	Number of Cities Served
1996	49
1997	51
1998	52
1999	56
2000	57
2001	58
2002	58
2003	58
2004	58
2005	61
2006	63
2007	64
2008	64
2009	68
2010	69

Source: Southwest Airlines. Forms 10-K filed with SEC.

SWA tried not to hire people who were humorless, self-centered, or complacent. Not surprisingly, there was no human resource department but, rather, a People Department at Southwest. The guiding principle for recruitment at SWA was "Hire for attitude and train for skills," which Kelleher believed was the most important principle. When an employee from the People Department said to him, "Herb, I'm getting a little embarrassed because I've interviewed 34 people for a ramp agent position in Amarillo," Kelleher replied, "If you have to interview 134 people to find the appropriate person to be a ramp agent in Amarillo, do it. Because the most important thing is to get the right people, and if you get the wrong ones they start poisoning everybody else."[10]

Kelleher's penchant for laughter and fun became a part of Southwest's culture. Prospective employees were asked how humor helped them out of a difficult situation. Prospective pilots were sometimes asked to pull on shorts, and the ones who saw fun in it passed the interview. All people at the company were to be treated with dignity and respect, and Kelleher did not believe in hierarchical barriers. When a vice president complained to the CEO that customers, gate agents, pilots, and baggage handlers had more access to the CEO than he did, Kelleher said to him, "Let me explain this: They're more important than you are." Kelleher recognized that the key to satisfied customers was having satisfied employees. So employees came first, and that orientation was embodied in the airline's mission statement (Exhibit 4).

The culture was put into operation through a number of policies and programs. The casual-dress policy reinforced the company's desire that people be themselves on the job. Celebrations such as spirit parties, culture parties, and weekly deck parties were organized at headquarters regularly to bring employees together. Activities at the events included gong shows, talent shows, dance contests, limbo contests, and famous-person look-alike themes. The culture committee at SWA welcomed new employees with a "New Hire Welcome Kit" that included a bag, T-shirt, badge holder, pen, and welcome letter. To build solidarity across all departments, there was an employee recognition program in which employees recognized each other's achievements. This practice helped community building within and across departments. For example, one work group committee recognized flight attendants 10 times a year with "Hokey Days," named for the broom apparatus used by flight attendants to sweep the cabin after the flights. Committee members chose two locations at which to honor flight attendants, greeted each arriving plane, waited until passengers got off, and then boarded with goodies. Flight attendants were asked to relax while the committee members cleaned the plane for them. There were similar programs to honor other departments as well.[11] There was also the "Walk a Mile Program," designed to foster problem solving and cooperation, in which an employee could do somebody else's job for a day (while operations people obviously could not fly the airplanes, pilots could do the

Exhibit 4   **Mission Statement of Southwest Airlines**

The mission of Southwest Airlines is dedication to the highest quality of Customer Service delivered with a sense of warmth, friendliness, individual pride, and Company Spirit.

To Our Employees

We are committed to provide our Employees a stable work environment with equal opportunity for learning and personal growth. Creativity and innovation are encouraged for improving the effectiveness of Southwest Airlines. Above all, Employees will be provided the same concern, respect, and caring attitude within the organization that they are expected to share externally with every Southwest Customer.

Source: Southwest Airlines. *www.southwest.com/about_swa/mission.html.*

work of operations agents).[12] Further, the company had the "Star of the Month," a program that recognized the distinct contributions of employees toward excellence in customer service—outstanding employees were featured in *Spirit*, Southwest's in-flight magazine.[13]

The company also expressed warmth toward its employees in other ways. At Southwest's headquarters in Dallas, the walls were covered with more than 10,000 picture frames that contained photos of employees' pets, of stewardesses in miniskirts, of Southwest planes gnawing on competitor's aircraft. Also there were teddy bears, jars of pickled hot peppers, and pink flamingos. There was cigarette smoking and lots of chuckling. "To me, it's comfortable," said Colleen Barrett, who was most responsible for nurturing the Southwest culture from its early days. "This is an open scrapbook. We aren't uptight. We celebrate everything. It's like a fraternity, a sorority, a reunion. We are having a party!" she said. Barrett also regularly traveled to meet the employees and personally sent them birthday cards, not so much to win their loyalty as to communicate the true spirit of a family. The company celebrated with its employees when good things happened and grieved with them when they had devastating experiences.[14] Barrett said, "What we do is very simple, but it's not simplistic. We really do everything with passion. We scream at each other and we hug each other."[15]

Cost consciousness was another important part of the culture. "Yes, our culture is almost like a religion," said Gary Kelly, the erstwhile CFO and the present CEO of Southwest. "But it's a dichotomy. In many ways we are conservative. Financially, for instance," he added.[16] According to Herb Kelleher, close attention to costs had produced the kind of financial success Southwest had seen. He said, "Even in the best of times, we kept our costs low and questioned every expenditure. For years, I used to approve every expenditure over $1,000. Why? To encourage a cost-conscious culture. I couldn't look at all of them, of course. But I would question them selectively, and that kept people paying attention."[17]

Treating employees well at Southwest did not mean that they were paid high salaries. By creating value through intangibles, the company kept wages lower than those of competitors. Officers at Southwest were paid about 30 percent less, on average, than their counterparts at other airlines. But the airline made stock options widely available, so all employees—not just executives—could share in the company's financial success. Southwest even had a policy that its officers received pay increases that were no larger, proportionally, than what other employees received. But employees were also expected to take pay reductions when times were not good. Job security was ensured, however, with a "no-furlough policy," and Southwest did not lay off a single employee during the economic downturn after the terrorist attacks on September 11, 2001, while many of its competitors did.[18] Caring for employee happiness showed positive results. Southwest had less employee turnover than its competitors. For years, Southwest enjoyed the loyalty of its employees despite the high level of employee unionization. "Once labor leaders realize that you're trying to take care of your people, most of the edge [in contract negotiations] is gone," said Kelleher.[19]

Southwest's employees worked more hours than their counterparts at other airlines. Southwest pilots flew nearly 80 hours a month, compared to United's 50 hours. Southwest pilots were paid by trip, not per hour, which created a strong interest in keeping flights on schedule. Also, the pilots tended to be cost-conscious because a big part of their compensation came from stock options. On some occasions, pilots even pitched in to help ground crews move luggage to ensure on-time flights—something virtually unheard of at Southwest's bigger rivals. Flight attendants at Southwest worked about 150 hours a month, compared with 80 hours at many other airlines, according to union president Thom McDaniel. Southwest attendants were required by contract to make a reasonable effort to tidy the airplane between flights, a job performed by maintenance personnel at rival airlines. According to an airline labor expert, senior flight attendants at United got as many as 52 vacation days a year (compared with 35 days for veterans at Southwest), and they never had to clean up after the passengers.[20]

Maintaining focus on the core business was another element for both controlling costs and pursuing a niche strategy. Kelleher consciously ensured that the company did not diverge into allied businesses, such as car rentals or reservations. Most of Southwest's growth had been organic; that is, it occurred by adding more flights on its existing routes and by connecting more dots (adding cities). The airline started complementing its short-haul flights with long-haul flights and began transcontinental services. According to Kelleher, the airline did not plan to have international flights, as they would require a total change in the way it operated and would involve training its 35,000 employees to handle that change.[21]

The cost consciousness and employee commitment translated into operational excellence and increased profitability (Exhibit 5). Southwest's planes flew about 10.9 hours per day, much more than any other airline except JetBlue, which flew close to 13.0 hours per day. Southwest could offer lower fares—as much as 50 percent lower than its major rivals—and still remain profitable. With such low costs, it created what was called the "Southwest effect," an explosion in the numbers of people traveling by plane, including many who would have gone by car before.[22] The term *Southwest effect* was coined by the U.S. Department of Transportation to refer to the consistent phenomenon of a decrease in average fares and a stimulation of demand that occurred when Southwest Airlines entered any market.[23]

In May 1988 Southwest became the first airline to win the coveted Triple Crown for a month: Best On-Time Record, Best Baggage Handling, and Fewest Customer

Complaints. Since then, Southwest has won it more than 30 times, as well as five annual Triple Crowns for 1992, 1993, 1994, 1995, and 1996. Southwest crossed its $1 billion revenue mark in 1990, thereby becoming a major airline, and topped the monthly domestic originating-passenger rankings for the first time in May 2003. It was also the largest carrier on the basis of scheduled domestic departures. Stories of Southwest employees providing excellent customer service abound, and Southwest even set up an internal TV system to show how its employees treated customers.[24]

The Changing Times and Challenges

Southwest Airlines had a change in leadership in August 2001 when Herb Kelleher relinquished power to two of his close aides. Colleen C. Barrett, vice president for customers, became the president and chief operating officer; and James F. Parker, general counsel, became the chief executive officer. Barrett and Parker had worked together for over 22 years, and both had worked with Kelleher for much longer—from the time he was a lawyer. In contrast to Kelleher's obtrusive personality, Parker was a quiet diplomat. He had been the company's lead labor negotiator for years, and his opponents said he pursued the company line quite forcefully, if politely, in talks. "He will surprise you because he doesn't look like he's tough, but he doesn't give anything away," said a former vice president of the airline's pilot association.[25] Unlike Kelleher, Parker was not as fond of celebrations, because he didn't see them as contributing to productivity. But he came to realize that the party preparations were a model of teamwork and employee bonding, and he started participating in the celebrations in 2002.[26]

Barrett had been the culture keeper of Southwest since the earliest days of the company. However, she was a reluctant public speaker. Thus, she let Parker take the lead with Wall Street and the media. It was too early to guess whether the lieutenants could replace the "rock star" personality of Kelleher, who had exuded warmth to his employees. Kelleher remained chairman of the board and focused on long-range strategy and government affairs. He maintained control of schedule planning and aircraft acquisitions, the backbone of Southwest's strategy during the period of transition.[27]

The growth of the company and the consequent increase in the number of employees also posed challenges to keeping the culture intact. The distance between the rank and file and top management was growing. While Colleen Barrett could reach all the employees through personally signed birthday cards when the company was small, the task was becoming increasingly unrealistic. Even though she continued to sign cards, she could reach only a fraction of Southwest's 35,000 employees dispersed in different cities. Keeping in close touch with employees was becoming

Exhibit 5   **Comparison with Key Competitors and Industry**

Measures of Comparison	Southwest	AMR Corp.	JetBlue	UAL	Industry (Regional Airlines)
Market cap	8.72B	2.17B	1.63B	7.65B	986.31M
Employees	34,901	78,250	11,121	N.A.	11.12K
Quarterly revenue growth (YOY)	14.80%	10.40%	13.00%	101.10%	20.30%
Revenue (TTM)	12.10B	22.17B	3.78B	23.23B	2.62B
Gross margin (TTM)	25.13%	23.03%	33.00%	29.44%	27.92%
EBITDA (TTM)	1.62B	1.40B	563.67M	2.60B	348.98M
Operating margins (TTM)	8.16%	1.39%	8.81%	7.22%	8.49%
Net income (TTM)	459.00M	−471.00M	97.00M	252.00M	N/A
EPS (TTM)	0.61	−1.41	0.31	1.08	0.69
P/E (TTM)	19.20	N/A	17.87	21.57	12.38
P/S (TTM)	0.72	0.10	0.43	0.33	0.45

Note: YOY = year over year; TTM = trailing 12 months.

Source: yahoofinance.com, March 2, 2011.

an increasingly challenging task. In earlier times of difficulty, Herb Kelleher personally addressed and rallied his troops, but such an exercise was no longer easy.

In addition, the warm employee relations at Southwest seemed to chill over time. Unions were becoming more aggressive in expressing their frustration, in contrast to earlier days when disputes were resolved more amicably and peacefully. In the summer of 2001, ramp workers picketed near company headquarters with signs that read "Record Profits Empty Pockets." They complained that staff shortages, combined with Southwest's record passenger loads and its drive to improve on-time performance, meant that they had to lift more bags and had to do so more quickly, which put them at risk of injury.[28] And, for the first time in company history, in July 2002 Southwest's mechanics union asked federal mediators to intervene to break a contract deadlock over pay. While the company was nowhere near a strike, the incident clearly signaled the strains appearing in employee relations.[29]

In 2002 the company was also engaged without much success in a contract renegotiation with flight attendants. In July 2003 a group of flight attendants staged a demonstration at the headquarters, carrying signs stating "Spread the LUV" and handing out cards to travelers that read "Give our flight attendants a break." The move was an expression of frustration over management's idea of increasing the flight attendants' work hours. Also, workers who had been working hard to boost the productivity of the company were not seeing much return from profit sharing and a stock value that was falling. After years of hard work, some long-time employees felt that they had no more to give. Karen Amos, a 26-year Southwest veteran, said, "We have been there for them. There comes a time when it becomes too much."[30] The company had to drop the move to increase work hours, but still could not get a deal made with the flight attendants. Some workers perceived that the company had been fairer in its negotiations in past years.

In November 2003, after 11 rounds of talks without success, the flight attendants threw a Thanksgiving party at Salt Lake City International Airport, primarily as a means of putting pressure on management to accept their demands for holiday pay and better working conditions. Kevin Onstead, a Southwest negotiator and flight attendant, said, "We are concerned about the culture of the airline. We are fighting for the recognition of our contribution to that culture. We've been key in Southwest Airlines' success. Flight attendants are prepared to strike as a last resort. We are willing to do whatever it takes to get a fair contract."[31] The negotiations had not borne fruit by early 2004. Thom McDaniel, president of the Transport Workers Union, said that the flight attendants were willing to return to the negotiating table. However, he made the point that the latest management offer fell short of their expectations. "We feel that our culture is at risk because of the actions taken by Southwest's management during these negotiations."[32] Many of the employee groups started feeling that Southwest Airlines was no longer the underdog and that their pay should match the profitability of the company. Love (LUV) alone no longer seemed to be enough. That meant a twin challenge in terms of culture and costs.

In July 2004 James Parker abruptly resigned as CEO of Southwest amid strained labor negotiations with the flight attendants. Some people said that Parker had spent too much time in the back offices of Southwest and was never really cut out for a job in the limelight.[33] Herb Kelleher stepped into the negotiations, and the flight attendants walked away smiling with a 31 percent pay raise.[34]

Gary C. Kelly, former chief financial officer of Southwest, took the helm. Kelly was certainly energetic, showing up at the office Halloween party in 2004 dressed as Gene Simmons, leader of the rock group Kiss.[35] He, of course, decided later that he was better off being Kelly than someone else. Kelly audaciously acquired six gates at Chicago's Midway Airport from bankrupt carrier ATA and signed Southwest's first ever code-share agreement with ATA, primarily in response to AirTran eyeing a move into Chicago. In December 2008, the airline agreed to provide an online link to WestJet's booking portal that helps its customers book flights to Canada. Later, Southwest formally filed an application with the Department of Transportation for rights to fly its own planes to Canada.[36] Southwest was already experiencing cost increases per average seat-mile (ASM), a key metric used to measure performance in the industry, primarily due to increases in fuel costs and wages. The cost per ASM went up from 7.07 cents in 1995 to 11.29 cents in 2010, with fuel costs, wages, and benefits as the major contributors (Exhibit 6). Southwest's cost per average seat-mile, however, remained below that of the big carriers. The company was already working hard on controlling costs. With more of its customers making reservations online and the labor cost advantage narrowing between major airlines after restructuring, further cost squeezing appeared to be a difficult proposition. Though Kelly did not concede it openly, he understood that further cost reductions would be hard to come by without modest fare increases and possible employee layoffs—something that was totally against Southwest's culture.[37] In 2007, a new fare structure was introduced that included Business Select, which gave customers priority in boarding.[38]

Intensifying competition in the low-fare segment was another factor that had become difficult to ignore. While competitors such as JetBlue and AirTran were not direct threats to Southwest on its existing routes, further expansion of those carriers could bring them head-on with Southwest. These new airlines offered far more attractive services, such as leather seats and in-flight entertainment systems, for almost the same fare. Therefore, these rivals could make the no-frills approach of Southwest pale before them. Whether Southwest's loyal customers would still stick with the airline when they could get

Exhibit 6 Southwest Airlines' Operating Expenses per Average Seat Mile, 2002–2010 (in cents)

Category	2010	2009	2008	2007	2006	2005	2004	2003	2002
Salaries, wages, and benefits	3.76	3.54	3.23	3.22	3.29	3.27	3.18	3.10	2.89
Fuel and oil	3.68	3.11	3.60	2.55	2.31	1.58	1.30	1.16	1.11
Maintenance materials and repairs	0.76	0.73	0.70	0.62	0.51	0.52	0.60	0.60	0.57
Aircraft rentals	0.18	0.19	0.15	0.16	0.17	0.19	0.23	0.25	0.27
Landing fees and other rentals	0.82	0.73	0.64	0.56	0.53	0.53	0.53	0.52	0.50
Depreciation and amortization	0.64	0.63	0.58	0.56	0.56	0.55	0.56	0.53	0.52
Other	1.45	1.36	1.34	1.43	1.43	1.41	1.37	1.37	1.47
Total	11.29	10.29	10.24	9.10	8.80	8.05	7.77	7.53	7.33

Source: Southwest Airlines. 2002–2010. Form 10-K filed with SEC.

more value for their money elsewhere was a significant question. Southwest's investments to automate and significantly streamline the ticketing and boarding process with computer-generated bag tags, automated boarding passes, and self-service boarding pass kiosks, and its investments to increase the functionality of its website, along with its moves to enhance aircraft interiors with leather seats, can hardly be described as *not* being motivated by competition.[39] That JetBlue caught Southwest's attention was clear by the comment that Southwest was studying the possibility of introducing an in-flight entertainment system, although at the time it was too costly to adopt. Thus, matching amenities with those of the emerging competition could pose additional challenges to SWA's low-cost strategy. Kelleher's reaction to the emerging competition was simple—he had seen that movie before.

Meanwhile, Southwest entered the Philadelphia market, a stronghold of US Air, in May 2004. The Philadelphia market was one of the most overpriced and underserved. Southwest aimed at capturing the market with its tried and tested low-cost, no-frills formula, albeit with leather seats on some of its newer planes. US Air responded, "We will be a vigorous competitor to Southwest in Philadelphia on every route they fly."[40]

In addition to establishing the ATA code share for Chicago's Midway,[41] Kelly added Phoenix to the code share in April 2005.[42] Then Kelly directed Southwest's entry into Pittsburgh in May 2005, announcing, "The Pittsburgh International Airport will be a great addition to our system."[43] In October 2005 Southwest began service out of Southwest Florida International Airport in Fort Myers,

making it the 61st Southwest city.[44] Robert M. Ball, executive director of Florida's Lee County Port Authority, said after courting Southwest for nearly a decade, "We have been working closely with Southwest for many years and are pleased they have selected Southwest Florida as their newest destination."[45] Kelly was on hand to wave the banner, and he said, "Now, our Southwest Florida customers have to look no further than their own backyard for Southwest's legendary low fares and great customer service." Denver, Colorado, and Washington Dulles International Airport were added to the list in 2006. From 2006 to 2010 the number of cities served increased from 63 to 69.[46]

Wright Amendment and Beyond

With legacy carriers achieving significant labor restructuring agreements and thus eroding SWA's once considerable wage-rate advantage, overcapacity in the East pushing down passenger yields lower than SWA would prefer, and other low-cost carriers such as JetBlue and AirTran carving their niches and reducing the "underserved and overpriced markets" that form the heart of Southwest's commercial strategy, further growth and even cost reductions have been difficult to come by.[47] Kelly pushed for the repeal of the Wright amendment.[48] Southwest entered into an agreement with the City of Dallas, the City of Forth Worth, American Airlines Inc. (which has its hub at Dallas–Fort Worth airport), and the DFW International Airport Board, following which these five parties sought enactment of legislation that would amend the original Wright amendment. Congress responded with a reform act that substantially reduced earlier restrictions.

This has worked to Southwest's advantage, because it can fly to many more destinations from Love Field than earlier, provided the flights stop first in a state within the Wright perimeter. This includes New Mexico, Oklahoma, Missouri, Arkansas, Louisiana, Mississippi, Kansas, and Alabama, along with Texas.[49] Southwest controls about 90 percent of the Love Field market. Southwest's passenger traffic at Love Field has risen by about 18 percent since the Wright restrictions were loosened in October 2006. This, of course, has a price war brewing between American and Southwest.[50]

None of the members of senior management would concede that Southwest is becoming a different creature. This is primarily because of the huge psychic investment the airline has in being the "underdog." "We're bigger, let's put it that way," says Kelleher. "I think the airline business is fundamentally an opportunistic business. . . . We suddenly have some opportunities materializing that are new to us."[51]

From being an underdog and a company pursuing a very conservative organic growth strategy, Southwest now looks to be compelled to grow through acquisitions. Southwest announced an agreement to acquire all outstanding shares of common stock of AirTran Holdings Inc., the parent company of AirTran Airways (AirTran), for a combination of $1.4 billion cash and Southwest Airlines's common stock in September 2010. This acquisition gave access to Atlanta, a Delta Air Lines fortress for decades, and more flights from New York and Washington, D.C. Whether or not Southwest overpaid for this acquisition is another matter for debate. Nevertheless, this acquisition will put the company more squarely in the sights of Delta, the major airline that turned Atlanta into the world's busiest airport with the "hub-and-spoke" system of funneling passengers to their destinations. In July Delta and its regional affiliates controlled 76 percent of passenger traffic at Hartfield-Jackson Atlanta, according to figures from the airport. AirTran's market share was 17 percent in the same month. To Kelly, that signifies a high-fare environment ripe for Southwest service. "We need more flights on a combined basis [in Atlanta] than AirTran has today," he says. "And I do mean significantly more flights—more than a couple." Such a move could spark a fierce response from Delta, akin to a "defend the fortress hub strategy," as Hudson Securities analyst Daniel McKenzie wrote in a note to clients.

It is a known fact that most M&A's end up destroying value for the acquiring company's shareholders. If Southwest's growth is going to be driven by M&A's going forward, is this growth going to be profitable and will it be sustainable?

Endnotes

1. Schlangenstein, M., & Hughes, J. 2010. Southwest CEO risks keep-it-simple strategy to reignite growth. *Bloomberg,* September 28. *http://www.bloomberg.com/news/* 2010-09-27/southwest-airlines-agrees-to-buy-airtran-for-1-4-billion-in-cash-shares.html

2. Rappeport, A., & Lemer, J. 2010. Southwest acquires Airtran for $3.4 bn. Financial Times, September 27. *http://www.ft.com/cms/s/0/14ff99a0-ca2e-11df-87b8-00144feab49a.html#axzz1ODSbX63E*

3. Bachman, J., Schlangenstein, M., and Hughes, J. 2010. Southwest charts a new flight plan. *Bloomberg-Businessweek,* September 29. *http://www.businessweek.com/magazine/content/10_41/b4198022740823.htm*

4. Freiberg, K., & Freiberg, J. 1996. Nuts! Southwest Airlines' crazy recipe for personal and business success. Austin, TX: Bard Press, 20–27. *archives.californiaaviation.org/airport/msg15249.html.*

5. Ibid.

6. Ibid., 6.

7. Greylock Associates. 2003. Herb Kelleher, chairman, CEO and president, Southwest Airlines.

8. Southwest Airlines. 2003, 2006, 2010. 10-K filings.

9. McConnell, B. 2001. The wild, flying turkey with wings: Creating customer evangelists—A profile of Herb Kelleher. *www.creatingcustomerevangelists.com/resources/evangelists/herb_kelleher.asp.*

10. Kelleher, H. 2003. Interview with Mark Morrison of *BusinessWeek* at Texas McComb's School of Business. *BusinessWeek,* December 23. *www.businessweek.com.*

11. Serwer, A., & Bonamici, K. 2004. Southwest Airlines: The hottest ting in the sky through change at the top, through 9/11, in a lousy industry, it keeps winning most admired kudos. How? *CNNMoney,* 2004. *http://money.cnn.com/magazines/fortune/fortune_archive/2004/03/08/363700/index.htm*

12. Kelleher, H. 1997. A culture of commitment. *Leader to Leader,* no. 4. *www.leadertoleader.org/knowledgecenter/journal.aspx?ArticleID = 143.*

13. Southwest Airlines. *www.southwest.com/careers/stars/stars.html.*

14. Shinn, S. 2003. LUV, Colleen. *BizEd,* March–April.

15. Serwer. 2004. Southwest Airlines: The hottest thing in the sky. *Fortune,* March 8: 88–106.

16. Ibid.

17. *Knowledge@Wharton.* 2003. What makes Southwest Airlines fly? April 23. *knowledge.wharton.upenn.edu/article.cfm?articleid = 753.*

18. Ibid.; Kelleher. 1997. A culture of commitment.; Freedman, M. 2002. Non-stop growth? *ABCNews.com,* July 2.

19. *Knowledge@Wharton.* 2003. What makes Southwest Airlines fly?

20. Donnelly, S. B. 2002. One airline's magic. *Time.* October 28: 45–47.

21. Kelleher. 2003. Interview with Mark Morrison; McConnell. 2001. The wild, flying turkey with wings.

22. Zellner, W. 2001. Southwest: After Kelleher, more blue skies. *BusinessWeek,* April 2: 45.

23. Boehmer, J. 2008. NYC to test Southwest effect. *Business Travel News,* December 8. *www.businesstravelnews.com/Business-Travel/Airline-News/Articles/NYC-To-Test-Southwest-Effect/*

24. *www.southwest.com;* Serwer. 2004. Southwest Airlines.

25. Freedman. 2002. Non-stop growth?

26. Trotman, M. 2003. Inside Southwest Airlines, storied culture feels strains. *Wall Street Journal Online,* July 11. *online.wsj.com.*

27. Zellner. 2001. Southwest: After Kelleher; Zellner, W., & Arndt, M. 2003. Holding steady. *Business Week,* February 3: 66–68.

28. Trotman. 2003. Inside Southwest Airlines.

29. Roman, M. 2002. Southwest Air's family feud. *Business Week,* July 15. *www.businessweek.com*

30. Trotman. 2003. Inside Southwest Airlines.

31. Warchol, G. 2003. Southwest crews rally for their cause. *Salt Lake Tribune,* November 26. *www.sltrib.com/2003/ Nov/11262003/Business/Business.asp.*

32. *AIRwise News.* 2004. Southwest flight attendants may resume contract talks. February 18. *www.airwise.com/ news/airlines/southwest.html.*

33. *Economist.* 2004. Global agenda. July 16: 1. *www. economist.com.*

34. Gimbel, B. 2005. Southwest's new flight plan. *Fortune,* May 16: 93–97.

35. Southwest Airlines. From SEC filings.

36. Zellner, W. 2005. Dressed to kill . . . competitors. *Business Week,* February 21: 60.

37. Southwest Airlines. From company press releases.

38. Gimbel. 2005. Southwest's new flight plan.

39. Southwest Airlines. SEC Form 10-K filings.

40. Serwer. 2004. Southwest Airlines.

41. Zellner. 2005. Dressed to kill . . . competitors.

42. Southwest Airlines. 2005. Press releases, March 7 and June 28.

43. Southwest Airlines. 2005. Press release, May 4.

44. Southwest Airlines. 2005. Press release, July 14.

45. Southwest Airlines. 2005. Press release, June 27.

46. Southwest Airlines. SEC Form 10-K filings.

47. Flint, P. 2005. Southwest keeps it simple. *Air Transport World,* April: 26.

48. The federal law that limited airlines operating at Dallas Love Field to serving destinations in Texas and seven nearby states, primarily with an intention to protect the then-new Dallas–Fort Worth International Airport. Southwest was not initially a part of the agreement, and therefore its original quest for existence led to its "underdog" mentality.

49. Southwest Airlines. 2006. SEC filing.

50. Mutzabaugh, B. 2007. Southwest soars at Dallas Love following relaxed Wright rules. *USAToday,* March 23. *blogs.usatoday.com/sky/wright_amendment/index.html.*

51. Gimbel. 2005. Southwest's new flight plan.

Appendix A   Key Terms Used

Aircraft utilization. The average number of block hours operated per day per aircraft for the total fleet of aircraft.

Available seat-miles. The number of seats available for passengers multiplied by the number of miles the seats are flown.

Average fare. The average one-way fare paid per flight segment by a revenue passenger.

Average stage length. The average number of miles flown per flight.

Break-even load factor. The passenger load factor that will result in operating revenues being equal to operating expenses, assuming constant revenue per passenger-mile and expenses.

Load factor. The percentage of aircraft seating capacity actually used (revenue passenger-miles divided by available seat-miles).

Operating expense per available seat-mile. Operating expenses divided by available seat-miles.

Operating revenue per available seat-mile. Operating revenues divided by available seat-miles.

Revenue passenger-miles. The number of miles flown by revenue passengers.

Revenue passengers. The total number of paying passengers flown on all flight segments.

Yield per passenger mile. The average amount one passenger pays to fly 1 mile.

Case 22   eBay

Expanding into China*

By 2010, eBay faced the challenge of surviving in the Asian market. Like many U.S. Internet companies, eBay had repeatedly tried to broaden its reach in Asia, where local rivals had strong ties to users. With Asia's population exceeding 3.8 billion, more than half the world's population, and Internet usage in the region skyrocketing at 620 percent,[1] eBay needed to develop a strategy that would successfully adapt to Asian local markets and compete with Taobao, China's top auction site, and other major local competitors.

In March 2010, eBay announced that Paypal would team up with China UnionPay in a bid to expand in the market dominated by Chinese rival Alipay. Alipay, a unit of Taobao's parent company, Alibaba Group, had 300 million users, three times as many as PayPal in China.[2] The partnership would give customers of China UnionPay, a national electronic-payment network, the ability to make Internet purchases from websites overseas. Before this partnership, PayPal offered Chinese consumers and businesses two types of accounts: one that allowed domestic transactions in Chinese Yuan and a second that permitted purchases abroad through dual-currency credit cards. The new program allowed customers with a UnionPay credit or debit card to make overseas purchases.[3]

eBay announced in December 2010 that PayPal would set up an international ecommerce hub in Chongqing, China, as the company aimed to boost exports from the nation by helping merchants conduct faster cross-border trade. PayPal agreed with Chongqing's municipal government to set up the center to offer foreign exchange settlement, telesales, training, verification, and other services.[4]

"Helping local companies connect with global customers would boost eBay's transaction volume from China more than 80 percent to $4 billion," eBay CEO John Donahoe, said in 2010.[5] eBay had been counting on PayPal and local partnerships to expand revenue from China after failing to gain a foothold to compete against Alibaba Group. "eBay plans to focus on exports and cross-border trades involving China instead of competing in the domestic market," he added.

eBay

Since its inception in 1995, eBay has enjoyed strong revenue growth and been a dominant player in the online auction industry. The company posted net income of $1.8 billion and revenue of $9.15 billion for 2010 (see Exhibit 1.) "We are driving strong global growth at Pay-Pal and strengthening our core eBay business. And we are innovating quickly in areas such as mobile, which is helping to position us at the forefront of trends shaping the future of shopping and payments," commented CEO John Donahoe.

eBay's founder, Pierre Omidyar, envisioned a community built on commerce, sustained by trust, and inspired by opportunity. The company's mission was to "enable individual self-empowerment on a global scale" and employ "business as a tool for social good." Omidyar cited "trust between strangers" as the social impact tied to eBay's ability to remain profitable.

The company's unique business model, which united buyers and sellers in an online marketplace, had attracted over 221 million registered users. eBay enabled e-commerce at multiple levels (local, national, and international) through an array of websites, including eBay Marketplaces, PayPal, Skype, Rent.com, and Shopping.com. The company's range of products and services had evolved from collectibles to household products, customer services, automobiles, and so on. The variety of products attracted a range of users that included students, small businesses, independent sellers, major corporations, and government agencies.

Despite eBay's outstanding growth performance, the company still faced a number of challenges in both domestic and international markets. The low entry barriers in the online marketplace attracted a number of large dot-com competitors, including Amazon, Yahoo, uBid, and Overstock. Historically, the company had acquired other online competitors, such as Stubhub (tickets), but established players such as Yahoo and Amazon posed a major threat to eBay's market share and ability to sustain profitability. Still, eBay's top management felt that the company would end up as a specialty business, an idea suggesting that it would face little threat from these major competitors. The company had no plans for further big acquisitions but intended to expand and identify synergies within existing business lines.

eBay acknowledged its inability to grow and compete in certain international markets. The company created localized sites in 24 countries and established a presence in Latin America through its investment in MercadoLibre.com. However, eBay's numerous attempts to penetrate the Asia Pacific market, specifically China and Japan, ended in failure, with the company pulling out of Japan and buying out Chinese start-up Eachnet, essentially canceling years of invested work. According to many analysts, the company's recent interest in its South Korean rival

* This case was prepared by Professor Alan B. Eisner and graduate students David J. Morates and Shruti Shrestha of Pace University. This case was solely based on library research and was developed for class discussion rather than to illustrate either effective or ineffective handling of an administrative situation. Copyright © 2011 Alan B. Eisner.

Exhibit 1   **Income Statements** (in thousands, except per-share amounts; year-end December 31)

	2006	2007	2008	2009	2010
Net revenues	$5,969,741	$7,672,329	$8,541,261	$8,727,362	$9,156,274
Cost of net revenues	1,256,792	1,762,972	2,228,069	2,479,762	25,564,667
Gross profit	4,712,949	5,909,357	6,313,192	6,247,600	6,591,607
Operating expenses:					
Sales and marketing	1,587,133	1,882,810	1,881,551	1,885,677	1,946,815
Product development	494,695	619,727	725,600	803,070	908,434
General and administrative	744,363	904,681	998,871	1,418,389	1,079,383
Provision for transaction and loan losses	266,724	293,917	347,453	382,825	392,240
Amortization of acquired intangible assets	197,078	204,104	234,916	262,686	189,727
Restructuring	—	—	49,119	38,187	21,437
Impairment of goodwill	—	1,390,938	—	—	—
Total operating expenses	3,289,993	5,296,177	4,237,510	4,790,834	4,538,036
Income from operations	1,422,956	613,180	2,075,682	1,456,766	2,053,571
Interest and other income, net	130,017	154,271	115,919	1,422,385	44,867
Income before income taxes	1,547,057	750,851	2,183,564	2,879,151	2,098,447
Provision for income taxes	(421,418)	(402,600)	(404,090)	(490,054)	(297,486)
Net income	$1,125,639	$ 348,251	$1,779,474	$2,389,097	$1,800,961
Net income per share:					
Basic	$ 0.80	$ 0.26	$ 1.37	$ 1.85	$ 1.38
Diluted	$ 0.79	$ 0.25	$ 1.36	$ 1.83	$ 1.36
Weighted average shares:					
Basic	1,399,251	1,358,797	1,303,454	1,289,848	1,305,593
Diluted	1,425,472	1,376,174	1,312,608	1,304,981	1,327,417

Gmarket Inc. and joint venture with Beijing-based Tom Online were further indications that eBay couldn't compete in these countries. To remain successful and enjoy the same financial performance as it had in the past, eBay needed to develop an effective strategy to compete in major Asian markets and mitigate the risk of existing local competitors.

Evolution of Auctions

Traditional Auctions

According to Greek scribes, the first known auctions occurred in Babylon in 500 BC. At that time, women were sold on the condition of marriage, and it was considered illegal for daughters to be sold outside auctions. Auctions evolved during the French Revolution and throughout the American Civil War, where colonels auctioned goods that were seized by armies.[6] Although there were various types of auctions, they all provided a forum where sellers could find buyers or hobbyists who were looking to purchase rare items and collectibles. Auctions were considered one of the purest markets, since buyers paid what they were willing to spend for an item, thereby determining the true market value of the item. Over time, auction formats continued to evolve, and through technological advances and improved communication they found a new home— the Internet.

Online Auctions

The primary difference between traditional and online auctions was that the online auction process occurred over the Internet as opposed to at a specific location where both buyers and sellers were present. Online auctions offered strategic advantages to both parties that were not typically available in traditional auctions. Buyers could select from millions of products and engage in multiple auctions simultaneously. Given the massive inventory of an online auction market, items were usually available in multiple auctions, allowing buyers to compare starting bid prices and search for better prices. Sellers were exposed to millions of buyers, since more buyers had access to the Internet and felt comfortable making purchases online. The net impact was increased price competition, since there were more buyers who were willing to purchase items at a higher price. Thus, the Internet gave buyers and sellers access to a marketplace that spanned the world.

Online auctions also offered the following strategic advantages:

1. *No time constraints.* A bid could be placed at any time.
2. *No geographic constraints.* Sellers and buyers could participate from any location with Internet access.
3. *Network economies.* The large number of bidders attracted more sellers, which attracted more bidders, and so on. This created a large system that had more value for both parties. Online auctions also allowed businesses to easily sell off excess inventory or discontinued items. This was done through either business-to-business (B2B) or business-to-consumer (B2C) auctions. Offering products and services in an online auction helped small businesses build their brand and reputation by establishing a devoted customer base. Finally, some businesses used the online marketplace as an inexpensive yet effective way to test-market for upcoming products.

E-Commerce

Although Vannevar Bush originally conceived the idea of the Internet in 1945, it wasn't until the 1990s that the Internet became overwhelmingly popular. According to Internet World Stats, in September 2010 there were over 1.9 billion Internet users in over 150 countries. Exhibit 2 shows Internet usage growth between 1995 and 2010.

As of 2010, North America was considered the region most penetrated by the Internet, with approximately 77.4 percent of the population already online. However, Internet usage growth between 2000 and 2010 was considerably less in North America than in other regions. The regions with the highest Internet usage growth were developing countries, where penetration was low, such as Africa, Asia, Latin America, and the Middle East. Considering close to 80 percent of the world's population resides in these areas, it is inevitable that Internet usage growth will continue to increase dramatically in these regions. Exhibit 3 shows world Internet usage and population as of December 2010.

Although Asia constituted approximately 57 percent of the world's population, its penetration rate was only 21.5 percent. Compared to other regions with high usage growth rates, such as Africa and the Middle East, Asia invested more in its technology infrastructure and contained by far the most current Internet users, making it a more attractive market. Exhibit 4 provides more detail on how Asia stacks against the rest of the world in terms of Internet usage.

As the usage growth of the Internet increased, so did the popularity of e-commerce. E-commerce, or electronic commerce, was the concept of conducting business transactions over the Internet. As in the case with online auctions, e-commerce eliminated boundaries such as time and geography, allowing businesses and customers to interact with one another constantly. As more users were exposed to the Internet, they became comfortable with the idea of conducting transactions online. In correlation with Internet growth usage, revenue generated through e-commerce increased dramatically since the 1990s.

E-commerce grew rapidly in regions outside North America as well, especially in Asia since China's admission into the World Trade Organization (WTO) on December 11, 2001. Induction in the WTO allowed China to conduct business with other nations more freely by reducing tariffs and eliminating market and government impediments.

Company Background

Computer programmer Pierre Omidyar founded the online auction website in San Jose, California, on September 3, 1995. Omidyar was born in Paris, France, and moved to Maryland with his family when his father took on a residency at Johns Hopkins University Medical Center. Omidyar became fascinated with computers and later graduated from Tufts University with a degree in computer science. While living and working in the San Francisco Bay area, he met his current wife, Pamela Wesley, a management consultant, who later became a driving force in launching the auction website. The couple's vision was to establish an online marketplace where people could share the same passion and interest as Pamela had for her hobby of collecting and trading Pez candy dispensers.[7] Omidyar also envisioned an online auction format that would create a fair and open marketplace, where the market truly determined an item's value. To ensure trust in the open forum, Omidyar based the site on five main values:

1. People are basically good.
2. Everyone has something to contribute.
3. An honest, open environment can bring out the best in people.
4. Everyone deserves recognition and respect as a unique individual.
5. You should treat others the way you want to be treated.

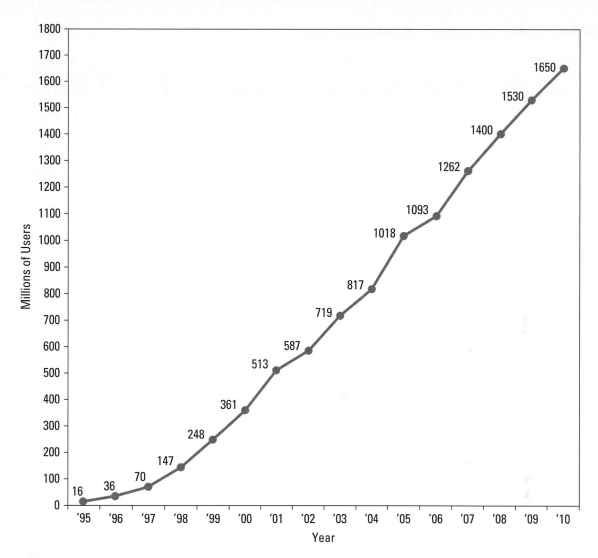

Exhibit 2 **Internet Usage Growth, 1995–2010**

Source: Internet World Stats. 2010. Global Village Online. *www.internetworldstats.com/*.

On Labor Day weekend in 1995, Omidyar launched Auction Web, an online trading platform. After the business exploded, Omidyar decided to dedicate more attention to his new enterprise and work as a consultant under the name Echo Bay Technology Group. When he tried to register a website for his company, Omidyar discovered Echo Bay was unavailable, so he decided to use the abbreviated version *eBay,* which also stood for "electronic bay area." The company's name was also selected to attract San Francisco residents to the site and prompt them to buy and sell items.

Initially, the company did not charge fees to either buyers or sellers, but as traffic grew rapidly, Omidyar was forced to charge buyers a listing fee to cover Internet service provider costs. When Omidyar noticed that the fees had no impact on the level of bids, he realized the potential for profitability of his business. To handle and manage the company's day-to-day operations, Omidyar hired Jeffrey Skoll (B.A.Sc. University of Toronto, MBA Stanford University). Skoll was hired as the company's first president, and he wrote the business plan that eBay later followed from its emergence as a start-up to its maturity as a financial success. The two worked out of Skoll's living room and various Silicon Valley facilities until they eventually settled in the company's current location in San Jose, California.

By the middle of 1997, less than a year under the name eBay, the company was hosting nearly 800,000

Exhibit 3 World Internet Usage and Population Statistics, 2010

World Regions	Population (millions)	Population (%)	Internet Usage (millions)	Percent Penetrated	Usage as % of World	Usage Growth, 2000–2010 (%)
Africa	1,013.8	14.8	110.9	10.9	5.6	2,357.3
Asia	3,834.8	56.0	825.1	21.5	42.0	621.8
Europe	813.3	12.0	475.1	58.4	24.2	352.0
Middle East	212.3	3.3	63.2	29.8	3.2	1,825.3
North America	344.1	5.0	266.2	77.4	13.5	146.3
Latin America	592.5	8.4	204.7	34.5	10.4	1,032.8
Australia	34.7	0.5	21.3	61.3	1.1	179.0
Total	**6,845.5**	**100.0**	**1,966.5**	**28.7**	**100.0**	**444.8**

Source: Internet World Stats. 2010. Usage and Population Statistics. *www.internetworldstats.com/*.

Exhibit 4 Internet Usage in Asia

Regions	Population (millions)	Internet %	Internet Users (millions)	Usage % Penetrated	Usage as % of World	Usage Growth, 2000–2008 (%)
Asia	3,834.8	56.0	825.1	21.5	42.0	621.8
Rest of world	3,010.8	44.0	1,141.4	37.9	58.0	362.7
Total	**6,845.6**	**100.0**	**1,966.5**	**28.7**	**100.0**	**444.8**

Source: Internet World Stats. 2010. Usage and Population Statistics. *www.internetworldstats.com/*.

auctions a day.[8] Although the rapid expansion of eBay's traffic caused the company to suffer a number of service interruptions, the site remained successful and continued to gain the confidence of its strong customer base. Skoll remained president until early 1998, when the company hired Meg Whitman as president and CEO. At the time, the company had only 30 employees and was solely located in the United States; in a decade the number of employees went up to over 15,000. In September 1998 eBay launched a successful public offering, making both Omidyar and Skoll instant billionaires. By the time eBay went public, less than three years after Omidyar had created the company, the site had more than a million registered users. The company grew exponentially in the late 1990s and, based on its 2010 performance, indicated no sign of stopping. Exhibit 5 highlights the company's recent growth performance by segments.

Whitman stepped down as the president and CEO of the company on March 31, 2008. Through a decade of her successful leadership, Whitman had managed to build an increasingly diversified portfolio of businesses and transformed a company with just 30 employees and $4.7 million in revenue into one of the fastest-growing companies in history, with revenues of $8.5 billion. "With humor, smarts and unflappable determination, Meg took a small, barely known online auction site and helped it become an integral part of our lives," said Omidyar, chairman of the board, about Whitman, who remained on the board of directors.[9] Both Omidyar and Whitman were confident that the new CEO, John Donahoe, was a good choice to lead eBay. Donahoe joined the company in 2005 as president of eBay's largest division, Marketplaces, and within three years managed to double the revenues and profits for this business unit. Before joining eBay, Donahoe served as the CEO of Bain & Company, an international consulting firm based in Boston.[10] "I'm extremely confident in John's skills and the abilities of John's veteran management team," Meg Whitman commented on the transition.[11]

Shortly after his election, Donahoe announced fundamental changes targeted at improving the overall buying experience and protection for eBay users. The changes

Exhibit 5 eBay Growth (in millions, year-end December 31)

Supplemental Operating Data	2008	2009	2010
Marketplace Segment:			
Gross merchandise volume*	$59,650	$57,206	$61,819
Payments Segment:			
Net total payment volume[†]	$60,146	$71,607	$91,956

* Total value of all successfully closed items between users on eBay Marketplaces trading platforms during the period, regardless of whether the buyer and seller actually consummated the transaction.

[†] Total dollar volume of payments, net of payment reversals, successfully completed through eBay payments network or on Bill Me Later accounts during the period, excluding the payment gateway business.

Source: eBay Inc., *www.ebayinc.com/*.

included lowering fees for listing items and raising minimum standards for the sellers, as well as offering incentives and discounts to reward sellers with the best buyer satisfaction ratings.[12] In addition, in June 2008 the company improved buyer and seller protection on eBay. First-time buyers were protected for 100 percent of an item's purchase price, while sellers would receive improved protection when items were paid for with PayPal.[13] Donahoe was confident that these changes would significantly reinforce healthy and frequent trading at eBay.

eBay Platforms

eBay's overall strategy comprised three primary components: products, sense of community, and aggressive expansion. All three components evolved around the various geographic and specialty platforms the company introduced.

Product Categories

eBay had an array of product categories and trading platforms that offered a range of pricing formats, such as fixed pricing. Relatively new for the company, establishing a fixed-price format allowed eBay to compete directly with major competitors such as Amazon.com and penetrate new market space. Before fixed pricing, selling prices were solely determined by the highest auction bid, and this took days or weeks depending on the length of the auction. eBay's different trading platforms also offered distinct services and target-specific market niches, which allowed eBay to broaden its customer base. The platforms included:

- *PayPal:* Founded in 1998 and acquired by eBay in 2002, PayPal enabled individuals to securely send payments quickly and easily online. PayPal was considered the global leader in online payments, with tens of millions of registered users. Paypal's president, Scott Thompson, expected revenue to double to $6 billion to $7 billion by 2013. He also predicted

that 75 percent to 80 percent of eBay transactions will be done through PayPal by 2013, up from 69 percent in 2010.[14]
- *Rent.com:* Acquired by eBay in February 2005, Rent. com was the most visited online apartment listing service in the United States, with more than 20,000 properties listed.
- *Skype:* Acquired by eBay in October 2005, Skype was the world's fastest-growing online communication solution, allowing free video and audio communication between users of Skype software. By November 2009, Skype connected more than 480 million registered users.[15]

Sale of Skype: eBay's acquisition of Skype was expected to enhance the customer experience by improving communication between buyers and sellers. When it acquired Skype, eBay said it hoped the service would support its auctions and its PayPal payment service by letting buyers and sellers discuss transactions. But eBay users were not so chatty. In November 2009 eBay sold Skype to a group led by Silver Lake Partners, a private equity firm in Silicon Valley. The deal was made at $2.75 billion with eBay retaining a 30 percent stake. Mr. Donahoe said eBay did not regret having bought Skype when company executives believed eBay was in a mortal struggle with Google, which was also pursuing the service. He said the spinoff would allow eBay to focus on its core e-commerce and online payment businesses and avoid extra distractions. "We don't regret having done this at all. We compete in a dynamic market, and you have to move quickly and take risks," Mr. Donahoe said. "When we bought Skype we thought it had synergies with our other two businesses, and it turns out it did not. But it also turned out that it's a great stand-alone business."[16]

In May 2011, Microsoft made an agreement to buy Skype for $8.5 billion from Silver Lake. eBay said it will earn more than a 50 percent return from the firm's initial investment of $2.6 billion in Skype six years ago with the latest Microsoft deal. "With this sale, we have realized a total return of $1.4 billion on our original investment in Skype" said John Pluhowski, a spokesman for eBay. Considering that eBay had bought Skype in a heavily criticized deal in 2005 and was considered a failed acquisition, the latest Microsoft agreement turned out to be good news for eBay making eBay one of the big winners in the Microsoft and Skype deal.

- *Online classifieds:* By January 2009, eBay had the world-leading portfolio of online classifieds sites, including Intoko, Gumtree, LoQUo.com, and mobile.de, as well as Netherlands-based Marktplaats.nl.[17] In 2007 eBay expanded its classifieds business through its acquisition of Kijiji.[18] In October 2008 eBay further diversified its classifieds portfolio by acquiring Den Bla Avis and BilBasen, providers of successful classifieds businesses in Denmark, for $390 million. "We are the global leader in classifieds, with top positions in Canada, Australia, Germany, Japan and the United Kingdom, and sites in more than 1,000 cities across 20 countries," said CEO John Donahoe after the latest acquisition.[19]
- *Shopping.com:* With thousands of merchants and millions of products and reviews, Shopping.com empowered consumers to make informed choices, which drove value for merchants.
- *Stubhub.com:* StubHub was an online marketplace for selling and purchasing tickets for sports events, concerts, and other live entertainment events.
- *eBay Express:* eBay Express behaved like a standard Internet shopping site but gave sellers access to over 200 million buyers worldwide. Sellers could design product categories within minutes, and buyers could purchase from multiple sellers by using a single shopping cart.
- *eBay Motors:* This specialty site was considered the largest marketplace for automobile buyers and sellers. Buyers could purchase anything from automobile parts to new or antique vehicles.

The use of product categories such as eBay Express and eBay Motors provided further depth in eBay's product offerings and enabled the company to target a broader market.

Sense of Community

The underlying key to all eBay sites and trading platforms was creating trust between sellers and buyers. The company created "community values," and this was why eBay users were willing to send money to strangers across the country. The Feedback Forum was created in February 1996 and encouraged users to post comments about trading partners. Originally, Omidyar handled disputes between buyers and sellers via e-mail by putting the disputing parties in touch with each other to resolve the issue themselves. He soon realized that an open forum where users could post opinions and feedback about one another would create the trust and sense of community the site required. Buyers and sellers were encouraged to post comments (positive, negative, or neutral) about each other at the completion of each transaction. The individual feedback was recorded and amended to a user profile, which ultimately established a rating and reputation for each buyer and seller. eBay users could view this information before engaging in a transaction. The company believed that the feedback forum was critical for creating initial user acceptance for purchasing and selling over the Internet and that it contributed more than anything else to eBay's success.

Aggressive Expansion

To compete effectively and create a global trading platform, the company continued to develop in U.S. and international markets that utilized the Internet. With intense competition in the online auction industry, eBay aimed to increase market share and revenue through acquisitions and partnerships in related and unrelated businesses. For example:

- In June 2000 eBay acquired Half.com for $318 million.
- In August 2001 eBay acquired MercadoLibre, Lokau, and iBazar, Latin American auction sites.
- On August 13, 2004 eBay took a 25 percent stake in Craigslist, an online central network of urban communities.
- In September 2005 eBay invested $2 million in the Meetup social networking site.
- In August 2006 eBay announced international cooperation with Google.
- In January 2007 eBay acquired online ticket marketplace Stubhub for $310 million.
- In June 2010 eBay acquired RedLaser, a mobile application that would let customers scan bar codes to list items faster on its online auction site and to compare prices.[20]
- In December 2010 eBay acquired Milo, a leading local shopping engine that would provide consumers access to accurate, real-time, local store inventory and pricing, giving them even more choice and flexibility when shopping online.[21]
- In December 2010 eBay acquired Critical Path Software Inc., a developer of smartphone applications, to accelerate its lead in mobile commerce.[22]

Company Business Model

eBay's business model was based on a person-to-person marketplace on the Internet where sellers conveniently listed items for sale and interested buyers bid on these items. The objective was to create a forum that allowed buyers and sellers to come together in an efficient and effective manner. The business model overcame the inefficiencies of traditional fragmented marketplaces, which tended to offer a limited variety of goods. According to former CEO Meg Whitman, the company started with commerce and what grew out of that was a community, essentially creating a community-commerce model.[23] The company's success relied primarily on establishing a trustworthy environment that attracted a large number of buyers and sellers. As eBay's reputation grew, so did the number of buyers and sellers, keeping the company in line with Omidyar's original vision. However, as new competitors entered the online auction business and the popularity of the Internet increased, eBay tweaked its business model to accommodate the changes in the fast-paced environment.

The company was aggressively expanding globally and looking for new products and services to offer to customers. It was also looking closely at the kind of merchants who sold on eBay. In the beginning, eBay focused on a consumer-to-consumer business model, but since some of the individuals became small dealers, the model changed to a mix of consumer-to-consumer and business-to-consumer. The sellers wanted to maintain their business on eBay, since it was their most profitable distribution channel. eBay wanted new ways to generate revenue as a result of more small dealers and businesses selling their products through the company's website.

eBay generated revenue through three main channels: marketplaces, payments, and, until 2009, communications. Marketplaces, which generated revenue by charging sellers a fee for every item they sold, accounted for over 65 percent of the company's revenue. As of December 2010 marketplace revenue was approximately $5.7 billion of the company's $9.15 billion total revenue. Another $3.4 billion of the company's revenue came from fees charged through electronic payments made through the company website, primarily via PayPal. The newest source of revenue, until November 2009, was communications (Skype), which produced $620 million of the company's revenue. Although free, eBay's communication software generated revenue through its premium offerings, such as making and receiving calls to and from landline and mobile phones, as well as voice mail, ring tones, and call forwarding. Exhibit 6 shows the company's recent revenue performance by type.

In addition to the primary revenue sources, there were specific elements of eBay's business model that made the company a success. eBay's dominance of the online auction market and the large number of buyers, sellers, and listed items were primary reasons for eBay's tremendous growth. The trust and safety programs, such as the Feedback Forum, continued to attract and retain new and current eBay users. The cost-effective and convenient trading, coupled with the strong sense of community, added further value to the company's business model. However, as the company continued to grow and new trends evolved, eBay had to continue to adjust its model to remain competitive. Exhibit 1 presents the company's consolidated income statement.

International Expansion

As competition intensified in the online auction industry, eBay expanded its international presence in an effort to create an online global marketplace. Gradually, eBay localized sites in the following countries:

- *Asia Pacific:* Australia, China, Hong Kong, India, Malaysia, New Zealand, Philippines, Singapore, South Korea, and Taiwan.
- *Europe:* Austria, Belgium, Denmark, France, Germany, Ireland, Italy, Netherlands, Poland, Spain, Sweden, Switzerland, and the United Kingdom.
- *North America:* Canada and the United States.

In many of the international websites, eBay provided local-language and -currency options to gain popularity and ensure the sense-of-community feeling. In most cases, eBay expanded its business by either acquiring or forming a partnership with a local company. This strategy helped eBay better understand local cultures and ensure that the company was meeting specific local needs. This approach proved successful with the company's equity investment in MercadoLibre.com, which targeted Argentina, Brazil, Chile, Colombia, Costa Rica, the Dominican Republic, Ecuador, Mexico, Panama, Peru, Uruguay, and Venezuela. At the end of 2006, MercadoLibre.com reported 18 million registered users who performed 15.8 million transactions worth $1.1 billion.[24] Other notable international growth acquisitions are listed below.

Asia Pacific

- Acquired China-based Eachnet for approximately $150 million. eBay's failure to manage the company resulted in its recent partnership with communications company Tom Online.
- Acquired all outstanding shares of India's Baazee. com, which later became eBay India.
- Acquired Korean rival Internet Auction Co. by purchasing nearly 3 million shares. Acquisition has not proved successful due to intense competition from top Korean auction site GMarket.

Europe

- Acquired Alando auction house for $43 million, a company that later became eBay Germany. Alando was previously considered Germany's leading online trading company. Germany became eBay's second-largest market, accounting for 21 percent of the company's total listings.
- Acquired Dutch competitor Marktplaats.nl, which had 80 percent of the Netherlands market share.
- Acquired Sweden's leading online auction company, Tradera.com, for $48 million.
- Acquired Denmark's leading online classifieds businesses, Den Bla Avis and BilBasen, for $390 million.[25]

Exhibit 6   Net Revenues by Type (in thousands, except percentage changes)

	Year Ended December 31, 2008	Percentage Change from 2008 to 2009	Year Ended December 31, 2009	Percentage Change from 2009 to 2010	Year Ended December 31, 2010
Net Revenues by Type:					
Net transaction revenues					
Marketplaces	$4,711,057	(5)	$4,461,845	8	$4,800,193
Payments	2,320,495	14	2,641,194	23	3,261,314
Communications	525,803	9	575,096	—	—
Total net transaction revenues	7,557,355	2	7,678,135	5	8,061,507
Marketing services and other revenues					
Marketplaces	875,694	(3)	849,169	8	920,434
Payments	83,174	86	154,751	13	174,333
Communications	25,038	81	45,307	—	—
Total marketing services and other revenues	983,906	7	1,049,227	4	1,094,767
Total net revenues	$8,541,261	2	$8,727,362	5	$9,156,274
Net Revenues by Segment:					
Marketplaces	$5,586,751	(5)	$5,311,014	8	$5,720,627
Payments	2,403,669	16	2,795,945	23	3,435,647
Communications	550,841	13	620,403	—	—
Total net revenues	$8,541,261	2	$8,727,362	5	$9,156,274
Net Revenues by Geography:					
U.S.	$3,969,482	—	$3,985,068	6	$4,214,215
International	4,571,779	4	4,742,294	4	4,942,059
Total net revenues	$8,541,261	2	$8,727,362	5	$9,156,274

Source: eBay Inc., *www.ebayinc.com/*.

For the most part, eBay was successful in expanding in Europe and Latin America, where it was able to quickly adapt to local needs through its partners. The company was also successful in countries it expanded to from the ground up, such as Canada and the United Kingdom. In 2007 the United Kingdom accounted for 15.5 percent of eBay's total listings. By engaging the local community in these countries, eBay customized its sites to meet specific local needs while providing access to the online global community.

eBay was considered the leader in each of its markets with the exception of Japan and China, in which it struggled repeatedly to gain market share. In 2002 eBay was forced to pull out of Japan due to rising costs and intense competition by rival Yahoo Japan. eBay also faced fierce competition in Korea, where GMarket, another investment of Yahoo, dominated the market.

Despite its lack of success in local Asian markets, eBay continued its attempts to expand into the region, recognizing the tremendous growth potential that was available. In June 2006 eBay formed a joint venture with PChome Online in Taiwan. PChome Online was an Internet service provider in Taiwan, with more than 10 million members.[26] The company offered services such as Internet portal, e-commerce platform, and telecommunications. The move was expected to provide eBay with the local e-commerce expertise it needed to launch a new trading website that catered to the needs of Taiwan's Internet users.

In 2006 eBay emphasized its commitment to the Chinese e-commerce market by announcing a new joint venture with Beijing-based Internet Company Tom Online Inc. Tom Online, which primarily sold cell phone add-on services, such as ring tones and avatars, put in $20 million for a 51 percent share and management control of eBay's online China site, Eachnet.[27] In 2002 eBay had purchased a 30 percent stake in Eachnet and within a year bought out local investors. Central management control of Eachnet was maintained in eBay's San Jose, California, location. Many believed the move to partner with Tom Online was a result of eBay's failure to adapt to local needs and successfully compete with China's online auction market leader Taobao, which controlled approximately 70 percent of the market. Jack Ma, the chief executive of Alibaba.com, Taobao's parent company, believed eBay's failure in China was due to an inability to build a community effect in the country, which, according to Ma, begins with customer satisfaction. Ma also felt that since eBay had to adhere to a global platform, meeting specific local needs was difficult because changes at a global level had to be approved in the United States, which further limited the company's ability to produce a website tailored to the Chinese market.[28]

In April 2009 eBay secured agreements to buy a 67 percent stake of South Korea's Gmarket in a deal estimated to be worth $1.2 billon. The move was part of Donahoe's effort to increase revenue in coming years. It was expected that Gmarket would help eBay's push into Asia.[29]

Competitors

As eBay's product offerings and pricing formats evolved, so did its range of competitors. Originally, the company faced competition from alternative auctions or other venues for collectors, such as flea markets and garage sales. However, as the company grew and introduced fixed pricing, the range of competitors included large companies like Walmart and Kmart that also had retail websites. eBay's product platforms, like eBay Motors, put the company in direct competition with auto dealers and other online auto sites, such as Autobytes. Still, eBay faced the harshest competition from major online companies, including Yahoo and Amazon, which also had online auctions that rivaled eBay's.

Yahoo!

eBay's larger online competitor was Yahoo, which also had a strong global presence, particularly in Asian markets. Yahoo originally started as a search engine and quickly evolved to include additional products and services, such as Yahoo! Mail, Yahoo! Maps, and Yahoo! Messenger. The company also offered e-commerce services through Yahoo! Shopping, Yahoo! Autos, Yahoo! Auctions, and Yahoo! Travel. Like eBay, Yahoo's e-commerce sites allowed users to obtain relevant information and make transactions and purchases online. However, Yahoo's business model primarily focused on generating revenue through search advertising. In the United States, in response to potential threats from web giant Google, Yahoo and eBay formed an alliance in which Yahoo utilized eBay's payment system, PayPal, and eBay gained additional advertising through Yahoo searches. Still, Yahoo posed a major competitive threat in foreign markets, particularly the Asia Pacific area, through its partnerships with GMarket and Taobao.

GMarket

Yahoo's stake in Korean auction site GMarket proved successful, with more than 17.2 million unique visitors. Founded in 2000, GMarket was a Korean online auction and shopping-mall website that generated its revenue by charging a fee based on selling price.[30] Like Taobao, GMarket offered fixed prices and provided an option to negotiate prices with sellers on an exclusive basis. This allowed buyers to conduct deals instantly instead of waiting until bids were completed. GMarket also offered cheaper listings. These options, along with constant new features, allowed GMarket to dominate the Korean online auction industry.[31] GMarket frequently introduced new marketing initiatives to provide sellers with various options to attract new customers. GMarket grew financially powerful in 2006 when it launched its IPO and Yahoo purchased a 9 percent stake in the company.

In 2009 eBay decided to secure an interest in its rival and was granted approval to purchase a combined 67 percent stake in Gmarket from Interpark Corp. and its chairman. In May 2010 eBay announced that it intended to work with Gmarket's founder to expand Gmarket's presence in Japan and Singapore. Lorie Norrington, president of eBay Marketplaces commented, "This joint venture is a sign of our continued commitment to help grow and lead ecommerce across Asia by offering more opportunities for sellers and extraordinary buying experiences for consumers."[32]

Taobao

In 2005 Yahoo entered a strategic partnership with Alibaba.com, Taobao's parent company, which created an instant threat in the Chinese market. The move created one of the largest Internet companies in China, one with a leading position in business-to-business e-commerce, consumer e-commerce, and online payments. Like GMarket, Taobao offered buyers and sellers quick and convenient ways to conduct business. Its instant messaging and fixed price arrangements allowed transactions to be conducted quickly. In 2006 the company partnered with Intel to offer customers a wireless platform. This further improved communication and convenience when customers were conducting transactions. In 2011 Taobao was eBay's largest competitor in China, controlling over 80 percent of the Chinese online auction market.[33]

In early 2010 eBay announced the partnership of PayPal with China UnionPay, a local intrabank card system operator, which would make it accessible for customers to make online purchases from overseas. This move was made to challenge Alipay, a unit of Alibaba Group that controlled about 50 percent of the market. This partnership would allow international retailers to sell to a large base of Chinese customers, who, combined, held 2.1 billon China UnionPay cards.[34] "After years of being the export hub for the world, now China is open for business as an import e-commerce market," said Scott Thompson, president of PayPal. "PayPal's partnership with China Union-Pay removes an important friction point that exists across borders, and we are thrilled to eliminate the payments barrier so merchants can welcome millions of new Chinese customers to their sites."[35]

Amazon

Despite not having a huge presence in the online auction industry, Amazon was still considered a fierce online global competitor. Amazon started as Earth's biggest bookstore and rapidly evolved to selling everything, including toys, electronics, home furnishings, apparel, health and beauty aids, groceries, and so on. Still, books, CDs, and DVDs accounted for more than 65 percent of the firm's sales. Although Amazon had a large international presence, the company's linkage to brick-and-mortar shops in the United States made it a greater threat locally than in foreign markets. Amazon's international local sites were in Canada, the United Kingdom, Germany, Japan, France, and China. Despite its large online presence, Amazon scaled back its online auction business, cutting staff and shutting down Livebid, as part of an overall corporate restructuring.

The Future of eBay

eBay had a number of opportunities in which it had already taken action. By 2011, eBay had made a number of strategic acquisitions that included Rent.com, international classified websites, Stubhub.com, and Shopping.com. These acquisitions added and complemented eBay's product offerings and further diversified the company's targeted market. With increased competition from Google and other major online companies, eBay had to continue to diversify and provide depth in its product offerings to remain competitive. Creating options and targeting distinct market niches would enable eBay to distinguish itself from competitors. This was particularly important because, as e-commerce and Internet usage rates continued to grow, so would the market opportunity for eBay. Because of its market-leading brand, eBay was in a unique position to capture a significant share of the market at an early stage.

eBay could also expand its existing products and services, such as PayPal. The product was relatively new and had the potential to grow and attract new customers, especially in international markets. Expanding PayPal into international markets would enable eBay to provide a simple way to conduct transactions across market borders. Considering the growth potential in developing markets, such as those in Africa, Asia, and the Middle East, expanding PayPal would attract many new customers, thus increasing eBay's revenue base. In line with e-commerce growth, as more customers felt comfortable with conducting transactions online, PayPal had the potential to be the preferred form of payment over the Internet.

However, for eBay to capitalize on these opportunities, the company would have to overcome the challenges of expanding into large foreign markets such as China and Japan. With almost 77 percent of the North American population using the Internet and only a 21.5 percent usage rate in the Asia Pacific area, eBay had a tremendous opportunity to expand and gain new customers. Considering that the Asia Pacific region had more than 50 percent of the world's population and was experiencing some of the largest online usage growth percentages in the world, tapping into this market was critical for eBay to expand.

eBay's operations in China remained small compared to Alibaba Group and other Chinese e-commerce companies, but, like PayPal, the company had refocused its energies on export-oriented merchants in China who wanted to reach overseas buyers on its international websites.[36] Experts viewed eBay's strategy of forming a partnership with former rival Alibaba Group as the best way to generate sales from China. All hopes were on Paypal's acceptance by China partners who were looking to expand international sales. It was critical for eBay to partner with local Chinese companies rather than going alone in the world's biggest Internet market in order to proceed in the local market.

Endnotes

1. Internet World Stats. 2010. Internet Usage Statistics. *www.internetworldstats.com/stats.htm.*
2. Galante, J. 2010. PayPal teams with China UnionPay to challenge Alipay. Bloomberg News, March 17. *www.bloomberg.com/apps/news?pid=newsarchive&sid=au4i5vaUlMNQ*
3. Ibid.
4. Bloomberg News. 2010. EBay's Paypal to set up global e-commerce hub in China. December 29. *www.businessweek.com/news/2010-12-29/ebay-s-paypal-to-set-up-global-e-commerce-hub-in-china.html.*
5. Ibid.
6. Doyle, R. A. 2002. The history of Auctions. *Auctioneer.* November 1. *www.absoluteauctionrealty.com/history_detail.php?id=5094*
7. *Internet Based Moms.* 2007. Pierre Omidyar—The Man behind eBay. April.
8. Academy of Achievement. 2005. Biography—Pierre Omidyar. November 9. *www.achievement.org.*

9.   eBay Inc. 2008. Meg Whitman to Step Down.
10. eBay corporate website, *ebayinc.com.*
11. eBay Inc. 2008. Meg Whitman to Step Down.
12. eBay Inc. 2008. eBay Announces Bold Changes.
13. eBay Inc. 2008. eBay and PayPal increase protections for buyers and sellers to shop with confidence. June 19. *www.ebayinc.com/content/press_release/20080619005753.*
14. Galante, J. 2011. PayPal's revenue will double by 2013, Thompson says. Bloomberg News, February 10. *www.businessweek.com/news/2011-02-10/paypal-s-revenue-will-double-by-2013-thompson-says.html.*
15. eBay Inc. 2009. Annual report, 2009.
16. Stone, B. 2009. In a sale, Skype wins a chance to prosper. *New York Times,* September 1. *www.nytimes.com/2009/09/02/technology/companies/02ebay.html?_r=1.*
17. eBay Inc. 2008. eBay acquires leading classifieds sites in Denmark. October 6. *www.ebayinc.com/content/press_release/20081006005606.*
18. eBay corporate website, ebayinc.com.
19. eBay Inc. 2008. eBay Inc. buys leading payments and classifieds businesses, streamlines existing organization to improve growth. October 6. *www.ebayinc.com/content/press_release/20081006005605.*
20. MacMillan, D. 2010. EBay buys bar-code app. *Bloomberg Businessweek,* June 23. *www.businessweek.com/technology/content/jun2010/tc20100623_901174.htm.*
21. eBay Inc. 2010. eBay acquires Milo, a leading local shopping engine. December 2. *www.ebayinc.com/content/press_release/20101202006358.*
22. eBay Inc. 2010. eBay acquires industry leading mobile application developer. December 15. *www.ebayinc.com/content/press_release/20101215006520.*
23. Himelstein, L., & Whitman, M. 1999. Q&A with eBay's Meg Whitman. *BusinessWeek Online,* May 31. *www.businessweek.com/1999/99_22/b3631008.htm.*
24. *IT Digest.* 2007. Argentina: MercadoLibre has 18mil registered users. January 25. *www.infobae.com.*
25. eBay Inc. 2008. eBay Acquires Leading Classifieds Sites in Denmark.
26. eBay Inc. 2006. eBay and PChome Online to Form Joint Venture in Taiwan. June 5. *www.ebayinc.com/content/press_release/20060605199313.*
27. Knowledge@Wharton, 2007. Ebay's deal with Tom Online offers some timely lessons for managers of global online companies. February 14. *www.knowledgeatwharton.com.cn/index.cfm?fa5viewArticle&articleID51562&languageid51*
28. Ma, J. 2005. Alibaba CEO says Taobao will dominate China online auctions. *Forbes.com,* May 5. *www.forbes.com/feeds/afx/2005/05/20/afx2043109.html.*
29. Cho, K., & Galante, J. 2009. EBay offers to buy Korea's Gmarket for $1.2 billion. *Bloomberg.com,* April 16. *www.bloomberg.com/apps/news?pid=newsarchive&sid=asyO3.3yVdnE&refer=home.*
30. Ihlwan, M. 2006. Gmarket eclipses eBay in Asia. *BusinessWeek Online,* June 28. *www.businessweek.com/globalbiz/content/jun2006/gb20060628_910393.htm.*
31. *BusinessWeek Online.* 2006. Out-eBaying eBay in Korea. July 17. *www.businessweek.com/magazine/content/06_29/b3993080.htm.*
32. Caverly, D. 2010. eBay announces new joint venture in Asia. WebProNews.com, May 7. *www.webpronews.com/ebay-announces-new-joint-venture-in-asia-2010-05.*
33. Epstein, G. 2010. eBay chief visits his Chinese conqueror. Blogs.Forbes.com, September 9. *blogs.forbes.com/gadyepstein/2010/09/09/ebay-chief-visits-his-chinese-conqueror/.*
34. *China Tech News.* 2010. PayPal works with China UnionPay for online payment services. March 23. *www.chinatechnews.com/2010/03/23/11777-paypal-works-with-china-unionpay-for-online-payment-services.*
35. BusinessWire.com. 2010. PayPal and China UnionPay open the global marketplace to Chinese consumers. March 17. *www.businesswire.com/news/home/20100317005661/en/PayPal-China-UnionPay-Open-Global-Marketplace-Chinese.*
36. Chao, L. 2010. EBay sees a market in China yet. *ChinaRealtimeReport,* May 19. blogs.wsj.com/chinarealtime/2010/05/19/ebay-sees-a-market-in-china-yet/.

Case 23   Mattel's Misfit Toys*

It was early March and over 25,000 buyers, sellers, manufacturers/licensors, and entertainment moguls had just converged at the Toy Fair 2011 held in New York City's Javits Center. Robert (Bob) Eckert, Mattel's chairman and chief executive, reflected on events since the recalls, the financial fallout, new industry cooperation, and increased government regulation, and considered Mattel's reputation and strategy. Within weeks the U.S. Consumer Product Safety Commission (CPSC) officially would be launching its new website and database for members of the public to submit descriptions of injury or damage caused by products. The Toy Industry Association, led by Mattel's own President-International Bryan Stockton, would be hosting a webinar and other updates to educate industry members about *www.saferproducts.gov*. In addition, traditional toy sales had not rebounded to levels before the 2007 recall crisis.

Considered a role model for offshoring and outsourcing to China, Mattel had also recently changed its inspection strategy. The company ended its long-term relationship with Dr. Prakash Sethi to monitor its worker conditions[1] in favor of industry-wide monitoring. Eckert gazed at the Sarge sitting next to his daughter's photo. How could he balance competitive pressures and restore consumer confidence in his company founded on creativity, fun, safety, and, above all, trust? Looking further out, did participation in industry monitoring efforts diminish the company's ability to further differentiate Mattel from the others, like RC2, that had also suffered recalls?

Mattel Becomes a Role Model

Ruth and Elliott Handler and Harold (Matt) Matson founded Mattel in a Southern California garage workshop in 1945. Mattel became a major player in the toy industry with the 1959 launch of the Barbie doll. By 2006 Mattel owned such brands as Barbie, Hot Wheels, American Girl, and Fisher-Price and licensed products from Disney and Harry Potter movies. Mattel was the world's largest toy maker, with 2006 revenue of $5.65 billion.

Mattel's use of offshoring and outsourcing predated the recent globalization and labor arbitrage trend. In fact, the first Barbie dolls were made in Japan in 1959. According to an industry expert, "Mattel was in China before China was cool, and they learned to do business there in a good way. They understood the importance of protecting their brand, and they invested."[2]

* This case was prepared by Professor Naomi A. Gardberg and Professor Donald H. Schepers of Baruch College, CUNY. Research assistance was provided by graduate students Meg Joseph, Jenny Rea, Edward Acevedo, Mike Gambale, Isaac Hefez, Audrey Pouvreau, and Monique Sampson. This case was solely based on library research and was developed for class discussion rather than to illustrate either effective or ineffective handling of an administrative situation. Copyright © 2011 Naomi A. Gardberg and Donald H. Schepers.

During the 1980s Mattel decided to take more control over its toy production. In particular, Mattel executives were concerned about a flood of imitation Barbie dolls if the icon was outsourced. They also thought that they could produce toys more efficiently by building large plants with greater economies of scale. Thus, Mattel's outsourcing strategy took shape. The company would produce and protect its core brands rather than use less costly outsourcing to the lowest-cost local manufacturer. However, short-term products featuring characters from movies and television shows other than Mattel's own brands would be outsourced.[3]

According to SEC filings, Mattel had found its bargaining power with retailers eroding during the 2000s. Mattel sold nearly half of its toys through only three mass merchandisers, Target, Toys "R" Us, and Walmart. To reduce dependence on these retailers, Mattel created a direct-mail catalog and website to sell directly to consumers.

Worker Safety

In 1996 *Dateline* broadcast an exposé on Mattel's alleged use of sweatshop labor in Indonesia during the holiday shopping season. The story alleged that Mattel hired underage workers and overworked them.[4] *U.S. News and World Report* published a cover story with the headline "Sweatshop Christmas" the same month. The company called the allegations unfounded.

Yet in response, Mattel hired Dr. Prakash Sethi, a professor at Baruch College–CUNY, and created the International Center for Corporate Accountability (ICCA), a not-for-profit, independently incorporated organization, to monitor Mattel sites for working conditions. Dr. Sethi, who had a reputation as a critic of worker mistreatment, agreed to monitor Mattel only if the firm allowed him to post his reports "publicly and uncensored."[5] As a result, Mattel was considered one of the most successful companies manufacturing in China.

> In 1997, Mattel created an extensive independent monitoring program, which provides objective checks and balances to evaluate compliance to our GMP [Global Manufacturing Principles] standards. The system is overseen by an independent monitoring organization that proactively and thoroughly inspects the company's owned-and-operated facilities around the world, as well as those of our suppliers, on aspects of day-to-day operations. Independent and internal auditors are continuously assessing our performance with GMP.[6]

In 2007 Dr. Prakash Sethi told the *New York Times* that "Mattel is the gold standard" for worker conditions. Sean McGowan, managing director and toy analyst at Wedbush Morgan Securities, told the *New York Times,* "Mattel talks about this with a passion, and it is not just lip service."[7]

Mattel gradually shifted production from the United States to lower wage countries. In 2002 Mattel closed its last U.S. manufacturing facility and offshored its production to Mexico.[8]

The company generated about 50 percent of revenues from core products in 12 company-owned and -operated factories, including five in China by 2006. This was among the highest proportions in the industry and reflected its emphasis on its core brands. Mattel made or sourced about 65 percent of its toys in China. The 35 percent of toys produced outside of China included Barbie dolls made in Indonesia and large Fisher-Price Little People toys made in Mattel's plant in Tijuana, Mexico. In an article written on July 19 and published on July 26, 2007, *The New York Times* had featured Mattel as a role model for manufacturing in China for the toy industry.[9]

Toy Safety

Despite its care in factory conditions, Mattel was not immune to toy safety recalls. The firm, including Fisher-Price and American Girls, issued 26 recalls between 1982 and August 2007, due primarily to consumer misuse or design flaws. For example, its 1998 recall of 10 million Fisher-Price Power Wheels electronic cars stemmed from consumer misuse rather than design flaw. The cars, made in the United States, were subject to teenagers and young adults purposely overriding the safety features.

Elisha Chan, Mattel's director of product integrity and corporate responsibility, was responsible for inspecting for dangerous product defects such as lead-based paint in 2007. He told the *New York Times* that suppliers were monitored closely and that Mattel had canceled contracts with firms who submitted fake or tainted supplies. In its own factories Mattel produced small batches of new toys before ramping up production. After full-scale production commenced, supplies were tested as they arrived at the factory and toys were periodically removed from the assembly line for testing. The company safety lab in Shenzen, China, tested toys made by outside companies.

In contrast, many Western companies operating in China did not test their raw materials, although suppliers were known to use cheaper material to increase their profit. Dane Chamorro, regional director of Control Risks, a global consulting firm concurred "This is very common. . . . The samples you get are always fantastic; but once they rope you in, they can cut back. And a lot of Chinese companies will do anything to cut costs."[10] During July 2007, Jim Walter, a senior vice president at Mattel, stated, "We are not perfect; we have holes. But we're doing more than anyone else."[11] McGowan, the Wedbush Morgan Seucrities analyst, told the *New York Times,* "All the toy testing and safety measures cost money. But the Mattel brand can command a premium price."[12]

Misfit Toys

A European retail partner notified Mattel that it found lead paint on some of its subsidiary Fisher-Price's toys, prompting Mattel's investigation in its distribution chain in early July 2007. The U.S. government began regulating the use of lead in consumer products, such as paint, furniture, and toys, in the 1970s.[13] Lead paint had been banned for use in toys in 1977 because of its harmful effect on child development, such as causing learning difficulties and anemia (a deficiency of hemoglobin, a molecule found inside red blood cells, that carries oxygen throughout the body).[14] Eckert ordered Mattel's own safety lab to begin additional testing. Some toys were tested in Mattel labs in China; other products outsourced to Chinese manufacturers were rerouted to its Mexican plant for testing. The company's own safety labs found hazardous lead paint on toys from several vendors. On August 1, 2007, Mattel announced the largest toy recall in units in its history, including the Elmo, Big Bird, Diego, and Dora characters, licensed by Sesame Street and Nickelodeon. Mattel stated that the lead-tainted toys were made from May to July 2007 and found during routine safety checks.[15] How did lead paint slip into Mattel's production line? How did tainted toys slip past Mattel's inspections?

Eckert surmised that the European retailer may have discovered the lead paint as a part of a broader reaction to the April toy recall issued by RC2, a Mattel competitor and the licensor for HIT Entertainment Limited's Thomas & Friends. Swiftly, he had ordered Mattel's units and subcontractors to review inputs, processes, and inventory. The results startled Eckert, the firm, retailers, and consumers. Several of Mattel's Chinese subcontractors bought less expensive lead paint from suppliers not on Mattel's approved list of eight suppliers.[16]

In addition to tracking, inspecting, and recalling toys, Eckert faced an onslaught of negative media coverage. Cartoons disparaging nontainted toys had appeared. Just three weeks after the recall, on August 23, Dana Parker, a California mother, appeared in Eckert's lobby at Mattel's El Segundo headquarters with her two children and several garbage bags filled with Fisher-Price and Mattel toys. In a CNN broadcast, she reportedly told Mattel personnel, "I need you guys to inspect my toys because I cannot do it."[17] Two employees from Mattel's Consumer Products Division inspected each of her toys in a company conference room and found all were safe. Eckert worried to what degree this mother's frustration represented the rest of Mattel's consumers.

Meanwhile, Mattel's executives rerouted toys from China to its Mexico factory for additional testing. Longtime Mattel supplier Lee Der produced 937,000 of the toys recalled due to excessive amounts of lead. Typically, Chinese firms have long supply chains that hinder tracing the exact origin of components, chemicals, and food additives.[18] However, in this instance, the paint was sold to the firm by the best friend of Lee Der's CEO, Zhang Shuhong. On August 13, Zhang Shuhong hung himself in the toy factory.

Two days later, Eckert issued additional recalls of another 19 million toys from China, citing excessive lead paint on 436,000 die-cast toy cars and too-easily removed small, powerful magnets on the remaining 18.2 million toys—9.5 million toys in the United States and 11 million in foreign countries. In fact, most of the toys were recalled due to the magnets. The recall of the Sarge character from *Cars* for lead paint raised the ire of Pixar and its corporate parent, Disney. The two recalls involved different manufacturers. Eckert stated, "We have had recalls every year since I've been here," but "the second recall was different; it was going to receive a different level of scrutiny."[19] He told CNN, "I'm disappointed, I'm upset, but I can ensure your viewers that we are doing everything we can about the situation." "Every production batch of toys is being tested, and we'll continue to enforce the highest quality standards in the industry."[20] Mattel's stock price dropped on news of the recall but recovered in after-hours trading.

In a full-page ad published in *The New York Times, The Wall Street Journal,* and *USA Today,* Eckert, a father of four, said that "nothing is more important than the safety of our children." "Our long record of safety at Mattel is why we're one of the most trusted names with parents," Eckert wrote. "And I am confident that the actions we are taking now will maintain that trust."[21]

With each recall, Eckert attributed the flaws to Chinese subcontractors. In a move that shocked the industry, on September 21, Thomas Debrowski, Mattel's executive vice president for worldwide operations, met with the Chinese product safety chief, Li Changjiang, and apologized for the company's own weak safety controls. "Our reputation has been damaged lately by these recalls," Mr. Debrowski told Li. "And Mattel takes full responsibility for these recalls and apologizes personally to you, the Chinese people, and all of our customers who received the toys."[22] The "vast majority of those products that were recalled were the result of a design flaw in Mattel's design, not through a manufacturing flaw in China's manufacturers," Debrowski said. "We understand and appreciate deeply the issues that this has caused for the reputation of Chinese manufacturers."[23] Hence, Mattel took responsibility for the recalls, blaming a design flaw rather than manufacturing mishap. In October 2007 Mattel announced a sales decline of $30 to $50 million and a charge of $40 million due to product scares, delayed shipments and revoked import licenses.[24]

The U.S. Toy Industry

In 2010 the United States toy market was valued at $40.4 billion (Exhibit 1). However, Euromonitor International estimated that the traditional toys and games segment, which represented 53.4 percent of the market, was expected to increase by only 1.4 percent from 2008–2013 (Exhibit 2). The toy industry was segmented into two main categories: traditional toys and games, such as cars and trains, dolls and accessories, and board games; and video games. It segmented people into four age groups: 8 and under, 9–12, 13–17, and 18 plus. During 2009, the 8-and-under age group accounted for 69 percent of toy sales; however, both market share and absolute dollar sales increased for the 9-to-12 age group.[25]

Exhibit 1 U.S. Retail Sales of Toys and Games by Sector, 2001–2010 (in millions of U.S. dollars)

	Traditional Toys and Games	Video Games	All Toys and Games
2001	23,295.7	9,447.0	32,742.7
2002	23,558.1	10,212.5	33,770.6
2003	23,470.2	10,316.9	33,787.1
2004	22,946.6	10,220.9	33,167.5
2005	22,282.6	10,812.3	33,094.9
2006	22,508.2	12,748.5	35,256.7
2007	22,191.8	18,143.7	40,335.5
2008	21,600.0	21,400.0	43,000.0
2009	21,460.0	19,700.0	41,160.0
2010	21,780.0	18,580.0	40,360.0

Source: Official statistics, trade associations, trade press, company research, store checks, trade interviews. Euromonitor estimates.

Exhibit 2 Forecast Sales of Toys and Games by Sector, 2011–2014*

	Traditional Toys and Games	Video Games	All Toys and Games
2011	24,762.7	43,401.3	68,164.0
2012	26,280.9	47,466.3	73,747.2
2013	27,799.0	50,544.2	78,343.2
2014	29,401.0	64,288.4	93,689.4
Sales growth			
2009–14 CAGR†	5.2%	21.7%	14.8%
2009–14 total	28.8%	166.7%	99.7%

Source: Official statistics, trade associations, trade press, company research, store checks, trade interviews. Euromonitor estimates.

* Sales numbers reported in millions of U.S. dollars.

† Compound annual growth rate.

In line with other industries, the toy industry was using less domestic production. In 2004 73 percent of U.S. toys were imported, with over 72 percent of imports coming from the People's Republic of China (PRC). By 2010 over 89 percent of U.S. toy imports were from China. Exhibit 3 contains data on toy manufacturing and imports from 2000 to 2007. The shift in manufacturing raised little attention until 2007, when a series of recalls due mainly to lead paint, attracted the attention of consumers, retailers, and regulators.

Industry Regulation

The toy industry was governed by both U.S. federal government monitoring and regulation and industry self-regulation. The Federal Hazardous Substances Act and its amendments, such as the 1969 Child Protection and Toy Safety Act, were the basic laws covering toy safety. In 1973 the Consumer Product Safety Act created the Consumer Product Safety Commission (CPSC). The CPSC, headquartered in Bethesda, Maryland, maintained teams of field inspectors to monitor both domestic and foreign-made toys for (1) paint and other similar surface-coating materials, (2) pacifiers and rattles choking and suffocation hazards, (3) toy-cap noise levels, (4) electrical-thermal toys, (5) contents of chemistry sets, (6) sharp edges and points, (7) small parts that could be swallowed or inhaled, (8) use and abuse testing, (9) hazardous substances, (10) flammability, and (11) toxic art materials.

The role of the CPSC is both proactive and reactive. The five parts to its powers are (1) develop voluntary industry standards, working with industry; (2) issue and enforce mandatory standards or ban products if no standards would protect the public; (3) force recalls or product repairs; (4) conduct research on potential product hazards; and (5) inform and educate consumers through media, state and local governments, private organizations, and responding to consumer inquiries.[26] For known hazards, the CPSC works with the industry to establish voluntary standards to protect the public. The CPSC then expects the industry to abide by those standards and could force a recall if a company distributed a product in violation of the voluntary standards. But the only time the CPSC can ban a product before it is marketed is when no standard would protect the public from the harm.

Exhibit 3   **U.S. Toy Imports** ($ millions)

	2000*	2001	2002	2003	2004	2005†	2006	2007
Total imports								
Wheeled toys	486	256	331	367	407	420	449	na
Dolls and accessories	1,475	1,219	1,258	1,226	1,005	1,038	1,053	na
Toys	7,631	7,267	7,654	7,769	7,937	8,272	8,295	10,512
Games	3,475	5,124	5,479	4,985	5,199	6,746	7,460	11,494
Festive articles	2,083	2,215	2,329	2,402	2,654	2,766	2,793	2,958
Total	15,150	16,081	17,051	16,749	17,202	19,242	20,050	24,964
Imports from China								
Wheeled toys	292	109	124	171	219	220	251	na
Dolls and accessories	1,295	1,073	1,160	1,119	925	962	966	na
Toys	6,300	5,948	6,424	7,769	7,937	7,300	7,326	9,253
Games	1,129	1,406	2,517	4,985	5,199	4,857	5,981	10,118
Festive articles	1,685	1,856	2,005	2,402	2,654	2,487	2,540	2,674
Total	10,700	10,392	12,227	16,446	16,934	15,826	17,064	22,045

Sources: * 2000–2004 data from Lauzon, M. 2005. China: The world's *toy* makers. *Plastic News,* 17(42): 16–18.and

† 2005–2007 data US Bureau of the Census: Foreign Trade Division USA Trade ® Online. Source: U.S. Import and Export Merchandise trade statistics *http://data.usatradeonline.gov.remote.baruch.cuny.edu/View/dispview.aspx*, accessed on June 1, 2011.

With regard to the toy recalls, the CPSC's jurisdiction covered paint, hazardous materials, and small magnets that could be swallowed. Warren noted, "With lead poisoning known to be a danger to all children, the United States undertook a remarkable, if still far from complete, purging of environmental lead, resulting in a reduction in average blood-lead levels to less than two micrograms per deciliter at century's end, from almost 15 in the mid-1970s.[27] Yet, as Warren noted, other countries have not acted as vigorously to ban or enforce legislation regarding lead and other toxic substances. These lax product-safety and environmental regulations lowered manufacturing costs in these countries but also prolonged the risk to U.S. children, as well as to the workers and children in those countries.

Leading up to 2007, the CPSC had received diminishing budgets. The number of personnel involved in the "Children's and Other Hazards" division had dropped from 228 in 2003 to 168 in 2006. Likewise, its budget dropped from $27.7 million to $25.6 million.[28] During the 1997–2006 timeframe, however, the pace of imports accelerated, with a 200 percent increase from 1997–2006. Over 85 percent of all recalls came from those imported products.[29] On July 31st, 2008, the U.S. Congress reauthorized and modernized the CPSC via H.R. 4040, Consumer Product Safety Improvement Act (CPSIA) of 2008.[30] The act increased CPSC funding to $136 million for 2009 and strengthened regulations surrounding toy regulation in particular. The allowable level of lead in children's products was further reduced, third-party testing and certification became mandatory, tracking labels would be affixed to children's products, websites and catalogues selling children's products would post new warnings, the voluntary industry standard ASTMF-963 became mandatory, and temporary bans on some phthalates were imposed pending additional testing.

In addition to federal regulations, the U.S. toy industry had established voluntary safety standards. The Toy Industry Association Inc. (TIA), a not-for-profit trade association for producers and importers of toys and youth entertainment products sold in North America, represented over 500 companies who accounted for approximately 85 percent of domestic toy sales (see Appendix A). TIA members included licensors, designers, inventors, safety consultants, testing laboratories, communications professionals, and the media. According to its website, "Our long history of leadership in toy safety includes the development of the first comprehensive toy safety standard. We continue to work with government officials, consumer groups and industry leaders on ongoing programs to ensure safe play."[31] The TIA posted a separate website with safety tips for parents, *www.toyinfo.org/*.

The TIA was itself a member of the International Council of Toy Industries (ICTI), which consisted of toy trade associations from Australia, Austria, Brazil, Canada, China, Chinese Taipei, Denmark, France, Germany, Hong Kong, Hungary, Italy, Japan, Mexico, the Netherlands, Russia, Spain, Sweden, the United Kingdom, and the United States. ICTI's website stated, "The health and safety of children throughout the world is the driving force behind ICTI, which promotes international toy safety standards and a responsible attitude to advertising and marketing to children."

ICTI developed its CARE (Caring, Awareness, Responsible, Ethical) Process "to promote ethical manufacturing, in the form of fair labor treatment, as well as employee health and safety, in the toy industry supply chain, worldwide. Its initial focus is in China, where 70% of the world's toy volume is manufactured. Its intent is to provide a single, fair, thorough and consistent program to monitor toy factories' compliance with ICTI's Code of Business Practices."[32] The ICTI CARE Process engaged toy companies and individual factories producing toys. To be considered an ICTI CARE member, a company must commit to purchasing products only from factories enrolled in the CARE Process. Factories were audited by independent auditing firms that were specially trained with regard to ICTI's code.

Toy Industry Trends

From 2010 to 2015 the number of children under five and age five to nine was predicted to increase nearly 3 percent and about 5 percent, respectively, in the United States (Exhibit 4). In 2006 American grandparents spent more than $30 billion, or $500 per child per year, on their grandchildren, a two-fold increase over what was spent a decade earlier.[33] The number of U.S. grandparents swelled from 70 million to well over 115 million in 2010 due to Baby Boomers achieving this milestone. Grandparents represented 25 percent of the annual toy dollars spent. As a result, manufacturers have targeted baby-boomer grandparents with nostalgic toys such as Fisher-Price's Snoopy Sniffer pull toy.[34]

To be profitable, toy makers have had to keep pace with the rapidly changing world, to stay on the edge of technology, to provide youngsters with appropriate toys for their enjoyment, and to challenge their creativity and imagination. According to the NPD Group's 2006 *Kids Leisure Time Study,* over 81 percent of children ages 5–12

Exhibit 4 U.S. Population Projections
(in millions)

Age	2015	2020	2025
Under 5	22,076	22,846	23,484
5–9	21,707	22,732	23,548
10–14	21,658	22,571	23,677

Source: U.S. Census Bureau, Population Division. 2008. Table 12: Projections of the Population by Age and Sex for the United States: 2010 to 2050 (NP2008-T12). August 14.

played with toys each week. Yet playing with toys, which accounted for 9 percent of their free time, was second to TV and movies at 16 percent.[35] A 2009 follow-up study indicated that kids ages 2–12 enjoyed 68 hours of leisure time per week, 49 percent of which was spent on entertainment. The percentage of free time spent watching TV and movies had not changed in three years, but the percentage of time playing with toys had increased to 12.8 percent (see Exhibit 5). Children were also being exposed to technology at an early age. The average age that children began using consumer electronic (CE) devices declined from 8.1 years in 2005 to 6.7 years in 2007.[36] This age compression challenged traditional toy manufacturers to maintain interest in their products and to incorporate technology in toys at an earlier age.[37]

Innovative toys incorporated voice recognition and animatronics as well as infrared vision and artificial intelligence. Some systems used motion-capture technology to place the child on-screen and literally "in" the game. Concerns over childhood obesity increasingly have pressured parents to provide toys that promote a more active lifestyle (such as *Dance, Dance Revolution*). At the same time, parents seek toys to aid in their children's creative and intellectual growth.

Competition

The U.S. toy industry consists of manufacturers and retailers. *Manufacturers* is a loose term, as the majority of the products in certain segments are outsourced to offshore subcontractors. Three manufacturers, Mattel, Hasbro, and JAKKS Pacific, dominated the U.S. toy industry. In addition, some smaller manufacturers such as RC2 produced a smaller range of toys for specific niches. A large number of smaller players who competed in new-product development also existed. When these companies stumbled onto a unique idea and enjoyed temporary success, they were usually acquired by a market leader.

Major foreign manufacturers, including such brands as Danish LEGO Group and Canadian MEGA Brands, also sold toys in the United States The growth of big-box retailer Toys "R" Us and discounter Walmart changed the balance of power in the industry, as each could demand concessions on price and other product features. The buyer power of these big-box retailers had driven smaller manufacturers, as well as retailers, nearly out of business. Appendix B provides a list of the major manufacturers, with important financial results for 2010.

Hasbro   Hasbro was founded by two brothers, Henry and Helal Hassenfield, in Providence, Rhode Island, in 1923. In 2010 Hasbro was the second largest toy maker behind Mattel, with revenue exceeding $3.84 billion. Its toys and brands included G.I. Joe, Tonka Toys, Nerf Balls, and Weebles, as well as board games such as Scrabble, Candy Land, and Monopoly. The firm also produced Marvel, Star Wars, Spider-Man, and Transformer toys under license from the filmmakers. These toys sell for higher prices than Hasbro's other products but also incur higher costs due to the licensing fees. Hasbro's Playskool line included both toys and baby-care items. The company viewed its core brand products as a more consistent revenue stream than its licensed products. Similar to Mattel, in 2009 almost 50 percent of Hasbro's sales came from three customers: Walmart (25 percent), Toys "R" Us (11 percent), and Target (13 percent).

Hasbro owned just two manufacturing facilities, in the United States and Waterford, Ireland. It outsourced most production to Chinese makers and a small amount

Exhibit 5   Ways Kids, Ages 2–12, Spend Their Free Time

	Average Weekly Hours	Percentage of Free Time Spent in This Activity
Watching TV/movies	12.2	16.1
Playing with toys	10.9	12.8
Being with friends	7.6	4.9
Physical activities	7.4	7.2
Listening to music	7.2	5.8
Video games	7.0	5.6
Extracurricular activities	6.7	5.8
Recreational computer	6.2	5.4
Reading	5.6	4.8

Source: NPD Group. 2009. *Kids Leisure Time* III study webinar. Available from Toy Industry Association or NPD Group.

of production to suppliers in Europe, other Asian countries, and the Americas. Its U.S. plant in Massachusetts produced games. The company first began manufacturing action figures in Hong Kong in the 1960s. In 2006 Hasbro reduced its manufacturing in Ireland while transferring production to Chinese suppliers. In addition, the company has begun product development and engineering in China. Hasbro partnered with Li & Fung to manage its Chinese supply chain and to act as its exclusive distributor in China. With Li & Fung, Hasbro has begun to sell toys in Chinese department stores (Isetan and New World) and hypermarkets as well. Hasbro required suppliers to meet international standards. Both Hasbro employees and approved ICTI auditors inspected vendors. During 2007 Hasbro had no product recalls due to lead paint. It did, however, have three recalls related to burn dangers with its Easy-Bake Oven. In 2010 Hasbro launched the U.S. cable network HUB with partner Discovery Communications.

JAKKS Pacific Although only 16 years old, JAKKS Pacific was one of the United States' top toy companies, making and selling action figures under exclusive license for World Wrestling Federation, die-cast and plastic cars (Road Champs, Remco), preschool toys (Child Guidance), pens and markers (Pentech), fashion dolls, and even pet products. In 2010 Jakks Pacific had revenue of $742.2 million. It employed 338 full-time employees in the United States, 255 in Hong Kong, 104 in China, 11 in Canada, and 3 in the UK. Target, Toys "R" Us, and Walmart accounted for nearly 60 percent of company sales.

JAKKS's growth strategy included expanding product lines through licensing agreements and acquisitions. The company partnered with Jelly Belly Candy Co. to create a line of art activities and stationery based on Jelly Belly jelly beans and HIT Entertainment to license Bob the Builder, Thomas & Friends, and Barney characters for a variety of arts and crafts products. JAKKS acquired Play Along, maker of plush toys, action figures, dolls, and preschool toys, in 2004. Play Along licenses include such brands as Care Bears, Teletubbies, and Cabbage Patch Kids. JAKKS Pacific Ltd., its Hong Kong division, oversaw overseas vendors' operations. In 2007 JAKKS Pacific avoided lead-paint-based recalls but did issue a recall for 245,000 battery packs for toy vehicles manufactured in China.

LEGO Group LEGO Group was the world's fourth largest toy maker, with 2009 sales of $2.2 billion. The company was still owned by grandchildren of its founder, Ole Kirk Christiansen. Since its founding in 1934, it has made over 200 billion building blocks. LEGO Group licensed and created products to complement television and movie releases, such as HIT Entertainment's *Bob the Builder, Star Wars,* and *Indiana Jones.* Until recently, LEGO Group manufactured toys in Denmark, the United States, and Switzerland. It shifted production from the United States and Switzerland to the Czech Republic,

Hungary, and Mexico and began outsourcing electronic components of certain toys primarily to electronics manufacturers, such as Flextronics (headquartered in Singapore), to reduce costs.

In an interview with *Plastics News,* LEGO Group spokeswoman Charlotte Simonsen explained that the company used centralized, highly automated production to produce its standardized plastic building blocks.[38] Plants in Eastern Europe, including the Czech Republic, were close to its headquarters in Billund, Denmark, allowing for oversight and rapid response. These highly automated plants made LEGO Group less sensitive to labor costs than other makers.

As a result, LEGO Group made only 3 percent of its products in China. Analysts believed that the company could benefit from the recalls, as parents searched for alternatives to products made in China. In 2006 LEGO Group recalled about 358,000 plastic trucks containing LEGO Duplo bricks. A wheel on the truck could come off, exposing a metal axle that could injure a toddler; the bricks were not recalled. Between 2006 and 2011 the company's revenues almost doubled to $2.2 billion and the group moved from the 4th largest to the 3rd largest toy manufacturer in the world.

RC2 Founded in 1989 as Racing Champions Corporation, RC2 grew to be one of the larger toy companies in the United States by 2010. Although RC2's 2010 revenue of $427.3 was a fraction of Mattel's, the firm's recall of 1.5 million Chinese-made Thomas & Friends wooden trains, popular with preschoolers, set off the wave of recalls and a near panic among preschoolers' parents. In contrast to Mattel and Hasbro, much of RC2's revenue was from production of licensed products, such as Thomas & Friends, Bob the Builder, and NASCAR vehicles. In addition, RC2 owned the Learning Curve family of brands (Eden and Lamaze) and First Years and produced various replicas of cars and trucks.

In contrast to typical recalls of toys from China, Thomas & Friends were usually "purchased in upscale toy stores for $10 to $70 apiece, often by politically empowered parents who are extremely averse to exposing their children to contaminants of any kind."[39] More than two-thirds of RC2's products targeted young children. Of the affected U.S. toy makers, RC2 was least dependent on the major retailers. In 2010, Walmart, Toys R Us, and Target accounted for only 38.9 percent of sales.

RC2 primarily served as an intermediary, linking content and characters to manufacturers. It had told analysts that it would prefer not to own its own plants. In 2010, 87.1 percent of RC2's products were manufactured in China. According to its financial filings, RC2 had long-term relationships with seven Chinese companies that produced about half its products. The recalled products were made in Dongguan, where half of China's toys originate. Ironically, the second recall in 2007 included green trees.

Retailers

Toy retailing in the United States radically changed with the birth of Toys "R" Us and the growth of Walmart. Walmart, Target, and Toys "R" Us accounted for about 50 percent of worldwide toy sales in 2010. Few independent toy retailers remained, as many lifelong specialty stores had been forced out when retailers, especially Walmart, demanded discounted prices. Exhibit 6 contains data on sales by distribution channel. Online toy sales continued to increase, more than doubling since 2003 to 7.4 percent of U.S. sales. These sales come from traditional retailers' sites, such as Target; e-retailers, such as *Amazon.com*; and manufacturers, such as Mattel. Appendix C provides a list of the major retailers, with important financial results for 2010.

Walmart   Walmart had been the world's largest toy retailer since 2000. Its estimated 2006 toy sales reached $18 million in the United States.[40] However, toys accounted for just 7 percent of the company's sales, based upon estimated square footage in 2009.[41] Walmart's market share provided it with the ability to negotiate with suppliers to discount prices. If a manufacturer's product lines were not offered at Walmart store locations, the company's sales often fell below expectations due to Walmart's growing market share. Walmart's wholesale low prices forced competitors to outsource production overseas to reduce their overhead costs. In addition, Walmart's deep discounting of toys in October acted as a preemptive strike to undercut its competitors.

Toys "R" Us   Once the largest toy retailer in the United States, Toys "R" Us reported the second highest 2006 toy sales of $5.7 billion. Sales had declined from $6.2 billion in 2005 due to its reorganization and severing of its relationship with *Amazon.com*. In 2005 two private investment firms (KKR and Bain Capital) and a real estate company (Vornado Realty Trust) bought Toys "R" Us for $6.6 billion. The firm owned, operated, or leased 866 Toys "R" Us stores, 200 leased stores, and 510 Babies "R" Us stores by the end of 2010. Company sales reached $13.6 billion in 2010.

Target   In 2006 Target's $3.45 billion in toy and games sales and 23 percent market share placed it in fourth place when games-only retailer GameStop was excluded. Target's online store ranked third behind eBay and *Amazon.com* in terms of visits. In 2006 Target launched "Time to Play!" toy boutiques inside the toy departments of each of its stores and introduced its own line of toys, called PlayWonder, for children ages two to five years. In addition, Target stocked a larger assortment of high-margin specialty toys than Walmart stocked. In 2009 electronics, entertainment, sporting goods, and toys accounted for 22 percent of sales.

Exhibit 6   U.S. Sales of Toys and Games by Distribution Format, 2003–2009

	% Retail Value						
	2003	**2004**	**2005**	**2006**	**2007**	**2008**	**2009**
Store-based retailing	**94.8**	**92.6**	**91.7**	**91.4**	**90.9**	**90.8**	**90.3**
Grocery retailers	3.0	3.6	4.1	4.6	4.8	4.9	5.0
Nongrocery retailers	82.8	80.4	79.3	78.4	76.3	75.5	75.6
Mixed retailers	48.0	50.3	52.7	53.4	50.7	48.7	48.9
Leisure and personal goods retailers	34.8	30.1	26.5	25.0	25.6	26.8	26.7
Other store-based retailing	9.0	8.6	8.3	8.4	9.7	10.4	9.8
Nonstore retailing	**5.2**	**7.4**	**8.3**	**8.6**	**9.1**	**9.2**	**9.7**
Vending	0.2	0.2	0.2	0.2	0.2	0.3	0.3
Home shopping	1.8	2.0	2.1	2.1	2.1	2.0	1.9
Internet retailing	3.2	5.1	5.8	6.1	6.7	6.8	7.4
Direct selling	0.1	0.1	0.1	0.1	0.1	0.1	0.1
Total	**100.0**	**100.0**	**100.0**	**100.0**	**100.0**	**100.0**	**100.0**

Source: Official statistics, trade associations, trade press, company research, store checks, trade interviews, Euromonitor estimates.

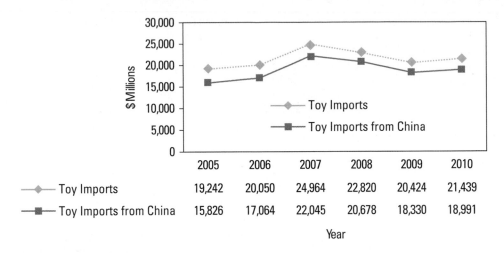

	2005	2006	2007	2008	2009	2010
Toy Imports	19,242	20,050	24,964	22,820	20,424	21,439
Toy Imports from China	15,826	17,064	22,045	20,678	18,330	18,991

Year

Exhibit 7 **U.S. Toy, Dolls, and Games Imports, 2005–2010**

Source: US Bureau of the Census: Foreign Trade Division USA Trade ® Online. Source: U.S. Import and Export Merchandise trade statistics *http://data.usatradeonline.gov.remote.baruch.cuny.edu/View/dispview.aspx*, accessed on June 1, 2011.

China Supplies the World's Toys

China was the world's largest toy producing and exporting nation, with more than 8,000 companies employing more than 3.5 million people in 2006. More than 30,000 different toys were made in China and exported to 100 countries and territories.[42] Exports to the United States peaked at over $24 billion in 2007, with 2010 exports of $18.9 billion (see Exhibit 7).

Toy manufacturing in China was shaped by two competing pressures: quality enhancement and cost reduction. On one hand, many export-oriented manufacturers had worked to increase product quality and quality control and had been certified by major international business standards groups. Over 300 toy makers had applied for Code of Business Practices certification developed by the ICTI.[43]

On the other hand, foreign firms had forced Chinese toy makers to reduce costs. As noted above, in the United States, toys were increasingly sold through mass merchandisers. "Retailers force prices down. It's relentless. It forces toy companies to manufacture as inexpensively as they can," said Frank Clarke, a spokesman for the Toy Industry Association, in an interview in *Plastic News*.[44] As costs for plastics and energy soared, manufacturers perceived labor as a potential source of cost savings.

Several factors made China an attractive toy supplier. First, the average wage in China was $200 per month. The Chinese government believed that China would stay competitive on the world market as long as wages remained below $600 per month. Second, China's currency, the yuan, was considered undervalued relative to the dollar. The yuan floated in a narrow band near 8.1 to the U.S. dollar. The Chinese government was under increasing pressure from the U.S. and European governments to increase

the yuan's value to stem the flood of Chinese exports across product categories. Either inflation in China or a revaluation of the yuan could decrease China's attractiveness as a manufacturer.

Another trend in China was a transition from merely serving as outsourcing partners in a foreign manufacturer's value chain to creating domestic research and design activities. With the support of the Chinese Ministry of Labor and Social Security, the China Toy Association created a certification for trained toy designers to improve the nation's product design capability.[45] Some Chinese firms began registering their own intellectual property with regard to toy design at home and abroad.

Surprisingly, some toy manufacturing has left China much as it shifted from Taiwan there in the 1990s. Labor shortages in some parts of China have driven up wages to the point that some Chinese manufacturers have invested in even-lower-wage countries, such as Viet Nam. In addition, threats by the U.S. government have made makers wary. Still, in 2009 toy exports from the rest of Asia to the United States were only about 9 percent of what China exported to the United States.[46]

Interestingly, the Chinese domestic toy market remains virtually untapped. The nation has 300 million children under the age of 14.

Recalls and Aftermath

In 2007 a safety and public relations crisis gripped the United States toy industry. Through mid-November 2007, toy manufacturers and the U.S. Consumer Product Safety Commission recalled over 25 million units through 60 recalls. Most of these recalls were due to lead paint found on products manufactured in China. From Thomas, the cheeky tank engine, to Diego and Barbie, some of the most loved toy brands were affected.

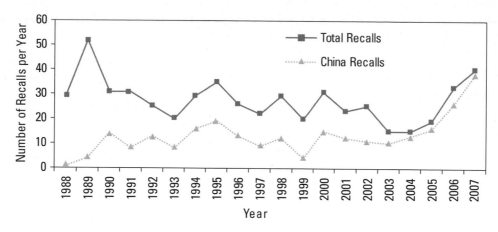

Exhibit 8 **Toy Recalls from 1988–2007**

Source: Bapuji, H., & Beamish, P. W. 2007. Toy recalls—Is China really the problem? *Canada-Asia Commentary,* 45:1–8.

The tipping point for the recall crisis seemed to be RC2's June 2007 recall of 1.5 million Chinese-made wooden railroad toys and set parts due to lead paint. The maker, Hansheng Wood Products Factory, was later included in an August 2007 export ban announced by the General Administration for Quality Supervision, Inspection and Quarantine, a China quality watchdog.[47] Toy recalls were not, however, a new problem for the industry and consumers. Exhibit 8 contains recall data for 1988–2007. The number of recalls involving toys made in China had increased along with the percentage of toys manufactured there. Most of the 2007 toy recalls were for traditional toys targeted to the most vulnerable age group: toddlers.

Following the 2008 CPSIA, however, the number of toy recalls declined dramatically. The CPSC noted a dramatic decline in toy recalls since 2008: "There were 46 toy recalls in fiscal year 2010, down from 50 recalls in 2009 and 172 recalls in 2008. Toy recalls related to lead in 2010 were down to 3, well below the 9 recalls reported in 2009 and 19 in 2008."[48]

In a 2007 editorial, the *Wall Street Journal* described the Chinese environment that spawned the product safety recalls and left Chinese consumers vulnerable to unsafe products.[49] Possible explanations included an ideological vacuum in postcommunist China due to Mao's destruction of traditional Chinese values and beliefs and the absence of any values other than wealth, or the current business environment, in which fierce competition and thin margins make every dollar count. A more comprehensive explanation was that "a political system without popular elections or an effective system of checks and balances has helped create a culture in which the Chinese are not accountable to *each other*" (italics in original).[50] As a result, no codified set of ethics to guide national behavior existed.

In a *New York Times* interview that same year, Sean McGowan, managing director and toy analyst at Wedbush

Morgan Securities, contended that toy recalls were not over. "If I went down to the shelves of Walmart and tested everything, I'm going to find serious problems. The idea that Mattel—with its high standards—has a bigger problem than everybody else is laughable. If we don't see an increase of recalls in this industry, then it's a case of denial."[51] Dr. S. Prakash Sethi, who independently monitored working conditions in Mattel's factories, agreed, "If Mattel, with all of its emphasis on quality and testing, found such a widespread problem, what do you think is happening in the rest of the toy industry, in the apparel industry and even in the low-end electronics industry?" However, Dr. Sethi added, "There is something to be said about the pressure that American and European and multinational companies put on Chinese companies to supply cheap products. The operating margins are razor thin, so you really should not be surprised that there is pressure to cut corners."[52]

Additionally, in 2007 several companies that license characters to toy makers announced additional inspection protocols. For example, Nickelodeon, which owns Dora the Explorer and Diego, hired a third-party monitor to check on all of the companies who licensed its characters, including Mattel[53] and RC2.[54] Sesame Workshop and Disney both announced additional testing programs.[55] Walmart revealed that one of the biggest concerns of its shoppers was the safety of toys manufactured in China.[56] Disney said that tests of its character toys for lead paint would include randomly testing toys taken from retail shelves.

In addition, Toys "R" Us hired engineers to randomly choose toys on its shelves for testing by an independent lab. In a *New York Times* interview, Ron Boire, president of Toys "R" Us, stated, "Trust but verify. We have to be confident. I have to be able to put my head on the pillow and say, 'I've done everything I can.' "[57]

The Chinese government initiated a crackdown on product safety for numerous industries. It revoked the export licenses of about 300 toymakers, closed approximately 2,000 unlicensed factories, and banned lead paint completely for use in U.S. toy exports.[58]

Nonetheless, the toy recalls threatened sales of Chinese products during the 2007 holiday season.[59] A Harris Poll found that over 90 percent of Americans were aware of the recalls, yet only 6 percent were confident that they had a recalled toy in their home, and even fewer reported taking action. Most respondents overestimated the number of recalls on lead paint rather than design flaws. Almost 50 percent of respondents reported that they would avoid products or toys from China that holiday season. Only about 10 percent of respondents stated that they would not avoid Chinese products or toys. Interestingly, the CPSC was the public's most trusted source of product safety information.

The U.S. toy recalls affected the industry elsewhere.[60] The EU threatened a ban on Chinese goods, including toys, if China failed to comply with EU health and safety measures. Beginning August 17, Brazil's government banned Mattel toy imports until it verified that Mattel's toys met local safety regulations.

On September 19 toy industry representatives testified before a U.S. Senate subcommittee and a U.S. House subcommittee on the question of the safety of toys sold in the United States and the possibility of tighter government control. In addition, critics called for the U.S. government to restore the CPSC's budget to pre-Bush levels. From 2005–2007, the Bush administration had cut the commission's budget by 10 percent, forcing a reduction in the number of investigators and agents.[61]

Consumer Product Safety Commission (CPSC) commissioner Thomas H. Moore told Congress that a number of parties, including the Bush Administration, U.S. Congress, regulators, manufacturers, importers, retailers, and "anyone else who may have been active or inactive participants in enabling the policy decisions and priorities that have led us to this point" shared blame for the recent wave of toy recalls. At a hearing of the U.S. House of Representatives Subcommittee on Commerce, Trade and Consumer Protection, Moore said those who stood by and "quietly acquiesced while the [CPSC] was reduced to a weakened regulator, largely relying on the regulated to regulate themselves, must examine and correct the role that they played in putting the commission in its current state."[62]

Moore also said that Congress had been right in rejecting the Bush Administration's staffing and budget proposal for fiscal year 2008, which would have reduced the CPSC staff by 19 full-time employees. However, Moore added that simply throwing resources at the CPSC in response to public alarm over the recent recalls would not resolve the situation. Instead, Moore endorsed an incremental approach to increasing the CPSC's budget and staff. "It has taken years for the commission to get to

its present position and it will take years to correct," said Moore.[63]

On November 19, 2007, California Attorney General Jerry Brown sued 20 toy makers and retailers, including Mattel and Toys "R" Us, due to "unlawful quantities of lead." The state accused the companies of knowingly exposing children to lead and failing "to provide warning of the risk, which is required under the Safe Drinking Water and Toxic Enforcement Act of 1986, known as Proposition 65."[64] And in January 2008, 56 members of Congress sent a letter to Eckert reminding him to "do the right thing" following reports that a Fisher-Price brand blood-pressure cuff was tainted by lead. Mattel had refused to issue a nationwide recall. The company launched an informal recall not under the auspices of the CPSC.

The 2008 CPSIA had changed the regulatory environment in which Mattel operated. The CPSC received more authority, and industry organizations such as TIA and ICTI gained more power as well. Eckert caught himself staring at Sarge. Mattel and its competitors needed to develop a new strategy for dealing with challenges in their competitive environment and the loss of consumer confidence. He felt fairly comfortable in the manner in which Mattel had dealt with the crisis as it unfolded. Not everything had been perfect, but it was a crisis, after all, and he thought Mattel's reputation would survive. He thought it was important to review how they had come to this crisis, review all strategic elements, and revise their strategy going forward. And with all the dynamics in the industry and consumer base changing as rapidly as they were, he wondered how Mattel would continue to differentiate itself to create value for consumers and investors alike.

Endnotes

1. Dee, J. A Toy Maker's Conscience. December 23, 2007, *New York Times Magazine,* 34–40.
2. Barboza, D. & Story, L. 2007. Toymaking in China, Mattel's way. *New York Times,* August 26.
3. Story, L. 2007. Lead paint prompts Mattel to recall 967,000 toys. *New York Times.* August 2: C1.
4. Barboza & Story. 2007. Toymaking in China.
5. Ibid.
6. Mattel Inc. website.
7. Barboza & Story. 2007. Toymaking in China.
8. Lauzon, M. 2001. Mattel Inc. ending U.S. production. *Plastics News.* 13(6): 1–2.
9. Barboza & Story. 2007. Toymaking in China.
10. Ibid.
11. Ibid.
12. Ibid.
13. Warren, C. 2007. The little engine that could poison. *New York Times.* June 22: A21.
14. U.S. Consumer Product Safety Commission (CPSC). 1977. Press release: CPSC announces final ban on lead-containing paint.
15. Story, L., & Barboza, D. 2007. Mattel recalls 19 million toys sent from China. *New York Times.* August 15: A1.

16. Story. 2007. Lead paint prompts Mattel to recall 967,000 toys.

17. *ABC7.com*. 2007. Mom confronts Mattel at corporate HQ over toy recall. August 23. *abclocal.go.com/kabc/story?section=local&id=5599290.*

18. Associated Press. 2007. Toy company CEO kills self. August 13. *www.cnn.com/2007/WORLD/asiapcf/08/13/china.toymaker.ap/index.html.*

19. Story, L. 2007. After stumbling, Mattel cracks down in China. *New York Times.* August 29.

20. CNN. 2007. Mattel CEO: "Rigorous standards" after massive toy recall. August 14. *www.cnn.com/2007/US/08/14/recall/index.html.*

21. Ibid.

22. Thottam, J. 2007. Why Mattel Apologized to China, *Time,* September 21.

23. Ibid.

24. Pimlott, D. 2007. Mattel earnings dented by recall of 21m toys. *Financial Times,* October 16: 28.

25. NPD Group. 2010. U.S. toy industry sales generate $21.47 billion in 2009. *www.npd.com/press/releases/press_100201a.html.*

26. CPSC. *www.cpsc.gov/about/faq.html.*

27. Warren. 2007. The little engine that could poison.

28. CPSC. 2007. 2007 Performance & Accountability Report. November. *www.cpsc.gov/cpscpub/pubs/reports/2007par.pdf.*

29. CPSC. 2008. 2009 Performance Budget Request. *www.cpsc.gov/cpscpub/pubs/reports/2009plan.pdf.*

30. U.S. Department of Commerce. 2009. U.S. Department of Commerce Industry Report: Dolls, Toys, Games, and Children's Vehicles. December 4. *www.ita.doc.gov/td/ocg/toyoutlook_09.pdf.*

31. Toy Industry Association Inc. *2001–2002 Toy Industry Fact Book. www.toyassociation.org/AM/Template.cfm?Section=About_TIA&Template=/TaggedPage/TaggedPageDisplay.cfm&TPLID=3&ContentID=2546.*

32. International Council of Toy Industries (ICTI). 2007. The International Council of Toy Industries CARE Process. *www.toy-icti.org/info/care_process.pdf.*

33. Kaplan, D. 2006. Grand-scale grandparents. *Houston Chronicle,* November 5. *www.chron.com/disp/story.mpl/front/4310259.html.*

34. Ibid.

35. NPD Group. 2006. *Kids Leisure Time Study.* Commissioned by the Toy Industry Association.

36. NPD 2007. *Kids & Digital Content* study. Available from the NPD Group.

37. NPD Group. 2009. *Kids Leisure Time* III study webinar. Available from Toy Industry Association or NPD Group.

38. Lauzon, M. 2005. China: The world's *toy* makers. *Plastic News,* 17(42): 16–18.

39. Warren. 2007. The little engine that could poison.

40. French, D. 2007. Top 25 retailers. *Playthings,* November 11. *www.giftsanddec.com/article/521779-Top_25_Retailers.php.*

41. Deprez, E. E. 2010. Walmart spurs sustainable toy animals into $1 billion market. *Bloomberg Businessweek. www.businessweek.com/news/2010-03-26/wal-mart-spurs-sustainable-toy-animals-into-1-billion-market.html.*

42. Liang, M. 2006. Bigger and better: The continued growth of China's toy industry. *Playthings,* October 2006: 14.

43. Ibid.

44. Lauzon. 2005. China: The world's *toy* makers.

45. Liang. 2006. Bigger and better.

46. U.S. International Trade Administration. 2009. U.S. imports for consumption.

47. Associated Press. 2007. Toy company CEO kills self.

48. CPSC. 2010. New data shows toy recalls declining, toy injuries increasing. November 18. *cpsc.gov/cpscpub/prerel/prhtml11/11042.html.*

49. Parker, E. 2007. Made in China. *Wall Street Journal,* July 12: A15.

50. Ibid.

51. Story & Barboza. 2007. Mattel recalls 19 million toys sent from China.

52. Ibid.

53. Story. 2007. Lead paint prompts Mattel to recall 967,000 toys.

54. Barboza, D., & Story, L. 2007. RC2's train wreck. *New York Times,* June 20.

55. Story, L. 2007. Disney to test character toys for lead paint. *New York Times.* September 10: C1.

56. Story. 2007. After stumbling, Mattel cracks down in China.

57. Story. 2007. Disney to test character toys for lead paint.

58. *Playthings.* 2007. Recall news briefs. September 12. *www.giftsanddec.com/article/526973-Recall_News_Briefs.php.*

59. HarrisInteractive. 2007. Recent toy recalls threaten sales of Chinese products this holiday season. The Harris Poll #114, November 14.

60. *Playthings.* 2007. Recall news briefs.

61. Warren. 2007. The little engine that could poison.

62. *Business and the Environment.* 2007. Blame for toy recall problems shared by many. 18(10): 11.

63. *Business and the Environment.* 2007. Blame for toy recall problems shared by many.

64. Associated Press. 2007. California sues Mattel over tainted toys. *www.msnbc.com/id/21886363.*

Appendix A   Toy Industry Association Mission

Our Mission

Our mission is to lead the growth and health of the toy industry. We are committed to addressing the needs of our diverse membership, building on our history of leadership in safety standards, advocacy on legislative and trade issues, visibility in the media, and philanthropy to children.

Developing the highest universal standards

We have a dedicated team leading the industry's safety initiatives, and we fulfill the role of chair in the ongoing review process for ASTM F963, the comprehensive toy safety standard.

Ensuring safe play for children

We educate manufacturers on safety and quality standards, and we lead public initiatives to educate consumers on safe play.

Protecting the rights of factory workers

We educate members on compliance with ethical manufacturing standards to ensure compliance with the ICTI CARE Program.

Enhancing the image and growth of the toy industry

We generate major feature stories and broadcast segments on the latest toys and trends, and we serve as industry spokesperson on vital issues in the news.

Supporting free trade and fair representation on regulatory issues

We voice issues with regulators in the U.S. and internationally. Our advocacy helps prevent unwarranted legislative or regulatory actions and ensure fair representation.

Source: Toy Industry Association Inc. Our mission. *www. toyassociation.org/AM/Template.cfm?Section=Mission.*

Appendix B Toy & Games Manufacturers Key Numbers 2010

Key Numbers	Mattel	Hasbro	JAKKS Pacific	LEGO* 2009	RC2	Industry Median	Market† Median
Annual sales ($ mil.)	5,856.19	3,837.6	742.2	2,245.91	427.34		
Employees‡	31,000	5,900	711	7,058	713		
Market cap ($ mil.)	8,866.98	4,054.9	503.16	—	471.24		
Profitability							
Gross profit margin	50.46%	58.90%	32.78%	—	42.32%	39.72%	30.37%
Pre-tax profit margin	14.46%	12.20%	6.72%	—	10.51%	5.71%	9.38%
Net profit margin	11.69%	8.50%	6.30%	11.6	6.95%	(1.23%)	4.03%
Return on equity	26.55%	25.60%	(68.90%)	—	13.71%	(1.49%)	6.11%
Return on assets	13.43%	10.40%	(46.39%)	—	7.57%	(0.68%)	1.01%
Return on invested capital	19.26%	13.79%	(57.48%)	—	10.18%	(0.89%)	2.79%
Valuation							
Price/earnings ratio	13.48	12.19	16.89	—	16.72	36.63	—
Per share data ($)							
Revenue per share	16.80	29.37	27.10	—	19.74	17.78	18.90
Dividends per share	0.83	0.76	—	—	—	0.35	0.53
Cash flow per share	1.45	2.53	2.58	—	1.19	2.80	2.78
Long-term debt per share	2.73	5.10	3.24	—	1.91	8.80	12.15
Book value per share	7.54	9.74	14.93	—	12.70	15.00	13.15
Total assets per share	15.54	24.47	22.93	—	17.36	32.54	77.89

Source: *www.Hoovers.com*

* Data unavailable.

† Public companies trading on the New York Stock Exchange, the American Stock Exchange, and the NASDAQ National Market.

‡ JAKKS Pacific and RC2 employee data are for 2009.

Appendix C Toy & Games Retailers Key Numbers 2010

Key Numbers	Walmart	Target	Toys "R" Us
Annual sales ($ mil.)	408,214.0	63,357.0	13,568.0
Employees	2,100,000	351,000	68,000
Market cap ($ mil.)	190,317.35	36,303.35	Private
Profitability			
Gross profit margin	25.37%	30.26%	
Pre-tax profit margin	5.41%	5.92%	
Net profit margin	3.51%	3.81%	2.24%
Return on equity	21.08%	17.12%	
Return on assets	8.58%	5.61%	
Return on invested capital	13.06%	7.70%	
Valuation			
Price/earnings ratio	12.35	13.66	
Operations			
Inventory turnover	9.00	6.57	
Days cost of goods sold in inventory	40.54	55.59	
Net receivables turnover flow	101.43	8.69	
Per share data ($)			
Revenue per share	112.28	90.43	
Dividends per share	1.21	0.84	
Cash flow per share	6.98	7.71	
Working capital per share	(2.03)	10.02	
Long-term debt per share	10.22	21.35	
Book value per share	18.40	21.01	
Total assets per share	47.92	62.89	

Source: *www.hoovers.com*

Case 24   Nintendo's Wii*

Does it make sense to buy a Nintendo Wii? For four years the answer was yes!

Since its release, the Wii had led video games' return to the cultural mainstream. Neither the Microsoft Xbox 360 nor the Sony PlayStation 3 offered the sorts of game controls that could truly appeal to a mass audience, and particularly to families that wanted to have fun together at home. Only the Wii had intuitive, motion-sensitive game controllers so gamers could sway the controller around and swing and twist it in space to bowl or throw or evoke some other action on the screen. With just a little more than 4,000 employees and 2010 revenue of $15.7 billion,[1] Nintendo was the market leader of the generation in video console sales growth, ahead of Microsoft and Sony. Microsoft had more than 89,000 employees, and its 2010 revenues were $62.48 billion.[2] Sony had more than 167,900 employees, and its 2010 revenues were over $77 billion.[3]

However, by the fall of 2010 the playing field was level, with Sony and Microsoft offering competition for the Wii motion-sensitive controllers. Looking at Kinect from Microsoft for the Xbox 360 and the Move system from Sony for PlayStation 3, it was clear that the two leading competitors had finally caught up with the Wii's lead in engineering and its ingenious human interface. For almost four years, the Wii had reshaped the home-entertainment experience. But by 2011, some observers feared that the Wii no longer did anything unique that the PS3 or Xbox 360 would not do even better[4]. PlayStation 3 and Xbox 360 already had superior graphics to the Wii, but now they were gaining motion-sensing controllers as well.

Background

Although Nintendo dates back to 1889 as a playing-card maker, Nintendo's first video-game systems were developed in 1979 and were known as TV Game 15 and TV Game 6.[5] In 1980 Nintendo developed the first portable LCD video game with a microprocessor. In 1985 Nintendo created the Nintendo Entertainment System (NES), an 8-bit video game console. The original NES was very successful, as its graphics were superior to any home-based console available at the time, and as a result more than 60 million units were sold worldwide.[6] The NES set the bar for subsequent consoles in platform design, as well as for accepting games that were manufactured by third-party developers. As competitors began developing 16-bit devices, such as Sega's Genesis system or NEC's PC Engine, Nintendo knew that it had to respond and develop its own 16-bit system.

The Super Nintendo Entertainment System (SNES) was developed to stay current with the competitors. The Super Nintendo was released in 1991 and, when purchased, came with one game, *Super Mario World*. This was the successor to the previous Mario Brothers games that were played on the original 8-bit NES. In 1996 Nintendo released Nintendo 64, which caused the popularity of the Super Nintendo to decline. The Nintendo 64 was Nintendo's third-generation video game console and was named after the 64-bit processor. During its product lifetime, more than 30 million Nintendo 64 units were sold worldwide.[7]

The Nintendo 64, like its predecessors, used cartridges to play its games, but at the time, the competing systems of Sony and Sega were using CDs for game storage. Cartridges could store 64 megabytes of data, while CDs could store around 700 megabytes of data. Also, CDs were much cheaper to manufacture, distribute, and create; thus, many game developers that traditionally supported Nintendo platforms began creating games that would support the other platforms to increase profits.[8] At the time, the average cost of producing a Nintendo 64 cartridge was cited as $25, compared to 10 cents to produce a CD. Therefore, game producers passed the higher expense to the consumer, which explains why Nintendo 64 games tended to sell for higher prices than Sony PlayStation games. While most Sony PlayStation games rarely exceeded $50, Nintendo 64 titles could reach $70.[9] Third-party developers naturally switched to the systems that used a less expensive CD platform (such as the PlayStation).

In 2001 Nintendo released its GameCube, which was part of the sixth-generation era of video game systems. These systems included Sony's PlayStation 2, Microsoft's Xbox, and Sega's Dreamcast. Although the GameCube did not use cartridges, Nintendo began producing its games using a proprietary optical-disk technology. This technology, while similar in appearance to CDs, was actually smaller in diameter and could not be played using a standard CD player.

Genyo Takeda, general manager of Integrated Research and Development for Nintendo, explained that innovation and creativity were fostered by giving several different development teams "free rein to couple a dedicated controller or peripheral with a GameCube title, and then see whether or not the end result was marketable. This project gave rise not only to the Donkey Kong Bongos and the Dancing Stage Mario Mix Action Pad, but also to a number of ideas and designs that would find their way into the Wii Remote."[10]

When Nintendo released the Wii video game console in 2006, it was already in the midst of a very competitive market. The previous generation of video game consoles consisted of the Sega Dreamcast, Sony PlayStation

*This case was prepared by Professor Alan B. Eisner and graduate student Eshai J. Gorshein of Pace University. This case was based solely on library research and was developed for class discussion rather than to illustrate either effective or ineffective handling of an administrative situation. Copyright © 2011 Alan B. Eisner.

2, Nintendo GameCube, and Microsoft Xbox. These systems were all released between 1999 and 2001 in the United States, and although the GameCube sold more systems than the Sega Dreamcast, it fell into third place behind the PlayStation 2 and the Xbox. The PlayStation 2 sold more than 115 million units worldwide, more than twice the combined unit sales of the GameCube and Xbox (21 million and 24 million, respectively). The next generation of video game consoles was about to become even more competitive.

As of 2010, Nintendo's revenues and income were on attractive upward trajectories (see Exhibits 1 and 2). Exhibit 3 shows that Nintendo's stock price was soaring compared to that of its larger competitors until mid-2010.

The Launch of the Wii

In 2006 Nintendo released its direct successor to the Game-Cube, the Wii (pronounced "we"). There were many reasons cited as to why the name *Wii* was chosen, but perhaps the most compelling reason was that "'Wii' sounded like 'we,' which emphasized that the console was for everyone. Wii could be remembered easily by people around the world, no matter what language they spoke. No confusion."[11] Initially the system was known by its code name, Revolution, but later the name was changed to Wii. Nintendo stated that it wanted to make the Wii a system that would make anyone who tried it talk to his or her friends and neighbors about it.[12]

The Wii was created to establish a new standard in game control, using an innovative and unprecedented

Exhibit 1 Income Statements (in millions of yen, except per-share items; year-end March 31)

	2010	2009	2008	2007	2006
Revenue	1,434,365	1,838,622	1,672,423	966,534	509,249
Total Revenue	1,434,365	1,838,622	1,672,423	966,534	509,249
Cost of Revenue, Total	859,131	1,044,981	972,362	568,722	294,133
Gross Profit	575,234	793,641	700,061	397,812	215,116
Selling/General/Administrative Expenses, Total	169,736	192,725	172,433	131,414	92,410
Research & Development	45,461	42,211	37,000	37,706	30,588
Depreciation/Amortization	3,469	3,438	3,405	2,664	1,764
Unusual Expense (Income)	−3,057	589	10,740	−3	−2,227
Operating Income	359,625	554,678	476,483	226,031	92,581
Gain (Loss) on Sale of Assets	59	−56	3,671	−132	−20
Other, Net	1,582	−2,839	1,777	3,087	2,398
Income Before Tax	367,443	448,137	433,780	289,605	166,472
Income Tax, Total	138,896	169,134	176,532	115,348	68,138
Income After Tax	228,547	279,003	257,248	174,257	98,334
Minority Interest	89	91	99	37	46
Net Income Before Extra. Items	228,636	279,094	257,347	174,294	98,380
Net Income	228,636	279,094	257,347	174,294	98,380

Source: *moneycentral.msn.com.*

Exhibit 2 **Balance Sheets** (in millions of yen, except per-share items; year-end March 31)

	2010	2009	2008	2007	2006
Assets					
Cash and Short-Term Investments	1,252,321	1,220,148	1,252,321	1,078,168	876,351
Cash & Equivalents	886,995	756,201	899,251	962,197	812,064
Short Term Investments	365,326	463,947	353,070	115,971	64,287
Total Receivables, Net	130,809	135,149	145,611	87,780	42,312
Accounts Receivable—Trade, Net	130,809	135,149	145,611	87,780	42,312
Accounts Receivable—Trade, Gross	131,876	139,174	147,787	89,666	43,826
Provision for Doubtful Accounts	-1,067	-4,025	-2,176	-1,886	-1,514
Total Inventory	124,673	144,752	104,840	88,609	30,835
Other Current Assets, Total	83,582	148,673	144,060	140,114	69,231
Total Current Assets	1,591,385	1,648,722	1,646,832	1,394,671	1,018,729
Property/Plant/Equipment, Total—Net	79,584	71,062	55,149	57,597	55,968
Intangibles, Net	4,111	2,169	2,009	505	319
Long-Term Investments	44,057	54,726	73,756	92,412	60,213
Other Long-Term Assets, Total	41,843	34,081	24,737	30,405	25,470
Total Assets	1,760,980	1,810,760	1,802,483	1,575,590	1,160,699
Liabilities and Shareholders' Equity					
Accounts Payable	264,613	356,774	335,820	301,080	83,817
Accrued Expenses	2,174	1,930	1,848	1,779	1,732
Notes Payable/Short-Term Debt	125	0	0	0	0
Current Portion of Long-Term Debt/ Capital Leases	65	9	0	0	0
Other Current Liabilities, Total	140,558	182,199	229,553	165,576	96,724
Total Current Liabilities	407,535	540,912	567,221	468,435	182,273
Total Long-Term Debt	157	15	0	0	0
Capital Lease Obligations	157	15	0	0	0
Minority Interest	174	25	98	138	176
Other Liabilities, Total	16,706	15,905	5,292	5,141	4,160
Total Liabilities	424,572	556,857	572,611	473,714	186,609
Common Stock	10,065	10,065	10,065	10,065	10,065
Additional Paid-In Capital	11,733	11,726	11,640	11,586	11,585
Retained Earnings (Accumulated Deficit)	1,527,315	1,432,958	1,380,430	1,220,293	1,096,073

(*continued*)

Exhibit 2 **Balance Sheets** (in millions of yen, except per-share items; year-end March 31) (*continued*)

	2010	2009	2008	2007	2006
Treasury Stock—Common	−156,585	−156,516	−156,184	−155,396	−155,112
Unrealized Gain (Loss)	1,661	3,100	5,418	8,898	10,717
Other Equity, Total	−57,778	−47,428	−21,495	6,432	762
Total Equity	1,336,411	1,253,905	1,229,874	1,101,878	974,090
Total Liabilities & Shareholders' Equity	1,760,983	1,810,762	1,802,485	1,575,592	1,160,699

Source: *moneycentral.msn.com.*

interface, the Wii Remote.[13] The Wii Remote was what made the Wii a unique home console. The remote acted as the primary controller for the Wii. Its motion-sensor capabilities allowed the user to interact and manipulate objects on the screen by moving and pointing the remote in various directions.[14] The Wii Remote was the size of a traditional remote control, and it was "limited only by the game designer's imagination."[15] For example, in a game of tennis it served as the racket when the user swung his or her arm, or in a shooting game it served as the user's gun. Not only did the remote serve as a controller, but it also had a built-in speaker and a rumble feature for even greater tactile feedback and game involvement.

The Wii Remote came with an arm strap that could be tied to the user's wrist so that the remote couldn't fly away when being used. The remote was powered by two AA batteries, which could power it for approximately 30 to 60 hours.[16] Exhibit 4 shows the Wii and Wii Remote.

The second part of the Wii Remote innovation was the Wii Nunchuk. The Nunchuk was designed to perfectly fit the user's hand, and it connected to the remote at its expansion port. The Nunchuk had the same motion-sensing capabilities that the remote had, but it also had an analog stick to help the user move his or her characters. The ambidextrous nature of the Wii controllers was something seldom seen in other game controllers; the Wii controllers permitted the user to hold the remote and Nunchuk whichever way felt most comfortable.[17] In addition to the analog stick, the Nunchuk had two buttons that gave the user quick access to other game functions. Thus, the Nunchuk offered some of the benefits of a standard game controller coupled with the high-technology motion sensors of the remote. Users could hold a Nunchuk in one hand and the Wii Remote in the other while playing the Wii Sports Boxing game and be transported into the boxing ring with on-screen opponents. The game controls were intuitive for jabs and punches; however, a missed block did not hurt as much as if one were really in the boxing ring.

Features

In addition to the Wii Remote, there were other features unique to the Wii. One was the Wii Menu, which was the first screen that appeared on the television when the Wii was turned on. According to Nintendo, the Wii Menu easily integrated itself into the everyday lives of its users.[18]

The menu displayed several different icons; one of them was the Mii Channel (pronounced "me"). This channel gave users the ability to create and personalize a 3-D caricature of themselves. Another icon was the Everybody Votes Channel, which permitted individuals to vote in national and worldwide polls on a variety of topics. There

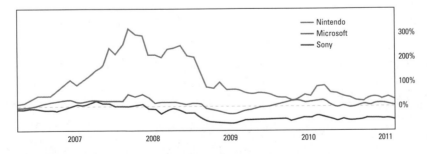

Exhibit 3 Game Console Manufacturers' Stock Prices

Exhibit 4 Wii and Wii Remote

was also the New Channel, which gave the individual up-to-date breaking news from around the world, organized into a variety of topics. The Forecast Channel allowed the individual to view weather reports from anywhere around the world. Users also had the ability to download older Nintendo games from the Wii Shopping Channel. A Wii Message Board allowed users to leave messages on the Wii for other users of the same console or leave reminders for themselves. The Internet Channel allowed individuals to surf the Internet from their Wii. The Photo Channel allowed the user to view photos stored on a standard SD memory card. And lastly there was the Disc Channel, which gave the user the ability to play Wii games or Nintendo GameCube disks.[19] The Wii was backward-compatible with the Nintendo GameCube's games, memory cards, and controllers.

Online Capabilities

Nintendo's Wii was the first Nintendo console that had online capabilities. The Wii could connect to the Internet in several different ways. One way was via a standard wireless protocol—a consumer's home high-speed Internet hookup (usually from a cable TV service or telephone company DSL). Another way the Wii could connect to the Internet was via the Nintendo DS, which had wireless capability built in. The Wii could also be connected to the Internet via an optional wired USB–Ethernet adapter.

According to Nintendo of America's president and COO, Reggie Fils-Aime, the Wii would "offer online-enabled games that consumers will not have to pay a subscription fee for. They'll be able to play right out of the box. . . . It will not have any hidden fees or costs."[20] By 2010, Nintendo had tried to catch up with its competitors Microsoft Xbox 360 and Sony PlayStation 3 by offering individuals the capability to play games interactively with other Wii users online.

The Wii was released in North America on November 19, 2006, and worldwide cumulative sales as of December 31, 2010, were in excess of 84 million units (see Exhibit 5).[21] In 2006, Wii units were simultaneously released in Japan, the Americas, Oceania, Asia, and Europe. Two years later, Nintendo expanded the Wii market to South Korea and Taiwan.[22] Although the sales numbers were quite large, however, Nintendo had been experiencing production problems with the Wii. Nintendo was unable to meet demand during 2007 and also struggled throughout 2008. By 2009, though, Nintendo had fully worked out the supply chain issues.)

Demographics

According to Nintendo, one of the key differences between the Wii and the competitors' systems was the broad audience that the Wii targeted.[23] Many of the Wii games could be played by people of all ages, and the Wii Remote and Nunchuk were easier to use than the complicated controllers of the Sony PlayStation 3 or Microsoft Xbox 360. Nintendo's TV commercials for the Wii showed people of different ages and social classes playing the Wii. According to Nintendo, the Wii Remote allowed people of all ages to enjoy its use. Nintendo had tried to create a controller that was "as inviting as it was sophisticated."[24] Nintendo's goal was to create games that everyone could play and a system that would appeal to women and people who had never played video games in the past. Shigeru Miyamoto, a senior director at Nintendo, explained, "Most of the game business is going down a similar path toward hyper-realistic graphics which re-create sports or movies. . . . We want to put a little more art into it in a way that casual consumers can enjoy the game."[25] The Wii offered something for both the advanced gamer and the person who had never played a video game before. The advanced gamer would enjoy the remote's unique features, whereas the novice gamer could use the remote as his or her hand and wouldn't need elaborate instructions on how to play a new game straight out of the box.

Although the Nintendo games were easily played by a greater range of ages, the graphics were undoubtedly a relative weakness of the product.[26] It was widely believed that the Wii had 2.5 times the power of the GameCube, but that was hardly enough to compete with the Xbox 360 or PlayStation 3.

Exhibit 5 Wii Cumulative Unit Sales (in millions)

Region	Units Sold	First Available
The Americas	40.53	11/19/06
Japan	11.45	12/2/06
Other Regions	32.67	12/8/06
Total	**84.65**	

Source: Nintendo.

Also, while Nintendo had been able to target a large range of age groups, it seemed to lack the lineup of games offered by other systems. Nintendo had focused on its proprietary Mario Brothers series games, as well as low-graphic, low-complexity games that could be played by people in a wide range of age levels. PlayStation 3's top-selling game was *Resistance: Fall of Man,* which had won many awards; but more important, it had a rating of Mature (a rating given by the Entertainment Software Rating Board), which meant that it was suitable for audiences of 17 and older only. Xbox's best-selling game was *Gears of War,* which also had a rating of Mature. The Wii's best-selling games were *The Legend of Zelda: Twilight Princess,* which had a rating of Teen, which meant it was suitable for ages 13 and up, and *Wii Sports,* which was rated Everyone, suitable for all audiences. Thus, while Nintendo hoped to target people of all ages, it had long been seen as a system that made video games for children, as evident from its Mario, Zelda, and Donkey Kong series. It was going to be difficult for Nintendo to position itself as a console for gamers of all ages and tastes.

Gaining the Interest of Game Developers

As evident from the history of game consoles, game developers have tried to make games more and more complex with each new generation of systems. This meant that more money was invested in the production of each subsequent generation of games. Because game developers were spending more money on developing games, they were at great financial risk if games did not succeed. Thus, many developers felt more secure in simply creating sequels to existing games, which in turn restricted innovation. The Wii's innovative controller, the Wii Remote, required a rethinking and reengineering of the human interface for game developers and programmers. Another issue with developing games for the Wii was that its graphics were not quite as good as those of the PlayStation 3 and Xbox 360, and therefore game developers were required to be more creative and develop special Wii editions of their games.

Many game developers used virtual-machine software in developing new games. It was believed that game developers could develop games for the Wii and then make them for other platforms on the basis of the same programming, thereby reducing production costs. However, while the Wii Remote distinguished itself from its competitors, it created a hurdle for developers. When developers created a game for the PlayStation 3, they could create the same game for the Xbox 360 and vice versa, whereas when developers created a game for the Wii, it required significant rework to deploy the title for the other platforms. Converting a title from the Xbox 360 or PlayStation 3 also required significant work to modify the game to incorporate code for the Wii Remote's special features.

The Competition

The launches of the Wii and the PlayStation 3 in November 2006 were the beginning of the battle for market share in the fierce competition of the seventh generation of video game consoles (see Exhibit 6). Although the Xbox 360 was released in 2005, Microsoft re-launched the Xbox 360 after some minor enhancements in 2006.

The price of $199 for the Wii included the Wii Remote, the Nunchuk attachment, the sensor bar, and the *Wii Sports* software title. The *Wii Sports* title included tennis, baseball, golf, bowling, and boxing games. This retail price was much less than the prices of the PlayStation 3 and Xbox 360, possibly because the Wii did not have as advanced a central processor unit or a high-definition video player.

Xbox 360

The Xbox 360 by Microsoft was released in November 2005, giving it a year lead over Nintendo's and Sony's new systems. While the configurations were changed several times, the Xbox 360 came in two different prices $299.99 for 250 GB and $199.99 for 4 GB as of 2011.

Although the prices were quite expensive to the retail consumer, in reality Microsoft was losing money on each sale. Take, for example, Microsoft's cost of producing the Premium System. It cost Microsoft $470 before assembly and an additional $55 for the cost of the cables, power cord, and controllers, bringing Microsoft's cost to $526. Thus, Microsoft was losing $227 on the sale of each system. This was the case not only with the Xbox 360 but also with its predecessor, the Xbox. There, too, Microsoft was selling a system for $299 that cost Microsoft $323 to produce.

One of the important features of the Xbox 360 was Xbox Live. According to Microsoft, Xbox Live was the "premier online gaming and entertainment service that enables you to connect your Xbox to the Internet and play games online."[27] This feature allowed individuals to play online against other users from around the world. Thus, Microsoft had created a community of individuals who were able to communicate with one another by voice chats and play against each other in a video game. It even allowed users to "see what their friends are up to at any time" and to look not only at their friends' lists but also their friends' friends lists.[28] Another service offered by Xbox Live was the Xbox Live Marketplace, which enabled users to download movies, game trailers, game demos, and arcade games. It was estimated that more than 70 percent of connected Xbox users were downloading content from the Xbox Live Marketplace, totaling more than 8 million members.[29] According to Microsoft, there were more than 12 million downloads in less than a year and, due to this popularity, major publishers and other independent gamers had submitted more than 1,000 Xbox Live games.[30] Similar to the Wii, the Xbox 360 had a dashboard that showed up when the system was powered up. This gave the user the ability to play either DVDs or games.

The Xbox 360 had the capability to play high-definition DVDs.[31] The CPU of the Xbox 360 was a custom triple-core PowerPC-based design manufactured by IBM and known as the Xenon. The Xbox 360 played all its games in 5.1-channel Dolby Digital surround sound, and, along with the IID display, the Xbox 360 could truly

Exhibit 6   Game Systems Comparison, 2011

	Nintendo	Sony	Microsoft
Console name	Wii	PlayStation 3 (with Move)	Xbox 360 (with Kinect)
Game format	12-cm Wii optical disk	Blu-Ray disc, DVD, CD	Game Discs, DVD, and CD
Hard drive	None	160 GB or 320 GB	120 GB or 250 GB
Price	$199	$299.99 (160 GB) $349.99 (320 GB) $400 (PS3 with Move)	$199.99(4GB), $299.99(4GB with Kinect), $299.99(250GB), $399.99(250GB with Kinect)
Ethernet	Wi-Fi	Ethernet, Wi-Fi, Bluetooth	Wi-Fi
Online services	Online game play, WiiConnect24, Wii Channels	Online game play, High Definition Blue-Ray player, stream movies and TV	Online game play, stream HD movies or TV
Controller	Wii Remote (wireless, motion sensing)	PlayStation Move Motion Controller	Xbox 360 wireless controller, Kinect Sensor
Backward compatibility	Yes (Nintendo GameCube)	Yes (certain models)	Yes (certain Xbox games)
Game count	860	806 (including Move games)	782 (including 23 Kinect games)

Source: Company reports; *Gamestop.com;* and author estimates.

display excellent picture and sound quality. However, a consumer who did not have a high-definition-enabled television set was not able to enjoy the high-definition features of the system. The Xbox 360 played all its games on dual-layer DVDs, which could store up to 8.5 GB per disc but also had the ability to play many other formats.[32] The system had an Ethernet port and three USB ports but could also connect to the Internet via a wireless network.

Microsoft began producing the Xbox 360 only 69 days before the launch date.[33] As a result, Microsoft was unable to supply enough systems to meet the initial demand, and, therefore, many potential customers were not able to purchase a console at launch.[34] However, according to Bill Gates, Microsoft had over 10 million units out in the market by the time Sony and Nintendo launched their systems.[35]

Kinect for Xbox 360   In November 2010 Microsoft introduced Kinect for Xbox 360, which was based around a webcam-style add-on peripheral for the Xbox 360 console. It enabled users to control and interact with the Xbox 360 without the need to touch a game controller, through a natural user interface using gestures and spoken commands. Kinect allowed the Xbox 360 to "see" the user and act according to the motions and gestures of the user. Kinect took the concept of the Wii and pursued it to its natural culmination, making the user the game controller. The Wii rescued gaming from being in a perpetual niche by

introducing a controller that was simple to use for the whole family. Kinect drove gaming into the future by literally seeing and listening to the users. Kinect used software technology that enabled advanced gesture recognition, facial recognition, and voice recognition. Some critics believed that the concept used by Kinect had potential far beyond games and might even become a new way of controlling computers of all kinds. It automatically identified who one player was and paused when the player left its vicinity, so it was not hard to imagine this ingenuity controlling all kinds of devices, like a PC, smartphone, or tablet.[36]

Sony Playstation 3   The PlayStation 3 was Sony's seventh-generation video game console. The PlayStation 3 had many advanced features, including a Cell Broadband Engine 64-bit processor that features a main power-processing element and up to eight parallel-processing elements. This was a multiprocessing unit that provided advanced support for graphics-intense games. Another notable feature of the PlayStation 3 was its ability to play Blu-Ray discs. Blu-Ray was a form of high-definition video, which enabled game developers to create games of higher sophistication.[40] Another key feature of the PlayStation 3 was the SixAxis wireless controller. This controller had sensors that could determine when a player maneuvered or angled his or her controller, which allowed game play to become a "natural extension of the player's body."[41] Although this was a more advanced remote than a standard wired remote, it lacked the true motion-sensing capabilities of the Wii Remote in its first version.[42]

The PlayStation 3 could play music CDs, connect to the Internet, copy CDs directly to its hard drive, play Blu-Ray discs and DVDs, connect to a digital camera, view photos, and more. However, a consumer who did not have a high-definition-enabled television set was not able to enjoy the high-definition features of the system.

Sales in North America were initially strong but tapered off rapidly, with 1.3 million units sold during the first six months of sales.[43] The United Kingdom also saw record-breaking sales of PlayStation 3, with more than 165,000 units (through heavy preordering) in its first two days on the shelves,[44] although the total European sales for the first six months of availability were only 920,000 units.[45] Sony CEO Howard Stringer attributed the slowing sales to a lack of software titles and said that Sony expected at least 380 new PlayStation 3 games to hit the market by 2008.[46] However, halfway into 2009, there were only 354 titles available. Sony introduced new 40 GB and 80 GB versions of the PlayStation 3, and, thanks to new features, cumulative sales rose to 9.2 million units by March 2008.[47] As of 2011, there were 160 GB and 320 GB versions of the PlayStation 3 available.

Part of the PlayStation Network's success was the ability to play games online. This allowed individuals to play with other players located in other parts of the world. The PlayStation Network allowed users to download games, view movie and game trailers, send text messages, and chat with friends. Users were also able to browse the Internet and open up to six windows at once.[48]

Since the launch of the PlayStation 3, there have been mixed reports about it. On the positive side, CNET stated that the PlayStation 3 was a "versatile and impressive piece of home-entertainment equipment that lives up to the hype . . . the PS3 is well worth its hefty price tag."[49] However, *PC World* magazine ranked the PlayStation 3 eighth out of the "Top 21 Tech Screwups of 2006."[50]

While Sony and Microsoft envisioned long-term profits on software sales of PlayStation 3 and Xbox 360, both companies experienced losses producing their seventh-generation consoles. Among the three rivals, Nintendo was the only one earning a significant profit margin on each Wii unit sold. According to David Gibson at Macquarie Securities, sales of the Nintendo Wii bring $6 of operating profit per console.[51]

PlayStation Move In September 2010, Sony released PlayStation Move, which basically copied the Wii's wand-like controller but with more accuracy. As with the Wii, users could wave the Move's controller around and swing it like a bat and hit the ball on the screen. The PlayStation Move combined a video camera with a physical controller packed with motion-sensing electronics, making it the technological cross between Kinect and the Nintendo Wii. The Move Motion Controller, or "wand," combined a gyroscope, accelerometer, and magnetic sensor to track

the controller in three dimensions, while the glowing ball at the end gave the PlayStation Eye camera a visual reference for handling aiming, cursor movement, and other motion.[52] While Wii's graphics were of low resolution and inferior detail, PS3 was a high-definition powerhouse. As one user said, "On the Wii, golf looks like a video game. On the PS3, golf looks like a golf course." Moreover, the PS3 played Blu-Ray movie discs and could display 3-D images, two things the Wii could not do. Also, the PS3 had a full lineup of great traditional games. Sony had shipped 4.1 million units of PlayStation Move worldwide in the first two months since its release. Although Sony was criticized for merely imitating Wii's technology, it turned out to be a successful imitation.[53]

The only obvious difference from Wii was the cost. While the Wii cost $199 and came with both the *Wii Sports* and *Wii Sports Resort* compilations. (A second controller cost around $40.), the PS3 with Move cost twice as much, $400, and came with only one game compilation, called *Sports Champions*. A second Move controller cost around $50. The least expensive version of the PlayStation 3, which did not include Move, cost $350. Thus, Nintendo and Sony offered comparable controllers rigged to machines with far different technical power and with quite different prices.[54]

The Future of Wii

There were 235 games for the Nintendo Wii by the end of its release year. By early 2011, however, the total number of games for the Wii (860 games) exceeded the total number of games available for its main competitor, Xbox 360 (782 games), depending on whether one counted backward compatibility with previous-generation games. The number of games indicates that the Wii was obviously a successful system—one that had drawn a good amount of interest from game developers and gamers around the world.

However, with Microsoft shipping record number of Kinect units within the first few months of its release, some analysts had started predicting that the Nintendo's dominance in video-game consoles was over. Microsoft was spending a reported $500 million advertising Kinect, more than it spent launching the first Xbox. The obvious goal was to repeat the Nintendo Wii's success in expanding the market to more casual gamers.[55] During the first half of 2010, Wii had started to see its shipments stumble. And some analysts expected that trend to continue through 2012. "It's not like Nintendo is going to go broke anytime soon, but its days of dominance are over," one analyst said.[56]

Microsoft and Sony had started to invade the casual family-user market, a key market for Nintendo's Wii, expanding beyond their former customer base of mainly hardcore gamers. The Xbox and PS3 were becoming more like an entertainment hub for families. Unless the user just needed the Nintendo fix, there were more innovative and exciting options, and Wii had to compete with tough competitors. Despite all the criticisms of Wii losing its momentum, there was no news from Nintendo about new versions of the Wii. The question remained as to what Nintendo would plan next.

Endnotes

1. Nintendo. 2010. Annual report. March 31.
2. Microsoft. 2010. Annual report. June 30.
3. Sony. 2010. Annual report. March 31.
4. Schiesel, S. 2010. A real threat now faces the Nintendo Wii. *New York Times.* December 3: F7.
5. Nintendo. 2008. Annual report. March 31.
6. Nintendo. *www.nintendo.com/systemsclassic?type=nes.*
7. Nintendo. 2008. Annual report, March 31.
8. Bacani, C., & Mutsuko, M. 1997. Nintendo's new 64-bit platform sets off a scramble for market share. *AsiaWeek,* April 18. *www.asiaweek.com/asiaweek/97/0418/cs1.html.*
9. *GamePro.* 2005. Biggest blunders. May: 45.
10. Nintendo. *wii.nintendo.com/iwata_asks_vol2_p1.jsp.*
11. Morris, C. 2006. Nintendo goes "Wii" . . . *CNNMoney.com,* April 27. *money.cnn.com/2006/04/27/commentary/game_over/nintendo/index.htm.*
12. Surette, T. 2006. Nintendo exec talks Wii Online, marketing. *GameSpot.com.* August 17. *www.cnet.com.au/games/wii/0,239036428,240091920,00.htm.*
13. Nintendo. 2006. Annual report.
14. See *wii.nintendo.com.*
15. Nintendo. *wii.nintendo.com/controller.jsp.*
16. *IGN.com.* 2006. Wii controllers: Unlocking the secrets. July 14. *wii.ign.com/articles/718/718946p1.html.*
17. Nintendo. *wii.nintendo.com/controller.jsp.*
18. See *wii.Nintendo.com.*
19. See *wii.nintendo.com.*
20. Surette. 2006. Nintendo exec talks Wii Online.
21. Nintendo. 2008. Consolidated financial statements. October 30.
22. See *wii.Nintendo.com.*
23. Nintendo. 2007. Annual report. March 31.
24. *wii.nintendo.com/controller.jsp.*
25. Levine, R. 2006. En garde! Fight foes using a controller like a sword. *New York Times,* October 30. *www.nytimes.com/2006/10/30/technology/30nintendo.html.*
26. *PC Magazine.* 2006. Nintendo Wii. November 13. *www.pcmag.com/article2/0,1895,2058406,00.asp.*
27. *www.Xbox.com/en-US.*
28. *web.archive.org/web/20080822104219/http://www.xbox.com/en-US/live/globalcommunity/fosteringcommunity.htm*
29. Microsoft. 2007. As Xbox LIVE turns five, Microsoft announces next wave of social fun. November 13. *www.microsoft.com/Presspass/press/2007/nov07/11-13XboxLIVEFivePR.mspx.*
30. Ibid.
31. Microsoft. 2007. Xbox 360 HD DVD player moves to $179, adds five free HD DVDs. July 26. *www.microsoft.com/Presspass/press/2007/jul07/07-26ComicConXboxHDDVDPR.mspx.*
32. *web.archive.org/web/20080822024003/http://www.xbox.com/en-AU/support/xbox360/manuals/xbox360specs.htm*
33. Morris, C. 2006. Nintendo's Wii may get early launch. *CNNMoney.com,* July 5. *money.cnn.com/2006/07/05/commentary/column_gaming/index.htm?section_money_latest.*
34. BBC News. 2005. Nintendo Wii sells out within hours. December 2. *news.bbc.co.uk/2/hi/technology/4491804.stm.*
35. Microsoft. 2006. Bill Gates declares 10 million-unit head start for Xbox 360 and outlines future of interactive entertainment. May 9. *www.microsoft.com/presspass/press/2006/may06/05-09E32006BriefingPR.mspx.*
36. Boehret, K. 2010. Xbox Kinect: Just how controlling can a body be? *Wall Street Journal,* November 24. *online.wsj.com/article/SB10001424052748704369304575632723525779384.html.*
37. Ibid.
38. Kessler, S. 2011. Microsoft Kinect sales set new Guinness World Record. *Mashable.com,* March 10. *www.cnn.com/2011/TECH/gaming.gadgets/03/10/kinect.sales.record.mashable/index.html.*
39. Peckham, M. 2011. Kinect breaks Guinness record, sells 10 million systems, tops iPhone and iPad. *PC World,* March 9. *www.pcworld.com/article/221738/kinect_breaks_guinness_record_sells_10_million_systems_tops_iphone_and_ipad.html.*
40. Sony. *www.us.playstation.com/PS3/About/BluRay.*
41. Sony. *www.us.playstation.com/PS3/About/WirelessController.*
42. Sony Computer Entertainment. 2006. SCE announces new controller for Playstation®3. May 8. *www.scei.co.jp/corporate/release/pdf/060509be.pdf.*
43. Slagle, M. 2007. Sony ships 1 million PS3s in North America. *MSNBC,* January 7. *www.msnbc.msn.com/id/16517299/ns/technology_and_science-games/t/sony-ships-million-pss-north-america/*
44. BBC News. 2007. PlayStation breaks sales records. March 27. *news.bbc.co.uk/1/hi/technology/6499841.stm.*
45. Ibid.
46. Layne, N., & Hamada, K. 2007. Sony promises more games to boost PS3 demand. *Reuters.com,* June 21. *www.reuters.com/article/2007/06/21/us-sony-ps-idUST28081120070621?sp_true.*
47. Sony. 2008. Annual report. March 31.
48. Sony. *www.us.playstation.com/PS3/Network.*
49. Carnoy, D. 2007. Review: PS3 pricey but impressive. January 8. *www.cnn.com/2007/TECH/fun.games/01/04/ps3.review/index.html*
50. Tynan, D. 2006. The top 21 tech screwups of 2006. *PCWorld,* December 20. *www.pcworld.com/article/128265-4/the_top_21_tech_screwups_of_2006.html.*
51. Schoenberger, C. R. 2008. Wii's future in motion. *Forbes,* December 12. *www.forbes.com/2008/11/28/nintendo-wii-wii2-tech-personal-cz-cs-1201wii.html.*
52. Greenwald, W. 2010. Kinect vs. PlayStation Move vs. Wii: Motion-control showdown. *PC Magazine,* November 6. *www.pcmag.com/article2/0,2817,2372244,00.asp.*
53. Schiesel, S. 2010. A real threat now faces the Nintendo Wii. *New York Times,* December 2. *www.nytimes.com/2010/12/03/technology/personaltech/03KINECT.html.*
54. Ibid.
55. Chiang, O. 2010. The Xbox moves in. *Forbes,* December 20. *www.forbes.com/forbes/2010/1220/technology-microsoft-xbox-kinect.html.*
56. Kawamoto, D. 2011. Is the era of Nintendo Wii leadership coming to an end? *DailyFinance.com,* January 7. *www.dailyfinance.com/story/is-the-era-of-nintendo-wii-leadership-coming-to-an-end/19790760/.*

Case 25   Weight Watchers International Inc.*

"Weight Watchers' profits have jumped off the scale."[1] So read the investment news headlines in February 2011 applauding Weight Watchers' prediction that 2011 revenue would grow by 15 to 20 percent. Weight Watchers, while the undeniable industry standard, had lost some of its luster in recent years as many potential consumers considered it the prior generation's answer to weight loss or simply not the right weight-loss choice for them. Originally started in 1963 by Jean Nidetch as a support group for women in her home, Weight Watchers International Inc. had grown into a multibillion-dollar weight-loss goliath in a matter of four decades' time. Aware of this stigma, Weight Watchers had set out to reinvent itself. In November 2010 Weight Watchers introduced the new Points Plus system. This replaced the old calorie-counting system by considering where the calories come from. Even though calories still counted, Points Plus encouraged people to eat a wide variety of healthy foods—split between three meals plus snacks within an individualized calorie level. With a counting system based on 2010 dietary guidelines, dieters were encouraged to maximize their Points Plus allowance by choosing more "Power Foods," the healthiest, most filling foods, such as whole grains, lean meats, low-fat dairy, and unlimited quantities of fresh fruit and nonstarchy vegetables. Doctors and nutritionists gave the new program a thumbs up: "I always loved the peer support aspect of the Weight Watchers program but it concerned me that the old points could be used for anything," Keri Gans, an American Dietetic Association spokeswoman said. "The new Points Plus program addressing where calories come from is a huge improvement."[2]

The market for weight-loss products was growing and obesity levels were on the rise in more and more parts of the world, which made weight management an attractive industry for firms, especially deeply entrenched firms such as Weight Watchers. However, faced with increased competition from other firms, most notably NutriSystem Inc., Weight Watchers had to increase customer value and seek new target segments to preempt the competition and stay on top of its promising industry. In the highly competitive weight-management industry, Weight Watchers International Inc. was in a position where it had to remain cognizant of the major trends that, at the time, had the potential to adversely affect industry and firm profitability and revenues. Those trends, as they related to Weight Watchers and the weight-loss industry, included the temporary emergence of fad diets, decreased effectiveness of marketing and advertising programs, the need for developing new and innovative products and services, the development of more favorably perceived or more effective weight management methods (such as pharmaceuticals and surgical options such as the Lap-Band), and the threat of impairment of the Weight Watchers brand and other intellectual property.[3]

The challenge for Weight Watchers was repositioning itself and creating a forward-focused diet plan for the 21st century while staying true to the mission initially established by Jean Nidetch, Weight Watchers's founder. The brand needed to remain relevant and, at the same time, pursue additional medium- to long-term initiatives, such as reaching out to new market segments.[4] How could Weight Watchers retain market leadership while staying hip, relevant, and preemptive? While Weight Watchers had made the effort to introduce new products for several years and had been in the process of shifting its strategic focus from narrow- to broad-based differentiation, the question still remained whether the company could stay true to its core values, mission, and models and, at the same time, embrace effective expansion.

Going into 2011, Weight Watchers attempted to reinvent itself by introducing marketing and product innovations both in the United States and abroad. It began to look beyond its core market of women, expanded its business model, launched new programs, and rejuvenated its brand. However, the continued expansion and innovation initiatives raised several concerns. Will this expansion in scope move Weight Watchers too far from its original mission and core philosophy? Will the extensions of the Weight Watchers brand succeed at attracting new members without losing the existing ones?

History and Expansion

Jean Nidetch began Weight Watchers in an unlikely, and unintended, way. The origins of Weight Watchers started when Jean invited six women into her home to help both herself and her neighbors and friends lose weight by communally discussing their weight-loss issues. Nidetch's belief, which became the core of the Weight Watchers philosophy, was that anyone could be given a "diet" but the group and social setting of "talk therapy" was the true component not only to losing weight but also *to keeping it off*. She believed in fostering success through group support, and she created a simple reward system that included pins and tie bars to reward increments of weight loss. The idea was simple, yet very effective![5]

The basic concept of the Weight Watchers plan, as it existed in 2011, consisted of two components. First, there was the Weight Watchers program, and second, there was the group support. The program was essentially a food plan and an activity plan. The food plan was intended to provide people with the educational tools they needed for weight loss as well as to provide control mechanisms

* This case was developed by Professor Alan B. Eisner, Pace University; Professor Helaine J. Korn, Baruch College–City University of New York; and graduate student Jennifer M. DiChiara, Pace University. Material has been drawn from published sources to be used for class discussion. Copyright © 2011 Alan B. Eisner.

so that individuals could find their way to healthier food choices. The company radically simplified the food selection process involved in dieting by assigning each food a corresponding point value, which eliminated the need to tally calories.[6] In the past, Weight Watchers had been recognized more for its food plan, but by 2011 it was getting noticed for its activity and cause marketing plans as well. Weight Watchers' Lose For Good campaign, an initiative that fought hunger both locally and globally by increasing awareness of this important issue and helping to provide access to healthy food for those in need, donated more than $2 million to its charitable partners, Share Our Strength and Action Against Hunger. Weight Watchers' new spokesperson, Academy Award–winning actress and Grammy Award–winning recording artist Jennifer Hudson, visited a New York City school as part of the campaign to help educate families on how to prepare healthy, low-cost meals. She also helped to spread the message that increasing access to healthy food is an important step in fighting both hunger and obesity.[7]

Nidetch had accomplished what she set out to do and much more. Weight Watchers, targeting primarily women, ages 25 to 55, experienced a rapid expansion. Of the behemoth that Weight Watchers came to be, Nidetch said, "My little group became an industry. I really didn't mean it to—it was really just a club for me and my fat friends." She continued by commenting on something a lecturer once said, "It's a place where you walk in fat and hope nobody notices you, and four or five months later you walk out thin and hope that everyone sees you." Nidetch believed that the love, information, companionship, and commiseration of fellow overweight individuals were the key components needed for the effective formula many people needed to succeed at weight loss. This idea has been perpetuated at Weight Watchers and has been translated into meeting leadership—all employees who now lead meetings are formerly overweight individuals who were successful on the plan.[8]

What Weight Watchers evolved into was a global branded consumer company providing weight-management services worldwide. By 2011, each week, approximately 1.3 million members attended almost 50,000 Weight Watchers meetings around the world. Weight Watchers was selling a wide range of branded products and services, including meetings conducted by Weight Watchers International and its franchisees (and the products sold at the meetings), Internet subscriptions to *WeightWatchers.com* (the company's Internet answer to weight management), licensed products sold by retailers, magazine subscriptions, and other publications.[9] In addition, the company had put its name and Point values on a variety of food products sold in supermarkets, such as Progresso soups,[10] and it had created a separate Weight Watchers menu for Applebee's restaurants, among other things.[11] Gradual expansion and the onset of the dot-com era inevitably led to the creation of *WeightWatchers.com*, an Internet-based version

of the Weight Watchers plan designed to increase brand awareness.

WeightWatchers.com

WeightWatchers.com, as it existed in 2011, offered two subscription options: Weight Watchers Online and Weight Watchers eTools.[12] At the time, *WeightWatchers.com* was the leading Internet-based weight-management provider in the world.[13] It held the position of market leader in the Internet category, with a growing business that still had relatively low awareness in the mind of the average weight-loss consumer.[14] However, the company also initiated TV advertising for Weight Watchers Online, as well as launching Weight Watchers Online for Men.[15]

In 2011 *WeightWatchers.com* was not only the leading subscription-based weight-loss site on the Internet but also the official website for Weight Watchers International Inc. It offered information on the Weight Watchers plan, provided several paid and free weight-loss tools, and housed an online messaging board, a series of fitness videos, and so on. Weight Watchers eTools, which could be accessed through the site, offered an integrated, multifeature food diary with a database of over 31,000 foods, along with their corresponding Point values, a recipe database, a restaurant guide, and a personal weight tracker. All of these tools helped Weight Watchers to foster its primary mission: helping people lose weight.[16] *WeightWatchers.com* allowed the company, for the first time, to bring in an entirely new group of customers who might not have considered the program otherwise.[17]

Industry and Competitive Environment

While Weight Watchers International Inc. had experienced stock price volatility in the past, as had the majority of its competitors, because of rival weight management options—such as the over-the-counter weight-loss drug *Alli,* launched by GlaxoSmithKline in June 2006, and the development of Allergan's Lap-Band device. However, there had never been a widely supported "magic pill" or surgical option to weight management to date. In the absence of a safe and effective pharmaceutical or surgical alternative for weight loss, Weight Watchers and its competitors had faced a weight-management industry characterized by not only competition but great opportunity as well. Along with expanding waistlines had come an expanding market for weight-management companies, and the time had come for such companies to be creative and innovative in sustaining and increasing market positions. At that time, no firm had been able to fare so well for so long in an industry plagued with fad diets and "the next best thing" as Weight Watchers had been.

Obesity was on the rise in the developed countries, especially in North America, and Weight Watchers was well positioned to help consumers as they began their weight-loss battles. In 2011 weight loss, including the health and fitness industry, constituted a $60 billion-a-year industry in the United States alone.[18] Nearly one-third of

Exhibit 1 Competitors for Weight Watchers

Diet Name	Weight Watchers	Competitors					
		Jenny Craig	Slim-Fast	eDiets	Zone Diet (Men's Menu)	Atkins Diet	Ornish Diet	Volumetrics
What it is	Venerable program that uses weekly meetings and weigh-ins for motivation and behavioral support for diet and exercise changes, or you can sign up for similar support online. Dieters either earn or spend "points" with food and exercise or consume specified foods on a "Core" plan. A vegetarian menu is available.	Dieters sign up for individual counseling and meal plans at company outlets, by phone, or online. Centerpiece of the diet is eating Jenny Craig–prepared foods of single-serving entrees and snacks, supplemented by dairy, salads, and other vegetables you prepare yourself. Vegetarian menu is also available.	Brand line of controlled-calorie shakes and bars, widely available in drugstores and supermarkets. Company website provides weekly menus. On standard meal plan, a bar or shake for breakfast and lunch with additional food. For dinner, a low-calorie meal you fix yourself.	Well-established online subscription diet site offers 24 meal plans customized for various eating preferences and desired weight loss. Membership includes access to support groups, experts, menu plans, and recipes. The standard eDiets.com weekly menu we analyzed met dietary guidelines and delivered the number of calories promised.	The "Zone" was created to be the ideal balance of food to keep blood sugar and hormones ready to fight obesity and diseases. To stay in the Zone, every meal must consist of 30% fat calories, 30% protein, and 40% carbs. Diet allows many fruits but practically no grains.	One of the more widely known low-carb diets starts with a two-week induction period that bans practically all carbs. The longer "ongoing weight loss" phase is only slightly less restrictive, gradually adding more fruits, vegetables, and wines.	Ultra low-fat vegetarian regimen bans all meat, fish, oils, alcohol, sugar, and white flour. Ornish's clinical studies have shown that strictly following the diet can prevent or reverse disease. He believes it is easier to make drastic changes in the diet than small ones.	Based on research at Penn State, diet aims to maximize the amount of food available per calorie, mainly by use of reduced-fat products, liberal addition of vegetables, and low-fat cooking techniques. Encourages first course of broth-based soup or low-calorie salad to take the edge off appetite.

(continued)

Exhibit 1 Competitors for Weight Watchers (*continued*)

Diet Name	Weight Watchers	Competitors						
		Jenny Craig	Slim-Fast	eDiets	Zone Diet (Men's Menu)	Atkins Diet	Ornish Diet	Volumetrics
Pros and cons	Behavioral support is proved to increase adherence to any diet. Scored average on weight loss in this group but first in long-term adherence. Recipes judged to be appetizing and fairly easy to prepare.	Diet requires minimal food preparation and meets dietary guidelines. Published study of actual client histories revealed high dropout rate, though those who stuck with the plan lost considerable weight. Clinical trial had better adherence.	Menu we analyzed meets dietary guidelines. Convenient for people with little time or desire to cook. Clinical studies show above-average long-term weight loss but high long-term dropout rate.	Customizable plans are appealing, especially for those with wheat or lactose intolerances, but clinical studies find average adherence and below-average weight loss.	The recipes were judged simple to prepare. The meal plan had a good nutritional profile, but figuring out the diet without a meal plan involved a lot of math. Weight loss below average.	There's growing evidence that dieters on Atkins aren't as hungry as on some other diets. Many find it too restrictive, so long-term adherence is below average. Long-term weight loss is average. Its nutritional profile is far outside dietary guidelines.	Provides the most food per calorie of any diet evaluated. Lower in fat than guidelines recommend. Studies show average long-term weight loss and below-average long-term adherence.	Recent clinical trials show best overall weight loss of any diet evaluated. The recipes were judged to be appetizing but somewhat time-consuming to prepare.

Source: *Consumer Reports.* 2007. Diet plans. June: 16–17.

Americans were reported to be on a diet, according to a *Restaurants & Institutions* New American Diner Study.[19] Particularly noteworthy was the rise of U.S. baby boomers as a significant proportion of the dieting population as they came to be more health conscious and proactive in their weight management than prior generations had been, and they were looking for new ways to gain control of their weight.[20] The obesity problem was not confined to the United States, however, and this made geographic expansion a possibility for weight-loss firms. Worldwide, the World Health Organization predicted 2.3 billion people would be overweight by 2015 and more than 700 million would be obese.[21] Overall, the statistics proved there were tremendous opportunities in the weight-loss industry, and that made it much harder to compete for the market share.

Weight Watchers was attempting to reinvent itself while still paying close attention to the moves of its weight-loss rivals. Competition for Weight Watchers International Inc. had included both price competition and competition from self-help, pharmaceutical, surgical, dietary supplement, and meal replacement products, as well as other weight-management brands, diets, programs, and products.[22] The main competitors for Weight Watchers included Jenny Craig, Slim-Fast, NutriSystem (Nasdaq: NTRI), eDiets (Nasdaq: DIET), The Zone, South Beach Diet, and Medifast, as well as programs from fitness gurus such as *The Biggest Loser* star Jillian Michaels.[23]

CEO Kirchhoff believed that most competitors were essentially in a different business than Weight Watchers was. He said, "Most of the companies that are out there aggressively marketing are in the business of providing and delivering meals. Weight Watchers is in the business of helping people change behavior. So in that sense, we're teaching people how to fish, and they are selling people fish."[24]

According to an article in *Consumer Reports,* it was determined that Weight Watchers offered dieters the best staying power. Weight Watchers earned the highest overall rating, on account of its nutritionally based diet, weekly meetings, and weigh-ins for behavioral support. *Consumer*

Reports liked the facts that the plan did not exclude any food group and that its Point system encouraged low-fat, high-fiber meals. Slim-Fast came in second and was recommended for dieters who did not like to spend time in the kitchen. The Zone was recommended for those who wanted a short-term, high-protein diet plan, while the Ornish plan was found to provide fairly large portions for low calories. Atkins' nutritional difficulties dropped its rating below those of the other diets. Exhibit 1 outlines the company's main competitors, their specialties, and their competitive advantages as presented by *Consumer Reports.* Jenny Craig, eDiets, South Beach Diet, and Volumetrics were also studied, but they were not ranked in the follow-up article, which cited a "lack of long-term, published clinical trials" on which to base the rankings.[25]

Business Model

Revenues for Weight Watchers International Inc., as shown in Exhibit 2, were principally gained from meeting fees (members paid to attend weekly meetings), product sales (bars, cookbooks, and the like, sold as complements to weight-management plans), online revenues (from Internet subscription products), and revenues gained from licensing (the placement of the Weight Watchers logo on certain foods and other products) and franchising (franchisees typically paid a royalty fee of 10 percent of their meeting fee).[26] The costs of running meetings were low, with part-time class instructors paid on a commission basis, and many meeting locations were rented hourly in inexpensive local facilities such as churches. This lean organizational structure allowed wide profit margins.[27] Meeting fees were paid up front or at the time of the meeting by attendees, resulting in net negative working capital for Weight Watchers—an indication of cash-flow efficiency.[28]

What was perhaps most important about Weight Watchers' business model was its flexibility. The number of meetings could be adjusted according to demand and seasonal fluctuations. The business model's reliance on a variable cost structure had enabled the company to

Exhibit 2 **Weight Watchers' Revenue Sources** (in millions)

	2010	2009	2008	2007	2006	2005
Meeting fees	$ 819.6	$ 817.5	$ 908.0	$ 880.7	$ 723.1	$ 681.1
Product sales	305.0	292.1	339.8	337.7	293.3	285.5
Online revenues	238.8	196.0	185.8	151.6	129.4	109.7
Licensing, franchise royalties, and others	88.6	93.3	102.2	97.1	87.5	75.0
Total	$1,452.0	$1,398.9	$1,535.8	$1,467.2	$1,233.3	$1,151.3

Source: Weight Watchers 10K filings.

maintain high margins even as the number of meetings over the same time period was expanded. When attendance growth outpaced meeting growth, the gross margins of Weight Watchers typically improved. Since fiscal year 2005, Weight Watchers International had maintained an annual gross margin in the operating segment of 50 percent or more.[29] However, although Weight Watchers' business model yielded high profit margins and strong cash flow as a result of the company's low variable expenses and low capital expenditure requirements, some analysts worried that the margins were dropping—between 2005 and 2010 gross margin had peaked at 55.5 percent, operating margin peaked at 30.8, and net margin peaked at 17 percent, while the 2010 trailing 12 months' numbers came in at 52.1, 24.5, and 11.7 percent, respectively.[30]

UBS analyst Andrew McQuilling commented on Weight Watchers' achievement of a near-perfect business model. McQuilling said, "There are three things we can always count on: death, taxes, and people's tendency to overeat. Since 1977, sales [for Weight Watchers] have compounded at a 13 percent rate. It's a profitable business that satisfies a growing market, so to speak. Weight Watchers is not just a fad. It's a perfect business. It's as if it sells air. The company has a 40 percent return on invested capital. People pay a fee to join and then pay to attend meetings."[31]

Unlike the privately owned Jenny Craig and Curves, which maintained their own centers with food inventories, Weight Watchers kept its capital costs low by allowing its meetings to be held anywhere. This model has allowed Weight Watchers to gain entry into the workplace at wellness-minded companies via its Weight Watchers at Work Program.[32]

Performance

Despite high leverage, Weight Watchers' financial health was considered "decent," according to a statement by Morningstar analyst Kristan Rowland. Bank of America analyst Scott Mushkin agreed, touting Weight Watchers' classroom-based approach as the only one with empirical evidence of success. The strong brand and doctor-recommended methods, it was expected, would help increase business for Weight Watchers as the fad diets faded out of fashion.[33] Exhibits 3 to 5 show financial statements of the firm.

Innovation

Domestically and abroad, Weight Watchers was fortunate enough to build on a foundation of four decades of weight management expertise that had allowed the company to become one of the most recognized and trusted brand names among weight-conscious consumers worldwide.[34]

The innovation initiatives at Weight Watchers were focused on three main objectives: (1) rejuvenating the brand through more effective marketing, (2) providing more customer value by introducing new products, and (3) broadening the customer mix by targeting new customer segments.

The Brand

With regard to its brand, Weight Watchers had been fortunate to have consumers consider its brand credible and

effective. The company needed to more adequately differentiate its lifestyle-based approach from the strictly dieting orientation utilized by many of its competitors. In a focus group for Weight Watchers, a woman who had considered joining expressed concern that her weight would be called out in public and that she would have to tell her whole weight-loss struggle as if she were at an Alcoholics Anonymous meeting. Thus, one of the primary challenges for Weight Watchers was to correct these types of misperceptions as to what Weight Watchers actually was.[35] Weight Watchers had the challenge of dispelling concerns that the meeting experience would be something akin to a *Biggest Loser* weigh-in and competition.

The second thing that Weight Watchers was trying to do was to reenergize the brand with more effective and differentiated marketing. In order to sustain Weight Watchers' brand image and combat some of the misconceptions in the consumer market, Weight Watchers International Inc. hired McCann Erickson, the U.S. advertising agency that reignited the MasterCard brand, to bring the same vitality to the Weight Watchers brand. It was hoped that by taking a fresh perspective on the way that Weight Watchers advertises and markets, McCann Erickson could differentiate Weight Watchers from the other, mostly unsuccessful, weight-loss and diet aids in order to position the company as more empathetic and contemporary to the consumer.[36] Of marketing, David Kirchhoff said, "I think we do a very good job of marketing to people who have been with us before, so-called rejoins, but I think we could do a much better job of marketing to people who have never been with us before."[37]

Weight Watchers believed that its advertising must accomplish three basic tasks. First, it had to be noticed when it was seen. Second, on noticing it, people had to associate the advertising with the Weight Watchers brand. Third, it had to accomplish both the first and the second aims while communicating something new about Weight Watchers that would cause consumers to reconsider Weight Watchers as their *solution*—a plan at which they could be successful.[38] Weight Watchers realized that it had not been doing a very good job of communicating any newness or innovation coming from within the company. Only by creating marketing activities that did a better job of relaying the meaningful benefits of Weight Watchers to consumers could the company convince people to join up. Consumers already had a perception of what Weight Watchers was. Accordingly, Weight Watchers had to actively emphasize the innovative things that it was doing in order to overcome consumers' preconceived notions.[39] The company needed to show its consumers that it was different from the other diets out there to unleash the power that Weight Watchers believed had become a little dormant in its brand.[40] Weight Watchers also had to consider the potential of marketing to relay relevant information that would appeal to a wider net of demographic groups.

The Program

To increase customer value, Weight Watchers introduced three new programs that provided members with more

Exhibit 3   Income Statements (in thousands)

	2010	2009	2008	2007	2006
Total revenue	1,452,000	1,398,913	1,535,812	1,467,167	1,233,325
Cost of revenue	661,400	670,939	700,835	653,231	557,165
Gross profit	790,600	727,974	834,977	813,936	676,160
Operating expenses:					
Selling, general, and administrative	400,300	371,324	409,930	378,329	296,112
Operating income or loss	390,300	354,650	425,047	435,607	380,048
Income from continuing operations:					
Other income/expenses net	900	228	1,969	161	126
Earnings before interest and taxes	313,200	356,878	427,016	435,768	380,174
Interest expense	76,200	66,722	92,667	109,277	49,532
Income before tax	313,200	290,156	334,349	326,491	330,642
Income tax expense	120,700	115,585	132,002	125,311	120,817
Minority interest	—	2,773	1,984	—	—
Net income from continuing ops	192,500	177,344	204,331	201,180	209,825
Net income	194,200	177,344	204,331	201,180	209,825

Source: Yahoo Finance; Weight Watchers 10K filings.

Exhibit 4   Balance Sheets (in thousands)

Assets	2010	2009	2008	2007	2006
Current assets:					
Cash and cash equivalents	40,534	46,137	47,322	39,823	37,504
Net receivables	43,722	57,864	70,181	62,472	43,767
Inventory	40,571	32,488	40,121	44,607	38,548
Other current assets	65,615	63,462	67,417	39,434	34,927
Total current assets	190,400	199,951	225,041	186,336	154,746
Property plant and equipment	30,900	36,038	37,508	37,649	31,033
Goodwill	51,425	51,373	51,296	51,364	51,329
Intangible assets	847,300	790,250	777,103	751,730	712,930

(*continued*)

Exhibit 4 **Balance Sheets** (in thousands) (*continued*)

	2010	2009	2008	2007	2006
Assets					
Other assets			3,120	3,229	3,127
Deferred long-term asset charges	23,400	6,563	12,684	15,913	49,227
Total assets	**1,091,987**	**1,087,509**	**1,106,752**	**1,046,221**	**1,002,392**
Liabilities and Stockholders' Equity					
Current liabilities:					
Accounts payable	168,567	174,979	211,046	209,920	138,262
Short/current long-term debt	197,524	255,947	224,032	45,625	18,922
Other current liabilities	159,886	105,129	60,046	102,886	79,348
Total current liabilities	**539,135**	**536,055**	**495,124**	**358,431**	**236,532**
Long-term debt	1,167,561	1,238,000	1,485,000	1,602,500	830,237
Other liabilities	13,300	15,342	11,459	9,834	3,990
Deferred long-term liability charges	62,800	34,624	2,685	1,786	—
Total liabilities	**1,782,711**	**1,824.021**	**1,994,268**	**1,972,551**	**1,070,759**
Stockholders' equity:					
Retained earnings	1,103,817	1,260,349	1,131,080	950,213	770,539
Treasury stock	(1,794,066)	(1,684,323)	(1,684,828)	(1,570,054)	(540,318)
Other stockholders' equity	(4,517)	(312,518)	(333,768)	(306,489)	(298,588)
Total stockholders' equity	**(694,766)**	**(736,512)**	**(887,516)**	**(926,330)**	**(68,367)**
Net tangible assets	**(690,724)**	**(1,578,135)**	**(1,715,915)**	**(1,729,424)**	**(832,626)**

Source: Yahoo Finance; Weight Watchers 10K filings.

Exhibit 5 **Cash Flow Statements** (in thousands)

	2010	2009	2008	2007	2006
Net income	**192,522**	**177,344**	**204,331**	**201,180**	**209,825**
Operating activities, cash flows provided by or used in:					
Depreciation	29,012	29,972	25,959	20,746	14,880
Adjustments to net income	46,152	55,648	29,769	39,744	47,335
Changes in accounts receivables	(6,964)	(1,322)	(343)	(2,099)	(10,656)
Changes in liabilities	22,225	(2,638)	7,408	70,728	22,936
					(*continued*)

Exhibit 5   Cash Flow Statements (in thousands) (*continued*)

	2010	2009	2008	2007	2006
Changes in inventories	(15,490)	1,624	(7,469)	(12,220)	(9,250)
Changes in other operating activities	14,027	7,651	(18,489)	466	(9,292)
Total cash flow from operating activities	**281,484**	**265,506**	**241,166**	**318,545**	**265,778**
Investing activities, cash flows provided by/used in:					
Capital expenditures	(9,137)	(12,349)	(16,281)	(18,030)	(14,329)
Other cash flows from investing activities	(19,509)	(11,278)	(55,905)	(30,799)	(157,042)
Total cash flows from investing activities	**(28,646)**	**(23,627)**	**(72,186)**	**(48,829)**	**(171,371)**
Financing activities, cash flows provided by/used in:					
Dividends paid	(53,409)	(54,078)	(55,045)	(58,524)	(51,792)
Sale/purchase of stock	2,513	5,546	(107,898)	(1,015,081)	(146,354)
Net borrowings	(205,916)	(194,500)	(625)	793,549	101,054
Other cash flows from financing activities	—	—	3,507	10,879	6,234
Total cash flows from financing activities	**(256,812)**	**(246,964)**	**(160,061)**	**(269,177)**	**(90,858)**
Effect of exchange rate changes	(1,629)	3,900	(1,420)	1,780	2,479
Change in cash and cash equivalents	**(5,603)**	**(1,185)**	**7,499**	**2,319**	**6,028**

Source: Yahoo Finance; Weight Watchers 10K filings.

flexibility and satisfaction. One innovation was a Monthly Pass payment option. When a member became a Monthly Pass subscriber, he or she participated in an eight-month recurring billing commitment in exchange for complete access to the full range of product offerings, including meetings and eTools. So the underlying benefit was customization—members could utilize the different options as they saw fit in meeting their weight-loss needs. And it seemed to work! People on the Monthly Pass were losing 30 percent more weight since the pass's implementation.[41] Further, there was a higher attendance intensity for Monthly Passers than for those that used pay-as-you-go.[42] If a member canceled his Monthly Pass because he had reached his goal weight, and then later regained weight, he knew that he could always return to Weight Watchers because the plan had worked in the past. Accordingly,

Weight Watchers International Inc. attempted to offer a better weight-loss proposition, which was hoped to drive more referrals and better return rates.

The Monthly Pass commitment plan not only was important to innovativeness but also represented an overall better and more effective way for members to approach weight loss. Monthly Pass allowed members to move away from a week-to-week focus in favor of a more holistic approach to incorporating Weight Watchers into their lives, complemented by the free inclusion of Weight Watchers eTools, a hallmark feature of the Weight Watchers Online program.[43]

Weight Watchers CEO David Kirchhoff touted the implementation of the Monthly Pass as a sign of the company's commitment to continually offering better value to its consumers. Aside from the plan's financial benefits, Kirchhoff said that the most important thing about Monthly Pass was that it provided a better weight-loss proposition and created a completely new way for customers to interact with Weight Watchers in a couple of different areas—first, in meetings, and second, through the Internet.[44] Kirchhoff believed that Monthly Pass had become the "new gold standard in weight loss."[45]

In addition, Monthly Pass was also beneficial to the company in that it gave Weight Watchers a salable proposition. Before the development of Monthly Pass, when potential customers called to make an inquiry, there was no way to sell them something at that moment to get them committed. With the development of Monthly Pass, the call center could now sell the product over the phone to consumers, in addition to the pass's availability on the Weight Watchers website.[46] However, Weight Watchers also wanted to continue to offer its conventional pay-as-you-go plan, because the company aimed to appeal to the widest variety of consumers with the most payment options available.[47]

Another creative program that Weight Watchers implemented was the new and improved TurnAround Program, which allowed members to personalize their daily target Points by gender, age, weight, height, and daily activity, while leaving no food off-limits. Following results of a consumer survey on dieting, Weight Watchers also added new foods to the Core Food List, snack options, information about knowing your hunger signals, more recipe and meal ideas, tips for eating out, success stories, and the like.[48] The lower-carbohydrate-focused Core Plan, of which the Core Food List was a part, was Weight Watchers' answer to the ease of use that low-carb diets provided—it eliminated the need to count Points and did not restrict portion sizes.[49] The Core Plan offered an alternative to the Flex Points Plan under the umbrella of the TurnAround Program.

The newest program, introduced at the end of 2010, was a revision to the traditional "Points" program. Renamed "Points Plus," the program was designed to educate and encourage people to make choices that favored foods the body worked harder to convert into energy, resulting in fewer net calories absorbed. Users were encouraged to focus on foods that create a sense of fullness and satisfaction and are more healthful, nudged toward natural foods rather than foods with excess added sugars and fats, while still allowing flexibility for indulgences, special occasions, and eating out. While calorie-counting had been the foundation of many weight-loss programs, including the Weight Watchers original Points System, the new Points Plus program went beyond just calories to help people make healthful and satisfying choices. The new formula took into account the energy contained in each of the components that make up calories—protein, carbohydrates, fat, and fiber—and it also factored how hard the body worked to process them (conversion cost) as well their respective eating satisfaction (satiety).[50]

The Customers

Innovation at Weight Watchers also involved broadening the customer mix and targeting new customer segments. Weight Watchers began to actively consider expanding beyond its target consumer market of women, ages 25 to 55.[51] In the company's attempt to appeal to other demographic groups, such as men and the Hispanic community in the United States, Weight Watchers needed to retool its offerings and approach to appear more relevant to weight-loss consumers who sought different methods of weight management.

In terms of the Hispanic community, the company was working to better serve the growing Hispanic population in California—for example, by offering improved Spanish-language meeting materials as well as by increasing the number of Spanish meetings offered.[52] Concurrently, Weight Watchers undertook a comprehensive market segmentation study aimed at yielding valuable insights intended to drive its new strategy.[53]

Men, another attractive market segment, appeared to be more the self-help type and were not as much in favor of a group-support experience.[54] Weight Watchers meetings were attended mostly by women, with men making up only 5 percent of members. Morgan Stanley analyst Catherine Lewis said, "Weight Watchers has a pipeline of unpenetrated and underpenetrated markets" and, thus, was testing home weight-loss services for men.[55]

Atkins, the low-carbohydrate-focused diet plan, held great appeal for men in the beginning of the new millennium.[56] By 2011, Atkins was much less popular in the weight-conscious community, and there existed a void in weight-management services for men that Weight Watchers International was hoping to fill.

To do so, Weight Watchers Online, the step-by-step online guide to following the Weight Watchers plan, and Weight Watchers eTools, the Internet weight-loss companion to conventional meetings, were being intentionally customized for men and their unique set of weight-loss challenges.[57] The *WeightWatchers.com* for Men customization was born of the realization that Weight Watchers should appear to be more culturally relevant to more groups of people who want different things.[58] Launched in late March 2007,[59] the customized products were targeted to attract men, who were estimated in 2003 to represent only 5 percent of Weight Watchers' members.[60]

A research study showed that about 70 percent of men are overweight and about 30 percent of men are obese. Yet, according to the study, only 28 percent of men were actively engaged in weight loss. Weight Watchers sought to provide the weight-loss answer for men by applying its 40 years of experience to its newly customized Internet offerings for men. While the fundamental concepts of weight loss—eat less and exercise more—were the same for both genders, the approach to weight loss for each gender was different. The chief scientific officer for Weight Watchers International, Karen Miller-Kovach, noted, "Men and women are biologically and emotionally different, and multiple variables factor into how each loses weight." However, the same underlying motivators for weight loss were shared between the genders: "appearance and health."[61] So, while the preferred means may have been different, the desired end was the same.

In regard to *WeightWatchers.com* for Men, Alexandra Aleskovsky, general manager of *WeightWatchers.com*, said, "Men have been losing weight with Weight Watchers for over 40 years, and hundreds of thousands are on [the] plan right now. Weight Watchers can help so many more men get in shape by offering our Internet products in ways that are more directly relevant to them, which is why we customized our offerings for men." As such, Weight Watchers Online for Men allowed men to follow the Weight Watchers plan and get food and fitness ideas and other content and resources tailored specifically to them.[62] The new products afforded Weight Watchers a new opportunity to appeal to a large market segment that might not have otherwise considered giving the program a try.[63]

The launch of Weight Watchers Online for Men was considered by the executives to be a "new product for a new market," and the company focused on getting the product experience right, delivering on consumer expectations, and doing a good job. Once the company felt that it was delivering the product correctly, it planned to be more aggressive in marketing it. However, even before the active targeting to men, the percentage of men as a percentage of the Weight Watcher's total market had been on the rise. For example, if the overall online business was up 22 percent, the growth in men's business was up quite a bit more than that. Weight Watchers was pleased with the early results of the male-focused products and was working toward identifying the proper levers for building that part of the business.[64]

Questions Remain

Following the onslaught of fad diets such as the low-carbohydrate-focused Atkins Challenge and South Beach Diet, Weight Watchers attempted to reinvent itself in several ways. It began to look beyond its core market of women, to include men, as well as to branch out to characteristically underserved weight-loss markets. Weight Watchers expanded its business model to include not only in-person meetings but also online weight-management tools. Building off a solid foundational business model, Weight Watchers hoped not only to expand its core consumer base but also to appeal to a wider range of consumers from both genders and to a larger span of age and demographic groups. Weight Watchers had been successful in introducing several innovations, including Monthly Pass, Weight Watchers for Men, and Points Plus. Through those and other means, Weight Watchers attempted to achieve broad differentiation that had "something for everyone." Especially with the launch of the Points Plus program in November 2010, Weight Watchers in North America had seen a substantial growth in the number of new members. As CEO David Kirchhoff, the president and CEO of Weight Watchers, noted, "The one area of our business that we have continued to struggle with is to improve our ability to bring newer-members into meetings. This had been a drag on the top line of our business, despite our success in significantly increasing retention, revenue per enrollment, and product sales. . . . Prior to the [Points Plus] program launch, newer-member enrollment growth had already moved into positive territory. After the program launch, even before we turned on our advertising for the new program, it increased dramatically."[65]

Kirchhoff expressed his delight with the results, and noted, "the advertising we've created is having some of the highest impact I've seen during my career at Weight Watchers."[66] Kirchhoff continued, "We've entered 2011 with our best January in years. We're seeing terrific enrollment volumes in our North American, UK, and Australian businesses and we've seen even further acceleration of the *WeightWatchers.com* business. In short, the Weight Watchers brand is showing a level of vitality and resonance in these markets that we have not seen in years. As we look forward, we're very much focused on building on momentum in this business by continuing to press forward on our strategy to bring Weight Watchers to a new level of performance."[67]

The question remains, then: Will Weight Watchers be effective in staying true to the core of Jean Nidetch's goals while still expanding to different target groups, different dieting platforms, and different means of offering them? Only time will tell, but one thing is certain: The weight-loss industry is not going away, and members of Weight Watchers' senior management have many tough and exciting decisions to make.

Endnotes

1. Dominguez, R. 2011. Weight Watchers' stock skyrockets amid membership increases, program makeover. *Daily News,* February 18. *articles.nydailynews.com/2011-02-18/news/28628749_1_stock-skyrockets-weight-watchers-weightwatchers-com.*

2. Zelman, K. M. Weight Watchers diet. *WebMD Expert Review. www.webmd.com/diet/features/weight-watchers-diet.*

3. Weight Watchers International Inc. (Weight Watchers). 2011. Form 10-K, 2010 annual report.

4. Ibid.

5. Nidetch, J. T., & Rattner, J. 1979. *The Story of Weight Watchers.* New York: Penguin Group.

6. Weight Watchers. 2010. Weight Watchers introduces revolutionary new program to help Americans improve their eating habits and successfully lose weight. November 29. *www.weightwatchersinternational.com/phoenix.zhtml?c=130178&p=irol-newsArticle&ID=1500758.*

7. Weight Watchers. 2010. This June 6 declared Weight Watchers Walk-It Day. June 3. *www.*

weightwatchersinternational.com/phoenix.zhtml?c=
130178&p=irol-newsArticle&ID=1434334;
and Weight Watchers. 2010. Weight Watchers launches
third annual Lose For Good campaign to help fight obesity
and hunger—brand ambassador Jennifer Hudson encourages Americans to lose weight for greater gain. September 7. www.weightwatchersinternational.com/phoenix.
zhtml?c=130178&p=irol-newsArticle&ID=1467784.

8. Weight Watchers. 2011. Form 10-K, 2010 annual report.
9. Ibid.
10. Let the Countdown to Soup Begin! *Business Wire,*
August 14, 2007.
11. G. Perrenot and K. Durnan. Lunch Ladies: Applebee's
Weight Watchers Menu. *Dallas Morning News,* April 11,
2005.
12. Weight Watchers. 2011. Form 10-K, 2010 annual report.
13. Weight Watchers. 2011. Press release: Weight Watchers declares quarterly dividend. PRNewswire, March 17.
www.weightwatchersinternational.com/phoenix.
zhtml?c=130178&p=irol-newsArticle&ID=1540487.
14. Weight Watchers. 2011. Form 10-K, 2010 annual report.
15. Ibid.
16. Weight Watchers. 2006. New fitness videos on
WeightWatchers.com go live: Comprehensive fitness
offerings round out online weight-loss plan from
Weight Watchers. *PR Newswire,* December 11. www.
weightwatchers.com/about/prs/wwcom_template.
aspx?GCMSID=1038431.
17. Weight Watchers. 2011. Form 10-K, 2010 annual report.
18. Williams, G. 2011. Made in the USA: The weight-loss
industry makes huge gains. *AOL Small Business,* February
16. smallbusiness.aol.com/2011/02/16/made-in-the-usa-
the-weight-loss-industry-makes-huge-gains/.
19. *Restaurants & Institutions.* 2007. Healthcare weighs in.
April 15: 17.
20. *Market Watch: Food.* 2003. Weight Watchers: Booming
Revenues. April: 12-13.
21. Weight Watchers. 2010. Tackling the Growing
Obesity Epidemic: New Research Shows
Weight Watchers Works Globally. July 13. www.
weightwatchersinternational.com/phoenix.
zhtml?c=130178&p=irol-newsArticle&ID=1446897.
22. Weight Watchers. 2011. Form 10-K, 2010 annual report.
23. Lee, J. 2010. Diet plan review: Best ways
to lose 20 pounds. *MoneyWatch,* January 4.
moneywatch.bnet.com/saving-money/article/
diet-plan-review-best-ways-to-lose-weight/377880/.
24. Weight Watchers. 2007. Event brief of Q4 2006 Weight
Watchers International, Inc. earnings conference call—
final. *Fair Disclosure Wire,* February 15.
25. Shaver, J. 2005. Weight Watchers tops list. *Fitness Business
Pro,* June: 8.
26. Weight Watchers. Form 10-K, annual reports.
27. Florian, E. 2002. When it comes to fat, they're huge.
Fortune, October 14: 54.
28. Choe. 2004. Weight Watchers' attractive figures.
29. Weight Watchers. Form 10-K, annual reports.
30. Jayson, S. 2010. Here's how Weight Watchers may be
failing you. *Motley Fool,* December 30. www.fool.com/

investing/general/2010/12/30/heres-how-weight-watchers-
may-be-failing-you.aspx.
31. Rynecki, D., & McQuilling, A. 2004. Keep an eye on
Weight Watchers Inc. *Fortune,* February 9: 138.
32. Serafin. 2006. The fat of the land.
33. Hogan, M. 2006. Heavy debt, big worries? *BusinessWeek
Online,* July 27: 13.
34. Weight Watchers. Form 10-K, annual reports.
35. Weight Watchers. 2007. Event brief of Q2 2007 Weight
Watchers International, Inc. earnings conference call—
final. *Fair Disclosure Wire,* August 1.
36. Weight Watchers. 2007. Event brief of Q1 2007 Weight
Watchers International, Inc. earnings conference call—
final. *Fair Disclosure Wire,* May 3.
37. Weight Watchers. 2007. Event brief of Q4 2006 Weight
Watchers International, Inc. earnings conference call—
final. *Fair Disclosure Wire,* February 15.
38. Weight Watchers. 2007. Event brief of Q1 2007 Weight
Watchers International, Inc. earnings conference call. *Fair
Disclosure Wire,* May 3.
39. Ibid.
40. Ibid.
41. Ibid.
42. Ibid.
43. Ibid.
44. Ibid.
45. Ibid.
46. Ibid.
47. Ibid.
48. Weight Watchers. 2006. Americans resolve to focus on
health in 2007: New Weight Watchers survey reveals 92
percent have a health-related resolution. *Business Wire,*
December 26.
49. Choe. 2004. Weight Watchers' attractive figures.
50. Weight Watchers. 2010. Weight Watchers introduces
revolutionary new program to help Americans improve
their eating habits and successfully lose weight.
November 29. www.weightwatchersinternational.
com/phoenix.zhtml?c=130178&p=irol-newsArticle&ID=
1500758.
51. Sunoo, B. P. 1997. Changing behavior at Weight Watchers.
Workforce, July: 27–29.
52. Weight Watchers. 2006. Event brief of Q4 2006 Weight
Watchers International, Inc. earnings conference call.
53. Weight Watchers. 2007. Event brief of Q2 2007 Weight
Watchers International, Inc. earnings conference call. *Fair
Disclosure Wire,* August 1.
54. Ibid.
55. Marcial, G. G. 2002. Hefty gains for Weight Watchers?
BusinessWeek, October 21: 168.
56. Gower, T. 2004. Medicine: Healthy man: Exercise without
dieting—it's a losing battle. *Los Angeles Times* (home
edition), April 12: F3.
57. Weight Watchers. 2007. Weight loss: Announcing the
launch of Weight Watchers Online for Men and Weight
Watchers eTools for Men. *Women's Health Law Weekly,*
April 22: 251.
58. Weight Watchers International Inc. Form 10-K, Annual
Reports.

59. Weight Watchers. 2007. Event brief of Q2 2007 Weight Watchers International, Inc. earnings conference call—final. *Fair Disclosure Wire,* August 1.

60. Wahlgreen. 2003. The skinny on Weight Watchers.

61. Weight Watchers. 2007. Weight loss: Announcing the launch of Weight Watchers Online for Men.

62. Ibid.

63. Weight Watchers. 2007. Event brief of Q1 2007 Weight Watchers International, Inc. earnings conference call—final. *Fair Disclosure Wire,* May 3.

64. Weight Watchers. 2007. Event brief of Q2 2007 Weight Watchers International, Inc. earnings conference call—final. *Fair Disclosure Wire,* August 1.

65. Weight Watchers. 2011. Weight Watchers International CEO discusses Q4 2010 results—earnings call transcript. February 17. *seekingalpha.com/article/253508-weight-watchers-international-ceo-discusses-q4-2010-results-earnings-call-transcript.*

66. Ibid.

67. Ibid.

Case 26 Pixar*

When nominations for the Academy Awards were announced in January 2011, *Toy Story 3* received nominations for best picture and for best animated feature. This represented the second consecutive film from Pixar

*This case was developed by Professor Jamal Shamsie, Michigan State University, with the assistance of Professor Alan B. Eisner, Pace University. Material has been drawn from published sources to be used for class discussion. Copyright © 2011 Jamal Shamsie and Alan B. Eisner.

Animation Studios that was nominated in both categories. The latest offering from the studio had already been heralded by almost all of the critics as soon as it had been released during the prior summer. It had also become the first animated feature to gross more than $1 billion in theatres worldwide, landing it in the top spot among the highest earning animated films of all time (see Exhibit 1). Although Pixar has not won for the best picture, it has already claimed four Oscars for best animation, which

Exhibit 1 Leading Animated Films

All 11 of Pixar's films released to date have ended up among the top animated films of all time based on worldwide box office revenues in millions of U.S. dollars.

Title	Year	Studio	Revenues
1. *Toy Story 3*	2010	Pixar	$1040
2. *Shrek 2*	2004	Dreamworks	$920
3. *Ice Age: Dawn of the Dinosaurs*	2009	Fox	$887
4. *Finding Nemo*	2003	Pixar	$868
5. *Shrek 3*	2007	Dreamworks	$799
6. *The Lion King*	1994	Disney	$784
7. *Up*	2009	Pixar	$731
8. *Shrek Forever After*	2010	Dreamworks	$712
9. *Ice Age: Meltdown*	2006	Fox	$655
10. *Kung Fu Panda*	2008	Dreamworks	$632
11. *The Incredibles*	2005	Pixar	$631
12. *Ratatouille*	2007	Pixar	$624
13. *Madagascar: Escape 2 Africa*	2008	Dreamworks	$604
14. *Madagascar*	2005	Dreamworks	$533
15. *The Simpsons Movie*	2007	Fox	$527
16. *Monsters, Inc.*	2002	Pixar	$525
17. *Wall-E*	2009	Pixar	$521
18 *Aladdin*	1992	Disney	$504
19. *Toy Story 2*	1999	Pixar	$485
20. *How to Train Your Dragon*	2010	Dreamworks	$484
21. *Shrek*	2001	Dreamworks	$483
22. *Cars*	2006	Pixar	$462
23. *Tarzan*	1999	Disney	$448
24. *Happy Feet*	2006	Warner Bros.	$384
25. *Ice Age*	2002	Fox	$383
26. *Monsters vs Aliens*	2009	Dreamworks	$382
27. *Beauty and the Beast*	1991	Disney	$377
28. *A Shark's Tale*	2004	Dreamworks	$367
29. *A Bug's Life*	1998	Pixar	$363
30. *Toy Story*	1995	Pixar	$362

Sources: Internet Movie Database (IMDb), *imdb.com*; and *Variety*.

represents half of the eight trophies that have been handed out since the category was added in 2001.

The recent string of successful releases—*Ratatouille, Wall-E* and *Up*—suggests that Pixar has continued to flourish despite its 2006 acquisition by the Walt Disney Company for the hefty sum of $7.4 billon. The deal was finalized by Steve Jobs, the Apple Computer chief executive who also heads the computer animation firm. Jobs had developed a production and distribution pact with Disney, under which the two firms split the profits that Pixar films generated from ticket sales, video sales, and merchandising royalties. But the deal was set to expire after the release of *Cars* in the summer of 2006. Disney CEO Bob Iger worked hard to clinch the deal to acquire Pixar, whose track record has made it one of the world's most successful animation companies.

Both Jobs and Iger realized, however, that they must try and protect Pixar's creative culture while they also try to carry some of this over to Disney's animation efforts. Even though Pixar has continued to operate independently of Disney's own animation studios, its key talent has overseen the combined activities of both Pixar and Disney. As part of the deal, Jobs gained considerable influence over Disney by assuming the position of a non-independent director and becoming its largest individual stockholder.

In order to ensure that Pixar manages to preserve its free-wheeling entrepreneurial culture, Jobs sits on a committee that includes other top talent from the animation studio, whose key task is to protect its unique approach to making movies. Pixar's lengthy process of crafting a film stands in stark contrast to the production line approach that has been pursued by Disney. This contrast in culture is best reflected in the Oscars that the employees at Pixar have displayed proudly, but which have been painstakingly dressed in Barbie doll clothing.

Above all, everyone at Pixar remains committed to making films that are original in concept and execution, despite the risks involved. They have begun to make some sequels, but only when they are able to come up with a new and compelling story that can make use of the old characters. However, it is not clear how long Pixar can keep generating hits, given their reliance on a high level of creativity. These concerns have continued to grow since no other studio has managed to generate such an unbroken string of successful films.

Pushing for Computer-Animated Films

The roots of Pixar stretch back to 1975 with the founding of a vocational school in Old Westbury, New York, called the New York Institute of Technology. It was there that Edwin E. Catmull, a straitlaced Mormon from Salt Lake City who loved animation but couldn't draw, teamed up with the people who would later form the core of Pixar. "It was artists and technologists from the very start," recalled Alvy Ray Smith, who worked with Catmull during those years. "It was like a fairy tale."[1]

By 1979, Catmull and his team decided to join forces with famous Hollywood director George W. Lucas Jr. They were hopeful that this would allow them to pursue their dream of making animated films. As part of Lucas's filmmaking facility in San Rafael, California, Catmull's group of aspiring animators was able to make substantial progress in the art of computer animation. But the unit was not able to generate any profits, and Lucas was not willing to let it grow beyond using computer animation for special effects.

Catmull finally turned in 1985 to Jobs, who had just been ousted from Apple. Jobs was reluctant to invest in a firm that wanted to make full-length feature films using computer animation. But a year later, Jobs did decide to buy Catmull's unit for just $10 million, which represented a third of Lucas's asking price. While the newly named Pixar Animation Studios tried to push the boundaries of computer animation over the next five years, Jobs ended up having to invest an additional $50 million—more than 25 percent of his total wealth at the time. "There were times that we all despaired, but fortunately not all at the same time," said Jobs.[2]

Still, Catmull's team did continue to make substantial breakthroughs in the development of computer-generated full-length feature films (see Exhibit 2). In 1991 Disney ended up giving Pixar a three-film contract that started with *Toy Story*. When the movie was finally released in 1995, its success surprised everyone in the film industry. Rather than the nice little film Disney had expected, *Toy Story* became the sensation of 1995. It rose to the rank of the third highest grossing animated film of all time, earning $362 million in worldwide box-office revenues.

Within days, Jobs had decided to take Pixar public. When the shares, priced at $22, shot past $33, Jobs called his best friend, Oracle CEO Lawrence J. Ellison, to tell him he had company in the billionaire's club. With Pixar's sudden success, Jobs returned to strike a new deal with Disney. Early in 1996, at a lunch with Walt Disney chief Michael D. Eisner, Jobs made his demands: an equal share of the profits, equal billing on merchandise and on-screen credits, and guarantees that Disney would market Pixar films as they did Disney's own.

Boosting the Creative Component

With the success of *Toy Story*, Jobs realized that he had hit something big. He had obviously tapped into his Silicon Valley roots and turned to computers to forge a unique style of creative moviemaking. In each of their subsequent films, Pixar has continued to develop computer animation that has allowed for more lifelike backgrounds, texture, and movement than ever before. For example, because real leaves are translucent, Pixar's engineers developed special software algorithms that both reflect and absorb light, creating luminous scenes among jungles of clover.

In spite of the significance of these advancements in computer animation, Jobs was well aware that successful feature films would require a strong creative spark. He

Exhibit 2 Milestones

1986	Steve Job buys Lucas's computer group and christens it Pixar. The firm completes a short film, *Luxo Jr.,* which is nominated for an Oscar.
1988	Pixar adds computer-animated ads to its repertoire, making spots for Listerine, Lifesavers, and Tropicana. Another short, *Tin Toy,* wins an Oscar.
1991	Pixar signs a production agreement with Disney. Disney is to invest $26 million; Pixar is to deliver at least three full-length, computer-animated feature films.
1995	Pixar releases *Toy Story,* the first fully digital feature film, which becomes the top-grossing movie of the year and wins an Oscar. A week after release, the company goes public.
1997	Pixar and Disney negotiate a new agreement: a 50-50 split of development costs and profits of five feature-length movies. Short *Geri's Game* wins an Oscar.
1998–99	*A Bug's Life* and *Toy Story 2* are released, together pulling in $1.3 billion in box office and video.
2001–04	A string of hits from Pixar: *Monsters Inc., Finding Nemo,* and *The Incredibles.*
2006	Disney acquires Pixar and assigns responsibilities for its own animation unit to Pixar's creative brass. *Cars* is released and becomes another box office hit.
2009	*Wall-E* becomes the fourth film from Pixar to receive the Oscar for a feature-length animated film.

Source: Pixar.

understood that it would be the marriage of technology with creativity that would allow Pixar to rise above most of its competition. To get that, Jobs fostered a campuslike environment within the newly formed outfit similar to the freewheeling, charged atmosphere in the early days of his beloved Apple, where he also returned as acting CEO. "It's not simply the technology that makes Pixar," said Dick Cook, president of Walt Disney Studios.[3]

Even though Jobs has played a crucial supportive role, it is Catmull, now elevated to the position of Pixar's president, who has been mainly responsible for ensuring that the firm's technological achievements help to pump up the firm's creative efforts. He has been the keeper of the company's unique innovative culture, which has blended Silicon Valley techies, Hollywood production honchos, and artsy animation experts. In the pursuit of Catmull's vision, this eclectic group has transformed their office cubicles into tiki huts, circus tents, and cardboard castles, with bookshelves that are stuffed with toys and desks that are adorned with colorful iMac computers.

Catmull has also been working hard to build upon this pursuit of creative innovation by creating programs to develop the employees. Employees are encouraged to devote up to four hours a week, every week, to further their education at Pixar University. The in-house training program offers 110 different courses that cover subjects such as live improvisation, creative writing, painting, drawing, sculpting, and cinematography. The school's dean is Randall E. Nelson, a former juggler who has been known to

perform his act using chain saws so students in animation classes have something compelling to draw.

It is such an emphasis on the creative use of technology that has kept Pixar on the cutting edge. The firm has turned out ever more lifelike short films, including 1998's Oscar-winning *Geri's Game,* which used a technology called subdivision surfaces. This makes realistic simulation of human skin and clothing possible. "They're absolute geniuses," gushed Jules Roman, cofounder and CEO of rival Tippett Studio. "They're the people who created computer animation really."[4]

Becoming Accomplished Storytellers

A considerable part of Pixar's creative energy goes into story development. Jobs understands that a film works only if its story can move the hearts and minds of families around the world. His goal is to develop Pixar into an animated movie studio that becomes known for the quality of its storytelling above everything else. As he put it, "We want to create some great stories and characters that endure with each generation."[5]

For story development, Pixar relies heavily on 43-year-old John Lasseter, who goes by the title of vice president of the creative. Known for his Hawaiian shirts and irrepressible playfulness, Lasseter has been the key to the appeal of all of Pixar's films. Lasseter gets passionate about developing great stories and then harnessing computers to tell these stories. Most of Pixar's employees believe it is this passion that has allowed the studio to ensure that each of its films has been a commercial hit. In fact, Lasseter is being regarded as the Walt Disney for the 21st century.

When it's time to start a project, Lasseter isolates a group of eight or so writers and directs them to forget about the constraints of technology. The group bounces ideas off each other, taking collective responsibility for developing a story. While many studios try to rush from script to production, Lasseter takes up to two years just to work out all the details. Once the script has been developed, artists create storyboards and copy them onto videotapes called reels. Even computer-animated films must begin with pencil sketches that are viewed on tape. "You can't really shortchange the story development," Lasseter has emphasized.[6]

Only after the basic story has been set does Lasseter begin to think about what he'll need from Pixar's technologists. And it's always more than the computer animators expect. Lasseter, for example, demanded that the crowds of ants in *A Bug's Life* not be a single mass of look-alike faces. To solve the problem, computer expert William T. Reeves developed software that randomly applied physical and emotional characteristics to each ant. In another instance, writers brought a model of a butterfly named Gypsy to researchers, asking them to write code so that when she rubs her antennae, you can see the hairs press down and pop back up.

At any stage during the process, Lasseter may go back to potential problems that he sees with the story. In *A Bug's Life*, for example, the story was totally revamped after more than a year of work had been completed. Originally, it was about a troupe of circus bugs run by P. T. Flea that tries to rescue a colony of ants from marauding grasshoppers. But because of a flaw in the story—Why would the circus bugs risk their lives to save stranger ants?—codirector Andrew Stanton recast the story to be about Flik, the heroic ant who recruits Flea's troupe to fight the grasshoppers. "You have to rework and rework it," explained Lasseter. "It is not rare for a scene to be rewritten as much as 30 times."[7]

Pumping Out the Hits

In spite of its formidable string of hits, Pixar has had difficulty in stepping up its pace of production. Although they may cost 30 percent less, computer-generated animated films do still take considerable time to develop. Furthermore, because of the emphasis on every detail, Pixar used to complete most of the work on a film before moving on to the next one. Catmull and Lasseter have since decided to work on several projects at the same time, but the firm has not been able to release more than one movie in a year.

In order to push for an increase in production, Pixar has more than doubled its number of employees over the last decade. It is also turning to a stable of directors to oversee its movies. Lasseter, who directed Pixar's first three films, is supervising other directors who are taking the helm of various films that the studio chooses to develop. *Monsters Inc., Finding Nemo, The Incredibles,* and *Ratatouille* were directed by some of this new talent. But there

are concerns about the number of directors that Pixar can rely upon to turn out high-quality animated films. Michael Savner of Bane of America Securities commented, "You can't simply double production. There is a finite amount of talent."[8]

To meet the faster production pace, Catmull has also added new divisions, including one to help with the development of new movies and one to oversee movie development shot by shot. The eight-person development team has helped to generate more ideas for new films. "Once more ideas are percolating, we have more options to choose from so no one artist is feeling the weight of the world on their shoulders," said Sarah McArthur, Pixar's vice president of production.[9]

Finally, Catmull is also turning to new technology in order to help ramp up production. His goal is to reduce the number of animators to no more than 100 per film. Toward this end, Catmull has been overseeing the development of new animation software, called *Luxo,* that has allowed fewer people to do more work. While the firm's old system did allow animators to easily make a change to a specific character, Luxo adjusts the environment as well (see Exhibit 3). For example, if an animator adds a new head to a monster, the system would automatically cast the proper shadow.

Catmull is well aware of the dangers of growth for a studio whose successes came out of a lean structure that wagered everything on each film. It remains to be seen whether Pixar can keep drawing on its talent to increase production without compromising the high standards that have been set by Catmull and Lasseter. Jobs has been keen to maintain the quality of every one of Pixar's films by ensuring that each one gets the best efforts of the firm's animators, storytellers, and technologists. "Quality is more important than quantity," he recently emphasized. "One home run is better than two doubles."[10]

In order to preserve its high standards, Catmull has been working hard to retain Pixar's commitment to quality even as it grows. He has been using Pixar University

Exhibit 3   **Pixar's Proprietary Software**

Marionette	An animation software system used for modeling, animating, and lighting.
Ringmaster	A production-management software system for scheduling, coordinating, and tracking a computer-animation project.
Renderman	A rendering software system for high-quality, photo-realistic image synthesis.

Source: Pixar.

to encourage collaboration among all employees so that they can develop and retain the key values that are tied to their success. And he has helped devise ways to avoid collective burnout. A masseuse and a doctor now come by Pixar's campus each week, and animators must get permission from their supervisors if they want to work more than 50 hours a week.

To Infinity and Beyond?

The continued success of Pixar's films clearly indicates that it has continued to turn out quality films even after it was acquired by Disney in 2006. This has managed to settle some of the concerns that arose at the time of the acquisition about its possible effect on Pixar's rather unique creative culture. David Price, author of a recent book on the animation firm, stated, "Most acquisitions, particularly in media, are value-destroying as opposed to value-creating, and that certainly has not turned out to be the case here."[11]

Along the same lines, Jobs expressed his satisfaction with the close relationship that the two animation studios have developed with each other: "Disney is the only company with animation in their DNA."[12] In fact, the acquisition of Pixar was viewed as an attempt by Disney to boost its own animation efforts by acquiring a group in which the talent of the individuals and the quality of the finished product are valued above everything else.

In order to ensure this, Ed Catmull and John Lasseter have been given charge of the combined animation business of both Pixar and Disney. In fact, *Tangled* represents the first Disney film that was completed under the supervision of these Pixar heads. For Lasseter, the new responsibilities for Disney have represented a return to his roots. He had been inspired by Disney films as a kid and started his career at Disney before being lured away to Pixar by Catmull. "For many of us at Pixar, it was the magic of Disney that influenced us to pursue our dreams of becoming animators, artists, storytellers and filmmakers," Lasseter stated.[13]

But Catmull and Lasseter continue to face a challenging task. They must ensure that they keep developing hits for Pixar even as they try to turn things around at Disney. Both of them, however, are confident of their ability to instill and maintain a strong sense of creativity. Part of their success lies in their faith in the talent that they recruit and train to work together. This leads to a continuous exchange of ideas and fosters a collective sense of responsibility on all their projects. "We created the studio we want to work in", Lasseter recently remarked. "We have an environment that's wacky. It's a creative brain trust: It's not a place where I make my movies—it's a place where a group of people make movies."[14]

Endnotes

1. Burrows, P., & Grover, R. 1998. Steve Jobs: Movie mogul. *BusinessWeek,* November 23: 150.
2. Ibid.
3. Ibid.: 146.
4. Ibid.
5. Graser, M. 1999. Pixar run by focused group. *Variety,* December 20: 74.
6. Ibid.
7. Burrows. & Grover. 1998. Steve Jobs: Movie mogul: 146.
8. Bary, A. 2003. Coy story. *Barron's,* October 13: 21.
9. Tam, P. 2001. Will quantity hurt Pixar's quality? *Wall Street Journal,* February 15: B4.
10. Burrows, P., & Grover, R. 2006. Steve Jobs' magic kingdom. *BusinessWeek,* February 6: 66.
11. Barnes, B. 2008. For Disney and Pixar, a smooth (so far) ride. *International Herald Tribune,* June 2: 9.
12. Holson, L. M. 2006. Disney agrees to acquire Pixar in a $7.4 billion deal. *New York Times,* January 25. *www.nytimes.com/2006/01/25/business/25disney. html*
13. Solomon, C. 2006. Pixar creative chief to seek to restore the Disney magic. *New York Times,* January 25: C6
14. Bary. 2003. Coy story.

Case 27   Procter & Gamble*

Even though Procter & Gamble has already claimed the status of the world's biggest maker of consumer products, CEO Robert McDonald claimed that there were still plenty of opportunities for the firm to grow its business. "There's plenty of room to keep growing," he recently told investors at the company's headquarters in Cincinnati.[1] In fact, McDonald expected P&G to achieve a 3 to 5 per cent net sales growth in the fiscal year that will end in June 2011. The firm had also just announced that it had increased or maintained its market share in most product categories in all regions of the world for the first time in 11 quarters.

These results are impressive, given that P&G had posted its first annual sales decline since 2001 when McDonald took over the firm in the summer of 2009. In order to achieve these results, the firm has cut prices on many of its products as consumers have cut back on their spending to cope with the economic downturn. At the same time, P&G has also been trying to maintain its profits by promoting the features of their higher-priced brands. The firm points to the success of Gillette's *Fusion Pro-Glide* razors as evidence of the willingness of consumers to continue to buy premium products.

P&G has also decided to pursue growth by embarking on its most ambitious plan to expand into emerging markets such as Brazil and India, which have long been

* This case was developed by Professor Jamal Shamsie, Michigan State University, with the assistance of Professor Alan B. Eisner, Pace University. Material has been drawn from published sources to be used for class discussion. Copyright © 2011 Jamal Shamsie and Alan B. Eisner.

dominated by Unilever and Colgate-Palmolive. "We're late to those markets," said McDonald, who spent much of his career overseas. "As a result, we've got to do things smarter."[2] Although emerging markets have accounted for about 30 percent of P&G's annual sales, they have delivered more than 50 percent of its recent growth.

Like his predecessor, A. G. Lafley, McDonald has been working hard to push out new products and build on P&G's well-known brands. The firm has managed to increase its number of "superbrands," each of which represents global annual sales of over $1 billion. In part by its acquisitions of firms such as Clairol and Gillette, the firm has increased the number of such brands to 23 over the past decade (see Exhibit 1). P&G continues to carefully build on each of these brands, relying on innovation to keep adding new products to expand each of them to reach out to more and more customers.

But McDonald has been developing many more ideas about how to make P&G relevant in the 21st century. He has continued to shift the focus of his firm away from its traditional reliance on household care. P&G has been making aggressive inroads into health and beauty products, making these areas account for the majority of the firm's sales and profits. Over the past year, the firm has even branched out into services by using franchises to enter the car-wash and dry-cleaning businesses. In pushing for these changes, P&G is undertaking the most sweeping transformation of the company since it was founded by William Procter and James Gamble in 1837 as a maker of soap and candles.

Exhibit 1   Business Segments

	Key Products	Billion-Dollar Brands
Fabric Care & Home Care	Air care, batteries, dish care, fabric care, surface care	*Ace, Ariel, Dawn, Downy, Duracell, Gain, Tide*
Baby Care & Family Care	Baby wipes, bath tissue, diapers, facial tissue, paper towels	*Bounty, Charmin, Pampers*
Beauty	Cosmetics, deodorants, hair care, personal cleansing, fragrances, skin care	*Head & Shoulders, Olay, Pantene, Wella*
Grooming	Blades and razors, face and shave products, home small appliances	*Braun, Fusion, Gillette, Mach 3*
Health Care	Feminine care, oral care, personal health care	*Always, Crest, Oral B*
Snacks, Coffee, & Pet Care	Pet food, snacks	*Iams, Pringles*

Source: P&G.

An Attempted Turnaround

For most of its long history, P&G has been one of America's preeminent companies. The firm has developed several well-known brands, such as *Tide,* one of the pioneers in laundry detergents, which was launched in 1946, and *Pampers,* the first disposable diaper, which was introduced in 1961. P&G built its brands through its innovative marketing techniques. In the 1880s, it was one of the first companies to advertise nationally. Later on, P&G invented the soap opera by sponsoring *Ma Perkins* when radio caught on and *Guiding Light* when television took hold. In the 1930s, P&G was the first firm to develop the idea of brand management, setting up marketing teams for each brand and urging them to compete against each other.

But by the 1990s P&G was in danger of becoming another Eastman Kodak or Xerox, a once-great company that might have lost its way. Sales on most of its 18 top brands were slowing, as it was being outhustled by more focused rivals such as Kimberly-Clark and Colgate-Palmolive. The only way P&G kept profits growing was by cutting costs, which would hardly work as a strategy for the long term. At the same time, the dynamics of the industry were changing as power shifted from manufacturers to massive retailers. Retailers such as Walmart were starting to use their size to try and get better deals from P&G, further squeezing its profits.

In 1999 P&G decided to bring in Durk I. Jager to try and make the big changes that were obviously needed to get P&G back on track. But the moves that he made generally misfired, sinking the firm into deeper trouble. He introduced expensive new products that never caught on, while letting existing brands drift. He also put in place a company-wide reorganization that left many employees perplexed and preoccupied. During the fiscal year when he was in charge, earnings per share showed an anemic rise of just 3.5 percent, much lower than in previous years. And during that time, the share price slid 52 percent, cutting P&G's total market capitalization by $85 billion. The effects were widely felt within the firm, where employees and retirees hold about 20 percent of the stock (see Exhibits 2 to 4).

But Jager's greatest failing was his scorn for the family. Jager, a Dutchman who had joined P&G overseas and worked his way to corporate headquarters, pitted himself against the P&G culture. Susan E. Arnold, president of P&G's previous beauty and feminine care division, said that Jager tried to make the employees turn against the prevailing culture, contending that it was burdensome and insufferable. Some go-ahead employees even wore buttons that read "Old World/New World" to express disdain for P&G's past.

A Renewed Emphasis on People

In 2000 Alan G. Lafley received a call from John Pepper, a former CEO who was a board member. He was asked to take over the reins of P&G from Jager, representing a

Exhibit 2   Income Statement

Years Ended June 30 (in $ millions)	2010	2009	2008
Net sales	$ 78,938	$76,694	$79,257
Cost of products sold	37,919	38,690	39,261
Selling, general and administrative expense	24,998	22,630	24,017
Operating income	16,021	15,374	15,979
Interest expense	946	1,358	1,467
Other non-operating income/(expense), net	(28)	397	373
Earnings from continuing operations before income taxes	15,047	14,413	14,885
Income taxes on continuing operations	4,101	3,733	3,594
Net earnings from continuing operations	10,946	10,680	11,291
Net earnings from discontinued operations	1,790	2,756	784
Net earnings	$ 12,736	$13,436	$12,075

Source: Procter & Gamble 10-K report 2010.

Exhibit 3 **Balance Sheet**

	Period Ending		
	June 30, 2010	June 30, 2009	June 30, 2008
Assets			
Current Assets:			
Cash And Cash Equivalents	2,879,000	4,781,000	3,313,000
Short-Term Investments	—	—	228,000
Net Receivables	6,325,000	7,045,000	8,773,000
Inventory	6,384,000	6,880,000	8,416,000
Other Current Assets	3,194,000	3,199,000	3,785,000
Total Current Assets	**18,782,000**	**21,905,000**	**24,515,000**
Property, Plant, and Equipment	19,244,000	19,462,000	20,640,000
Goodwill	54,012,000	56,512,000	59,767,000
Intangible Assets	31,636,000	32,606,000	34,233,000
Other Assets	4,498,000	4,348,000	4,837,000
Total Assets	**128,172,000**	**134,833,000**	**143,992,000**
Liabilities			
Current Liabilities:			
Accounts Payable	15,810,000	14,581,000	7,977,000
Short/Current Long-Term Debt	8,472,000	16,320,000	13,084,000
Other Current Liabilities	—	7,768,000	9,897,000
Total Current Liabilities	**24,282,000**	**30,901,000**	**30,958,000**
Long-Term Debt	21,360,000	20,652,000	23,581,000
Other Liabilities	10,189,000	9,146,000	8,154,000
Deferred Long-Term Liability Charges	10,902,000	10,752,000	11,805,000
Minority Interest	324,000	283,000	—
Total Liabilities	**67,057,000**	**71,734,000**	**74,498,000**
Stockholders' Equity			
Preferred Stock	1,277,000	1,324,000	1,366,000
Common Stock	4,008,000	4,007,000	4,002,000
Retained Earnings	64,614,000	57,309,000	48,986,000
Treasury Stock	(61,309,000)	(55,961,000)	(47,588,000)
Capital Surplus	61,697,000	61,118,000	60,307,000
Other Stockholder Equity	(9,172,000)	(4,698,000)	2,421,000
Total Stockholder Equity	**61,439,000**	**63,382,000**	**69,494,000**
Net Tangible Assets	**(24,209,000)**	**(25,736,000)**	**(24,506,000)**

Source: Yahoo Finance.

Exhibit 4 **Financial Breakdown** (in billions of U.S. dollars)

Business Segment	Net Sales		Net Earnings	
	2010	2009	2010	2009
Fabric care & home care	23.8	23.1	3.3	3.0
Baby care & family care	14.7	14.1	2.0	1.8
Beauty	19.5	18.9	2.7	2.6
Grooming	7.6	7.4	1.5	1.4
Health care	11.5	11.3	1.9	1.8
Snacks & pet care	3.1	3.1	0.3	0.2

Source: P&G.

boardroom coup unprecedented in the firm's history. In a sense, Lafley, who had risen up through the ranks of P&G, had been preparing for this job his entire adult life. By the time he had taken charge, Lafley had developed a reputation as a boss who steps back to give his staff plenty of responsibility and to help shape decisions by asking a series of keen questions. As CEO, Lafley refrained from making any grand pronouncements on the future of P&G. Instead, he spent an inordinate amount of time patiently communicating to his employees about the types of changes that he wanted to see at P&G.

Lafley began his tenure by breaking down the walls between management and the employees. Since the 1950s, all of the senior executives at P&G had been located on the 11th floor at the firm's corporate headquarters. Lafley changed this setup, moving all five division presidents to the same floors as their staff. Then he turned some of the emptied space into a leadership training center. On the rest of the floor, he knocked down the walls so that the remaining executives, including himself, would share open offices.

Indeed, Lafley's charm offensive so disarmed most P&Gers that he was able to make drastic changes within the company. He replaced more than half of the company's top 30 managers, more than any P&G boss in memory, and trimmed its workforce by as many as 9,600 jobs. And he moved more women into senior positions. In fact, Lafley skipped over 78 general managers with more seniority to name 42-year-old Deborah A. Henretta to head P&G's then-troubled North American baby-care division.

In fact, Lafley was simply recognizing the importance of people, particularly those in managerial roles at P&G. Back in 1947, Richard Dupree, who was CEO at the time, had said, "If you leave us our buildings and our brands, but take away our people, the company will fail."[3] For years, the firm has been known to dispatch line managers rather than human resource staffers to do much of its recruiting.

For the few that get hired, their work life becomes a career-long development process. At every level, P&G has a different "college" to train individuals, and every department has its own "university." The general manager's college holds a week-long school term once a year when there are a handful of newly promoted managers.

P&G also maintains a comprehensive database of all of its more than 130,000 employees, each of which is tracked carefully through monthly and annual talent reviews. All managers are reviewed not only by their bosses but also by lateral managers who have worked with them, as well as on their own direct reports. Every February, one entire board meeting is devoted to reviewing the high-level executives, with the goal of coming up with at least three potential candidates for each of the 35 to 40 spots at the top of the firm, including that of the CEO. For those who might aspire to rise to the executive ranks, P&G tries to give them as broad an experience as possible. "If you train people to work in different countries and businesses, you develop a deep bench," said Moheet Nagrath, head of human resources.[4]

A New Strategic Focus

Above all, Lafley had been intent on shifting the focus of P&G back to its consumers. At every opportunity that he got, he tried to drill his managers and employees to not lose sight of the consumer. He felt that P&G has often let technology, rather than consumer needs, dictate its new products. He wanted to see the firm work more closely with retailers, the place where consumers first see the product on the shelf. And he wanted to see much more concern with the consumer's experience at home.

Under McDonald, P&G has continued to emphasize the ability of its brands to serve consumers' needs. Over the previous decade, the firm has updated all of its 200 brands by adding innovative new products. It has begun to offer devices that build on its core brands, such as *Tide*

StainBrush, a battery-powered brush for removing stains, and *Mr. Clean AutoDry,* a water pressure–powered car-cleaning system that dries without streaking. P&G has also begun to approach its brands more creatively (see Exhibit 5). *Crest,* for example, which used to be marketed as a toothpaste brand, is now defined as an oral care brand. The firm now sells *Crest*-branded toothbrushes and tooth whiteners.

Even in a tough economic climate, McDonald has been pushing even harder for P&G to continue to develop its brands by coming up with new ideas that would appeal to consumers. "There's nothing more important that we can do in these tough times than to keep our brands strong, to continue leading innovation and to win the consumer value equation every day," he told shareholders at the last annual meeting.[5] In fact, McDonald insisted that P&G has introduced more new products over the past year than at any other time in his 30 years at the firm. That includes items like *Gillette* razors with a less irritating shave, *Crest* toothpaste with a sensitive shield, and *Downy* fabric softener that promises to keep smelling fresh for a week.

In order to ensure that P&G continues to come up with innovative ideas, McDonald has also been committed to a practice that was introduced by Lafley. The former CEO had confronted head-on the stubbornly held notion that everything must be invented within P&G, asserting that half of its new products should come from the outside. Under the new "Connect and Develop" model of innovation, the firm has begun to get almost 50 percent of its new product ideas from outside the firm. This can be compared to the 10 percent figure that existed at P&G when Lafley took charge.

A key element of P&G's strategy, however, has been to move the firm away from basic consumer products such as laundry detergents, which can be knocked off by private labels, to higher-margin products. This has been leading McDonald to focus even more strongly on the firm's beauty and personal-care business. Under Lafley, P&G made costly acquisitions of Clairol, Wella, and Gillette to complement its *Cover Girl* and *Oil of Olay* brands. But P&G's most dramatic move has been to move into prestige fragrances through licenses with Hugo Boss, Gucci, and Dolce & Gabbana. Although the beauty products division now accounts for about a third of the firm's total revenues, its sales growth has begun to slow down.

A Revolution Still in the Making

Even as P&G has been trying to build on its well-known brands by introducing new products, it is now moving into services through franchising. The idea to diversify beyond products came from FutureWorks, a unit that the firm set up to expand sales of its brands, particularly in saturated markets such as the United States. Four years ago, Future-Works began considering franchise opportunities, looking for service industries where ownership was fragmented and consumers were not satisfied. It came up with several ideas, starting with car washes and dry cleaning. "I think service is yet an untapped area for us," said McDonald in a recent interview.[6]

The car washes build on *Mr. Clean,* P&G's popular cleaning product. The *Mr. Clean* line, in fact, now stretches from toilet bowl cleaners to do-it-yourself car-wash kits. In expanding the brand to car washes, the firm has worked hard to distinguish its outlets from others by offering additional services, such as *Febreze* odor eliminators, lounges with Wi-Fi and big-screen televisions, and spray guns that children can aim at cars passing through the wash. The firm has been expanding slowly, starting with a test market in Cincinnati, where P&G is based.

Exhibit 5   **Significant Innovations**

- *Tide* was the first heavy-duty laundry detergent.
- *Crest* was the first fluoride toothpaste clinically proven to prevent tooth decay.
- *Downy* was the first ultra-concentrated rinse-add fabric softener.
- *Pert Plus* was the first 2-in-1 shampoo and conditioner.
- *Head & Shoulders* was the first pleasant-to-use shampoo effective against dandruff.
- *Pampers* was the first affordable, mass-marketed disposable diaper.
- *Bounty* was the first three-dimensional paper towel.
- *Always* was the first feminine protection pad with an innovative, dry-weave topsheet.
- *Febreze* was the first fabric- and air-care product that actually removed odors from fabrics and the air.
- *Crest White Strips* was the first patented in-home teeth-whitening technology.

Source: P&G.

The firm is even more enthusiastic about its entry into dry cleaning outlets that are named after *Tide,* its best-selling laundry detergent. P&G believes that consumers will be drawn to its franchise stores by the brand name and by the superior service. The stores will include drive-through services, 24-hour pickup, and environmentally benign cleaning methods. The firm also intends to infuse the stores and its dry-cleaning fluids with the scent of the brand that is cozily familiar to most U.S. households. "It smelled really good in there," said a customer. "When I think of *Tide,* I have so many good feelings. I'm surprised that they didn't think of it sooner."[7]

P&G had tried an at-home dry-cleaning product during the late 1990s, which was eventually withdrawn because of lackluster sales. It had also opened dry-cleaning stores, called Juvian, in Atlanta, which were eventually closed. But the firm believed that it had learned from these failures in the launch of its new franchise outlets. An early pilot store in Kansas generated more than $1 million in annual sales, four times the industry average.

In order to overcome its lack of franchising experience, P&G broke its decades-old practice of internal promotions to hire William Van Epps, who had managed franchising at Pepsico. "We're not stepping into this for spare change," said Nathan Estruth, vice president of FutureWorks. "We believe we can create a sizeable service business for P&G using the franchise business model as a platform across P&G brands."[8]

Daunting Challenges

Since he has taken over from Lafley, McDonald has continued to make the same type of bold moves that he had initiated in order to remake P&G into a company that is admired, imitated, and uncommonly profitable. This has forced him to pay close attention to every aspect of the firm's strategy and organization. As a result of this, McDonald has introduced the concept of "purpose-inspired growth," which is meant to help P&G employees believe that that they are not merely pushers of detergents and deodorants but that they are helping to improve people's daily existence. "It's more than a noble idea," he proclaimed at the firm's recent analyst meeting.[9]

But analysts have pointed to the risk that P&G is taking with some of its recent moves, such as its aggressive push into beauty products, including fragrances. They have questioned the ability of a firm that uses a very methodological approach to make and sell mass-market goods to be successful in a business that is known to be quirky and fickle. Unlike the conventional practice of established firms to keep trying to come up with new brands as older ones lose their cachet, P&G hopes to apply its

brand-development methods to sustain its beauty brands over time. "We need to find ways to do brand building," said Hartwig Langer, the firm's president of global prestige products.[10]

The firm is taking even bigger risks with its use of franchises to move into the service business. P&G has not considered using any partners to enter into a new area, despite the threats that it might pose to its carefully developed image. "It's much easier for a bad experience to happen with a service brand than a product brand," said Julia Beardwood, a partner of a consulting firm that has worked with P&G on many projects. "It's harder to have quality control."[11] But the firm insists that it is minimizing its risks by forcing its franchise owners to undertake five weeks of training and requiring some coaching for all of the employees of these outlets.

Above all, McDonald is aware that P&G must seek out new avenues for expansion. Finding new avenues to grow could be the only way to counter P&G's growing reliance on Walmart. Former and current P&G employees say the discounter already accounts for about one-third of P&G's global sales. Meanwhile, the pressure from consumers and competitors to keep prices low will only increase. In a recent conference call with reporters, McDonald commented on the moves that P&G has been making to confront these challenges: "This is a period of what we would describe as continuity with change."[12]

Endnotes

1. Byron, E. 2010. P&G stays firm on sales outlook. *Wall Street Journal,* December 17: B4.
2. Reingold, J. 2011. Can P&G make money in places where people earn $2 a day? *Fortune,* January 17: 89.
3. Kimes, M. 2009. A tough job for P&G's new CEO. *CNNMoney.com,* June 10.
4. Kimes, M. 2009. P&G's leadership machine. *Fortune,* April 13: 22.
5. The Procter & Gamble Company. 2010. Press release: Purpose-inspired growth strategy is working, P&G CEO tells shareholders. *PR Newswire,* October 12.
6. Neff, J. 2010. P&G plots growth path through services. *Advertising Age,* March 22: 2.
7. Martin, A. 2010. Smelling an opportunity. *New York Times,* December 9: B1.
8. McKeough, K. 2010. Procter's gamble. *Crain's Chicago Business,* November 8: 2.
9. Reingold. 2011. Can P&G make money in places?
10. Byron, E. 2007. P&G's push into perfume tests a stodgy marketer. *Wall Street Journal,* November 12: A15.
11. McKeough. 2010. Procter's gamble.
12. Kimes. 2009. A tough job for P&G's new CEO.

Case 28 Zhejiang Geely Automotive's Purchase of Volvo*

In 2011 Geely Automotive was still a relatively unknown Chinese carmaker, but it had put in place a plan designed to catapult it to international standards. Geely had started off manufacturing home appliances in 1986, and it had only been manufacturing automobiles since 1997. But Geely's founder and chairman of the board, Shufu Li, had ambitious plans for Geely. In a relatively short period of time, he had steered Geely into becoming the largest privately owned carmaker in China. But he would not stop there—he hoped to bring Geely up to world-class standards. He wanted Geely to be able to compete with Daimler, Ford, and Toyota. Mr. Li believed that only by becoming as good as the best foreign brands could Geely compete both in China as well as internationally. He knew this would be difficult, as independent Chinese automakers are known to have problems in operations, design, safety, quality, and brand-building. As part of this plan, Geely's parent company, Zhejiang Geely Holdings, acquired the iconic Swedish automaker Volvo from Ford Motor Company in 2010. This case presents the situation and challenges faced by Geely as it attempts this epic transformation from refrigerator manufacturing to world-class automaker.

Geely's History

Geely Motors was based in the historically important city of Hangzhou, the capital city of Zhejiang province. Geely, whose name denotes fortune and luck (吉利) in Chinese, was founded by Mr. Shufu Li in 1986. Geely's motto is "passion in professional dedication, innovation, communication and hard work."[1] The company initially began by manufacturing refrigerators and related accessories and began to manufacture motorcycles in 1993. In 1997 the company entered the automotive industry as the first private Chinese company approved by the central government to produce automobiles. In 2005 Geely Automobile Holdings Limited listed on the Hong Kong Stock Exchange.

By 2011 Geely was among the top 10 automakers in China in terms of market share. The company operated six power-train and car assembly plants. They were located in Lanzhou (Gansu province), Linhai (Zhejiang province), Luqiao (Zhejiang province), Ningbo (Zhejiang province), Xiangtan (Hunan province), and Shanghai (see Exhibit 1). This gave the company a production capacity of approximately 300,000 cars per

year. The firm employed 12,000 workers, including more than 1,600 engineers and technical personnel. In addition, Geely had gotten the governmental approval to establish a new base in Jinan of Shandong Province in eastern China. Geely was planning to set up a complete vehicle production base in Harbin, capital of Heilongjiang Province, in northeastern China. It was nearing the conclusion of talks with the Heilongjiang government. The first phase of the project would have capacity of around 100,000 to 150,000 vehicles annually. This would be the automaker's eighth manufacturing facility in China. Additionally, Geely had signed an agreement with Cixi city government of Zhejiang Province to build a RMB18.8 billion (US$2.81 billion) auto industrial city with annual production capacity of one million units in the Cixi economic development zone.[2]

Geely produced automobiles under five key brand groups: Geely, Maple, Gleagle, Emgrand, and Englon. The firm was the only Chinese car manufacturer to have developed its own range of engines, which had capacities ranging from 1 liter to 1.8 liters, supporting automatic and manual transmissions. By 2010 Geely was ranked as one of the country's top 500 firms. It was a fully integrated independent auto firm with a complete auto ecosystem from design and R&D to production, distribution, and service. Geely began to attract attention as the company experienced rapid growth. Through a broad distribution network consisting of 500 4S (sale, spare-parts, service, and survey) shops and nearly 600 service stations all over China, Geely sold over 330,000 vehicles in 2009.

The Global Automobile Industry

2009 was the worst year for U.S. auto sales in nearly 30 years. The U.S. auto industry underwent a radical transformation in 2009, one of the most turmoil-filled years in its more than 100-year history. In 2009 auto sales in the United States amounted to 10,431,509 vehicles, which was a 21 percent decrease compared to 2008 sales, 35 percent compared to 2007. The Big Three leading American automakers were facing historic challenges both operationally and financially. GM and Chrysler took the biggest hits after both went through bankruptcy court and stayed alive with government aid. For the year, GM sales were off 33 percent from 2008. Chrysler showed some signs of progress at showrooms and was helped by less-profitable sales to fleets, such a rental companies and municipalities, but still sold only 931,000 vehicles for the year, its worst performance since 1962.

Although Ford reported a sales decline of 15 percent in 2009, it had its first gain in U.S. market share since 1995 thanks to strong demand for midsize cars like the Ford Fusion and crossovers like the Ford Escape. In the

* This case was written by Yuan Yi Chen, Michael N. Young, and Allan K. K. Chan from Hong Kong Baptist University. The development of this case was partially supported by the *Chinese Business Case Research Centre* at Hong Kong Baptist University. The purpose of the case is to serve as a basis for classroom discussion rather than to illustrate either effective or ineffective handling of an administrative situation. Copyright © 2011 Michael N. Young.

Exhibit 1 Geely's Manufacturing Locations

summer of 2009, the government's "Cash for Clunkers" program helped somewhat with US$2.85 billion in government-backed rebates. Americans responded, buying nearly 700,000 vehicles. But for the most part, 2009 was a dismal year for new vehicles. Foreign automakers Honda, Nissan, and Toyota also saw sharp declines for 2009. Honda's sales were off 22 percent, while Nissan was down 19 percent. Nissan's increase in December came from higher sales of its Versa compact car. Toyota sales were down just over 20 percent for the year. Sales of smaller, cheaper vehicles, however, helped drive gains for some manufacturers. Hyundai continued its surge, with an 8 percent yearly gain, while its low-cost Kia brand reported 2009 sales gains of nearly 10 percent. Japanese automaker Subaru, famous for small all-wheel-drive cars and sport utility vehicles, said 2009 was its best year ever for sales and market share. They reported a 15 percent sales gain for the year and called 2009 an unqualified success.

But by 2010, U.S. auto sales were sputtering back to life, and analysts were projecting sales to continue increasing into 2011. With sales of around 11.5 million new cars and trucks, 2010 was still the second-worst year in almost three decades, after 2009. This was quite a drop from the heights of the early 2000s, when credit was cheap, incentives were rampant, and sales topped 17 million. In 2010 Ford sold 1.9 million cars and trucks, an increase of 15 percent over 2009. It was able to capture market share from rivals GM and Toyota. Ford's sales rose thanks to strong demand for its pickups, as construction companies and other small businesses began buying trucks again. The F-150 pickup was the best-selling vehicle in the United States in 2010. GM sold 2.2 million vehicles in 2010, for an increase of 6.3 percent over 2009. Chrysler sold 1.1 million vehicles in 2010—a year-on-year increase of 17 percent. This was an impressive rebound, considering the company had emerged from a bankruptcy restructuring in 2009.

For foreign automakers, winners included South Korea's Hyundai, which said its sales rose 24 percent for the year to 538,000 vehicles, a record for the company. Nissan reported an 18 percent sales increase for 2010 to nearly 909,000 vehicles. Honda sold over 1.2 million vehicles in 2010, a 7.6 percent increase. However, Toyota continued to struggle. Its sales were flat in 2010, a casualty of the company's tarnished safety record.

Toyota had recalled more than 10 million vehicles since late 2009 for various issues, including sticky gas pedals. In early 2011, it was too early to tell whether the Japanese manufacturers would be significantly affected by the March 12 earthquake and tsunami that struck northeastern Japan.

Car companies had downsized and they were producing fewer vehicles, so they didn't have to resort to costly incentives in order to clear out inventory. Big incentives—like the employee-pricing-for-everyone program in the summer of 2005—were one reason buyers flocked to dealerships. Also, buyers had been spooked by falling home prices and stubbornly high unemployment. But the economy was improving, and car companies were more confident about 2011. The recovery in global car sales also remained on track, with volumes advancing 6 percent above a year earlier in January 2011.

The Rise of China's Auto Market

Although the global auto market was sputtering, this was not the case in China, where automobile sales increased by an explosive 32.4 percent in 2010. China had already overtaken the United States as the largest car market in 2009, and it was also the largest market for General Motors vehicles[3]. This was indicative of China's epic transformation to a market economy and meteoric economic rise that had seen double digit growth rates for most of the past 20 years. China's middle class was expanding rapidly, and its large land mass and infrastructure could support a huge car fleet. Moreover, as China emerged as an economic power, the Chinese authorities were hoping to reduce reliance on exports and encourage more growth from domestic consumer spending.

China's auto industry produced 18.06 million units in 2010. This was up from 13.79 million units in 2009, of which 8 million were passenger cars (sedans, sport utility vehicles, multipurpose vehicles, and crossovers) and 3.41 million units were commercial vehicles (buses, trucks, and tractors). In 2009, 13,644,800 cars were sold in China. The total revenue was RMB512.81 billion (US$76.67 billion) and profit rose to RMB117.28 billion (US$17.53 billion). The growth in the auto industry was driven by increases in demand for cars in both the domestic and overseas markets.

The growth of China's auto industry was nothing short of astounding. China produced one million cars in 1992 and two million cars per year by 2000. After China's entry into the World Trade Organization (WTO) in 2001, the development of the automobile market accelerated. Between 2002 and 2007, China's national automobile market grew by an average of 21 percent, or one million vehicles, year-on-year. In 2006 China's vehicle production capacity successively exceeded six, then seven million, and in 2007 China produced over eight million automobiles. In 2009, 13.759 million motor vehicles were manufactured in China, surpassing Japan as the largest automobile maker in the world. In 2010 both sales and production topped 18 million units, with 13.76 million passenger cars delivered. Likewise, the number of registered cars, buses, vans, and trucks on the road in China is projected to exceed 200 million units by 2020. For this reason, Geely, along with other car makers, had begun paying increasing attention to the China market.

China's automobile manufacturers could be classified into two types: joint ventures and domestic independent manufacturers. Of the automobiles produced, 44.3 percent were local brands (BYD, Lifan, Chang'an, Geely, Chery, Hafei, Jianghuai [JAC], Great Wall, Roewe, etc.). The rest were produced by joint ventures with foreign car makers such as Volkswagen, Mitsubishi, General Motors, Hyundai, Nissan, Honda, Toyota, and so on. Most of the cars manufactured in China were sold within China, with only 369,600 cars being exported in 2009. These joint ventures were so prevalent that they hardly left any market share for other independent manufacturers. Even so, Geely was determined in its resolve to become a major player.

One reason that independent car companies had difficulty competing was the perception that they lacked innovative designs. Market observers at the Detroit Auto Show in 2006 were unimpressed by the simple curves of mainland cars. They also commented on the shoddy finish and the tinny sounds of the doors[4]. Although Geely engineers were trying to modify car designs and engineering, Mr. Li knew that Chinese engineers still had a long way to go before they could satisfy the sophisticated tastes of Western buyers. Furthermore, Chinese products had a reputation for infringing upon others' intellectual property rights. For instance, Chery and Geely were accused of copying technology from GM and Toyota, respectively. GM said that Chery's popular small QQ model was a rip-off of its Chevrolet Spark. Although neither GM nor Toyota prevailed in court, the lawsuits inevitably tarnished the image of Chinese car makers. In 2011 Geely was sued by the British car maker Land Rover over a trademark dispute. Land Rover said it had been using two Chinese characters "Lu Hu" in China for its "Land Rover" brand since the early 1990s, but that in 1999 Geely registered the "Lu Hu" trademark knowing that Land Rover was using it.[5] Exhibit 2 shows total automobile sales by region.

Geely's Operations

With the motto of "passion in professional dedication, innovation, communication and hard work," Geely had created a corporate culture that encouraged innovation and growth. Geely was founded on a culture of entrepreneurship, research, and innovation, and this continued into 2011 with ongoing investments in education, training, and R&D. Geely had grown its workforce with a commitment

Exhibit 2   **International Automobile Sales by Region**

	1990–1999*	2000–2007*	2008#	2009#
Total Sales (millions of units)	39.20	49.19	62.33	51.03
North America	16.36	19.41	15.85	12.68
Canada	1.27	1.60	1.64	1.46
United States	14.55	16.79	13.19	10.40
Mexico	0.54	1.02	1.02	0.82
Western Europe	13.11	14.59	13.54	13.62
Germany	3.57	3.30	3.09	3.81
Eastern Europe	1.18	2.55	4.17	3.12
Russia	0.78	1.37	2.90	1.47
Asia	6.91	10.45	15.07	17.68
China	0.43	2.91	4.98	7.32
India	0.31	0.78	1.20	1.43
South America	1.64	2.19	3.70	3.93
Brazil	0.94	1.37	2.23	2.53

Source: Global Auto Report, Global Economic Research.

Note: * average annual sales

    # annual sales

to hard work and quality. Stakeholders had come from all across China with diverse nationalities or overseas experiences. In short, Geely had developed a strong track record amid changing circumstances.

Research and Development   Geely was well aware of the importance of R&D to corporate sustainability in automotive manufacturing. Therefore, Geely had been putting more than 10 percent of its annual sales revenue into R&D. For example, in 2009 Geely invested over RMB1.2 billion (US$179.4 million) in R&D to back up its independent development path. Geely's R&D capabilities were shaped by its team of engineers. The company had more than 1,600 engineers who came from all over China, as well as a number of foreign engineering experts and Chinese who had experience overseas. The research team expanded by more than 200 people during the first three quarters of 2009 and represented more than 13 percent of the firm's overall workforce. Geely had established the Geely Automobile Research School and the Geely Engine Research School. A new R&D center was planned to be built in Hangzhou, with a Phase 1 investment of RMB350 million (US$52.3 million).

Geely had mastered most of the key technologies that were crucial to an automaker, including knowledge about engines, drive trains, ancillary power systems, and interior and exterior equipment. The company claimed to be the first Chinese automaker that independently researched automobile transmissions. As of September 2009 Geely had achieved more than 1,200 patents, 30 of which were granted internationally. One technological advancement was the creation of the world's first Blow-Out Monitoring and Braking System ("BMBS"), a unique technology that helped to control a car when a tire blows out. In addition, Geely had invested in the research of new environmentally sound technologies and operated a self-developed Energy Efficient Building System ("EEBS") that reduced noise during the production process and cut gas emissions by up to 35 percent. Mr. Li believed that by mastering technology Geely would be able to maintain its competitive advantage when facing foreign rivals.

Geely placed significant emphasis on training. Geely's training program involved all employees and included regular lectures and educational sessions. To improve product design and quality, Geely began cooperating with many foreign automakers, from such countries as South Korea, Germany, and Italy. Experts from foreign companies and institutes were invited to Geely to share their experience and provide training. Meanwhile, Geely's employees were sent abroad to receive professional training. Such opportunities for knowledge exchange gave Geely's employees opportunities to fulfill individual growth. The R&D initiatives enabled Geely to gain a more advantageous position in the local market, and it lifted its international profile. These factors increased Geely's confidence in its ability to compete in China as well as overseas.

Product Positioning in the China Market Chinese carmakers have not provided data on overseas sales by country. But in general, exports paled in comparison to production for the domestic Chinese market. Besides Geely, a few other Chinese automakers also considered tackling overseas markets, including Chang'an Automobile Group, Beijing Automotive Holding Co., and Chery Automotive[6]. In 2008 the mainland exported 644,000 vehicles (worth US$8.88 billion) according to the China Association of Automobile Manufacturers, which was an increase of approximately 9.4 percent and 32.5 percent respectively over 2007. However, because of the financial crisis and resulting decrease in automobile demand internationally, only 370,700 vehicles (worth US$5.19 billion) were exported in 2009.

Initially, Geely competed on price in China, providing a series of models ranging in price from RMB30,000 (US$4,485) to RMB80,000 (US$11,960). These prices put the dream of owning an automobile within reach of consumers in China's rural areas, where incomes were lower. Geely had developed an effective cost-control system. First, each product had its own specialized manufacturing base to enhance efficiency. For instance, the plant in Shanghai focused primarily on mid-level automobiles, whereas the operations at Ningbo of Zhejiang Province manufactured the lower-end models, with price ranging between RMB50,000 (US$7,475) to RMB70,000

(US$10,465). The target market of the models manufactured at Taizhou of Zhejiang Province was even lower, with prices around RMB30,000 (US$4,485). In addition, cost-saving was achieved through vertical integration; by producing many components in-house, Geely was able to further reduce costs and keep information regarding its manufacturing processes proprietary.

Although Geely primarily began as a price leader, it slowly began to produce higher quality cars. Management realized that it was difficult to compete on price in the long-term, because the profit margins for low-end products were razor thin. Thus, in 2004, having cemented its leading position in the low-end segment, Geely ventured into the middle- to high-end market. Prior to this, all of Geely's models in China targeted the low-end of the market, priced from RMB30,000 (US$4,485) to RMB80,000 (US$11,960). By the end of 2004, Geely introduced its first middle-level model, Beauty Leopard, which ranged from RMB80,000 (US$11,960) to RMB120,000 (US$17,940). Then they targeted the sports segment and mid-level portions of the market. For instance, 23 new models were introduced at China's automotive exposition in April 2008. Geely introduced the Emgrand EC8, a limousine model with distinct Chinese elements at the Auto China Show 2010 (see Exhibit 3). The presence of the Emgrand EC8 at the auto show, which was a sign of the booming Chinese automobile industry, indicated that the independent Chinese national automakers had begun to manufacture luxury cars. Moreover, in order to represent a new image, Geely paid RMB3.6 million (US$0.54 million) for a design contest for its new logo, including RMB2 million (US$0.30 million) for the designer. The new logo (see Exhibit 4) was put into use at the end of 2007.

The company reiterated in 2011 that its objective was to move to the upper end of the market and break from a traditional reliance on lower-cost models to boost average

Exhibit 3 Emgrand EC8 Display at Auto China 2010 Show

Exhibit 4 Geely Logo

revenue and profit per car sold. "We are not the Geely of five or six years ago," chief executive Gui Shengyue said. The firm would start production on the Emgrand EX7 SUV by June at a newly built factory in Chengdu with an initial annual capacity of 50,000 units, Gui said. They were also in the process of developing eight new upper-end models.[7]

By 2010 there were more than 8 million Geely cars on the road, and the company's trademark was well recognized throughout China. To further increase sales and provide after-sale service, Geely had built a dealership and service network across China and in each of its new markets. As customer satisfaction was critical, Geely became the first Chinese auto manufacturer to establish a call center providing around-the-clock service. In December 2010, Geely became the first domestic automaker to sell cars on *Taobao* Mall (see *www.taobao.com.cn*) China's largest online shop[8].

Geely faced tough competition from strong joint venture competitors and on several occasions was nearly driven out of business, but Mr. Li Shufu remained resilient and optimistic. He did not attempt to obtain a foreign partner like many of his competitors. He believed that partnering with a foreign firm was a losing proposition in the long run. The Chinese partners had little bargaining power over their larger, more established foreign partners, and they participated very little in the decision making. Furthermore, the alliances often did not bring about the advanced technology that was promised by the foreign partner. Instead, foreign partners often maintained tight control, with the goal of maximizing their return. Mr. Li liked the independence of financial and operational decisions that came from remaining free of a foreign partner.

Overseas Market Development Historically, Chinese vehicle exports had primarily been limited to buses and trucks and other heavy equipment. But Chinese manufacturers had steadily been upgrading their

Exhibit 5 An Iconic London Black Cab Being Assembled at the Coventry Plant

technology and production efficiency in an attempt to compete overseas in private passenger vehicles. The import and export unit of Geely Holding Group, Shanghai Geely International Corporation, was founded in July 2002. Offices were established in five strategic markets: the Middle East, Africa, Southeast Asia, Central America, and South America. Geely exported about 19,000 vehicles in 2009, making it the second largest automobile exporter from China.

After its participation in the 2005 Internationale Automobil-Ausstellung (IAA) in Frankfurt, Germany, Geely began to design and build a car model just for export to Western countries. Geely had established strong international partnerships and also made a variety of international investments. It had begun working with Magna Steyr of Austria, but the start date for exporting vehicles to Europe was not confirmed.[9] The company had set up production plants in Indonesia and Russia, each with the capacity to produce 50,000 cars. It was reported that Geely was in talks with four to five countries for future cooperation, citing discussions to set up assembly plants in Africa, Europe, and the United States. In addition, Geely signed an agreement with Manganese Bronze Holdings in October 2006. Manganese manufactured the distinctive London black taxi (see Exhibit 5). Under the agreement, Geely became the largest shareholder of the British automaker. At the same time, the Shanghai LTI Automobile Components Co. Ltd., a joint venture with Manganese, was established in 2007. This venture came into production in mid-2008. By 2011 executives were confident that the London black cab manufacturing venture could turn profitable that year. The Shanghai plant started shipping knocked-down car kits to the Coventry plant for assembly instead of making them on site, a move that could save nearly US$5000 per car in costs.

In 2009 Geely acquired Drive Train Systems International Pty Ltd., a leading global transmission developer headquartered in Australia. In March 2011 the Geely MK became the first Chinese passenger car to enter the Australian market, with retail prices beginning at $11,990 Australian dollars (see Exhibit 6). Geely saw Australia as an ideal test market for the car-savvy Western consumers before launching in the United States and Europe. The MK appeared to be a good value, but it was only the beginning for Geely's ambitious plans for the Western markets.

Geely had developed a network of more than 500 retail distributors in 45 countries across five continents and nearly 600 service stations. In addition, Geely sourced components both domestically and internationally, with many of its 650 suppliers supplying the firm from their operations elsewhere in the world. Geely's Enterprise Resource Planning (ERP) after-sale service information system ensured that Geely was intimately involved with

Exhibit 6 The Geely MK, Which Went on Sale in Australia in March 2011

its network and able to respond quickly to market demand as well as analyze customer patterns. Geely planned to expand this global footprint with additional manufacturing facilities, dealer networks, and customer support systems.

Questions about Quality and Safety China was world-renowned as the world's workshop—dominating industries from shoes and toys to tools and basic electronics. However, when it comes to cars, China is a relatively late entrant. Although Geely received encouragement from the Chinese government, there were numerous challenges that had to be overcome in order for the company to succeed. Other things equal, low price is associated with low quality, and products from China had a reputation for shoddy workmanship. For example, the Landwind SUV made by Chinese automaker Jiangling Motors had gained a reputation for being of extremely poor quality,[10] and this had tarnished the image of Chinese automobiles. The result of the German Allgemeiner Deutscher Automobil-Club (ADAC) test, which was comparable to European New Car Assessment Programme (NCAP) safety standards in passenger cabin protection, was *zero* out of 5. The passenger cabin completely collapsed upon collision. Since safety was an important factor in consumers' decision to buy, the test result seriously eroded Western consumers' confidence in the safety of Chinese cars.

Geely still had a long way to go on the safety and quality fronts[11]. On December 12, 2006, at the Chinese Car and Technology Research centres crash test laboratory, CNAP, the body responsible for Chinese car safety, carried out a crash test on *Zi You Jian* (also translated as Freedom Vessel), a small sedan from Geely. The crash test was conducted on all aspects of the car's outer shell. Results showed that the pillar between the driver door and rear left-hand side door was extremely weak[12]. *Zi You Jian* also took part in a Russian crash test in 2008. The crash test was conducted by the Russian magazine *Automotive*

Review, which bought the car for just under US$12,000. Although this test was conducted two years after the first test, the car scored zero stars. The editors of the magazine began calling the car the "Death Vessel."[13] (See YouTube videos; search "Geely Crash Test.")

For this reason, Geely was determined to make technological breakthroughs in the areas of safety and quality control, as well as energy efficiency and environmental protection, and it was believed the Volvo acquisition could help in these areas. All new Geely cars needed to pass tests from independent testing centers with standards specified by the New Car Assessment Programme (NCAP) in China. Geely also took quality control seriously. All Geely facilities were ISO9000 compliant, and the Ningbo plant was certified ISO/TS16949:2002. Moreover, the Geely team launched a five-year energy efficiency and environmentally friendly auto development program to develop cars not powered by standard gasoline engines. Furthermore, the company intended to develop five hybrid models in the near future that would incorporate plug-in, stop-run, hybrid, and electric-only systems.

The Volvo Acquisition

Details of the Merger In 2009 Geely's parent company, Zhejiang Geely Holdings, made a big step toward international expansion by announcing it would acquire Volvo Car Corporation from Ford Motor Company. This US$1.8 billion acquisition was, at that time, the largest cross-border acquisition by a Chinese privately owned enterprise. The transaction agreements included, in addition to the stock purchase agreement, further agreements on intellectual property rights, supply, and R&D arrangements between Volvo Cars, Geely Group, and Ford.

Although initially the two companies would operate independently, future potential synergies could be envisioned. For example, it was hoped that Geely could benefit from Volvo's advanced safety, quality, and environmental technologies. In particular, Volvo was known as a leader in automobile safety. This appealed to Geely, which was particularly stung by having their car labeled a "death vessel" by overseas crash testers. It was thought that Volvo could benefit by the infusion of new resources and greater access to the burgeoning China market. Geely hoped to preserve Volvo's existing manufacturing facilities in Sweden and Belgium. The collaborative relationships that Volvo had built with employees, unions, suppliers, dealers, and customers were also valuable for Geely. On completion of the merger, Volvo would be a separate company with its own management team and a new board of directors based in Gothenburg, Sweden. The board and the management would have a mandate to develop Volvo's leadership in safety and environmental technologies, expanding the company as a world-leading premium brand with a presence in more than 100 markets with ambitious plans for the fast-growing Chinese market.

Li Shufu would become chairman of the board at Volvo Car Corporation and Hans-Olov Olsson, a former president and chief executive of Volvo, would become vice chairman. In February 2011, Volvo established its China headquarters in Shanghai and announced that it would build its first Chinese plant in the western city of Chengdu, scheduled to open in 2013 with an annual capacity of 100,000 units. A year after the merger, Volvo managed to make a profit in 2010—a first since 2005. Volvo sold nearly 374,000 units globally, up 11.2 percent from the previous year; sales in China increased 36 percent to 30,522 cars.

In China, Volkswagen was the first foreign automaker to set up a joint venture in 1984. As a result, Audi cars were viewed as a made-in-China luxury brand among government officials. Geely's strategy was to grab market share from Audi, and to boost Volvo's China sales to over 200,000 units annually by 2015. Geely wanted to sell Volvos to wealthy Chinese consumers and especially government officials in China, at prices ranging from US$40,000 for basic models to US$100,000 for high-end luxury models (see Exhibit 7). Although foreign-brand cars sold in China were made in China, the brands were owned by the foreign companies. It was hoped that this would work in Volvo's favor, as patriotic Chinese consumers might prefer buying a car from a Chinese-owned company. It was the same strategy that Chinese computer maker Lenovo used when it bought IBM's PC business and became a world-class player. However, while this strategy might benefit Volvo in China's domestic market, it might harm the Volvo brand in foreign markets, where the association with Chinese-made automobiles might signify lower quality or safety. It remained to be seen whether the gains would offset the losses.

Turnaround and Branding Challenges Geely's parent company faced a challenge in restoring Volvo to long-term profitability. Volvo posted revenue of US$12.4 billion in 2009 by selling 334,000 cars, but it recorded a pretax loss of US$653 million.[14] Geely planned to double Volvo's sales in Europe and North America and gave primary importance to building the brand's market share in China and other emerging markets. As the history of General Motors, Ford, and Chrysler show, the auto industry was one of the most ferociously competitive industries. This was especially true in mature markets like the United States and Europe, where entrenched incumbents would fight to the death to defend their turf. Geely had little experience selling cars outside of China, let alone running major manufacturing operations in a country as far away and as different as Sweden. Geely lacked experience in the developed countries in how to market and sell upscale cars. Turning Volvo around would require Geely to make upfront investments to increase production capacity and in advertising and brand building. Many industry analysts predicted that 13-year-old Geely, barely known abroad, would have a difficult time turning around Volvo.

Geely also faced challenges regarding brand management. An important reason for the Volvo acquisition was the value of the Volvo brand. In China, Volvo was considered as luxurious and safe as Mercedes-Benz and BMW. Geely wanted to improve its brand name by acquiring Volvo, so as to move to the higher end of the market. As Mr. Li Shufu put it, "From my perspective, Volvo's product is already in very good demand. Our real challenge is how we are going to evolve and develop the Volvo brand further." However, the ability to buy is not the same as the ability to manage. The facts were that Geely was known as a manufacturer of cheap cars with a short history that included poor safety and questionable quality, while Volvo was a premier European luxury brand. As a Chinese company, Geely hoped to localize Volvo cars for the Chinese market without diluting the global image and positioning of the Volvo brand.

Furthermore, it was likely that costs would have to be cut at Volvo, which was still losing money at the time of the acquisition. But this would be difficult, given that Volvo is known as a leader in safety and environmental technologies. If Geely began to use more Chinese-made components in Volvo cars, it could tarnish Volvo's high-end or safety reputations. Meanwhile, Geely sold subcompact cars in emerging markets like Russia, Turkey, and Venezuela. It did not enter the U.S. market, because its quality standards didn't match U.S. safety and other standards. Geely's basic cars were sold for US$6,000 each, and the company was still viewed as a low-end car maker.

Three months after the merger, Volvo and its new owner admitted to differences. Mr. Li, the new chairman of Volvo, disagreed with the product and brand strategy of company executives back in Sweden. He wanted Volvo to develop larger cars for China, while Volvo wanted to develop small, fuel-efficient vehicles in keeping with their

Exhibit 7 The Volvo S40

reputation for being environmentally friendly. Should the company target the Chinese consumers' tastes for ostentatious luxury cars or stick to its mandate of environmental protection and safety?

Potential Culture Clash

Postacquisition cultural integration has always been a challenge, even when the companies came from the same country. This challenge is compounded in cross-border acquisitions, where there are differing national cultures on top of differing corporate cultures. Lenovo's acquisition of IBM's PC Division was a vivid example. Lenovo faced enormous challenges as it attempted to incorporate its U.S. division into its predominantly Chinese organization. Similarly, although Geely Holdings had accumulated some international experience from their export activities, the company had limited experience in cross-cultural management. In this case, the acquirer was smaller and less experienced than the acquired. Volvo had a long and proud tradition and a deeply entrenched corporate culture that reflected its proud Scandinavian heritage. This situation had the potential for wounded pride on the Swedish side, loss of face on the Chinese side, and policy disagreements all around.

Future Growth

Geely had consistently achieved strong sales growth. Its revenues rose roughly 55 percent to RMB9.24 billion (US$1.41 billion) in the first half of 2010, while net income surged to RMB804.85 million (US$122.69 million) from RMB595.91 million (US$90.84 million) for the same period of 2009[15]. Geely was never shy about its ambitions for international expansion. Geely bought shares in Coventry, England–based Manganese Bronze Holdings and owned 20 percent of the iconic London black cab manufacturer. Traditionally seen as a mass-market car maker, Geely entered the luxury car market by acquiring Volvo in 2010.

Geely planned to continue increasing its international presence over the coming five years, with a goal to build 15 production bases worldwide. In addition, it hoped to sell two-thirds of its cars outside of China and to double the global sales of the newly acquired Volvo brand. To do so, the company was growing both organically through its existing car brands and through acquisitions and partnerships. By 2015 Geely planned to have developed several new car models, all compliant with international emissions requirements and suitable for sale overseas, and all of which would be designed with both domestic and international markets in mind. Among these new models would be five hybrid cars, which were currently under development. Geely also hoped to release eight new series of gasoline and diesel engines as well as seven new series of manual and automatic transmissions.

In order to do this, it would have to successfully integrate its new acquisition, which still faced many challenges. "Volvo cannot fail," said David Zhao, auto industry analyst of Frost & Sullivan, noting that the government would lose face if Geely's acquisition proved unprofitable[16].

Endnotes

1. *www.geely.com.*
2. *Financial Times Information.* 2006. "Geely on fast lane for expansion." October 18.
3. Allison Jackson, *China Daily.* 2010. "China overtakes US as world's largest auto market." January 11.
4. Bernard Simon, "Eastern carmakers fine-tune their strategies to ensure a slice of the lucrative western market," *Financial Times,* 2007. January 4.
5. "Short Critique," *China Daily.* 2010. November 15.
6. Andy Cheng, "Chery to Set Up Three Assembly Plants Abroad," *SinoCast China Transportation Watch.* 2007. January 2.
7. Neil Gough, "Geely's new SUVs to boost profit," *South China Morning Post.* 2011. Geely's new SUVs to boost profits. March 24.
8. Toru Shimoharaguchi, "Young China execs challenge world," *Nikkei Weekly.* 2011. January 17.
9. Alysha Webb, Crain Communications. 2006. "Despite obstacles, Chinese carmakers are keen to come to Europe: Players to watch in the race to export from East to West." December 11.
10. China Business Infocentre, The WTO Column. 2005. Can Chinese products survive a crash test? *http://www. afroshanghai.com/forums/index.php?topic=130.0.*
11. *The Cars Guide.* 2010. "Moving forward in the motoring world." August 20.
12. China Car Times. 2006. "Geely crash test—Zi You Jian— Free Vessel." December 13.
13. China Car Times. 2008. "Geely 'Death Vessel.'" February 4.
14. *Gazette* (Montreal). 2010. "China's Geely hopes to turn around Volvo." August 3.
15. Vinicy Chan, "Asiamoney best managed company awards: China," *Asiamoney.* 2010. December.
16. Miho Nagano, Geely's Volvo Management Challenge: Selling Made-In-China Volvos," *Investor's Business Daily,* July 16th 2010.

Case 29   Ann Taylor

Survival in Specialty Retail*

In March 2011, when Ann Taylor announced its 2010 year-end financial results, it was rewarded with glowing headlines—profits had gone up sharply. Especially the fourth quarter results had beaten analysts' expectations, rising to $14 billion from just above breakeven a year earlier. However, these sales comparisons were "among the easiest compares in the industry" because of the company's poor sales during the last three years.[1] Did Ann Taylor deserve kudos?

2010 had been an uphill battle after 2009—the "worst holiday season in four decades"—had generated a "wave of retail closures" among many well-known companies, including Zales, Gap, Talbots, and Ann Taylor.[2] The chief executive of JCPenney had called the situation "the most unpredictable environment in his 39-year retail career."[3] One analyst noted that the women's clothes retailers, especially, had felt the downturn and lost customers overall since 2008, as the weak economy caused shoppers to cut back on purchases.[4]

Although most forecast a modest recovery in spending in 2011, at least some retailers had seen their customers splurge in the fourth quarter of 2010—luxury destinations such as Neiman Marcus, Nordstrom, and Saks saw double-digit growth. The feeling going into spring 2011 was that customers had shown "a clear preference for select high-end apparel brands such as Gucci," and were "willing to pay a premium on something that delivers on luxury." At the same time, shoppers were also "hunting down designer brands at steep discounts" at stores such as TJ Maxx or Target, causing one businessman to label this the "barbell effect": "high-end brands are holding ground among consumers, while spending at value-oriented stores has also been pretty stable. [But] it's a tough place for mid-tier right now," namely those retailers such as Gap, Chico's, and Ann Taylor. Luxury fashion spending was up 35 percent in 2010, while mainstream fashion gained just 8 percent overall.[5]

In addition, the global economic picture was not pretty, especially in China, where wage increases were causing cost inflation in merchandise manufacturing. With most specialty apparel retailers sourcing product out of Asia, this made it difficult to predict merchandise margins going forward. One group of analysts pointed out that "the competitive environment is much more challenging today than it was just five years ago when most specialty retailers achieved their operating margin peaks. . . . The fact is that over the next few years it will be rare for a specialty apparel retailer to return to its historical level of profitability."[6]

What might this mean for Ann Taylor? CEO Kay Krill felt it was "a good day for Ann" in January 2011, as she considered her company's strong quarterly and year-end report, saying, "I think we are in a very healthy situation on many, many fronts."[7] However, as one group of analysts commented, "It's amazing to think that for an industry that has not experienced sourcing cost inflation in 30 years, most retailers expect to raise prices and report at least flat merchandise margins in FY2011 . . . beware the irrationally exuberant management teams that have suggested [gross profit margins] could rise . . . (e.g., Ann Taylor or Chico's FAS)."[8] Why might Krill be accused of heading up an "irrationally exuberant management team"?

Krill had been appointed president of Ann Taylor Stores Corporation (ANN) in late 2004, and she succeeded to president/CEO in late 2005 when J. Patrick Spainhour retired after eight years as CEO. At that time, there was concern among commentators and customers that the Ann Taylor look was getting "stodgy," and the question was how to "reestablish Ann Taylor as the preeminent brand for beautiful, elegant, and sophisticated occasion dressing."[9]

Krill's challenge was based on the ANN legacy as a women's specialty clothing retailer. Since 1954, Ann Taylor had been the wardrobe source for busy, socially upscale women, and the classic basic black dress and woman's power suit with pearls were Ann Taylor staples. The Ann Taylor client base consisted of fashion-conscious women from age 25 to age 55. The overall Ann Taylor concept was designed to appeal to professional women who had limited time to shop and who were attracted to Ann Taylor stores by their total wardrobing strategy, personalized client service, efficient store layouts, and continual flow of new merchandise.

ANN had two branded divisions focused on different segments of this customer base:

- Ann Taylor (AT), the company's original brand, provided sophisticated, versatile, and high-quality updated classics.
- Ann Taylor LOFT (LOFT) was a newer brand concept that appealed to women who had a more relaxed lifestyle and work environment and who appreciated the more casual LOFT style and compelling value. Certain clients of Ann Taylor and LOFT cross-shopped both brands.

ANN also carried both brands in factory outlet stores. The merchandise in each branded division's store was specifically designed to carry the brand label. The stores featured the previous years' top fashions and were located in outlet malls, where customers expected to find Ann Taylor

* This case was prepared by Professor Pauline Assenza of Berkeley College, Professor Alan B. Eisner of Pace University, and Professor Jerome C. Kuperman of Minnesota State University–Moorhead. This case is solely based on library research and was developed for class discussion of strategies rather than to illustrate either effective or ineffective handling of the situation. An earlier version of this case was published in *The CASE Journal* 5, no. 2 (Spring 2009). Copyright © 2009 The CASE Association. Current copyright © 2011 Pauline Assenza and Alan B. Eisner.

and other major-label bargains. Both brands were also increasingly retailed online, on their respective websites.

ANN had regularly appeared in the *Women's Wear Daily* Top 10 list of firms selling dresses, suits, and evening wear and the Top 20 list of publicly traded women's specialty retailers. These listings recognized the total company, that is, the combined results of both divisions. Since 2005, the LOFT division, with more square footage per store, had outsold the flagship Ann Taylor (AT) division stores.[9] Since its emergence as a distinctly competitive entity, LOFT had been such a success for the company that some analysts credited the division for "keeping the entire ANN corporation afloat."[10] However, missteps at LOFT in 2009 and 2010 had once again put AT on a stronger footing. Financial data from 2006 to 2010 show the performance of LOFT compared to AT. (See Exhibit 1.)

Krill acknowledged the ongoing challenge: "To be successful in meeting the changing needs of our clients, we must continually evolve and elevate our brands to ensure they remain compelling—from our product, to our marketing, to our in-store environment."[11] Although Krill believed that, overall, Ann Taylor still had its historic appeal; the question remained whether that appeal could be sustained indefinitely in the risky and uncertain specialty retail environment, where success depended on the "ability to predict accurately client fashion preferences."[12]

Ann Taylor Background

Ann Taylor was founded in 1954 as a wardrobe source for busy, socially upscale women. Starting out in New Haven, Connecticut, Ann Taylor founder Robert Liebeskind established a stand-alone clothing store. When Liebeskind's father, Richard Liebeskind Sr., a designer himself, as a good-luck gesture, gave his son exclusive rights to one of his best-selling dresses, "Ann Taylor," the company name was established. Ann Taylor was never a real person, but her persona lived on in the profile of the consumer.

Ann Taylor went public on the New York Stock Exchange in 1991 under the symbol ANN. In 1994 the company added a mail-order catalog business, a fragrance line, and free-standing shoe stores positioned to supplement the Ann Taylor (AT) stores. The mail-order catalog attempt ended in 1995, and the lower-priced apparel concept, Ann Taylor LOFT, was launched. LOFT was meant to appeal to a younger, more casual and cost-conscious, but still professional, consumer. CEO Sally Kasaks incorporated more

Exhibit 1 AT versus LOFT Financial Performance, FY 2006–2010

	Fiscal Year Ending				
	Jan. 29, 2011	**Jan. 30, 2010**	**Jan. 31, 2009**	**Feb. 2, 2008**	**Feb. 3, 2007**
Net Sales (in millions)					
Ann Taylor stores	$ 503.1	$ 462.0	$ 694.8	$ 866.6	$ 912.8
Ann Taylor e-commerce	92.6	61.4	70.2	NA	NA
Ann Taylor Factory Outlet	268.0	248.0	254.9	NA	NA
Total Ann Taylor brand	863.7	771.3	1,019.9	866.6	912.8
LOFT stores	943.3	947.8	1,098.2	1,174.4	1,146.5
LOFT e-commerce	96.9	60.2	61.8	NA	NA
LOFT Outlet	76.3	49.3	14.7	NA	NA
Total LOFT brand	1,116.5	1,057.2	1,174.7	1,174.4	1,146.5
Other*				355.6	283.7
Total company	$1,980.2	$1,828.5	$2,194.6	$2,396.5	$2,343.0
Comparable-Store Sales Percentage, increase or (decrease)					
Ann Taylor	18.7	(23.8)	(17.0)	(3.7)	3.1
LOFT	5.0	(11.9)	(10.2)	(5.4)	1.9
Total company	10.7%	(17.4%)	(13.4%)	(3.3%)	2.8%

* "Other" includes Ann Taylor Factory and Internet sales before these were substantial enough to be broken out separately.

(*continued*)

Exhibit 1   AT versus LOFT Financial Performance, FY 2006–2010 (*continued*)

	Fiscal Year Ending				
	Jan. 29, 2011	Jan. 30, 2010	Jan. 31, 2009	Feb. 2, 2008	Feb. 3, 2007
Net sales	100.0%	100.0%	100.0%	100.0%	100.0%
Cost of sales	44.2	45.6	51.9	47.8	46.3
Gross margin	55.8	54.4	48.1	52.2	53.7
Selling, general, and administrative expenses	49.4	52.9	47.8	44.4	44.1
Restructuring and asset/ goodwill impairment	0.3	2.8	17.2	1.4	—
Operating income (loss)	6.1	(1.3)	(16.9)	6.5	9.6
Interest income	0.0	0.1	0.1	0.3	0.7
Interest expense	0.1	0.2	0.1	0.1	0.1
Income before income taxes	6.0	(1.4)	(16.9)	6.7	10.2
Income tax provision	2.3	(0.4)	(1.7)	2.6	4.1
Net income	3.7%	(1.0%)	(15.2%)	4.1%	6.1%
Percentage change from prior period:					
Net sales	8.3%	(16.7%)	(8.4%)	2.3%	13.0%
Operating income	600.1	(93.6)	(339.2)	(30.6)	70.8
Net income	503.1	(94.5)	(443.3)	(32.0)	74.6

Source: ANN Inc. 10K filings.

casual clothing, petite sizes, and accessories in an attempt to create a one-stop shopping environment to "widen market appeal and fuel growth."[13] Following losses in fiscal 1996 that could be attributed to a fashion misstep—cropped T-shirts didn't fit in with the workplace attire—Kasaks left the company. New ANN CEO Patrick Spainhour, who had been chief financial officer at Donna Karan and also had previous experience at Gap, shelved the fragrance line and closed the shoe stores in 1997.

Originally, the LOFT stores were found only in outlet centers, but in 1998 the LOFT stores in the discount outlet malls were moved to a third concept, Ann Taylor Factory (Factory). The Factory carried clothes from the Ann Taylor (AT) line. This "outlet" concept offered customers direct access to the AT designer items "off the rack" without elaborate promotion and with prices regularly 25 to 30 percent less than at the high-end Ann Taylor stores. The LOFT concept was revamped, and stores were opened in more prestigious regional malls and shopping centers. By 1999 LOFT clothes were a distinct line of "more casual, yet business-tailored, fun, and feminine" attire, and they were about 30 percent less expensive than the merchandise at the flagship Ann Taylor division's stores.[14] At that time, the LOFT was under the direction of Kay Krill, who had been promoted to the position of executive vice president of the LOFT division.

Ann Taylor attempted a cosmetics line in 2000, which it discontinued in 2001. In 2000 the online store at *www. anntaylor.com* was launched, only to be cut back in late 2001 when projected cash-flow goals were not met. In early 2001 Spainhour restructured management reporting relationships, creating new president positions for both the AT and LOFT divisions, and Kay Krill was promoted from executive vice president to president of LOFT. In 2004 Krill was made president of the entire ANN corporation, bringing both Ann Taylor and LOFT under her control.

In February 2005 Kay Krill announced that LOFT had reached $1 billion in sales; and in June 2005 ANN completed a move to new corporate headquarters in Times Square Tower in New York City.[15] In the fall of 2005 chairman and CEO J. Patrick Spainhour retired and President Kay Krill was elevated to the CEO position. In a conference call following her promotion, Krill stated her goals as "improving profitability while enhancing both brands . . . restoring performance at the Ann Taylor division and restoring the momentum at LOFT."[16]

Krill felt that the outlook for fiscal year 2006 was cautiously positive, and she announced continued plans for expansion and related capital expenditures. The stock responded with new highs, moving to a peak of over $40 in late 2006. At that time, analysts were mainly supportive, citing "confidence in the retailer's strong management team, improving store products, and conservative inventory management."[17] ANN's stock price subsequently retreated in 2007 and 2008, along with the rest of the retailing sector.

Challenges in the macroeconomic climate had prompted Krill to announce a restructuring plan in 2008.[18] However, after a posted loss of $333.9 million in 2008 and the continuing economic uncertainty going into 2009, ANN

was reluctant to give any profit forecast for the coming quarters. At the end of 2009 net sales had reached the lowest point since 2005, and in 2010 had still not rebounded enough to surpass 2005 figures. (See Exhibit 2.) At the end of 2010, the fourth quarter results indicated sales had jumped 10 percent from 2009, and although gross margins fell to 51.7 percent from 52.5 percent a year earlier, earnings per share, excluding restructuring charges, had nearly quadrupled. (See Exhibits 3, 4, and 5.) This made the stockholders happy, but, as one analyst said, to really fire up shareholders, "you need to forecast *future* results that are higher than hoped."[19] CEO Krill did just that, stating that the company expected "fiscal 2011 total net sales of approximately $2.175 billion, reflecting a total Company comparable sales increase in the mid-single digits." In addition, signaling a more focused strategy moving forward, Krill announced a name change for the company going into 2011:

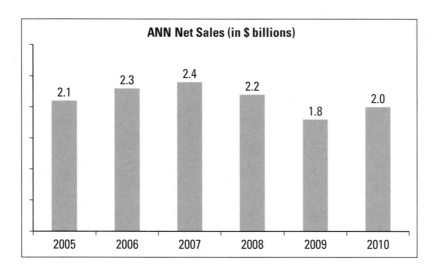

Exhibit 2 ANN Net Sales (in $ billions)

Exhibit 3 **Income Statements** (in thousands of dollars)

	Period Ending		
	Jan. 29, 2011	Jan. 30, 2010	Jan. 31, 2009
Total Revenue	1,980,195	1,828,523	2,194,559
Cost of Revenue	876,201	834,188	1,139,753
Gross Profit	1,103,994	994,335	1,054,806
Operating Expenses			
Selling, General, and Administrative	978,580	966,603	1,050,560
			(*continued*)

Exhibit 3 Income Statements (in thousands of dollars) (*continued*)

	Period Ending		
	Jan. 29, 2011	**Jan. 30, 2010**	**Jan. 31, 2009**
Nonrecurring	5,624	51,686	375,883
Operating Income or Loss	**119,790**	**(23,954)**	**(371,637)**
Income from Continuing Operations			
Total Other Income/Expenses Net	964	935	1,677
Earnings before Interest and Taxes	120,754	(23,019)	(369,960)
Interest Expense	1,632	3,091	1,462
Income before Tax	119,122	(26,110)	(371,422)
Income Tax Expense	45,725	(7,902)	(37,516)
Net Income	**73,397**	**(18,208)**	**(333,906)**

Source: ANN Inc. 10K filings.

Exhibit 4 Balance Sheets (in thousands of dollars)

	Period Ending		
	Jan. 29, 2011	**Jan. 30, 2010**	**Jan. 31, 2009**
Assets			
Current Assets:			
Cash and Cash Equivalents	226,644	204,491	112,320
Short-Term Investments	—	5,655	—
Net Receivables	72,277	79,995	74,773
Inventory	193,625	169,141	173,447
Other Current Assets	57,367	45,613	63,056
Total Current Assets	549,913	504,895	423,596
Property Plant and Equipment	332,489	365,934	469,687
Other Assets	12,523	6,656	12,628
Deferred Long-Term Asset Charges	31,895	24,656	54,528
Total Assets	**926,820**	**902,141**	**960,439**
Liabilities			
Current Liabilities:			
Accounts Payable	232,805	227,819	260,001

(*continued*)

Exhibit 4   **Balance Sheets** (in thousands of dollars) (*continued*)

	Period Ending		
	Jan. 29, 2011	**Jan. 30, 2010**	**Jan. 31, 2009**
Liabilities			
Short/Current Long-Term Debt	—	—	2,200
Other Current Liabilities	49,103	47,555	45,582
Total Current Liabilities	**281,908**	**275,374**	**305,583**
Long-Term Debt	—	—	3,400
Other Liabilities	22,997	14,652	18,832
Deferred Long-Term Liability Charges	198,470	194,929	219,512
Total Liabilities	**503,375**	**484,955**	**543,927**
Stockholders' Equity			
Common Stock	561	561	561
Retained Earnings	487,691	414,294	432,502
Treasury Stock	(863,569)	(771,297)	(800,701)
Capital Surplus	801,140	777,786	791,852
Other Stockholder Equity	(2,378)	(4,158)	(7,702)
Total Stockholder Equity	**423,445**	**417,186**	**416,512**
Net Tangible Assets	**423,445**	**417,186**	**416,512**

Source: ANN Inc. 10K filings.

Exhibit 5   Statement of Annual Cash Flows

	Period Ending		
	Jan. 29, 2011	**Jan. 30, 2010**	**Jan. 31, 2009**
Net Income	**73,397**	**(18,208)**	**(333,906)**
Operating Activities, Cash Flows Provided by or Used in			
Depreciation	95,523	104,351	122,222
Adjustments to Net Income	26,526	68,371	347,000
Changes in Accounts Receivables	5,130	(5,186)	2,863
Changes in Liabilities	(7,680)	(26,059)	370
Changes in Inventories	(25,919)	4,306	77,250
Changes in Other Operating Activities	(2,666)	6,128	(42,981)
Total Cash Flow From Operating Activities	**164,311**	**133,703**	**172,818**

(*continued*)

Exhibit 5   **Statement of Annual Cash Flows** (*continued*)

	Period Ending		
	Jan. 29, 2011	Jan. 30, 2010	Jan. 31, 2009
Investing Activities, Cash Flows Provided by or Used in			
Capital Expenditures	(61,213)	(38,573)	(110,342)
Investments	5,322	(376)	8,227
Other Cash Flows from Investing Activities	(1,331)	(617)	—
Total Cash Flows from Investing Activities	**(57,222)**	**(38,949)**	**(102,115)**
Financing Activities, Cash Flows Provided by or Used in			
Sale/Purchase of Stock	(97,094)	1,654	(96,873)
Net Borrowings	1,622	(4,557)	5,402
Other Cash Flows from Financing Activities	3,377	—	—
Total Cash Flows from Financing Activities	(84,936)	(2,583)	(92,408)
Change in Cash and Cash Equivalents	**22,153**	**92,171**	**(21,705)**

Source: ANN Inc. 10K filings.

I am pleased to announce today that, in order to better reflect the multi-channel focus we have on our business, we have decided to change our corporate name from Ann Taylor Stores Corporation to ANN INC. Today, our Company is far more than a traditional "store-based" retailer. We have two distinct brands—Ann Taylor and LOFT—each of which operates across three channels and enables us to reach our client whether she is making her purchases at our stores, online or at our factory outlet locations.[20]

The Apparel Retail Industry
Industry Sectors

Practically speaking, industry watchers tend to recognize three separate categories of clothing retailers. Industry publications such as the *Daily News Record* (DNR—reporting on men's fashion news and business strategies) and *Women's Wear Daily* (WWD—reporting on women's fashions and the apparel business) as well as industry associations such as the National Retail Federation (NRF) report data within the clothing sector, which is divided into three categories:

- *Discount mass merchandisers:* Chains such as Target, Walmart, TJX (TJ Maxx, Marshall's, A.J. Wright, Bob's Stores), and Costco.
- *Multitier department stores:* Those offering a large variety of goods, including clothing (e.g., Macy's and JCPenney), and the more luxury-goods-focused stores (e.g., Nordstrom and Neiman Marcus).

- *Specialty store chains:* Those catering to a certain type of customer or carrying a certain type of goods, for example, Abercrombie & Fitch for casual apparel.

More specifically in the case of specialty retail, many broadly recognized primary categories exist, such as women's, men's, and children's clothing stores (e.g., Victoria's Secret for women's undergarments,[21] Men's Wearhouse for men's suits, Abercrombie Kids for children ages 7 to 14[22]). Women's specialty stores are "establishments primarily engaged in retailing a specialized line of women's, juniors' and misses' clothing."[23]

Specialty Retailer Growth: Branding Challenges

Unlike department stores that sell many different types of products for many types of customers, specialty retailers focus on one type of product item and offer many varieties of that item. However, this single-product focus increases risk, as lost sales in one area cannot be recouped by a shift of interest to another, entirely different product area. Therefore, many specialty retailers constantly seek new market segments (i.e., niches) that they can serve. However, this strategy creates potential problems for branding.[24]

Gap Inc. is an example of a specialty retailer that had added several brand extensions to appeal to different customer segments. In addition to the original Gap line of casual clothing, the company offered the following: Old Navy with casual fashions at low prices, Banana

Republic for more high-end casual items, Athleta performance apparel and gear for active women, and Piperlime as an online shoe store. In 2005 Gap spent $40 million to open a chain for upscale women's clothing called Forth & Towne, which closed after only 18 months. The store was supposed to appeal to upscale women over 35—the baby-boomer or "misses" segment—but, instead, the designers seemed "too focused on reproducing youthful fashions with a more generous cut" instead of finding an "interesting, affordable way" for middle-aged women to "dress like themselves."[25]

Chico's FAS Inc. was another specialty retailer that tried brand expansions. Chico's focused on private-label, casual-to-dressy clothing for women age 35 and older, with relaxed, figure-flattering styles constructed out of easy-care fabrics. An outgrowth of a Mexican folk art boutique, Chico's was originally a stand-alone brand. Starting in late 2003, Chico's FAS decided to promote two new brands: White House/Black Market (WH/BM) and Soma by Chico's (Soma). Chico's WH/BM brand was based on the acquisition of an existing store chain, and it focused on women age 25 and older, offering fashion and merchandise in black-and-white and related shades. Soma was a newly developed brand offering intimate apparel, sleepwear, and active wear. Each brand had its own store-front, mainly in shopping malls, and was augmented by both mail-order catalog and Internet sales. The idea was that the loyal Chico's customer would be drawn to shop at these other concept stores, expecting the same level of quality, service, and targeted offerings that had pleased her in the past.

Although Chico's had been a solid performer during the decade, surpassing most other women's clothing retailers in sales growth, a downturn in 2006 caused Chico's shares to fall more than 50 percent when the company reported sales and earnings below analysts' expectations. Chico's had seen increasing competition for its baby-boomer customers, and it said it had lost momentum, partly because of "fashion missteps" and lack of sufficiently new product designs. The company's response was to create brand presidents for the three divisions to hopefully create more "excitement and differentiation."[26]

In an attempt to better manage the proliferation of brands, many firms, similar to Chico's, created an organizational structure in which brands had their own dedicated managers, with titles such as executive vice president (EVP)/general merchandise manager, chief merchandising officer, or outright "brand president."[27] Because each brand was supposedly unique, companies felt the person responsible for a brand's creative vision should be unique as well.

An alternative to brand extension was the divesti-ture of brands. In 1988 Limited Brands[28] acquired Aber-crombie and Fitch (A&F) and rebuilt A&F to represent the "preppy" lifestyle of teenagers and college students ages 18 to 22. In 1996 Limited Brands spun A&F off as a separate public company. Limited Brands continued divesting brands: teenage clothing and accessories brand The Limited TOO in 1999, plus-size women's clothing brand Lane Bryant in 2001, professional women's clothing brand Lerner New York in 2002, and in 2007 the casual women's clothing brands Express and The Limited. Paring down in order to focus mostly on its key brands Victoria's Secret and Bath & Body Works, the corporation made it clear that it was still not done reconfiguring itself.[29]

Women's Specialty Retail: Competitors and the "Misses" Segment

The National Retail Federation, a trade group based in Washington, D.C., reported that the retail niches showing the greatest growth were department stores, stores catering to the teenage children of baby boomers, and apparel chains aimed at women over 35.[30] The four major women's specialty retailers that were trying to target older upscale shoppers were Ann Taylor, Chico's FAS, Coldwater Creek, and Talbots. Ann Taylor was the only one of these with a significant brand extension for the younger professional, but all four were pursuing a shopping environment and merchandise that were clearly focused on women over 35. (See Exhibit 6.)

This group of "older" women was part of the baby-boomer demographic, born between 1946 and 1964, and the purchasing power of these women had not gone unnoticed.[31] Historically, this "misses" market had been challenging to define, and therefore the category had been slow to innovate. Accounting for nearly $45.9 billion of the total $108.7 billion women's clothing purchases in 2009, these women were diverse, ranging from "traditional types who prefer flat shoes and ankle-length skirts to women who resemble characters from *Desperate Housewives*."[32]

To respond to this diversity in the marketplace, women's specialty retailer Talbots Inc. had acquired catalog and mail-order company J.Jill Group in 2006. J.Jill was a women's clothing specialty retailer offering casual fashion through multichannel mail-order, Internet, and in-store venues. J.Jill targeted women ages 35 to 55, while Talbots focused on the 45 to 65 age group. Although the acquisition had supposedly positioned Talbots as a "leading apparel retailer for the highly coveted age 35+ female population,"[33] Talbots subsequently decided to sell off this division in 2009, in the wake of retailing's "abysmal holiday season." Analysts were not surprised, because Talbots had never made an acquisition before and had encountered problems integrating the two businesses.[34] Going into 2011, Talbots was struggling with merchandise that was perceived as too "mature," with stores that looked old-fashioned, and with vacancies in key upper management positions. Overall sales at Talbots had dropped in 2010 by 1.6 percent, but online and direct (catalog) sales had increased 9.8 percent and 6.7 percent, respectively, and CEO Trudy Sullivan was expecting that the web channel would spark growth.[35]

Exhibit 6   Selected Retail Performers: Descriptions

Company Ticker Symbol	Number of Stores	Locations Served	Merchandise Market Served	Comments
Ann Taylor*ANN*	907	46 states plus Puerto Rico	Specialty women's— private-label "total wardrobing strategy" to achieve the "Ann Taylor look" in suits, separates, footwear, and accessories	Brands are Ann Taylor for updated professional classics; LOFT for lower-priced, more casual wear; and Ann Taylor Factory & LOFT Outlet for outlet-priced items.
Talbots *TLB*	580	46 states plus Canada and the UK	Specialty—women's apparel, shoes, and accessories via store, catalog, and Internet	Brands are Talbots and Modern Classics for women. Brands target high-income, college-educated professionals over 35 years old.
Chico's FAS*CHS*	1,080	48 states plus U.S. Virgin Islands and Puerto Rico	Specialty women's— privately branded clothing, intimate garments, and gifts for fashion-conscious women with moderate to high income	Brands are Chico's for women over 35, White House/Black Market for women over 25, and Soma intimates.
Coldwater Creek Inc.*CWTR*	356	48 states	Specialty women's— apparel, accessories, jewelry, and gifts via store, catalog, Internet, and day-spa locations	Offers Coldwater Creek brand of clothing and jewelry, cosmetics, and personal care products to women over 35 with income in excess of $75,000; socially responsible.

Source: Mergent Online; company reports.

Coldwater Creek, with its large jewelry, accessory, and gift assortment in addition to apparel, targeted women over 35 with incomes in excess of $75,000 by appealing with a Northwest/Southwest lifestyle approach that included a group of spa locations. Coldwater's customer was not considered "trendy" by any means: "She's never going to be a fashion leader . . . but she wants to look modern."[36] Coldwater Creek had created a common brand identity for its three distribution channels: catalog, Internet, and in-store shopping, but it too was having trouble finding the right mix of merchandise and presenting items properly in the stores, and also suffering from key gaps in upper management. Since 2009 Coldwater Creek had posted losses in every quarter except one, and even though its online and

direct sales channels had seen more traffic than its competitors Talbots, Ann Taylor, and Chico's, these venues had seen a two-digit percentage reduction in volume in 2010.[37]

Chico's FAS was one of the first to introduce the concept of apparel designed for the lifestyle of dynamic mature women who were at the higher-age end of the boomer demographic.[38] Chico's had always been aware of the need to focus its branding on the older women's segment. As a result of this focus, Chico's had ended the difficult 2008 year with "strong brand equity," one of the few specialty retailers with "staying power."[39] However, by 2010 Chico's was having trouble as well, perhaps going "too young" with the fashion selection.[40] In 2011, of the four retailers focused on the "mature women" segment, Chico's was the only one focused on inventory, supply-chain management, and moving out of a reliance on China's manufacturing power. Analysts therefore saw Chico's as having good prospects for maintaining positive margins going forward. In fact, based on 2010 results, Chico's and Ann Taylor were both among the top five in the Apparel Retail industry as ranked by gross margin.[41] (See Exhibit 7.)

In August 2007 Kay Krill announced that ANN would be creating a new chain of stores, expected to launch sometime in 2008 or 2009, targeting this "older-women" segment. Some analysts wondered about this move into an overlooked but risky market that had "tripped up several competitors." They pointed out that although ANN's clothes were expected to be more fashionable, the company still faced stiff competition, made even tougher given the uneven performance of AT and LOFT.[42] In 2008, as a result of the overall economic conditions, Krill announced that this new concept offering would have to be delayed at least until 2009,[43] and by 2010 there was no more mention of this initiative. Instead, Krill announced that the "boomer" terminology was outdated: "We never called ourselves 'misses.' We're timeless, modern and ageless, and we had to adjust and become more relevant to what modern consumers want today. It's been an evolution. I feel like we are on the right track."[44]

Instead of a new store concept, Krill had moved to further differentiate LOFT and Ann Taylor by creating outlet (discount) stores and online channels for both brands. The online venue allowed ANN to develop marketing segments for petites, for special occasion dressing, for maternity, and for fragrances—all concepts previously considered, launched, and ultimately dropped from the in-store channel. In 2010 e-commerce accounted for about 12 percent of ANN's total quarterly sales, while the outlet channel contributed 17 percent. Therefore, it was no wonder Krill stated, "One of our key priorities in 2011 is to further capitalize on the enormous potential of the e-commerce channel."[45] ANN also planned to accelerate its outlet store growth plans, opening up to 44 new factory stores, serving either the LOFT or AT divisions, in the first half of 2011. These stores offered merchandise for 25 to 30 percent less than the cost at the AT or LOFT regular stores. In addition, the LOFT stores were slated for an overhaul, adding warmth and creating a less "lofty" look, and the Ann Taylor stores were being downsized to a more productive, smaller store format.[46]

Exhibit 7   Selected Retail Performers: Financial Results

Company Name*	Total Revenue (millions)	Net Income (millions)	Inventory Turnover	Revenue per Employee($)
Abercrombie & Fitch	2,929	254.00	3.06	36,708
Ann Taylor Stores Corp.	1,828	−23.95	4.87	97,529
Charming Shoppes Inc.	2,064	−77.96	3.89	76,667
Chico's FAS Inc.	1,713	69.65	5.56	106,041
Coldwater Creek Inc.	1,038	−56.13	4.74	109,268
Limited Brands Inc.	8,632	448.00	4.74	93,982
Talbots Inc.	1,235	−29.41	4.70	136,157

	ROI % (Operating)	Gross Margin (%)	Operating Margin (%)	Net Profit Margin (TTM) (%)
Abercrombie & Fitch	6.15	64.32	4.03	0.01
Ann Taylor Stores Corp.	−5.76	54.38	−1.31	−1.00
Charming Shoppes Inc.	−12.36	49.58	−4.24	−3.78
Chico's FAS Inc.	11.51	56.02	6.31	4.07
Coldwater Creek Inc.	−16.69	32.19	−4.35	−5.40
Limited Brands Inc.	17.8	35.08	9.95	5.19
Talbots Inc.	−2.91	33.53	−0.70	−2.38

* All results are stated in U.S. dollars, using the filings as of January 2010.

Source: Mergent Online.

ANN Operational Information

At the end of fiscal year 2010, ANN had 896 stores in 46 states, the District of Columbia, and Puerto Rico, with flagship locations in New York and Chicago. (See Exhibit 8A and 8B.) The company had also had an online presence since 2000, transacting sales at *www.anntaylor.com* and *www.anntaylorLOFT.com*. This "very profitable" Internet channel was considered "a meaningful and effective marketing vehicle for both brands," representing a 119 percent increase in AT and LOFT sales for 2010, and was a way for ANN to reach out to the international market.[47]

Substantially all merchandise offered in ANN's stores was exclusively developed for the company by its in-house product design and development teams. ANN sourced

Exhibit 8A Stores' Operational Data

	FY2010	FY2009	FY2008	FY2007
Employees, total	19,400	18,800	18,400	18,400
Inventory turns*	4.8	4.9	5.4	4.7
Net sales per sq ft	$337	$311	$372	$435
Net sales (revenue) per employee	$102,072	$97,529	$119,597	$130,603
Average sq ft per store:				
Ann Taylor	5,500	5,300	5,300	5,300
LOFT	5,800	5,900	5,900	5,700
Ann Taylor Factory	7,300	7,300	7,300	6,700
LOFT Outlet	6,500	6,800		

* Inventory turns can be calculated differently, depending on whether yearly average or year-end inventory values are used.

Source: ANN Inc. 10K filings; Mergent Online.

Exhibit 8B Specific Store Detail (in number of stores)

	Total Open at Beginning of Fiscal Year	Opened during Fiscal Year*				Closed during Fiscal Year	Open at End of Fiscal Year*					Expanded during Fiscal Year
		ATS	ATL	ATF	LOS		ATS	ATL	ATF	LOS	Total	
2003	584	8	61	1		6	354	268	26		648	8
2004	648	10	77	8		5	359	343	36		738	6
2005	738	9	73	15		11	357	416	51		824	12
2006	824	11	52	7		25	348	464	57		869	16
2007	869	14	52	11		17	349	512	68		929	14
2008	929	4	25	23	14	60	320	510	91	14	935	8
2009	935	—	9	1	4	32	291	506	92	18	907	1
2010	907	—	10	0	14	34	266	502	92	36	896	1

* ATS = Ann Taylor; ATL = Ann Taylor LOFT; ATF = Ann Taylor Factory; LOS = LOFT Outlet Stores.

Source: ANN Inc. company reports, available at *investor.anntaylor.com*.

merchandise from approximately 145 manufacturers and vendors, none of whom accounted for more than 10 percent of the company's merchandise purchases in fiscal 2010. Merchandise was manufactured in over 19 countries, including China (42 percent of purchases, 50 percent of total merchandise cost), the Philippines, Indonesia, India, and Vietnam.

ANN's planning departments analyzed each store's size, location, demographics, sales, and inventory history to determine the quantity of merchandise to be purchased for, and then allocated to, the stores. The company used a centralized distribution system with a single warehouse in Louisville, Kentucky. At the store level, merchandise was typically sold at its original marked price for several weeks. After that, markdowns were used if inventory did not sell. Store planners recognized that the lack of inventory turnover could have been the result of poor merchandise design, seasonal adaptations, changes in client preference, or incorrectly set original prices. Recent challenges had included planning for inventory fluctuations caused by online channel demand.

ANN used a real-estate expansion program designed to reach new clients either by opening new stores, relocating stores, or expanding the size of existing stores. Store locations were determined on the basis of various factors, including:

- Geographic location.
- Demographic studies.
- Anchor tenants in a mall location.
- Other specialty stores in a mall or in the vicinity of a village location.
- The proximity to professional offices in a downtown or village location.

Two potential concerns were emerging for ANN as a result of its recent investments in store expansion and remodeling. First, the increasing sales volume threatened to put stress on the company's internal distribution system. The distribution center in Louisville had been investing in incremental improvements through automation and software integration. However, the distribution center had sufficient capacity to supply only 1,050 stores. After that, ANN's logistical experts cautioned that the building footprint would have to be expanded.[48] A second concern was whether projected earnings, given economic uncertainty, would actually be able to cover the projected long-term lease obligations.[49]

Ann Taylor's Historic Issues: Brand Identity & Management Turnover

As with other specialty retailers, ANN had struggled with erratic performance in one division or the other and had suffered from excessive turnover in top management ranks. When ANN went public in 1991, the Ann Taylor brand, with its historically loyal following, was a candidate for brand extension. At one point in its history, the company had five separate store concepts: Ann Taylor (AT), Ann Taylor's Studio Shoes, Ann Taylor LOFT, Ann Taylor Petites (clothing for women 5 feet 4 inches and under), and Ann Taylor Factory. In addition, ANN's management had experimented with a makeup line and children's clothes. By 2005, the company had closed the shoe stores, reduced the accessories inventory that stores carried, and eliminated the makeup line.

Since 1999 analysts had warned that ANN needed to be wary of cannibalization within the brands. The analysts speculated that customers might turn away from AT in order to buy at LOFT. ANN had always tried to respond to the customer with "wardrobing," a philosophy of "outfitting from head to toe," combining relaxed everyday wear with more dressy pieces.[50] Since LOFT sold more relaxed but still tailored items at a lower price than AT, some of AT's customers might shop at LOFT for things that they previously would have bought at AT.

Therefore, in 2005 Krill asked her staff to spend time with ANN customers and develop "brand books," or profiles, of the typical Ann Taylor (AT) and LOFT clients.[51] The "Ann" (AT) marketing profile was of a married 36-year-old working mother with two children and a household income of $150,000. She would lead a busy, sophisticated life. When giving a presentation to a client, she'd wear a formal suit with a blouse, not a camisole, underneath, and her idea of dressing down at work might be a velvet jacket with jeans.

In contrast, the typical LOFT client was in her 30s and married, with children, worked in a laid-back, less corporate environment, and had a household income between $75,000 and $100,000. She would call her style "casual chic" and might wear pants and a floral top with ruffled sleeves to work, while on the weekend she would wear a printed shoulder-baring halter top with cropped jeans.

Also in 2005, Krill tried to reconfigure ANN's top management, creating three positions that reported directly to her—COO, executive vice president (EVP) of planning and allocation, and EVP/chief marketing officer. These three additional positions provided specific expertise while still allowing Krill to "lead both divisions [AT and LOFT] in a more hands-on-way." Krill then focused on merchandising and marketing, especially brand differentiation.[52] AT and LOFT continued to have separate EVPs for merchandising and design and separate senior vice presidents for divisional marketing, design, sourcing, and store direction.

In 2006 Krill lost her recently hired COO, Laura Weil, who left abruptly after only a few months on the job. Weil's many responsibilities at ANN had included merchandise planning; information systems; all supply chain operations, including sourcing, logistics, and distribution; real estate; construction and facilities; and purchasing; as well as finance, accounting, and investor relations.[53] Krill decided not to replace Weil and eliminated the position on the organizational chart. Krill assumed leadership of LOFT again, playing a dual role while searching for a new divisional president.

Krill commented, "I believe that building a winning team is critical to fully realizing our company's full potential."[54] However, it appeared that creating that "winning team" was taking longer than anticipated. One source wondered about the pressure on Krill, especially because she didn't have a strong operating partner to help with merchandising and other creative decisions.[55]

Even though Krill had made differentiation between AT and LOFT a top priority, analysts continued to challenge Krill's efforts, noting that it had been hard to get both divisions moving forward simultaneously. As one analyst said, "It just seems like it's a struggle to get both of these divisions firing on all cylinders at the same time."[56] Krill responded to the comment that consistency had been a problem: "The notion that Ann Taylor got soft because I was supporting the LOFT team is really a completely inaccurate comment. As CEO of the company I have to spend my time on many things, and if one of our businesses is softening in any way I will focus extra time on it."[57]

In August 2007 long-time CFO James Smith and Chief Marketing Officer Elaine Boltz both resigned, and then in July 2008 long-time Chief Supply Chain Officer Anthony Romano also left to "pursue other interests."[58] Although she had hired a new CFO and chief marketing officer in late 2007, these departures left Krill once again without a lot of depth at the top.[59] However, Krill had had experience with management turnover, as she had dealt with seven resignations, seven new hires, and two promotions in her upper-management team over two years' time. As of the end of 2008, she had finally filled the AT and LOFT divisional president positions, and these individuals had remained in place, at least into 2011.

Future Initiatives

By 2011, Krill appeared to have conquered both the branding and the management turnover issues. Acknowledging that differentiating LOFT from Ann Taylor had always been a challenge, she believed that "we have evolved both brands to be highly differentiated and distinct. . . . Absolutely, the number-one challenge is to sustain the momentum of both brands and all channels."[60] Outlining ANN's strategic priorities for 2011, Krill commented, "We are focused on continuing to deliver high-quality fashion at tremendous value for our client." The 2011 priorities included the following:

- Increasing traffic to the Ann Taylor brand and further enhancing the brand experience.
- Improving the LOFT brand stores channel and continuing to capitalize on the potential of the online and outlet channels.

- Investing in the continued growth of the e-commerce channel, facilitating international and mobile commerce and personalizing the website; improving multichannel inventory capabilities.
- Renovating stores at both Ann Taylor and LOFT to increase productivity.
- Carefully managing product costs throughout the supply chain.
- Implementing technology enhancements for inventory and mark-down management and international shipping for e-commerce.
- Maintaining a strong balance sheet and free cash flow to enhance shareholder value.

Krill felt the transition to a "world-class multi-channel retailer" would allow Ann Inc. to serve "two distinct segments of the market with two differentiated brands" across three channels: "We want to reach our clients seamlessly wherever they shop, whether it is in our stores, online or in factory-outlet centers."[61] Krill was excited about the future. Did she have reason to be, or was she "irrationally exuberant"?

Endnotes

1. Covert, J. 2011. So richly rewarding. *New York Post,* March 12. *www.nypost.com/p/news/business/so_richly_ rewarding_h2gKcSqaRqVp91URBIeEdK.*

2. Hill, C. 2008. Retailers such as Ann Taylor, Sears and Talbots face clogins, bankruptcies, takeovers in 2009. *New York Daily News,* December 29. *www.nydailynews. com/money/2008/12/29/2008-12-29_retailers_such_as_ ann_taylor_sears_and_t.html.*

3. Maestri, N. 2008. Retailers try to thrive in tumultuous climate. *Reuters.com,* June 16. *www.reuters.com/article/ email/idUKN1332245620080616.*

4. Bhattacharjee, N. 2011. Ann drops Taylor tag to pursue multichannel plans. *Reuters,* March 11. *www.reuters.com/article/2011/03/11/us-anntaylor- idUSTRE72A2K620110311.*

5. Dickler, J. 2011. Consumers: We want Gucci or Target. Forget the Gap. Shoppers are once again showing a preference for high-end brands. *CNN Money,* March 9. *money.cnn.com/2011/03/09/pf/consumers_prefer_luxury/.*

6. The Retail Geeks. 2011. No chance for New York & Company's operating margin to peak again. *SeekingAlpha.com,* March 31. *seekingalpha.com/ article/261157-no-chance-for-new-york-company-s- operating-margin-to-peak-again.*

7. Moin, D. 2011. Growing Ann Taylor gets a new moniker. *WWD,* March 14: 8.

8. The Retail Geeks. 2011. The big short: A view on retail in 2011. *SeekingAlpha.com,* March 25. *seekingalpha.com/ article/260245-the-big-short-a-view-on-retail-in-2011.*

9. Warner, B., director, corporate communications, Ann Taylor Stores Corporation. 2007. ANN representatives noted that there was no apparent cause-and-effect relationship between AT sales decline and the growth of LOFT. Personal communication, July.

10. Tucker, R. 2004. LOFT continues to pace Ann Taylor. *Women's Wear Daily,* August 12: 12.

11. Ann Taylor Stores Corporation. 2007. Letter to shareholders. *Ann Taylor Stores Corporation 2007 Annual Report. investor.anntaylor.com/phoenix.zhtml?c=78167&p=irol-reportsAnnual.*

12. Ann Taylor Stores Corporation. 2008. Q1 2008 Ann Taylor Stores earnings conference call. *SeekingAlpha.com,* May 22. *seekingalpha.com/article/78473-ann-taylor-stores-corp-q1-2008-earnings-call-transcript.*

13. Wilson, M. 1995. Reinventing Ann Taylor. *Chain Store Age Executive with Shopping Center Age,* January: 26.

14. Summers, M. 1999. New Outfit. *Forbes,* December 27: 88.

15. Ann Taylor Stores Corporation. 2005. Ann Taylor announces LOFT division reaches $1 billion in sales. *Investor.AnnTaylor.com,* February 12. *investor.anntaylor.com/news/20060213-187405.cfm?t=n.*

16. Krill, K. 2005. As quoted in "Q3 2005 Ann Taylor Stores earnings conference call."

17. Associated Press. 2006. Ann Taylor Stores jumps on strong earnings. *MoneyCentral.MSN.com,* March 10. *news.moneycentral.msn.com/ticker/article.asp?Feed=AP&Date=20060310&ID=5570346&Symbol=US:ANN.*

18. Ann Taylor Stores Corporation. 2007. Letter to shareholders.

19. Koppenheffer, M. 2011. Ann Taylor shares popped: What you need to know. March 11. *www.fool.com/investing/general/2011/03/11/ann-taylor-shares-popped-what-you-need-to-know.aspx.*

20. Ann Taylor Stores Corporation. 2011. Ann Taylor reports substantially higher sales and earnings for fourth quarter and fiscal 2010. *Investor.AnnTaylor.com,* March 11. *investor.anntaylor.com/phoenix.zhtml?c=78167&p=irol-newsArticle&ID=1538446.*

21. Victoria's Secret is a division of Limited Brands, which also operates Pink (a subbrand of Victoria's Secret focused on sleepwear and intimate apparel for high school and college students), Bath & Body Works, C.O. Bigelow (personal beauty, body, and hair products), The White Barn Candle Co. (candles and home fragrances), Henri Bendel (high-fashion women's clothing), and La Senza (lingerie sold in Canada and worldwide).

22. Abercrombie & Fitch, as of 2011, had three brand divisions in addition to the flagship Abercrombie & Fitch stores: abercrombie (the brand name is purposely lowercase) for kids ages 7 to 14; Hollister Co. for southern California surf-lifestyle teens; and Gilly Hicks: Sydney, launched in 2008, specializing in women's intimate apparel. RUEHL No. 925, launched in 2004 with more sophisticated apparel for ages 22 to 35, closed on January 31, 2010.

23. *www.census.gov/svsd/www/artsnaics.html.*

24. According to the American Marketing Association (AMA), a brand is a "'name, term, sign, symbol or design, or a combination of them intended to identify the goods and services of one seller or group of sellers and to differentiate them from those of other sellers.' . . . Branding is not about getting your target market to choose you over the competition, but it is about getting your prospects to see you as the only one that provides a solution to their problem." A good brand will communicate this message clearly and with credibility, motivating the buyer by eliciting some emotion that inspires future loyalty. From *marketing.about.com/cs/brandmktg/a/whatisbranding.htm.*

25. Turner, J. 2007. Go forth and go out of business. *Slate,* February 26. *www.slate.com/id/2160668.*

26. Lee, G. 2007. Chico's outlines plan to improve on results. *Women's Wear Daily,* March 8: 5.

27. The responsibilities of these positions include "creative vision" for the brand: marketing materials, store design, and overall merchandising (developing product, ensuring production efficiency, monitoring store inventory turnover, and adjusting price points as needed).

28. See endnote 21.

29. *Columbus Business First.* 2007. Limited Brands cutting 530 jobs. June 22. *columbus.bizjournals.com/columbus/stories/2007/06/18/daily26.html.*

30. Jones, S. M. 2007. Sweetest spots in retail. *Knight Ridder Tribune Business News,* July 31: 1.

31. See, for instance, the website *www.aginghipsters.com,* a "source for trends, research, comment and discussion" about this group.

32. Agins, T. 2007. The boomer balancing act: Retailers say new looks for middle-age women are both youthful and mature. *Wall Street Journal* (Eastern edition), November 3: W3; and Moin, D. 2010. Scoring some hits: Misses' market sees marked turnaround. *WWD,* March 31: 1.

33. Talbots Inc. 2006. Talbots completes the acquisition of the J.Jill Group. *Business Wire,* May 3. *phx.corporate-ir.net/phoenix.zhtml?c=65681&p=irol-newsArticle&ID=851481.*

34. Abelson, J. 2008. Talbots is seeking a buyer for J.Jill. *Boston Globe,* November 7. *www.boston.com/business/articles/2008/11/07/talbots_is_seeking_a_buyer_for_j_jill.*

35. Talley, K. 2011. Talbots swings to 4Q loss; accelerates store plan. *Wall Street Journal Online,* March 24. *online.wsj.com/article/BT-CO-20110324-709615.html;* Brohan, M. 2011. Talbots' annual web sales grow but not in Q4. *InternetRetailer.com,* March 25. *www.internetretailer.com/2011/03/25/talbots-annual-web-sales-grow-not-q4;* and Demery, P. 2010. Talbots eyes the web channel for growth. *InternetRetailer.com,* October 6. *www.internetretailer.com/2010/10/06/talbots-eyes-web-channel-growth.*

36. Edelson, S. 2007. Coldwater Creek brings natural vibe to Manhattan. *Women's Wear Daily,* August 13: 4.

37. Reuters. 2011. Coldwater Creek posts weak Q4 results, shares drop. *Reuters.com,* March 9. *www.reuters.com/article/2011/03/09/coldwatercreek-idUSL3E7E92SZ20110309;* Benzinga.com. 2011. Piper Jaffray comments on Coldwater Creek following Analyst Day. March 30. *www.benzinga.com/analyst-ratings/analyst-color/11/03/962766/piper-jaffray-comments-on-coldwater-creek-following-analy#ixzz1IE6akb3p;* and *Wall Street Journal Online.* 2011. Coldwater Creek 4Q loss widens more than expected on sharp sales drop. March 9. *online.wsj.com/article/BT-CO-20110309-714200.html.* See also The Top Internet Retailer 500, which ranks

business-to-consumer retailers in the United States and Canada based on online sales, including retail chains, catalogers, web-only merchants, brand manufacturers, and digital content sellers, at *www.internetretailer.com/top500/list/.*

38. Some marketers believe that the boomers are a bifurcated demographic: Although the boomer market encompasses those born between 1946 and 1964, boomers born between 1946 and 1954 have slightly different life experiences than those born between 1955 and 1964.

39. *Wall Street Transcript Online.* 2009. Investor interest in specialty apparel companies examined in Wall Street transcript specialty retail report. March 25. *finance.yahoo.com/news/Investor-Interest-in-twst-14741666.html.*

40. Steigrad, A. 2009. Misses' customers proving a tough target to hit. *WWD,* April 13: 12.

41. Chico's FAS Inc. 2011. Chico's Q4 2010 earnings call transcript. February 23. *www.morningstar.com/earnings/22554464-chico-s-fas-inc-chs-q4-2010.aspx;* Chokkayelu, A. 2010. How cheap is Coldwater Creek's stock by the numbers? *Motley Fool,* December 6. *www.fool.com/investing/small-cap/2010/12/06/how-cheap-is-coldwater-creeks-stock-by-the-numbers.aspx;* Smith, A. 2011. Shares of JOS A Bank Clothiers rank the highest in terms of gross margin in the apparel retail industry. *Mysmartrend.com,* March 13. *http://www.mysmartrend.com/news-briefs/news-watch/shares-jos-bank-clothiers-rank-highest-terms-gross-margin-apparel-retail-ind-2*

42. Kingsbury, K., & Moore, A. 2007. Ann Taylor tries for a better fit.*Wall Street Journal* (Eastern edition), August 25: B6.

43. Barbaro, M. 2007. Ann Taylor said to plan boomer unit. *New York Times,* August 13: C3.

44. Moin. 2010. Scoring some hits.

45. Bharracharjee, N. 2011. Ann drops Taylor tag to pursue multichannel plans. *Reuters.com,* March 11. *www.reuters.com/article/2011/03/11/us-anntaylor-idUSTRE72A2K620110311:* "Online sales have been a strong growth driver for most retailers. Maintaining and running an online store needs less overhead costs and lets retailers make more margins on sales."

46. Ann Taylor Stores Corporation. 2011. Ann Taylor reports substantially higher sales and earnings for fourth quarter and fiscal 2010. *Investor.AnnTaylor.*com, March 11. *investor.anntaylor.com/phoenix.zhtml?c=78167&p=irol-newsArticle&ID=1538446.*

47. Information in this section comes from Ann Taylor Stores Corporation 10K filing as of FY2010.

48. *Modern Material Handling* (warehousing management edition). 2006. Ann Taylor: Upgrade with style. March: 38.

49. Jones, S. D. 2006. Moving the market—tracking the numbers/outside audit. *Wall Street Journal* (Eastern edition), July 17: C3.

50. Kennedy, K. 2000. This is not your momma's clothing store—not by a longshot. *Apparel Industry Magazine* (Altanta), December: 22–25.

51. Merrick, A. 2006. Boss talk: Asking "What would Ann do?" In turning around Ann Taylor, CEO Kay Krill got to know her customers, "Ann" and "Loft." *Wall Street Journal* (Eastern edition), September 15: B1.

52. Moin, D. 2005. Ann Taylor Stores taps two to fill out executive ranks. *Women's Wear Daily,* March 3.

53. Moin, D. 2006. Laura Weil exits Ann Taylor. *Women's Wear Daily,* May 5: 2.

54. Ann Taylor Stores Corporation. 2006. Ann Taylor Stores 2005 Annual Report. *investor.anntaylor.com/phoenix.zhtml?c=78167&p=irol-reportsAnnual.*

55. Moin, D. 2006. Rebound at Ann Taylor: CEO Kay Krill fashions retailer's new career. *Women's Wear Daily,* June 26: 1.

56. Ann Taylor Stores Corporation. 2008. Q4 2007 Ann Taylor Stores earnings conference call. *SeekingAlpha.com,* March 14. *seekingalpha.com/article/68606-ann-taylor-stores-corporation-q4-2007-earnings-call-transcript?page=8.*

57. Ann Taylor Stores Corporation. 2008. Q1 2008 Ann Taylor Stores earnings conference call.

58. Ann Taylor Stores Corporation. 2008. Ann Taylor announces executive management changes. *Investor.AnnTaylor.com,* July 15. *investor.anntaylor.com/phoenix.zhtml?c=78167&p=irol-newsArticle&ID=1174968.*

59. Poggi, J. 2007. Specialty retailers see high exec turnover. *Women's Wear Daily,* August 20: 2–2.

60. Moin. 2011. Growing Ann Taylor gets a new moniker.

61. Ann Taylor Stores Corporation. 2011. AnnTaylor Stores' CEO discusses Q4 2010 results—earnings call transcript. *SeekingAlpha.com,* March 11. *seekingalpha.com/article/257806-anntaylor-stores-ceo-discusses-q4-2010-results-earnings-call-transcript?source=thestreet.*

Case 30 Jamba Juice*

In early 2011, Jamba Juice, already known for its healthy fruit smoothies, introduced its first ever vegetable smoothie: three flavors, each containing three full servings of fruits and vegetables in a 16-ounce cup, all under 250 calories. How would you like to enjoy a Berry Topper smoothie with organic granola for breakfast, and a Berry UpBEET drink blending strawberries and blueberries with the juices from carrots, beets, broccoli, and lettuce for lunch to get your daily recommended servings of fruits and vegetables? Or how about a Coldbuster smoothie packed with antioxidants when you get the sniffles, a Protein Berry Workout smoothie when you get back from the gym, and a Peanut Butter Moo'd chocolaty treat when your sweet tooth starts to ache? Add to that a Whirl'n frozen yogurt, a Grab-and-Go salad or flat-bread sandwich, an Ideal Meal of yogurt and fruit or hot oatmeal, with Hot Blends, made-to-order organic coffee, brewed by the cup, and Jamba Juice had something to satisfy your every taste and nutritional desire.

The Jamba Juice Company had gradually expanded its product line since 1994 to offer Jamba products that pleased a broader palate. In addition, Jamba had been pursuing an aggressive expansion program, evolving from a made-to-order smoothie company into a healthy, active lifestyle company, but was it biting off more than it could chew? After all, the new menu items put Jamba Juice in play against the likes of McDonald's and Starbucks. In light of four straight years of net financial losses, CEO James White had his work cut out for him.

Jamba Inc.'s results reported in March of 2011 had not impressed the analysts. Bottom line results had missed expectations for all four quarters of 2010. However, one analyst noted that the investment in Jamba's expanded product line might translate into larger profits later on.[1] This expansion might please the analysts, but employees had been troubled, believing all these new initiatives coming at the same time made it "hard to focus on a moving target," and possibly confused the loyal customers: "There is no time to wow our customers when we are constantly pushed to sell the food and hot beverages."[2] In January 2009, just after his arrival as the new Jamba Juice CEO, White had instituted a new set of strategic priorities.

Believing it was necessary to revitalize the company, White had outlined the following goals:[3]

- Deliver improved comparable sales in company-owned stores.
- Build a retail food capability across all four day parts (breakfast, lunch, afternoon, dinner).
- Accelerate the development of franchise and nontraditional stores.

* This case was developed by Professor Alan B. Eisner, Pace University; Jerome C. Kuperman, Minnesota State University–Moorhead; and Professor James Gould, Pace University. Material has been drawn from published sources to be used for class discussion. Copyright © 2011 Alan B. Eisner.

- Implement a disciplined expense-reduction plan.
- Build a consumer products licensing growth platform.

Entering 2011, Jamba Juice had made some headway in some of these growth goals, but the economic conditions were not yet favorable, especially in California, where most Jamba Juice retail operations were located. Could Jamba Juice succeed with its strategic growth plans, especially now that McDonald's, Starbucks, and Tim Hortons were selling smoothies?

Background

Juice Club was founded by Kirk Perron and opened its first store in San Luis Obispo, California, in April 1990.[4] While many small health-food stores had juice bars offering fresh carrot juice, wheat germ, and protein powder, dedicated juice and smoothie bars were sparse in 1990 and didn't gain widespread popularity until the mid- to late 1990s.

Juice Club began with a franchise strategy and opened its second and third stores in northern and southern California in 1993. In 1994 management decided that an expansion strategy focusing on company stores would provide a greater degree of quality and operating control. In 1995 the company changed its name to Jamba Juice Company to provide a point of differentiation as competitors began offering similar healthy juices and smoothies in the marketplace.

In March 1999 Jamba Juice Company merged with Zuka Juice Inc., a smoothie retail chain with 98 smoothie retail units in the western United States. On March 13, 2006, Jamba Juice Company agreed to be acquired by Services Acquisition Corp. International (headed by Steven Berrard, former CEO of Blockbuster Inc.) for $265 million.[5] The company went public in November 2006. In August 2008 Jamba Juice faced significant leadership changes. Steven Berrard agreed to assume the responsibilities of interim CEO, replacing Paul E. Clayton.[6] In December 2008 James White was named CEO and president, while Berrard remained chairman of the board of directors. Prior to joining Jamba Juice, White had been senior vice president of consumer brands at Safeway, a publicly traded Fortune 100 food and drug retailer.

Jamba Juice stores were owned and franchised by Jamba Juice Company, which was a wholly owned subsidiary of Jamba Inc. As of December 28, 2010, Jamba Juice had 743 locations consisting of 351 company-owned and operated stores and 392 franchise stores.[7] During fiscal year 2010, Jamba Inc. had over $260 million in revenue, a huge increase compared to the just over $23 million in revenue during fiscal year 2006 but still a net loss overall (see Exhibits 1 and 2).[8]

Company Culture

Jamba attempted to provide a unique company culture in which team members could execute at high levels while expressing their passion for the brand. Jamba believed its vision and values were more than bulletin-board postings; they were embodied in the store teams, the support staff, and the leadership team. Jamba's ability to execute its growth strategy depended on maintaining and enhancing its unique culture. To

Exhibit 1 Income Statements

	Fiscal Year Ended		
	Dec. 28, 2010*	Dec. 29, 2009	Dec. 30, 2008
Revenue:			
Company stores	$254,491	$295,607	$ 333,784
Franchise and other revenue	8,162	5,946	9,106
Total revenue	262,653	302,553	342,890
Costs and operating expenses:			
Cost of sales	61,307	72,669	89,163
Labor	85,189	100,589	120,251
Occupancy	38,561	43,888	44,868
Store operating	38,358	38,734	43,714
Depreciation and amortization	14,610	18,271	24,717
General and administrative	37,262	37,044	48,057
Store preopening	648	516	2,044
Impairment of long-lived assets	2,778	12,639	27,802
Store lease termination and closure	4,255	1,234	10,029
Trademark and goodwill impairment	—	—	84,061
Other operating	(4,292)	(3,924)	3,817
Total costs and operating expenses	278,676	321,660	498,523
Loss from operations	16,023	(20,107)	(155,633)
Other income (expense):			
Gain (loss) on derivative liabilities	—	1,597	7,895
Interest income	73	404	365
Interest expense	(547)	(6,905)	(2,064)
Total other income (expense)	(474)	(4,904)	6,196
Income (loss) before income taxes	(16,497)	(25,011)	(149,437)
Income tax benefit (expense)	(159)	1,066	274
Net income (loss)	$ (16,656)	$ (23,945)	$(149,163)

Source: Jamba 10-K reports.

* Estimate.

ensure that the culture continued to drive business execution, Jamba's leadership team attempted to focus on the following:

Leadership capability: Jamba focused on attracting and retaining quality individuals who executed the business strategy while building the platform for future growth.

Store-level capability: Jamba stores were the foundation of the business and had to execute flawlessly;

leadership ensured that stores were fully staffed and trained in order to provide the energetic and memorable Jamba store experience.

Community: An employee-shared appreciation of community involvement was a key to developing and sustaining emotional connections with customers; commitment to the communities where Jamba operated was vital to maintaining customer loyalty and sustaining the passion of Jamba team members.

Exhibit 2 **Balance Sheets** (in thousands of dollars)

	2010*	2009	2008
Assets			
Current assets:			
Cash and cash equivalents	30,664	30,081	25,881
Net receivables	6,377	10,440	4,594
Inventory	2,486	3,732	3,435
Other current assets	6,508	4,170	7,183
Total current assets	**46,035**	**48,423**	**41,093**
Long-term investments	—	—	520
Property, plant, and equipment	49,215	70,266	95,154
Intangible assets	1,341	1,850	2,998
Other assets	3,423	4,281	4,520
Deferred long-term asset charges	40	998	1,435
Total assets	**100,054**	**125,818**	**145,720**
Liabilities and Stockholders' Equity			
Current liabilities:			
Accounts payable	56,530	64,115	58,594
Short/current long-term debt	—	240	2,344
Other current liabilities	—	—	1,922
Total current liabilities	**56,530**	**64,355**	**62,860**
Long-term debt	166	1,163	23,110
Other liabilities	—	—	2,659
Deferred long-term liability charges	15,416	14,695	16,670
Total liabilities	**72,112**	**80,213**	**105,299**
Stockholders' equity:			
Redeemable preferred stock	20,554	31,069	—
Common stock	64	53	55
Retained earnings	(358,493)	(341,837)	(317,892)
Capital surplus	365,817	356,320	358,258
Total stockholders' equity	**7,388**	**14,536**	**40,421**

Source: Jamba 10-K reports.

* Estimate.

Store Management and Personnel

Jamba Juice Company's operations team was the foundation for its performance and vital to long-term growth. Jamba recruited and retained leaders with broad experience in management and industry. The company also supported its store operations with a combination of regional directors of operations, district managers, and store general managers.

Attracting and developing team members who provided superior service was paramount to producing the positive customer experience that Jamba strived for. Jamba sought to hire customer-service-oriented people and provided team members with extensive training, financial incentives, and opportunities for advancement when they fulfilled service expectations. To monitor the level of customer service, Jamba instituted a system-wide mystery-shopper program, which gave valuable feedback on store performance.

Maintaining the Jamba Juice Company corporate culture was essential as the company continued to expand. Jamba Juice Company carefully screened potential team members to ensure they held many of its core values and fit into the culture. By emphasizing its mission statement and values and encouraging responsibility and accountability at every level, Jamba believed that it had created a sense of team member loyalty and an open and interactive work environment, resulting in a highly passionate workforce.

At the franchise level, Jamba used a number of regional franchise consultants to assist with rollouts of new products and marketing campaigns, providing best practices and franchise feedback to the company. In addition, technology and procedural enhancements in areas such as labor management and scheduling relieved store managers from unnecessary administrative reporting and enabled them to focus on customer service.

Store Design

The color scheme employed by Jamba Juice stores was consistent among stores, providing a bright and cheerful theme with colors that embodied Jamba's commitment to fresh and healthy juices, smoothies, and other energizing products. The highly interactive Jamba experience was designed to attract customers with the enticing aroma of fresh fruit, vegetables, and wheatgrass and the high-energy sounds of whirring blenders and team members calling out greetings.

To highlight Jamba's commitment to providing a memorable and pleasant customer experience, and to facilitate high foot traffic through its stores, Jamba worked with a retail design consultant to formulate a model plan for its stores that would showcase natural materials used in construction, highlight the high-quality natural ingredients used in Jamba's products, and provide for efficient customer flow. Additional focus was placed on the "theater" aspect of smoothie making by providing an environment in which all food preparation could be conducted behind glass and in the open so that customers could watch as their order was freshly made with all-natural ingredients. The layout offered a casual bar-type atmosphere featuring interior stools and exterior tables and chairs, glass cases displaying baked goods, and shelving in front of cash registers. Supported by the theater of the fully displayed production process, Jamba Juice Company believed that the Jamba experience was a competitive advantage.

Advertising and Marketing

According to Jamba Juice Company's top management, the Jamba brand communicated the passion and positive energy of the Jamba experience. The company's focus on its brand was designed to ensure that customers were aware of the positive product attributes and the vision and values of the Jamba team. Jamba Juice Company believed that the branding efforts were instrumental to generating strong same-store sales growth and laying the foundation for new-unit growth. The brand initiatives encompassed the following:

Brand communications: Generating awareness and loyalty through the communication of the product benefits and the eventual development of an emotional connection with the customer.

Product: Optimizing and innovating—devoting additional resources to optimizing the current menu and developing new, appealing menu items.

Store environment: Presenting a store environment that was an energizing and memorable experience for customers.

Jamba Juice Company's marketing focused on communicating the benefits of the products and the brand's values through many creative and nontraditional avenues. Marketing efforts were concentrated on store locations to build unique and pleasant experiences that would generate positive word of mouth. As Jamba Juice Company entered new markets, it had to communicate the Jamba story, the benefits of its products, and their usage occasions. Jamba augmented its in-store communications with small promotional events, community involvement, and opportunistic grassroots marketing.

Jamba Juice Company believed that it benefited from international media attention, which provided it with a significant competitive advantage. Historically, Jamba had not engaged in any mass-media promotional programs, relying instead on word of mouth, trade-area marketing, and in-store promotions to increase customer awareness. However, Jamba was featured in stories appearing in the *Wall Street Journal,* the *New York Times, USA Today,* and a host of local newspapers and magazines, as well as profiled spots on TV news shows such as *Good Morning America.*

Jamba also capitalized on the openings of new sites as opportunities to reach out to the media and secure live local television coverage, radio broadcasts, and articles in local print media. Openings were also frequently associated with a charitable event, thus serving to reinforce Jamba Juice Company's strong commitment to its communities. For instance, the 2011 media event at the opening of the first international Jamba Juice location in South Korea highlighted the appearance of the official spokesperson for Jamba Juice in South Korea, Olympian Tae-Hwan Park, who won the gold medal in the men's 400 meter freestyle event and silver in the men's 200 meter freestyle event in the 2008 Olympics. A popular figure in South Korea for his active, healthy lifestyle and energetic, outgoing personality, Mr. Park, was profiled on the Jamba Juice South Korean website, *www.jambajuice.co.kr.*[9]

Building a Retail Food Capability

Jamba Juice stores offered customers a range of blended beverages, baked goods and meals, nutritional supplements, and healthy snacks. Jamba smoothie and juice options were made with real fruit and 100 percent fruit juices, were blended to order, and provided four to six servings of fruits and vegetables. Jamba smoothies were rich in vitamins, minerals, proteins, and fiber. In addition to the natural nutrients in Jamba smoothies, Jamba offered supplements in the form of Boosts and Shots. Boosts included 10 combinations of vitamins, minerals, proteins, and extracts designed to give the mind and body a nutritious boost. A complimentary Boost was offered with each Jamba smoothie. Shots included three combinations of wheatgrass, green tea, orange juice, and soymilk designed to give customers a natural concentrate of vitamins, minerals, and antioxidants.

As a complement to its smoothie and boost offerings, Jamba also offered baked goods and other meal items. Each of these items was made with natural ingredients and was high in protein and/or fiber. One popular item added was steel cut hot oatmeal with fruit, a low calorie organic product that captured a "best of" rating by nutritionists when compared against offerings from McDonald's, Starbucks, Au Bon Pain, and Cosi.[10] Also added were a variety of "grab-and-go" wraps, sandwiches, and California flatbread food offerings. In 2010 Jamba added the Hot Blends beverages to the list. These Hot Blends products included three tea latte flavors and a Classic Hot Chocolate made with premium natural and organic ingredients, as well as six varieties of Mighty Leaf organic tea pouches. In addition, an organic brew-by-the-cup coffee service and a line of Whirl'ns frozen yogurt and sorbet bar treats, with probiotic fruit and yogurt blends, were added in select locations.

Then, in 2011, Jamba introduced its first line of fruit and vegetable smoothies with three offerings: the Berry UpBEET combining the delightful flavors of strawberries and blueberries with the juices from carrots, beets, broccoli, and lettuce; the Apple 'n Greens blend of apple-strawberry juice with the juice from dark leafy green vegetables, carrots, and lettuce, and adding spirulina (a microscopic blue-green algae used as a dietary supplement), peaches, mangos, and bananas; and the Orange Carrot Karma—a simple blend of carrot juice, orange juice, mangos, bananas, and ice.

Supplies

Smoothie and juice products depended heavily on supplies of fresh and fresh-frozen fruits and vegetables. The quality of each smoothie depended to a large degree on the quality of the basic produce ingredients from which it was made. It was therefore essential that the supply of produce was of the highest quality and was consistent throughout the year. To achieve these dual goals and realize the lowest possible purchase costs, Jamba Juice Company purchased all of its projected requirements for the coming year from suppliers at the height of the season for that particular type of produce.

Jamba conducted quality assurance testing at the time of packing to ensure that the produce met its high standards, which matched or exceeded USDA grade-A standards. The produce was then flash-frozen and stored by the suppliers for shipment to distributors throughout the year. Jamba contracted with independent distribution companies to distribute produce to the stores. Jamba believed that by clustering future store development, it could begin to lower distribution costs and therefore reduce the cost of goods sold.

All of Jamba's nutritional supplements (e.g., boosts) and baked goods were created to exacting specifications. After quality-control checks at the support center, all products were shipped directly to stores by outside distributors. Jamba did not maintain central warehousing facilities.

Competitors

Jamba was the smoothie industry leader and had several fairly strong competitors with similar health and fitness focuses, such as Juice It Up!, Planet Smoothie, and Smoothie King, but by 2009 that had changed. Starbucks and Panera Bread had entered the smoothie market, and McDonald's brought its marketing machine into the frozen drink category, launching its line of smoothies in the summer of 2010 with a value pitch. McDonald's introduced a 12-ounce smoothie for $2.29, while Jamba Juice's berry smoothies started at $3.55 for 16 ounces. When asked about the McDonald's push into its competitive space, Jamba Juice's CEO White said, "We view the entry of McDonald's into the smoothie category as an overall validation of the potential of smoothies. Their advertising will expand interest in the category." White felt Jamba Juice offered consumers "a trade-up option to McDonald's smoothies with more ingredients like mangos and pomegranate juice, and more customizable options, like vitamin or protein additions."[11]

On the international market, Canadian-based Tim Hortons had been offering smoothies in its U.S. market since mid-2010 and in 2011 was beginning to sell berry smoothies in Canada. Analysts there believed the smoothie market was "hot," growing 8 percent in 2010, with relatively small consumption.[12] Jamba Juice had signaled its intent to expand into Canada, with franchise development of up to 125 locations by 2020.

In addition to being a past leader in the smoothie industry, Jamba was also a competitor within the broader quick-service restaurant (QSR) arena. On QSR Magazine's 2007 Top 50 Quick-Service and Fast-Casual Chains list, Jamba Juice had ranked 47th overall (compared against all burger, sandwich, Mexican, chicken, pizza/pasta, Asian, seafood, and snack segments). However, by 2010, Jamba had fallen to 57th. Tim Hortons (number 49), Cold Stone Creamery (47), Baskin-Robbins (36), Dunkin' Doughnuts (7), and Starbucks (5) were the only "specialty food" companies in the "Snack" QSR market segment that ranked higher on the list than Jamba Juice.[13]

Customers

The Jamba Juice Company's increasingly broad product selection made it a competitor against a variety of "snack" providers (coffee houses, doughnut shops, ice cream parlors), as well as fast-food meal establishments (burgers, pizza, tacos, fried chicken). Jamba's core customers were health-conscious consumers who led, or aspired to lead, a healthy lifestyle. Therefore, Jamba positioned its products as healthy alternatives to conventional fast-food fare. Due to vast options in size, calorie content, and relative sweetness,

Jamba smoothies, baked goods, and meals could serve as a light snack, a sweet treat, or even a meal replacement for on-the-go customers who wanted to avoid highly processed or sugar-rich convenience foods. The company's commitment to fresh produce and natural products bolstered its image as a leading provider of premium natural food and beverages and positioned it well to benefit from the healthy alternatives trend, especially in the wake of First Lady Michelle Obama's initiative to combat childhood obesity.

Smoothie as Fast-Food Alternative Smoothies have been called the fast food of the new millennium. Consumers who once grabbed a hot dog or hamburger for lunch were now choosing a fresh-fruit smoothie or organic snack as a healthy alternative. For example, a Jamba Juice 30-ounce Protein Berry Workout with Whey smoothie provided 21 grams of protein and 7 grams of fiber for only 480 calories and 1.5 grams of fat. In contrast, a McDonald's Quarter Pounder and small french fries provided 26 grams of protein and 6 grams of fiber but also had 660 calories and 32 grams of fat. In addition to being easier on the waistline and arteries, the Jamba smoothie also provided 110 percent of the USRDA for calcium, 120 percent of vitamin C, and 80 percent of vitamin D, while the McDonald's meal offered only nominal mineral value and a host of artificial preservatives. This type of comparison by educated consumers was what helped Jamba draw in new customers as they looked to "clean up" their diets.

Treat Alternative The growing number of consumers focused on living a healthy lifestyle had a major impact on the grocery, restaurant, and health care industries. Consumers increasingly demanded products that supported their interests in fitness and nutrition while also providing high-quality taste and a "treat" they could feel good about. Jamba's Creamy Indulgences line provided customers with a treat they could perceive as being as decadent as ice cream but one they could enjoy while consuming fewer calories and less sugar.

Functional Foods Functional foods included ingredients that provided extra benefits beyond basic nutrition—such as antioxidants to fight free radicals or plant sterols to block cholesterol. Jamba believed that consumers increasingly looked for products that offered specific health benefits in addition to great taste. In order to cater to these multidimensional desires, Jamba Juice had introduced the Blended with a Purpose line of smoothies, including Coldbuster, Protein Berry Workout, Acai Super-Antioxidant, and Fit n' Fruitful.

Energy Beverages With consumers increasingly living highly active and on-the-go lifestyles, demand for a convenient source of energy and refreshment had grown dramatically. The energy beverage market captured a significant amount of this growth because the beverages were more convenient and portable than traditional hot coffee and tea drinks. But most retail ready-to-drink energy beverages were high in both sugar and caffeine. For consumers seeking a healthy source of energy, Jamba Juice introduced beverages and Boosts that combined natural caffeine sources, such as Matcha Green Tea and Guarana, with the nutritional benefits of fruit to provide a healthy and flavorful source of sustained energy.

Jamba's Growth Strategy

The Jamba Juice Company's growth strategy was to expand its existing markets and develop new markets, while leveraging its support infrastructure. Understanding that it required strong unit-level economics across regions and platforms to continue growth, Jamba strove to achieve three things: unit economics (i.e., continue to improve on store profitability), new-unit growth (i.e., continue to expand in existing markets as well as emerging and new markets), and leveraged infrastructure (i.e., continue to build on and leverage existing infrastructure to improve profitability).

Developing New Stores Jamba generally characterized its stores as either traditional or nontraditional locations. Traditional locations included suburban strip malls and various retail locations in urban centers. Traditional stores averaged approximately 1,400 square feet in size and were designed to be fun, friendly, energetic, and colorful to represent the active, healthy lifestyle that Jamba Juice Company promoted.

Nontraditional stores were located in areas that allowed Jamba to generate awareness and try out new products to fuel the core business. Jamba's nontraditional opportunities included store-within-a-store locations, airports, shopping malls, and colleges and universities:

Store-within-a-store: Jamba Juice Company was developing franchise partner relationships with major grocers and retailers to develop store-within-a-store concepts. The franchise partnerships provided it with the opportunity to reach new customers and enhance the brand without making significant capital investments. Jamba's premium brand appealed to major retailers that focused on enhancing their customers' in-store experience. The company was confident that the flexibility of the Jamba concept to fit into many formats enabled Jamba to build awareness outside its traditional locations.

Airports: Jamba operated several airport locations and had the opportunity to develop stores in numerous additional airports. Jamba Juice Company's highly portable product appealed to travelers on the go and provided an energizing boost to tiring air travel.

Shopping malls: Jamba had opportunistically established stores in shopping malls that presented attractive expansion opportunities. In addition, as with the airport locations, the indoor setting helped to alleviate weather and seasonal vulnerabilities that challenge traditional locations.

Colleges and universities: The Jamba brand was believed to be extremely appealing to the average college student's active, on-the-go lifestyle, and Jamba expected to continue to develop on-campus locations.

Other potential nontraditional store locations:
Additional high-traffic, nontraditional locations existed for Jamba to explore. Many large health clubs included a juice and smoothie bar within their buildings, and new gyms were popping up every day as the American culture became more health and fitness conscious. There was an opportunity for Jamba to partner with a major gym chain or individual private gyms with high membership rates. Another possibility was to partner with a large school district. Schools across the country were under increasing scrutiny to offer healthy alternatives to the traditional fat-, carbohydrate-, and preservative-rich foods served in cafeterias. Many schools had other fast-food kiosks within the school (which attracted additional criticism); therefore, offering a Jamba kiosk might be a viable option that was economically profitable for Jamba and politically profitable for the schools.

Jamba Juice Company had followed a strategy of expanding its store locations in existing markets and opening stores in select new markets. During 2007, Jamba began acquiring the assets of Jamba Juice franchised stores in an attempt to gain more control over growth direction. Over 30 franchise stores were acquired during the first three quarters of 2007, and Jamba expected to continue making additional franchise acquisitions as part of its ongoing growth strategy. In 2006 approximately 33 percent of Jamba's stores were franchised, but franchises accounted for only about 4 percent of its revenue.[14] By April 2008, 71 percent of Jamba stores were company owned. In early 2008 a financial analyst predicted that Jamba's widely recognized brand poised it to "expand in an under-penetrated and growing health food market."[15] However, the same analyst recognized that Jamba was experiencing declines in store traffic and store-level margins due to the subprime crisis and that Jamba therefore planned to slow its expansion until the economy had a chance to recover.[16] In May 2008 Jamba announced its plans to close 10 underperforming company-owned stores by the end of the year and terminate signed leases for seven unbuilt locations.[17]

In August 2008 CEO Paul E. Clayton stepped down after eight years in the role and was ultimately replaced by James White in November 2008. White subsequently reversed the trajectory of the growth strategy, focusing on the acceleration of franchise and nontraditional store growth. By 2011 franchisees outnumbered company-owned stores (see Exhibit 3). International growth was also on the horizon. Starting with the first South Korean location in January 2011, Jamba Juice was poised to open more than 200 stores in South Korea and 125 stores in Canada by 2020.

Increasing Customer Frequency One of the key objectives of Jamba's growth strategy was to increase the frequency of customer visits, which averaged fewer than two per month for 80 percent of Jamba customers.[18] Jamba viewed the conversion of "light users" (two or fewer times per month) to "heavy users" (eight or more times per month) as a significant opportunity to increase sales year-round and significantly decrease weather and seasonal vulnerabilities.

The main driver of Jamba's revenue and profit was the sale of smoothies during hot weather. In southern states (e.g., California), where the weather remained warm year-round, Jamba experienced fairly steady sales. However, in the northern states (e.g., New York), where there was a cold and fairly lengthy winter season, Jamba experienced severe seasonal variability. Jamba Juice Company intended to continue developing fresh concepts that appealed to customers at any time of day and in any weather or season. One way Jamba was doing this was by using fast-cook ovens (installed to heat hot-pocket sandwiches) to make soup, hot tea, and coffee products. In addition, the push toward increasing the presence of nontraditional stores inside existing venues in the Northeast was a move to counter the seasonal slump.

Expense Reduction Plan

As a major part of CEO White's strategic initiative, and partly due to the weakness of the consumer spending environment, Jamba planned to increase operating margins by eliminating approximately $25 million in store-level costs. This would be done over several years by reducing costs of goods sold, simplifying operations to reduce labor costs, better managing wages and benefits, implementing a labor planning system, increasing occupancy savings, and improving management of controllable costs, store costs, and marketing expenditures. In addition, Jamba took measures to reduce general and administrative costs.[19]

Exhibit 3 **Store Types and Locations**

	Company-Owned Stores	Franchise Stores	Total Stores	Nontraditional Stores*
2010	351	392	743	
2009	478	261	739	127
2008	511	218	729	119
2007	501	206	707	99

* Out of the Total Stores, all stores could be in nontraditional locations

Building a Licensing Growth Platform

Jamba Juice Company's strong association with premium, flavorful beverages translated well into ready-to-drink beverages available in a variety of retail locations.

Jamba Juice Company had reached a licensing agreement with Nestlé under which Nestlé would manufacture six of Jamba's juice and smoothie ready-to-drink products for distribution in eight western states.[20] Nestlé planned to gradually expand distribution of the Jamba drinks into other U.S. markets and possibly even into overseas markets. The products would contain nonfat milk, which would differentiate them from other juice-drink competitors, including Naked Juice (owned by Pepsi) and Odwalla (owned by Coca-Cola). Kraft had a similar deal with Starbucks to distribute its Frappuccino drinks. Nestlé Jamba All-Natural Energy Drinks were rolled out in multiple retail locations in the Northeast, and in 600 Jamba Juice retail stores in March 2011. Both Nestlé and Jamba Inc. continued to explore other joint opportunities to extend the Jamba brand.[21]

During 2010, Jamba expanded licensing agreements to include a line of fruit-infused coconut water, to be distributed through the Pepsi Beverage Company, functional wellness Brazilian super fruit shots, and all-natural fruit cups to be produced in partnership with Zola and Sundia Corporation. Other Jamba-branded consumer products included yogurt and sorbet frozen novelty items manufactured under license by Oregon Ice Cream LLC out of Eugene, Oregon, and made available in select retailers; and Jamba-branded apparel, including cotton T-shirts, beanies, and a canvas tote bag, developed in partnership with licensee Headline Entertainment.

Can Jamba Grow without Losing Its "Healthy Alternatives" Brand Identity?

Jamba Juice Company's desire to grow by expanding its selection of nonjuice menu items seemed to follow the Starbucks model. Once only coffee houses, most Starbucks stores now offered a variety of muffins, fruit plates, sandwiches, quiches, and desserts. This menu expansion helped Starbucks attract customers who were looking for a light meal or dessert to go with their coffee and also attracted noncoffee drinkers who just came in for the food. Offering iced coffees and teas helped Starbucks overcome some of its seasonal variability, giving customers a cool-drink offering during hot-weather months. Offering ready-to-go-drinks in grocery and convenience stores also enabled Starbucks to get its products to a wider customer base.

Likewise, Jamba set out to strengthen its customer reach by offering ready-to-drink products, hot food and drink items to attract customers during the cold-weather months, and a range of breakfast and lunch food items to complement its juice-based offerings and satisfy customer desires all day and all year-round. Could Jamba attract the Dunkin' Doughnuts breakfast business, the McDonald's lunch crowd, the Baskin-Robbins dessert seekers, and perhaps even the Starbucks afternoon energy fixers? By expanding its menu very broadly, would Jamba run the risk of being categorized as a fast-food restaurant, rather than being viewed as a fast-food alternative? Or could Jamba follow Starbucks's path of broadening its menu base but still maintaining its stature as a higher-end establishment? CEO James White had some tough decisions to make, particularly given Jamba's slow pace of recovery.

Even though the turnaround seemed to be on track, with expenses finally coming under control, the bottom line still wasn't improving fast enough for some analysts. There was speculation that a buyout offer might come along. After all, several food, beverage, and fast-food giants, Starbucks and McDonald's among them, might be able to amplify Jamba's brand and make the most of what appeared to be the early stages of CEO White's turnaround effort.[22]

Endnotes

1. Munarriz, R. A. 2011. 7 reasons not to worry this week. *Motley Fool,* March 7. *www.fool.com/investing/general/2011/03/07/7-reasons-not-to-worry-this-week.aspx.*

2. Employee feedback from *www.glassdoor.com/Reviews/Jamba-Juice-Reviews-E11191.htm.*

3. Jamba Inc. 2010. Jamba Inc. Form 10K annual report, for period ending December 29, 2009. Available at *ir.jambajuice.com/phoenix.zhtml?c=192409&p=irol-sec.*

4. *FundingUniverse.com.* n.d. Jamba Juice Company (company history). *www.fundinguniverse.com/company-histories/Jamba-Juice-Company-Company-History.html.*

5. Jamba Juice Company. 2006. Jamba Juice Company and Services Acquisition Corp. International announce merger. March 13. *www.sec.gov/Archives/edgar/data/1316898/000110465906015960/a06-6826_1ex99d1.htm.*

6. Jamba Inc. 2008. Jamba, Inc. announces changes to its senior management team. *Business Wire,* August 6. *ir.jambajuice.com/phoenix.zhtml?c=192409&p=irol-newsArticle&ID=1189166.*

7. Jamba Inc. 2011. Jamba, Inc. to announce fourth quarter and fiscal year 2010 financial results on March 10, 2011. Business Wire, February 28. *ir.jambajuice.com/phoenix.zhtml?c=192409&p=irolnewsArticle&ID=1533589.*

8. Jamba Inc. 2011. Jamba Inc. Form 10K annual report, for period ending December 28, 2010. Available at *ir.jambajuice.com/phoenix.zhtml?c=192409&p=irol-sec.*

9. Jamba Inc. 2011. Jamba Juice and SPC Group celebrate first store opening in South Korea. *Business Wire,* January 31. *ir.jambajuice.com/phoenix.zhtml?c=192409&p=irolnewsArticle&ID=1521600.*

10. Jamba Inc. 2011. Jamba Juice oatmeal favorite pick on Good Morning America today. ABC News, February 8. *ir.jambajuice.com/phoenix.zhtml?c=192409&p=irol-news&nyo=0;* video clip available at *abcnews.go.com/GMA/video/fast-food-oatmeal-how-healthy-is-it-12865436.*

11. Ziobro, P. 2010. McDonald's smoothie launch may juice up entire category. *Wall Street Journal,* July 12. *online.wsj.com/article/NA_WSJ_PUB:SB10001424052748704288204575363261168521980.html.*

12. QSRweb.com. 2011. Tim Hortons rolling out smoothies in Canada. March 4. *www.qsrweb.com/article/179756/Tim-Hortons-rolling-out-smoothies-in-Canada.*

13. QSR. n.d. 2010 QSR 50. *www.qsrmagazine.com/ reports/2010-qsr-50.*

14. Lee, L. 2007. A smoothie you can chew on: To appeal to diners as well as drinkers, Jamba Juice is adding heft to its concoctions. *BusinessWeek,* June 11: 64.

15. Zacks Investment Research. 2008. Zacks analyst blog highlights: Jamba Juice, Krispy Kreme, Starbucks and PeopleSupport. January 10. Retrieved from *news. moneycentral.msn.com/ticker/article.aspx?symbol=US:JMB A&feed=BW&date=20080110&id=8018383.*

16. Ibid.

17. Jamba Inc. 2008. Jamba announces organizational changes and store development reductions. *Business Wire,* May 15. *ir.jambajuice.com/phoenix. zhtml?c=192409&p=irol-newsArticle&ID=1189172.*

18. Lee. 2007. A smoothie you can chew on.

19. Jamba Inc. 2009. Jamba announces its 2009 "BLEND" Plan: Build, license, expense-reduction, non-traditional, development - defines strategic priorities for 2009. Business Wire, January 21. *ir.jambajuice.com/phoenix. zhtml?c=192409&p=irol-newsArticle&ID=1246899.*

20. Swarts, W. 2007. Jamba's juice deal with Nestle froths up shares. *SmartMoney. www.smartmoney.com/invest/stocks/ Jambas-Juice-Deal-With-Nestle-Froths-Up-Shares-22223/*

21. *Drinks Business Review.* 2011. Nestlé Jamba All-Natural Energy Drinks to land at 600 Jamba Juice stores in U.S. March 11. *energysportsdrinks.drinks-business-review.com/ news/nestl-jamba-all-natural-energy-drinks-to-land-at- 600-jamba-juice-stores-in-us-110311.*

22. Munarriz, R. 2011. Is Jamba good to the last slurp? *Motley Fool,* January 7. *www.fool.com/investing/general/ 2011/01/07/is-jamba-good-to-the-last-slurp.aspx.*

Case 31 Build-A-Bear Workshop*

By 2011, Build-A-Bear Workshop had continued to reinvent itself by introducing new stuffed animal characters, wardrobes, and accessories. The company tried to keep its products fresh and interesting by launching temporary themed product lines and opening pop-up stores to lure the customers to revisit Bearville (what the company affectionately called its stores). In May 2010 Build-A-Bear created a one-month zoo novelty themed product line. The interactive entertainment retailer of customized stuffed animals provided "zoorrific" fun for guests. Families could find a new collection of furry friends plus zoo-themed activities in stores and at *buildabearville.com*, where guests could receive exclusive virtual zoo rides. Seven different furry animals, a giraffe, tiger, flamingo, leopard, monkey, panda, and parrot, were included in the collection.[1] Similarly, April 2010 saw a "fairytales come to life" theme. The stores were transformed into enchanted palaces where every guest was treated like royalty and given a free crown. After reciting the royal promise, guests could dress up new animals, like Enchanted Pony and Enchanted Dragon, or add various enchanted theme accessories, such as a knight costume, gold wings, a castle, and so on. "Build-A-Bear Workshop has always been a magical place for families, where imagination and adventure come to life," said Maxine Clark, Build-A-Bear Workshop founder and chief executive bear. "Our whimsical furry friends, enchanted store experience, and online fun fairytale-themed adventure provide our Guests with endless ways to play happily ever after."[2]

Continuing its strategy of product revitalization, in September 2010 Build-A-Bear introduced Star Wars products, including a Star Wars bear, Star Wars theme song sound chip that could be added to any animal, and Princess Leia, Han Solo, Darth Vader, and Jedi Knight costumes.[3] The year 2010 was also the year of pop-up stores for Build-A-Bear, when the company took advantage of the holiday season and opened 10 pop-up stores in time for the Christmas season. This expansion made the experience of Build-A-Bear Workshop available to many holiday shoppers and gave consumers a chance to make great personalized gifts with an extensive assortment of the latest holiday animals, fashions, and accessories. The pop-up stores provided the company with a great opportunity to attract customers to Bearville, because there would be a natural increase in mall traffic and consumers would be focused on gift spending.[4]

Build-A-Bear continued its year-long series of charitable activities and events across the nation. The company had successfully projected the image of a socially conscious firm by reaching out to a wide range of organizations,

including the Juvenile Diabetes Research Foundation, programs to stop cyber-bullying, and programs supporting domestic pets, youth education, autism, and marine mammals affected by oil spills to name a few.[5] Build-A-Bear extended its charities internationally as well by providing support for children and families affected by the earthquake in Haiti in 2010 and contributing to Japan earthquake relief efforts in 2011. "People have been asking me for years how we will maintain our teddy bear culture as we grow," said Maxine Clark. "I think the answer is simple. It's about teddy bears and it's about heart. And it's about being good people and good bears. The language of teddy bears is understood in every country and by all ages."[6]

After a decade of existence, Build-A-Bear Workshop was ranked no. 94 in *Fortune*'s "100 Best Companies to Work For" list in 2009 and moved up to no. 80 in the 2010 list. "We are honored to be included for the second consecutive year on the FORTUNE '100 Best Companies to Work For' list. Build-A-Bear Workshop was founded 13 years ago on a simple but powerful idea: to create a successful company with heart. Our associates' spirit, dedication, hard work and commitment have made us the world's leading interactive retail-entertainment brand. Every associate is able to participate in making Build-A-Bear Workshop the best place to work and play," said Maxine Clark in 2010. "We've accomplished so much in such a short period of time by putting the heart—and the fun—back into retail."[7]

However, not everything looked so rosy in Bearville; the company financials looked quite grizzly. Like all retailers, Build-A-Bear was greatly affected by shifting markets and the fluctuating economy in 2009–2010. Although the firm announced significant improvement in fourth quarter 2010, the year-end results showed decreased revenue (see Exhibits 1 and 2). Ms. Clark announced at the end of 2010, "We drove double digit increases in our e-commerce sales in the fourth quarter and the year. We have begun working with an outside consulting firm to review our supply chain, logistics and other expense areas and expect to generate savings in the latter half of fiscal 2011. We are also working with the consultants to identify opportunities for revenue growth. With a strong balance sheet that includes no debt, no borrowings on our credit facility and $59 million in cash at year end, we believe we are well positioned to capitalize on growth opportunities in the year ahead."[8] However, her announcement seemed in stark contrast to what the stock market suggested in February 17, 2011, when Build-A-Bear Workshop Inc. topped the list of "Biggest Percentage Price Decliners" among common stocks on the New York Stock Exchange.[9] The analysts questioned whether Build-A-Bear had reached its potential and what new products and strategies the company could offer to step up its financial performance.

* This case was developed by Professor Alan B. Eisner, Pace University; Professor Helaine J. Korn, Baruch College–City University of New York; graduate student Lucia Vojtkova; and Professor Dan Baugher, Pace University. Material has been drawn from published sources to be used for class discussion. Copyright © 2011 Alan B. Eisner.

Exhibit 1 Income Statements

	Fiscal Year		
	2010	2009	2008
Revenues:			
Net retail sales	$387,163	$388,552	$460,963
Franchise fees	3,043	3,353	4,157
Commercial revenue	11,246	4,001	3,196
Total revenues	401,452	395,906	468,316
Costs and expenses:			
Cost of merchandise sold	239,556	247,511	270,918
Selling, general, and administrative	163,910	161,692	185,608
Store preopening	708	90	2,410
Store closing	—	981	2,952
Interest expense (income), net	(250)	(143)	(799)
Total costs and expenses	403,924	419,746	461,089
Income before income taxes	(2,472)	(23,840)	7,227
Income tax expense	(2,576)	(11,367)	2,663
Net income	$104	($12,473)	$4,564
Earnings per common share:			
Basic	$0.01	($0.66)	$0.24
Diluted	$0.01	($0.66)	$0.24
Shares used in computing common per share amounts:			
Basic	18,601,465	18,874,352	19,153,123
Diluted	19,034,048	18,874,352	19,224,273

Source: Build-A-Bear Workshop Inc. Form10-K reports.

Exhibit 2 Balance Sheets (in thousands of dollars, except share and per-share data)

	January 1, 2011	January 2, 2010
Assets		
Current assets:		
Cash and cash equivalents	$58,755	$60,399
Inventories	46,475	44,384
Receivables	7,923	5,337
Prepaid expenses and other current assets	18,425	19,329
Deferred tax assets	7,465	6,306
Total current assets	139,043	135,755
		(*continued*)

Exhibit 2 **Balance Sheets** (in thousands of dollars, except share and per-share data) (*continued*)

	January 1, 2011	January 2, 2010
Property and equipment, net	88,029	101,044
Goodwill	32,407	33,780
Other intangible assets, net	1,444	3,601
Other assets, net	14,871	10,093
Total Assets	$275,794	$284,273
Liabilities and stockholders' equity		
Current liabilities:		
Accounts payable	$36,325	$32,822
Accrued expenses	15,488	11,185
Gift cards and customer deposits	28,880	29,301
Deferred revenue	6,679	8,582
Total current liabilities	87,372	81,890
Deferred franchise revenue	1,706	2,027
Deferred rent	28,642	34,760
Other liabilities	361	816
Commitments and contingencies		
Stockholder's equity:		
Preferred stock, par value $0.01, Shares authorized: 15,000,000: No shares issued or outstanding at January 3, 2009 and December 29, 2007	—	—
Common stock, par value $0.01. Shares authorized: 50,000,000. Issued and outstanding: 19,478,750 and 20,676,357 shares, respectively	196	204
Additional paid-in capital	76,582	80,122
Accumulated other comprehensive (loss) income	(9,959)	(6,336)
Retained earnings	90,894	90,790
Total stockholders' equity	157,713	164,780
Total Liabilities and Stockholders' Equity	$275,794	$284,273

Source: Build-A-Bear Workshop Inc. Form10-K reports.

Build-A-Bear Background

It all started on a simple idea that Maxine Clark heard over 30 years ago from Stanley Goodman, former CEO of May Department Stores, "Retailing is entertainment and the store is a stage—and when the customers are happy, they spend more money." On the basis of this idea, Build-A-Bear Workshop brought the teddy bear alive and was the only global company that offered an interactive make-your-own-stuffed-animal retail-entertainment experience. Inspired by Goodman's statement, Clark brought the brand experience to the toy industry in 1996 and established Build-A-Bear headquarters in St. Louis, Missouri.[10] Clark created a custom-teddy-bear empire built with "heart" and was personally involved in setting the strategic agenda, building the organization, and maintaining the strategic leadership. As the former president of Payless Shoe Source, Clark based the Build-A-Bear concept on two of the hottest trends in retailing—entertainment and customization. Her years of retailing experience paid off and gave Clark unique insights into creating her own successful concept for mall-based retailing.[11] Having no children of her own, Clark took every opportunity to interact with her customers, employing both low- and high-tech methods to communicate with Build-A-Bear fans.[12] Weekly store visits and numerous e-mails provided Clark with valuable customer feedback that she put into practice to build a truly customer-centered organization.

Since the opening of the first store in 1996, Build-A-Bear Workshop capitalized on its unique experience and attracted a strong base of loyal customers. The company's target market consisted mainly of families with children, primarily ages 3 to 12. Build-A-Bear stores also appealed to grandparents, aunts, and uncles of children and to teen girls who occasionally brought along their boyfriends as well. The Build-A-Bear experience was also sought by child-centric organizations, such as scouting organizations and schools, that were looking for interactive entertainment options of the type Build-A-Bear Workshop could provide. Overall, it has been the company's belief that "our stores, which are primarily located in malls, are destination locations and draw guests from a large geographic reach."[13]

The theme-park-environment stores operated as specialty retailers of plush animals and related products, including approximately 30 styles of teddy bears as well as various clothing, shoes, and accessories for the stuffed animals. Build-A-Bear Workshop stores generated strong sales wherever they opened. The company differentiated itself from the competition with marketing initiatives that facilitated stronger connections with its customers.[14] Approximately 3,000 square feet in size, every Build-A-Bear store stood out thanks to a highly visual and colorful appearance, with custom-designed fixtures featuring teddy bears and other themes relating to the Build-A-Bear Workshop experience.

Build-A-Bear Experience

Build-A-Bear Workshop provided a unique and exceptional approach to the entertainment retail industry. The company's core concept was based on allowing its customers, uniquely termed "guests," to make, personalize, and customize stuffed animals of their choosing. The customization feature provided customers with more value than they would receive from mass-produced products. In addition, personalizing the product stimulated customers' creativity and gave them a feeling of empowerment. This concept "capitalizes on what we believe is the relatively untapped demand for experience-based shopping as well as the widespread appeal of stuffed animals."[15] As Maxine Clark pointed out, "We [at Build-A-Bear] don't think about ourselves as a toy store— we think of ourselves as an experience. Unlike the rest of the industry, Build-A-Bear Workshop sales don't peak around holidays; they are evenly distributed."[16]

The Build-A-Bear Workshop atmosphere was based on a highly visual environment, with the teddy bear theme carried throughout the store, creating a fantasy land where stuffed animals came to life. "Shopping at one of the Build-A-Bear's colorful, [brightly] lit stores [was] one part consumption, ten parts entertainment,"[17] and this entertainment factor provided Build-A-Bear Workshop with a competitive edge in the toy industry.

The culture at Build-A-Bear Workshop encouraged employee contribution and collaboration, and the resulting above-average employee retention rates at Build-A-Bear contributed to the quality of the guest experience, the foundation stone of the company's differentiation.[18] Maxine Clark recognized that Build-A-Bear's success was largely dependent on the support of her employees, also known as "associates."[19] Therefore, Build-A-Bear was highly selective in the hiring process and ensured that the chosen associates stayed actively involved in what was happening with the company. For instance, fewer than 4 percent of the applicants for store manager were hired in 2008.[20] Build-A-Bear's excellent customer service largely contributed to the chain's overall customer satisfaction, which was close to 90 percent.[21]

The primary role of the associates, also referred to as the "Master Bear Builders," was to share the experience with the guests and guide them at each phase of the bear-making process. The process itself consisted of eight steps carried out on the Build-A-Bear "assembly line," which comprised different bear-making stations.

1. At the *Choose Me* stage, customers were introduced to all the furry characters in the store and would select one, which soon became their new friend. Each store usually carried over 30 different stuffed animals, which varied with the season. The prices of the Build-A-Bear furry friends ranged from $10 to $25.

2. At the *Hear Me* station, customers could personalize their new friend with a sound selected from several choices, including giggling, barking, meowing, or growling, which would be placed inside their stuffed animal during the stuffing process. Guests could even record their own 10-second Build-A-Sound message for an additional $8.

3. The *Stuff Me* station allowed customers to stuff their new friend with the help of one of the Master Bear Builders. At this stage, customers would bring their stuffed animal to life by selecting a small satin heart and placing it inside their new furry friend. Each animal was also given a special bar code that would allow it to be reunited with its owner if ever lost.

4. The furry friend would then be neatly pulled shut at the *Stitch Me* station.

5. Next, customers could brush their animal at the *Fluff Me* station to make sure their new friend was well groomed.

6. At *Dress Me,* customers were able to express the true personality and style of their new best friend by choosing from hundreds of outfits and accessories. Build-A-Bear provided the "beary" latest furry fashions, thanks to partnering with fashion leaders such as Limited Too, Skechers, Hello Kitty, Disney, and Harley-Davidson. Build-A-Bear Workshop also licensed a variety of college and university logos that were placed on Tiny Tees shirts, and it sold bear-sized MLB, NBA and WNBA, NFL, NHL, and NASCAR sports stuff.

7. At the *Name Me* stage, customers registered their new friend on one of the in-store computers. This information was used to create a personalized birth certificate and enter their friend in the Find-A-Bear ID program.

8. Finally, customers concluded their bear-making process at the *Take Me Home* station, where they received their customized birth certificate, and each new furry friend was then placed in its own Cub Condo carrying case.[22]

Build-A-Bear Workshop provided a unique shopping experience, as customers created an emotional bond with the toy through the interactive process of bringing it to life. As CEO Maxine Clark commented, "The store offers a total experience from start to finish. It's about so much more than just coming in and buying an off-the-shelf bear, although you can do that too if you want. But most people prefer to make their own—even if they have to stand in line to do it. Shoppers are, and typically desire to be, involved in the entire bear-making process."[23]

To emphasize the strength of its brand, Build-A-Bear Workshop instituted the Fur Stuff Club (a loyalty rewards program),[24] as well as a bear identification system that aimed to unite children with their lost Build-A-Bear stuffed animals.[25] The company's CIO, Dave Finnegan, believed that the "experience starts with the [stuffed animal's] barcode." As customers registered their furry friends at a designated kiosk, each consumer would be prompted to scan the bar code and add his or her name, mailing address, and e-mail address—information that would later be stored in the corporate database. Build-A-Bear also launched an automated Stuff Fur Stuff Club, which served as an electronic history of the guests' preferences and purchases. The program tracked the purchased products, the frequency of the customers' visits, as well as their response to certain offers. The Stuff Fur Stuff Club encouraged loyalty and attracted shoppers by awarding them 1 point for every $1 they spent. After earning 100 points, customers would receive a $10 reward. Thanks to the automated program, the company could analyze purchase patterns and history trends and learn who was redeeming their points and what they were using the points for.[26] Both the bear identification system and Stuff Fur Stuff were differentiating features that allowed Build-A-Bear to recognize and communicate important information to its guests, as well as stay ahead of changing customer preferences.[27]

Expansion and Innovation

In November 2004 the company expanded the make-your-own concept from stuffed animals to dolls with the opening of its first Friends 2B Made stores, where guests could make their own doll friends. By the end of 2006, Build-A-Bear Workshop operated one stand-alone Friends 2B Made store and eight other Friends 2B Made stores adjacent to, or within, Build-A-Bear Workshop stores in the United States.[28] The company also expanded its merchandise assortments by establishing licensing agreements with professional baseball, basketball, hockey, and football teams and with NASCAR.

In 2005 Build-A-Bear Workshop partnered with Ridemakerz, allowing fathers and sons to customize their own toy cars.[29] In the same year, the company introduced Build-A-Bear Workshop On Tour, with a bear-covered mobile trailer that opened up into a complete 800-square-foot Build-A-Bear Workshop store. The On Tour idea was part of the company's integrated marketing strategy to bring the Build-A-Bear Workshop brand and experience to places other than malls where families go and have fun, such as various sporting and entertainment venues across the country.[30]

Build-A-Bear Workshop teamed up with Major League Baseball to provide fans across the country with opportunities to support their favorite teams in unique ways. Build-A-Bear opened five Build-A-Bear Workshop ballpark stores across the country. The ballpark stores were open during the teams' home games and included the same experience and interaction as the mall-based stores, with exclusive animals, outfits, and accessories. Clark also believed that the promotion of Scott Seay in 2006 to president and chief operating "bear" would allow Build-A-Bear to gain efficiencies throughout the organization.[31]

In March 2009 John Haugh joined Build-A-Bear Workshop as president and chief marketing and merchandising bear. Prior to joining Build-A-Bear Workshop, Haugh served as president of It's Sugar LLC, a candy and confectionary retailer. Haugh stepped in at a difficult time to be a retailer, amid the economic recession of 2008–2009. Meanwhile, Tina Klocke was named chief operations and financial bear. Klocke assumed formal responsibility for store operations in addition to her continuing role as chief financial bear.

Changing Industry

Although Build-A-Bear Workshop's interactive experience was unique in the toy retail industry, this didn't make the competition any less intense. Kids changed their preferences at a rate so fast that a phenomenon one year could be gone the next year. To compete with others in catching children's new preferences and activity time, a specialty retail store such as Build-A-Bear Workshop had to face competition from all different directions, including toy manufacturers like Hasbro and Mattel, which sell their products through giant retail chain stores—Walmart, Toys "R" Us, Target, Kmart, Sears, and other discounted chains. Other competitors included, but were not limited to, American Girl, Vermont Teddy Bear, Russ Berrie, Ty, Fisher-Price, Mattel, Ganz, Applause, Boyd's, Commonwealth, and Gant. Maxine Clark considered her competition to be every company that tried to attract the customer's time and entertainment money.[32] As products in the toy industry became more commoditized, many companies searched for new ways to differentiate their offerings beyond simply manufacturing and delivering the toys to the customers. Following the Build-A-Bear example, some of the company's main competitors, including Vermont Teddy Bear and American Girl, began initiatives to recast their traditional products and services in ways that would create experiences for their customers.

Vermont Teddy Bear, established in Burlington in 1981, marketed its product as the "only bear made in America and guaranteed for life." Struggling to find customers in the local area, the company developed the unique "Bear-Gram" concept of mailing customized teddy bears to visiting tourists. The new concept had huge success, and the company experienced tremendous growth. In 1993 the Vermont Teddy Bear Company hit number 58 on the *Inc. Magazine* list of the fastest-growing private companies in the United States. Because the customers received their furry friends through the mail, Vermont Teddy Bear needed to find innovative ways to create an experience for the bear owners. To involve customers in the bear-making process, the company invited all of its fans to regularly scheduled Vermont Teddy Bear plant tours. Each tour featured many fun activities for the young visitors and their friends and families, including a lunch at the Hungry Bear Café or a visit to the Bear Shop, the Bear Museum, and the Vermont Teddy Bear Hospital. The company also created a "wow!" experience for the recipients of its teddy bears thanks to its unique packaging. The gift box included an airhole for the bear and a warning not to turn the box upside down lest the bear get a headache, as well as a sweet treat and a personalized card with a colorful drawing of the headquarters and all the employees' first names. In the Vermont Teddy Bear locations, bear counselors assisted customers in selecting and personalizing their bears. The company also let its customers be creative by customizing a teddy bear look-a-like that captured the personality and appearance of someone special to them.

Another Build-A-Bear competitor, American Girl Inc., also decided to move to a new level in providing value for its customers. Founded in 1986, American Girl specialized in manufacturing high-end dolls, books, and magazines for young girls. Since it was acquired by Mattel Inc. in 1998, American Girl started a rapid retail expansion and concentrated on further product development. To create additional customer value, American Girl took steps to develop new engaging experiences between the dolls, the girls, and their families. In 2005 the company opened its first American Girl (AG) Places, in New York, Los Angeles, and Chicago, providing visitors with a unique retail experience through which they could engage in many exciting activities and bond with their new doll friends. Every AG Place included a theater showing a live play concentrated on the doll collection, a café for grown-up dining experiences or birthday parties, and a doll hair salon or a photo studio. Encouraged by the success of the AG Places, in 2007 American Girl opened two American Girl Boutique and Bistros, in Dallas and Atlanta. These new locations were the company's latest way to connect with girls by allowing them to celebrate special times with their families and friends in a fun and casual environment. According to Ellen L. Brothers, the president of American Girl and the executive vice president of Mattel, the company became much more than a place that sells dolls. "It's the place where imaginations soar—from boutiques to special events, from the café to the theater and beyond."[33]

Changing Market

While providing unique experiences for the customers became an important competitive advantage in the toy industry, there were also other factors shaping the competitive environment that required attention. While the Internet had helped bolster the retail toy industry, it had also intensified competition dramatically. The Toy Industry Association reported that increasingly popular electronic gadgets, video, and online games, such as the Nintendo Wii game console and the *www.webkinz.com* online community, could easily attract children's attention and thus reduce the time kids spent with their plush animals. This shift has changed the focus of some companies, such as Hasbro, which turned to the web to bring attention to new editions of its board games Monopoly and Trivial Pursuit.[34] Furthermore, according to the technology-loving experts, electronic toys had the potential to provide the best educational applications, thanks to interactive displays of pictures, lights, and sounds. Electronic toys were deemed to be very helpful when teaching young children about cause and effect and hand-eye coordination—two important behavioral learning skills.[35]

According to leading market research company The NPD Group, U.S. retail sales of toys generated $21.87 billion in 2010, in which online/Internet sales grew 22 percent from 2009, while the sales of plush toys were flat, at $1.73 billion.[36] Build-A-Bear Workshop recognized the need to infuse more technology into its product line offerings to stay ahead of its competitors. One way in which Build-A-Bear attempted to expand on technology was by offering a technology-based platform for its customization experience through the introduction of a Build-A-Bear video game for Nintendo DS. The Nintendo DS simulation, a game in which players could customize a digitized bear (or character) on screen, attempted to re-create the in-store experience by reproducing the process of shopping and creating a bear in a Build-A-Bear Workshop as a video. Through the use of a touch screen, wireless technology, enhanced graphics, and innovative control mechanisms, the game simulated the same bear-building process as the one in the stores. The game featured eight different characters to be played with and cared for, as well as a kitchen and a dining room to prepare meals for the video characters. The users could also design the room of their favorite character.[37]

Maxine Clark stated that 80 percent of the customers were repeat guests who planned their visit in advance, which meant people who had visited the stores loved them.[38] Build-A-Bear Workshop's special mix of products and highly interactive, theme-park-like environment inside the malls were what kept customers coming back and were the key components in the franchises' rapid success. But declining comparable same-store sales meant that sales based on the repeat customers were not enough. To attract more people to its stores, the company organized Build-A-Party events for kids' birthday parties and scout outings. The company stayed true to its differentiation strategy by not following the example of its competition, which often used markdowns to sell products. Instead, Build-A-Bear

Workshop tried to increase its brand awareness as an experienced retailer by allocating large portions of its budget to national television advertising, direct mail, and other types of publicity (4.2 percent of total revenues in 2010).[39]

At the same time, there was only so much the company could do when most of its stores were inside malls, where traffic was declining partly because of the rising price of gasoline and the weak economy. To cope with this issue, Build-A-Bear Workshop had already tried to explore other options such as opening new stores outside the malls and relying more on the online storefront and licensing.

Besides its dependency on mall traffic, Build-A-Bear Workshop also faced constraints that were related to children's ages and preferences. Even as management was strategically trying to lure more customers to the stores, the company was facing a generation of kids that got older younger. The "kids getting old younger (KGOY)" phenomenon was noted on the Toy Industry Association's website: "Kids are seeking more sophisticated entertainment . . . and doing so at younger and younger ages." Tastes were maturing and becoming more sophisticated at a younger age, reducing the available time slot for products designed for children. The KGOY generation was familiar with what technology could offer. Given that children ages 1 to 14 were the recipients of approximately 80 percent of Build-A-Bear's stuffed animals, the Wellbeing study of kids ages 8 to 15 revealed valuable information for the company. According to the findings of the study, announced on Nickelodeon and MTV in November 2006, children throughout the world were growing up younger and appeared to be experiencing higher levels of stress in their daily lives. Despite their young age, kids already felt pressure to succeed. Thus, getting a good grade in school was their top priority. Those who were growing up in an environment with more news media outlets generally felt less safe regardless of where they came from in the world.[40] All the findings related to age compression were based on the current generation of children and therefore could be valuable to the toy industry if translated into business-specific strategies. In other words, with the kids' concerns and priorities on the table, what could Build-A-Bear do to make its brand more appealing to them?

The Toy Industry Association's report contained another interesting finding related to the age factor: The heart of the toy industry belonged to kids seven and under. This segment accounted for over 60 percent of total industry dollar volume, and the reason was simple: These children had more time to spend with toys because they faced fewer school hours, had less homework, and were not as diverted by youth electronics and video games.[41] Considering the new trends in children's preferences, should Build-A-Bear Workshop look into having multiple strategies targeting different age groups?

Financials and the Future

The early years of Build-A-Bear Workshop were marked with great success. The company's physical locations grew from 150 stores at fiscal year-end 2003 to 344 company-owned stores in the United States, Canada, the United Kingdom, and Ireland by 2010. Due to this expansion, Build-A-Bear Workshop saw an increase in its revenues from $301.7 million in fiscal year 2004 to $437.1 million in 2006. Its compound annual revenue growth rate reached 20.4 percent, and its net income jumped from $18.5 million in fiscal year 2004 to $29.5 million in 2006, ultimately resulting in a compound annual net income growth rate of 26.5 percent.[42]

Because new stores generated much higher sales per square foot, part of the company's growth came from opening up more stores. New stores typically paid for themselves in their first year of operation, and comparable same-store sales began to decline in the second and third years. Before 2009, Build-A-Bear Workshop had planned to open 25 to 30 new stores per year so that 75 percent of the U.S. population would be within 30 miles of a Build-A-Bear Workshop. In addition, the company signed licensed product agreements with leading manufacturers to use the Build-A-Bear Workshop brand to develop products for retailers. Internationally, the company's expansion plan was to have well-capitalized franchisees with retail or real estate expertise. Build-a-Bear Workshop operated 290 stores, primarily in major malls, throughout the United States and Canada, 54 stores in the United Kingdom and Ireland, and an Internet store (see Exhibit 3).[43]

Unfortunately, the initial successful performance did not last. Build-A-Bear Workshop's comparable-store sales declined steadily from 2004 to 2008 and more so during the economic recession of 2009–2010.[44] As of 2010, new-store development was placed on hold until the economy had a chance to recover from the recession.

Because Build-A-Bear Workshop could not efficiently capitalize in the market, there was speculation on Wall Street that the firm's current cash flow could support a buyout price much higher than its present value. One of the potential buyers might have been Disney, which already had a partnership with the company and could leverage the Build-A-Bear brand to promote Disney movies and TV shows. To evaluate alternative strategies that could increase its share value, possibly including the buyout option, Build-A-Bear Workshop hired the investment bank Lehman Brothers, but the findings of the analysis have yet to be released.[45]

Clark, who was aware of the strategic challenges that Build-A-Bear was facing, was optimistic about the future and stated, "We [at Build-A-Bear] believe that through our highly profitable business model and unique retail-entertainment concept, we will continue to grow total revenues, increase net income, and generate excess cash flow."[46] Had Build-A-Bear Workshop reached a mature stage in the domestic market, as indicated by its slower comparable-store sales and decreases in profit? To sustain its domestic market position in such a dynamic competitive industry, Build-A-Bear Workshop will have to continue building on its creativity and boost innovation in its offerings, such as the temporary themed product lines and seasonal pop-up stores.

Exhibit 3 Store Data

Store Data	Fiscal Year				
	2010	2009	2008	2007	2006
Number of stores at end of period					
North America	290	291	292	272	233
Europe	54	54	54	49	38
Total stores	344	345	346	321	271
Square footage at end of period					
North America	841,600	846,373	856,504	810,208	712,299
Europe	77,870	77,520	77,520	70,577	56,701
Total square footage	919,470	923,893	934,024	880,785	769,000
Average net retail sales per store	$1,030	$1,044	$1,329	$1,576	$1,761
Net retail sales per gross square foot, North America	$356	$358	$445	$516	$573
Consolidated comparable-store sales change	(2.0%)	(13.4%)	(14.0%)	(9.9%)	(6.5%)

As Maxine Clark said, "Ray Croft didn't invent hamburgers. Howard Schultz didn't invent coffee. And Oprah didn't invent talk shows. They just invented how to do it and how to do it better." Clark would have to invent a way to turn the Build-A-Bear experience into a lasting legend. Despite the grizzly financials, Clark remained upbeat about the future of Build-A-Bear. Only time will tell whether Build-A-Bear will grin and bear it.

Endnotes

1. Build-A-Bear Workshop Inc. 2010. Press release: Explore the wild side of Build-A-Bear Workshop. *Business Wire*, May 28. *phx.corporate-ir.net/phoenix. zhtml?c=182478&p=irol-newsArticle&ID=1432265*.
2. Build-A-Bear Workshop Inc. 2010. Press release: Fairytales come to life at Build-A-Bear Workshop. *Business Wire*, April 06. *phx.corporate-ir.net/phoenix. zhtml?c=182478&p=irol-newsArticle&ID=1409941*.
3. Build-A-Bear Workshop Inc. 2010. Press release: Build-A-Bear Workshop introduces out of this world Star Wars products. *Business Wire*, September 21. *phx.corporate-ir.net/phoenix. zhtml?c=182478&p=irol-newsArticle&ID=1473280*.
4. Build-A-Bear Workshop Inc. 2010. Press release: Build-A-Bear Workshop to open pop-up stores in time for the 2010 holiday season. *Business Wire*, September 17. *phx.corporate-ir.net/phoenix. zhtml?c=182478&p=irol-newsArticle&ID=1472604*.
5. See Build-A-Bear Workshop press releases at *phx. corporate-ir.net/phoenix.zhtml?c=182478&p=irol-news*. The charities mentioned are from various press releases from 2009–2011.
6. Build-A-Bear Workshop Inc. 2007. Press release: Build-A-Bear Workshop surpasses $10 million mark in charitable giving as it cele-bear-ates 10th birthday. *Business Wire*, January 30. *phx.corporate-ir.net/phoenix. zhtml?c=182478&p=irol-newsArticle&ID=955609*.
7. Build-A-Bear Workshop Inc. 2010. Press release: Build-A-Bear Workshop named one of Fortune's "100 Best Companies to Work For." *Business Wire*, January 21. *phx.corporate-ir.net/phoenix. zhtml?c=182478&p=irol-newsArticle&ID=1377527*.
8. Build-A-Bear Workshop Inc. 2011. Press release: Build-A-Bear Workshop, Inc. reports significant improvement in fiscal 2010 fourth quarter and full-year results. *Business Wire*, February 17. *phx.corporate-ir.net/phoenix. zhtml?c=182478&p=irol-newsArticle&ID=1529994*.
9. *Wall Street Journal*. 2011. Build-A-Bear Workshop, Princeton National Bancorp: Biggest price decliners (BBW, PNBC). March 17. *online.wsj.com/article/SB10001424052 748704657704576150551956521540.html*.
10. Clark, M. 2007. Build-A-Bear's founder shares her story. *BusinessWeek Online*, September 17. *www.businessweek. com/smallbiz/content/sep2007/sb20070912_785676.htm*.
11. *PR Newswire*. 2006. Leading entrepreneur shares secrets of success in innovative new book." April 20.
12. Tsiantar, B. 2005. Not your average bear. *Time*, July.

13. Build-A-Bear Workshop Inc. 2011. Form 10-K, filed March 17. This statement has appeared in numerous previously SEC filings and in the company profile; see *phx.corporate-ir.net/phoenix.zhtml?c=182478& p=irol-homeprofile.*

14. Ibid.

15. Ibid.

16. Conley, L. 2005. Customer-centered leader: Maxine Clark. *Fast Company,* October 1.

17. Mithers, C. L. 2003. A bear of a business. *Ladies Home Journal,* November.

18. Build-A-Bear Workshop Inc. 2006 annual report, Form 10-K: 7.

19. Ibid.: 14.

20. Build-A-Bear Workshop Inc. 2008 annual report, Form 10-K.

21. Howell, D. 2000. Retailers attribute success to out-of-box innovations. *DSN Retailing Today,* October 2: 4–58.

22. Build-A-Bear Workshop Inc. 2006 annual report.

23. Wilson, M. 1998. This bear market toys with success. *Chain Store Age,* January: 50–53.

24. Build-A-Bear Workshop Inc. 2006 annual report.

25. Imbs, C. 2004. Maxine Clark: A beary good idea. *St. Louis Commerce,* July.

26. Amato-McCoy, D. M. 2007. Levels of loyalty. *Chain Store Age,* April: 51–53.

27. Build-A-Bear Workshop Inc. 2006 annual report: 9.

28. Build-A-Bear Workshop Inc. 10-K reports.

29. Kaufman, J. 2007. After Build-A-Bear, build-a-toy-car. *New York Times,* May 29.

30. Build-A-Bear Workshop Inc. 2005. Press release, January 10.

31. Build-A-Bear Workshop Inc. 2006 annual report.

32. Logue, A. C. 2005. Warm, fuzzy and business savvy. *NYSE Magazine,* October–November.

33. *www.americangirl.com.*

34. *New Media Age* (London). 2005. October 20: 18.

35. *toy-tma.com.*

36. NPD Group. 2011. Press release, January 27.

37. *www.estarland.com/index.asp?page=NintendoDS&product=29856.*

38. Clark, M. 2006. Build-A-Bear chief Maxine Clark discusses changing the retail industry. *Webster University's School of Business & Technology Newsletter,* Summer.

39. Build-A-Bear Workshop Inc. 2010 Form 10-K.

40. Feely, P. 2005. The toy industry and youth marketing today: Going beyond "KGOY." *Toy Industry Association,* April 10.

41. Ibid.

42. Build-A-Bear Workshop Inc. 2006 annual report, Form 10-K: 4

43. Build-A-Bear Workshop Inc. 2010 Form 10-K.

44. Ibid.

45. *BusinessWeek Online.* 2007. Build-A-Bear brings out the bulls. June 29.

46. *M2PressWIRE.* 2007. Build-A-Bear Workshop, Inc. announces it is evaluating strategic alternatives for enhancing long-term shareholder value. June 28.

Case 32   JetBlue Airlines

Getting "Blue" Again?*

JetBlue posted a net income of $97 million in 2010. The airline continues to pursue its goal of becoming "the Americas' Favorite Airline" and aims to attain positive free cash flow and long-term sustainable growth while maintaining adequate liquidity. Financially, the airline was far better than after the Valentine's Day fiasco in February 2007 and subsequent loss of $84 million in 2008. It focuses on controlling costs, maximizing unit revenues, and managing capital expenditures and aims to achieve disciplined growth (see Exhibit 1).[1]

However, in recent years, JetBlue appears to be moving away from its core strategy, in quite interesting ways, of being a low-cost player providing the distinctive "JetBlue experience." In its efforts to boost revenues, the airline began charging $10 to $20 for seats with extra legroom, doubled its ticket-change fee to $100, and introduced

* This case study was prepared by Professor Naga Lakshmi Damaraju of The Indian School of Business, Professor Alan B. Eisner at Pace University, and Professor Gregory G. Dess at the University of Texas at Dallas. The purpose of the case is to stimulate class discussion rather than to illustrate effective or ineffective handling of a business situation. The authors thank Mrs. Shefali Mittal, Indian School of Business, for her research assistance and Professor Michael Oliff at the University of Texas at Dallas for his valuable comments on an earlier version of this case. Several parts of the case are from an earlier version. Copyright © 2011 Damaraju, Eisner, and Dess.

refundable tickets that cost more than nonrefundable ones. Further, the airline began charging $7 for a pillow-and-blanket kit, an amenity usually provided free of charge by other airlines.[2] Breaking another low-cost rule, JetBlue moved away from ticket sales through its own website and signed up with travel agencies and the Galileo and Sabre global distribution systems in August 2006 and with online travel agencies such as Orbitz in January 2008. Further, it sold approximately 42.6 million shares of common stock to Deutsche Lufthansa, the German carrier, in January 2008, which indicates a move away from its "growing alone" strategy,[3] and also forged an interline agreement with Virgin Atlantic. With the interline agreement, passengers on JetBlue will be able to connect through Boston, New York, or Washington to catch flights to London Heathrow on Virgin Atlantic. JetBlue customers connecting in Orlando will be able to fly to London's Gatwick airport, Manchester, England, or Glasgow, Scotland.[4] While this is not a strict "hub-and-spoke" model, it nearly amounts to the same thing. These moves raise the question: Will JetBlue be what it was envisaged to be?

The U.S. Airline Industry[5]

There are three primary segments in the airline industry: major airlines, regional airlines, and low-fare airlines. Major U.S. airlines, as defined by the Department of Transportation,

Exhibit 1 JetBlue's Stock Performance vs. S&P 500

Source: *finance.yahoo.com.*

are those with annual revenues of over $1 billion. As of the end of 2010, 18 passenger airlines belonged to this category, the largest of which were American Airlines, Continental Airlines, Delta Air Lines, Northwest Airlines, and United Airlines. These airlines offer scheduled flights to most large cities within the United States and abroad and also serve numerous smaller cities. Most major airlines adopted the hub-and-spoke route system. In this system, the operations are concentrated in a limited number of hub cities, while other destinations are served by providing one-stop or connecting service through the hub.

Regional airlines typically operate smaller aircraft on lower-volume routes than do major airlines. Unlike the low-fare airlines, the regional airlines do not have an independent route system. They typically enter into relationships with major airlines and carry their passengers on the "spoke"— that is, between a hub or larger city and a smaller city. There were six chief regional U.S. airlines at the end of 2010.

In 1971 Southwest initiated service as a regional carrier, but by 1990 it had become a major airline when its revenues crossed the $1 billion mark.[6] The Southwest model was based on operating a single-type aircraft fleet with high utilization, having a simplified fare structure with single-class seating, and achieving high productivity from its human and physical assets. In contrast, the "hub-and-spoke" system, increased labor costs, and increases in multitype aircraft fleets bloated the cost structure of the major airlines.

Deregulation of the U.S. airline industry in 1978 ushered in competition in the previously protected industry. Several low-cost, low-fare operators entered the competitive landscape that Southwest had pioneered.

The low-fare airlines operate from "point to point" and have their own route system. The target segment of low-fare airlines is fare-conscious leisure and business travelers who might otherwise have used alternative forms of transportation or not traveled at all. Low-fare airlines stimulated demand in this segment and also have been successful in weaning business travelers from the major airlines. There are four chief low-cost U.S. airlines. The main bases of competition in the airline industry are fare pricing, customer service, routes served, flight schedules, types of aircraft, safety record and reputation, code-sharing relationships, in-flight entertainment systems, and frequent-flier programs.

The economic downturn in the late 1990s and the terrorist attacks on the World Trade Center and the Pentagon on September 11, 2001, severely affected the airline industry. The demand for air travel dropped significantly and led to a reduction in traffic and revenue. Security concerns, security costs, and liquidity concerns increased. Lower fares and also increased capacity of the low-cost airlines created a very unprofitable environment for traditional networks. Most of the traditional network airlines, since 2001, have filed for bankruptcy or undergone financial restructuring, mergers, or consolidations. With these restructurings, many of them have been able to significantly reduce labor costs, restructure debt, and generally gain a more competitive cost structure. This has enabled the major airlines to provide innovative offerings similar to those of low-cost airlines while still maintaining their alliances, frequent-flier programs, and expansive route networks. The gap between low-cost airlines and traditional network airlines has been diminishing drastically.

Neeleman and JetBlue[7]

Born in São Paulo, Brazil, and brought up in Salt Lake City, David Neeleman dropped out of the University of Utah after his freshman year to move back to Brazil and become a missionary. After two years of missionary work, he made his modest beginning in establishing his own business by renting out condominiums in Hawaii. He then established his own travel agency and began chartering flights from Salt Lake City to the islands to bring in prospective clients for his rental services. Neeleman's sales prowess caught the attention of June Morris, who owned one of Utah's largest corporate travel agencies. Soon after, in 1984, Neeleman and Morris launched the Utah-based Morris Air, a charter operation. Morris Air was closely modeled after Southwest Airlines, the legendary discount airline in the United States.

Neeleman considered Herb Kelleher, Southwest's founder, his idol. He studied everything Kelleher accomplished and tried to do it better, which meant keeping costs low and turning planes around quickly, among a host of other operational and strategic activities and choices. While following the Southwest model, Neeleman brought his own innovations into the business. He pioneered the use of "at-home reservation agents," routing calls to agents' homes to save money on office rent and infrastructure expense. He also developed the first electronic ticketing system in the airline industry. By 1992, Morris Air had grown into a regularly scheduled airline and was ready for an initial public offering (IPO) when Southwest, impressed by Morris's low costs and high revenue, bought the company for $129 million. Neeleman became the executive vice president of Southwest. However, Neeleman could not adjust to Southwest's pace of doing things. By 1994, he was at odds with the top executives and left after signing a five-year noncompete agreement. In the interim between leaving Southwest and establishing JetBlue, Neeleman developed the electronic ticketing system he had initiated at Morris Air into one of the world's simplest airline reservation systems: Open Skies. He sold Open Skies to Hewlett-Packard in 1999. During the same period, he was also a consultant to a low-fare Canadian start-up airline, WestJet Airlines.[8] In 1999, after the noncompete agreement with Southwest Airlines ended, Neeleman launched his own airline. He raised about $130 million of capital in two weeks, an unprecedented amount for a start-up airline.[9] Weston Presidio Capital and Chase Capital, venture capital firms that had backed Neeleman's prior ventures, were return investors, and financier George Soros was also brought into the deal. "David's a winner; I knew anything David touched would turn to gold," said Michael Lazarus of Weston Presidio Capital, which had earlier funded Morris Air. "We were intrigued with his ideas about a low-cost airline."[10] With such strong support from venture capitalists, JetBlue began as the highest-funded start-up airline in U.S. aviation history.

JetBlue commenced operations in August 2000, with John F. Kennedy International Airport (JFK) as its primary base of operations. In 2001 JetBlue extended its operations to the West Coast with its base at Long Beach Municipal Airport, which served the Los Angeles area. In 2002 the company went public and was listed on Nasdaq as JBLU. JetBlue had expected to sell 5.5 million shares at about $24 to $26 in its initial public offering. Instead, it sold 5.87 million shares at $27 per share through its lead underwriters Morgan Stanley and Merrill Lynch. The shares closed at $47, up by $20, on the first day of trading. JetBlue's stock offering was one of the hottest IPOs of the year.[11] JetBlue had been established with the goal of being a leading low-fare passenger airline that offered customers a differentiated product and high-quality customer service. It was positioned as a low-cost, low-fare airline providing quality customer service on point-to-point routes. JetBlue had a geographically diversified flight schedule that included both short-haul and long-haul routes. The mission of the company, according to David Neeleman, was "to bring humanity back to air travel." To stimulate demand, the airline focused on underserved markets and large metropolitan areas that had high average fares. The "JetBlue effect" aspired to bring about three effects in the markets it entered: fares going down, traffic going up, and JetBlue capturing a big chunk of that traffic (see Exhibit 2).

JetBlue was committed to keeping its costs low. To achieve this objective, the company originally operated a single-type aircraft fleet comprising Airbus A320 planes as opposed to the more popular but costly Boeing 737. The A320s had 162 seats, compared to 132 seats in the Boeing 737. According to JetBlue, the A320 was cheaper to maintain and also more fuel efficient. Because all of JetBlue's planes were new, the maintenance costs were also lower. In addition, the single type of aircraft kept training costs low and increased personnel utilization. JetBlue was the first to introduce the "paperless cockpit," in which pilots, equipped with laptops, had ready access to flight manuals that were constantly updated at headquarters. As a result, pilots could quickly calculate the weight, balance, and takeoff performance of the aircraft instead of having to download and print the manuals to make the calculations. The paperless cockpit thus ensured faster takeoffs by reducing paperwork and helped in achieving quicker turnarounds and higher aircraft utilization.[12] No meals were served on the planes, and pilots even had to be ready, if need be, to do the cleanup work on the plane to minimize the time the aircraft was on the ground. Turnaround time was also reduced by the airline's choice of less congested airports.[13] Innovation was everywhere; for example, there were no paper tickets to lose and no mileage statements to mail to frequent fliers.

With friendly, customer service–oriented employees; new aircraft; roomy leather seats with 36 channels of free LiveTV, 100 channels of free XM satellite radio, and movie channel offerings from FOXInflight; and wider legroom (one row of seats was removed from its A320 aircraft to create additional space), JetBlue promised its customers a distinctive flying experience, the "JetBlue experience." With virtually no incidences of passengers being denied boarding; high completion factors (99.6 percent as compared to 98.3 percent at other major airlines); the lowest incidence of delayed, mishandled, or lost bags; and the third-lowest number of customer complaints, the company was indeed setting standards for low-cost operations in the industry. The company was voted the best domestic airline in the *Conde Nast Traveler*'s Readers' Choice Awards for five consecutive years. It was also rated the World's Best Domestic Airline by readers of *Travel + Leisure Magazine* in 2006. In addition, it earned the Passenger Service Award from *Air Transport World*.[14]

Expansion and Growth

JetBlue grew to serve 63 destinations in 21 states, Puerto Rico, and 11 countries in the Caribbean and Latin America by the end of December 2010 (see Exhibit 3). It operated 650 daily flights on average and was the sixth largest

---

Exhibit 2   **The JetBlue Effect***

Route	Increase in Daily Passengers, %	Decrease in Average Fare, %	JetBlue's Share of Local Traffic, %
New York to Miami/Ft. Lauderdale	14	17 (to $121.50)	23.1
New York to Los Angeles Basin	2	26 (to $219.31)	18.0
New York to Buffalo	94	40 (to $86.09)	61.2

Source: Data from BACK Aviation Solutions, adapted from Zellner, W. 2004. Is JetBlue's flight plan flawed? *BusinessWeek*, February 16.

* Figures as of second quarter, 2003.

passenger carrier in the United States based on revenue passenger miles by the end of 2010.[15]

However, divergence from JetBlue's original model was evident. From operating a single aircraft type, which was the basis of having low training costs, flexibility in personnel management, and so on, the airline moved to include a second type of aircraft, the Embraer 190, which it was not comfortable operating. Also, JetBlue acquired LiveTV LLC in 2002 for $41 million in cash and the retirement of $39 million of LiveTV debt.[16] Further, the company embarked on other paths where it did not necessarily have prior experience. On February 6, 2007, *USA Today* announced that JetBlue planned to enter into an alliance with Aer Lingus, an Irish flag carrier. The alliance was expected to facilitate easy transfers for both airlines' customers, but unlike traditional code-share alliances, it would not allow either airline to sell seats on the other airline, meaning customers would have to make individual reservations with both carriers.[17] On February 14, 2007, JetBlue's first code-share agreement, with Cape Air, was announced. Under this agreement, JetBlue passengers from Boston's Logan Airport would be carried to Cape Air's destinations throughout Cape Cod and the surrounding islands, and customers would be able to purchase seats on both airlines under one reservation. While Lufthansa's January 2008 acquisition of a minority equity stake in JetBlue did not automatically lead to any code-share agreements, Lufthansa expected to have "operational cooperation" with JetBlue.

Nevertheless, high fuel prices, the competitive pricing environment, and other cost increases made it increasingly difficult to fund JetBlue's growth profitability. The airline suffered its first-ever losses after its IPO in 2005. It posted net losses of $1 million and $20 million for 2006 and 2005, respectively, and an unprecedented $76 million loss for 2007, with the primary reason being rising fuel costs (see Exhibits 4 and 5). In July 2008 the company modified its growth plans by deferring a total of 21 aircraft deliveries from between 2009 and 2011 to between 2014 and 2015 and sold several of its Airbus A320s from 2006.[18]

Despite the airline's much touted unique culture, in 2006 the International Association of Machinists (IAM) attempted to unionize JetBlue's ramp service workers. Though the union organizing petition was dismissed by the National Mediation Board because fewer than 35 percent of eligible employees supported an election, unionization is a possibility going forward.[19] What this means to JetBlue's cultural fabric remains to be seen.

The Operations Meltdown and Beyond[20]

Valentine's Day 2007 is the nightmare in JetBlue's hitherto glorious history for more than one reason. Not only did the event destroy JetBlue's reputation for customer friendliness and cost Neeleman his job, but it also exposed the critical weaknesses in the systems that had kept the airline's operations going.

There was trouble in the Midwest for several days before the Valentine's Day storm reached the East Coast. Unlike the blowing snow and frigid temperatures in cities such as Chicago, the storm turned into freezing rain and sleet as it slammed the mid-Atlantic region, causing havoc on major highways and virtually shutting down airports. Most other airlines canceled dozens of flights

Exhibit 3 **JetBlue's Growth**

| Year | Destinations | Employees | Operating Aircraft | | |
			Owned	Leased	Total
2000	12	1,174	4	6	10
2001	18	2,361	9	12	21
2002	20	4,011	21	16	37
2003	21	5,433	29	24	53
2004	30	7,211	44	25	69
2005	33	9,021	61	31	92
2006	49	10,377	70	49	119
2007	53	11,632	77	57	134
2008	52	11,852	83	59	142
2009	60	12,532	92	59	151
2010	63	12,948	96	64	160

Source: JetBlue SEC filings.

Exhibit 4 Statements of Operations Data (in millions of dollars, except per-share data; year-end December 31, 2010)

	2010	2009	2008	2007	2006
Operating revenues	3,779	3,292	3,392	2,843	2,364
Operating expenses:					
Salaries, wages, and benefits	891	776	694	648	553
Aircraft fuel	1,115	945	1,397	968	786
Landing fees and other rents	228	213	199	180	158
Depreciation and amortization	220	228	205	176	151
Aircraft rent	126	126	129	124	103
Sales and marketing	179	151	151	121	104
Maintenance materials and repairs	172	149	127	106	87
Other operating expenses	515	419	377	350	294
Total operating expenses	3,446	3,007	3,279	2,673	2,236
Operating income:	333	285	113	170	128
Government compensation	—	—	—	—	—
Other income (expense)	(172)	(181)	(202)	(139)	(129)
Income (loss) before income taxes	161	104	(89)	31	(1)
Income tax expense (benefit)	64	43	(5)	19	6
Net income (loss)	**97**	**61**	**(84)**	**12**	**(7)**
Earnings (loss) per common share:					
Basic	0.36	0.24	(0.37)	0.07	(0.04)
Diluted	0.31	0.21	(0.37)	0.06	(0.04)

Source: JetBlue SEC filings.

Exhibit 5 Operating Statistics (year-end December 31, 2010)*

	2010	2009	2008	2007	2006
Revenue passengers ($ thousands)	24,254	22,450	21,920	21,387	18,565
Revenue passenger-miles ($ millions)	28,279	25,955	26,071	25,737	23,320
Available seat-miles (ASMs) ($ millions)	34,744	32,558	32,442	31,904	28,594
Load factor (%)	81.4	79.7	80.4	80.7	81.6
Aircraft utilization (hours per day)	11.6	11.5	12.1	12.8	12.7
Average fare ($)	140.69	130.67	139.56	123.23	119.73
Yield per passenger-mile (cents)	12.07	11.30	11.73	10.24	9.53
Passenger revenue per ASM (cents)	9.82	9.01	9.43	8.26	7.77
Operating revenue per ASM (cents)	10.88	10.11	10.45	8.91	8.27
Operating expense per ASM (cents)	9.92	9.24	10.11	8.38	7.82

(*continued*)

Exhibit 5 **Operating Statistics** (year-end December 31, 2010)* (*continued*)

	2010	2009	2008	2007	2006
Operating expense per ASM, excluding fuel (cents)	6.71	6.33	5.80	5.34	5.07
Airline operating expense per ASM (cents)[†]	9.71	8.99	9.87	8.27	7.76
Departures	225,501	215,526	205,389	196,594	159,152
Average stage length (miles)	1,100	1,076	1,120	1,129	1,186
Average number of operating aircraft during period	153.5	148.0	139.5	127.8	106.5
Average fuel cost per gallon ($)	2.29	2.08	3.08	2.18	2.08
Fuel gallons consumed (millions)	486	455	453	444	377
Full-time equivalent employees at period end[†]	11,121	10,704	9,895	9,909	9,265

Source: JetBlue SEC filings.

* See the appendix at the end of this case for a glossary of the terms used in this table.
† Excludes results of employees and operations of LiveTV, LLC, that are unrelated to the airline operations.

in preparation for the storm. However, JetBlue management opted to wait it out. With its policy of doing whatever it can to ensure a flight is completed, even if this means waiting for several hours, the airline sent outbound flights to the runway at John F. Kennedy airport in New York at about 8 a.m. This was done to ensure that the planes would be ready to take off as soon as the weather let up. However, instead of letting up, the weather deteriorated further. The federal aviation guidelines do not allow planes to take off in ice-pellet conditions, and so the JetBlue planes and equipment were soon literally freezing to the tarmac. By about 3 p.m., with no hope of getting the planes off the ground, the airline began calling in buses to bring the passengers back to the terminal. By then, however, the damage had been done. Airport terminals, more so in the JFK hub, were filled with passengers still expecting to get on flights, and, compounding the problem, they were now being joined by hundreds of infuriated passengers returning from the JetBlue planes. "Things spiraled out of control. We did a horrible job," said Neeleman in a conference call early the next week. "We got ourselves into a situation where we were doing rolling cancellations instead of a massive cancellation. Communications broke down, we weren't able to reach out to passengers and they continued to arrive at the airports. . . . It had a cascading effect." The chaotic situation could not be brought under control for another week.

A number of shortcomings in the company's information systems were responsible for this debacle, according to Charles Mees, the new CIO who had joined the company a few months before the event. The reservation system, for example, was not expanded enough to meet the extreme customer call volume. As the seriousness of the Valentine's Day situation became apparent, managers with JetBlue's

Salt Lake City–based reservation office began calling in off-duty agents to assist with the expected high volume of calls. These agents normally work primarily from their homes, using an Internet-based communications system to tap into the company's Navitaire Open Skies reservation system. (Headquartered in Minneapolis, Navitaire hosts the reservation system for JetBlue and about another dozen discount airlines.) The passengers who were bumped off the planes or arrived at JFK and other East Coast airports to find their JetBlue flights had been canceled had only one option for rebooking their flights: Call the JetBlue reservation office. JetBlue customers did not have the option of using airport kiosks to rebook their flights via its website. The company had been working on the online rebooking issue since December 2006, but the new feature was not yet ready in February 2007. As a result, the Salt Lake City reservation agents were suddenly flooded with calls from irate passengers trying to get on another flight or to find out about compensation possibilities. With Mees's emergency call to Navitaire, the system could be boosted to accommodate up to 950 agents at one time (up 300 from the original 650), but then it hit a wall. Even with the boosted capacity, there was difficulty finding enough bodies to staff the phones. Off-duty crews and airport personnel volunteered for the task, but they were not trained in how to use the system.

Also in a mess was the baggage-handling mechanism. As passengers struggled through terminals to make new reservations, their bags piled up in huge mounds at airports. JetBlue did not have a computerized system in place for recording and tracking lost bags. Because the airline hardly ever canceled flights, if there were bags left over at the end of a flight, airport personnel figured out ownership by looking up a passenger's record. However, such a process became

Exhibit 6   **Direct-Competitor Comparison**

Performance Indicators	JetBlue	AMR Corp.	Southwest Airlines	UAL Corp.	Industry
Market cap	1.65B	2.07B	8.83B	7.39B	205.21M
Employees	N/A	78,250	34,901	N/A	7.48K
Quarterly revenue growth (YOY)	12.60%	10.40%	14.80%	101.10%	8.30%
Revenue (TTM)	3.78B	22.17B	12.10B	23.23B	2.65B
Gross margin (TTM)	33.24%	23.03%	25.13%	29.44%	23.47%
EBITDA (TTM)	591.00M	1.40B	1.62B	2.60B	348.98M
Operating margins (TTM)	9.55%	1.39%	8.16%	7.22%	5.66%
Net income (TTM)	97.00M	−471.00M	459.00M	252.00M	N/A
EPS (TTM)	0.31	−1.41	0.61	1.08	0.69
P/E (TTM)	17.92	N/A	19.36	20.84	9.32
PEG (5-yr expected)	2.33	−4.26	2.46	1.58	2.07
P/S (TTM)	0.43	0.09	0.73	0.31	0.11

Source: *finance.yahoo.com*, as of March 7, 2011.

Note: YOY = year over year; TTM = trailing 12 months.

totally unmanageable with massive cancellations happening. The airline had entered into an agreement in 2003 with Lufthansa to purchase a system called BagScan, but the system was never implemented. Mees admits, "We didn't prioritize it—probably because it is so focused on the [Enterprise Resource Planning] project." JetBlue was growing fast and needed increased capabilities in the Enterprise Resource Planning system to handle its human resource functions.

There were also other system headaches to deal with. JetBlue uses several applications from Sabre Airline Solutions of Southlake, Texas, as part of its core operations infrastructure. This is in addition to the Navitaire reservation system. The application, Sabre Flight Control Suite, provides the airline with utilities to manage, schedule, and track its planes and crews, while Sabre's Dispatch Manager is used to develop actual flight plans. Another application, Flite Trac, within the Flight Control Suite, interfaces with the Navitaire reservation system. This application provides real-time information to managers on factors such as flight status, fuel information, passenger lists, and the original, revised, estimated, and actual arrival times. The Sabre CrewTrac application tracks crew assignments, ensures legal requirements are met, and provides pilots and flight attendants with access to their schedules via a secure web portal. During the disastrous Valentine's Day event, there was a glitch between these Sabre applications and Navitaire's SkySolver, which JetBlue uses to figure out the best way to emerge from flight disruptions.

Neeleman said, "We had so many people in the company who wanted to help who weren't trained to help. We had an emergency control center full of people who didn't know what to do. I had flight attendants sitting in hotel rooms for three days who couldn't get a hold of us. I had pilots e-mailing me saying, 'I'm available, what do I do?'" Mees said he did not have any idea why the information could not be transferred or why the system incompatibility could not be discovered beforehand. He, of course, added that there were other day-to-day priorities to manage. "In the heat of battle at any rapidly growing company, you're always trying to address your most immediate needs," Mees said. "But you've got to continually remind yourself that you have to take a step back and look at the things that aren't right in front of you—find out what the tipping points are—before they can impact you." Southwest, by contrast, handled the Valentine's Day weather disaster with ease by simply canceling most services during the disrupted period. It looked as if JetBlue had completely missed out on this obvious solution (see Exhibit 6 for a direct-competitor comparison).

The airline's reputation hit rock-bottom. To limit the damage, JetBlue announced huge compensations to customers—refunds and future flights, which were to cost the airline about $30 million. Neeleman quickly followed up with a new Customer Bill of Rights. The Customer Bill of Rights basically outlined self-imposed penalties for JetBlue and major rewards for its passengers if the airline experienced operational problems and could not adjust to weather-related cancellations within a "reasonable" amount of time. For example, the bill contained provisions for notifying customers, prior to scheduled departure, of delays, cancellations, and diversions and their causes. It also promised that the airline would take necessary action to deplane customers if an aircraft is ground-delayed for five hours. Further, if a flight landed and was unable to taxi in to a gate right away, customers were to receive compensation ranging from $25 to the full amount of their one-way fare (in vouchers redeemable toward a future JetBlue flight), depending on the extent of delay. All these announcements and even a public apology could, of course, not restore things to normalcy. Neeleman was pushed out as CEO on May 10, 2007. Dave Barger, the president, assumed the position of chief executive officer.

JetBue sold approximately 42.6 million shares of common stock to Deutsche Lufthansa, the German carrier, in January 2008. Lufthansa paid $300 million, net of transaction costs, for this stake in JetBlue, whose stock had lost about two-thirds of its value since its operational meltdown on February 14, 2007. The stock purchase could be a precursor to an eventual takeover of JetBlue by Lufthansa if U.S. laws restricting foreign ownership of domestic airlines to 25 percent change at a later point in time. JetBlue's CEO, David Barger, said, "There was never really any dialogue about 'what if,'" and added that the deal doesn't change JetBlue's strategy of avoiding takeover and growing alone.[21]

JetBlue significantly reduced its capital expenditures in 2010 compared to previous years. It modified the airbus A320 purchase agreement in February and October 2010, deferring 16 aircraft previously scheduled for delivery in 2011 through 2013 to 2015 and 2016. It also modified the Embraer 190 purchase agreement in August 2010 and cancelled two Embraer 190 aircraft previously scheduled for delivery in 2012. JetBlue may also modify fleet growth further in the future.[22]

In the midst of these developments, it is forging a number of interline agreements. JetBlue has announced interline agreements with LAN, South African, American, and Aer Lingus, and in March 2011 it announced the interline agreement with Virgin Atlantic. While the relationship expands JetBlue's catchment, the odd thing worth noting in the case of Virgin Atlantic is that Virgin Atlantic and Virgin America have some shared ownership, with Virgin Group owning 25 percent of Virgin America. Virgin America is a major competitor of JetBluc. How JetBlue manages these "coopetition" relationships will be interesting to watch.[23]

Endnotes

1. JetBlue SEC filings 2011.
2. Associated Press. 2007. Lufthansa pays $300 million for JetBlue stake. December 13. *www.msnbc.msn.com/id/22248073.*
3. Maynard, M. 2008. JetBlue starts selling blankets and pillows. *NewYork Times,* August 5. *www.nytimes.com/2008/08/05/business/05pillow.html.*
4. Associated Press. 2011. JetBlue partners with Virgin Atlantic. March 22. *www.pressdemocrat.com/article/20110322/WIRE/110329891*
5. This section draws heavily on the SEC filings of JetBlue for the years 2008 and 2009. Other sources include Zellner, W. 2003. Look who's buzzing the discounters. *BusinessWeek,* November 24; Zellner, W. 2004. Folks are finally packing their bags. *BusinessWeek,* January 12; and a joint study by A. T. Kearney and the Society of British Aerospace Companies, *www.atkearney.com/shared_res/pdf/Emerging_Airline_Industry_S.pdf.*
6. *www.southwest.com/about_swa/airborne.html.*
7. This section draws heavily on Gajilan, A. T. 2004. The amazing JetBlue. *Fortune Small Business. www.fortune/smallbusiness/articles/0.15114,444298-2,00.html.*
8. Brazilian-American Chamber of Commerce of Florida. 2004. 2004 Excellence Award. *Chamber News. www.brazilchamber.org/news/chambernews/ExcellenceAward2004.htm.*
9. Gale/Cengage Learning. n.d. JetBlue Airways Corporation. In *International directory of company histories. galenet.galegroup.com.*
10. Gajilan. 2004. The amazing JetBlue; DiCarlo, L. 2001. Management and trends, Jet Blue skies. *Forbes.com,* January 31. *www.forbes.com/2001/01/31/0131jetblue.html.*
11. *CNNMoney.* 2002. JetBlue IPO soars. April 12. *money.cnn.com/2002/04/12/markets/ipo/jetblue.*
12. *BusinessWeek.* 2003. WEBSMART50. November 24: 92.
13. Bay, W., & Neeleman, D. 2002. JetBlue reaches new heights in airline industry (interview with David Neeleman by Willow Bay of CNN Business Unusual). Aired June 23. *www.cnn.com/TRANSCRIPTS/0206/23/bun.00.html.*
14. JetBlue SEC filings, 2006.
15. JetBlue SEC filings, 2007.
16. From the company's press releases, *www.jetblue.com.*
17. *USAToday.* 2007. JetBlue, Aer Lingus to forge world's first international discount alliance. *USAToday.com,* February 6.
18. Field, D. 2008. AirTran and JetBlue scale back growth. *Airline Business,* June 17. *www.flightglobal.com/articles/2008/06/17/224704/airtran-and-jetblue-scale-back-growth.html.*
19. Schlangenstein, M. 2006. No union vote for JetBlue. *Bloomberg News*, July 19. *findarticles.com/p/articles/mi_qn4188/is_20060719/ai_n16541848.*
20. This section draws heavily on the following sources: Bartholomew, D., & Duvall, M. 2007. What really happened at JetBlue? *www.baselinemag.com,* April 5; and Bailey, J. 2007. Long delays hurt image of JetBlue. *New York Times,* February 17: 1.
21. Associated Press. 2007. Lufthansa pays $300 million for JetBlue stake.
22. JetBlue SEC filings 2011
23. Associated Press. 2011. JetBlue partners with Virgin Atlantic; and Blank, D. 2011. JetBlue and Virgin Atlantic (finally) announce interline agreement. *Online Travel Review,* March 22. *www.onlinetravelreview.com/2011/03/22/jetblue-and-virgin-atlantic-finally-announce-interline-agreement/.*

Appendix A   Glossary of Key Terms Used*

aircraft utilization The average number of block hours operated per day per aircraft for the total fleet of aircraft.

available seat-miles The number of seats available for passengers multiplied by the number of miles the seats are flown.

average fare The average one-way fare paid per flight segment by a revenue passenger.

average stage length Average number of miles flown per flight.

break-even load factor The passenger load factor that will result in operating revenues being equal to operating expenses, assuming constant revenue per passenger mile and expenses.

* From JetBlue SEC filings, 2008.

load factor The percentage of aircraft seating capacity that is actually utilized (revenue passenger-miles divided by available seat-miles).

operating expense per available seat-mile Operating expenses divided by available seat-miles.

operating revenue per available seat-mile Operating revenues divided by available seat-miles.

passenger revenue per available seat-mile Passenger revenue divided by available seat-miles.

revenue passenger-miles The number of miles flown by revenue passengers.

revenue passengers The total number of paying passengers flown on all flight segments.

yield per passenger-mile The average amount one passenger pays to fly 1 mile.

Case 33 The Casino Industry in 2011*

Casinos across the United States have suffered as the economic crunch forced people to cut back on their spending. The major casinos in Las Vegas and Atlantic City are therefore working hard to try and recover from their first ever back-to-back losses during 2009 and 2010. "The picture is not good," said Michael Lawton, senior research analyst for the Nevada Gaming Control Board. "The golden goose is hurting."[1] However, early estimates indicate that casino losses were much smaller during the last year, and analysts expect that the industry will return to profitability in 2011(see Exhibit 1). Over the five years to 2016, IBISWorld forecasts that casino revenues and profits will grow around 3 percent each year.

At the same time, there are increasing concerns about the growth potential of places such as Las Vegas and Atlantic City over the longer term. The economic slowdown forced potential visitors to put off their travel plans and find some type of casino activity closer to where they live. Even as economic conditions improve, it is not clear how many of these patrons will return to these two major casino destinations. With some form of casino now allowed in over half the states, competition is developing all over the country, led by riverboat casinos and Native American casinos (see Exhibit 2). In addition, slot machines are being added at a variety of venues, such as racetracks.

* This case was developed by Professor Jamal Shamsie, Michigan State University, with the assistance of Professor Alan B. Eisner, Pace University. Material has been drawn from published sources to be used for class discussion. Copyright © 2011 Jamal Shamsie and Alan B. Eisner.

Exhibit 1 U.S. Casino Industry Gaming Revenues*
(in billions of dollars)

2009	30.74
2008	32.54
2007	34.13
2006	32.42
2005	30.37
2004	28.93
2003	27.02
2002	26.50
2001	25.70
2000	24.50

* Gaming revenues include the amount of money won by casinos from various gaming activities, such as slot machines, table games, and sports betting.

Source: State gaming regulatory agencies.

Similar concerns are being raised about the growth of competition in various locations outside the United States. Over the years, casinos have been developed in various parts of Europe and Asia, which may compete for the high rollers who have been frequent visitors to Las Vegas and Atlantic City in the past. In 2007 Macau replaced Las Vegas as the leading casino gambling center, after the opening of *Sands Macau*, the first Las Vegas–style casino, three years earlier. Other Las Vegas–based casinos have also entered this market with lavish properties, such as *MGM Grand Macau* and *Wynn Macau*.

In order to deal with this growing competition, casinos in Las Vegas have been developing extravagant new properties. MGM Mirage is just completing work on the *City Center* at an expense of more than $8 billion. Covering 67 acres, this mini city bordering the Las Vegas Strip includes luxury hotels, condominium units, a convention center, and retail space. Construction is also expected to resume on *Echelon Place*, which is being built by Boyd Gaming on the former site of *Stardust*. At $4.4 billion, the 5,000-room *Echelon Place* is eventually expected to be far more expensive than the previous record for a single casino, which was set when Steve Wynn built his $2.7 billion resort.

Casinos in Atlantic City are also vying to retain and grow their business. *Trump Marina* was sold off to Landry's in order to be rebranded as the *Golden Nugget* after a $150 million renovation. Work has also resumed on the $2.8 billion renovation of the *Revel* casino, one of the first to open in Atlantic City after casinos were legalized. New laws have also been passed to allow the development of two smaller boutique casinos.

Riding the Growth Wave

Although some form of gambling can been traced back to colonial times, the recent advent of casinos can be traced back to the legalization of gaming in Nevada in 1931. For many years, this was the only state in which casinos were allowed. As a result, Nevada still retains its status as the state with the highest revenues from casinos, with annual gambling revenues rising to over $10 billion by 2004. After New Jersey passed laws in 1976 to allow gambling in Atlantic City, this allowed the large population on the East Coast easier access to casinos. However, the further growth of casinos has only been possible since 1988, as more and more states have begun to legalize the operation of casinos because of their ability to help generate more commercial activity and create more jobs, in large part through the growth of tourism (see Exhibit 3).

The greatest growth has come in the form of waterborne casinos that have begun to operate in six states that have allowed casinos to develop at waterfronts such as rivers and lakes. By 2010 about 80 such casinos were generating over $10 billion in annual revenues. Several of the casinos along the Gulf Coast were destroyed or severely

Exhibit 2 **Breakdown of Gaming Revenues by State, 2009** (in billions of dollars)

	Revenues	Gambling Locations
Nevada	10.34*	260 land-based
New Jersey	3.94†	11 land-based
Indiana	2.80	1 land-based, 10 riverboats, 2 racinos
Mississippi	2.47	30 land-based dockside
Louisiana	2.46	1 land-based, 13 riverboats, 4 racinos
Pennsylvania	1.97	3 land-based, 6 racinos
Missouri	1.73	12 riverboats
Illinois	1.43	9 riverboats
Iowa	1.38	7 land-based, 7 riverboats, 3 racinos
Michigan	1.34‡	3 land-based
New York	1.02	8 racinos
West Virginia	0.91	4 racinos
Colorado	0.74	40 land-based
Delaware	0.56	3 racinos
Rhode Island	0.46	2 racinos
New Mexico	0.24	5 racinos
Florida	0.22	4 racinos
South Dakota	0.10§	35 land-based (limited stakes)
Oklahoma	0.09	2 racinos
Maine	0.06	1 racino
Kansas	0.02	1 land-based

* 5.50 of this revenue comes from the Las Vegas strip.

† All of this revenue comes from Atlantic City.

‡ All of this revenue comes from Detroit.

§ All of this revenue comes from Deadwood.

Source: 2010 AGA Survey of Casino Entertainment.

damaged by Hurricane Katrina. To encourage casinos to rebuild, Mississippi lawmakers passed a law in 2005 allowing casinos to operate up to 800 feet from the shore, allowing them to have a stronger foundation to withstand future hurricanes. Most of the damaged casinos in the area had reopened by early 2007.

As casinos have spread to more states, there has also been a growing tendency to regard casino gambling as an acceptable form of entertainment for a night out. Although casinos have tended to draw players from all demographic segments, a recent national survey found that their median age was 47 and their median household income was around $50,000. On the whole, casino gamblers tended to be better educated and more affluent than those who bought lottery tickets. In fact, the bigger casinos attracted a high-roller segment, which could stake millions of dollars and included players from all over the world. Many of the casinos work hard to obtain the business of this market segment, despite the risk that the sustained winning streak of a single player could significantly weaken the earnings for a particular quarter.

The growth of casino gambling has also been driven by the significantly better payouts that they give players compared with other forms of gambling. Based on industry estimates, casinos typically keep less than $5 of every $100 that is wagered. This compares favorably with racetrack betting, which holds back over $20 of every $100 that is wagered, and with state run lotteries, which usually

Exhibit 3   States with Native American Casinos, 2009

State	Number of Casinos
Alabama	3
Alaska	3
Arizona	25
California	68
Colorado	2
Connecticut	2
Florida	8
Idaho	7
Iowa	1
Kansas	6
Louisiana	3
Michigan	20
Minnesota	38
Mississippi	2
Missouri	2
Montana	16
Nebraska	6
Nevada	3
New Mexico	22
New York	8
North Carolina	2
North Dakota	12
Oklahoma	106
Oregon	9
South Dakota	11
Texas	1
Washington	33
Wisconsin	33
Wyoming	4

Source: 2010 AGA Survey of Casino Entertainment.

coin-operated slot machines typically account for almost two-thirds of all casino gaming revenues. A major reason for their popularity is that it is easier for prospective gamblers to feed a slot machine than to learn the nuances of various table games. Major slot-machine manufacturers, such as International Game Technology, have been making the transition to cashless or coin-free gaming by switching to the use of tickets. With the advent of new technology, server-based gaming will allow games on these machines to be changed or updated from a central system (see Exhibit 4).

Betting on a Few Locations

Although casinos have spread across much of the country, two cities have dominated the casino business. Both Las Vegas and Atlantic City have seen a spectacular growth in casino gaming revenues over the years. Although Las Vegas has far more hotel casinos, each of the dozen casinos in Atlantic City typically generates much higher revenues. Over the last couple of decades, these two locations accounted for almost a third of the total revenues generated by all forms of casinos throughout the United States.

Las Vegas clearly acts as a magnet for the overnight casino gamblers, offering several high-end casino hotels, with many choices for fine dining, great shopping, and top-notch entertainment. This allows the casinos to generate revenues from offering a wide selection of activities apart from gambling. At MGM Mirage, for example, revenue from nongaming activities has typically accounted for almost 60 percent of net revenue in recent years. Visitors find it easy to travel to Las Vegas, as it is linked by air to many major cities both in the United States and around the world.

During the 1990s, Las Vegas had tried to become more receptive to families, with attractions such as circus performances, animal reserves, and pirate battles. But the city has been very successful with its recent return to its sinful roots with a stronger focus on topless shows, hot night clubs, and other adult offerings that have been highlighted by the new advertising slogan "What happens in Vegas, stays in Vegas." Paul Cappelli, who creates

Exhibit 4   Favorite Casino Games, 2009

Slot Machines	59%
Blackjack	18%
Poker	7%
Roulette	6%
Craps	5%

Note: This is from a poll which asked people what their favorite casino game was.

Source: 2010 AGA Survey of Casino Entertainment.

keep about $45 of every $100 that is spent on tickets. Such comparisons can be somewhat misleading, however, because winnings are put back into play in casinos much faster than they are in other forms of gaming. This provides a casino with more opportunities to win from a customer, largely offsetting its lower retention rate.

Finally, most of the growth in casino revenues has come from the growing popularity of slot machines. These advertising messages, believes that Las Vegas lost its way with the effort to become family friendly. "People don't see Vegas as Jellystone Park. They don't want to go there with a picnic basket," he explained.[2]

For the most part, Las Vegas has continued to show a consistent pattern of growth in visitors. "We still compete with Orlando and New York," said Terry Jicinsky, head of marketing for the Las Vegas Convention and Visitors Authority. "But based on overnight visitors, we're the top destination in North America."[3] In order to accommodate this growth, several of the major resorts, such as *Bellagio, Venetian,* and *Mandalay Bay,* have added new wings. Even some of the older properties have been expanded. For example, *Caesers Palace* has been extensively renovated and expanded to include a new Colosseum and a new Roman Plaza.

By comparison, Atlantic City cannot compete with Las Vegas in terms of the broad range of dining, shopping, and entertainment choices. It does, however, offer a beach and a boardwalk along which its dozen large casino hotels are lined. Atlantic City attracts gamblers from various cities in the Northeast, many of whom arrive by charter bus and stay for less than a day. Atlantic City officials point out that one-quarter of the nation's population lives sufficiently close so that they can drive there with just one tank of gas.

The opening of the much-ballyhooed *Borgata Hotel Casino* in 2003 was part of a push to make Atlantic City more competitive with Las Vegas. "There's no question that this is a Las Vegas–style mega-resort," said Bob Boughner, the CEO of the *Borgata.*[4] After a brief lull, the renovation of the *Revel* casino and the conversion of the *Trump Marina* into the *Golden Nugget* is expected to draw in new visitors.

Raising the Stakes

The gradual rise in the number of casinos, including those on riverboats, has led each of them to compete more heavily with each other to entice gamblers. Casinos have had to continuously strive to offer more in order to stand out and gain attention. This is most evident in Las Vegas and Atlantic City, the two destinations where most of the largest casinos are located next to each other. Potential gamblers have more choices when they visit either of these cities than they have anywhere else.

In Las Vegas, each of the casinos has tried to deal with this competition by differentiating itself in several ways. A large number of them have tried to differentiate on the basis of a special theme that characterizes their casino, such as a medieval castle, a pirate ship, or a movie studio. Others have tried to incorporate the look and feel of specific foreign destinations. *Luxor*'s pyramids and columns evoke ancient Egypt, *Mandalay Bay* borrows looks from the Pacific Rim, and the *Venetian*'s plazas and canals recreate the Italian resort city.

Aside from ramping up the appeal of their particular properties, most casinos must also offer incentives to keep their customers from moving over to competing casinos. These incentives can be particularly helpful in retaining those high rollers who come often and spend large amounts of money. Casinos try to maintain their business by providing complimentary rooms, food, beverage, shows, and other perks each year that are worth billions of dollars. Gamblers can also earn various types of rewards through the loyalty programs that are offered by the casinos, with the specific rewards being tied to the amount that they bet on the slot machines and at the tables.

Some of the larger casinos in Las Vegas are also trying to fend off competition by growing through mergers and acquisitions. In 2004 Harrah's announced that it was buying casino rival Caesars, allowing it to become the nation's leading operator of casinos, with several properties in both Las Vegas and Atlantic City (see Exhibit 5). This deal came just a month after MGM Mirage had stated that it was buying the Mandalay Resort Group, allowing it to double the number of casinos it held on the Las Vegas Strip. Firms that own several casinos can also pitch each of their properties to a different market and allow all of their customers to earn rewards on the firm's loyalty program by gambling at any of these properties.

Such a trend toward consolidation, however, does not seem to make a serious dent on smaller firms that operate just one or two resorts that appeal to particular types of customers. Steve Wynn's success with *Wynn* led him to open *Encore,* another glitzy casino resort next to his original property. Similarly, the recently opened 455-room *Palms* hotel and casino has already become one of the hottest and most profitable properties in Las Vegas. "There will always be a market for a person who doesn't feel comfortable in a big casino setting," said George Maloof, a co-owner of the *Palms Resort.*[5]

Responding to Growing Threats

The growth of Las Vegas and Atlantic City has been matched by the spread of casinos in many other parts of the United States. Among these, the largest volume of business is generated by the riverboats that have sprung up in Iowa, Illinois, Mississippi, Louisiana, Missouri, and Indiana. However, the growth of these casinos has not had much effect on the growth of visitors to Las Vegas and Atlantic City. Tom Graves, stock analyst at Standard & Poor's, has expressed his confidence in the attractiveness of Las Vegas: "There's a perception among gamblers that Las Vegas is still the foremost gaming market."[6]

However, all of these casinos are facing growing competition from a variety of sources. Foremost among these is the rise in the number of Native American casinos. The Indian Gaming and Recreation Act of 1988 authorized Native Americans to offer gaming on tribal lands as a way to encourage their self-sufficiency. Of the approximately 550 Native American tribes in the United States, more than 200 have negotiated agreements with states to allow gaming on tribal land. Native American casinos are exempt from federal regulations and are not required to pay any

Exhibit 5   Leading Casino Operators

2009 Revenue	2009 Income	
		Caesars Entertainment
$8.9 billion	$828 million	One of the largest casino operators in the world. Operates casinos across the U.S., including several in Las Vegas and Atlantic City. Runs several upscale casinos such as *Caesers Palace, Bally's, Paris, Flamingo, Harrah's,* and *Rio* in Las Vegas. Also manages several Native American casinos.
		MGM Resorts
$5.9 billion	($1.3 billion)	Most of its casinos are located in Las Vegas and other parts of Nevada. Runs casinos under the name of *MGM Grand, Bellagio, New York-New York, Mirage, Luxor,* and *Monte Carlo,* which cater to the high end of the market. Developed the City Center project in Las Vegas. Also operates casinos on the Gulf Coast and in Illinois and Michigan. Has developed MGM Grand Macau.
		Las Vegas Sands
$4.5 billion	($355 million)	Operates the *Venetian* and *Palazzo* in Las Vegas. Has also developed casinos in Macau, spearheaded by the *Sands Macau* and the *Venetian Macao,* and a casino in Singapore.
		Wynn Resorts
$3.0 billion	$21 million	Operates the higher end *Wynn Resort* and *Encore* casino, both in Las Vegas. Also operates the *Wynn* and *Encore Macau.*
		Penn National Gaming
$2.37 billion	($265 million)	Merged with Argosy Gaming in 2005. Operates mid-priced casinos spread over the U.S., including riverboats in different states. No properties in Las Vegas or Atlantic City. Also operates several racetracks.
		Boyd Gaming
$1.6 billion	$156 million	Operates casinos in various U.S. states. Las Vegas properties that target the middle-income segment include *Gold Coast, Orleans,* and *Sam's Town.* Is developing a higher-end casino, *Echelon Place,* in Las Vegas. Runs the *Borgata* in Atlantic City.
		Isle of Capri Casinos
$1.1 billion	$43.6 million	Primarily operates riverboat casinos across the U.S. Also operates casinos in Grand Bahamas and UK.
		Station Casinos
N/A	N/A	Operates mid-priced casinos in and around Las Vegas. Leading casinos are *Palace Station, Sunset Station,* and *Boulder Station.* Currently reorganizing under bankruptcy protection.

taxes on their revenues, but they generally pay a percentage of their winnings to the state in which they are located.

Over the past decade, a large share of the growth in U.S. gaming revenues has come from Native American casinos. The impact of these casinos on the traditional casino industry is likely to increase over the next few years. Several states are reaching agreements to allow the introduction or expansion of Native American casinos because of the additional revenues that they can provide. This has created fears that the growth of these Native American casinos is likely to draw away gamblers from the other types of casinos. In particular, the growth of these casinos in states such as California and Minnesota may reduce the number of gamblers that make trips to gambling destinations such as Las Vegas and Atlantic City.

The casino industry is also facing growing competition from the introduction of gaming machines at racetracks. Installing gaming machines at racetracks—sometimes referred to as "racinos"—has being growing in popularity in the six states where they are already allowed. According to the American Gaming Association, gaming activity at these racetracks has shown considerable growth over the last five years. Seeing these results, several additional states are considering legislation that would allow racetracks to raise their revenues by providing slot machines to their visitors.

Finally, all casinos are closely observing the growth of gambling on the Internet. Although Internet gambling is not allowed under legislation in the United States, some 2,000 offshore sites generate about $15 billion in revenue. Electronic payment systems have made it possible for gamblers in the United States to make bets on these sites without cash, checks, or credit cards. Most casino operators believe that Internet gambling could represent both a threat and an opportunity for them. Placing bets through home computers offers convenience for prospective gamblers and a potentially low-cost business model for firms that already operate casinos. It is widely believed that gambling on the Internet might eventually be legalized, regulated, and taxed. "We frankly find attempts at prohibition to be very shortsighted," said Alan Feldman, senior vice president of the MGM Mirage in Las Vegas.[7]

Gambling on the Future

The competitive pressures that had forced many firms to build new casinos or to renovate existing ones made it difficult for them to deal with the drop in revenues that accompanied the recent economic downturn. In many cases, the heavy spending burdened casino operators with large amounts of debt that became harder to manage when demand for casino gambling began to decline. A few firms around the United States, including some in Las Vegas and Atlantic City, ran into financial problems, forcing them to sell off some of their casinos and seek bankruptcy protection. Over the past few years, Trump Entertainment, Tropicana Entertainment, and Station Casinos have all filed for bankruptcy.

So far, such isolated failures have not dampened the enthusiasm of most of the firms that are continuing to invest heavily into casinos. Many of these gaming firms view the current economic conditions as a temporary setback that has forced them to place some of their plans for growth on hold. Even as casino revenues have dropped since 2008, 28 percent of the U.S. adult population still visited a casino, making this form of gaming second in popularity only to lotteries.

If the attraction of gaming continues to show the same level of growth that it has over the past decade, this should allow Las Vegas and Atlantic City to thrive even with the rise of new casinos in other locations. Some observers even believe that the spread of this form of gaming has created a bigger market for the casino resorts in these locations. As more and more people are drawn to casinos, they will be pulled to these centers of gaming. Few places, including Macau, can match Las Vegas or Atlantic City in terms of other forms of entertainment, such as shopping, fine dining, and theatre shows.

Nevertheless, there are questions about the possible impact of the proliferation of casinos and the availability of Internet gambling on the revenue growth of gaming centers such as Las Vegas and Atlantic City. But many industry observers believe that these gaming centers will continue to thrive as people who gain a taste for gambling will eventually want to visit Las Vegas or Atlantic City in order to experience the real thing. Jan L. Jones, senior vice president for Harrah's Entertainment, remarked, "Counting Las Vegas down and out, given the entrepreneurial spirit at work here, is just foolish."[8]

Endnotes

1. Ryan, C. 2011. Las Vegas Strip casinos post $2.5 billion loss last fiscal year. *Tribune Business News*, January 31.
2. McCarthy, M. 2005. Vegas goes back to naughty roots; Ads trumpet return to adult playground. *USA Today*, April 11: B6.
3. Ibid.
4. Sloan, G. 2003. Atlantic City bets on glitz: Down-at-the-heels resort rolls the dice, wagering a cool $2 billion that it will one day rival Las Vegas. *USA Today*, August 29: D1.
5. Palmeri, C. 2004. Little guys with big plans for Vegas. *BusinessWeek*, August 2: 49.
6. Woodyard, C., & Krantz, M. 2004. Latest Vegas marriage: Harrah's, Caesers tie knot; $5 billion deal marks strategy to reach more gamblers. *USA Today*, July 16: B1.
7. Woellert, L. 2004. Can online betting change its luck? *BusinessWeek*, December 20: 67.
8. Friess, S. 2009. Las Vegas sags as conventions cancel. *New York Times*, February 15: 20.

Case 34 Dippin' Dots Ice Cream and Coffee?*

By 2010, Dippin' Dots had expanded its product line from ice creams to uniquely brewed coffees. Founder Curt Jones took a similar colder-than-cold instant-freezing process that made Dippin' Dots ice creams so delectable and redirected that technology to fresh brewed coffee. Just as he had dubbed Dippin' Dots the "ice cream of the future" two decades earlier, he said the new "coffee dots" would adopt the slogan "coffee of the future."[1] Real espresso was made from fresh, high-quality Arabica beans then flash frozen into dots immediately, capturing the flavor and aroma. Named "Forty Below Joe edible coffee," the coffee dots could be eaten with a spoon, heated with water and milk to make a hot "fresh-brewed" coffee without brewing, or blended with Frappé beads to make a Dippin' Dots Frappé.[2] Jones's once-kid-targeted dots now had a very adult twist. As of April 2011, four flavors of edible coffee dots—Espresso, Caramel Frappé, Mocha Frappé, and Vanilla Frappé—were available at various locations of Dippin' Dots.[3] Jones hoped that this new product would take Dippin' Dots outside the arena of seasonal treats.

However, Jones was also thinking about more kid-friendly treats. For years Jones had been thinking of coming out with low-cal, low-fat Dippin' Dots that could meet the nutrition requirements and regulations to be sold at public schools. The result was "Chillz," a lower-calorie alternative to ice cream introduced in 2010. Dippin' Dots Chillz was a low-fat frozen-beaded dessert made with Truvia, an all-natural sweetener. This healthier alternative to ice cream was also an excellent source of Vitamin C and was available in three flavors: Sour Blue Razz, Wango Rainbo, and Chocolate.[4] "We're starting to distribute Chillz through the vending channel. We already have two contracts underway and expect to get more. Vending companies know and love the Dippin' Dots brand. With Chillz and other products, it's a great opportunity for them. Schools need that revenue. They've thrown out a lot of products in recent times that have no nutritional value. So we feel bullish about Chillz," said Dippin' Dots' vice president of sales, Michael Barrette, in 2010.[5]

Dippin' Dots was back from the brink of bankruptcy the firm had faced in 2009. Founder Curt Jones returned to the firm as CEO and also headed up new product development. Jones would now have to balance two large responsibilities, company operations and product development, if the "Ice Cream of the Future" was to have one.

History

Founded by Curt Jones and incorporated in 1988, Dippin' Dots Inc., headquartered in Paducah, Kentucky, was the company that made the "ice cream of the future."[6] The company's chief operation was the sale of BB-size pellets of flash-frozen ice cream in some two dozen flavors to franchisees and national accounts throughout the world. As a Six Flags customer commented, "I gotta say, man, they're pretty darn good. . . . Starts off like a rock candy but ends up like ice cream."[7]

Dippin' Dots was the marriage between old-fashioned handmade ice cream and space-age technology. Dippin' Dots were tiny round beads of ice cream that were made at super-cold temperatures, served at subzero temperatures in a soufflé cup, and eaten with a spoon. The super-cold freezing of Dippin' Dots ice cream, done by liquid nitrogen, cryogenically locked in both flavor and freshness in a way that no other manufactured ice cream could offer. The process virtually eliminated the presence of trapped ice and air, giving the ice cream a fresh flavor and a hard texture. Not only had Jones discovered a new way of making ice cream, but many felt his product proved to be much more flavorful and richer than regular ice cream. According to Jones, "I created a way . . . [to] get a quicker freeze so the ice cream wouldn't get large ice crystals. . . . About six months later, I decided to quit my job and go into business."

Jones was a microbiologist by trade, with an area of expertise in cryogenics. His first job was researching and engineering as a microbiologist for ALLtech Inc., a bioengineering company based in Lexington, Kentucky. During his days at ALLtech, Jones worked with different types of bacteria to find new ways of preserving them so that they could be transported throughout the world. He applied a method of freezing using super-cold temperatures with substances such as liquid CO_2 and liquid nitrogen—the same method used to create Dippin' Dots.

One process Jones developed was "microencapsulating" the bacteria by freezing their medium with liquid nitrogen. Other scientists thought he was crazy, because nothing like that had ever been done before. Jones, however, was convinced his idea would work. He spent months trying to perfect the process and continued to make progress. While Jones was working over 80 hours a week in ALLtech's labs to perfect the microencapsulating process, he made the most influential decision of his life. He took a weekend off and attended a family barbeque at his parents' house. It just so happened that his mother was making ice cream the day of the barbeque. Jones began to reminisce about homemade ice cream prepared the slow, old-fashioned way. Then Jones wondered if it was possible to flash-freeze ice cream. Instead of using a bacteria medium, was it possible to microencapsulate ice cream?

The answer was yes. After virtually reinventing a frozen dessert that had been around since the second century BC,[8] Jones patented his idea to flash-freeze liquid cream, and he opened the first Dippin' Dots store.[9] Once franchising was offered in 2000, the "Ice Cream of the Future"

* This case was prepared by Professor Alan B. Eisner of Pace University and graduate student Brian R. Callahan of Pace University as a basis for class discussion rather than to illustrate either effective or ineffective handling of an administrative situation. Copyright © 2011 Alan B. Eisner.

could be found at thousands of shopping malls, amusement parks, water parks, fairs, and festivals worldwide. Dippin' Dots ice cream was transported coast to coast and around the world by truck, train, plane, and ship. In addition to being transported in specially designed cryogenic transport containers, the product was transported in refrigerated boxes known as pallet reefers. Both types of containers ensured fast and efficient delivery to franchisees around the world. The product was served in 4-, 5-, and 8-ounce cups and in 5-ounce vending prepacks.

Product Specifics

Dippin' Dots were flash-frozen beads of ice cream typically served in a cup or vending package. The ice cream averaged 90 calories per serving, depending on the flavor, and had 9 grams of fat. The ice cream was produced by a patented process that introduced flavored liquid cream into a vat of−325-degree liquid nitrogen, where it was flash-frozen to produce the bead or dot shape. Once frozen, the dots were collected and either mixed with other flavors or packaged separately for delivery to retail locations. The product had to be stored at subzero temperatures to maintain the consistency of the dots. Subzero storage temperatures were achieved by utilizing special equipment and freezers supplemented with dry ice. Although storage was a challenge for international shipping, the beads could maintain their shape for up to 15 days in their special containers. To maintain product integrity and consistency, the ice cream had to be served at 10 to 20 degrees below zero. A retail location had to have special storage and serving freezers. Because the product had to be stored and served at such low temperatures, it was unavailable in regular frozen-food cases and could not be stored in a typical household freezer. Therefore, it could be consumed only at or near a retail location, unless stored with dry ice to maintain the necessary storage temperature.

Industry Overview

The frozen dairy industry has traditionally been occupied by family-owned businesses such as Dippin' Dots, full-line dairies, and a couple of large international companies that focused on only a single sales region. The year 2008 was a relatively flat year for the production and sale of ice cream, as volume in traditional varieties remained flat and new types of ice cream emerged. Despite higher ingredient costs, manufacturers were continually churning out new products, though at a slower rate than in the previous year. These ranged from super-premium selections to good-for-you varieties to cobranded packages and novelties. Most novelty ice creams could be found together in supermarket freezer cases, in small freezers in convenience stores, and in carts, kiosks, or trucks at popular summertime events. Ice cream makers had been touched by consolidation trends affecting the overall food and beverage industry that extended beyond their products, as even the big names were folded into global conglomerates.

The ice cream segment in the United States had become a battleground for two huge international consumer-product companies seeking to corner the ice cream market. Those two industry giants were Nestlé SA of Switzerland, the world's largest food company, with more than $90 billion in annual sales, and Unilever PLC of London and Rotterdam, with over $52 billion in annual revenues. Both had been buying into U.S. firms for quite a while, but Nestlé, which already owned the Häagen-Dazs product line, upped the ante with its June 2003 merger with Dreyer's Grand/ Edy's Ice Cream Inc. of Oakland, California. But even as the two giants dominated the U.S. ice cream industry, about 500 small businesses continued to produce and distribute frozen treats. As one commentator said, "Like microbrewers and small-scale chocolate makers, entrepreneurs are drawn to ice cream as a labor of love."[10] Some of the better-known brands were regional ones, such as Blue Bell, based in Brenham, Texas (see Exhibit 1).

More than $21 billion was spent on ice cream in 2010, and ice cream and related frozen desserts were consumed by more than 90 percent of households in the United States.[11] Consumers spent $8.9 billion on products for at-home consumption, while $13.9 billion went toward away-from-home purchases. Harry Balzar, of the market research firm NPD Group, said about ice cream in general, "It's not a small category, but one that has remained flat for more than a decade, and is not likely to grow."[12] The challenge for producers was to woo customers away from competitors and sustain a loyal fan base by continuing to innovate. The trend toward more healthy treats had spurred the major players, Nestlé and Unilever, to develop reduced-fat product lines that still had the taste and texture of full-fat ice cream. Edy's/ Dreyer's, Breyers, and Häagen-Dazs had all continued to experiment, and the "slow churned," "double-churn," and "light" products were seeing increased sales since their introduction in 2004.[13]

In October 2002 it was announced that Good Humor–Breyers Ice Cream of Green Bay, Wisconsin, and Ben & Jerry's of Vermont had formed a unified retail sales division named Unilever Ice Cream. The new organization brought together both companies and represented the five Unilever North American ice cream brands, which include Ben & Jerry's, Breyers, Good Humor, Popsicle, and Klondike. Good Humor–Breyers had created several new cobranded novelties specifically for convenience-store and vending locations. The company had also set out to expand the availability of single-serve novelties by placing freezers of its products in Blockbuster video stores and Breyers-branded kiosks in 30 Chicago-area Loews theaters. In addition to prepackaged products, freshly scooped ice cream was served at the kiosks. The new sales team would focus solely on the out-of-home ice cream business and, therefore, exclude grocery channels.

Another novelty product delivery system in the independent scoop shop was the "slab" concept. Employees at franchises such as Marble Slab Creamery, Cold Stone Creamery, and Maggie Moo's worked ingredients on a cold granite or marble slab to blend premium ice cream

Exhibit 1   Top 10 Brands*

Top 10 Ice Cream/Sherbet Brands[†]				
	Sales ($ millions)	Percentage Change vs. Year Ago	Unit Sales (millions)	Percentage Change vs. Year Ago
Total category	$4,403.00	−0.30%	1,370.00	−0.40%
Private label (ice cream)	812.8	−2.7	285.9	−0.4
Breyers	638.8	7.5	196.7	10.0
Dreyer's/Edy's Grand	445.1	−1.0	130.9	−4.7
Häagen-Dazs	287.3	12.1	83.4	7.2
Dreyer's/Edy's Slow Churned	284.0	100.8	76.8	93.3
Blue Bell	253.2	2.0	75.0	1.0
Ben & Jerry's	207.6	8.7	67.8	10.1
Wells' Blue Bunny	122.0	14.0	34.6	17.1
Turkey Hill	116.9	13.8	41.8	14.1
Private label (sherbet/sorbet/ices)	59.8	−4.0	27.3	−2.7

Top 10 Frozen Novelty Brands[†]						
	Sales ($ millions)	Percentage Change vs. Year Ago Dollar Share	Dollar Share	Unit Sales (millions)	Percentage Change vs. Year Ago	Unit Share
Total category	$2,470.70	2.30%	100	819.4	−0.10%	100
Private label	317.9	−4.0	12.9	134.5	−3.2	16.4
Nestlé Drumstick	131.3	−0.6	5.3	38.0	−3.8	4.6
Weight Watchers	127.4	57.3	5.2	28.9	54.1	3.5
Klondike	126.2	−5.0	5.1	42.7	−7.5	5.2
Popsicle	113.3	10.4	4.6	41.5	5.0	5.1
Dreyer's/Edy's Whole Fruit	103.4	−1.3	4.2	31.6	−9.9	3.9
Carvel	93.2	6.0	3.8	5.9	2.4	0.7
The Skinny Cow	84.3	16.2	3.4	19.5	12.8	2.4
Dreyer's/Edy's Dibs	83.6	97.8	3.4	25.2	91.6	3.1
Häagen-Dazs	57.4	7.6	2.3	19.0	8.1	2.3

* Total sales of all forms of ice cream/sherbet brands in supermarkets, drug stores, and mass merchandisers (excluding Walmart).
[†] Total sales of all forms of frozen novelty brands in supermarkets, drug stores, and mass merchandisers (excluding Walmart).

Source: Information Resources Inc.

with the customer's choice of tasty additives, such as crumbled cookies, fruits, and nuts, before serving it in a cup or cone. The novelty was the entertainment of watching the preparation. All three chains ranked in *Entrepreneur* 's list of the top-500 franchise opportunities in 2006, but commentators were skeptical of sustainability once the novelty wore off, especially since the average price was $5 for a medium serving.[14] As of 2011, both Cold Stone Creamery and Marble Slab Creamery were able to maintain spots in *Entrepreneur* magazine's list of the top 500 franchises, ranked in the 54th and 147th positions, respectively.[15]

Industry Segmentation

Frozen desserts come in many forms. Each of the following foods has its own definition, and many are standardized by federal regulations:[16]

- **Ice cream** consists of a mixture of dairy ingredients, such as cream, milk, and nonfat milk, and ingredients for sweetening and flavoring, such as fruits, nuts, and chocolate chips. Functional ingredients, such as stabilizers and emulsifiers, are often included in the product to promote proper texture and enhance the eating experience. By federal law, ice cream must contain at least 10 percent butterfat before the addition of bulky ingredients, and it must weigh a minimum of 4.5 pounds to the gallon.
- **Novelties** are separately packaged single servings of a frozen dessert, such as ice cream sandwiches, fudge sticks, and juice bars, which may or may not contain dairy ingredients.
- **Frozen custard** or **french ice cream** must also contain a minimum of 10 percent butterfat as well as at least 1.4 percent egg yolk solids.
- **Sherbets** have a butterfat content of between 1 and 2 percent and have a slightly higher sweetener content than ice cream. Sherbet weighs a minimum of 6 pounds to the gallon and is flavored either with fruit or other characterizing ingredients.
- **Gelato** is characterized by an intense flavor and is served in a semifrozen state. Gelato contains sweeteners, milk, cream, egg yolks, and flavoring.
- **Sorbet** and **water ices** are similar to sherbets, but they contain no dairy ingredients.
- A **quiescently frozen confection** is a frozen novelty such as a water-ice novelty on a stick.
- **Frozen yogurt** consists of a mixture of dairy ingredients, such as milk and nonfat milk, that have been cultured, as well as ingredients for sweetening and flavoring.

Dippin' Dots Growth[17]

The growth of Dippin' Dots Inc. had been recognized in the United States and the world by industry watchdogs such as *Inc.* magazine, which ranked Dippin' Dots as one of the 500 fastest-growing companies two years in a row, 1996 and 1997. Dippin' Dots Franchising Inc. ranked number four on *Entrepreneur* magazine's 2004 list of the top 50 new franchise companies, and it achieved the 101st spot on *Entrepreneur*'s Franchise 500 for 2004. In 2005 Dippin' Dots ranked number two as a top new franchise opportunity and climbed to number 93 on the Franchise 500 list. By the end of 2009, Dippin' Dots had slid to 175th position on *Entrepreneur*'s Franchise 500 list.[18] And by 2011 Dippin' Dots had fallen off the Franchise 500 list. Exhibit 2 shows the growth of franchises for Dippin' Dots.

Despite the company's initial success, the achievements of Curt Jones and Dippin' Dots have not come without obstacles. Once Jones had perfected his idea, he needed to start a company for the new process of flash-freezing ice cream. Like many new entrepreneurs, Jones enlisted the help of his family to support his endeavor. It was essential to start selling his product, but he had no protection for his idea from competitors.

The first obstacle confronting Jones was the need to locate funding to accomplish his goals. He needed money

Exhibit 2 **Dippin' Dots Franchise Growth**

Year	U.S. Franchises	Canadian Franchises	Foreign Franchises	Company Owned
2009	486	1	0	1
2008	420	0	0	2
2007	441	0	0	3
2006	448	1	0	2
2005	635	1	0	2
2004	618	1	0	2
2003	598	0	0	2
2002	580	0	0	2
2001	569	0	0	3
2000	525	0	0	1

Source: *Entrepreneur.* n.d. Dippin' Dots franchising. *www.entrepreneur.com/franchises/dippindotsfranchising/289468-0.html.*

for the patent to protect his intellectual property and needed seed money to start manufacturing the ice cream once the patent was granted. At the same time that Jones was perfecting the flash-freezing process for his ice cream, he was also working on a Small Business Association (SBA) loan to convert the family farm into one that would manufacture ethanol. However, instead of using the farm to produce the alternative fuel, Jones's parents took out a first, and then a second, mortgage to help fund Jones's endeavor. Thus, Jones initiated the entire venture by self-funding his company with personal and family assets.

Unfortunately, the money from Jones's parents was only enough to pay for the patent and some crude manufacturing facilities (a liquid nitrogen tank in his parent's garage). He next had to open a store, and doing so required even more money—money that Jones and his family did not have. They were unable to get the SBA loan because, while the product was novel and looked promising, there was no proof that it would sell. So Jones and his newly appointed CFO (his sister) went to an alternative lender who lent them cash at an exorbitant interest rate that was tacked onto the principal weekly if unpaid.

Now in possession of the seed money they needed, Curt Jones and his family opened their first store. Its summertime opening created a buzz in the community. The store was mobbed every night, and Dippin' Dots was legitimized by public demand. With the influx of cash, Jones was able to move his manufacturing operation from his family's garage into a vacant warehouse. There he set up shop and personally made flash-frozen ice cream for 12 hours every day to supply the store.

After the store had been operating for a few months, the Joneses were able to secure small business loans from local banks to cover the expenses of a modest manufacturing plant and office. At the same time, Jones's sister made calls to fairs and other events to learn whether Dippin' Dots products could be sold at them. Luckily for the Joneses, the amusement park at Opryland in Nashville, Tennessee, was willing to have them as a vendor. Unfortunately, the first Dippin' Dots stand was placed in front of a roller coaster, and people generally did not want ice cream before they went on a ride. After a few unsuccessful weeks, Jones moved the stand and business picked up considerably. Eventually, the Joneses were able to move to an inline location, which was similar to a store, where Dippin' Dots had its own personnel and sitting area to serve customers.

Through word of mouth, interest in Curt Jones and Dippin' Dots spread. Soon other entrepreneurs contacted Jones about opening up stores to sell Dippin' Dots. In 1991 a dealership network was developed to sell ice cream to authorized vendors and provide support with equipment and marketing. During that time, Jones employed friends in corporate jobs. Dippin' Dots grew into a multimillion dollar company with authorized dealers operating in all 50 states and internationally (see Exhibit 3).

By the end of the 1990s, Jones was happy with his company, but he felt as if Dippin' Dots had hit a plateau and needed to reach the "next level" to continue to prosper. He began working with his friend and now controller and director of franchising, Chad Wilson, to develop the franchise system. By January 2000, all existing Dippin' Dots dealers were required to sign a franchise agreement and pay the associated franchise fees for any location they operated or planned to operate.

A franchise location was any mall, fair, national account, or large family entertainment center. According to the franchising information in 2011, the initial franchise fee was $12,500, with an estimated initial investment range from $80,428 to $235,250.[19] The result was a cash inflow for Dippin' Dots franchising. Franchisees were required to pay a 4 percent royalty fee and contribute one-half percent of their gross incomes to an advertising fund, which Jones said had greatly enhanced marketing.

The Ice Cream of the Future

Dippin' Dots was counting on youthful exuberance to expand growth. "Our core demographic was pretty much 8- to 18-year-olds," said Terry Reeves, former corporate communications director. "On top of that, we're starting to see a generation of parents who grew up on Dippin' Dots and are starting to introduce the products to their kids." Although Dippin' Dots seems to appeal more to youngsters, the product still has to have staying power as customers grow older. As one individual commented, "How can this stuff keep continuing to call itself the 'ice cream of the future'? Well the future is now, folks, and they have been pushing this sorry excuse for ice cream off on me at amusement parks and zoos since I was a little kid."[20]

In 2002 McDonald's reportedly spent $1.2 million on advertising to roll out Dippin' Dots in about 250 restaurants in the San Francisco area. Jones called the deal "open-ended" if it worked favorably for both firms. "I think both companies are proceeding with the impression that nothing was going to be overcommitted," he said. "We're growing at a 10 to 15 percent annual rate and we're excited about the potential of McDonald's, but it's too early to tell." However, by 2007 Dippin' Dots was available only at a few McDonald's franchises in southern California. Storage and transportation issues were problematic, and the price of the product, 5 ounces for $5, was too steep for all but the die-hard Dippin' Dots fans.

In other marketing efforts, Dippin' Dots ads had been running in issues of *Seventeen* and *Nickelodeon* magazines. Reeves said the company had been "inundated with e-mails" after the June 2002 issue of *Seventeen* hit the newsstands. Additionally, Dippin' Dots had hired a Hollywood firm to place its ice cream in the background of television and movie scenes, including the 2003 *Cheaper by the Dozen*. In 2002 the Food Network's *Summer Foods: Unwrapped* showcased Dippin' Dots as one of the most unique and coolest ice cream treats. 'N Sync member Joey Fatone ordered a Dippin' Dots freezer for his home after seeing a Dots vending machine at a theater the band rented in Orlando. Caterers also sought Dippin' Dots

Exhibit 3 Milestones

1988	Dippin' Dots is established as a company in Grand Chain, Illinois.
1989	First amusement park account debuts at Opryland USA in Nashville.
1990	Production facility moves to Paducah, Kentucky.
1991	Dealer network is established for fair, festival, and commercial retail locations.
1994	First international licensee is set up (Japan).
1995	New 32,000-square-foot production facility opens in Paducah.
1997	Production facility expands by 20,000 square feet; company earns spot on *Inc.* 500 list of fastest-growing private companies in the United States.
2000	Dippin' Dots Franchising Inc. is established, and first franchise is offered; litigation against competitors is initiated to protect patent.
2001	Dippin' Dots enlists 30 new franchisees. *Franchise Times* magazine lists Dippin' Dots third in the United States in number of ice cream franchise locations behind Baskin Robbins and Dairy Queen.
2002	Dippin' Dots Franchising Inc. achieves 112th spot on *Entrepreneur* magazine's Franchise 500 list, ranks 69th on their list of the fastest-growing franchise companies, and is named the number 1 new franchise company. Dippin' Dots becomes a regular menu offering at McDonald's restaurants in the San Francisco Bay area.
2003	Dippin' Dots Franchising Inc. achieves 144th spot on *Entrepreneur* magazine's Franchise 500 list and number 4 on *Entrepreneur*'s list of the top 50 new franchise companies. Dippin' Dots opens the Ansong manufacturing plant, 80 miles south of Seoul, South Korea.
2004	Dippin' Dots Franchising Inc. ranks number 4 on *Entrepreneur*'s Top 50 New Franchise Companies list and achieves 101st spot on *Entrepreneur* magazine's Franchise 500 list. Curt Jones and Dippin' Dots are featured on a segment of the *Oprah Winfrey Show*, appearing in 110 countries. Dippin' Dots is featured among the top 10 ice cream palaces on the Travel Channel. Curt Jones is quoted in Donald Trump's best-selling *The Way to the Top* (p. 131).
2005	International Dairy Foods Association names Dippin' Dots Best in Show for Dot Delicacies. Dippin' Dots also wins three awards for package design. Dippin' Dots Franchising Inc. ranks number one on *Franchise Times* magazine's Fast 55 list of the fastest-growing young franchises in the nation. Ice cream cake and ice cream sandwiches (Dotwiches) are introduced to launch the Dot Delicacies program.
2006	Company leadership is restructured. Curt Jones becomes chairman of the board. Tom Leonard becomes president of Dippin' Dots Inc. Dots 'n Cream, conventional ice cream enhanced by beads of Dippin' Dots, is introduced for market testing in Kroger stores in the Midwest. The 200th franchisee begins operations.
2007	Dippin' Dots is available in Colombia, and *www.dippindots.com* V.5 is launched.
2008	Dippin' Dots Franchising Inc. ranks 112th on *Entrepreneur*'s Franchise 500 list.
2009	Curt Jones returns to running the day-to-day operations of the firm. Dippin' Dots slides to 175th on *Entrepreneur*'s Franchise 500 list.
2010	Dippin' Dots has 3 million Facebook fans

Source: Dippin' Dots Inc. n.d. History. *www.dippindots.com/more-info/history.html*.

for their star clients. A recent birthday party at the home of NBA star Shaquille O'Neal featured Dippin' Dots ice cream. Dippin' Dots continued to pursue the celebrity word-of-mouth route by serving Dippin' Dots products at events such as the MTV awards and celebrity charity functions.

According to Jones, almost half of Dippin' Dots sales came from national accounts such as stadiums, theaters, and theme parks like Six Flags; the rest of the estimated $50 million income came from approximately 150 franchisees, many with multiple locations.[21]

Dippin' Dots had met increased competition in the out-of-home ice cream market. The major threats to Dippin' Dots were other franchise operations, such as Ben & Jerry's, Häagen-Dazs, Baskin-Robbins, Carvel, Dairy Queen, and newcomers such as Cold Stone Creamery, Maggie Moo's, and Marble Slab Creamery (see Exhibit 4).

In addition, a very similar type of flash-frozen ice cream called Frosty Bites was introduced in the spring of

Exhibit 4 Ice Cream Franchises, 2010

Franchise Name and Description	Start-Up Costs ($ thousands)	Number of Franchises
Abbott's Frozen Custard *Frozen Custard*	120–126.8	20
All American Specialty Restaurants Inc. *Ice cream, frozen yogurt, deli sandwiches, espresso*	171–485	30
Applegate Inc. *Ice cream*	137.7–322	7
Baskin-Robbins USA Co. *Ice cream, frozen yogurt, frozen beverages*	46–401	2,597
Ben & Jerry's *Ice cream parlor*	143.3–446.2	340
Blue Sky Creamery *Ice cream, gourmet coffees, desserts*	98.8–157.5	7
Bruster's Real Ice Cream *Homemade ice cream*	201–1,273	225
California Quivers *Carts and kiosks serving fresh-fruit ices*	45–149.3	3
Carvel *Ice cream, ice cream cakes*	261.8–350.7	417
Cefiore *Frozen yogurt*	196.5–425	27
Cold Stone Creamery *Ice cream, Italian sorbet*	292.4–440.2	1,163
Culver Franchising System Inc. *Frozen custard, specialty burgers*	1,600–2,800	412
Dairy Queen *Soft-serve dairy products, sandwiches*	382–1,800	4,451
Dippin' Dots Franchising *Specialty ice cream, frozen yogurt, ices, sherbet*	80.4–235.3	486
Fiji Yogurt *Frozen yogurt*	163.3–368.5	0
Freddy's Frozen Custard LLC *Frozen custard, steakburgers, hot dogs*	332–788	22
FreshBerry Natural Frozen Yogurt *Natural frozen yogurt, smoothies, yogurt popsicles*	165.7–386.2	16
Golden Spoon Franchising *Frozen yogurt*	365.5–442.5	2
Häagen-Dazs Shoppe Co. Inc. *Ice cream, frozen yogurt*	143.9–428.1	250
Happy Joe's *Pizza, pasta, ice cream*	113.7–1,200	50
La Paletera Franchise Systems Inc. *Fruit bars and cups, smoothies, ice cream*	94.5–185.7	35
MaggieMoo's Intl. LLC *Ice cream, smoothies, cakes*	225.7–354.5	139

(*continued*)

Exhibit 4   Ice Cream Franchises, 2010 *(Continued)*

Franchise Name and Description	Start-Up Costs ($ thousands)	Number of Franchises
Marble Slab Creamery Inc. *Ice cream, frozen yogurt, baked goods*	250–403	261
Melt Inc. *Gelato, Italian coffees, crepes*	200–400	8
Menchie's *Self-serve frozen yogurt*	241.5–574.5	38
Paciugo Gelato & Caffe *Gelato*	177.7–475.5	42
Red Mango Franchising Co. *Frozen yogurt*	252.1–496.6	65
Repicci's Italian Ice *Italian ice*	50–143.3	48
Ricky's Italian Ice *Italian ice, soft serve ice cream, desserts*	98.7–195	0
Rita's Italian Ice *Italian ices, frozen custard, gelati*	199.4–378.4	561
Ritter's Frozen Custard *Frozen custard*	249–818	62
Scandinavian Shave Ice *Shaved ice, ice cream, coffee*	131.4–297.7	0
Shake's Frozen Custard *Frozen custard*	168–800	30
Spoon Me Franchising LLC *Frozen yogurt*	183–491	8
Strickland's *Homemade ice cream, related products*	253.7–431.4	14
Sub Zero Ice Cream *Frozen desserts*	98.5–202.5	7
Tasti D-Lite *Frozen desserts*	253.7–431.4	51
TCBY *Frozen yogurt*	143.8–343.4	438
Yogurtland Franchising Inc. *Self-serve frozen yogurt*	228.9–521.5	96

Source: *Entrepreneur*. n.d. Ice cream franchises. *www.entrepreneur.com/franchises/categories/ffqicecr.html.*

2000 by eight disenfranchised former dealers of Dippin' Dots. Another company, Mini Melts, was also manufacturing a similar product, and two brothers who were formerly part of the Dippin' Dots dealer network brought this flash-frozen ice cream into the competitive mix. In 2002 Jones had thought that introducing a formal franchising agreement would provide protection against copycats and unify the company's public image, since Dippin' Dots was often unrecognizable under its unstructured dealership network of locations. Terry Reeves said,

> The stronger and more unified Dippin' Dots retail offering became through franchising, the more [franchisees] were able to be considered for better retail properties (high-end malls, better locations, and so on). This obviously strengthened our system and bolstered overall sales for the company and for our franchisees. While franchise fees and royalties were a new income source, much of the profit was put back into the business to promote future growth.

Although one dealer commented that Dippin' Dots used incoming franchise fees from royalties on sales for its own corporate means rather than to improve franchise support, most dealers did convert to the new franchise system. Dippin' Dots Franchising Inc. grandfathered existing dealers' locations by issuing a franchise and waiving the franchise fee for the first contract period of five years. Many dealers had to renew their contracts in 2004; while many were initially apprehensive of converting to a franchised system, less than 2 percent left the system, and the firm showed franchise growth.

Meltdown?

In an attempt to counteract the copycat threats from Frosty Bites and Mini Melts, Dippin' Dots brought a patent infringement lawsuit against them in 2005. However, during the jury trial, Dippin' Dots testimony in support of the original patent revealed that Jones had made sales of the beaded ice cream product to over 800 customers more than a year before submitting the patent application.

Even though Jones argued that these sales were for the purpose of market testing and that the production method had subsequently been further refined, therefore deserving of a patented process, the court rendered the patent non-enforceable because these sales were not disclosed to the Patent Office. An appeal by Dippin' Dots was denied in 2007, and the patent was declared invalid.[22]

Mini Melts, released from the lawsuit, continued to expand manufacturing facilities throughout the world; it had plants in South Korea, the Philippines, the United Arab Emirates, Hong Kong, and China as well as the United Kingdom and the United States. Instead of having franchises, Mini Melts sold dealerships for vending machines and kiosks carrying its products. Mini Melts CEO Tom Mosey was nominated by Ernst and Young as Entrepreneur of the Year and has been listed in the *Inc.* 500 for two separate ventures over the years.[23]

By 2009 Dippin' Dots had billed itself as the ice cream of the future for over 20 years. However, Dippin' Dots was close to a meltdown. Founder Curt Jones said, "[Dippin' Dots] just got hit by a perfect storm" of soaring operating costs and plummeting sales. Jones has resumed daily control over financially troubled Dippin' Dots after a three-year break from operations. Jones let go of President Tom Leonard, who had run Samsonite before joining Dippin' Dots in August 2006, and Operations Vice President Dominic Fontana, who had spent about 17 years with Häagen-Dazs. Jones described the separations as amicable and regrettable.[24]

In spite of these challenges, Jones, always the inventor, was investing in R&D to create a conventional ice cream product that had super-frozen dots embedded in it. He was developing a new product that could withstand conventional freezers while preserving the super-frozen dots in the ice cream. Called Dots 'n Cream and available in berry crème, caramel cappuccino, mint chocolate, orange crème de la crème, vanilla bean, vanilla over the rainbow, wild about chocolate, and banana split, this product was introduced for market testing in Kroger stores in the Midwest in 2006. Thus, Dippin' Dots could finally have a take-home ice cream option. As of April 2011, the Dots 'n Cream product was still only available in a few locations and could be bought online.[25]

The other new product introduced by Dippin' Dots was Dot Delicacies. The new product to be introduced in this category was named Dot Treats. As of April 2011, there were seven different Dot Treats: Solar Freeze, sundaes, floats, shakes, Clusterz, Quakes, and LOL (lots of layers).[26] These products were available at most of the retail locations where Dippin' Dots ice cream was sold.

By 2010, Dippin' Dots had started an online venture by selling some of its products through its website. Customers could order ice creams, yogurts, and sherbets online, and they would be delivered to their doors. The company had also branched out and released a series of coffee-based products. The "coffee dots" were new concepts in coffee—frappé and espresso that could be eaten by spoon or could be made into hot coffee drinks by just adding water and milk. Another untapped market Jones and his team tried to enter was the market of healthy ice cream. The low-fat frozen beaded dessert named "Chillz," made with all-natural sweetener, was introduced by Dippin' Dots as a healthier alternative to ice cream. This product was developed with public schools in mind and was being distributed in schools through vending channels.

Despite the development of new products, the company's experience and resource base are clearly in the ice cream manufacturing and scoop-shop retailing businesses. Dealing with supermarket chains and vending distribution firms was a challenge for this relatively small firm. However, opportunities might still be pursued by enlarging the franchise and national-account businesses for scoop shops and vending machines. Jones has continued to assess his company's situation, identifying and choosing among the best strategic options for Dippin' Dots's growth.

Endnotes

1. Horovitz, B. n.d. Dippin' Dots does Coffee Dots. *chefsblade.monster.com/news/articles/714-dippin-dots-does-coffee-dots.*
2. Dippin' Dots Inc. 2010. Forty Below Joe. *DippinDots.com,* September 23. *www.dippindots.com/news/2010/07/dippin-dots-coffee.html.*
3. Dippin' Dots Inc. n.d. Forty Below Joe edible coffee. *www.dippindots.com/products/lines/coffee.html.*
4. Dippin' Dots Inc. 2010. Dippin' Dots Chillz frozen treat. *VendingMarketWatch.com,* January 7. *www.vendingmarketwatch.com/product/10110602/dippin-dots-chillz-frozen-treat.*
5. Perna, G., & Fairbanks, B. 2010. From the future to the present. *Food and Drink Digital,* March 24. *www.foodanddrinkdigital.com/reports/dippin'-dots-future-present.*
6. Information, unless otherwise stated, is derived from the Dippin' Dots website (*www.DippinDots.com*), the Dippin' Dots 10-year anniversary video, and the self-published Dippin' Dots Corporate Profile.
7. Associated Press. 2006. Business blazing for supercold Dippin' Dots. July 23. *www.msnbc.msn.com/id/14001806.*
8. Ice cream's origins are known to reach back as far as the second century BC, although no specific date of origin is known and no inventor has been indisputably credited with its discovery. We know that Alexander the Great enjoyed snow and ice flavored with honey and nectar. Biblical references also show that King Solomon was fond of iced drinks during harvesting. During the Roman Empire, Nero (AD 54–86) frequently sent runners into the mountains for snow, which was then flavored with fruits and juices. Information from International Dairy Foods Association, Ice Cream Media Kit.
9. The idea of using liquid nitrogen to make ice cream had been around in scientific circles for some time. To learn how to make ice cream this way at home, see *www.polsci.wvu.edu/henry/icecream/icecream.html.* See also *Scientific*

American. 1994. April: 66–71; and *www.subzeroicecream. com/press/coldfacts2006.pdf.*

10. Anderson, G. 2005. America's favorite ice cream. *CNN/ Money.com,* July 29. *money.cnn.com/2005/07/25/pf/ goodlife/summer_ice_cream.*

11. Author estimates; and *Dairy Facts,* International Ice Cream Association, *www.idfa.org.*

12. Murphy, K. 2006. Slabs are joining scoops in ice cream retailing. *New York Times,* October 26. *www.nytimes. com/2006/10/26/business/26sbiz.html.*

13. Moskin, J. 2006. Creamy, healthier ice cream? What's the catch? *New York Times,* July 26. *www.nytimes. com/2006/07/26/dining/26cream.html.* Note: *Slow churned* and *double churned* refer to a process called low-temperature extrusion, which significantly reduces the size of the fat globules and ice crystals in ice cream.

14. Murphy. 2006. Slabs are joining scoops in ice cream retailing.

15. *Entrepreneur.* 2011. 2011 Franchise 500 rankings. *www. entrepreneur.com/franchises/rankings/franchise500-115608/2011,-2.html.*

16. All definitions are taken from International Dairy Foods Organization (IDFA). n.d. What's in the ice cream aisle?

http://www.idfa.org/news--views/media-kits/ice-cream/ whats-in-the-ice-cream-aisle/.

17. Dippin' Dots 10th anniversary promotional video.

18. *Entrepreneur.* 2009. 2009 Franchise 500 rankings. *www.entrepreneur.com/franchises/rankings/franchise500-115608/2009,-4.html.*

19. Dippin' Dots Inc. n.d. Franchising. *www.dippindots.com/ business/franchising.html.*

20. Michelle, S. 2006. *Yelp Reviews–Chicago,* November 17. *www.yelp.com/biz/qnA4ml7Lu-9W4SDJOF1YPA.*

21. Associated Press. 2006. Business blazing for supercold Dippin' Dots.

22. Jones, L. 2010. Dippin' Dots spends millions on patent invalidity. Noro IP, November 15. *www.noroip. com/news-blog/dippin-dots-spends-millions-on-patent-invalidity/*

23. See *www.minimelts.com.*

24. Walker, J. 2009. Dippin' Dots founder takes control of company after management layoffs. *Paducah Sun* (Kentucky), March 13.

25. See *www.dippindots.com/products/lines/ dotsNCream.html.*

26. See *www.dippindots.com/products/lines/treats.html.*

Case 35   Microfinance

Going Global . . . and Going Public?*

In the world of development, if one mixes the poor and nonpoor in a program, the nonpoor will always drive out the poor, and the less poor will drive out the more poor, unless protective measures are instituted right at the beginning.

–**Dr. Muhammad Yunus,** founder of the Grameen Bank[1]

More than 2.5 billion people in the world earn less than $2.50 a day. None of the developmental economics theories have helped change this situation. Less than $2.50 a day means that these unfortunate people have been living without clean water, sanitation, or sufficient food to eat, or a proper place to sleep. In Southeast Asia alone, more than 500 million people live under these circumstances. In the past, almost every effort to help the very poor has been either a complete failure or at best partially successful. As Dr. Yunus argues, in every one of these instances, the poor will push the very poor out!

In 1972 Dr. Muhammad Yunus, a young economics professor trained at Vanderbilt, returned home to Bangladesh to take a position at Chittagong University. Upon his arrival, he was struck by the stark contrast between the developmental economics he taught in the classroom and the abject poverty of the villages surrounding the university. Dr. Yunus witnessed more suffering of the poor when, in 1974, inclement weather wiped out food crops and resulted in a widespread and prolonged famine. The theories of developmental economics and the traditional banking institutions, he concluded, were completely ineffectual for lessening the hunger and homelessness among the very poor of that region.

In 1976 Dr. Yunus and his students were visiting the poorest people in the village of Jobra to see whether they could directly help them in any way. They met a group of craftswomen making simple bamboo stools. After paying for their raw materials and financing, the women were left with a profit of just two cents per day. From his own pocket, Dr. Yunus gave $27 to be distributed among 42 craftswomen and *rickshaw* (human-driven transport) drivers. Little did he know that this simple act of generosity was the beginning of a global revolution in microfinance that would eventually help millions of impoverished and poor begin a transition from destitution to economic self-sufficiency. Dr. Yunus was convinced that a nontraditional approach to financing is the only way to help the very poor to help themselves.

*This case was developed by Brian C. Pinkham, LL.M., and Dr. Padmakumar Nair, both from the University of Texas at Dallas. Material has been drawn from published sources to be used for class discussion. Copyright © 2011 Brian C. Pinkham and Padmakumar Nair.

The Grameen Project would soon follow—it officially became a bank under the law in 1983. The poor borrowers own 95 percent of the bank, and the rest is owned by the Bangladeshi government. Loans are financed through deposits only, and there are 8.35 million borrowers, of which 97 percent are women. There are over 2,500 branches serving around 81,000 villages in Bangladesh with a staff of more than 22,000 people. Since its inception, the bank has dispersed more than $10 billion, with a cumulative loan recovery rate of 97.38 percent. The Grameen Bank has been profitable every year since 1976 except three years and pays returns on deposits up to 100 percent to its members.[2] In 2006 Dr. Yunus and the Grameen Bank shared the Nobel Peace Prize for the concept and methodology of microfinance, also known as microcredit or microloans.[3]

What Is Microfinance?

Microfinance involves a small loan (US $20–$750) with a high rate of interest (0 to 200 percent), typically provided to poor or destitute entrepreneurs without collateral.[4] A traditional loan has two basic components captured by interest rates: (1) risk of future payment, and (2) present value (given the time value of money). Risk of future payments is particularly high when dealing with the poor, who are unlikely to have familiarity with credit. To reduce this uncertainty, many microfinance banks refuse to lend to individuals and only lend to groups. Groups have proven to be an effective source of "social collateral" in the microloan process.

In addition to the risk and time value of money, the value of a loan must also include the transaction costs associated with administering the loan. A transaction cost is the cost associated with an economic exchange and is often considered the cost of doing business.[5] For banks like the Grameen Bank, the cost of administering ($125) a small loan may exceed the amount of the small loan itself ($120). These transaction costs have been one of the major deterrents for traditional banks.

Consider a bank with $10,000 to lend. If broken into small loans ($120), the available $10,000 can provide about 83 transactions. If the cost to administer a small loan ($120) is $125, its cost per unit is about 104 percent (!), while the cost of one $10,000 loan is only 1.25 percent. Because of the high cost per unit and the high risk of future payment, the rate of interest assigned to the smaller loan is much higher than the larger loan.

Finally, after these costs are accounted for, there must be some margin (or profit). In the case of microfinance banks, these margins are split between funding the growth of the bank (adding extra branches) and returns on deposits for bank members. This provides even the poorest bank member a feeling of "ownership."

Microfinance and Initial Public Offerings

With the global success of the microfinance concept, the number of private microfinance institutions exploded. Today there are more than 7,000 microfinance institutions, and their profitability has led many of the larger institutions to consider whether or not to "go public." Many microfinance banks redistribute profits to bank members (the poor) through returns on deposits. Once the bank goes public through an initial public offering (IPO), however, there is a transfer of control to public buyers (typically investors from developed economies). This transfer creates a fiduciary duty of the bank's management to maximize value for the shareholders.[6]

For example, Banco Compartamos (Banco) of Mexico raised $467 million in its IPO in 2007. The majority of buyers were leading investment companies from the United States and United Kingdom—the geographic breakdown of the investors was 52 percent U.S., 33 percent Europe, 5 percent Mexico, and 10 percent other Latin American countries. Similarly, Bank Rakyat Indonesia (BRI) raised $480 million in its IPO by listing on multiple stock exchanges in 2003; with the majority of investors who purchased the available 30 percent interest in the bank were from the United States and United Kingdom. The Indonesian government controls the remaining 70 percent stake in BRI. In Kenya, Equity Bank raised $88 million in its IPO in late 2006. Because of the small scale of Equity Bank's initial listing on the Nairobi Stock Exchange, the majority of the investors were from Eastern Africa.[7] About one-third of the investors were from the European Union and United States.[8]

Banco Compartamos[9]

Banco started in 1990 as a nongovernmental organization (NGO). At the time, population growth in Latin America and Mexico outpaced job growth. This left few job opportunities within the largest population group in Mexico—the low-income. Banco recognized that the payoffs for high-income opportunities were much larger (dollars a day), relative to low-income opportunities that may only return pennies a day. Over the next 10 years, Banco offered larger loans to groups and individuals to help bridge the gap between these low-income and high-income opportunities. However, their focus is to serve low-income individuals and groups, particularly the women who make up 98 percent of Banco's members.

The bank offers two microfinance options available to women only. The first is the *credito mujer* (women's credit). This loan ranges from $115–$2,075, available to groups (12–50) of women. Maturity is four months, and payments are weekly or biweekly.

If a group of women demonstrates the ability to manage credit through the *credito mujer,* they have access to *credito mejora tu casa* (home-improvement loans). This loan ranges from $230–$2,300 with a 6- to 24-month maturity. Payments are either biweekly or monthly.

The average interest rate on these loans is 80 percent. Banco focuses on loans to *groups* of women and requires the guarantee of the group—*every* individual in the group is held liable for the payment of the loan. This provides a social reinforcement mechanism for loan payments typically absent in traditional loans. The bank also prefers groups because they are more likely to take larger loans. This has proven effective even in times of economic downturn, when banks typically expect higher demand for loans and lower recovery of loans.

In 2009, with Mexico still reeling from the economic recession of 2008, Banco provided financing to 1.5 million Mexican households. This represented a growth of 30 percent from 2008. The core of the financing was *credito mujer,* emphasizing the bank's focus on providing services for the low-income groups. The average loan was 4.6 percent of GDP per capita ($440), compared with an average loan of 54 percent of GDP per capita ($347) at the Grameen Bank in Bangladesh.[10] With pressure from the economic downturn, Banco also reduced its cost per client by more than 5 percent, and continues (in late 2010) to have a cost per client under $125.

Consider two examples of how these microloans are used. Julia González Cueto, who started selling candy door-to-door in 1983, used her first loan to purchase accessories to broaden the image of her business. This provided a stepping stone for her decision to cultivate mushrooms and *nopales* (prickly pear leaves) to supplement her candy business. She now exports wild mushrooms to an Italian restaurant chain. Leocadia Cruz Gómez has had 16 loans, the first in April 2006. She invested in looms and thread to expand her textile business. Today, her workshop has grown, she is able to travel and give classes, and her work is widely recognized.

Beyond the Grameen Bank

These are just a few examples of how capitalistic free-market enterprises have helped the world to progress. It is generally accepted that charitable contributions and government programs alone cannot alleviate poverty. More resources and professional management are essential for microfinance institutions to grow further and sustain their mission. An IPO is one way to achieve this goal when deposits alone cannot sustain the demand for loans. At the same time, investors expect a decent return on their investment, and this expectation might work against the most important goal of microfinancing, namely, to help the very poor. Dr. Yunus has recently reemphasized his concern of the nonpoor driving out the poor, and talks about microfinance institutions seeking investments from "social-objective-driven" investors with a need to create a separate "social stock market."[11]

The Grameen Bank story, and that of microfinancing, and the current enthusiasm in going public raise several concerns. Institutions like the Grameen Bank have to grow and sustain a long-run perspective. The Grameen Bank has not accepted donor money since 1998 and does not foresee a need for donor money or other sources of external capital. The Grameen Bank charges four interest rates, depending on who is borrowing and for what purpose the money is being used: 20 percent for income-generating loans, 8 percent for housing loans, 5 percent for student loans, and *interest-free* loans for struggling members (unsympathetically called beggars). (Although these rates would appear to be close to what U.S. banks charge, we must point out that the terms of these loans are typically three or four months. Thus, the annualized interest rates would be four or five times the aforementioned rates.)

The Grameen Bank's "Beggars-As-Members" program is a stark contrast to what has been theorized and practiced in contemporary financial markets—traditional banking would assign high-risk borrowers (like beggars) the highest interest rate compared to more reliable borrowers who are using the borrowed money for generating income. Interestingly, the loan recovery rate is 79 percent from the "Beggars-As-Members" program, and about 20,000 members (out of 110,000) have left begging completely.[12] However, it is difficult to predict the future, and it is possible that the Grameen Bank might consider expanding its capital base by going public just like its Mexican counterpart.

Most developmental economists question the wisdom of going public, because publicly traded enterprises are likely to struggle to find a balance between fiduciary responsibilities and social good.[13] The three large IPOs mentioned above (Banco, BRI, and Equity First) all resulted in improved transparency and reporting for stockholders. However, the profits, which were originally distributed to bank members as returns on deposits, are now split between bank members (poor) and stockholders (made up of mostly EU and U.S. investors). Many of these microfinance banks are feeling the pressure of NGOs and bank members requesting lower interest rates.[14] This trend could potentially erode the large profit margins these banks currently enjoy. When faced with falling profits, publicly traded microfinance institutions will have to decide how best to provide financial services for the very poor and struggling members of the society without undermining their fiduciary duties to stockholders.

Endnotes

1. Yunus, M. 2007. *Banker to the poor: Micro-lending and the battle against world poverty.* New York: PublicAffairs.
2. The Grameen Bank removes funding for administration and branch growth from the initial profits and redistributes the remaining profits to bank members. This means that a poor bank member who deposits $1 *in* January may receive up to $1 on December 31! Grameen Bank, *www.grameen-info.org.*
3. Grameen Bank, *www.grameen-info.org.*
4. Microfinance banks vary to the extent that the rates of interest are annualized or specified to the term. Grameen Bank, for instance, annualizes the interest on its microloans. However, many other banks set a periodic rate where, in extreme cases, interest may accrue daily. Grameen Bank, *www.grameen-info.org.*
5. Chapter 6, pages 213–214.
6. Khavul, S. 2010. Microfinance: Creating opportunities for the poor? *Academy of Management Perspectives,* 24(3): 58–72.
7. Equity Bank, *www.equitybank.co.ke.*
8. Rhyne, E., & Guimon, A. 2007. The Banco Compartamos initial public offering, *Accion: InSight,* no. 23: 1–17. *resources.centerforfinancialinclusion.org/insight/IS23en.pdf.*
9. Unless otherwise noted, this section uses information from Banco Compartamos, *www.compartamos.com.*
10. We calculated all GDP per capita information as normalized to current (as of 2010) U.S. dollars using the International Monetary Fund (IMF) website, *www.imf.org.* The estimated percentages are from Banco Compartamos, *www.compartamos.com.*
11. Yunus. 2007. *Banker to the poor.*
12. Grameen Bank, *www.grameen-info.org.*
13. Khavul. 2010. Microfinance.
14. Rhyne & Guimon. 2007. The Banco Compartamos initial public offering.

Case 36 Green Mountain Coffee Roasters and Keurig Coffee*

On March 10, 2011, Starbucks and Green Mountain Coffee Roasters (GMCR) announced the formation of a strategic relationship for the manufacturing, marketing, distribution, and sale of Starbucks and Tazotea branded K-Cup portion packs for use in GMCR's Keurig single-cup brewing system. The new relationship was designed to provide owners of Keurig single-cup brewers with the additional choice of Starbucks-branded super-premium coffees for their brewers. This strategic relationship furthered Starbucks's stated goals of expanding its presence in premium single-cup coffee, making its premium coffees conveniently available to consumers whenever, wherever, and however they wanted it. Howard Schultz, president, CEO, and chairman of Starbucks Corporation stated,

> Today's announcement is a win for Starbucks, a win for GMCR and most importantly a win for consumers who want to enjoy Starbucks coffee with the Keurig Single-Cup Brewing system. Our research shows that more than 80 percent of current Starbucks customers in the U.S. do not yet own a single-cup brewer and our relationship will enable Starbucks customers to enjoy perfectly brewed Starbucks coffee at home, one cup at a time.

Jeff Hansberry, president, Starbucks Global Consumer Products Group, added, "We are proud to be the exclusive super-premium licensed coffee brand produced by GMCR for the Keurig Single-Cup Brewing system, and we are looking forward to working with our colleagues at GMCR to further accelerate growth in single-serve coffee." Lawrence J. Blanford, GMCR president and CEO stated, "This relationship is yet another example of GMCR's strategy of aligning with the strongest coffee brands to support a range of consumer choice and taste profiles in our innovative Keurig Single-Cup Brewing system."[1]

GMCR appeared on a roll with the Starbucks development following similar news in February with Dunkin' Donuts announcing a promotion, manufacturing, and distribution agreement making Dunkin' Donuts coffee available in single-serve K-Cup portion packs for use with Keurig Brewers.[2] Beginning in the summer of 2011, Dunkin' Donuts will offer 14-count boxes of Dunkin' Donuts coffee in single-serve K-Cup portion packs exclusively at participating Dunkin' Donuts restaurants in the United States and Canada. GMCR will exclusively package the new Dunkin' K-Cup portion packs using coffee sourced and roasted to Dunkin' Donuts exacting specifications. Nigel Travis, Dunkin' Brands CEO and Dunkin' Donuts president stated,

> We believe customers will be delighted to learn that 'America's Favorite Coffee' will soon be able to be prepared in America's fastest-growing single-cup brewing system. By introducing Dunkin' K-Cup portion packs and making them available exclusively in our restaurants, we are giving people more occasions to enjoy Dunkin' Donuts coffee and more ways to enjoy using the Keurig Single-Cup Brewing System. We believe this alliance of two brand leaders means incremental sales of GMCR, for Dunkin' Donuts and for our Dunkin' Donuts franchisees.

GMCR president and CEO Larry Blanford stated,

> Dunkin' Donuts has top quality coffee, an extremely loyal customer base and impactful advertising programs. Combine those assets with consumers' enthusiastic response to Keurig's Single-Cup Brewing technology and we believe this alliance represents a truly exciting opportunity for both companies, with the potential to strengthen Keurig brewer adoption by consumers in one of the fastest-growing categories of the coffee industry.

According to The NPD Group/CREST, Dunkin' Donuts served the most hot traditional and iced coffee in America (for quick-serve restaurants, year ending October 2010), selling more than one billion cups of hot and iced coffee every year. Dunkin' Donuts was recently ranked number one in customer loyalty in the coffee category for the fifth consecutive year by the 2010 Brand Keys Customer Loyalty Engagement Index. Additionally, in 2010 Dunkin' Donuts opened more net new locations globally than any other quick-serve brand.

While Wall Street rewarded the stock price of GMCR on the news of the strategic relationships, Larry Blanford could not ignore the risks related to GMCR's Keurig business. Although GMCR was based in Waterbury, Vermont, with a geographic footprint weighted almost exclusively to the U.S. and Canada, several global developments posed risks to Keurig's future growth. Blanford was concerned about several issues. including product liability, protecting GMCR's intellectual property, GMCR's ability to integrate their acquisitions, and the effect of commodity costs on Keurig brewers.

Coffee Consumption in the United States

The U.S. population consumed more coffee than soft drinks in 1969. According to Jack Maxwell of *Beverage Digest,* U.S. consumption of coffee in 1969 was approximately 40 gallons per capita versus 20 gallons of soft drinks. By

* This case was prepared by doctoral student Keith F. Moody and Professor Alan B. Eisner of Pace University as a basis for class discussion rather than to illustrate either effective or ineffective handling of an administrative situation. Material has been drawn from published sources. Copyright © 2011 Keith F. Moody and Alan B. Eisner.

1998, coffee consumption had fallen to 20 gallons per capita annually compared to more than 50 gallons of soft drinks consumed. But consumer preferences can and did change, responding to the availability of higher-quality coffee by drinking more coffee and reversing a three-decade decline. The National Coffee Association conducted a survey revealing that 80 percent of Americans drink coffee occasionally and over 50 percent drink coffee daily. The U.S. per capita consumption of coffee was estimated to be 424 servings, which included in-home and out-of-home consumption of roast, ground, instant, and ready-to-drink (bottled/canned) coffee.[3] While the average consumption per drinker rose to over three cups per day, 18- to 24-year-olds who drink coffee averaged 4.6 cups per day, whereas those over 60 years old averaged only 2.8 cups per day.[4]

The total coffee market in 2010 was estimated to be 105 billion cups or $34 billion (see Exhibit 1).[5] Specialty coffee has become a mainstream staple as younger drinkers have come of age with Starbucks virtually omnipresent. Given the proliferation of specialty coffee and a palate less tolerant of Robusta coffee from a can, the Millennial Generation provides a robust outlook for specialty coffee demand (see Exhibit 2).

The Keurig K-Cup Single-Serve Brewing System

Keurig single-serve systems are designed to quickly brew a single cup of coffee, tea, hot chocolate, or other hot beverage such as apple cider. The coffee grounds or other brew material are supplied in a prepared, single-serving unit called a "K-Cup." Once the brewer has warmed up, the Keurig user inserts a K-Cup into the brewer, places a mug under the spout, and invokes the brew feature. Within 20 to 60 seconds, the beverage is brewed. Keurig machines brew by piercing the foil seal on top of the plastic K-Cup with a spray nozzle, while simultaneously piercing the bottom of the K-cup with a discharge nozzle. Grounds

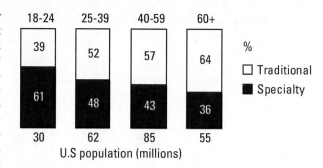

Exhibit 2 Coffee Preference Percentages by Age

Source: National Coffee Association, 2010 Drinking Trends.

contained inside the K-cup are embedded within a paper filter. A measured quantity of hot water is forced through the K-Cup, passing through the brew material and the filter into a cup or mug. A brewing temperature of 192 degrees Fahrenheit (89 Celsius) is the default setting, with some models permitting users to reduce the temperature per preference.

"Pod" Brewing Market

The Keurig brewer utilizes patented, innovative brewing and single-cup technology to deliver a fresh-brewed cup of coffee, tea, or cocoa at the touch of a button. Brewers with Keurig Brewed technology were the top five selling coffeemakers in the United States on a dollar basis for the period of October through December 2010 and represented 49 percent of total coffeemaker dollar sales for that period according to the NPD Group. At the KeyBanc Capital Markets investor presentation, Larry Blanford reported that Keurig brewer and accessories sales increased 58 percent in the first quarter of 2011 versus first quarter 2010. During this same time period, K-Cup portion pack net sales increased 89 percent to $332.9 million. As a percentage of total coffeemaker dollar sales, Keurig's percentage has increased quarter on quarter every quarter since 2007 (see Exhibits 3–6).

While the coffeemaker category sales excluding Keurig declined over 5 percent in 4Q 2010 versus 4Q 2008, sales of the Keurig brewers actually increased over 400 percent during the period, fueling total category dollar sales growth in excess of 53 percent for the period. As of year-end 2010, Keurig and Keurig-licensed brewers were approaching the point where sales would account for over 50 percent of total coffeemaker category sales (see Exhibit 7).

During the first quarter of 2011, Keurig-branded brewers continued to gain market share in the coffeemaker category. According to NPD, in GMCR's fiscal first quarter, Keurig-branded brewers (without third-party brewers) remained the number one dollar-share leader in the U.S. coffeemaker category, with the four top-selling brewers and over 45 percent dollar share, compared to 36.4 percent

Exhibit 1 Total U.S. Coffee Market Value

Traditional $17 - $19 B

Specialty $15 – $17 B

Exhibit 3 GMCR Keurig Percentage of Total Coffeemaker Dollar Sales, 2007–2010

Source: NPD Group.

Note: Includes all coffeemakers and espresso makers. NPD data do not include all retailers and are estimated to represent 35 percent to 40 percent of the total marketplace.

Exhibit 4 Green Mountain Coffee Roasters Income Statement

	Period Ending		
	Sept. 25, 2010	Sept. 26, 2009	Sept. 27, 2008
Total Revenue	1,356,775	786,135	500,277
Cost of Revenue	931,017	540,744	323,372
Gross Profit	425,758	245,391	176,905
Operating Expenses:			
Research Development	—	—	—
Selling General and Administrative	286,986	169,005	134,493
Operating Income or Loss	138,772	93,386	42,412
Income from Continuing Operations:			
Total Other Income/Expenses, Net	(269)	16,338	(235)
Earnings before Interest And Taxes	138,503	92,724	42,177
Interest Expense	5,294	4,693	5,705
Income before Tax	133,209	88,031	36,472
Income Tax Expense	53,703	33,592	14,173
Net Income from Continuing Operations	79,506	54,439	22,299
Net Income	79,506	54,439	22,299
Preferred Stock and Other Adjustments	—	—	—
Net Income Applicable to Common Shares	79,506	54,439	22,299

Source: Yahoo Finance.

Exhibit 5 Green Mountain Coffee Roasters Balance Sheet

	Period Ending		
	Sept. 25, 2010	Sept. 26, 2009	Sept. 27, 2008
Assets			
Current Assets:			
Cash and Cash Equivalents	4,756	242,091	965
Short-Term Investments	—	50,000	—
Net Receivables	204,547	101,710	60,928
Inventory	262,478	132,182	85,311
Other Current Assets	23,488	11,384	4,886
Total Current Assets	**495,269**	**537,367**	**152,090**
Property, Plant, and Equipment	258,923	135,981	97,678
Goodwill	386,416	99,600	73,953
Intangible Assets	220,005	36,478	29,396
Other Assets	9,961	3,979	4,531
Total Assets	**1,370,574**	**813,405**	**357,648**
Liabilities			
Current Liabilities:			
Accounts Payable	214,669	118,156	72,214
Short/Current Long-Term Debt	19,009	5,030	33
Other Current Liabilities	4,377	3,257	673
Total Current Liabilities	**238,055**	**126,443**	**72,920**
Long-Term Debt	335,504	73,013	123,517
Other Liabilities	5,191	—	—
Deferred Long-Term Liability Charges	92,579	26,599	21,691
Total Liabilities	**671,329**	**226,055**	**218,128**
Stockholders' Equity			
Common Stock	13,282	13,081	2,549
Retained Earnings	213,844	134,338	81,280
Treasury Stock	—	—	(7,336)
Capital Surplus	473,749	441,875	63,607
Other Stockholder Equity	(1,630)	(1,944)	(580)
Total Stockholder Equity	**699,245**	**587,350**	**139,520**
Net Tangible Assets	**92,824**	**451,272**	**36,171**

Source: Yahoo Finance.

a year ago. For the same fiscal first quarter 2011 period, NPD estimated that, including third-party Keurig-branded brewer sales, Keurig brewers represented 49.3 percent of total coffeemaker dollar sales. In Canada, Keurig brewers (without third-party brewers) were the second leading dollar-share leader of all coffeemakers, with the brand increasing its dollar share to 14.6 percent in GMCR's fiscal first quarter 2011 from 8.1 percent in 2010. On a unit

Exhibit 6 Segment Summary

Specialty Coffee business unit(SCBU): Sources, produces, and sells more than 200 varieties of coffee, cocoa, teas, and other beverages in K-Cup portion packs and coffee in more traditional packaging, including whole bean and ground coffee selections in bags and ground coffee in fractional packs, for use both at-home (AH) and away-from-home (AFH). In addition, SCBU sells Keurig single-cup brewers and other accessories directly to consumers and to supermarkets.

Keurig: Sells AH single-cup brewers and accessories and coffee, tea, cocoa, and other beverages in K-Cup portion packs produced by SCBU and other licensed roasters to retailers by principally processing its sales orders through fulfillment entities for the AH channels. Keurig sells AFH single-cup brewers to distributors for use in offices. Keurig also sells AH brewers, a limited number of AFH brewers and K-Cup portion packs directly to consumers via its website, *www.keurig.com*.

	Net Sales ($ millions)			Growth (%)	
	2010	2009	2008	2010	2009
SCBU	629	383.8	285.9	64	34
Keurig	727.8	402.3	206.6	81	95
Corporate	—	—	—	—	—
Total company	1,356.8	786.1	492.5	73	60

	Income before Taxes ($ millions)			Growth (%)	
	2010	2009	2008	2010	2009
SCBU	119.5	53.5	27.8	123	92
Keurig	72.3	40.4	28	79	44
Corporate	(44.1)	(2.8)	(18.7)	(1475)	85
Intercompany eliminations	(14.5)	(3.1)	(1.7)	(368)	(82)
Total company	133.2	88.0	35.4	51	149

Source: GMCR 2010 annual report.

basis, Keurig-branded brewers (without third-party brewers) gained ground, increasing share to 6.8 percent in 2011 from 3.2 percent in 2010 for all coffeemakers.

Approximately 18.5 million coffee brewers were sold each year in the United States, and Keurig's goal was to convert over half of the 90 million American homes with coffee brewers to Keurig.[6] As recently as 2007, research by the NPD Group indicated that the single-serve proposition wasn't compelling enough for consumers to replace their existing coffeemakers with pod machines. NPD's research indicated that a significant proportion of purchasers were unsatisfied and cited unreliable machines as a problem as well as the coffee itself. The pods available, consumers complained, were pricey, often hard to find, and limited in terms of flavor and blends. In their survey, the NPD Group found some consumers were dissatisfied with the performance of pod machines, with 17 percent of

machines returned, thrown out, or given away. John Block, director for the NPD Group, said, "Manufacturers and retailers have a great opportunity to improve their position in the marketplace by listening to consumer feedback, and integrating all three attributes that customers want most into their product offering: a reliable pod machine, easy-to-find refills, and a variety of coffee flavors."[7]

A Multichannel Strategy for the Away-from-Home (AFH) Market

Keurig initially focused on the AFH commercial segment of office users. Increasing demand and brand awareness enabled Keurig to pursue a multichannel strategy, providing widespread exposure to consumer trial. Starbucks and other specialty coffee purveyors laid the groundwork for launching into the AFH office coffee service (OCS) market by educating consumers about gourmet coffee and moving

Total Coffeemaker Dollar Sales in millions Oct. - Dec. 2010
(includes third-party brewers)

Exhibit 7 **Total Coffeemaker Dollar Sales, October–December 2008 through October–December 2010 (in millions)**

Source: NPD Group.

Note: Data include third-party brewers. "Total coffeemaker" category includes all coffeemakers and espresso makers. NPD data do not include all retailers and are estimated to represent 35 percent to 40 percent of the total marketplace.

coffee beyond a commodity. Starbucks may be responsible for a paradigm shift regarding the price elasticity for coffee. The paradigm that applied to price elasticity affecting consumer purchases of Robusta coffee by the can shifted with the proliferation of fresh-ground Arabica beans served in a coffeehouse, often for $2 or more per cup. This paradigm shift enabled Keurig to offer a single-cup brewing system into offices, capitalizing on consumer demand to replicate their coffeehouse quality java in the office.

There were approximately 2.6 million coffee brewers in offices nationwide serviced by a network of approximately 1,700 distributors. Of those offices, GMCR estimated that 12 percent had single-cup brewers, and about half of those were Keurig brewers.[8] While Keurig brewers were estimated to be in 30 percent of offices in New England, national penetration in the office channel was only about 6 percent.

Keurig continued working with its network of Keurig Authorized Distributors (KADs) to execute office acquisition plans, conduct lead generation, demonstrations, and sampling programs to build Keurig's office coffee business. In addition to Keurig's traditional distributor network, customers such as Office Depot and Staples were helping Keurig grow through their business-to-business solutions for both large and small office applications.

Another AFH single-serve opportunity Keurig identified was the hotel market. There were approximately five million coffeemakers in hotel rooms across North America. Keurig believed that 40 percent of these rooms

catered to travelers who would appreciate the benefits of single-serve brewing. The Keurig team went through a rigorous process to develop new brewer concepts for the market. The development of a new "hotel in-room" brewer was one example (see Exhibit 8).

Single-Cup Brewer System Competition

Consumers had many options of single-cup brewing systems to choose from in North America and internationally. Competition in the single-cup brewing system market was increasing, as relatively low barriers to entry encouraged new competitors to enter the market, particularly with typically lower-cost brewers that brewed coffee packaged in nonpatented pods. Many current and potential competitors had substantially greater financial, marketing, and operating resources versus Keurig. According to Keurig, their primary competitors were Flavia Beverage Systems (manufactured by Mars), the Tassimo beverage system (manufactured and marketed by Kraft), the Senso brewing system (manufactured and marketed by Philips and Sara Lee), and a number of additional single-cup brewing systems and brands. Kraft's Tassimo system was made primarily for at-home use, while the Mars's Flavia system targeted offices.

A January 2009 *Consumer Reports* article on coffeemakers covered pod machines. The article stated, "With pod machines, you simply drop in a sealed packet of coffee—no grinding, no scooping, and no mess. But many lock you into the company's coffee, which tends to be pricey, and the results have been unimpressive." According to *Consumer Reports,* "Cuisinart's Cup-O-Matic SS-1, $200, did best among the pod models tested. It took standard pods or your own grind and lets you pick regular or bold in five cup sizes. It was reasonably quick: about three minutes for the first cup, one minute thereafter. But the model occasionally leaked extra water into the cup, diluting the coffee." *Consumer Reports* also tested the Keurig Breville BKC600XL, $300. *Consumer Reports* commented that the Keurig machine, "accepts any K-cup as well as loose coffee grounds. It was fairly quiet but that first cup takes almost four minutes." *Consumer Reports* recommended, "If you want coffee for one in a hurry and you insist on the neatness and convenience of a pod machine, consider the Cuisinart for its flexibility and speed. Otherwise, we recommend our top-scoring to-go model, the Melitta Take2 ME2TM. It's quick, brewed superbly, and costs just $25."

The History of Keurig

Named for the Dutch word for excellence, Keurig was launched in 1990 by Peter Dragone and John Sylvan, with the belief that coffee should always be served fresh, whether at home or at the office, just as in a gourmet coffeehouse. Dragone and Sylvan noticed that people were leaving the office in search of a fresh cup of coffee and asked themselves, "Why do we brew coffee by the pot when we drink it by the cup?" From this question, the revolutionary concept of Keurig K-Cup portion pack brewing was born. In 1994 Keurig secured a patent and came

THE STEPS TO BRINGING A
KEURIG® BREWER TO MARKET

The Keurig team goes through a rigorous process to develop new brewer concepts and bring them to market. Our development of the B130 hotel in-room brewer is a good example.

1 The process started with a marketing analysis of industry segments that might benefit from gourmet single-cup brewing. Hotel made sense, as for gourmet coffee in-room, and Keurig's speed and convenience would be attractive to guests.

2 Next came meeting with hotel companies to get customer feedback. Keurig placed commercial brewers in several hotels, free of charge, to capture guests' experiences with the brewer.

3 Armed with this insight, the Keurig marketing team developed a detailed specfication for an in-room hotel brewer. Key factors were identified, such as brewer size (it needed to be small), and a design to avoid having water remain in the brewer between guests. The Keurig engineering team kicked into high gear to determine new technology needed for a hotel room brewer, than designed an engineering prototype.

4 Now the fun could begin: product ID work. Keurig takes the look and feel of its brewers very seriously. Several have won design awards. Keurig's outside product ID firm presented dozens of potential looks for the in-room brewer. Once a design was chosen, it was time to turn the product over to Keurig's manufacturing partners.

The result? A brewer that has been a major success and is now found in over 40,000 hotel rooms in North America!

3 Minutes until fresh brewed coffee

PLACE CUP
HEATING
BREW
POWER

Exhibit 8 Keurig "Hotel In-Room" Brewer

up with a prototype. Two venture capital firms kicked in $1 million and gave Dragone and Sylvan one year to prepare a model for mass production. When they missed that deadline, the venture capitalists offered more money but demanded that Nick Lazaris, a veteran executive who once served as chief of staff to West Virginia Governor (now Senator) Jay Rockefeller, be brought on. In 1998, after eight years of development, Keurig released an industrial-strength, single-serve machine that delivered a perfect cup of coffee or tea every time.

Keurig was a technology company in the coffee industry. Keurig brewers represented a fusion of technology and design. To maintain and enhance its position as a leader in the gourmet single-cup market, Keurig invested significant resources and capital in engineering and research and development. This led to a strong and growing portfolio of market-leading, proprietary technology. Keurig's integrated engineering team drove fast and innovative product development in all three areas that supported Keurig's

single-cup system: brewers, portion packs, and high-speed packaging lines that manufactured the portion packs. Keurig's integrated approach to new-product development resulted in accelerated new-product launches since 2004. Keurig employed over 30 degreed engineers from varied disciplines. The engineering team at Keurig included mechanical, software, and nutritional science, as well as quality assurance and industrial engineering. As of 2007, Keurig held 26 U.S. and 65 international patents covering a range of its portion packs, packaging line, and brewer technology, and Keurig had additional patent applications in process. Of these, 72 were utility patents and 19 were design patents. The Keurig system was based on three fundamental elements:

1. A patented and proprietary portion-pack system ("K-Cup") using a specially designed filter, sealed in a low-oxygen environment to ensure freshness (see Exhibit 9).

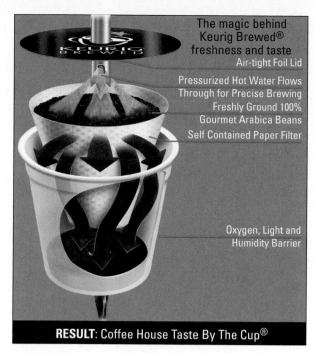

The magic behind
Keurig Brewed®
freshness and taste
Air-tight Foil Lid

Pressurized Hot Water Flows
Through for Precise Brewing
Freshly Ground 100%
Gourmet Arabica Beans
Self Contained Paper Filter

Oxygen, Light and
Humidity Barrier

RESULT: Coffee House Taste By The Cup®

Exhibit 9 The Keurig K-Cup

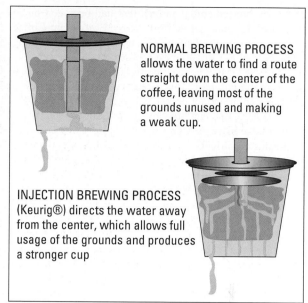

NORMAL BREWING PROCESS allows the water to find a route straight down the center of the coffee, leaving most of the grounds unused and making a weak cup.

INJECTION BREWING PROCESS (Keurig®) directs the water away from the center, which allows full usage of the grounds and produces a stronger cup

Exhibit 10 Normal versus Injection Brewing Process

2. Specially designed, proprietary high-speed packaging lines that manufactured K-Cups at the coffee roaster's facilities using fresh roasted and ground coffee (or tea)

3. Brewers that precisely controlled the amount, temperature, and pressure of water to provide a consistently superior cup of coffee or tea in less than a minute when used with K-Cups.

Keurig's patented system eliminated the need to measure coffee or water—the two primary culprits for suboptimal java. With the Keurig system, pressurized hot water was filtered through a small plastic pod, called a K-Cup, that combined both filter and coffee (see Exhibit 10).

Keurig maintained a sizeable quality control team to assist engineering in establishing quality standards; to communicate standards to all manufacturing partners, roasters, and suppliers; and to audit compliance with Keurig's established standards. This emphasis on quality products, easy-to-use features, and innovative technologies earned Keurig high marks in customer satisfaction, with 94 percent customer satisfaction from tracked brewer purchasers.

A licensing agreement enabled Green Mountain Coffee Roasters to package its high-quality Arabica beans in Keurig's patented container, the K-Cups. GMCR started distributing the new single-cup Keurig Premium Coffee System to office-coffee-service (OCS) and food-service providers in 1998. GMCR and Keurig sold the system through select distribution channels. The system featured the single-cup Keurig brewer and eight varieties of Green

Mountain coffee, including blends, flavored, decafs, and estate coffees. Keurig's K-Cup packaging guaranteed that each cup of coffee was as fresh as "the first cup of every pot." Keurig's strategy to gain market share in the office market was to sell machines to distributors and encourage them to give the machines away or lease them for a small fee. The economics of the strategy worked for distributors, because the real profit was in selling K-Cups. If an office went through 30 or 40 K-Cups per day, a distributor recouped the cost of the machine in less than six months of K-Cup sales.

When Keurig launched its first single-cup brewer for the office market in 1998, it partnered with Green Mountain Coffee to manufacture and sell Keurig's patented K-Cups. Although Green Mountain Coffee was the first roaster to sell its coffee in Keurig's single-cup brewing system, by 2003 GMCR was competing for Keurig's sales with three other North American roasters: Diedrich Coffee, Timothy's, and Van Houtte, a vertically integrated roaster and office coffee distributor in Canada and the United States. Since 2003, Keurig had licensed several additional coffee roasters to package gourmet coffee and teas into K-Cups, all of whom paid royalties to Keurig based on the number of K-Cups shipped. For each K-Cup shipped, roasters paid Keurig a royalty of approximately $.04. This unique licensing agreement system enabled Keurig to offer the industry's widest selection of gourmet branded coffees and teas in a proprietary single-cup format. This wide coffee selection proved to be a key differentiator for Keurig's brewing system. Consumers could choose from 11 gourmet brands and over 130 varieties of coffees and teas in K-Cups. Of the more than 2 billion cups of Keurig brewed coffee and tea that had been consumed since Keurig launched in 1998,[9] Green Mountain Coffee continued to be the leading K-Cup roaster, representing 57 percent of K-Cups shipped in fiscal 2008.[10]

In 1998 GMCR held a minority investment of less than 5 percent in Keurig Inc. This partnership with Keurig developed into an important growth driver in fiscal 2000, as the unique Keurig one-cup brewing system gained momentum in the marketplace. K-Cup sales made up 15.7 percent of total sales at GMCR in fiscal 2000. GMCR's partnership with Keurig Inc. continued to be an important growth driver in fiscal 2001, with K-Cup sales comprising 20.4 percent of total revenue for GMCR. Keurig's ownership structure changed in 2002 as a result of agreements with GMCR and Van Houtte. Keurig sold stock to Van Houtte, raising $10 million to seed Keurig's at-home business launch. The investment secured Van Houtte a 28 percent ownership position in Keurig. Simultaneously, GMCR invested $15 million, by acquiring and executing stock options, to purchase 42 percent of Keurig. These strategic moves resulted in GMCR and Van Houtte joining Memorial Drive Trust (MDT) as the top three shareholders of Keurig. MDT, an investment advisory firm, had been the primary venture investor in Keurig since 1995 and led Keurig's board of directors. Separate shareholder agreements with MDT, however, restricted both GMCR and Van Houtte from holding a seat on Keurig's board of directors. However, in June 2006, GMCR completed its acquisition of Keurig for $104.3 million.

Expanding Keurig's Family of Brands

In addition to Green Mountain Coffee and GMCR's affiliated Newman's Own Organics and Celestial Seasonings Tea brands, which were packaged and sold by Green Mountain Coffee, Keurig's other North American K-Cup brands offered as of year-end 2006 included Diedrich, Gloria Jean's, Coffee People, Timothy's, Emeril's, Van Houtte, Bigelow, Tully's, and Twinings.

In January 2007, Keurig Inc. and Caribou Coffee, the second largest publicly traded gourmet coffee company in the United States in terms of number of retail stores, announced a partnership to market Caribou's gourmet coffees in Keurig K-Cups. "We are proud to welcome Caribou to the Keurig family," stated Nick Lazaris, former president of Keurig. "Caribou is an exceptionally strong brand with a loyal following among gourmet coffee lovers. Our office and home Keurig users will be delighted with Caribou in K-Cups."[11] Under license from Caribou Coffee, Keurig served as the wholesale distributor and a direct retailer for Caribou Coffee K-Cups. In addition, many Keurig premium retail partners added Caribou Coffee K-Cups to the selection of K-Cups already carried in 6,700 stores coast to coast. For the office coffee channel, Caribou Coffee K-Cups were offered through Keurig's authorized distributors for marketing to offices where Keurig brewers were installed. Caribou marketed both Caribou Coffee K-Cups and Keurig brewers in many of its coffeehouses.

As Keurig gained momentum across the United States, the diversity of the K-Cup brand portfolio increased in importance because regional preferences could not be underestimated as national penetration progressed. The addition of Caribou Coffee, a strong Midwest brand, helped build K-Cup sales and introduce Green Mountain Coffee to areas beyond its core market.

In September 2008 GMCR announced an asset purchase agreement to acquire the Tully's coffee brand and wholesale business. Tully's was a well-respected specialty coffee roaster with Pacific Northwest roots and heritage. The Tully's wholesale business division distributed coffee to over 5,000 supermarkets, located primarily in the western states, and also sold coffee in K-Cup portion packs. The Tully's acquisition was designed to provide GMCR with a complimentary West Coast brand and business platform to facilitate future geographic growth and brand expansion. In March 2009 GMCR completed the acquisition of the Tully's Coffee brand and wholesale coffee business from Tully's Coffee Corporation for the purchase price of $40.3 million. GMCR financed the purchase through its existing $225 million senior revolving credit facility. Larry Blanford stated, "This acquisition strengthens our leadership in specialty coffee and will support our plans to establish our proprietary Keurig Single-Cup system as the preferred way to enjoy coffee throughout North America." Tully's retail locations continued to operate under license and supply agreements with GMCR. Tully's retail and international business remained an independent company, operating under the name of TC Global Inc., owned by its existing shareholders and managed by its existing management team.

In November 2009 GMCR announced the acquisition of Timothy's Coffees of the World Inc. for a cash purchase price of approximately $157 million, in U.S. dollars. The acquisition included the Timothy's World Coffee brand and wholesale business (but did not include retail operations) and was maintained as a wholly owned Canadian subsidiary, with operations integrated into GMCR's Specialty Coffee Business Unit. Headquartered in Toronto, Ontario, Timothy's was a premium coffee company that produced specialty coffee, tea, and other beverages in a variety of packaged forms. Additionally, Timothy's produced K-Cup portion packs for the Keurig single-cup brewing system sold under the Timothy's World Coffee, Emeril's, and Kahlua Original K-Cup brands. Timothy's became a licensed roaster of Keurig Inc., a wholly owned subsidiary of GMCR, in 2000. Regarding the acquisition, Larry Blanford stated,

> Timothy's is a great addition to GMCR's family of brands. We have been collaborating together since they became a Keurig licensee and know the company is a great strategic and cultural fit. We believe that Timothy's, along with our Green Mountain Coffee brand, will contribute meaningfully to our future success in Canada and throughout North America. It will accelerate GMCR's geographic expansion with a Canadian brand platform

that includes manufacturing and distribution synergies. The retail portion of the Timothy's business has been purchased by Bruegger's Enterprises, Inc. and will continue to support the Timothy's brand across Canada. Our acquisition includes a five-year coffee supply agreement with Bruegger's Canadian affiliate and we look forward to our expanding relationship with them as we already supply all of their 290 locations in the U.S. . . . Timothy's wholesale business and brand is a landmark international acquisition for GMCR—representing the accomplishment of a key goal: to further optimize the Keurig opportunity and our family of brands across North America.

In May 2010 GMCR announced that it had acquired Diedrich Coffee Inc. for $35 per share of common stock in cash, pursuant to a cash tender offer and a "short form" merger, in a transaction with a total value of approximately $300 million. Diedrich Coffee became a wholly owned subsidiary of GMCR and was integrated into GMCR's Specialty Coffee business unit. Diedrich Coffee specialized in sourcing, roasting, and selling the world's highest quality coffees. The company marketed its three leading brands of specialty coffees, Diedrich Coffee, Coffee People, and Gloria Jean's Coffees, through office-coffee-service distributors, restaurants, and specialty retailers and via the company's web stores. Diedrich Coffee was one of the few roasters under license to produce K-Cups for Keurig's top-selling single-cup brewing system. Regarding this acquisition, Larry Blanford stated,

> By taking the next logical step beyond our already successful licensing agreement with Diedrich Coffee, we are bringing in house three strong, complementary brand platforms—Diedrich, Gloria Jean's and Coffee People—and augmenting the growing GMCR beverage brand portfolio. In addition, we are gaining manufacturing and distribution facilities in California, which will enable us to more effectively, reach consumers in this region.

The combined company operated manufacturing and distribution facilities in Waterbury and Essex, Vermont; Castroville, California; Knoxville, Tennessee; Sumner, Washington; and Toronto, Ontario. GMCR also announced that it amended its Amended and Restated Revolving Credit Agreement to provide for a new term loan for $140 million, a new uncommitted revolver increase option of up to $100 million, and increases in the permitted amounts of certain forms of indebtedness and investments. In connection with the closing, GMCR executed the $140 million new term loan to pay for a portion of the Diedrich Coffee acquisition purchase price.

In December 2010 GMCR announced that it had successfully completed its acquisition of LJVH Holdings Inc. ("Van Houtte") for an aggregate cash purchase price of CAD $915 million, or USD $905 million, subject to adjustment for final exchange rate and future adjustment based on Van Houtte's working capital, net indebtedness, and preclosing taxes as of immediately prior to the acquisition's

closing. Headquartered in Montreal, Quebec, Van Houtte was a leading gourmet coffee brand in Canada in the home and office channels. Van Houtte's last 12 month's net sales were CAD $445 million as of August 21, 2010, or approximately USD $433 million based on the exchange rate as of September 13, 2010. Van Houtte roasted and marketed gourmet coffee for home and office consumption and distributed it through Van Houtte's direct-to-store delivery and coffee-services networks in Canada and the United States. GMCR expected to continue operations from Van Houtte's location in Montreal, Quebec, under the leadership of Gerard Geoffrion, Van Houtte's president and CEO. Van Houtte's Canadian brands included Van Houtte, Brûlerie St. Denis, Les Cafés Orient Express Coffee, and Brûlerie Mont Royal. Van Houtte also produced K-Cup portion packs for the Keurig single-cup brewing system under the Van Houtte, Bigelow, and Wolfgang Puck K-Cup brands. Regarding the acquisition, Gerard Geoffrion, Van Houtte president and CEO stated, "As a result of our long-term relationship as a Keurig licensee, we know there is a strong cultural and strategic fit between GMCR and Van Houtte. We believe the combination of our brands, employees and our respective geographic strengths makes for a stronger overall company and will enable us to continue to grow our presence in Canada." Larry Blanford stated, "We are very pleased to welcome Van Houtte and its approximately 1,800 employees into the GMCR family. We are confident that Van Houtte, with its well-known portfolio of brands and strong management team, will help drive GMCR's future success in Canada and throughout North America." GMCR financed the Van Houtte acquisition through a combination of cash on hand and new debt financing. GMCR entered into $1.45 billion in senior credit facilities, consisting of:

1. A term loan A facility in an aggregate amount of $250 million,
2. A term loan B facility in an aggregate amount of $550 million,
3. A U.S. revolving-credit facility in an aggregate amount of $450 million, and
4. An alternative currency revolving credit facility in an aggregate amount of $200 million.

GMCR used a portion of the proceeds from these senior credit facilities to repay GMCR's borrowings under its former credit facility and to pay the Van Houtte acquisition purchase price. GMCR also planned to use a portion of the proceeds from these senior credit facilities to support GMCR's ongoing growth.

Subsequent to the closing of the transaction, GMCR anticipated conducting a strategic review of Van Houtte's U.S. coffee-services business, Filterfresh, in contemplation of a potential divestiture of Filterfresh, given GMCR's current sales and marketing structure and its existing network of independent Keurig authorized distributors throughout the United States. The proceeds from any divestiture would be used to reduce GMCR's outstanding indebtedness.

Corporate Social Responsibility Shaped the Organizational Culture at GMCR

Green Mountain was committed to conducting its business in a socially responsible manner. The company believed that doing well financially could go hand in hand with giving back to the community and protecting the environment. In their 2010 annual report, GMCR stated that their success was supported by their long-standing commitment to social and environmental responsibility (see Exhibit 11). That commitment, combined with GMCR's entrepreneurial spirit and highly engaged workforce, enhanced their competitive advantage and provided GMCR an "opportunity to create better coffee, and brew a better world." GMCR allocated 5 percent of their pretax profits to support social and environmental projects every year. GMCR posted their Corporate Social Responsibility Report at *www.Brewing-ABetterWorld.com.*

GMCR worked to protect the environment. Waste reduction and responsible energy use were two of GMCR's top priorities and had been since 1983, when GMCR began composting in their retail coffee shops. In 1989 GMCR developed Earth-Friendly coffee filters. More recent examples of GMCR's commitment to protecting the environment included working with International Paper to bring to market the world's first to-go cup made with renewable materials, installing an on-site biodiesel fueling station, and embracing carbon offsets.

Exhibit 11 GMCR's Corporate Social Responsibility Initiatives

Partnering with Supply-Chain Communities and Supporting Local Communities	FY10	FY09	FY08
Total resources allocated to social and environmental programs as a percentage of income before taxes	5.2%	5.0%	5.2%
Total resources allocated to social and environmental programs (in thousands)	$6,931	$3,666	$1,910
Total cash contributions (in thousands)	$5,946	$2,686	$1,155
Average hours volunteered per full-time employee	6.3	7.4	6.0
Total number of employee volunteer hours	14,878	9,981	6,208
Dollars allocated to workplace volunteerism programs (in thousands)	$355	$255	$139
Donations of products, equipment, and administrative supplies (allocated dollars at cost; in thousands)	$630	$346	$280
Protecting the Environment			
Solid waste to landfill as a percentage of revenue (tons/$1,000,000)*	1.1	1.6	2.2
Direct energy use as a percentage of revenue (therms/$1,000)**	3.2	3.5	4.7
Tons of greenhouse gases emitted and offset (direct and indirect from operations, estimated)***	66,132	40,455	30,137
Building Demand for Sustainable Products			
All Fair Trace Certified™ lbs. (organic and nonorganic) shipped as a percentage of total lbs. shipped	28%	30%	29%
Creating a Great Place to Work			
Average hours in training/continuous education per full-time employee	38	50	49
Percentage employees agreeing that Green Mountaing Coffee Roasters is an "Overall Great Place To Work"	☺	93%	86%

* Specialty Coffee business unit only.

** FY10 includes facilities in CA, MA, TN, VT, WA and a facility in Toronto, Ontario. FY09 includes facilities in TN, VT, and WA. FY08 includes facilities inTN and VT.

*** We are committed to offsetting 100% of estimated emissions from our measured carbon footprint. Our FY10 estimate of total greenhouse gas emissions includes the benefit of our purchase of approximately 26,000 megawatt-hours in renewable energy certificates, which reduces our estimated emissions by approximately 6,600 tons.

☺ The next "Overall Great Place to Work" survey will be administered in spring 2011.

As the single-cup coffee market and Keurig brewing systems grew in popularity, GMCR understood that the impact of the system was one of their most significant environmental challenges. Finding a more environmentally friendly approach to the packaging challenge represented by the K-Cup portion pack waste stream was a big priority for GMCR. GMCR actively researched alternatives to the petroleum-based materials that made up the majority of Keurig K-Cup packaging. GMCR commissioned Life-Cycle Analysis in 2008 to help quantitatively understand the environmental impact of the K-Cup portion pack as it compared to using a typical drip-brewer and identify the best opportunities to reduce its impact. GMCR worked to identify the right definition of "environmentally friendly" for the Keurig system and all their packaging. Because the term "environmentally friendly" can mean many things (carbon-neutral, biodegradable, compostable, petroleum-free, etc.), GMCR was researching what was possible today and tomorrow, taking into account the current state of packaging technology, consumer preferences, community infrastructure, performance requirements, and the demands of the marketplace. GMCR continued to offer the My K-Cup product, a reusable filter assembly that could be refilled by the consumer, was easily cleaned, and was compatible with all Keurig home brewers currently sold. On the brewer side, all Keurig engineers had been trained on the European RoHS directive, which restricted the use of certain hazardous substances in electrical and electronic equipment, and all Keurig brewers were RoHS compliant.

Keurig-Fueled Sales Growth at GMCR

For fiscal 2010, the Keurig single-cup brewing system (brewers and K-Cups) were driving growth and value creation for GMCR. Approximately 88 percent of consolidated net sales for GMCR were derived from the Keurig Brewing System (brewers, K-Cup portion packs, and royalties).

While net sales for GMCR's specialty coffee business rose 64 percent in 2010 to $629 million, the Keurig business unit sales increased 81 percent to $728 million for total net sales of $1,357 for GMCR. Sales were forecast to increase by 45–53 percent in 2011 to $1,968 to $2,076. As a reseller, Keurig placed K-Cups and brewers side-by-side in outlets such as Bed Bath & Beyond, Macy's, Target, and many more. Keurig merchandised brewers and K-Cups in over 19,000 retail outlets plus 14,000 supermarket locations in fiscal 2010 (see Exhibit 12). For the 12 weeks ended December 26, 2010, the GMCR 12-count K-Cups had penetrated 61 percent of the grocery stores in the United States.[12]

Risks Brewing at Keurig
Manufacturer and Trade Risks

Because all Keurig single-cup brewers were made by a single manufacturer in China, GMCR was exposed to significant risks that could materially adversely affect the supply or cost of Keurig machines. Any disruption in production or inability of GMCR's manufacturer to produce adequate quantities to meet consumer demand, whether as a result of a natural disaster or other causes, would significantly impair GMCR's ability to operate their business on a day-to-day basis. Furthermore, GMCR faces the possibility of product supply disruption and increased costs in the event of a number of other occurrences, including changes in the policies of the Chinese government, political unrest or unstable economic conditions in China, changes in foreign exchange rates, or developments in the United States that are adverse to trade, such as the enactment of protectionist legislation.

Quality and Liability Risks

Product recalls and product liability were also potential dangers. If GMCR's manufacturer of brewers does not adhere to product safety requirements or quality-control standards, GMCR might not identify a deficiency before

Exhibit 12 GMCR Sales Growth

brewers ship to Keurig customers. This could damage Keurig's reputation, and thus GMCR's reputation and brands, and even lead to customer litigation against GMCR. Of course, GMCR maintains a reserve for product warranty costs, which is based on estimates and their knowledge of current conditions, but GMCR's actual costs could exceed that reserve, resulting in higher costs and a need to increase their reserve for future warranty costs. For example, during fiscal 2010, GMCR experienced higher than expected warranty returns for certain brewer models. (They believed a component used in certain Keurig brewer models during late 2009 to be at fault.) To correct the issue, GMCR replaced the affected brewers and made changes to their hardware and software. However, it is possible that GMCR will experience warranty expenses related to this or similar quality issues in the future.

Proprietary Technology Risks

GMCR's ability to compete effectively depends, in part, on their ability to maintain the proprietary nature of Keurig technologies, which include the ability to obtain, protect, and enforce patents and other trade secrets and know-how relating to Keurig technology. GMCR owns patents that cover significant aspects of their products, and certain patents of GMCR will expire in the near future. In the United States, patents associated with GMCR's current-generation K-Cup portion packs will expire in 2012 and 2017. GMCR also has pending patent applications associated with current K-Cup portion pack technology which, if ultimately issued as patents, would extend coverage over all or some portion of K-Cup portion packs and have expiration dates extending to 2023. These applications may not issue, or if they issue, they may not be enforceable, or may be challenged, invalidated, or circumvented by others. Additionally, GMCR has a number of portion-pack patents that extend to 2021 but which GMCR has elected not to commercialize yet and may never commercialize. In addition, Keurig has continued to invest in further innovation in portion packs and brewing technology that would enhance their current patents or could lead to new patents. GMCR takes steps to protect all such innovation and is prepared to protect their patents vigorously. Given the complex technical issues and inherent uncertainties in litigation, however, there can be no assurance that GMCR would prevail in any intellectual property infringement litigation they instituted to protect their intellectual property rights.

Risks of Integrating Acquisitions

Integrating GMCR's acquisitions into their business presents significant challenges and risks to their business, including: distraction of management from regular business concerns; assimilation and retention of employees and customers; managing the operations and employees of those businesses, none of which have been near their current headquarters and operation locations; or GMCR might fail to successfully integrate the acquired businesses into their business and, as a result, fail to realize the expected benefits of these acquisitions. Diedrich had a history of operating losses, and

GMCR's ability to achieve and then maintain the profitability of this business line depended on GMCR's ability to manage and control operating expenses and to generate and sustain increased levels of revenue. GMCR might fail to grow and build profits in business lines or achieve sufficient cost savings through integrating customer service or administrative and other operational activities. If GMCR was not able to successfully achieve these objectives, the anticipated benefits of these acquisitions would not be realized, or it might take longer to realize them than expected. As a result, their operations could be materially adversely affected.

Risks from Fluctuating Commodity Costs

Significant fluctuations in the cost of other commodities, such as steel, petroleum, and copper, influence prices of plastic and other components used in manufacturing Keurig coffee brewers. Approximately 96 percent of the Keurig brewers shipped in fiscal 2010 were sold to the at-home channel approximately at cost, or sometimes at a loss, when factoring in the incremental costs related to sales (including fulfillment charges, returns reserve, and warranty expense). With respect to the Keurig single-cup, at-home system, GMCR continued to pursue a model designed to penetrate the marketplace, a component of which was to sell brewers at affordable consumer price points in order to attract new customers into single-serve coffee. Any rapid, sharp increases in their cost of manufacturing at-home brewers would be unlikely to lead GMCR to raise sales prices to offset their increased cost, as GMCR's strategy was to drive penetration and not risk slowing down the rate of sales growth as compared to GMCR's competitors or before realizing cost reductions in GMCR's purchase commitments. There was no assurance that GMCR would be able to sell at-home brewers approximately at cost when such fluctuations occur.

Risks of Coffee Availability

Decreased availability of high-quality Arabica coffee beans could jeopardize GMCR's ability to maintain or expand their business. GMCR roasted over 50 types of green coffee beans to produce more than 100 coffee selections. If one type of green coffee bean were to become unavailable or prohibitively expensive, GMCR believed they could substitute another type of coffee of equal or better quality meeting a similar taste profile. However, a worldwide supply shortage of the high-quality Arabica coffees GMCR purchases could materially adversely affect their business. Worldwide or regional shortages of high-quality Arabica coffees could be caused by multiple factors, such as weather, pest damage, or economics in the producing countries. In addition, the political situation in many of the Arabica-coffee-growing regions, including Africa, Indonesia, and Central and South America, can be unstable, and such instability could affect GMCR's ability to purchase coffee from those regions. If Arabica coffee beans from a region became unavailable or prohibitively expensive, GMCR could be forced to discontinue particular coffee types and blends or substitute coffee beans from other regions in GMCR's blends. Frequent substitutions and changes in GMCR's coffee product lines could lead to cost increases, customer alienation, or fluctuations in gross margins. While the production of commercial-grade coffee was generally increasing, many industry experts were concerned about the ability of specialty coffee production to keep pace with demand. Arabica coffee beans of the quality GMCR purchased were not readily available on the commodity markets. GMCR depended on their relationships with coffee brokers, exporters, and growers for the supply of their primary raw material, high-quality Arabica coffee beans. In particular, the supply of Fair Trade Certified coffees was limited. GMCR might not be able to purchase enough Fair Trade Certified coffees to satisfy the rapidly increasing demand for such coffees, which could materially adversely affect revenue growth.

Endnotes

1. Green Mountain Coffee Roasters Inc. (GMCR) & Starbucks Corp. 2011. Press release: Starbucks Corporation and Green Mountain Coffee Roasters, Inc. enter into strategic manufacturing, marketing, distribution and sales relationship. *Business Wire,* March 10. *investor.gmcr.com/releasedetail. cfm?ReleaseID=555937.*

2. GMCR & Dunkin' Brands Inc. 2011. Press release: Green Mountain Coffee Roasters, Inc. and Dunkin' Donuts to make America's favorite coffee available in K-Cup portion packs for Keurig Single-Cup Brewers. *Business Wire,* February 22. *investor.gmcr.com/releasedetail.cfm?ReleaseID=551547.*

3. *Javataza Specialty Coffee.* Coffee is one of America's favorite beverages. *www.javataza.com/index.php? option=com_content&view=category&layout=blog&id= 4&Itemid=26&lang=en&limitstart=15*

4. Black, K. 2009. Business statistics: contemporary decision making. 6th ed. Wiley. p. 268.

5. Starbucks 2010 Annual Report. Coffee facts and statistics. 2011. Specialty Coffee Association of America. *www. scaaevent.org/PDF/Press%20Kit/2011/Facts%20and%20 Figures.pdf*

6. Marquardt, K. 2008. Brewing profits, a cup at a time: Green Mountain heats up the single-serve coffee market. *U.S. News & World Report,* 145, no. 11 (November 17): 55.

7. Duff, M. 2007. Latest brewers may serve up sales, good coffee. *Retailing Today,* April 23: vol. 46, iss. 6, page 18.

8. GMCR. 2007 annual report.

9. Keurig Coffee, 2008. Press release: Keurig celebrates 10th anniversary –providing gourmet single cup coffee brewing to homes and offices. January 21. *www.keurig.com.*

10. GMCR. 2008 annual report.

11. Business Wire. Keurig and Caribou coffee announce single cup coffee partnership. 2007. January 8. *www. businesswire.com/news/home/20070108005606/en/ Keurig-Caribou-Coffee-Announce-Single-Cup-Coffee*

12. GMCR, 2011. Press release: Fiscal Q1 2011 performance. February 2. *www.gmcr.com.*

photo credits

Chapter 1: page 6, NOAA; page 23, The McGraw-Hill Companies, Inc./John Flournoy, photographer

Chapter 2: page 40, Brand X Pictures/PunchStock; page 70, ONOKY - Photononstop/Alamy

Chapter 3: page 84, © Keith Eng 2007; page 90, The McGraw-Hill Companies, Inc./Andrew Resek, photographer

Chapter 4: page 139, Ingram Publishing; page 148, © Lars A. Niki

Chapter 5: page 165, Geostock/Getty Images; page 168, Pamela Carley

Chapter 6: page 200, The McGraw-Hill Companies, Inc./Jill Braaten, photographer; page 222, C Squared Studios/Getty Images

Chapter 7: page 246, Royalty-Free/CORBIS; page 253, Digital Vision/Getty Images

Chapter 8: page 298, The McGraw-Hill Companies, Inc./Jill Braaten, photographer; page 302, The McGraw-Hill Companies, Inc./John Flournoy, photographer

Chapter 9: page 313, Royalty-Free/CORBIS; page 321, The McGraw-Hill Companies, Inc./John Flournoy, photographer

Chapter 10: page 366, Photodisc/Getty Images; page 368, Mark Steinmetz

Chapter 11: page 389, © M. Blinnikov; page 413, The McGraw-Hill Companies, Inc./Jill Braaten, photographer

Chapter 12: page 438, Tom Grill/Corbis; page 451, The McGraw-Hill Companies, Inc./Andrew Resek, photographer

Chapter 13: page 478, Digital Vision/Getty Images; page 479, PhotoDisc Imaging/Getty Images

company index

Page numbers followed by n refer to footnotes.

b

B. Dalton, 100
Baazec.com, C173
Babies "R" Us, 295, C185
Baby Bells, 57
BAE, 266
BagScan, C274
Bain & Company, 131, 438, C170
Bain Capital, C185
Baltic Beverages Holding, C37
Banana Republic, C241–C242
Banco Compartamos, C293, C294
Banc of America Securities, C218
Bank of America, 203–204, 230, C15, C107
Bank Rakyat Indonesia, C293, C294
Barclay's Capital, C63
Barnes & Noble, 99, 180, 304
Barrons.com, 230
Baskin-Robbins, C254, C257, C288, C289
Bassett Furniture, 459
Basset-Walker, 209
Bath & Body Works, C62, C242
Bayer AG, 266
BBAG, C37
Bear Stearns, 4, C15
Bebo, 202
Bed Bath & Beyond, C307
Beecham Group, 223
Beijing Automotive Holding Company, C230
Bellagio, C280
Bellows & Samson, C13
BellSouth, 220
Ben & Jerry's, C284, C285, C289
Beneficial, 223
BenQ, 400
Bentley, sales and market share, C117
Berkshire Hathaway, 84, 231, 335
Best Buy, 92, 398, 458, C71, C72
    corporate social responsibility at, 457
    new direction for, 397
Best Practices LLC, 461
Beth Israel Deaconess, 413
Better Business Bureau Wise Giving
    Alliance, C25
Better Homes and Gardens, C88
Beverly Hills Rent-a-Car, 175
Bigelow, C304
Bil Basen, C172, C173
BI-LO, C135
Bing, C58
BizRate, 65, 117
Blackberry, 432, 439
Blockbuster Inc., 41, 180, 303, C250
Bloomingdales, 305
Blue Bell, C284, C285
Blue Cross of California, 66
Blue Sky Creamery, C289
BMG, C150
BMW Group, 68, 70–71, 169, 170–171, C113,
    C233
    dependability ranking, C118
BMW of North America Inc., sales and market
    share, C116–C117
Bob's Stores, C241
Body Shop, 296
Boeing Company, 6, 247, 302, 303, 327, 375, 483,
    C104, C110–C111, C121, C156

Bombay Company, 459
Bonnier Corporation, C90
Book Industry Study Group, 64
Books-A-Million, 64
Books Are Fun Ltd., C96, C97
Booz Allen Hamilton, 334
Borders Group, 118
Borgata Hotel Casino, C280
Boston Consulting Group, 165, 216–218, 274, 301
Boston Market, C41, C42
Boston Scientific, 220
Bowls: A Cereal Joint, 173
Boyd Gaming, C277, C281
Boyd Group, 167
Boyd's, C263
Boys & Girls Clubs, C23
BP Amoco, 30, 266
Brand Keys Customer Loyalty Engagement Index,
    C296
Brenton Brothers, C9, C10
Breyer's Ice Cream, C284, C285
Bridgestone, 266
Brinker International, 29, 368
British Airways, 448
British Petroleum (BP), 21, 204, 335
    oil spill of 2010, 5, 7
British Sky Broadcasting, 344
Brocade, 332
Bruegger's Enterprises, C305
Brunswick, 6
Bruster's Real Ice Cream, C289
BTIG, C82
BTR, 214
Buckman Laboratories, 145–146
Buena Vista, C78, C79
Bugati, 175
Build-A-Bear Workshop, case
    assembly line process, C262–C263
    balance sheet, C260–C261
    in changing market, C264–C265
    charitable activities, C259
    company history, C261–C262
    employee retention, C262
    in entertainment retailing, C262–C263
    expansion and innovation, C263
    financial performance, C265–C266
    future prospects, C265–C266
    hiring policy, C262
    impact of financial crisis, C259
    income statement, C260
    organizational culture, C262
    product revitalization, C259
    store atmosphere, C262
    store data 2006–2010, C265–C266
    in toy retail industry, C263–C264
Burdines, 86
Burger King, C42
Business Roundtable, 334, 375, 376

c

Cable Value Network Shopping, C60
Cabot Corporation, 218–219
Cadbury Schweppes, 220, 328, 483
Caesars Entertainment, C281
Caesar's Palace, C280
California Bay Area United Way, C23

California Quivers, C289
Callaway Golf, 269
    strategic alliance, 270
CalPERS, 337–338
Calvin Klein, 190
Campbell Soup Company, 84, 90
Canadean Ltd., C35
Canadian Football League, 309
C&S Wholesale Grocers, C130
Cannondale, 169, 177
Canon, 28, 266
Cape Air, C271
Cargill, 97
Caribou Coffee, C304
Carling O'Keefe Breweries, 226
Carlsberg, C34, C36
Carmike, C76, C78, C80, C81, C82
Carnival Cruise Line, 333
Carrefour, 222
    problems at, 240
Carvel, C285, C289
Casino, 240
Casio, 206
Caterpillar, Inc., 169, 188, 364
Cathay Pacific Airlines, 49, 305
Catholic Charities, C23
Cayuse Technologies, 256
CBS network, 302, 376
CCU, C35
Cefiore, C289
Celanese Chemical Corporation, 254
Celestial Seasonings Tea brands, C304
Celestica, 378
Cemex, 347
Center for Automotive Research, 67
Center for Progress, 60
Central Airlines, C155
Century, C76
Cerberus Capital Management, 203
Cereal Bowl, 173
Cereality, 173
Cessna, 327
Challenger Electrical Distribution, 376
Champion International, 215
Chang'an Automotive Group, C228, C230
ChangeOne, C96
Charity Navigator, C25
Charity Organization of Denver, C19
Charles Schwab & Company, 222–223
Charming Shoppes Inc., C244
Chartwell Investments, 399
Chase Capital, C269
Chemical Bank, 424
Chery Automobile Company, 70–71, C228, C230
Chesapeake Energy, problems at, 318
Chevrolet, 294
Chick-fil-A Inc., C41
Chico's FAS Inc., C235, C242, C243, C244
Chili's Restaurants, 29
China Association of Automobile Manufacturers,
    C230
Chipotle Mexican Grill, C41, C42
Christie Digital Systems, C82
Chrysler Corporation, 70, 193, 203, 209, 309,
    C111, C226, C227, C233
    dependability ranking, C118
    sales and market share, C114
Chrysler/Dodge/Jeep, C113
Ciba-Geigy, 205, 218

Page numbers followed by n refer to footnotes.

a

Aaker, David A., 198, 276
Abelson, J., C248
Abelson, R., C69
Abraham, M., 114
Acevedo, Edward, C178
Ackerman, E., C58
Ackerman, Jason, C124, C125, C126
Ackerson, Daniel F., C30, C33
Adams, S., 155
Adamy, J., C44, C45
Adler, P. S., 157
Afuah, A., 75, 119n, 120, 390
Agins, T., C248
Ahlstrom, D., 345, 346, 353
Aiman-Smith, L., 466
Aime, F., 158
Akula, V., 275
Albrinck, J., 466
Aldag, R. J., 491
Aldrich, H. E., 313
Aleskovsky, Alexandra, C212
Alessandri, T. M., 352
Alexander, M., 236
Ali, R., C102
Allard, M. J., 157
Allen-MacGregor, Jacqueline, C24
Alpeyev, P., 378
Alsever, J., 256
Alston, Alyce, C101
Alvarez, Ralph, C42
Alvarez, S. A., 73
Alvin, Mike, 250
Amabile, T. M., 157
Amato-McCoy, D. M., C267
Amburgey, T. L., 389
Amelio, Gilbert, C143, C144, C145
Amit, R., 116
Amos, Karen, C161
Amram, M., 467
Anaptyxi, Constantine, C11
Anaptyxi, Nikolas, C11, C13
Anard, B. N., 237
Andersen, M. M., 100, 115, 427
Andersen, R. A., 389
Anderson, E., 115
Anderson, G., C292
Anderson, J. C., 114
Anderson, P., 155
Anderson, S., C27
Andre the Giant, C48, C51
Angel, R., 110, 116
Angeletti, N., C102
Angevine, R., 186
Angle, Kurt, C51
Angwin, J. S., 237
Anmuth, Douglas, C63
Anslinger, P. A., 236
Ansoff, H. Igor, 74

Ante, S. E., 203
Anthony, Scott, 416
Arai, H., 155
Aramony, William, C23, C24
Arar, Y., C153
Argawal, A., 351
Argyris, Chris, 319, 349
Arikan, A. M., 35, 115
Arino, A., 237
Arison, Micky M., 333
Armstrong, R. W., 198
Armstrong, Tim, 202
Arndt, B., 465
Arndt, M., 236, 237, 353, C44, C45, C164
Arno, A., 237
Arnold, D., 277
Arnold, Susan E., C221
Arnott, D. A., 350
Arregale, J.-L., 116, 158
Ashkenas, R., 373
Assenza, Pauline, C18, C88, C141, C235
Aston, A., 35, 74
Augustine, Norman R., 10, 35, 199, 326, 350, 380
Aumann, Yonatan, 369
Austin, R. D., 35, 198
Austin, Steve, C46, C51, C52

b

Baatz, E. B., 428
Bacani, C., C201
Bachman, J., 276, C163
Bader, P., 158, 159
Bahrami, H., 382
Baier, J., 156
Baig, E. C., 148
Bailey, J., C275
Baker, Kevin, C34–C35
Baker, S., 74, 139, 350
Bakke, Dennis, 420–421, 429
Balfour, F., 252
Ball, B., C52
Ball, Robert M., C162
Ballou, J., 289
Balmer, Steven, 415
Bamford, C. E., 74
Bansal, P., 156
Bapuji, H., C187
Barbaro, M., C249
Barboza, D., C188, C189
Barger, Dave, C275
Barkema, H. G., 199, 237
Barman, Emily, C27
Barnes, B., C275, C219
Barnes, Christopher, 376, 390
Barnes, L. A., 491
Barnett, M. L., 75
Barnevik, Percy, 37, 157
Barney, J. B., 35, 73, 94, 101, 115, 156, 198

Baron, R. A., 156, 313, 466
Barrera, Luz, C18
Barrett, A., 237, C69
Barrett, Colleen, C155, C159, C160
Barrett, W. P., C26
Barrette, Michael, C283
Barringer, B. R., 391
Barry, Stephanie, 447
Bart, C. K., 37
Bartholomew, D., C275
Bartlett, C. A., 199, 275, 362, 389
Bartness, A., 391
Barton, N., C26, C27
Bartz, Carol A., 409, C53, C55, C56, C57–C58
Barwise, P., 157
Bary, A., C219
Bashkoff, Lara, C103
Basker, E., 247
Bateman, Graeme, C71
Baugher, Dan, C259
Baum, J. A. C., 237
Baumgarter, P., 75, 198
Bauwhede, H. V., 331
Bay, Willow, C275
Bayers, C., 118n
Baysinger, B. D., 352
Beamish, P. W., 275, 313, C187
Bearden, W. O., 199
Beardwood, Julia, C225
Becker, G. S., 155
Beckhard, R., 35, 37, 373, 426
Begley, T. M., 35, 262
Bell, Charles H., C42
Beller, P. C., 350
Belton, C., 275
Ben-Aaron, D., 35
Benioff, Marc, 439
Bennett, J., C69
Bennett, James, 172
Bennett, N., 351
Bennett, Stephen M., 195
Bennett, Steve, 440
Benoist, Marc, 256
Benoit, Chris, C50
Bensaou, B. M., 115
Bensinger, G., 305
Benz, M., 36
Berfield, S., C122
Bergen, M. A., 197, 314
Berggren, F., 114
Bergstrom, B., 211
Berkowitz, E. N., 199, 276, 277
Berle, Adolf, 333
Berman, P., 361
Berman, Todd, 399
Bernanke, Ben, 45
Bernardino, Joseph, 229
Berner, Mary G., C88, C90–C91, C97, C101, C102
Berner, R., 303
Bernoff, J., 96, 428
Berns, Gregory, 142

subject index

Cash coverage ratio, 105, 476, 496–497
Cash cows, 217, 218
Cash ratio, 105, 476, 496
Casino industry, case
   bankruptcies, C282
   competition for Las Vegas, C277
   competitive environment, C280
   demographics of customers, C278
   favorite games, C279
   future of, C282
   growth since 1931, C278–C279
   impact of financial crisis, C277
   leading operators, C281
   locations, C279–C280
   mergers and acquisitions, C282
   payouts, C278–C279
   response to growing competition,
      C280–C282
   revenues 2000–2009, C277
   revenues by state, C278
   run by Native Americans, C279
Causal ambiguity
   definition, 98
   and employee exit costs, 103
Causality, 401, 402
Celebrity endorsements
   for Dippin' Dots, C287–C288
   at QVC, C63
Cell phones
   Apple Inc., C147–C149
   market shares, C148
Center for Auto Safety, 343
Center for Study of Responsive Law, 343
Centralization, in functional structure, 360
CEO duality
   and agency theory, 339–340
   controversy, 339–340
   decline in, 340
   definition, 339
   succession problem, 340
   unity of command, 339
CEOs
   changes at Apple Inc., C144–C145
   of FreshDirect, C125
   policies to maximize value of the firm, 338
   Sarbanes-Oxley Act on, 342
   succession plan at Apple Inc., C151–C152
CEO turnover
   forced by board of directors, 334–335
   problem for companies, 335
Chaebols, 346
Change, barriers to, 402–404
Change management, 432
Chapter 11 bankruptcy
   General Motors, C31
   Reader's Digest, C88, C91
Charitable activities, Build-A-Bear Workshop,
   C259
Chief financial officers, Sarbanes-Oxley Act on,
   342
Child Protection and Toy Safety Act, C181
China
   admission to World Trade Organization, C168
   air cargo revenue, 49
   auto production 2010, C228
   challenge for eBay, C176
   demand for luxury goods, 49
   eBay's position in, C166, C176
   economies of scale, 246
   Geely Automotive, case, C226–C234

General Administration for Quality Supervision,
   Inspection and Quarantine, C187
middle class, 244–246
middle class market, 40
Ministry of Labor and Social Security, C186
National Economic Research Institute, 244
New Car Assessment Program, C232
population, 246
product safety in, C188
reduced population growth, 168
rise of auto market, C228
soft drink competition, 100
source for toy industry, C178, C179, C180,
   C181, C186
China Toy Association, C186
Chinese culture, 400
Clean water, access to, 436
Climate change, 375
Closure, 140
Closure relationships, 139, 140
Code of Ethics Guidelines on Competitive
   Intelligence, United Technologies, 44
Codified knowledge, 147–149
Coercive power, 405
Coffee availability risk, C308–309
Coffee consumption, C296–C297
Coffee preferences, C297
Collaboration
   among business units, C68
   overcoming barriers to, 141
College tuition, 58
Collusion, 309
Combination strategies, 161
   definition, 176
   effect of Internet, 185–187
   exploiting profit pool, 177, 178
   extended value chain, 177–178
   and five-forces model, 178
   flexible manufacturing, 176–177
   mass customization, 176–177
   in new ventures, 299–300
   pitfalls
      demands on management time, 179
      ending stuck in the middle, 178–179
      miscalculating revenue sources, 179
      underestimating value chain
         challenges, 179
Commission-based business model, 119, 120
Commitment to excellence, 292
Commoditized products, 65
Commodity cost fluctuations, C308
Common-size balance sheet, 490–491
Common-size income statement, 492–493
Common stock sale by JetBlue Airways, C275
Communications, organizational, 383
Companies; *see also* Organizations
   alumni networks, 139
   array of technologies used by, 88
   book vs. market value, 125–126
   environmental values, 24
   fallen stars, 4–5
   global dispersion of value chains, 254–255
   global vs. regional, 266
   information sources, 501–506
   intellectual capital, 123
   motives for international expansion, 244–249
   perspective of balanced scorecard, 108
   risks of international expansion
      currency risks, 252–253
      economic risk, 251–252

   management risks, 253–254
   political risk, 249–251
Company rankings, 504
Comparison shopping, online, 117, 186
Compensation
   incentive, 370
   large bonuses at AIG, C15–C17
   sales commissions, C8
   Southwest Airlines, C159
Competencies
   in-house at modular organizations, 378
   in innovation partners, 442
   for new ventures, 451
   ought for innovation partners, 442
Competing for the Future (Hamel & Prahalad), 40
Competition
   based on price, 61
   and blue ocean strategy, 296
   deceiving, 303
   Dippin' Dots response to, C291
   dysfunctional, 362
   globalization of, 255
   innovation for, 431
   intensifying for Southwest Airlines, C161–C162
   in maturity stage, 189
   soft drink industry, 100
   in toy industry, C183–C184
   for World Wrestling Entertainment, C52
Competitive actions
   defensive actions, 308
   forms of, 309
   frontal assault, 306
   guerrilla offensive, 307–308
   selective attacks, 307–308
   strategic, 307
   tactical, 306, 307
Competitive advantage
   from bundle of resources, 79
   and business performance, 163
   creating, 8–9, 180–181
   by creating factors of production, 243
   criteria for firm's resources, 95–101
   in diamond of national advantage, 241–244
   and diversion of firm's profits, 103–104
   from dynamic capabilities, 151–152
   eroded at Dell Inc., 101–102
   exploiting profit pool for, 177, 178
   focus of business-level strategy, 161
   forces eroding, 180
   from general administration, 89
   generic strategies for
      combination strategies, 176–179
      differentiation, 162, 169–174
      focus, 162, 174–176
      overall cost leadership, 162, 164–169
   in global markets
      cost reductions, 255–257
      global strategy, 259–260
      international strategy, 257–259
      local adaptation, 255–257
      multidomestic strategy, 260–263
      transnational strategy, 263–265
   goal in global start-ups, 367
   from Internet, 116–120
      business model types, 119–120
      customer feedback, 118
      entertainment programming, 118
      evaluation activities, 117
      expertise, 118
      problem-solving activities, 117–118

Operating income
   Reader's Digest, C97
   World Wrestling Entertainment, C49
Operational effectiveness, 8–9
Operational efficiency and effectiveness, 328
Operations
   Apple Inc., C146
   assessment factors, 83
   definition, 84
   in differentiation strategy, 170
   environmentally friendly, 84
   of JetBlue Airways, C272–C273
   in overall cost leadership, 164
   QVC, C61–C62
   in service organizations, 92–93
Opportunistic behavior
   forms of, 340–341
   and market for corporate control, 341
Opportunities; *see also* SWOT analysis
   opened by Internet, 184
   recognizing, 40–41
Opportunity analysis framework, 284
Opportunity evaluation, 284–286
Opportunity recognition, 279
   awareness, 284
   definition, 284
   deliberate search, 284
Opposable Mind (Martin), 401
Options
   embedded, 452–453
   types of, 452
Oral case presentation, 479
Organizational boundaries, 15
Organizational capabilities
   at Apple Inc., 95
   definition, 95
   kinds of, 94, 95
Organizational control, 398
Organizational culture
   boundaries and constraints, 325–328
   Build-A-Bear Workshop, C262
   Chinese vs. Western practices, 400
   common shared values, 383
   definition, 323
   entrepreneurial, 448
   environmental values, 24
   ethical, 398–400
   evolving from boundaries to, 439–440
   examples, 323
   at Geely Automotive, C228–C229
   at General Parkelite Corporation, C4–C6
   Green Mountain Coffee Roasters,
      C306–C307
   implicit boundaries, 324
   Jamba Juice, C250–C251
   lax at Rainbarrel Products, C7–C10
   reasons for emphasis on rewards, 322–323
   Southwest Airlines, C156–C160
   sustaining effectiveness of
      culture committee, 324
      rallies and pep talks, 324
      storytelling, 324
   wolf culture, 398–399
Organizational design, 15
   ambidextrous, 383–385
   in case analysis, 489
   composition of, 355
   leadership task, 398
Organizational ethics
   definition, 417

fraud potential, 418
   versus individual ethics, 417–419
Organizational flexibility argument, 136
Organizational goals, 9
   aligned with reward systems, 330
   analysis of, 12
   in case analysis, 487
   flexibility in meeting, 416
   strategic–financial comparison, 450–451
   3M Corporation, 6
Organizational integrity, 419
Organizational learning, 321
Organizational resources, 94
Organizational structure, 15
   ambidextrous designs, 383–385
   boundaryless designs, 372–383
      barrier-free organizations, 373–376
      factors to consider, 382–383
      modular, 377–379
      virtual organization, 379–382
   created by leadership, 398
   definition and function, 357
   divisional structure, 361–366
   functional structure, 359–361
   at General Motors, C30
   at Heineken, C36
   horizontal, 383
   independent action in, 456
   influence on strategy formulation, 368
   in international operations, 366–368
   matrix structure, 364–365
   patterns of corporate growth
      conglomerate strategy, 359
      functional structure, 358
      holding company structure, 359
      for international markets, 358
      simple structure, 358
      strategic business units, 359
      vertical integration, 358–359
   problems at Sun Microsystems, 363
   reward and evaluation systems, 368–372
      business-level strategy, 369–371
      corporate-level strategy, 371–372
   simple structure, 359
   and strategy, 355
   strategy–structure relationships, 357–359
   types of, 355
Organizational vision; *see* Vision
Organizations; *see also* Companies
   barriers to change, 402–404
   boundaryless, 355
   code of conduct, 421–422
   conflicting demands on, 18
   conflicts within, 326
   diversity management, 136
   dynamic capabilities, 151–152
   entrepreneurial orientation, 431
   environmentally aware
      competitive intelligence, 42–44
      environmental forecasting, 44–45
      environmental monitoring, 42
      environmental scanning, 41–42
      scenario analysis, 45–46
      SWOT analysis, 46–47
   external boundaries, 373
   geographic boundaries, 373
   hierarchy of goals, 26–32
   horizontal boundaries, 373
   integrative view of, 24
   key stakeholders, 17

long- vs. short-term perspective, 9–10
mission statements, 29–30
performance evaluation
   balanced scorecard, 107–110
   financial ratio analysis, 104–107
permeable boundaries, 357
protecting intellectual assets, 149–151
protection of human capital, 127
resource-based view of, 93–104
strategic management perspective, 24–26
strategic objectives, 30–32
structural holes, 141
subcultures in, 325
tribal loyalty, 134
understanding stakeholders, 397–398
value-chain analysis, 81–93
vertical boundaries, 373
vision, 26–29
Outbound logistics, 84–85
   assessment factors, 83
   definition, 84
   in differentiation strategy, 170
   electronic networks, 84
   in overall cost leadership, 164
   in service organizations, 92–93
Outside consultants, 473
Outside directors, 335, 336, 343
Outsiders, to neutralize biases, 416
Outsourcing, 213, 291
   in boundaryless organizations, 357
   definition, 254
   manufacturing volume of industries, 255
   by Mattel, C178, C179–C180
   Microsoft strategy, 378
   by modular organizations
      advantages, 377
      strategic risks, 378–379
   recent explosion in, 254–255
Overall cost leadership, 163
   absolute cost advantage, 168
   basis of, 162
   in combination strategies, 176–179
   competitive parity, 166–167
   effect of Internet, 182–183
   from electronic invoice system, 186
   experience curve, 165
   and five-forces model, 168
   in new ventures, 297
   often unattainable for start-ups, 297
   pitfalls
      common inputs with rivals, 168
      easily imitated, 168–169
      erosion of cost advantage, 169
      lack of parity on differentiation, 169
      too much focus on few value chain
         activities, 168
   reward and evaluation systems, 370
   at Ryanair, 167
   summary of, 174
   tactics, 164–165
   value chain activities, 164
   at Vizio, Inc., 298

p

Parenting advantage, 214–215
   in unrelated diversification, 206
Partnerships
   Apple Inc., C150–C151

Revenues
  Apple Inc., 105–106
  of casino industry, C278
  decline at Reader's Digest, C88
  decline at Yahoo!, C55
  enhanced by sharing activities, 208–209
  Geely Automotive, C234
  generated by Mattel, C179
  in growth stage, 189
  Hangzhou Wahaha Company, 102
  from Internet gambling, C282
  of main casino operators, C281
  miscalculating sources of, 179
  movie industry, C76–C77
  and movie theater growth, C86
  movie theater sources
    box office sales, C80–C81
    concessions, C80
    preshow advertising, C80
  of QVC, C60
  Reader's Digest, C95–C96
  Samsung Electronics, C72
  of U.S. casino industry 2000–2009, C277
  Weight Watchers, C206
  World Wrestling Entertainment
    breakdown by category, C48
    percentage breakdown, C49
Reverse innovation
  characteristics, 248–249, 250
  examples, 250
Reverse positioning
  at Commerce Bank, 190
  definition, 190–191
Reward and evaluation systems
  business-level strategy, 369–371
  corporate-level strategy, 371–372
  dysfunctional, 396
  in ethical organizations, 423–424
  motivational role, 368–369
Reward power, 405
Rewards, redistribution of, 413–414
Reward systems
  aligned with company goals, 330
  characteristics, 325
  in corporate governance, 338–339
  definition, 324
  effective, 325
  evolving from boundaries to, 439–440
  financial and nonfinancial, 135
  as motivator, 324
  with multiple divisions, 325
  potential downside, 324–325
  reasons for emphasis on, 322–323
    building loyalty, 323
    competitive environment, 323
    at Starbucks, 324
  and subcultures, 325
Risk reduction
  goal of diversification, 218–219
  by value chain location, 248
Risk–return trade-off for new ventures, 450
Risks
  of exporting, 268
  in global strategy, 260
  in international strategy, 258–259
  of joint ventures, 270–271
  for Keurig
    coffee availability, C308–C309
    fluctuating commodity costs, C308

integrating acquisitions, C308
  manufacturer and trade, C307
  proprietary technology, C308
  quality and liability, C307–C308
  of licensing and franchising, 269
  in multidomestic strategy, 262–263
  of strategic alliances, 270–271
  in transnational strategy, 264–265
  of vertical integration, 212–213
Risk sharing, 333
Risk taking, 455
  dangers and pitfalls, 462
  definition, 461
  encouraging, 416
  techniques
    assess risk factors, 462
    use workable approach, 462
  types of, 461
Rivalry, 244
  and competitive dynamics, 300
Rivals, copying ideas of, 8
Role models, 420–421
  managerial, 330
Role playing, in case analysis, 472–473
Romantic view of leadership, 5–6
Rules-based controls, 328
Rural outsourcing, 256
Russia, currency devaluation 1998, 253

S

Safe Drinking Water and Toxic Enforcement Act,
  California, C188
Safety issues, Geely Automotive, C232
Sales
  Ann Taylor Stores, C238
  Apple Inc., C141–C142
  box-office revenues, C80–C81
  coffeemakers, C301
  definition, 85
  in differentiation strategy, 170
  examples, 85–86
  Ford Motor Company, C104, C112, C119,
    C120
  Geely Automotive, C234
  General Motors, C28, C30
  Green Mountain Coffee Roasters, C298
  growth for Green Mountain Coffee Roasters,
    C307
  growth from sharing activities, 208
  in growth stage, 189
  legal/unethical actions, 86
  by McDonald's 2011, C39
  movie industry, 247
  Nintendo Wii, C196
  online grocery business, C128
  in overall cost leadership, 164
  by QVC 1989–2010, C59
  in service organizations, 92
  of toys and games 2003–2009, C185
  U.S. automakers 2010, C227
Salience, 401, 402
Sarbanes-Oxley Act, 48, 50, C24
  as control mechanism, 342
  on financial statements, 328
  on outside directors, 343
  on whistleblowers, 424

Scenario analysis
  definition and functions, 45–46
  at PPG Industries, 46
Scent of a Mystery, 293
Search activities, 117
Search barrier, 141
Search costs, 213
Search engines, 506
  market shares, C56
  number of U.S. visits 2010, C57
Securities and Exchange Commission
  company disclosure reports, 503–504
  and Countrywide Financial, 332
  EDGAR database, 503–504
  financial disclosure to, 342
  suit against KPMG, 341
Seeds vs. weeds dilemma, 437
Selective attacks, 307–308
Selective demand, 189
Self-awareness, 407, 408
Self-censorship, 482
Self-management skills
  motivation, 407, 408
  self-awareness, 407, 408
  self-regulation, 407, 408
Self-regulation, 407, 408
Sell-offs, 225n
Senate Finance Committee, C24
Senior incentive programs, 370
Separation of ownership and control,
    332–334
  agency theory, 333
  managerial self-interest, 333–334
  and role of board of directors, 334–336
Service organizations, applying value chain
    to, 92–93
Services
  definition, 86
  in differentiation strategy, 170
  examples, 86
  outsourcing, 255
  in overall cost leadership, 164
Setting a direction, 396
  at Best Buy, 397
  definition, 397
  leadership task, 397–398
Seventeen magazine, C287
Shared value concept, 3
  definition, 22
  examples, 22–23
  fair trade movement, 22
  and new concept of capitalism, 21
  and value chain productivity, 22
Shareholder activists, 336–338
  definition, 337
  institutional investors, 337–338
  power to direct corporations, 337
  and shareholder rights, 337
Shareholder rights plans, 232
Shareholders
  and corporate governance, 15
  in Latin America, 347
  long-term returns to, 330n
  power to direct corporations, 337
  rights of, 337
Shareholder value
  generating, 16–17
  portfolio management for,
    217–218

A Summary of Five Types of Financial Ratios

I. Short-term solvency, or liquidity, ratios

$$\text{Current ratio} = \frac{\text{Current assets}}{\text{Current liabilities}}$$

$$\text{Quick ratio} = \frac{\text{Current assets} - \text{Inventory}}{\text{Current liabilities}}$$

$$\text{Cash ratio} = \frac{\text{Cash}}{\text{Current liabilities}}$$

II. Long-term solvency, or financial leverage, ratios

$$\text{Total debt ratio} = \frac{\text{Total assets} - \text{Total equity}}{\text{Total assets}}$$

$$\text{Debt-equity ratio} = \text{Total debt/Total equity}$$

$$\text{Equity multiplier} = \text{Total assets/Total equity}$$

$$\text{Times interest earned ratio} = \frac{\text{EBIT}}{\text{Interest}}$$

$$\text{Cash coverage ratio} = \frac{\text{EBIT} + \text{Depreciation}}{\text{Interest}}$$

III. Asset utilization, or turnover, ratios

$$\text{Inventory turnover} = \frac{\text{Cost of goods sold}}{\text{Inventory}}$$

$$\text{Days' sales in inventory} = \frac{365 \text{ days}}{\text{Inventory turnover}}$$

$$\text{Receivables turnover} = \frac{\text{Sales}}{\text{Accounts receivable}}$$

$$\text{Days' sales in receivables} = \frac{365 \text{ days}}{\text{Receivables turnover}}$$

$$\text{Total asset turnover} = \frac{\text{Sales}}{\text{Total assets}}$$

$$\text{Capital intensity} = \frac{\text{Total assets}}{\text{Sales}}$$

IV. Profitability ratios

$$\text{Profit margin} = \frac{\text{Net income}}{\text{Sales}}$$

$$\text{Return on assets (ROA)} = \frac{\text{Net income}}{\text{Total assets}}$$

$$\text{Return on equity (ROE)} = \frac{\text{Net income}}{\text{Total equity}}$$

$$\text{ROE} = \frac{\text{Net income}}{\text{Sales}} \times \frac{\text{Sales}}{\text{Assets}} \times \frac{\text{Assets}}{\text{Equity}}$$

V. Market value ratios

$$\text{Price-earnings ratio} = \frac{\text{Price per share}}{\text{Earnings per share}}$$

$$\text{Market-to-book ratio} = \frac{\text{Market value per share}}{\text{Book value per share}}$$